EUROPEAN HISTORY

SINCE 1870

EUROPEAN HISTORY

SINCE 1870

By

F. Lee Benns

INDIANA UNIVERSITY

Fourth Edition

APPLETON-CENTURY-CROFTS, Inc.

NEW YORK

PREFACE TO FOURTH EDITION

IT is becoming more and more recognized that the period since 1870 in European history constitutes a distinct epoch, one in which the increasing envolement of Europe in affairs throughout the world has converted the history of that continent, especially its international relations, into a history of world politics. The global nature of Europe's history in the past half-century has been shockingly emphasized by two destructive world wars. This volume presents the history of Europe in such a way that the reader should obtain a clear insight into the economic, social, and political forces which led to these world wars and an appreciation of the profound changes which have occurred in the life of Europe—and the world—since 1870.

Part One lays the foundation for an understanding of Europe's history by explaining the economic and social trends of the period. Part Two traces the history of the European states down to 1914. Each country's internal problems and developments, imperialistic ambitions and achievements, and foreign policy have been woven together in order to show how they interacted upon one another. Inevitably the chapters in this part of the book reveal the driving power of nationalism, the sharp clash of imperialisms, the gradual growth of entangling alliances, the huge expansion of armaments, and the rise of international fear and suspicion which brought on the First World War. Part Three discusses that war, the revolutionary forces released by it, the Paris peace settlement which followed it, and the gradual breakdown of that settlement. Part Four deals primarily with national problems in the period between the two world wars and describes the various political experiments—Communist, Fascist, Nazi, and the like—which profoundly altered the life of many countries. Part Five examines the tragic collapse of collective security during the interwar years, seeks to give some idea of the terrible destructiveness of the Second World War, and shows how mankind's postwar efforts to re-establish life as it had been before that war were complicated by the world conflict between "Communist totalitarianism" and "Western Democracy."

In this fourth edition Chapters XXVI–XXX have been rewritten and a new chapter, "Collective Security on Trial," has been added to provide a discussion of the Korean War and the various diplomatic, economic, and

military measures taken by the Free World since 1947 in an effort to
defend itself against the threat of Communism. The author continues to
be indebted to many who have made studies of special topics and upon
whose writings he has freely drawn. The extensive, freshly compiled
bibliography to some extent indicates his debt.

F. LEE BENNS

CONTENTS

vii

PART THREE: THE FIRST WORLD WAR AND ITS
INTERNATIONAL AFTERMATH

ILLUSTRATIONS

MAPS AND CHARTS

Part One

❦

ECONOMIC FORCES AND

SOCIAL TRENDS

ALTHOUGH statesmen and political leaders usually appear as the principal *dramatis personae* in any general history, more frequently than they realize the roles which they enact are dictated for them by the economic and social forces of their period. The chapters in Part One therefore explain briefly how the years from 1870 to 1914 were marked by a rapid spread of industrialism, a lively interest in a new and intensified imperialism, a tremendous increase and concentration of wealth, a marked growth in population and a steady movement of people into urban centers, a general rise in the standard of living, and a noticeable improvement in the rights and power of labor. In general, the period may be characterized as one of bourgeois ascendancy.

Chapter I

INDUSTRIALISM, IMPERIALISM, AND

WORLD POLITICS

AN understanding of the history of Europe since 1870 requires at the outset an appreciation of the fact that during this period new inventions and improved methods of manufacture brought the swift expansion of industry and commerce; that cheaper and more rapid means of transportation and communication opened the way for the economic exploitation of regions far removed from Europe; that desire for increased supplies of raw materials and for wider markets for the products of an expanded and accelerated industry resulted in a new outburst of imperialism; in short, that in an era of world politics the history of Europe after 1870 was not merely the history of that continent but to a large extent the history of the world.

The Acceleration of Industrial Development after 1870

The great importance of the Industrial Revolution of the late eighteenth and early nineteenth centuries has been repeatedly emphasized. It is well known that the changes in industry and transportation inaugurated in Great Britain during that period laid the foundations for the radical economic transformation through which the world passed in the succeeding century. Mechanical power supplanted hand power; the factory system superseded domestic manufacture; and railways and steamships, by increasing the speed and decreasing the cost of transportation, bound distant regions more closely together. Nevertheless, it appears that more attention should be given to the unprecedented expansion and acceleration of industry which came in the years after 1870. These were the years in which industrialism spread most widely throughout the world, in which industrial output was most rapidly increased, in which industrial and commercial rivalry between the great powers became most keen.

Although by 1870 the new industrialism had pretty thoroughly transformed the economic life not only of Great Britain but of France and Belgium as well, it had only begun to make itself felt in an effective way in

3

Germany, Austria, and northern Italy. Prussia's large-scale iron and steel plants were not established until after 1850, and it was only in the seventies and eighties that the great industrial development of Germany really began. In the United States the era of tremendous industrial expansion came after the Civil War (1861–1865), and the establishment of modern industry in Russia and Japan did not occur until the eighties and nineties. But in both Germany and the United States, the industrial movement, once begun, worked with extraordinary rapidity; in a single generation these countries advanced into the ranks of the great industrial nations of the world. The last quarter of the nineteenth century, therefore, witnessed a vast extension of the industrialized area of the globe.

This expansion is clearly revealed by statistics for the production of iron. In 1870 Great Britain was smelting half of the world's iron, three times as much as any other country. By the close of the century, however, her share of the iron industry had diminished in a startling way. The United States had won first place, and in 1903 Germany forged ahead of Great Britain into second place. This change in position was caused not by a decline in Great Britain's production—she was smelting more iron than in 1870—but by the tremendous expansion in world production of the metal.

Prior to 1870 the chief metallic materials of construction were cast iron and wrought iron, which, because of their limitations, were not entirely satisfactory. After that date, however, new methods of manufacture greatly increased the production of steel. In the seventies the Bessemer process [1] and the Siemens open-hearth process [2] came to be generally adopted. By the former, after the iron ore had been heated until it was a molten mass, it was purified by blowing a blast of air through it while it was in a "converter." The air oxidized the carbon and some of the impurities which had been in the ore; the correct proportion of carbon was then added to the molten mass to convert it into steel. By the Siemens process, which was developed in the late sixties, the iron ore was smelted in a gas furnace, through which gas and hot air were forced, at a constant and controlled pressure, in order to oxidize the impurities in the ore.

Although these processes revolutionized the metal industries by greatly reducing the cost of steel as well as increasing the speed with which it could be produced, they could be used only with ores which contained no phosphorus. Fortunately, in the late seventies two British chemists, Sidney G. Thomas and Percy G. Gilchrist, perfected a method of removing the baneful phosphorus from the ore by lining the converter with a basic

---

[1] This process, although invented by Sir Henry Bessemer in 1856, required further years of experimentation before it became a commercial success.

[2] Invented by Sir William Siemens.

material—consisting chiefly of lime and magnesia—with which the phosphorus would unite. Their invention had momentous results, for it not
only made phosphoric ores like those of Lorraine available for steel production,[3] but again greatly increased the speed of smelting.

Throughout the world the new processes of steel production combined
to lessen the cost of steel. The price of steel rails, for example, was cut in
half between 1874 and 1883, and the price of other steel commodities fell
in a similar way. Superior to iron in lightness, hardness, and durability,
steel came to be extensively substituted for iron. In the case of both iron
and steel, however, production experienced a tremendous increase. Between 1870 and 1910 the world's production of pig iron rose from approximately 12,000,000 to more than 60,000,000 tons. In 1870 the world's steel
production was only 692,000 tons; by 1910 it had increased to more than
55,000,000 tons. The Age of Steel, it appears, actually began in the years
after 1870. The expansion which took place in the iron and steel industry
is typical of that which occurred to a greater or less degree in the manufacture of staple products. In practically all of the older industries there
came in the period after 1870 a pronounced acceleration in production.

But the great increase in the world's industrial production did not result
merely from the application of new inventions and new processes to the
old established industries. It was also caused in part by the rise of many
new industries, which sprang into existence as the result of inventions
made in the latter part of the century. The manufacture of electrical
equipment is a good example of this new type of industry. In the fifties
the Morse telegraph—the first practical recording telegraph—was introduced in Europe, and in the late seventies and eighties the telephone made
its appearance. About 1866 the modern dynamo-electric machine was invented almost simultaneously by three men working independently of
one another. Twelve years later the first efficient electric arc light was invented (1878), and in the following year Thomas Edison's incandescent
lamp was produced.[4] Edison's invention of the bipolar dynamo in 1878
and his introduction of the "Edison system" of central-station power production four years later gave the first commercial importance to electric
generator and power development, which thereafter progressed rapidly.
Electric tramways developed in the eighties and during the last decade of
the nineteenth century were introduced in the larger cities. In many cases
electric power, generated near waterfalls, rapid streams, coal mines, or peat
bogs and transmitted cheaply over wires, supplanted steam power in
transportation and manufacturing.

[3] Introduced into Germany in 1879, the Thomas-Gilchrist process helped to speed that
country on its later spectacular industrial career.
[4] By 1927 the world consumption of electric lamps had reached 950,000,000 a year.

The rise of the new electrical industry may be illustrated by figures from Germany. In 1882 the number employed in this industry was so insignificant that it was not listed separately in official statistics. In the last decade of the nineteenth century, however, the number of establishments manufacturing electrical machinery and equipment nearly quadrupled. The number employed in this industry increased to 15,000 by 1895, to approximately 50,000 by 1902, and to nearly 100,000 by 1910. Seventeen years later one single electrical concern in Germany employed more than 110,000 workmen. A development and expansion analogous to that of the electrical industry occurred also in the chemical and, somewhat later, in the automotive industries as well. In the early 1920's, for example, the General Motors Corporation was acclaimed the greatest industrial corporation in the world.

The years after 1870, furthermore, saw the application of capital to industry on a scale formerly unknown. Huge sums were raised by the sale of stock to thousands of investors throughout the world. The phenomenal growth of industry, with its resultant increase in competition, also gave an impetus to a movement toward closer organization and concentration of industrial enterprise. While not unknown to Great Britain and France, industrial consolidation was most pronounced in the United States and Germany. In the former, competing enterprises in the same industry often amalgamated under one direction in a "trust" in order to eliminate duplication, control raw products, crush out weaker competitors, regulate prices, and increase profits. In Germany "cartels" were organized. In a cartel the various businesses remained independent in management and retained their own profits. They sought by business agreements, however, to regulate output, fix prices, and assign sales territory, and thus again to increase profits.

More and more, too, science was applied to industry, and industrial laboratories came to play an increasingly important role. In this development Germany took the lead toward the close of the nineteenth century, and eventually in that country scarcely an industry of any size and importance considered itself complete without some kind of laboratory for the carrying on of research. The movement spread to other countries, especially to the United States, which ultimately surpassed Germany in its use of laboratories and scientists in industry. Great enterprises spent large sums on expensive and complicated apparatus and employed hundreds of university-trained scientists to carry on experimental research in problems connected with industry. Countless inventions and startling advances resulted from the co-operative work of industrial scientists.

In the industrial laboratories the chemist occupied the chief position. As a result of his work substances were analyzed, altered, and imitated. By means of synthetic chemistry many products such as nitrates, indigo, leather, and rubber were made artificially. New products were manufactured from what had formerly been considered waste substances—dyes, medicines, perfumes, oils, and explosives, for example, from coal tar. Furthermore, in such processes as steel-making, glass-making, bleaching, dyeing, and tanning, chemistry wrought a sweeping revolution.

In the twentieth century a system of mass production, developed first in the United States, was gradually inaugurated in the chief industrial countries of the world. This system sought to produce large quantities of goods cheaply and well by the extensive use of automatic machinery, the extreme division of labor, and the saving of time and energy. Its essential features were the manufacture of standardized interchangeable parts and the assembling of these parts into a completed whole with the least possible use of handicraft labor. In some enterprises automatic machinery became so highly developed that human labor was practically eliminated.

To summarize, then, the years after 1870 saw the marked expansion of most of the older industries and the establishment of new ones of equal or greater importance; the building-up of huge units of production through the large-scale application of capital and the eventual adoption of the system of mass production; the tendency toward consolidation of individual units into cartels, syndicates, or trusts; and, as an inevitable consequence of all these developments, a notable increase in the volume of industrial production.

Improvements in Transportation and Communication

Simultaneous with the industrial expansion discussed above, and intimately connected with it, were the astonishing changes which occurred in the world's means of transportation and communication. Railways were enormously extended. Between 1870 and 1914 Great Britain's fifteen thousand miles grew to nearly twenty-four thousand, while France's railway system expanded from eleven thousand miles to more than thirty-one thousand. In the single generation after 1875 Germany's railway mileage more than doubled. In 1885 Russia had sixteen thousand miles of railway; two decades later she had within her empire more than forty thousand miles. By the close of the first decade of the twentieth century the trans-Siberian railway—5500 miles in length—had been built by the Russian government to link St. Petersburg on the Baltic with Vladivostok on the Pacific; Hamburg on the North Sea had been connected with Constantinople, and another line was under construction to unite the Otto-

man capital with the Persian Gulf—the two systems to constitute the famous Berlin-Bagdad railway; [5] and imperialists had even dared to dream
of joining South Africa with Egypt by means of a Cape-to-Cairo railway.

Mountains were tunneled and rivers were bridged in an effort to bind
Europe together. In 1871 engineers completed the Mt. Cenis tunnel through
the Alps to connect France and Italy by rail; ten years later the St. Gothard
tunnel united the railway systems of Italy and Germany and gave the latter
a railway connection with the Mediterranean. The longest railway tunnel
in Europe—more than twelve miles in length—in 1905 pierced the Alps
beneath the lofty Simplon pass. By the opening of the twentieth century
Europe was traversed by more than 200,000 miles of railways; and overseas,
by the close of the first quarter of the present century, European capitalists
and engineers had constructed nearly 150,000 more miles of railways in
Africa, Asia, and Australasia.

Furthermore, in the period after 1870 railway service and facilities were
vastly improved. The use of rolled steel rails made possible about 1870 the
construction of a track capable of withstanding the strain of much faster
and heavier trains, and thereafter the weight and capacity of freight cars
were considerably increased. The introduction of the air brake reduced by
90 per cent the time and distance required to stop a train by hand brakes, and
the installation of electrically controlled automatic block signals greatly
increased the safety of railway operations. Both of these improvements came
in the last quarter of the nineteenth century. The powerful locomotives and
mile-long trains of the twentieth century were a far cry from Stephenson's
light train of 1825.

The facilities for land transportation were further extended in the years
after 1900 as a result of the introduction of the automobile. In the closing
years of the nineteenth century Gottlieb Daimler, a German, invented a
"horseless carriage" which was propelled by an internal combustion engine
using gasoline. Soon thereafter inventors in other European countries
and in the United States were building automobiles, but it was not until
the twentieth century that they were manufactured in great numbers.
The first to build a cheap, serviceable car was Henry Ford of the United
States, who introduced the system of mass production in the manufacture
of automobiles and thus gave a great impetus to the industry. Although no
other countries nearly equaled the United States in the manufacture and
use of automobiles, transportation in all of them was revolutionized as
cities gradually became linked together with hard, smooth, concrete highways. By 1929, largely as a result of the influence of the automobile, the
highways of the world had been extended to more than 6,500,000 miles;
by 1936 the total mileage had risen to 9,900,000.

[5] See page 76.

INNOVATIONS IN TRANSPORTATION

An early automobile and one of the first airplanes built by the Wright brothers.

By the latter year an 8000-mile automobile road had been completed across Africa from the Cape to Cairo, and another crossed that continent from east to west. Regular automobile service was maintained on the deserts between Damascus and Bagdad, and in China automobile roads were being rapidly pushed into the interior. "Between the English Channel and the Bosporus, between mystic Saigon and teeming Shanghai, the Strait of Gibraltar and the Suez Canal," there were passable motor roads by 1937.[6]

Meanwhile great strides had been made in the improvement of ocean transportation. Down to 1870 the merchant fleet of the world consisted chiefly of sailing ships, and as late as 1880 there was as much tonnage driven by wind as by steam. The relatively slow adoption of the steamship had been caused largely by the limitations of the marine engine, which greatly restricted the amount of space available for cargo. After 1870, however, a new type of engine—the compound engine—reduced the consumption of coal by at least half, and an improved condenser not only made it possible to use the same water in the boilers for two months, but also caused a diminished consumption of coal. These two inventions reduced the cost of operating steamships and, equally important, by reducing the space required to carry coal and water, increased the space available for cargo. In the eighties steel hulls—lighter than those of iron or wood—were introduced. Since the displacement of steel ships was less in proportion to their carrying capacity than that of iron or wooden ships, they could take on more cargo than the latter before their load lines were reached. Moreover, steel ships were safer than wooden ones and cheaper than those made of iron. The compound engine, the improved condenser, and the use of steel for hulls thus greatly increased the cargo-carrying capacity of ships, and led in consequence to a phenomenal decrease in the cost of ocean transportation.

Further improvements in steamships came with the succeeding years. The introduction of the triple-expansion engine brought still greater economy in fuel. More powerful engines made possible the use of screw propellers, which, although invented as early as 1836, were not extensively used until after 1870. The invention of the steam turbine to drive the screw propellers made possible, early in the twentieth century, a further development in speed, size, and economy. In this century, too, oil—cleaner, less bulky, and more economical of labor—began to displace coal as a fuel for marine engines.

To facilitate marine transportation, fueling stations, where steamships could replenish their supplies, were established along the principal routes, and mechanical appliances for rapidly loading and unloading were installed

[6] Report of the highways committee of the Automobile Manufacturers Association.

in the important harbors. Furthermore, two great obstacles to ocean transportation were removed. The Isthmus of Suez, which formerly barred the way from the Mediterranean to the Indian Ocean, was pierced in 1869 when the Suez Canal was opened in November of that year. By connecting the Mediterranean with the Red Sea, this 100-mile canal shortened by thousands of miles the sea voyage from the North Atlantic and the Mediterranean to the East. In the summer of 1914 the route to the Pacific was similarly shortened when the Panama Canal was opened through the Isthmus of Panama between North and South America. A twentieth-century commercial map of the world showed the globe crossed in every direction by definite lanes over which innumerable freight and passenger ships were regularly plying from port to port.

But man's means of transportation were not limited to land and water; the twentieth century saw him utilizing the air also. The first attempt in modern times to sail in the air had occurred in 1783 when two Frenchmen named Montgolfier launched a balloon filled with gas. One hundred and twenty years later (1903), at Kittyhawk, North Carolina, a heavier-than-air machine, propelled by its own power and carrying a man, made a sustained flight when the airplane launched by Orville and Wilbur Wright flew for less than a minute and then landed safely. After this exploit, aviation advanced rapidly. Improvements were made in the construction of airplanes, in their motors, in methods of flight, and in the study of atmosphere. The development of a light air-cooled engine prepared the way for long sustained flights, and the magnetic compass and later the invention of an earth-inductor compass provided instruments for finding direction.

In 1909 Louis Blériot, a Frenchman, flew across the English Channel; ten years later John Alcock and Arthur W. Brown, British army officers, flew from Newfoundland to Ireland, a distance of about two thousand miles. American airplanes in 1924 flew from California around the world by way of Alaska, Japan, China, India, Europe, Greenland, and Boston, covering the distance in 175 days. Two years later Richard E. Byrd, an American naval officer, flew over the North Pole, and in 1927 Charles A. Lindbergh, an American, astonished the world by making a sensational nonstop transatlantic flight alone from New York to Paris, a distance of 3610 miles, in slightly more than thirty-three hours. In the same year an airplane flight was made across the Pacific from California to Honolulu, and in 1928 the first westward flight across the North Atlantic was made by two German aviators, who were forced down on an island off the coast of Labrador after a flight from Dublin. Thereafter new airplane records were made almost yearly.

The twentieth century saw, too, the balloon transformed into an airship when Count Ferdinand von Zeppelin, a German, invented a dirigible with a rigid frame, immense gas bag, and hanging cabins. Although the airship never became so common as the airplane, it soon began to establish travel records. In 1919 the Atlantic was crossed for the first time in the air by a British airship; ten years later the *Graf Zeppelin,* a German dirigible commanded by Hugo Eckener, circumnavigated the globe in less than twelve days of actual flying.

By this time aviation had been put upon a commercial basis. In 1919 an air line was started between London and Paris. Eventually regular passenger, mail, and express service was established not only between the chief cities on each continent, but also between the continents. In 1937 airplanes were regularly flying between Europe and Africa, South America, Asia, and Australia and between the United States and South America and the Far East. In 1936 a German dirigible, the *Hindenburg,* carried passengers regularly between Germany and the United States during the summer months and continued the service in 1937 until an explosion wrecked it, with the loss of a considerable number of lives. Dirigible service was then suspended, pending a decision regarding the use of noninflammable helium. In this same year, however, satisfactory experimental airplane flights were made between the United States and Great Britain over the North Atlantic, and it was not long until regular mail and passenger service was inaugurated over the Atlantic and the Pacific. In 1937, too, the possibility of an entirely new route of travel was opened up when Russian airplanes made nonstop flights from Moscow by way of the North Pole to the United States.

Until about the middle of the nineteenth century the speed of communication was limited to the speed of transportation, for messages had, in general, to be carried from one place to another. The second half of the century, however, saw communication emancipated from its age-long dependence upon transportation. In 1866 electric communication was successfully established between Europe and North America by means of a cable laid on the floor of the Atlantic. By 1870 two more transatlantic cables were in operation, and eventually the continents came to be linked together by some thousands of cables covering hundreds of thousands of miles. In the late seventies the telephone was introduced in Europe, and by 1900 hundreds of thousands of them were in operation. The last quarter of the nineteenth century saw men transmitting messages with undreamed-of speed across oceans, seas, and continents.

But the end was not yet. In the nineteenth century Heinrich Hertz, a German physicist, confirmed the theory advanced by a British physicist that invisible electric "waves" in the ether permeate all space and matter.

In 1896 Guglielmo Marconi, an Italian, availing himself of Hertz's discoveries, invented a mechanism to send and receive messages without wires by means of "Hertzian waves." In 1901 Marconi sent a wireless message across the Atlantic. Within a few years the wireless became an established and accepted means of communication. It not only enabled Europe to send messages to the most isolated places with almost lightning speed, but, applied to ships, it made possible constant contact between vessels and distant ports. Utilization of the wireless to broadcast storm warnings and to summon speedy aid to ships in distress resulted in saving the lives of thousands of voyagers.

With the development of locomotives capable of drawing heavy trains at a rate of sixty or seventy miles an hour, with the invention of engines powerful enough to drive huge ships across the Atlantic in five days, with the invention of devices to give almost instantaneous communication between the most distant places of the globe, space and time appeared to be nearly eliminated so far as the peoples of the earth were concerned. In the half century after 1870 the progress of the nations was accompanied by a notable "shrinking" of the globe.

The Revival of Interest in Colonial Expansion

This rapid "shrinking" of the world was accompanied by a revived interest in colonial expansion. During the half century preceding 1870 there had been among European statesmen a distinct distrust of colonies. Between 1776 and 1823 Great Britain, Spain, and Portugal had all seen their great and hard-won colonial empires shattered by declarations of independence. The truth of Turgot's eighteenth-century prediction, "Colonies are like fruits which cling to the tree only till they ripen," seemed borne out by the facts, and statesmen came to view colonial dependencies with a definite aversion. Furthermore, the doctrines of free trade and *laissez faire,* which swept Europe in the first half of the nineteenth century, logically undermined the economic foundations of colonial imperialism. Colonies were, so to speak, *territoria non grata.*

But the tremendous industrial expansion and the veritable revolution in transportation and communication which came after 1870 changed all this. Each of the great industrial countries soon reached the place where it was manufacturing more than its own people could consume. Each, in other words, sought foreign markets. But none of the great industrial countries wished to be the dumping ground for another's surplus, and consequently all except Great Britain erected protective tariff barriers during the last quarter of the nineteenth century. To manufacturers looking for markets for their surplus goods, therefore, the prospect of colonies whose markets could be monopolized by the mother country began to have a great appeal in the eighties and nineties of the last century.

With the expansion of industry came, too, the need for assured and easily accessible supplies of those raw materials which went into the manufacture of finished products. Vegetable oils were required for the production of such commodities as tin plate, paint, and lubricants. Manganese was needed for steel mills, and jute for the manufacture of the millions of bags in which goods are packed for shipment. The introduction of the bicycle and later of the automobile led to a growing demand for rubber, and the development of oil-burning and internal-combustion engines tremendously increased the consumption of petroleum. Added sources of food supplies were needed, also, for the sustenance of the increased millions who were devoting themselves no longer directly to the raising of foodstuffs but to the production of manufactured goods. The rise in the general standard of living, moreover, brought an increased demand for tropical and subtropical products—fruits, coffee, cocoa, tea, and sugar. To the desire for colonies as new markets for surplus manufactures was added, therefore, the desire to have them as assured sources of foodstuffs, minerals, and raw materials.

The revolutionary changes in the means of transportation and communication which came after 1870 provided an added incentive for the acquisition of colonies. The cheapness, speed, and dispatch with which bulky and heavy goods could be transported in large and swift steamships made it increasingly profitable to bring such goods to Europe. Cheap transportation, furthermore, greatly widened the area in which Europe's manufactured products could be profitably marketed. During the eighties refrigeration was successfully installed in steamships, and a new era was opened for the tropics and for regions far distant from Europe. Without deterioration frozen or chilled meats, fresh fruits, butter, cheese, and eggs could now be brought to Europe from far-flung colonial empires.

The punctuality and regularity introduced into ocean transportation by lines of steamships which plied between important points according to stated time schedules brought a greater degree of certainty into overseas trade. This was further increased by means of the telegraph and the cable, which closely knit far-distant lands with Europe. Business communications became easier, and transactions were shortened. Consignments became less of a speculation, goods were shipped to order, and the contact between buyer and seller became more direct.

Furthermore, the lessened cost of railway construction and operation after 1870 greatly accelerated the opening up of vast new areas overseas. Railways could circumvent rapids, could cross deserts, and could surmount or tunnel through mountains. They were not, like draft animals, killed by the tsetse fly of tropical Africa. They were not vitally affected by ice or snow, tropical heat, or malaria. The fact that goods could be profitably transported to and from distant interiors encouraged the penetration of unexploited continents in the search for raw materials and markets.

In the closing years of the nineteenth century still another factor provided an incentive for the acquisition of colonies. Vast accumulations of "surplus capital," resulting from the profitable industrial and commercial expansion of the period, called for reinvestment. The same capital which would earn 3 or 4 per cent in agricultural improvements in a settled country like France, it was pointed out, would bring from 10 to 20 per cent in an agricultural enterprise in South America, Canada, Australia, or New Zealand. Sums invested in new railway construction in a country like Great Britain would earn scarcely more than 2 or 3 per cent, but they would earn up to 20 per cent in similar undertakings in new lands. The desire for opportunities to invest surplus profits in the backward places of the earth, therefore, prompted bankers to join merchants and mill-owners in the demand for colonies.

Many who were not directly concerned in the financial side of colonial expansion—who were not manufacturers, exporters, shipowners, or bankers—often came to favor the acquisition of colonies. Christian missionaries and those interested in Christian missions frequently advocated imperial expansion. David Livingstone, the famous missionary to Africa, for instance, sought to have Great Britain extend her rule over that Dark Continent in order that slavery might be destroyed and Christianity and Western civilization introduced. Sometimes missionaries in heathen lands called upon their homeland to raise its protecting flag above them; at other times they persuaded converted chieftains to swear allegiance to the government of the country from which they themselves came. At home, missionary societies and religious leaders became interested in Africa, Asia, and the Pacific isles and frequently urged statesmen to extend their own Christian government over pagan lands. Unwittingly, often, the missionary advanced the cause of the economic imperialist by teaching heathen tribes to wear Western clothes and to use Western tools. Sometimes, too, a missionary's death at the hands of pagan savages provided statesmen of the homeland with a reason or a pretext for conquest.[7]

Finally, many patriots sought to gratify their possessive instinct by increasing the "national wealth" of the homeland through the acquisition of colonies or profitable concessions abroad. They sought the confidence which came with the knowledge that their country controlled essential raw materials, that their cannon would never lack shells, their warships

[7] See page 73.

never be without fuel, their laboratories never seek vainly for ingredients of explosives. They sought, too, the comfort which came from the belief that overseas colonies provided added reservoirs of man power as well as naval bases for use in future defensive wars. They believed that colonies could serve as outlets for their country's surplus population,[8] and that their emigrants might be diverted from foreign countries to the colonies and thus retained within the empire as producers of wealth and as potential soldiers in time of war. They sought, as well, the satisfaction which came from their ability to point with pride, on the map of the world, to the various territories controlled by their particular country.

Economic Imperialism after 1870

In the closing decades of the nineteenth century, accordingly, there occurred in Europe an extraordinary revival of colonial imperialism. French patriots announced that the conquest of colonies was France's *mission civilisatrice;* Italian statesmen proclaimed it a "sacred duty"; and Englishmen considered it as "the white man's burden" which no civilized people should shirk. Germany, after at first abstaining from empire-building, ultimately plunged boldly into the quest for colonies and economic concessions. Austria-Hungary strove valiantly to gain the ascendancy in the Balkans, while Russia, not content with her great realm in Europe and Siberia, "stretched acquisitive hands into Central Asia, Persia, Manchuria, and Mongolia, and looked hungrily on Turkey, Tibet, and Afghanistan." The frenzied scramble for colonies which ensued among the chief powers of the world brought conflicts far greater than those of the eighteenth century.

Down to the last quarter of the nineteenth century more than 90 per cent of Africa was as yet unappropriated by the European powers, and it constituted still an unknown and impenetrable land—the Dark Continent. The earlier period of colonization had done little more than trace the coastline of central Africa and had resulted merely in the establishment of European trading posts along the coast at the mouths of some of the rivers. In the interior most of the natives still lived in small tribal units, with here and there a little despotic kingdom. In the second quarter of the nineteenth century, however, the desire to convert these heathen Negroes prompted Christian organizations to send in missionaries, probably the most famous of whom was the Scotsman, David Livingstone.

Livingstone went to Africa in 1840, but, becoming more interested in exploration than in exhortation, he ultimately decided to give up his

---

[8] For a discussion of the rapid growth of population in Europe in the nineteenth century, see page 27.

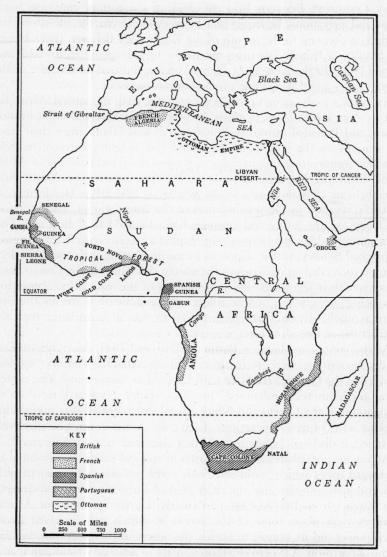

ATLANTIC
OCEAN

E U R O P E

Black Sea

Caspian Sea

MEDITERRANEAN
SEA

Strait of Gibraltar

FRENCH
ALGERIA

A S I A

OTTOMAN
EMPIRE

LIBYAN
DESERT

TROPIC OF CANCER

S A H A R A

Nile R.

RED SEA

SENEGAL

Senegal
R.

GAMBIA

GUINEA

FR.
GUINEA

SIERRA
LEONE

Niger R.

S U D A N

OBOCK

TROPICAL

PORTO NOVO

FOREST

IVORY COAST

GOLD COAST

LAGOS

C E N T R A L

EQUATOR

SPANISH
GUINEA

GABUN

R.

A F R I C A

ATLANTIC

Congo R.

ANGOLA

Zambesi R.

MOÇAMBIQUE

OCEAN

MADAGASCAR

TROPIC OF CAPRICORN

KEY

British
French
Spanish
Portuguese
Ottoman

Scale of Miles
0   250   500   750   1000

CAPE COLONY   NATAL

INDIAN
OCEAN

AFRICAN POSSESSIONS OF EUROPEAN POWERS ABOUT 1870

position as a missionary and devote the rest of his life to opening up the Dark Continent. Between 1854 and 1871, at the cost of countless hardships and privations, he explored central Africa from the mouth of the Congo on the west to the mouth of the Zambesi on the east. Later Henry M. Stanley, a British-American journalist, in attempting to find Livingstone (1871) for the *New York Herald*, became himself an explorer of the Congo basin and Livingstone's most famous successor.

As, thanks to the efforts of the explorers, the map of tropical Africa began to show rivers, lakes, plateaus, and mountains, Great Britain, France, Spain, and Portugal moved their national claims inland from their trading stations on the west coast. Germany and Belgium entered the field as added competitors, and, in order to prevent the rapid partition of Africa from disturbing the general peace of Europe, international conferences were held in 1876 and again in the winter of 1884–1885. The former, at Brussels, resulted in the organization of the International Association of the Congo by the astute and grasping King Leopold II of Belgium. This association had as its purpose the exploitation of central Africa, and dispatched Stanley to that region as its agent. During the years 1879–1882 Stanley succeeded in persuading the native chieftains of the Congo basin to convert their territories into protectorates of the association—protectorates being areas where native rulers were permitted to retain the outward symbols of power but were forced to rule in accordance with the instructions of a resident foreign agent.

At the conference held in Berlin in 1884 and 1885 the rights of Leopold's association were recognized, and its African territory was organized as the Congo Free State with Leopold as "sovereign." The conference, furthermore, condemned the slave trade, advocated freedom of navigation on the Congo and Niger rivers, and required due notification to other states of new annexations of territory. A region must be effectively occupied, it declared, before it could be recognized as a protectorate.

Africa, an unexploited continent, rich in tropical products, inhabited by backward tribes which could offer only feeble resistance to modern military conquest, now became the chief field of Europe's colonial endeavors. In the years from 1890 to 1900, particularly, a great scramble for African territory took place, some of the details of which will be given later.[9] Each power did its utmost to outwit the others in the great and thrilling game of partition. A Negro chieftain's "mark" on a treaty blank, no matter how obtained, was cited as conclusive evidence that his lands had become a protectorate of the power which held the treaty. Bribes and gifts were freely bestowed, and intimidation was far from unknown. Within a very short time, in consequence, nearly the entire continent had been ap-

[9] See pages 117–122, 139–140, 170–173.

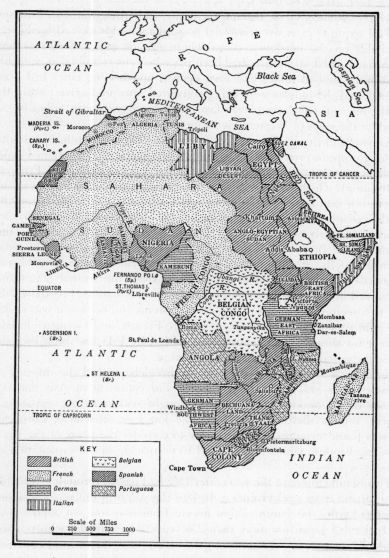

ATLANTIC
OCEAN

EUROPE

Black Sea

Caspian Sea

MEDITERRANEAN

Strait of Gibraltar

ASIA

MADERIA IS.
(Port.)   Morocco

Algiers Tunis

ALGERIA TUNIS

Tripoli

SEA

CANARY IS.
(Sp.)

Fez
MOROCCO

LIBYA

Cairo SUEZ CANAL

RIO
DE
ORO

LIBYAN
DESERT

EGYPT

TROPIC OF CANCER

SAHARA

SENEGAL
GAMBIA
PORT GUINEA

SUDAN

Khartum

Asmara ERITREA

FR. SOMALILAND
BR. SOMA-
LILAND

Freetown
SIERRA LEONE
Monrovia

NIGERIA

ANGLO-EGYPTIAN
SUDAN

LIBERIA
Akkra

DAHOMEY
Lagos

KAMERUN

Addis Ababa
ETHIOPIA

FERNANDO PO I.
(Sp.)
ST. THOMAS I.
(Port.) Libreville

Ubangi R.

UGANDA
BRITISH
EAST
AFRIC

EQUATOR

FRENCH CONGO

R.
Congo

Victoria
Nyanza

ASCENSION I.
(Br.)

BELGIAN
CONGO

GERMAN
EAST
AFRICA

Mombasa
Zanzibar
Dar-es-Salem

St. Paul de Loanda

Boma

L.
Tanganyika

ATLANTIC

ANGOLA

OCEAN

RHODESIA

L.
Nyasa

Mozambique

MADAGASCAR

ST HELENA I.
(Br.)

Salisbury

Tanana-
rive

GERMAN
SOUTHWEST
AFRICA

Windhoek

BECHUANA-
LAND

MOZAMBIQUE

TROPIC OF CAPRICORN

Pretoria
TRANS-
VAAL

ORANGE
FREE STATE

Pietermaritzburg
Bloemfontein

CAPE
COLONY

Cape Town

INDIAN

OCEAN

KEY

British	Belgian
French	Spanish
German	Portuguese
Italian	

Scale of Miles
0   250 500 750 1000

AFRICAN POSSESSIONS OF EUROPEAN POWERS IN 1914

propriated by European powers, though vast areas of the hinterland were as yet ineffectively occupied.

By 1914 France, Great Britain, Germany, Italy, Belgium, and Portugal had all acquired extensive territorial possessions in Africa, and Spain had footholds on the northwest coast. Thousands of miles of railway had been constructed, steamships had been placed on rivers and lakes, valuable gold and diamond mines had been opened up, thriving cities had been erected, and the jungles were being converted into productive farmlands. In the interior, tribal wars were fast disappearing as savage tribes began to adopt the ways of Western civilization.

Although in many places native rulers still exercised nominal authority under European protection, only two regions in all Africa retained independent governments. One of these was the isolated empire of Ethiopia (Abyssinia), which was saved from incorporation in Italian Eritrea in the nineteenth century largely by the rugged nature of the country and the warlike character of its inhabitants.[10] An agreement between Great Britain, France, and Italy assured the political independence of this country, but in matters of finance and industry it was more or less dependent upon French and British capitalists. The other independent state was Liberia, founded largely by liberated Negro slaves from the United States and organized in 1847 as a free republic. But even this state was partially subject to foreign tutelage, for in matters of customs and finance it was under the joint supervision of American, British, French, and German officials. Except for these two states, however, Africa, by 1914 had been brought completely under the domination of Europe.

But Africa was not the only part of the globe to feel the impress of Europe's new imperialistic impulse; the vast continent of Asia and the islands of the South Seas were also brought within its ever-expanding sphere. But, in their exploitation of the Far East after 1870, European powers found it increasingly necessary to consider the plans of the virile Japanese Empire, which wished itself to participate in the exploitation of Asia.

This island empire in the years after 1867 had passed through a veritable political and economic revolution. In 1867 the youthful mikado Mutsuhito was freed from the domination of his chief officer or *shogun*, whose family had ruled Japan for more than 250 years. The mikado, who reigned until 1912, inaugurated a regime of progress and enlightenment. Feudalism was abolished, the government was centralized and made more efficient, and a national army and a modern navy were established under the direction of European officers. In an attempt to make Japan the equal of the Western powers, foreigners were invited into the country, and Japanese

[10] See page 140.

commissions were sent abroad to study European institutions. Western learning was introduced, Western codes of law were adopted, religious toleration was granted, and in 1889 a written constitution, based on European models, was promulgated. Western methods of industry were introduced, and in the last quarter of the nineteenth century Japan became a modern industrial power. And, as happened in Europe, so in Japan, imperialists were soon demanding colonial expansion to obtain markets, foods, raw materials, and outlets for the country's dense population.

Prior to 1870 the European powers had already taken some steps to establish their control in the Far East. Great Britain had set up her rule in India, France had occupied Cochin-China and Cambodia in Indo-China, Russia had appropriated the vast but dreary expanse of Siberia, the Netherlands and Great Britain had established themselves in the East Indies, and Spain in the Philippine Islands. A beginning had also been made in opening up China to European merchants and missionaries. As the result of wars waged against the Chinese Empire by Great Britain and France in 1840–1842 and in 1856–1860, eleven ports had been opened to foreign traders, foreign ministers had secured the right to reside in Peiping (then called Peking), Europeans had been granted the right to travel in the interior, Christian missionaries had been assured the protection of the Chinese government, and Great Britain had acquired the island of Hongkong and a foothold on the mainland adjoining.

During the succeeding years the vast Chinese Empire with its three hundred million inhabitants was a constant temptation to the imperialistic powers. Unlike Japan, her sister empire, China was long deterred by prejudice, a notion of self-sufficiency, and conservatism from embarking upon a program of modernization in the Western sense. Her armies and navies were therefore helpless before the powerful military and naval machines of modern imperialism and were unable to prevent the exploitation and spoliation of the empire. Gradually, however, an intense resentment developed among the Chinese, resulting, toward the close of the nineteenth century, in popular attacks on missionaries and other foreigners who were accused of undermining the ancient traditions of China.

In the year 1900 the local riots grew into an anti-European rebellion, led particularly by members of the secret society of Boxers. The latter insisted that China's misfortunes were due to the displeasure of their ancestors, whose memory was desecrated by locomotives speeding over their graves. They denounced the recently introduced machinery for throwing workmen out of employment, and called upon all patriotic Chinese to rise in defense of their country. A large part of the population of northern China was won over, and soon the European legation quarters in Peiping were crowded with frightened foreigners, besieged by the fanatical Chinese.

Great Britain, Germany, Russia, Japan, and the United States rushed troops to rescue the legations and to punish the Boxers. A relief expedition fought its way from Tientsin to Peiping and brought assistance to the beleaguered foreigners. Unfortunately, the scandalous conduct of European troops, who wantonly pillaged Peiping, sorely disgraced the Western world. The attempt of the Chinese to expel foreign influences from their country in the so-called Boxer War was severely punished. A heavy indemnity of $320,000,000 was levied,[11] and a promise to repress all antiforeign societies was exacted. The futility of attempting to shut out Western powers without borrowing from them the political, economic, and military methods which gave them their superiority was deeply impressed upon many of the Chinese.

In 1905 the dowager empress gave up her opposition to the Westernization of China and began the reorganization of the Chinese army on European lines. The building of railways under Chinese control was encouraged. The ancient classical system of education was abolished, and Western science and modern languages were substituted. In 1907, yielding to pressure from the progressive group, she promised a constitution and announced that representative government would be gradually introduced. Unfortunately, the dowager empress died in 1908, leaving the throne to a two-year-old boy. The regent who was appointed was a weakling, incapable of handling the national assembly which was convened in 1910. The government's attempt to suppress certain radicals in the South, where secret societies had been organized to work for the establishment of a democratic republic, led to the outbreak of revolution in the Yangtse valley. In 1912 the struggle resulted in the deposition of the boy-emperor and the establishment of a republic.

Foreign powers immediately took advantage of the confusion in China to advance their own interests. Russia compelled the new Chinese government to recognize most of Mongolia, referred to as Outer Mongolia, as an autonomous province under conditions which made it practically a Russian protectorate. Great Britain took steps somewhat similar. When Tibet revolted against the Chinese republic, the British government forbade the Chinese to suppress the revolt, and China accordingly lost actual authority in that great province, which tended more and more to become a British sphere of influence.

By 1914 China's tributary kingdoms of Burma, Annam, Tonkin, and Korea and the great island of Formosa had been wrested from her. Four

[11] Part of her share of the indemnity was renounced by the United States and was used by China to educate Chinese students in America. In 1925 the United States renounced the balance of her share in the indemnity in order that it might be used to advance scientific education in China. The balance of Russia's share of the indemnity was renounced by the Soviet government soon after it came into power in Russia in 1917.

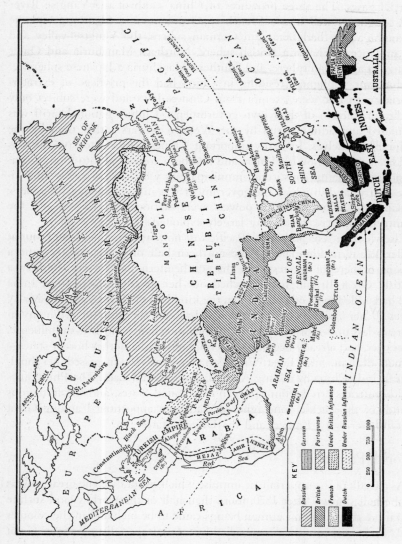

ASIATIC POSSESSIONS OF EUROPEAN POWERS IN 1914

important ports had been leased to foreign powers as naval and commercial bases. The three provinces of China south of the Yangtse River had been converted into a French sphere of interest. Shantung and the Hoangho valley had become a German sphere, the Yangtse valley and the province of Shansi a British sphere, Northern Manchuria and Outer Mongolia a Russian sphere, and Southern Manchuria a Japanese sphere.

Moreover, foreigners residing in China had the privilege of extraterritoriality, that is, were exempt from Chinese laws and were subject only to the jurisdiction of their own governments. China's national tariff was regulated and administered by the Western powers rather than by the Chinese themselves. In many important Chinese cities extensive districts had been acquired by foreigners and had been converted into foreign concessions. The latter constituted municipalities which were free from Chinese control and in which the government was in the hands of foreigners. Troops of various Western powers were stationed in China, and the country's resources were being largely exploited by foreign capital.

Elsewhere in Asia and in the Pacific vast new stretches had been brought under Western domination. The northern half of Persia had become a Russian sphere of interest and the southeastern part of the country a British. Great Britain had stretched out her greedy fingers from India and had added most of Baluchistan, the kingdom of Burma, and the Malay states to her Asiatic empire, and had brought the amir of Afghanistan more or less under British control. British merchants and British influence, moreover, had already begun to penetrate into India's other border states— Nepal, Bhutan, and Tibet. France had extensively increased her holdings in Indo-China by adding Annam, Tonkin, and Laos. The Philippines had been transferred from Spain to the United States, and the numerous islands of the Pacific, long ignored, had been apportioned among Great Britain, Germany, France, and the United States.

World Politics

As a result of the imperialistic impulse which swept over the great powers in the half century after 1870, more than half of the world's land surface and more than a billion human beings came to be included in the colonies and "backward countries" controlled by a few imperialistic nations. Great Britain had ten times more colonial subjects of other races than she had British citizens. France had twenty times as great an area in her territories overseas as she had in Europe. Italy was one sixth as large as her colonies, Portugal, one twenty-third, Belgium, one eightieth. The nations of western Europe became dwarfs beside their colonial possessions." [12]

[12] The above statements and much of the concluding discussion in this chapter are based upon Parker T. Moon's enlightening volume, *Imperialism and World Politics*, pages 1–4.

As imperialism had given birth to world-wide empires, so, too, it brought into being world-wide diplomacy. As the succeeding chapters will show, European statesmen became actors on a stage as broad as the earth. Bargains struck by European diplomats and secretly signed in some European capital often affected the destinies of unwitting millions scattered over the globe. In 1904, for instance, Great Britain and France entered into an agreement which dealt with Newfoundland in America, Morocco and Egypt in Africa, Siam in Asia, and the New Hebrides Islands in the Pacific.[13] Three years later Russia and Great Britain struck a bargain which affected the future of Persians in the Middle East, Afghans on the borders of India, and the inhabitants of Tibet on the outskirts of the Chinese Empire.[14]

Alliances and ententes came to have a new meaning. Desire to protect imperial interests was the key to the Anglo-Japanese alliance of 1902.[15] Desire to increase imperial holdings was the basis of the Anglo-French entente of 1904.[16] Fears aroused by Germany's imperialistic ambitions in the Ottoman Empire were the explanation of Great Britain's willingness to drop her century-long opposition to Russia in favor of an entente with that country.[17] Common desire to advance their imperialistic schemes of aggrandizement constituted the reason for Franco-Italian agreements in 1900 and 1902.[18]

The international crises which shook Europe from time to time during the two decades before the First World War were but surface manifestations of the swift, deep current of imperialism. In 1898 Great Britain and France trembled on the verge of war in the famous Fashoda crisis,[19] and the cause was their rivalry for a million or more square miles of territory in the African Sudan. The Moroccan crises of 1905 and 1911,[20] which so nearly plunged all Europe into war, were merely two more of those explosions which were caused from time to time when the aims of imperialistic nations chanced to cross. The war of 1914 itself was in part the product of imperialism. The alignment of the European powers in that conflict was dictated not by race or democracy or kinship of culture, but by imperialism. Germany, Austria-Hungary, and Turkey were brought together by Teutonic domination of the Near East. Latin France and Teutonic Britain were united by their imperialistic bargain of 1904; liberal Britain and autocratic Russia, by their imperialistic agreement of 1907.

[13] See page 117.
[14] See page 190.
[15] See page 179.
[16] See page 117.
[17] See page 190.
[18] See pages 116, 117.
[19] See page 116.
[20] See pages 117–122.

Europe's history after 1870 became, thus, a history not merely of that continent but of the world; her statesmen were forced to concern themselves not with continental affairs alone, but with world politics. And the root and *raison d'être* of world politics was imperialism.

Chapter II

SOCIAL CHANGES, PROBLEMS, AND

PROGRAMS

THE vast industrial expansion discussed in the preceding chapter not only brought a tremendous increase in manufactured goods, a re-awakened interest in imperialism, and an era of world politics, but also contributed to the enormous increase and urbanization of population, the appearance of new economic and social evils, the clash of antagonistic social classes, and the formulation of new programs for the social and economic betterment of mankind. Any full comprehension of the domestic history of the chief countries of Europe after 1870 requires, therefore, a realization that, wherever modern industrialism gained a foothold, there occurred a social revolution which was in its effects both far-reaching and profound.

Growth and Urbanization of Population

The nineteenth and twentieth centuries witnessed an amazing growth in the population of Europe, a growth which was considerably accelerated in the years after 1870. During the century ending in 1870 the increase in Europe's population had been at the rate of approximately 16 per cent for each twenty-year period. In the years from 1870 to 1890, however, the rate rose to 20 per cent, and in the succeeding twenty-year period (1890–1910) it mounted to 26 per cent. By 1901 Great Britain's population, which stood at 23,000,000 in 1871, had increased to 40,000,000. Similarly, in the forty years after 1871 Germany's population rose from 41,000,000 to 65,-000,000, while that of Italy grew from less than 27,000,000 to 36,000,000.

At the opening of the nineteenth century the total population of Europe was 175,000,000; at the outbreak of the First World War it stood at approximately 450,000,000 despite the fact that some 40,000,000 Europeans had emigrated to other parts of the world. Were Europe's rate of population increase for the period from 1890 to 1910 to continue without further emigration, the end of the twentieth century would see some 1,230,000,000 persons crowded into that small continent. The relation between this rapidly increasing population and the demand for colonial expansion after 1870 has already been discussed.[1]

Two important factors made possible this phenomenal increase in population. In the first place, the conquest of disease and the throttling of pestilence brought a marked decline in the death rate and an equally notable lengthening of the span of life. Thanks to Joseph Lister's introduction of the techniques of antisepsis and to Louis Pasteur's discovery of micro-organisms and the resultant acceptance of the germ theory of disease, a relentless warfare upon bacteria was inaugurated in the eighties of the nineteenth century. The patient work of thousands of keen-eyed and painstaking men, working in clinics and laboratories, gradually exposed disease to light; vaccination and inoculation, general sanitation, and personal hygiene did much to vanquish it, especially among the infantile, juvenile, and early adult groups.

Astounding results ensued, particularly in the reduction of the rate of infant mortality. In the last fifty years of the eighteenth century half of the children born in London died before they were two years old. By 1925, however, the infantile death rate had been so reduced by modern hygiene and medicine that London was losing only about seven babies in a hundred during their first year. This was also true for England as a whole; and altogether, by 1925, thirteen countries in the world had succeeded in reducing their infantile mortality rate for the first year to not more than 10 per cent.

At the same time the campaign against infectious diseases brought down the figures for deaths from that cause in a truly marvelous way. Diphtheria, scarlet fever, and typhoid fever, it was discovered, could be largely eliminated by inoculation, yellow fever could be wiped out, and epidemics of cholera, typhus, and plague could be prevented. Cures were found, likewise, for some goiters and for syphilis; a means of relieving the symptoms of diabetes was found; and tuberculosis, though not eliminated, was lessened. In 1850 some 94 per cent of all deaths were caused by infections; in 1925 only about 50 per cent came from that cause. Gradually, therefore, the span of life was lengthened.[2] During the seventeenth and eighteenth centuries, it is said, human life was being extended in Europe at the rate of about four years a century. In the first three quarters of the nineteenth century, the rate was increased to nine years a century; the last quarter of the century saw it rise to seventeen. One of the chief

[1] See page 16.

[2] "Whereas in England today at the age of fifteen the expectation of life for boys is forty-five and for girls forty-eight years, in Rome it was twenty and fifteen years respectively; whereas in England at the age of thirty the expectation of life for men is thirty-three and for women thirty-six years, in Rome it was nineteen and fourteen years respectively." E. A. Ross, *Standing Room Only?*, page 73.

reasons for Europe's rapid growth in population after 1870 was, accordingly, not an increasing birth rate but a decreasing death rate.

But people, in order to live, must have something upon which to subsist, and this was the contribution of the Industrial and Agricultural Revolutions. The vast increase in the world's wealth—that is, in goods which may be used to satisfy human needs—which resulted from the Industrial Revolution has already been pointed out.[3] Although agriculture did not keep pace with industry in the application of science to production, great strides were nevertheless made after 1870 in opening up and cultivating immense wheat areas in the Americas and elsewhere. Large farms in these regions stimulated invention, and beginning in the latter part of the nineteenth century agricultural machinery was considerably improved. Rotary plows, combination harvesting and threshing machines, and tractors brought not only an increase in cultivated area but a decrease in the man power required for farming. These developments resulted in a lowered cost of production, which, combined with cheap transportation, made it possible for Europe to import large quantities of foodstuffs, paying for them in manufactured goods. The application of chemistry to agriculture in Germany and other countries, furthermore, helped to improve the productiveness of the soil and to increase the yield of foodstuffs in Europe itself. Increased food supplies, in conjunction with the extensive transportation facilities available after 1870, effectively did away with the danger of famine in most of Europe, and accordingly removed one of those checks upon population which in the Middle Ages had been so powerful.

But the Industrial and Agricultural Revolutions not only made possible the existence of a much larger population; they were responsible likewise for the great growth of cities in Europe in recent times. The building of huge factories necessitated the dwelling together in a small area of thousands of workmen, and the tendency of allied industries to locate in the same place accelerated this movement. The artisans, in turn, required others to serve them, and the consequent addition of "the butcher, the baker, the candlestick maker" still further increased the population of the community. Strategically located places became the centers of transportation systems, and thus still greater numbers congregated from among the transport workers. The quest for higher wages, the desire for superior industrial, social, and educational opportunities, and the lure of the city's companionships and amusements, furthermore, drew thousands from the farm to the city. A marked concentration of people in large urban centers resulted, especially in the more highly industrialized areas.

In 1871 England and Wales had thirteen cities with more than 100,000

[3] See pages 5–7

population; twenty years later they had twenty-four. In the same period the number of their cities with 20,000 or more inhabitants increased from 103 to 185. A similar development took place also in Prussia. In 1871 the latter had only four cities of over 100,000 population; by 1895 the number had increased to eighteen. In fact, the growth of cities was pronounced throughout all Europe. At the beginning of the nineteenth century there were only fourteen European cities with more than 100,000 inhabitants; a century later there were 140 such cities.[4] Several cities came to have a population of considerably more than a million.[5] In western Europe during the nineteenth and twentieth centuries, as in the civilized centuries of antiquity, city life came to predominate over rural life.

But the growth of large cities came to constitute perhaps the greatest of all the problems of modern civilization. Out of it arose such new questions and problems as those of diminished rural labor supply, urban labor organization and unrest, dwindling district schools and overcrowded and half-time city schools, municipal transit and sanitation and taxation, poverty, the tenement house, and the "submerged tenth"—in short, a very large share of the maladjustments and physical and moral wastes of civilization.[6] On the other hand, closer association in urban communities made men's minds more open and alert, readier to question existing evils, more insistent upon changes to remedy them, and more able through combination and co-operation to alter them. The great political, economic, and educational reform movements of recent times had their beginnings in the cities.

Changes in Social Classes

Wherever factories made their appearance, there too appeared inevitably the capitalist and the workingman. Machinery and factories were costly. Raw materials, furthermore, had to be purchased and wages paid before any return could be received from the sale of goods. The ordinary artisan was usually in no position to make these advances, and so, consequently, a small number of moneyed men everywhere came into possession of the new means of production and were enabled thereby to reap the financial rewards of the new era. Industrial profits were frequently large, and im-

[4] Of only two cities—Paris and Constantinople—can it be affirmed with confidence that their population at any time during the Middle Ages exceeded one hundred thousand, although it is possible that London also attained this figure. F. A. Ogg and W. R. Sharp, *Economic Development of Modern Europe*, page 13.

[5] London grew from less than a million (1801) to over seven million (1911), Berlin from 826,000 (1871) to over two million (1910), Moscow from 751,000 (1882) to 1,617,157 (1914), and Leningrad (then St. Petersburg) from less than a million (1882) to over two million (1914).

[6] Ogg and Sharp, *op. cit.*, pages 336–337.

mense fortunes were accumulated by those who were clever and bold. Soon the industrial capitalists were in control of wealth far beyond the fondest dreams of the most avaricious aristocrats and merchants of the old regime.

Modern industrialism produced, however, not only a new capitalist class but a new wage-earning class, the proletariat. Under the factory system the machine workers, drawn largely from the farm or from the old type of handicraft, became almost wholly dependent upon the industrial capitalists for their means of livelihood. Facing the alternative of working or starving, they toiled for long hours at wages arbitrarily fixed by the factory owner. When factories came to employ hundreds of workmen, the individual was lost in the mass and became merely a numbered "hand." Between the worker and his employer there came to be no personal contact, only a "cash nexus," as it has been called. The factory-owner paid a definite sum—wages—for a definite amount of work, and, having paid it, he felt under no further obligation to his men. Furthermore, as industry expanded, the huge factories were owned no longer by a single capitalist but by great corporations which consisted of hundreds or even thousands of stockholders. Under such conditions most of the owners knew little about the business, which they entrusted to managers; they were interested in it only as a source of dividends. That their large dividends were sometimes made possible by the evil conditions under which their workmen labored, such owners often never realized.

The new industrial capitalists became a part of the bourgeoisie and by their wealth and power tipped the scales decisively in favor of this group, which had been rising into prominence since the Commercial Revolution. The influence of the old landed aristocracy, already on the wane, in the period after 1870 definitely gave way in western Europe to the power of the wealthy bourgeoisie.[7] In fact, in many cases the landed nobleman of the later nineteenth century began to invest a portion of his wealth in the stocks of corporations managed or directed by the bourgeoisie, and thus came to be partially identified in his economic interests with this group. As the years went by, tradesmen, professional men, skilled artisans, and even some of the more thrifty peasants were occasionally able to invest small amounts in industrial stocks or bonds, and thus, almost unwittingly, linked their interests with those of the capitalist class.

The influence and power of the industrial capitalists in the years after 1870 were enormous. Millions of factory workers and their families were dependent upon them for their livelihood. Thousands of clerks and other "white-collar" office workers were hardly more free. The welfare of trades-

---

[7] In eastern Europe the decline of the landed aristocracy came more especially after the First World War.

men and professionals in hundreds of industrial centers rested largely in turn upon the workers in factory and office to whom they catered. The closing down of a great industry was a calamity not to the factory workers of the community alone, but to thousands of others indirectly dependent upon it. Grocers and bakers, barbers and tailors, doctors and dentists, plumbers and tinsmiths, landlords and clergy all discovered that their own prosperity was linked, indirectly at least, with that of the "captains of industry." Even the peasant learned that the price of his farm products was in some way related to the prosperity of the bourgeoisie. The power which the latter wielded in directing national policies, therefore, was exceedingly great. In western Europe they became the ruling class, carrying on the nation's business, dominating its society, and in general lording it over the workingmen.

The Bourgeoisie versus the Proletariat

The early industrial capitalists readily adopted the economic philosophy of Adam Smith and the French physiocrats, and advocated that the government should remove all artificial restrictions which interfered with the processes of production and distribution, that the state should pursue a policy of "no interference" (*laissez faire*). Obviously, if the government could be prevailed upon to abandon its regulative program, the bourgeoisie would be free to develop in their own way the natural resources of the world, and this was exactly what they desired. Manufacturers and capitalists believed, furthermore, in the philosophy of man's "natural rights" and held that one of these was his right to make money in whatever way he might choose. They were firmly convinced of the soundness of economic individualism, and maintained that life was, after all, essentially a struggle in which the unfit must perish and the best inevitably come to the top.

Industrial liberty, which was largely achieved for a time in the nineteenth century, was undoubtedly a great boon to the capitalists. To the new class of industrial laborers, however, it was something quite the reverse. Practically everywhere, in the early transitional stages of the modern industrial era, the factory worker was exploited and depressed. His helpless condition, without either land or tools, compelled him to accept work on such terms as were offered. Wages were accordingly low and hours of labor long. Ill-ventilated, poorly lighted, unsanitary factories menaced health and morals. The threat of unemployment, resulting from recurring industrial crises, further technological improvements, or the displacement of men by cheaper women and children, was ever present. Usually the workmen and their families were crowded together in dirty slums near the factory, where cheerless homes in cheap tenements only too often drove them to spend their "free" time in the corner saloon. Drunkenness and immorality were rife. Disease, the result of filth and the lack of hygienic necessities, periodically swept off its victims by the hundreds.

When the factory workers learned by bitter experience that they could not as individuals successfully bargain with their employers in regard to their hours, wages, and working conditions, they sought naturally to combine in self-defense with their fellow-workmen. But everywhere they encountered hostile legislation. Everywhere trade unionism in the beginning was looked upon by the governing classes as a criminal movement, and workers who joined unions or took part in strikes were liable to punishment. Not until 1824–1825 did it become lawful to organize a trade union in Great Britain, and not until the seventies were the legal restrictions removed which long interfered with the effective use of the strike. Prior to 1869 the right of labor to combine was legally denied in all German states, and in France, although trade unions were tolerated by the government after 1864–1868, it was only in 1884 that they received full recognition. During the first half of the nineteenth century, therefore, in industrial disputes between workers and employers, the former found themselves almost helpless.

If laws stood in the way of trade unions and the workers' right to combine, then, concluded the workingmen, the laws must be changed. But here again the proletariat was handicapped. Although the middle class of France and Great Britain gained political rights in the thirties, nowhere in Europe in the first half of the nineteenth century did the workingman have power in the government which ruled him. Inevitably arose the demand for political reform. The Chartists of Great Britain, for example, during the decade from 1838 to 1848, insisted that every adult man should be given the franchise, that voting should be by secret ballot, that property qualifications for membership in the House of Commons should be abolished, and that members should receive salaries. By such reforms workingmen hoped to gain for themselves not only the right to elect members of Parliament but the right to be elected themselves. In this way, they believed, they could safeguard themselves against legislation hostile to their interests. But the Chartist movement and similar efforts failed, and not until about 1870 did workingmen gain the ballot, and then only in Great Britain, Germany, and France.[8] The struggle for democratic government, therefore, was one of the great movements carried over into the period after 1870.

[8] For Great Britain, see page 154; for Germany, see page 50; for France, see page 99.

The Rise of Socialism

Meanwhile, one of the results of the misery, inequality, and discontent caused by the new industrial conditions was the rise of socialism.[9] Although it is practically impossible to define socialism accurately because of the wide diversity of ways in which the term has been used, certain of its essential beliefs and objectives are fairly clear.

The socialist ascribes a very large measure of the world's economic ills to the fact that great masses of men have been deprived of the possession of land and capital and thus of first-hand access to the sources of wealth. Millions of men, in consequence, have been made altogether dependent for a living upon the wages they receive in the employ of men who benefit "unjustly" from their labor. The fundamental objective of socialism is the prevention of this exploitation of the workers by the capitalists and landlords. To this end they demand the abolition of private property as a basis of capitalistic production, and the transfer to the state of its ownership and control. In other words, land in general, factories, workshops, railways—all the means of production and distribution in this capitalistic era—and all forms of private wealth that might give rise to an "unearned increment" should cease to be owned by private individuals,[10] and be handed over to the state.

In the matter of government the socialists have usually regarded democracy as a necessary concomitant of their system. It follows, then, that, if all land, forests, and minerals, and all means of production, transportation, trade, and banking were nationalized, they would belong to the people as a whole. All profits which formerly went to landlords and capitalists would then accrue to the state—that is, to the people. Rent and interest would be abolished, and the only form of income would be that paid by the state to its employees. Every person in the state would contribute to the community's productiveness in accordance with his ability or capacity, and the so-called leisure class would cease to exist.

Although certain elements which enter into it may be traced back through the centuries even to Plato's *Republic*, socialism is essentially a nineteenth-century product. The founder of British socialism was the manufacturer-philanthropist, Robert Owen, a Welshman who in 1800 became manager and part owner of large cotton mills at New Lanark in Scot-

[9] The term "socialism" was apparently coined in England in 1835 in connection with discussion aroused by the organization of a workers' association under the auspices of Robert Owen. In 1840 it found its way into a book published in France and became accepted in the general vocabulary of economics.

[10] In general, socialists would permit the individual to have his own clothing, household possessions, money, and perhaps even his own house and a bit of ground. Early communists, however, advocated that all property be owned in common.

land, which employed more than two thousand men, women, and children. Here he improved factory sanitation, rebuilt his workmen's houses, raised wages, reduced hours of labor, and founded primary schools, with the result that what had been a degenerate and wretched population was transformed into a healthy, industrious, and contented community.

Owen maintained that the development of machine production, when organized entirely for private profit, must inevitably entail the poverty and degradation of the working class. Beginning in 1817, he proposed co-operation as a remedy. Men, he advocated, should be organized in groups—consisting of from five hundred to three thousand people—which should own and use in common all the means of production necessary for the welfare of the members of the group. The community should be chiefly agricultural, but should carry on a variety of occupations so as to be as nearly as possible self-sufficing. His scheme envisaged the whole country, even the world, organized on the basis of such communities, but several attempts to put his ideas into operation ended only in complete failure.

In France in the early nineteenth century several men advocated schemes which were socialistic. The founder of French socialism is usually considered to have been Count Henri de Saint-Simon. A contemporary of Owen, he was not, like Owen, a successful business man, but instead a student of political and social problems. Between 1817 and 1825 he published the socialistic program which had gradually taken form in his mind, namely, state ownership of the production and distribution of goods and payment to each man in strict proportion to his industry and skill. He did not, like many socialists, advocate the idea of equal distribution to all. During his lifetime Saint-Simon had little influence; in vain he waited for that opportunity to test his plan which never came. Charles Fourier, a younger French contemporary of Saint-Simon, was somewhat more explicit in his proposals. He proposed the reorganization of society into democratic, self-governing units of about four hundred families, which should, like Owen's, be economically as nearly self-sufficient as possible. A complicated system of distribution was outlined in which each should receive a liberal minimum, the balance of the community's profits to be given in definite proportions to capital, labor, and talent. Attempts to establish Fourier's communities, however, were, like those of Owen, usually failures.

The early socialists were essentially imaginative and utopian and apparently thought little, if at all, of making use of political machinery to facilitate the attainment of their ends. Far more practical was the French journalist, Louis Blanc, whose proposals came to have a wide appeal to the workers of France. Blanc proposed that the state, reconstructed on a democratic basis, should supply workingmen with the instruments of labor. Every man, he maintained, has a natural right to work for his own support, and, if he cannot find employment on just terms at the hands of private individuals, the state should come to his assistance. National workshops should be established by the state and placed in the control of the workers. Such factories, he believed, would gradually displace privately owned establishments, and competition would thus give way to co-operation. When that day arrived, production would no longer be carried on by capitalists who hired laborers for wages and retained the profits for themselves, but would be managed by the workers in their own interests. Blanc gained a considerable following among French workingmen, and in the revolution of 1848 he was able to force the provisional government in France to recognize in principle his program. But the attempt to inaugurate what was said to be his scheme failed.[11] In France the socialistic movement was temporarily discredited, and the socialists themselves were suppressed.

The most eminent exponent of nineteenth-century socialism, however, was none of the above-mentioned men but the gifted German Jew, Karl Marx. Born in 1818 of a middle-class family in Rhenish Prussia, Marx was given an excellent education in the universities of Bonn, Berlin, and Jena, and in 1841 received the Ph.D. degree. From his university career he emerged a bourgeois liberal, and for about a year as editor of a Rhineland newspaper he vigorously attacked the reactionary government of Frederick William IV. When his newspaper was suppressed in 1843, Marx betook himself to Paris. There he came to know Louis Blanc and, mingling with other socialists and radical exiles, formed an enduring friendship with Friedrich Engels, a fervent advocate of socialist doctrine. As the result of his environment and of his own study, Marx became a firm believer in social reform and an ardent champion of the cause of the proletariat. In 1848 he and Engels published the now famous *Communist Manifesto*,[12] which has come to be considered the first great pronouncement of modern socialism. Expelled from Brussels and again from Prussia, Marx in 1849 sought refuge in London, where he lived until his death in 1883. The latter half of his life he spent elaborating and expounding his economic views. In 1867 he published the first volume of his fundamental work, *Capital*, and left at his death two more volumes which were subsequently edited and published by Engels.

The inevitable result of modern industrialism, Marx declared, was the division of men into two great groups—the relatively small capitalist class, or bourgeoisie, and the more numerous wage-earning class, or proletariat.

[11] Blanc vigorously denied that what was done in 1848 was in accord with his proposals.

[12] Terminology in the new field of economic and social reform was not yet fixed, and "communist" was here used by Marx to indicate something which was later called socialist.

The former by its monopolistic control of industry waxed wealthy, while the latter, without land or capital and wholly dependent upon wages, was subjected to harsh and arbitrary exploitation. Labor, he maintained, was the source of all value, and the chief defect in the existing order was that the worker received a wage barely sufficient for the subsistence of himself and his family, the surplus product of his labor being unjustly appropriated by capitalists.

But to the workingmen Marx held out hope. Capitalism was not the final stage of economic organization, he insisted, but merely a transitional stage which would be succeeded by socialism. Final socialization of the means of production would follow the seizure of political power by the proletariat, and this step, though it might be delayed, could not be permanently prevented. In fact it was inevitable, for the proletariat was constantly increasing its numerical superiority over the bourgeoisie and sooner or later would be in a position to assert its economic will. The new socialist society could thus be brought about by peaceful steps—by evolution rather than by revolution—and to this end he emphasized the need for political democracy as its indispensable antecedent.

Marx sought to make socialism international and cosmopolitan. "Workers of the world, unite!" had been the clarion call of his early *Manifesto*. At a great public meeting of workers of many nations held in London in 1864 it was decided to establish a permanent international organization. The constitution of the International Workingman's Association, drafted by Marx, declared that the emancipation of labor was not a local or national problem but one which embraced all modern countries. This emancipation, it asserted, had hitherto failed of achievement because of (1) the lack of solidarity of the various branches of labor within individual countries, and (2) the lack of unity between the laboring classes of different countries. Elaborate machinery for the new association was created, comprehensive plans for its work were formulated, and from time to time international congresses were held.

But the International, as it came to be called, was never very successful. It was weakened from within by factional quarrels between the anarchists and the socialists, and weakened from without by the pronounced impetus given to nationalism by the Franco-German War (1870–1871),[13] and by the excesses of the Communard uprising in Paris (1871),[14] with which Marx sympathized.

After the breakup of the International, the socialist movement proceeded in the several countries independently. In order to wage an effective fight against the bourgeoisie, the socialists organized into political parties

[13] See page 90.
[14] See pages 91–92.

on the model of the Social Democratic Party of Germany.[15] By 1914 practically every civilized country had its socialist party. With the continued growth of socialism came in 1889 the founding of the Second International, with which the various socialist parties of the world soon became affiliated. At the time of the outbreak of the First World War this association had 12,000,000 members in twenty-seven different countries. Socialism, therefore, was a force which had to be taken into account in the years after 1870.

Anarchism and Syndicalism

Far more revolutionary than socialism, though in the popular mind often confused with it, was anarchism, another movement which developed during the nineteenth century. Actually, socialism and anarchism are as far apart as the poles, for while, as already pointed out, the former is the acme of collectivism, the latter is the extreme of individualism. Socialists would have the state control everything for the common good of all; anarchists, on the other hand, would destroy all authority in order to establish complete individual freedom. "The only revolution that can do any good to the people," the anarchists preached, "is that which utterly annihilates every idea of the state and overthrows all traditions, orders, and classes."

Anarchism was first propounded in a way to attract attention by the Frenchman, Pierre Joseph Proudhon, who, as a matter of fact, was the one to coin the term "anarchist." Proudhon came into prominence in 1840 when he published a book entitled, *What is Property?* His answer was brief and to the point—"Property is theft." Why? Because, he asserted, "it appropriates the value produced by the labor of others without rendering an equivalent." During the next quarter century, despite occasional imprisonment or exile, he continued through his writings to formulate and promulgate his doctrines. The capitalist system he would supplant by co-operative productive associations which would assure to the worker the product of his labor. The state he would abolish in favor of mutual protective associations. Religion, a restriction upon human freedom, he would replace with altruism. Proudhon was fundamentally a kindly and humane theorist who believed in human perfectibility. He held that man was capable of an infinite amount of self-betterment, and that he could gradually be educated to see the abuses of the capitalist system and to desire the advantages of anarchism. Proudhon therefore opposed the use of violence.

But, based upon extreme individualism, anarchism could hardly be

[15] See page 54.

expected to have a common platform of policies to which all anarchists adhered. Another and more aggressive group of anarchists, led in the beginning by the Russian revolutionist, Michael Bakunin, believed that violence should be used to achieve their ends. Not through peaceful political action would economic reforms be secured, they asserted, but through the "direct action" of terrorism and strikes. The dissension engendered within the International by the conflicting views of Marx and Bakunin has already been mentioned. Nevertheless, although the anarchists were expelled from that association by the Marxian socialists, they continued to gain adherents and to conspire to bomb and to assassinate. "Our task," they announced, "is destruction, terrible, total, inexorable, and universal." [16] Anarchism, however, never became popular, rarely established in any country a regular political party, and utterly failed to win the great body of workmen away from its implacable enemy, socialism.

In the latter part of the nineteenth century, however, socialism was considerably affected by a radical movement which developed among its own members. Disappointed by the failure to attain at an early date many of the things held out by earlier socialists, and alarmed at the growing moderation of some of their more practical leaders, a few socialists—more impatient and more uncompromising than the others—decided that socialism's existing methods would never achieve the sweeping changes which they sought. They determined, therefore, to adopt different methods. It was futile, they declared, to expect slow, patient work and calm, persuasive logic alone to attain the great goal of socialism. Resort should be had not to parliaments, the instruments of the bourgeoisie, but to force and violence, to direct action through trade unions, the agencies which belonged peculiarly to the workers themselves. Because of its emphasis upon trade unions (*syndicats,* in French), the new movement was called syndicalism.

The syndicalists advocated that workers should be organized by whole industries, rather than by particular trades or crafts. For instance, a building-trades union should include all carpenters, plumbers, tinsmiths, ironworkers, painters, and the like. Then, when strikes were called, not one group but the members of the whole union would cease work. Through gigantic strikes the transportation and industry of any country could be paralyzed and the will of the proletariat imposed. A relentless warfare should be waged against the capitalists, but even in times of "peace" capitalist enterprises could be damaged and capitalism weakened by *sabotage* [17] —loafing on the job, injuring the machinery, spoiling the finished product.

[16] In the years after 1870 rulers or statesmen in several states were assassinated by anarchists.
[17] The origin of this term is said to have been the act of certain French workmen who at the opening of a strike threw their wooden shoes (*sabots*) into the machinery to ruin it.

Many of the ultimate aims of syndicalism—such as the overthrow of capitalism and the operation of the means of production for the benefit of the workers—were those of the socialists. Others, however, were quite different. It envisaged, for example, a state organized not on a democratic basis but on the basis of industries or trade unions, in which case it would be controlled by the laborers alone.[18] In its anti-government bias and its program of violent destruction of the political state it was suggestive of anarchism. Syndicalism, however, was more successful than anarchism in appealing to the workingmen, especially those in France, Italy, and Spain. Nevertheless, in Europe as a whole socialism, despite its more radical rivals, continued after the eighties steadily to increase its following.

Bourgeois-Proletarian Compromise

To many it seemed that the lining-up of the rival forces of the bourgeoisie and the proletariat must inevitably lead to bitter civil strife between these antagonistic social classes. Although in 1917 such a struggle did occur in Russia,[19] and at the close of the Second World War in some other countries, in general prior to 1914 civil and class warfare was avoided. Willingness on the part of the opposing groups to lessen somewhat their extreme demands operated in the interest of social peace. Leaders of socialism, when they found themselves at the head of large political parties with some prospect of political preferment, tended to moderate their views and to become willing to co-operate with other parties in the gradual solution of national problems. At the same time leaders of the bourgeoisie, fearful of movements more radical than socialism, became willing to surrender some of their own doctrines and to concede some of the things for which the socialists contended.

The history of Europe from 1870 to 1914 clearly reveals the fact that each group obtained some of its objectives while it abandoned or indefinitely postponed the attainment of others. The bourgeoisie gave up their earlier determined opposition to the extension of political privileges to the workingmen, and a gradual progress toward political democracy ensued. By 1914 in most of the countries of western Europe the proletariat had secured a close approximation to that full manhood suffrage which they had long sought.

Similarly, the bourgeoisie relinquished their "right" to industrial "liberty" and put aside their demand to be "let alone" in the management of their businesses. In consequence the proletariat secured, without overmuch resistance on the part of the middle classes, legislation improving

[18] Somewhat on the order of the Soviet government established in 1917 in Russia.
[19] See pages 375–376.

their conditions of labor. Laws were enacted to regulate the employment of women and children and to control hours and conditions of labor.
Factory inspectors were appointed to protect the workers in matters of
light, ventilation, and sanitation. By the end of the century elaborate
provisions guarded against the most patent evils of the industrial system.
Furthermore, the workingmen ultimately won not only the right to combine in trade unions but the capitalists' consent to enter with them into
"collective bargaining."

Free public-school education, one of the prime tenets of the socialists,
was also largely secured with the "benevolent" support of the bourgeoisie,
who perhaps hoped thus to wean the masses away from radicalism. In the
first half of the nineteenth century Prussia alone among the great powers
of Europe had a public-school system that successfully reached the children of workers. In the other countries education was largely left to
churches and to private enterprises and only half-heartedly supported by
the state. During the last part of the century, however, the other leading
powers began to establish public and compulsory systems of primary education. Great Britain made a feeble beginning in 1870,[20] and France went
much further in 1881.[21] By 1914 great strides had been made in most of
the countries of western Europe toward wiping out illiteracy.

The workingmen secured, too, the enactment of laws to assure themselves at least a minimum degree of material comfort. Although at first
bitterly opposed by the socialists, who feared that their strength would be
undermined, social-insurance laws were enacted by Germany in the
eighties and gradually adopted later in one country after another. The
bourgeoisie, with the idea of increasing social efficiency and at the same
time of weakening the socialists, threw their support to such legislation.
National insurance against death, illness, and unemployment was introduced; old-age pensions were provided; and even minimum wages in
certain industries were established.

On the other hand, the socialists were in general prevented from carrying
out their program of nationalization of industry and commerce. Instead,
the bourgeoisie, by availing themselves of their powerful economic position
and the growing conviction among other classes that their own prosperity
and welfare were indissolubly linked with that of the capitalists, were
able to secure considerable legislation favorable to private industry. Despite
the fulminations of the socialists, protective tariffs were erected and subsidies granted to aid capitalistic industries in practically every country but
Great Britain.[22] Advantageous corporation laws were enacted, and taxation

---

[20] See page 159.
[21] See page 101.
[22] The 1930's saw the introduction of protective tariffs even in Great Britain.

systems were, in general, drafted so as to injure business as little as possible. Finally, the policy of economic imperialism was adopted by the great powers after 1870 largely in response to the demands of the industrialists and over the protest of the socialist parties.

Rise in the Standard of Living

Every upward movement of economic progress, it is said, has been accompanied by greater social inequality, and doubtless it is true that in 1914 the contrast between the economic and social status of the British multimillionaire class and that of the poverty-stricken proletariat in the East End of London was greater than that which existed between the medieval noble and his serfs. Nevertheless, for the population of Europe as a whole the period from 1870 to the outbreak of the war brought a gradually rising standard of living, a change which, though nowhere so radical as the transformation which occurred in the United States during the same period, was nevertheless very appreciable. Living conditions in Europe in the first quarter of the twentieth century were on a distinctly higher plane of convenience and comfort than they had been a century earlier. This, of course, was particularly true of the bourgeoisie, but it was also true to a lesser degree of the proletariat and even of the peasantry. Doubtless standards of living would have been raised even higher had it not been for the rapid increase in Europe's population during the period.

Modern inventions and the industrial progress of the nineteenth century introduced into housing facilities innumerable improvements. In general, hygienic and sanitary conditions became far better. Plentiful supplies of good water, often brought to urban centers from miles away, were piped into individual houses and apartments. For most urban dwellers the simple turning of a faucet supplanted the old-time trip to the well or the cistern and the burdensome carrying of water buckets. Cheap transportation facilitated the use of coal for domestic purposes and resulted in better heating; and the latter, in turn, made possible more adequate supplies of hot water. Gradually bathtubs were introduced, and bathing became more of a pleasure and less of an arduous duty. Electric lighting, gas cooking, and the introduction of many new appliances not only greatly reduced the burden of housekeeping, but also increased the comforts of life. In many modern apartment houses elevators removed the necessity for climbing long flights of stairs, and the telephone greatly reduced the need for leaving the apartment at all unless one so desired.

Cheap transportation, modern large-scale canning, and refrigeration profoundly altered the problem of food supplies. Fresh vegetables and fruits, brought from all parts of the world, became obtainable throughout the year. Fresh meats and fish could be had in abundance regardless of location. In general, man's diet was greatly enriched by the advance of modern industry and science. At the same time, large-scale production and the resultant decline in prices brought within the range of even the poor man's pocketbook numerous articles which in earlier centuries only the wealthy could afford. In fact, even the so-called "average man" of the twentieth century had many things far beyond the dreams of medieval nobles, while the elegantly appointed limousines, large and commodious private yachts, and luxuriously furnished mansions of the twentieth-century capitalists would have been the envy of all kings of the old regime.

The outlook of the people of Europe was greatly broadened. The application of steam and later of electricity to the printing press, the introduction of swift typesetting by means of the linotype—a mechanism, invented in 1885, by means of which type is set by manipulating a keyboard similar to that of a typewriter—and the manufacture of newsprint paper by the chemical treatment of wood pulp, all reduced the price of newspapers and brought them within means of even the poorest. At the same time, the telegraph, the cable, and the wireless made possible the quick collection of news and enabled editors to place before their readers daily—almost hourly —accounts of the happenings of the world. For many, indeed, the radio in the home eventually brought immediate contact with the world at large, enabling them at will to listen to addresses and concerts given hundreds or even thousands of miles away. Thousands of "movie" theaters brought to millions of people weekly vivid and enlightening pictures of world events. The horizon of the European became as wide as the universe.

Modern means of transportation greatly reduced the time and effort needed to cover distance. Within the cities tramcars and autobuses enabled the masses to move from one section to another with a minimum of effort, while motorcars provided the upper classes with facilities for speeding from apartment or suburban home to office swiftly and with little effort. For hundreds of thousands of workers the humble bicycle—which came into general use in the late eighties—abolished the weary trudging to and from the factory and the shop. The modern European became far more mobile than his ancestors.

With the passing of the years the amount of leisure was increased and extended to greater and greater numbers of people. The working day was gradually shortened, holidays became more frequent, and vacations more general. Athletic sports, first popularized in Great Britain, were ultimately taken up in other industrial countries, and organized games came to play a greater part in the life of Europe than at any time since the Greeks. For many of even the "ordinary" people the coming of cheap automobiles in the twentieth century brought the opportunity to spend holidays and weekends in the countryside, and for those less fortunate reduced railway "excursion fares" and the bicycle afforded similar opportunities.

 The rise of the conservative peasantry to new standards of living, however, was considerably slower than that of the urban population. Nevertheless, some of the advances which altered city life affected also the rural districts. Many a lowly peasant cottage, for example, came to be lighted by electricity. In general, the outlook of the peasant was broadened. Although he did not change his habit of staying close to home, others by motorcars, bicycles, and railways invaded his community and forced upon him some of the contacts of travel. Rural mail delivery, cheap daily newspapers, and an occasional radio, moreover, did much to end his isolation.

The Progress of Woman

The position of no class of society, perhaps, was more profoundly altered by the rise and spread of modern industrialism than that of woman. Before the Industrial Revolution woman was, as now, usually married and consequently called upon to perform the many tasks connected with the running of the old-time household. In addition to the bearing and rearing of children—often many—her time was generally devoted to cooking, cleaning, spinning, weaving, and sewing for the family. The unmarried woman found it practically impossible to engage in business or to obtain employment outside the home and was therefore driven to the necessity of living in the household of some relative. There she helped with the daily tasks, frequently devoting her time to the family's weaving and spinning—a forlorn and dejected spinster. But married or unmarried, woman in the old days, being engaged in no gainful occupation, was usually dependent for her support on some man—her husband, her father, or her brother.

Woman's inferior economic position was but one aspect, though perhaps the fundamental cause, of her general status of inferiority to man. The legal position of the unmarried woman was in no sense on a plane with that of man, while that of the married woman was even lower. In fact, the married woman had practically no rights of her own. She could not make a legal contract, could not hold property in her own name, could neither sue nor be sued in court. She had no legal existence apart from her husband, who was responsible for her as though she were a minor. She was almost completely under his authority and could legally be beaten by him for disobedience. Her property went to him upon marriage, and children born of that marriage were legally his. Possessed, supposedly, of inferior brains, the married woman led a secluded existence, rearing children, "keeping house"—in many respects little more than a domestic serf of her "lord and master."

The Industrial Revolution and the factory system, however, paved the way for a change in the status of woman by undermining or destroying the economic dependence which so long held her in a position subordinate to man. Many types of factory work could be performed as well by women as by men; some, indeed, could be better done. Women would work for less pay and were more docile, so that the new employers often preferred to hire them instead of men. Women in industrial communities, consequently, left their homes by the thousands to enter the factories. There, as earlier in the home, they engaged in spinning, weaving, canning, and the making of clothes. But there was this important difference, that, whereas formerly their toil had brought them no fixed monetary income but merely their subsistence, now they received a definitely stipulated wage. And, although in the early stages of modern industrialism this wage was pitifully low and the conditions under which it was earned were thoroughly deplorable, gradually factory legislation and economic competition led to an improvement in both wages and conditions. In the end the factory, by providing woman with an opportunity to become a wage-earner, did much to emancipate her.

For employment in the factory was only the entering wedge. Soon women began to be admitted into the semiskilled occupations and even the professions. By the close of the first quarter of the twentieth century millions of them were employed as wage-earners in factories, offices, and stores; and many types of employment, too, even began to show a tendency toward no discrimination in wages because of sex. With woman's advance into the ranks of the wage-earners came for her a measure of economic independence. No longer need the unmarried woman play the role of the humble, dependent spinster; she had advanced to the status of the "bachelor girl," independent and free.

Furthermore, hundreds of thousands of married women joined their unmarried sisters as wage-earners and, by contributing to the family budget, not only raised their standards of living but won a degree of independence morally, if not at first legally, in the home. The lot of the middle-class married woman, moreover, likewise improved, though in another way. To her modern industry brought not an opportunity for work in a factory but a release from many of the irksome tasks in the home. With improved household appliances and conveniences, and with factories doing her spinning, weaving, clothes-making, laundry, and canning, she was enabled to enjoy a life of leisure such as her eighteenth-century predecessor had never known.

The improvement of woman's economic status strengthened her demand for an advance in her social and political status as well. Feminists, as they came to be known, inaugurated a movement to reorganize the world "upon a basis of sex-equality in all human relations; a movement which would reject every differentiation between individuals upon the ground of sex, would abolish all sex-privileges and sex-burdens, and would strive to set up the recognition of the common humanity of woman and man as the foundation of law and custom." As the result of their efforts and other influences, gradually in the course of the nineteenth century, and especially in the period after 1870, the position of woman was vastly improved.

Considered mentally inferior to man, woman was long denied access to higher education. In 1848, however, was founded Queen's College in Great Britain for the education of young women. Sweden opened the study of dentistry and surgery to women in 1861, the Swiss University of Zurich opened all its departments to them in 1863, and two years later a woman for the first time was granted a medical diploma in Great Britain. In subsequent years the institutions of higher learning throughout the world gradually opened their doors to women on equal terms with men, and ultimately were graduating thousands of them annually.

Gradually, too, woman's legal and political rights were extended. In Great Britain, for example, legislation in 1882 gave the married woman a right to hold property in her own name, and in 1886 another law finally gave the mother equal rights with the father in the control of their children. Although woman has not yet won complete legal equality with man throughout the world, the repeal of many obsolete laws and the enactment of much progressive legislation after the First World War went far toward placing her on the same legal plane with man.

Politically, though slow to come, sweeping advances were eventually made in the position of woman. Despite more than a half century of education and agitation, despite the vigorous campaigns of hundreds of woman suffrage societies and a host of militant suffragettes, by 1914 only Norway and Finland among the states of Europe, had extended the national franchise to women. Beginning in 1918, however, there came a rapid extension of political rights to them. In a score of states not only was the suffrage conferred upon them but public offices were opened to them as well. The years after 1920 saw many women elected to national parliaments and some even elevated to places of importance in national cabinets. The day when woman was expected to play no part in the public life of the world was past.

EUROPE
1871

ATLANTIC OCEAN

HEBRIDES
ORKNEY IS.
CHRISTIANIA
NORWAY
Stavanger
Christiansand

BRITISH ISLES
SCOTLAND
Aberdeen
Glasgow
Edinburgh
Newcastle
NORTH SEA
DENMARK

IRELAND
Belfast
Dublin
Cork
IRISH SEA
Manchester
Liverpool
WALES
ENGLAND
Birmingham
Bristol
Plymouth
LANDS END
London
NETHERLANDS
Amsterdam
The Hague
Rotterdam
Antwerp
HELIGOLAND (GER.)
Kiel
Bremen
Hanover
Leipzig

CAPE CLEAR
ENGLISH CHANNEL
CHANNEL IS. (BR.)
ST. OF DOVER
Le Havre
BELGIUM
Brussels
Cologne
Frankfurt
LUX.
Metz
Nuremberg
GERMANY
RHINE R.
DANUBE R.
Munich

Brest
Nantes
Paris
Orleans
SEINE R.
Strasbourg
Basel
Berne
SWITZERLAND
ALPS
Geneva

CAPE FINISTERRE
Santander
San Sebastian
Bordeaux
Bayonne
FRANCE
LOIRE R.
St. Etienne
Lyons
RHONE R.
THE
Milan
Venice
Trie

Vigo
Oviedo
Oporto
PORTUGAL
GARONNE R.
Toulouse
Turin
Genoa
PO R.
ITALY

DUORO R.
EBRO R.
PYRENEES MTS.
Saragossa
Nice
Marseilles
Toulon
Florence
CORSICA (FR.)
Ajaccio

SPAIN
Madrid
TAGUS R.
Toledo
Lisbon
TAGUS R.
Valencia
Barcelona
Rome
Naples

Seville
Granada
Malaga
Cadiz
STRAIT OF GIBRALTAR
GIBRALTAR (BR.)
Cartagena
BALEARIC IS. (SP.)
MINORCA
MAJORCA
Palma
SARDINIA (IT.)
Cagliari

MEDITERRANEAN
Palermo
SICI

A F R I C A

TRM
0°
10°E

Part Two

FOUR DECADES OF PEACE

IN THE period from 1871 to 1914 the only wars which occurred in Europe were fought in the Balkans. In each case the conflict was of relatively short duration, and only once was a great power directly involved. Generally speaking, therefore, after 1871—although some of the great powers waged imperialistic wars outside the Continent—Europe as a whole enjoyed forty years of international peace. The preceding chapters have already pointed out some of the notable economic and social trends of these years.

The chapters in Part Two, dealing with the national histories of the European states, disclose still other characteristics of the period. They reveal the advance of constitutionalism, the widening of the suffrage, and real progress toward political and social democracy. They tell of the growth of interest in popular education, of the increased reverence for science and materialism, of the diminishing loyalty to the church and the resultant rise of anticlericalism. They point out how nationalism continued to be exalted, how it entered the field of business and emerged as economic nationalism, how it operated more and more as a dynamic force in Europe's history. Finally, these chapters make crystal-clear how during four decades of peace forces were generated which in 1914 produced the most terrible war that the world had yet known.

Chapter III

THE GERMAN EMPIRE

BETWEEN 1866 and 1871, thanks to the skillful diplomacy of Prussia's great minister, Otto von Bismarck, and to the unexcelled military genius of her generals, Roon and Moltke, the situation in what had been the German Confederation was completely altered. During the first half century of its existence the confederation had been dominated by the Austrian Habsburgs. But as a result of Prussia's decisive victory in the Austro-Prussian War (1866), the Austrian Empire was expelled from the confederation and a new North German Confederation, which included all of the German states north of the Main, was organized under the hegemony of a greatly enlarged Prussia. Next, by taking advantage of a wave of chauvinism in France, Bismarck contrived to bring about the Franco-German War (1870–1871), in which the German states south of the Main fought as allies against France, and at the close of which they joined (January, 1871) with the states of the North German Confederation to establish the German Empire.

The Structure of the Imperial Government

The constitution of this German Empire was that of the North German Confederation revised to meet the changed conditions resulting from the events of January, 1871. By virtue of this document the empire became a federation of twenty-five states—four kingdoms, six grand duchies, five duchies, seven principalities, and three free cities.[1] As in the United States, the powers of the federal government were specifically enumerated, while those of the states were broad, undefined, and residual. Nevertheless, the scope of the enumerated powers was very broad, including the control of taxation and customs duties, the army and navy, foreign and interstate commerce, postal and telegraph systems, coinage, weights and measures, patents and copyrights, banking and the issuing of paper money, and civil and criminal law. Federal laws, however, were to be executed not by federal officials but by those of the several states.

The federal legislative power was vested in two houses, the Bundesrat

[1] In addition, there was the imperial domain of Alsace-Lorraine, which until 1911 occupied the position of a purely dependent territory.

49

and the Reichstag. The former, in which the sovereignty of the empire resided, represented the constituent states and consisted of delegates appointed by the princes of the monarchical states and by the senates of the free cities. The votes in the Bundesrat were distributed more or less arbitrarily, little attempt being made to apportion them in exact relation to population, wealth, or importance.[2] Had these been considered, Prussia would have received an absolute majority. The apportionment was designed by Bismarck to convince the lesser states that they need have no fear of Prussian domination. Legally the status of the delegates was that of diplomats who spoke and voted not at their own discretion but under specific instructions of the governing authorities by whom they were appointed and by whom, also, they might be recalled and replaced at any time. Each state's vote was cast as an indivisible block, regardless of the individual opinions of the delegates.

The Reichstag, in contrast with the Bundesrat, was organized on a broadly national basis, representing not the states but the people of the empire as a whole. Its members were elected for five-year terms by the direct and secret ballot of male citizens over twenty-five years of age. The number of seats was fixed at 397, of which 235 belonged to Prussia. Although legally the legislative power of the empire rested jointly in the Bundesrat and Reichstag, actually the Reichstag came to occupy a purely subordinate position. Under normal procedure bills were prepared, discussed, and voted in the Bundesrat, submitted to the Reichstag for consideration and acceptance, and returned for further examination by the Bundesrat before their promulgation by the Kaiser. In a sense, it was the Bundesrat that made law with merely the assent of the Reichstag.

The constitution stipulated that the king of Prussia should be president of the federation and should bear the title of *Deutscher Kaiser* (German Emperor). Although technically considered merely as *primus inter pares* in a federation of territorial princes, the Kaiser was entrusted with extensive powers. He had authority to convene and adjourn both the Bundesrat and the Reichstag, the power to appoint and remove the chancellor and all subordinate officials of the administrative hierarchy, the right to make treaties with other nations, appoint and receive ambassadors, and declare defensive war.[3] In him was vested the control of the army and navy.

The place filled in some political systems by a ministry or cabinet was, in the German Empire, occupied by a single official known as the imperial chancellor. The chancellor has been described as the Kaiser's

---

[2] Prussia had seventeen, Bavaria six, Saxony four, Württemberg four, Baden three, Hesse three, Mecklinburg-Schwerin two, Brunswick two, and the seventeen other states one each.

[3] Treaties relating to matters controlled by imperial legislation, and the declaration of offensive war, required the consent of the Bundesrat.

"other self." He was appointed, and might be dismissed by the Kaiser, to whom alone he was responsible. In Germany there was no ministerial responsibility to the legislature as in Great Britain, France, and Italy. The chancellor held a position of great power. He presided over the Bundesrat; he proposed most of the legislation; he had the right to address the Reichstag; and he usually named the heads of the departments of imperial administration and supervised their work, for the various ministers were, in effect, only the heads of various bureaus of the imperial chancellory.

In order to gain the adherence of some of the larger states Bismarck had offered certain special privileges. The imperial constitution stipulated, for example, that the supreme court of the empire was to be held in Saxony; that Bavaria should have the chairmanship of the Bundesrat's committee on foreign affairs and that Saxony and Württemberg should be represented on that committee; that Bavaria should have her own postal and telegraph system and, in time of peace, should manage her own army; that Bavaria, Württemberg, and Baden should not be subject to the federal taxes on beer and brandy.

Nevertheless, it was to Prussia, the state which had created the empire and which in area and population overshadowed all the others put together, that the predominance fell. Prussia's king was *ipso facto* German Kaiser with all the extensive powers which have been enumerated. In the powerful Bundesrat Prussia was practically supreme. Her representative, as chancellor, was president of that body; the chairmanships of all permanent committees except that on foreign affairs were held by her; her votes were sufficient to block any amendment to the constitution; her delegation could prevent any change in regard to military affairs, the navy, the tariff, and the various consumption taxes; in any tie vote her representatives had the right to cast the deciding ballot. Of the Reichstag seats she held an overwhelming majority.

Early Political History

From the era before 1870 the German Empire inherited three major political parties—the Conservative, the Progressive, and the National Liberal. The Conservative Party, organized in the fifties by Bismarck and other Junkers (the Prussian aristocracy), remained distinctly Prussian. Drawn almost entirely from the agricultural classes of that state, it opposed liberalism and loyally supported the king, the army, and the Lutheran Church. On the other hand, the Progressive Party, founded in the sixties, rigorously championed true parliamentary government and with equal zeal opposed the development of militarism. Drawn largely from the professional and bourgeois classes of Prussia it stood for individual rights and

limited monarchy. It had opposed Bismarck during the years when he
was preparing to unify Germany "by blood and iron," and had consequently lost some of its popular appeal as a result of Bismarck's success in
creating the German Empire.

3 The National Liberal Party, the first important German—as distinct
from Prussian—party to make its appearance, was organized after the
Austro-Prussian War and the formation of the North German Confederation. Delighted with the outcome of Bismarck's German policy, and grati-
fied by his incorporation in the new constitution of provisions for the
election of the Reichstag by direct and universal manhood suffrage, this
party aimed to support Bismarck in his further national endeavors. Prior
to 1871 it worked to promote the cause of German nationalism in South
Germany. The National Liberals came chiefly from the industrial classes
and were drawn in many instances from the Progressive Party. They were
willing to postpone further constitutional development for a time while
the central government was being consolidated and strengthened. In general, they supported the army, favored free trade, and were anticlerical.

It was upon the National Liberals that Bismarck chiefly leaned during
his early years as chancellor. The Conservatives, he knew, would not be
likely to oppose his policies so long as the latter did not threaten Prussia's
ascendancy in Germany or their own ascendancy in Prussia. With the
active support of the National Liberals, therefore, Bismarck proceeded
to consolidate the empire. Believing that military strength must be the
future defense of the German Empire, as it had been the chief instrument
in its creation, the chancellor at once turned his attention to the army.
A considerable portion of the huge French war indemnity was devoted
to the construction of fortifications and to the replacement of military
equipment and stores destroyed during the Franco-German War. In 1872
a uniform system of military jurisprudence, based upon Prussia's principle
of compulsory military service, was adopted for the whole empire except
Bavaria, and the military efficiency of the German army was assured. The
peace strength of the army was placed at about 400,000 men, and the Reichstag after determined opposition was persuaded to make financial grants
for the military not annually but for seven-year periods.[4]

In 1873 an imperial railway bureau was created to assist in unifying the
various systems of state railways. Two years later the control of banking
was transferred from the states to the federal government, and in 1876
the Reichsbank (Imperial Bank) was established under the management
of the empire. Facilities were thus provided for the expeditious conduct
of the nation's financial operations as well as for its economic stability. At
the same time new and uniform coins, stamped with the arms of the

---

[4] Bismarck had wished them to be made in perpetuity.

empire and bearing the effigy of William I, silently proclaimed through-out the realm a united Germany. The North German Confederation's code of criminal law and common code for trade, commerce, and banking, promulgated in 1869, were made applicable to the whole empire, and new codes for civil and criminal procedure were drawn up and adopted.

In the early seventies a fourth political party—the Center [5] or Catholic Party—made its appearance. Having its strength principally in the South German states and in Rhenish Prussia, and being therefore essentially a states' rights party, it was from the beginning hostile to Bismarck's centralizing policies. A conflict which might eventually have arisen be-tween the chancellor and the Catholics was made almost inevitable by other circumstances. Bismarck was suspicious of the Catholics. When many of them sought to have Germany intervene in Italy in order to restore to the pope his temporal power, he accused them of trying to cause trouble between Italy and the newly established empire. Furthermore, the chancellor apparently feared that Pius IX's *Syllabus of Errors* (1864), denouncing liberty of conscience, secular education, civil marriage, and divorce as "modern errors," and the enunciation by the Vatican Council (1869–1870) of the doctrine of papal infallibility, were but foundation stones for subsequent papal interference in the domestic affairs of Germany. Firmly determined to centralize and unify the empire at all costs, Bis-marck decided to attack the Catholics, who to him were the personifica-tion of separatism and localism. The conflict which he waged against them was looked upon by many liberals as a defense of contemporary civilization against a medieval church that had declared war against modern tend-encies. It came to be known, therefore, as the *Kulturkampf* (Battle for Civilization).

The opening gun in the battle against the church was fired by Bis-marck in 1872 when he prevailed upon the Reichstag to pass a law ex-pelling the Jesuits from the empire. Then followed, after the breaking-off of diplomatic relations between Prussia and the Vatican, a regular barrage of laws ("May Laws" or "Falk Laws") against the church. Enacted by the Prussian Landtag, they applied not to the empire as a whole but only to Prussia; but the latter constituted two thirds of all Germany. By these laws it was stipulated that no one but a German might be appointed to an office in the Catholic Church in Prussia, that priests must have at-tended state schools and universities and have passed government exam-inations, that all ecclesiastical seminaries must be under state control, that seminaries for boys must be abolished, and that civil marriage should thereafter be compulsory. Many religious orders, furthermore, were sup-pressed.

[5] So-called because in the Reichstag it sat between the Right and the Left.

An open conflict between Prussia and the church ensued when the pope declared the "May Laws" null and void and urged the clergy not to obey them. Led by Bismarck, the state fined and imprisoned disobedient priests, suspended its financial payments in several dioceses, confiscated church property, and closed over a thousand Catholic churches. The National Liberals, the Progressives, some Lutheran Conservatives, and a small minority of "Old Catholics"—schismatics who refused to accept the recently announced doctrine of papal infallibility—gave Bismarck their approval. Extreme nationalists of various types rallied to the chancellor's support against the pope, who was accused of seeking to undermine the Hohenzollern empire in the nineteenth century as his predecessors had the Hohenstaufen empire in the Middle Ages.

The great bulk of the German Catholics, however, remained staunchly loyal to the pope despite the so-called "Diocletian persecution" to which the church was subjected. To register their determined opposition to Bismarck's policies, they flocked to the support of the Center Party, which, in 1874, was consequently able to increase its representation in the Reichstag from 63 to 91, with a total poll of nearly 1,500,000 votes.

Meanwhile, another minor opposition party had made its appearance to worry Bismarck. As early as 1863 Ferdinand Lassalle, a brilliant but somewhat erratic social reformer and politician, had sought to unite the German workingmen in the cause of social regeneration. Under his leadership was founded in Leipzig in that year the Universal German Workingman's Association, designed to be developed into a great national party. A membership of less than five thousand had been obtained, however, when Lassalle's career was suddenly cut short in 1864 by a duel resulting from a love affair. In that same year, it chanced, Karl Marx commissioned one of his ablest followers, William Liebknecht, a scholar and a revolutionist in 1848, to undertake in South Germany the formation of workingmen's societies based upon Marxian principles. Liebknecht became acquainted with August Bebel, a forceful young organizer of the proletariat, and a comradeship was established which was broken only by the former's death in 1900.

In 1869 these two socialist leaders succeeded in founding the Social Democratic Workingman's Party, and six years later they persuaded Lassalle's Workingman's Association to merge with their new organization. While the Social Democrats sought ultimately to establish in Germany a Marxian socialist regime on a democratic republican basis, they announced that their first objective would be the attainment of a "free state," since political freedom was the necessary antecedent of economic freedom. They advocated reforms to bring about parliamentary government, secular education, individual liberty, and the elimination of military and clerical

"BISMARCK HAS RESIGNED AGAIN!"

The Iron Chancellor used to threaten to resign whenever William I objected to
his policies, whereupon the aged Kaiser would give way to him.

influences from political life. They favored the introduction of heavy income taxes, inheritance taxes, and free trade; and, being Marxians, they
emphasized the desirability of internationalism rather than nationalism.
In many respects their aims were the very antitheses of Bismarck's.

In the general election of 1877 the Social Democrats polled nearly half
a million votes and elected twelve members to the Reichstag. Bismarck
and William I viewed with alarm these triumphs of the party, and the
former sought an opportunity to destroy it. In 1878 two unsuccessful
attempts by socialists to assassinate the Kaiser provided the chancellor
with the desired excuse. In October of that year, accordingly, the Reichstag
was persuaded to pass a law of remarkable severity against them. Socialist
societies were to be disbanded, socialist meetings prohibited, and socialist
newspapers suppressed. The circulation of socialist literature and all efforts
to spread socialist doctrine were made penal offenses, punishable by fines
and imprisonment. Police were empowered to supervise labor organizations
and to expel from the empire any person accused of being a socialist. Martial law might be proclaimed where considered to be expedient. Many saw
in such legislation the reappearance of the reactionary spirit of the Carlsbad
Decrees (1819),[6] and Bismarck was denounced as the very reincarnation
of Metternich himself. Progressives and Centrists joined the Social Democrats in their invectives.

Realizing that he could not wage a destructive campaign simultaneously
against both the Catholics and the socialists without running the danger
of having them unite to block his cherished plans for the empire, Bismarck
decided that he must make peace with one of the groups. As between the
"black internationalists" and the "red internationalists," he considered the
former less dangerous, and he therefore determined to come to terms with
the Catholics. Pope Leo XIII, elected in 1878, was known to hold more
moderate views than his predecessor, and to him the chancellor offered
terms of peace which the church accepted. Diplomatic relations were
again established between Prussia and the Vatican, and King William was
empowered to administer the "May Laws" at his own discretion. Between
1878 and 1887 most of the anti-Catholic legislation was repealed, and the
latter year saw the church once more occupying virtually its former position
in Germany.

Perhaps the chief result of Bismarck's *Kulturkampf* was a permanently
solidified Center Party, which thereafter played an important role in
German political history. In general it opposed excessive militarism and
imperialism and threw its support to legislation in favor of the Catholic
Church, states' rights, social and political reform, and indirect taxation.
In 1912 it was the second largest political party in the empire, first place

6 These were enacted to suppress liberalism in the German Confederation.

being held by the Social Democrats. For Bismarck's campaign against the
socialists was no more successful than that against the church. Despite his
vigorous efforts to destroy the Social Democratic Party, the latter preserved
its organization and carried on an effective propaganda in Germany from
the Swiss city of Zurich. Although at the first election after the enactment
of the repressive legislation the socialist strength declined, thereafter it
steadily rose until by the First World War it was receiving practically a
third of the total popular vote. Bismarck failed to defeat his opponents
within the empire with the same thoroughness and dispatch with which
he had defeated those abroad in the years from 1864 to 1871.

Economic Progress and Social Legislation

Although in the thirty years preceding the establishment of the empire
German industry passed through those fundamental changes which are
associated with the Industrial Revolution, it was only after 1870 that the
growth of industry and industrial organization in that country reached
such proportions as to entitle it to be called "one of the capital economic
phenomena of modern times."

A number of factors contributed to Germany's startlingly rapid industrial
and commercial expansion in the years immediately after the Franco-
German War. In the first place, the very establishment of the empire was
a great boon to German industry because of the uniform and beneficent
legislation which it made possible under Bismarck. In the second place, the
annexation of Alsace-Lorraine contributed a double impetus. The thriving
textile industries of Alsace brought an enormous increase of resources and
output and at the same time a higher standard of excellence to the manufacture of German textile goods; and the iron mines of Lorraine, thanks
to the Thomas-Gilchrist process, greatly increased the empire's mineral
resources and helped to lay foundations for Germany's later advance in
the heavy industries. In the third place, the receipt from France of a war
indemnity of five billion francs made suddenly available for German industrial expansion a vast amount of new capital.

The close of the Franco-German War, therefore, was followed by a
period of tremendous industrial activity and speculation in Germany.
While in the twenty-year period preceding that war only 295 stock companies with a capital of some $600,000,000 had been organized, the four-
year period from 1870 to 1874 saw the establishment of 857 such companies
with a capital of $800,000,000. During these "foundation years" (Gründer-
jahre), as they were known in Germany, new factories were constructed
so rapidly that chimneys appeared to spring up like weeds. In 1874 this
exceptional outburst of industrial activity and overspeculation culminated,

however, in a severe financial and industrial crisis. The boom collapsed, and during the next decade and a half the empire was called upon to devote its energies largely to recovering its equilibrium and to building more solidly the foundation of its new economic life.

Economic depression naturally gave rise to an insistent demand for the restoration of the protective tariffs which had been gradually abandoned in the preceding two decades.[7] Free trade had never been fully accepted in Germany and had always been opposed by various powerful industrial interests. In the late seventies the demands of these industrial leaders were reinforced by those of the landowners, who, formerly favorable to free trade, were converted to protection by the competition of American and Russian grain. Both the Conservative Party, representative of the great landed interests, and the Center Party, consisting largely of peasants, pronounced in favor of protection.

Originally an ardent believer in free trade, Bismarck gradually came to the conviction that the interests of the German Empire required a return to protection. He observed, he said, that protectionist countries were prospering while free-trade countries were retrograding, that Germany, on account of her free-trade policy, was becoming the dumping ground for other countries' surplus products. Furthermore, he saw that for the rapid increase in imperial expenditures the existing fiscal system was coming to be inadequate. Increases of the customs duties, it appeared to him, not only would afford protection for Germany's economic interests but would at the same time increase the federal government's income and correspondingly lessen its dependence upon the states. Bismarck therefore decided to champion the cause of protection.

In 1878 the chancellor abandoned his alliance with the National Liberal Party, which was committed to free trade; and in the following year, with the support of the Center and Conservative Parties, he succeeded in enacting a tariff to protect both farm products and domestic manufactures. Although from the viewpoint of protection the new tariff was not wholly satisfactory, the customs duties, together with excise taxes and a high duty on sugar and tobacco which he secured at this time, provided the federal government with adequate income and gave it a new strength.

Bismarck's abandonment of free trade was only one aspect of his reaction against that doctrine of *laissez faire* which was so dear to the National Liberals. His repudiation of that principle was further shown by his intervention in the affairs of capital and labor through the enactment of social insurance laws, a type of legislation in which the German Empire, under Bismarck's leadership, became the pioneer. The policy of government alleviation and prevention of social distress appealed to the chancellor

---

[7] In 1877 ninety-five per cent of all imports entered the German Empire duty-free.

not only because of its broadly humanitarian aspects but because he believed it would both strengthen the empire and undermine the socialists, against whom he was then waging his repressive campaign.

Bismarck held that, according to modern Christian ideas, the state had not only the defensive duty of protecting existing rights but the positive duty of promoting the welfare of all its members, especially those who were weak and in need of help. Such activities of the state were, he believed, not only a duty of humanity and Christianity but a matter of self-interest to the state, for the unpropertied classes, constituting the most numerous and the least educated part of the population, must be led to regard the state not as an institution contrived for the protection of the better classes of society but as one serving their own needs and interests. Should not the workingman as a soldier of industry, Bismarck inquired, receive a pension as much as the soldier who had been disabled or the civil servant who had grown old in the service? If the state would show a little more Christian solicitude for the workingman, give him the right to work as long as he was healthy, assure him care when he was sick and maintenance when he was old, then, he declared, the socialists would sing their siren song in vain, and the workingmen would cease to throng to their banner.

Humanitarian desire to ameliorate the hardships of the proletariat and political desire to wean the workingmen away from socialism to the support of the empire, then, were the dominant factors which led Bismarck to adopt the policy of social legislation. This policy had already been urged by others. As early as 1878 a small group of Conservatives in the Reichstag had advocated the establishment of a system of compulsory insurance against poverty and old age, and August Bebel had even gone so far as to formulate a scheme for direct insurance by the state. The next year the Reichstag was informed that the government accepted the principle of social insurance, and in 1881 Bismarck announced his famous program. The local and voluntary workingmen's insurance systems which already existed in Germany he proposed to combine into a great national system to which should be added the compulsory feature.

Bismarck's proposal encountered vigorous opposition from two distinctly different groups. The Social Democrats, after a futile attempt to amend the first bill in order to make it more extensive in its application, finally ended by denouncing it and refusing to give it their support. The various acts they considered to be only halfway measures, and they professed to see in them nothing but bribes offered to the workers in order to win them from socialism. On the other hand the Progressives, believers in the doctrines of *laissez faire,* vigorously denounced the bills as the very essence of socialism itself. It was not until 1883 that the first of Bismarck's measures became a law; the second and third were passed in 1884 and 1889 respectively.[8]

The sickness insurance law, after amendments in subsequent years, ultimately covered all workers whose annual wages were less than two thousand marks. The insurance fund was in general sustained by the employers and the employees, and was administered by a board representing both groups. The former contributed one third and the latter two thirds, the expense to the worker rarely exceeding 3 per cent of his wage. In return the worker received free medical and surgical treatment, hospital or home care, burial money in case of death, and a sick allowance ranging from one half to three fourths of his wage. If illness continued more than six months, the burden was transferred to the accident insurance fund.

The accident insurance law as later amended applied to practically every industry of importance, and nearly all workingmen, regardless of the amount of their wages, were required to be insured. In this instance the funds for the system were contributed entirely by the employers. Compensation for injury included free medical and surgical treatment plus a cash benefit depending upon the seriousness of the disability. In cases of accidental deaths compensation consisted of burial money together with pensions for widows, children, and other dependents. The system of invalidity and old-age insurance as finally revised and extended included in 1914 practically every person over sixteen years of age who worked for wages. The cost of this insurance was met chiefly by contributions from the workers and their employers in equal amounts, supplemented by payments from the federal government. The law entitled all contributing wage-earners to an invalidity annuity in case of permanent disability and to an old-age annuity after the seventieth year.

Bismarck's social legislation had far-reaching effects not only in Germany but abroad. At first looked upon by foreign governments as radical and socialistic, it came eventually to be copied and even extended by most of the other countries of Europe. Had he during his whole chancellorship succeeded in doing no more than initiate his scheme of social insurance, Bismarck would yet have been entitled to rank among the empire's greatest statesmen.

Diplomatic Ascendancy under Bismarck

Bismarck's greatest claim to statesmanship rests, however, not upon his record in legislation but upon his achievements in diplomacy, a realm

[8] In 1911 the Workmen's Insurance Code, containing nearly two thousand articles, replaced the earlier separate laws or series of laws in regard to sickness, accident, and invalidity insurance. This code covered practically the whole industrial population of the empire.

in which he stood without a peer. His spectacular success in unifying Germany and establishing the empire has already been mentioned. During the years from 1862 to 1870 his matchless skill was devoted primarily to the task of precipitating wars under circumstances which would be favorable to Prussia. Wars he sought not because he desired military glory for itself, but because he believed that they were essential to the consummation of his plan for a united Germany. During the next two decades, however, his inimitable ability as a diplomat was devoted not to the causing of wars in Europe but to their prevention. Peace, not war, he now believed to be indispensable, for the newly created empire needed most of all to consolidate the gains which had been made by the three preceding wars.

Unfortunately for the peace of Europe, Bismarck's unification of Germany had been accompanied by the annexation of Alsace-Lorraine, an act which was denounced by Frenchmen as a crime—"the brutal dismemberment of a nation." Although the German chancellor hoped to win the French eventually to accept the loss of these provinces as a *fait accompli,* he realized that in the years immediately following the Franco-German War resentment against Germany and desire for revenge were strong among the French. Of France alone he had no fear, but the possibility of France's constructing a coalition of powers hostile to the German Empire constituted for him a veritable nightmare. If he could successfully isolate France diplomatically, however, such a coalition might be prevented and the possibility of an attack upon Germany removed. In order to keep them out of the French orbit he determined, therefore, to establish close relations with the other two great powers adjoining Germany, namely, Austria and Russia.

Within a few months after the signing of the treaty of Frankfort, accordingly, Bismarck brought about friendly personal meetings on Austrian soil between William I and Francis Joseph. In the next year the latter planned to return the visit at Berlin, and Tsar Alexander II, fearful lest the two emperors might reach agreements inimical to the interests of Russia, practically invited himself also to the imperial reunion. In September, 1872, the three rulers and their foreign ministers met in Berlin for conferences. Although no definite commitments were made, the meeting served as a demonstration of reconciliation and friendship as well as an exhibition of monarchical solidarity against the rising tide of socialism. Moreover, the simultaneous visits to Berlin of Francis Joseph and Alexander indirectly strengthened Germany's position by revealing to France the latter's diplomatic isolation.

More definite steps were taken by the three rulers in 1873. Russia and Germany in a secret convention promised military assistance to each other in case either were attacked by another power. A second convention, signed at first by Russia and Austria and later by Germany also, bound all three (1) to consult one another concerning questions in which they might have divergent interests, and (2) to come to an understanding regarding a common line of action in case aggression by any other power menaced the peace of Europe. The entente of 1872 was thus transformed into the so-called League of the Three Emperors.

Unhappily for the cordial relations established by the agreements of 1873, Austria's new policy of seeking to extend her influence southeastward into the Balkans—a policy resulting from her expulsion from Germany and Italy in 1866—brought her into direct conflict with Russia's ambitions in that part of Europe. Germany was thus placed in the embarrassing position of having to choose between two friends. In 1878 at the Congress of Berlin [9] Bismarck threw his support largely to Austria, thus enabling her to secure control of Bosnia and Herzegovina and causing Russia to have to modify the treaty of San Stefano. Russia was blocked in her plan to advance in the Balkans. The tsar was not only deeply resentful but firmly convinced that Russia's misfortunes were caused by Bismarck's action. A violent outburst against Germany occurred in the Pan-Slav press, increases were ordered in Russian armaments, and Russian troops were pushed westward toward the German frontier.

In view of the danger from Russia, Bismarck at once sought a defensive alliance with Austria. He originally desired an agreement in which each would promise to aid the other in case of attack by any third power, but Austria was unwilling to undertake such a far-reaching obligation. The treaty which was signed on October 7, 1879, therefore, was directed primarily against their great Slav neighbor. If either should be attacked by Russia or any power supported by Russia, it stipulated, the other was bound to come to the assistance of the one attacked with its whole war strength. If either, furthermore, should be attacked by any power except Russia, the other was bound to observe a benevolent neutrality. The Austro-German alliance, it is seen, thus gave Bismarck a double assurance. If Russia attacked Germany, Austria would aid Germany; if France attacked Germany, Austria would at least not aid France. From the day of its consummation until the collapse and disappearance of the Dual Monarchy in 1918, this alliance constituted the cornerstone of German foreign policy.

But Bismarck had by no means permanently turned his back upon Russia, for he could never wholly rid himself of the fear that France might form a coalition with that power against Germany. Consequently, when in 1880 Russia sought to gain Germany's support for the closure of the

---

[9] See page 224.

Straits, Bismarck utilized the situation to restore the old harmony between the three empires which had been destroyed by the Congress of Berlin. In June, 1881, a secret convention was finally signed by Germany, Russia, and Austria. By its provisions it was agreed that, if one of the three found itself at war with a fourth power (except Turkey), the other two would

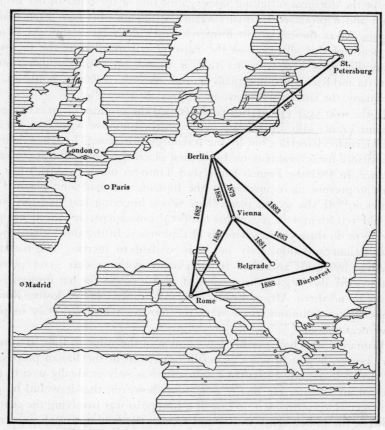

AUSTRO-GERMAN SYSTEM OF ALLIANCES, 1887–1890

preserve a benevolent neutrality toward it and devote their efforts to localizing the conflict. In an attempt to settle the Balkan problem, it was further agreed to respect Austria's rights in Bosnia and Herzegovina under the treaty of Berlin, to make no change in the territorial status of Turkey in Europe except by common consent, to offer no opposition to the eventual reunion of Bulgaria and Eastern Rumelia, and to insist upon the closure of the Straits as laid down in the treaties on that subject. Austria, however, reserved the right to annex Bosnia and Herzegovina whenever she deemed such action opportune.

This alliance of the three emperors had definite advantages for Germany. It re-established monarchical solidarity; it tended to remove causes of conflict between Austria and Russia and thus enabled Germany to escape the dilemma of taking sides against one or the other of her neighbors; and it protected Germany against an alliance between France and Russia. All of these were, in Bismarck's eyes, desirable results. As a consequence of this alliance and the Austro-German alliance, the German chancellor now had assurance that, if France attacked Germany, both Austria and Russia would remain neutral, and that, if Russia should attack Germany, the latter would have in Austria an active ally.

In the next year (1882) Bismarck secured the promise of an active ally against France also. In this case, however, the initiative was taken not by the German chancellor but by the Italian government. The latter desired an alliance for several reasons. In the first place, there was hostility toward France. In 1881 the French had seized Tunis in northern Africa just in time to prevent its occupation by the Italians, who had long planned to annex it.[10] In the second place, there was a lingering fear that the pope would yet attempt to regain his temporal possessions, as indeed he was trying to do through the channels of diplomacy. In the third place, there was Italian ambition. Italy not only wished to increase her national prestige by being associated in an alliance with another great power; she wished also to gain the support of such a power for her imperialistic plans in northern Africa. Enmity toward France, fear of losing Rome, imperialistic ambitions, these were the motives which led Italy to propose negotiations.

Bismarck, who had a rather low opinion of the value of Italy as a military power, was at first not especially interested in the Italian proposals. Reluctant to assume an Italian liability, he was only gradually won to the idea of an alliance. He finally concluded, however, that it would be advantageous to Germany if, in case of a European war involving the central powers, the Italian army was bound to take the field against France and not against Austria. Upon his suggestion, therefore, negotiations were initiated between Italy and Austria. The latter, perceiving the benefit which would come to herself if Italy were bound to remain neutral in case of an Austro-Russian conflict, finally acquiesced in the plan for an alliance. On May 20, 1882, therefore, Germany, Austria, and Italy united in the Triple Alliance.

Under the terms of the treaty, if Italy without direct provocation on her

---

[10] See map on page 19; for discussion of the incident, see page 103.

part were attacked by France, the other two powers were bound to come to her assistance with all their forces. On the other hand, if Germany were attacked by France without direct provocation, Italy was bound to come to the assistance of Germany. If one or two of the signatory powers were attacked and engaged in war with two or more great powers, all three were pledged to assist one another. Finally, it was stipulated that, if a great power should threaten the security of one of the signatory powers and the threatened party should find itself forced to make war, the other two powers were bound to observe a benevolent neutrality.

The Triple Alliance continued in force until 1915 and was therefore one of the most important and most stable of the European alignments. By it Bismarck still further increased the security of the German Empire. In return for the promise to come to the assistance of Italy against a French attack (a contingency very unlikely to happen), Germany obtained very real benefits. Should France attack her, French forces would have to contend also against an Italian army on the Alpine frontier. Should France and Russia jointly attack her, Germany would have the assistance of both Austria and Italy. Finally, should Russia alone attack Germany the latter would benefit from the fact that Austria, not having to fear for her Italian frontier, could send her whole strength against Russia and thus relieve the pressure on Germany's eastern front.

But the Triple Alliance did not complete the network of treaties by means of which Bismarck sought to assure the peace of Europe. With the Austrian government the German chancellor raised the question whether the "League of Peace" could be extended to include Rumania and possibly Serbia and Turkey. In a sense Serbia was already linked with the Triple Alliance by a secret treaty which she had signed with Austria in 1881, agreeing that, without previous understanding with the Dual Monarchy, she would neither negotiate nor conclude any political treaty with another government, and would not admit to her territory a foreign armed force, regular or irregular, even as volunteers.[11]

No such connections existed between Rumania and the central powers, however, and so, upon Austria's approval of the step, Bismarck opened negotiations with Bucharest. The defensive Austro-Rumanian treaty which was signed on October 30, 1883, became the basis of Rumania's adherence to the Triple Alliance. Although Russia was not named in the document, it provided in substance that if Austria or Rumania were attacked by Russia, the two would assist each other against the aggressor. Germany in another agreement signed the same day undertook the same obligations respectively toward Austria and Rumania that they had taken toward each

[11] For a fuller discussion of this treaty see page 262.

other, and in 1888 Italy also adhered to the Austro-Rumanian treaty. The so-called Quadruple Agreement which resulted was regularly renewed and continued in force until the First World War.

But the alliance of the three emperors, created in 1881 and renewed for three years in 1884, suffered a less happy fate. Once again Austro-Russian rivalry in the Balkans smashed Bismarck's diplomatic plans when, in 1887, Tsar Alexander III refused to renew the alliance because of his distrust of Austria and her policy in southeastern Europe. When Bismarck discovered that the tsar was unshakable in his determination to break with Austria, he accepted with alacrity Russia's proposal for a Russo-German defensive treaty. In 1887 the two powers agreed that, if either of them were at war with a third great power, the other would maintain toward it a benevolent neutrality and would seek to localize the conflict. This provision was not to apply, however, to a war in which Russia attacked Austria or Germany attacked France. This so-called reinsurance treaty further recognized Russia's position in the Straits and in the Balkans in much the same way as it had been recognized in the alliance of the three emperors. Again Bismarck had advanced the security of the German Empire, for by the reinsurance treaty France was effectively blocked from securing Russia as an ally in an attack upon Germany.

A glance at the diagram (on page 63) of the network of defensive alliances which the German chancellor created in the two decades after 1871 quickly reveals the extent of France's isolation and the corresponding measure of Bismarck's diplomatic success. The peace of the German Empire was assured, for no power cared to risk a war against a country which was supported by secret alliances assuring it of the co-operation of Austria, Russia, Italy, and Rumania. The German chancellor had cured his nightmare of alliances by inoculation.

Beginnings of Colonial Expansion

Meanwhile, the rise of German industry and trade had created "a veritable hothouse atmosphere for the culture of the colonial idea." Since Germany had made herself supreme in Europe, why, asked many German patriots, should she not extend her power upon the sea and overseas? Unfortunately, the backward and feudal condition of the German states at the time of the Commercial Revolution and the *laissez-faire* doctrines of their various rulers during the first part of the nineteenth century had militated against the acquisition of colonial territory. Although German missionaries and German merchants had settlements and trading posts in Africa and the South Sea isles, not one of the component states which united to form the German Empire in 1871 brought with it a single square mile of overseas dominion.

With the establishment of the empire, however, political disunion and economic weakness ceased to be deterrents to German maritime and colonial expansion. In the very first year of the empire the imperial admiralty was created and a naval base was established at Wilhelmshafen on the North Sea. Increasing commerce demanded naval protection, and as navalism grew it paved the way for colonies. "For a growing people," asserted Prince Albrecht, "there is no prosperity without expansion, no expansion without an overseas policy, and no overseas policy without a navy." During the early years of the empire, however, Bismarck and the ruling classes generally opposed firmly the policy of imperialism. In 1874, for example, the chancellor declined to accept Zanzibar as a German protectorate even though it was voluntarily offered by the native ruler himself.

A number of factors explain Bismarck's unwillingness to encourage colonial undertakings during the early years of his chancellorship. In general, he believed that colonial expansion would involve too great expense, would cause friction with other powers, and would interfere with his efforts to attain German security in Europe. He particularly desired to maintain friendship with Great Britain and was opposed to any activity which would be likely to cause friction with that power while Germany was young and her navy weak. Furthermore, during the period immediately after 1870, he was relying upon the support of the National Liberals to carry through domestic policies, and the latter were in those days still believers in the doctrines of *laissez faire*. Finally, Bismarck believed that there was no general popular demand or support for colonialism within Germany herself.

Nevertheless, by 1876 the chancellor had come to the conclusion that a great state like Germany could not entirely dispense with colonies, and during the next eight years he apparently played a double game. Openly and officially he continued to repudiate the policy of colonial expansion; secretly and indirectly he pursued that very policy. Governmental protection was extended to all overseas commercial enterprises, and a series of commercial treaties both inaugurated a system of overseas trade protection and endorsed the acquisition of naval stations.

Gradually circumstances came to favor Bismarck's open adoption of a policy of overseas expansion. Within the country itself there came an increase of colonial sentiment as advocates of imperialism flooded the empire with propaganda. In 1882 the Colonial Society was founded, and in January, 1884, its official organ, the *Kolonialzeitung,* was launched. By

1884 the organization had some thousands of members scattered in hundreds of places throughout Germany. By that year, furthermore, with Germany's security in Europe apparently attained, the international situation seemed more favorable to German overseas expansion. Although Bismarck still believed it wise to subordinate his colonial policy to the exigencies of foreign relations, he now decided that it was no longer necessary to subordinate it to the point of negation as he had done prior to 1875. On April 24, 1884, accordingly, the chancellor publicly inaugurated the German colonial empire by telegraphing to Lüderitz, a Bremen merchant, that the latter's settlements in Southwest Africa were under imperial protection.

During the next five years Bismarck steadily pursued his new policy of expansion. In the course of the year 1884 the German Empire established four protectorates: Southwest Africa, Kamerun, Togoland, and East Africa. Early in the following year territory was gained in the Far East. A quarter of New Guinea (rechristened Kaiser Wilhelmsland), a group of the Solomon Islands and other islands north of New Guinea (later named the Bismarck Archipelago), and the Marshall Islands were recognized by Great Britain as German protectorates. Within an astonishingly short time, therefore, the foundations of a very respectable colonial empire were laid.[12] General recognition of Germany's new status as a colonial power was in a sense conceded when the first international colonial congress met in Berlin in November, 1884. Over this gathering Bismarck presided and, with France, dictated the provisions of the Congo Act [13] determining the commercial and legal future of a large part of western Africa.

When, in March, 1885, the Steamship Subsidy Bill passed the Reichstag with a large majority, Bismarck announced that at last there was manifest in Germany the "popular support" which he considered indispensable to a colonial policy. A new tone crept into his utterances. He now talked not merely of the empire's duty to protect commercial settlements but of the desirability of colonies for their own sake. Indeed, he began to emphasize their economic value and to urge that Germany should through them be made economically independent. Colonies, he pointed out, would open new markets to German industries, cause further expansion of German trade, and provide a new field for German activity, civilization, and capital.

But Bismarck did not permit his colonial ambitions to interfere with the attainment of the ends sought by his foreign policy. When relations became strained between Germany and Great Britain because of the latter's resentment of his new colonial policy, the German chancellor at once took

---

[12] For the location of Germany's colonies, see the maps on pages 19 and 23.
[13] See page 18.

steps to smooth away all causes of friction so that no *rapprochement* might result between Great Britain and France. So successful were his efforts that Gladstone, British prime minister, in the end even went so far as to welcome Germany as "our ally in the execution of the great purposes of Providence." The Anglo-German "colonial honeymoon" which began in 1885 Bismarck sought to transform into a lasting bond by negotiations for a British alliance in 1889, but in this case without result.

William II and the "New Course"

On March 9, 1888, the aged William I died and was succeeded by his son, Frederick III. The latter, however, was fatally ill at the time of his accession and died on June 15 of the same year. As a result of these circumstances there mounted the imperial throne a young man of twenty-nine years, William II, the grandson of William I. Like his grandfather a firm believer in the value of military power, William II's first imperial messages were issued not to the German people but to the army and navy. Like his grandfather, too, a loyal adherent to the divine-right theory of kingship, he did not hesitate upon occasion to assert that "the king's will is the supreme law of the land." Characterized by his own father as inclined to be vain and conceited, he was also impulsive and strongly influenced by moods. Vigorous, aggressive, and possessed of exceptional ability as a public speaker, he developed a tendency to use pompous language and to resort to spectacular public display, a tendency which seriously embarrassed the imperial government from time to time in the succeeding years. Nevertheless, he played such an important role in German and world affairs that "the Kaiser" came to be synonymous in the popular mind with "William II."

Although the new ruler resembled his grandfather in many respects, he differed profoundly from him in his attitude toward Bismarck. Despite his deep respect for the veteran chancellor's ideas and achievements, William II was himself ambitious for power and eager to rule as well as reign. He was not at all attracted by the prospect of becoming a mere imperial figurehead under the domination of Bismarck. Almost inevitably differences in viewpoint and policies developed between the young, impulsive, ambitious Kaiser and the old, conservative, powerful chancellor whom he had inherited. William II, for example, although he disliked the socialists no less than Bismarck, refused to approve or support the latter's futile antisocialist legislation, which was accordingly permitted to lapse. Bismarck, on the other hand, refused to accept a cabinet order which destroyed his position as intermediary between the other ministers and the Kaiser. Each hesitated to take the final step to sever their relations, but

in 1890 William II finally demanded Bismarck's resignation. For years
Bismarck had assiduously preached that the chancellor was responsible
to the Kaiser and to him alone, and his words now rose to mock him.
In the light of his earlier assertions, when William II withdrew his support, no course was open to him except to resign. Thereafter, until his
death in 1898, Bismarck lived in retirement at Friedrichsruh.

The new chancellor was Count von Caprivi, a veteran soldier, but one
who was unfamiliar with politics, largely dependent on the information
and advice of others, and incapable of effective leadership. To a considerable extent William II became his own chancellor. Although many of
Bismarck's policies were retained in the ensuing years, in some respects
the "dropping of the pilot" appeared to be followed by the charting of
a "new course." This was particularly noticeable in the realm of foreign
affairs, where, despite William II's declaration that his foreign policy
would remain the same as that of his grandfather, fundamental changes
were soon introduced.

William I had repeatedly emphasized the need of keeping the friendship of both Russia and Great Britain, and this aim had been a cardinal
point in Bismarck's successful diplomacy. When the question of renewing
the reinsurance treaty with Russia was raised in 1890, however, counselors
in the German foreign office, hostile to Bismarck, argued against it. The
Russian treaty was, they said, contrary to the spirit of the Triple Alliance,
and it might, furthermore, alienate Great Britain if its existence became
known to that country. William II and Caprivi were won over by these
arguments, and negotiations for a renewal of the reinsurance treaty were
dropped. Thus came almost immediately the first break in the network
of alliances which Bismarck had so laboriously constructed to isolate
France. Russia, herself isolated, grew suspicious of the policy of the new
Kaiser and soon thereafter became receptive to the solicitous proposals
of France.[14]

Eventually Great Britain, too, was alienated from Germany. In this case
the alienation came not as the result of the severing of treaty relations but
in consequence of a fundamental change in the aims of German foreign
policy. Whereas Bismarck had been content to have the German Empire
a military power and the dominant state in continental Europe, William II
was determined through colonial and naval expansion to make it a world
power. But the aims of German world policy inevitably conflicted with
the aims of Great Britain, gradually aroused the latter's suspicions and
fears, and finally drove her, too, into the arms of France.[15]

[14] For the Franco-Russian alliance which resulted in 1894, see page 104.
[15] For these developments, see page 117.

To a certain extent Germany's new world policy was the natural consequence of her astounding economic development after 1890. By that year the empire had fully recovered from its economic collapse of 1874, and in the succeeding years a combination of factors carried it rapidly to the front. Little handicapped by the existence of inefficient and out-of-date industrial plants, the Germans profited by the experience of others and adopted the latest and most improved methods of manufacture. The application to industry of the excellent scientific and technical training provided by German schools and universities, furthermore, frequently brought the discovery of new methods and the introduction of greater efficiency. And the natural industriousness of the German workingman, coupled with the well-known German capacity for organization, made possible the building up of industrial enterprises that could successfully meet all competition. In the two decades after 1890 German industrial and commercial expansion was truly spectacular. The production of steel during that period, for example, increased seven times faster in Germany than in Great Britain.

Germany's industrial expansion in turn demanded world markets for her increased production, raw materials for her almost insatiable machines, and foodstuffs for her rapidly growing urban population. To obtain these William II considered it necessary for Germany, because of her late entrance into world trade, to pursue a vigorous foreign and colonial policy. New colonies were essential if Germany's European hegemony were to be transformed into world power; in fact, to the Kaiser's mind colonial policy was only a branch of that world policy which the German Empire must adopt for the protection of its continental position. He accordingly placed himself at the head of the colonial movement and boldly embarked upon the "new course," departing without apparent hesitation from Bismarck's more cautious policy of subordinating colonial expansion to the exigencies of continental foreign policy.

Furthermore, to support the new world policy William II demanded the building of a powerful navy. Such a navy, he believed, would give expression to the greatness of the new Germany. It would provide the empire's growing commercial and colonial interests with adequate protection, and in case of war would remove from the German people the danger of being cut off from indispensable food supplies and raw materials. Moreover, a powerful navy might be used to back up German diplomatic arguments in the struggle for commercial and colonial advantages; it might, in fact, compel even Great Britain to make concessions in the colonial world rather than "risk" a naval struggle.

The Scramble for Overseas Territory

The "new course" as applied to colonial policy was particularly noticeable during the decade after 1894. This period witnessed a feverish
activity on the part of the Kaiser, who apparently sought by taking advantage of the embarrassments of other countries to gain for Germany a
"place in the sun." During these years, according to one distinguished
specialist in the diplomacy of imperialism, "the Germans made something
of a nuisance of themselves by interjecting themselves into every problem
and by demanding compensation everywhere and at all times." [16]

To facilitate the carrying-out of this policy, William II sought to have
about him ministers who endorsed his views. For example, in 1894, when
he appointed the aged Prince Hohenlohe to the chancellorship, the latter
at once announced that the "support of our colonial possessions is a command of national honor and a manifestation of our national prestige."
In his quest of new territories the Kaiser had also the encouragement of
"big business," the Colonial Society, the Navy League, and the Pan-German
League. The latter—a patriotic organization of teachers and professors,
business and professional men, and officials—was founded in the early
nineties, when it announced as one of its prime aims "the promotion of
an active colonial policy." It sought to further an energetic German
policy of might in Europe and overseas, and above all to carry forward
the German colonial movement to tangible results.

The technique of the Kaiser's "new course" was at once revealed when
friction developed between Great Britain and the Boers of the Transvaal Republic during the years 1894–1895. German warships were sent
to Delagoa Bay, which the British were hoping to obtain from Portugal
in order to control the Boer republic's outlet to the sea; German protests
were raised against Jameson's raid into the republic; and finally the
famous "Kruger telegram" was sent by the Kaiser to the Boer president
congratulating him on "preserving the independence" of his country.[17]
Back of all these actions, apparently, was William II's real desire to land
troops in order to bring about an annexation of territory for Germany, a
step from which he was deterred only by the opposition of his chancellor
and foreign secretary. German activities on this occasion failed to secure
any territory, but they did succeed in bringing to an unhappy end the
Anglo-German "honeymoon" so felicitously arranged by Bismarck.

The Kaiser's next move was in the Far East. With Germany building
a bigger navy and extending her economic interests throughout the world,

---

[16] W. L. Langer, *The Diplomacy of Imperialism, 1890–1902*, Volume II, page 531.
[17] For a fuller discussion of these incidents, see pages 170–172.

the possibility of securing a naval base in the Far East had been discussed for some time in German naval and colonial circles. An ice-free port which would give access to a useful hinterland was sought, and in 1897 Kiaochow on the Shantung peninsula of China was selected as a desirable site. Fortunately for the Kaiser's plans, two German missionaries were murdered by the Chinese in this very Shantung province. "We must take advantage of this excellent opportunity," William II telegraphed to the foreign office, "before another great power either dismembers China or comes to her help! Now or never!" A German squadron was immediately dispatched to Kiaochow, and in March, 1898, a treaty was wrested from China leasing to Germany for ninety-nine years some two hundred square miles of territory on the shores of Kiaochow Bay. Germany thus acquired not only a naval base in the Far East but a valuable economic sphere of influence in the great Chinese Empire.[18] As significant by-products, however, she incurred the increased hostility of Great Britain, the suspicion of France, and the indignation of the rising Far Eastern power, Japan.

The acquisition of one naval base in the Pacific only whetted the Kaiser's appetite for more, and the outbreak of the Spanish-American War in 1898 appeared to offer further possibilities. At first the idea of establishing a German protectorate over the Philippine Islands was seriously considered, but the ultimate decision was to demand adequate compensations for Germany in case the islands fell into the hands of another power. Admiral von Diederichs was dispatched to Philippine waters with a large squadron in the hope of his being able to seize a naval station, but the outburst of anti-German feeling in the United States following disagreements between Admiral von Diederichs and Admiral Dewey in Manila Bay prevented such a step. Instead, Germany sought a division of the colonial spoils in co-operation with the United States, and ultimately, in return for the payment of $4,200,000 to Spain, acquired the Caroline, Palau, and Marianas Islands.[19] Although the islands might serve as naval stations and cable landings, they were of little value economically. Nevertheless, their acquisition was described to the Reichstag by the chancellor as a milestone "along the road of *Weltpolitik*."

Germany next took advantage of Great Britain's isolation and colonial conflicts with France and Russia [20] to try to advance her colonial program. In the view of Joseph Chamberlain, British colonial secretary at that time, she seized the occasion to "blackmail" Great Britain into making conces-

[18] The lease carried with it the right (1) to fortify and administer the territory as if it were Germany's, (2) to build railways into the interior to join the projected Chinese system, (3) to exploit all mines found near the railways, and (4) to enjoy special preference for German capital and materials in the construction of public works in the whole province of Shantung.

[19] Except for Guam, which went to the United States.

[20] See pages 116 and 177.

sions in order to induce her "not to interfere where she has no right of interference." In 1898 Portugal was in need of financial assistance, and it was thought that she might be obliged to mortgage her colonies in Africa. Germany accordingly persuaded the British government to sign a treaty providing for the division of the Portuguese colonies—Angola and Mozambique [21]—between herself and Great Britain as spheres of influence, should Portugal become insolvent and offer her colonies as collateral for a loan. Nothing came of the venture, but it is indicative of the Kaiser's frantic attempts to extend Germany's overseas empire.[22]

In 1899, however, Germany did manage to secure additional territory at Great Britain's expense. In that year a tripartite condominium in Samoa, participated in by Germany, Great Britain, and the United States, came to an end with the death of the native ruler. Out of the tangled negotiations which ensued, in the course of which Germany threatened to break off diplomatic relations with Great Britain, came a new arrangement for Samoa, in consequence of which Germany was enabled to add the islands of Opolu and Sawai to her empire.[23] Great Britain was obliged to be satisfied with compensations elsewhere, giving way only because of Germany's threats at a time when she was embarrassed by her own isolation.

Although in the ensuing years Germany rapidly extended her commercial activities and economic penetration in various parts of the world, she made no further territorial gains until 1911. In that year she precipitated what is known as the second Moroccan crisis [24] by seeking territorial compensation for permitting France to establish a protectorate over Morocco in northwestern Africa. At first Germany demanded that the whole French Congo be given to her; but, when France refused to make any such sweeping cession of territory and when Germany discovered that Great Britain was strongly supporting France in the crisis, Germany was obliged to moderate her demands. In the end she had to be content with a strip of the French Congo which would give German Kamerun access to the Congo River.

Taken altogether, the territory which was added to Germany's overseas empire during William II's reign was pitifully small in extent and in no wise comparable either in area or in importance to the vast stretches which Bismarck had acquired in Africa and the East Indies. And, unfortunately for Germany, in contrast with the great chancellor, who had secured his colonies without engendering much friction or arousing the serious hostility of other countries, William II had made his territorial acquisitions

[21] See the map on page 19.
[22] Unknown to Germany the British government practically nullified the Anglo-German treaty by a treaty of alliance negotiated with Portugal in the following year.
[23] The United States took Tutuila
[24] See pages 121–122.

at the high cost of antagonizing three great powers: Great Britain, France, and Japan.

Mittel-Europa and the *Drang nach Osten*

Meanwhile, the Pan-German League looked with longing eyes upon the 16,000,000 people of German race in central Europe outside the empire and envisaged the day when they might be absorbed into the fatherland and make the latter a mighty state with 80,000,000 citizens of homogeneous nationality. Leaders of the league talked also of a central European customs union and even of a closer connection with Holland, Belgium, Switzerland, and Austria-Hungary, perhaps also Rumania. Such a *Mittel-Europa* would knit together under German leadership the basins of the Rhine, Elbe, Oder, and Danube. Extending from the North Sea and the Baltic to the Black Sea and the Adriatic, it would lie in a strategic position to advance German opportunities for commercial expansion.

Although the Pan-German League never had an immense membership and never gained any tremendous following in the Reichstag, it was "one of the most strident jingo societies in the world and its noise was quite incommensurate with its size." Those who have studied its activities admit that its "indirect influence was probably larger than its direct importance." [25] The theories of the Pan-Germanists found their way into much of the German political writing of the decade before the First World War and caused some alarm abroad, especially among the British, who feared that German economic expansion might open the way for German political domination of the Continent.

Though the Pan-German aspirations to dominion over the Low Countries and over the Adriatic were openly disavowed by the responsible statesmen of Germany, the Kaiser's project of opening up and exploiting the rich resources of the Ottoman Empire was not. Within a year of his accession William II had made an ostentatious visit to the sultan despite the opposition of Bismarck, who maintained that Germany's relations with Turkey must be kept subordinate to her Russian policy. Throughout his chancellorship Bismarck had never forgotten that the price of Russian friendship was a free hand in the Near East, and he had deeply prized that friendship. Bismarck's cautious and skillful diplomacy was cast to the winds, however, by William II. The latter saw in the exploitation of Turkey—one of the few large and potentially rich areas of the world which had not yet been "staked out" by some great power—compensation for Germany's limited colonial opportunities outside Europe.

As early as 1888 a German syndicate had received a concession from

[25] M. Wertheimer, *The Pan-German League*, pages 210 and 217.

Turkey to build a railway from the Bosporus to Angora, and the Anatolian Railway Company had been organized to carry out this project. In the following year the same German syndicate had also secured control of the Oriental Railway connecting Austria-Hungary with Constantinople. In 1893 the Anatolian Railway Company had obtained a further concession to construct a branch line to Konia in southern Anatolia, and this new project was completed three years later. Originally the German syndicate had been given to understand that it would ultimately be granted the right to extend the Anatolian Railway to Bagdad. Bismarck, however, had opposed such an extensive project, maintaining that no one should "lay on the German people the obligation to fight Russia for the future of Bagdad."

But the Kaiser was not deterred by any such ideas. In 1898 he definitely launched his plan for creating a German-Ottoman economic entente which might ultimately be transformed into a political alliance. In that year he made a second spectacular visit to the sultan, and out of that visit came the promise from Turkey of a concession to build the Bagdad Railway to connect Konia with Bagdad and the Persian Gulf. What the Kaiser and his advisers had in mind, apparently, was the construction of a unified railway system extending from the Bosporus across Anatolia to Aleppo, with one branch running from there through Syria to Arabia and Egypt and another running through Mesopotamia to the Persian Gulf.[26] When completed according to the plans, this Bagdad Railway, linked with the Anatolian Railway, the Oriental Railway, and railways of *Mittel-Europa,* would establish a gigantic road of steel, largely under Teutonic control and stretching from the North Sea to the Persian Gulf. Such a railway system—often referred to as the Berlin-Bagdad railway—would enable German capitalists to tap the rich mineral and agricultural resources of the Ottoman Empire and go far toward giving Germany political ascendancy in that part of the world.

Although in the beginning the German bankers had been interested in the Turkish railway concessions primarily for commercial reasons, after 1899 the attitude of the German government and the German public gave the Bagdad Railway project a definitely political complexion in the eyes of foreign statesmen. Russia objected to the further construction of railways in northern Anatolia, and consequently it became necessary to alter the plan for the railway to Bagdad. In 1899 it was decided that the extension to Bagdad should start not from Angora, as originally planned, but from Konia. The British also were disturbed by the project and apprehensive for the safety of their interests in Persia and India. Great

[26] See the map on page 369.

Britain accordingly took prompt steps to block the southern end of the proposed railway by making an agreement (1899) with the sheik of Koweit on the Persian Gulf. The sheik accepted British protection and promised to make no international agreements without British approval. The one possible exit to the Persian Gulf for the Bagdad Railway was thus effectively blocked.

Nothing was done by the German syndicate with the concession received in 1899 until 1903, when a new agreement was made with Turkey, and the Bagdad Railway Company was incorporated to construct and operate the proposed line from Konia to the Persian Gulf. The German promoters of the railway planned to construct it with the aid of a subsidy from Turkey and with loans floated in Germany, Great Britain, and France. According to their plans, representatives from each of these countries would be on the railway company's board of directors, but control would be in the hands of Germans.

Although the British prime minister and foreign secretary favored participation in the project and the formation of a tripartite syndicate, opposition in the cabinet and the hostile attitude of the press eventually forced the British government to abandon the plan to co-operate with the German syndicate. Possibly views expressed in a German book, *Die Bagdadbahn* (1903), may have increased British opposition. The author, Paul von Rohrbach, declared: "England can be attacked and mortally wounded by land from Europe in only one place—Egypt.... We can never dream, however, of attacking Egypt until Turkey is mistress of a developed railway system in Asia Minor and Syria, and until through the extension of the Anatolian Railway to Bagdad she is in a position to withstand an attack by England upon Mesopotamia." The French government, at first benevolently neutral regarding the railway, in 1903 also turned against the project and forbade trading in the securities of the railway on the Paris Bourse. Perhaps its attitude was strongly influenced by its eagerness at that time to win Great Britain to an Anglo-French entente.

In 1908 the German syndicate surrendered to the Turkish government its concession to build the section of the Bagdad Railway from Bagdad to the Persian Gulf and thereby removed the chief ground for British hostility to the project. Directors of the syndicate, eager for British co-operation, recommended giving to the British the section of the railway from Bagdad south. The "dream of the German Bagdad Railway to the Gulf is dreamed away," wrote one of the directors. Negotiations were opened between the German and British governments, but great difficulty was experienced in reaching any agreement. The British suggested a conference of the four powers—Germany, Great Britain, France, Russia—but

Germany declared that in such a conference she would be outvoted three to one.[27] The Germans, for their part, proposed that the section of the railway from Bagdad to Koweit be given over to Great Britain, provided the latter would grant Germany some concession as a *quid pro quo*. Early in 1910 the British foreign secretary declined this proposal as "one which His Majesty's Government cannot entertain."

Some progress was made in solving the Bagdad Railway problem later in 1910, however, when the tsar visited the Kaiser in November of that year. As the result of the so-called Potsdam conversations carried on at that time, Germany came to a general understanding with Russia regarding the railway. By the agreement Russia promised to put no obstacles in the way of the building of the railway and in return secured Germany's recognition of Russia's sphere of interest in Persia.[28] Early in 1914 Germany reached an agreement with France also. In this case the two powers recognized that northern Anatolia and Syria were French spheres of railway construction and that the regions served by the existing Anatolian and Bagdad Railways were German spheres. Finally, in June, 1914, the Germans and the British initialed an agreement. The latter "in recognition of the general importance which the construction of the Bagdad Railway possesses for international trade," promised not to obstruct the building and management of the railway. However, no railway connection between Basra and the Persian Gulf was to be constructed unless a complete understanding had been reached by the British, the German, and the Ottoman governments.

Although before the outbreak of the war in 1914 understandings were thus eventually reached regarding the Bagdad Railway by Germany, Russia, France, and Great Britain, the project had already done much to poison the international atmosphere. Germany had come to believe that the opposition of the three Entente powers was only part of their general policy of encirclement, which was designed to restrict and ultimately crush the German Empire. On the other hand, Russia, Great Britain, and France had become deeply suspicious of Germany's plans in the Near East and had become alarmed by her increasing influence in the Ottoman Empire. Russia, especially, had considered Germany's strong support of Austria-Hungary during the Bosnian crisis of 1908 as proof of the Kaiser's determination to persist in the *Drang nach Osten* at any cost. Russia's realization that the Austro-German advance into the Balkans and Turkey must be checked if her own plans for securing control of the Straits at Constantinople were not to be thwarted had much to do with the course of events during the fateful days of July, 1914.

[27] France, Russia, and Great Britain had in 1907 entered into the Triple Entente. See pages 119 and 190.

[28] A specific agreement was signed in August, 1911.

The Rapid Rise of German Naval Power

Even before William II had become the ruler of Germany he had been deeply interested in naval affairs. After ascending the throne he became increasingly convinced of the need for a larger and more powerful German navy, and in the succeeding years he constantly agitated in favor of increasing the size of the fleet. Throughout the empire it was generally felt, however, that, since Germany was maintaining such a large military establishment, she could not hope to rank as a first-class naval power. Therefore, despite William II's desire for a more powerful fleet—which was at first looked upon as merely one of his whims—Germany in 1895 stood only fifth in naval strength among the powers. Although by that time the German Empire had risen to second place in the world in foreign trade, in sea power she ranked below even Italy.

But by the middle of the nineties the Kaiser began to be joined in his demand for a larger navy by others from many quarters. Merchants from Hamburg, professors from the universities, members of the Colonial Society, and the Pan-German League began to agitate for more warships to protect German commerce. History, it was asserted, could not offer a single example of a great commercial state that had been able to maintain its position for any length of time without the support of sea power. Gradually the members of the Reichstag became less hostile to expenditures for the navy. Hoping to take advantage of the rising sentiment in favor of naval expansion, the Kaiser in 1896 appointed as minister of marine Alfred von Tirpitz, "probably the ablest naval man produced by any country in modern times."

Tirpitz at once began to make his plans for giving Germany a modern fleet, and by October, 1897, he had put his program into form and had secured the approval of the Kaiser. His projected naval bill called for the construction by 1905 of eleven battleships, five first-class cruisers, and seventeen small cruisers. In case of a war against Russia or France or both, such a naval force, it was maintained, would enable Germany to prevent a blockade of the German coasts and thus keep open the lanes of commerce and food supply. Such a fleet, though far from being able to challenge Great Britain on the sea, might lead the latter to take a more favorable attitude toward the German Empire. When the bill was laid before the Reichstag, it received the support of the National Liberals, the Conservatives, and a majority of the Centrists, and in March, 1898, it was finally passed by the lower house.

This act, however, did not in itself provide Germany with a naval force comparable to that of Great Britain or even of France. Consequently, by the summer of 1899, even before his first program was completed, Tirpitz concluded that a new program must be prepared. It was decided to take advantage of sentiment aroused by the Boer War,[29] when a British warship seized a German merchant ship, to introduce a second naval bill, and in December, 1899, the chancellor in an important speech in the Reichstag explained that Germany must have a navy so powerful that even the strongest naval power could not attack it without grave risk. The government's program had the support of those groups which had advocated the enactment of the first bill, but it also had the enthusiastic backing of the recently organized Navy League. The latter, heavily financed by the great steel interests of the empire, had at that time a membership of more than 100,000, a publication, *Die Flotte,* with a circulation of some 250,000, and an active corps of lecturers. The Germans were soon won to a belief in the political value of a great navy as an instrument of *Weltpolitik*.

The second naval bill was rapidly pushed through the Reichstag during the first half of 1900. Only the Social Democrats and a few of the Centrists and Progressives voted against the measure, which was passed in June of that year. The new act provided for a fleet of thirty-eight battleships to be completed in twenty years and to be built regardless of cost. Apparently what the Kaiser and his ministers desired was a fleet large enough to meet the British home fleet, which was at that time about thirty-two ships. Then, they evidently believed, Germany would appear as an attractive possible ally of Great Britain, or, failing this, of Russia or France. Unfortunately, they did not foresee that Germany's naval programs would not attract Great Britain into a German alliance but would ultimately drive her into the arms of France and Russia.

In 1905 Great Britain, taking heed of the value of powerful battleships as demonstrated in the Russo-Japanese War,[30] laid the keel of a new type of fighting craft known as dreadnoughts. The introduction of such large and powerful ships inevitably made all previous battleships largely obsolete, and at once opened the way for Germany to compete on an equal footing with Great Britain in the new category of fighting ships. Of what particular value would Britain's large fleet of obsolete ships be if Germany could have a fleet of dreadnoughts as large as the British? In 1906, accordingly, Germany passed a new navy law providing for six large cruisers of the dreadnought type to be completed in 1918.

As early as 1889 the British government had adopted the policy of maintaining a two-power naval standard, that is, the policy of having a navy as powerful as that of the next two naval powers combined. Naturally, therefore, Germany's determination to construct a powerful fleet disturbed

[29] See page 173.
[30] See pages 237–240.

the British. In 1907 the latter at the Second Hague Conference asked to
have the question of armaments considered, but Germany opposed the
proposal. Instead, Germany steadily progressed with her naval program—
largely, it seems, to satisfy the ego of the Kaiser, who got great satisfaction
from possessing and reviewing his fleet. In 1908 still another German
naval law accelerated the retirement of old warships and authorized the
building of four dreadnoughts yearly from 1908 to 1911 and two yearly
from 1912 to 1917. When the British in 1908 attempted to reach some naval
agreement with Germany, the Kaiser indignantly declared that he would
fight before he would accept dictation in such matters from a foreign
government. In consequence Great Britain was thrown into what has
been called the naval panic of 1909,[31] and in turn proceeded to accelerate
her own construction of dreadnoughts.

In 1909 Bülow, who since 1900 had played an aggressive role in international affairs as German chancellor, resigned and was succeeded by
Theobald von Bethmann-Hollweg. The latter was very eager to improve
relations between Germany and Great Britain. Believing that naval rivalry
was largely the cause of friction between the two powers, he speedily took
up with the British government the question of making some naval
agreement. He proposed that each country should retard its building program in the hope of modifying public opinion in the direction of fewer
ships. But he declared that the naval agreement must be accompanied by
a political agreement in which Great Britain should promise not to attack
Germany and to remain neutral if Germany were attacked by a third
power. Unfortunately for the success of Bethmann-Hollweg's proposals,
officials in the British foreign office doubted the chancellor's sincerity,
professed to believe that his proposal was merely designed to get Great
Britain out of the Triple Entente, and suspected that, once Great Britain's
hands were tied, Germany might feel free to move against other countries.
Sir Edward Grey, British foreign secretary, finally replied that the proximity of parliamentary elections made it inadvisable to discuss naval limitation at that time.

After the second Moroccan crisis [32] German imperialists argued that their
government had been weak in the face of British threats, and demanded
that the German navy should be further increased until it would be
powerful enough to dissuade the British from interfering with German
plans. A sort of Anglophobia spread through Germany in 1911 and 1912,
and many came to believe that Great Britain was the fatherland's most
dangerous enemy. General von Bernhardi's book, *Germany and the Next
War* (1912), voiced the feeling of German chauvinists and was designed

[31] See page 191.
[32] See pages 121–122.

largely to awaken Germans to the urgent need to prepare for the coming conflict. Early in 1912 the Kaiser announced to the Reichstag that a supplementary naval bill would soon be introduced.

By this time, however, certain business men in Germany and Great Britain had come to the conclusion that some effort should be made to reach an Anglo-German understanding. In January, 1912, Sir Edward Cassel, a London banker, had gone to Berlin to open the way for future discussions. Germany appeared willing to consider the British proposals and invited the British foreign secretary to confer with the Kaiser. Sir Edward Grey did not care to make the visit, however, and so Lord Haldane, the British war minister, was sent in his place. As a result of conversations between Haldane and the Kaiser, the latter agreed to retard the construction of the recently proposed ships. But again Bethmann-Hollweg desired to link the naval understanding with a political agreement of some kind. He proposed that the two countries should each promise not to join any combination of powers directed against the other, and that each should remain neutral in case the other was forced into war.

Both in Germany and in Great Britain there were those who desired the Haldane mission to fail. In Germany Tirpitz and his followers strongly opposed any change in Germany's naval program, while in the British foreign office there was great reluctance to accept the political formula suggested by the German chancellor lest it antagonize Russia and France. In April, 1912, Asquith, the British prime minister, declared that the wisdom of prolonging the discussions "about a formula" was doubtful, and in the end nothing tangible came of the Haldane mission.

In May, 1912, Germany's supplementary naval law—creating a new squadron which would eventually include three new dreadnoughts—was passed. Although thereafter Germany slowed down her naval construction slightly, she had risen by 1914 to second place among the naval powers of the world. Unfortunately for the peace of Europe, however, without actually building a navy powerful enough to challenge Great Britain on the seas, the Kaiser by his speeches and by his various navy bills had by 1914 succeeded in thoroughly alarming and antagonizing the British, in whose opinion control of the seas was a matter of national existence.

Efforts to Expand the Triple Alliance

During the nineties William II, like Bismarck in the eighties, sought to draw Great Britain into an alliance with Germany. Twice in 1895 he invited the British to join the Triple Alliance under an implied threat of possible opposition by the continental powers if Great Britain continued her policy of isolation. Apparently, too, his favorable attitude toward the

Boers in 1895 and 1896 was designed in part to frighten Great Britain into closer relations with that alliance. But all his invitations and threats were of no avail. Although the British were willing in 1898 to conclude an Anglo-German alliance to protect their interests in the Far East,[33] they were not willing to enter into any alliance having to do with Europe. Germany on her part declined at that time to ally herself with Great Britain against Russia in the Far East, and continued to hope that the pressure of other countries might yet drive the British to link themselves with the Triple Alliance. During the Boer War, when the possibility of a continental coalition against Great Britain was being discussed, Germany stood by the British in the hope of winning their good will. Unfortunately for Germany's hopes, her own naval law of 1900 apparently had more effect upon Great Britain and doubtless hastened the consummation of the Entente Cordiale between that country and France.

After 1904 the Kaiser turned his attention to the task of securing an alliance with Russia. He had given diplomatic support to the latter in her demand that Japan withdraw from the Asiatic mainland in 1895 and had urged the tsar forward in his advance into Manchuria in 1898.[34] In 1904, after Russia with Germany's encouragement had become involved in the Russo-Japanese War, the Kaiser outlined to the tsar a plan for a continental alliance of Germany, Russia, and France against Great Britain. Relations between the last and Russia were severely strained at the time, and matters actually progressed to the point where a treaty was drafted in which Germany and Russia promised mutual aid in case either should be attacked by a European power. Unfortunately for the Kaiser's scheme, however, the two rulers disagreed as to whether the treaty should be signed first and France be later informed or vice versa, and in the end the project was dropped.

In 1905, after an armistice had been signed in the Russo-Japanese War, the Kaiser again conferred with the tsar—this time near Björkö in the Gulf of Finland—and on this occasion he won the tsar over to his point of view. A treaty was signed (July 24, 1905) with terms as outlined above, and it was agreed that, after the new pact became effective, Russia should notify France of its terms and should attempt to gain her adherence also. "At last," William II joyfully informed his chancellor, "the fatherland is free from the clutch of the Franco-Russian Alliance." But much to the Kaiser's surprise, both Chancellor von Bülow and Baron von Holstein, political director of the German foreign office, severely criticized the treaty which he had so high-handedly concluded.

The somewhat simple-minded tsar was likewise astonished to discover

[33] See pages 178–179.
[34] For these developments, see pages 235–236.

that France would have nothing to do with the Björkö pact. Furthermore, the tsar's foreign minister did not hesitate to point out the incompatibility of the Russo-German agreement and the Franco-Russian alliance of 1894. It appeared that the friendship of France would be lost if the Björkö agreement were carried through, that Russia would have to choose between Germany and France. Financial reasons, if no others, dictated friendship with the latter, for the expenditures in connection with the Russo-Japanese War and the Russian revolution which began in 1905 made foreign borrowing absolutely necessary. Nicholas II therefore declined to let the Björkö treaty become effective, and the Kaiser's grandiose scheme for a continental alliance against Great Britain dissolved into thin air. But, obviously, if the treaty had been ratified, and if France had acceded to it, the Entente Cordiale would have been destroyed, and Great Britain would have become isolated among the European powers.

The Eve of the First World War

Meanwhile William II's determination to pursue a course of *Weltpolitik* had not gone unchallenged within Germany. In the opening years of the twentieth century the Center, Progressive, and Social Democratic Parties organized in the Reichstag a solid bloc in opposition to the Kaiser's colonial policy. The Centrists resented the expense connected with the policy, deplored the accompanying cruelties and ill treatment of the natives, and denounced the maladministration of the colonies. The Social Democrats vigorously opposed the policy on the ground that it tremendously enriched a few capitalists but brought to the mass of German workers only an increasingly heavy tax.

From 1903 to 1906 the conflict was waged in the Reichstag. Opponents of imperialism argued that Germany's trade with her colonies was so small in comparison with that with other countries that it did not warrant the expense of having them. They showed, for example, that Germany's colonial trade in 1904 constituted only half of one per cent of the country's total foreign trade, that in 1906 Togoland alone of all the German colonies was self-supporting. They pointed out, further, that most of the country's overseas territories were unsuitable for European settlement and produced figures to show that in 1903 there were in all the colonies a total of only 5125 Germans, of whom 1567 were officials and military.

Eventually, in 1906, the Reichstag drastically reduced the amounts demanded by the government for imperial purposes and thus precipitated a parliamentary crisis over Germany's colonial policy. The deadlock brought the dissolution of the Reichstag by Chancellor von Bülow, who declared that "the issue involves the question of our entire colonial policy and, what is more, of our position in the world." "Germany's position in the world is menaced," declared the *Norddeutsche Allgemeine Zeitung.* "The forthcoming election will decide whether Germany is capable of developing into a world power." The electoral campaign which ensued witnessed an unprecedented interference on the part of the imperial administration, which had the support of the various nationalist societies. The Navy League, the Pan-German League, the Colonial Society, and the Association for the Suppression of Socialism utilized their nation-wide organizations to appeal to German "patriotism" to support the government. The Progressive Party ultimately shifted over in favor of imperialism, so that only the Centrists and the Social Democrats were left in the opposition. The election returns revealed that these two parties combined had suffered a loss of more than 20 per cent of their Reichstag seats, and constituted, therefore, a decisive endorsement of the Kaiser's policy of *Weltpolitik.* Said Bülow, quoting the great and beloved Bismarck, "You have placed Germany in the saddle and now she can ride."

One explanation of the seemingly overwhelming defeat of the Centrists and Social Democrats in the election of January, 1907, was to be found in the fact that there had never been a reapportionment of the Reichstag seats since the founding of the empire. In the thirty-six years since 1871 great shifts had occurred in Germany's population as a consequence of the industrialization of the country, and the failure to recognize these changes in the empire's population resulted in a Reichstag which was no longer truly representative of the German people. Densely populated urban communities were grossly underrepresented, while sparsely settled rural regions like those in Pomerania and East Prussia were tremendously overrepresented. Such a condition, of course, constituted a very serious handicap to the parties representing the more densely populated areas. The Social Democrats vigorously demanded a redistribution of the Reichstag seats in proportion to Germany's population as it was in the industrial twentieth century.

There was in fact an increasingly widespread desire that the German Empire be democratized, a desire which was voiced not alone by the Social Democrats. The National Liberal, Progressive, and Center Parties all favored a reapportionment of representation in the Reichstag. But the Social Democrats went further by demanding that women be given the franchise, and that the chancellor be made responsible to the Reichstag, that is, that ministerial responsibility be introduced in the empire. In this last demand the Social Democrats were supported by the Progressives also. Finally, the Social Democrats, the National Liberals, and the Progressives all advocated the abolition of the three-class system of voting which had prevailed in Prussia since 1850 in the election of that state's local Landtag.[35] In the years just before the First World War, accordingly, Germany's semi-autocratic system of government was being more and more openly attacked by her own citizens.

In 1908 an indication that the Kaiser's irresponsibility might not long go unchallenged was forthcoming when William II permitted the *London Daily Telegraph* to publish an interview dealing with Anglo-German relations. Although the Kaiser had apparently hoped by his statements to reduce the ill feeling which existed between the British and German peoples, his tactlessness resulted in infuriating them both. Bülow, the chancellor, seized the occasion to exact a promise from William II that in the future he would make no public statements without the previous approval of the chancellor. The Reichstag also, by a decisive vote, condemned the Kaiser's irresponsible action. Had all those who desired to introduce ministerial responsibility stood loyally together at this time, parliamentary government might have been obtained. But the National Liberals hung back, and no step was taken.

In 1909 the coalition of Conservatives and National Liberals which had been supporting Bülow split on the issue of his finance bill, which, to meet the rising costs of the army and navy, included an inheritance tax. The latter was distasteful to the Conservatives, who therefore deserted the chancellor and helped to defeat his budget. In July, 1909, Bülow resigned as chancellor and was succeeded by Bethmann-Hollweg. In order to dispel any rising hope that Bülow's resignation might constitute a precedent for ministerial responsibility, the new chancellor hastened to announce that, even if he should fail to secure the support of the Reichstag, he would remain at his post as long as he retained the confidence of the Kaiser. By concessions to the Conservatives in matters of taxation, however, he managed to create a bloc including them and the Centrists which lasted until 1912.

The elections of that year revealed the growing opposition to the government. Despite the chancellor's promises of future political reform and despite his vigorous attacks upon the Social Democrats, the latter won their greatest electoral victory up to that time, increasing their representation in the Reichstag from 43 to 110 seats. They now constituted the largest single group in the Reichstag and failed of electing their candidate for the presidency of that body by only twenty-one votes. Eventually the government was enabled to carry on, but only by forming a Reichstag bloc which included practically all groups except the Social Democrats. Nevertheless, one fact must have caused considerable concern to the Kaiser and his chan-

---

[35] By this ingenious system, in which voters were divided into three classes according to the amount of taxes they paid, the wealthier citizens in the first two classes—though constituting a relatively small minority of the total population of Prussia—were able to defeat the bulk of the voters who composed the third class.

cellor—in 1912, for the first time in the history of the empire, the elections had gone decisively against the government.

Nor did developments in the Reichstag in the succeeding months bring much comfort. In 1912 Bethmann-Hollweg's government attempted to enforce a law against the Poles living in eastern Germany. This law, which had been enacted in 1908 under Bülow as part of the government's program to "Germanize" the Polish districts, provided that Polish landowners might be dispossessed of their holdings by a government commission, in case they refused to sell, so that German colonists might be settled in that region in their stead. The price to be paid to the Polish landowner would be determined by German courts. The act had originally encountered vigorous protests, but, influenced by the demands of Pan-Germans and extreme chauvinists, Bethmann-Hollweg undertook to force the sale of a few estates. The repercussion in the Reichstag was immediate and loud. In January, 1913, by a vote of more than two to one, the Reichstag resolved that the policy of the chancellor was contrary to its views, and thus passed the first vote of "no confidence" in the history of that body.

Before the year was out another vote of "no confidence" had been passed, this time as a result of events in Alsace. The German government had never succeeded in "Germanizing" or conciliating the bulk of the inhabitants of Alsace-Lorraine. At the time of their annexation in 1871 the elected representatives of the provinces had unanimously protested against being torn from France and had demanded a plebiscite on the question. Their demand had been refused, and the provinces, treated like a conquered territory, had been converted into an imperial territory (*Reichsland*) ruled by a government responsible to the Kaiser. After 1874 Alsace-Lorraine was permitted fifteen representatives in the Reichstag, and for years these deputies continued to denounce the annexation. When in the late eighties the possibility of reunion with France began to appear chimerical, the inhabitants of the provinces launched a demand for rights as Germans. They sought to obtain for Alsace-Lorraine a local government such as the other states of the empire had. For a generation their demand went unheeded, while hundreds of thousands of Germans were settled in the provinces in an attempt to "Germanize" them.

Eventually, in 1910, Alsace-Lorraine was informed that it would be given its own government, and in the next year a new constitution was voted by the German parliament. It stipulated that a bicameral legislature should be the sole source of legislation for the provinces, but the political machinery was so constructed as to retain most of the control in the hands of the imperial government. The governor of Alsace-Lorraine was appointed by the chancellor, and the ministry of the local government was responsible to this governor. Although the lower house of the legislature was popularly elected, enough members of the upper house were appointed to give the government control of that body. If the lower house attempted to impose its will by refusing to pass the budget, the government might use that of the preceding year. The fifteen Reichstag representatives of Alsace-Lorraine were popularly elected, but the three Bundesrat representatives were appointed by the governor. The constitution was a deep disappointment to the people of Alsace-Lorraine.

Relations between the appointed government of the provinces and the local legislature were far from amicable. In 1912 and in 1913 votes of censure were passed against the government. The fact that the imperial authorities kept a large army in the provinces further antagonized the inhabitants, and the overbearing attitude of the military was a constant source of complaint. In 1913 the latter were especially obnoxious in the Alsatian town of Zabern, making arbitrary arrests and imprisoning civil judges who protested against military violence. On one occasion a lieutenant slashed with a saber the forehead of an unoffending lame Alsatian cobbler. When a civil court sentenced the lieutenant to forty-five days' imprisonment, a military court promptly canceled the sentence and released the officer. This incident resulted in the Reichstag's passing another vote of "no confidence," this time by more than five to one. Although the chancellor did not resign, these votes in 1913 appeared to be symptomatic of the increasing strength and confidence of the popularly elected branch of the imperial government. It seemed that in time democratic reform must inevitably come in the German Empire.

To ward off such an eventuality as long as possible, the conservative groups began to appeal to patriotism and to cite the increasingly threatening international situation in Europe. The opportunity offered by the rise in nationalistic spirit in 1911 was immediately seized upon by the German general staff to demand an enlargement of the military forces. Those interested in further building up the army founded in 1912 the Security League, which was designed to propagandize the German people systematically with militarism. The military, although at first opposed by the civil authorities, eventually won out, and in May, 1912, a law was passed providing for a reorganization and increase in man power of the army during the succeeding five years. But the militarists were not yet satisfied. They continued to demand a still larger army because of "recent changes in the Balkans," [36] because of the "growing menace of Russian Pan-Slavism," [37] and because of "France's desire for war." [38] In April, 1913, the government introduced a new army law, which was passed on

[36] For the Balkan wars, see pages 309–312.
[37] For Russian Pan-Slavism, see page 251.
[38] For the situation in France, see page 123.

June 30. By the provisions of the new law the peacetime army of Germany would consist of about 870,000 men when the military plans were completed in April, 1914.

Within the German Empire there were, of course, great numbers who desired peace.[39] But unfortunately for the peace of Europe, the militaristic utterances of the extreme chauvinists and the above-mentioned programs of military and naval expansion almost completely overshadowed this fact. In consequence, there was steadily developing in other countries during 1913 and 1914 a profound distrust and increasing fear of Germany. The growing alarm eventually led President Wilson of the United States to send Colonel House, his personal representative, to Europe in 1914 to explore the possibilities of preventing the outbreak of a great war. When Colonel House visited Berlin in May of that year, he discovered a condition which he described as "militarism gone mad."

[39] In 1912 the Union for International Understanding was organized to denounce war agitation and to work for peace. Other peace societies were founded, and it is said that pacifist literature was being more widely read between 1912 and 1914 than that of the militarists.

Chapter IV

THE THIRD FRENCH REPUBLIC

AT the opening of the year 1870 France was a monarchy presided over by Emperor Napoleon III, nephew of the famous Napoleon Bonaparte. For some time Napoleon III's prestige had been declining, as a result of his ill-fated intervention in Mexico and his failure to play an important role during and after the Austro-Prussian War of 1866. In July, 1870, therefore, the French government, in the hope of restoring the waning prestige of the Bonapartist dynasty and of weakening the position of Prussia, seized the opportunity created by an offer of the Spanish throne to a Hohenzollern prince to launch a war against Prussia. This, of course, was exactly what Bismarck ardently desired it to do. The French expected that the ensuing hostilities would occur on German soil and that the South German states would join with France in administering a decisive defeat to a common foe.

Disaster and Recovery

But the French armies never reached German territory, the South German states fought on the side of Prussia, and in September at Sedan the French suffered a crushing defeat, the emperor himself being taken prisoner. The news of the disaster was followed in Paris by an immediate demand for the abolition of the empire and ultimately by the proclamation of the republic and the establishment of a provisional Government of National Defense. The latter placed upon the deposed emperor all blame for the war and announced that it was willing to end hostilities immediately on condition that no territory should be taken from France. But since it was the intention of German leaders to make annexations of territory as a result of the German victories, the war continued with the Germans laying siege to Paris.

Eventually the Parisians were starved into submission, and in January, 1871, an armistice was signed to permit the election of a National Assembly to decide whether or not France should make peace at the cost of losing territory. Gambetta, the outstanding leader of the republicans, favored a continuance of the war in the vain hope of preventing the loss of territory, and most of the other republican candidates took a similar stand.

As a majority of the French people, especially the peasants, wanted peace and could see no possible gain to be made in waging a hopeless struggle, they voted against republican candidates, with the result that the new National Assembly consisted of a majority of royalists, who had stood for peace. The Assembly, when it met at Bordeaux, voted overwhelmingly to end the war, and elected the liberal-monarchist Thiers as "Chief of the Executive Power," with authority to negotiate with Bismarck for peace. Being predominantly royalist in its membership, the Assembly took no formal step to recognize the republic, but rather to the dismay of republicans voted to move the seat of government to Versailles, so long unfavorably connected in the popular mind with the monarchy.

But, before Thiers could conclude the negotiations for peace, he was faced with a serious insurrection at home. During the time when Paris was besieged, a new government had been organized in that city by committees of workingmen and middle-class republican national guardsmen. This was the Commune of Paris. The various elements constituting and supporting the Commune differed widely in the matter of ultimate aims, but they were agreed on at least one point, namely, that the monarchy should not be restored. Naturally, therefore, the Commune came to look with suspicion upon the newly elected, predominantly royalist National Assembly, which had hastened to make Versailles the seat of its government and had authorized the negotiation of what was bound to be a humiliating peace. Nor was this all. To the masses of Parisians, who had already suffered severely in the war, it appeared that the National Assembly was determined to heap further hardships upon them. It ordered, for instance, that the government's payment of wages to the National Guard—which included all able-bodied men in Paris—should be stopped; and at the same time it decreed that the payment of rents and debts—upon which there had been a moratorium during the war—should be resumed. To the lower classes of the city, unable to obtain employment because of the dislocation of industry and commerce resulting from the war, it appeared that the National Assembly was the instrument of the wealthy creditor classes against the suffering masses.

The Commune of Paris therefore raised the red flag of socialism, launched a revolt against the National Assembly, and urged other communities to organize similar "communes," to join in a general movement to repudiate the Assembly's authority, and to establish a federated state in which each commune should be self-governing. In such a decentralized state, it was hoped, the industrial centers would not be outweighed by conservative peasants, and socialism might be established by the urban workingmen. Communes were set up in a number of other cities, but they were quickly suppressed. The Commune of Paris, however, was able to defend itself for weeks, thanks to the military experience of its adherents among the national guardsmen and thanks to the enthusiastic support which it received from various radical groups in the city—anarchists, socialists, and embittered republicans. The conservative elements of Paris were for a time pushed unceremoniously into the background.

In the provinces most Frenchmen were alienated by the radicalism of the Parisians and alarmed at the prospect of a bloody civil war. They therefore threw their support whole-heartedly to the National Assembly when the latter decided to use the French armies recently returned from the front to put down the Commune. In April, 1871, French troops laid siege to Paris, and after six weeks of fighting finally forced their way into the city. From then on the conflict became a bitter fratricidal struggle in which neither side showed much mercy. Outnumbered and outgeneraled, the Communards resorted to frightful acts of revenge and destruction. Prominent persons held as hostages were slain in cold blood, and famous buildings, including the Tuileries, were destroyed by fire. In retaliation, the troops of the National Assembly frequently shot down the prisoners whom they captured.

In the end the forces of the Versailles government won, and order was gradually restored in the city, which had passed through two sieges within nine months. Severe measures were taken by Thiers' government against the defeated Communards. Imprisonment, exile, and death were meted out in a sort of judicial terrorism which was inaugurated after the collapse of the revolt. By 1875, it has been estimated, over thirteen thousand Communards had been imprisoned or deported. Consequently, one result of the uprising of the Paris Commune was that the republic, with most of the radical leaders of Paris dead or in exile, was left in the hands of leaders who were for the most part moderate. Another result was that for a decade or two economic and political radicalism of any kind was held in suspicion not only in France but in other bourgeois countries as well.

In the midst of its struggle with the Paris Commune Thiers' government had concluded its negotiations with Bismarck, and on May 10, 1871, had signed the treaty of Frankfort. By the provisions of this treaty France was compelled to cede Alsace and a large part of Lorraine to the new German Empire. She was, furthermore, to pay an indemnity of five billion francs within three years and to submit to and support a German army of occupation until the indemnity was paid. In the eyes of all Frenchmen the peace terms were both severe and humiliating, and it was only with great reluctance that the National Assembly eventually ratified the treaty.

By the summer of 1871 France was again at peace both at home and abroad and in a position to turn her attention to measures of reorganization and recovery. The National Assembly, which had been elected for the purpose of making peace with Germany, declined, however, to dissolve after peace was secured. Instead, it assumed by the Rivet law of August, 1871, power both to govern France and to prepare a new constitution. For various reasons, discussed below, the latter task was difficult and somewhat long delayed. But in matters of ordinary legislation and administration the National Assembly and the government of Thiers made considerable progress.

One task which confronted the government was that of liberating the country from the occupation of German troops. The presence of foreign soldiers on French soil was a constant reminder of the nation's recent defeat. Furthermore, it constituted a financial drain on the republic's budget. But the occupying forces would not be removed until the indemnity had been paid, and might in fact be increased if payments were not forthcoming. Thiers, therefore, immediately turned his attention to the raising of funds to pay the indemnity, and through popular loans floated both in France and abroad the needed money was secured. France was happily freed of German troops six months before the end of the stipulated three-year period, and Thiers was enthusiastically hailed as the "liberator of the territory."

But the French were concerned not only in getting the German troops out of France but in keeping them out in the future. The military system of the Second Empire had been seriously discredited by a defeat which, the French believed, had been caused not by lack of heroism or fighting ability on their part but by the superiority of the Prussian system. In 1872, therefore, a law was enacted introducing in France the Prussian principle of universal compulsory military service. In theory every able-bodied Frenchman was to serve five years in the active army and a longer period in the reserve. Actually, because of financial difficulties, the system was not fully enforced. Part of those subject to military training were chosen by lot for the five-year period; the rest received only six months of training in the active army. Other measures were taken, too, to strengthen France. New forts were constructed along the new German frontier, and the powerful fortifications about the capital were further strengthened. The French were still determined that, so far as military might was concerned, France should continue to be a great power. Some, in fact, even envisaged the day when France might undertake a successful war of *revanche*.

The Establishment of the Republic

When on September 4, 1870, France was proclaimed a republic by Gambetta and his associates, the step was taken without consulting the French people. Although the action was in accord with the desires of those staunch republicans who had long sought to restore a republic of the type that had been proclaimed in 1792 and again in 1848, it was obviously distasteful to the royalists. The latter were, in general, of three types, differentiated by their ideas regarding the dynasty which should sit on the throne of France: (1) Legitimists, conservative or reactionary royalists who desired to enthrone Henry, Count of Chambord, grandson of the last Bourbon monarch, Charles X; (2) Orleanists, liberal royalists who sought to elevate to the throne the Count of Paris, grandson of the last Orleanist ruler, Louis Philippe; and (3) Bonapartists, imperialists who sought to continue the Napoleonic dynasty which had only recently been overthrown.

Royalist Groups

It has already been pointed out that the National Assembly, elected in February, 1871, to decide upon the question of war or peace, had a strong majority of royalists. It is not surprising, therefore, that, when it first convened at Bordeaux, the Assembly took no step committing itself to a permanent continuance of the republic which had been proclaimed. Under Thiers' guidance a temporary political truce was voted in the "Pact of Bordeaux," in which the Assembly agreed that the republican government should continue temporarily without prejudice to the later claims of any party. Doubtless the thought was that, once peace had been made with the enemy, the question of France's permanent government could be settled by a test of strength of the various groups.

But when by the early summer of 1871 peace had been concluded and order restored in France, the royalist majority in the Assembly refused to permit the election of a new constituent assembly to draft a permanent constitution. Apparently the royalists were reluctant to submit the political future of France to a popular plebiscite. Instead, they forced through the Assembly the Rivet law conferring upon that body constituent powers. That is to say, the Assembly which was elected to decide upon peace or war, now, without further consulting the people of France, assumed or usurped the authority to draft a constitution. At the same time it gave Thiers, a liberal monarchist, the title of "President of the French Republic," stipulating, however, that the president should be responsible to the Assembly and presumably removable by it. Thus a crude parliamentary system of government was inaugurated, but without constitutional basis.

When the royalists next sought to restore the monarchy, they soon discovered that, though they constituted a majority in the Assembly, they were, as stated above, fatally divided among themselves. Consequently, little progress was made in the drafting of a constitution. The Legitimists were inclined to desire a France which should be reminiscent of the old regime, which should faithfully protect the interests of the aristocracy and the Catholic Church. The Orleanists, on the other hand, desired to establish a liberal constitutional monarchy somewhat on the order of the British,

"VIVE THIERS!"

French rejoicing at Belfort over the departure of the German army of
occupation in 1873.

in which the king should reign but not rule. Obviously, it was difficult to reconcile these incompatible ideas in one constitutional document. And it was equally difficult to arrange a settlement satisfactory to the two major claimants to the throne. The Count of Chambord could not forget that his grandfather had been driven from his throne by the very revolution which had enthroned the grandsire of the Count of Paris.

The delays and uncertainties contingent upon the political maneuvering of the Legitimists and Orleanists, each group seeking to advance its own cause at the expense of the other, ultimately led Thiers to abandon his liberal monarchist ideas and to decide that a republic was after all the type of government which would least divide the French people. Thiers therefore began to advocate a conservative republic. Such views were, of course, anathema to the royalists, who, though unable to agree on many subjects, did agree that Thiers should be removed from the presidency. That aged and veteran statesman was consequently forced to resign, and to his place a dyed-in-the-wool royalist, Marshal MacMahon, was elected by the Assembly. It was believed that MacMahon would willingly resign the presidency when the royalist impasse was ultimately overcome.

Alarmed, perhaps, by Thiers' conversion to the republic and by Gambetta's active campaigning in its behalf, the royalists now redoubled their efforts to achieve their end. Eventually they persuaded the Count of Paris to seek a compromise with his cousin. Pocketing his pride, the Orleanist candidate consented to visit the Count of Chambord, who was living in Austria, and to recognize him as the head of the family. The two royalist candidates agreed that the Legitimist Count of Chambord should mount the throne as Henry V and that, since he had no children, he should be succeeded by the Orleanist Count of Paris and his heirs. The impasse, it appeared, had at length been overcome; the republic seemed doomed.

But, unfortunately for the plans of the royalists, the Count of Chambord was the type of Bourbon who had learned nothing. He had not been in France for forty years and was completely out of touch with the country; he was still thoroughly permeated by the political and religious ideas of the old regime; he was an ardent believer in the divine right of monarchs and a loyal standard-bearer of the Bourbon white flag. When all these facts were emphatically brought home to the Orleanist liberal monarchists by the Count of Chambord's announcement of his divine-right ideas and by his insistence upon the restoration of the Bourbon flag in place of the beloved tricolor, the liberal monarchists themselves drew back. The compromise plan thus came to naught.

The Orleanists now decided that it would be to their best interest to co-operate with the republicans until such time as the reactionary Count of Chambord should be removed from the scene by death. Then, they reasoned, their liberal Count of Paris might ultimately come to the throne. In November, 1873, accordingly, the Orleanists joined with the republicans to the extent of passing through the National Assembly a bill fixing President MacMahon's term of office definitely at seven years. The liberal royalists hoped that within this period events might so shape themselves that the way would be cleared for an Orleanist restoration. As it eventually proved, however, this was the first constitutional step in the definite establishment of the republic.

General distrust and more political maneuvering delayed further steps in constitution-making until 1875. Meanwhile, Gambetta and other republican leaders were busily agitating in favor of the republic. Gradually some of the royalists became alarmed lest the unsettled conditions in the country should encourage a Bonapartist revival or even lead to some radical republican regime. To them a conservative republic was much to be preferred to either of these alternatives. Consequently, by January, 1875, enough of the royalists had been won over by the republicans so that it was possible by the slim margin of one vote to enact a law making definite provision for the method of election and the re-eligibility of the president of the republic. In the succeeding months of that year the Assembly at last gave itself definitely to the drafting of further "constitutional laws." By the close of 1875 the organic laws constituting the new republican government had been completed, with provision for a president, a cabinet of ministers, a popularly elected Chamber of Deputies, and an indirectly elected Senate. With the structure of the new government completed, the National Assembly, which had governed France since 1871, was thereupon dissolved.

But the dissolution of the royalist Assembly did not bring to an end the struggle between royalists and republicans. The former had by no means given up the fight. Although, as a result of the first parliamentary elections in 1876, the republicans controlled the Chamber of Deputies, the royalists controlled the Senate. And the president, too, it must be remembered, was a royalist. President MacMahon, who sincerely believed that France should have a monarchical form of government, did his utmost to advance the royalist cause, working particularly through the army and the Catholic clergy. But the republican leaders, especially the dynamic lawyer-politician, Gambetta, were not slow in counterattacking. Throughout the length and breadth of France Gambetta, the "traveling salesman of the republic," denounced the alliance between the royalists and the church, and gradually won many anticlericals to the republican cause by his repeated assertion, "Clericalism is the enemy!"

In May, 1877, President MacMahon made another move to advance the royalist cause when, despite the republican control of the Chamber of

Deputies, he forced the resignation of the republican ministry, replaced it with one consisting of royalist and clerical sympathizers, dissolved the Chamber, and called for new elections. President MacMahon asserted that he had the right to select such ministers as he chose, regardless of the wishes of the Chamber of Deputies, which asserted that the cabinet must be satisfactory to the Chamber. In the ensuing campaign the issue, therefore, was not merely royalism versus republicanism but also parliamentary versus presidential government. In other words, whether France was to be a republic or a monarchy, the question was: Should the ministry be responsible to the popularly elected Chamber, as in Great Britain, or to the titular executive of the state, as in the German Empire? In the exciting electoral campaign which ensued the various groups of republicans were fused by Gambetta into a "Federation of the Left," which, thanks largely to his enthusiasm, energy, and oratory, won a decisive victory. The new Chamber at once forced the resignation of the royalist ministry, and President MacMahon recognized the situation by appointing a cabinet which was satisfactory to the Chamber. The issue was thus settled in favor of parliamentary government.

When, in 1879, elections to the Senate gave the republicans control of that body also, President MacMahon apparently recognized the futility of his royalist campaign. Faced by a republican Senate, a republican Chamber, and a republican ministry, the royalist president resigned his office. Jules Grévy, a staunch bourgeois republican with a reputation for dignified and sound statesmanship, was at once elected president, and at last the government of the French Republic was actually in the hands of loyal republicans.

The political framework of the Third Republic, though merely pieced together by a succession of "constitutional laws" and though planned by a goodly number of those who drafted it to be only a stop-gap affair, proved to have unexpected strength and permanence, lasting with comparatively little change down to 1940. The constitution upon which it rested consisted not of a single document, as in the former German Empire, but simply of a number of organic laws enacted by a National Assembly which never had been empowered to draft a constitution. It was neither systematic in its arrangement nor comprehensive in what it covered. There was nothing in it regarding the sovereignty of the people. Nevertheless, of all the great powers on the Continent, the French Republic was the only one which in the years after the First World War continued its political structure unchanged.

The National Assembly did not fundamentally alter the administrative system established by Napoleon I, and the Third Republic, in contrast with the former German Empire, was a highly centralized state, divided for administrative purposes into units called departments. In each department the executive officer was a prefect, an appointee of the central government, who was assisted by an elected council with somewhat meager powers. The departments were subdivided into districts, the latter into cantons, and the cantons into communes, of which there were some 36,000 in the republic.

The legislative power of the republic rested in a bicameral parliament consisting of a Chamber of Deputies, elected directly for a four-year term by universal manhood suffrage, and a Senate, elected indirectly for nine years, one third being retired every three years. The senators were chosen by electoral colleges, one in each department, consisting of the deputies of the department, members of the local councils of the department and its districts, and representatives from each of its communes. It was originally provided that seventy-five senators should hold office for life, but this provision was later repealed. The Chamber of Deputies was the more powerful of the two houses, for, though in theory the Senate had equal authority with the Chamber, in reality it acted more as a brake on hasty action of the popularly elected house. The Chamber was the body which usually controlled the rise and fall of ministries. When the Chamber and the Senate met in joint session they constituted the National Assembly, which had power to amend the constitution by a majority vote, provided the proposal for the amendment had previously been made by the president or by a majority vote of each house.

The president of the republic was elected for a seven-year term by the National Assembly. His powers were distinctly limited. He had no veto power over legislation passed by parliament, and all his acts had to be countersigned by a member of the cabinet. Under the constitution he had the authority, with the consent of the Senate, to dissolve the Chamber. So much discredit was cast upon the use of this power by President MacMahon in 1877, however, that no president later exercised this right. As has been pointed out many times, the President of France did not reign like the hereditary King of Great Britain, nor did he rule like the elected President of the United States. He was the titular head of the republic, but neither ruled nor reigned. When, in the period after the First World War, a president overstepped the precedents in this respect, he was compelled to resign by the Chamber of Deputies.[1]

The actual executive power of France was in the hands of a cabinet of ministers officially appointed by the president but actually named by the leaders of parliament and directly responsible to that body. The Third Republic thus adopted the British system of parliamentary government rather than the German system with an executive not responsible to the national legislature. But the parliamentary system operated quite differently in

[1] See page 546.

France than in Great Britain. Whereas some one party usually controlled the British House of Commons, the French ministry, because of the many political groups in France, had to rely on coalitions or blocs. Furthermore, the French political groups were neither so well organized nor so clear-cut in their differences as the British parties, with the result that blocs once formed were forever disintegrating and permitting a ministry to fall. By resorting to his right of "interpellation" a deputy might at any time force a vote of "lack of confidence" and the resignation of the ministry. Between 1870 and 1914 the Third Republic had a kaleidoscopic succession of at least fifty different ministries. There was never any question in France of a ministry's dissolving the Chamber of Deputies to avoid resigning; the Chamber was supreme. On the other hand, the rapid change in ministries did not entail a rapid change in policies. Frequently the new cabinet, with ministers reshuffled and with possibly a few added, supported the same policies as the one which fell. Instability of ministries and relative stability in policies usually obtained.

Early Republican Measures

Following the triumph of republicanism, Gambetta's "Federation of the Left" dissolved, and the republican groups which emerged fell, generally speaking, into two categories: the Moderates and the Radicals. The Moderates appealed more especially to the possessing classes, definitely favored a policy of overseas expansion in order to restore French power and prestige, and were only moderately anticlerical. Jules Ferry, serving as premier or minister of education in the years immediately after 1880, was their outstanding leader. The Radicals, on the other hand, appealed more particularly to the masses, deplored colonial expansion as likely to weaken France in Europe, and were inclined to be strongly anticlerical. Their chief spokesman and leader was Georges Clemenceau, formerly mayor of Montmartre, a radical section of Paris. During the first two decades of the republic Clemenceau was a member of the Chamber of Deputies, where he gained the title of "Tiger" because of the number of ministries he overturned. His vitriolic attacks were launched not against royalists alone but against conservative and moderate republicans as well. The republic's political situation was further complicated by the fact that the royalists and clericals constituted a Right group which seized every opportunity to embarrass the successive republican ministries. Nevertheless, the government, under Jules Ferry's guidance, was able to enact a number of important measures.

Following the triumph of the republicans, the capital of France was moved from royalist Versailles to revolutionary Paris (1880), the anniversary of the popular attack on the Bastille—July 14—was made the national holiday, and the stirring "Marseillaise" was restored as the national anthem of the republic. In 1884 the "constitutional laws" of France were modified to strengthen the republic and lessen the influence of those who might be opposed to its permanence. Proposals to modify the republican form of government were made illegal, members of former ruling families were declared ineligible for the presidency of the republic, and provision was made for the gradual abolition of the life senatorships which had originally been created.

No provision had been made in the "constitutional laws" for a bill of rights, and so the republicans enacted a number of measures to safeguard the individual liberties of the French people. In 1881 laws were passed granting freedom of speech and permitting the holding of public meetings without the necessity of securing official authorization from the government. Freedom of the press was also established. In 1884, largely through the influence of Waldeck-Rousseau, one of Gambetta's followers, full freedom to organize and to strike was granted to workingmen by a law which has been characterized as the "charter of liberties" of organized labor in the Third Republic. Under this law French trade unions expanded until their membership came to include millions of workers.

The success of the Third Republic, Ferry and his associates believed, required an intelligent, enlightened, and loyal electorate. Since the privilege of the ballot had been extended to all male adults, it was now felt that all of the youth of the country must be educated. Ferry believed, furthermore, that the best way to inculcate loyalty to the republic was through schools which were free from royalist and clerical influence. The inauguration of a system of secular schools would entail a considerable change in French education, however, for in the preceding years of the nineteenth century Catholic religious instruction had been given in most of the schools of the country, and great numbers of schools had been conducted and controlled by various Catholic teaching orders.

Nevertheless, under Ferry's inspiration and guidance, laws were enacted and administrative decrees were issued during the eighties which had, in general, two major aims: to wipe out illiteracy and to weaken the control of the Catholic Church over education. To accomplish the first of these objectives, a state-supported public-school system was established, and education in the public schools was made free. Elementary education in some school was made compulsory for all children from six to thirteen years of age, but it was left to the parents to decide whether their children should attend public or private schools. A system of secondary schools for girls was established, and higher education for women, formerly neglected, was now encouraged. Equal opportunities with men were conceded to women in most of the educational institutions of the republic. An attempt was made to guard against the influence of the clergy in the public-school system. No religious instruction might be given in the state-supported schools, and only those lay persons who held diplomas from the state's normal schools might teach in them.

To weaken the position of the Catholic Church in the field of education, religious schools were denied financial support from the state, and it was hoped that many parents might be won to send their children to the public schools because attendance at the latter was free. The Jesuit order, whose members were bitterly opposed to secular schools, was dissolved, and its members were expelled from the country. Various other teaching orders which had not been "authorized" by the state were likewise disbanded, and their members were forbidden to conduct schools. Higher institutions of learning controlled by the church were deprived of the right to grant degrees or to call themselves universities.

The anticlerical spirit of the republicans, especially of the Radicals, was further shown by legislation regarding marriage. In 1816 the influence of the clericals had resulted in the abolition of divorce in France as contrary to the doctrines of the Catholic Church. The republicans now insisted that marriage was merely a civil contract, and enacted a law stipulating that all marriages, to be legal, must be performed by civil magistrates. In 1884 they also re-established divorce by passing a law providing that marriages might be dissolved or annulled by the civil courts.

Colonial Expansion and Emergence from Isolation

As pointed out above, Jules Ferry and his moderate republicans favored a vigorous colonial policy. Success in this field might do much to obliterate the humiliation of the Franco-German War and might even disguise the fact that the Third Republic was being forced to play a minor role on the international stage of Europe. For, during the first two decades after the establishment of the German Empire, France stood isolated among the powers of Europe, condemned to this position by Bismarck's skillful diplomacy, by her own military weakness, and by the suspicion with which the apparently unstable Third Republic was viewed by the monarchs of Europe. Although French patriots fervently hoped and ardently planned to regain for their country its lost position in Europe, although many of them were patently dominated by the idea of *revanche,* responsible French leaders clearly realized that an isolated and weak France was in no position to regain her lost provinces or to wage a successful war against the republic's powerful neighbor on the east. The day of *revanche* had therefore to be postponed.

In the meantime, within France there were strong advocates of a vigorous policy of overseas expansion. Not long after the humiliating treaty of Frankfort Professor Pierre Leroy-Beaulieu published a famous essay on modern colonization. "Colonization," he concluded, "is the expansive force of a nation, its power of reproduction, its dilation and multiplication across space. ... The nation that colonizes is the premier nation; if it is not today, it will be tomorrow." Almost simultaneously with the publication of Leroy-Beaulieu's work, Jules Ferry and his Moderate associates, perhaps confusing colonization with imperialism, began a campaign to extend the overseas territory controlled by France. In their efforts they had the blessing of the German chancellor, Bismarck, who believed that the French people needed "satisfactions for their pride" and who hoped that such satisfactions in the form of new colonies might lead the French to forget and possibly even to forgive the loss of Alsace-Lorraine. Consequently, in the decade after 1871 he advocated for France a policy of colonial expansion and frequently assured French statesmen of his willingness to support the Third Republic diplomatically if the latter sought to extend her overseas territory. In other words, Bismarck attempted to direct France's reviving energies away from *revanche* by turning them into the field of colonial expansion.

The Third French Republic inherited a colonial empire of some 375,000 square miles, which included principally Algeria in northern Africa, Cochin-China and Cambodia in southeastern Asia, and scattered footholds on the west coast of Africa, in India, in the Pacific, and in the western hemisphere. The first imperial venture undertaken by the republic was in southeastern Asia, where Cochin-China and Cambodia were used as bases of operation. As a result of a series of military operations begun in 1874 and eventually concluded in 1887, Annam and Tonkin were secured at the expense of China and Laos from Siam. In consequence, the republic by the close of the eighties had carved out an imposing empire in southeastern Asia with an area nearly half again as large as France itself and with a population of some 20,000,000 industrious natives.[2]

Before these conquests had been completed, the Third Republic had also launched its campaign to secure more territory in Africa. Assured of both German and British good will, in 1881 it annexed Tunis to the east of Algeria. Although this step antagonized Italy and helped to drive her into the Triple Alliance, it extended French control along the Mediterranean and improved the republic's claim to the hinterland of Africa when the time for the inevitable partition of that great continent should occur. A few years later France began to extend her control over the island of Madagascar, off the east coast of Africa. In 1885 the ruler of the island was forced to give France a port and to entrust to the republic the control of Madagascar's foreign relations. Five years later, as the result of a colonial

[2] For the places mentioned in these paragraphs, see the maps on pages 19 and 23.

bargain, Germany and Great Britain recognized Madagascar as a French protectorate, and in 1896 the native ruler was expelled and the island definitely annexed. Again an area greater in extent than France itself was obtained.

Meanwhile, other gains had been made at scattered points. In 1888 Jibuti, a port in Somaliland on the Gulf of Aden, had been acquired, and a foothold for expansion into Ethiopia was thus provided. On the west coast of Africa, also, the French had further extended their holdings by annexing Dahomey and establishing themselves on the Ivory Coast and in Guinea. By the close of the century the upper Niger territory had been connected with the coastal regions on the west, and the isolated French colonies there had been converted into possible commercial outlets for the extensive empire which France had carved out in the Sahara and in the western Sudan. Incidentally, France had successfully hemmed in and limited the further expansion of Kamerun, much to the chagrin of German imperialists.

But French statesmen were interested not alone in territorial expansion overseas; they were eager to remove the republic from its condition of international isolation. Consequently, they were not slow to seize the opportunity which was offered when Russia was set adrift by the German Kaiser after the dismissal of Bismarck in 1890. Immediately they determined to seek an alliance with the tsarist empire. Naturally certain obstacles had to be overcome if this was to be accomplished. Russian prejudice was strong against an alliance with the country whose Emperor Napoleon I had occupied Moscow and whose Emperor Napoleon III had helped to bring defeat to Russia in the Crimean War. Tsarist reluctance to be bound in any way with revolutionary democratic France was also a factor to be overcome.

On the other hand, Russia was as isolated as France. She likewise feared the increasingly powerful and aggressive German Empire, which had apparently decided to support its ally Austria in her imperialistic ventures in the Balkans. Furthermore, in the nineties Russia was embarking upon an industrial program which required extensive loans from abroad, and French bankers were very willing to make the necessary loans. The logical consequence of all these factors was that Russia and France came together in an entente (1891) which culminated later in a military convention creating the Franco-Russian alliance of 1894. In this convention it was provided that, if France were attacked by Germany or by Italy supported by Germany, Russia would aid France; and that, if Russia were attacked by Germany or by Austria supported by Germany, France would aid Russia. Quite evidently France was emerging from her isolation and beginning again to assume her role among the great powers.

The Weakening of the Royalists and Clericals

Meanwhile, within France various groups had become seriously discontented with the course of events after 1879. The Radicals vigorously denounced French colonial expansion because of the great expenditures involved and because such enterprises tended to divert the government's attention from numerous domestic problems which, to their minds, urgently demanded a solution. The clericals, alarmed by the laws which had been enacted to weaken the influence of the church, were firmly convinced that the republic would have to be overturned if the Catholic Church in France were to escape from further legislation of a similar type. The royalists, continuing to lament the establishment of the republic, were quick to join with the clericals in seizing any opportunity which might present itself for discrediting or undermining the republican regime.

Conditions within France in the late eighties were such as to invite criticism. Following the death of Gambetta in 1882 and the downfall of Ferry in 1885, no outstanding personality for a time was able to dominate the political stage. Ministries succeeded one another with what appeared to be an alarming rapidity, and the efficacy of parliamentary government seemed open to question. The national budget was unbalanced, and deficits caused serious concern to those who advocated sound financial policies. On top of all this, political corruption was discovered in republican circles, involving even President Grévy's son-in-law, who had sold his influence to persons desiring to obtain membership in the coveted Legion of Honor. The resultant scandal forced the resignation of President Grévy in 1887, even though he himself was not personally involved. Jules Ferry appeared to be the logical successor to Grévy in the presidency, but the Radicals were opposed to him and were able to force the election of a compromise candidate, Sadi Carnot, who, though a Moderate, was less repugnant to the Radicals.

Many conservatives, fearful lest a republican government was too weak to meet the needs of France, began to believe that some type of "strong government" might perhaps be preferable. Moreover, many French patriots among the younger generation, dissatisfied with the peaceful policies of the Third Republic, grew more and more impatient with statesmen who would not let themselves be swayed by the idea of *revanche*. Chauvinistic Frenchmen organized societies like the "League of Patriots" to keep alive a burning desire to regain the lost provinces of Alsace-Lorraine. Naturally, they, too, desired a "strong government," though for reasons somewhat different from those which actuated the royalists, clericals, army officers, and conservatives. Among several large groups in France, therefore, the psychological state in the eighties was in many respects analogous to that preceding the establishment of fascist dictatorships in Europe in the years following the First World War.

The one who for a time seemed destined to lead the forces of discontent against the republic was General Georges Boulanger, a cousin of Clemenceau. Upon the latter's recommendation, Boulanger, who was believed to be a staunch republican, was appointed minister of war. In this position he sought by various moves to win the favor of the soldiers and soon began to use his office for personal ends. He was a dashing figure on horseback and utilized the military reviews to disclose this fact. Through newspapers which he controlled he repeatedly intimated that France under his leadership might secure her *revanche* upon Germany. In order that the executive power might be strengthened, he began to advocate a revision of the constitution. Republican leaders, including Clemenceau, became alarmed at Boulanger's growing popularity and his increasingly apparent personal ambition. Fearful of the rise of another "Napoleon," they combined in 1887 to force the general not only from the ministry but also from the army as well.

Around Boulanger the various discontented groups—except the Radicals—now rallied, and ultimately the general organized the National Party, largely financed by the royalists, who hoped that he might be used to overturn the republic. Bonapartists, clericals, and even some chauvinistic republicans flocked to his support. For a time he became the storm center of France. Six times during 1888 he was elected to the Chamber of Deputies. In January, 1889, a Paris constituency elected him once again by a huge majority. At that time his friends advised him to arouse the Paris mob and with the aid of the League of Patriots to seize the government of France by force. But apparently Boulanger lacked the necessary boldness to become a dictator, for he made no overt move against the government.

The republicans, however, decided that the time for action had arrived. Temporarily laying aside their differences, they combined to defend the republic against its foe. The government ordered Boulanger's arrest on charges of conspiracy. Boulanger did not wait to be arrested, however, but fled in haste from the country. In his absence he was convicted of conspiracy against the state, and the League of Patriots which had supported him was ordered dissolved. In the general elections of September, 1889, a popular reaction against his movement gave the anti-Boulanger republicans a sweeping victory. Two years later the general committed suicide in Brussels.

Whether the republic was as much endangered by the Boulanger affair as the frightened republicans believed is uncertain. Certain it is, however, that it was definitely strengthened by the outcome and by measures taken by the government subsequently. In the first place, the belief that the republic could not be "strong" in time of need was dispelled by the government's aggressive action against Boulanger, action which went far toward destroying any lingering hope that a military dictatorship might be established. The danger of an army plot was lessened when the government retired many royalists in high military positions and filled their places with loyal republicans. In the second place, the royalists, by openly supporting Boulanger, were in the end discredited along with the general, and their cause was therefore further weakened. Moreover, although this development was not directly a result of the Boulanger affair, many clericals deserted the royalist cause in consequence of an encyclical letter in which Pope Leo XIII urged French Catholics to accept the republic and, instead of seeking to overturn it in order to protect the interests of the Catholic Church, to attempt by constitutional means to secure the repeal of republican legislation obnoxious to the church.

The inability of the royalists to overturn the republic when presented with an opportunity like that in 1889 appeared to indicate that the royalist cause was doomed to failure. The son and heir of Napoleon III had died in 1879, thus weakening the Bonapartist cause. Four years later the Count of Chambord had died and carried with him to his grave the hopes of the Legitimists. Although the Count of Paris still lived and still asserted his right to the throne, the Orleanists were too discredited and too discouraged to make any open attempt to place him on it.

In the succeeding years the royalists and clericals were further discredited and weakened by their connection with an anti-Semitic campaign and with a notorious army scandal. In the nineties France experienced a strong wave of anti-Semitism, which was carefully fostered by a writer and journalist, Édouard Drumont. According to him the anticlerical laws of the republic were the result of Jewish influence, the oppressors of labor were Jewish capitalists and industrialists, and the reason why the army was in no position to drive the German forces out of Alsace-Lorraine was that it was constantly thwarted and betrayed by Jewish renegades. A financial scandal (1894) in connection with a French corporation engaged in constructing a canal across the Isthmus of Panama involved several Jewish bankers and members of parliament and seemed to offer ground for anti-Semitic charges. Further substantiation of the charges appeared to be forthcoming when in the same year a Jewish captain of artillery in the French army was convicted of selling military secrets to Germany.

Alfred Dreyfus, the condemned captain, was a wealthy Alsatian Jew who had been attached to the general staff. In October, 1894, he was suddenly arrested, accused of treason, convicted in a secret session by a court-martial, and sentenced to expulsion from the army and to life imprisonment on Devil's Island, a penal colony off the coast of French Guiana. The evidence against him was an unsigned document which was said to be in Dreyfus' handwriting, but later developments indicated that he was apparently being made the victim of a plot to cover the irregularities of some of his military associates and superiors. In January, 1895, he was publicly and dramatically degraded in the presence of a large detachment of the French army. So hysterical was the anti-Semitic feeling in the country at this time that mob violence was invoked against some who dared to assert that Dreyfus was innocent of the charges upon which he had been convicted.

A few Frenchmen were dissatisfied with the verdict, however, and sought to ascertain the real truth regarding the "Dreyfus affair." In 1896 a Colonel Picquart became convinced that the document in question was written not by Dreyfus but by a certain Major Esterhazy. When Picquart informed the minister of war of his belief, he was at once transferred to the army in northern Africa, and nothing was done to reopen the case. When rumors of what had happened became known, a group of radical republicans began to demand a new trial. The resultant discussions divided the French people generally into two groups: the anti-Dreyfusards, consisting of anti-Semitics, clericals, royalists, reactionaries, and chauvinists, who believed that the Dreyfus agitation was an attack on the honor of the army, and the Dreyfusards, consisting of the Radicals, certain liberal idealists among the intellectuals who opposed race hatred and believed in "fair play," and those who maintained that the army should be definitely subordinated to the civil authority.

Despite the wish of government and army leaders, the case could not be dismissed as a closed affair, and eventually Major Esterhazy was tried by a court-martial, only to be enthusiastically acquitted (1898). The distinguished novelist, Émile Zola, next sought to have the Dreyfus case reopened and ultimately forced the government to defend its action. The minister of war then produced further evidence of Dreyfus' guilt, but, unfortunately for the strength of his case, one of his documents was soon proved to be a forgery. In 1899 Major Esterhazy, who had fled from France, admitted that he had written the document which had originally been ascribed to Dreyfus. Again the latter was tried by a court-martial, with high army officers bending every effort to secure a second conviction, and again the court condemned Dreyfus. But this time President Loubet at once pardoned him and ordered his release. The Dreyfusards were still dissatisfied, however, and in 1906 succeeded in having the case submitted to the court of cassation, the highest court in France. That court ultimately ruled that the charges against Dreyfus were utterly unfounded, and that the second court-martial before which the captain had been tried had been guilty of gross injustice. Dreyfus was restored to the army with the rank of major and was invested with a decoration of the Legion of Honor.

The spectacular Dreyfus affair, which disturbed French equanimity for so many years, was significant in a number of respects. The outcome discredited and weakened still further the royalists and clericals, who were suspected of using the "honor of the army" as a screen to hide what was actually a conspiracy against the republic. Furthermore, the Dreyfus affair provided an opportunity for the civil authorities to assert their supremacy over the military. The army, still largely officered by men from the upper classes who at heart were royalists, constituted the chief instrument for the possible overthrow of the republic by a *coup d'état.* Now the army was further republicanized and made definitely subordinate to the civil authority. Both the Boulanger and the Dreyfus affairs, accordingly, not only greatly weakened the royalist cause but revealed that the republican forces were sufficiently strong to maintain the republic in the time of crisis.

The Separation of Church and State

During the struggle to rehabilitate Dreyfus the Moderates and Radicals had organized in parliament a bloc of "republican defense" which included also the Socialists. Although the reaction which followed the uprising of the Paris Commune had militated against the rise of a socialist party in France, a beginning had been made in 1876 when the Labor Party had been founded by Jules Guesde upon his return from exile. In 1880 the party had become definitely socialist when it adopted a program drafted in co-operation with Karl Marx. During the eighties a number of other socialist parties had appeared, and by the nineties the various socialist groups had made considerable progress in France. The leaders of the new movement included a number of young men—among them Alexandre Millerand, Aristide Briand, René Viviani, and Jean Jaurès—who were destined to play important roles in the history of the republic. Their immediate demands were for social legislation in the interests of the workingmen, but their ultimate goal was the socialization of French industry. Through the co-operation of Briand and Jaurès a socialist newspaper, *L'Humanité,* was established in Paris to advance the cause. In the parliamentary elections of 1893 the various socialist groups gained a combined representation of about fifty in the Chamber.

In 1899 the Socialists were forced to decide to what extent they would co-operate with other parties, for in that year the bloc of "republican defense" secured control of the ministry. Pierre Waldeck-Rousseau, the new premier, wished to have a broad foundation for his government and so sought to include representatives of the Moderates, Radicals, and Socialists. On this issue the Socialists split. Although they were ready to support the bloc's program in its general outlines, the majority, led by Guesde and Jaurès, were opposed to participating in a ministry with "bourgeois" parties. Millerand, Briand, and others, however, were willing to accept office, and, when the former became the minister of commerce in Waldeck-Rousseau's cabinet, he and his supporters were expelled from the Socialist Party.

The Radicals in return for their support of Waldeck-Rousseau demanded that anticlericalism be made the foundation stone of the new ministry's policy. They openly attacked the Catholic Church, which, despite the pope's encyclical calling for support of the republic, was widely suspected of antirepublican sentiments. The church schools were accused not only of providing inadequate education for the children who attended but of deliberately inculcating royalist doctrines. Furthermore, the concordat of 1801, which regulated the relations between church and state in France, was vigorously denounced on the ground that it gave the pope excessive power within the republic and because payment of the salaries of the clergy by the government was said to constitute a heavy and unnecessary drain on the budget of the state.

In 1901 the attack against the church began with the enactment of the Associations Law, which was aimed at the religious orders, or congregations, of monks and nuns. The premier pointed out that these orders had been growing in membership and wealth at an astonishing rate, that during the last quarter of the nineteenth century the number of nuns had increased fivefold, that the property of the orders had risen in half a century from fifty million francs to more than a billion. The orders were therefore denounced on economic, educational, and political grounds, and the Associations Law was designed to alter the situation. According to the provisions of this act every congregation must be "authorized" or incorporated. Those that failed to receive authorization from the government were to be dissolved, and their property was to be confiscated. Apparently the new law was approved by large numbers of Frenchmen, for parliamentary elections in 1902 resulted in a sweeping victory for the radical republicans who came to hold a dominant position in the Chamber of Deputies.

A ministry of Radicals now took over the reins of government, and to the new premier, Émile Combes, an extreme anticlerical, was entrusted the enforcement of the Associations Law. Nearly all of the religious orders that applied for authorization were refused on the ground that they served no useful purpose socially. Both these and the orders that failed to seek authorization—some five hundred in all—were at once suppressed. The government was particularly drastic in dealing with the teaching

orders. Most of their schools were closed, and their members were forbidden to teach or preach. Tens of thousands of monks and nuns thus
found themselves homeless. In 1904 the Radical campaign to remove education from the hands of "royalist" clergy led to the enactment of a law
directed against even the authorized orders, which were forbidden to recruit new members. Furthermore, although the act permitted authorized
orders to continue their activities in the French overseas empire, it was
decreed that within France all teaching by members of religious orders—
whether in public or in private schools—must cease within ten years. The
result sought by the Radicals was obtained; the number of children attending the public schools increased until by 1914 more than 80 per cent of
them were thus included.

The next step in the anticlerical program of the Radicals was to secure
the abrogation of the concordat of 1801, and in 1903 a parliamentary committee headed by Briand was appointed to draft a measure to provide
for the separation of church and state. Naturally there was friction between the papacy and the French government over the suppression of
religious orders, and ill feeling reached a climax in 1904 when Pope Pius X
protested to the Catholic powers of Europe because the President of France
paid an official visit to the King of Italy, a "usurper" in the eyes of the
papacy. The Socialists in the parliament seized this occasion to denounce
the pope's interference in French political affairs, and the French ambassador was recalled from the Vatican. With diplomatic relations thus
broken off, a bill for abrogating the concordat was introduced, and in 1905
the Separation Law was enacted.

By the provisions of this law the concordat of 1801 was finally abrogated. No longer was the state to pay the salaries of the Catholic, Protestant,
or Jewish clergy, though provision was made for payments to aged clergy
and, temporarily, to those who had but recently entered the priesthood.
Title to all church property remained vested in the state, where it had
been since 1789, but it was stipulated that associations of laymen might
make arrangements with the government for the use of church buildings
for public worship. The state was to surrender all control over the appointment of Catholic bishops in France; both state and church were to be
. "free."

Protestants and Jews accepted the Separation Law more or less readily,
and even many Catholics felt that it might be to the best interests of the
church to be free from state interference and control. But Pope Pius bitterly denounced the law. In the first place, by the unilateral action of
the state it abrogated an agreement originally reached through negotiation
between two sovereign parties. In the second place, the act was declared
contrary to canon law, which was opposed to the management of church

affairs by laymen. In the third place, it was asserted that the refusal to continue state financial support to the clergy was unjust because that support
was the logical consequence of the state's earlier confiscation of clerical
property. Finally, the pope announced that the principle of separation of
church and state was "an absolutely false thesis, a very pernicious error."
The pope therefore forbade members of the church to observe the law,
with the result that no associations for public worship were formed by
the Catholics.

Eventually, after more than a year of friction and chaos, a new law
—largely the work of Briand—was enacted by the parliament. By the
provisions of the act of 1907 the use of churches was made free and was
to be regulated by contracts between priests and government officials without resort to the associations of laymen which were so objectionable to the
pope. In the end the religious situation for Catholics in France came to
be not unlike that in the United States; that is, church and state were
completely separate, the state making no contributions to the support
of the clergy, and the church being free to manage its own affairs in
accordance with canon law.

Economic and Social Progress

Industrial expansion in France under the Third Republic was in no
wise comparable to that which occurred in Germany under the empire.
For one thing, French industry suffered a severe blow from the cession
of Alsace-Lorraine. By that transfer of territory Germany had secured valuable iron deposits, important iron and steel plants, and large textile mills.
Germany's gain was France's loss. It took the iron industry of France
more than two decades to recover from this blow. The republic's industrial development was further handicapped in two important respects.
France lacked sufficient coal, and what she had was, generally speaking,
poor in quality—not good for coking. In the second place, France had no
great surplus of cheap labor which might be used in industrial development. Beginning in the eighties the population of France became nearly
stationary. There was a shortage of labor rather than a surplus, so that it
was practically impossible to supply the workers for a large industrial
system.

In two types of industry, however, there was a considerable development. When Germany required the cession of part of Lorraine, she did
not—through ignorance—make her demands extensive enough to include the whole iron basin. In the northeastern part of France, therefore,
the republic did possess valuable iron deposits, and here also it had some
coal. In this district, accordingly, after the Thomas-Gilchrist process made

these ores available for the manufacture of steel, the French made notable advances in the metallurgical industries, partly with the aid of cheap labor imported from Belgium and Italy. In steel production before the war in 1914 the republic made greater progress relatively than any other country on the Continent, though its total output was still below that of either Germany or Great Britain. During these years, too, French production of coal increased threefold and that of iron approximately fivefold. Nevertheless, because of the lack of adequate coal resources, much French iron ore was exported to the Ruhr region of Germany, there to be smelted into steel.

In another district of the country—that about Lyons—a second type of industry flourished, namely, the manufacture of silk. For a time France led the world in the production of this commodity, but ultimately she came to have a serious competitor in the Italian silk industry, and still later an even more damaging rival in rayon, a fiber made from wood pulp. Some expansion occurred also in the country's cotton textile industry. Outside the metal and textile trades, however, the typical industrial unit of France remained, down to the twentieth century, the small workshop and not the huge factory. French industrialists were slow to adopt mass methods of production, and at the opening of the century 80 per cent of the country's 600,000 industrial establishments still employed four workers or less.

With the rise of industrial labor came the demand for the right to have trade unions, a demand which was met in 1884, as pointed out above, by legislation legalizing and protecting labor combinations. Labor unions grew rapidly, and in 1895 most of them came together into the General Confederation of Labor, which aimed to unite all workers and to develop a feeling of class solidarity. At the opening of the twentieth century French trade unions became extremely radical, adopted the socialist theory of class struggle, and opposed "political" action in favor of "direct" action. In other words, the syndicalists, as French labor unionists were called, sought by strikes, sabotage, and other "direct" attacks on the captains of industry to overturn the capitalist system.

In the decade before the First World War France was repeatedly and seriously disturbed by attempts to inaugurate "general" strikes when all labor was supposed to cease. Probably the most spectacular of these attempts was made in 1910, when a strike of railwaymen almost completely stopped traffic on the country's railway system. Much to the surprise and chagrin of the strikers, Premier Briand, who himself in his younger days had advocated resort to the general strike, turned against them. The government called the railwaymen, most of whom were reservists, to the colors, and then ordered them as soldiers under military discipline to operate the railways. The strike was thus broken, and the workers decided that, since the government could play such a decisive part in the class struggle between capital and labor, the latter had better seek to gain control of the government.

The Socialist Party was the chief gainer from this decision. In 1905 the various factions of Socialists had come together into one political group, the Unified Socialist Party, led by the able Jean Jaurès. By 1914 the representation of this party had increased in the Chamber to more than one hundred, and at that time it was believed by many that Jaurès might soon be elevated to the premiership. Although he was doomed to be only a minority leader in the years before 1914, his growing influence was constantly thrown on the side of those policies which aimed to bring social and industrial democracy at home and international peace abroad.

Thanks, in part, to Jaurès' efforts, in the two decades after 1890 the government enacted a number of laws for the benefit of the workingmen. Hours of labor were gradually reduced, a weekly rest day was made compulsory, minimum age limits were established for industrial workers, factory hygiene and safety were made matters of state concern, a system for the voluntary arbitration of industrial disputes was established, free medical attendance for workers and their families was introduced, a workmen's compensation law was enacted, and a system of old-age pensions was adopted. In other words, France followed somewhat tardily in the footsteps of Germany and Great Britain in the matter of social legislation and factory laws, and by 1914 she had not advanced so far in these matters as had these other countries.

Perhaps one reason for French slowness in social legislation was the fact that fundamentally, even in the twentieth century, France was an agricultural country. Before the First World War more than half of the population of the republic still lived in communes which were classified as rural. The country had between five and six million landed proprietors, 99 per cent of whom owned less than one hundred acres. Contrary to the general impression abroad, although most of the *holdings* were small and were owned and tilled by the peasants, most of the arable land was held in relatively large units by landowners who rented it to tenants or let it out to workers "on shares." French agricultural products were varied and plentiful enough to make France practically self-sufficing. In addition to the staple crops, the French peasants produced for export such products as olive oil, wines, and brandies. When, because of increased and cheaper facilities for overseas transport, French agriculture began to suffer because of the import of agricultural products from abroad, protective tariffs were introduced, and government bounties were frequently extended to certain types of agricultural production. Further to assist the peasants, agricultural schools were established, co-operative societies were encouraged, and mutual loan banks and insurance agencies were given government guarantees.

At the time that the Third Republic came into being, the French, as a result of their own frugality and a period of prosperity under the Second Empire, had accumulated a large amount of capital. A considerable part of the French people had risen into the class of *rentiers,* that is, they were not compelled to engage in any productive activity but could live—sometimes rather frugally—on the income from their investments. Most of the *rentiers* had invested rather heavily in the government bonds floated by the Third Republic and therefore were vitally concerned with its perpetuation and sound financial condition. Not all of the wealth of *rentiers* could be placed in government bonds, however. In a great industrial country with rapidly expanding enterprises it might have been readily absorbed by industry, but France did not fulfill these conditions. Consequently, French investors loaned large sums of money abroad—sometimes to governments in need, sometimes to prosperous expanding industrial enterprises. As early as 1882 French foreign investments amounted to four or five billion dollars, and each year thereafter saw that figure rise markedly. This outward flow of capital in the nineties played a part in removing France from her position of international isolation. It also increased popular interest in France's role as a colonial and world power.

The Creation of the Entente Cordiale

Meanwhile, with confidence increased by French emergence from isolation in 1894, French imperialists were becoming ever more ambitious. In the nineties they envisaged an empire which should not only include all of northwestern Africa but actually extend from the Atlantic to the Red Sea, from the Mediterranean to the Gulf of Guinea. With this in mind they planned to build a railway from Jibuti on the Gulf of Aden across Ethiopia to the Nile and to connect this vast region with French territory in central Africa. Such plans naturally conflicted with those of the imperialists of Great Britain, who, in turn, had visions of a great British empire extending unbroken from South Africa to Egypt. Great Britain therefore sought to check French expansion by encouraging Italian colonial ambitions. Italy had already secured footholds in Eritrea on the Red Sea and in Somaliland, and the British now encouraged them to conquer Ethiopia. The military disaster which overtook the Italians at Adowa in 1896 is discussed elsewhere.[3]

Even before this Italian defeat, however, the French had begun their

[3] See page 140.

campaign to unite their territories in western and eastern Africa. Early in 1896 two forces were organized and sent out. From French Conge Marchand with a number of French officers and some two hundred natives set out for the Sudan, while a stronger French force was ordered to march inland from Jibuti to join forces with Marchand on the upper Nile. A little later, after the battle of Adowa, Great Britain ordered Kitchener with an Egyptian army to move south to occupy the Sudan. A clash between French and British imperialism seemed inevitable, especially in view of the fact that Kitchener's progress was greatly retarded because of his decision to build a railway as he advanced.

In July, 1898, after a two-year struggle through the trackless tropical regions of central Africa, Marchand reached Fashoda on the Nile and there raised the French tricolor. Unfortunately for the strength of his position, however, the stronger French columns which were to join him from the east were delayed by swamps and fever and did not arrive. On the other hand, in the fall of 1898 Kitchener and his forces did arrive on the scene, to be welcomed to "French territory" by Marchand. Great Britain refused to recognize the region as belonging to France, an acute international crisis resulted, and the two countries came to the verge of war. But when France consulted her ally, Russia, regarding a course of action, she was advised by no means to risk an actual break with Great Britain. Furthermore, the French foreign minister, Théophile Delcassé, who had in mind the creation of a Franco-British entente as a means to other ends, believed that it would be to the best interest of France to yield at this time to the British. The French government therefore repudiated Marchand's action and ordered him to withdraw from Fashoda. A serious cause of friction between Great Britain and France was thus removed, and the crisis passed.

One reason for Delcassé's conciliatory policy at this time was that he had in mind the addition of Morocco to the French empire in northern Africa and for the successful accomplishment of this step needed a free hand. In 1900 Delcassé availed himself of the fact that Italy's ill will toward France had been subsiding to bring about a Franco-Italian understanding. In that year Italy agreed to give France a free hand in Morocco in return for the latter's giving her a free hand in Tripoli and Cyrenaica. The resultant good feeling between the two Latin countries led to a further agreement two years later. The two powers promised (1902) that, should either be the object of a direct or indirect aggression on the part of one or more powers, or should either, as a result of a direct provocation, find itself compelled in defense of its honor or its security to take the initiative of a declaration of war, the other would maintain a strict neutrality. In other words, should Germany attack France or should

France "in defense of her honor or her security" declare war upon Germany, Italy would remain neutral. The international position of the Third Republic was considerably improved by these two agreements.

Delcassé also turned to French advantage the changing viewpoint in Great Britain, where Germany's rapid strides in industry and commerce, her adoption of a policy of vigorous colonial expansion, and her increasing demand for a place in the sun were causing uneasiness. This uneasiness was transformed into alarm after Great Britain's proffer of an alliance with Germany had been declined and the latter's apparent unfriendliness had been revealed by her encouragement of the Boers.[4] These circumstances led Great Britain to abandon her previously unfriendly attitude toward France and, skillfully used by Delcassé, resulted in the establishment of the Entente Cordiale (1904), which the French foreign minister had so ardently desired. Although a number of questions which had disturbed Franco-British relations were adjusted in the treaties signed at this time, perhaps the most important result was the agreement that Great Britain should have a free hand in Egypt and France a free hand in Morocco. No definite alliance or military convention was entered into, but an era of good feeling began which led Great Britain and France into closer and closer co-operation in international affairs and thus increased the Third Republic's influence as a great power.

These treaties are good examples of what President Wilson of the United States later denounced as "secret diplomacy," for certain secret agreements in regard to Morocco and Egypt were not published. In other words, while French and British citizens rejoiced over what they thought had been signed by their responsible ministers, in reality they were being duped by those very officials. The published treaties stated that the French had no intention of altering the political status of Morocco and that the British likewise did not intend to change the political condition of Egypt. The secret clauses, on the contrary, stated that, if it became necessary to change the status of Morocco and Egypt, the former should be divided between France and Spain and Great Britain should be given a free hand in Egypt. In 1904 France also signed a secret treaty with Spain agreeing upon a future division of Moroccan territory.

The Moroccan Crises

While Delcassé had taken secret steps to assure France of the diplomatic support of Italy, Great Britain, and Spain in case he decided to carry through his plan to convert Morocco into a French protectorate, he had neither informed Germany of his plans nor asked for her approval.

[4] See pages 171–172.

Although the German chancellor, Bülow, was warned by his ambassador at London that negotiations of some sort were being carried on by Great Britain and France, the officials at Berlin firmly believed that Franco-British enmity was of too long standing to permit any pacific settlement of all their disputes. They were somewhat surprised and taken aback, therefore, when shortly before the conclusion of the negotiations Delcassé informed the German ambassador at Paris that Great Britain and France were about to conclude a general colonial agreement. Since the French foreign minister omitted the courtesy of officially informing the German government of the contents of the treaties, the latter had to obtain its information from reports in the press. It has been asserted by some that Bülow through devious channels learned of the unpublished secret agreements, and, although this fact has never been proved, his subsequent actions appear to lend color to this suspicion.

However that may be, Delcassé apparently felt so secure after the Moroccan agreements with Italy, Great Britain, and Spain that he began to prepare the way for the so-called reforms which he expected to force upon the Moroccan sultan. Bülow and Holstein, his adviser in the German foreign office, believed, on the other hand, that France's position was so weakened by Russia's war in the Far East that they might successfully utilize the occasion to advance Germany's prestige and at the same time to test the strength of the recently achieved Entente Cordiale between France and Great Britain. They therefore attempted to block Delcassé's program by encouraging the ruler of Morocco to reject the proposed reforms. Furthermore, although the Kaiser personally wished Germany to pursue a policy of hands-off so far as Morocco was concerned, the German chancellor practically forced William II to make a visit to Tangier, the chief port of Morocco on the Mediterranean. At Tangier on March 31, 1905, the Kaiser, as he was so likely to do upon occasion, in his public address said too much and said it too emphatically. His statement that he considered the Sultan of Morocco as an independent sovereign was regarded in France as an insult to the Third Republic. The international situation at once became strained.

Apparently what Bülow desired to do was to increase German prestige as a world power by indicating that nowhere on the globe was it safe to make imperialistic bargains without considering Germany's interests. The French popularly believed, however, that the German chancellor was seeking to destroy the Franco-British entente and to embarrass France in order to receive some *quid pro quo*. Shortly after the Kaiser's speech, therefore, the French premier, Rouvier, took it upon himself to ask Bülow what Germany desired in compensation for giving France a free hand in Morocco. Bülow did not ask for territorial compensation but declared that, since the status of Morocco had been fixed by the Madrid conference of 1880, France must permit her position there to be determined by an international conference of the signatory powers. The French premier, who was by no means so aggressive as his foreign minister, then suggested to the German chancellor that France and Germany might conclude a general colonial settlement similar to that which France and Great Britain had recently signed. But Bülow was at this time apparently more interested in raising German prestige than he was in settling colonial disputes, for he failed to notify the Kaiser of the French premier's proposal.[5]

Meanwhile, Delcassé had flatly refused to accept Bülow's demand for a conference, and in his stand was given full diplomatic support by the British foreign secretary, the Marquis of Lansdowne, who likewise opposed the conference. Nevertheless, the milder Rouvier, fearing the possibility of war, opposed Delcassé, with the result that the French cabinet had to choose between its premier and its foreign minister and chose to support the former. In June Delcassé was obliged to resign, and his portfolio was assumed by the more cautious Rouvier. In the face of Bülow's continued insistence upon a conference, the French premier at last gave way, and a conference was called to meet at Algeciras in Spain. It thus appeared that Germany had won a decisive diplomatic victory.

At the Algeciras conference, which convened on January 16, 1906, Germany found, however, that instead of isolating France she was herself practically isolated. Italy, Russia, Great Britain, Spain, and the United States supported France, and only Austria-Hungary voted on the side of Germany. Although the last appeared to have won her point when the fiction of Moroccan independence was preserved, France was left in a position where she could continue to increase her influence in the sultanate, and she was not compelled to give Germany compensation. The French, nevertheless, felt extremely bitter toward Germany because of the way she had forced the matter before an international conference.

In 1907 France's position as a great power was further strengthened when Russia, united with France in the alliance of 1894, and Great Britain, linked with France in the Entente Cordiale of 1904, adjusted their differences and came to an understanding.[6] Again, no binding alliance was consummated between these two powers, but the good feeling and close understanding which followed led to the designation of France, Russia, and Great Britain as the powers of the Triple Entente. Thus the great powers of Europe came to be pretty definitely divided into two groups— the Triple Alliance, created by Bismarck, and the Triple Entente, created by France. The Third Republic had successfully emerged from its long

[5] The Kaiser later stated that such a settlement would have been acceptable to him.
[6] See page 190.

isolation and had come to occupy that central position in a system of powerful alliances and ententes which Bismarck during his chancellorship had so successfully sought to prevent.[7]

Meanwhile, despite the events of 1905 and 1906, France continued her efforts to secure control of Morocco. In the very next year after the Algeciras

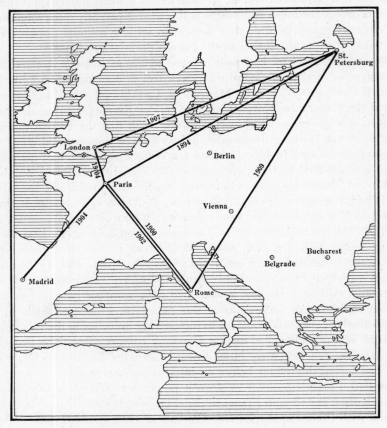

FRANCO-RUSSIAN SYSTEM OF ALLIANCES AND ENTENTES, 1894–1909

conference she used a civil war in the sultanate with accompanying outrages against Frenchmen as an excuse to land her marines at Casablanca. The renewed friction which developed between Germany and France over the continued presence of French troops in Morocco was greatly increased in 1908 when the German consul at Casablanca sought to aid

[7] A comparison of the drawings on pages 63 and 120 will reveal graphically France's emergence from isolation. In 1909 Russia and Italy also made an imperialistic bargain and entered into an entente. See page 145.

deserters from the French foreign legion to escape. A minor crisis was precipitated, but it was soon adjusted by referring the questions at issue to arbitration by the Hague Tribunal.[8] Early in 1909 Germany and France negotiated a convention in which the former stated that her interests in Morocco were merely "economic" and in which she promised to recognize France's political ascendancy in the sultanate, provided economic equality for all nations was assured.

Although the Moroccan convention of 1909 seemed to presage calm relations between France and Germany, friction between the two foreign offices continued. French and German concessionaires quarreled about their respective rights, and each group looked to its own government for support. Moreover, conditions within Morocco also caused trouble. The lives and property of Europeans were endangered by repeated uprisings within the sultanate, and France was particularly disturbed because the unrest there appeared to spread contagiously across the frontier into Algeria. In 1911 France decided that protective steps must be taken and notified the powers that her troops would occupy certain towns "to restore order." In May of that year the Moroccan capital, Fez, was occupied by French troops.

The Germans regarded this step as a violation of the agreements made at Algeciras; in fact, they considered it merely a move toward the establishment of a French protectorate. Apparently the German government had little real expectation of being able to prevent France from taking this step; its chief concern was to secure for Germany something in the nature of compensations. The French, on their part, were willing to consider the matter of compensations, and in June discussions were begun. The Germans at once made rather extravagant claims as to the value of the concessions they would have to surrender in Morocco if France established her protectorate. Kiderlen, the German foreign secretary, was especially aggressive and suggested to the chancellor that the dispatch of a German warship to "protect" German interests in Morocco might facilitate the Franco-German negotiations. The Kaiser and Chancellor Bethmann-Hollweg reluctantly gave their consent to his plan, and on July 1 the German gunboat *Panther* entered the harbor of Agadir, a Moroccan Atlantic port.

Three days before the *Panther's* arrival at Agadir a new ministry had come into power in France. The new premier was Joseph Caillaux, one of the younger Radicals, a capable financier and a good administrator. He was of the opinion that France should seek a *rapprochement* with Germany as a step toward preserving the peace of Europe as well as toward lessening the heavy burden of militarism. Although Caillaux was eager

[8] For the creation of the Hague Court, see page 322.

to reach a pacific settlement with Germany, he was determined that the latter should receive no part of Morocco. He was willing to make concessions to her elsewhere in return for her recognition of France's protectorate, but, because of divisions within the French ministry on this subject, France delayed in making any definite offers. Eventually, on July 15, Germany demanded the French Congo. War seemed near when France refused to make any such sweeping cession of territory.

If Russia had given France any encouragement, war might actually have resulted, but Russia stated that she would not fight for Morocco and suggested that France grant suitable compensation to Germany. Officially, the British government took no steps to increase France's intransigence, though there was some concern in Britain over Germany's demand for compensation. The British, not knowing exactly what Germany wanted, jumped to the conclusion that Germany was seeking territory in Morocco, and at once feared for the safety of Britain's lines of communication with South Africa and India. On July 21, when it appeared that the Franco-German negotiations might collapse, the British foreign secretary, Sir Edward Grey, proposed that Great Britain might join Germany and France in discussing the matter of compensation. With the stage thus set, Lloyd George, a member of the British ministry, declared in a public address that Great Britain would not allow herself to be excluded from negotiations on subjects which touched her vital interests, that peace at such a price would be too great a humiliation. The natural effect of this speech was to convince both the French and the Germans that Great Britain would support France.

Although the Germans, in the face of this apparent British threat, felt that they could not retreat, the German foreign secretary did abandon his idea of driving a hard bargain with the French and therefore moderated his demands. He would, he admitted, be content with much less than the whole French Congo. Negotiations still dragged, but eventually a settlement was reached, and a treaty was signed in Berlin in November, 1911. France received recognition of her right to establish a protectorate over Morocco, provided she agreed to maintain the "open door" policy in that country. In return she ceded to Germany a portion of her Congo territory so that German Kamerun might have access to the Congo River.[9] In March, 1912, France announced her establishment of a protectorate over Morocco and began the unenviable task of pacifying the country.[10]

[9] Germany at the same time ceded to France territory in Africa near Lake Chad. See the map on page 19.

[10] In November, 1912, a Franco-Spanish treaty handed over to Spain about 12,000 square miles of Morocco just across from Gibraltar and a small strip in the southern part of the sultanate. The important port of Tangier with some surrounding territory was internationalized.

Agitation over "Preparedness"

In France, as a result of the crisis of 1911, the nationalists felt that Germany had interfered in matters that did not concern her and that France must be made better prepared for war so that she could take a stronger stand in defense of her rights in future crises. Caillaux's policy toward Germany, nationalists declared, had been "too conciliatory." In the Senate opposition to the Franco-German treaty which his government had signed was so strong that the Caillaux ministry was forced to resign. In January, 1912, Raymond Poincaré became premier in a ministry which was distinctly conservative and nationalistic. Poincaré, a highly successful corporation lawyer, was perhaps the outstanding spokesman of those nationalists who believed that Germany's increasing threat to French security must be met by a policy of "preparedness"—military and diplomatic—for war. He had the support of the Right and Center parties and also of those Radicals who followed the Tiger, Clemenceau. A native of Lorraine— though not of the part ceded to Germany—he was known to be unreconciled to the treaty of Frankfort, and therefore was a popular figure with French prewar chauvinists. As premier and minister of foreign affairs he devoted himself to strengthening France's system of alliances and ententes.

In the critical year 1913, when the international situation was tense and the fear of war was increasing, Poincaré was elected President of France. In his inaugural address he announced his belief that it was "impossible for a people to be really peaceful, except on the condition of being always prepared for war." In 1912 conscription had been extended to Algeria and West Africa, and preparations had been made to incorporate into the French army the republic's colored colonial troops. Early in 1913 the French war minister apparently learned of Germany's plans to expand her army. To meet this "threat" a new military bill was introduced in the Chamber of Deputies on March 6. To compensate for the fact that France's small and stationary population prevented a natural increase of the army under the old law, the new act proposed to raise the term of active service from two to three years.[11] The bill was strenuously opposed in the Chamber by the Radicals and Socialists, and Jaurès made a number of eloquent attacks upon it. An alternative scheme for national defense through the use of a popular militia was offered by him, but it failed to secure the approval of the military leaders. Although huge mass meetings were held by French workingmen to denounce the measure, the bill finally became

[11] In the preceding years, largely because of the demands of the Radicals and Socialists, the period of active service had been reduced from five years to two.

a law in 1913, and for a short period France had a larger peace-time army than Germany.

But the opponents of the new law did not cease their activity with its enactment. Peace demonstrations were organized, and threats of a general strike were made. In the bitterly contested parliamentary election of 1914 the new military law was the chief issue. The outcome of the election indicated that the act was exceedingly unpopular in France, for the new Chamber was perhaps the most radical that the republic had yet had. Although Poincaré's policy appeared to be repudiated, the president resolutely refused to appoint anyone as premier unless he would first agree to retain the three-years law. After a long ministerial crisis such a government was organized. Before the rival groups in the Chamber could come to grips over the issue of militarism and presidential power, however, the crisis of 1914 broke, and the French of all types rallied to the support of the republic. When, during the crisis, Jaurès dared to raise his voice against the approaching war, he was deliberately shot down and killed by a fanatical nationalist.

Chapter V

THE KINGDOM OF ITALY

PRIOR to 1861 the Italian peninsula was politically divided and largely dominated by the Austrian Habsburgs and the Roman Catholic popes. There was no Italy in the political sense of the word; Italy was merely a "geographical expression." The transformation of this "geographical expression" into a political entity was largely the work of three famous Italians —Joseph Mazzini, Count Camillo di Cavour, and Joseph Garibaldi. The first by his inspired voice and his "Young Italy" society aroused Italian youth and awakened a nationalistic enthusiasm to liberate and unify Italy. The second by his consummate statesmanship and clever diplomacy gained French aid for Sardinia's attempt to drive the Habsburgs out of Italy in the Austro-Sardinian War (1859). The third by his dashing boldness and with his "Thousand Red Shirts" speedily conquered (1860) the Two Sicilies in the cause of a united Italy. On March 17, 1861, the Kingdom of Italy was proclaimed with Victor Emmanuel II of the house of Savoy as king. The new state did not include, however, Venetia and the Patrimony of St. Peter—the latter being a small district surrounding and including Rome. Venetia was secured from the Habsburgs as a result of the Austro-Prussian War (1866), in which Italy was Prussia's ally; Rome was taken from the pope and made the capital of the Italian kingdom during the Franco-German War (1870), when the pope was deprived of the protection of French troops.

The New State

In 1870, therefore, for the first time since the destruction of Theodoric's kingdom in the sixth century, the Italian peninsula constituted a united and independent state. Unfortunately for this new state, however, it was from the very outset of its history seriously handicapped by its economic limitations, for it was inferior in mineral wealth, natural resources, and capital to Great Britain, Germany, and France. The coal and iron which the latter had in abundance, Italy, if she were to become an industrial country, would have to import. Even her agriculture failed to produce sufficient foodstuffs for her rapidly increasing population, for Italy, when it came to rich arable land, was less favored than Russia, Austria-Hungary,

125

and France. Large areas of the Italian peninsula consisted of bleak, barren mountain ridges or low unhealthy swamplands. In the south, where the land reforms of the French Revolution had little penetrated, the *latifundia* were farmed in a primitive fashion by poverty-stricken agricultural laborers. In the north the peasants, though industrious, were generally too poor or too backward to use scientific methods of farming. In 1870, therefore, Italy, with a population of about 26,000,000, already had a "surplus population" in the sense that it could not be adequately supported by the existing agriculture and industry of the kingdom.

The citizens of the new state—divided by the physical features of the peninsula, separated by the previous centuries of conflict between their petty rulers, isolated by the lack of modern means of transportation and communication—were not yet fused into one people. Marked contrasts existed between different sections of the new kingdom, so marked, in fact, that Italy was once described as a country in which two stages of civilization existed simultaneously. In the north there was some modern industry and a number of large and progressive cities inhabited by a prosperous bourgeoisie and an intelligent and aggressive proletariat. In the region south of the former Grand Duchy of Tuscany, however, conditions were quite otherwise. The popes and the former Bourbon rulers had done little to improve their lands. Facilities for travel were distinctly backward; in 1860, for example, Naples had less than sixty miles of railways. There were few large cities, and the rural regions were infested with brigands who made travel a hazardous undertaking. Secret criminal societies like the *Camorra* of Naples and the *Mafia* of Sicily flourished unchecked. Everywhere the standard of living of the Italians was relatively low, and the great bulk of the population in the south was illiterate.

The government of the new kingdom was based on the constitution which King Charles Albert had granted to Sardinia in 1848. In the representative monarchical government which Italy in a sense thus inherited the king occupied a position similar to that of the British monarch, that is, he reigned but did not rule. Supreme authority was vested in a parliament of two houses and in a ministry appointed by the king but responsible to the parliament. The latter consisted of a Senate, composed of members appointed for life, and a Chamber of Deputies, elected on a franchise so restricted that not more than 2½ per cent of the population were entitled to vote. Italy resembled France and Germany in having, not two major political parties, but a considerable number of minor factions. Her political parties were, indeed, even less organized and stable than those of France, and in the early years of the kingdom constituted little more than loosely organized groups attached to different political leaders.

After the proclamation of the Italian kingdom the Marquis of Azeglio,

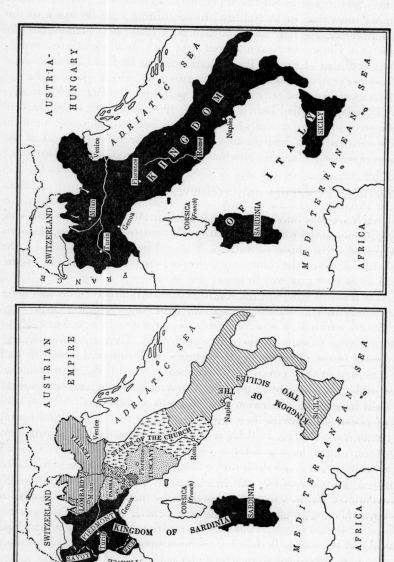

THE KINGDOM OF ITALY IN 1871

THE ITALIAN PENINSULA IN 1858

Cavour's predecessor as Sardinian premier, had declared, "We have made Italy; we must now make Italians." In conformity with the spirit of this pronouncement, the new kingdom had been made not a federation like the German Empire but a centralized state with an administrative system analogous to that of France. In the years between 1861 and 1870 the country had been arbitrarily divided into provinces which ignored the old boundaries of such earlier political units as Naples, Venetia, and Tuscany; a loyal civil service had been introduced; the public debt had been consolidated; a uniform system of taxation had been inaugurated; uniform legal codes had been brought into being; and the military forces of the various previously existing states had been fused into one Italian army.

Immediate Problems and Achievements

By 1871 a whole series of objectives, which Italian patriots had long sought to attain, had been realized; and Italy stood at the opening of a new period in her history. As King Victor Emmanuel pointed out, the heroic age was over; the commonplace era of practical work must be begun. Poetry must now give way to prose.

To the political groups of the Right were first confided the difficult tasks with which Italian statesmen were called upon to wrestle. These were the groups which had achieved national unification and brought about administrative reforms in the years after 1859. They were chiefly representative of the upper and middle classes of Piedmont, Lombardy, and Tuscany, and in their policies were inclined to be patriotic, dignified, cautious, and somewhat antidemocratic. Unfortunately, the one who would naturally have been their leader, Count Cavour, had died in 1861 soon after the proclamation of the Italian kingdom, so that this capable and liberal statesman was no longer available to help solve the many difficult problems which confronted the new state.

Probably the most pressing immediate problem after 1870 was that of adjusting the relations between the kingdom and the papacy. Although the seizure of the states of the church and the elevation of Rome to a position as the capital of the new state were entirely satisfactory to the great bulk of the Italian people, the pope vigorously and consistently maintained that he had been illegally deprived of his temporal possessions. In default of a general international agreement regarding the papacy's new status, an agreement in which other powers were apparently reluctant to become involved, the Italian government decided to deal with the question by domestic legislation. In 1871 parliament enacted the Law of Papal Guarantees to serve as the basis of relations between the papacy and the Italian kingdom.

By the provisions of this law the pope and his successors were guaranteed possession of St. Peter's, the Vatican and its gardens, the Lateran Palace, and the Villa of Castel Gandolfo. The head of the church was accorded sovereign rights within these possessions, including the inviolability of his own person and the authority to receive and send ambassadors. He was further granted free use of the Italian telegraph, railway, and postal systems, and guaranteed an annual subsidy from the state of approximately $645,000. Pope Pius IX refused to recognize the Law of Papal Guarantees, however, because it was a simple legislative act of the Italian government, a unilateral arrangement rather than a concordat. He and his successors refused to accept the annual subsidy, declared that they had been deprived of sovereign territory and were unable to exercise their legitimate prerogatives as sovereigns, and proclaimed themselves "prisoners of a usurping power" which they refused to recognize. From 1870 to 1929 no pope ever left the Vatican.

When successive appeals to the Roman Catholic powers failed to bring intervention, the papacy eventually adopted a policy of obstruction. In 1874 Pope Pius by a decree, *Non Expedit,* urged that Catholics should not participate in parliamentary elections nor hold office under the Italian government; and twelve years later another papal decree, *Non Licet,* expressly forbade the political activities which had earlier been declared inexpedient. These decrees were strongly resented by many Catholics who were Italian patriots, and they were never generally observed. Nevertheless, the Roman question remained, and the kingdom in its early years was deprived of the public services of many capable men who did observe the pope's injunction.[1]

Strange to say, the government continued to maintain Roman Catholicism as the state church of Italy. It paid the salaries of the clergy and passed upon the appointment of Catholic bishops. It also permitted religious instruction to be given in the public schools and even went so far as to support the church's view regarding divorce. Doubtless these policies were viewed by the government as minor concessions to satisfy the great majority of the Italian people, who were at heart sincerely loyal to Catholicism. On the other hand, the state did not hesitate to make a number of reforms which "seemed to be demanded in the interests of civil society." These included the confiscation of church property, the suppression of theological faculties in Italian universities and of spiritual directors in the public schools, the establishment of state inspection of Catholic schools, and the introduction of compulsory civil marriage.

A second problem for Italy's statesmen was economic, and, although seriously handicapped by the great expense involved, the government set

[1] For the final settlement of the Roman question by Mussolini, see pages 487–488.

resolutely to work to improve the economic conditions of the country. Highway construction was pushed as old roads were repaired and new ones built. More railways were opened until the kingdom's railway mileage increased from slightly more than 1000 in 1861 to nearly 4500 in 1876. Harbors were developed, and government subsidies were given to the country's mercantile marine. The 10,000 tons of steamships which Italy possessed in 1862 rose by 1877 to approximately a million tons. Though some progress was thus made in the years immediately after 1870, the gigantic task of bringing the various districts of the country up to an approximate level in economic well-being and Italy as a whole up to the standards of a modern state was one to engage the brains of the kingdom's most capable statesmen for decades to come.

Meanwhile, the government was moved by the desire to have Italy ranked among the great powers of Europe. Such "greatness," of course, demanded impressive military and naval forces. As the result of reforms which were made, Italy by 1873 had a peace-time army of 350,000 men, capable of being more than doubled in size in time of war. Warships were constructed, arsenals were established at Spezia and Taranto, and in 1881 an academy was opened at Leghorn for the training of naval officers.

Not unconnected with the foregoing problems, naturally, was the paramount problem of national finance. The new kingdom had assumed the debts of the various states which it had absorbed, and this indebtedness had been increased by heavy necessary expenditures coupled with the government's inadequate revenues in the decade after 1861. The national debt in 1871 amounted to the relatively huge sum of more than $1,600,-000,000. An important task for the government of the Right, therefore, was that of securing a balanced budget so as to escape from the ever-embarrassing national deficits. "The great question which eclipses all others, however important," wrote one Italian statesman in 1873, "is the question of finance. All the chief problems—credit, the currency, the army, national defense, political institutions, economic development—are bound up with it." In the five years after 1870 the ordinary revenues of the Italian kingdom were increased until the Italians became the most heavily taxed people in all Europe, but in the end the fiscal battle was won—at least temporarily—and the government on March 16, 1876, was able to announce that a balanced budget had at last been achieved. Two days later the government of the Right was driven from power.

The Left in Power under Depretis and Crispi

The parliamentary elections of 1876 had gone in favor of the Left, for a number of factors had conspired to make the Right groups unpopular.

In the first place, they had refused to extend the franchise beyond its exceedingly narrow limits and so were accused of trying to keep the mass of Italians "in bondage." The Left groups, on the other hand, stood for "democracy and progress." In the second place, a demand for educational reform had arisen which the Right group, handicapped financially, had ignored. Then, in its efforts to balance the budget, the Right had necessarily imposed heavy taxes and thus of course had aroused much hatred and opposition. Finally, the Right was denounced for its reputed favoritism toward the people of northern Italy at the expense of the rest of the country.

The Left groups now took over the reins of government with a ministry headed by Agostino Depretis, a native of Lombardy who had in his youth been a member of "Young Italy." With short interludes he was in power from 1876 to 1887, when he was succeeded by a Left colleague, Francesco Crispi, a Sicilian who headed the government during most of the time until 1896. These men derived their political support chiefly from the middle classes of Sicily and Naples, but their two decades in power were partly the result of their corrupt political "system." Depretis and Crispi developed methods of controlling parliamentary elections that were, from their own point of view, most efficient. Bribery of electors was openly practiced; registration lists were frequently altered to eliminate the names of political opponents; and gangs of ruffians—sometimes even the *Mafia* and the *Camorra*—were utilized to terrorize the opposition. Such methods usually resulted in the election of a majority of supporters. The Left leaders were also masters of parliamentary intrigue and frequently bought off an opposition leader by appointing him to a post in the cabinet. Since from that moment the new minister's main objective was to keep the government in power as long as possible so that he himself might reap material rewards, his opposition to the premier usually subsided.

The Italian people hailed the elevation of the Left to power as the coming of a new era in which a reforming government would right all the wrongs and heal all the ills from which the masses suffered. Such a program was beyond the ability of any statesman or group of statesmen to fulfill. Nevertheless, under Depretis and Crispi a number of reforms were made. In 1877 an act was passed making education compulsory between the ages of six and nine, but because of financial difficulties no adequate provision was made to carry it out. Five years later a new franchise law was enacted which lowered the age, tax, and educational requirements for voters. By this reform the Italian electorate was increased from approximately 600,000 to more than 2,000,000. The possibility of a gradual but continuous expansion of the electorate was offered by the provision that the franchise would be extended, regardless of property qualification, to all males over twenty-one years of age who had received a primary school education. Under Crispi a new communal and provincial law was also enacted, extending slightly the control of the voters over local affairs. The mayors of the larger communes, for example, were thereafter to be elected locally.

But Italy's chief problem remained economic, and all governments, whether Left or Right, were compelled to wrestle with it in the succeeding years. If adequate food supplies for Italy's growing population were to be provided by the nation, agriculture must be vastly improved. An exhaustive agrarian inquiry, authorized in 1877, brought home to the government the natural poverty of the country and led to the adoption of a far-reaching program for improvement. Though still handicapped by the lack of necessary funds, the government took a number of steps. Instruction in agrarian subjects was introduced in some of the higher schools; special agricultural schools were opened; and experimental farms and agricultural exhibitions were established. Hundreds of thousands of acres of swampland were drained and opened to agriculture. New health laws were enacted; the number of local physicians was increased; measures were taken to combat pellagra and malaria; and epidemics were considerably checked. Co-operative purchasing societies were organized among the peasants, and the importation of agricultural implements and fertilizers was increased to a marked degree. With improved methods, better seeds, and modern implements, a considerable rise in the country's agricultural production resulted, especially in northern Italy. Nevertheless, Italy still remained unable to feed her people adequately.

In industry, too, much progress was made, especially after a system of protective tariffs was erected in 1887. By the close of the century northern Italy had become considerably industrialized, the chief gains being made in the metallurgical, textile, electrical, and chemical industries. Progress in the first of these in time reached the place where the country's industries were able to take care of the nation's steel requirements so far as railway construction and naval and military supplies were concerned. In the cotton textile industry the number of operatives rose nearly 300 per cent during the two decades after 1882. The chief textile industry, however, was silk; eventually Milan surpassed Lyons as the silk-producing center of the world. But modern industry was long dependent upon steam for power, and, for the production of steam, coal—which Italy lacked—was necessary. To lessen the country's dependence upon foreign coal, Italy early embarked upon the development of hydroelectric plants. The use of electricity for industrial purposes rapidly increased, though the greatest development in this field came after the opening of the twentieth century.

By 1905, however, Italy had the largest and best hydroelectric plants in Europe. Nevertheless, with a rapidly growing industry the country was still obliged to import great amounts of coal.

Although Italy's industries thus expanded, the lot of the Italian industrial workers remained hard. Because of the dependence upon foreign coal, Italian industries had to pay more for this essential commodity than those of Germany, Great Britain, and the United States. This was true also in regard to other raw materials. Italian industries could compete with those of other countries, therefore, only if Italian labor and capital received smaller returns. In general, Italian industrialists sought to hold down the costs of production by low wages. On the other hand, the protective tariff tended to increase the cost of various products within the country. As a result of these factors, Italian industrial workers were worse off than those in most of the other countries of western Europe.

In an attempt to secure sufficient foreign exchange to pay for her needed imports of raw materials and foodstuffs, Italy made special efforts to increase her exports and to improve her merchant marine. The country's foreign trade was greatly injured by a ten-year tariff war which Italy began with France in 1887, but on the other hand it was aided by the growing importance of the Mediterranean as an avenue of commerce after the opening of the Suez Canal and by a favorable commercial treaty with Germany in 1892. The latter became Italy's best customer, and the commercial and financial ties between the two countries tended to make Italy an economic satellite of the German Empire toward the close of the nineteenth century. In 1898 the Franco-Italian tariff war was brought to a close with the signing of a new commercial treaty between the two countries, and Italy's commerce benefited accordingly. During the first decade of the twentieth century the country's foreign trade practically doubled in value.

Nevertheless, because of Italy's great need to import food and raw materials, she constantly had an unfavorable balance of trade. If, like France and Great Britain, she had had millions of dollars invested in foreign countries, this would not have constituted a particularly difficult problem, for invisible returns from these foreign investments would have enabled the country to meet its need for foreign exchange. But Italy was poor and had little income from the foreign investments of her citizens. She was, on the contrary, herself a debtor nation. Fortunately for her, however, she did possess two sources of invisible income. Hundreds of thousands of Italian emigrants by their remittances to relatives "back home" sent a steady stream of foreign exchange into the country. At the same time the thousands of tourists, who came yearly to visit the historical sites of Italy or to inspect her magnificent art galleries and museums, spent in the country a considerable sum which also thus became available for foreign payments. Further to reduce the demand for foreign exchange, the government by subsidies encouraged the building of an Italian merchant marine to carry the country's overseas commerce. By 1914 Italy's mercantile shipping was surpassed in tonnage by that of only five other nations in the world.

The Left leaders in the beginning accepted the principle of a balanced budget, and for a number of years after they came into power the national government had slight surpluses. Eventually, however, the increasing expenditures for constructing public works, for maintaining the army and navy, and for inaugurating a program of colonial expansion overtook the state's increasing revenues, and deficits again became the rule. Although expenditures for schools and for social betterment were curtailed, although taxes were increased until they became an excessive burden for the mass of the Italian people, the years between 1887 and 1898 saw accumulating deficits, which amounted by the latter year to a total of approximately $610,000,000. The Italian state appeared to be always on the verge of bankruptcy.

The economic gains enumerated above were largely offset, so far as a rise in the general standard of living was concerned, by the very high birthrate which prevailed and by the increasing pressure of population upon resources which resulted. The hard economic conditions of millions of Italians and the rather hopeless outlook which confronted so many of them, especially in southern Italy where the masses were landless and poverty-stricken, drove hundreds of thousands out of the country as emigrants. Many of them were in a sense transient laborers, who left Italy for a number of months each year to seek work in the neighboring countries of Europe or in South America. Great numbers of them, however, sought to establish homes in countries like the United States, Brazil, and Argentina, where they hoped to find more favorable conditions and greater opportunities for themselves and for their children. In the generation after 1876, according to official figures, more than eight million emigrants left Italy, though the net loss was of course not so great as this. In fact, in 1910 the figure for those who were permanently lost to Italy was officially put at about 5,500,000.

Emigration, while it helped to relieve the pressure of population in Italy, aided the country in other ways. In the regions where emigrants settled abroad they provided an expanding market for Italian commodities. Then, as stated above, Italy's international financial position was strengthened by the money sent back by many emigrants to their relatives. Naturally, also, the lot of these fortunate Italian relatives was often improved as a result of the remittances. Furthermore, many Italians, having amassed a small competence abroad, returned to Italy and introduced higher living standards in the communities where they settled.

Economic hardships in Italy had, also, an effect upon the political situation in the country and aided greatly in the rise of the Socialist Party and other radical organizations. Although both Marx and Bakunin had sought to introduce their ideas into Italy even before the country had completed its unification, it was not until the nineties that socialism made great progress. In 1882, the year in which the suffrage was widened, the Independent Workers Party was organized in Milan, but it was suppressed by Depretis four years later. About 1890, however, Antonio Labriola, in his lectures on the philosophy of history in the University of Rome, began to expound with great enthusiasm the Marxian concept of historical materialism. *Das Kapital,* translated into Italian, was also made more easily accessible to Italian readers. But more influential than Labriola in the rise of Italian socialism was Filippo Turati, who in 1891 became editor of a review in Milan which he made the medium for popularizing the *Communist Manifesto* along with other writings of Marx and Engels.

In 1891 the Italian Socialist Party was organized in Milan, and in the next year it succeeded in electing ten deputies to the Chamber. Crispi, like Bismarck, sought to destroy socialism by rigorous repressive measures. In 1894 he ordered the dissolution of all socialist organizations. Many socialists were imprisoned, and others had their names struck off the election lists. Newspapers were prosecuted, and after the end of the session of parliament in that year Socialist deputies were arrested and imprisoned. But Crispi was no more successful than Bismarck in his similar campaign. At by-elections some of the imprisoned Socialists were elected as deputies, and in the general election of 1895 the Socialist representation in the Chamber rose to twelve.

In that same year the party published its "minimum program," which, though denounced at the time, appears mild indeed today. In fact, much of what it sought had already been obtained in some of the more progressive countries of the West. For the workers it demanded the inclusion of a minister of labor in the cabinet and legislation to protect woman and child labor, to compel a day of rest each week, to provide accident and sickness insurance, to prohibit night work. For Italians generally it sought to obtain effective compulsory education, universal suffrage, payment of members of the Chamber of Deputies, and liberty of conscience, speech, press, and assembly. In the economic realm it advocated national ownership of mines and railways and the inauguration of arbitration of disputes between capital and labor. In 1896 was established the first daily newspaper of the party, *Avanti!,* edited by Leonida Bissolati, and named after the chief Socialist paper in Germany, *Vorwärts.*

Early Attempts to Play the Role of a Great Power

Meanwhile, in international affairs Italy had been attempting to play the role of a great power. Her first venture was directed toward extending her territory to the north and the northeast. Although exalted by the achievement of national unification, Italian patriots were not slow to realize that there was still an *Italia Irredenta*, that is, territory just outside Italy's national boundaries inhabited by Italians. The Trentino in the Alps and the region around Trieste at the head of the Adriatic were the principal places now coveted by nationalistic Italians. Attempting to take advantage of the Balkan situation in 1877–1878, Depretis' government sought to acquire *Italia Irredenta* in compensation for Austria's occupation of Bosnia and Herzegovina.[2] In fact, during the summer of 1877 Francesco Crispi made a tour of the major European capitals in an effort to make such an arrangement, but without success. At the ensuing Congress of Berlin the Italian representative raised objections to Austria's occupation of Bosnia-Herzegovina and put forward a claim to the Trentino as a fair compensation for such occupation. But Italy received no support for her contention. Instead, Crispi lamented, the Italians "were humiliated at Berlin as the last people in Europe." They returned to Rome, he declared, "slapped and despised." *Italia Irredenta* and its redemption by Italy remained for more than a generation an unsolved problem.

In another sphere—that of colonial expansion—Italy was also balked in the early days of the kingdom. She was especially eager to annex Tunis, a territory in northern Africa just across from Sicily, which already contained a considerable number of Italians. In the seventies, as a result of the fiscal difficulties of the ruler of Tunis, a commission consisting principally of Frenchmen and Italians took control of the ruler's financial affairs. It seemed likely that political intervention might follow foreign financial control, and Italy sought to prepare for that intervention. But before Italy got around to intervene, France with the support of Germany and Great Britain in 1881 transformed Tunis into a French protectorate. France's action at once aroused a strong feeling of hostility in Italy and for almost two decades embittered relations between the two states.

A popular demand was now raised in Italy in favor of some alliance so that the kingdom would not be limited to the role of an unimportant neutral state. Some Italian statesmen believed that the prestige of Italy would be more likely to be enhanced if Italy would devote herself to the improvement of her economic, financial, and military strength and not seek alliances for the present. Such leaders believed that it would not be long until one of the great powers would voluntarily seek an alliance

2 See page 225.

VICTOR EMMANUEL II AND FRANCIS JOSEPH
The king of Italy (left) playing host to the emperor of Austria at Venice
in 1875.

with a strengthened Italy. But Italian patriots could not wait. Consequently, Italy herself made the overtures to Germany which in the end resulted in the formation of a defensive alliance, including on Bismarck's insistence the Dual Monarchy also. The Triple Alliance [3] definitely linked Italy with two of the great powers of Europe, but otherwise Italy's gains from it were relatively unimportant. One consequence for Italy was that, now that she was allied with Austria-Hungary, it was necessary for some years to soften the demand for the acquisition of *Italia Irredenta,* and irredentist societies were therefore frequently suppressed.

In 1886 Italy sought to use the negotiations leading to a renewal of the Triple Alliance to pave the way for future Italian expansion in the Balkans and in northern Africa. In the former Italy was jealous of Austria's position and sought to check further Habsburg expansion there. Consequently, as a condition of her own renewal of the Triple Alliance she insisted upon Austria's signing a separate convention (February, 1887) in which the two powers stated their desire to maintain the *status quo* in the Balkans and promised to forestall any territorial modifications which would be injurious to either. They further agreed, however, that, if either power should be obliged to change the *status quo* "by a temporary or a permanent occupation, such occupation would take place only after previous agreement between the two powers, which would have to be based upon the principle of a reciprocal compensation for all territorial or other advantages that either of them might acquire over and above the existing *status quo,* and would have to satisfy the interests and rightful claims of both parties." This agreement became Article 7 of the treaty by which the Triple Alliance was again renewed in 1891.

In 1887, also, Italian statesmen succeeded in linking Germany with Italy's ambitions in northern Africa. In order to block France in any possible further expansion in that region and at the same time to prepare the way for her own aggression there, Italy sought to make the renewal of the Triple Alliance contingent upon German aid to Italy. Although Bismarck at first refused to consider the Italian proposal, the somewhat strained international situation in 1886–1887 eventually influenced him to accede to Italy's demand. In consequence, when the Triple Alliance was renewed in 1887, a supplementary convention was also signed by Germany and Italy. In this convention it was agreed that, if France should move to extend her hold in northern Africa and in consequence Italy should feel that she must herself take action in northern Africa "or even have recourse to extreme measures in French territory in Europe," the ensuing state of war between Italy and France would call for the aid of Germany against France. This agreement became Article 10 of the Triple Alliance when

[3] For the terms of the alliance, see pages 64–65.

it was next renewed in 1891, and obviously by it that alliance lost its original defensive character.

In January, 1887, Italy, desiring further to block possible French expansion in northern Africa, sought a treaty with Great Britain in which the two states would agree that the *status quo* in the Mediterranean, the Adriatic, the Aegean, and the Black Sea should so far as possible be maintained, but that, if this was impossible, no modification should be permitted without a previous agreement between the two powers. Italy further desired an agreement that, in return for her support of Great Britain in Egypt, Great Britain would support Italy in Tripoli and Cyrenaica in case of encroachments on the part of a third power, and that in general the two governments would give each other support in the Mediterranean against any third power.

The British preferred a secret understanding rather than a formal treaty, however, and in February the two governments by an exchange of notes agreed on the maintenance of the *status quo* in the four seas as Italy had suggested. The British government, however, contented itself with the statement that, if it should become impossible to maintain the *status quo,* both powers desired that there should be no extension of the domination of any other great power over any portion of these coasts. The character of the two powers' co-operation, Great Britain asserted, must be decided by them, when the occasion for it arose, according to the circumstances of each case. Quite clearly, though Italy gained something by the exchange of notes, she failed at that time to secure Great Britain's definite support for her future expansion in northern Africa. The Italo-British Mediterranean agreement was further extended in 1887 by Austria-Hungary's adherence to it and by a secret exchange of notes between Italy and Spain. The last two powers agreed to attempt to maintain the *status quo* in the Mediterranean, and each promised not to co-operate with France against the other in regard to northern Africa.

Meanwhile, Italy with Great Britain's blessing had made a beginning of her colonial expansion elsewhere in Africa. Her activity had gradually centered along the Red Sea, whose importance had been increased by the opening of the Suez Canal in 1869. In 1881 Assab, which for some time had been held by an Italian navigation company, was taken over by Italy, and four years later Massaua was similarly occupied. But the kingdom's first colonial expeditions were frequently marked by incompetence and serious blunders. One instance—that of providing heavy military coats for soldiers destined to tramp the burning shores of the Red Sea—became notorious.

Italian imperialists, ardently desirous of carving out an empire in northeastern Africa, coveted Ethiopia, and Italy's subsequent attempt to extend her occupation of Massaua into the interior eventually precipitated a war with this strong empire. In 1887 Italy suffered her first colonial disaster when an Italian force was surprised and annihilated at Dogali. This tragedy was shortly succeeded by the death of Agostino Depretis and by the elevation to the premiership of his colleague Francesco Crispi.

Although Crispi had opposed the expedition to Massaua, once the occupation had occurred he was reluctant to withdraw Italian forces. In fact, in 1889 the occupation was extended, and in the next year the colony was organized and christened Eritrea. In 1889, too, the imperialistic impulse in Italy drove the government on to further steps. A new colony was founded in Somaliland on the east coast of Africa, southeast of Ethiopia. In the same year Italy aided Menelik, a local Ethiopian chieftain, to usurp the imperial throne of Ethiopia, and in return persuaded him to sign a treaty of friendship (treaty of Ucciali) which Italy at once interpreted as transforming Ethiopia into an Italian protectorate. In 1891 Great Britain signed a treaty with Italy recognizing Ethiopia as within Italy's sphere of influence.

Two years later Menelik, becoming suspicious of Italy's intentions, denounced the treaty of Ucciali. France encouraged him to take this step, and in return a French company was given the right to build a railway from Jibuti through Ethiopia to the Nile. Italy, in turn, encouraged by Great Britain, decided to force her protectorate upon Ethiopia, and in 1895 Italian armies began an advance into that country from Eritrea. Menelik long delayed giving battle, but eventually near Adowa (March 1, 1896) he disastrously defeated the Italian forces. Two Italian generals and 4600 Italian officers and men were killed, and 1500 others were taken prisoners. Overwhelmed by a wave of national grief and indignation, Crispi at once resigned. In the succeeding months Italy made peace with Ethiopia, paid Menelik an indemnity of some $2,000,000, recognized his absolute independence, and withdrew from the province which the Italian forces had occupied. Again it appeared that Italy lacked the aptitude, experience, and resources to become a great colonial power. Thereafter Adowa was to patriotic Italians a synonym for humiliating disaster.

Although the two decades prior to 1896 are usually looked upon as an unfortunate period in Italian foreign policy, nevertheless, in the view of the distinguished Italian historian, Benedetto Croce, Italy during those years "by means of Irredentism, her African ambitions, her understandings with England, the pledges given and received with regard to the Triple Alliance, and the contingent clauses contained in the treaty, laid down all the premises of her future international policy which issued at last in her participation in the [First] World War."

The Era of Giolitti

The downfall of Crispi in 1896 was followed by a short period of rule by the Right groups under a number of premiers. These ministries had the task of liquidating the war with Ethiopia which Crispi had begun. They also were obliged to deal with serious outbreaks of disorder within the country arising from widespread social discontent and the increasing radicalism of anarchists and syndicalists. In 1898 trouble arose among the workers of Milan, and in the ensuing conflict between the proletariat and government troops nearly one hundred persons were killed. Harsh punishments were the lot of the leaders of the insurrection, but popular unrest still continued, culminating in the assassination of King Humbert I by an anarchist on July 29, 1900. Humbert had succeeded his father, Victor Emmanuel II, upon the latter's death in 1878; he was now succeeded by his thirty-year-old son, who mounted the throne as Victor Emmanuel III. The new king early endeared himself to the Italian people, and remained a popular figure until he became identified with the rise of Fascism.

In the decade before the First World War the chief statesman-politician in Italy was Giovanni Giolitti. Back in the eighties of the nineteenth century he had been a member of the Chamber of Deputies. In 1889, because of his extensive knowledge of the country's financial problems—and perhaps also because of his attacks upon Crispi—he had been made secretary of the treasury in the latter's government. In 1892 he had even risen to be prime minister, but his government had become involved in bank scandals and had soon fallen. At the opening of the new century his influence again began to increase; in 1901 he was made minister of the interior, and in 1903 he once more became the head of the government. From then until early in 1914 Giolitti was the dominant personality in Italian political life, though not continuously the premier.

Giolitti, whether from his democratic nature or from his desire to win the political support of the masses, was sympathetic with the sufferings and needs of the poorer classes. In his efforts to aid the urban proletariat he adopted many of the planks of the Socialists for his own. To improve the lot of the workers, he recommended social legislation; to lessen the heavy burden which rested on their shoulders, he advocated tax reform. In the conflicts between capital and labor he urged the neutrality of the state and thus indirectly encouraged the workers to resort to strikes. The result was an epidemic of strikes not only among the urban proletariat but among agricultural laborers as well. In 1904 a general strike in northern Italy for a time paralyzed the economic life of that part of the country.

The trade-union movement rapidly spread during the era of Giolitti and resulted in the formation of the General Confederation of Labor with its headquarters at Turin. Railwaymen and government employees organized unions, and even university professors and public-school teachers formed associations. Radicals came to the fore with their plans for political and social revolution, and the Socialists increased their representation in the Chamber until by 1913 it totaled seventy-two. In addition, the Republicans—the political heirs of Mazzini—who advocated universal suffrage, repeal of the Law of Papal Guarantees, military preparedness, and political decentralization, in the decade before 1914 controlled twenty-three members in the Chamber and usually co-operated with the Socialists to form an extreme Left.

Gradually the conservative groups became alarmed. In an effort to win over the Socialists Giolitti in 1904 offered Turati a cabinet post, but the latter declined because of the Socialist Party's principle of opposition to co-operation with the bourgeoisie. A similar invitation was extended to Bissolati in 1911, but he, too, was forced to decline. The growth of radicalism eventually had its effect upon the pope, who threw his support to Giolitti's groups against the Socialists in the elections of 1904 and in the following year by an encyclical practically withdrew the earlier Non Licet. Catholics were now permitted to participate in politics in critical cases which affected "the highest interests of society, which must at all costs be protected." The party situation was further complicated when a Catholic political party—the Popular Party—was at once organized and soon began to play a role in the Chamber of Deputies, where in 1913 it held thirty-five seats.

Nevertheless, in the two decades before the First World War many reforms were inaugurated, and considerable progress was made in improving the economic position of the masses. A great amount of social legislation was enacted. In 1898 the insurance of workers against accident was made compulsory for employers, and a voluntary system of pensions for old age and invalidity was inaugurated with government subsidies. Ten years later another of the Socialists' planks became an actuality when a weekly day of rest was ordered for industrial workmen. In 1910 a system of maternity insurance for women workers was introduced to aid in the expenses attendant upon childbirth. Further steps with a decidedly socialistic tinge were taken. In 1905 the railways of the country were nationalized, and seven years later private insurance companies experienced the same fate. The country's municipalities, moreover, were empowered to own and operate their public utilities, and the government definitely encouraged the organization of co-operative banking and commercial associations. In an effort to improve education, national legislation in 1904 required every commune to establish public schools to be maintained by local taxes, and eventually (1911) elementary education was taken over by the central government with a view to its improvement. The results were distinctly encouraging. Whereas at the opening of the twentieth century illiteracy was nearly 50 per cent, by 1914 it had been reduced to approximately 25 per cent.

In 1912 further steps toward political democracy were taken when laws were enacted providing for the payment of members of the Chamber and for the extension of the franchise. At the opening of that year, out of a population of more than thirty-four million, only 3,247,772, or less than one in ten, were entitled to vote in parliamentary elections. A new electoral law received its approval on June 30 of that year, however, and granted the suffrage to practically all adult male citizens,[4] raising the number of eligible voters to 8,635,148, of whom, it was estimated, the majority could neither read nor write. But in the ensuing elections of 1913 great numbers of the newly enfranchised citizens failed to vote, either because they feared that the electoral system was beyond their comprehension or because they felt it was not worth the trouble to cast their ballots. Many argued that the result indicated that Italy was not yet ready for manhood suffrage.

The Rising Tide of Nationalism and Imperialism

Meanwhile, various factors were combining to wipe out the feeling of sectionalism in the different parts of the kingdom. The thousands of miles of new railways, which increased the ease and frequency of travel within the peninsula for business men and others; the rise of modern newspapers, with their ever-widening circles of readers; the spread of business enterprises across old state boundaries, giving workers and others engaged in the same efforts an increasing feeling of solidarity; the one national capital and the one national parliament, from which emanated uniform laws for the whole country; the new administrative system, with its civil servants drawn from all parts of the peninsula; the military service, which ignored the former provincial lines and threw peasants and city-dwellers together in the same units; all of these in the course of years gradually built up in the kingdom a spirit of Italian nationalism at the expense of the older provincial loyalties.

It is not surprising, perhaps, that with a growing national consciousness there should come a recrudescence of irredentism, despite Italy's membership in the Triple Alliance. Although the statesmen of the Left had attempted to keep the question of *Italia Irredenta* in the background be-

[4] Besides those who had the right to vote because of their elementary school education, the new measure extended the franchise to those who had completed their military service and to those who were at least thirty years of age.

cause of its possible effect on Italy's international relations, the opening
years of the twentieth century saw the irredentist movement again gaining
ground. Anti-Austrian demonstrations occurred in Italy from time to
time,[5] and in 1905 friction between the Austrian and Italian governments
became pronounced when the latter declined to give Austria the satisfaction
demanded after the president of the Italian Chamber of Deputies had
alluded to "our Trentino."

Furthermore, Italian nationalism, carefully nurtured by patriotic writers
like Gabriele d'Annunzio, began to contemplate the possibility of transforming the Adriatic into an Italian lake and the Balkans into an Italian
economic sphere of influence. But obviously neither these achievements
nor the redemption of the Trentino and Trieste could be accomplished
without bringing Italy into conflict with Austria-Hungary. To many
nationalists such an eventuality was not looked upon as altogether impossible or even undesirable, for, in the words of one Italian historian,
"Italy still bore in her bosom the open sores of Custozza and Lissa, always
dreaming of wiping out the disgrace which she had suffered."

Therefore, although Italy's unnatural alliance with Austria-Hungary
continued to exist—partly, perhaps, through inertia—in the closing years
of the nineteenth century her ill will toward France subsided, and she
began to gravitate toward the Triple Entente. France very definitely
encouraged a *rapprochement,* and as early as 1896 signed a convention
with Italy safeguarding the rights of the tens of thousands of Italians
resident in Tunis. Two years later, as mentioned above, a favorable commercial treaty ended the harmful tariff war between the two Latin countries. In 1900 Italy, already casting greedy eyes upon Tripoli in northern
Africa, signed a convention with France in which she gave the latter a
free hand in Morocco, receiving in return the promise of a free hand for
herself in Tripoli and Cyrenaica. Two years later she moved still closer
to France when the two powers agreed that, should either be the object of
a direct or indirect aggression on the part of one or more powers, the
other would maintain a strict neutrality. Victor Emmanuel's visit to Paris
and that of President Loubet to Rome in 1904 gave outward expression
to the new friendship between their two countries. At the Algeciras conference in 1906 [6] France received even more tangible evidence of Italy's
good will when the latter openly supported France rather than Germany.

For a time efforts were made by both Austria and Italy to ward off the
almost inevitable conflict arising between them in the Balkans. As early
as 1887 in the renewal of the Triple Alliance mutual pledges had been
given. In 1900 the two states agreed to respect the *status quo* in Albania

[5] For example, when the University of Innsbruck refused to appoint Italian teachers in 1903.
[6] See page 119.

or, if it could not be maintained, to unite to establish her autonomy. Two years later, in order to conciliate Italy, Austria agreed not to oppose the former's action in Tripoli and Cyrenaica. In the succeeding years Italy continued in many ways to advance her economic penetration of the Balkans. By 1908 considerable progress had been made in Montenegro, where the tobacco monopoly of the country was in the hands of one Italian company, a concession for navigation on Lake Scutari was held by another, and the port of Antivari and a railway had been constructed by still a third. Italian business firms were also established in the Albanian towns of Scutari and Durazzo.

In 1908 the possibility of cordial relations between Italy and Austria was made more remote when the latter announced her annexation of Bosnia and Herzegovina.[7] The effect of Austria's action upon Italy's foreign policy was immediately shown when at Racconigi (1909) the latter agreed with Russia to attempt to maintain the *status quo* in the Balkans to the exclusion of all foreign domination, and in return for Russia's favorable attitude toward Italian interests in Tripoli and Cyrenaica further agreed to consider favorably Russian interests in the question of the Straits at Constantinople. Italy thus became still more closely linked with the states of the Triple Entente.

The indignation aroused in Italy by the annexation of Bosnia and Herzegovina further kindled the spirit of Italian nationalism. In 1910 the nationalists held a congress in Florence, where they demanded that the government adopt a "practical" rather than a "sentimental" policy. They established a daily newspaper, which advocated militarism and attacked liberalism. Liberty, they asserted, was a hindrance to a nation which "aspires to conquer for itself the largest share in the rule of the world." They urged a sweeping educational reform, which should include the rejection of books with timid morality and their replacement by the works of Kipling and Theodore Roosevelt as representative of "the morality of men who do things."

Although the more abundant fruit of this nationalist movement was not forthcoming until the Fascist period of Italian history, it had its influence on events in the years that preceded 1914. For some time Italy had been pursuing the path of economic penetration in Tripoli and had been attempting through secret agents to reach understandings with the Arab chiefs of that region. After 1908 the nationalists began to urge the conquest of this "land of promise" as a sound business proposition for Italian capitalists and as a suitable field for the colonization of "as many as two million" Italian emigrants. Others like the Socialists, however, asserted what was more nearly the truth, namely, that Tripoli had no good

[7] See page 303.

harbors for possible naval bases, that it had an inadequate rainfall and little possibility of irrigation, that it was merely a burning desert dotted with occasional oases, and that the long period of fighting which would be necessary to pacify the country would entail an expense far out of proportion to the value of the conquest.

But in September, 1911, Giolitti gave way before the rising tide of nationalism and imperialism. Citing the "disorder and neglect" in Tripoli and the opposition to Italian economic activities there, the Italian government on September 28 sent an ultimatum to Turkey demanding her consent to Italy's military occupation of that territory. On the next day Italy declared war. When the powers later attempted to mediate between the belligerents, Italy, in order to ward off proposals for a compromise, proclaimed Italian sovereignty over Tripoli (November, 1911). Nearly a year later Turkey in the peace of Lausanne (October, 1912) renounced her sovereignty over Tripoli and Cyrenaica, which were at once organized as an Italian colony named Libya. Turkey also left the Dodecanese Islands, which Italian forces had occupied, in Italian hands as a guarantee until all Turkish military and civil representatives were withdrawn from Tripoli. As later events proved,[8] Italy by her venture gained these islands also, and thereafter had footholds both in northern Africa and in the eastern Mediterranean.

Naturally, the Tripolitan War threw the national budget once more completely out of balance, and the increased national debt in turn required an increase in national taxes. Although the imperialistic enterprise had been enthusiastically hailed by the nationalists, the parliamentary elections of 1913 appeared to leave the matter of its general popularity open to question. The Socialists, opponents of imperialism, increased their representation in the Chamber from 40 to 72, while, on the other hand, Giolitti's bloc suffered a reverse. In 1914 he was succeeded as premier by the Conservative, Antonio Salandra.

Conditions during the few months of Salandra's ministry which preceded the outbreak of the war in 1914 were hectic. Irredentism was fanned into fever heat by the dismissal of Italians from office by the governor of Trieste in 1913 and by fierce street fighting in the same city the next year between Italians, financially encouraged by the Italian government, and Slavs, encouraged by Austria. At the same time, influenced by the radical writings and speeches of the new editor of *Avanti!,* Benito Mussolini, the Socialists and Syndicalists of Italy became ever more aggressive. The government's forcible suppression of disorders in June, 1914, precipitated a general strike throughout Italy. Fighting occurred in several places, but the most radical steps were taken in Romagna and the marches, where

[8] See page 490.

extremists went so far as to proclaim a republic. Although this movement was quickly suppressed by Salandra's government and repudiated by Turati in the name of the Socialist deputies, it is obvious that Italy was in a weakened condition at the fateful hour when the First World War broke out. How that great conflict was eventually utilized by Italian nationalists and imperialists to advance toward their goals is discussed in the later pages of this book.[9]

[9] See page 354.

Chapter VI

THE UNITED KINGDOM AND THE

BRITISH EMPIRE

IN 1870 what is usually referred to briefly as Great Britain included England, Scotland, Ireland, and Wales. The last of these had been absorbed by England in the sixteenth century; England and Scotland had united in the early years of the eighteenth century to form the Kingdom of Great Britain; and by the Act of Union (1800) Ireland had been joined with Great Britain to constitute the United Kingdom of Great Britain and Ireland. The United Kingdom therefore comprised the British Isles. In area it was much smaller than Russia, Austria-Hungary, Germany, or France; in fact, it was smaller, even, than Spain or Sweden. Of the so-called great powers only Italy stood below it in area and population.

But the importance of Great Britain in European and world affairs did not rest merely upon the resources and population of the British Isles. The United Kingdom was the heart and center of the most extensive and populous empire the world has ever known. Compared with its huge overseas realm, the kingdom was a tiny dwarf. The British at home and their English-speaking cousins within the empire were overwhelmingly outnumbered by the heterogeneous population which inhabited British territory in Asia, Africa, and the islands of the seas. In every section of the globe were territories and peoples which constituted parts of the British Empire.

The British Empire in 1870

The various parts of this empire differed noticeably in their political relation to the government at Westminster. A large share of the empire, territorially speaking (but only a small part in population), was in 1870 self-governing. These self-governing areas were in general the regions which had been colonized by the British, the parts where British settlers and their descendants outnumbered the native population. Prominent in this category was the Dominion of Canada, which had been created by the British North America Act of 1867, and which after 1878 had jurisdiction over all British territory north of the United States except Newfoundland and its dependency Labrador. Newfoundland constituted a separate self-governing colony. In Australasia there were in 1870 seven self-governing colonies: Western Australia, South Australia, Victoria, New South Wales, and Queensland in Australia proper; Tasmania, an island just south of Australia; and New Zealand, lying some 1200 miles to the southeast.[1]

In Africa there was one self-governing colony. During the Napoleonic wars the British had conquered the Dutch colony in South Africa, and at the conclusion of the wars the Congress of Vienna had ratified their possession. Most of the white inhabitants of the colony were Dutch Boers (farmers), who held a considerable number of native slaves. When Great Britain in the thirties abolished slavery in all her colonies, several hundred Boers had moved northeast and north from Cape Colony in search of new homes where they might be free from Britain's control. Natal, the colony which they established along the coast to the northeast, had been annexed by the British in 1843, but the Orange Free State and the South African Republic (the Transvaal) north of the Vaal River had been recognized as independent Boer republics in the fifties. Although Great Britain's Cape Colony had not actually been granted self-government in 1870, it obtained that privilege in 1872.

These self-governing parts of the empire had their own parliaments and ministries and managed their own domestic affairs largely as they pleased. Theoretically, Great Britain held the right to veto legislation enacted by their parliaments and to decide in the British Privy Council such judicial cases as might be appealed to it; actually, however, the British government interfered but little in their internal affairs. The various governors-general who were sent by the British government to these parts of the empire were about as powerless there as the king was in the United Kingdom itself.

By far the largest part of the population of the empire, however, lived in territories which did not have self-government. Most of this population —perhaps 80 per cent of the total of the empire—lived in India, that great triangular peninsula lying south of Afghanistan and the Himalaya Mountains in Asia. Here dwelt perhaps as many as 300,000,000 people, who differed among themselves in race, religion,[2] language,[3] cultural standards, and economic status. Britain's hold on India had been forged during the seventeenth, eighteenth, and nineteenth centuries by representatives of

[1] The first six of these in 1900 agreed upon a plan of confederation, and each then became a state in the Commonwealth of Australia. The seventh remained outside the Commonwealth and in 1907 was raised to a rank equal to that of Canada and Australia and was thereafter called a dominion.

[2] Hindus and Moslems, each group divided into many sects, predominated.

[3] More than two hundred languages were spoken.

the British East India Company, which until 1858 had held political sway over India. In the latter year, however, Parliament had deprived the company of its political powers and had transferred control of Indian affairs to the British government. In 1876 another act of Parliament designated British India as the Empire of India, of which the British sovereign was to be the emperor or empress. During most of the period after 1870, therefore, India was an "empire."

Supreme authority in the Empire of India resided in a British viceroy who ruled from Calcutta with the aid of an executive council and with practically dictatorial powers. The viceroy was responsible to the secretary of state for India, a British cabinet member, who was assisted by a small council in London. But not all of India was included within the Empire of India. Several hundred "native states"—including perhaps as much as 40 per cent of the total area—were governed by native princes who recognized British suzerainty over them and who agreed to amicable relations with the Empire of India and to a degree of supervision by the British viceroy. Although most of the native princes were content with their relation to the British Empire, many intellectuals among the natives came to desire home rule or even complete independence for the Empire of India. Increasingly, as the nineteenth century came to a close, the British government was forced to reckon with the rising spirit of nationalism within India.

In addition to the self-governing colonies and the Empire of India the British Empire embraced a great number of other territories scattered over the globe.[4] These, like the Empire of India, were inhabited principally by non-English peoples, and, though differing somewhat among themselves in the way in which they were governed, they had as a group little home rule. Most of these possessions held in 1870 the status of "crown colonies." Their governors were appointed by and responsible to the colonial ministry in London, and were assisted by "advisory" bodies chosen from the British residents in their respective colonies. Many of the "crown colonies" provided strategically located stations for the British navy; others were of great importance to British commercial interests; still others proved their value later by serving as bases for the further extension of the British Empire.

For Great Britain's empire overseas was tremendously enlarged in the years after 1870. Although British statesmen differed noticeably in the degree of aggressiveness with which they protected or extended the empire,

---

[4] The more important of these scattered territories were: Bermuda, the Bahamas, the Windward Islands, the Leeward Islands, Jamaica, Trinidad, Barbados, British Honduras, British Guiana, and the Falkland Islands in the western hemisphere; Gold Coast, Gambia, Sierra Leone, and Natal in Africa; Gibraltar and Malta in the Mediterranean; and Ceylon, the Straits Settlement, Hongkong, and Mauritius in Asia and the South Seas.

the forces of economic imperialism in the end drove them all to acquire ever more and more territory. Asia, Africa, and the South Seas were the chief scenes of British imperialistic activity in the ensuing years; peaceful penetration, military occupation or conquest, and diplomatic negotiation were the means used.

By 1914 Great Britain had obtained an overseas empire so vast in territorial extent and so rich in natural resources as to be a constant source of envy to the less fortunate nations of the globe. Within this empire rested the control of a large share of the world's supply of diamonds, gold, coal, iron, wool, cotton, and wheat, not to mention such other important raw materials as antimony, asbestos, copper, graphite, lead, manganese, nickel, rubber, tin, and zinc. Much of the territory was favorably located in the temperate zones. An avenue of escape for Great Britain's surplus population was thus provided within its confines, and by 1914 some 17,000,000 descendants of British stock were living in the dominions and colonies overseas. And this great empire provided a constantly expanding market for British goods. In the years immediately preceding the First World War more than half of Great Britain's export trade was with her possessions. Even as early as 1870 the British Empire was absorbing 25 per cent of the goods exported from the United Kingdom.

The United Kingdom in 1870

That Great Britain in 1870 was in the very heyday of her economic golden age, standing without a peer as an industrial and commercial country, was not the result of her possession of vast territories overseas, however. Her supremacy was the result primarily of two other circumstances: her possession of valuable natural resources in coal and iron and her leadership in the inauguration of the Industrial Revolution. Although other countries had adopted and were adopting the modern industrial system, the early start which Great Britain had made in this field gave her an ascendancy which in 1870 had not yet been seriously challenged. She was at that date largely the workshop of the world; from her factories and mills a steady stream of exports flowed to the uttermost parts of the globe.

In the five years beginning in 1870 the average annual value of exports from the British Isles was approximately £230,000,000—almost as much as the export trade of France and Germany combined, and more than the total for Germany and the United States. Nearly 90 per cent of the value of British exports—which consisted chiefly of cotton yarns and cloth, woolen and linen goods, pig iron, steel, rails and plate, machinery, and coal—was in goods manufactured in whole or in part in Great Britain, and to this export trade the textile, iron, and steel industries contributed most extensively. The textile mills of Lancashire and Yorkshire surpassed those to be found in any other country, and the iron and steel industries about Sheffield and Birmingham were the largest in the world. Coal production, too, was an important element in Britain's prosperity, for she not only mined enough to supply her own industrial needs but had a surplus for export to less fortunate countries.

In the early seventies the United Kingdom's foreign trade—exports and imports combined—reached the tremendous total of £669,000,000—an amount which completely dwarfed the foreign trade of any other country. And almost two thirds of the shipping which was engaged in carrying this trade was British, for in the shipping trade the United Kingdom's ascendancy was even more striking than in commerce. In 1870 the total tonnage (5,617,693) of the kingdom's merchant navy exceeded that of the mercantile fleets of the next five ranking maritime countries combined; in fact, in steam tonnage the British merchant fleet was more than twice that of the other five countries taken together. British merchantmen carried not only most of the cargoes of the homeland and the empire but a good share of those of other countries also. In the early seventies, for example, British ships carried approximately 46 per cent of the foreign trade of the United States, 37 per cent of that of France, and 33 per cent of that of Germany. Profits from the carrying trade constituted an important item in the national income.

The ascendancy of British shipping was naturally reflected in the kingdom's shipbuilding industry, for the latter constructed ships for registry both in the United Kingdom and in foreign countries as well. The Clyde district of Scotland led the world in the building of ships. But British ships contributed not only thus to British industry but also to the increase of British commerce. By their established routes and their connections with British warehouses they helped to develop a great *entrepôt* trade. Many British vessels brought their cargoes of overseas goods to British warehouses and markets, and from these centers the goods were distributed among European buyers. In a similar way European goods were brought to Britain, whence they were re-exported in British ships to many parts of the world. Of Britain's foreign trade in 1872, for example, re-exports accounted for £58,000,000.

In 1870 London was the greatest commercial port in the world; and it was also recognized as the world's financial center. British capitalists had invested great sums—as much as £1,500,000,000 in 1875—throughout the empire and in many foreign lands. Interest and dividends from these overseas investments provided a steady stream of income for the country, an income which was further supplemented by the large earnings of British bankers, brokers, and insurance companies, which served foreigners as well as the British themselves. In summary, then, it may be said that in 1870 Great Britain earned most of her national income by serving as the manufacturer, merchant, shipper, and banker for a large part of the world.

Politically, this "workshop of the world" was a constitutional monarchy in which the sovereign reigned but did not rule. In 1870 the British ruler —Queen Victoria—was a mere figurehead in the government. Although in theory she had many powers, in actual fact the powers that she appeared to exercise were controlled by her cabinet. The latter, a political device originated by the British, was a committee of members of Parliament, apparently appointed by the ruler but in reality chosen by the majority party in the House of Commons. The executive power of the kingdom was exercised by this cabinet. But the duties of the cabinet were not limited to the appointment of officials and the supervision of administration; it also assumed responsibility for and guided national legislation. All important bills were introduced in Parliament by cabinet members. The cabinet was in turn responsible to Parliament; that is, it was not appointed for a fixed term but might be forced out of office by a vote of "no confidence" in the Commons or by the failure of the latter to pass an important bill sponsored by the ministers. Two courses were open to the cabinet in case of its repudiation by Parliament. It might forthwith resign and permit the leader of the opposition to form a cabinet, or it might dissolve Parliament and call for a new election. In the latter case the voters of the kingdom decided whether or not the cabinet should resign. If a majority of the members of the new Parliament favored the cabinet, the latter continued at the head of the government; if not, it resigned.

The legislative body of the kingdom was a bicameral parliament, consisting of the House of Lords and the House of Commons. The former consisted for the most part of hereditary English peers; there were also a number of elected Scottish and Irish peers and the bishops of the established Anglican Church. Despite the fact that the Lords were not directly responsible to the voters, they exercised considerable power of a negative type in national legislation. Although by threatening to create new peers a ministry might, as in 1832, force the Lords to pass desired legislation, this device was reserved for only the most critical occasions. In general, therefore, the Lords were in a position to tone down or defeat bills that appeared to them radical or inimical to the interests of the groups they represented—socially, the landed aristocracy; politically, the Conservative Party. When the latter was not in control of the cabinet, the Lords tended to obstruct legislation. The threat "to mend or end" the House of Lords was often muttered by those who sat on the Liberal benches in the House of Commons. One power the Lords had by 1870 apparently surrendered to the Commons, namely, the power to enact the national budget. Although in principle the upper house had co-ordinate power in the drafting and adoption of the budget, precedent had established the rule that the Lords must enact money bills passed by the House of Commons.

The latter during the preceding centuries had gradually risen in influence until by 1870 it was generally recognized as the predominant—although not the all-powerful—branch of the government. Its consent was necessary for all legislation; it dominated the ministry; and through its control of the "purse strings" it could, if it willed, completely paralyze the government. The House of Commons represented the British "people," and was chosen from time to time by popular election. Although elected for a maximum term of years, it might be dissolved in the name of the king by the cabinet when the latter wished to test the opinion of the electorate. Prior to 1832 the Commons had been largely controlled by the aristocracy, but the Reform Act of that year had so widened the electorate and changed the representation as to shift control into the hands of the middle classes. There it had remained for a generation until in 1867 a second Reform Act again altered the situation. Once more the franchise had been widened and the representation redistributed. As a consequence, in 1870 almost all townsmen, and in rural districts practically all men but the farm laborers, could vote. The act of 1867 thus for the first time had placed the Commons under the control of the mass of the people. Nevertheless, the franchise in Great Britain was not yet open to all men as in France and Germany after 1870; perhaps as many as a third of the men in the kingdom were still denied the vote.

Despite the reform measures of 1832 and 1867 the British government in 1870 was still largely dominated by the upper and wealthier classes. Obviously the House of Lords was in their control. But a large share of the seats in the Commons, most of the places in the cabinet, and the important positions in the administrative system were also held by them. Furthermore, the leadership in the two most important political parties was for the most part in their hands. In the ensuing years, however, these classes were forced more and more to cater to the desires of the masses, for without the electoral support of the latter the retention of political power was not long possible.

The two major political parties in the kingdom in 1870 were the Liberals and the Conservatives. The former, the spiritual heirs of the Whigs, had increased in strength as a consequence of the Reform Act of 1832. The Liberal Party was largely the medium for expressing the desires of the bourgeoisie, though the enfranchisement of the urban workingmen in 1867 temporarily brought into the party most of the voters from that class also. In theory the Liberals favored free trade, the further extension of the franchise, and the alleviation of the ills of Ireland; they were critical of the position and power of the established church, were not enthusiastic about imperial expansion, and usually were not particularly aggressive in foreign affairs. The Liberals have been characterized as the party of "peace, retrenchment, and reform."

The Conservatives were the successors of the Tories of the pre-1832 era. The party was dominated by the aristocracy and was to a considerable extent the champion of the interests of the landed classes. It had, for instance, long supported a protective tariff on agricultural products. It was in general hostile to "progressive" legislation and usually favored the maintenance of the *status quo*. Consequently, it supported the established church, the established peerage, the established landowning system, and the established relations with Ireland. It was more nationalistic and imperialistic than the Liberal Party and accordingly, when in power, pursued a more aggressive foreign policy and a more vigorous imperialistic program. It must be emphasized, however, that the Conservative Party was not the agent of reaction. It sought rather to apply the brakes to radical or overspeedy legislation. When, despite their opposition, progressive measures were adopted, the Conservatives acquiesced in the situation and gave up their resistance. In fact, upon occasion the Conservative Party itself championed measures which were liberal and progressive. The Reform Act of 1867 had been passed under a Conservative government.

In the seventies a third political group, the Irish Nationalists, made its appearance in the British parliament. This party drew its support from Ireland and was interested almost solely in improving the lot of the Irish. Although Ireland constituted part of the United Kingdom, it was not happy in that association. Ireland was different from Great Britain. Whereas England, Scotland, and Wales were predominantly Protestant, Ireland was largely Catholic. Whereas Great Britain had become chiefly industrial, Ireland had remained for the most part agricultural. Whereas the problems confronting the three parts of Great Britain were largely similar, those of Ireland were felt to be distinctly different. Whereas the Welsh and the Scots were generally happy in their union with the English, most of the Irish had never ceased to resent their political absorption into the United Kingdom. Their political goal was "home rule" for Ireland.

Hatred of the English had been bred into the Irish by centuries of economic exploitation and religious and political oppression. In the seventeenth century Englishmen and Scots had been "planted" in northern Ireland on lands which were taken from the native Irish; and in the seventeenth and eighteenth centuries most of the rest of Ireland had been transferred from the Irish to British landlords. The Irish had been forced to become agricultural laborers or tenants on the estates of these land-lords—many of whom lived in England. As tenants—and there were 600,000 of them in 1870—they were subject to the arbitrary exploitation of their landlords, for the British government had sought to force upon Ire-land a system of *laissez faire* in land. In other words, the landlords had been conceded the right to dispose of their property as they pleased, with the result that Irish peasants had been subjected to the "withdrawal of customary privileges, the ceaseless demand for higher rents, the peren-nial notice to quit, and the cruel eviction."

Since most of the peasants had no alternative other than to farm, the landlords could exact almost any rent they desired and could always find new tenants to succeed those evicted. Furthermore, according to the law the landlords were under no obligation to compensate evicted tenants for improvements which the latter had made during their tenancy.[5] The most pressing problem for the Irish peasants was that of securing protection against oppressive landlords. They sought legislation which would pro-vide for fair rent, fixity of tenure, and "free sale"—the latter meaning the right to sell to their successors improvements which they had made. These demands were popularly referred to as the "three F's." The ultimate goal of the Irish peasants was, of course, the destruction of landlordism and the return of the land which had once been theirs.

Religious differences also undoubtedly played a part in the attitude of the Irish toward the British. The former had for the most part remained Catholic at the time when Great Britain broke away from the Catholic Church. But Protestant leaders in Britain had sought to win the Irish to their faith and had established in Ireland the Church of Ireland, which was in essence only the Anglican Church under another name. Irish Catholics were long forced to contribute to this established church which none of them attended and which none of them desired. Prior to 1829, also, the Catholic Irish—that is, most of the Irish—had been denied the right to represent Ireland in the parliament of the United Kingdom.

The century preceding 1870 had witnessed a notable rise of Irish national-ism, which had expressed itself in a succession of organizations under one name or another. At the close of the eighteenth century there had been formed the society of United Irishmen, including both Catholics and Protestants. Their rebellion in 1798 had precipitated the decision to absorb Ireland into the United Kingdom. Next, in the first quarter of the nine-teenth century, had come the Catholic Association, led by Daniel O'Connell. This organization had made some gains for Irish Catholics by securing

---

[5] Although the lot of agricultural laborers and tenants of England was none too happy, nevertheless among them there was lacking the feeling that prevailed among the Irish—that their exploitation was at the hands of an alien people.

the removal of many civil disabilities and the granting to Catholics of the right to hold seats in the British parliament. In 1843 the Catholic Association had been dissolved and its leader imprisoned by the British government. But the suppression of O'Connell's organization had been followed almost at once by the appearance of a new and more radical society known as Young Ireland, whose members were pledged to try to establish an independent Irish republic. During the wave of nationalistic revolts on the Continent in 1848 the Young Irish had made an attempt to throw off British control, but their revolt had merely brought the suppression of their society and the punishment of their leaders.

Late in the fifties still another organization, the Fenian Brotherhood, had been formed—this time among the Irish in the United States. Although it never secured much of a following among the peasants of Ireland, the society received considerable support from Irish outside the island. In 1866 Fenians in the United States had made a foolish and abortive raid on Canada, and in 1867 other Fenians in the industrial cities of Lancashire had precipitated riots which were so serious as to lead the British government to call out troops to maintain order. Any history of the United Kingdom after 1870, it is obvious, must accordingly give attention to the situation in Ireland and to the role of the Irish Nationalist Party, which was organized in that year.

William Ewart Gladstone

In 1870 William Ewart Gladstone was British prime minister. He had already had a long career in Parliament, having entered the House of Commons as a Conservative in 1833. While still a student at Oxford he had attracted attention by his speeches against the Reform Bill of 1832, and as a result had been sent to Parliament for a pocket borough through the influence of the Duke of Newcastle. Almost immediately Gladstone was included in one of the Conservative ministries in a minor office, and from then on he was almost regularly a member of the ministry when the Conservatives were in power. He supported Sir Robert Peel in seeking the repeal of the Corn Laws in 1846, and thereafter became more and more liberal in his views. In 1853 Gladstone became chancellor of the exchequer in a coalition government, and at once disclosed not only his understanding of budgetary matters but his ability to explain and clarify the intricacies of state finance with an eloquence which could hold the House of Commons enthralled for hours.

In 1859 Gladstone became the chancellor of the exchequer in a purely Liberal government and thereafter was identified with the more progressive wing of the Liberal Party. For several years he supported the various efforts to secure further parliamentary reform, but to no avail, largely because Lord Palmerston, the leader of the Liberals, was opposed to such a step. Upon the death of the latter in 1865, Gladstone became the real leader of the party despite the fact that Lord Russell, an older man, held the office of prime minister. Following Palmerston's death Gladstone sponsored a parliamentary reform bill, but it was defeated in the House of Commons, and the Liberal government was forced to resign. The Reform Bill of 1867 was then passed under a Conservative government, thanks largely to the influence of Gladstone's rival, Benjamin Disraeli. The first election held under the new franchise, however, resulted in a majority not for the Conservative Party, under whose government it had been enacted, but for the Liberals.

Accordingly, Gladstone—destined in the succeeding quarter of a century repeatedly to serve Great Britain as prime minister—became head of the government for the first time (1868–1874). The Liberal leader at once turned his attention to the Irish situation and by two acts sought to alleviate the ills of Ireland. In 1869 an act of Parliament disestablished the Church of Ireland. Church and state were completely separated, and the church was dispossessed of much of its property other than church buildings. The Irish were also released from their obligation to support the church—with the result that many parishes at once ceased to exist—and bishops of the Church of Ireland were deprived of their seats in the House of Lords. This measure went far toward removing all religious grounds for complaint on the part of the Irish Catholics.

A second act, the Land Act of 1870, dealt with the Irish agrarian situation. The British government abandoned its *laissez-faire* principle in regard to land and repudiated the landlords' doctrine of an absolute and infallible right in property in land. The new act forbade the arbitrary increasing of rents and stipulated that an evicted tenant should be compensated for whatever improvements he had made. It also provided that the state should lend peasants who desired to buy land a certain percentage of the purchase price. Unfortunately, the act largely failed to improve the lot of the tenants because selfish landlords were quick to discover and avail themselves of huge legal loopholes in it. While in principle it antagonized the landlords, in operation it failed to satisfy or relieve the Irish peasants.

But Gladstone was not unmindful of the need for more general reform. As in France after the establishment of the Third Republic, so in Great Britain after the wide extension of the franchise in 1867, it was felt that better provision must be made for popular education. Prior to 1870 the kingdom had no compulsory education and no state system of free education. In fact, nearly half of the children were receiving no formal instruction whatsoever. The schools that did exist were voluntary; that is, they were denominational schools, which received some slight aid from the national government, or private schools—called "public" in England—like Rugby, Eton, and Harrow. The Forster Education Act of 1870 provided for the establishment of board schools—so-called because they were put in charge of locally elected boards—to supplement the existing educational facilities. These schools, in which no denominational religious instruction was to be given, were to be supported by national grants, by local taxes, and by student fees. Although the act made no requirement of compulsory school attendance, this decision being left to the discretion of each school board, the general tendancy thereafter was toward some form of compulsory education. In 1871 the doors to institutions of higher learning were also opened wider by an act abolishing the existing religious tests for admission to Oxford and Cambridge. Thereafter these institutions accepted as students dissenters and Roman Catholics as well as Anglicans.

In addition to his educational reform Gladstone favored the recently enfranchised workingmen by still other measures. The Trade Union Act of 1871 finally conferred legal status upon trade unions by authorizing them to own property and giving them the right to undertake and defend actions at law. As a consequence, trade unionism rapidly expanded in the ensuing years. In 1872 the political freedom of the masses was safeguarded when the secret or "Australian" ballot was introduced in place of voting by word of mouth. Some attention was given, also, to the condition of the workers, for in the same year a law was passed forbidding the underground employment of women and children under twelve years of age. Gladstone also struck at the privileged position of the aristocracy by placing the British civil and military services more directly on a merit basis, thus opening them to others than the upper classes. In 1870 a system of civil-service examinations was introduced, and in the following year the purchase system, by which the wealthy had formerly been able to buy commissions and promotions in the army, was abolished.

Naturally, so many reform measures could not be introduced without antagonizing the affected classes. Many high-church Anglicans and some nonconformists were alienated by the education act with its apparently hostile attitude toward religious education. Others of the upper classes were antagonized by the reforms in the civil service and in the army. Many denounced the government's conciliatory attitude in foreign policy as pusillanimous and weak. Russia, Britain's traditional enemy, had successfully abrogated (1870) the provisions of the treaty of Paris forbidding Russian ships in the Black Sea. She had also continued practically unhindered her steady advance in central Asia toward the frontiers of India.[6] Furthermore, in 1871 Gladstone's government had agreed to express to the United

[6] See pages 209–210.

States its regret at the escape of the *Alabama* and other Confederate cruisers and to refer the assessment of damages to an international tribunal,[7] and Great Britain had been compelled to pay the United States £3,250,000 in damages. Although the method of settling this international dispute was undoubtedly enlightened and progressive, many in Great Britain felt that the outcome was a national humiliation. Disraeli, the Conservative leader, declared: "It would have been better for us all if there had been a little more energy in our foreign policy, and a little less in our domestic legislation."

Benjamin Disraeli

It is perhaps not surprising therefore that in the general election of 1874 the Liberals were decisively defeated. A Conservative ministry, headed by Disraeli, then took over the reigns of government. In 1837 Benjamin Disraeli, like Gladstone four years earlier, had entered Parliament as a Conservative, but, unlike Gladstone, he had remained a Conservative through all the intervening years. At the beginning of his political career he had been handicapped by his Jewish descent [8] and by his striking peculiarities of manner and appearance, but he was an able man and a brilliant speaker, and in less than two decades he came to be the real head of the Conservative Party. Like Gladstone, he frequently held the office of chancellor of the exchequer, but he lacked the former's unusual ability to serve in this capacity. Disraeli enthusiastically supported the monarchical principle of government and was a firm believer in the imperial destiny of Great Britain. In 1867 he had sought to strengthen the Conservative Party by uniting the nobility and the urban workingmen against the bourgeoisie, and had accordingly sponsored the measure which in the end became the reform act of that year. In 1868 Disraeli had been prime minister for some ten months just preceding Gladstone's first ministry.

Disraeli was a man of seventy when he entered upon his second term as prime minister in 1874. His primary interest was in foreign and colonial affairs, and he felt, furthermore, that the country was in need of a period of rest from disturbing legislation after the great number of reform measures which had been enacted in the preceding seven years. Nothing particularly startling, therefore, was done in the field of domestic legislation. Nevertheless, under his government laws were enacted (1) forbidding

---

[7] During the American Civil War a number of cruisers were built in Great Britain for the Confederate government and allowed to sail out to the high seas to destroy American merchant ships. The most notorious instance was that of the *Alabama,* which was allowed to sail despite the protests of the United States government.

[8] He had received Christian baptism when a boy.

children under ten to work in textile factories, (2) forbidding children under fourteen who lacked a certain amount of education from working in any industries, (3) forbidding—to protect British sailors—the use of overloaded or unseaworthy ships, (4) placing all establishments using mechanical power in the same category without respect to size, (5) permitting "peaceful picketing" by strikers, and (6) codifying the existing social legislation.

Far more striking were the achievements of Disraeli's government in the realm of colonial and foreign affairs. Queen Victoria was proclaimed Empress of India (1877); Baluchistan on the northwestern boundary of India was converted into a protectorate; and by means of the second Afghan War (1878–1881) Russia's threatening advance toward British India was checked. Steps were taken, also, to safeguard Britain's most direct route to India.

In 1869 the Suez Canal, connecting the Mediterranean with the Red Sea through Egyptian territory, had been opened and had inevitably altered the trade routes of the world. The canal had been constructed by a French engineer, Ferdinand de Lesseps, and had been largely financed by a French company. Because of the difficulty of securing sufficient funds for the project,[9] however, Lesseps had had to enlist the support of the khedive of Egypt, who had eventually subscribed to nearly half of the shares of the company. Once the canal was constructed and in successful operation, it soon became obvious that it constituted an important link in the British Empire's "lifeline," for in the seventies two thirds of the tonnage passing through the canal was British. Great Britain, therefore, could not well be indifferent to its control. Consequently, when in 1875 the khedive found himself in financial difficulties, Disraeli, without waiting for parliamentary consent, boldly and quickly purchased his canal shares for Great Britain at the cost of £4,000,000. By this coup he at once secured for the British government an influential position on the canal's board of directors.[10]

In 1878 at the Congress of Berlin [11] Disraeli not only helped to halt Russia's advance into the Balkans but strengthened Britain's own position relative to the Suez Canal. In return for the promise of British support against Russia, the sultan ceded to Great Britain the island of Cyprus, strategically located in the eastern Mediterranean. In the following years Great Britain's ability to control and protect the Suez Canal was further increased as the result of developments in Egypt. The khedive had been so extravagant in his expenditures as ultimately to destroy his credit and

[9] Great Britain, Russia, Austria, and the United States declined to subscribe to the shares of the company.

[10] Great Britain obtained 176,602 of the total 400,000 shares.

[11] See page 224.

place him in an embarrassing position financially. He was accordingly forced to accept British and French financial advisers, and, when he rebelled at this, he was in 1879 removed from the throne. The new khedive was forced to accept Anglo-French financial advice, and from 1879 Egypt was subjected to the "dual control" of France and Great Britain. Elsewhere in Africa the Conservative government's imperialism was evident. In 1877 the Transvaal Republic was annexed, and two years later the British were plunged into a formidable war against the Zulus, in which they suffered a number of reverses before the natives were finally overcome.

By the close of 1879 Disraeli, now known as the Earl of Beaconsfield, was becoming unpopular. Expensive wars abroad, economic depression at home, relative inattention to domestic legislation, and increasing parliamentary obstruction by the Irish Nationalists, all reacted against his ministry. In the general election of March, 1880, the Conservatives went down in defeat, and a few weeks later Beaconsfield resigned without waiting to face the new Parliament. In 1881 the Conservative leader died and thus brought to an end the parliamentary and ministerial rivalry which had so long existed between himself and Gladstone.

GLADSTONE'S LATER MINISTRIES

The latter, himself seventy years old, in 1880 became prime minister for the second time. He was at once compelled to deal with the situation in Ireland, which was becoming more and more difficult as the result of the activities of Charles Stewart Parnell and his Irish Nationalists. Strange to say, Parnell was not a native Catholic Irishman but a Protestant of English descent. He had developed, however, an intense hatred of the British, and the attainment of home rule for Ireland had become his highest ambition. In 1877 he and his followers had inaugurated in the House of Commons a policy of obstructing all legislation until their demand for home rule should be heeded. Though Parnell himself opposed the use of force, unrest and outbursts of violence prevailed in Ireland and led Gladstone's government to push through Parliament a number of coercive measures.

At the same time, in the hope of conciliating the Irish, Gladstone had Parliament pass a new land act (1881). This act, designed to remedy the defects of the law of 1870, provided for a land court to fix the rent for a fifteen-year period during which the tenant might not be evicted except for nonpayment of rent and for certain other specified reasons. It also provided that the tenant might dispose of his interest in his holding at the best price he could get. With its adoption of the "three F's," the act thus safeguarded the tenants' rights to remain upon the land, to pay only "fair" rent, and to dispose of their interest in their holdings. It was obviously

THE EARL OF BEACONSFIELD

Disraeli addressing a meeting of the Conservative Party at the Carlton Club
shortly before his death in 1881.

based on the principle of dual ownership and was a triumph for the Irish peasantry.

Although Gladstone's second ministry saw the enactment of laws providing for compulsory elementary education and for employers' liability, the chief legislation of this period had to do with political and parliamentary reform. In 1883 the Corrupt Practices Act limited the amount which a parliamentary candidate might spend for election expenses and made bribery for political purposes a criminal offense. In 1884 the third Reform Act was passed, extending the franchise to farm laborers and to a number of other smaller groups which had not before been included. The electorate was thus increased by some two million voters; thereafter domestic servants, bachelors living with their parents without paying rent, and those having no fixed residence were the only classes of men excluded. In the following year the Redistribution Act was passed, depriving more than a hundred towns of their separate representatives and including them for purposes of representation as parts of the counties in which they lay, and reducing the representation of many others. On the other hand, more populous cities and counties were awarded increased representation. The act also provided for the division of the counties and most of the large towns and cities into electoral districts of approximately equal population, each with one representative in Parliament. After 1885, therefore, Great Britain had equal electoral districts, the secret ballot, and almost manhood suffrage for the election of Parliament. In 1882, also, the Municipal Corporations Act had given the right to vote for city officials to all men inhabiting the city, regardless of property-holding.

By this time, despite his own aversion to imperialistic ventures, Gladstone had become deeply involved overseas—thanks largely to the legacy which he had inherited from Disraeli. Popular opposition in the Transvaal against its annexation by Great Britain was strong and had eventually led to open revolt by the Boers. A brief military campaign ensued, and in February, 1881, the British were decisively defeated in a minor engagement at Majuba Hill. Gladstone had waged his election campaign in 1880 against imperialism and was prepared to recognize the independence of the Transvaal Republic. A peace treaty (1881) therefore restored self-government to the Boers under British suzerainty. A later convention (1884), however, omitted the clause regarding suzerainty and merely stipulated that the Transvaal could not conclude treaties with foreign powers without the approval of the British government. In Britain these steps were viewed with indignation by many who interpreted them as a weak surrender in the face of force.

In Egypt, too, Gladstone encountered difficulties. A strong nationalist movement soon developed in that country against the dual control of

Great Britain and France. In 1881 the standard of revolt was raised, and the slogan "Egypt for the Egyptians" resounded. The British government proposed to France joint military intervention in Egypt, but France declined to participate. Great Britain then decided to proceed alone, and in 1882 a British fleet bombarded and captured Alexandria. Ultimately British troops advanced to Cairo, and the nationalist movement thereupon collapsed. Although Gladstone's government formally notified the powers that the British army would be withdrawn "as soon as the state of the country, and the organization of the proper means for the maintenance of the Khedive's authority, will admit of it," British troops continued to be stationed in Egypt. The real ruler of the country came to be the British consul-general and high commissioner, and British imperialists soon considered the Nile valley as part of the British Empire.

From Egypt the British were soon drawn into difficulties in the eastern Sudan. Egypt had attempted to establish her authority in this region along the upper Nile but had aroused strong opposition by her edicts against the slave trade and by her heavy taxes. Led by Mohammed Ahmed, who claimed to be divinely ordained to drive out both Egyptians and Europeans, the Sudanese rose in the early eighties and annihilated an Egyptian army. Gladstone's government decided that Egypt should withdraw from the Sudan and sent a small force of British troops commanded by General Charles Gordon to aid in the evacuation. Before Gordon could accomplish his task, however, he and his troops were surrounded at Khartum. Gladstone's government was dilatory in sending reinforcements, with the result that, before the latter arrived, Khartum was captured early in 1885 and Gordon was killed by native "dervishes."

Gladstone's failure to take prompt measures to relieve Gordon roused a storm of fury in Great Britain. Discontent was further increased by his government's apparently ineffective policy toward Russia's advance upon Afghanistan.[12] Even Gladstone's domestic legislation reacted against him, for his land act antagonized many of the British without fully satisfying the Irish Nationalists. In June, 1885, Parnell and his followers turned against Gladstone, who resigned and was succeeded by Lord Salisbury, the new leader of the Conservative Party. But in January, 1886, the Irish Nationalists in turn repudiated Salisbury, and Gladstone again became prime minister.

But Gladstone's third ministry was of short duration, chiefly because he espoused the cause of the Irish Nationalists. Soon after coming into power he introduced a bill to give Ireland a separate parliament for her own affairs, hoping thus to obtain peace and contentment in Ireland and

[12] In 1885 the Russians occupied Penjdeh in Afghanistan. Instead of ousting them by military measures, Gladstone's government submitted the matter to arbitration.

the end of Irish obstruction in the British parliament. Unfortunately for his hopes, however, more than a fourth of the Liberal members of Parliament were opposed to home rule. Led by John Bright and Joseph Chamberlain, they seceded from the Liberal Party and formed the Liberal Unionist Party, which joined with the Conservatives to oppose Gladstone's Home Rule Bill. Although the eighty-six Irish Nationalist members threw their support to Gladstone, the bill was defeated in the House of Commons. Parliament was then dissolved in order that new elections might test the feeling of the country on the question. The Liberals were defeated, Gladstone was forced to resign, and for the next six years the Conservatives were in power.

In the parliamentary election of 1892 Gladstone again made home rule the chief issue of his campaign. Although the Liberals failed to gain a majority of the seats in Parliament, the combined strength of the Liberals and the Irish Nationalists provided such a majority. Consequently, Gladstone for the fourth time became prime minister, and in 1893 he introduced his second Home Rule Bill. The measure, though vigorously denounced and opposed by the Conservatives and the Liberal Unionists, was this time passed by the House of Commons. But this achievement brought little satisfaction to the Irish Nationalists, for the bill was decisively rejected by the House of Lords and therefore failed to become law. Early in 1894 Gladstone at the age of eighty-four resigned the premiership and retired from public life. Four years later the "Great Commoner" died. He alone of all British statesmen had had the distinction of four times holding the office of prime minister.

The Conservatives in Power

Except for the brief interlude of Liberal government from 1892 to 1895, the Conservatives were in power for practically two decades after 1886. Until 1902 Lord Salisbury served as prime minister and as foreign secretary when the Conservatives were in office. His chief interest was in foreign affairs, and, from the viewpoint of an aristocrat and an imperialist, Britain's foreign policy was ably conducted during his period. In 1902 Salisbury was succeeded as prime minister by his nephew, Arthur James Balfour, who had been the Conservative leader in the House of Commons, and who remained at the head of the government until the Conservatives went out of power in December, 1905. Balfour was more of a philosopher than a politician or statesman. Though his parliamentary speeches were acclaimed for their scholarly open-mindedness and their philosophic and literary qualities, he did not distinguish himself particularly as a party leader.

The third outstanding figure in this period of Conservative rule—and probably the most important—was Joseph Chamberlain, who had led the Liberal Unionist secession in 1886. Chamberlain was a successful Birmingham business man. He had played an active role in the political life of his city and was well known for the political reforms he had introduced while mayor of that municipality. From 1886 to 1892 he was informally allied with the Conservatives, but, when Salisbury formed his third ministry in 1895, Chamberlain accepted the post of colonial secretary. Generally speaking, Chamberlain favored colonial expansion, closer relations between the mother country and the colonies, the erection of protective tariffs for the kingdom in conjunction with a system of imperial preference for the empire, and the enactment of further social legislation. In 1885, before he left the Liberal party, he had published a proposed program of reform which included free education, small agricultural holdings, and more democratic local government. Gladstone's indifference to these proposals had helped to pave the way for the final break which came in the following year over Irish home rule. Chamberlain's influence is apparent in the domestic legislation of the Conservative period.

In 1888 the Conservatives passed the County Councils Act transferring most of the administrative powers of the counties from the frequently old and inefficient justices of the peace to elected councils. This act had for counties much the same significance that the Corporation Act (1835) had had for towns and cities. In the realm of education two steps were taken. In 1891 the Elementary Education Act provided for the making of grants from the national treasury to denominational schools as well as to board schools in England and Wales, and made possible the practical abolition of tuition fees in the elementary schools. Eleven years later (1902) the Conservatives further strengthened the denominational schools by an act stipulating that the latter should be placed on the same footing with board schools in respect to both national grants and local taxation. Since nearly 90 per cent of the thousands of voluntary schools were controlled by the Church of England, the act was particularly distasteful to dissenters.

In the realm of labor and social legislation some slight advances were made. In 1887 the Mines Act forbade the employment of either girls or boys under twelve years of age. Five years later (1892) the Small Holdings Act authorized the county councils to buy land, to sell it in blocks of less than fifty acres each, and to loan to the purchaser as much as three quarters of the purchase price. The measure was designed to increase the number of small independent farmers in the kingdom. Steps were taken, too, to protect the workers in case of accident. In 1897 the Workmen's Compensation Act obligated employers in industry to insure their employees against accident, and three years later the act was extended to include agricultural employees also. In 1901 a comprehensive factory code was drafted to serve as the basis of Britain's industrial system.

Although the Conservatives were unalterably opposed to home rule for Ireland and did not hesitate to resort to coercion to quell the Irish Nationalists, they did enact legislation to alter the land situation in that part of the kingdom. Gladstone's land act of 1881 had applied the principle of "dual ownership," a principle which had proved to be unsound economically as well as socially. The act had been a triumph for the Irish peasantry; nevertheless, the latter remained discontented—they wanted the land. But the landlords were even more dissatisfied, for they soon discovered that "fair" rents were lower rents, and that lower rents, in the face of an organized peasantry, were just as difficult to collect as high rents. Dual ownership broke the landlords financially; for them it brought "a regime of force, fraud, and folly." From this intolerable situation they were ultimately enabled to retire with a minimum of loss as a result of a series of land purchase acts sponsored by the Conservatives.

The first of these acts was passed during Salisbury's first ministry in 1885, and other acts of a similar nature were passed in 1887, 1891, 1896, and 1903. These measures were designed to facilitate the transfer of land in Ireland from the landlords to the tenants. The act of 1903, known as the Wyndham Act, though it went further than the earlier measures, was typical. It provided that £100,000,000 should be set aside by the British government to enable Irish tenants to buy out their landlords, money being loaned to the peasants on very easy terms. By repaying annually to the government 3¼ per cent of the principal amount borrowed, a tenant could extinguish his debt—both principal and interest—in less than sixty-nine years. At the same time, in order to induce the landlords to sell at prices the tenants could or would pay, the government gave the landlords a bonus of 12 per cent of the purchase price. During the early years of the twentieth century great numbers of Irish tenants availed themselves of this act to become owners of their holdings.[13] To further placate the Irish the Local Government Act (1898) extended to Ireland the system of county and district councils which prevailed in England. Despite these measures, which were designed to "kill home rule with kindness," the Irish Nationalists nevertheless refused to withdraw their demands for a separate Irish parliament.

[13] By 1922 only 70,000 holdings were as yet unpurchased by their occupiers. After the establishment of the Irish Free State the latter enacted a sweeping agrarian law compelling landlords to sell their estates and tenants to purchase their holdings.

Resurgent Imperialism

The fiftieth anniversary of Queen Victoria's accession to the throne, joyously celebrated throughout the kingdom, witnessed a rising tide of nationalism and imperialism. The chief ministers of the self-governing colonies, in London for the queen's jubilee, were invited to confer with British ministers on matters which concerned the empire as a whole, and their meeting blazed the way for a series of colonial conferences during the ensuing years. Also, for the "protection" of the imperial interests the Conservatives in 1889 committed Great Britain to the two-power naval standard; that is, they decided that the British navy must be as great and powerful as any other two navies combined. The building program which they inaugurated in that year called for the construction of some seventy new fighting ships.

Overseas, during this Conservative period, vast stretches of new territory were added to the empire. Although some additions were made in the Far East—notably in Borneo—the chief gains were in Africa. With Great Britain controlling territory in South Africa as well as along the lower Nile, British imperialists began to dream of a railway to connect Cape Colony with Cairo in Egypt. For a time it appeared that it might indeed be possible to construct such a "Cape to Cairo" railway through a continuous strip of British territory, for by means of protectorates or chartered commercial companies British control was established over Nigeria (1886), Somaliland (1887), British East Africa, later called Kenya Colony (1888), Rhodesia (1889), British Central Africa, later called Nyasaland (1893), and Uganda (1896).[14]

Obviously, if the British were to control an unbroken strip of territory from Cape Colony to the Mediterranean, they could not be indifferent to the fate of the region along the upper Nile, from which they and the Egyptians had been driven by the Sudanese in 1885. Moreover, having practically converted Egypt into a British protectorate, Great Britain was inevitably forced to take an interest in the Sudan, for ownership of this territory entailed control of the waters of the Nile, which were indispensable to the agricultural life of Egypt. Consequently, although the British

[14] International disagreements and boundary disputes were the inevitable accompaniment of such tremendous territorial expansion, but these were adjusted by various international bargains. One of the most famous of these was that with Germany in 1890. Great Britain recognized that German East Africa extended westward to the confines of the Congo Free State, and ceded to Germany (1) the island of Helgoland in the North Sea, (2) a long narrow strip of territory to connect German Southwest Africa with the Zambesi River, and (3) territory to extend German Kamerun north to the shores of Lake Chad. In return, Germany relinquished all claim to Uganda, Nyasaland, the islands of Zanzibar and Pemba off the east coast of Africa, and some disputed territory on the border of German Togoland. For the location of the territories mentioned in this paragraph, see the map on page 19.

in the eighties were themselves unwilling to undertake the conquest of the Sudan, they were determined not to let it fall into the hands of the French. Great Britain's futile attempt to thwart French efforts to secure the Sudan by encouraging Italy's plans in Africa,[15] and the subsequent British decision to send General Kitchener with an Egyptian force to occupy the Sudan, with the resultant Anglo-French crisis over Fashoda (1898),[16] have been discussed. British imperialism triumphed, and in March, 1899, France agreed to withdraw. Great Britain then arranged with Egypt that the Sudan should be an Anglo-Egyptian condominium under the joint sovereignty of the two countries. In reality, however, the governor-general and most of the important officials were British army officers, and in the eyes of British imperialists the Sudan was British.

The way was now open for a British Cape to Cairo project, for in 1894 King Leopold, as sovereign of the Congo Free State, had made a bargain with Great Britain, by the terms of which the latter received a perpetual lease of a narrow strip of territory extending from Lake Tanganyika to Uganda. Since northern Rhodesia touched the southern shores of Lake Tanganyika, this corridor between the Congo Free State on the west and German East Africa on the east opened the way for the British to establish a system of land and water communication under their control from Cape Colony to the Mediterranean.

By this time Great Britain had become involved in a struggle with the Boers of South Africa. Friction had been developing for some time. In the eighties British imperialists—notably Cecil Rhodes, who had come to South Africa in 1870 and had there become a dominant economic figure —had brought vast regions in Bechuanaland and Rhodesia under British control and had thus succeeded in hemming in the two Boer republics. When the Boers then sought to secure a corridor to the Indian Ocean through Tongaland, their plans had been blocked by British annexation of the latter in 1894. The only other non-British port which might be of use to the Boers was in Mozambique on Delagoa Bay. The Boers had vainly tried to secure control of this bay in 1891 and in 1893, and the British suspected that in their attempts they had had the sympathy and support of Germany. This seemed to be borne out in 1894 when a native insurrection in the vicinity of the bay led to the landing of British troops to protect British nationals. This step was immediately followed by a protest from the German government and by the arrival of two German warships. Germany's apparent interest in the Boers disturbed Great Britain, which went so far as to warn Germany about interfering in that part of Africa. Although a few months later Germany was further warned against

15 See page 140.
16 For the Fashoda affair, see page 116.

"coquetting" with the Transvaal, German warships took a prominent part in the formal opening of the Delagoa Bay Railway in June, 1895.

The Boers, naturally antagonized by British aggressiveness in South Africa, were also irritated by the great influx of foreign miners, promoters, and adventurers—largely British—which had followed the discovery of gold in the Transvaal about 1886. The Boers became alarmed lest they should be overwhelmed in their own state by the thousands of prospectors, laborers, and others who were rushing into the Transvaal, and ultimately sought to retain political control in their own hands by restricting the privileges of citizenship. The Uitlanders (Outlanders), as they were called by the Boers, were in turn angered by this discrimination and by the fact that their enterprises were handicapped by laws of the republic imposing tariff duties, establishing dynamite and railway monopolies, and preventing importation of cheap labor. Friction between the Uitlanders and the Boers soon developed.

Eventually some of the British gold-producers and business men in the Transvaal conspired with Cecil Rhodes, then prime minister of Cape Colony, to overthrow the Boer government. A revolution was to be precipitated in Johannesburg, and then an armed force was to invade the republic. Unfortunately for Rhodes' plans, before all the arrangements had been perfected, Leander Starr Jameson, administrator of Rhodesia, with a force of about six hundred men invaded the Transvaal in December, 1895, only to be surrounded and captured within a few days. The raid proved to be a miserable fiasco, and was denounced and repudiated by the British government. Rhodes was compelled to resign the premiership (1896) and was later condemned and censured by the British Parliament. His political influence was largely ended, and in 1902 he died.[17]

The Jameson raid put a strain upon Anglo-German as well as upon Anglo-Boer relations. Before the outcome of the venture was known, the British ambassador at Berlin was informed that Germany must insist on the independence of the Transvaal, and the German ambassador at London was instructed to inquire whether the British government approved the raid. If it did, he was to demand his passports. The Kaiser desired that marines should be landed at Delagoa Bay in case of trouble in the Transvaal, but, before this could be done, the Boer government had asked that the landing of German forces be deferred pending negotiations with the British. The Kaiser apparently still harbored visions of an alliance with the Transvaal against the British with a possible protectorate over the Boer republic as the goal. The German chancellor and foreign minister, however, devoted all their efforts to dissuading the Kaiser from landing

[17] Rhodes left most of his huge fortune to endow scholarships at Oxford University for students from the British colonies and from the United States and Germany.

troops or seeking a protectorate and in the end were successful. As a sop
to the Kaiser, he was permitted to send a telegram to President Kruger
of the Transvaal expressing his "congratulations that you and your people, without appealing to the help of friendly powers, have succeeded
... in restoring peace and in maintaining the independence of the country
against attacks from without." The Kruger telegram was looked upon
in Great Britain not only as "unfriendly" but as an "ingeniously worded
insult," "a deliberate affront" to the British, "a piece of gratuitous in-
solence." It obviously helped to turn British public sentiment against the
German Empire. The telegram has been characterized as "one of the
greatest blunders in the history of modern diplomacy."

The Jameson raid also operated to hasten the Anglo-Boer struggle for
supremacy in South Africa. The Boers thereafter were convinced that
there was a plot to deprive them of their country and that the British were
only awaiting a pretext for war. President Kruger accordingly became
increasingly anti-British, made an alliance with the Orange Free State,
and strongly encouraged the Afrikander Bond, a Boer organization in
Cape Colony which sought a union of the European races of South Africa
on the basis of South African nationality and independence. On the other
hand, British mining interests in the Transvaal remained dissatisfied with
their position and sought British intervention in their behalf. Although
fundamentally their grievance was economic,[18] the British in the Transvaal
emphasized their political disabilities, complaining that the Boers insisted
upon a residence requirement of fourteen years for the franchise.

In the early summer of 1899 a conference was held between President
Kruger and Sir Alfred Milner, the imperialistic British high commissioner of Cape Colony, in the course of which the former offered to reduce
the franchise requirement from fourteen years to seven. Milner demanded
that it be made five years. In August the Boers next offered a five-year
franchise plan, with the proviso that Great Britain should drop her claim
to suzerainty, cease interfering in the domestic affairs of the Transvaal,
and agree to refer minor questions in dispute to arbitration. If Milner had
been sincerely desirous of reaching an agreement, this proposal might
have been used as a basis for further discussion. But Milner believed that
Great Britain should remain firm. "They [the Boers] will collapse if we
don't weaken, or rather if we go on steadily turning the screw," he informed Chamberlain, the British colonial secretary. The latter, therefore,
in his reply to the Boer proposal accepted it *without* the proviso; in other
words, from the Boer viewpoint he rejected it.

Apparently by the beginning of September, 1899, Chamberlain had

[18] British capitalists hoped, if they got control of the Transvaal government, to save
£2,500,000 annually by securing an unrestricted labor supply with resulting lower wages.

decided upon war, and the subsequent negotiations were merely drawn out in order to give the British time to get troops to South Africa. He accordingly demanded the five-year franchise without conditions, but this demand Kruger rejected. The Boer government, after having asked for further British proposals and having been put off, concluded that the continuation of negotiations would be useless. Apparently hoping for victory with the possible help of Germany and other powers, Kruger in October demanded that all controversies be arbitrated and that British military preparations in South Africa be stopped. Great Britain refused to discuss this ultimatum, and on October 11, 1899, war began. In the ensuing struggle the Orange Free State made common cause with the Transvaal against the British.

In the Boer War (1899–1902) the British were forced to put into the field a greater number of troops than had ever before been used by Great Britain in a foreign war. Although the Boers never had more than 40,000 soldiers under arms at one time, the British eventually concentrated in South Africa a force of some 350,000 men—largely volunteers from Great Britain, Canada, Australia, and New Zealand. But the Boers were well acquainted with the vast territory in which they fought, they were accustomed to the use of firearms, they were led by resourceful commanders, and they fought with a courage that was indomitable. When eventually Lord Roberts with an overwhelming force succeeded in defeating the organized Boer armies and in capturing the capitals of the two Boer republics, the Boer soldiers resorted to guerrilla warfare. The British had to summon Lord Kitchener from Egypt and then had to resort to systematic "drives" and concentration camps to pacify the Boer country in small sections at a time.

Eventually the greater resources and man power of the British turned the scales, and in May, 1902, the Boers signed the treaty of Vereeniging accepting British sovereignty. In return for this acknowledgment, however, Great Britain promised to permit the use of the Dutch language in schools and courts, to grant self-government to the former republics at the earliest possible opportunity, and to pay £3,000,000 to the Boers in compensation for their destroyed farms. The Boer War brought an extensive and economically rich region into the British Empire, but the price was exceedingly high. The struggle had cost the British 30,000 lives and £250,000,000.

Increasing Trade Rivalry and British Policy

It was hardly to be expected that Great Britain could maintain indefinitely the dominant industrial and commercial position which she held as the "workshop of the world" in the first three quarters of the nineteenth century. Attention has already been called to the great expansion and acceleration in industry which occurred in various countries in the years after 1870.[19] To this development Great Britain had directly contributed, in fact, by exporting between 1848 and 1877 capital goods—machinery and the like—valued at more than £800,000,000. Though Great Britain for a time had profited heavily by thus selling "the sinews of the Industrial Revolution" abroad, obviously her former monopoly of the new mechanical methods of production was thereby destroyed. In the end the new industries which arose in Europe and America seriously challenged Great Britain's own production.[20]

The realization of this fact first burst upon the British during the economic depression which engulfed the world in the later seventies. Exports from Great Britain fell alarmingly, while consular reports called attention to the inroads being made in foreign markets by French, Belgian, and German manufactured goods. This competition was in no sense the cause of Britain's existing economic depression, but the depression hastened her discovery of the increasing trade rivalry abroad. Though the British were somewhat disturbed by this new competition and by the rising tide of tariff protectionism in Europe and America, they were confident that their own colonies and the "half-civilized countries" of the world would provide them with markets for the continued expansion of their trade.

But the next great depression (1884–1888) shook British confidence. The reports of foreign trade rivalry of the seventies were given grim substantiation in the eighties when the products of French, Belgian, German, American, and other national industries rapidly penetrated into markets formerly controlled by the British. Europe herself was fast shaking off her dependence on Great Britain for both capital and consumption goods. Outside Europe the trade rivalry of other countries was less keen, but it was growing rapidly because of the relative decline in the effectiveness of British methods and equipment for withstanding it.

The manufacturers and merchants of Great Britain tended to cling to methods which often were old-fashioned and obsolete in contrast with those used by their competitors in the newer industial countries. Technical and commercial education was being stressed in Europe, frequently with resultant reductions in the cost of manufacturing. Knowledge of foreign languages, careful study of markets, and superior ability to exploit them successfully were powerful aids to the expansion of German, French, and Belgian commerce. In the eighties, indeed, foreign manufacturers began to compete with the British even within the United Kingdom. "Our

---

[19] See pages 3–7.
[20] Much of the discussion in this section of the chapter is based on R. J. S. Hoffman's study, *Great Britain and the German Trade Rivalry, 1875–1914.*

former customers," lamented a Sheffield industrialist, "have become our competitors, and not only sell against us, but undersell us, not merely in neutral markets, but under our very noses at home."

In the eighties, too, Great Britain began to lose some of her valuable *entrepôt* trade. One reason for this decline was the increasing use of the Suez Canal. "The Commercial Revolution was reversed. The Canal did to nineteenth-century England what Vasco da Gama's voyage did to sixteenth-century Italy: it cut much of the ground from under the position of the British middleman. Trieste, Venice, Genoa, Marseilles, Odessa, and other south European ports were enabled to increase greatly their direct trade with distant lands, and instead of buying Asiatic goods in the British market they imported more and more directly from the places of origin." [21] Furthermore, as already pointed out, the world was being knit together by telegraphic communication, so that the need of laying up great supplies of Eastern goods in warehouses in Great Britain was lessened. The British were ceasing to be the great distributors and warehousemen of the world. Between 1872 and 1886, for example, Great Britain's *entrepôt* trade in raw silk declined by more than 80 per cent.

Eventually the British awoke to the fact that their most formidable competitors in the struggle for markets were the Germans. In every quarter of the globe the latter were extending their commercial activity with steady and successful persistence. Ever keener competition, resulting in part from the rising tide of protectionism, operated to throw British and German business men against each other in various parts of the world. The press in Great Britain repeatedly cited evidences of German gains, while British commerce languished; by 1896 Germany had been singled out in the popular mind as Britain's most dangerous trade rival.

In January of that year the report of a British commission disclosed that Britain's leadership in the supply of iron and steel was passing, and it explained the advantages which the German industry had over their own. This report, coming almost simultaneously with the Kaiser's telegram to President Kruger, caused great excitement, which was increased by a book, *Made in Germany,* published in the same year. The British were severely shaken by the author's statement that "the industrial glory of England is departing and England does not know it." Germany, he warned, had entered into a deliberate and deadly rivalry with Great Britain and was battling with might and main for the extinction of the latter's supremacy. It is evident, he declared, "that on all hands England's industrial supremacy is tottering to its fall and that this result is largely German work." Perhaps it is not surprising that during the summer of 1896 the British passed through a period of hysteria over the threat of German trade rivalry. By the end of

[21] Hoffman, *op. cit.,* pages 70–71.

the year the alarm had largely subsided, but feeling was still so strong in 1897 that the writer of an article in a well-known weekly declared: "If Germany were extinguished tomorrow, the day after tomorrow there is not an Englishman in the world who would not be the richer."

Although in the succeeding years there was no outburst of public alarm over German trade comparable to that of 1896, nevertheless, the British steadily grew more and more acutely aware of the relentless commercial struggle with Germany. Occasionally certain definite matters served to focus attention upon the economic antagonism. Between 1899 and 1902, for instance, news of German shipping subsidies and of the German absorption of several British steamship lines caused a shipping scare and grave concern over the possible destruction of Britain's hitherto lucrative maritime carrying trade.

Chamberlain believed that one way to meet the increasing trade rivalry which Great Britain was encountering was to bind the British colonies more closely with the mother country and to link the self-governing dominions with the United Kingdom by means of a system of "imperial preference." According to his plan the dominions should reduce their tariff rates on goods coming from Great Britain, while retaining higher rates for goods from outside the empire. Such a scheme would, of course, operate to the advantage of British manufacturers and merchants. In 1897 Chamberlain utilized the occasion of Queen Victoria's second jubilee to convoke another colonial conference of the governors of the dominions in the hope that something might be done about imperial preference. Although Canada adopted a measure embodying this principle, the movement as a whole made relatively little headway. The dominions saw little to be gained for themselves by opening their doors to United Kingdom goods as long as Great Britain gave their export products—chiefly raw materials—no preference in her markets over goods from outside the empire. Imperial preference seemed logically to demand the adoption by Great Britain of some scheme of protective tariffs.

In 1903, when Germany passed Great Britain in the production of iron, thus relegating the latter to third place in world production of this commodity, Chamberlain moved on to the second point in his program and demanded a protective tariff for the United Kingdom. Under his auspices the Tariff Reform League was organized to carry on propaganda to educate the public in the need for a change in Britain's free-trade policy. But the free-traders rallied their forces, and the country was subjected to a vigorous debate in the press and on the platform regarding the respective merits of the two policies. Although Balfour finally accepted the principle of protection, the Conservatives split on the issue because the prime minister declined to recommend the laws which Chamberlain demanded. The latter thereupon resigned from the cabinet but devoted his energy to the task of converting the Conservative Party to his program. Inevitably the tariff question played an important part in the next parliamentary election and contributed to the defeat which the Conservatives sustained at that time.

The Abandonment of "Splendid Isolation"

Although Great Britain was slow to abandon her venerated policy of free trade, world affairs did convince her that she must modify the basis of her foreign policy. During most of the latter half of the nineteenth century she had followed the policy of playing a lone hand in international affairs. Upon occasion, to be sure, she had co-operated with other powers to achieve a common end—when that end was consonant with the advancement of her own colonial and maritime interests. In the fifties, for instance, she had joined with France in the Crimean War to prevent Russian ascendancy in Turkey.[22] Again, in 1878, she had united with Austria-Hungary to force the tsar to submit the Balkan situation to the Congress of Berlin after Russia's decisive defeat of the sultan in that year.[23] And in 1887 she had entered into an agreement with Austria-Hungary and Italy to maintain the *status quo* in the Mediterranean and Black seas.[24] On each of these occasions, which appear to mark departures from Britain's policy of isolation, the agreements had been designed to safeguard or advance the interests of the British Empire. So far as continental complications were concerned, Great Britain had steadfastly adhered to her policy of no entanglements. When in the eighties Bismarck had pressed her to enter into an alliance with Germany, she had firmly declined to become involved.[25]

By 1898, however, the international situation overseas had become so complicated that the British government began to question the wisdom of longer pursuing the policy of "splendid isolation." Germany and Russia were pushing into northern China,[26] threatening Chinese territorial integrity. France was pushing eastward in the Sudan,[27] apparently aiming to secure control of the region of the upper Nile. Friction was increasing in South Africa between the Boers and British imperialists, with the Boers receiving obvious encouragement from Germany.[28] The latter, in turn, was seeking for her own purposes to capitalize British embarrassment by pushing colonial claims in Africa and the South Seas. If Great Britain could have

[22] See page 209.
[23] See page 224.
[24] See page 139.
[25] See page 69.
[26] See pages 73 and 235–236.
[27] See page 116.
[28] See pages 170–172.

dealt with Russia, France, and Germany singly and at different times, the situation would not have been so alarming to the British, but in 1898 it appeared that in a sense all three were closing in upon her and that she stood without a friend, isolated among the great powers.

For some time there had been growing in Great Britain the feeling that the kingdom must abandon its isolation and seek positive support among the other great powers. As early as 1896 one influential journal had declared: "We frankly can go no further alone, in the face of the obstacles which it is now within the power of Germany, Russia, and France to pile up in our path." Some declared that the cornerstone of British policy should be an agreement with Russia, and in 1898—when Russia was pushing into South Manchuria—Great Britain sought to reach an understanding with the tsarist government. She proposed a definition of Russian and British spheres of preponderance in both China and Turkey, but on condition that existing rights should not be altered, existing treaties violated, or the integrity of China or Turkey impaired. The British proposal was, of course, a thinly disguised move to commit Russia to a program which the latter had no intention of adopting. According to Tsar Nicholas, it merely revealed to Russia that Great Britain sought the former's friendship in order to block Russian advances in the Far East. Since the tsar's government was determined to operate with a free hand in China, nothing tangible in the way of an agreement resulted.

But Great Britain was equally determined to stop, if possible, any further Russian encroachments upon China, and next sought to secure an agreement to that end with Germany. Chamberlain, who was thoroughly convinced that Britain's isolation had become dangerous, opened negotiations in 1898 by proposing to Germany an Anglo-German alliance. The German government was at once interested, but, when it learned that the purpose of such an alliance would be to check Russia's advance beyond Manchuria, its interest perceptibly declined. Apparently what Chamberlain suggested was that China should be divided into British, German, and Russian spheres of predominance. The British sphere (in South China) would be the largest, most populous, and farthest removed from the Russian; the German sphere would serve as a buffer between the British and the Russians. But Germany had no intention of being used as a cat's-paw to protect British interests in the Far East. Furthermore, she was very willing to have Russia become involved in China; she had, indeed, deliberately encouraged Russia to take steps leading in that direction.

What the Germans on their part wanted was an alliance with Great Britain which would leave France isolated and would give a guarantee of reinsurance against Russia. But the British were not interested in any agreement having to do with Europe. Without such an alliance, however, the Germans were opposed to an Anglo-German treaty as outlined by Great Britain, for its very submission to the British Parliament—even though rejected—would increase the hostility of Russia and France toward Germany. The Germans believed, furthermore, that such an alliance with Great Britain would shift to the German frontier much of the pressure that Russia was then exerting on China. This to the Germans was altogether undesirable. Germany, therefore, concluded that she might better wait until Great Britain was still harder pressed before entering into any British alliance. Undoubtedly, future developments would make Great Britain's abandonment of isolation even more imperative, and, when the British need of an alliance became more pressing, perhaps Germany could secure better terms. Germany was little disturbed by Chamberlain's threat that, if Germany rejected Great Britain's offer, the latter might find it necessary to make separate agreements with France and Russia.

Nevertheless, Great Britain did not wholly despair of a German alliance, and in 1899 the possibilities were again explored by Chamberlain and Bülow. When the latter appeared favorable, Chamberlain in a famous speech at Leicester went so far as to broach the subject publicly—only to have Bülow in a subsequent speech in the Reichstag apparently turn his back on the suggestion. Again in 1901 formal negotiations for an alliance were actually begun. Germany then insisted that Great Britain must join the Triple Alliance in order to afford Germany protection against Russia, but this Great Britain refused to do. According to Salisbury, the liability of having to defend the German and Austrian frontiers against Russia was too heavy in proportion to the benefit which Great Britain might derive from such an alliance. So once more the negotiations came to naught.

Meanwhile Japan, too, had become alarmed by Russia's advance into South Manchuria.[29] In 1901 Japan tried through diplomacy at both St. Petersburg and London to see what she could obtain to protect her interests in the Far East. At London the advances of the Japanese ambassador were cordially received, for Great Britain feared the conclusion of an agreement between Russia and Japan which might make the British position in the Far East almost hopeless. Largely to prevent such a Russo-Japanese understanding, it appears, Great Britain signed a treaty of alliance with Japan on January 30, 1902.

By the terms of the agreement the two powers recognized the independence of China and Korea and declared that they were not motivated in their agreement by aggressive tendencies. They recognized, however, that each had special interests—Great Britain in China, Japan in both China and Korea—which it would be admissible for either to safeguard if threatened by the aggressive action of any other power or by disturb-

[29] See page 236.

ances in China or Korea. If either party, in defense of its interests as defined, became involved in a war with a third power, the other party was to remain neutral; but, if the enemy were actively supported by a fourth power, the other party was to join its ally and make war in common. In other words, should Great Britain go to war with Russia over her interests in China, Japan would stay neutral. But if Russia should be joined by France or Germany, Japan would come to the aid of Great Britain. The alliance was to last for five years, or longer unless denounced one year in advance by either party.

The Anglo-Japanese alliance constituted a landmark in British foreign policy, for it marked the abandonment of Great Britain's principle of isolation. But the Anglo-Japanese alliance was only the first step in Great Britain's new foreign policy. The next came in 1904 when she and France adjusted their various colonial difficulties in different parts of the world. Probably Britain's chief gain by these agreements was the relinquishment by France of her rights and interests in Egypt in favor of Great Britain, and the declaration by France that she would afford Great Britain her diplomatic support in case the British position in Egypt was challenged. The Entente Cordiale which resulted from these friendly agreements augered well for the future co-operation of Great Britain and France in case Germany should attempt, as in preceding years, to play one of them off against the other in order to secure something for herself.

The Rejection of the Conservatives

During the opening years of the twentieth century the Conservatives steadily declined in popularity. Although at the outset the Boer War had the general support of the British people, before it was won a revulsion had set in against such imperialistic ventures and against those responsible for them. Conservatives were not only blamed for getting the kingdom into difficulties; they were also accused of incompetency in the waging of the conflict which resulted from their aggressiveness. At home the Education Act of 1902 by its favor to the Anglicans had alienated many dissenters, and the Taff Vale decision of the Conservative House of Lords (1901) had antagonized labor. This decision maintained that trade unions could be held responsible for financial losses suffered by employers as a result of strikes, and that trade-union funds could be attached for payment of such damages. On top of all this, Chamberlain's advocacy of a protective tariff for the kingdom was out of accord with the views of most Englishmen, the issue even causing dissension within the Conservative Party itself. After the Conservatives had lost steadily in by-elections during 1904 and 1905, Balfour in December of the latter year resigned the premiership.

Sir Henry Campbell-Bannerman then formed a ministry of Liberals and dissolved Parliament. The Liberals appealed to the country with a platform which called for the maintenance of free trade, the alteration of the Education Act of 1902 in the interest of the dissenters, the enactment of a law to modify the Taff Vale decision, more stringent national regulation of the liquor traffic, extensive legislation for social and industrial betterment, and reconciliation with the Boers of South Africa. In the ensuing election (January, 1906) the Liberal Party won a decisive victory, securing a comfortable majority over all the other parties combined. Counting the Irish Nationalist and Labor Parties as anti-Conservative, Balfour's government was repudiated by a parliamentary ratio of approximately 500 to 157.

One of the significant results of this election was the winning of twenty-nine parliamentary seats by the recently organized Labor Party. Workingmen had occasionally been returned to Parliament during the preceding generation, but they had been elected as candidates of the Liberal Party. Although in 1893 the Independent Labor Party had been founded to put forward candidates pledged to a socialistic program, its platform had been too radical to attract many workingmen, and in 1900 it had won only one seat. After the Taff Vale decision, however, representatives of the trade unions and of a number of socialist societies determined to take more effective steps politically to safeguard the interests of the workers, and so they had organized the Labor Party. Its success in the election of January, 1906, was the first of a series which in the course of the succeeding generation made the Labor Party one of the two major political parties of the kingdom.[30]

Reform under the Liberals

The ministry which Campbell-Bannerman had organized in December, 1905, had been one of exceptional talent, reflecting the various shades of Liberal opinion and including for the first time in British history a representative of labor. The prime minister himself had entered Parliament in 1868 and thirty years later had been chosen leader of the Liberal Party. He had never shown the outstanding ability of Gladstone, but he typified the nineteenth-century liberalism of that great leader. The older group of Liberals was represented by a few other members, also. Prominent among them was John Morley, a well-known editor and author, who had only

[30] See pages 526 and 530.

recently published his monumental life of Gladstone. Morley had entered Parliament in 1883 and had served in Gladstone's ministry three years later. Another was James Bryce, a lawyer, professor, and scholarly writer on historical and political subjects, who had entered Parliament in 1880 and had been a member of Gladstone's cabinet in 1892.

Destined to be more important in British history and in the development of the Liberal Party were several younger men in the ministry, the leader of whom was Herbert H. Asquith, a distinguished lawyer, nonconformist, and free-trader, who had entered Parliament in 1886 and had been a member of Gladstone's ministry in 1892. Since Campbell-Bannerman, the titular head of the party, was in feeble health, Asquith was the virtual leader of the Liberals. When in April, 1908, ill health forced the former to retire from public life, he was succeeded as prime minister by Asquith, who continued to serve in that capacity until late in 1916. Associated with him as representatives of the younger group were Richard Haldane, Sir Edward Grey, John Burns, Winston Churchill, and David Lloyd George.

Richard Haldane, a Scottish lawyer, statesman, and philosophical writer, who had entered Parliament in 1885, became secretary for war. Sir Edward Grey, scion of a famous family of Whigs, a Liberal member of Parliament during the preceding two decades, assumed the portfolio for foreign affairs. John Burns, who had entered Parliament in 1892, was a famous labor leader in London who had frequently clashed with the government in his efforts to defend the rights of the workers. He became president of the Local Government Board. Winston Churchill was the youngest member of the group. He had had a rather adventurous career in his twenties, having served as a soldier or war correspondent in various parts of the world. At the age of twenty-nine he had entered Parliament as a Conservative (1900), but had opposed Chamberlain's tariff policy and had soon withdrawn from that party. Churchill held various positions in the new ministry, eventually becoming (1911) first lord of the admiralty.

The one who was to become the most influential figure in the Liberal Party was David Lloyd George, a Welshman, the son of a humble schoolmaster who had died when David was a young boy. Denied the advantages of a university education, Lloyd George had studied law and had become a lawyer. He was an outspoken Welsh nationalist, and in 1890 he had been elected to Parliament to represent the "common people." In general he was bitterly opposed to the landed aristocracy, to Chamberlain's imperialism and protectionism, and to the privileged position of the Anglican Church. A brilliant and courageous speaker, during the Boer War he had not hesitated to denounce the government for its aggression against the Boers. At that time he had been extremely unpopular throughout the country, but the reaction against imperialism which came as a result of the war eventually brought him back into favor. Lloyd George was at first president of the Board of Trade, but upon the reorganization of the cabinet in 1908 he assumed the important post of chancellor of the exchequer.

The Liberals at once turned their attention to the situation in South Africa. After 1902 tens of thousands of Chinese coolies had been imported into the Transvaal to provide cheap labor for the mine owners. Further importation of Chinese was stopped by the Liberals. Self-government was granted to the former Boer republics, with the result that the Boers immediately gained control of the governments in the Transvaal and in the Orange River Colony. Moreover, the Boer organization in Cape Colony —the Afrikander Bond—won the elections there also.

With the Boers in political control of three of the four British South African colonies, a movement to unite them all into one union was inaugurated. A federal constitution was drafted by a convention representing the colonies, and in 1909 it was approved as the South Africa Act by the parliament of Great Britain. In the following year the Union of South Africa—a federation consisting of Cape Colony, Natal, the Transvaal, and Orange River Colony—was established. General Louis Botha, who had fought against the British in the Boer War and had later been the prime minister of the Transvaal, at once became prime minister of the Union and served in this capacity until his death in 1919. The Boer leaders ultimately concluded that the interests of their people could best be served by co-operating with the British in South Africa under the effective protection of the British Empire.

Within the United Kingdom a number of important measures were enacted in rapid succession. The Trades Disputes Act (1906) reversed the Taff Vale decision by providing immunity for the funds of trade unions, by legalizing peaceful picketing, and by declaring that what was lawful for an individual was lawful also for a combination. In the same year the Workmen's Compensation Act made employers liable for compensation to all manual laborers and to practically all other employees receiving less than £250 a year. The Old Age Pension Act (1908) provided pensions for all resident British citizens over seventy years of age, provided they had incomes of less than £31½ yearly. The Labor Exchange Act of the same year provided for a nation-wide organization of labor exchanges to assist in bringing employers and unemployed workers together to their mutual benefit.

In 1911 the National Insurance Act, applying only to the building and engineering trades, introduced in an experimental way health and unemployment insurance. Funds for the scheme were to be subscribed partly by the employers, partly by the workers, and partly by the state. In case

of sickness the benefits included weekly payments, free medical attendance, and free hospital treatments; in case of unemployment not caused
by strikes or lockouts, the benefits included payments for a maximum of
fifteen weeks. The unemployment feature of the act was frankly in the
nature of an experiment. Attempts to pass bills regarding education, plural
voting, and the liquor traffic, though successful in the House of Commons,
were blocked by the Conservatives in the House of Lords. Earlier statements that the upper house would have to be "mended or ended" again
began to be heard.

These somewhat abstract statements about the need for altering the
House of Lords were transformed into positive demands by the Lords'
rejection of the budget passed by the Commons in 1909. The budget of
that year was no ordinary budget. Added naval expenditures resulting
from the armaments race with Germany plus the cost of the recently enacted pension system greatly increased the need for revenues. The Conservatives asserted that the taxable resources of the kingdom were already
overburdened and advocated tariffs as the only new way to expand the
national revenues. Their arguments had no appeal for Lloyd George,
however.

The chancellor of the exchequer was determined to use his budget not
merely to provide added revenues for the state but to improve the social
conditions of the kingdom. For one thing, he desired to shift the burden
of taxation "from the producers to the possessors of wealth." Although
Great Britain in proportion to size was probably the wealthiest country
in the world, her wealth was concentrated in the hands of a relatively few.
Half of the national income, it was estimated, went to 12 per cent of
the people. According to Salvation Army estimates, 3 per cent of the
British people were rich, 9 per cent were comfortably well off, and 88
per cent were poor. Millions were found to be living constantly on the
verge of starvation. Lloyd George sought to use taxation to help change
these conditions. He therefore drafted what he called a "war budget,"
that is, one which was designed "to wage war against poverty" in Great
Britain. To strike at the wealthy his budget called for (1) increased income and inheritance taxes, (2) supertaxes on the larger incomes, and
(3) higher tax rates on unearned incomes.

But Lloyd George desired particularly to use the budget as a weapon
against the landed aristocracy and large landed proprietors. Great Britain
was not, like France, a country of petty peasant proprietors. In England
and Wales the number of persons holding more than one acre of land
constituted less than ⅗ of 1 per cent of the total population. Twenty-seven
lords, it was asserted, owned one tenth of England, and almost half of all
the cultivated land of the country belonged to some 2250 landed aristocrats.

In Scotland, according to estimates, approximately 90 per cent of the land was the property of some 1700 persons. But the concentration of land-ownership was not the only evil in the agrarian situation. The land was being used less and less for agricultural or grazing purposes and was being converted more and more to unproductive use in the form of lawns, gardens, hunting preserves, and the like.

One reason for this change was that agriculture in Great Britain was not in the twentieth century so profitable as it had been before 1870. The greatly decreased costs of transportation and the introduction of refrigeration on railways and steamships had adversely affected it. Distant parts of the world were able to sell their grains, meats, and dairy products in Britain at prices lower than were profitable to British farmers—largely tenants who were obliged to pay relatively high rents and were unable to use the more modern and large-scale methods of the newer lands. Since free-trade Britain did not give farmers the aid of protective tariffs to help meet this competition, as did Germany, France, and other countries, many of them were forced to give up the struggle. In the years just before the First World War Britain was producing only one fifth of the food consumed by her people.

Lloyd George's budget was in part designed to help alter the land and agricultural situation in the kingdom by the imposition of certain types of taxes. Obviously, the proposed taxes discussed above might force some landowners to sell parts of their great holdings in order to pay the levies and thus lead gradually to a breaking up of the large estates. In addition, however, the budget called for (4) heavy taxes on unearned increments of land values, that is, on increases in the value of land not the result of improvements made by the owner, (5) new taxes on undeveloped idle land (formerly not taxed), particularly on game preserves, in the hope of forcing more land back under cultivation, and (6) a special tax of 5 per cent on income derived by landowners from the companies that operated mines on their properties. Although the budget included various other items of revenue, these were the chief innovations.

As might have been expected, the possessing classes at once attacked Lloyd George's finance bill on the ground that it was unfair and that it struck at the security of property. For nearly six months the measure was hotly debated in Parliament, in the press, and on the platform. Early in November it was passed by the House of Commons, but before the month was out it had been decisively rejected by the Lords. Though the latter had never formally surrendered their right to veto a budget, they had long ceased to use that right, and Prime Minister Asquith at once denounced their action as a "wanton breach of the settled practice of the Constitution."

Parliament was dissolved to ascertain the will of the voters, and the Liberals campaigned on a platform calling for the enactment of the budget, the abolition of the veto power of the Lords, and the granting of home rule for Ireland. These last two proposals were made largely to hold the support of the Irish Nationalists, who were firmly determined to weaken the House of Lords so that a home-rule bill could be enacted. In the election of January, 1910, the Liberals lost more than a hundred seats to the Conservatives, but, since they received the support of the Irish Nationalists and the Laborites, they were enabled to continue in office. The budget was then reintroduced, and this time it was passed by the House of Lords.

With the budget safely out of the way, the Liberals next undertook to carry out their pledges to the Irish Nationalists. The Parliament Bill was introduced with three major provisions. (1) The right of the Lords to veto any money bill was abolished; any bill declared a money bill by the speaker of the Commons would become a law one month after it was submitted to the Lords, regardless of their failure to enact it. (2) Any measure not a money bill, if passed in the Commons in three successive sessions, would become a law, in spite of the veto of the Lords, provided that two years had elapsed since its first introduction. (3) The maximum life of Parliament was to be reduced from seven to five years. The House of Lords refused to accept these proposals, so again Parliament was dissolved, and for the second time in 1910 a general election was held.

Practically no change in the relative number of seats in Parliament resulted from the second election. The Liberals lost two seats, but their allies in the Commons gained four. So long as the Irish Nationalists and the Laborites supported them, therefore, the Liberal ministry was safe. Again Asquith introduced his Parliament Bill. The Lords amended the measure, but, when Asquith refused to accept the amendments and announced that the king was ready to create enough new peers to carry the measure through the Lords, the latter finally gave way and enacted the bill as passed by the Commons. The House of Lords thus ceased to be a coordinate part of the legislature, for it could no longer control the budget and at most could only delay for two years other legislation desired by the Commons. The Parliament Act constituted, therefore, a political revolution against the aristocracy.

The Liberal government next proceeded to reward its political allies of 1910–1911. Up to that time membership in Parliament had carried no remuneration, and therefore a workingman dependent upon his wages alone could hardly afford to accept a seat. To meet this situation the various labor unions had paid union wages to those of their members who were elected to Parliament. In 1909 the Conservative House of Lords, in what was known as the Osborne judgment, had held that it was illegal for trade unions to use money raised by the compulsory contributions of their members to pay salaries to men representing the workers in Parliament. Obviously this decision struck a severe blow at the Labor Party. To overcome the handicap under which the Labor members operated, Parliament in 1911 enacted a law providing that members of the House of Commons should receive salaries of £400 a year. Two years later another Trade Union Act empowered the unions to use their funds for political purposes if so authorized by a general ballot of their members. The labor unions were thus strengthened in their efforts to build up an adequate representation of the British workers in Parliament.

The Parliament Act of 1911 opened the way for Lloyd George to carry through his cherished plan for the disestablishment of the Anglican Church in Wales, where most of the population consisted of dissenters. In 1912 the House of Commons passed a bill separating church and state in Wales, disendowing the church of much of its property, and depriving the Anglican bishops in Wales of their seats in the House of Lords. The Lords refused to pass the measure, but, since they now had only a suspensive veto, the bill became a law in 1914. Although, because of disturbed conditions during the First World War, the act was temporarily suspended, it eventually became effective at the close of the war.

The Irish Home-Rule Crisis, 1912–1914

The Liberals were indebted to the Irish Nationalists for support in the crisis of 1910–1911 and were committed to the introduction of a third Home Rule Bill. In April, 1912, a bill providing for an Irish parliament but not for complete autonomy was introduced in the Commons, where it was passed in January, 1913, only to be immediately rejected by the House of Lords. Again it was passed by the Commons, and again it was rejected by the Lords. Under the provisions of the Parliament Act of 1911 it appeared, however, that nothing could prevent the eventual enactment of the law in 1914 if the Commons again passed it.

But by this time the prospect of home rule for Ireland had caused a furor in that island. The Protestant Ulsterites of northeastern Ireland, largely descendants of English and Scottish settlers, opposed home rule and were determined to do everything in their power to prevent it. In their stand they were actuated to some extent by deep-seated emotions. Conflicts dating from the days of the Reformation had bred in the Protestants of Ulster a profound hatred and fear of the Catholic Irish. In view of the treatment which had earlier been meted out to the Irish Catholics when the Protestants had been in the ascendancy, the latter now dreaded possible reprisals at the hands of an Irish parliament dominated by Catholics. There was, too, an economic fear. Ulster, the industrial section of Ireland, was the wealthier and more progressive part of the island. The industrialists of that region were apprehensive lest an Irish parliament, controlled by representatives from the more backward agricultural parts of Ireland, might contrive to shift the burden of taxes to industrial Ulster or might otherwise enact legislation harmful to the economic life of that region. Racial antipathy, religious hatred, and economic fear thus led the Ulsterites to oppose home rule and to demand instead that Ireland should remain part of the United Kingdom.

Sir Edward Carson, leader of the Ulsterites,[31] believed that the Liberal government might be frightened into dropping the home-rule project if Ulster showed its determination not to submit. "We will stop at nothing," he declared, "if an attempt is to be made to hand the Loyalists of Ireland over to those whom we believe to be the enemies of our country." In Ulster great mass meetings and demonstrations were held; a volunteer army of 100,000 was organized; and over 237,000 Unionist men bound themselves by a "solemn covenant" never to submit to an Irish parliament. In his decision to organize demonstrations among the Protestants of Ulster, Carson was supported by the leaders of the Conservative Party, who not only favored the maintenance of the United Kingdom but hoped to embarrass the Liberals and possibly put a stop to their "socialistic" legislation by driving them from power.

Carson believed that any government would ponder long before it dared "to shoot a loyal Ulster Protestant devoted to his country and loyal to his King." Asquith did ponder long, and eventually he sought to find some compromise which might be acceptable to both the Unionists and the Irish Nationalists. But as soon as the Liberals began to waver, the Irish Nationalists, led by John Redmond, in turn started to raise a force of "Irish volunteers" to support their demand for the granting of home rule to the whole island. Civil war appeared to threaten in Ireland if the Home Rule Bill should actually be passed. The situation for the Liberal government was made still more difficult and perplexing when several high officers of the British army which was destined for service in Ireland resigned their commissions rather than fight against the Unionists of Ulster.

Nevertheless, despite the threatening situation in Ireland, the Home Rule Bill was passed for the third time by the Commons in May, 1914. In July, with conditions in Ireland growing constantly more menacing, King George[32] went so far as to call a conference at Buckingham Palace

[31] Carson was not an Ulsterite. In Parliament he represented the University of Dublin—an Episcopalian institution.
[32] Queen Victoria was succeeded in 1901 by her son, Edward VII, and the latter in turn by his son, George V, in 1910.

of the representatives of the Liberals, Conservatives, Irish Nationalists, and Ulster Unionists. "For months," he said, "we have watched with deep misgivings the course of events in Ireland. The trend has been surely and steadily towards an appeal to force, and today the cry of civil war is on the lips of the most responsible and sober-minded of my people." Despite the king's anxiety, however, no agreement could be reached at the conference, and the crisis continued.

When the First World War broke out in August, the seriousness of the international situation led the various groups involved in the home-rule struggle to reach a compromise agreement. The Irish Nationalists gained their point—the Home Rule Bill was enacted into law in September. But the Ulster Unionists and British Conservatives secured the simultaneous enactment of a law suspending the Home Rule Act for the duration of the war. Actually, therefore, the existing political status of Ireland was left undisturbed, and the settlement of the home-rule problem was merely postponed until a later time. Before that time had arrived, however, the demands of the Irish Nationalists had gradually become so extreme that they were then unwilling to accept a settlement such as that proposed in the Home Rule Act of 1914.[33]

The Triple Entente

Meanwhile, in the decade before the First World War, Great Britain—having abandoned her isolationist policy—had been drawn ever deeper into international understandings and entanglements. During the first Moroccan crisis, precipitated by Germany in part to test or even destroy the Entente Cordiale,[34] France had sought to transform the Entente into an alliance by securing from Great Britain the latter's promise of assistance. The British government, however, desiring to keep its hands free, had declined to accede to the French request. But Sir Edward Grey, the foreign secretary, had gone so far as to authorize the carrying on of military conversations between the general staffs of the two countries, so that, if Great Britain should ever decide to go to the aid of France in time of war, the French and British armies could co-operate effectively. Thereafter, in the words of Winston Churchill, "the relations of the two staffs became increasingly intimate and confidential." The British army was reorganized to prepare it for participation in a European war, and conversations were even inaugurated with the Belgian general staff regarding military aid which Great Britain might extend to Belgium if the latter's neutrality should be violated by Germany.

[33] See pages 537–538.
[34] See pages 118–119.

In 1906 the British government took still another step in its program
of adjusting Britain's colonial difficulties with other powers. It has already
been pointed out that Great Britain as early as 1898 had sought to reach
an understanding with Russia, only to be rebuffed. Other overtures—
equally futile—had been made to Russia in 1903 and 1904. But Sir Edward
Grey believed that an understanding with Russia was desirable, and in
the spring of 1906 negotiations between the British and Russian governments were again inaugurated. By this time circumstances had been so
altered as to make Russia more ready to consider an understanding. She
had been checked in the Far East by Japan,[35] and was once more casting
her eyes on the Near East in search of a possible outlet to the seas.

What Russia now desired was to secure the opening of the Straits at
Constantinople to Russian warships. But in the Ottoman Empire by 1906
the ascendancy had passed from Great Britain to Germany. If Russia was
to be successful in carrying through her Straits policy, therefore, it appeared that she must smooth away the causes of friction between herself
and Great Britain in order to strengthen her position against Germany.
She was given to understand that, if Great Britain and Russia could adjust their differences over Tibet, Afghanistan, and Persia, "the effect upon
British public opinion would be such as very much to facilitate a discussion
of the Straits question if it came up later on."

The negotiations between the two countries dragged on for months,
and it was not until August, 1907, that an agreement was finally reached.
By it disputes between the two powers were adjusted in the Middle East.
Neither was to attempt to seize Tibet, which was recognized as part of
the Chinese Empire. Russia further agreed that Afghanistan was outside
her sphere of influence. But the most important provision of the settlement had to do with Persia, which was divided into three spheres of influence. It was agreed that northern Persia was a Russian sphere, southeastern Persia a British sphere, and central Persia a neutral zone. Both
powers recognized in principle the territorial integrity and political independence of Persia. Russia, furthermore, recognized Great Britain's
special position in the Persian Gulf. Great Britain, it is apparent, gained
more by the settlement than did Russia.

Although the Anglo-Russian agreements in no way constituted an alliance and Germany was not mentioned in them, the two signatory powers
had established cordial relations between themselves and were thus free
to unite against Germany if their interests were challenged by her. The
Anglo-Russian understanding of 1907, together with the Anglo-French
agreements of 1904, constituted what came to be called the Triple Entente.

Developments in other fields also tended to drive the British into closer

[35] For the Russo-Japanese War, see pages 237–240.

relations with France and Russia. Although Great Britain shared in the tremendous expansion of world trade which occurred in the decade before the war in 1914 to such an extent that from 1910 to 1913 her export trade yearly reached a new record peak, German commercial rivalry was nevertheless a powerful factor in shaping British national policy. It not only provided a source of fear which alarmists exploited; it also engendered suspicion, jealousy, and alarm. J. Ellis Barker, a distinguished British writer on Germany's economic life, declared in 1908 that fate "has placed Great Britain and Germany in the same reciprocal position into which it put Rome and Carthage two thousand years ago. Germany wishes to possess that which Great Britain wishes to keep, and it is difficult to see how, under the circumstances, a collision between the two countries can be avoided." There seems little doubt that German trade rivalry bred resentment and fear in Great Britain and that these in turn caused a dislike of Germany that rose in time to the level of hatred.

Anti-German sentiment was further fed by Germany's naval laws of 1906 and 1908 providing for the construction of dreadnoughts.[36] In Great Britain the Liberal government, upon coming into power, had abandoned the existing plan of constructing four dreadnoughts annually and instead had ordered only three in 1907 and two in 1908. Many Englishmen were thrown into something like a panic by the fear that Germany might be able successfully to challenge Great Britain's supremacy on the sea. In 1909 a wave of naval agitation swept the kingdom, and in response to it the Liberals again presented naval estimates calling for the construction of four dreadnoughts. Although Sir Edward Grey informed Parliament that Great Britain's relations with Germany were excellent, the Conservatives moved a vote of censure of the government on the ground that it was neglecting the defense of the empire. Chauvinists raised the cry, "We want eight, and we won't wait," and in the end the Liberal government was forced to give way and order eight dreadnoughts for 1909.

Meanwhile, in the Bosnian crisis of 1908–1909 Great Britain had given Russia full diplomatic support when the latter demanded that Austria-Hungary's annexation of Bosnia-Herzegovina should be submitted to a conference and that Serbia should be given compensation.[37] Similarly, as already pointed out, she loyally supported France at the time of the second Moroccan crisis in 1911. In the latter year the Anglo-French military conversations, which had been begun in 1906, were completed, and the details of the plan for the British to fight by the side of the French were settled. In 1912, after the failure of the Haldane mission [38] and the decision of

[36] See pages 80–81.
[37] For the Bosnian crisis, see pages 303–305.
[38] See page 82.

the German government to continue to expand its navy, Great Britain moved still closer to France by entering into a naval understanding with her. Disturbed by Germany's naval program, the British decided to withdraw some of their ships from the Mediterranean so that they might successfully meet any possible challenge of the German navy in the North Sea. In order that the combined forces of Austria-Hungary and Italy might not thereby gain the ascendancy in the Mediterranean, Great Britain induced France to concentrate her whole fleet in that sea.

The French, in turn, sought some promise of protection for their northern coast and persuaded the British government to an exchange of notes on this subject. It was agreed that, if either government had grave reason to expect an unprovoked attack by a third power, it should at once discuss with the other whether both countries should act together to prevent aggression and, if so, what measures they would take in common. If the latter involved action, it was agreed, the plans of the general staffs would immediately be considered, and the governments would then decide what effect should be given to them. Plans for naval co-operation were subsequently drafted by the French and British admiralties.

In 1914 Russia sought to bring about a still closer union of the powers of the Triple Entente by having it converted into a formal and public alliance. The British government opposed this step as being not then feasible, but did inform the Russian government of the contents of the notes exchanged by France and Great Britain in 1912. Great Britain thus revealed to Russia the plans for probable close co-operation between the other two members of the Entente. She went even further, however, and permitted the inauguration of Anglo-Russian naval conversations similar to those held earlier between the French and British admiralties. But when, early in July, 1914, the Russian government again urged an alliance, the matter was once more postponed on the ground that the British government was then too busy with the Irish situation to give the question the necessary consideration.

It is thus obvious that, although by 1914 Great Britain had actually entered into no alliance so far as treaties were concerned, she had established cordial relations with both France and Russia and by exchanges of notes had largely transformed—in spirit, at least—the Entente Cordiale into a defensive agreement against Germany. It is also very clear that, although in the decade before 1914 the British government considered it had retained freedom of action in time of crisis, morally it had obligated Great Britain to take certain steps in defense of France. The British position was misleading and dangerous. The government's declaration that Britain's hands were free led Germany to think that the former would remain neutral in case of a European war. The Anglo-French exchange of notes and the military and naval conversations, on the other hand, convinced French leaders that "the principle of an eventual co-operation of the military and naval forces of France and England" had been established. When the great crisis came in 1914, events proved that the French view was correct. Great Britain was no longer isolated and free but was rather entangled in the plans and ambitions of Russia and France.

Chapter VII

THE LESSER STATES OF WESTERN

EUROPE

IN western Europe in addition to the four great powers—Germany, France, Italy, and Great Britain—there were before the First World War eight "lesser" powers. Most of them, however, were inferior only in respect to total resources, population, military and naval establishments, and ability to play a dominant role in international affairs. In personal liberty, economic well-being, achievements in science and literature, and progress in political, social, and economic institutions, some of them were not surpassed by any of the great powers. The lot of the citizens of many of these lesser states was far happier than that of their contemporaries in some of their more powerful neighbors.

The Scandinavian Monarchies

Among the more progressive states of Europe were the three Scandinavian countries—Denmark, Norway, and Sweden—which had much in common. The inhabitants of all three were "Nordics"; they spoke Teutonic languages which were closely related; and most of them were Lutheran Protestants in their religion. The economic life of all three was based primarily upon agriculture, commerce, and fisheries, though they differed slightly in the emphasis given to each. In all of them popular education was exalted and illiteracy reduced to the vanishing point. Although they all retained the monarchical form of government, they nevertheless introduced democratic principles and were among the first to grant full political and civil rights to women. In all three countries the twentieth century saw socialism become an influential force in their political and economic life. Their producers' co-operatives, consumers' co-operatives, and dairymen's associations were carefully studied and frequently imitated by even the great powers. Although ranked among the lesser states, they stood in the vanguard of Western civilization.

In 1870 the Danish kingdom, the smallest of the Scandinavian countries,[1] consisted of the Jutland peninsula, the neighboring islands in the Baltic, and the Faroe Islands lying midway between the Shetlands and Greenland. It was then governed under a constitution, adopted in 1866, which provided for a bicameral legislature. In the upper house a minority of the members were appointed for life by the king, and the rest were chosen by the large taxpayers. The lower house was elected by a wide but not manhood suffrage. Denmark thus had a constitutional form of government, but the constitution was frequently ignored by King Christian IX, who ruled until 1906.[2] Throughout most of his reign a struggle was waged by the lower house to force the king to recognize the principle of ministerial responsibility, but not until 1901 did Christian finally yield on this point. After that year, however, parliamentary government prevailed in Denmark.

In the decade before the war of 1914 strenuous efforts were made by the Liberals and the rising Socialists to bring about the democratization of the government. Ultimately, in 1914 and 1915, constitutional amendments were adopted introducing manhood and womanhood suffrage in the elections for both houses of parliament, the age requirement being twenty-five for the lower house and thirty-five for the upper. Moreover, the life memberships in the latter were abolished, and a system of proportional representation was adopted. Denmark thus took her place among the most democratic countries of the world.

Meanwhile, progress had also been made in the country's economic life. Although some attention was given to fisheries and, increasingly with the passing years, to industry, the greatest percentage of the population derived its livelihood from agriculture. Danish peasants specialized in the production of butter, eggs, and bacon for export to neighboring countries, particularly to Great Britain—which took more than two thirds of the kingdom's exports—and to Germany. To aid the peasants in marketing their products, borrowing money, and securing expensive equipment, numerous co-operative societies were organized. Also, with the increase in the number of employees in industry [3] and commerce, social legislation was enacted to provide labor exchanges and accident, sickness, old-age, and unemployment insurance.

After 1870 some changes were made in the territorial and political status of the kingdom's overseas possessions, which at the opening of the period consisted of Iceland, Greenland, the Faroe Islands, and three islands in the West Indies. In 1874 Iceland was granted home rule and was thereafter

---

[1] Denmark's population in 1945 was estimated at 4,024,000.

[2] Christian IX was succeeded by Frederick VIII (1906–1912), Christian X (1912–1947), and Frederick IX.

[3] Industrial factories in 1925 employed 392,000 persons.

governed by her own parliament; in 1918 her complete independence was recognized by Denmark, and thereafter Iceland was united with the former only because they both had the same king. In 1917 the Danish West Indies (the Virgin Islands) were sold to the United States. The Faroe Islands being an integral part of the kingdom, Denmark's only colony today is Greenland. In 1920 the kingdom's area in Europe was slightly increased by the addition of a strip of territory in northern Schleswig.[4]

In 1870 Norway and Sweden [5] were united in a personal union. Each kingdom had its own parliament and own ministry, but they had a common ruler and common ministers of war and foreign affairs. Generally speaking, the Norwegian government was more liberal than that of Sweden, probably because Sweden had a strong aristocracy and a dependent peasantry, while Norway was largely a land of peasant proprietors and sturdy fishermen. Supreme authority in Norway was vested in an indirectly elected parliament over whose acts the king had only a suspensive veto; in Sweden the parliament was controlled by the aristocracy, and the king had an absolute veto over its acts.

This union of the two kingdoms had existed ever since the Congress of Vienna had transferred Norway from the King of Denmark to the King of Sweden at the close of the Napoleonic wars. At that time Norwegian nationalism had been so strong that the inhabitants of Norway consented to the transfer only after the Swedish king had agreed to recognize Norway as "a free, independent, and indivisible kingdom united with Sweden under one king." And in the succeeding years Norwegian nationalism had continued to be strong. Eventually the Norwegians demanded their own flag and their own consular service, separate from Sweden's. These demands arose in part from the fact that by the opening of the twentieth century Norway had become an important commercial country.

But King Oscar II (1872–1907) refused to sanction the appointment of Norwegian consular agents, alleging that such a step might ultimately lead to a double foreign policy. Consequently, in 1905, after the consular question had been discussed for more than a decade, the Norwegian parliament voted unanimously to separate Norway from Sweden and to depose Oscar II. In many cases such a step might have precipitated war, but this was averted when the Swedish government decided to recognize the dissolution of the union if the step was approved by a popular plebiscite in Norway. The plebiscite was held and resulted in an almost unanimous vote in favor of separation. In the subsequent treaty of dissolution the two powers agreed (1) to demilitarize their common frontiers and (2) to refer

---

[4] See page 398.

[5] Norway is a little larger than Italy and in 1947 had a population of 3,000,000; Sweden is only slightly less in area than Germany in 1920 and in 1946 had a population of 6,673,956.

to the Hague Tribunal any future disputes between them which could not be settled through the ordinary channels of diplomacy.

Norway offered her throne to a Swedish prince, but, when he declined, she turned to the royal family of Denmark. In 1906 a Danish prince was crowned as Haakon VII.[6] The kingdom was then further democratized. Direct elections for the parliament were introduced in 1906; women were granted suffrage on the same basis as men in 1913; the suspensive veto of the king was abolished in the same year; and women were made eligible for membership in the cabinet in 1915. With direct and proportional representation, universal manhood and womanhood suffrage, ministerial responsibility, and a merely honorary king, Norway became a thoroughly democratic country.

Although Norway is large, most of it is barren and mountainous. Over 72 per cent of her territory is unproductive, and less than 4 per cent is under cultivation. But forests constitute one of the kingdom's chief sources of wealth; almost one fourth of Norway is in forests, and among her chief exports are wood pulp, paper and cardboard, and timber. Of her population 30 per cent gained their livelihood in 1930 from agriculture and forestry and 28 per cent from industries related largely to forestry. Navigation and transportation provide the economic basis for 10 per cent of the country's population, for Norway's merchant marine has long been important. In 1939 among European countries it was exceeded in total tonnage by only Great Britain and Germany. Approximately 100,000 Norwegians are engaged in the fisheries industry, cod and herring constituting an important export commodity. The working people of Norway have gained considerable political influence; in the years after 1918 the Laborites were by far the largest political party in the kingdom.

Meanwhile, Sweden, too, had entered the ranks of the democratic nations. After the death of Oscar II and the accession of his son, Gustavus V, universal manhood suffrage was introduced for the election of the lower house of the parliament; the property qualification for electors of the upper house was decreased; proportional representation was provided for both houses; and ministerial responsibility was inaugurated. Following the First World War the suffrage was extended to women, also, on the same basis as to men.

In the years after 1870 Sweden became increasingly industrialized. At the opening of the period only 12½ per cent of her population depended for their livelihood upon industry and commerce, but fifty years later the percentage had increased to 44. By 1933 nearly 400,000 workers

[6] This title was assumed to indicate the continuity of the independent kingdom of Norway, Haakon VI having been the last king of Norway before she was united with Denmark in the Middle Ages.

were employed in factories. Iron mining also was important, especially in the arctic regions of the country. Politically, with the increase of industrial workers came the rise of the Socialist Party. In the parliamentary elections of 1914 it obtained more than a third of the seats in the lower house, and eighteen years later the kingdom had its first Socialist ministry. During the economic depression of the 1930's Sweden attracted the attention of the world by her experiment with a "managed" currency.

Holland and Belgium

Although each of these states is smaller than Denmark, Norway, or Sweden, the population of each is considerably larger than that of the most populous Scandinavian country. In fact, the Netherlands—popularly referred to as Holland[7]—and Belgium are the two most densely populated countries in Europe, each having in 1930 more than 8,000,000 inhabitants. Special circumstances accounted for the ability of these two small kingdoms to support such relatively large populations.

Holland possessed an overseas empire of approximately 788,000 square miles with more than 60,000,000 inhabitants. Most of this empire was located in the East Indies, where the Netherlands controlled rich and populous Java, Sumatra, Celebes, most of Borneo, and approximately half of New Guinea, besides innumerable small islands.[8] In the western hemisphere she possessed Dutch Guiana on the northern coast of South America and Curaçao and a number of smaller islands in the Caribbean. The East Indian empire provided the Netherlands with a steady stream of wealth in the form of rubber, coffee, palm oil, tea, and tobacco. Moreover, the administration of the islands offered profitable careers to many Netherlanders, while the exploitation of their resources was very profitable to Dutch merchants and bankers.

But Holland's economic life was based, in part, upon two other factors also. The country was strategically located not only from a military but from a commercial viewpoint. Rotterdam and Amsterdam served as entrepôts for a considerable amount of trade between central Europe and countries overseas. This exchange of goods across Holland's territory brought income to Dutch carriers and middlemen and provided a livelihood for many Netherlanders. Furthermore, Holland was also a rich agricultural land and was advantageously located between Great Britain and Germany. Neither of these countries produces sufficient foodstuffs for its population, and therefore they provided the Dutch peasants with ready markets for their agricultural and dairy products. Holland's wealth

---

[7] Holland is only one—but the largest and richest—of the eleven provinces in the Kingdom of the Netherlands.

[8] For the location of the Dutch East Indies, see the map on page 23.

and her economic importance in world affairs were therefore much greater than her limited area in Europe would seem to indicate.

Political democracy was somewhat slower to develop in Holland than in some of her neighbors. In 1870 the kingdom had a bicameral parliament with ministerial responsibility, but the ruler [9] still held an absolute veto over all legislation. The upper house of the parliament was elected by the legislatures of the eleven provinces, and the lower house was chosen by those who paid a heavy property tax. The government, therefore, was largely in the hands of the wealthier classes. The succeeding years saw some progress, however. In 1887 and again in 1896 the electorate was enlarged by modifying somewhat the property qualifications. Ultimately, in 1917, further reforms introduced proportional representation and manhood and womanhood suffrage at the age of twenty-five for the election of the lower house. In the years after 1918 the two most important political parties were the Catholic and the Social Democratic.[10]

The economic foundation upon which Belgium rested was quite different from that of her neighbor to the north. Although some 60 per cent of the country was under cultivation and, thanks to the use of intensive methods and co-operative enterprise, agriculture had continued to be profitable, only a small percentage of the Belgians gained their livelihood from farms. For Belgium was rich in coal and iron, and early in the nineteenth century she experienced the Industrial Revolution. She was not only the first continental country to become industrialized, but she became the most highly industrialized of them all. Eventually, those engaged in industry came to outnumber those employed in agriculture by four to one (1930). In trade and commerce, too, Belgium came to occupy an important place. Before the First World War the volume of her foreign trade—chiefly with France, Great Britain, Holland, and Germany—was almost a third again as large as that of Italy. In 1930 the number of Belgians engaged in commerce and transportation exceeded the number of agriculturists by more than 15 per cent.

Belgium had an extensive colonial realm, which, although not so rich perhaps as that of the Netherlands, was still of considerable value to the kingdom. The establishment of the Congo Free State under the sovereignty of Leopold II has already been discussed.[11] At first Belgium as a state

[9] King William III ruled until 1890, when he was succeeded by his minor daughter, who became Queen Wilhelmina.

[10] From 1815 to 1890 the rulers of the Netherlands were also the rulers of the Grand Duchy of Luxembourg, a tiny state lying between France and Germany just east of Belgium. In 1890 the grand duchy did not pass to Queen Wilhelmina, however, but went to one of her father's male relatives, Adolphus of Nassau. The little state was included in the German customs union, and its industrial life was largely dominated by Germany. In 1867 Luxembourg had been neutralized and forbidden to have any armed force except local police.

[11] See page 18 and the map on page 19.

had no control over this territory. But the cruel treatment of the natives in attempts to force them to provide exploiting companies with ivory and rubber was later reported by the missionaries, and the disclosures led to insistent demands that reforms be introduced. In 1908, accordingly, the sovereignty of the region was transferred from Leopold to the Kingdom of Belgium, which ruled it thereafter as a colony. Belgium's economic strength was thus further increased, for the Congo was particularly rich in rubber and also supplied the kingdom with gold, diamonds, copper, palm oil, cotton, coffee, and ivory.[12]

The Belgians are not, like the people of the Scandinavian countries and Holland, homogeneous linguistically and racially. Those in the southern part of the kingdom are Walloons, who are closely akin to the French and speak French. Those in the north are Flemings, who are closely related to the Dutch in race and language. The Flemings are more numerous than the Walloons, but the Belgian bourgeoisie up to 1914 spoke only French, though Flemish was an official language to the extent that both French and Flemish had to be used in government publications. During the First World War, Germany sought to weaken Belgian resistance by encouraging the Flemings to make more demands for cultural rights. King Albert thereupon promised the Flemings equality of language and the creation of a Flemish University of Ghent. In 1921, Belgium was divided into two parts; in one all administrative matters were to be conducted in Flemish and in the other, in Walloon. A later law provided that beginning with the academic year 1930–1931 all instruction in the University of Ghent was to be in Flemish.

In 1870 Belgium was a constitutional monarchy with a bicameral parliament and ministerial responsibility but with a suffrage limited by a relatively high property qualification. Only a small percentage of the population could vote, and most of the urban workers were disfranchised. The two most important political parties were the Liberals and the Catholics. The former were anticlerical and accordingly favored secular education; the latter desired to have religious instruction in the schools and wished it to be controlled by the Catholic clergy. Until 1884 the Liberals were generally in power, with the result that religious instruction was not given in the schools.

In the eighties, however, the Liberal Party began to lose many of its members to the Socialists, and in 1884 the Catholic Party came into power and thereafter retained control of the government until after the First World War. As might be expected, religious instruction was introduced in most of the schools. But the Catholic Party also responded to the de-

[12] After the First World War a small part of German East Africa was added to the Belgian Congo as a mandate of the League of Nations and was rechristened Ruanda-Urundi.

mand for political reform and social legislation. After the country had experienced a great general strike (1893) in which the workers demanded manhood suffrage, the government in 1894 made a concession and extended the franchise to practically all men twenty-five years of age. But in order to protect the propertied class somewhat, the principle of plural voting was introduced; that is, additional votes were allotted to those men who could meet certain property qualifications. Under this law a man might have as many as three votes. In the succeeding years the Socialists raised the slogan "one man, one vote."

To appease the workingmen as well as to improve their condition, legislation was enacted to regulate factories, legalize trade unions, provide old-age pensions, and erect workers' dwellings. To satisfy the Flemish-speaking peasants and workingmen, Flemish was in 1898 made the official language of the state along with French. Thereafter both Flemish and French had to be used in governmental publications and the like. In the next year proportional representation was introduced for the election of members of the parliament. Eventually, in 1921, the constitution was further revised to provide for manhood suffrage at twenty-one years of age for both houses of the parliament and to grant the ballot to a limited number of women.[13] The reforms of 1899 and 1921 weakened the Catholic Party.[14]

Situated as she is between France and Germany and just across the Channel from Britain, Belgium occupies a highly strategic military position in Europe. Through her territory run the easiest routes over which either France or Germany may invade the other, and from her shores may an offensive against Britain be most easily launched. Fear that one of the great powers might gain the ascendancy in the little kingdom and eventually utilize it for military purposes had led Great Britain, France, Prussia, Russia, and Austria to sign a treaty in 1839 neutralizing Belgium. By the provisions of this agreement Belgium was to be an independent and perpetually neutral state, and was bound to observe such neutrality toward all other states. The great powers placed this article of the treaty under their guarantee.

Nevertheless, in the opening years of the twentieth century, Belgium became alarmed by the growing tension between the great powers and by Germany's construction of strategic railways up to the Belgian frontiers. To protect her neutrality Belgium strengthened the fortresses around Liége and Namur until they were considered almost impregnable. She

[13] The franchise was extended to widows whose husbands or sons had been killed in the war and to women who had suffered imprisonment at the hands of the German authorities.

[14] In 1919 it lost the parliamentary majority which it had held since 1884, and six years later it lost first place to the Socialists, who secured places in the ministry. For a time their able leader, Émile Vandervelde, was prime minister of the kingdom.

also carried on negotiations with Great Britain and France looking to the defense of her neutrality in case of a German invasion. Finally, in 1913, she introduced compulsory military service for all of her young men.

Switzerland

In the years before 1914 Switzerland was probably the most democratic country in the world. This small republic was a confederation of twenty-two cantons [15] which had gradually come together for mutual protection during the preceding centuries. The confederation as a whole was not homogeneous in its population, however. Of its inhabitants approximately 65 per cent (1914) were German; 23 per cent French, and 12 per cent Italian. Besides differing in language and customs the Swiss also differed in religion, 57 per cent (1930) being Protestant and 41 per cent Roman Catholic. Furthermore, in the years after 1870 the Swiss came to differ noticeably in their economic activities. To the herdsmen of the mountains and the petty farmers of the valleys were added increasingly the industrial workers of the cities.

The ability of these diverse groups to live together contentedly within one state was the result in part of three circumstances. In the first place, the cantonal governments had extensive powers, for in the confederation only certain delegated powers belonged to the national government. Although all of the cantons recognized the principle of popular sovereignty, they differed among themselves in the organization of their local governments. While some of the more populous adopted the representative type of government, some of the smaller cantons long retained a type of pure democracy—all the electors meeting at one time in one place to make political decisions by oral voting. Extensive local government, therefore, made it possible for each canton to manage its own local affairs as it chose. In the second place, the confederation was divided into so many cantons that in each of them the population was fairly homogeneous racially and linguistically, and so there was lacking the feeling that one racial group was being dominated or exploited by another. In the third place, no one of the racial groups was distinctly favored by or in the national government. All three languages were recognized as official; any one of them might be used in discussions in the parliament; the presidency of the confederation went by rotation to the different nationalities; and the central government usually sought to exercise its authority in such a way as not to antagonize any of the cantons on racial, linguistic, or religious grounds.

Under the constitution of 1848, as amended in 1874 and again in 1891,

---

[15] Three of the cantons were divided so that technically there were nineteen cantons and six half-cantons.

the federal legislature consisted of an upper house with two representatives from each canton and a lower house popularly elected in proportion to population. The republic had a plural executive, called the Federal Council, which was chosen by the parliament, and the chairman of this council —though differing little from the other members in power—bore the title of President of the Swiss Confederation. But the legislative power of the national government was not entirely or finally in the hands of the parliament, for, by means of the referendum, laws passed by the parliament might be rejected by popular vote, and, by means of the initiative and referendum,[16] laws might be popularly adopted even though not enacted by the parliament.

The economic life of Switzerland had for the most part a three-fold basis. Agriculture and dairying predominated in many of the cantons, and the manufacture of cheese and condensed milk constituted one of the republic's chief industries. In a number of the cities—notably Zurich, Basel, Geneva, and Bern—a considerable amount of modern industry developed and provided employment for some hundreds of thousands of Swiss workers.[17] Silk and artificial-silk goods, watches, embroidery, coal-tar dyes, and electrical goods were among the exports from this little state. In addition to agriculture and dairying and industry and commerce, the third important source of income for the Swiss was the tourist trade. Hotel-keeping provided a livelihood for thousands of people, and it might well be said that one of Switzerland's chief businesses was the sale of scenery.

Spain and Portugal

In the half century before the First World War Spain and Portugal were undoubtedly the most backward of the lesser states of western Europe. In 1870 Spain was in the midst of a political upheaval which had resulted from the overthrow of the Bourbon ruler, Queen Isabella II, in 1868. At that time universal manhood suffrage had been proclaimed, and freedom of religion and of the press had been guaranteed, and subsequently the Cortes had drafted a constitution providing for a liberal monarchy based upon the principle of popular sovereignty. A new monarch was then sought, and eventually Prince Leopold of Hohenzollern was selected. Although in the end Leopold declined the throne, the Prussian minister, Bismarck, so manipulated events that out of Leopold's candidacy emerged the Franco-German War of 1870–1871. In November, 1870,

[16] The principle of the popular referendum was adopted in 1874, that of the initiative in 1891.
[17] In 1929 factories employed 409,083 workers in Switzerland.

Amadeo—the second son of King Victor Emmanuel of Italy—finally accepted the Spanish throne. But continual political strife, occasioned by the opposition of republicans, Carlists,[18] and legitimists, soon discouraged the new monarch, and in 1873 he abdicated.

In February, 1873, the Cortes proclaimed a republic, but the new government from its very inception was denounced and opposed by the royalists of all types, by the clergy, and eventually by the military leaders. It was furthermore embarrassed by wars with the Carlists and regionalists at home and with the Cubans overseas. Late in 1874 the army declared in favor of the restoration of the Bourbons, and early in the next year the son of Isabella II returned to Spain to rule as Alfonso XII. In 1876 a new constitution was adopted providing for a parliamentary government with ministerial responsibility and with a franchise based upon a property qualification.

Although parliamentary in name, the government of Spain during the ensuing years was really controlled by cliques of politicians and military leaders, who fell generally into two opposing groups: the Conservatives, organized and led by Canovas del Castillo, who had worked to overthrow the republic; and the Liberals, led by Mateo Sagasta. There was relatively little difference between the views and policies of the two groups, although perhaps the Conservatives were more sympathetic with the nobility and clergy of the old regime. The two leaders ultimately reached an agreement in accordance with which their parties rotated in office by controlling the elections. This rotation of office-holding, with its privilege of distributing patronage, continued down to the opening of the twentieth century. Political corruption and coercion were general. In protest against this type of regime Canovas was assassinated in 1897.

But corruption and inefficiency were not limited to the kingdom alone; they were found also in Spain's colonies overseas. In 1878 a revolt which had raged in Cuba for ten years was put down partly by military force and partly by the promise to introduce reforms in that island. But the reforms had not been forthcoming, and so in 1895 the Cubans again raised the standard of rebellion. In attempting to suppress this revolt Spain was handicapped by an uprising in the Philippines and ultimately defeated by the intervention of the United States. At the close of the Spanish-American War (1898) Spain gave Cuba her independence and ceded Puerto Rico and the Philippines to the United States. In the next year she sold her other islands in the Pacific to Germany. Of her once proud overseas

---

[18] The Carlists were the successors of those who in 1833 had asserted, on the basis of the Salic law, that the legal successor of Ferdinand VII was not his daughter, Isabella, but his brother, Don Carlos. The chief supporters of Don Carlos during the so-called Carlist wars of the thirties had been the nobility, the clergy, and those who favored royal absolutism.

empire Spain at the opening of the twentieth century possessed only small strips of territory in Africa and a few islands in the eastern Atlantic.

In 1902 Alfonso XIII came to the throne.[19] Although he was personally popular, the new king's reign was almost continually disturbed by social unrest and the demand for far-reaching reform. To a large extent the latter was the result of changing economic conditions within the country. Spain was predominantly agricultural, and hard-working peasants constituted the bulk of her population. In the nineteenth century, however, the landed aristocracy and the numerous and privileged clergy were the most influential classes. But Spain also had considerable deposits of iron, copper, coal, zinc, and lead, and the closing years of the nineteenth century saw the introduction of some modern industrialism, especially in the regions around Barcelona, Madrid, Seville, and Bilbao. They saw, too, the rise of an industrial and financial bourgeoisie and an urban proletariat.

The industrial workers were soon attracted by the doctrines of the socialists, syndicalists, and anarchists and consequently became more and more radical in their views. And since manhood suffrage had been introduced in 1890, the radicals were able to make their influence felt in politics. The twentieth century, therefore, witnessed increasing conflict between the upholders of the old regime and those who sought to modernize Spain and bring her institutions abreast of those in the more progressive countries. The former consisted largely of nobility, clergy, and adherents of the *status quo* generally; the latter included most of the bourgeoisie, intellectuals, and proletariat.

In 1902 state supervision of elementary schools was authorized, and seven years later elementary-school attendance was made compulsory. Nevertheless, the facilities for popular education were inadequate and inefficient, and a large percentage of the Spanish people continued to be illiterate. Some progress was made in the realm of social legislation—trade unions were authorized, factories regulated, employers' liability for accidents introduced—but here, too, Spain lagged behind the progressive states. In 1907 the Conservatives, in an attempt to nullify the radicalism of the proletariat by the conservatism of the peasantry, made the exercise of manhood suffrage compulsory.

Despite this step, anticlerical sentiment began to make itself felt, and in 1910 a Liberal government, pledged to an anticlerical program, came into office. Diplomatic relations with the papacy were thereupon severed, taxes were placed on industrial enterprises conducted by religious orders, and the establishment of additional religious houses without the sanction

[19] He was the posthumous son of Alfonso XII, who had died in 1885. During the years from 1885 to 1902 Maria Christina, the queen-mother, had ruled as regent.

of the government was forbidden. But, when it was rumored that church
and state were to be separated and education secularized, the reactionary
and conservative groups organized such strong opposition that the Liberal
government was forced to give way, and the Conservative premier who
came into power resumed relations with the pope and prevented further
anticlerical legislation. The struggle between the clericals and the anticlericals was carried over into the postwar period.[20]

With the growing differentiation between industrial Catalonia and the
agricultural sections of the kingdom, an autonomist movement began
to develop in the northeastern section of the country. The regional consciousness of this district was deep-rooted, for it had emerged as a separate
entity back in the ninth century when Charlemagne created the Spanish
March. Not until the fourteenth century had it been conquered and
gradually merged into what became the Spanish monarchy, and during the
intervening centuries it had developed a separate language and literature
and its own parliament. Even down until the nineteenth century many of
its liberties had been retained, though during this century the last vestiges
of its former independent existence were destroyed by the highly centralized government at Madrid. But Catalan nationalism survived and in the
years before the First World War a states' rights program was being advocated. On the eve of the war, therefore, the permanence of the centralized Bourbon monarchy in Spain was being challenged by those favoring republicanism, socialism, syndicalism, and regionalism.

But in the neighboring kingdom of Portugal the Braganza line of rulers
was not permitted to remain on the throne even down to the war. Political life in Portugal in the years from 1870 to 1910 was very similar to
that in Spain with its corresponding manipulation of elections and rotation in office of leaders of the two principal political parties. As in Spain,
too, there was the gradual growth of radicalism, which expressed itself in
the programs of the republicans, socialists, syndicalists, and anarchists.

Although under Louis I (1861–1889) conditions appeared to be fairly
stable, popular discontent was being engendered by the prevalence of
political corruption, the burden of heavy taxes, and the government's
indifference to social reform and popular education. Under Carlos I (1889–
1908), who was inclined to resort to dictatorial methods to accomplish
his ends, unrest became greater and more widespread. Eventually, in
1908, both the king and the crown prince were assassinated. Carlos'
second son then mounted the throne as Manuel II. But the new ruler's reign
was short. The republicans redoubled their efforts to bring about the
downfall of the monarchy and sought especially to win over the organized
armed forces.

[20] See pages 562–567.

In 1910 a republican revolt broke out when both the army and the navy mutinied and seized the capital. Manuel fled from the country, and a provisional government proclaimed a republic. In 1911 a democratic constitution, closely resembling that of the Third French Republic, was adopted, and Manuel Arriaga, long a leader of the Portuguese republicans, was elected president. Then followed a series of anticlerical laws, which resembled those enacted earlier in France. Diplomatic relations with the pope were broken off; church and state were separated; religious orders were suppressed and their property confiscated; and a system of free, secular education was introduced.

But the establishment of the republic brought neither political stability nor general content. Socialists were dissatisfied with the bourgeois character of the new regime; monarchists intrigued to restore the old regime; and army leaders repeatedly meddled in political affairs. Great strikes, frequent riots, and occasional insurrections and coups prepared the way for the establishment of the fascist dictatorship which was eventually inaugurated in Portugal after the First World War.

Although one of the smaller states of Europe, Portugal possessed one of the largest overseas empires. Before the war only the empires of Great Britain, France, and Germany exceeded it in area. Most of this overseas territory was located in Africa, but some of it was in India and the Far East.[21] Unfortunately for Portugal, her empire was not so rich as that of the Netherlands, and by many the expenses entailed in administering so large a colonial realm were considered beyond her financial ability. Germany's prewar interest in the possibility of obtaining some of this territory, in case the Portuguese government went bankrupt, has already been discussed.[22]

---

[21] The Cape Verde Islands off the west coast of Africa; Portuguese Guinea, Angola, and Mozambique in Africa; Goa, Damaun, and Diu in India; part of Timor in the Malay archipelago; and Macao in China. The Azores and the Madeira Islands were not colonies but were considered integral parts of Portugal.

[22] See page 74.

Chapter VIII

THE RUSSIAN EMPIRE

WITHIN Russia, the great Slavic power of northern and eastern Europe, the half century before the First World War witnessed an unending struggle between liberals and radicals, on the one hand, who sought to bring the institutions of the empire more nearly into harmony with those of the progressive countries of the West, and conservatives and reactionaries, on the other, who were determined to perpetuate the old regime as long as possible. In this struggle the Romanov dynasty and government were as a general rule closely aligned with the latter group. Plots and counterplots, assassinations and executions, imprisonment and exile, revolution and repression were the accompaniments of the conflict, which was hard-fought and bitter. Although some progress was made, the empire in 1914 was still far from the goal which liberals and radicals envisaged.

In international affairs Russia's role during this period was dominated largely by the centuries-old desire to obtain a suitable warm-water outlet to the high seas. In the quest for such a port her statesmen schemed and intrigued both in Europe and in Asia, but on each occasion their plans were thwarted by one or more of the great powers. In 1914 Russia's renewed determination to gain an outlet through the Straits had much to do with precipitating the First World War.

The Vastness of Russia

In 1870 the Romanov Tsar Alexander II ruled over the largest country in Europe both in area and in population. But his empire was not limited to Europe any more than the British Empire was limited to the British Isles. Across the Ural Mountains intrepid trappers, gold-seeking miners, aggressive merchants, political refugees, escaped serfs, and adventurers generally had pushed the Russian frontier ever onward into Siberia. Long before the nineteenth century they had extended Russian territory to the northern Pacific Ocean; in fact, they had even appropriated in the name of the tsars the Alaskan region [1] of North America. By the time of Alexander II the tsar ruled an empire second in size only to the British, an

[1] Alaska was sold to the United States in 1867.

empire which had been created not by overseas expansion but by constantly advancing its frontiers over land.

From the days of Peter the Great Russia's diplomacy and policy of territorial expansion, so far as they may be said to have had a conscious dominating motive, had been directed toward the acquisition of a satisfactory outlet to the high seas. Peter himself had secured an access to the Baltic, and Catherine the Great had gained a foothold on the Black Sea. Neither of these outlets was satisfactory, however; the former because it was not an ice-free port throughout the year, and the latter because the fortified Bosporus and Dardanelles, connecting the Black Sea with the Mediterranean, were in the control of the Ottoman Empire and might be closed to Russian commerce or to the passage of Russian warships almost at the whim of the sultan's government.

One of Russia's major aspirations, accordingly, was to secure the control of the Straits, and during the nineteenth century she schemed in various ways to attain this end. At times it appeared that her interests could best be advanced by partitioning or destroying Turkey and bringing under Russian control the territory along the Straits. At other times it seemed that the desired outlet could best be secured by maintaining the territorial integrity of the Ottoman Empire and at the same time gaining for Russia a privileged position as a sort of guardian of Turkey. In pursuing the former policy Russia eagerly sought to avail herself of unrest among the sultan's subject races in the Balkans in order by intervention to gain territory for herself and the good will of the Balkan peoples. In pursuing the second policy she posed either as the defender of Turkey—in return for privileges in respect to the Straits (as in 1833)—or as the protector of the Greek Christians in Turkey—in order to secure opportunities to interfere in Turkish affairs.

At the time when Alexander II mounted the throne (1855) Russia was engaged in the Crimean War, a struggle which had been precipitated by her attempt to carry out the second of these policies. Great Britain and France had come to the aid of Turkey, and in 1856 the tsar was compelled to withdraw from the struggle. By the subsequent treaty of Paris Russia was compelled to cede to Moldavia (later called Rumania) a valuable strip of Bessarabia at the mouth of the Danube, and was forced to agree to the neutralization of the Black Sea. No warships were thereafter to be stationed in that sea, and no arsenals were to be permitted on its shores.[2] The treaty appeared to constitute a definite check, at least temporarily, to any Russian advance in the Near East.

Blocked in that direction, the empire's energies were next turned to ex-

[2] During the Franco-German War Russia announced her abrogation of these provisions regarding the Black Sea.

pansion into other regions, particularly into the Middle East and the Far East. South of the Russian Empire, between Chinese Turkestan on the east and the Caspian Sea on the west, lay a vast territory which was organized into Moslem khanates and peopled largely by nomadic tribesmen. The latter occasionally conducted raids northward into Russian territory and from time to time attacked Russian caravans. They thus provided the tsar's foreign minister, Gorchakov, with an opportunity to justify Russia's subsequent conquests on the ground that the constant inroads of lawless tribes made Russian advances unavoidable until the frontiers of some well-ordered states should be reached. In an apparent effort to reach such frontiers Russia pushed steadily southward toward Persia, Afghanistan, and India.

In 1865 a number of strongholds, including Turkestan and Tashkend, were captured, and the conquered region was eventually organized (1867) into a governor-generalship named Turkestan. Almost at once a conflict began between the Russian governor-general of Turkestan, General Kauffmann, and the ruler of the neighboring khanate of Bokhara. In 1868 the Russians captured the sacred city of Samarkand and forced the ruler of Bokhara to recognize the suzerainty of the tsar. Five years later Russian troops under the command of General Kauffmann invaded Khiva from Turkestan and from the Caspian Sea and soon completed its conquest. Part of the Khivan territory was annexed to Russia outright, and part became a vassal state. Next, in the middle seventies, a civil war in the khanate of Kokand was seized upon by the Russians as an opportunity for an attack, and in 1876 Kokand was incorporated in the Russian Empire as a province with the name Fergana.

Still pushing southward, a Russian army leader entered Kabul, the capital of Afghanistan, and persuaded the ruler of that country to sign a treaty (1878) placing his country under Russia's protection. This, at last, had the effect of moving the British to action, for, despite Gorchakov's efforts to allay their fears, they had for some time been alarmed at Russia's steady advance toward India. The British had hoped that a neutral zone might be established in the Middle East between their possessions and Russia's and had urged the tsar to recognize the Amu River as the boundary between his territory and Afghanistan, the latter supposedly being in the British sphere of influence. As soon as the Russian treaty with Afghanistan became known, therefore, Great Britain launched a war against the Afghan amir and eventually (1881) succeeded in placing on the throne of Afghanistan a ruler who was favorable to Great Britain's interests. Russia's further southward expansion was therefore checked in this part of the Middle East by British troops and diplomats.

Meanwhile, in the Far East other important territories had been acquired. In 1858 the governor-general of Eastern Siberia annexed the region on the left bank of the Amur River together with the great stretch of territory on the right bank lying between the Amur and the Pacific and extending south as far as the present city of Vladivostok. Here was a good harbor which was ice-bound only three or four months of the year, and here Russia planned to build a new city and port to provide a better outlet to the Pacific. In 1860 all this territory was formally ceded to the tsar by China. In the same year Russia also secured the northern half of the valuable island of Sakhalin, and fifteen years later the rest of the island, which had been in Japanese possession. As a result of these acquisitions of territory Russia was thereafter in a position to play an increasingly important role in the affairs of the Far East. Incidentally, she now possessed an empire variously estimated as including from one seventh to one sixth of the land surface of the globe.

The Backwardness of Russia

Although by far the largest of the states of Europe, Russia, when judged by the standards of Western civilization, was decidedly the most backward of the great European powers. In fact, if the institutions of the empire are considered as they existed when Alexander II began to rule, it is obvious that the Russians were lagging far behind the peoples of the other great powers, were, in fact, actually living amid conditions which were not greatly different in many respects from those which had existed in western Europe centuries before.

The social life of the empire was organized in a distinctly medieval fashion. As in western Europe in the Middle Ages, the great bulk of the population consisted of peasants who lived in village communities known in Russia as *mirs*. The great majority of these peasants were serfs. Most of them were bound to the soil. They worked on the great estates of the landed aristocracy and in their personal lives were in many ways subject to the demands of their overlords. Some, however, had been released from agricultural work but were still obligated in various other ways to their lords and masters. As in medieval times, the privileged group in Russia consisted of the aristocracy and the clergy. Relatively speaking, the bourgeois class was small and of little influence; at the middle of the nineteenth century less than 8 per cent of the population lived in towns or cities.

In her economic life, too, Russia was still largely medieval. Despite its wealth of mineral resources, the empire was chiefly dependent upon agriculture for its economic well-being. And in agriculture the system of cultivation was that of the inefficient and out-of-date three-field system, with the serfs working dispersed or scattered holdings which were periodically redistributed by the mir. A large share of the peasant's time was spent on the lord's domain, the rest on his own strips. The Agricultural Revolution had not yet reached Russia.[3] Industry was largely of the type found under domestic and guild systems, since the Industrial Revolution had as yet made practically no headway in the empire. Domestic commerce was carried on largely over water and caravan routes, for facilities for travel and trade were still not greatly different from those which existed in medieval times. In the middle of the nineteenth century, according to one Russian authority, the total length of the railways in operation in the vast Russian Empire was not more than 660 miles.

Politically, Russia was still back in the age of Louis XIV—in the period of the old regime. The government was an absolute monarchy, supposedly controlled entirely by the divine-right Autocrat of all the Russias, who from 1855 to 1881 was Alexander II. There was no constitution to restrict the tsar. There was no national legislature to determine the laws which were to govern the Russians and bind their ruler. Although the tsar was assisted by a sort of cabinet, the Council of the Empire, ministerial government in the Western sense of the term did not exist; the ministers were appointed by and were responsible to the tsar, whose decrees constituted the law of the land. Naturally, in an empire as far-flung as the Russian, the government, although centralized in St. Petersburg, was administered chiefly by a large number of officials, with most of whom the tsar never came in contact. Unfortunately for the permanence of the tsarist regime, many of these officials not only oppressed the people but administered the government with gross inefficiency and widespread corruption. Probably one reason why the autocratic regime lasted as long as it did was the naïve belief of the Russian peasants that their ills were not the fault of their "little father," the tsar, but were caused by those corrupt officials whom he himself would remove from office if he but knew the real situation.

As in the Middle Ages, education and culture in Russia were the privilege of the few. Illiteracy was largely the rule, and even those who received education were sometimes thwarted in their search for truth by the interference of the tsar's government, which occasionally dictated what might and might not be studied. In religion the dominant faith was the Greek Orthodox, and there was a close union between this church and the state. The tsar himself appointed the procurator of the holy synod, who in turn dominated the church. Although in Russia's great population there were also Roman Catholics, Uniates, Protestants, Jews, Moslems, and others, the government openly favored the Greek Orthodox Church

---

[3] Even as recently as the second decade of the twentieth century the average yield of wheat in Russia was per acre only two thirds of that in the United States and less than half of that in France.

and frequently persecuted those of other faiths. Among the Greek Orthodox believers there was much that was suggestive of the Middle Ages. "The pilgrims, dressed like Tannhäuser in the third act, with staves in their hands and wallets at their sides, who wander through Russia on their way to pray at the Holy Sepulchre, belong to the age of the Crusades. The ascetic who spends his life in prayer and fasting and wears chains about his body seems to have found his way into modern Russia from the Egyptian Thebaid of the fourth century."

Finally, the Russian Empire, like most states in early medieval times, was not a homogeneous nation but was inhabited by a conglomeration of races and varying linguistic groups. The Slavic Russians—the Great Russians, the Little Russians (Ukrainians), and the White Russians, who spoke languages that were akin—constituted more than 70 per cent of the empire's population. They inhabited most of the central and eastern provinces of European Russia and were the predominant element in the central part of the empire in Asia. The other 30 per cent of Russia's population consisted of Poles in Poland, Lithuania, and the Ukraine; Jews in Poland, Lithuania, and the Ukraine; Finns and Swedes in Finland; Germans, Lithuanians, Letts, and Estonians in the Baltic provinces; Rumanians in Bessarabia; Tatars in the Crimea and the southeastern provinces; Armenians, Georgians, and Circassians in the Caucasus; Mongols in Siberia; Moslem tribes in central Asia; and many other groups like the Lapps and Eskimos in northern Siberia. Although among the Poles and Finns—and to a less extent, perhaps, among the Rumanians, Lithuanians, Estonians, and Letts—there was some feeling of national rebellion against being ruled by the alien tsar, most of the other subject groups were as yet undisturbed by the dynamic spirit of nationalism which existed in the West.

Alexander II—Liberal or Conservative?

In the early years of his reign Alexander II by various measures gained the reputation of being a reformer, a ruler who was desirous of liberalizing Russian institutions so that they might be brought into harmony with those of the other great states of the West. Whether in the beginning the tsar was a sincere liberal or was merely moved to modernize the empire so that it might escape in the future a disastrous defeat like that suffered in the Crimean War, it is difficult to say. According to some Russian historians, Alexander in his political views did not differ greatly from his father, Nicholas I, and at heart held the ideal of enlightened despotism.

The young tsar opened his reign most auspiciously by attacking the institution of serfdom. For more than a century there had been an increasing realization in Russia that serfdom should be abolished, a realization which was hastened from time to time by the outbreak of peasant disorders. While many were influenced by the moral and social evils inherent in a servile system, perhaps more were swayed by the economic and military defects. It was found that forced labor was inefficient and wasteful, and that lack of the incentive which usually comes from private ownership of property dampened the serfs' zeal for labor. In the army it was emphatically brought home by the Crimean War that Russian servile soldiers were no match for the free men of western Europe in the matter of intelligence and initiative. The military strength of Russia, resting largely on servile troops, was found to be greatly exaggerated. The old regime in Russia had proved to be incapable of organizing an effective defense of the empire. It was therefore decided that the system of serfdom must be abolished.

In the reign of Alexander I the serfs of the Baltic provinces had been set free without any land and had immediately become an agricultural proletariat. By many this was considered to be an unsatisfactory solution of the problem. Alexander II was determined that land allotments should be provided for the emancipated peasants, but the adjustment of relations between freedmen and landed aristocrats and the setting of the price to be paid for the land given to the peasants called for careful study. For three years a committee worked on the general plan of emancipation and on the details of its execution. In a manifesto issued in March, 1861, the project was eventually confirmed by the tsar.

By the terms of Alexander's edict household serfs were given their personal freedom without redemption and without any form of compensation. But all the millions of serfs who had worked on the land were to receive in addition to their personal freedom their homesteads and certain allotments of land. Generally speaking, about half of the cultivated land was handed over to the peasants. The land allotments were not given to the peasants directly in full personal ownership, however, but to the mirs, which consisted of the heads of the families in the peasant villages. The mirs, in turn, were periodically to divide the land among the peasants roughly in proportion to the size of the different families. Nor were the land allotments surrendered by the estate-owners without compensation. In most cases the government paid the landowner for the land which he surrendered to the mir, and the latter was obligated to repay the government over a period of forty-nine years. The millions of serfs on the royal appanages and on the state lands were given their freedom in 1863 and 1866 respectively.

Although Alexander's edict of emancipation gained for him the title of "Tsar Liberator," the provisions and execution of the edict of emancipation were unsatisfactory to most of those involved. In the first place, the peasants maintained that all the land of the proprietor should have been given to the peasants. In general the peasants received allotments of land which before 1861 had absorbed only half of their labor.⁴ In the second place, the peasants asserted that the land should have been given to them as individuals rather than to the mirs. The incentive of private ownership was still largely lacking when the peasants did not know how long they would retain their own particular strips of land. Furthermore, in a sense the peasant still found himself unfree, for the mir not only allotted him his strips of land but determined his portion of the land tax and even decided whether or not he might leave the mir. On the other hand, the landed proprietors often had difficulty in obtaining satisfactory labor to till the land which they still held after the peasants were no longer required to work for them.⁵ Many proprietors gave up the attempt to exploit their own domains, sold parts or all of their holdings,⁶ and moved to the cities.

After the emancipation of the serfs, other reforms were made which went far, it was thought, toward modernizing the character of the Russian state. In 1864 the tsar took a step which was believed by many to be second in importance only to his freeing of the serfs. By an imperial decree of that year he introduced a system of local self-government by the creation of *zemstvos* or assemblies. In each county of the thirty-four administrative provinces, or "governments," of Russia, a local zemstvo was created and empowered to levy local taxes and to look after such matters as roads, hospitals, education, public health, and public welfare generally.⁷ For the purpose of choosing the zemstvos the electorate of each county was divided into three classes—the private landowners, the mirs, and the townspeople— each of which elected representatives. The local zemstvos in turn chose provincial zemstvos. Although the zemstvos were authorized to deal only with matters with which the central government had not concerned itself, they provided political training in responsible administration and came in time to serve as critics of the tsar's regime. In 1870 town government was likewise reformed, and municipal *dumas* or councils, elected on a three-class system analogous to that in Prussia,⁸ were established.

In the sixties, too, reforms were made in the judicial system of Russia, which had stood almost untouched since the days of Catherine the Great. By decrees of Alexander II civil and criminal cases were taken out of the

---

⁴ Though the size of the peasant holdings after emancipation varied in different provinces, the average was slightly more than twenty-two acres.

⁵ Apparently the small allotments of land to the peasants were designed in part to make the latter willing to work for the landed proprietors in order to supplement their own incomes.

⁶ It has been estimated that by 1905 half of the land possessed by the nobility after emancipation had passed into peasant hands.

⁷ The central government in St. Petersburg reserved to itself all police and military authority.

⁸ See footnote on page 86.

hands of local administrators—usually landed proprietors—and turned over to a system of lower courts, which were freed of all class distinction and made independent of the administrative officials. The tsar's purpose appeared to be to institute in his empire a judicial system similar in its general outlines to that which existed in western Europe. Provision was therefore made for jury trial in criminal cases, for public rather than secret trials, for the appointment of prosecuting attorneys, for adequate remuneration of the judges, and for the use of private lawyers. The system, as completed, provided for justices of the peace, elected by the local zemstvos,[9] district and circuit judges, and a senate, the latter serving as the empire's highest court of appeal.

While reform was still the order of the day, the tsar also gave permission for travel abroad, restored a considerable measure of academic freedom to the universities, made easier of access the institutions of higher learning, encouraged the establishment of primary and technical schools, and considerably weakened the censorship of the press. The results of these steps, however, were not particularly pleasing to Alexander. Numerous publications at once began to use their liberty to criticize the gross incompetence of the tsar's administrative system; the views of the intelligentsia began to be expressed through new magazines which catered to the professional and educated classes; and the wider opening of the doors of the universities tended to make more democratic and more critical the student bodies of those institutions.

If, as many aver, Alexander II was not at heart a true liberal, it is probably not surprising that he was easily and rather quickly turned against reform when incidents occurred to frighten or alarm him. Perhaps the first incident which led him to question the advisability of continuing as a liberal was the revolt which occurred in Russian Poland (1863), where groups of poorly armed patriots sought to throw off the Russian yoke. Although the insurrection was quickly suppressed by the tsar's army, Russian reactionaries and Slavophiles—those who cherished Russia's ancient institutions and opposed the introduction of Western ideas—were not slow to argue that the difficulties in Poland were the inevitable result of the tsar's liberal concessions. If he continued with his reform program, they declared, similar unrest and possibly insurrections might be expected in Russia proper. Their arguments were doubtless given added potency in the tsar's mind when an unbalanced communist attempted to shoot him in 1866.

In the ensuing years, therefore, Alexander II pursued a policy of reaction, as a result of which some of the chief reforms which he had introduced were greatly curtailed. The zemstvos, whose institution had been so gladly wel-

---

[9] Actually, however, the peasants in most cases involving small civil litigations were not allowed to use the new courts.

comed by public-spirited Russians, were within two years of their creation placed under the control of local governors, were restricted in the matter of publicity for their debates, and in 1868 were considerably limited in the matter of taxation. The reform of the judiciary was likewise never carried to its completion. The government failed to observe the principle that local judges were irremovable, and gradually different types of offenses were withdrawn from the jurisdiction of local courts. In 1878, for instance, it was ordered that political cases should be referred to courts-martial. The press, too, was increasingly subjected to new restrictions entailing limitation of subscribers and the necessity for advance censorship.

Attempts were also made to control advanced education in order to prevent the too widespread dissemination of dangerous ideas. History, modern languages, and geography were definitely subordinated to such supposedly nonrevolutionary subjects as Latin, Greek, and mathematics. Science, on the other hand, was taken out of the curriculum altogether. In an effort to crush not only tendencies toward liberalism but tendencies toward nationalism as well, the government sought to suppress everything having to do with the Ukrainian (Little Russian) language and literature. It was ordered, for example, that Ukrainian should not be used in printing or on the stage, and that specialists in the study of the Ukrainian language and literature should be removed from university faculties. Similar steps were taken also against the Poles.

Nihilism and Terrorism

But at the very time when Alexander's government was becoming more and more reactionary, certain groups in the empire were seeking and demanding further liberal reforms. These demands were in part the rather natural consequence of the critical spirit which had been developed among the younger intellectuals during the sixties by the writings of two Russians, Alexander Herzen and Michael Bakunin. In 1857 the former, an exile in London, had founded a weekly journal—the *Kolokol* (*Bell*)—which was smuggled into Russia and which came to have a limited circulation among the intellectuals of that country. Through the *Kolokol* Herzen attacked various Russian institutions and advocated something in the nature of utopian socialism. But he was, after all, rather moderate in his demands, and so he has been called the father of Russian liberalism. Bakunin, on the other hand, was an extreme radical who is usually considered to have been the father of both Russian anarchism and terrorism. A member of an aristocratic Russian family, after his term of service in the army he had traveled and studied in Europe. While a student in Germany he had come under the influence of the philosopher, Hegel, and later in Paris under that of the anarchist, Proudhon. During the fifties he had spent some years in Russian prisons, but he eventually escaped from Siberia and lived the rest of his life an exile from Russia. Through his writings Bakunin advocated the breaking of the restrictive bonds of religion, the state, and even the family in order that mankind might stand forth free and unshackled by conventions or authority. Such a change could be brought about, he declared, only by violence.

Although the Russian intellectuals did not at once take up Bakunin's program of violence, they did adopt a critical attitude toward Russian institutions and ideals. According to them, reason and science must be the yardsticks for judging institutions, and nothing of the old regime in Russia should be respected or accepted unless it measured up to these standards. The Russians who held these views became known as nihilists (*nihil* being the Latin for nothing). "A nihilist," wrote the Russian novelist, Turgenev, "is a man who does not bow down before any authority, who does not take any principle on faith, whatever reverence that principle may be enshrined in." In their role, therefore, the Russian nihilists of the nineteenth century were not unlike the French enlightened critics of the preceding century. Although they were not primarily interested in altering the political institutions of Russia, the critical attitude which they exalted inevitably reacted against the tsarist regime.

Before long many of the young intellectuals threw off the restraint of bureaucratic tradition and conservatism and began to demand civil equality, bona fide trial by jury, complete freedom of conscience and of the press, police reform, popular control of legislation and finance, and ministerial responsibility. Strange as it may seem, the intellectuals received some support from the nobility. Many of the latter believed that, since the nobles had been deprived of social and economic privileges by the abolition of serfdom, they should receive in exchange a part of the governing power of the empire. During the seventies there was a steadily increasing demand that elective representation should not be limited to the local zemstvos and dumas but should be extended to some national legislative body as well.

The younger intellectuals eventually came to the conclusion that to gain results, they must first propagandize the masses, who were, of course, the peasants. In the seventies, therefore, hundreds of students went out to live among the peasants as teachers, laborers, physicians, nurses, clerks—in fact, they took any kind of job they could obtain. But the mission of these *narodniki* (men of the people) proved to be an utter failure. The government at once arrested and imprisoned or exiled several hundred participants in the movement. It was not difficult to identify them, of course, because radical intellectuals were bound to be conspicuous in a peasant village. The peasants themselves had little realization of the significance of the doctrines advocated by the *narodniki* and remained largely inert. It soon became evident to the intellectuals that the peasants were not interested in politics, or in socialism, but only in acquiring more land.

Thwarted in their efforts to enlighten the masses, many of the members of the *narodniki* became radical revolutionists and turned definitely to the use of terrorism as advocated earlier by Bakunin. "Terrorist activity," wrote one radical, "consists in the destruction of the most harmful persons in the government, the protection of the party from spies, and the punishment of official lawlessness and violence in all the more prominent and important cases in which such lawlessness and violence are manifested. The aim of such activity is to break down the prestige of governmental power, to furnish continuous proof of the possibility of carrying on a contest with the government, to raise in that way the revolutionary spirit of the people and inspire belief in the practicability of revolution, and, finally, to form a body suited and accustomed to warfare." In pursuance of this program spies and policemen were frequently assassinated, but gradually the terrorist campaign turned to high officials and ultimately came to center on Alexander himself. In 1873 a second futile attempt was made on his life. But when, shortly thereafter, the tsar embarked on another venture designed to gain for Russia the coveted outlet to the Mediterranean, it was hoped by many that a foreign war and an aroused national enthusiasm might ultimately engulf and destroy the menacing terrorists.

Intervention in the Balkans

In the middle seventies conditions in the Balkans were such as again to encourage Russia to hope that she might benefit by intervention in that troubled part of Europe. Although, as the Ottoman flood had receded during the first half of the century, some of the Christian peoples had begun to emerge as national states, the sultan in 1870 still controlled the greater part of the Balkan peninsula. Despite the fact that the Greeks had established a small independent kingdom in the south, and the Rumanians, Serbs, and Montenegrins had carved out autonomous principalities in the north, the Ottoman Empire stretched across the Balkans from the Black Sea on the east to Austrian Dalmatia and the Adriatic on the west. Included within this Turkish realm was a heterogeneous population of Bulgarians, Macedonians, Greeks, Serbs, Albanians, and Bosnians, the great bulk of whom were Christians.

The Turks had never succeeded in assimilating these various peoples, largely because of the differences in religious faith and more lately because of the strong national sentiment which had begun to develop among them. On the other hand, the mutual jealousies and rival territorial ambitions which divided and weakened the subject peoples had enabled the sultan to retain his hold in the Balkans much longer than might otherwise have been expected. Because the subject Christian peoples, the *"rayahs"* (cattle), had been almost continuously exploited by their Moslem over-lords, the powers, in the treaty of Paris (1856), had forced the sultan to promise to introduce reforms to safeguard the rights of these subjects. In practically every case, however, the half-hearted attempts at reform had broken down because of the inefficiency of Turkish officials and because of the opposition of the Moslem population.

In the summer of 1875 affairs in the Balkans reached a crisis when, as a result of the Moslem attempt to collect extortionate taxes, the Yugoslav populace of the little province of Herzegovina raised the standard of rebellion. Soon other uprisings occurred in Bosnia, where the rebels were strengthened by volunteers from the neighboring Yugoslav state, Serbia. The Bulgarians, probably the most downtrodden of the sultan's subject peoples, next took heart and seized the occasion to rise against their Turkish masters, only to be slaughtered without mercy by Ottoman forces. A tremendous wave of popular indignation swept through the Yugoslav peoples of the Balkans, and in response to it the rulers of the small principalities of Serbia and Montenegro declared war on Turkey, and the former immediately invited a Russian general to command the Serbian army. At once there arose the fear that from the Balkan war a general European conflict might develop.

In accordance with agreements reached in 1873 when the League of the Three Emperors had been created,[10] the emperors of Austria, Russia, and Germany, in January, 1876, sent a joint note to the sultan demanding reforms in the interests of the latter's Christian subjects, but the Balkan insurgents were not satisfied with the sultan's promises and continued to fight on. In May the three emperors again intervened to demand an armistice, but without effect. Two months later Emperor Francis Joseph and Tsar Alexander met at Reichstadt to consider the Balkan situation. At that time they agreed not to intervene for the present, but further agreed that if Russian intervention with resultant territorial changes should occur, Austria should receive the provinces of Bosnia and Herzegovina. Apparently, too, it was agreed that Russia should regain the strip of Bessarabia which she had lost in 1856 and should make additions of territory along the eastern shores of the Black Sea. Provision was also made for the territorial enlargement of Serbia, Montenegro, and Greece, for the establishment of Bulgaria and Rumelia as autonomous states, and for the transformation of Constantinople into a free city.

Military operations had meanwhile continued in the Balkans, and by

[10] See pages 61–62.

the autumn of 1876 it appeared that the Turkish forces would capture Belgrade, the capital of Serbia. In October, therefore, Russia intervened with an ultimatum demanding an armistice, which was this time accepted. Great Britain now concluded that, unless the plight of the Christian subjects of the sultan was at once alleviated, Russia would probably declare war upon Turkey. In a war in behalf of fellow-Christians against what the British Liberal leader, Gladstone, called the "unspeakable Turk," Russia would undoubtedly have the popular sympathy of Europe and might therefore be in a position to recover that informal protectorate over Turkey which she had sought and lost in 1853–1856. Great Britain accordingly invited the powers to a conference at Constantinople to consider means of adjusting the Balkan situation without territorial gains to any of the great powers.

Such a conference opened in December, 1876, but when Sultan Abdul Hamid II refused to weaken his independence by giving the powers any authority in his empire, the conference disbanded two months later without tangible result. In March, 1877, the powers, meeting in London, reached another agreement looking to the protection of the Turkish Christians, but the sultan obstinately refused to consider even this more moderate proposal, citing the treaty of Paris to prove that Turkey was absolutely independent of outside intervention. Feeling was by this time so high in Russia that, despite a warning of bankruptcy by his minister of finance, Alexander II declared war against Turkey on April 24, 1877. Russia was later joined in the war by the neighboring principality of Rumania.

For a time Russia's military progress was not great, for she was handicapped by the fact that her army reforms had not yet been completed.[11] She was also hampered by the perennial evils of incapable leadership, peculation in army contracts, and administrative abuses. Nevertheless, victories finally came. In November, 1877, Kars was taken; in December the main Turkish army was captured with the fall of Plevna, and the Russian troops began to cross the Balkan Mountains; in February, 1878, the tsar's forces were approaching Constantinople and were at last in sight of their long-sought goal.

But unfortunately for Russia's plans, the nearer her forces approached the coveted Turkish capital, the more other powers appeared to prepare to intervene. Austrian forces were moved into the Carpathians, where, if called upon, they could strike at the flank of the Russian army; and a British fleet, at first concentrated in the eastern Mediterranean, in February entered the Straits, where it would be in a position to bombard the tsar's forces if they attempted to take Constantinople. Furthermore, the

[11] In 1874 Alexander II had begun reforms which were designed to organize the Russian army according to the Prussian system of universal military service.

British government let it be known that Russia's entrance into that city would constitute a cause for war. Accordingly, when Abdul Hamid offered to open peace negotiations, the tsar considered it the better part of wisdom to accept without actually entering the Ottoman capital. The treaty which resulted took its name from San Stefano, a village not far from Constantinople.

Ignoring the agreements which had been reached by Alexander and Francis Joseph at Reichstadt in 1876, Russia now dictated a treaty which left to the sultan in Europe only an area in the vicinity of the Straits, including Constantinople and Adrianople, and the detached district of Albania along the Adriatic in the west. Rumania, Serbia, and Montenegro were to be enlarged territorially and to be recognized by the sultan as entirely independent politically. A new Christian state, Bulgaria, was to be created with boundaries to include not only Bulgaria proper but most of Macedonia from the Aegean to Albania. Such a Bulgaria would be the largest of all the Balkan states. It would still in theory belong to the Ottoman Empire and would pay an annual tribute to the sultan in recognition of this status, but it would have its own prince and make its own laws. Bosnia and Herzegovina were also to receive a measure of autonomy in the interests of their Christian subjects; nothing was said about handing these provinces over to Austria-Hungary.

But the tsar was not unmindful of the interests of his own empire. Russia was to obtain part of Armenia, where her armies had been victorious, a strip of the Dobrudja adjoining Rumania,[12] the destruction of all Turkish fortifications along the Danube, the opening of the Straits to the commerce of all nations, and a large war indemnity. In addition to advancing his empire in the region across the Caucasus, he had, he hoped, greatly increased his influence if not his territorial holdings in the Balkans, for it was rather to be expected that the new Bulgaria, brought into being by the tsar and not yet completely independent of the sultan, would become a satellite of the Russian Empire. It was hoped, too, that the other Balkan states which would benefit by the treaty of San Stefano might out of gratitude be loyal to the tsar's interests. Finally, it is possible that the tsar expected that the sultan's inability to pay the large war indemnity would provide Russia with an excuse to interfere in Turkish affairs. The net result of the treaty of San Stefano seemed particularly favorable to the tsar.

That fact was also abundantly clear to both Austria-Hungary and Great Britain. Quite apparently the tsar had flagrantly violated the agreement reached with Francis Joseph at Reichstadt. The Habsburg hope of even-

---

[12] Russia planned to exchange the strip of the Dobrudja for the strip of Bessarabia which had been transferred from Russia to Rumania by the treaty of Paris (1856).

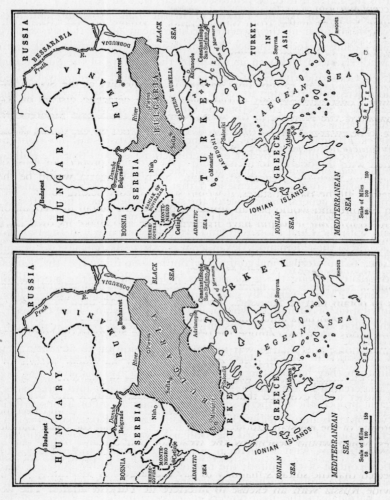

THE BALKANS BY THE TREATY OF SAN STEFANO

THE BALKANS BY THE TREATY OF BERLIN

tually securing a suitable port on the Aegean now seemed blocked by the creation of a big Bulgaria. Austria-Hungary, therefore, was bitterly opposed to the treaty of San Stefano. But so also was Great Britain. Statesmen of the latter feared, or professed to fear, that an advance of Russia's interests either in Asiatic Turkey or in the Balkans would endanger British dominance in the eastern Mediterranean and seriously menace Britain's route to India. In fact, British desire to keep Russia back from the Mediterranean had been increased by the opening of the Suez Canal in 1869. Consequently, Great Britain and the Dual Monarchy decided to block Russia by refusing to accept the treaty of San Stefano and in this decision were supported by Serbia and Greece, both of which were alarmed by the creation of a big Bulgaria.

Austria-Hungary, therefore, announced that Russia had no right to revise the treaty of Paris by her unilateral action, asserted that the Balkan situation was one which concerned all the powers that were signatories of that earlier treaty, and demanded that the treaty of San Stefano be submitted to a general conference of the signatory powers. The aggressive, imperialistic Lord Beaconsfield (Disraeli) immediately aligned Great Britain with the Dual Monarchy and even threatened war if the tsar did not accede to their demand. Alexander was extremely reluctant to submit his treaty to an international conference, but he soon discovered that Russia stood isolated among the great powers and, mindful of the outcome of the Crimean War, eventually gave way to Austro-British pressure. Upon the invitation of Bismarck, who promised to act as an "honest broker" for the interested powers, the ensuing congress met at Berlin in the summer of 1878.

In general, the Balkan states fared worse under the new treaty of Berlin than they had by the treaty which Russia had dictated. The big Bulgaria created by the San Stefano agreement was split into three parts: Bulgaria proper, the northern section, was made an autonomous principality subject to annual tribute to the sultan; Eastern Rumelia, the southeastern section of the proposed big Bulgaria, was granted some administrative autonomy with a Christian governor but under the military and political control of the sultan; the rest of the proposed big Bulgaria was restored to the sultan without restrictions. Thus, at the expense of Bulgarian nationalism, the great powers endeavored to thwart Russia's hopes of increased influence in the Balkans. Rumania, Serbia, and Montenegro were formally recognized as independent, but the last two received less in territory than Russia had planned to give them. Of all the Balkan states, perhaps Greece fared best, for the congress recommended that Turkey cede her Thessaly, and this was done in 1881.

Russia, the victor in the war, received from Rumania [13] the small strip of Bessarabia, which she had lost by the treaty of Paris, and the region around Batum, Ardahan, and Kars, which she had conquered in the Caucasus. Austria-Hungary and Great Britain each took part of the spoils. The former gained the right to occupy and administer Bosnia and Herzegovina, the right to garrison Novibazar, and special commercial privileges in Serbia and Montenegro. The latter, in a separate Turco-British convention, obtained the island of Cyprus in the eastern Mediterranean in return for her promise to uphold the territorial integrity of the Ottoman Empire against any future Russian attack. To Russia it appeared that, though she had sacrificed thousands of lives and spent millions of rubles to improve her position in the Balkans, the Austrians and British, merely by cleverly playing the game of diplomacy, had secured in the final settlement greater gains.

Russia's humiliation at the Congress of Berlin contributed not at all to Alexander's popularity among Russian patriots, nor did the reactionary measures which his government had begun to take even before the Russo-Turkish War add to his popularity among the liberals and radicals. In fact, the liberal desire for a constitution was still further accentuated when Bulgaria, the little Slavic state created largely as a result of the tsar's efforts, received a constitution. In 1879 the terrorists published the tsar's "death sentence," and thereafter pursued more vigorously than ever their campaign of violence. Late in that year an attempt was made to wreck the tsar's train while it was on the way from the Crimea to the capital; and in February, 1880, the dining room of the Winter Palace was blown up, the tsar escaping death only because his expected guest was a half hour late. On the other hand, during these years the government redoubled its efforts in a countercampaign of oppression.

Ultimately Alexander decided that he must give way to liberal sentiment. He therefore appointed a commission headed by the minister of the interior, Loris Melikov, conferred upon it dictatorial powers, and authorized it to find a solution for the situation. Melikov believed that revolutionary activities could not be stopped by repressive measures alone. He argued that, if the government could placate the liberals by granting a moderate constitution, it could at the same time deprive the radicals of the moral support of this group. In February, 1881, the minister of the interior submitted to the tsar a scheme for associating popularly elected representatives with the government in legislative work. On March 13 the tsar signed Melikov's project, but later that same day, while driving on

[13] Rumania was forced to content herself with the annexation of part of the Dobrudja, with a population largely non-Rumanian.

the Catherine Canal, he was assassinated by a nihilist's bomb. "The bomb that killed Alexander put an end to the faint beginnings of Russian constitutionalism."

Reaction, Repression, and "Russification"

The new tsar, Alexander III, although undoubtedly courageous, industrious, and honest, was by intellect and education greatly limited in his outlook. He had opposed his father's return to a policy of liberalism in 1881, and for him his father's assassination was sufficient proof of the futility of such a course. Furthermore, by his intimate advisers—especially by Constantine Pobiedonostsev, his former tutor—Alexander III was strongly urged to abandon liberalism and to withhold from publication the projected scheme for political reform. It is not surprising, therefore, that the new tsar departed from his father's course and in his accession manifesto openly proclaimed his faith in the power and right of autocracy. The plan for establishing a sort of representative government, which had been devised by Melikov and accepted by Alexander II, was accordingly never executed. Instead, a policy of reaction and repression, at once inaugurated, was vigorously pursued throughout his reign.

Upon his death in 1894 Alexander III was succeeded by his twenty-six-year-old son, who ascended the throne as Nicholas II. Lacking most of the qualities of a statesman and leader, Nicholas was not particularly interested in political matters, but he was firmly determined to maintain the principle of autocracy unchanged. He was easily influenced by those surrounding him, and since in the early years of his reign many of his intimate advisers were inherited from his father, it is not surprising that he adopted and put into effect the political program of Alexander III. The granting of a constitution and the establishment of an imperial parliament were, in the words of Nicholas II, only "senseless dreams." From 1881 to 1917, therefore, Russia was subjected almost continuously to a policy of reaction, repression, and "Russification," though in the last decade of this period the accumulated popular discontent was usually at or near the explosive point.

The directing genius in this policy of repression was Pobiedonostsev, who held the office of procurator of the holy synod. He formulated for the tsarist policy of reaction a political theory based on a deep distrust of human intellect and human nature. "If all representatives of the people were saints," he wrote, "a parliamentary regime would be the very best kind of all; but as the morality of popular representatives is usually more than dubious, a parliamentary regime is the worst." To his mind democracy of the Western type was rotten, and only the Russian patri-

The T. F. Healy Collection

THE VICTIM OF A NIHILIST'S BOMB

The wounded Alexander II being conveyed to the Winter Palace.

archal system of government was still sound. Parliaments, freedom of the press, secular education, jury trials were all to him anathema. His position as lay chairman of the governing body of the Russian Orthodox Church he deliberately utilized to crush liberalism and foster reaction. Sermons of clergymen were censored, and village priests were instructed to report to the police any of their parishioners who appeared to be "politically untrustworthy."

Assisting Pobiedonostsev in the execution of the policy of repression was Viatscheslav Plehve, the director of the department of secret police in the ministry of the interior. Through the agency of the so-called "Third Section," which was authorized to make arrests without warrants and to punish without trials, Plehve sought to crush all opposition to the tsarist regime. Ubiquitous spies and secret police diligently ferreted out and mercilessly suppressed the liberals and radicals. Imprisonment, exile, or death was the lot of those who dared to oppose the government. Thousands were sent to penal colonies in the wilds of Siberia, while other thousands sought safety by flight to foreign countries.

In accordance with Alexander III's "cold storage" policy for Russia— that is, his policy of preserving Russian autocratic institutions by keeping them from being contaminated by contact with Western ideas—the program of repression was directed particularly against education and the press, the avenues through which a free public opinion might be expected to manifest itself. Children of the lower classes were excluded from the secondary schools, and Pobiedonostsev even made a futile attempt to have the primary schools transferred from the control of the local zemstvos to the church. The universities were deprived of all autonomy, and student clubs were forbidden. Courses of study were modified by government decree, and many well-known books by foreign authors were excluded from use by Russian intellectuals. When student demonstrations were staged against such measures, they were ruthlessly suppressed by troops. Many students were expelled from the universities; many were sent into exile. Intellectuals who were suspected of "revolutionary" political tendencies were placed under police supervision, while control of the press was made complete by subjecting most magazines and newspapers to a "preliminary censorship" of government agents.

To strengthen itself against the forces of liberalism and radicalism, the government sought to win the support of the nobles. Special privileges were extended to them in the realm of local government, and steps were taken to bring the peasants partly back under their control. For this purpose, apparently, the office of land captain was created. These land captains were appointed by the government from the nobility and were placed under the direct control of the tsar's minister of the interior. They were given not only administrative power in local affairs but also authority to act as judges over the peasants. Moreover, the system of representation in the zemstvos and dumas was deliberately altered so as to increase the influence of the nobility and of the wealthier classes, and at the same time other measures were inaugurated which were designed to weaken the influence of the peasants. After 1890, for instance, the latter were permitted to elect only candidates for the zemstvos, the actual peasant representatives being finally chosen by the governors from the list of candidates. Despite this alteration in the system of representation, however, the zemstvos and dumas continued to be suspected by the government, which deliberately weakened their powers while increasing those of the government-appointed provincial governors.

Accompanying the government's policy of reaction and repression was that of "Russification." It has already been pointed out that a considerable part of the population of the Russian Empire consisted of non-Russians. To Alexander III and his Slavophile ministers this situation constituted a challenge, and they inaugurated measures which were designed to meet it. They sought to achieve within the empire uniformity in such matters as language, religion, and general cultural ideals, and to this end vigorous steps were taken to crush all national feeling in the non-Russian parts of the realm—particularly in Finland, Poland, and the Baltic provinces.

Finland at the time of her conquest had been granted autonomy by Alexander I, and in the minds of the Finns their country was bound to Russia only by a personal union through the tsar. In accordance with the policy of "Russification," however, Finland's political rights were progressively ignored. In the nineties Russians began to supplant Finns in the higher administrative offices, and ability to use the Russian language became necessary for an officeholder in even the lower ranks of the administration. By an imperial decree (1899) the diet of Finland was arbitrarily reduced to the status of a mere consultative body, and a Russian was appointed secretary of state for Finland in defiance of the Finnish constitution. Eventually, Russian was made the official language of Finland (1900), the independent Finnish army was abolished and replaced by the Russian military system (1901), all administrative offices in Finland were opened to Russians (1902), and the tsarist system of espionage, arbitrary arrest, and imprisonment was extended to that grand duchy (1903).

Even under Alexander II repressive measures against the Poles had been initiated as a result of the Polish uprising of 1863, and under Alexander III further steps were taken to crush Polish nationalism. As a consequence, the use of the Polish language was made illegal, and all teachers were compelled to use Russian—even when they were giving instruction in Polish literature and language! The use of the Russian language on business and trade signs was made obligatory. Public offices in Poland were closed to Poles, and for more than a decade after 1885 Poles might not legally sell land to non-Russians. In the Baltic provinces of Estonia and Latvia, where German barons had long held an ascendancy over the peasants, the Slavophile goal was the destruction of the cultural dominance of the Germans. Russian was made the official language instead of German, and eventually in these provinces "Russification" went so far as to force the change of German place names to Russian and to forbid the use of German in both public and private educational institutions.

"Russification" also led to various measures of repression against the adherents of religious faiths other than Russian Orthodoxy. In the Baltic provinces, for example, the erection of Lutheran churches was made dependent upon the consent of the procurator of the holy synod, and Lutheran schools were placed under the control of the tsarist government. In Poland the government interfered with the Roman Catholic Church, depriving it of its revenues and converting parish priests into salaried state officials. Following the Polish uprising of 1863, many Roman Catholic monasteries had been suppressed and their property confiscated. In Lithuania and White Russia the "uniate" Catholics [14] were persecuted, their marriages and their children being officially considered as illegitimate.

The five million Jews who lived within the empire suffered particularly from the policy of "Russification." Since they differed from the great bulk of the Russians in race, religion, language, and social customs, their loyalty was suspected by the government, and they were openly discriminated against. During the eighties and nineties a number of anti-Jewish measures were introduced which definitely marked the Jews as a class apart. As a consequence, they became legally restricted in respect to their residence, their political rights, their educational opportunities, and their economic status.

In the matter of residence, all Jews were expected to live within the so-called Jewish Pale, which comprised the Ukraine, Poland, and Lithuania. Exceptions were offered for certain classes of Jews—university graduates, wealthy merchants, professional men, and artisans—who might, if they were fortunate, obtain special licenses from the government permitting them to reside outside the Pale. Within the Pale the Jews were generally compelled to live in towns and cities under the surveillance of the government. They were forbidden to move into the smaller villages. Their political rights were definitely restricted, for they could not vote for mem-

---

[14] The Uniates—members of the United Greek Church—retained many of the practices of the Greek Orthodox Church, but recognized the leadership of the pope at Rome.

bers of the dumas in the cities in which they lived but had to be content with such representatives as the governor might appoint. In the matter of education the number of Jews who might enter secondary schools and universities was limited to a fixed percentage of the student body which ranged from 3 per cent to 10 per cent, depending upon the location of the institution. Many were forced to leave Russia in order to obtain the education which they desired.

Economically, the Jews were subjected to numerous restrictions. They could not legally buy or lease land in rural districts. Practically all public employment was closed to them. Authority had to be secured from the government before a Jew could become a lawyer, for the government sought to limit the number of Jews in the various professions. The number of Jewish stockholders in any industrial corporation was definitely limited. Although obliged to serve in the army, they might not rise to the rank of officer. As a result of these restrictions, many Jews became, almost of necessity, bankers or retail merchants. In these capacities they frequently won the hatred of the peasants because of their high rates of interest or high mercantile profits.

It must not be thought, of course, that all of these laws were always and everywhere enforced. Russian officials were frequently open to corruption, and Jews by "paying the price" might gain a certain precarious immunity. On the other hand, Russian officials sometimes went to the other extreme and did not afford the Jews the protection to which they were legally entitled. At times anti-Jewish riots—pogroms—broke out, at which time Jews were more or less systematically subjected to plundering and even massacre while the police looked on with toleration. Perhaps the most notorious of these pogroms occurred in 1903 in the Bessarabian city of Kishinev, when the Jewish quarter of the city was raided and hundreds of Jews were killed or wounded. Anti-Jewish legislation and pogroms such as this led hundreds of thousands of Jews to migrate from Russia to the United States, carrying with them their deep-seated and bitter hatred of the tsarist regime.

The Introduction of Modern Industrialism

Despite the government's policy of reaction and repression, economic developments during the reigns of Alexander III and Nicholas II were producing certain classes which were destined eventually to challenge and destroy the government responsible for that policy. Until about the time of Alexander III, Russia had remained almost exclusively an agricultural country, a land of peasants dominated by a landed aristocracy and an Orthodox clergy. There was no strong and ambitious bourgeois class and no numerous and aggressive group of industrial workers. Beginning in the eighties, however, this condition was gradually altered by the introduction of modern industrialism of the Western type.

A number of factors made possible Russia's relatively rapid industrial development in the succeeding years. In the first place, the empire possessed considerable quantities of such basic raw materials as coal, iron, and petroleum. In the second place, an abundant supply of cheap labor was available during these years because of the rapid growth of the peasant population after emancipation, with the consequent pressure of rural population on the inadequate land-holdings.[15] In the third place, in the late eighties Russia began to borrow extensively from abroad and thus secured funds not only for stabilizing her currency and for military purposes, but also for railway construction and for loans to private industrial enterprises as well. And what the Russian government did in these respects Russian bankers and private industrialists did also. By 1914 foreign loans totaling billions of dollars had been utilized, in part, to provide the needed capital for the development of Russia's resources.

The one who did most, perhaps, to hasten the advent of modern industrialism in Russia in the years before the First World War was Sergius Witte, "the Colbert of Russia." After having served as head of the government's department of railways and as minister of communications, in 1892 he became Alexander III's minister of finance, a post in which he was retained by Nicholas II until 1903. Not without considerable opposition from Slavophiles—who looked upon the development of Russian industrialism as an injury to the peasants and a menace to autocracy— Witte did his utmost to encourage the rise of industry and the expansion of railway facilities within the empire. He assiduously sought foreign loans to finance both industry and transportation and deliberately pursued a policy of high protective tariffs to aid the former.

The economic consequences of Russia's adoption of modern industrialism soon became obvious. By 1895 the railway mileage within the Russian Empire had risen to approximately 22,000; by 1914 it had increased to more than 40,000. Railways transformed the economic situation in Russia, for with railways it became possible to link together the vast resources of the empire, to transport commodities from places of abundance to areas of scarcity, to get goods more readily and assuredly to markets both at home and abroad. In consequence, mines were opened, factories were constructed, and commerce was increased. From the Donets basin by 1914 came annually millions of tons of coal; from the region about Baku came other millions of tons of petroleum. By 1914, too, Russia was producing more than four million tons of pig iron being exceeded

15 Between 1850 and 1900 the population of Russia doubled.

in this respect only by Great Britain, the United States, and Germany. But the most important branch of Russia's industries was the manufacture of textiles. By 1914 Russia was able not only to satisfy her home demand for cotton goods but to compete successfully in foreign markets as well. In the production of cotton goods she stood fourth in the world.[16]

The introduction of modern industrialism into Russia and the consequent need for obtaining large loans from abroad had an influence also upon the government's foreign policy. Before the eighties Russia's foreign loans had been floated largely in Germany, but during that decade the increased demand for funds to advance Germany's own industrial and imperial progress began to absorb German capital. Furthermore, Bismarck sought to bring political pressure on Russia by excluding her bonds from the Berlin stock exchange. But Russia was increasingly in need of foreign financial assistance, and when a group of French bankers offered in 1888 to grant a loan to her, she turned to France as the source of her future borrowings. Naturally, the relations between the two governments became more cordial. Consequently, when in 1890 Germany declined to renew the existing reinsurance treaty with Russia [17] and the latter found herself cast adrift and isolated among the powers, it was almost inevitable that she should look with favor upon suggestions of a *rapprochement* when they were made by French statesmen. The result, as has already been pointed out,[18] was the Franco-Russian entente of 1891, which led in 1894 to the Franco-Russian defensive alliance against Germany.

Connected, also, with Russia's industrialization were the efforts made under Witte's direction to advance Russia's economic penetration of regions adjoining the empire. In the early nineties, for instance, Witte called attention to the economic opportunities which were open to Russia in Persia. In consequence, a Russo-Persian bank was organized, and, supported by the tsarist government, it undertook to finance Russian concessions and Russian trade in Persia. In the succeeding years Persia became the principal foreign market for Russia's cotton industries, which were able successfully to compete there with British goods.

But Witte's attention was not focused merely on the Middle East. Under his direction the construction of a trans-Siberian railway was begun in the nineties in order that European Russia might have a railway connection with Vladivostok, her port on the Sea of Japan. For more than a decade thereafter the work was pushed forward with funds provided largely by loans floated in France. In 1905 the 5000-mile, single-track railway was

[16] Because of the protective tariffs, however, the great bulk of the Russians—the peasants—had to pay higher prices for many commodities than they had paid before the advent of industrialism in Russia.

[17] See page 70.

[18] See page 104.

finally completed, and railway communication between St. Petersburg and Vladivostok was actually inaugurated.

Imperialism in the Far East

The construction of the trans-Siberian railway constituted part of Russia's century-long search for a suitable outlet to the high seas. Her attempts to advance to the Mediterranean, made earlier in the nineteenth century, had been resolutely checked by the great powers. Her move southward through central Asia had likewise been stopped—at least temporarily —by Great Britain in the eighties. In the nineties Russia temporarily laid aside her ambitions in the Balkans [19] and determined to seek a warm-water port in the Far East. She saw no reason why, if the powers were bent upon dismembering China, she should not secure her share, especially since by pushing southward through Chinese territory she might obtain an all-year ice-free port. Russia apparently marked out for her immediate expansion the Chinese territories of Manchuria and Korea. These, if annexed to the Russian Empire or if converted into Russian spheres of influence, would provide excellent ports to supplement Vladivostok, which was closed for part of each year. Control of Manchuria, moreover, would enable Russia to build across that province a shorter and more direct line to Vladivostok.

Probably, if Russia had had to deal only with the "backward" Chinese, she would have succeeded in carrying through these plans in the Far East with a large degree of success. But unfortunately for Russia's ambitions, she was forced to deal not only with the Chinese but with the Japanese as well. As already pointed out, Japan in the second half of the nineteenth century had been rapidly adopting many Western ideas and institutions, had rapidly industrialized herself, and by the closing decade of the century was ready to embark upon a program of imperial expansion. She was especially desirous of securing Korea, a tributary kingdom of China lying on the Asiatic mainland just across Tsushima Strait from Japanese territory. As a result of Japanese interference in Korean affairs a war was precipitated between China and Japan in 1894.

The Sino-Japanese War of 1894–1895 quickly revealed that the Chinese were no match for the Japanese, who had modernized their military and naval forces. By the treaty of Shimonoseki, which Japan dictated to China, the latter agreed (1) to cede to Japan the island of Formosa and the Liaotung peninsula in southern Manchuria, (2) to pay an indemnity of $150,000,000, and (3) to recognize Korea as an independent kingdom. Independence for Korea was generally recognized as merely a step prelim-

---

[19] For the Austro-Russian treaty of 1897, see page 300.

inary to absorption by Japan. Naturally, Japan's acquisition of a foothold on the Asiatic mainland in territory desired by Russia was particularly distasteful to the latter. If Korea came into the hands of Japan, the latter would control both sides of Tsushima Strait, the southern outlet of the Sea of Japan upon which Vladivostok was located. Should Japan also secure Port Arthur and the Liaotung peninsula, Russia would be prevented from obtaining a warm-water port in that region.

Russia therefore determined to force Japan to withdraw from the Asiatic mainland and turned to France and Germany for support in this program. France, which had only recently succeeded in securing Russia as an ally, naturally responded with alacrity to the Russian request for joint intervention in the Far East. At the same time the Kaiser, desiring Russia's support for Germany's contemplated plans in the Far East,[20] willingly lent his support to the Russian plan of intervention. Possibly the Kaiser even hoped to weaken the Franco-Russian alliance by helping one member of that alliance to become so deeply involved in the Far East that it would be unable to play an aggressive role in the West.[21]

Soon after the conclusion of the treaty of Shimonoseki the three powers in a joint note "advised" Japan to refrain from annexing any part of the Chinese mainland. Japan had not yet proved her mettle against any of the great powers of the West and could not contemplate with equanimity a clash between herself and a coalition consisting of Russia, Germany, and France. She therefore gave up her claim to territory on the Asiatic mainland and in return received from China an additional indemnity of $22,500,000.

Russia, posing as the defender of Chinese territorial integrity, next sought to advance her own position in China. In 1896 a treaty of friendship was concluded between Russia and China in which the former undertook to aid the latter in case she were attacked by a third power. China, on her part, was persuaded to permit the establishment of the Russo-Chinese Bank,[22] which was to assist the Chinese government to meet its indemnity payments to Japan and which was also authorized to embark upon various types of financial and economic enterprises in China. Later in the same year this newly organized bank secured a concession to build the Chinese Eastern Railway from Chita in Siberia across Manchuria to Vladivostok. Such a railway would obviously connect Russia's port in the Far East with inland Siberia and European Russia by a much shorter and more direct route than that of the circuitous trans-Siberian railway.

[20] See page 73.
[21] "We must try," wrote the Kaiser in 1895, "to nail Russia down in eastern Asia, so that she may occupy herself less with Europe and the Near East."
[22] It was organized as a Russian corporation.

The political nature of the proposed railway was indicated by the fact that its bonds were to be guaranteed by the Russian government and that Russian military guards could be stationed along the railway to maintain order even in time of peace.

In 1898 Russia further strengthened her position in the Far East by securing (1) a twenty-five-year lease of about five hundred square miles of territory—including part of the region surrendered by Japan in 1895 —at the end of the Liaotung peninsula, and (2) the right to construct a branch line to connect this territory with the Chinese Eastern Railway at Harbin.[23] Subsequently the harbor of Dairen was improved for commercial use, and a powerful fortress and a naval base were constructed at Port Arthur. At last Russia had a warm-water outlet for her trans-Siberian railway. Moreover, Manchuria, it appeared, must inevitably come under Russia's economic and military dominance, for the railways would largely control the commerce of the province,[24] and would greatly facilitate the movement of Russian troops. Furthermore, the stationing of Russian guards along the railway routes and the presence of Russian military and naval forces at Port Arthur presaged ill for Chinese sovereignty in Manchuria. During the Boxer rebellion (1900), in fact, Russia sent troops into the province apparently with a view to detaching it from China, and after the rebellion she neglected to withdraw them.

Russia's apparent decision to annex Manchuria was particularly distasteful to the Japanese. The latter therefore protested against the former's military occupation of the province, and Russia promised to withdraw her forces—but again neglected to do so. Actually Russia was determined to hold Manchuria and even had visions of adding Korea also. Russians were already trying to gain concessions and political influence in that kingdom. But Korea, though nominally independent, had since 1895 been considered by the Japanese as their special sphere. They naturally became alarmed. For a time, however, Japanese statesmen were divided as to the correct policy to pursue. Some argued that Japan might better come to a compromise agreement with Russia and permit the latter to seize Manchuria. Others held that a war against Russia was inevitable and that Japan should seek to secure an anti-Russian alliance with Great Britain.

In 1901 Japan opened negotiations with both St. Petersburg and London. As it chanced, Great Britain also was alarmed by Russia's activities

[23] Great Britain attempted through diplomacy to prevent Russia's acquisition of these bases, but Russia was supported by Germany and France and secured Japan's acquiescence by concessions to the latter in Korea. In the end Great Britain had to be content with the lease of Weihaiwei on the northern coast of the Shantung peninsula, on the southern coast of which Germany had just secured a foothold at Kiaochow (see page 73). France joined in the scramble for leases and obtained a concession on the shores of Kwangchow Bay.

[24] The Chinese Eastern Railway was given mining rights along its route.

in the Far East and was ready to abandon her long-cherished policy of isolation for an Anglo-Japanese alliance. The treaty concluding such an alliance was signed in January, 1902.[25] The terms of the alliance assured Japan that, if war occurred between herself and Russia, Great Britain would remain neutral, and that, if any power assisted Russia in such a war, Great Britain would come to the aid of Japan. By thus choosing to ally herself with Great Britain, Japan, it appeared, had determined to check Russian expansion in the Far East even at the cost of war.

The Russo-Japanese War

In 1903 Japan attempted to reach an agreement with Russia. As a preliminary she demanded that the latter withdraw her troops from Manchuria. She suggested, however, that she might be willing to recognize Russia's ascendancy in the greater part of that province if Russia would recognize Japan's right of intervention in Korea and if Japan might build a railway from Korea into Manchuria to connect with the Chinese Eastern. When Russia hesitated to commit herself and delayed making a definite reply, the Japanese government became impatient and broke off diplomatic relations. Japanese statesmen apparently believed that Russia by her dilatory tactics was merely trying to postpone the inevitable conflict until her strategic railways in the Far East should be completed and until her Pacific war fleet should be freed from the handicap of winter's ice. They decided not to wait for Russia's convenience and on February 8, 1904, Japan launched a surprise attack upon the Russian warships at Port Arthur. Two days later she formally declared war. A struggle to determine which power should dominate the Far East was thus inaugurated.

To the casual observer it appeared that the war was to be a conflict between a powerful giant from the West and an inexperienced, weak pigmy from the East. But superficial appearances were altogether deceiving. Although Russia was vastly superior in man power and resources, she was seriously handicapped from the very outset by her inability to bring her full strength to bear. The scene of the conflict was far distant from the heart of Russia, and her troops and supplies had to be transported thousands of miles over the single-track trans-Siberian railway. Furthermore, although the Russian troops were probably not greatly inferior to the Japanese, they lacked enthusiasm for the war, whose purpose they either did not understand or did not approve. In fact, the war never received the whole-hearted support of the Russian people. Moreover, the twin evils of inefficiency and corruption, which had so often undermined Russian armies in the past, were again present and operative. Finally, it

[25] For the terms, see pages 179–180.

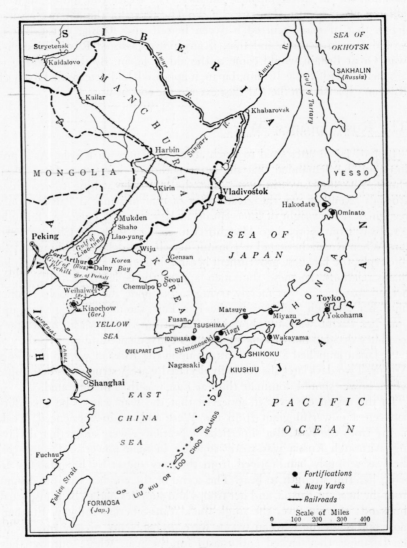

THE FAR EAST IN 1904

was Russia's misfortune to have a supreme command which lacked initiative and strategic ability.

Japan, on the other hand, had a highly disciplined, efficient, and enthusiastic military force, which was ably directed by its commanding officers and loyally supported by the populace at home. Furthermore, she was in close proximity to the seat of hostilities and in a position to place her forces in the field with a minimum of difficulty. Perhaps most important of all, as a result of her surprise stroke against the Russian warships Japan was in complete control of the sea. Without such control, in fact, she could hardly have maintained an army on the Asiatic mainland. It was the realization of this fact that had led her to cripple Russia's fleet by a surprise attack before war was formally declared.

With the Russian fleet at Port Arthur severely damaged, Japan proceeded to rush her troops into southern Manchuria. There they cut off Port Arthur, drove the tsar's forces back to the north, and in the autumn of 1904 succeeded in defeating the main Russian army under General Kuropatkin in a great battle at Liaoyang. Early in 1905 Port Arthur, besieged by land and blockaded by sea, surrendered to the Japanese. In March the Russian army was again decisively defeated, this time in a ten-day battle farther north at Mukden. Following this disaster, the possibility of a Russian victory in the war appeared to hang on the fate of a Russian fleet which was even then on its way to engage the Japanese.

In September, 1904, thirty-six Russian warships, commanded by Admiral Rozhestvensky, had left the Baltic bound for Japanese waters. Part of the fleet had gone eastward through the Mediterranean while the main detachment had proceeded around Africa, and not until the spring of 1905 had the reunited fleet eventually reached Far Eastern waters. At the time of the defeat at Mukden it was slowly feeling its way northward through the South China Sea and up the Chinese coast. If the Russians could win the impending naval engagement and gain control of the sea, they would be in a position to isolate the Japanese army in Manchuria and even to bombard Japanese coast cities and towns. Japan might be forced to withdraw from the war. But an increasing sense of despair prevailed among the men in the Russian fleet, who realized that an incompetent government had sent them on a mad naval venture. Already absent eight months from their Baltic bases, having steamed halfway around the world, they were destined to meet in its home waters an efficient modern fleet of proved mettle and with a capable commander in the person of Admiral Togo.

On May 15 the Russian warships encountered Admiral Togo's whole fleet off the coast of the Japanese island of Tsushima. In the ensuing battle the Russians were outnumbered, outmaneuvered, and outshot. Almost before they knew what had struck them they were disastrously defeated. Most of the Russian ships were sunk or captured by the Japanese. A half dozen or so escaped to neutral ports, where they were interned. Only three of the smallest vessels succeeded in reaching their destination in the harbor of Vladivostok. Russia's dramatic effort to wrest the control of Far Eastern waters from Japan had proved a dismal failure; the naval disaster rang the death knell on Russia's hope of final victory.

Both the German Kaiser and the American President Roosevelt now urged peace upon the belligerents. Although Russia with her vast resources and man power might possibly have sent new armies to continue the struggle in the Far East, popular discontent and revolutionary outbreaks at home were alarming the tsar's ministers, who were therefore not unwilling to consider peace proposals. On the other hand, the Japanese by their military efforts had nearly bankrupted themselves and so were quite ready to halt their military operations. On President Roosevelt's invitation a peace conference was opened at Portsmouth, New Hampshire. Sergius Witte ably represented the tsar at the conference and succeeded in saving Russia from the worst consequences of her disastrous defeat. By the treaty of Portsmouth (September 5, 1905) Russia's lease of the Liaotung peninsula, Russia's railway from Port Arthur north to Changchun, and Russian coal-mining rights in southern Manchuria were all transferred to Japan, thus converting southern Manchuria into a Japanese sphere of influence. Russia recognized Japan's preponderant interest in Korea and her right to control and protect the Korean government. In addition, Russia surrendered to Japan the southern half of the island of Sakhalin, which Japan had occupied during the war. Clearly the Japanese had administered a definite check to Russian expansion in the Far East. They had furthermore demonstrated not only to the tsar but to the world at large that a new great power had appeared which must thereafter be considered in dealing with affairs in that part of the globe.

The Revolution of 1905

Perhaps the chief reason why the tsarist government gave up so soon its struggle against Japan in the Far East was that it was being confronted at home by widespread unrest and revolutionary outbreaks. As between the loss—perhaps only temporary—of prestige and power and territory in the Far East and the complete collapse of autocratic government within Russia the tsar considered the former as the less of the two evils. And in 1905 the downfall of Russian autocracy seemed imminent. The repressive policies of Alexander III and Nicholas II had signally failed to crush out liberal and radical opposition to the tsarist regime. Discontent had remained general and had grown with the passing years. And the introduction of modern industrialism in Russia had further contributed to the growth of unrest, for it had increased both in number and in strength the bourgeois capitalist class and the industrial proletariat.

In the opening decade of the twentieth century there were several distinct groups which sought to introduce political and economic changes in Russia. The proletariat, deprived of any real voice in the government and oppressed by an industrial system which forbade the organization of trade unions,[26] had offered a fertile field for socialist propaganda. Marxian socialists had soon gained the attention of the factory workers, and in the nineties industrial strikes had begun to occur. Eventually, in 1898, the Social Democratic Party was organized in Russia, and its members began to plan for the time when political power might be theirs, when factories might be seized, the capitalists turned out, and a millennium of shorter hours, increased wages, and better conditions ushered in. They therefore sought to overthrow the empire in order to erect in its stead a socialist republic.

In 1903 the Social Democratic Party, at a congress held outside Russia, split into two wings: the *Bolsheviki* or majority, led by Nicholas Lenin, and the *Mensheviki* or minority, led by George Plekhanov. Originally they differed only in matters of party organization, but in the course of years they came to differ fundamentally on the question of party tactics as well. The Bolsheviks were the extremists, opposed to any co-operation with bourgeois parties, opposed to the policy of gradual reform, in favor of a cataclysmic upheaval which should establish the regime of the proletariat. The Mensheviks, on the other hand, were the moderates, willing, if necessary, to bring in the socialist regime gradually through the slow education of the masses, even with the co-operation of the moderately liberal groups. In other words, the Bolsheviks were more "revolutionary," the Mensheviks more "evolutionary."

Another socialist group, founded about 1900 and known as the Socialist Revolutionary Party, undertook to advance the interests of the peasants. Its members were interested chiefly in the land problem and sought to transform the land from private property into "the property of the whole people." The lands which the peasants had been permitted to buy at the time of their emancipation had been inadequate to support them, and the steady increase in population and subsequent subdivision of estates had considerably reduced the per capita holdings. In consequence, millions of land-hungry Russians gazed enviously upon the remaining estates of the

[26] Although the government restricted the development of trade unions, it did attempt to improve the lot of the industrial workers. Various laws limited hours of work, regulated the employment of children, and provided for accident compensation.

crown, the church, and the aristocracy and longed for the time when they might be seized and parceled out. The Socialist Revolutionary program, therefore, aimed at the destruction of both the political and the social regime of Russia for the benefit of the peasant masses.

What may be called a liberal group was also eventually organized and consisted largely of the professional classes of the cities and the more progressive elements of the nobility, who had been active in the district and provincial zemstvos. Utilizing the latter as a medium for discussion, these nobles had sought to secure better educational facilities, a fairer electoral system, removal of restrictions upon the zemstvos, and the crowning of the zemstvo system by the establishment of an elective national zemstvo. In 1903 secret conferences held outside Russia resulted in a union of the bourgeois liberals with the progressive zemstvo leaders in an organization called the Union of Liberation. The liberals, as well as the Socialist Revolutionaries, were interested in the land question, and they advocated a policy of compensated expropriation of the holdings of the aristocracy and the state in order to improve the lot of the peasants. Their political program called for a democratic, parliamentary monarchy like that of Great Britain. The "unifying influence of tsardom," they believed, was essential for the preservation of Russian national unity.

But discontent was not limited to the Russians proper. It was inevitable that the government's policy of "Russification" should also arouse strong opposition among the oppressed national groups within the empire. This was particularly true of the Finns, who never ceased to demand that the domestic independence of their grand duchy be respected. It was likewise true of the Poles and Jews, who had suffered severely at the hand of the tsarist government. Groups like these awaited only a favorable opportunity to implement their discontent and could be counted upon with a fair degree of certainty to align themselves with or take advantage of any Russian revolutionary movement in order to force the tsar to make concessions to them.

The outbreak of the Russo-Japanese War in 1904 had greatly increased popular discontent in Russia, partly because most of the people had no clear idea why it was being fought, and partly because evidences of corruption and inefficiency were at once revealed in the lamentable failure to provide the army with adequate munitions, equipment, and supplies. The growing unrest within the country received a startling confirmation when, in July, 1904, the tsar's reactionary minister of the interior, Plehve, was assassinated. Temporarily it seemed that Nicholas II might become less reactionary. Prince Mirsky, a liberal, was appointed to succeed Plehve, and in November, 1904, the government even permitted representatives of the zemstvos and dumas to meet informally in a national congress.

From the latter came a petition requesting Nicholas II not only to guarantee individual liberties, but to extend local self-government and to establish a national parliament. In response to this petition the tsar's government did grant a few reforms but very carefully refrained from taking any step to provide for a national parliament. The liberal and radical groups remained, therefore, far from satisfied, and popular agitation continued unchecked.

In the early days of 1905 St. Petersburg was paralyzed by a strike which involved tens of thousands of workers. A priest, Father Gapon, sought to lead some of the strikers and drafted a petition to Nicholas requesting a number of moderate economic and political reforms. On Sunday, January 22, 1905, Father Gapon led a procession of several thousand people—men, women, and children—to the Winter Palace to present this petition to the tsar personally. Although the priest and his followers gave no indication of desire to provoke disorder or to start a revolt, the procession was fired upon by the military as it approached the palace. As a consequence, several hundred persons were killed and nearly three thousand were wounded. When news of the events of "Bloody Sunday" became known, it was at once answered by further strikes and political demonstrations. The government now became genuinely alarmed and decided to suppress popular unrest by resort to force. The liberal Mirsky was therefore summarily dismissed from office, and the reactionary General Trepov was instructed to restore order in the capital.

But the brutal measures of the latter failed to cow the radicals. In February Grand Duke Sergius, the tsar's uncle, was assassinated, and others less prominent in government circles from time to time suffered a similar fate. The popular movement for reform—now become, in fact, revolutionary—continued unabated. Political meetings and banquets were held despite police activities. Influenced by Social Democratic leaders, workers in nearly every type of industry struck. The transportation and communication systems were disrupted. At the height of the movement the strange spectacle was presented of restaurant waiters, university professors, chorus girls, drug clerks, newspapermen, college students, skilled workers, manual laborers all striking in an attempt to force the tsar to grant reforms. In rural regions the peasants under Socialist Revolutionary leaders showed their dissatisfaction by attacking the landed aristocracy, burning their homes, and pillaging their barns. Subject nationalities in Poland and in the Caucasus seized upon the occasion to try to secure national concessions. Revolt spread even into the imperial navy, where the crew of the battleship *Potemkin* joined the revolutionary movement.

With the greater part of his armed forces thousands of miles away in Manchuria, the tsar was in no position to suppress such a widespread movement by force and decided that he must bend before the revolutionary storm. In an attempt to weather the popular hurricane—without actually surrendering his autocratic power—Nicholas II in a succession of decrees granted religious toleration, relaxed the enforcement of anti-Jewish legislation, remitted the land payments of those peasants who were in arrears, conceded the right of Poles and Lithuanians to use their languages in private schools, placed the trial of political offenders in the hands of the regular courts, promised to call a national assembly, dismissed Trepov, Pobiedonostsev, and many others, and called Witte—who had just negotiated peace with Japan—to serve as his chief minister. Such concessions, designed to win the support of the peasants, subject nationalities, and moderate liberals, left the political structure of Russia practically unchanged, however, and were themselves subject to arbitrary alteration in the future if the tsarist autocracy continued. The revolutionary storm, therefore, did not subside. Instead, the empire's economic life was brought almost to a standstill. Faced by this crisis, the tsar was at length forced to give way.

In October, 1905, Nicholas II issued a manifesto granting freedom of speech, of the press, and of association, promising the institution of a national legislature, the Duma, to represent all classes of the people, and proclaiming the "immutable rule" that no law would thereafter be considered binding without the consent of the Duma, that to the people would be given "the power to exercise an effective supervision over the acts of the officials." In an effort to win greater popular support a decree was issued reducing by 50 per cent the peasants' land payments for 1906 and canceling all payments after January 1, 1907.[27] Further to strengthen the government, another decree in December, 1905, made suffrage for the new Duma practically universal. To appease the Finns, who had inaugurated a general strike, their grand duchy was given back its right of local autonomy, and the Finns were conceded the authority to draft a constitution to take the place of the one suppressed by the tsar in 1899.

It is quite obvious that the popular movement which had forced the tsar thus to grant concessions rested upon the support of many and diverse elements of the Russian people, and that, once some of the groups had attained their ends, the united front would begin to disintegrate. Many of the more moderate liberals, for instance, were willing to accept the tsar's October manifesto as satisfactory and final. The Octobrists, as they were soon called, consisted chiefly of liberal nobles and industrial capitalists who favored a government in which the Duma should play a role subordinate to the divine-right monarch, somewhat as did the Landtag of Prussia. They advocated the continuation of a centralized regime and

[27] According to the calculations of the government these payments would not have ended legally until 1931.

were somewhat sympathetic with the Slavophile policy of "Russification." Their most outstanding leader was Alexander Guchkov. *Octobrists*

On the other hand, the more pronounced liberals, who organized the Constitutional Democratic Party under the leadership of the distinguished Russian historian, Paul N. Miliukov, considered the tsar's manifesto only the beginning of necessary political reform. The Constitutional Democrats or "Cadets," as they were called, advocated a constitutional government based on the doctrine of popular sovereignty. They urged that the first Duma should not confine itself to legislative functions but should act as a constituent assembly to draft a constitution for Russia. This constitution, according to them, should transform the tsar into a mere titular head of the empire and give real executive power to a ministry responsible to the Duma. In short, the Cadets envisaged the conversion of Russia into a democratic, parliamentary monarchy like the British. Many of them, moreover, advocated a federal structure of government which would make possible a greater degree of cultural and political autonomy for the subject peoples of Russia. The Cadets were drawn chiefly from the professional classes, university men, and more progressive bourgeoisie.

Naturally the October manifesto failed to satisfy the Social Democrats. But among the latter there were differences of opinion as to what should be done, now that the tsar had made concessions. The Mensheviks believed that Russia was not yet ready for socialism, that the most that could be expected at that time was the establishment of a democratic republic in which the masses could through a national parliament work for socialist institutions and the improvement of the lot of the working people. A soviet or council of workers' delegates—largely Mensheviks—had been organized in St. Petersburg and had played an important role in directing the general strike which had paralyzed the economic life of Russia. This soviet, which came largely under the influence of Leon Trotsky after his arrival in October, 1905, planned to push the political revolution still further by renewed strikes.

But many of the Bolshevik leaders, including Nicholas Lenin, who returned to Russia in November, held aloof from the soviet movement. They were not so much interested in democracy under capitalist auspices as they were in the overthrow of capitalism itself. These Bolshevik leaders condemned the Mensheviks' willingness to co-operate with the liberals, and Lenin's attitude did much to undermine the soviet. In fact, the first experiment with a workers' soviet was short-lived. A second general strike called by it in November was a failure, and in December another attempt to launch such a movement met with little response. Following Witte's arrest of nearly two hundred leaders of the workers, the soviet movement utterly collapsed. An armed insurrection in Moscow, instigated by the

Bolsheviks near the end of the year, was likewise eventually suppressed.

By this time many of the moderate elements in Russia, genuinely alarmed by the continued violence of the radicals, had begun to rally to the side of the tsar, who naturally received also the support of most of the beneficiaries of the old regime. Eventually, with the gradual return of Russian troops from the Far East after the signing of the treaty of Portsmouth, the moment of fear which had impelled the tsar to make his liberal concessions passed away, and then—in spite of Count Witte's opposition— came a systematic attempt on the part of the governmental clique to restore as much as possible of the autocratic system. The nationalistic revolts in the Caucasus and in Poland were violently suppressed. To intimidate opposition in other quarters a veritable reign of terror was inaugurated through the agency of pogroms and the activities of the "Black Hundreds" —gangs of hoodlums who were encouraged to attack the people. In the rural regions the peasants were forcibly pacified by troops loyal to the government. Thousands of Russians were arrested or executed in the ensuing months.

In March, 1906, the tsar undertook to annul the October manifesto so far as its most important features were concerned. By a further decree an upper house, the Council of the Empire, was created and given power co-ordinate with the Duma. Of two hundred members, half were appointed by the tsar and the rest were chosen by various institutional organizations. Obviously, the purpose of this second house was to act as a check upon the popularly elected Duma in the interest of tsarist autocracy. It was also decreed that the fundamental laws of the empire were not to be within the power of the Duma, and that foreign affairs, the army, and the navy belonged exclusively to the tsar's jurisdiction. It was provided that between sessions of the Duma any matter might, in case of emergency, be dealt with by executive decree, the latter to become law in case the Duma did not enact legislation on the subject during the first two months of its next session. Finally, in case the budget or laws concerning army recruits had not been passed by May 1 of any year, the government might legally use the figures for the preceding period. Thus the Duma was effectively blocked in advance if it should attempt to use "the power of the purse strings" to coerce the tsar. The increasing influence of the reactionaries was further revealed when on May 2, 1906, shortly before the first Duma was to convene, Witte was dismissed as prime minister and was succeeded by Goremykin, an old man who was largely the tool of the supporters of autocracy. Another strong reactionary, Peter Stolypin, was given the important position of minister of the interior.

Meanwhile, elections for the first Duma had been held. The Social Democrats and the Socialist Revolutionaries as parties both boycotted the elections because they wanted not a legislative but a constituent assembly. A group of radicals, called the Labor Party, however, secured somewhat more than a hundred seats, and unorganized peasants, chiefly interested in agrarian reform, obtained about two hundred. The supporters of the government consisted chiefly of a small number of Octobrists and a few conservatives and reactionaries. Of all the organized groups the Constitutional Democrats held the most seats and largely dominated the Duma. The outcome of the elections might possibly have been more alarming to the tsar except for the fact that shortly before his resignation Count Witte had secured from French and British bankers a loan of $450,000,000. With this sum available the government was in a position to treat somewhat cavalierly the demands of the Duma.

The latter soon after convening petitioned the tsar to abolish the Council of the Empire, to recognize ministerial responsibility to the Duma, to permit the expropriation of the estates of the landlords for the benefit of the peasants, and to grant amnesty for political prisoners. Since the tsar had no intention of granting such reforms, a deadlock ensued, for the Duma on its part then refused to enact the few laws requested by the government. In the end the Duma was dissolved by the tsar. In a futile attempt to rally popular support for the Duma, the Cadet deputies and a few others thereupon assembled in Viborg in Finland and issued a manifesto appealing to the Russian people to refuse taxes and military service. When a few spasmodic antigovernment revolts occurred, however, they were quickly suppressed by tsarist forces, and many revolutionaries were executed or exiled to Siberia. The signers of the Viborg manifesto themselves were disfranchised, with the result that the Constitutional Democratic Party lost many of its more aggressive leaders.

Elections were eventually held for a second Duma, and, despite the government's efforts to influence the vote, the result was practically the same as before. Opponents of the system of autocracy controlled an overwhelming majority of the seats. And the fate of the second Duma was the same as that of the first; in June, 1907, it was likewise arbitrarily dissolved. The tsar thereupon issued what amounted to a constitutional amendment drastically altering the electoral system. The representation of the subject nationalities was greatly reduced, in some cases abolished altogether; and the political influence of the landlord class was much increased by the introduction of a system of indirect representation on a class basis something like that existing in Prussia. As a result of these measures, the third Duma, elected in the autumn of 1907, was satisfactory to the tsarist government. The Cadets and the Left groups altogether controlled less than seventy-five seats, while the Octobrists and others on the Right held approximately four times as many. The new Duma was accordingly permitted to function until the expiration of its term; the fourth Duma, elected in 1912, was also acceptable to the government and was still in existence when Russia entered the First World War.

Looking back upon the events of 1905 and the two succeeding years, opponents of the autocratic regime felt that all their efforts to secure for Russia a liberal parliamentary government had been largely futile. With the tsar reserving to himself the right arbitrarily to alter at any time the constitutional basis of the imperial government, as he had done in 1907, Russia could hardly be said to have a constitutional government in the true sense of the term. With the imperial ministers responsible to the tsar alone, parliamentary government as it was understood in the West was entirely lacking in Russia. Finally, with so many state matters excluded from the jurisdiction of the Duma, the latter could hardly be considered even a legislative body in the full meaning of the term. Thanks largely to the military support of a loyal army, the financial and moral support of foreign governments, and the division among the revolutionists, Russian autocracy came through the upheaval of 1905 with only minor political losses.

The Eve of the First World War

In the years from 1906 to 1914 the situation in Russia largely resembled that which had preceded the revolutionary movement of 1905. On the side of the government reaction and repression were again in the ascendancy. Year by year scores—sometimes hundreds—were sentenced to death for their political activities, while a more or less steady stream of Russians passed as exiles into Siberia or fled in desperation to foreign countries. Once more, too, the policy of "Russification" was vigorously pushed, particularly against the Jews, the Finns, the Poles, and the subject nationalities in the Caucasus. On the other hand, the revolutionists, slowly recovering from their despair, began again to lay plans and hatch plots to assassinate officials and ultimately to bring about the overthrow of the tsarist regime. Eventually, Social Democratic propagandists once more aroused the industrial workers to strikes and riots with political as well as economic purposes.

Stolypin, who had succeeded Goremykin as prime minister in 1906, hoped to rally the bulk of the Russians to the tsar's side. Most of the nobility—who, however, were declining in importance—could be counted upon for support. In addition, most of the industrial capitalists, who looked upon autocracy as protection against labor unions, labor unrest, and socialism, appeared willing to uphold the tsarist regime. Their political representatives, the Octobrists, largely dominated the Duma in the succeeding years and usually threw their influence in favor of government measures. The peasants, the overwhelming majority of the population, Stolypin sought to win by his agrarian reforms.

During the revolution Witte had secured a decree canceling further land payments to the government after 1906, and this measure had of course removed a heavy burden from the shoulders of the peasants. Stolypin now sought to increase the amount of land available for the peasants and to create a class of independent petty landowners who, like those in France, might come to constitute a conservative force within the country. In October, 1906, accordingly, a decree was issued giving the peasants the right to purchase crown lands. To facilitate the transfer of not only the crown lands but those of the nobles as well, the Peasants' Bank was authorized to loan peasants the necessary funds at low rates of interest. Since, after the events of 1905 and 1906, many nobles were alarmed lest their estates should be seized without compensation, much of their land subsequently passed into peasant hands.

Another decree, in November, 1906, permitted peasants to withdraw completely from the control of the mir. The head of any peasant family might demand that his share of the common land be given to him in a solid block, which thereafter would be his to do with as he pleased. In other words, collective ownership was to give way to individual ownership, with a resultant increased incentive to improved methods of agriculture. By 1914 more than a third of the heads of peasant families had become petty landed proprietors. Greater inequalities among the peasants soon developed, however, as a result of this decree. Some—less capable or more restless—sold their lands and moved to the cities, while others—more competent or more ambitious—bought up the land of those who wanted to leave and rose to the level of fairly well-to-do farmers (the *kulaks*). The average peasant, however, was still land-hungry and continued to look with covetous eyes upon the remaining lands of the crown, the nobility, and the church. Many of the dissatisfied, with the encouragement of the government, sought to better their condition by emigrating to Siberia. In the years between 1906 and the First World War some 350,000 peasants yearly moved into Asiatic Russia.

Although unrest among the peasants was somewhat lessened by these developments, that among the urban workers was not. After 1910 strikes became more frequent, and political assassinations once more began. In September, 1911, Stolypin was killed, but his removal from the premiership in no way altered the general trend of policy. The ministers who succeeded him were of the same type as he. Although in 1912 a law was enacted giving the peasants the benefit of the general judicial system of the empire by displacing land captains with justices of the peace, and

1912

although in the same year the industrial proletariat was conceded an employers' liability act with provision for accident and sickness insurance, the policies of the government continued to be basically repressive and reactionary. Popular unrest therefore continued to grow. By 1914 the industrial strikes had taken on a definite political complexion. In the early summer of that year the working people of St. Petersburg were filled with revolutionary ideas, the capital was convulsed by revolutionary strikes and even open street fighting. "Demonstrations and meetings were held, tramway cars were overturned, telephone and telegraph poles were cut down, and barricades were built." According to Alexander Kerensky, head of the provisional government after the downfall of the tsar,[28] if the First World War had not broken out, revolution "would have come not later than the spring of 1915, perhaps even at the end of 1914."

In Russian foreign policy, meanwhile, developments had occurred of deep significance. In 1906 Alexander Izvolsky had become foreign minister. The latter had as his chief objectives the strengthening of Russia's position in Constantinople, the opening of the Straits to Russian warships, and perhaps ultimately the acquisition by Russia of control of the Straits themselves. The Straits had become vitally important to Russia economically, for through them was exported a great part of the country's wheat crop. But Izvolsky realized that Russia could not successfully pursue such a policy in Europe if she were handicapped by misunderstandings and clashes in Asia. Accordingly, he sought to reach agreements in the Far East in order that Russia's hands might be free in Europe. To this end he concluded in 1907 a convention with Japan, which was followed by a second and fuller treaty in 1910. By the terms of these agreements Japan was recognized as having a preponderant influence in southern Manchuria and Russia in northern Manchuria. Japan and Russia thus came to an amicable agreement regarding their positions in the Far East.

Izvolsky felt, however, that Russia was still too involved in Asiatic complications to make it safe for her to pursue a vigorous policy in the Balkans. Friction and rivalry disturbed the relations between Russia and Great Britain in the Middle East, particularly in Persia, Afghanistan, and Tibet. But Russia, Izvolsky believed, could not afford to quarrel with Great Britain if she desired to strengthen her position in Europe. Consequently, when Great Britain suggested an Anglo-Russian agreement which should settle all difficulties between the two countries, Izvolsky readily fell in with the idea. Moreover, the members of the Duma, hoping that liberalism might be advanced in Russia if the latter co-operated with Great Britain, willingly approved such a step. In 1907, accordingly, an Anglo-Russian treaty was signed in which the two powers came to an under-

[28] See pages 374–375.

standing regarding their positions in the Middle East.[29] This agreement and the others already made between Russia and France (1894) and France and Great Britain (1904) completed what came to be called the Triple Entente.

Beginning in 1908 Izvolsky's foreign policy was chiefly concerned with advancing Russia's position in the Near East. In other words, thirty years after the treaty of Berlin had decisively checked the expansion of Russian power in the Balkans, the tsarist government once more directed its attention to that part of Europe. Thwarted in the Far East by Japan and in the Middle East by Great Britain, Russia in 1908 was more than ever determined to secure her long-coveted outlet to the sea through the Near East. It was in accordance with this policy that Izvolsky attempted to make a bargain with Austria-Hungary in 1908, only in the end to suffer a diplomatic reverse.[30] It was in pursuance of this plan that, having been checked in 1908, he reached in the following year an agreement with Italy (1909),[31] by the terms of which the two powers promised to co-operate in blocking Austria-Hungary's further advance in the Balkans.

It was in accordance, too, with Russia's desire to advance in the Balkans that Pan-Slavists assiduously sought to cultivate the friendship of Slavs outside the empire. Russia was held up as the great elder brother of oppressed and thwarted Slavs everywhere, but special efforts were made to win the Slavs within the Habsburg realm to this viewpoint. With Russia's benediction Pan-Slavic congresses, attended particularly by the Slavs of Serbia, Bulgaria, and Austria-Hungary, were held during the years from 1908 to 1911. As a result of this policy, in the years before 1914 great numbers of Slavs in central and southeastern Europe came to consider Russia as their natural protector and possible benefactor.

When Izvolsky was transferred from the foreign office to the Russian embassy at Paris (1910), he used his new position to advance his Balkan policy. Under his personal direction determined efforts were made to "Balkanize" the Franco-Russian alliance in order that the French should be won to support Russia's policy in the Near East. At the same time, in the foreign office at St. Petersburg, Izvolsky's successor, Sergius Sazonov, Stolypin's brother-in-law, largely continued Izvolsky's Balkan policy. Under Russia's tutelage the Balkan League [32] was created in 1912 chiefly for the purpose of thwarting Austria-Hungary's attempt to advance through Macedonia to the Aegean. During the Balkan crisis of 1912–1913 [33] Russia strongly supported Serbia's attempt to gain an outlet on the Adriatic be-

[29] For the terms, see page 190.
[30] For these negotiations and the Bosnian crisis of 1908, see pages 301–305.
[31] See page 145.
[32] See pages 308–309.
[33] See pages 310–311.

cause that little Slavic country had become an anti-Habsburg pawn of the tsarist empire. But again, chiefly because of Austria-Hungary's opposition, Russian diplomacy was obliged to recede from the stand which it had taken.

The diplomatic defeat which Russia suffered at that time, as well as the one which had occurred four years earlier in connection with Austria's annexation of Bosnia, Russian patriots and Pan-Slavists ascribed to the military unpreparedness of the empire. Stolypin's government had sought to rebuild the Russian navy as rapidly as possible after the Russo-Japanese War and had endeavored to reorganize and strengthen the Russian army, but in 1912 the Russian military and naval forces were still far from adequate for a great war. In 1912 and again in 1913, however, large loans were secured in France for the improvement of the army and the construction of strategic railways, and in 1914 a five-year program of military and naval expansion, involving billions of dollars, was inaugurated. In the latter year, also, the term of active service in the Russian army was lengthened by six months, and more than a hundred thousand recruits were added to the peace-time army. To observers of international affairs it appeared that the foreign policies of Russia and Austria-Hungary must inevitably lead to a clash in the Balkans, and Russia was doggedly determined to be prepared to defend her interests when the next crisis should occur.

Chapter IX

THE AUSTRO-HUNGARIAN DUAL

MONARCHY

IN the early centuries of modern European history the German Habsburg dynasty had expanded its territorial holdings to include many non-German peoples at a time when the latter were incapable of fulfilling their mission as states. The result was that in the last half century preceding the First World War that dynasty ruled over a polyglot empire which had become an anachronism. The history of Austria-Hungary, therefore, differed from that of most of the countries of western Europe in that it was "not so much the history of a people or a country as the history of a state."

Within the state, during these years, the Habsburg dynasty was compelled to struggle almost constantly with what the distinguished Austrian historian, Alfred Pribram, called "the irreconcilable antagonism of the different nationalities which aimed at an independence incompatible with the idea of imperial unity and of the ascendancy which the Germans had enjoyed for hundreds of years." Abroad, during the same time, the dynasty felt compelled to push its influence into the Balkans in order to check the disruptive forces of Yugoslav nationalism both within and without the empire. When the propaganda of the Serbian Yugoslavs increased in fervor and eventually appeared actually to menace the integrity of the Habsburg realm, Austro-Hungarian leaders were won to the belief that only by military measures against Serbia could the Dual Monarchy be preserved.

The Habsburg Ruler

The head of the Habsburg dynasty was Francis Joseph. Born in 1830, elevated to the throne as a result of the inundating wave of revolt that swept over the Austrian Empire in 1848, he held the throne for almost "three score years and ten." Death brought his reign to a close (1916) during the fateful war of 1914–1918, which paved the way for the complete disintegration of his realm only two years later. During all these years

253

he was, in the last analysis, responsible for all important decisions of the government.

From the beginning of his reign Francis Joseph apparently held the divine-right idea of kingship, and to his last days he firmly believed that the ruler's will should consistently be the strongest political force in the realm. Proud of the dynasty which he represented, he was never content that as its head he should become a mere figurehead, a shadow ruler. He took his position seriously, was an industrious monarch, conscientiously rising at an early hour to take care of the routine work of his empire. The later hours of his days were almost regularly occupied with audiences to ministers and other high officials, for he sought to keep in close contact with his responsible political servants. In matters of policy Francis Joseph could upon occasion display a watchful patience that was admirable, and at other times could show a firmness, even a stubbornness, which brought dismay to his ministers. What he lacked in intellectual ability and imagination, he in part made up for as his reign progressed by his long years of experience in dealing with perplexing political problems. The fact that the complicated machinery of the Dual Monarchy actually functioned with a fair degree of smoothness would seem to testify to the emperor's political ability.

Throughout his reign Francis Joseph's major political aim was that of preserving his realm intact despite the friction which occasionally developed between the two halves of his empire, and despite the ever-rising tide of nationalistic opposition among the subject races. When driven to extremities, he sought to overcome his difficulties by compromises, but even here his innate conservatism led him to depart as little as possible from established tradition. He had little real comprehension of the political significance of the changes which were taking place in the world as a result of the transformation in industry, transportation, and communication which came in the late nineteenth and the early twentieth centuries, for his emphasis upon the proprieties of social distinction and his somewhat rigid isolation through his system of court ceremonials prevented him from coming into close touch with the bourgeoisie or with public opinion. Nevertheless, there is little doubt that in his later years the venerable Habsburg ruler constituted a personal bond of union for his millions of subjects, who could not be held together as in most countries by the abstract tie of nationalism.

A second aim to which Francis Joseph seemed to cling after 1867 was that of peace. Having in his early years seen his empire lessened in extent and in international prestige by the wars of 1859 and 1866, the emperor was determined at almost any price to prevent the Dual Monarchy from being drawn into war. Even as an old man in his eighties, when confronted by men like Conrad von Hötzendorf, chief of staff, and Count Berchtold, foreign minister, who sought to precipitate a war against Serbia, Francis Joseph had to be tricked by a forged telegram before a declaration of war could be wrung from him.[1]

The Habsburg Realm

Despite the losses sustained in the wars of 1859 and 1866,[2] Francis Joseph after 1867 ruled a realm which in area stood second among the states of Europe, being surpassed in this respect only by the Russian Empire. From north to south it stretched from the plains of the Vistula to the shores of the Adriatic; from east to west, from the bounds of Rumania to the heart of the Alps. The greater part of this territory—the Danube valley—constituted a geographic, economic, and military unit. But the realm as a whole was not so completely unified. Galicia and Bukowina, cut off by the Carpathian Mountains, seemed more naturally to belong to Poland or Russia than to the Dual Monarchy. Similarly, the Adriatic coastlands, cut off from the Danube valley by the Dinaric Alps, were probably more easily accessible to Italy than to those living in the heart of the Habsburg empire. The Adriatic territory, however, did provide the Dual Monarchy with valuable outlets to the sea at Trieste and at Fiume.

Racially, Austria-Hungary was inhabited by a very heterogeneous population. The two most numerous races were the Germans and the Magyars,[3] who, generally speaking, occupied the center of the empire, although they also constituted large minorities in various other sections of the country. The next most numerous element were the Czechs, who dwelt chiefly in Bohemia, Moravia, and Silesia, where in the beginning they constituted the lower classes, largely controlled by a minority of Germans. To the east of Moravia were the Slovaks, akin to the Czechs but dominated by the Magyars. Across the Carpathian Mountains to the north were the Poles in western Galicia, and in eastern Galicia the Ukrainians, who were largely exploited by the Poles. In Bukowina, Transylvania, and the Banat of Temesvar the majority of the inhabitants were Rumanians, largely

---

[1] See page 339.
[2] See page 125.
[3] The census of 1910 showed the races divided approximately as follows:

Germans	12,011,081	Serbs	2,041,889
Magyars	10,067,917	Croats	2,888,171
Czechs	6,643,059	Slovenes	1,371,256
Slovaks	1,967,520	Italians	771,054
Poles	4,977,642	Mohammedan Slavs	612,137
Ukrainians	3,999,100	Others	367,853
Rumanians	3,224,728		

For the distribution of the races in the monarchy, see the map on page 571.

tenants and workers on the estates of the great Magyar landlords. To the south of the Magyars dwelt the Serbs, Croats, and Slovenes—Yugoslavs who were akin to the peoples living farther south in Serbia, Bosnia-Herzegovina, and Montenegro. In the Trentino, in Trieste, in part of Istria, and in some towns along the Dalmatian coast the Italians predominated. Although in a general way the population of the Habsburg empire was grouped in large national blocks, the races were so interspersed that it would be impossible to draw political boundaries for national states in such a way as not to leave fairly large minorities as ethnic islands in most of the states.

Politically, this Habsburg realm had been divided in 1867 into two almost completely separate states by the *Ausgleich* or compromise of that year. By the terms of the *Ausgleich* the former Austrian Empire had been transformed into the Dual Monarchy. Under this unique political system the whole realm was divided into two autonomous parts: the Empire of Austria, which included Lower Austria, Upper Austria, Salzburg, Tirol, Vorarlberg, Bohemia, Moravia, Silesia, Galicia, Bukowina, Styria, Carinthia, Carniola, Gorizia and Gradisca, Istria, Trieste, and Dalmatia; and the Kingdom of Hungary, which included Hungary proper, Transylvania, Croatia-Slavonia, and the district of Fiume.

The two countries constituted separate states, each with its own constitution, parliament, ministry, courts, administration, and language. They were, however, united under one flag and had one common sovereign, who in Austria was known as emperor and in Hungary as king. Certain interests common to both, notably foreign affairs, war, and finance, were controlled by joint ministers, appointed by the emperor-king but responsible to a body known as the Delegations. The latter consisted of 120 members, half elected by the Austrian parliament and half by the Hungarian parliament, and they not only supervised the joint ministers but voted the budget for the army and for foreign affairs. The Delegations met alternately at Vienna and Budapest, the capitals of the respective states. Usually they sat separately, meeting in joint session only in case of failure to agree, and then simply for the purpose of voting and not for debate. Matters concerning tariffs, trade, currency, and railways were settled between the two countries by treaties renewed every ten years by the Delegations.

Each half of the Dual Monarchy had its own constitution. In Austria a parliament known as the Reichsrat consisted of an aristocratic upper house of nobles and officials and a lower house elected by the seventeen provincial diets. In Hungary the upper house was aristocratic and largely hereditary, and the lower house was elected on a franchise so highly restricted as also to keep power in the hands of the upper classes of the Magyars. In neither half of the Dual Monarchy was the government democratic.

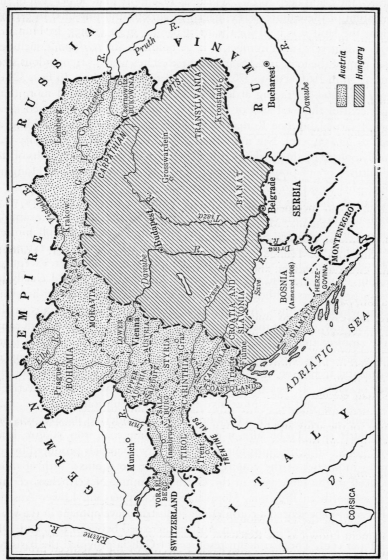

RUSSIA

GERMAN EMPIRE

ROUMANIA

Austria

Hungary

Pruth R.

Danube R.

Lemberg

GALICIA

Dniester R.

BUKOWINA

CZERNOWITZ

CARPATHIAN Mts.

TRANSLYVANIA

Kronstadt

Bucharest

Danube R.

Krakow

Vistula R.

Grosswardein

Budapest

BANAT

Belgrade

SERBIA

SILESIA

MORAVIA

LOWER AUSTRIA

Vienna

Tisza R.

R.

Danube R.

Drave R.

Save R.

Drina R.

BOSNIA
(Annexed 1908)

MONTENEGRO

HERZE-GOVINA

Prague

BOHEMIA

Elbe R.

UPPER AUSTRIA

Salzburg

STYRIA

Graz

CARNIOLA

CARINTHIA

Trieste

Fiume

CROATIA AND SLAVONIA

DALMATIA

COASTLAND

ADRIATIC SEA

Munich

Inn R.

Innsbruck

SALZBURG

TIROL

COTIC ALPS

TRENTINE

Trent

VORARLBERG

SWITZERLAND

Rhine R.

ITALY

CORSICA

The Austro-Hungarian Dual Monarchy

Economically, the realm over which the Habsburg ruler presided was essentially an agricultural state, possessed of rich grain fields, extensive pasture lands, and deep forests. As late as 1910 more than 56 per cent of the population of the empire was engaged in agricultural pursuits. In certain regions the land was held for the most part in great estates. In Hungary proper a relatively small number of large holdings, the *latifundia,* included 40 per cent of the total area.[4] Some of these estates were of tremendous size, running from 186,000 up to 570,000 acres in a single holding. In fact, 324 of these *latifundia,* averaging at least 41,000 acres each, included more than 19 per cent of the total area of Hungary. The church also possessed great areas of farm land, one Roman Catholic bishop, for instance, holding as much as 266,000 acres. Not more than a third of the land in Hungary was actually owned by those who personally cultivated it; and four fifths of the agricultural population—nearly half of the total population of Hungary proper—held less than 20 acres per family.

Although the great estates were most numerous in Hungary, they were found also in Croatia-Slavonia and Bohemia. In the latter, for example, Prince Schwartzenberg owned 437,000 acres, and Francis Joseph himself held an estate of 86,000 acres. Here, too, the church holdings were extensive. In certain regions like Salzburg, Tirol, and Carinthia, however, except for the church holdings and the state forests, the land was owned chiefly by peasant proprietors. Although there was much dissatisfaction with a land system which permitted the concentration of such large holdings in the hands of a few, much of the increase in agricultural production which came in the empire after 1870 was the result of the activities of the great landowners. It was the latter who took the lead in introducing improvements in agricultural technique, and in these respects they set an example for the lesser peasantry. It was the great landowners, too, who most effectively voiced the demand for a protective tariff on agricultural goods.

In mineral resources the Habsburg realm, considering its size, was not particularly rich. To be sure, it did possess some coal, iron, copper, lead, silver, gold, and petroleum; but in 1907 the raw materials produced by the mining industries of the empire were in value not quite a fifth of those produced in the same year in the German Empire. Nevertheless, certain regions—northern Bohemia, Moravia, Silesia, Upper and Lower Austria, and Styria—experienced a considerable industrial development in the years after 1870. The output of coal in Austria increased between 1876 and 1913 by 370 per cent. The petroleum resources of Galicia provided the basis for Austria's production of refined oil and paraffin. Bohemia, possessed of a large share of the empire's coal and iron, became a great manufactur-

---

[4] These figures for landholding are for the year 1913, and are based on statements in O. Jaszi's *The Dissolution of the Hapsburg Monarchy, passim.*

ing region, producing, in addition to such staples as machinery and textiles, commodities like glassware, porcelains, chemicals, and paper. By the opening of the twentieth century Austria had become largely a capitalist country, and the economic, social, and political differences between the industrial regions and the other sections of the empire were distinctly noticeable.

For the exchange of goods between the industrial and agricultural parts of the realm an extensive railway system was constructed, the railway mileage increasing from less than 4000 at the time of establishment of the Dual Monarchy to more than 27,000 at the outbreak of the war in 1914. In a sense the regions of the empire which were less developed industrially—Galicia, Hungary, and the Yugoslav territories—became agricultural colonies of the more advanced industrial sections. The industrial leaders, running true to form, soon demanded and obtained protective tariffs for their infant industries and thus practically forced the agricultural regions to buy their manufactured goods. When eventually efforts were made to establish industries in Galicia, Bukowina, Hungary, Transylvania, and the Yugoslav regions, the capital was to a considerable extent furnished by the German bankers of Austria, so that the inhabitants of these districts felt that they were still largely subject to the "exploitation" of Viennese financiers. Eventually the great landowners struck back and demanded and secured a protective tariff on agricultural products. After 1887, therefore, both industrial and agricultural products were protected, and the cost of living for both urban and rural classes became in consequence greater than it might otherwise have been.

By the opening of the twentieth century the numbers of the bourgeoisie and of the proletariat had greatly increased, not only in the essentially industrial regions of the empire but also in various more or less isolated districts elsewhere. In Austria-Hungary as in other countries the workers were soon demanding the introduction of universal, equal, and direct suffrage. But industrialism not only helped to strengthen the demand for democratic reform; it also accentuated the differences between the Germans and the subject races. In the great majority of cases the leaders of the new large-scale industries established in the non-German parts of the empire were Germans. Frequently the proprietors of the already existing small industrial enterprises were of non-German stock. Naturally, the latter feared and opposed the new great industrialists and, in an effort to maintain their own positions, appealed to their fellow nationalists to support them by buying their products. In the second place, the workers in the new factories were generally of non-German stock, so that the anticapitalist feeling which was present among the proletariat in all countries was in Austria-Hungary further sharpened by a nationalistic rebellion against "exploitation by foreign capitalists." Finally, in the more advanced industrial region of

Bohemia a prosperous bourgeoisie developed among the Czechs. The children of these bourgeois Czechs were privileged to secure an advanced education in high schools and in the Czech university in Prague, and as a result became more and more permeated by Czech national ideals. Industrialism, therefore, although it tended in many ways to unite the Habsburg realm, also helped to complicate the problems arising from the nationalism of the subject races. These problems were made still more difficult by the acquisition of new territory in 1878.

Austria's Advance into the Balkans

By the treaties resulting from the Austro-Prussian War of 1866 the Habsburgs had been effectively ousted from their earlier positions of influence in both Germany and Italy. For a time Francis Joseph nursed the faint hope of revenge against the Hohenzollerns, but the weakening of France in the Franco-German War and the establishment of the powerful German Empire in 1871 definitely ended the possibility of any future Habsburg ascendancy in central Europe. Similarly, the completion of Italian unification by the acquisition of Rome in 1870 seemed to auger ill for any further meddling by the Habsburgs in that region. In fact, it even raised the question as to how long they themselves might retain their remaining Italian subjects against a rising irredentist movement on the other side of the Alps.

Shut out of Germany and Italy, the statesmen of the Dual Monarchy were not slow to realize that Austria-Hungary's hope of future expansion must be to the southeast into the Balkans. Indeed, as early as 1868 Count Beust, Francis Joseph's chancellor, had expressed this view. Such a policy was not, of course, altogether new, for ever since the days of Prince Eugene the Habsburgs had pursued more or less consistently a policy of southeastern penetration. After 1871 the idea of extending the empire in that direction again came to the fore and with it the realization that for such a policy a reconciliation between the Habsburg and Hohenzollern rulers was essential. This reconciliation, sought also by Bismarck, was brought about in 1872 and 1873.[5] Within two years thereafter uprisings among the Christian populations of the Balkan peninsula provided an opportunity for Austro-Hungarian diplomats to begin fishing in troubled waters.

After the Balkan uprisings against Turkish oppression broke out, Francis Joseph and Alexander II of Russia, each doubtless suspicious of the other's projected plans in southeastern Europe, met for a conference in July, 1876, at Reichstadt. The former persuaded the tsar to agree that Austria-Hungary should receive the provinces of Bosnia and Herzegovina, adjoining the Dual Monarchy on the south, if Russia should intervene in the Balkans

[5] See pages 61–62.

THE CONGRESS OF BERLIN

Bismarck, in the center, towers above the other delegates; Disraeli stands with a cane in his hand.

and territorial changes should result. When, however, Russia after her victorious war against Turkey (1877–1878) completely ignored her commitments to Austria-Hungary in the subsequent treaty of San Stefano, the Dual Monarchy united with Great Britain in a determined effort to prevent Russia from carrying through her Balkan program.[6]

In the new settlement which was reached at the Congress of Berlin (1878) Austria-Hungary for all practical purposes gained two new provinces in the Balkans, a fact which Andrássy admitted in private when he declared that the occupation of Bosnia-Herzegovina was only an annexation "very badly disguised." Furthermore, in securing the right to garrison the province of Novibazar, she not only succeeded in driving a territorial wedge between Serbia and Montenegro but gained control over what was then thought to be an excellent route for a railway to Saloniki. In addition, she secured commercial privileges in Serbia and Montenegro, including the right to use Antivari in the latter as a "free" port for her mercantile and naval ships. Incidentally, of course, she succeeded in thwarting Russia's attempt to secure the ascendancy in the Balkans. It is obvious, therefore, that Austria-Hungary strengthened her position and influence in southeastern Europe as a result of events between 1875 and 1878.

In 1881 the Habsburg government further improved its Balkan position diplomatically by linking Serbia with the Dual Monarchy. Serbia, as a consequence of the outcome of events at Berlin in 1878, was temporarily alienated from Russia. Moreover, cut off from Montenegro by the Austrian-garrisoned province of Novibazar and almost enclosed on three sides by Austro-Hungarian territory, she had been made extremely dependent upon the Habsburg empire for her economic well-being. Francis Joseph's government hastened to take advantage of the situation created by these circumstances and persuaded Serbia to sign a convention which made the latter almost a protectorate of the Dual Monarchy. In return for Austria-Hungary's future support of Serbia's claims in Macedonia, Serbia agreed to abandon her aspirations in Bosnia-Herzegovina. She promised, further, that she would conclude no political treaties with other states without a previous understanding with Austria-Hungary, and would not admit to her territory any foreign armed forces of any kind. This treaty, one Serbian statesman indignantly pointed out, placed Serbia in the same relation to Austria as Tunis to France. Serbia's need of Habsburg assistance was made abundantly clear in 1885, however, when it was necessary for Austria-Hungary to intervene to prevent the destruction of the little kingdom at the hands of Bulgaria.[7]

Meanwhile, although Russia's reaction to events at Berlin had been

[6] For a fuller account of this crisis of 1878, see pages 222–225.
[7] See page 286.

so threatening that Germany and Austria-Hungary had concluded a defensive alliance in 1879,[8] thanks to Bismarck's skillful diplomatic maneuvers the three eastern empires were again brought together in 1881. In the treaty signed at that time Russia agreed to respect Austria-Hungary's recently acquired rights in Bosnia-Herzegovina, and the two powers promised to make no territorial changes in European Turkey in the future except by common consent.[9] Two years later Austria-Hungary's position in the Balkans appeared to be still further strengthened when Rumania, alienated from Russia by her loss of Bessarabian territory to that country by the treaty of Berlin, was persuaded by Bismarck to make a defensive alliance with the Habsburg empire against the tsar.

By the close of 1883, therefore, Austria-Hungary appeared to have advanced far toward obtaining for herself a dominating position in the Balkans and had apparently mapped out the course which she was to attempt to follow thereafter in southeastern Europe. The Dual Monarchy contained millions of Yugoslavs and Rumanians who would naturally be more and more drawn toward Serbia and Rumania, the adjoining states of their kinsmen. It therefore became the Habsburg policy after 1878 to endeavor to keep these increasingly nationalistic little states under Austria-Hungary's influence. By so doing Francis Joseph hoped to prevent that disintegration of his polyglot realm which might otherwise result from an active propaganda launched among the subject nationalities of his monarchy by Serbs and Rumanians.

The Problem of Nationalism in Austria

Francis Joseph had made his first compromise with the spirit of nineteenth-century nationalism within his realm when he signed the *Ausgleich* of 1867 recognizing the Kingdom of Hungary as a separate political entity under the domination of the Magyars. But this concession failed to end his difficulties. Within the German-dominated Austrian half of the Dual Monarchy, the Slavs were grievously disappointed that no provision had been made to recognize their separate statehood. The Czechs and Poles, especially, protested against the new settlement and demanded an autonomy similar to that which had been granted to the Magyars. The Poles, in fact, refused outright to send representatives to the Austrian Reichsrat.

In an effort to satisfy the national yearnings of at least one of the Slavic groups the Austrian government, controlled by the German Liberals, made another concession to nationalism in 1869 by granting the province

---

[8] See page 62.
[9] For other terms of the agreement, see pages 63–64.

of Galicia complete autonomy. It was thereafter to have a Polish governor appointed by the emperor, an autonomous Polish school system with eventually two Polish universities, a Polish bureaucracy, and recognition of the Polish language as official within the province. Furthermore, in accordance with the well-established Habsburg policy of *divide et impera,* the Poles were given political and economic ascendancy over the Ukrainians of eastern Galicia, and were thus largely won to a loyal support of the government at Vienna.

But the Czechs continued to rebel against their status under the Austrian constitution of 1867. They asserted that the Reichsrat in Vienna had no right to legislate for Bohemia and Moravia, and declared that Bohemia was historically an independent kingdom joined with the rest of the Habsburg realm only by a common sovereign. They refused to attend the Bohemian provincial diet which had been authorized by the new Austrian constitution, and vehemently demanded that the Bohemian kingdom be restored with its own independent central government located in the ancient capital, Prague. Eventually, to placate the Czechs and to win their loyalty, Francis Joseph went so far as to promise to recognize the existence of the Kingdom of Bohemia by coming to Prague to be crowned and by giving the Prague government legislative control over all questions distinctly Bohemian. To win the numerous Germans of Bohemia to accept this new arrangement, he promised that in Bohemia the German language would be placed on an equality with the Czech, and that so far as possible the administrative districts of the kingdom would be arranged to separate the Germans from the Czechs.

But strong opposition was immediately voiced by powerful elements in the Dual Monarchy. Naturally, the Germans of Bohemia sought to prevent an arrangement which would subject them to the domination of the more numerous Czechs, and they were strongly supported in their efforts by the Germans elsewhere in the empire. The Magyars, too, perhaps for fear of the influence of such a move on their own minor nationalities, strongly opposed the carrying out of the emperor's promises. In the face of these developments Francis Joseph reversed his position and quickly withdrew his promises to the Czechs. So thoroughly did the emperor change his views that it was later made a crime to circulate the message which he himself had voluntarily sent to the Czechs! In deep disgust, the latter decided to resort to passive resistance and so refused to send representatives to either the Austrian Reichsrat or the Bohemian diet. They failed, however, to alter the emperor's latest decision.

But the boycotting of the Reichsrat by the Czechs and some of the other subject peoples appeared to cast discredit upon the imperial regime. In 1873, accordingly, a new electoral system was inaugurated which provided for the election of deputies to the Reichsrat not in a block by the diet of each province but directly by the voters themselves. Under the already existing electoral law the right to vote for members of the provincial diets was vested in four different classes: landowners, cities, chambers of commerce, and rural districts. By the reform of 1873 it was provided that each of these four classes should elect directly a certain number of deputies to the Reichsrat. The system was quite definitely weighted in favor of the landowning and upper bourgeois classes, however. For instance, deputies elected in the rural districts each represented 11,600 voters (1890) while those elected by the landowners each represented only 63 voters. The new electoral system made it practically impossible for the dominant national group to control the election of all the deputies from any province and thus largely prevented a 100-per-cent boycott of the Reichsrat by any province.

1873

For fourteen years, from 1879 to 1893, the Austrian government was headed by Count Taafe, a boyhood friend of the emperor and of all the Austrian ministers after 1867 perhaps the one who most nearly represented the views of Francis Joseph himself. His long ministry was doubtless the result in part of this fact, but it was also in part the result of his success in placating some of the nationalities and in cleverly playing off at times one group against another. There were those, too, who felt that bribery was a factor in his long retention of power. However that may be, he managed to persuade the Czechs to take their seats in the Reichsrat and, aided by the political divisions among the Germans, succeeded in creating a parliamentary majority of Poles, Czechs, Slovenes, and Christian Socialists.

The latter—members of a Catholic party somewhat like the Center Party in the German Empire—consisted principally of peasants and lower bourgeoisie of German stock with a sprinkling of Poles and Czechs. They favored greatly extending the franchise, enacting social legislation, and increasing the rights and privileges of the subject nationalities. Beginning in the eighties they exerted considerable influence in favor of imperial legislation to improve the status of the factory workers. Between 1884 and 1888, for instance, laws were enacted to regulate hours and conditions of labor in factories and mines, to limit the industrial employment of children and women, to legalize labor unions, and to provide at least a start in social insurance.

Meanwhile, to retain the support of the Czechs, Count Taafe was repeatedly compelled to make concessions of one sort or another. The Czech language, for example, was placed on an equality with German in the administrative system of Bohemia. In the realm of education, particularly, the Czechs made national gains. The number of Czech elementary schools was increased, Czech high schools and technical schools were established, and eventually (1882) a Czech university was founded in Prague. Politically, the Czechs obtained an electoral law which enabled them to control a majority in the Bohemian diet, and were further given so many positions in the bureaucracy that the Germans of Bohemia in protest took their turn at boycotting the diet in Prague.

But Taafe's position was ultimately undermined by the rise in Bohemia of the "Young Czechs," a group whose leaders were politically more democratic and economically more radical than the "Old Czechs" who had been supporting his government. The distinguished intellectual leader of this new group was a professor of philosophy in the Czech university in Prague, Thomas G. Masaryk,[10] who had risen to this position from the humble home of a Slovak blacksmith on one of the large estates in the empire. Under his guidance the Young Czechs devoted themselves enthusiastically and energetically to improving the cultural and economic conditions of Bohemia and Moravia as a means of increasing the political influence and power of the Czechs. Their strength was disclosed when, in 1890, Taafe attempted to satisfy the Germans of Bohemia in the matter of the bureaucracy of that province by a compromise arrangement. His plan, which provided for two sets of officials—one of Germans, and one of Czechs—in all districts with mixed populations, at once encountered the vigorous opposition of the Young Czechs, who were instrumental in having the scheme rejected. His position, thus weakened, was later made altogether untenable by the attacks which were made upon his government by certain groups when he proposed to widen the suffrage to include the lower classes. In 1893 Count Taafe resigned the premiership.

In 1897, however, a slight electoral reform was made during the ministry of the Polish Count Badeni, as the result of which a fifth electoral class, which included all men at least twenty-four years of age, was to elect seventy-two deputies to the Reichsrat. Obviously, the new system bestowed a double vote upon those who were already included in one of the other four classes. Its inconsistency with democracy is further revealed by the fact that, whereas the 1,700,000 voters in the first four classes together chose 353 deputies, the 5,500,000 voters in the fifth class were permitted to elect only 72. The measure was far from popular with those interested in advancing the cause of democracy.

In an effort to keep the Czechs satisfied, Badeni issued orders that brought his downfall. In 1897 he decreed that all Bohemian officials should know both German and Czech. The Germans, most of whom had not gone to the trouble of learning the Czech language, immediately denounced his order and demanded its withdrawal. To enforce their demand, the

[10] At the close of the First World War he became the first president of the new Republic of Czechoslovakia. See page 575.

German deputies in the Reichsrat deliberately resorted to obstruction in order to prevent that body from carrying on its work. Epithets and ink-stands were hurled with abandon in the legislative halls, while riots occurred in the streets outside. In despair Badeni's government resigned, and his orders were withdrawn. The Czechs, dissatisfied with the outcome of the affair, now in turn resorted to riots, until peace was restored by the proclamation of martial law in Prague. One of the paradoxes of the Austrian situation seemed to be that the more the national claims of any group were granted the more that group considered itself oppressed.

The success of the German parliamentary obstruction at this time set a precedent for years to come. Thereafter dissatisfied groups of deputies by their noise and disorder frequently prevented the Reichsrat from going on with its work until a ministry in desperation resigned or resorted to a dissolution of the ineffective legislative body. A visitor to the Reichsrat in 1914 was told that each faction in the national legislature had transformed its committee room into an arsenal in which were locked away a complete assortment of such noise-makers as whistles, sleigh bells, cow bells, harmonicas, and trombones for use in making impossible the conduct of business when it so desired. It thus appeared that the principle of parliamentary government could not succeed in a state where an increasing nationalism repeatedly drove the various parties to a mutual hostility.

Francis Joseph had long maintained that Austria could not be governed parliamentarily, and now more or less readily resorted to the use of Article 14 of the Austrian constitution, which gave the government the authority to issue emergency decrees if they became necessary when the Reichsrat was not in session. In the succeeding years, therefore, the government usually dissolved the Reichsrat when it became altogether obstructive and then resorted to legislation by way of emergency decrees. In the leading universities constitutional lawyers were soon found who constructed a right on the part of the state to defend itself against obstruction, and so the system went merrily on.

As a result, while Austria in the years preceding the war of 1914 nominally had a constitutional parliamentary government, in actual fact she had a government which was a bureaucratic absolutism functioning under a "constitutional cloak." Parliament became largely a sham affair. In it the national groups continued to voice their demands and to obstruct legislation; outside it, by means of emergency decrees and the granting of occasional concessions to some of the opposition groups, the government continued to function more or less unhindered. In theory Austria possessed a government in which the ministry was responsible to the Reichsrat; in actuality she had one in which the responsibility was to the emperor. And to help him maintain his dominant position above parliamentary obstruction, Francis Joseph had (1) a powerful German-officered imperial army, (2) a reliable and loyal bureaucracy, and (3) a Roman Catholic clergy who used their influence to strengthen the Habsburg hold on the lesser nationalities.

The Russian revolution of 1905 excited the subject races and the more radical elements in Austria and resulted in popular demonstrations, long parades, and, when the government attempted to use repressive measures, bloodshed. In 1906 a new prime minister, Baron Beck, decided to see what the effect of introducing universal suffrage would be. A number of political leaders believed that the lower classes were really far less influenced by nationalism than the upper enfranchised groups, and that the nationalistic movements within the empire might be weakened by granting universal suffrage. By the reform measure of January, 1907, the old class system was abolished, and all men twenty-four years of age were given the right to vote. The most startling result of the first exercise of the new franchise was the election (1907) of eighty-seven Social Democratic deputies to the Reichsrat.[11]

But the new electoral law in no wise lessened the government's difficulties with the various nationalities. The Slav groups took to holding Pan-Slavic congresses to keep alive their nationalistic objectives. After the government of the German Empire enacted its laws to dispossess the Poles of their land in Germany;[12] the Poles in Galicia turned their wrath against all things German, and resorted to a boycott even of goods made by Austrian Germans. The government, in order to embarrass the Poles, thereupon began to encourage Ukrainian nationalism, with the result that acute friction developed between the Ukrainians and the Poles in Galicia, where riots became of frequent occurrence. In 1912 the Ukrainians took their turn at paralyzing the Reichsrat by resorting to noise-making devices, and not until after the government had promised to establish a Ukrainian university in Lemberg did the few Ukrainian deputies cease their obstruction. Eventually even the Polish government of Galicia had to make concessions to the Ukrainians in order to secure a cessation of their obstructionist activities in the provincial diet.

A veritable wave of nationalistic obstruction swept over Austria just before the First World War. In 1912 the Italians by resort to such measures forced the government to dissolve the diet in the province of Tirol. In 1913 street riots broke out among the Italians of Trieste when the provincial governor began dismissing Italians from office, and in an effort

---

[11] The effect of introducing universal manhood suffrage is seen in other figures on parliamentary deputies. Counting the Liberals, the Christian Socialists, and the Social Democrats as "German" parties, the Germans controlled only eighteen more seats than the subject nationalist groups taken together.

[12] See page 87.

at conciliation the government was led to promise to establish an Italian university in that city. In Bohemia the Germans succeeded in paralyzing the provincial diet because of their dissatisfaction with concessions which had been made to the Czechs. Finally, to cap the climax, the Czechs themselves in 1914 returned to the use of obstruction [13] and by their measures forced a dissolution of the Reichsrat. Thereafter Austria functioned without the Reichsrat until, in the third year of the First World War, the exigencies of that conflict made necessary its convocation.

The Program of Magyarism in Hungary

Although it is usually asserted that the *Ausgleich* of 1867 gave control of Austria to the Germans and that of Hungary to the Magyars, each a minority in its own realm, it is obvious from what has been written about the Taafe ministry in Austria that at times the subject races had considerable political influence in that half of the Dual Monarchy. This was never the case in Hungary. The government of the latter was almost entirely in the hands of the Magyar aristocracy, a very small minority of the total population of the kingdom. The upper house of the national legislature was frankly aristocratic and mostly hereditary, and the lower house, too, was largely responsive to the desires of the landed aristocrats. Elected on a franchise so restricted that only about 6.5 per cent of the population had the ballot (1914), it consisted to a large extent of representatives of the aristocrats and of those who might be called the gentry. In addition to the limited franchise, the aristocracy in order to protect itself resorted to gerrymandering of electoral districts, open voting, official pressure, and bribery. As might be expected, the bureaucracy, too, consisted almost wholly of Magyars. So far as Hungary was concerned, therefore, the result of the *Ausgleich* was to confer home rule upon the Magyars and for all practical purposes upon only a small fraction of them—the aristocracy.

The Magyar aristocrats presided over a country which as late as 1914 was largely a land of the old regime. Although the revolution of 1848 had legally destroyed feudalism and had given land to some of the peasantry, a relatively small number of leading families still dominated the political,

[13] The following is a description by an eye-witness of a session in the lower house of the Reichsrat in March, 1914: "About a score of men, all decently clad, were seated or standing each at his little desk. Some made an infernal noise violently opening and shutting the lids of these desks. Others emitted a blaring sound from little toy trumpets; others strummed jew's-harps; still others beat snare drums. And at their head, like a bandmaster, stood a grey-bearded man of about 65, evidently the leader of this wilful faction, directing the whole pandemonium in volume and in tempo. The sum of uproar thus produced was so infernal that it completely drowned the voice of a man who was evidently talking from his seat in another part of the house, for one could see his lips moving and the veins in his temples swelling. Bedlam let loose! That was the impression on the whole."

economic, and social structure of the monarchy. A great part of the peasants lacked land of their own and as an agricultural proletariat continued in economic dependence upon the large landed proprietors. And the latter were nearly all Magyars, for of the 1657 owners of estates of more than 1420 acres in Hungary (1914), only 142 were not Magyars. According to one distinguished Hungarian historian, three or four leading families dominated in most of the counties, and all of the more prominent officials of the kingdom were related to one another directly or by marriage.[14]

At first it appeared that the government of the restored Hungarian kingdom might be inclined to deal liberally with its racial minorities. In 1868 an enlightened law drafted by Francis Deák was enacted, guaranteeing the equal rights of nationalities in the matters of languages and schools, and in the same year a compromise was reached with the Croats which granted autonomy to Croatia (Croatia-Slavonia) under a Magyar governor. The official language of this province was to be Croatian, and the Hungarian government was to be limited in its control of Croatia to such matters as trade, finance, and the army. The Croats, furthermore, were conceded the right to have five of the sixty Hungarian representatives in the Austro-Hungarian Delegations, and three members in the upper house and forty members in the lower house of the Hungarian parliament. When, however, the Rumanians, the Slovaks, and the Ukrainians sought to secure similar separate institutions, they met with stern refusals. Even the proclamation of a federation of the non-Magyars by representatives of these three peoples (1869) failed to move the dominant Magyar leaders.

Following the death of the liberal Deák in 1875, all pretense of compromise with the minority races of Hungary was dropped by the Magyar leaders, prominent among whom were Count Julius Andrássy and Count Stephen Tisza. The liberal law guaranteeing the equal rights of nationalities soon became a dead letter. Instead, an intensive campaign of "Magyarization" was inaugurated. Innumerable steps were taken to wipe out the non-Magyar languages. Except in Croatia no high schools or universities were permitted unless instruction was in Magyar, and figures for 1913 reveal that 82 per cent of those who graduated from high schools and nearly 90 per cent of the students in colleges and universities were Magyars. In some parts of the kingdom even primary schools using a non-Magyar language were closed.[15] Only the use of Magyar was permitted in the

---

[14] A Hungarian publicist, writing at the close of the nineteenth century, likened the Schönborn estate with its more than 340,000 acres and its two hundred villages to a small medieval state. Although the estate was inhabited by some 70,000 Ukrainian peasants, the two representatives from this district in the lower house of the Hungarian parliament were regularly chosen by the owner of the estate.

[15] The effect of such a policy is seen in the figures for illiteracy. As late as 1910 more than 31 per cent of the population over six years of age in Hungary proper was illiterate.

postal, telegraph, and railway services, and even family names and place names were subject to "Magyarization." The press was also utilized to advance this program, for more than 80 per cent of all the newspapers and periodicals published in Hungary were (1909) limited to the Magyar language. Upon occasion even the funds raised to keep alive the language and literature of the subject nationalities were ruthlessly confiscated by the Magyar government.

Because of the highly restricted franchise in Hungary, the lesser nationalities were largely excluded from the parliament and therefore precluded from using that body to set forth their grievances. In 1881, however, Rumanian representatives drafted demands for the restoration of political autonomy to Transylvania, the appointment of Rumanians as officials in that region, and state aid for Rumanian schools, but their demands received little consideration. When later they made an attempt to go over the head of the Hungarian government to present their grievances to Francis Joseph himself, the chief result was that they themselves were brought to trial on the charge of "incitement against the Magyar nationality." Evidence of the deep dissatisfaction which prevailed among the subject nationalities is seen in the heavy emigration of these classes from the Hungarian kingdom after the policy of "Magyarization" became effective. Between 1876 and 1910 more than 3,500,000 left the country.

Although the Magyar leaders could almost unanimously agree on the policy of Magyarizing the subject peoples in the kingdom, the last decade of the nineteenth century saw a serious split among the Magyars over the question of maintaining the *Ausgleich* unchanged. One group, the Liberals, continued to be satisfied with the benefits which the Magyars derived from that "compromise." Another, organized as the Independence Party, became increasingly dissatisfied with the *Ausgleich*. Its members were the spiritual heirs of those who had stood with Louis Kossuth in 1848–1849 and were now led by his son, Francis Kossuth. They demanded the end of the *Ausgleich,* the destruction of the dual structure of Austria-Hungary. They sought the abolition of the Delegations and the joint ministers, and desired instead a purely personal union with Austria through the Habsburg Francis Joseph.

Consequently, though the Hungarian parliament escaped the obstructionist activities of subject nationalities such as paralyzed the Austrian Reichsrat, it was seriously handicapped at times by the Independents. The latter joyfully resorted to obstructionist tactics whenever it came time to renew the decennial agreements with Austria. In the nineties they denounced the proposed commercial treaty with Austria with such force that they brought the downfall of the Liberal government, which under one premier or another had been in power since 1867. But this proved to be a futile achievement, for the commercial agreement was completed nevertheless.

The Independents next directed their attack against the use of the German language in the Austro-Hungarian army. They demanded that Magyar should be made the language of service and command in all regiments recruited in Hungary, despite the fact that more than half of the soldiers from Hungary were Slovaks, Ukrainians, Rumanians, Croats, Serbs, or Germans. If they could carry their point in this matter they stood to gain in two ways. Magyar nationalism would be exalted by having the Magyar language placed on a plane of equality with German in the army. And, in the second place, the army could thereafter be used as an efficient instrument for the "Magyarization" of the subject races of Hungary.

Although Francis Joseph had apparently cared not at all what the Magyars did to the minor national groups in Hungary so long as they adhered to the Dual Monarchy, he did object strenuously to the destruction of the unity of the Habsburg army and to the loss of his unlimited imperial and royal command over the military forces of his realm. He therefore refused to consider this proposal of the Independents and insisted that the command of the Austro-Hungarian army was his special royal prerogative. Again the Independents by their obstructive tactics brought the dissolution of the parliament; and later, in 1905, Count Tisza, the Liberal premier, was forced out of office when the Liberals were defeated in an election in January of that year. But Francis Joseph refused to surrender. On the contrary, he himself took the offensive. First he prorogued the parliament, and next he proposed a scheme for universal suffrage in Hungary. Obviously such an innovation would be a boon for the subject races and a disaster for the Magyars. Then, early in 1906, he actually dissolved the existing parliament but issued no call for the election of another.

These steps secured the desired results for the Habsburg ruler. The Independents—chiefly Magyars—decided to make a bargain with the Hungarian king in order to rid themselves of the menace of universal suffrage. In return for Francis Joseph's promise to call new elections and to postpone indefinitely his plan for universal suffrage, the opposition agreed to pass the budget, renew another commercial treaty with Austria, and postpone indefinitely further discussion of the army language question. A coalition government, largely representative of the Magyar aristocracy but containing a number of Independents also, was then organized under Wekerle. On the important matter of his supreme control of the Austro-Hungarian army, however, Francis Joseph had triumphed. As late as 1910 some 85 per cent of the officers in the Habsburg army were Germans.

But the Independents soon found other matters about which to agitate. In 1908 the charter of the Austro-Hungarian Bank, with its head office in Vienna, was due to expire. The Independents speedily seized this occasion to demand that there should not be one Austro-Hungarian Bank for the whole Dual Monarchy but a separate bank for each of the two states. Again they met the opposition of Francis Joseph, who once more threatened to bring forward his proposal for universal suffrage. Parliamentary life in Hungary during the ensuing months became exceedingly hectic; but when, in 1909, the parliament failed to pass the budget, the government carried on as usual regardless of that fact.

Meanwhile, conditions both at home and abroad had begun to give the more moderate Magyars cause for concern. Nationalism among the subject races, especially the Slavs, was noticeably on the increase. Russia's growing interest in and encouragement of the Pan-Serb movement seemed to threaten the very existence of the Hungarian kingdom. In the international crisis of 1908–1909 [16] Austria-Hungary had seemingly won against Serbia and Russia only because of the vigorous support which she had received from the German Empire. To many thoughtful Magyars the situation seemed wholly unfavorable for a conflict within the Dual Monarchy. The Independence Party, accordingly, was weakened by defections of the more moderate Magyars, and in the election of 1910 the Liberals once more won control of the parliament. Nevertheless, again in 1912 the Independents returned to the attack by renewing their efforts to limit Francis Joseph's supreme command over the army, and again they resorted to parliamentary obstruction. Count Tisza, in June, 1913, once more became premier, and this time he defeated the obstructionists, though he had to resort to police action to do it. From 1913 until after the death of Francis Joseph this iron-handed premier, despite occasional attempts to assassinate him, remained at the head of the Hungarian government.

Grave concern over the rising nationalism of Hungary's subject races led Tisza in his last ministry to attempt to conciliate the 3,000,000 Rumanians living in Transylvania. Ever since the establishment of the Dual Monarchy the Rumanians had sought autonomy. The government's refusal to consider their demands, together with its policy of "Magyarization," its efforts to control the Rumanian Church, and its refusal to recognize the Rumanian intelligentsia in the state government or in the local administration had led eventually to an irredentist movement which aimed at the union of Transylvania with the Kingdom of Rumania. Although Rumanian irredentism was never so aggressive as the Yugoslav—partly because it was discouraged by King Carol of Rumania—it was increasing rapidly among the intelligentsia and the middle classes in the second

[16] See pages 301–305.

decade of the twentieth century. Tisza's negotiations with the Rumanians in 1914, in a half-hearted effort to conciliate them, therefore proved futile.

The Yugoslav Question

The most threatening menace to the territorial integrity of the Dual Monarchy in the twentieth century came from the Serbs, Croats, and Slovenes, who were collectively referred to as Yugoslavs. As early as 1848 Croat leaders had envisaged the creation of some kind of Yugoslav state, linked with the rest of the Habsburg realm in a personal union through Francis Joseph. In the revolution of that year they had aided the emperor to put down the Magyar movement for independence in Hungary, but had themselves obtained little from Francis Joseph in return for their support. Not until late in the sixties did they receive any encouragement. In 1867 a Yugoslav Academy was created to keep alive their cultural heritage; in the next year they were given a limited political autonomy by the Magyar government at Budapest; and in 1874 they secured a Slavic university at Agram. Meanwhile, a National Party had grown up in Croatia, aimed at the creation of a large Yugoslav state to include, besides Croatia-Slavonia, the Serbs in southern Hungary, the Austrian province of Dalmatia, and the Hungarian port of Fiume.

The acquisition of Bosnia and Herzegovina, whose inhabitants consisted chiefly of Serbs and Croats, further complicated the Yugoslav problem. At the very beginning there was strong opposition to Habsburg rule, and several army corps had to be sent into the provinces before Austro-Hungarian control could be actually established. The provinces were never annexed to either of the partners of the Dual Monarchy but remained apart as a sort of colonial realm governed by the imperial minister of finance. Although in the years after 1878 some material improvements were made—such as the construction of roads and railways, and the abolition of brigandage—the provinces were denied self-government, and remained largely in a condition of feudalism and illiteracy. In 1910 more than four fifths of the population of Bosnia and Herzegovina over six years of age were unable to read and write. The Habsburg government, in order to offset the influence of the Croats, had sought in a way to create a feeling of Bosnian nationalism, but it only succeeded in building up a pro-Serb sentiment instead. Increasingly with the passing of the years the Bosnians dreamed of union with a greater Serbia.

As early as 1878 Austro-Hungarian leaders had begun to fear the rise of a greater-Serbia movement, and at the Congress of Berlin they had insisted that the narrow province of Novibazar should be turned over to the military occupation of the Habsburg army. This they had demanded partly in order to prevent direct contact between the two Yugoslav states, Serbia and Montenegro. In the eighties Austria-Hungary had taken advantage of Serbia's exigencies at that time to make her almost a dependency in order to bring her into line with Austro-Hungarian policies. The treaty of 1881 had never been popular in Serbia, and the pro-Austrian Obrenovich ruler who had signed it was denounced in Serbia for his action. A group in the little kingdom was soon plotting to overthrow the reigning dynasty in favor of a member of the rival Karageorgevich line.

Although even before 1903 the Serbs had begun to turn from Austria to Russia, the revolutionary seizure of the throne of Serbia by the pro-Russian Karageorgevich King Peter in that year gave a great impetus to Pan-Serbianism and to the rise of a strong anti-Habsburg sentiment. The latter was further increased in 1906 when Magyar landlords managed to prevent the renewal of the commercial treaty between Austria-Hungary and Serbia. As a result of the tariff war that followed, Serbia lost practically all of the market for her products in the Dual Monarchy, and since the Serbs exported chiefly pork, the quarrel was popularly referred to as the "pig war." Serbian peasants suffered greatly from this loss of markets, and as might be expected the denunciation of the Habsburgs was extremely bitter. Serbia's need of an outlet to the sea was realistically brought home to the Serbs. Added fuel was thus provided for the already burning desire of many Serbs to create a great Yugoslav kingdom which would embrace the Yugoslavs of Serbia, Montenegro, Bosnia, and the Habsburg empire as well.

While Serbian propagandists sought to inculcate these ideals among their kinsmen across the border, the repressive measures of the Magyar government of Hungary helped the movement along by alienating the Yugoslavs within the Dual Monarchy. In 1905 deputies from Croatia, Dalmatia, and Istria, meeting at Fiume, demanded, in total disregard of the dividing line between the Austrian Empire and the Kingdom of Hungary, that Dalmatia and Croatia-Slavonia be united in one state. In the same year this Yugoslav movement was further strengthened when Dalmatian Serbs and Croats, meeting at Zara, proclaimed that the Serbs and Croats constituted one nation, and demanded that steps be taken by the Habsburg government to give substance to the Fiume resolutions. Those who supported these resolutions came to be known as the Serbo-Croat coalition. Apparently the repressive measures of the Magyars had led most of the Roman Catholic Croats and the Greek Orthodox Serbs to waive their differences in order to present a united front to the Magyars.[17] In 1906

---

[17] The Croatian Nationalists, who feared future domination by the Serbs, were bitterly opposed to the Serbo-Croat coalition.

the coalition elected a majority of the diet of Croatia. Two years later it again won control, and the governor, unable to secure support in the diet, dissolved that body and ruled autocratically.

In an effort to discredit the Serbo-Croat coalition, Magyar leaders sought to prove that many Serbs in Hungary had actually become traitors to the kingdom by becoming linked with the Serbian government at Belgrade. During 1908 and 1909 scores of Serbs were brought to trial, and many were condemned to prison. In the latter year, too, an article based on documents in the government archives and written by Heinrich Friedjung, a well-known Austrian historian, appeared in a Vienna newspaper. The writer described Serbia's intrigues against the Dual Monarchy, and, at least by implication, accused the leaders of the Serbo-Croat coalition of treason. The article proved to be a boomerang against the government, however, for, in the celebrated Friedjung trial which resulted when the leaders of the coalition sued for libel, it was proved that some of the documents which the historian had used were forgeries. Furthermore, Professor Masaryk, the leader of the Young Czechs, investigated the documents later and in 1911 announced his conviction that both the Austrian minister at Belgrade and Aehrenthal, the Austro-Hungarian foreign minister in Vienna, had been involved in the forgery.[18] Although the Magyars by their accusations of treason had succeeded in largely destroying the influence of Supilo, the leader of the Serbo-Croat coalition, they brought down on the Habsburg government a veritable hornet's nest of criticism, which further alienated the Yugoslavs within the empire and made Europe as a whole suspicious of the policies and purposes of the Dual Monarchy. This was especially so after the somewhat discredited Austro-Hungarian minister at Belgrade was elevated to the position of under-secretary of state in the Habsburg foreign office.

The government still wrestled valiantly, if perhaps mistakenly, with the Yugoslav problem. The railway systems and economic interests of Bosnia-Herzegovina and Dalmatia were deliberately separated to hinder co-operation between these two districts. In 1910 a constitution was granted Bosnia, and a diet, with a franchise so contrived as to prevent the appearance of any national party, was established. But, though the government managed to control the diet, Yugoslav enthusiasts caused trouble in other ways. In the very year that the constitution was granted, an unsuccessful attempt was made on the life of the governor. It was not long till the new constitution was suspended and Bosnia was temporarily put under military rule.

In Yugoslav districts outside Bosnia the situation became still worse.

---

[18] It is probable that both of these men had been deceived by a Serbian adventurer regarding the authenticity of the documents involved.

Eventually, in 1912, even the more passive Slovenes of Austria became aroused to the extent that they proclaimed their determination to attempt to unite their district with Croatia-Slavonia. In the latter, although the Serbo-Croat coalition declined in strength after the discrediting of Supilo, it did not give up the fight. The Croatian schools were filled with Yugoslav propaganda. In 1912 the Croatian university at Agram had to be closed for a time because of nationalistic activities among its students, and many high schools suffered a similar fate. More and more the tendency to resort to violence became evident. The governor of Croatia dissolved the diet and established a dictatorship, with the result that in 1912, in 1913, and in 1914 attempts were made to assassinate him and his successor. The spirit of violence spread also to the neighboring city of Fiume, where in 1913 an attempt was made to blow up the governor's residence.

There were some within the Dual Monarchy who felt that perhaps the best way to meet the Yugoslav menace was to permit the creation of a large Yugoslav state within the empire and to concede to this state a status equal to that of Austria and Hungary. That is to say, such reformers advocated changing the Habsburg empire from a dual to a "trial" or triple monarchy. They urged that such a step would go far toward drowning out the siren song of the Yugoslavs outside the empire, who were advocating that all Yugoslavs should be gathered into a greater Serbia. The Croats had a civilization and an economic well-being which was undoubtedly on a higher plane than that which prevailed in the Serbian kingdom. Because they were the literary and cultural leaders of the Yugoslavs, they had an influence out of all proportion to their numbers. Give them political equality within the Habsburg empire, the advocates of "trialism" declared, and their desire to be part of a Serbian-dominated state would soon disappear. Archduke Francis Ferdinand, the heir-apparent to the Habsburg throne, was drawn more and more to favor some such reorganization of the Habsburg realm in the early years of the twentieth century.

But the Magyar leaders, who were chiefly responsible for the alienation of the Yugoslavs, were not willing to consider any reform which might decrease the importance of the Hungarian kingdom or lessen their own power within it. They were therefore opposed to any experiment in the matter of "trialism," and were more inclined to favor those in the Dual Monarchy who in desperation concluded that the only way to save the empire from disintegration as the result of Yugoslav propaganda was utterly to destroy Serbia or at least to bring her definitely under Habsburg domination. An advocate of such measures was Conrad von Hötzendorf, who became chief of staff of the Habsburg army late in 1906. Until the outbreak of the war in 1914 he steadily urged an attack upon the little

Serb kingdom as the only way to end the menace of Yugoslav nationalism. To prepare the Habsburg army for such a war—which, of course,
might involve Russia—two years of peace-time service in the army were
made compulsory (1912), with the result that the standing army of the
Dual Monarchy was increased to 450,000 men. Perhaps the concluding
tragedy of Francis Joseph's long reign was that it was Hötzendorf's ideas
rather than those of Francis Ferdinand which were in the ascendancy in
Austria-Hungary just prior to 1914.

Chapter X

TURKEY AND THE BALKANS

ALTHOUGH the territory which is usually referred to as the Balkans constitutes a small part of Europe, within that region before the First World War there existed such a tangle of conflicting nationalistic programs and clashing imperialistic ambitions as to make peace within the peninsula almost an impossibility. The difficult problem of handling this complex Balkan situation in such a way as to satisfy the interested powers —large and small—has frequently been reduced to the two words, "Eastern Question." A German historian, writing in the nineteenth century, grasped the importance of the Balkan situation in a way that was almost uncanny. "Amongst the great problems of our age," he wrote, "none is more fitted to occupy the thoughts, not only of the professional statesmen but of every keen-sighted individual who takes an interest in politics, than the so-called Eastern Question. It is the pivot upon which the general politics of the century now drawing to an end are turning, and it will be so for the coming century also." How correct he was in his historic prophecy the events recorded in this and the next succeeding chapter offer abundant proof.

Political Geography of the Balkans, 1878–1908

As a result of changes made by the treaty of Berlin [1] and by events in the immediately succeeding years, the political map of the Balkan peninsula after 1878 was far different from that which had existed a few years earlier. The northernmost of the Balkan states, the one which adjoined both Russia and Austria-Hungary, was Rumania, which was bounded by the Pruth and Danube rivers on the northeast, the Carpathian Mountains on the west, the Danube River on the south, and the Black Sea on the east. In 1878 it was the largest and strongest of the Balkan states. South of Rumania, extending from the Black Sea on the east to Serbia on the west and to the Balkan Mountains on the south, was the newly created principality of Bulgaria, which was still a tributary state of the sultan. It was a very disgruntled state in 1878 because the Congress of Berlin had

[1] It would be profitable for the student to reread here the account of events leading to the treaty of Berlin. See pages 219–225.

deprived it of territory running down to the Aegean which the treaty of San Stefano had originally allotted to it. South of the Balkan Mountains was the autonomous district of Eastern Rumelia, ruled by a Christian governor appointed by the sultan. Its inhabitants were largely Bulgarians and ardently desired to have their territory incorporated in Bulgaria.

To the west of Bulgaria was the little independent principality of Serbia, which was separated from Austria-Hungary on the north by the Save and Danube rivers. On the east it bordered on Rumania and Bulgaria; on the west and southwest it was hemmed in by the Habsburg-administered province of Bosnia and by the narrow strip of Novibazar, which was occupied by Austro-Hungarian military forces. One reason for Austria's insistence upon her military occupation of this little province had been that a way might be open for the possible construction of an Austrian railway to the port of Saloniki. A second reason had been the Habsburg determination to keep Serbia and Montenegro, the neighboring little Yugoslav principality, from having direct contact with each other. Serbia was a landlocked state—the only one in the Balkans—and therefore largely dependent commercially upon Austria-Hungary. To the west of Serbia, separated from her by Novibazar, was the tiny principality of Montenegro, which for all practical purposes had been independent for more than three quarters of a century, though that fact had not been legally recognized until 1878. In the treaty of Berlin it had been given a seaport on the Adriatic, though with conditions attached which made it somewhat subordinate to Austria-Hungary.

The southernmost part of the peninsula and a number of the islands adjoining it in the Mediterranean and Aegean seas constituted the independent kingdom of Greece, the first of the Balkan states to gain legal recognition of its freedom. In 1881, as a result of agreements made at the Congress of Berlin, Greece received additions of territory in Thessaly. All of the territory from Greece's northern boundary to the southern limits of Montenegro, Novibazar, Bulgaria, and Eastern Rumelia belonged in 1878 to the Ottoman Empire, as did Crete and most of the other Greek-inhabited islands in the Aegean. On the European mainland the sultan's realm included the important cities of Constantinople, Adrianople, and Saloniki, and extended from the Black Sea through Thrace, Macedonia, Epirus, and Albania to the Adriatic.

Although the great powers at Berlin had solemnly pledged themselves to guarantee the integrity of the remaining territorial holdings of the Ottoman Empire, some of them apparently did not take their pledges very seriously. Within three years after the treaty of Berlin, Russia, Austria-Hungary, and Germany agreed (1881) not to oppose the eventual union of Bulgaria and Eastern Rumelia. With three of the great powers in this

THE BALKANS, 1885–1913

tolerant state of mind, it is not surprising that the national leaders of Bulgaria and Eastern Rumelia should conspire to overturn the Berlin settlement. In 1885 the two states united to form one principality.[2]

For a quarter of a century after 1885 the national states in the Balkans continued to maintain the *status quo* territorially. Perhaps this was in part the result of the increasing jealousies and rivalries of a number of the great powers, each of which feared that another might advance its position and prestige if any further change did occur in the Balkan peninsula. In 1887 agreements looking to the maintenance of the *status quo* in the Balkans were made by Italy and Austria-Hungary and by Italy and Great Britain,[3] and a decade later by Russia and Austria-Hungary. Fear that any territorial change or any war in the Balkans might precipitate a general European conflict also led the great powers for a time to oppose any attempt to change the *status quo*.

Internal History of the Balkan National States

Although, in the minds of many, Rumania, Bulgaria, Greece, Serbia, and Montenegro in some vague way constituted before 1914 a sort of amorphous mass in southeastern Europe which was called the Balkans, in reality each of these states in the years before the First World War had its own individuality, its own problems, its own hopes and aspirations. Before an account is given of further changes in the political geography of the Balkans, it would be wise to learn something of the domestic history of these states which played such an important role in reducing the territory of the sultan in Europe.

RUMANIA

During the quarter century from 1856 to 1881 numerous changes had been made in the political status of the Rumanians who dwelt in Moldavia and Wallachia. After the Crimean War the treaty of Paris (1856) had made these two provinces of the Ottoman Empire autonomous but separate political units; three years later the provinces had each elected the same man, Alexander Cuza, as its prince; and in 1862 the sultan had accorded legal recognition to the principality of Rumania formed by their union. Finally, at the close of the Russo-Turkish War of 1877–1878, the treaty of Berlin had recognized the complete independence of Rumania, which in 1881 proclaimed herself a kingdom. Meanwhile, the native prince who had first ruled Rumania had been forced to abdicate (1866) because he

[2] For a fuller discussion of this step, see pages 285–286.
[3] See pages 138–139.

had made reforms which were unpopular with the powerful landed aristocracy and clergy. The one who became the first king of Rumania was Carol (Charles), of the German family of Hohenzollern-Sigmaringen, a younger brother of the one who was offered the throne of Spain in 1870.[4] In 1881 this Hohenzollern prince was crowned King Carol I of Rumania.

Carol rather naturally was inclined to pursue a pro-German policy and to align his kingdom with the two great Germanic empires. Furthermore, Rumanian public opinion—what there was of it—was in the eighties opposed to Russia because the latter had forced Rumania to surrender a valuable strip of Bessarabia in 1878. It is not surprising, therefore, that Rumania signed a defensive alliance with Austria-Hungary against Russia and that almost to the day of Carol's death (1914) she remained a loyal satellite of the Austro-German alliance. In her domestic political institutions, too, Rumania under Carol imitated the Hohenzollern kingdom of Prussia in having a government which was largely aristocratic and which conferred great power upon the monarch. Another Prussian institution which King Carol admired was the army. He accordingly increased his own army in numbers, installed German instructors, and modernized its equipment, with the result that Rumania in the succeeding years had the largest military force of all the Balkan states.

Three causes of popular dissatisfaction and unrest existed within Rumania during the years from 1878 to 1914. One was economic. The country was predominantly agricultural, and the majority of its inhabitants were peasants. But the land was held for the most part by powerful landed proprietors who were reluctant to make any concessions which might weaken their positions. Rumania therefore had an agrarian problem. With the steady increase of the rural population the danger of peasant uprisings became imminent. In an attempt to improve the agrarian situation—without antagonizing the landed proprietors—the government provided (1889) for the sale of public lands to the peasants, but this step naturally failed to solve the problem permanently. So strong did the unrest become that a great uprising occurred in 1907, when the peasants demanded sweeping land reforms. A large part of the army was mobilized to suppress the revolt, but following its collapse a number of measures were enacted in an effort to placate the peasants. Nevertheless, in 1914 nearly half of the total agricultural area of the country was still in the hands of large landowners, who constituted scarcely more than half of one per cent of the total number of agriculturists. On the other hand, a million peasant proprietors in 1914 each had farms of less than twenty-five acres. Not until after the First World War was agrarian legislation

[4] See page 203.

enacted to put more of the country's land in the hands of the peasants.[5]

A second cause of popular dissatisfaction was political, for the Rumanian government was far from democratic. The kingdom had a national parliament which was very similar to the Prussian Landtag in that the lower house was elected on a three-class system of suffrage which gave a small percentage of the wealthier Rumanians a predominant voice in legislation. Out of a population of approximately 7,500,000 in 1914 fewer than 200,000 were entitled to participate in national elections. Furthermore, King Carol, like the ruler of Prussia, had an absolute veto on all laws which the parliament might enact. Despite agitation in behalf of a more liberal system of government, little progress was made, and it was not until the closing years of the First World War that the franchise was widened.

A third cause of unrest was the presence within Rumania of a considerable number of Jews. They lived for the most part in the towns, where they were often the chief merchants and moneylenders, and as a group they constituted the bourgeoisie of the country, as they did in parts of Russia. The Congress of Berlin, in order to protect the Jews, had stipulated when it recognized Rumania as an independent state that all citizens must be granted equal rights regardless of their religion. But Rumania, in order to destroy any political power of the Jews, passed a law which classified Jews as aliens [6] and therefore not entitled to the rights of citizenship. Naturally, this caused great dissatisfaction among the Rumanian Jews. Furthermore, in order to turn criticism from themselves, the landed proprietors occasionally aroused the peasants against the "money-lending, anti-Christian" Jews. This was not particularly difficult to do when anti-Jewish pogroms were occurring at frequent intervals in neighboring Bessarabia. Not until 1917 were the Rumanian Jews admitted to citizenship, but even this step failed to stop the agitation of the anti-Semites within the kingdom.

Despite these disturbing factors, noticeable economic—if not cultural—progress was made in the kingdom in the period before 1914. As in Hungary, the great landowners led the way in introducing improved agricultural methods and machinery, and the soil was naturally rich. The country therefore came to be one of the important grain-producing regions of Europe. As a result of cordial relations with Germany and Austria-Hungary, capital from these states entered Rumania and helped to develop railway facilities and the country's rich oil fields. As part of the ramifications of the famous Berlin-Bagdad railway scheme, Rumania was linked by rail with Constantinople, and by 1914 she had more than two thousand miles of state-owned railways.

[5] See page 599.
[6] Somewhat as Nazi Germany did in 1935. See page 515.

BULGARIA

By the terms of the treaty of Berlin, establishing Bulgaria as an autonomous principality tributary to the sultan, this new state was to be administered by a Russian commissar until a constitution had been drafted and adopted by a popular assembly. In 1879 the Russian commissar submitted the draft of a conservative constitution to an assembly of Bulgarians, who immediately transformed it into a democratic instrument of government, providing for universal manhood suffrage, a one-house parliament, and ministerial responsibility. The assembly next turned to the matter of selecting a ruler for the new state and unanimously chose Alexander of Battenberg, twenty-two years old, an intelligent and honest but obviously inexperienced German prince. Perhaps the most important reason for his election was that he was a nephew of Tsar Alexander II and was favored by him for the throne.

Starting with a provisional directive position in Bulgaria, the tsar apparently hoped to transform the new principality into something like a Russian protectorate to serve as a Romanov outpost in the Balkans. To accomplish this end he relied on the gratitude and political inexperience of the Bulgarians and upon the subservience of the young prince, who could not help feeling that in a sense he was a representative of the tsar. The democratic constitution of Bulgaria had never been popular with Prince Alexander's Russian advisers, and after a number of conflicts between the parliament and the prince, the latter with Russian support in 1881 suppressed it. For two years Prince Alexander ruled as a quasi autocrat —on the surface. But he knew, and many of his subjects suspected, that he was only a figurehead for the tsar, for during this period two Russian generals dominated his ministry, and other Russians held high positions not only in the army but in the government as well.

Eventually the young ruler became irritated by his position of subordination to Russia, and looked about for a way of escape. He thought he found it in the presence within Bulgaria of a group of patriots who were hostile to his domineering Russian advisers. To free himself from absolute dependence upon the Russian tsar, Prince Alexander sought a reconciliation with his patriotic subjects. In 1883 he restored the democratic constitution, replaced many of his Russian advisers with Bulgarians, and regained popular favor—at the cost of incurring the tsar's enmity. Thereafter, for a time, Russia's policy was designed to keep Bulgaria weak. Events in 1885, however, further strengthened the principality.

In that year a group of conspirators expelled the governor of Eastern Rumelia, proclaimed the union of this district with the principality of Bulgaria, and sent a delegation to invite Prince Alexander to become the sovereign of Eastern Rumelia. The prince was momentarily deterred by fear of the displeasure of the tsar, but in the end, moved by the national enthusiasm of his Bulgarian subjects, he accepted the throne of Eastern Rumelia and sent Bulgarian military forces to occupy that district. Obviously all this was in flagrant violation of the treaty of Berlin, and among the great powers an exchange of diplomatic notes at once began in an effort to decide upon a course of action. The tsar, to show his displeasure, immediately ordered the withdrawal of all Russian officers from the Bulgarian army.

But the repercussion of events in Bulgaria was greater in the Balkan states than among the great powers. Both Greece and Serbia announced that the Balkan equilibrium had been upset by Bulgaria's enlargement and consequently demanded territorial increases for themselves as compensation. Serbia, in fact, went so far as to mobilize her army and invade Bulgaria, hoping perhaps that the latter's army would be demoralized by its recent loss of Russian officers. Contrary to all the expectations of the powers, Serbia, the older and supposedly the better-organized state, more than met her match in the war that ensued. The Bulgarians valiantly rallied to defend their recently enlarged national state, and, three days after the invasion of Bulgaria began, the Serbs were overwhelmed by a disastrous defeat. The victorious Bulgars then drove the Serbs back across the frontier and started for Belgrade. They had hardly launched their invasion, however, when they were met by an ultimatum from Austria-Hungary. Under pressure from the latter, Bulgaria was compelled to sign a truce, which was later followed by a peace treaty. Thanks to Habsburg intervention Serbia neither lost territory nor had to pay an indemnity, and thus escaped from what might have been the disastrous results of her attack upon her neighbor.

Bulgaria's defeat of Serbia apparently had its effect also upon any plans which the great powers may have been formulating to prevent the union with Eastern Rumelia. Although the powers at first protested and stated that they would not recognize the union, in the end they did nothing to prevent what the Bulgarian people had so enthusiastically achieved. In fact, Great Britain's desire to utilize the Balkan states to check Russia's future expansion toward the Mediterranean led British statesmen to exert pressure upon the sultan in favor of recognizing the union of the two principalities now that enmity existed between Bulgaria and the tsar. By April, 1886, the sultan, in need of Great Britain's friendly support, had formally recognized the *fait accompli*, and the other powers had acquiesced. Bulgaria thus emerged from the crisis greatly increased in area and population. On the other hand, Prince Alexander's position was weakened, for by strengthening his principality he had further antagonized the tsar.

In the end the latter's opposition cost Alexander his throne. Utilizing the discontent of certain Bulgarian army officers, the Russian government succeeded in hatching a conspiracy which resulted (1886) in the seizure of the prince, who was compelled to sign his abdication and was then carried off to Russian Bessarabia. Although he was later released and was recalled to the throne by those who had driven the pro-Russian conspirators from the capital, Prince Alexander apparently had lost his nerve. When he learned from the tsar that the latter would not approve his return to Bulgaria, he appointed a regency, in September, 1886, and then rather abjectly resigned his throne.

Within Bulgaria a political struggle now ensued. On the one side the pro-Russians wished to consult the tsar regarding a new ruler and were in general content to have the principality constitute a sort of Russian protectorate. On the other side the Bulgarian nationalists desired to pursue a policy of freedom and independence from outside control. The latter were led by Stefan Stambulov, president of the parliament, a somewhat coarse Bulgarian peasant but a man of vigor, courage, and intelligence. Stambulov's group eventually won, and the second Russian attempt to gain the ascendancy in Bulgaria was thus thwarted. Almost a year passed, however, before the parliament chose a new ruler. Again they turned to Germany, this time electing Prince Ferdinand of Saxe-Coburg, who, though young, apparently had sufficient courage and self-reliance to accept a difficult position among an alien people. That he understood the national sentiment of his adopted land seemed evident when he chose as his prime minister Stefan Stambulov.

The election of Prince Ferdinand had been made against the protest of Russia, and consequently the tsar's government would not formally recognize the new ruler. Russia's attitude in turn deterred the other powers from taking such a step. Despite Russian conspiracies against him, however, Ferdinand managed to hold his throne. During the first seven years of his reign he was apparently content to study the Bulgarian situation and to let Stambulov manage the government. The latter, a Russophobe at heart, energetically devoted himself with every means at hand to advancing the independence and security of Bulgaria. Inclined to use highhanded measures to achieve his ends, when he considered them necessary, he naturally created numerous bitter enemies within the country.

By 1894 Prince Ferdinand had arrived at the place where he desired to be recognized by the governments of Europe, and he was clever enough to realize that, if he could win the support of the Russian tsar, his quest for recognition would be facilitated. Furthermore, he had begun to grow weary of Stambulov's rather arbitrary rule. Consequently, it was not difficult for friction to develop between the ruler and his Russophobe prime minister, and eventually (1894) Stambulov submitted his resignation.[7] Prince Ferdinand next availed himself of a change of rulers in Russia to seek a reconciliation with the new tsar, Nicholas II. In this he was successful, and, following recognition by the Russian government, Prince Ferdinand's position as ruler of Bulgaria was speedily accepted by the other states of Europe. In 1908, after the Young Turk revolution,[8] Ferdinand successfully proclaimed the complete independence of Bulgaria and changed his title from Prince to King.

Bulgaria, in contrast with Rumania, was a land of petty peasant proprietors and so was not disturbed by agrarian agitation advocating the seizure of great estates. She was, also, politically democratic, though the peasants were all too often inclined to permit politicians to manage the government. Economically, the country advanced steadily in the generation before the Balkan wars. Roads and railways were constructed to facilitate communication within the country, and Varna on the Black Sea and ports on the Danube were improved to take care of the foreign trade. A good public-school system was established, and education was made compulsory for boys and girls. By 1914 the percentage of illiterates in the Bulgarian army was much lower than that in any other Balkan state. Her army, too, at the opening of the Balkan wars, was one of the strongest to be found in the Balkan peninsula.

GREECE

When the Ottoman flood began to recede in the Balkans in the nineteenth century, Greece was the first national state to emerge and to receive legal recognition of its independence by Turkey and the European powers. In the thirties it was established as a kingdom, and Otto I, the second son of King Louis I of Bavaria, reigned in Greece from 1833 to 1862. In the latter year nationalistic dissatisfaction with the king's numerous German advisers and with his lack of strong aggressive efforts to secure additional territory for Greece led to a popular uprising which drove him from the country. In 1863 a new monarch, secured this time from Denmark, mounted the throne of Greece as George I. In order to help popularize the new ruler with his subjects at the very outset of his reign, Great Britain in 1864 ceded to Greece the Ionian Islands off the west coast of the Balkan peninsula. In 1881, as already explained, Greece also secured Thessaly from Turkey as a result of the recommendation of the Congress of Berlin.

[7] In the following year Stambulov met death at the hands of an assassin.
[8] See page 306.

Soon after the accession of King George a new constitution was adopted which laid the foundation for the political life of the Greek state until after the First World War. Greece established a one-chamber parliament (*Boulé*) elected by universal suffrage. Unfortunately, the widespread illiteracy and political inexperience of the masses and the tendency of many Greek leaders to resort to political corruption in the interests of their diverse factions militated against stability in government. The reign of George I saw on an average at least one ministry come and go each year.

Arnold J. Toynbee, an English historian well versed in the history of the Near East, succinctly summed up the history of Greece before the war of 1914 when he stated: "The Greek nation's present was overshadowed by its future, and its actions paralyzed by its hopes." Patriotic Greeks, it appeared, were more concerned with adding to the kingdom the many Greeks who lived under the Turkish flag than they were in improving the lot of those that already lived under the Greek flag. Fundamentally, Greece was a poor agricultural country, and in the seventies its rural population was illiterate and backward. In the early days of King George's reign the country was lacking in railways and inadequately provided with roads, bridges, and means of communication. This had the effect of encouraging brigandage in some of the isolated districts. Although the kingdom was advantageously situated for playing a mercantile role in the eastern Mediterranean, for years its port facilities were neglected and its commerce remained insignificant. The national treasury was almost continuously on the verge of bankruptcy.

Crete was one of the territories which frequently held the attention of the Greeks to the detriment of progress in Greece herself. Crete was a large island lying to the southeast of Greece and was inhabited almost entirely by Greeks. The Cretans were as eager to become part of the Greek kingdom as the patriots of Greece were to bring about their annexation. Uprisings and insurrections against the Turkish government were of frequent occurrence on the island, and at the Congress of Berlin the great powers had attempted to remove the cause of Cretan unrest by compelling the sultan to grant the islanders a local assembly with a Christian majority.

But the Turkish government failed to carry out its promises, and the Cretans refused to be satisfied with their new status. Doubtless, even if the sultan had faithfully lived up to his agreements, unrest would have continued because of the strong national sentiment which had been aroused in favor of union with Greece. In February, 1897, the Cretans once more rose against their Turkish overlords, and in Greece a great outburst of national sentiment compelled King George to send warships and troops to aid the insurgents. A little later, on the mainland, other Greeks, organized as irregular troops, began raiding across the border into Turkish territory in the Balkans. The Ottoman government thereupon declared war, and its troops began an invasion of Greece.

In May, 1897, the great powers intervened and compelled the belligerents to sign an armistice, and in the course of the succeeding months a treaty was negotiated. To pay for her ill-prepared and hot-headed attack upon the Turks, Greece was compelled to cede to the sultan a small strip of Thessaly and also to pay an indemnity. For Greece the outcome of the venture, therefore, was harmful both to her national prestige and to her national treasury. The insurrection did bring some improvement in the status of the Cretans, however. The four great powers—Great Britain, Russia, France, and Italy [9]—persuaded the sultan to retain only nominal suzerainty in Crete and to withdraw from the island all Turkish troops and civil officials. The protecting great powers, apparently sympathetic with Greek nationalism, then appointed as governor of Crete Prince George, the second son of the Greek king.

The insurrection of 1897 helped to raise to prominence a Cretan who was destined to play a prominent role in Greek affairs for more than a quarter of a century. This was Eleutherios Venizelos, whose ancestors had migrated from Greece, after a futile revolt in the eighteenth century, while that country was still part of the Ottoman Empire. As a youth he had come under the influence of Greek nationalism, for he had received his collegiate degree from the University of Athens. Following his graduation from the university, Venizelos had returned to Crete thoroughly imbued with a determination to advance the Pan-Hellenic program by adding his island to the Greek kingdom. As might be expected, therefore, he had played a prominent part in the uprising of 1897, and in recognition of his political importance in Crete Prince George gave Venizelos a position in his government. But since the former sought to maintain the autonomous status of Crete while the latter aimed to bring about its union with Greece, they naturally disagreed on policies. Venizelos ultimately organized a political opposition to Prince George's government and in 1906 was instrumental in forcing the latter's resignation as governor. Prince George was then succeeded in his office by a Greek who, the great powers permitting, received his appointment at the hands of King George of Greece. Further recognition was thus accorded by the powers to Greek nationalism.

In the Greek parliamentary elections of 1910 Venizelos—who because of his ancestry was considered a citizen of Greece—entered the campaign as a candidate from a district in Athens and was elected. A strong national-

[9] Apparently in deference to the Kaiser's desire to secure the ascendancy in Turkey, both Germany and Austria-Hungary declined to be involved in the new settlement.

ist organization in the country then forced King George to accept Venizelos as his prime minister. During the years immediately preceding the First World War, therefore, Venizelos was the guiding genius in Greek history. He apparently had two principal aims: in domestic affairs to modernize and strengthen the kingdom; in foreign affairs to bring about a system of alliances which could be utilized to advance Greece toward the ultimate consummation of her Pan-Hellenic dream. To accomplish the first of these aims he made many changes in Greek institutions. These included the revision of the constitution, the creation of an efficient civil-service system, the improvement of the nation's finances, the inauguration of free and compulsory education, the enactment of progressive social legislation, and the reorganization of the army and navy. His successful efforts to secure alliances and to obtain further territory for Greece are discussed in later pages of this chapter.

SERBIA AND MONTENEGRO

Serbia, a small, primitive, agricultural country—cut off from the high seas in every direction by the intervening territory of other states—had inaugurated her revolt against the Ottoman Empire as early as 1804, when she was led by a swineherd known as "Black" ("Kara") George. Kara George, however, had been defeated and driven from the country by the Turks, but another insurrection occurred a few years later under the leadership of Milosh Obrenovich. In 1830 the little country was granted its autonomy by the sultan and from then on had practically an independent status, an independence which, as already pointed out, was formally conceded in the treaty of Berlin. In 1882 Serbia was raised to the rank of a kingdom.

Two important questions disturbed the history of Serbia down into the opening years of the twentieth century. Within the country there was the question whether the Obrenovich or the Karageorgevich dynasty should sit on the Serbian throne. In 1817 Milosh Obrenovich had murdered his rival for power, Kara George. Milosh then ruled in Serbia until 1839, when he was forced from power by adherents of the rival dynasty. In 1842 a Karageorgevich prince gained the throne, but in 1858 he in turn was driven from power to be succeeded by the aged Milosh Obrenovich. The latter lived only two years. In 1868 his son, Michael, was murdered by the Karageorgeviches, but the latter failed to secure the throne. In 1870 the Prince of Serbia was Milan Obrenovich.

Milan's abortive war against the Turks in 1876–1877 did not enhance his popularity with his subjects. Neither did Serbia's meager gains at the subsequent Congress of Berlin. A few years later his popularity suffered a further distinct decline when his secret convention (1881) surrendering Serbian aspirations in Bosnia and converting the principality into a satellite of Austria-Hungary became known. Whatever rise in popular favor resulted from his assumption of the title of king in 1882 was wiped out three years later by his disastrous attack upon Bulgaria, especially since the war brought increased taxation for the Serbs. Had his personal life been above reproach, his situation might not have been quite so hopeless, but his life was known to be scandalous, and there was little popularity to be gained by referring to it. From time to time, too, the king had to deal with anti-Obrenovich conspiracies and attempts at insurrection. Eventually, in 1889, after having proclaimed a liberal constitution for his kingdom, he resigned in favor of his son, who mounted the throne as King Alexander I.

Unfortunately the new king was not much of an improvement on his father. Apparently he had no thought of being a liberal monarch, for he abrogated the constitution which his father had granted and sought to rule without restraint. In the early years of his reign he increased his unpopularity because, like his father, he aligned Serbia in international affairs with Austria-Hungary. Finally, he shocked and antagonized a good share of his subjects by allowing his personal life to take precedence over his official position. While on a vacation at Biarritz the king chanced to fall in love with Draga Masin, an older woman, the divorced wife of a Serbian army officer; and despite the objection of his people, he married her and placed her on the throne as Queen Draga. From the beginning the new queen was unacceptable to those at court, and Alexander's tendency to favor her relatives added to his own unpopularity. Some army officers finally entered into a conspiracy with partisans of the Karageorgevich line to get rid of the Obrenovich dynasty. In 1903 King Alexander, Queen Draga, and a considerable number of their ministers and attendants were foully murdered in a palace revolution.

The throne of Serbia was now offered to Peter Karageorgevich, who accepted it and was crowned as King Peter I, but many of the European powers for a time refused to recognize the new government because of the manner in which it had come to power. The new monarch restored the constitution of 1889, with modifications widening the franchise, introducing proportional representation, and providing for special representation of the educated classes. King Peter accepted the idea of parliamentary government and chose his ministers from the majority party in the national legislature. The new king and his able premier and adviser, Nicholas Pashich, at once set out to strengthen the nation's financial condition and to increase its military forces so that Serbia might be prepared to grasp any favorable opportunity to redeem the Yugoslavs living beyond the kingdom's borders. So far as the question of dynasty was concerned, however, it appeared to be settled, for the murdered Alexander had been the last legitimate representative of the Obrenovich line.

The second important question which long disturbed the prewar history of Serbia was that of deciding whether the little state should align itself with the neighboring Dual Monarchy or with the more distant Russian Empire. In favor of the former was the fact that it was close at hand and could offer a favorable market for Serbia's products. Against an alliance with Austria-Hungary, however, was the fact that the latter included within her bounds great numbers of those who were akin to the Serbs. It appeared almost inevitable that a conflict must ensue between the powerful Austro-Hungarian monarchy and the little Serbian state when the Habsburgs, on the one hand, should try to extend their influence and territory down toward Saloniki, and the Serbs, on the other, should seek with increasing nationalism to redeem their Yugoslav kinsmen. For this reason it seemed to many Serbs more logical that their country should seek the backing and support of the great Slavic Russian Empire.

It has been pointed out that the outcome of the Congress of Berlin temporarily alienated Serbia from Russia and that in the following decade Serbia by treaty and otherwise became a sort of dependency of the Dual Monarchy.[10] This course of events was not particularly favored by the Serbian people, who showed their displeasure with the policy increasingly with the passing of the years. The Austrian alliance was one of the factors contributing to the unpopularity of both Milan and Alexander. So strong had become the nationalistic sentiment against Austria that even King Alexander shortly before his assassination had begun to turn in his international outlook from Austria to Russia. It was quite clear to King Peter when he assumed the crown that the only popular foreign policy for him would be one which was firmly anti-Austrian. This policy, accordingly, he adopted as his own, and from 1903 Serbia became more and more anti-Austrian and increasingly pro-Russian in her sentiment.

Serbia's change in foreign policy had a very real effect upon the domestic conditions of the country. In 1905, when the Serbian government was reorganizing its army and was about to purchase big guns, Austria-Hungary demanded that they should be bought from Austrian manufacturers instead of from French. Apparently the Habsburg government hoped to control the little kingdom's munitions supply and thus indirectly dominate its foreign policy also. When Pashich refused to permit Austria-Hungary to decide where Serbia should buy her munitions, the Dual Monarchy as punishment raised a customs barrier against Serbian exports and initiated the already discussed "pig war." This step only in-

[10] See page 262.

creased Serbian nationalism to a higher pitch than ever, and in the end it led to an improved economic status as well. In 1906 the Ottoman government granted Serbia a lease on part of the harbor at Saloniki and conceded her the right of free entry and export. With a way thus opened to the high seas, Serbian exporters eventually found new markets in other countries, and Serbia to a considerable extent gained her military and economic freedom from Austria-Hungary. But Serbian patriots fully realized that they were still without a seaport of their own and that their free access to overseas countries continued to depend upon the good will of some one of Serbia's neighbors. So far as the question of foreign policy was concerned, however, it had been almost unanimously decided in favor of co-operation with Russia.

This was also the foreign policy of Prince Nicholas, the ruler of the diminutive Yugoslav state of Montenegro. Inhabited by Serbs, Montenegro was inclined in foreign affairs to co-operate with Serbia as she had done in 1875 and as she was destined to do again in 1912, in 1913, and in 1914. Until 1905 Montenegro was ruled in a patriarchal manner, but in that year her ruler so far gave way to the spirit of the times as to grant his subjects a democratic constitution. Five years later Nicholas sought to exalt his small country by raising it to the rank of a kingdom. In the years before the war of 1914 the King of Montenegro, like the King of Serbia, was enamored of the idea of bringing all the kinsmen of the Serbs into some kind of Yugoslav state.

National Aspirations of the Balkan Peoples

None of the Balkan peoples organized in independent states after 1878 were content with the national boundaries which had been forced upon them largely as the result of the decisions of the great powers. The annexation of Eastern Rumelia by Bulgaria in 1885 and the attempted annexation of Crete by Greece in 1897—discussed in the pages above—were both indicative of the strong nationalist sentiment which existed in Bulgaria and Greece. But the Bulgarians and the Greeks were not the only Balkan peoples to be moved by nationalist aspirations. The people of every Christian state in the Balkans were ambitious to liberate and unite within the bounds of their own state the great numbers of kinsmen who dwelt outside their political frontiers; and each felt that their right to do this was as justifiable as had been the unification of Italy and Germany a few decades earlier or the consolidation of France and Great Britain some centuries before. For a clear understanding of subsequent developments in the Balkans and in Europe, a knowledge of the nationalist aspirations of each of the Balkan states is therefore essential.

On the surface it appeared that the Rumanian nationalists had a very difficult problem to solve, for their kinsmen were not all located in one foreign country, like those of Greece, for example. In Russian Bessarabia, to the north of Rumania across the river Pruth, the bulk of the population —the peasants—was chiefly Rumanian in the twentieth century despite the Romanov policy of "Russification." To the west of Rumania, in the Austrian province of Bukowina and in the Hungarian district of Transylvania,[11] the greater part of the people—again the peasants—were also Rumanians. Obviously, if Rumanian nationalists were to attain their goal completely, it would have to be won at the expense of both the Dual Monarchy and the Russian Empire.

To a minor state like Rumania this appeared to be an impossible task. A partial nationalist success, it was believed, must temporarily suffice. That is to say, Rumania by allying herself with either the Habsburgs or the Romanovs must be content for the time to gain territory at the expense of the other. There was some division of opinion within the country as to which policy should be adopted, but Rumania's loss of territory to Russia in 1878 turned the scale in favor of an alliance with Austria-Hungary against Russia. Such an alliance was signed in 1883.[12] Furthermore, the Rumanian King Carol I was staunchly pro-German in his sentiment, and so down until 1913 Rumania remained a faithful ally of the Hohenzollern and Habsburg rulers, and fondly dreamed of a future opportunity to wrest Bessarabia from Russia.

The program of the Bulgarian nationalists appeared more likely to be realized at the opening of the twentieth century than that of the Rumanians, for the territory which they coveted lay within the already decadent Ottoman Empire. Their program had in a sense already been outlined for them in the treaty of San Stefano which Russia had dictated in 1878. In 1885, to be sure, the Bulgarians had achieved part of their ambition, but they still aspired to "liberate" and annex Macedonia, of which they had been deprived by the Congress of Berlin. After 1878 a "map marking the lost territory of Macedonia hung in every Bulgarian school, and every Bulgarian peasant brooded over its loss and resolved in his sullen, dogged fashion to win it back." [13] Macedonia had not constituted a separate political unit for centuries, and its boundaries in consequence were somewhat difficult to define. In general, it included the valleys of the Vardar and Struma rivers and the peninsula of Saloniki. It extended from Thrace on the east to Albania and Epirus on the west, and in the north it merged into the Sanjak of Novibazar.

[11] See the linguistic map on page 571.
[12] See page 65.
[13] H. W. V. Temperley, *History of Serbia*, page 315.

Meanwhile, south of Macedonia the nationalists of Greece had become thoroughly permeated and dominated by Pan-Hellenic dreams of a "greater Greece," which should bring within the bounds of their kingdom the millions of Greeks who lived in what had once been the Hellenic world around the Aegean. Their nationalistic program included the eventual acquisition of Epirus, parts of Macedonia, Thrace, Constantinople, parts of Asia Minor including the important city of Smyrna, the islands of the Aegean, and Crete. If and when their nationalist dreams came true, the Greeks would once more have a realm which might rival that of the former Byzantine Empire. Although the territorial ambitions of Greece all lay within the realm of the Ottoman Empire, part of what the Greeks sought fell within the bounds of the territory coveted by Bulgaria.

It has been repeatedly indicated in connection with other topics that the closing years of the nineteenth century saw the rise of a strong national sentiment among Serbian patriots, who envisaged the creation of a great Yugoslav state under the leadership of Serbia. In the twentieth century, before the First World War, this desire for Yugoslav unification became a burning passion among chauvinistic Serbs. The "greater Serbia" would include not only Serbia herself but Montenegro, the Austrian provinces of Dalmatia and Carniola, the Hungarian kingdom of Croatia-Slavonia, the Austro-Hungarian imperial territory of Bosnia-Herzegovina, and part of Turkish Macedonia. The Yugoslav threat to the territorial integrity of the Dual Monarchy has already been discussed.[14] It should be observed here that the "greater Serbia" program constituted a menace, also, to Bulgaria's ambitions in Macedonia.

It will be obvious, therefore, that Macedonia constituted a veritable apple of discord for at least three of the Christian states of the Balkans. Bulgaria, Greece, and Serbia all laid claim to the district on historic grounds. The successive Balkan migrations had all passed through the Vardar valley, and each had left its impress on the population. Furthermore, as any student can see by consulting a historical atlas, at one time or another Macedonia had been within the political bounds of states dominated by Greeks, Serbs, or Bulgarians. Historic grounds alone could not settle the problem. Serbia and Bulgaria laid claim to the territory also on linguistic grounds. But, since the Serbs and Bulgars were themselves kindred nationalities, speaking similar languages, it was difficult to determine to which of them the intermediary dialects belonged. Furthermore, the Greeks claimed that in Saloniki and the coastal towns a majority of the people were Greeks; while, to make the situation still more complicated, even the Rumanians entered the controversy by claiming kinship with isolated groups of Vlachs.

By the closing years of the nineteenth century a triangular struggle for

---

14 See pages 274–278.

possession of Macedonia—when finally the Turks should be ousted—had developed, with Bulgaria, Greece, and Serbia as the contestants. Because of the earlier and more vigorous activities of the Bulgarian Church, it appeared that Bulgaria had won a majority of the Macedonians to favor union with her, though here again the situation became more complicated in 1893 when a Macedonian revolutionary committee began to agitate for complete autonomy for a Macedonia which should be independent of any one of the three claimants.[15] But the fate of the region was to a considerable extent connected with the course of events within the Ottoman Empire, to the history of which it is now necessary to turn.

Abdul Hamid and His Decadent Empire

The ruler who held the throne of Turkey throughout most of the period included in this chapter was Sultan Abdul Hamid II, who had mounted the throne in 1876 after his two immediate predecessors had both been deposed within a few months, and who held it for more than a generation until he himself was deposed in 1909. Abdul Hamid had been elevated to his position by a small group of liberals who hoped that by reform the national unrest within the Balkans might be quieted and the empire be freed from threatening international intervention. But, unfortunately for their liberal hopes, they chose the wrong man to be sultan. "Dry, unimaginative, and pedantically devoted to labor of a purely clerical sort, ... an old-fashioned Turk with a mentality bounded by the Koran," Abdul Hamid developed an absolutism "of which the main elements were deceit and fear, and which to operate ... required a tireless subterranean plotter, a creature half fox, half rat." [16]

To be sure, when, shortly after his accession, the great powers had intervened in Ottoman affairs, the wily sultan had hastily promulgated a constitution which seemed designed to Westernize and liberalize his realm. But his trick had failed to convince the powers that the millennium had arrived in Turkey, and so they had demanded that the sultan undertake a program of reform in the Balkans under foreign supervision. When Abdul Hamid refused thus to compromise his independence, war with Russia had resulted, and further territory had been lost by the Ottoman Empire in the resultant treaty of Berlin.[17]

[15] "It [the Macedonian question] presents, on the one hand, such a medley of jarring races, long-standing animosities, and ever-recurring atrocities, and, on the other hand, such a jumble of ethnographic riddles, philological controversies, psychological uncertainties, unreliable statistics, assertions and counter-assertions flatly contradictory on every point, that one almost despairs of an idea as to how it ought to be settled, or of the hope of ever seeing it settled at all." C. H. Haskins and R. H. Lord, *Some Problems of the Peace Conference,* pages 267–268.

[16] F. Schevill, *History of the Balkan Peninsula,* page 423.

[17] For an account of events in Turkey from 1870 to 1878, see pages 219–225.

Probably it was inevitable that a far-flung empire like that of the sultan would disintegrate in an age which was coming to be dominated by the forces of nationalism, industrialism, and imperialism. To begin with, it was a polyglot state, necessarily subject to the devastating ravages of the rising and dynamic nationalism of its subject peoples, aided and abetted as they were by their kinsmen who resided in the neighboring national states. If ever the latter could lay aside their national jealousies and enmities long enough to unite against their common foe, they were almost bound to bring disaster upon Turkey in Europe.

In the second place, the empire was so located that in 1878 it presented a tempting morsel to at least three imperialistic powers. Its territory commanded the Suez Canal, the vital link in the trade routes between the Western world—especially Great Britain—and the East. It stood athwart the important Straits connecting the Black and Mediterranean seas, and thus blocked Russia in her "historic mission" to acquire control of the Bosporus and Dardanelles. Its territory intervened between the Dual Monarchy and Saloniki, the port on the Aegean which Austria-Hungary hoped eventually to acquire to free her from dependence upon the Adriatic. In fact, one reason for Austria-Hungary's stipulation at Berlin (1878) that her military forces should be permitted to occupy Novibazar—the narrow strip of Ottoman territory lying between Serbia and Montenegro—was that she thought it offered a good railway route to Saloniki.

In the third place, the Ottoman Empire was economically in no position to defend itself against the great powers. It was still predominantly an agricultural country, having been hardly touched by the Industrial Revolution. Moreover, its agriculture was carried on largely by methods which were primitive and inefficient. Aside from agriculture, its natural resources were, in the nineteenth century, largely undeveloped. A backward country, therefore, inhabited by a population both sparse and poor, it was totally unable to raise enough revenues to enable an inefficient and corrupt government to support military and naval forces adequate for defense against the great industrial powers.

As a result of territorial losses to the great powers and to the national states established by the subject races, the Ottoman Empire by 1878 had shrunk to a mere shadow of what it had been in the seventeenth century. The sultan's loss of sovereignty over Rumania, Serbia, Montenegro, and Thessaly and his loss of all control—though technically retaining sovereignty—over Bulgaria, Bosnia, Herzegovina, and Cyprus—all in consequence of arrangements made at the Congress of Berlin—have been pointed out. But further losses were soon forthcoming. In 1881 France converted Tunis into a French protectorate, and in the next year Great Britain, in order to strengthen her hold on the Suez Canal, established a virtual protectorate over Egypt,[18] which was at least in name a dependency of the sultan. Again in 1897, as mentioned above, the sultan, for all practical purposes, also lost Crete when that island was granted autonomy under a Greek governor.

That Turkey in Europe was not entirely destroyed during the nineteenth century was the result not of her ability to defend herself militarily but of her policy of playing one great power against another. From 1854 to 1856 she had relied upon British and French support to defeat an aggressive Russia in the Crimean War. Two decades later she had escaped almost complete expulsion from Europe at the hands of Tsar Alexander II only because Austria-Hungary and Great Britain came to her assistance diplomatically— for a price. After the British became less vitally interested in checking Russia's expansion into Turkey—they themselves having obtained Cyprus and Egypt to safeguard their interest in the Suez Canal—Turkey turned more and more to Germany as a possible protector against the Russian Empire. William II's increasing interest in Turkey has already been discussed.[19]

Thus Abdul Hamid, in order to meet the threat to his empire from abroad, continued the old policy of double-dealing with the great powers. His domestic policies were no more admirable. As soon as he again felt secure on his throne, the powers at Berlin having solemnly sworn to uphold the integrity of his empire, he adjourned the recently created parliament and firmly and indefinitely suspended the constitution of 1876. As someone has pointed out, the sultan's interest in liberal reform appeared to fluctuate directly with the danger of foreign intervention. For thirty years Abdul Hamid ruled as an absolute autocrat.

So far as popular unrest was concerned, his aim was not to nurse and coddle it but to suppress it with every means at hand. To ferret out individual political enemies he relied on an elaborate system of espionage; to rid himself of them, he did not hesitate to resort to assassination. When unrest appeared among groups of his Christian subjects, he resorted to a system of terrorism by encouraging the less civilized Moslems to massacre them. An instance of the latter came in the nineties when his Christian Armenian subjects in Anatolia rebelled (1894) and were punished by having the Moslem Kurds turned loose upon them. All Europe shuddered at the fearful butchery of tens of thousands of Armenians, and Abdul Hamid came to be known as "Abdul the Damned."

The situation which finally brought Turkish affairs to a crisis developed in Macedonia, to which the sultan in the treaty of Berlin had promised to grant an autonomous regime. But Abdul Hamid, perhaps fearing that the

[18] See page 165.
[19] See pages 75–78.

grant of local autonomy was but the first step toward an inevitable surrender of authority, failed to carry out his promise, and the great powers
for various reasons never took any steps to force his observance of the
treaty. Doubtless one reason for the lack of activity among the great
powers was the fear that any real intervention might again lead to complications, as in 1875–1878, and to the advancement of the Balkan interests of
one power at the expense of some other. A *rapprochement* between the two
great powers most directly interested in the Balkan problem—Russia and
Austria-Hungary—came about in 1897 when they avowed their determination to maintain the *status quo* and abjured for the time being any designs
of conquest in the Balkans.

Meanwhile, conditions in Macedonia improved not at all; in fact, they
grew steadily worse. Unrest in this region continued unabated, fomented
to a considerable extent from Bulgaria, where the hope of eventually creating a "big Bulgaria" still survived. It was fomented, too, by Turkish mis-
government, by brigandage, and by widespread misery. The list of murders, the names of victims of kidnapers, and the story of burning villages
were spread far and wide by the foreign newspapers. Eventually, in the
face of another Macedonian insurrection (1903), the statesmen of Europe
were forced to turn their attention once more to the Balkans. Under pressure from Great Britain, what became known as the Mürzsteg program was
drafted by Russia and Austria-Hungary. Since this program was supported
by all the great powers of Europe, it was perforce accepted by the sultan.
The plan provided for maintaining peace in Macedonia by means of an
international mounted police, each of the five great powers being responsible for its allotted sector. The scheme never succeeded in completely
pacifying Macedonia, however, largely because of the activities of Bulgars,
Serbs, and Greeks, who continually plotted to redeem their kinsmen.

By this time, among the Turks themselves forces were being engendered
which were to topple Abdul Hamid from his throne. The sultan's efforts
to suppress all liberals within the empire drove many Turks to other countries. These liberals gathered in some of the democratic centers of western
Europe and there became more than ever determined to liberalize and reform the Ottoman Empire. By resort to propaganda through secret agents
as well as through newspapers and pamphlets, they ultimately gained a considerable following among the younger generation of Turks. In fact, the
Young Turks, as they came to be called, made such headway in winning
over the officers of the sultan's army that they dared in 1906 to transfer the
headquarters of their organization, the Committee of Union and Progress,
from Paris to Saloniki.

The Young Turks were still discussing plans for a possible insurrection
against the sultan when in 1908 they learned that the great powers were once

again considering intervention in anarchic Macedonia. Fearful that this region, too, might be lost to the Ottoman Empire unless steps were taken at once to reform conditions there, they launched a revolt in the army in Macedonia and at the same time voiced demands for a constitution. So widespread was the military revolt that Abdul Hamid at once saw the futility of resistance. In July, 1908, he again proclaimed the constitution of 1876, and issued a writ summoning the national parliament. Thus with almost no bloodshed a political revolution was consummated in the empire. Everywhere and among all classes there was deep rejoicing "while Christians and Mohammedans, Bulgars and Greeks, Albanians and Serbs passionately embraced in church, mosque, and public square, comporting themselves as if they verily believed that all men had become brothers."

The Bosnian Crisis

The leaders of the Young Turks, while residing in western Europe, had absorbed not only liberalism but nationalism as well. The Committee of Union and Progress therefore did not limit its pronouncements to such topics as liberty and democracy; it likewise discussed with what appeared to be great assurance its plans for removing the foreign-imposed restrictions upon Turkey's authority in such regions as Bosnia, Herzegovina, Crete, Macedonia, and even Bulgaria. In some quarters of Europe it actually began to be feared that the Ottoman Empire might be rejuvenated and under the guidance of the Young Turks become a power of some consequence. Such a development did not fit in with the plans of certain European governments, notably those of Austria-Hungary and Russia.

In the years just before 1908 developments within the Dual Monarchy were such as to lead the Habsburg government to increase its activity in the Balkans. In 1906 Count Aehrenthal, who hoped to meet the Yugoslav menace within Austria-Hungary by more aggressive action in the Balkans, became the Habsburg foreign minister, and Conrad von Hötzendorf, who urgently advocated a protective war against Serbia, became the new chief of staff. As part of Austria-Hungary's more aggressive Balkan policy plans were outlined for the construction of a new railway through Novibazar to link Vienna and Budapest with Saloniki and Constantinople.[20] In January, 1908, before the Young Turk revolt, Aehrenthal announced his plan for the new railway which would give the Dual Monarchy access to the Aegean through territory which was wholly Turkish.

Later in the year, however, the Austro-Hungarian general staff ap-

[20] The principal existing railway—through Serbia—was no longer considered secure for Austria-Hungary after the latter lost Serbia's favor in the opening years of the twentieth century.

parently came to the conclusion that the province of Novibazar was in no way suitable for a military railway, that the best military route to Saloniki was that followed by so many migrations in earlier centuries, that is, through Belgrade, Nish, and the Vardar valley.[21] In other words, Belgrade constituted the real gateway from Austria-Hungary into the Balkans. Obviously, an Austrian advance toward Saloniki through Serbia could be successfully executed only if Serbia were a Habsburg dependency or were crushed by overwhelming force. Austrian military plans therefore called for the weakening of the little Serb kingdom if not for its actual absorption by the Dual Monarchy.

This military decision seemed to coincide very closely with the desires of Habsburg diplomats, for Aehrenthal's foreign policy called for similar action in order to put an end to the pro-Serb agitation which was being carried on among the Yugoslav subjects of the Dual Monarchy. Apparently Aehrenthal believed that one effective way to check the spread of revolutionary fever from Serbia into the Habsburg provinces to the west "was to sterilize Bosnia-Herzegovina by the antiseptic process of annexation." So long as these provinces were formally recognized as being under the sultan's sovereignty, so long would the Serbs carry on their propaganda in the hope that, when Turkish rule in the Balkans finally and completely crumbled, the Yugoslavs of Bosnia-Herzegovina might be united with their kinsmen in Serbia. Aehrenthal hoped that the outright annexation of the provinces by Austria-Hungary might give the death-blow to the "greater Serbia" idea. By various agreements Austria-Hungary's right to annex the provinces at her own discretion had already been recognized. She had secured Russia's consent in 1876 and again in 1881, Germany's approval in 1881, and Italy's promise (1887 and 1905) that their annexation would not be considered a change in the Balkan *status quo* in the meaning of the terms of the Triple Alliance.[22]

Meanwhile, Russia's defeat in the Far East by Japan (1905) [23] and her subsequent agreements with Great Britain in regard to the situation in the Middle East (1907) [24] had had the effect of turning her attention once more to the Near East. Her diplomats now increased their activity in the Balkans and were eager to advance their Pan-Slavic program and to take advantage of Serbia's recently regained friendship. Shortly after Aehrenthal's announcement of plans for the new railway through Novibazar, for example, Izvolsky, the tsar's foreign minister—probably to win Serbia's good will—announced Russia's intention to build a railway across the

[21] Since the cost of building a railway through mountainous Novibazar was too great to warrant its construction for other than military reasons, the project was dropped.

[22] For these various agreements, see pages 63–64, 138, 220.

[23] See pages 237–240.

[24] See page 190.

Balkan peninsula from the Danube to the Adriatic and thus not only to provide Serbia with her long-sought access to the sea but also to link the Slavic countries more closely together.

The primary aim of Izvolsky's foreign policy in 1908, however, was to secure for Russia the right to send her warships through the Straits. In July of that year he suggested to Aehrenthal that they might discuss in the spirit of reciprocity their countries' desires in respect to Bosnia-Herzegovina and the Straits. After the Austro-Hungarian ministerial council had actually decided (August 19) to annex the provinces, Aehrenthal informed Izvolsky that, although Austria-Hungary considered the provinces her own, an Austro-Russian agreement might possibly be made. Russia might promise to show a benevolent attitude if circumstances should compel Austria-Hungary to annex the provinces, and in return Austria-Hungary might promise that, if the question of the Straits was raised, she would be willing to have a confidential exchange of views on the subject with Russia.

In the middle of September Izvolsky and Aehrenthal met at Buchlau and reached a number of agreements. The former gave his consent to the annexation of Bosnia-Herzegovina, provided Austria-Hungary withdrew from Novibazar; the latter agreed to the opening of the Straits to Russia's warships, provided the same right was extended to the warships of the other countries bordering on the Black Sea, and provided Turkish territory was left inviolate. Izvolsky now set out to secure international approval for altering the status of the Straits, but, before he had made any headway, Aehrenthal announced (October 6) the annexation of the provinces.

Naturally, this step caused great resentment at Constantinople, though even the Young Turks must have realized in their hearts that Bosnia and Herzegovina were already lost to the Ottoman Empire. Nevertheless, to show their opposition, the Turks began a boycott of Austro-Hungarian goods. Serbia's reaction to the annexation was much more vigorous than that of Turkey, for the little kingdom now saw rapidly disappearing all its own hopes of eventually annexing the provinces. Public opinion in both Italy and France was inclined to be indignant, but the governments of these states did not go so far as that of Great Britain. The latter at once denounced Austria-Hungary's action as a violation of the treaty of Berlin —though it must be admitted that this was not the first violation.

The Kaiser, on his part, feared that the annexation might alienate Turkey from the Teutonic powers and thus ruin their project for a *Drang nach Osten*. Ultimately, however, Bülow, his chancellor, won him to the view that Germany must stand by Austria-Hungary now as the latter had stood by Germany at Algeciras in 1906.[25] The German government made

[25] For the Algeciras conference, see page 119.

every effort to pursuade Turkey to recognize the annexation in return for the payment of an indemnity by Austria-Hungary, and in February, 1909, the Ottoman government did sign a protocol to that effect.

Meanwhile, among the diplomats of the great powers probably the loudest protests against Aehrenthal's step had come from Izvolsky. Apparently the latter, when he had thought that by co-operating with Austria-Hungary he might gain for Russia the coveted freedom of passage through the Straits, had cared little about the national aspirations of the Serbs. But Premier Stolypin in St. Petersburg saw the situation in a different way. What particularly worried him was the possible reaction of the Russian Pan-Slavists if they discovered that Russia's foreign minister had consented to betray Serbia's interest in Bosnia. He therefore sent specific instructions to Izvolsky not to abandon Serbia, but instead to protest against the annexation and insist that again, as in 1878, the Balkan situation must be dealt with by a general European congress. Stolypin maintained, too, that Aehrenthal's step was a violation of the understanding between Russia and Austria-Hungary that neither would disturb the *status quo* in the Balkans.

During the winter of 1908–1909 the international situation was particularly strained. On the one hand, the Serbs and the Pan-Slavs denounced Austria-Hungary; on the other, the Habsburg government attempted to scotch the Yugoslav peril by its notorious trial of Austrian Yugoslavs for treason at Agram.[26] Feeling ran high, and the danger of war was great. But Austria-Hungary was comforted by assurance from Germany that, if the former invaded Serbia and Russia in consequence attacked her, Germany would join the war on the side of the Habsburgs.

For a time it looked as though war might actually break out between Serbia and Austria-Hungary. The Serbian parliament by a unanimous vote demanded that Turkish sovereignty be maintained over Bosnia-Herzegovina. In view of the annexation, Serbia's "irreducible minimum" demand was that a strip of Bosnian territory should be ceded to her in order to give her contact with Montenegro and at the same time afford both states an outlet to the Adriatic. When news of the Austro-Turkish protocol of February, 1909, reached Belgrade, the Serbian army was mobilized, and an appeal was made to the Entente powers for assistance. The latter were inclined to give Serbia their support, but Austria, with the backing of Germany, stood firm. Since British and French support of Serbia was limited to diplomatic measures, the question of military assistance rested wholly with Russia.

The latter's decision not to give Serbia military aid at this time was doubtless hastened by a note from Bülow. The German chancellor had agreed

[26] See page 276.

to give the powers signatory to the treaty of Berlin an opportunity to sanc-tion the recently concluded Austro-Turkish protocol, provided Izvolsky would first promise that Russia's approval would be forthcoming when requested. In this way the fiction that the treaty of Berlin could not be altered, except with the consent of all of the signatories, would be main-tained. When Izvolsky appeared to hesitate to commit himself on this proposal, Germany notified him that, if he declined to accept it, she would "let things take their course." At St. Petersburg this statement was in-terpreted to mean that Germany would not restrain Austria from attacking Serbia (as the Austrian general staff was eager to do), and that, if Russia attacked Austria in behalf of Serbia, Germany would enter the war against Russia. The Russian government, realizing that it must fight alone and that its military recovery from the Russo-Japanese War was not yet com-plete, decided not to intervene.

Serbia was therefore left without military support and was placed almost at the mercy of Austria-Hungary. Had the Austrian military leaders been given free rein, a preventive war against Serbia might have been fought in 1909, but Francis Joseph firmly opposed such a conflict. Furthermore, Great Britain through diplomatic channels sought to save Serbia from military disaster by discovering some formula for a note which Serbia might send to Austria-Hungary in order to mollify the latter. In March the Brit-ish foreign secretary, Grey, finally secured a formula which Aehrenthal agreed to accept if Serbia used it. Perhaps his willingness to accept the formula was influenced by the fact that consent to Austria-Hungary's modification of the treaty of Berlin had been secured from all the powers signatory to the treaty except Great Britain. On March 31, 1909, Serbia in a note to Austria-Hungary recognized without reservation the latter's an-nexation of Bosnia and Herzegovina, and pledged herself "to live in the future on terms of good neighborliness" with the Dual Monarchy. Aehren-thal declared the Serbian note acceptable, and Great Britain then agreed to Austria's alteration of the treaty of Berlin.

After nearly six months of severe strain on the international situation, the crisis thus passed. Russia had been obliged to postpone her plan to aid Serbia, and Austrian chauvinists had been compelled to abandon, at least temporarily, their plan to smash Serbia. But the crisis was particularly un-fortunate, for it intensified Serbia's hatred of Austria-Hungary and led Russia to bend every effort to improving her position so that in the future she might thwart the plans of the Teutonic powers for a *Drang nach Osten*. In fact, Russia at once laid plans not only to create some kind of Balkan league but to "Balkanize" the already existing Franco-Russian alliance.

Ottoman Losses to Nationalism and Imperialism, 1908–1913

Austria-Hungary was not the only state to take advantage of the weakness of the Ottoman government following the Young Turk revolution. Urged on by Aehrenthal, Bulgaria, which was still tributary to the sultan, seized the occasion to forestall any future steps to reintegrate her territory with a rejuvenated Ottoman Empire. On October 5, 1908, Prince Ferdinand proclaimed Bulgaria's complete independence of the sultan, and to indicate his country's new status he himself assumed the title King. The Young Turks, who probably realized the absolute impossibility of holding Bulgaria within their empire, merely demanded the payment of an indemnity in return for the sultan's surrender of his legal prerogatives under the treaty of Berlin. As was to be expected, the governments of Bulgaria and Turkey could not agree on the amount to be paid, but thanks to Russia's mediation and apparent generosity [27] an agreement was reached, and in April, 1909, the sultan signed a treaty recognizing the complete independence of Bulgaria.

In October, 1908, anti-Turkish steps were taken in Crete also. On October 12, after a bloodless revolution had been staged five days earlier, the assembly of the island formally proclaimed the union of Crete with Greece. The office of high commissioner was abolished, and the government was entrusted temporarily to a committee of Cretans which included Eleutherios Venizelos. Although the union was not actually effected at this time, Turkey's shadowy claim to Crete faded still more, for the great powers in 1909 withdrew their troops from the island and left Venizelos in full control. All that remained for the Cretans and the Greeks was to secure eventually the formal acknowledgment of the sultan's loss of sovereignty.

At Constantinople, meanwhile, the situation was confused and uncertain. Although the foxlike Abdul Hamid had promptly proclaimed a constitutional government, he was not content to surrender his autocratic power without a struggle. When he saw the Young Turks embarrassed by the actions of Austria-Hungary, Bulgaria, and Crete, when he saw that many of those about him were tempted to question the wisdom of entrusting the fate of the empire to the inexperienced and, it appeared, unsuccessful Young Turks, he sought to arouse among his subjects a movement in his own behalf. In April, 1909, he was able to stage a counterrevolution—but

[27] Russia, again seeking to build up her influence in Bulgaria, agreed to pay the difference between what Turkey demanded and what Bulgaria offered. Of course, Russia's payment was to come out of her own claims on Turkey.

it was only short-lived. Troops loyal to the Young Turks soon arrived from Saloniki, and on April 27 Abdul Hamid was deposed. A new sultan, Abdul Hamid's brother, was proclaimed as Mohammed V. During the succeeding years the real power in the Ottoman government, however, was in the hands of the Young Turk ministry which assumed power upon the deposition of Abdul Hamid. The ministry, in turn, was practically the tool of the Committee of Union and Progress, which, in turn, was supported by the military. Probably the most influential leader in Turkish affairs was the strongly nationalist Enver Bey.

Those at the head of the Ottoman government after the downfall of Abdul Hamid were extremely nationalistic and soon embarked upon a vigorous policy of "Turkification." Their plan called for the revival of the empire by the joint process of nationalization and centralization. Armenians in Anatolia; Arabs in Syria, Mesopotamia, and Arabia; Greeks, Bulgars, and Serbs in Macedonia; the herdsmen of Albania; all these were to be "Turkified." This, to the extreme nationalists, necessitated the use of Turkish alone as the official language of the empire and the institution of a system of Turkish national schools. To strengthen the empire for its new role in international affairs, they decided to adopt the principle of compulsory military service, and secured German officers to reorganize the army. Similarly, they sought to improve the naval forces of the empire with British assistance.

Thus it was that the subject nationalities of the Ottoman Empire, after their first thrill of joy over the proclamation of a constitution and the subsequent deposition of the hated and feared Abdul Hamid, awoke to find their lot not better but perhaps even worse than before 1908. Centralization under the Young Turks appeared to mean, so far as the subject races could see, merely a continuation of the despotism of the deposed sultan. "Turkification" was soon found to entail repression of the non-Turk nationalities, accompanied by bloody measures as of old. In the spring of 1909 several thousand Armenians were massacred in cold blood at the instigation of Turkish authorities. Naturally, such Young Turk policies and measures not only failed entirely to win the loyalty of the subject groups but quickly drove them into active opposition. A home-rule movement was begun by the Arabs in Syria, and an insurrection in behalf of complete independence broke out in Arabia. In Macedonia and Albania nationalistic plots and conspiracies, accompanied by severe repressive measures at the hands of the Ottoman government, once more became the rule.

With the Ottoman Empire thus violently shaken by the nationalistic reactions of its subject peoples, the Turkish government had next to meet an imperialistic attack on its territorial integrity—this time at the hands

of Italy. The Tripolitan War, which began in 1911, has already been discussed,[28] as has Turkey's recognition of her loss of sovereignty over Tripoli
and Cyrenaica by the treaty of Lausanne in 1912. The sultan's government
was thus ousted from control of the last sections of that great empire in
northern Africa which it had once ruled.

The Tripolitan War had its effect, also, in Russia. Shortly after the war
began, the tsar's ambassador to Turkey proposed a Russo-Turkish league
in which, in return for Russia's guarantee of Turkey's territorial integrity,
the latter was to grant free passage of the Straits for Russian warships. The
proposal failed, however, because both the British and the German government secretly opposed it, and the sultan in consequence refused to grant
the right of passage. Russia's inability to solve her problem by direct negotiations with Turkey naturally increased her desire to create a Balkan
league which might be used indirectly to help change the *status quo* of
the Straits. This desire was further strengthened when during the war
the Ottoman government closed the Straits because Italian warships
bombarded the forts along the Dardanelles. The closing of the Straits,
in turn, prevented the accustomed flow of Russian exports from the Black
Sea area, and entailed the loss of millions of rubles to Russian merchants.

Another effect of the Tripolitan War was to increase the likelihood that
a Balkan league would be established, for the small Balkan states reasoned
that, if Italy could despoil the Ottoman Empire with impunity, perhaps
they could do the same. Furthermore, if the great powers could not or
would not force reforms in Macedonia to lessen the burdens borne by their
despairing kinsmen, why should not the Balkan states undertake to "liberate" them? Success would, of course, necessitate some sort of understanding among the Balkan states in order to bring effective co-operation.
Russia readily gave her blessing and assistance when the rulers and statesmen of Bulgaria, Greece, and Serbia sought to come to an understanding.

Negotiations for an alliance between Bulgaria and Serbia, begun in
October, 1911, resulted in a secret treaty in March, 1912, in which the two
states mutually guaranteed their political independence and territorial integrity and agreed to oppose with all their forces any attempt by a great
power to seize any part of the Ottoman Balkan territory if either of them
considered such action hostile to its interests. Annexed to the treaty of
alliance was an agreement on the future division of Turkish Macedonia.
Here Bulgaria made some concessions, for she had formerly demanded
autonomy for Macedonia in the hope that she herself might eventually
secure it all. The Serbo-Bulgar delimitation agreement assigned Struga,
Uskub, and Kumanova to Serbia, and Okhrida, Monastir, and Ishtip to
Bulgaria. A "contested zone" was left for future delimitation and was

[28] See page 146.

to be settled by the arbitration of the Russian tsar in case the two powers could not agree. In May, 1912, a secret military convention was signed by the two powers. In the same month Bulgaria and Greece also agreed on united action in case of war with Turkey, but reached no definite understanding regarding a division of Macedonian territory. Apparently Montenegro, too, became linked more or less formally with the other three powers in this Balkan league.

No precise time had been set by the Balkan states for their contemplated war on Turkey. Nevertheless, events so shaped themselves during the summer of 1912 as to hasten an attack. In the first place, Turkey was engaged in a war with Italy which was rapidly turning into a decisive defeat. If the Balkan powers wished to strike while Turkey was embarrassed elsewhere, they must strike soon. In the second place, Turkish concessions to the Albanians greatly alarmed the Balkan allies. Soon after the Young Turk revolution the Albanians had begun to agitate in favor of an autonomous national state. In 1909 their separatist policy had led the Turks to attempt to suppress them by military force, but the Turks soon discovered that it was an extremely difficult task to carry on a successful war against the herdsmen in the Albanian hills. When, in 1911 and 1912, Turkey found herself compelled to deal also with Italian imperialism, the Ottoman government decided to treat with the Albanians, and in the summer of 1912 the latter were conceded extensive home rule under the suzerainty of the sultan. But the part of the treaty which particularly alarmed the Balkan states was that which delimited Albania so as to include the four districts of Scutari, Janina, Monastir, and Kossovo. If this plan for an autonomous Albania should actually be executed, each of the four Balkan states would find itself excluded from a district which it had planned to annex.

The Balkan allies accordingly decided upon an immediate war against Turkey. Formal demands for Macedonian reforms were dispatched to Constantinople. On September 30, 1912, Bulgaria, Greece, and Serbia all ordered mobilization; eight days later little Montenegro made the fateful plunge and declared war. Although Russia and Austria-Hungary in a joint note thereupon announced that they would permit no modification of the territorial status of European Turkey at the end of the conflict, Serbia, Greece, and Bulgaria declared war on October 18. Meanwhile, Turkey had made peace with Italy, and now planned to hurl all her German-trained forces against the Balkan allies. It was apparently expected by the great powers and even feared by the Balkan states themselves that the Ottoman army would be formidable.

But the actual course of events proved the very opposite. Each of the allies operated in a separate area, and each was soon successful. The Bulgars, advancing in the Maritza valley, at once defeated the main Turkish army at Kirk Kilissé. After a second defeat at Lule Burgas the Ottoman forces fled until they reached the Chatalja line of fortresses only twenty miles from Constantinople. Siege was laid by the Bulgars to the fortified city of Adrianople. The Greeks successfully bottled up the Turkish navy in the Dardanelles, occupied most of the Turkish islands in the Aegean, and captured Saloniki. The Serbs, operating in the Morava and upper Vardar valleys, were also victorious, capturing Uskub and advancing into Macedonia as far as Monastir. Then, seeing her way to the sea down the Vardar valley blocked by Greek and Bulgarian forces, Serbia turned west in search of an outlet to the Adriatic, and late in November her forces occupied Alessio and Durazzo on the Albanian coast. The Montenegrins, at the same time, laid siege to the strong fortress of Scutari. The Albanians, now thoroughly alarmed, declared their independence of Turkey in a last-minute attempt to preserve their district from being divided among the victorious allies.

By this time developments in the Balkans had ceased to be a concern of Turkey and the Balkan allies alone, for the attack on Turkey precipitated another crisis among the great powers of Europe. Austria-Hungary feared that, if Serbia got an outlet to the Adriatic, the excitement and enthusiasm for the little kingdom which would be aroused in the Yugoslav districts of the Dual Monarchy would endanger the territorial integrity of the Habsburg realm. At the very outbreak of the Balkan conflict, therefore, Austria-Hungary had decided that she would go to war if necessary to prevent Serbia from gaining an outlet to the Adriatic. On the other hand, Russia feared that the Dual Monarchy might utilize the war as an occasion to seize more territory in the Balkans or might avail itself of this new opportunity to attack Serbia. The tsar's government accordingly decided that it would go to the aid of Serbia if Austria-Hungary attacked.

The crisis among the great powers was actually precipitated when the Serbs finally fought their way to the Adriatic. To check the Serbs, Austria-Hungary and Italy at once proclaimed the establishment of a new state, Albania. Some years earlier the Habsburg government had secured the approval of both Russia and Italy for this projected step.[29] Serbia had naturally never been consulted on this matter, however, and now persisted in her determination to secure an adequate outlet to the sea. Russia, despite her earlier agreement, was inclined to sympathize with Serb aspirations, and France gave Serbia strong support throughout the ensuing crisis. Germany, France, and Great Britain were all eager, however, to keep the

---

[29] In 1897 Austria-Hungary and Russia had agreed that such a state should be created if the territorial status in the Balkans could not be maintained, and three years later Italy had acceded to this agreement.

Balkan War from spreading to the rest of Europe and engulfing the great powers. Upon Poincaré's suggestion, therefore, Sir Edward Grey proposed that informal discussions should be held in London by himself and the ambassadors of Russia, Austria-Hungary, Germany, France, and Italy, and his proposal was accepted.

Accordingly, when Turkey—with her holdings in Europe practically reduced to Constantinople and the three besieged cities of Adrianople, Janina, and Scutari—signed an armistice on December 3, 1912, the subsequent peace conference was held in London under the supervision of the diplomats of the great powers. The peace conference was broken up in January, 1913, however, when the aggressive Enver Bey by a *coup d'état* seized power in Constantinople and resumed the war. On March 6 the Greeks captured Janina; on March 26 the Bulgars and Serbs entered Adrianople; and on April 22 the Montenegrins occupied Scutari in defiance of the orders of the London conference of ambassadors, which had meanwhile continued to hold frequent meetings.

The action of the Montenegrins increased the international tension. At London the statesmen of the six great powers had been attempting to reach an agreement on the size of the new Albania. Russia, representing Serbia, and Italy, hoping to dominate a weak Albania, desired to create a small state, while Austria-Hungary, desiring to check Serbia and to make Albania strong enough to repel Italy's penetration, argued for a large state. France supported Russia's views. Germany and Great Britain were chiefly interested in achieving a compromise which would prevent the spread of the Balkan War. But when little Montenegro went so far as to refuse to evacuate Scutari in the face of a joint note from the six great powers, it appeared that the war might engulf at least one great power, for in May Austria-Hungary decided to attack Montenegro. Her decision, however, quickly led the king of Montenegro to announce that he would at once withdraw his forces from Scutari, and so Austria-Hungary withheld her hand. But the course of events had taught her that the threat of force might thereafter prove effective in dealing with the Yugoslav states.

Meanwhile, in April, Turkey—now holding in Europe little more than the district about Constantinople—again sued for an armistice. Negotiations were resumed, and a treaty was signed in London on May 30, 1913. By the treaty of London—which was never ratified—Turkey lost all territory in Europe except a narrow strip extending from Constantinople to a line drawn from Enos on the Aegean to Midia on the Black Sea. If all the territory taken from the sultan had been turned over to the victorious Balkan allies, perhaps the latter could have pacifically reached a more or less satisfactory division of the spoils. But, as pointed out above, the great powers had intervened to create Albania, to which Montenegro and Serbia were to be compelled to surrender territory and ports captured by their military forces.

As a consequence of the loss of territory which she had conquered to give herself an access to the Adriatic, Serbia demanded that the territorial agreements reached with Bulgaria before the war should be revised. She now desired that her territory should be extended through Macedonia to the northern boundary of Greece so that she might be able to have at Saloniki an access to the sea through territory of a friendly power. Serbia and Greece held the territory which now came into dispute, for, while Bulgaria had been engaged in driving the Turks back through Thrace toward Constantinople, these two powers had occupied most of Macedonia. They now urged Bulgaria to be satisfied with the acquisition of Adrianople and Thrace.

But Bulgaria, whose desires in Thrace had been partly thwarted at London by Russia, was determined to acquire Macedonia and refused to consider any change in the original Serbo-Bulgar agreement. The immediate result of Bulgaria's attitude was the conclusion (June 1, 1913) of a defensive military convention against her by Serbia and Greece. Russia was alarmed at the possibility of the destruction of her Balkan league and urged restraint upon both Bulgaria and Serbia. The latter's future expansion, Russia pointed out, should be at the expense of Austria-Hungary rather than Bulgaria. "A break between Bulgaria and Serbia," Russia declared, "would be a triumph for Austria." The situation was further complicated by the attitude of Rumania, which during the First Balkan War had demanded that Bulgaria should surrender part of the Dobrudja to her in order to maintain the Balkan equilibrium.

Bulgaria's intransigence at this time was partly the result of encouragement from Austria-Hungary, whose statesmen were busily engaged in attempting to separate Bulgaria from her allies so that the Balkan league might be wrecked. Moreover, the Habsburg government was strongly opposed to a further material and moral strengthening of hostile Serbia at the expense of Bulgaria. Austria-Hungary was willing, in return for a friendly attitude on the part of Bulgaria, to give active support to the latter's aspirations in the Balkans, provided Bulgaria by compensations could keep Rumania neutral. Shortly after Bulgaria learned of the Habsburg attitude, she ordered her troops to attack the Serbs (June 29). The Second Balkan War—this time between the Balkan states—was thus launched. Greece and Montenegro at once entered the conflict against Bulgaria. And, although Bulgaria had agreed to cede some territory to Rumania, the latter also declared war against her. Bulgaria was therefore forced to fight against invading armies from the south, the west, and the north.

The Second Balkan War was of short duration, for Bulgaria was no

THE BALKANS IN 1914

match for her numerous foes. With the Bulgars sure to be defeated, Turkey also entered the fray and sent her army up the Maritza valley to retake Adrianople. King Ferdinand sued for peace, and an armistice was concluded on July 31. Ten days later a new peace treaty was signed by the Balkan states at Bucharest, and on September 29 another treaty was signed between Bulgaria and Turkey. Bulgaria suffered by the terms of both treaties. She was forced to hand over part of the Dobrudja to Rumania, to cede Adrianople and Kirk Kilissé to Turkey, and to content herself with a mere bit of Macedonia in the vicinity of Strumitsa and with central Thrace and an outlet to the Aegean at the unsatisfactory port of Dedeagach. And the boundary between Turkey and Bulgaria was so drawn that the only railway to Dedeagach was partly under Turkish control.

Greece got probably the best part of the spoils, for she acquired Epirus with the city of Janina, a large share of western and southern Macedonia with the two excellent ports of Saloniki and Kavalla, Crete, and most of the Aegean islands.[30] Serbia, although she did not secure the territory which she sought on the Adriatic, did obtain all of "Old Serbia," including Monastir and the Vardar valley down to Gevgeli. It was expected that she would secure an economic outlet to the Aegean through the Greek port of Saloniki. Serbia and Montenegro divided the district of Novibazar between them and thus at last came to have their long-desired common frontier.

In the western part of the Balkan peninsula, commanding the eastern shore of the Strait of Otranto and effectively cutting off Serbia from access to the sea, the great powers established the new sovereign state of Albania. To this new state—a principality—they gave a German ruler, Prince William of Wied. In March, 1914, the latter arrived in Albania, which as yet had nothing resembling a modern government. When the new ruler attempted to set up his authority, many of the Albanian mountaineers —long free from outside restraint of any kind—rebelled. The country was soon in a turmoil, and when, shortly after his arrival, the First World War broke out, Prince William withdrew from his recently acquired principality, never to return.

A comparison of the map of the Balkans in 1914 with that in 1870 will reveal the extent to which the Ottoman Empire had been driven from Europe during the intervening years; it had almost ceased to be a European power. A study of the maps will also show how the small Balkan states had been greatly enlarged at the expense of Turkey. Nevertheless, despite the considerable degree of success which each Balkan people had had in

---

[30] Rhodes and the Dodecanese—which from the viewpoint of nationalism belonged to Greece—had been occupied since the Tripolitan War by Italian troops. The great powers made no move to force them out in favor of Greece.

extending its national territory, in 1914 none was yet content. Bitterness was the lot of Bulgaria, which was still determined to gain the territory in Macedonia which the ill-fated treaty of San Stefano had allotted her. Restless ambition, whetted by partial success, still disturbed Greece, Serbia, and Rumania, each eyeing with longing the foreign territory occupied by her kinsmen. Increased hatred of Austria-Hungary for her part in forcing the creation of Albania poisoned the heart of Serbia. The Balkans in 1914 still constituted a region where a terrific explosion might occur at any time.

Part Three

❧

THE FIRST WORLD WAR AND ITS

INTERNATIONAL AFTERMATH

DURING the years from 1871 to 1911 Europe largely escaped the horrors of war. Nevertheless, as preceding chapters have shown, within this period forces were engendered which inevitably brought clashes between national aims and ambitions. Consequently, there occurred in the early years of the twentieth century a succession of international crises which ultimately culminated in that of 1914. The failure of Europe's statesmen to surmount this crisis, as they had successfully surmounted those of the preceding decade, let loose upon Europe and the world the most dreadful war yet known. The first two chapters in Part Three explain the basic causes of the First World War, discuss the tangled negotiations of July, 1914, consider the problem of "war guilt," trace the military and diplomatic history of the ensuing struggle, and show how the war released revolutionary forces which brought the downfall of three imperial dynasties. But during "the war to end war" mankind dreamed of a new international order, and many hoped that the ensuing peace conference would lay the foundation for this new era. The next two chapters point out the problems, achievements, and mistakes of this peace conference. They discuss the postwar efforts through international organizations and international treaties to reduce armaments and to lessen or abolish war, and they reveal how grievously mankind's hopes for the creation of a new world order were disappointed.

Chapter XI

THE OUTBREAK OF WAR IN 1914

D ESPITE the many hopes and plans for international peace which encouraged the world in the two decades before 1914, it is obvious that certain fundamental causes of international conflict seemed to be irresistibly drawing the great powers of Europe toward war. Crisis followed crisis in the years after 1904. Each left its heritage of suspicion, fear, and hatred; each led the nations to strengthen their armed forces to prepare to defend themselves against attack. By 1914 the tension between the powers had become so great that, in the face of Austria-Hungary's determination to crush Serbia, all efforts to preserve peace proved unavailing, and Europe found herself plunged into the most terrible war she had yet experienced. Until the very outbreak of the First World War, however, many still clung to their hopes of peace.

Hopes of Peace

To many people in the years before 1914 one of the most hopeful signs of peace among the nations was the fact that since 1871 no war had occurred between the great powers of Europe. Although some of the countries had carried on wars outside Europe, those who longed for world peace hoped that, once all the unclaimed areas on other continents had been appropriated and all the "backward" regions of the world had been Europeanized, war might finally be banished from the face of the earth.

These seekers after peace—the pacifists—pointed to many circumstances which seemed to indicate that the world might outgrow war. The nineteenth century, they argued, had witnessed the rise of businesses on such a scale that nations could no longer exist economically as isolated units but had become dependent upon one another for their economic well-being. The very magnitude of foreign investments, the rapid development of international credit and exchange, they declared, inevitably worked to promote mutual confidence among the nations. The improved means of communication and the introduction everywhere of cheap newspapers, they asserted, tended to create a world community and made possible the development of a world opinion against war. The interchange among the nations of professors and students and the spread of scientific discoveries across national borders helped to provide the peoples of the world with a common cultural background. In fact, the nineteenth and twentieth centuries, they pointed out, had gone far toward the development of a world community with increasingly uniform ideas and ideals.

They pointed out also—these advocates of peace—that the nations were becoming more and more accustomed to co-operation in spheres which were nonpolitical. In the seventies of the nineteenth century, for example, thirty states had organized the Universal Telegraph Union; twenty-three states had agreed to use the metric system of weights and measures; and sixty states had created the Universal Postal Union with its headquarters in Bern, the capital of Switzerland. Thanks to this last step, uniformity of postal laws, low rates, and speedy delivery had resulted for international mail. Soon hundreds of millions of letters and packages were being delivered throughout the world with a degree of safety that was remarkable. Other international agreements which helped to bring world solidarity were entered into by many nations. During the eighties conventions to standardize patent laws and copyright laws were ratified by a number of states.

The tendency toward world co-operation and world solidarity appeared, also, in many spheres of activity outside the control of national governments. Catholic Christians in 1881 began a series of eucharistic congresses, which were held successively in different parts of the world and were attended by clergy and laymen of many countries, and Protestant Christians likewise convened in world gatherings. In 1889 the Socialists organized the "Second International," and thereafter they held congresses of the workers of the world. In 1889, too, an international Parliamentary Union was set up to aid in spreading throughout the world the idea and practice of parliamentary government. Organizations such as the Rotary Club and the Boy Scouts extended across national lines, and they, also, held their world congresses. Especially significant were the numerous world gatherings of scholars and scientists with their resultant exchange of ideas in all realms of knowledge. By 1914 there were more than thirty international organizations that concerned themselves with "international science." It was hoped by pacifists that enlightened leaders everywhere might come to have a world outlook and that they, in turn, might exert their influence to lead mankind to think not merely in terms of one country but internationally.

To facilitate the growth of internationalism and to aid in the movement for world peace, the pacifists had begun early to organize. Prior to 1870 various peace societies had been established in Great Britain, the United States, Switzerland, and France. By 1914 the number of organizations of this type had increased until there "were 55 in Italy; 36 in France;

22 in Great Britain; 17 in the United States; 8 each in Austria and Sweden; 7 in Latin America; 4 in Australia; 3 each in Hungary, Norway, Russia, Spain, Japan, and Denmark; and 1 in Canada—a total of 160 organizations with many branches and an enormous membership." Probably one weakness in the peace movement was its failure to crystallize into one great international society with a definite and uniform program. After 1889, however, peace advocates held yearly international congresses, and in 1891 they located the permanent headquarters for their international peace movement at the capital of Switzerland.

Many were drawn into the peace movement not merely because of their hatred of the brutality and suffering which always accompany war, but also for economic reasons. In an effort to be "prepared" against an attack by another country, each of the great powers levied ever-increasing taxes. If war could be abolished, it was argued, a heavy financial burden could be lifted from the shoulders of mankind. Furthermore, it was maintained, the cost of a great war in the twentieth century would be so tremendous as to stagger the imagination. Writers of keen vision pointed out that such a conflict would be disastrous for even the victors. Ever since Bismarck had made the Franco-German War "pay" by successfully collecting an indemnity of five billion francs from defeated France, it had been thought in many quarters that, if a war was won, the cost of waging it could be placed on the shoulders of the defeated. In 1898, however, Ivan Bloch, a Polish Jew, revealed the futility of this fond hope by pointing out in his book, *The Future of War,* that war under modern conditions would inevitably bring general bankruptcy and starvation. His thesis received added support in 1910 when Norman Angell, an Englishman, asserted in his volume, *The Great Illusion,* that the economic and social conditions of the twentieth century made a military victory in war a mere illusion so far as improvement in the national well-being was concerned.[1] Other men like Alfred Nobel, a Swedish chemist and manufacturer of dynamite, Andrew Carnegie, an American steel manufacturer, Count Leo Tolstoi, a Russian novelist and social reformer, and Baron d'Estournelles de Constant, a French senator and publicist, gave abundantly of their wealth, their ability, and their time to advance the cause of peace.

Of course, it was realized that differences among nations would inevitably arise to cause ill feeling and friction. But, it was argued by peace-lovers, no differences could arise that could not be peaceably adjusted through diplomatic channels, use of arbitration, or resort to the mediation of other powers. A number of famous international controversies had been thus settled without recourse to war, perhaps the most famous being the *Alabama* case (1871–1872), the Bering Sea controversy (1892), and the

[1] Of course certain individuals—the war profiteers—might profit.

Alaskan boundary dispute (1903), all between the United States and Great Britain; the colonial differences between Germany and Spain (1886); the dispute over the Samoan Islands (1899), between Great Britain, Germany, and the United States; the boundary dispute between Argentina and Chile (1902); and the differences between France and Germany over Morocco (1905–1909). By 1909 some eighty treaties making arbitration compulsory had been concluded between the various countries, and it has been estimated that during the century preceding 1914 arbitration in some form had been used to settle nearly three hundred international disputes.

In 1899 what was considered to be a notable step forward in the cause of international arbitration occurred when the first Hague Peace Conference [2] created the Permanent Court of Arbitration, popularly referred to as the Hague Court because it met at the capital of the Netherlands. This court was hardly a permanent tribunal in the full sense of the term, for it consisted merely of a list of the names of 132 distinguished jurists from which disputing states might, if they wished, select arbitrators. It had, moreover, no compulsory jurisdiction over any state and no way to enforce its decisions. The court was eventually housed in a magnificent peace palace erected at The Hague with funds provided by Andrew Carnegie. By 1914 eighteen important cases and a number of lesser ones had been settled by this tribunal. On the other hand, even after the establishment of the Hague Court the great powers—Russia and Japan—resorted to war to settle their differences (1904–1905), Italy waged war against Turkey to gain colonial territory in northern Africa (1911–1912), and the Balkan states rose in arms against the sultan to advance their nationalist programs (1912–1913).

Causes of War

It is obvious from the foregoing statement that, at the very time when more and more attention was being given to the matter of preventing war, in the very years after machinery had been set up at The Hague for the pacific settlement of international disputes, wars were being fought in rapid succession by the nations of Europe. Why was this? In the first place, it was because the more deeply engrained spirit of competitive nationalism proved to be stronger than the more recently awakened ideal of international conciliation. In the second place, it was because various types of competition had developed among the nations, each of which was determined either to attain some objective or to prevent another power from attaining its objective, regardless of the justice of either's cause, and even at the cost of war if a reasonable chance of victory seemed present.

[2] See page 325.

3And in the third place, it was because the nations of the world in their international relations lived in a "state of anarchy."

Although since 1914 much has been written on the subject of "international anarchy," it may be well to explain what is meant by the term and what its significance was—and is—in the history of the world. In 1914 Europe consisted of some twenty-five sovereign states, each in theory the equal of every other. They were called sovereign states because each refused to recognize any authority higher than its own will and its own interests. Each claimed the right to make its own decisions and steadily refused to accept or adopt any procedure which seemed to encroach upon its complete independence—independence to enter into alliances, to make war, to conclude peace, to do as it pleased. None would concede the right of any higher international authority to make decisions binding it, and none would admit its obligation to appeal to any arbiter except force where matters of "national honor" or "territorial integrity" were involved. In other words, the states of Europe lived in a condition of anarchy in the sense that each recognized no authority outside itself.

In such circumstances war was very likely to occur whenever some ambitious "sovereign" power believed that the situation was favorable for it to obtain some objective for which it was competing with other powers. And international competition was present in many fields in the years before 1914. Rival national plans clashed in numerous places. The preceding chapters have given many instances of wars resulting from imperialism and of diplomatic conflicts—arising from the same cause—which at times brought Europe to the verge of war. Unfortunately for the peace of the world, in 1914 many imperialistic programs still remained unfulfilled to constitute a disturbing element to the course of international relations.

Austria-Hungary still sought to push her way into the Balkans in order to check the anti-Habsburg propaganda emanating from Serbia. Germany was inclined to support Austria-Hungary's Balkan program, for she herself planned to exploit the rich resources of Asia Minor and for the latter purpose needed a railway route through friendly territory in the Balkans as well as predominance in Constantinople. Obviously the German and Austrian plans for a *Drang nach Osten* conflicted with Russia's desire to accomplish her "historic mission" of acquiring Constantinople and the Straits, together with domination in the Balkans. The ambitions of the two Teutonic empires militated, also, against the realization of Italy's hopes for territorial expansion, for the latter—in addition to her ambitions in Africa and Asia Minor—desired to control the eastern coast of the Adriatic in order that she might transform that sea into an Italian lake. And Great Britain and France, despite the fact that they possessed the first and second

largest overseas empires respectively—or because of that fact—were disturbed lest some power might seek to obtain a "place in the sun" at their
expense. Imperialism thus produced conflicting national aspirations, bred
mutual fears and suspicions, and created an atmosphere which made a
great war possible.

Not unrelated to the clash of imperialistic programs had been the construction of numerous entangling alliances. By 1914 Europe had come to
be divided, in a general way, into two rival groups of heavily armed, ambitious powers. On the one hand, it will be recalled, there was the system of defensive alliances centering around Germany and Austria-Hungary
which Bismarck had created between 1879 and 1883.[3] These included the
Austro-German alliance (1879) and the Austro-Rumanian alliance (1883),
both against Russia, and the Triple Alliance (1882), which was aimed
primarily against France. On the other hand, there was the Franco-Russian
alliance (1894), defensive against Germany, and the Triple Entente (1904,
1907), which, though not specifically aimed against any particular power,
was largely facilitated by a common fear of Germany.[4] Italy was linked
with both sets of alliances, for, despite her membership in the Triple Alliance, she had made a colonial agreement (1900) and a military agreement
(1902) with France and an imperialistic bargain (1909) with Russia,[5]
which tended to wean her away from the Teutonic powers. Therefore,
although on paper Germany's system of alliances seemed more closely
and more definitely knit together than France's group of alliances and
ententes, it is doubtful if that was actually so.

These ententes, alliances, and counteralliances, though defensive in their
original character, eventually created an atmosphere favorable to war.
Naturally, the number of "danger spots" which might embroil all Europe
in a serious international conflict was increased as states became more and
more entangled in the plans and aspirations of their allies. At the same
time, believing that if attacked they would have the active assistance of
their allies, states became less willing to make concessions in times of
diplomatic clashes. Finally, as the international situation became more tense,
members of each alliance became reluctant to concede anything to members of the other lest their action be interpreted as weakness and their group
suffer a loss of prestige.

Accompanying the rise of entangling alliances, and undoubtedly accelerated by the fear engendered by these alliances, was the growth of huge
national armaments. After the Austro-Prussian and Franco-German wars,
the system of conscription which seemed to have enabled Prussia to gain

[3] For an account of the creation of Bismarck's system of alliances, see pages 61–66.
[4] For an account of France's alliances and ententes, see pages 104, 116–117, 119.
[5] For these agreements, see pages 116, 161.

an easy victory in each case was rapidly adopted by the other states on the Continent. One after another the national armies were reorganized on the Prussian model. Year by year the number of young men called to serve in the various national armies was increased until Europe came to be a veritable armed camp. All of this was done in the name of peace, for it was argued that the best insurance against war was national preparedness. Many taxpayers complained, however, of the ever-increasing tax burden laid upon them for armaments which some pacifists maintained would not assure peace but might rather provoke war. The latter viewpoint was well presented by H. N. Brailsford, an Englishman, who in *The War of Steel and Gold* (1914) asserted that preparedness inevitably brought war.

At the close of the nineteenth century a feeble attempt was made to limit armaments by international agreement. In 1898 Tsar Nicholas II of Russia invited the powers to assemble at The Hague to consider the possibility of some such agreement. Whether he was moved to this step by a sincere personal desire to promote the cause of peace or merely because the financial burden which armaments entailed was becoming too great for Russia to carry, is not clear. It soon became apparent, however, that some of the statesmen of the great powers were opposed to any international limitation on armaments. When the Hague Peace Conference convened in 1899 with delegates from twenty-six states present, no agreement was reached on this subject. In general, Germany stood out as the power most opposed to limitation of land armaments, and Great Britain blocked all steps which might weaken her control of the seas.

A second Hague Peace Conference, held in 1907, was attended by the representatives of forty-four states, but again the nations failed to agree upon any limitation of armaments. A number of rules were adopted to regularize and make more humane the conduct of war, but these, as the succeeding pages disclose, were largely ignored when the First World War came. Attempts to arrive at some agreement limiting naval armaments were also carried on by direct negotiations between Great Britain and Germany, but these, too, proved futile.[6] And so the armaments race went madly on. By 1914 the five major continental powers had millions of men in their peace-time standing armies, to say nothing of other millions trained and organized in the reserves.

Such a situation did much to create an atmosphere favorable to war. In the first place, it engendered international fear and suspicion. Although each power professed to be preparing merely to defend itself against aggression, each in turn suspected the others of preparing *for* aggression. In the second place, the knowledge that great military establishments were

[6] For these negotiations, see page 82.

back of them undoubtedly increased the reluctance of statesmen to make concessions which might appear in the nature of national diplomatic defeats and, conversely, increased their determination to press for some advantage which might appear to be a national diplomatic triumph. In the third place, in all countries to some extent, but more particularly in Germany, the growth of armaments contributed to the development of a state of mind usually summed up in the one word "militarism." [7] In the fourth place, with the growth of great military machines there developed in each country a general staff of leaders and experts, one of whose chief concerns was to prevent the army of another power from "getting the jump" on them in time of international crisis. These general staffs worked out carefully calculated "timetables" of what must be done if war should break out, and in every international crisis there was always the danger that some chief of staff, in an effort to maintain the schedule on his "timetable," might force an order for mobilization and thus precipitate a war. Finally, the existence of great military establishments produced a group of armament manufacturers in all of the important countries who were at times not averse to the spread of warlike ideas as a means of increasing their own profits.

A fourth factor which disturbed the course of European international affairs and constituted an ever-present potential cause of war was the increasing desire of certain groups of people of the same race, speaking the same language or kindred dialects, having in general the same customs and traditions, and inhabiting contiguous territories, to unite into one state independent of foreign domination. This was the goal of nationalism. The years before 1914 had witnessed a considerable advance toward this nationalist ideal in the creation of the German Empire and the Italian, Greek, Belgian, Serbian, Rumanian, and Bulgarian kingdoms. Nevertheless, in 1914 national statehood was as yet unattained or only partly attained in various parts of Europe. In general, Austria-Hungary and Russia constituted the chief obstacles to its consummation.

Although the desire for national unity was a force in Italy, which since her consolidation had cast longing eyes upon the Trieste and Trentino territories of Austria-Hungary wherein dwelt "unredeemed Italians," and in France, where the desire to regain the lost provinces of Alsace-Lorraine was

---

[7] "Militarism is an attitude of approval of war as an elevating, ennobling occupation, as the purifying salt in the otherwise nauseous human compound; . . . usually the approval rises to a desire for national glory as the product of military success, welcoming quarrel in order that war's beneficent influence may have full operation; and . . . the approval and desire have, as a result, the endowment of the military profession with a rank and worthiness higher and more meritorious than attaches to avocations of civil character." J. S. Ewart, *The Roots and Causes of the Wars (1914–1918)*, Volume I, pages 479–480.

still strong in the hearts of many, it constituted a more active factor in the Balkans. Here, though considerable advance toward national statehood had been made, each state was possessed of nationalist dreams as yet unfulfilled. Greece desired to obtain Thrace, some of the Aegean islands, and parts of Asia Minor in order to reconstruct the ancient Byzantine Empire. At the same time Bulgaria hoped to secure most of Macedonia and Thrace in order to round out her territory and gain an adequate outlet to the Aegean. Rumania longed to bring within her boundaries the millions of "unredeemed" Rumanians dwelling in Transylvania, Bukowina, and parts of Bessarabia. Serbia aspired to liberate her kinsmen who dwelt within the Habsburg empire and to gain a foothold on the Adriatic. Naturally, this unrest in the Balkans constituted a standing menace to the peace of Europe, the more so since states like Russia and Austria-Hungary sought to turn the Balkan aspirations to their own advantage. The possibility that some Balkan group would attempt to complete its "unification" and thus precipitate a war in which the great powers might participate was always present.

And if the statesmen of any power—great or small—led their country into war, they were almost certain to receive the enthusiastic support of the great majority of their fellow citizens. Patriotic history and literature magnified the former glory and future promise of each nation, while patriotic writers devoted themselves to extolling the superiority of their own racial group. "Patriotic state education taught unquestioning loyalty to state or dynasty as the first principle of moral conduct, carefully obscured any questionable occurrences or policies in the national past, and frowned on national criticism and proposals of radical reform." In every country some jingo or venal newspapers stood ready upon the least pretext to inflame public opinion by criticizing and misrepresenting the acts or policies of other states. In many countries international antipathies had been assiduously cultivated, with the result that national suspicions, fears, and hatreds were deep-seated. Such was the spirit of this type of nationalism that in each state the people felt that their government was always honest and upright in its dealings with others, that if war occurred it was because some other state was the aggressor.

Recurring International Crises

Many careful observers of the course of international events during the decade before 1914 were not wholly surprised by the outbreak of the First World War, for a series of international crises accompanied by an increasing tension among the great powers had revealed a noticeable drift toward war. These crises have been discussed in the preceding chapters, but it will be well to recapitulate briefly in order to get the international situation in 1914 clearly in mind.

The first crisis, it will be recalled, was precipitated in 1905, when the Kaiser landed at Tangier and proclaimed his support of the Moroccan sultan in maintaining the political sovereignty and territorial integrity of his country. War between France and Germany might have resulted from this step and the latter's subsequent demands, but it was avoided because the French government gave way and permitted the Moroccan situation to be settled at the Algeciras conference.[8] Although the outcome of this conference was largely favorable to France, the latter deeply resented Germany's interference in French plans. At the same time Germany was disturbed by finding herself and Austria-Hungary almost isolated in the deliberations of the Algeciras conference, for Italy had voted in favor of France against her own ally. Apparently this fact was not lost on the Kaiser, who, at the close of the conference, sent a telegram to Francis Joseph referring to Austria-Hungary as his "faithful ally," evidently implying that Italy had proved unfaithful to the Triple Alliance.

If the German government's plan in precipitating the crisis had been to destroy or weaken the recently consummated Entente Cordiale between France and Great Britain, it had failed miserably. At the very outset of the crisis British public opinion supported France, and the German ambassador at London had notified Berlin that British newspapers were even "more French than the French." In fact, during the crisis Sir Edward Grey, British foreign secretary, went so far as to inform the German ambassador that, if Germany actually attacked France, Great Britain could hardly keep out of the war. Furthermore, after consulting the prime minister and the minister of war, Grey permitted British army leaders to work out with French and Belgian military men provisional plans for British aid against a German attack in case Great Britain should ever decide to go to the aid of these two countries. The crisis therefore served to consolidate the Franco-British entente, while increasing the tension between France and Germany.

The next event which placed a severe strain upon the peaceful course of international relations came in 1908 when Austria-Hungary announced her annexation of Bosnia and Herzegovina.[9] From one viewpoint the ensuing crisis was of nationalist genesis, for the annexation aroused the Serbs almost to a frenzy because it appeared to block their plans for a "greater Serbia." From another viewpoint the crisis was imperialistic, for the Russian government was inclined to support Serbia's demand for an outlet

[8] For an account of the first Moroccan crisis, see pages 118–119.
[9] For an account of the Bosnian crisis, see pages 301–305.

to the sea in order to strengthen Russia's own position in the Balkans. Again war might easily have resulted between Serbia and Russia, on the one hand, and Austria-Hungary and Germany, on the other, had not Russia yielded and permitted the annexation of the provinces without a conference of the powers.

There is little doubt that in this crisis the Teutonic powers gained a decisive diplomatic victory. But the price they paid was high. Serbia now hated Austria-Hungary more bitterly than ever. By her promises to Austria-Hungary she had gained immunity from immediate attack; but in the following years she pushed the reorganization of her army with feverish activity, obtaining from France guns, munitions, and military advice. Although she had officially undertaken not to carry on propaganda inimical to Austria-Hungary, the promise had little likelihood of being fulfilled so far as the secret agitation of the various Serbian patriotic societies was concerned. The Yugoslav threat to the territorial integrity of the Dual Monarchy was not destroyed by the annexation of Bosnia-Herzegovina.

In the second place, Russia, after her humiliation, definitely began to make preparations for a war which she regarded as inevitable. In order to block the plans of the Teutonic powers and at the same time strengthen her own position in the Balkans, she at once turned her attention to the creation of a Balkan league. In 1909 she proposed to Bulgaria a military convention designed to protect each against the Teutonic powers and Turkey. Although the convention seems never to have been actually signed, Russia's attitude is disclosed in one article which stipulated "that the realization of the high ideals of the Slavic peoples in the Balkan peninsula ... is possible only after a favorable outcome of Russia's struggle with Germany and Austria-Hungary." In France, at the same time, Russia began a campaign to "Balkanize" the Franco-Russian alliance, that is, to convert the French to the view that developments in the Balkans which were vital to Russia were important likewise to France.

In the third place, the annexation strained relations between Italy and Austria-Hungary and led the former to take one more step toward the Triple Entente. During the crisis, when anti-Austrian agitation in Italy was so feverish, Austria-Hungary had concentrated forces in the Trentino. Apparently the Habsburg chief of staff had even contemplated an attack on Italy as well as on Serbia. Russia took advantage of the increasing anti-Habsburg feeling in Italy to come to an agreement with that power (October, 1909) in which each promised to attempt to maintain the *status quo* in the Balkans.[10] Apparently both had in mind the possibility of checking further Habsburg expansion to the southeast. Italy's double-dealing at this time becomes obvious when it is pointed out that only a few weeks

[10] For the agreement of Racconigi, see page 145.

later (December, 1909) she signed another Balkan agreement with Austria-Hungary in which each renewed professions of loyalty to the Triple Alliance.[11]

3 Within less than three years after the settlement of the Bosnian crisis Europe was again pushed to the verge of war by Germany's demand for extensive territorial compensation as her price for permitting France to transform Morocco into a French protectorate.[12] In this crisis Great Britain gave her whole-hearted diplomatic support to France. Had the French government positively refused to make any territorial concessions to Germany or had the latter failed to moderate her demands upon France, war might have followed, but fortunately neither government wanted war, and so eventually a pacific settlement was reached. But so strong was the feeling caused in France by this crisis that the pacific Caillaux ministry was overturned and was succeeded by one headed by the strong nationalist, Poincaré.[13] The latter immediately set out to strengthen the ties between France and Russia. In Germany many felt that their government had been blocked in its demands for compensation by Britain's control of the sea and consequently demanded further increases in the German navy. Germany's new naval program, in turn, increased the tension between Germany and Britain, especially after the Haldane mission failed to check their naval rivalry.[14]

4 Hardly had the statesmen of Europe regained their breath after the second Moroccan crisis before an equally grave crisis was precipitated, when, despite the opposition of the great powers, the Balkan league made a concerted attack upon Turkey in 1912. The two Balkan wars that ensued and the crisis which developed among the great powers in consequence were discussed in the preceding chapter.[15] Suffice it to point out here that the wars of 1912–1913 had far-reaching effects on the general European situation.

They nearly doubled the area and population of Serbia, greatly increased her self-confidence, and strongly stimulated her hope of a speedy realization of that dream of a "greater Serbia" which envisaged the ultimate acquisition of Bosnia-Herzegovina, Dalmatia, Croatia-Slavonia, and the Serb-inhabited districts of southern Hungary. They greatly increased the size and importance of Greece, where enthusiasm for a further advance toward

[11] Austria-Hungary agreed that, if she should be compelled to occupy Novibazar, either temporarily or permanently, the obligation to make territorial compensation to Italy would become effective.

[12] For an account of the second Moroccan crisis, see pages 121–122.

[13] See page 123.

[14] For an account of the Anglo-German naval rivalry and the Haldane mission, see pages 79–82.

[15] See pages 309–314.

the realization of its aims led the Greek government to purchase two war-ships from the United States in preparation for seizing any future oppor-tunity which might present itself for the reconstitution of the Pan-Hellenic empire. They converted Bulgaria into a defeated and humiliated power which was eager for revenge upon her erstwhile allies and was therefore prepared to join with any great power that seemed in a position to bring to her the Macedonia which she had twice lost within a single generation.

They turned over to Greece and Serbia former Turkish territory through which Austria-Hungary had planned to secure railway connection with the Aegean, at the same time placing in more powerful hands her exist-ing railway route to Constantinople. They obviously made more difficult of realization the proposed Berlin-Bagdad railway under German influ-ence. They revealed that Rumania was no longer a trusty satellite of the Teutonic powers, and at the same time smashed Russia's recently created Balkan league. The net result seemed unfavorable to the Teutonic powers. In fact, so alarmed was the Austrian government over developments in the Balkans at this time that in the summer of 1913 it seriously contem-plated a preventive war against Serbia in order to keep that country from becoming too powerful and too attractive to the Yugoslav people within the Dual Monarchy. The latter was on the point of launching an attack against the little Slav kingdom and was deterred only by the opposition of Germany and Italy.

Increasing International Tension

During the years 1912–1914, when the governments and peoples of Eu-rope displayed an "excessive nervosity," existing alliances and ententes were tightened up and new ones were projected. Definite steps were taken, for instance, to bring France and Great Britain into closer relations. After the failure of the Haldane mission,[16] Great Britain transferred most of her Mediterranean fleet to the North Sea in order quickly to balance there the increase in strength which Germany was planning to gain in the ensuing years by the execution of her naval program. In view of the weakening of the Entente naval power in the Mediterranean by the withdrawal of Brit-ish ships, Great Britain urged France to station most of her navy in that sea. Naturally, the latter was reluctant to leave her Atlantic coast unde-fended unless she received some guarantee from Britain. Eventually, with the consent of the British cabinet, personal notes were exchanged (No-vember, 1912) between Grey and Cambon, the French ambassador at Lon-don. Grey explicitly stated that, if either country suspected that it was about to be the victim of an unprovoked attack, "it should immediately

16 See page 82.

discuss with the other whether both governments should act together to prevent aggression and preserve the peace, and, if so, what measures they would be prepared to take in common." This correspondence, obviously, went far toward transforming the Entente Cordiale into a Franco-British alliance against Germany. Apparently the French government so regarded it, for it soon transferred its Atlantic fleet to the Mediterranean. Furthermore, Marshal Joffre later stated that French military plans were developed with the assumption of active British support.

In 1912, too, steps were taken to bring France and Russia into a closer understanding regarding the Balkans. Although in August of that year Poincaré informed Sazonov that France would not go to war over a Balkan question, he qualified his statement by adding the clause, unless Russia is attacked by Germany. Later in the year Izvolsky, the Russian ambassador at Paris, reported to St. Petersburg that Poincaré realized that an attack upon Serbia by Austria might force Russia to give up her passive attitude and take diplomatic steps followed by military measures against Austria. According to Poincaré, Izvolsky reported, Russia could count on French diplomatic support and, if Germany should come to the military aid of Austria, military support as well. Whether Izvolsky exaggerated or truly reported what Poincaré had said is not clear, but the effect upon the Russian government at St. Petersburg would have been the same in either case. The statement seemed to indicate that the Russian ambassador at Paris had at last succeeded in "Balkanizing" the Franco-Russian alliance. At the same time, in order to make the French people "Balkan-conscious," the French press was extensively subsidized by Izvolsky with funds secured from Russia. Meanwhile, to implement the alliance more effectively, a Franco-Russian naval convention was concluded, and the general staffs of the two countries conferred annually to perfect their plans for a joint offensive against Germany in case of war. Finally, in 1914 Russia was informed of the exchange of letters between Grey and Cambon in November, 1912, and negotiations were opened between Russia and Great Britain looking to a naval agreement.

Nor were the powers of the Triple Alliance inactive. Although that alliance was not due to expire until July, 1914, the treaty was renewed in December, 1912, and extended until July, 1920. Italy announced, however, that in case of war she would be unable to send any of her military forces north of the Alps, as she had always promised to do during the preceding quarter of a century. France's transfer of her whole navy to the Mediterranean, however, frightened her enough so that she was willing to sign a naval convention with the other partners in the Triple Alliance. In June, 1913, agreements were reached defining the action of the Mediterranean fleets of Germany, Austria, and Italy in case of war. Provision was specifically made for attacking French troop ships operating between North Africa and France. And in the spring of 1914 Italy once more promised to send troops into Germany to fight against France in case Germany should be attacked by the latter. So far as agreements on paper were concerned, therefore, the powers of both the Triple Alliance and the Triple Entente were more closely bound together in 1914 than they had ever been before.

In the Balkans, meanwhile, both Russia and Austria-Hungary were busily engaged in trying to construct or reconstruct alliances. During the wars of 1912–1913 Berchtold had managed to destroy Russia's Balkan league, but he was not content with this achievement. He next sought to overcome the threat of a "greater Serbia" by the creation of a Balkan alliance against Serbia, with Bulgaria as the pivot but with Greece, Turkey, and possibly Rumania also included. During 1914 negotiations were carried on between the Dual Monarchy and Bulgaria which had progressed far enough by July of that year so that Bulgaria was able to secure a loan from Berlin. On the other hand, Russia, whose diplomacy had received something of a blow by the destruction of her Balkan league, was desperately attempting to reconstruct the league by substituting Rumania for Bulgaria.

In 1913 and 1914 both sets of great powers were also attempting to improve their positions at Constantinople, where the Turkish government was trying to reorganize its military and financial departments after the Balkan wars. An Englishman was invited to reorganize the empire's finances; a Frenchman was asked to train the gendarmerie; a German general, Liman von Sanders, was invited to reorganize and train the army; and a British admiral was asked to do the same for the navy. The growing international tension in Europe is clearly revealed by the fact that, as soon as Sazonov learned of the Sanders mission, he entered a determined protest against giving a German command of an army corps in the Ottoman capital, where, he declared, the sultan would be deprived of all liberty of action. The Russian foreign minister wished to use the occasion to force Germany to draw back. But Great Britain, whose admiral's powers over the Ottoman navy were probably greater than those of Sanders over the army, declined to support Russia, and France likewise refused to exert pressure at Berlin.

In January, 1914, at a Russian council meeting Sazonov urged an immediate attack upon Germany unless the latter abandoned the Sanders mission. The council, however, decided for peace. The German government, in order to appease Russia, offered a compromise arrangement by the terms of which Sanders was not to command troops in Constantinople but was to function merely as inspector of the Turkish army. But Sazonov was still dominated by the idea that Russia must not permit Germany to secure control of Constantinople and the Straits, and during the early weeks of 1914 Russian military and naval officers worked on plans for seizing the Straits in case of necessity. In a council meeting in February of that year it was decided that Russian operations against the Straits could not be inaugurated with any assurance of success without a general European war.

Meanwhile, Russia's willingness to support Serbia in order to block Austria-Hungary's advance into the Balkans continued unchecked, as was indicated by the tsar's statement to Premier Pashich of Serbia when the latter had a conference with him in St. Petersburg in January, 1914. "For Serbia," declared Nicholas II, "we shall do everything." Russia directed her immediate efforts toward securing a union of Serbia and Montenegro and in 1914 began to bring pressure to bear on the ruler of the latter state. Such a union not only would increase the size and population of Serbia, but would at the same time provide the latter with an outlet to the Adriatic. The Austrian government, however, had come to the conclusion that, if this union were ever consummated, it would demand that the coast of Montenegro should go to Albania. Such a transfer of territory would have at least two significant results. It would again prevent Serbia from securing an outlet to the sea, and it would extend Albania's territory northward to the Austrian frontier. The latter possibility was particularly alarming to the Italians, because they believed it would increase Austria's influence over Albania, which the Italians themselves wished to dominate. Consequently, in the late spring of 1914 Italy again wavered in her loyalty to the Triple Alliance.

These brief glimpses of the diplomatic situation in Europe in 1913 and 1914 somewhat resemble the pieces of a jig-saw picture, none of which alone gives a complete or true idea of the picture as a whole. Possibly enough of the pieces have been fitted together, however, to indicate that just before the crisis of 1914 international rivalry and friction in Europe were being more and more localized and centered in the Balkans and the Near East. And as the fears and suspicions increased, so did the measures for expanding the various national armies and navies. Europe as a whole was perhaps never so well prepared to wage war as in the summer of 1914.[17]

Gradually the international situation became more tense. In Austria-Hungary "the feeling that the nations are moving toward a conflict, urged by an irresistible force," grew from day to day. In Russia the military began to realize that "we are preparing for a war in the West. Not only troops but the whole nation must accustom itself to the idea that we arm

[17] For the military and naval preparations of Germany, France, Russia, Austria-Hungary, and Great Britain, see the following pages, respectively: 88–89, 123–124, 252, 278, 191.

EUROPE
1914

HEBRIDES
ORKNEY IS.
NORWAY
Christiania
Stavanger Christian-
sand
BRITISH
ISLES
SCOTLAND
Aberdeen
Glasgow Edinburgh
NORTH
SEA
DENMARK
IRELAND
Belfast
Dublin
I R I S H
S E A
Newcastle
Copen-
ha...
HELIGOLAND
(GER.)
Kiel
Cork
CAPE
CLEAR
Manchester
Liverpool
THE
NETHERLANDS
Amsterdam
Ham...
ATLANTIC OCEAN
WALES
ENGLAND
Birmingham
Bristol
London
The
Hague
Rotterdam
Bremen
Ber...
Hanover
Leipzig
Plymouth
LANDS
END
ST. OF
DOVER
Antwerp
Cologne
Frankfurt
GERMAN
CHANNEL IS. □
(BR.)
ENGLISH CHANNEL
Le Havre
BELGIUM
Brussels
LUX.
Metz
RHINE R.
Nuremberg
CHANNEL IS. □
(BR.)
Brest
Paris
SEINE R.
Strasbourg
DANUBE R.
CAPE
FINISTERRE
Nantes
Orleans
LOIRE R.
FRANCE
Basel
Munich
Santander
San
Sebastian
Bordeaux
GARONNE R.
St. Etienne
Lyons
Berne
SWITZER-
LAND
A L P S
Geneva
Trie...
Oporto
Vigo
Oviedo
Bayonne
Toulouse
RHONE R.
Milan
Venice
PO R.
PORTUGAL
DUORO R.
EBRO R.
PYRENEES
MTS.
Saragossa
Turin
Genoa
ITALY
Lisbon
SPAIN
Madrid
TAGUS R.
Toledo
Marseilles
Toulon
Nice
Florence
CORSICA
(FR.)
Ajaccio
Rome
Seville
Valencia
Barcelona
Naples
Cadiz
Granada
Malaga
Cartagena
BALEARIC IS.
(SP.)
MINORCA
MAJORCA
Palma
SARDINIA
(IT.)
STRAIT
OF
GIBRALTAR
GIBRALTAR
(BR.)
M E D I T E R R A N E A N
Cagliari
Palermo
SIC...
A F R I C A
TRM
0°
10° E

ourselves for a war of annihilation against the Germans, and the German empires must be annihilated." In France the nationalists argued that Germany's threat to French security must be met by increased preparedness. "Russia is ready. France must be ready too," proclaimed the headlines of an article in the St. Petersburg *Bourse Gazette* in June, 1914, whereupon the Kaiser wrote: "Any German who still disbelieves that Russia and France are working full steam for an early war against us . . . is fit for the madhouse." "The whole of Germany is charged with electricity," wrote Colonel House, after visiting Berlin in May, 1914. "Everybody's nerves are tense. It only needs a spark to set the whole thing off." "Peace," the German ambassador in Paris reported, "remains at the mercy of an accident."

The Austro-Serbian Crisis of 1914

Such was the atmosphere in Europe when Francis Ferdinand, nephew of the Habsburg emperor and heir to the Austrian and Hungarian thrones, set out for his visit to the capital of Bosnia. In going to Sarajevo at this time the archduke took his life in his hands, for Bosnia was honeycombed with propaganda of two Serbian societies, "National Defense" and "Union or Death," and men were not lacking to undertake his assassination in the interest of the "greater Serbia" movement.[18] Even before the announcement of the proposed visit of the archduke, the latter of these societies had marked him for assassination. His presence in Sarajevo provided the sought-for occasion, and plans were laid under the direction of Colonel Dimitriyevich, a member of the society and chief of the intelligence division of the Serbian general staff. Three Bosnian young men who volunteered to carry out the plot were furnished with the necessary pistols, ammunition, and bombs in Belgrade, and smuggled back across the frontier into Bosnia. Apparently still others were in Sarajevo on that fateful day as "reserves" in case the attempts of these three should fail.

On the morning of June 28, 1914, the archduke's party arrived in Sarajevo shortly before ten o'clock. A few minutes later, when the party was on the way to the town hall to be welcomed by the mayor, a bomb was hurled by one of the trio of conspirators. It missed its mark, however, and exploded under the car behind the one in which Francis Ferdinand and his wife were riding. Later, when the archduke was returning from the town hall, a second conspirator suddenly jumped on the running-board of the car and assassinated both the archduke and his wife.

[18] Many Serbs feared that the archduke's scheme for transforming the Dual Monarchy into a Trial (triple) Monarchy with autonomy for the Slavs might wean their kinsmen in the empire away from the "greater Serbia" movement.

Once more events in the Balkans precipitated a European crisis. Count Berchtold, Austro-Hungarian foreign minister, determined to use this occasion for that final reckoning with Serbia which had been desired but postponed in 1913. The Austro-Hungarian government held that Serbian propaganda, seeking to unite all Yugoslavs under the Serbian flag, must encourage such crimes and endanger the Habsburg dynasty and empire if not stopped. Austria-Hungary's efforts must now "be directed to isolating Serbia and reducing her size." Austria-Hungary consulted her ally and learned that Germany would fully support her in *whatever* action she might decide to take. This promise, given shortly after the assassination (July 6), constituted what was later called Germany's "blank check" to Austria-Hungary. Germany, naturally, was anxious to have her one dependable ally maintain her strength undiminished, and concurred in her belief that this necessitated military action against Serbia. Austria-Hungary desired only a local war between herself and Serbia, and Germany in the beginning urged rapidity of action in order to forestall intervention. Both recognized, however, the possibility that Russia would intervene in Serbia's behalf.

Berchtold now proceeded to pave the way for the desired military action. On July 7 at a ministerial council [19] meeting in Vienna the foreign minister proposed a surprise attack upon Serbia. To this Count Tisza, the Hungarian premier, objected, and so the matter was postponed. One week later, however, Tisza consented to a short-term ultimatum purposely designed to be so severe that Serbia could not accept it. Said Berchtold after the ultimatum had been drafted, "The text of the note, to be sent to Belgrade, as it was settled today, is such that we must reckon with the probability of war."

The ultimatum asserted that Serbia had broken her promise "to live on good neighborly terms," with Austria-Hungary by encouraging propaganda aimed against the Dual Monarchy, and declared that the latter was thus compelled to abandon its attitude of benevolent and patient forbearance in order to put an end "to the intrigues which form a perpetual menace to the tranquillity of the monarchy." The ultimatum then made several peremptory demands, the most important of which were: (1) that the Serbian government officially condemn the anti-Austrian propaganda of its citizens; (2) that it suppress all publications and societies which incited hatred and contempt of the Dual Monarchy; (3) that all anti-Austrian teachers and books be eliminated from the public schools; (4) that the public officials implicated in the anti-Austrian propaganda be dismissed;

---

[19] Matters of foreign policy were usually settled by the ministerial council, which included the Austro-Hungarian joint ministers of foreign affairs, war, and finance, the prime ministers of both Austria and Hungary, and sometimes their finance ministers.

THE ARCHDUKE AT SARAJEVO

The arrival of Francis Ferdinand and his wife on June 28, 1914.

(5) that two Serbian officers, named in the ultimatum, be arrested at once; (6) that Serbia accept the collaboration of Austrian officials in the suppression of the anti-Austrian propaganda within her borders; and (7) that Serbia accept the help of Austrian officials in the investigation of those implicated in the Sarajevo crime. On July 23 the ultimatum, with a demand for an answer within forty-eight hours, was presented to Serbia.

The Entente powers' request that Austria-Hungary extend the time limit beyond the stipulated forty-eight hours was bluntly refused. Serbia consequently submitted her reply within the designated period. She offered to accede to all the demands of the ultimatum except the ones referring to the participation of Austro-Hungarian officials in the suppression of anti-Austrian propaganda and in the investigation of the Sarajevo crime. These, she asserted, would be a violation of her rights as a sovereign state. Serbia offered, however, to refer the whole matter to the Hague Court or to a decision of the great powers, if Austria considered the reply unsatisfactory. The reply was conciliatory, and most of the powers considered that it laid the basis for negotiation. The Kaiser himself believed that it removed "every reason for war." Nevertheless, Austria-Hungary asserted that the reply was unsatisfactory, severed diplomatic relations with Belgrade, and ordered partial mobilization against Serbia—which had already mobilized her army. "Vienna burst into a frenzy of delight, vast crowds parading the streets and singing patriotic songs till the small hours of the morning."

The Futile Efforts to Prevent War

Serbia's attempt to prevent war by having Austria-Hungary's ultimatum referred to the Hague Court or to a conference of the great powers had failed because of the Habsburg government's unwillingness to accept that means of settlement. Perhaps the latter still remembered how Germany had fared at the Algeciras conference. The great powers now offered various plans and made various proposals for a pacific settlement. On the day after the ultimatum was delivered to Serbia Sir Edward Grey, British foreign secretary, proposed that Great Britain, France, Germany, and Italy should exert a moderating influence simultaneously in Vienna and St. Petersburg. Nothing came of this plan, however, largely because of the attitude of France and Russia, which demanded pressure on Austria-Hungary.

In this crisis Russia was determined to support Serbia and asserted that she would agree to a settlement only in so far as it involved no humiliation of the latter as an independent state. Furthermore, she believed that her own position in the Balkans demanded a strong and independent Serbia to block the way of her rival, Austria-Hungary. Apparently the tsar's foreign minister, Sazonov, hoped to prevent war by bluffing Austria-Hungary into moderation by a show of force. On July 25 the Russian government issued orders for the "period preparatory to war," and on the next day notified Austria-Hungary that, if the latter's forces crossed the Serbian frontier, the Russian army would be mobilized against the Dual Monarchy. At the same time Sazonov requested Berchtold to discuss the ultimatum with him. Meanwhile, in St. Petersburg there were many who felt that war was inevitable and that now was Russia's chance for a final reckoning with Germany and the acquisition of Constantinople and the Straits. Sazonov characterized the Austrian ultimatum as highly provocative and expressed the hope that Great Britain would proclaim her solidarity with Russia and France.

As in 1913, so now, however, Grey was chiefly interested in mediation in the interests of peace. He believed that France, Germany, Italy, and Great Britain—the powers which had no direct interest in Serbia—might act jointly in Vienna and St. Petersburg. On July 26, therefore, he proposed that these governments instruct their ambassadors in London to meet in conference with him for the purpose of discovering an issue which would prevent complications. He contemplated a procedure similar to that followed during the Balkan crisis of the preceding year. France and Italy promptly accepted the proposal, but Germany declared that she could take part in mediation only at Austria-Hungary's express wish. The latter had no such wish, and so the plan was rejected.

Germany, in turn, advocated direct conversations between Russia and Austria-Hungary, and on July 26 such conversations were initiated between Sazonov and the Austro-Hungarian ambassador in St. Petersburg. Sazonov requested that the latter be authorized to discuss a redrafting of certain points in the Austro-Hungarian ultimatum in such a way as to satisfy Austria-Hungary's chief demands and at the same time be acceptable to Serbia. Berchtold, who was resolved not to enter into negotiations regarding issues between Serbia and Austria-Hungary, at first evaded Sazonov's request and later rejected it on the ground that war had already been declared against Serbia. The declaration of war had been issued on July 28 for the specific purpose of evading further proposals for mediation. Opposed to war to the very last, Francis Joseph was tricked into giving his consent by a forged telegram stating that Serbian forces had already entered Austria-Hungary. The bombardment of Belgrade, an unfortified city, began on July 29.

This action on the part of Austria-Hungary furnished further basis for Russia's belief that the former was planning "to gobble up Serbia." At the same time it gave Russian military officers an opportunity to exercise pressure for war preparation. They felt that a war between Austria-Hungary and Serbia was necessarily a war between Austria-Hungary and Russia, and therefore between Germany and Russia; while Sazonov believed that Germany was supporting Austria-Hungary and would continue to do so unless Russia made it clear that she would threaten Austria-Hungary with force in order to protect Serbia. On July 29 Russia declared mobilization against the Dual Monarchy. France approved the Russian policy and, far from exerting a moderating influence, telegraphed the promise of full French aid.

On July 29, also, Russia requested Great Britain again to press for mediation with a view to the suspension of military operations. The latter then suggested to Germany as a good basis for mediation that Austria should occupy Belgrade or other towns as pledges, while mediation should seek "to procure for Austria all possible satisfaction." This same plan had already been proposed by the Kaiser, and came to be known as the "pledge plan." Information on Russia's action together with Great Britain's attitude now caused Germany at once to address sharp warnings to Austria-Hungary, pointing out that the latter's refusal "to exchange views with St. Petersburg would be a grave mistake." Berchtold thereupon permitted the renewal of conversations at St. Petersburg the next day, but limited them to an explanation of the ultimatum and to a discussion of Austro-Russian—not Austro-Serbian—relations.

On July 30 the German ambassador at Vienna presented to Berchtold Great Britain's "pledge plan," together with Bethmann-Hollweg's urgent request for its acceptance. "If Austria refuses all intervention, we are thus faced with a conflagration in which England would go against us, and, according to all indications, Italy and Rumania not with us, and we two would have to face four great powers.... Austria's political prestige, the honor of her arms as well as her legitimate demands on Serbia, could be amply preserved by the occupation of Belgrade or other places.... Under these circumstances we most urgently and earnestly submit to the considerations of the Vienna cabinet that it should accept mediation under the honorable terms specified. The responsibility for the consequences which will otherwise result would be uncommonly serious for Austria and for ourselves." Later in the day the Kaiser also sent a telegram of somewhat the same tenor to Francis Joseph. The German government thus—a little late, perhaps—finally brought a moderating influence to bear upon its Habsburg ally.

The Habsburg foreign minister, however, declined to commit himself on the thirtieth, but ordered a meeting of the ministerial council for July 31. But before the council met on that day, the Austro-Hungarian government had received other messages from German officials. When on July 30 Moltke, the chief of the German general staff, learned that the tsar had declined to stop Russia's military preparations, he at once advised Austria to mobilize against Russia and promised German aid. When Berchtold saw Moltke's telegram, he exclaimed, "Who is in charge, Bethmann or Moltke?" After news of Russia's order of general mobilization reached Berlin on the morning of July 31, Moltke again urged Austria-Hungary to proceed at once with general mobilization.

When the Austro-Hungarian council met on the morning of July 31 to formulate its own plans, therefore, it had two types of messages from Germany to consider: Bethmann-Hollweg's urgent advice to accept Great Britain's pledge plan and Moltke's equally urgent advice to order immediate general mobilization. Berchtold himself believed that warlike operations against Serbia must continue, that Austria-Hungary could not negotiate concerning the British offer so long as Russian mobilization had not been stopped, and that Austria-Hungary's demands must be accepted integrally without negotiation. The council of ministers adopted Berchtold's views, and practically repudiated the mediation proposals, as Francis Joseph clearly realized when he wrote to the Kaiser: "I am aware of the implication of my decisions, and have made them with entire confidence in the justice of God and with the certainty that your armed forces will range themselves with unalterable fidelity in favor of my Empire and the Triple Alliance." On that day Austria proclaimed mobilization against Russia, some hours after the latter had herself ordered general mobilization against Austria and Germany.

As early as July 26 Russia had begun to take far-reaching measures preparatory to general mobilization. Three days later, after news of the bombardment of Belgrade, mobilization had been ordered against Austria-Hungary. Finally, in the afternoon of July 30, the consent of the tsar to general mobilization was obtained, and on the following morning public announcement of the mobilization was made. According to Russian army orders of 1912, mobilization was not the signal for beginning hostilities. Nevertheless, it was generally understood between the French and Russian experts that mobilization was equivalent to a declaration of war, and Great Britain had warned Russia as early as July 25 "that if Russia mobilized, Germany would not be content with mere mobilization or give Russia time to carry out hers, but would probably declare war at once." On July 30, France, her ally, had urged Russia to "take no immediate steps that may give Germany any pretext for the total or partial mobilization of her forces." Germany herself had warned Russia that mobilization was a highly dangerous form of diplomatic pressure since "the purely military consideration of the questions by the general staffs would find expression, and if that button were once touched in Germany, the situation would get out of control." Yet, despite all these warnings, and at a time when Germany was at length endeavoring to restrain her ally, and when the Kaiser and the tsar were in telegraphic communication, Russia proclaimed general mobilization.

Apparently Germany had at first decided to remain quiescent unless Russia actually attacked Austria-Hungary or actually commenced war preparations against herself. But Germany's chances for success in war depended upon rapidity of action, while Russia, because of her area and her deficient transportation facilities, needed time for mobilization and concentration of her troops. In the words of Jagow, German secretary for foreign affairs, Germany "had the speed and Russia had the numbers, and the safety of the German Empire forbade that Germany should allow Russia to bring up masses of troops from all parts of her wide dominions." The German military leaders naturally failed to see the wisdom of the tsar's suggestion that both Russia and Germany carry out their mobilizations without recourse to war, while the diplomats continued "to negotiate for the welfare of our two countries and the universal peace which is so dear to our hearts." Upon receiving news of Russia's general mobilization, therefore, Germany immediately proclaimed a "threatening state of war," and later the same day, upon the demand of Moltke, presented an ultimatum demanding that Russia stop every measure of war against Germany and against Austria-Hungary within twelve hours, or German mobilization would follow. No answer was forthcoming, and on August 1 Germany declared war upon Russia.

The system of entangling alliances now began to operate, for Germany well understood that France was bound to come to the aid of Russia in just such a contingency as now existed. The German general staff had years before planned that in case of a war against Russia and France, Germany's first thrust must be against France because the latter could mobilize much more rapidly than Russia. With France defeated by an overwhelming attack, German forces could then turn against more slowly moving Russia. It was the essence of the German military plan, therefore, that attack on France should not be delayed. Germany could not wait for France to decide to attack in accordance with the latter's treaty obligations. As early as July 31 she inquired from France what course the latter would pursue in the event of war between Germany and Russia. It is now known that she was prepared to demand the handing over for the duration of the war of Toul and Verdun in case France promised neutrality. Even if the French government had aimed to stay neutral, this demand for the two fortresses would have forced France into the war, for no French government would have consented to hand over to the Germans the fortresses. Germany had no opportunity to make her second demand, however, for France replied that she would consult her own interests, and began to mobilize. Although France carefully held her troops back ten kilometers from the German frontier, on August 3 Germany declared war on her.

Meanwhile, on July 31 Great Britain had asked France and Germany whether, in case of war, they would engage to respect the neutrality of Belgium, and France had given the desired assurance. Germany, however, had declined to state her attitude. Both France and Germany had signed treaties to respect the neutrality of Belgium and Luxembourg, but, as pointed out above, German military leaders years before had decided that in order to crush France quickly it would be better to violate the neutrality of Belgium than to make a frontal attack on the French fortified eastern frontier. On August 2 German troops occupied Luxembourg despite the protests of that little state. On the same day Germany presented an ultimatum to Belgium demanding within twelve hours permission to move her troops across that country into France. She promised, if permission were granted, to guarantee Belgian independence and integrity and to pay an indemnity. On the other hand, she threatened that, if any resistance were encountered, she would treat Belgium as an enemy, and the "decision of arms" would determine her subsequent fate. Belgium refused to grant Germany's request and appealed at once to Great Britain for diplomatic support in upholding her neutrality. On August 4 German troops crossed the Belgian frontier, and Bethmann-Hollweg admitted to the Reichstag that "this is a breach of international law ... the wrong we thereby commit we will try to make good as soon as our military aims have been attained."

The invasion of Belgium had its immediate effect in Great Britain, where up to this time public opinion had strongly opposed entrance into the war. Although Sir Edward Grey himself believed that Great Britain's interests demanded that she should range herself beside France and Russia if war came, the British cabinet was divided on the question. For a time, therefore, Great Britain kept her hands free and refused to commit herself regarding future action. On July 29 Bethmann-Hollweg made a strong bid for Great Britain's neutrality, promising that Germany if victorious would take no territory from France in Europe, would respect the neutrality of the Netherlands, and—if Belgium did not take sides against Germany—would respect her neutrality after the war. Grey's immediate reaction was that he could not for a moment entertain the chancellor's proposals.

Germany having failed in her effort to secure a promise of British neutrality, France next sought to attach Great Britain more closely to herself. On July 30 Cambon, the French ambassador at London, reminded Grey that their two countries had agreed in 1912 that, if peace was threatened, they would immediately discuss with each other what should be done. Cambon declared that now was the time for such discussions and suggested that the British government might promise to come to the aid of France in case of aggression by Germany. On the next day Grey stated that his government could not then give any pledge, and on August 1 he informed Cambon that "France must make her decision without reckoning on an assistance that we are not now in a position to promise."

On August 2, however, in view of Germany's declaration of war on Russia and her anticipated attack on France, Great Britain assured the latter that the British fleet would undertake to protect French coasts and shipping, should the German fleet come into the Channel or through the North Sea to attack them. This she did because as a result of her request in 1912 the French fleet was in the Mediterranean, and the northern and western coasts of France were undefended. Great Britain felt in honor bound to protect the latter, though the offer brought the resignation of two members of the cabinet.

On the following day came news of the German ultimatum to Belgium. This action threatened a cardinal principle of British foreign policy, namely, that the little countries across the narrow seas should not be absorbed by any great imperial system which might be hostile to Great Britain. In part because of this determination, Great Britain had fought against Louis XIV and Napoleon I, and had insisted during the Franco-German War that both sides respect Belgian neutrality. When, therefore, on August 4 news reached London that German troops had actually crossed the frontier into Belgium, Great Britain dispatched an ultimatum to Germany demanding assurance by midnight that Germany would respect Belgian neutrality. Germany, while admitting that Belgium's protest was just and that a wrong was being committed, refused on the ground that "necessity knows no law," and accused Great Britain of making war "just for a scrap of paper." The next day Great Britain announced that a state of war existed between herself and Germany.

By August 24 Austria-Hungary had declared war on Russia and Belgium; France and Great Britain had declared war on Austria; Serbia had declared war on Germany; and Montenegro had joined Serbia against Austria and Germany in another struggle to fulfill their common political aspiration. Early in September Russia, France, and Great Britain transformed their entente into a war-time alliance by signing the pact of London, in which each agreed not to conclude peace separately nor to demand peace terms without a previous agreement with the others.

The Question of War Guilt

Much time has been spent in trying to determine which country was primarily responsible for the outbreak of the First World War. Probably no decision will ever be reached which will satisfy all. It is obvious that the crisis of 1914 was precipitated as a consequence of propaganda carried on within the Dual Monarchy by Serbs who ardently sought to attain the national unification of all Yugoslavs. It is equally clear that fear of alienating the Magyars deterred the Habsburg government from giving the Yugoslavs within Austria-Hungary a place co-ordinate in political power with Austria and Hungary and led rather to repressive measures. The latter, in turn, made the Bosnians a fertile field for pro-Serbian propaganda, and from these disaffected Bosnians came the assassins of the Austrian archduke.

There is little doubt that after the assassination Count Berchtold and Conrad von Hötzendorf determined to end the Yugoslav menace by crushing Serbia with military force, and that Germany definitely encouraged Austria-Hungary to take military measures against the small Slav kingdom. It seems reasonable to believe that, if Austria-Hungary had not early in the crisis received this encouragement from Germany, she would never have dared to be so intransigent in the succeeding days. At the same time it is very clear that Russia, in order to thwart Austria's further advance into the Balkans, to enhance her own prestige, and to bring herself nearer the accomplishment of her "historic mission," was determined from the outset of the crisis to go to war if necessary to prevent Serbia from being weakened in her political sovereignty or territorial integrity. And early in the crisis Russia, in turn, was encouraged by the French government, which stated that it approved of Russia's stand and that it would give her loyal support.

Great Britain, while declining to commit herself to either set of powers, repeatedly sought, as in 1912–1913, to find some way out of the crisis short of war, and offered a number of plans for settlement. It appears, however, that this time Germany refused to co-operate with Great Britain as closely and as wholeheartedly as she had in the previous crisis. Nevertheless, it must be admitted that eventually—perhaps after it was too late to influence Russia effectively—Germany did apparently exert considerable pressure upon Austria-Hungary in favor of moderation and mediation. This is more than can be stated in regard to French influence upon Russia.

On the other hand, so far as mediation is concerned, both Russia and France appeared generally more willing to accept the various plans offered than did Austria-Hungary and Germany. Whether Russia's willingness to accept mediation was dictated by her belief that thus she might gain more time for her mobilization is not clear. What is clear, however, is the fact that Austria-Hungary steadily declined to accept any and all schemes for a pacific settlement of her dispute with Serbia, even when toward the end of the crisis her own ally, Germany, strongly urged her to accept, and even though she knew her attack on Serbia would probably precipitate a general war.

It is, of course, undisputed that Russia—perhaps seeing in Austria-Hungary's actions nothing but a determination to crush Serbia and in Germany's stand nothing but a decision to support her ally—was the first great power to order general mobilization with its inevitable fatal effect on the general staffs of all the other countries. On the other hand, it is perfectly evident that Germany was the first great power to declare war on another great power, thus automatically and unavoidably transforming the Austro-Serbian war into a great European conflict. There is so much evidence which may be used against at least four of the great powers that the decision as to primary responsibility seems to be largely a matter of arranging the evidence according to the already existing bias of each investigator.

Probably the truth is that each statesman and each country did about what could be expected under the circumstances, that the sole responsibility cannot be placed on any one person or state, that they were all being driven into the abyss of war by certain fundamental or underlying forces. Anyone who will carefully study the crisis cannot help seeing that those who directed the destinies of the nations were largely the victims of the forces about them. Nationalism, imperialism, militarism, and entangling alliances all played a part in the final denouement, and the development of a great war out of the crisis was made more easy and inevitable because the countries of the world lived in a state of international anarchy.

The Alignment of the Powers in 1914

Two of the countries which were linked with Germany and Austria-Hungary did not join those powers in the First World War. Berchtold had not taken Italy into his confidence in respect to his plans for sending an ultimatum to Serbia, and thus antagonized Italy at the very outset. Immediately upon learning of the ultimatum, however, the latter began to demand compensation under Article 7 of the Triple Alliance [20] and intimated that the Trentino might be considered as acceptable. Although Germany urged Austria-Hungary to offer some compensation to Italy, Berchtold was reluctant to cede any Austrian territory. In view of the Habsburg foreign minister's attitude, Italy informed her allies, just before the outbreak of hostilities between Germany and Russia, that, since the impending war was aggressive on the part of the Dual Monarchy, Italy was released from her obligations to them under the terms of the

[20] For this article, see page 138.

Triple Alliance. Although Berchtold stated that Austria-Hungary would be willing to consider a partition of Albania if Italy would join the Teutonic powers, the Italian government on August 3, 1914, formally declared its neutrality.

The secret Franco-Italian treaty of 1902 [21] had provided that in just such a contingency as existed in August, 1914, Italy should remain neutral. Nevertheless, it was not Italy's treaty obligations that dictated her policy so much as what her prime minister, Salandra, called "sacred egoism." In this respect, of course, she differed little from the other powers. She had always feared to lay her coasts open to attack by the British navy; her own army and navy had not yet recovered from the exhausting struggle in Tripoli; and *Italia Irredenta,* which she longed to incorporate within her own frontiers, lay within the territory of Austria-Hungary. During the opening weeks of the war Italy continued to carry on negotiations with both sets of powers to determine what she could gain from each, but her neutrality during this period contributed very materially, if indirectly, to the German defeat on the Marne by releasing French troops from the southeast for use against Germany.

Even before the outbreak of the war in 1914 the Austrians had decided that, despite the treaty of 1883,[22] Rumania could hardly be counted a loyal ally. She was, of course, in an advantageous position to receive bids for her aid from both sets of powers during the crisis. Russia started by offering Transylvania and a guarantee of the territory in the Dobrudja which Rumania had recently taken from Bulgaria. Austria-Hungary countered by offering Bessarabia. Although King Carol apparently advocated Rumania's entrance into the war on the side of Austria in accordance with her treaty obligations, Rumanian statesmen preferred a policy of watchful waiting. On August 3 the crown council decided in favor of neutrality, but Rumania, like Italy, continued to negotiate with both sides. Eventually, in fact, Rumania and Italy agreed (September 23, 1914) to follow the same course during the war.

Before the year was over, however, each set of belligerents was reinforced by one more power. Early in August Great Britain asked Japan for assistance under the terms of the alliance concluded in 1902 and renewed in 1905 and 1911. Germany was already busy with warlike preparations in Kiaochow, her naval base in the Shantung peninsula, and her warships in the Far East constituted a serious menace to British commerce. One of the objects of the Anglo-Japanese alliance was the defense of the special interests of the contracting parties in eastern Asia, and Japan decided to comply with the British request and, if necessary, declare

[21] See page 116.
[22] See page 65.

war upon Germany. Doubtless in reaching this decision Japan was more especially actuated by the desire to lessen by one the number of powers competing with her in the exploitation of China. On August 15, therefore, Japan sent an ultimatum to Germany demanding that the latter should withdraw all warships from Chinese and Japanese waters and deliver up the entire leased territory of Kiaochow before September 15 "with a view to the eventual restoration of the same to China." When Germany refused to comply with the demands of the ultimatum, Japan declared war on August 23.

The last country to be drawn into the conflict in 1914 was Turkey. In the years preceding the First World War, German influence—political, military, commercial, and financial—had steadily increased at Constantinople, so that it was almost inevitable that Turkey should enter the struggle on the side of the Teutonic powers. This was particularly likely in view of the fact that her traditional foe, Russia, was one of the Entente powers. Upon the assassination of the archduke the Ottoman government at once sought to connect itself with the Triple Alliance. The German government, at first reluctant to consider any definite commitment to Turkey, ultimately came to look with favor upon such an alliance; and a treaty, hurriedly drafted, was accordingly signed by Germany and Turkey on August 2 at the very height of the diplomatic crisis. Drawn up before the conflict had become one between the great powers, it provided that Turkey should enter the war on the side of the Teutonic powers in case Russia intervened.

While the Entente powers, unaware of this secret alliance, sought through diplomacy to secure Ottoman neutrality, the Turks utilized the weeks spent in futile negotiations to carry out extensive military preparations. Gradually Turkey's connection with the Teutonic powers became evident. Upon the outbreak of the war two German cruisers in the Mediterranean took refuge in the harbor at Constantinople. When their officers refused either to put to sea or to be interned, the Entente powers protested, but to no avail. Later in the year Turkey closed the Dardanelles to commerce, thereby cutting Russia's communication with the Mediterranean, and again protests had no effect. On October 29 one of the German cruisers, masquerading as a Turkish ship, shelled Russian towns on the Black Sea, and three Turkish torpedo boats raided the port of Odessa. In consequence Russia, on November 3, declared war on Turkey and was followed in this action two days later by both France and Great Britain. At the close of the year, therefore, the military alignment stood: Germany, Austria-Hungary, and Turkey against Russia, France, Great Britain, Japan, Belgium, Serbia, and Montenegro. The two conflicting groups soon came to be generally called the Central Powers and the "Allies."

Chapter XII

THE FIRST WORLD WAR

THE First World War differed from previous conflicts not only in the gigantic size of the armies directly engaged and the appalling numbers of casualties suffered, but in the tremendous mobilization of men and resources behind the lines for war purposes. The struggle was not confined to the battlefields alone, but was waged in factories, laboratories, and banks, on farms, railways, and merchant ships. In the First World War nations fought nations, and strained every nerve, utilized every resource for victory.

Relative Advantages of the Belligerents

For waging the war each side had certain distinct advantages. To begin with, the Central Powers possessed a much closer unity of command than did the Allies. Almost from the opening gun, and certainly after 1916, Germany overshadowed her allies, whose plans she came to direct, whose armies her officers frequently came to command. Among the Allies, on the other hand, until the very closing months of the war, lack of unity existed, and diversity of plans and lack of co-ordination resulted. The Central Powers, too, possessed a distinctly strategic advantage in their geographical position. Its compactness and the splendid network of railways made possible the prompt and efficient transfer of troops from one military front to another. The Allies, on the other hand, were widely separated geographically. From the beginning, Russia was almost completely isolated from her allies in the west. The resources of Great Britain's far-flung empire could be utilized only after they had been gathered from the seven seas and transported through the perils of the sea to the front where they were needed. Japan was thousands of miles from the main theaters of the war and confined her activities chiefly to the Far East.

Nevertheless, the Allies possessed several very important advantages, especially in the case of a long war. They greatly surpassed the Central Powers in man power and economic resources. Moreover, they possessed a naval supremacy which enabled them not only to marshal their own resources but to trade with neutral countries overseas. Thus they were able to utilize the food-producing and munition-producing facilities existing in extensive regions outside their own frontiers. At the same time Allied naval supremacy brought with it the power to blockade the coast lines of the Central Powers and, to a large extent, force them to depend on their own resources for the sinews of war. Throughout the conflict the Allies cheered themselves with the thought that time was on their side.

The Breakdown of German Plans for 1914

But Germany did not intend that the war should be of long duration. She aimed to strike a decisive blow at France immediately, then to wheel upon the slower-moving Russians and to defeat them in more leisurely fashion. With this end in view the "Schlieffen plan" called for the delivery of the blow not on the Franco-German frontier, which was lined with impregnable fortresses and defended by the Vosges Mountains, but through the neutral buffer states of Luxembourg and Belgium. On August 5 German troops attacked the Belgian fortified city of Liége, and, though temporarily halted by the stubborn defense of the Belgian army, they entered the city two days later. On August 23 the Germans captured the reputedly impregnable fortress of Namur after a three days' bombardment by heavy howitzers. The way was at length cleared for a German invasion of France, but, because of Belgian resistance, eighteen days had been required for the march to the French frontier.

France, meanwhile, had failed to concentrate her forces on the Belgian frontier and so was now faced with the necessity of shifting some of her armies to that front. The British Expeditionary Force crossed the Channel without mishap and on August 22 took up positions on the French left in accordance with prearranged plans. But French fighting at Charleroi and British at Mons failed to stop the German advance, and the Allied armies began a general strategic withdrawal.[1] Not until September 5, at the very gates of Paris, did Joffre give up his Fabian policy of retreat. On the next day came his order "to attack and repel the enemy." For seven days (September 6–12) the first battle of the Marne raged over a front extending from Paris to Belfort, engaging more than two millions of men. In the end —thanks to Joffre's strategy and the heroic efforts of Gallieni, Foch, Castelnau, and others—Paris was saved, the first German plan of campaign was wrecked, and the forces which were to have crushed France in a month were hurled back.

The main German armies now retreated to a strong position on the river Aisne, where trenches had been prepared for the infantry and concrete foundations for the big guns. From this position the Allies were unable to dislodge them. Next, the lines of both armies were extended westward

[1] For the French front, see the maps on pages 351, 380, and 389.

and northward, the French in an effort to outflank the Germans, the latter in an effort to protect themselves and to seize the Channel ports. Though the Germans succeeded in occupying Ghent, Bruges, and the coast towns of Zeebrugge and Ostend, their attempt to push on to Dunkirk, Calais, and Boulogne was thwarted by the determined resistance of the Allies, especially the British in the terrible first battle of Ypres. Thereafter the

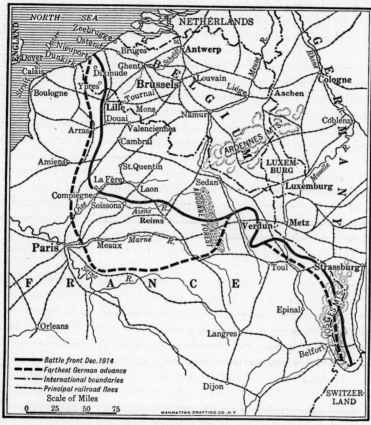

THE WESTERN FRONT IN 1914

conflict in the west ceased to be a war of movement and maneuver, and settled down to trench warfare over a line extending some six hundred miles from the Channel to the Alps. For nearly four years, since there were no flanks to be turned, the aim of the strategists on both sides was to force a "break-through" by frontal assaults against heavy guns and concrete "pill-boxes" bristling with machine guns.

Meanwhile, in the east the Russian armies had been mobilized more

rapidly than Germany had expected. Even before German troops had
reached the French frontier through Belgium, Russian soldiers were pour-
ing into East Prussia.[2] In alarm, the German government summoned from
retirement General Paul von Hindenburg, reputed to be a specialist in
the strategy and geography of a war with Russia, and appointed General
Ludendorff, chief quartermaster of the Second Army in the west, as chief
of the general staff of the Eighth Army in the east, with Hindenburg in
command. The battle of Tannenberg which followed (August 26–31)
put an end to Russian plans in East Prussia even more completely than
the Marne did to German plans in the west. The bulk of the Russian army
in this area was captured or destroyed; less than a third escaped. But
simultaneously with her advance into East Prussia Russia had driven
against the Austrians in Galicia, and by the end of the year she was in
complete occupation of nearly all of that province.

But fighting was not restricted to Europe. Great Britain was not in a
position in 1914 to be of great assistance to her allies with her armies, but
she played a vital role with her fleets. Almost immediately her naval superiority swept Germany's merchant marine from the seas. Furthermore,
the British navy, by hunting down and destroying isolated German warships, by forcing others into neutral ports, where they were interned, and
by blockading the German battle squadron in its own home waters, gradually cleared the seas of these threats to Allied shipping, and made possible
the gathering of Allied troops and supplies from the uttermost parts of
the earth.

Overseas, too, events went against Germany, owing largely to the fact
that the British navy made it impossible for her to send assistance to her
colonies. Immediately after her declaration of war on Germany, Japan
had begun a blockade of Kiaochow; a few days later troops were landed
and a siege was begun. On November 10, 1914, the German base was
surrendered to Japan. By this time, too, Germany's various island possessions in the Pacific had been captured by Japanese or British colonial
forces. In Africa, where the chief German colonies were located, operations were begun by Allied forces, and Togoland was soon conquered by
Anglo-French armies. The other colonies held out longer, but it was
only a question of time until they too would be captured.

German Successes of 1915

Early in 1915 Germany resolved to attempt to break Britain's control of
the seas, and decided upon the unrestricted use of submarines against all
vessels of the Allied countries. Her naval staff believed that the submarines

---

[2] For the Russian front, see the map on page 355.

would prevent Great Britain from bringing her military forces to play on the Continent to the same extent as hitherto, and that this would have the effect of breaking the fighting spirit of the other members of the Entente. Accordingly, on February 4, 1915, Germany designated the waters about the British Isles as a "war zone" in which enemy merchantmen would be sunk. This step she justified on the ground of self-preservation and as a justifiable countermeasure against "the war of starvation which had been initiated against the noncombatant population of Germany" by Great Britain's classifying as contraband all foodstuffs intended for consumption in that country.

In response to an American note on the subject, Germany asserted that, if Great Britain would permit the importation of food and raw materials in accordance with the declaration of London, Germany would abandon her unrestricted submarine campaign. Great Britain, while willing to permit the importation of food in case Germany lifted the submarine blockade, refused to allow the importation of raw materials, and announced on March 1 that she intended to intercept all overseas trade with Germany, to detain all goods, and to bring neutrals into British ports for search. The situation for neutrals came to resemble that at the time of the British and Napoleonic decrees in the early years of the nineteenth century. Anti-British feeling, which was rising in the United States, subsided, however, when a German submarine sank without warning the great British liner *Lusitania,* with a loss of some twelve hundred lives, of which over one hundred were American. A wave of anti-German sentiment swept over the United States.

Within a week an American note demanded that Germany disavow the sinking, make reparation, and take immediate steps to prevent the recurrence of such acts, and a second American note convinced Bethmann-Hollweg that the United States was determined to resist the submarine campaign as then being waged. Since Allied countermeasures and the scarcity of submarines had prevented the campaign from exerting any perceptible influence on Great Britain's warlike operations, Germany decided that the slight results did not warrant a policy which might bring the United States into the war, and accordingly ordered her submarine commanders to cease attacking passenger vessels. Germany's counteroffensive on the seas in 1915 thus proved to be a failure.

But the Allied attempt to open the straits connecting the Black Sea with the Mediterranean likewise failed. Early in 1915, upon Russia's suggestion, Great Britain and France decided to undertake an offensive at the Dardanelles.[3] A successful outcome here would be especially advantageous for the Allies, for it would open a much desired communication

---

[3] See map on page 313.

with Russia from the Mediterranean and would relieve her from Turkish pressure on the Caucasian front. It would also diminish the danger of attack on the Suez Canal and Egypt. The first plan called for a naval attack in the hope of forcing the heavily fortified strait. For this purpose a powerful fleet of British and French battleships was gathered; but when, on March 18, the Allied fleet attempted to force the narrows, a Turkish minefield in an unsuspected location led to the loss of three battleships and some two thousand men. Admiral de Robeck became alarmed at his losses and immediately ordered a general retirement.

It was next decided that the strait must be opened by troops rather than ships. On April 25 the Allied troops, chiefly Australian, New Zealand, Indian, and French colonial soldiers, began their Gallipoli campaign, forcing a landing on the peninsula at terrible cost. But the Turks had used the interval since the naval failure at the Dardanelles to strengthen the fortifications on the hills, so that the Allied soldiers were called upon to drive from almost impregnable positions a much stronger Turkish army under the command of a skillful German general. Three costly attempts to capture the peninsula netted the Allies nothing but the loss of some 55,000 men. The strait remained closed until the end of the war.

While the Dardanelles and Gallipoli campaigns were being waged, the Allies had hoped that Italy might be persuaded to join them and not only relieve Russia by engaging Austrian troops in the south but also contribute some forces for use against Turkey. During the early months of 1915 both sets of belligerents made bids for Italy's favor. Eventually, on April 26, 1915, Great Britain, France, and Russia signed with Italy the secret treaty of London, in which they promised Italy the Trentino and southern Tirol up to the Brenner Pass, Gorizia and Gradisca, Trieste and the Istrian peninsula, North Dalmatia and the islands facing it, Valona in Albania and a military zone about it, the Dodecanese in the Aegean, rights to the province of Adalia in case Turkey should be partitioned or divided into spheres of influence, and the extension of her possessions in Eritrea, Somaliland, and Libya in case Great Britain and France should gain colonial territory in Africa at the expense of Germany.

On May 23 Italy declared war on Austria, and on September 5 she signed the pact of London, further binding herself not to make peace except in concert with the Allies. But the military hopes of the latter, based on Italy's entrance into the war, were sadly disappointed in 1915. Italy sent no troops to aid in the Gallipoli campaign, asserting that they could not be spared from the home front. Furthermore, Italy's attacks along the Isonzo and in the Trentino made little headway because of the difficult terrain[4]

---

[4] For the Italian front, see the map on page 373.

and apparently contributed not at all to relieving the increasing Teutonic
pressure on Russia.

And Russia, by this time, was in dire need of all the assistance she
could get, for on May 1 a powerful Austro-German army had launched an
attack and pierced the Russian lines near Gorlice in Galicia. The Russians,

THE EASTERN FRONT IN 1915

inadequately equipped with heavy guns and insufficiently supplied with
munitions, could not check the attack; in less than two months most of
Galicia was regained by the Central Powers. But this was not all. On
August 4 the Russians were forced to evacuate Warsaw and Ivangorod in
Poland. By autumn the Central Powers had driven them out of Poland,
Courland, and part of Lithuania. These regions included one of Russia's

important industrial areas, and their loss greatly lessened her ability to wage a large-scale war.

In September, 1915, the Central Powers were free to look for other fields to conquer, and at length determined to administer to Serbia her long-delayed chastisement. Troops were accordingly shifted from the Russian to the Serbian front, and by the promise of receiving Serbian Macedonia, Bulgaria was persuaded to join the Central Powers in their attack on Serbia. The latter was in no position to hurl back the Central Powers when on October 7, 1915, they launched their invasion. Within two months Serbia and Montenegro were conquered; only on the Greek island of Corfu, where they were protected by Allied naval batteries, did the Serbs find a refuge from the Central Powers.

The Allied attempt to come to the aid of Serbia had been an inglorious failure. Trusting until too late that Bulgaria would not join the Central Powers or that, if she did, Greece would carry out her part of the Greco-Serbian alliance,[5] the Allies had made no preparations to aid Serbia before September, 1915. As soon as Bulgaria actually mobilized, Greece did likewise, and the Greek premier, Eleutherios Venizelos, asked the Allies to send a force of 150,000 men to co-operate with Greece in support of Serbia. But King Constantine later decided that the interests of Greece could best be served by neutrality, dismissed Venizelos, and refused to enter the war. The Allied forces which landed at Saloniki on October 5 were not only too few to render effective aid to Serbia; they were so few that their own position soon became precarious in view of the successes of the Central Powers.

Teutonic achievements in 1914 and 1915 had obviously done much to realize the German dream of a *Mittel-Europa* and a *Drang nach Osten*. The industrial regions of Belgium and northern France, Poland, parts of Lithuania and the Baltic provinces, Serbia, Montenegro, and northern Albania had all been successively conquered and held. Bulgaria and Turkey had become subsidiary allies, and seemed to be doing well. Apparently all that remained to be done was to defeat decisively the Allied forces in the west, and then dictate a peace commensurate with Teutonic achievements.

[5] In 1913 Greece and Serbia had signed a treaty and military convention in which it was provided that "in case of a sudden attack by ... the Bulgarian army against the Hellenic or Serbian army, the two states ... promise to each other mutual military support, Greece with all her land and sea forces, and Serbia with all her land forces." Constantine maintained that this applied only to a Balkan war, not to a general European war.

German Failure to End the War in 1916

The western front was therefore chosen as the area of attack in 1916, and Verdun was selected as the objective. The French lines at this point were only about ten miles from the German railway communications. An Allied drive here might conceivably render the whole German front in France and Belgium untenable. Furthermore, Verdun was an objective for the retention of which the French would be compelled to throw in every man they had. If they did so, Germany argued, the forces of France would bleed to death; if they did not do so, and Germany captured the city, the effect on French morale would be disastrous.

On February 21 the German attack was opened by a bombardment even more terrific than that which had preceded the campaign against Russia in the spring of 1915. Then, after scouts had ascertained that the bombardment had accomplished its work of destruction, after the German guns had changed their range and placed a "curtain of fire" behind the French trenches, the German infantry moved forward and occupied the French first line with comparative safety. The Germans expected to be in Verdun in four days. But the Germans had miscalculated the date of their entrance into Paris in 1914; they soon discovered that they had again erred in 1916. Responding to the battle cry, "They shall not pass," the French held on while the conflict raged back and forth about the city. With only a slight slackening of effort on either side, the struggle continued through March, April, and May. In June, when the Germans got within four miles of the city, even Joffre doubted whether Verdun could be held. But the French struck back and on June 30 recovered ground and neutralized the German advantage. Intermittent fighting continued in the Verdun sector during the summer and fall, but for all practical purposes the battle of Verdun was ended. The Germans had failed to achieve the results which they had expected from their attack; they had won a few square miles of territory, but the price they had paid in the irreparable loss of troops was out of all proportion to the gain which they had made.[6]

While the struggle for Verdun was in progress, the most important naval engagement of the war was fought in the North Sea. As already pointed out, German naval policy was not to risk a decisive action until, by the process of attrition, British forces had been so weakened as to give the German fleet good prospects of victory. With a view to destroying part of the British fleet, Vice-Admiral Hipper with scouting forces was ordered to demonstrate off the southwest coast of Norway in the hope of

[6] German casualties at Verdun were 427,000 killed, wounded, or missing; French casualties were 535,000.

luring a British squadron out. The German battle fleet, under Vice-Admiral Scheer, was to remain out of sight until the British squadron appeared, when it would rush in to annihilate it. Early in the morning of May 31, 1916, the German fleet sailed forth.

Unknown to the Germans, however, the British battle fleet on May 30 was ordered to concentrate in the North Sea. Early in the following afternoon the British scouting squadron under Vice-Admiral Beatty and the German squadron under Hipper made contact. The latter, hoping to draw the British on, fell back toward the German battle fleet some fifty miles distant. A running engagement occurred until Beatty discovered that he had encountered the more powerful German fleet, whereupon the British light squadron turned and attempted to draw the Germans toward the British high-seas fleet. Late in the afternoon the latter came in sight and succeeded in placing itself between the German fleet and its home base. The scene seemed to be set for a gigantic naval engagement. But the German fleet maneuvered with the sole object of avoiding an engagement and returning to its base. This the British prevented so long as it was light, but during the night the German fleet managed to cut its way through a weaker section of the British battle line, and returned to Helgoland. The question of victory was a matter of dispute at the time, and the battle of Jutland is still being fought by experts. Nevertheless, although the British lost fourteen ships to the Germans' eleven and suffered more than twice as many casualties, they were left in control of the sea.

Meanwhile, although German headquarters had vetoed the Austrian suggestion of a combined Austro-German attack upon Italy when the proposal had been made during the preceding winter, the Austrian general staff determined to carry out the plan with its own resources. It chose as its point of attack the salient of the Trentino, which ran down to the Lombard plain, threatening the Italian left flank. The Austrian objective was to be the Venetian plain, through which ran the two railway lines which were the main communications with the Isonzo front. If they could cut one, the Isonzo army would be crippled and compelled to retreat; if both, it might be pocketed and disastrously defeated.

On May 14 the preliminary bombardment began with over two thousand guns on a thirty-mile front. The Italians fell back, suffering heavy casualties. Cadorna, commander-in-chief of the Italian armies, immediately summoned his reserves to assemble around Vicenza, a stronghold protecting the northern railway line to the east, but the transfer of a new army of nearly a half million from the reserve lines of the Isonzo required time. The Italian brigades strove heroically to hold back the Austrians in the ensuing days, in some places sacrificing more than half of their strength. Nevertheless, on June 4 the Austrian troops were only eighteen miles from

Ewing Galloway, N. Y.

THE GERMAN HIGH COMMAND

Hindenburg, William II, Ludendorff.

Vicenza. But by this time Cadorna had received his reinforcements, and soon thereafter the Italian troops repulsed what proved to be the last of the great Austrian attacks. Within a few days Cadorna began to move forward in a counterstroke. The Austrian plan to force the retirement or capture of the Italian army on the Isonzo front had failed.

One of the chief reasons why the Austrians were forced to relax their efforts against the Italians was the unexpected launching of a Russian attack on the eastern front on June 4. The Austrian lines in the east had been weakened not only by the withdrawal of troops for use in the Trentino offensive but by the withdrawal of artillery as well. When, therefore, the Russians suddenly attacked along almost the entire front from the Pripet marshes southward to Rumania, they met relatively little resistance. Near Lutsk they broke through the Austrian lines and within two days opened a gap fully thirty miles wide. By June 16, in twelve days of fighting in this vicinity, they had taken Lutsk and Dubno, had advanced some fifty miles from their original lines, and had reached the Galician frontier. Meanwhile, in Bukowina, Czernowitz had been taken on June 10; and a week later the Russians were in possession of most of the province.

Teutonic forces were rushed to the threatened area from the French, Italian, and Balkan fronts, and Austrian operations were put more completely under the control of German headquarters. When opposed by German and more trustworthy Austrian divisions, the Russian advance slackened. Some Russian gains were made during July and August, but by the middle of the latter month the drive had spent itself, and it came to an end principally for lack of war materials with which to carry it on. Nevertheless, the effect of the Russian drive had been favorably felt by Allied armies before Verdun, on the Somme, in the Trentino, and along the Isonzo. On the latter front, in fact, the Italians launched an attack on August 4 which succeeded in capturing Gorizia.

By this time the western front was once more ablaze as the result of an Allied offensive. The Allies had created a military machine which they believed at last to be superior to that of the enemy. During all the last week of June they had subjected the German lines in the Somme valley to a terrific bombardment in an effort to wipe out the opposing trenches. In that week more munitions were used by the big guns each day than the total amount manufactured in Great Britain during the first eleven months of the war. Then, on July 1, along a twenty-five-mile front the Allied infantry leaped to the attack. From then until November 18, when the weather finally rang down the curtain on the drama in the west, the battle raged with only one intermission in September.

To the general public the Allied drive on the Somme seemed a failure, for it wrested only about 120 square miles of territory from the enemy.

Nevertheless, it did succeed in doing three things. It relieved Verdun, and transferred the offensive in the west from Germany to the Allies; it held the bulk of the German army on the western front; and it wore down the German forces tremendously, for the latter suffered some 445,322 casualties to the British 419,654.

The German failure at Verdun and the Austrian failure in the Trentino, followed by the Russian advance into Galicia and Bukowina, the Allied drive on the Somme, and the Italian capture of Gorizia, all had their effect on Rumania, which, up to this time, had remained a restless and uneasy neutral. Following Russia's spectacular drive against the Austrians in June, 1916, however, Allied statesmen once more negotiated with Rumania in the attempt to gain her support. In the end a secret treaty was signed by Great Britain, France, Russia, Italy, and Rumania, promising to the latter the Banat of Temesvar, Transylvania, and Bukowina. In addition the Allies promised the simultaneous assistance of both the Russian forces in Bukowina and the Allied forces at Saloniki. On August 27 Rumania declared war on Austria.

On the next day Rumanian troops, in an effort to close in on the Austrians from the north and the south, crossed the frontier into Transylvania at eighteen different points. But, for several reasons, they advanced not to victory but to defeat. In the first place, they were fatally short of heavy guns, airplanes, machine guns, and even rifles, and they had no great reserve of ammunition. Russia had guaranteed an ample supply of munitions, but the promise was not fulfilled. In the second place, they failed to receive the promised co-operation of the Allied armies. Russia's progress in the Carpathians was counted upon to divert the Austrian left wing in Transylvania, and Sarrail's advance from Saloniki was expected to engage the attention of Bulgaria; but neither of these developments occurred. Exhaustion of men and munitions, after a four months' campaign against Teutonic troops, prevented the Russian armies from carrying out their part of the bargain; and Sarrail, with a large but heterogeneous and poorly equipped army at Saloniki, hesitated to strike northward in a vigorous offensive lest a hostile Greek army attack him suddenly from the rear.

During the first three weeks of her campaign Rumania conquered about a quarter of Transylvania. But Mackensen was immediately dispatched to command a Bulgar-Teutonic army on the southern frontier of Rumania, while Falkenhayn took charge of the Austro-German forces facing the Rumanians in Transylvania. Heavy guns and immense supplies of munitions were rushed to the east. A simultaneous advance on the Transylvania and Dobrudja fronts then followed, and the Rumanian armies were soon in flight for safety. Bucharest fell on December 6, and by the middle of the following month, the Central Powers had occupied all the Dobrudja, all Wallachia, and a portion of southern Moldavia, and had driven the Rumanian government to Jassy.

The net result of Rumania's entry into the war thus seemed favorable to the Central Powers. The fertile grain fields and rich oil wells of that unfortunate country were added to *Mittel-Europa's* economic resources. The menace of Rumania's long-delayed intervention was removed, and the Central Powers now held their lines in the east with actually fewer men than had formerly been required. Teutonic prestige, which had been badly shaken by earlier events of the year, was once more restored. The Central Powers determined to capitalize this latest achievement and to seize the favorable position created by the fall of Bucharest to make a peace offer.

Peace Proposals of the Central Powers

For some months Germany had been hoping that the President of the United States would propose mediation. Almost from the beginning of the war President Wilson had considered mediation, and in January, 1915, he had sent Colonel E. M. House to Europe as his private and personal representative to discover, by conversations with persons of high authority in the belligerent countries, the possible attitude toward mediation. In 1915 Colonel House had found, however, that, although everybody seemed to want peace, nobody was willing to concede enough to get it; that none of the belligerents was willing to yield an iota of its aspirations; that France and Germany especially wanted annexations; and that both the Allies and the Central Powers expected to win the war and to impose their own terms. "Mothers and wives, fathers and brothers," he had discovered, desired peace, but not the governing groups.

A year later Colonel House again sounded out opinion and discovered that the Allies were determined to fight until the utter collapse of Germany, were confident of ultimate victory, and stated that the time was premature for mediation. But although the Allies were not interested in President Wilson's proposed mediation, the Central Powers had reached the place where they were favorably disposed toward peace proposals. When, for various reasons, President Wilson delayed making any open proposal of mediation, therefore, the Central Powers at length decided to make one themselves. They believed that, in view of their decisive defeat of Rumania, they would run little risk of damaging their prestige or showing signs of weakness, and that, if the Allies rejected their offer, the odium of continuing the war would fall upon them.

Accordingly, on December 12, 1916, less than a week after the fall of Bucharest, Germany transmitted a note to France, Great Britain, Russia,

Japan, Serbia, and Rumania. Animated "by the desire to stem the flood of blood and to bring the horrors of war to an end," the Central Powers proposed peace negotiations. They felt sure that the propositions which they would bring forward in the negotiations would be such as to serve as a basis for the restoration of lasting peace. But if, in spite of this offer of peace and conciliation, the struggle should continue, the four Central Powers, they stated, were resolved to carry it on to the end, "while solemnly disclaiming any responsibility before mankind and history."

The weak feature of the German note was the absence of any definite terms of peace. In respect to this matter Germany was in an embarrassing position. If she proposed terms which would be moderate enough to invite serious discussion by the Allies, the German people would question the much-advertised success of the Central Powers, and their morale might be weakened or destroyed. On the other hand, if she formulated terms in accordance with popular expectations and the demands of her military leaders, the Allies could assert that peace with victorious Germany would mean a Germanized world, and Allied morale would be enormously strengthened.

An official reply to Germany was presented on December 30 in the collective name of Russia, France, Great Britain, Japan, Italy, Serbia, Belgium, Montenegro, Portugal, and Rumania. The mere suggestion, without statement of terms, that negotiations should be opened, was not, they asserted, an offer of peace but a war maneuver, a calculated attempt to influence the future course of the war, and to end it by imposing a German peace. The object of Germany's overtures, they declared, was to create dissension in public opinion in Allied countries, and to stiffen public opinion in the Central Powers, "already severely tried by their losses, worn out by economic pressure and crushed by the supreme effort which has been imposed upon their inhabitants." They denied that the Central Powers had won the victory; the "war map" of Europe represented nothing more than "a superficial and passing phase of the situation, and not the real strength of the belligerents." The Allied governments, therefore, fully conscious of the gravity of the moment, but equally conscious of its requirements, refused to consider a proposal which was "empty and insincere."

Germany's Unrestricted Submarine Campaign

Even before the Allied rejection of their peace proposal both Hindenburg and Ludendorff had been urging the resumption of unrestricted submarine warfare. They had come finally to the conclusion that only by this means could Germany force the Allies to accept peace. But Bethmann-Hollweg had wished to try first his peace proposal, and general headquarters had consented. Toward the close of December, however, Hindenburg again insisted that Germany's dangerous economic and military position made the unrestricted submarine campaign absolutely essential. The chancellor at length gave way, and on January 9, 1917, a German crown council decided that unrestricted submarine warfare should be resumed on February 1. That this move on the part of Germany would force the

THE ZONE OF UNRESTRICTED SUBMARINE WARFARE, FEBRUARY, 1917

United States to join the Allies, they had little doubt; but they believed that the war would be ended long before the United States could raise, train, equip, and place in Europe any great number of troops. Furthermore, in an attempt to embarrass the United States in case of war, Zimmermann, secretary for foreign affairs, instructed the German minister in Mexico to propose an alliance with that country as soon as an outbreak of war appeared certain. He was to propose that Germany should give general financial support, and Mexico should "reconquer the lost territory of New Mexico, Texas, and Arizona."

On January 31, 1917, Germany announced that beginning the next day all sea traffic within certain zones adjoining Great Britain, France, and Italy and in the eastern Mediterranean would, "without further notice, be prevented by all weapons." All vessels, neutral or belligerent, were to be sunk by German submarines. Special permission was granted for one regular American passenger steamship to sail in each direction between the United States and Great Britain each week, provided a number of hard and fast rules were observed. Germany was confident that this measure would "result in a speedy termination of the war and in the restoration of peace which the Government of the United States has so much at heart."

American exasperation with the Central Powers had been increasing for some months. Both groups of belligerents had been eager to influence public opinion in the United States and had carried on an active propaganda by means of subsidized newspapers and public speakers. But the Central Powers had not been content with propaganda; their diplomatic representatives had further proceeded to organize and support a staff of conspirators. Passport frauds had been committed, strikes had been instigated in munition plants, and bombs had been manufactured for the destruction of factories and ships. Late in 1915 the United States had demanded the recall of the Austro-Hungarian ambassador and the military and naval attachés of the German embassy because of their improper activities. Now, on February 3, the German ambassador was handed his passports, and President Wilson announced to Congress the severance of diplomatic relations with Germany.

President Wilson did not believe that Germany would actually do with her submarines what she had announced, and preferred to await "overt acts" before taking further steps. Nevertheless, the immediate result of the German decree was a practical embargo on American shipping, since most shipowners refused to risk the loss of their vessels. On February 26 the President pointed out to Congress this practical embargo on American shipping and asked for authority to maintain armed neutrality "to protect our ships and our people in their legitimate and peaceful pursuits on the sea," but the measure was defeated in the Senate by the obstructionist tactics of a few members.

Meanwhile, the British steamship *Laconia* was sunk without warning on February 26 with the loss of eight American lives. Three days later the "Zimmermann note" to Mexico, which had been intercepted and deciphered by the British government, was published in the United States.

The President was therefore accorded popular support when, on March 12, the government issued an order for arming American merchant ships by executive authority. Then followed within a week the sinking (March 16–17) of three homeward-bound American ships with the loss of American lives; and by the first of April thirty-five more Americans had been drowned. These attacks undoubtedly constituted "overt acts," and anti-German sentiment rose to a high pitch in the United States.

Entrance of the United States into the War

On April 2 President Wilson went before a joint session of the Senate and the House of Representatives and advised that "Congress declare the recent course of the Imperial German Government to be in fact nothing less than war against the government and people of the United States." During the next two days Congress adopted a declaration of war by large majorities, and on April 6, 1917, President Wilson issued a proclamation declaring that "a state of war exists between the United States and the Imperial German Government."

The United States now began the task of preparing to aid the Allies and to defeat Germany. French and British missions to America pointed out that the United States could best assist by contributing (1) money, (2) food and ships to convey food, (3) help against the submarines, (4) men. In respect to the first, Congress on April 24 passed the War Finance Act authorizing the raising of seven billion dollars and the lending to the Allies of three billion. By the end of June over one billion dollars had been advanced to the Allies—chiefly for the purpose of purchasing food, cotton, metals, and other war materials. America's entry into the war saved the Allies serious financial difficulties during the early part of 1917. Every effort was made, also, to increase the quantity of foodstuffs and war materials which could be shipped to the relief of the Allies and to expedite their transportation to Europe. In July the President made Herbert Hoover "food-controller"; in August Congress passed food-control and shipping acts.

To counteract the menace of the submarine, the United States immediately seized all enemy merchant ships in American waters and inaugurated a tremendous shipbuilding program which called for the rapid construction of great numbers of standardized steel ships. In addition, a considerable flotilla of American destroyers was soon dispatched to co-operate with the British fleet against the German submarines in British waters. The submarine campaign, indeed, proved to be a bitter disappointment to the Central Powers. In the early months of 1917 Allied shipping losses were tremendous, and the Teutonic threat to the sustenance of the British people and to the munitioning of the Allied armies was extremely grave. But gradually in two ways the menacing blow was countered. In the first place, shipping losses were ultimately cut down. This was accomplished by weapons of offense against the submarine itself—the submarine chaser, the destroyer, the decoy ship, the submarine, the airplane, the bomb, and the depth charge; and by methods of defense—the camouflaged ship, the convoy system, and the barrage. In the second place, Allied shipping losses were made good by the rapid construction of new tonnage. In the end, German submarines were being destroyed about as rapidly as they could be built, and Allied shipping was being constructed faster than submarines could sink it.

At the time of the declaration of war upon Germany, the United States regular army consisted of only slightly more than 165,000 men, of whom more than 25,000 were scattered in outlying possessions and overseas posts. To remedy this situation the Selective Service Act was passed in May, authorizing the President (1) to increase the regular army by voluntary enlistment to the maximum war strength, (2) to draft into federal service the national guard, and (3) to raise by conscription a force of 500,000 men, with 500,000 more if deemed necessary. On June 5 some nine and a half million men between the ages of twenty-one and thirty years were registered, and on July 20 the drawing of 625,000 men to form the first selective army took place at Washington. During the summer the national guard was mobilized, but not until September was the mobilization of the new national army begun. Germany was correct in her calculation that it would be months after the resumption of the unrestricted submarine campaign before the military forces of the United States could play an effective role in Europe.

The Allied Offensives of 1917

Meanwhile, on the western front the year opened with the voluntary relinquishment of about one thousand square miles of French territory by the German armies. As early as November of the preceding year the retreat had been decided upon, and for various reasons. The Allied drive on the Somme had struck a deadly blow at Teutonic strength and had badly dented the German line. Further Allied gains at this point might endanger the whole Teutonic western front. Allied superiority in troops in the west had risen to thirty or forty divisions, and retirement to a shorter and more defensible line would enable the Central Powers to meet this situation more readily. Finally, a strategic retreat to a stronger line might nullify the extensive preparations which the Allies were making for a gigantic offensive in 1917. During the winter, therefore, a fresh system of trenches was constructed in front of Cambrai and St. Quentin, and the new bulwark of defense was christened the "Siegfried Line." The Allies, however, persisted in calling it the "Hindenburg Line." In March the Germans began to withdraw to their new position, devastating the surrendered territory as they went.

But the Germans were not left long undisturbed in their new positions. On April 9 the British opened a drive against the north end of the new line along a forty-five-mile front in the vicinity of Arras. At the end of the battle the British had gained some seventy-five square miles, had taken more than 20,000 prisoners, and had captured hundreds of heavy guns, trench mortars, and machine guns. The Hindenburg Line had proved to be no more impregnable than the old one, but the British had had to pay a terrific price to prove this—30,000 killed and 75,000 wounded.

While the battle of Arras was in progress, the French, commanded by General Nivelle who had succeeded Joffre as generalissimo in December, 1916, launched an attack in an effort to capture Laon. The first day's battle, April 16, ended in driving sleet; the second day's began in a hurricane of wind and snow. By the close of the fifth, the French had taken all the banks of the Aisne from Soissons to Berry-au-Bac and all the spurs of the Aisne heights. They had captured 21,000 prisoners and 183 guns. But the French themselves had suffered 75,000 casualties, of whom 15,000 were dead. And they were still very far from Laon. Nivelle had failed, and he fell from command as suddenly as he had risen. In May, Pétain was appointed to succeed Nivelle as commander-in-chief of the French forces, Foch becoming chief of the general staff.

The great sacrifice of men provoked a near-crisis in the French army. No adequate preparation had been made for the care of the wounded, who were sent to various parts of France where they spread despondency by the tale of their needless sufferings. The depression which resulted found vent in mutiny, which, beginning about May 20, broke out in ten divisions. Pétain immediately set to work to remedy this menacing situation. For the remainder of the year, however, the French limited themselves on the western front chiefly to the policy of attrition, seeking by minor attacks to wear the Germans down in man power, war materials, and morale. Although throughout most of the summer and fall the British carried on operations in Flanders, their offensives brought the Allies comparatively little new territory.

Allied disappointments in the West were to some extent balanced by successes in Mesopotamia and the Near East. In 1916 the British had suffered a humiliating defeat at the hands of the Turks when a small force commanded by General Sir Charles Townshend had been besieged in Kut-el-Amara and forced to surrender in April of that year. To retrieve

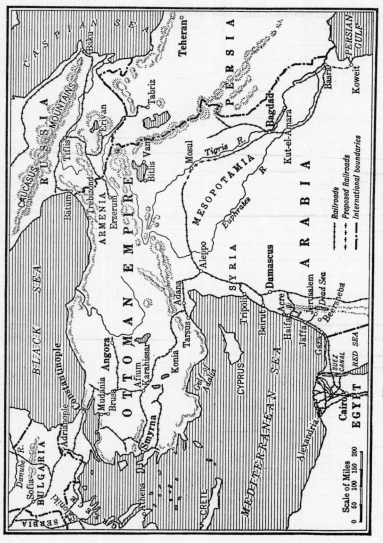

The map is labeled with the following:

CASPIAN SEA

RUSSIA

CAUCASUS MOUNTAINS

Baku

Teheran°

PERSIA

PERSIAN GULF

Tabriz

Erivan

Tiflis

Batum

Trebizond

ARMENIA

Erzerum

Van

Bitlis

Mosul

Tigris R.

Bagdad

Kut-el-Amara

Basra

Koweit

MESOPOTAMIA

Euphrates R.

OTTOMAN EMPIRE

BLACK SEA

Constantinople

Adrianople

Mudania

Brusa

Angora

Afium Karahissar

Konia

Tarsus

Adana

Aleppo

SYRIA

Tripoli

Damascus

Beirut

Haifa

Acre

Jerusalem

Dead Sea

Beersheba

ARABIA

Jaffa

Gaza

CYPRUS

MEDITERRANEAN SEA

SUEZ CANAL

RED SEA

Cairo

EGYPT

Alexandria

Smyrna

Gulf of Adalia

CRETE

Athens

SERVIA

BULGARIA

Sofia

Danube R.

Salonika

Scale of Miles
0 50 100 150 200

Railroads
Proposed railroads
International boundaries

THE OTTOMAN EMPIRE IN THE FIRST WORLD WAR

this disaster, the British forces at the head of the Persian Gulf had been strengthened and put under the command of General Sir Stanley Maude. In December, 1916, this force had begun an advance up the Tigris. In February, 1917, Maude recaptured Kut-el-Amara, and on March 11 he entered the coveted city of Bagdad. By so doing he restored British prestige in the East, deprived the Central Powers of one of the famous goals of their *Drang nach Osten,* raised the morale and enthusiasm of the Allies, and correspondingly depressed the spirits of the Turks.

Events elsewhere were similarly depressing for Germany's ally in the East. In November, 1916, the sherif of Mecca proclaimed the independence of the Arab kingdom of Hejaz and received the prompt recognition of the Allied powers. Beginning in 1917, therefore, the sultan's forces were compelled to fight not only against the invading Allies but against the revolting Arabs as well. The latter were of considerable indirect assistance to the British in their efforts to protect the Suez Canal and to build a railway across the Sinai peninsula, preparatory to an advance into Palestine. In October, 1917, General Allenby launched his offensive. On November 1, Beersheba was taken by a surprise attack, and five days later Gaza fell. The British continued to push northward, took Jaffa, the port of Jerusalem, on November 16, and on December 11 occupied the Holy City itself. The year closed with the British holding a line running from the Mediterranean to the Dead Sea north of Jaffa and Jerusalem, while in Mesopotamia they had advanced to within a hundred miles of Mosul. Turkey was beginning to crumble.

For a year and a half the Allied forces at Saloniki had been practically impotent to advance against the Central Powers largely because of their fear of the possible action of Greece in their rear. The year 1917 saw the Greek situation finally clarified and the Saloniki army freed from this handicap. In the closing months of the preceding year Greece had been subjected to various coercive acts of the Allies. Her navy had been seized, her coasts had been blockaded, and King Constantine had been compelled to transfer most of his military forces to the Peloponnesus. Early in June, 1917, Allied forces occupied strategic points in Thessaly to safeguard the rear of the Saloniki forces, and French troops seized the isthmus of Corinth. On June 11 an Allied high commissioner demanded both the abdication of Constantine and the renunciation of the crown prince's right of succession. The king bowed to the inevitable and on the following day abdicated the throne in favor of his second son, Alexander. Venizelos was recalled as premier, and early in July Greece joined the countries at war with the Central Powers. In the eyes of the latter the Allied treatment of neutral Greece differed little from their own treatment of Belgium.

War-Weariness

Meanwhile, three long years of fierce and bloody fighting had called into the trenches tens of millions of men. Over four million had already been compelled to lay down their lives, and other millions had been wounded or crippled for life.[7] National bankruptcy stared each country squarely in the face.[8] And to the masses it all seemed futile and empty. In all the belligerent countries the spring and summer of 1917 saw the masses war-weary and yearning for peace.

In the Austrian Empire this war-weariness was reflected in the report of the foreign minister, Count Czernin, to Emperor Charles [9] (April, 1917), pointing out that "the burden laid upon the population has assumed proportions that are unbearable," that the "dull despair of the population increases day by day," that "our military strength is coming to an end," that "another winter campaign would be absolutely out of the question," that "in the late summer or in the autumn an end must be put to the war at all costs," and that it "will be most important to begin peace negotiations at a moment when the enemy has not yet grasped the fact of our waning strength." It was seen in the downfall of the ministry, in the weakening of the Dual Monarchy's loyalty to Germany, and finally in Emperor Charles' secret overtures to France (March–May) looking toward a separate peace, even at the expense of granting Serbia access to the sea.

Within the German Empire the same feeling was revealed by the increase in the number of Socialists who opposed the war, by the Bavarian Prince Rupprecht's desire for peace, by the conversion of the Center Party's leader, Erzberger, from a peace of conquest to a peace without annexations, by unofficial statements in London and Paris that the Kaiser was disposed to peace, and finally by the Reichstag's resolution (July 19) that it strove "for a peace of understanding and the permanent reconciliation of the peoples," and that with such a peace "forced acquisitions of territory and political, economic, or financial oppressions are inconsistent." But since Germany, in the words of Bethmann-Hollweg, had now come to be governed by a military dictatorship, no definite steps were taken to give the resolution substance.

War-weariness in the Allied countries was manifested during 1917 in what has been called the "defeatist movement," the essence of which was that peace could not be won through victory, but must be attained through negotiations—a "peace without victory." In France and Italy the tendency

---

[7] The loss of life in the first two years of the war was greater than the total death toll of all the important wars from 1790 to 1914.

[8] The total cost of the war for the first three years was about $90,000,000,000.

[9] He had succeeded Francis Joseph in November, 1916.

was especially strong. The mutiny in the French army in 1917 has already been mentioned. But behind the lines newspaper proprietors, financiers, senators, and deputies became interested, and ex-Premier Joseph Caillaux was extremely active in spreading the doctrines. The reaction ultimately came, however, valiantly led by the aged veteran, Georges Clemenceau, who insisted upon a "peace through victory." Two ministries fell as a result of his fierce attacks, and he himself finally became premier and minister of war on November 16, 1917. Not many weeks later Clemenceau, in order to crush defeatism in France, took the drastic step of ordering Caillaux's arrest on the charge of having endangered the security of the state.

In Italy the defeatist movement was encouraged by secret agents of the Central Powers and by representatives of the Russian Bolsheviks. Both the illiterate peasants and the radical proletarian Socialists became imbued with the doctrines. Even the army became infected. In August rioting occurred in Turin, one of the chief munition centers, and mutiny broke out among the troops sent to quell the disorder. In consequence, exemption from military service was canceled for many of the munition workers, who were organized into battalions and sent to the Italian front. By chance they were placed in the very sector where the Central Powers had decided to strike in an effort to cut off the Italian Second Army, on the Isonzo north of Gorizia, and the Third Army, which held the line from Gorizia to the Adriatic.

On October 24, 1917, the Central Powers launched an attack in the Julian Alps. A breach was made in the Italian lines at Caporetto, and Teutonic troops rushed through. By the twenty-eighth the Austro-German troops had reached the Friulian plain, had taken Cividale, and were menacing Udine. The Italian Second Army, weakened by the discontent and treason of its recently acquired Turin battalions and broken by the impact of new Teutonic tactics, became "a fugitive rabble." The Italian Third Army, in a desperate effort to escape capture by retreat, precipitately withdrew from Gorizia.

The plight of this Third Army was most serious. The Tagliamento River was the first halting-place for Cadorna's retreat, and the Third Army was as far from that river as were the advance forces of the enemy. For a time it seemed doomed. "A million of men were retreating along the western highways, encumbered with batteries and hospitals and transport, while by every choked route peasants and townsmen fled for refuge from the Austrian cavalry." But the Third Army was not captured; with heavy losses and by the narrowest margin it escaped. On November 1 it was in position on the western bank of the Tagliamento with the river between it and the enemy. Its successful retreat made an Italian stand possible and deprived the Teutonic forces of their expected triumph. But on November 3 the enemy crossed the river and began to move west along the edge of the hills. On the seventh the Italians abandoned the Tagliamento, halted temporarily on the Livenza, and by the tenth were back on the Piave. Here the retreat ended.

French and British reinforcements were at once dispatched from the western front. Diaz supplanted Cadorna as commander-in-chief. Italian

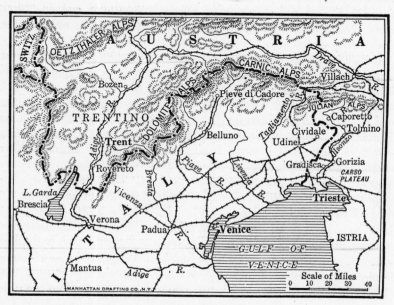

THE AUSTRO-ITALIAN WAR AREA

boys of seventeen and eighteen, many with little military training, were rushed to the battle line. Italian monitors off the coast contributed their constant shelling to the defense. During November and December desperate fighting continued, but the Teutonic advance was finally checked. The disaster had cost Italy some 600,000 men in addition to great quantities of war materials. Yet in the end it aroused Italy's fighting spirit, brought reforms in her commands, and forced the government to give more attention to the "civil front." Out of the defeat, too, came the movement for a unified western command. Early in November the premiers of France, Great Britain, and Italy met at Rapallo, and from their conference developed the Supreme War Council of Versailles.

The Bolshevik Revolution in Russia

War-weariness undoubtedly played a great part, also, in Russian developments in 1917. The Russian army was discouraged, discontented, and weary of the futile struggle, which seemed to be waged not only against the Central Powers at the front, but against the forces of inefficiency, corruption, and even treason in the rear. By the winter of 1916–1917 the army was already in process of dissolution. "Unwillingness to fight, decline of discipline, distrust and suspicion of officers, desertion in the rear" were present. One of the essentials for successful revolution—a discontented and disloyal army—thus existed in Russia by the spring of 1917.

Among the masses, meanwhile, discontent and unrest were greatly accentuated by the economic conditions. The relative cost of living increased during the war by leaps and bounds. During the winter of 1916–1917 a coal shortage developed which made itself felt in the progressive closing down of industries in which its use was essential. The transportation system, none too efficient at best, collapsed under the strain of the war. Finally, the shift of millions of peasants from the farms into the armies, the tremendous demand for food to feed these armies, the peasants' unwillingness to part with food for depreciating paper currency, and the collapse of the transportation system, all conspired to produce an acute food shortage in the larger towns and cities.

In March, 1917, bread riots, industrial strikes, and mutinies among the troops occurred in Petrograd (the name given to St. Petersburg in September, 1914), and within a few days the tsar had been forced to abdicate. A provisional government, which hoped to accomplish what the revolution of 1905 had failed to achieve, assumed control and prepared to carry the war to a "decisive victory" in conformity with Russia's past agreements with the Allies. Although an aggressive war was contrary to the desires of the soviets of workers, peasants, and soldiers which had been organized throughout Russia, War Minister Kerensky bent every effort to prepare for a successful offensive which was projected for July, 1917.

Kerensky's plan called for local attacks to hold the German troops in the north while the main blow was delivered against the weaker Austrian lines. But Russian deserters betrayed the plan to the enemy, and German reinforcements were sent to the Austrian rather than to the German front. After weeks of feverish activity on the part of Kerensky and his assistants, the Russian advance began. For a few days all went well. Thousands of prisoners and vast quantities of war material were captured, and an advance of some twenty miles was made. Wherever the Austrian lines were not stiffened by Germans, they gave way. But on July 19 a heavy concentration of German troops began a drive in the direction of Tarnopol. Not yet recovered from the exhaustion of their own attack, the Russians fell back under German pressure. Discipline and organization broke down; entire regiments shot their officers and refused to fight. The whole Russian line in Galicia precipitately took to flight, and the Russian gains of 1916 were completely wiped out.

Meanwhile the Bolsheviks, led by Nicholas Lenin who had returned to Petrograd from Switzerland in April, 1917, had made an almost irresistible appeal to the war-weary Russian masses with a program which called for: (1) immediate conclusion of a general peace; (2) immediate confiscation of landed estates without compensation and without delay for legal forms; (3) possession and operation of factories by the workmen; (4) national control of production and distribution; (5) the substitution of soviets of workmen, peasants, and soldiers for all existing agencies of government; (6) the exclusion of the propertied classes from political rights. Although a Bolshevik attempt at an armed uprising in Petrograd failed in July, their strength and numbers continued to increase, aided partly by General Kornilov's abortive attempt to set up a military dictatorship in September. Within a week after the crushing of the Kornilov rebellion, the Bolsheviks gained control of the executive committee of the Petrograd soviet for the first time.

Elsewhere, too, the Bolsheviks rapidly increased in numbers and strength. Throughout the country land-hungry peasants, who cared not so much for victory over Germany as for the overthrow of the landlords, began to approve the Bolshevik program. In the cities the workers, so long at the mercy of their government-protected employers, became enamored of the Bolshevik promise of complete control of industry. And the active soldiers, maltreated, betrayed in the war, compelled to endure untold hardships, and at the same time yearning for the war to end in order that they might return to claim their share of the confiscated lands, gladly enlisted under the Bolshevik banner of peace.

Lenin now made up his mind that the time to strike was at hand. The occasion was to be the assembling of the All-Russian Congress of Soviets, which was set for November 7. A large majority of those who had been elected to this congress were Bolsheviks, and there was thought to be little doubt that the congress would declare itself in favor of handing over power to the soviets. During the night of November 6 the public buildings of Petrograd were occupied by Bolshevik troops. Railway stations, telegraph and telephone offices, bridges, power plants, and even the Bank of Russia came into their control. On the morning of the seventh a Bolshevik proclamation announced that the provisional government had been overthrown. "Long live the revolution of the workers, soldiers, and peasants!" Late in the day the members of the provisional government, with the exception of Kerensky, who escaped, were arrested and imprisoned. That same night the All-Russian Congress of Soviets approved the *coup d'état* and passed a resolution formally taking over the government, which thereupon became the soviet government. On the next day the same congress established a new provisional government, called the "Soviet of the People's Commissars," of which Lenin was chairman and Leon Trotsky commissar for foreign affairs.

Nov. 8

The Treaty of Brest-Litovsk

Within two weeks after the November revolution Commissar for Foreign Affairs Trotsky sent to the foreign diplomats in Petrograd a note stating that the Soviet government intended "to propose to all peoples and their respective governments an immediate armistice on all fronts, with the purpose of immediately opening *pourparlers* for the conclusion of a democratic peace." The Allies ignored Trotsky's note but the Central Powers, which were naturally eager to have Russia withdraw from the war, responded with alacrity. Negotiations for an armistice were begun at Brest-Litovsk on December 3, and twelve days later a definite truce was signed between representatives of Russia on the one hand and of Germany, Austria, Bulgaria, and Turkey on the other.

On December 22, 1917, the first peace conference of the war was formally opened at the same place, but because of the dilatory tactics of the Bolsheviks real negotiations were not begun until January 10, 1918. An impasse then resulted and the conference broke up again four days later and adjourned *sine die,* the only positive achievement being the extension of the armistice to February 12. But Germany was determined to have a signed peace. On February 18, therefore, German armies on the eastern front once more began to advance into Russia. The following day Lenin and Trotsky capitulated and agreed to sign.

Peace negotiations were, accordingly, once more resumed and resulted in the treaty of Brest-Litovsk, signed on March 3, 1918. Russia agreed: (1) to give up Poland, Courland, and Lithuania, and to let Germany and Austria determine the future status of these territories in agreement with their populations; (2) to evacuate Livonia, Estonia, Finland, and the Åland Islands; [10] (3) to evacuate the Ukraine and to recognize the treaty

[10] These regions were soon brought within the orbit of the Central Powers. In April, 1918, German troops landed in Finland, and not long afterward the throne was offered to Prince Charles of Hesse, brother-in-law of the Kaiser. On April 21 the Kaiser himself "accepted" the invitation of Estonian Balts to be the ruler of that country. In March Germany recognized the independence of Lithuania, which in July received Prince William of Urach, a younger member of the ruling house of Württemberg, as king. In April German and Austrian troops, entering the Ukraine as allies, occupied the whole country and established a military dictatorship under the pro-German General Skoropadski.

signed between the Ukrainian People's Republic and the Central Powers; (4) to surrender to Turkey the districts of Ardahan, Kars, and Batum; (5) to discontinue all Bolshevik propaganda in the territory of the Central Powers and in the territories ceded by the treaty. Two months later Rumania, completely isolated, was forced to sign the unusually harsh treaty of Bucharest. For the Central Powers, the withdrawal of Russia and Rumania from the conflict ended the necessity of waging a war on two fronts and opened the way for the transfer of troops to the west, where the decisive battles of the war were to be fought in 1918.

German Repudiation of Allied War Aims

Meanwhile, early in 1918 the Allied war aims had been clarified and formulated as a result of two notable addresses—that of Premier Lloyd George before the British trade unions on January 5, 1918, and that of President Wilson before the United States Congress three days later. The two statesmen were in general agreement, and their aims may be discussed in the order of President Wilson's famous Fourteen Points, destined to play such an important part in the final settlement. They were:

1. "Open covenants of peace, openly arrived at."
2. "Absolute freedom of navigation upon the seas, outside territorial waters, alike in peace and in war."
3. "The removal, so far as possible, of all economic barriers and the establishment of an equality of trade conditions among all the nations."
4. Reduction of national armaments "to the lowest point consistent with domestic safety."
5. "A free, open-minded, and absolutely impartial adjustment of all colonial claims, based upon a strict observance of the principle that in determining all such questions of sovereignty the interests of the population concerned must have equal weight with the equitable claims of the government whose title is to be determined."
6. "The evacuation of all Russian territory and such a settlement of all questions affecting Russia as will secure the best and freest co-operation of the other nations of the world in obtaining for her an unhampered and unembarrassed opportunity for the independent determination of her own political development and national policy."
7. The evacuation and restoration of Belgium without any limit to her sovereignty.
8. The evacuation and restoration of French territory, and the righting of "the wrong done to France by Prussia in 1871 in the matter of Alsace-Lorraine."
9. A readjustment of Italian frontiers "along clearly recognizable lines of nationality."
10. "The freest opportunity of autonomous development" for the peoples of Austria-Hungary.

11. The evacuation and restoration of Rumania, Serbia, and Montenegro, with "free and secure access to the sea" for Serbia.

12. Secure sovereignty for the "Turkish portions" of the Ottoman Empire; security and autonomous development for "the other nationalities which are now under Turkish rule"; the permanent opening of the Dardanelles "as a free passage to the ships and commerce of all nations under international guarantees."

13. The erection of an independent Polish state including "the territories inhabited by indisputably Polish populations" with "a free and secure access to the sea," and with an international guarantee of her "political and economic independence and territorial integrity."

14. The formation of "a general association of nations ... for the purpose of affording mutual guarantees of political independence and territorial integrity to great and small states alike."

Wilson's Fourteen Points evoked no enthusiasm among the leaders of the Central Powers, whose spirits were buoyed by the Italian disaster of October, 1917, and by the Bolshevik Revolution in the following month. It appeared that the Russian collapse would nullify the Allied campaign of attrition, and that the Central Powers could once more confront the Allies in the west with a numerical superiority. These facts led Hindenburg and Ludendorff to lay their plans for 1918 with every expectation of final victory for the Central Powers in that year. It was this expectation of a speedy triumph that led the political leaders of the Central Powers to treat cavalierly the Allied announcements of war aims.

The views of the Central Powers were set forth on January 24 in addresses by Count Hertling, the German chancellor, and Count Czernin, the Austrian foreign minister. On the first four points they admitted that "an understanding might be reached without difficulty." The fourteenth point Czernin accepted much more whole-heartedly than did Hertling, the former stating his belief that it would "nowhere meet with opposition in the Austro-Hungarian Monarchy," the latter only grudgingly conceding that "the Imperial German Government is gladly ready, after all other pending questions have been settled, to approach the examination of the basis of such an association of nations." But not even a grudging acceptance was vouchsafed the remaining points. The Allied war aims, Count Hertling asserted, reflected the Allies' mistaken belief that they were the victors and that it was the Central Powers who were the vanquished.

GERMANY'S FINAL MILITARY EFFORT

In February Hindenburg and Ludendorff explained their military plans for 1918 to a secret session of the Reichstag, which approved the undertaking even though it called for Germany's loss of a million and a half men. Their aim was to obtain a decision in the field in four months, before the United States could bring her tremendous resources and man power fully to bear. As the first step in their campaign, they proposed to isolate the British army by rolling it up from its right and then driving it into the sea or holding it in an entrenched camp between the Somme and the Channel. The first drive, therefore, was to be directed against that point in the line where the British and French forces met, on the supposition that the lack of unified command among the Allies would lead to confusion here at the moment of attack. German divisions were withdrawn from the Italian and Balkan fronts, and some half million men were transferred from the east. By March Hindenburg was on the western front with the "whole German manhood for the first time united in a single theater of war, ready to strike with the strongest army that the world has ever known."

After preliminary threats on the Champagne and Ypres fronts, the Germans on March 21, 1918, suddenly hurled a force of over half a million men against a fifty-mile sector between Arras and La Fère. The British, outnumbered three or four to one, gave way and on the second day lost contact with the French on their right. It appeared that the Germans would succeed in breaking through the line as they had planned. But on the twenty-sixth the gap was again bridged, and, although the British continued to retreat, their line was neither broken nor pushed back into the sea. Nevertheless, when the battle finally ended in the latter part of April, the British had retreated some thirty-five miles and had suffered over 300,-000 casualties.

One reason for the extent of the British disaster on the Somme was Pétain's reluctance to shift immediately sufficient troops from the French lines to the British sector. One result of the defeat was the realization of the absolute necessity for a unified command of all Allied forces. In the midst of the retreat British and French statesmen met and unanimously decided, on March 26, to entrust at once the control of all forces in the west to General Foch, by universal consent the master mind among the Allied generals. Four weeks later he was given added authority by being made "Commander-in-Chief of the Allied Armies."

At the same time strenuous efforts were made to overcome the Allied inferiority in man power. Great Britain passed a more drastic conscription act, subjecting every British man between the ages of eighteen and fifty-five to military service, and within a month sent across the Channel 355,000 British troops which had been kept in England to meet a possible invasion. By herculean efforts, during May, June, and July over 675,000 American soldiers were rushed across the Atlantic to France—more than twice the number sent in the whole preceding year. On April 28 the first American regular army divisions, after long training in quiet sectors, began active fighting on the Picardy front.

Meanwhile, on April 9, shortly after the first offensive died down, the Germans struck their second blow against the depleted British left wing between La Bassée and Armentières, where there seemed to be a possibility of breaking through to the Channel ports. But the British troops responded to General Haig's plea that "there must be no retirement. With our backs to the wall ... each one of us must fight on to the end." And,

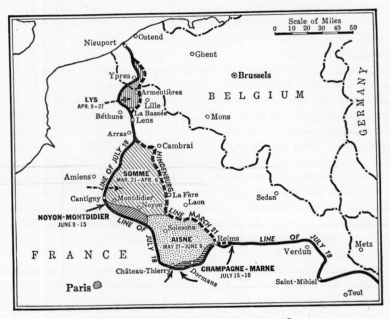

THE GERMAN OFFENSIVES OF 1918

although in some places they retreated from fifteen to twenty miles, the British stemmed the German flood, kept their lines intact, and held the enemy far back from the coveted Channel ports.

These two tremendous drives with their spectacular results temporarily encouraged the German people to make still further sacrifices, although the German armies had already incurred something over half a million casualties. Ludendorff's attempts to rebuild his forces with men returned from hospitals and with boys of the 1920 class were suffered in silent anguish in the hope that a "German peace" would be won before autumn. By the last week of May Ludendorff had succeeded in replacing more than 70 per cent of his losses. On the twenty-seventh he struck his third terrific blow, this time against the French between Soissons and Reims. Within two days the Germans captured Soissons, and on the thirty-first they reached the Marne valley, down which they hoped to advance toward Paris. But now at length the American forces began to play a decisive role. The second division and parts of the third and twenty-eighth divisions were thrown into the line and helped to bring the German drive to an end. Not only did they halt the Germans; they recaptured from them some of the positions which they had already taken.

But again the Germans had made a tremendous advance of over thirty miles in three days. They had seized the Marne bank for ten miles and had taken between 30,000 and 40,000 prisoners. Their position was such that it offered no safe resting place, however. They must continue the battle or relinquish their gains. So far they had established two salients threatening Paris; they now sought to convert them into one by a fourth attack (June 9–15) on a front of twenty-two miles between Montdidier and Noyon. But this time the French army, expectant and reinforced, resisted firmly and stopped the drive after an advance of only six miles. In this they were assisted by the American first division, which had proved its mettle earlier (May 28) by capturing and holding Cantigny.

No sooner had this offensive subsided in the west than the Austrians launched what they hoped would be a decisive drive against the Italians on the Piave. But General Diaz learned of the Austrian plans, and knew that the attack was to begin at three in the morning of June 15. He therefore anticipated the assault by an Italian bombardment of the Austrian troops and succeeded in seriously upsetting their assembly. Nevertheless, at the designated hour the advance began, the Austrians attempting to use the tactics which had been so successfully employed by the Germans in France. They had succeeded in crossing the river with nearly 100,000 men when suddenly, on the afternoon of the seventeenth, the flooding of the Piave turned that broad, shallow stream into a raging torrent which swept away ten of the fourteen bridges upon which the Austrians depended. On the next day Diaz with reinforcements began the counterattack. Within a week the whole of the west bank of the Piave was once more in Italian hands. Austria, instead of putting Italy out of the war, had lost 20,000 prisoners and had suffered at least 150,000 casualties. It was Austria's last great effort. She was broken in spirit, and great numbers of her people were starving. Mutinies and desertions menaced her armies, and disruptive nationalist aspirations threatened the empire. Germany must now continue the struggle practically alone.

But in the west the Germans were preparing to do this. They planned a great *Friedensturm,* or "peace offensive," which was to strike the French line to the east and west of Reims, capture that city, split the French front, cut the vital railway from Paris to Nancy, and enable German troops to sweep down the Marne valley to Paris. At midnight on Sunday, July 14, the sound of great guns to the east told Paris that the final struggle for her capture had begun. Four hours later, at dawn, the Germans began an advance, the importance of which was recognized by both sides. "If my offensive at Reims succeeds, we have won the war," said Ludendorff. "If the German attack at Reims succeeds, we have lost the war," admitted Foch. The Germans succeeded in crossing the Marne between Château-Thierry and Dormans, but they got little farther. On the southeast an Italian corps blocked their way, while on the southwest they encountered American troops who stopped them and pushed them back across the Marne. East of Reims French and American troops held back the German rush and prevented the capture of the city. In the three days' battle the Germans advanced barely six miles at the farthest point. The day of their terrific sledgehammer blows was past. Paris was again saved, and thereafter the offensive rested in Allied hands.

For Foch was now in a position to undertake a general advance. Thanks to American reinforcements, the Allies once more had superiority in rifle strength, a superiority which continued to increase during the rest of the war. The decisive turning point in the conflict had come. Thereafter the collapse of the Central Powers was speedy and sure. A series of Allied offensives rolled back the German armies without cessation until their final surrender in November. On August 8 a terrific British attack convinced Ludendorff that the war could not be won, and at a conference at general headquarters at Spa five days later he advised the initiation of "peace feelers." The German chancellor was given a free hand to act at his discretion. Early in September the German army chiefs informed Chancellor Hertling that they must have peace as soon as possible.

The Disintegration of Austria-Hungary

By this time, too, the Habsburgs were in dire straits, for they were waging a struggle not only against foes without their empire but also against disintegration within. The long pent-up national aspirations of the various subject peoples were seeking concrete expression. In January, 1918, Czech, Polish, and Yugoslav deputies in the Reichsrat had drafted a program calling for the establishment of a sovereign constituent assembly for every local area in which a specific language was spoken, the settlement of boundary disputes by means of plebiscites, and the right of each nation to form whatever political ties it desired. Three months later Czechs and Yugoslavs in a great public meeting in Prague had taken a solemn oath to "persist in the struggle for independence in all circumstances and unto the end."

Meanwhile, abroad, energetic steps had been taken to present the claims of the various subject nationalities. Before the war was a year old, national leaders of the Czechoslovaks, Yugoslavs, and Poles were busily at work seeking to gain the sympathy of the Allies and the official recognition of the justice of their cause. Representing the Czechoslovaks abroad were Thomas G. Masaryk, professor of philosophy in the Czech University of Prague and long the leading exponent of the Czech nationalist movement, Eduard Beneš, one of his young colleagues at the university, and Milan Štefánik, a distinguished Slovak scientist. By them the Czechoslovak National Council was organized in Paris, and "bureaus" were established in France, England, Italy, and the United States to create a sentiment favorable to Czechoslovak national aspirations.

Similarly, under the leadership of Ante Trumbich, a deputy in the Austrian Reichsrat, the Yugoslav Committee was organized in London. The aim of the Yugoslav leaders was set forth later in the declaration of Corfu (July 20, 1917), drawn up jointly by Trumbich and the Serbian premier, Pashich, and forecasting the "Kingdom of the Serbs, Croats, and Slovenes." These three peoples, according to the declaration, constituted a single nation, and it was definitely agreed that they should become united under the Karageorgevich dynasty in a constitutional, democratic, and parliamentary monarchy, the constitution for which should be drafted, after peace had been attained, by a constituent assembly elected by universal suffrage.

In the early years of the war somewhat less vigorous steps were taken abroad in behalf of the Poles under the leadership of Paderewski, world-renowned pianist, and Sienkiewicz, the famous Polish novelist. Eventually the Polish National Committee, seeking the resurrection of a free and united Poland, located its headquarters in Paris and appointed Paderewski to represent it in Washington. By the middle of 1918 the subject nationalities had succeeded in winning from the Allied governments official recognition of the justice of their cause.

But the military collapse of the Dual Monarchy was a necessary prerequisite of the final independence of the subject races, for the Habsburg government steadily refused to consider any such eventuality. To this collapse military developments in the Near East contributed. On September 15 the Allied forces on the Saloniki front finally began their oft-delayed advance. In the battle of the Vardar, Serbian, French, British, and Greek troops attacked the Bulgarians, who were routed and forced to retreat. As soon as the latter's territory was actually invaded, the Bulgarian government sued for an armistice, and on September 30 the first of the Central Powers went out of the war. Her means of transportation, now placed at the disposal of the Allies, opened the way for an attack upon Turkey from the west. But Turkey did not wait for any such eventuality. Cut off from the Central Powers, driven back three hundred miles by a rapid Allied advance which captured Damascus, Beirut, Tripoli, and Aleppo in the single month of October, fearful for the safety of Mosul in Mesopotamia and Adrianople in Thrace, the Turks likewise appealed for an armistice, and withdrew from the war on October 31.

The defection of Bulgaria threw the burden of maintaining the Balkan front on weakened Austro-German forces, which were further demoralized by events within the Dual Monarchy. Early in October the German-Austrian deputies of the Reichsrat constituted themselves a provisional national assembly and proclaimed the establishment of a new Austrian state. On October 5 representatives from all Yugoslav territories of the empire met at Zagreb and elected a Yugoslav national council to defend their interests. Two days later at Warsaw Polish representatives issued a manifesto promising a national government and a freely elected diet for a reunited Poland. On October 14 Beneš informed the Allied governments that the Czechoslovak National Council in Paris had been transformed into a provisional government with Masaryk as president, Beneš as foreign minister, and Štefánik as secretary for war; and France recognized the provisional government on the next day.

In a last desperate effort to save his realm from complete disintegration Emperor Charles issued a manifesto on October 16, 1918, announcing the policy of federalization. But in Hungary the issuing of the imperial manifesto was regarded as the destruction of the *Ausgleich,* and the Hungarian government at once declared that the Dual Monarchy was dissolved. This resulted, in turn, in the immediate assertion of the right of self-determination by the Rumanians and Slovaks of the Hungarian kingdom. During the succeeding ten days the empire went completely to pieces, and the various districts came under the political control and administration of different national councils—Ukrainian, Yugoslav, Czech, German, Magyar, and Rumanian. National popular governments supplanted the Habsburg dynasty.

On the field of battle, meanwhile, the Habsburg forces were being relentlessly driven back. On October 12 they lost Nish, and two days later Durazzo and Novibazar. By the nineteenth their line near the Rumanian frontier was back on the Danube. On the twenty-fourth the Allies launched an attack in the Trentino and on the Piave, which resulted a week later in the complete routing of the Austrian forces on these fronts. On November 1 the Serbians recaptured Belgrade; two days later the Italians made their triumphal entry into Trieste. On that same day (November 3) the Habsburgs, beset behind and before, capitulated and signed an armistice with the Allied Powers. Eight days later Emperor Charles formally surrendered his Austrian throne. Of *Mittel-Europa,* Germany alone remained a belligerent.

Downfall of the Hohenzollerns

Meanwhile, in the west the Germans by September had been driven back to the Hindenburg Line, having suffered a million and a half casualties since they had left it less than six months earlier. But the Allies continued their attacks unceasingly. In the middle of September over half a million American soldiers wiped out the long-standing St. Mihiel salient. Farther west the Allied troops smashed through the Hindenburg Line and drove the Germans back out of Péronne, Lens, and Dixmude. By September 28 Ludendorff concluded that all was lost and so informed the Kaiser at a conference at Spa the next day. On the thirtieth Hertling resigned as chancellor, and the Kaiser announced that "the German people shall co-operate more effectively than hitherto in deciding the fate of the Fatherland." On October 1 Hindenburg insisted that a peace offer should be made at once, and two days later made his demand more peremptory.

The Kaiser now appointed Prince Max of Baden German chancellor, with a coalition ministry admitting two Socialists into the government for the first time in the history of the empire. On the following day the new government sent a note to President Wilson appealing for a cessation of hostilities, and announcing Germany's readiness to accept the President's Fourteen Points together with his later pronouncements as a basis for the discussion of peace terms. But the obtaining of an early armistice was not the only nor perhaps the most important task which rested upon the shoulders of the new chancellor. He had also to attempt to preserve the Hohenzollern empire against the forces which were by now apparently determined to bring about its downfall.

To the Germans the war had brought ever-increasing hardships, privations, and sorrow. These in turn had led to disappointment, disillusionment, and a decline in enthusiasm for the war and for those who in the popular mind had come to be held responsible for its continuance. In 1916 this feeling had split the Social Democrats when Haase denounced the continuance of the war and was in consequence read out of the party. In the following year he and his followers had organized the Independent Social Democratic Party. Thereafter they had devoted their efforts to denouncing the war as a crime and had even begun to work for the overthrow of the empire. Even more destructive in their activities than the

Independents were the Spartacists, led by Karl Liebknecht and Rosa Lux-emburg, both of whom spent a considerable part of the war period in prison. This group had developed on the left wing of the Independents and took its name from the so-called Spartacus letters, the first of which had appeared in 1916 on the Kaiser's fifty-seventh birthday. These letters had denounced the war as one of imperialistic aggression and had summoned Germans to employ all possible obstructive tactics against it.

After the Russian Bolshevik revolution and subsequent peace of Brest-Litovsk the "poison gas of Leninism" was wafted back upon Germany. The leaders of the Spartacists and Independent Socialists were supplied with money, arms, and literature, and from the Russian embassy a staff of men worked to overthrow the very government to which it was accredited. The Spartacists now became definitely imbued with communistic doctrine and began to advocate the immediate socialization of industry and a world revolution of the proletariat. In preparation for the latter they sought to establish revolutionary workmen's and soldiers' councils throughout Germany and even at the front.

The German defeat in the second battle of the Marne and the fearful collapse of the entire western front during the following months had a disastrous effect on German morale. Everywhere was the belief that the nation had been duped and deceived, and that there was but one road to salvation—the overthrow of the regime which had brought this immense misery upon the people. The destruction of the military dictatorship of general headquarters and the democratization and parliamentarization of the empire became the program, late in September, of the National Liberals and Centrists, who signified their desire to work toward this end in co-operation with the Majority Socialists.[11]

A menacing situation thus confronted Prince Max when he assumed the chancellorship early in October. But the new chancellor hoped that by rapidly democratizing the constitution and the government he might save the Kaiser and the Hohenzollern dynasty. Reform was now the order of the day. Ministerial responsibility was established, the sanction of war and peace was placed in the hands of the Reichstag, the military was brought under the control of the civil authority, amnesty was granted to political prisoners, and freedom of press and assembly was established. Prince Max thus ended the personal regime of the Hohenzollerns and gave the German Empire its first parliamentary government. The Kaiser remained merely as the symbol of German unity.

But by this time William II was doomed. The Kaiser's position, already undermined by Socialist and enemy propaganda, became altogether un-

[11] After the founding of the Independent Social Democratic Party, those who remained in the original Social Democratic Party became known as Majority Socialists.

tenable when President Wilson demanded, as the prerequisite of peace negotiations, "the destruction or reduction to virtual impotency of the arbitrary power which has hitherto controlled the German nation." When the German people learned "that the nations of the world do not and cannot trust the word of those who have hitherto been the masters of German policy," that, if the United States "must deal with the military masters and the monarchical autocrats of Germany . . . , it must demand, not peace negotiations, but surrender," a revulsion of popular feeling set in against generals, emperors, and kings. Early in October the question of the Kaiser's abdication began to be discussed among the people, and by the end of the month the demand had apparently gained the support of the bulk of the nation as the only means to assure a cessation of hostilities and bearable terms of peace.

The final crisis was precipitated when the admiralty, realizing that the armistice terms would undoubtedly demand the surrender of the German navy, ordered the fleet to steam out to engage the British in a final decisive battle. When the men realized that, with armistice negotiations actually under way, the lives of 80,000 subordinates were to be recklessly sacrificed, their bitter opposition was aroused. "If the English attack us," they declared, "we will defend our coasts to the last, but we will not ourselves attack. Farther than Helgoland we will not go." This of course constituted only mutiny, not revolution.

But it soon became revolution. On November 4 the sailors' revolt became general. Soldiers' councils were elected, the red flag was hoisted, and the cry "Long live the Republic!" was raised. On the next day the workers of Kiel joined the revolt and formed workmen's councils. What had originally been a naval mutiny now became a great revolutionary movement, which spread rapidly through the coast towns, where the proletariat united with the sailors. By the close of the first week in November the revolution had triumphed along the German coasts. The success of these uprisings became known in the interior, and town after town raised the revolutionary standard.

On the night of November 8 Majority Socialist leaders instructed the workers of Berlin that, if the Kaiser's abdication was not announced in the early morning papers of the ninth, they were to leave their work and hold big demonstrations. The Independent Socialists, likewise, decided to begin their revolution on the same morning, announcing, "We do not demand one person's abdication, we demand the republic." By ten o'clock on the morning of the ninth, therefore, thousands of unarmed workmen were marching toward the center of the city, carrying placards inscribed, "Brothers, no shooting!" But the appeal was hardly necessary, for the troops in Berlin were already mutinying and forming soldiers' councils.

When no word came of the Kaiser's abdication, the Majority Socialists resigned from Prince Max's ministry and demanded that the government be entrusted to men who had the full confidence of the German people. Prince Max thereupon surrendered the chancellorship to Friedrich Ebert, leader of the Majority Socialists, and at two o'clock that afternoon the Majority Socialist leaders proclaimed the German Republic.

At general headquarters, on the same day, the Kaiser learned from the army heads that the troops would no longer fight either abroad or at home, that they would not defend the Kaiser's life against German republicans, and that there was little chance, therefore, of his being able to reconquer Germany with their help. Confronted with these facts, the Kaiser at length agreed to a conditional abdication. In the afternoon came the message that "His Majesty is ready to abdicate as German Kaiser, but not as King of Prussia." That night in a special train he fled to the Dutch frontier.

The End of the War

Meanwhile, during October, the Allied troops had completed their smashing of the Hindenburg Line by an "arpeggio" of attacks, which forced the Germans almost completely out of France and compelled them to surrender the Channel ports and a considerable portion of Belgium. At the same time, farther east a disastrous blow had been struck by the American forces in their Meuse-Argonne offensive, "beyond compare the greatest ever fought by American troops." [12] For nearly seven weeks the battle raged, with 1,200,000 American soldiers advancing through tangled woods and underbrush toward the Sedan-Mézières railway. This was the principal line of supply for most of the German forces in the west, and, if it were cut, a German retirement on the whole front must result. Slowly American troops pushed back the best of the German divisions until, on November 6, they reached the outskirts of Sedan, cut the Sedan-Mézières railway, and made the German line untenable.

The day before the Americans entered Sedan, President Wilson finally informed Germany that she might apply for an armistice to Marshal Foch. On the following day a delegation headed by Matthias Erzberger was dispatched to receive the terms which on November 8 were laid down by Foch, subject to rejection or acceptance without amendment within seventy-two hours. The position of the delegates was most difficult. Mutiny had already broken out in the navy. Even while they considered the armistice terms, the government of Prince Max was forced to give way to a So-

[12] "The actual weight of the ammunition fired was greater than that used by the Union forces during the entire Civil War."

cialist ministry headed by Friedrich Ebert, and the Kaiser fled precipitately
from general headquarters to Holland. Behind them was a Germany in
chaos; before them, a document which they were loath to sign.

According to the thirty-five clauses of the terms, Germany was to evacuate Belgium, Luxembourg, France, and Alsace-Lorraine within two weeks,
and all the territory on the left bank of the Rhine within one month. Allied
troops were to take over all of this territory and were to occupy the bridgeheads of the Rhine at Mainz, Coblenz, and Cologne to a depth of thirty
kilometers on the right bank. A neutral zone ten kilometers wide was to

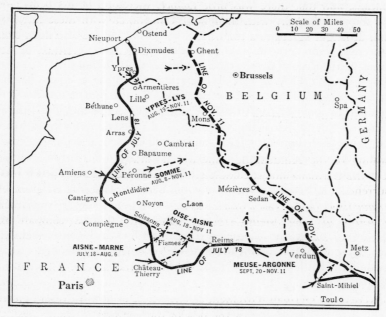

THE FINAL ALLIED OFFENSIVE OF 1918

extend along the right bank of the Rhine from Holland to the Swiss
frontier. All German troops in Russia, Rumania, and Turkey were to
be withdrawn. Within two weeks 5000 locomotives, 150,000 railway cars,
and 5000 motor trucks in good working order were to be delivered to the
Allies. A specified number of submarines and warships were to be surrendered, and the rest, together with the naval aircraft, were to be disarmed. There was to be an immediate repatriation, without reciprocity,
of all Allied prisoners. Finally, the existing blockade of Germany was to
continue unchanged, though the armistice stated that the Allies "contemplate" such provisioning of Germany as should be found necessary. These
terms were in no sense peace terms. They were designed merely to

bring about a cessation of fighting, and to render it utterly impossible for Germany successfully to resume hostilities. At five o'clock on the morning of November 11 the news was flashed to an anxious and expectant world that in a little clearing in the former royal forest of Compiègne these armistice terms had been accepted and signed by the German delegates, to take effect at 11 A. M.

Undoubtedly the First World War was the bloodiest that had ever been fought. The conflict mobilized the tremendous total of 65,000,000 men. Of these millions of the most able-bodied of the nations, nearly 9,000,000 lost their lives and about 22,000,000 were wounded in battle. In addition, it is estimated that the loss of civilian life due directly to war or to causes induced by war equaled or perhaps exceeded that suffered by the armies in the field. Nor does this take into account the terrible effects of war, famine, pestilence, and disease on the sufferers who did not die.

The First World War was also unquestionably the costliest that had ever been fought. The total direct war costs for the principal belligerents amounted to about $186,000,000,000,[13] and when to this are added the indirect costs due to destruction of property, depreciation of capital, loss of production, interruption of trade, and the like, the real economic cost is raised to the stupendous sum of $270,000,000,000. If to this is further added the estimated capitalized value of the human lives lost in the war ($67,000,-000,000), the astronomical figure of some $337,000,000,000 is reached. The statesmen who had been responsible for the war might well stand aghast at the cataclysm which they had brought upon Europe, and at the stupendous task of reconstruction and reorganization which confronted them when, at eleven o'clock on the morning of November 11, 1918, firing finally ceased on the battlefields of the First World War.

[13] The direct cost of the First World War to the United States was nearly enough to pay the entire cost of running the United States Government from 1791 up to the outbreak of the First World War.—U. S. General Staff, *The War with Germany: A Statistical Summary,* page 135.

Chapter XIII

THE PARIS PEACE SETTLEMENT:
THE TREATIES

T HE signing of the armistice was not followed immediately by the drafting of the peace treaties. For various reasons, two full months elapsed between the cessation of fighting and the first preliminary meeting of the peace conference, and twenty-one months elapsed before the last of the treaties comprising the Paris peace settlement was formally signed. Even so, the process of peace-making was much swifter in 1919–1920 than at the close of the Second World War. Before hostilities ceased in 1918 attempts had been made to gather and organize the great mass of information—historic, geographic, ethnographic, economic, and the like—which would be needed for the inevitable peace conference. Great numbers of experts had been working for months gathering facts which might have a bearing on the solution of the many intricate and complex problems which would have to be met.

The Paris Peace Conference

In recognition of the heroic part played by France in the war, Paris was designated as the seat of the peace conference, and early in 1919 the national delegations began to arrive. Although there was a noticeable absence of crowns and gold lace, the plenipotentiaries constituted a distinguished assemblage of the responsible statesmen of the world, including besides the President of the United States at least eleven prime ministers and twelve foreign ministers. Among them were such outstanding men as Clemenceau, Pichon, Tardieu, and Cambon of France; Lansing and House of the United States; Lloyd George, Balfour, and Bonar Law of Great Britain; Orlando and Sonnino of Italy; Hymans of Belgium; Dmowski and Paderewski of Poland; Pashich and Trumbich of Yugoslavia; Bratianu of Rumania; Kramář and Beneš of Czechoslovakia; Venizelos of Greece; and Smuts and Botha of South Africa. The Soviet government of Russia, which had signed a separate peace with the Central Powers in March, 1918, and which was not in good repute with the Allies because

of its repudiation of capitalism, was not represented. Nor were any delegations from the defeated powers present during the drafting of the peace
terms, for theirs was a role which called merely for the signing of the completed documents. This was to be a dictated, not a negotiated, peace.

On January 12, 1919, the two ranking delegates of the United States,
of Great Britain, of France, and of Italy in an informal meeting decided
that those states which had declared war on, or had broken off relations
with, Germany should be represented at the conference, and that the number of plenipotentiaries of each state should vary from one to five, the five
great powers to have the latter number. A plenary session of the conference was to consist of the plenipotentiaries of all the powers, but the
main organ was to be the Council of Ten. This council should consist of
two representatives of each of the five great powers,[1] and should have
the right to decide what questions were to be referred to the general conference, and to reserve to itself all questions which it considered needed
preliminary treatment. It was further decided that the great powers should
be represented on all committees or commissions, the others being represented only when questions directly affecting them were being discussed.
Although in theory all decisions of the conference required the approval
of a plenary session, as a matter of fact only six plenary sessions were held
before the treaty with Germany was signed. For all practical purposes,
therefore, the Council of Ten constituted the peace conference during
the first two months. Its meetings were secret, but representatives of the
other powers were given an opportunity to appear before the council in
order to present their claims.

The intricate facts that underlay most of the problems which it was called
upon to solve, facts which were constantly being made more difficult to
ascertain because of the steady stream of propagandist pamphlets, treatises,
ethnographic maps, and petitions which flooded the conference, soon convinced the Council of Ten that it must be assisted in its investigations. The
result was the appointment of special commissions, varying greatly in size,
to which difficult questions were referred for preliminary study and report.
France, Great Britain, Italy, and the United States always had representatives on each commission, and other powers had seats on some of the
larger ones. Although their reports were in no sense binding upon the
council, many of the articles in the final treaties were taken bodily from
the reports of commissions.

By the middle of March, two months after the opening of the conference,

---

[1] At the peace conference, the United States, Great Britain, France, Italy, and Japan were
designated as the "Principal Allied and Associated Powers," the rest being designated merely
as the "Allied and Associated Powers." For the sake of brevity, the former will be referred to
as the "principal Allies" or the "great powers," the latter as the "small powers."

the only parts of the treaty with Germany which had been finally agreed upon were the military, naval, and air terms. None of the important and complex territorial questions had yet been decided. But the alarming conditions in Europe seemed to urgently demand greater speed on the part of the conference. This desire for greater speed together with the need for secrecy during the period of compromise between the great powers led to a change in the organization of the conference. On March 25 it was announced that informal conferences of the chief plenipotentiaries would take the place of the former meetings of the Council of Ten. The "Big Four"—Wilson, Lloyd George, Clemenceau, and Orlando—beginning with purely personal and informal conversations, finally constituted themselves the supreme Council of Four, which made almost all the important decisions of the conference in respect to the treaty with Germany.

It was an interesting personnel which composed this council: Clemenceau, the dauntless Tiger, stolidly silent save when some remark disclosed his dry humor or stinging sarcasm, inclined to be cynical and dogmatic, inflexibly and courageously fighting for one object, the security of his beloved France; Lloyd George, the nimble-minded, responsive politician, shrewd, alert, dynamic, ingenious, more and more inclined to be lenient with the defeated powers, seeking by compromise and adjustment to bring speedily a peace which would facilitate Britain's much-needed revival of trade; Wilson, idealistic spokesman of the moral and spiritual forces of the world, clear-minded and resolute, tirelessly working to construct the League of Nations which he firmly believed would be the salvation of mankind; Orlando, learned, warm-hearted, eloquent, destined to play a relatively subordinate part in the general settlement, nevertheless struggling to satisfy the ambitions of his enthusiastic compatriots.

Almost inevitably conflict arose among these four statesmen when the time came for various secret treaties to be presented for fulfillment, for the abstract Fourteen Points to be transformed into definite treaty provisions. In the latter case, the very elasticity and vagueness which had made it easy for the powers to accept some of the points in principle made it likewise easy for differences in interpretation to arise when they came to be examined from the conflicting nationalistic points of view. In fact, even before the peace conference the Allies had made a number of reservations. The chief problem of the statesmen at Paris was to draft terms which would reconcile the opposing viewpoints of the Allied powers. No one man could dominate a group like the "Big Four." Agreement was possible only through compromise, though frequently affairs had to reach an actual crisis before a settlement was finally effected. On one occasion President Wilson in despair ordered his ship, the *George Washington,* to come for him; on another Orlando and his delegation went even so far as to withdraw from the conference and return to Rome. Despite the strain and stress which prevailed at such times as these, however, the peace conference managed to hold together and eventually completed its work.

The Treaty of Versailles

Although more than a dozen treaties and conventions were eventually drafted and signed in the attempt to settle the many and complex problems raised by the First World War—treaties between the Allies and the defeated powers, between the principal Allies and some of the newly created states, and even between some of the Allies themselves, undoubtedly the treaty with Germany was the greatest single achievement of the peace conference.

THE LEAGUE COVENANT

At the very outset of the conference an acute difference of opinion arose as to whether the Covenant of the proposed League of Nations should be included in the treaty with Germany or should constitute a separate document. There was little doubt, of course, that the conference was expected to create such an organization. Even before the war much thought had been given to the possible prevention of international wars, and various societies had been organized both in Europe and in America to work toward that ultimate goal. The First World War with its terrible bloodshed and suffering gave a great impetus to the movement, and during the final year of the conflict the idea of creating an international organization to prevent war made a tremendous appeal. By the time the peace conference assembled there was a general demand that this great international assembly should create some common agency for the prevention of war. The spokesman of world opinion on this subject was President Wilson, who was determined that the League Covenant should be an integral part of each of the peace treaties. On this point Wilson won out; the second plenary session of the conference adopted his viewpoint and entrusted the drafting of the Covenant to a special commission of which Wilson was chairman and upon which sat ultimately the representatives of fourteen states. This commission considered a number of drafts, among which the most important were undoubtedly those of General Smuts and Lord Robert Cecil, and the Covenant in its final form was definitely approved at another plenary session of the conference on April 28, 1919. It constituted the first twenty-six articles in the treaty with Germany as well as in the treaties with the other defeated powers.

THE "BIG FOUR" AT THE PEACE CONFERENCE IN 1919

Orlando, Lloyd George, Clemenceau, Wilson.

TERRITORIAL PROVISIONS

When the statesmen came to consider the territorial provisions of the treaty with Germany, it was readily agreed that Alsace and Lorraine should be restored to French sovereignty. Clemenceau demanded, in addition, that in the interest of French security Germany's western frontier should be fixed at the Rhine, that the ten thousand square miles of territory lying on the left bank of the Rhine between Alsace and Holland should be detached from Germany and erected into an autonomous and neutral state. A secret treaty of 1917 with Russia had, in fact, stipulated that such a state should be created and that it should be occupied by French troops until all the terms of the final treaty of peace had been fulfilled by Germany. Although it was admitted that the inhabitants of the territory were thoroughly German in speech and life, Clemenceau argued that the Rhine constituted the one advance line which could not be turned and which guaranteed France against invasion.

From the outset Lloyd George opposed the creation of such a buffer state, and repeatedly insisted that "another Alsace-Lorraine" must not be created. The French plan was also consistently opposed by President Wilson. In the end Clemenceau surrendered his demand for the creation of a separate state on the left bank of the Rhine. In return, however, he secured the occupation of this territory by an Inter-Allied force for at least fifteen years, as a guarantee of Germany's execution of the peace treaty, and the permanent demilitarization of the left bank together with a strip of territory fifty kilometers wide on the right bank. Finally, and in addition, Lloyd George and Wilson promised France a guarantee treaty of security which provided that their two countries would come to the aid of France in case of an unprovoked attack by Germany.

Clemenceau also advanced a claim to the Saar basin, a small but highly industrialized and densely populated area, most of which had been French before 1815. The basin was of economic value because it included a rich and concentrated coal bed. Furthermore, the Saar mines lay on the outer edge of Germany, they were within a dozen miles of the new French frontier, they were already linked with the industries of Lorraine which were to become French, and with two exceptions they were the state property of Prussia and Bavaria. Clemenceau demanded the political annexation of the territory which had been French before 1815 and the full ownership of the mines but not the political sovereignty of the rest of the basin.

In view of the deliberate destruction of French coal mines by the Germans in 1918, and in view of the fact that prewar Germany had a large surplus of coal, the Allied statesmen looked with favor upon French ac-

quisition of the Saar coal mines. The acquisition of these mines might
justly balance the destruction of the French mines, and any excess value
might be credited to Germany's reparations account. But neither Lloyd
George nor Wilson favored the political annexation of the district by
France. Again a compromise resulted. Germany for the time was to retain the political sovereignty of the region, but was to hand over the

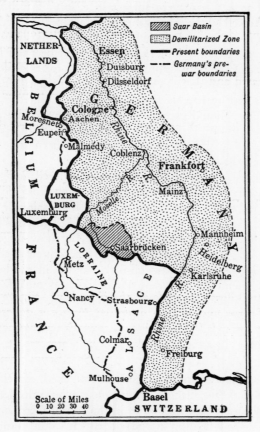

THE RHINELAND

government of the district to a commission under the League of Nations
for fifteen years. The coal mines were to be ceded to France, and the
district was to be within the French customs boundary. After fifteen
years the people of the basin should vote as to their future political status
—reunion with Germany, union with France, or continuance under the
League of Nations. If the popular vote favored permanent union with
Germany, the latter was to repurchase the mines of the basin at a price fixed

by three experts, a Frenchman, a German, and a representative of the League of Nations.

To the west of the Saar Germany renounced her rights over the railways of Luxembourg, and this grand duchy ceased to be part of the German Customs Union. Slight changes in the German-Belgian frontier line were made in favor of Belgium in the vicinity of Moresnet, Malmédy, and Eupen. The last two were subject to a sort of plebiscite, which—although denounced by the inhabitants as unfair in its procedure—resulted in favor of annexation to Belgium. The treaty also stipulated that the frontier between Germany and Denmark should be fixed in conformity with the wishes of the population, and provided for two plebiscite zones. This was because northern Schleswig, when taken from Denmark in 1864, had been promised by Prussia that it would be reunited with Denmark if the inhabitants "should express such a desire by a vote freely given." This "vote freely given" Prussia never had permitted. In accordance with the plebiscites, which were held in 1920, the northern zone was assigned to Denmark and the southern to Germany.

It was in the east, however, that Germany suffered her greatest losses, for here a considerable part of her territory, taken from Poland in 1772–1795, was allotted to the new Polish republic. It has already been pointed out that during the war the Allies had committed themselves to the restoration of a "united and independent Poland." But how large this Poland should be or where her boundaries should be placed none of the "Big Four" knew. The only thing that was definitely known in the beginning was the Allied statement that the new Poland should include the territory inhabited by a population indisputably Polish, and "should be assured a free and secure access to the sea." To provide the latter, experts recommended that a corridor through the province of West Prussia, including both banks of the lower Vistula and the city of Danzig, should be given to Poland.

But this recommendation was vigorously attacked, especially by Lloyd George. He argued that such an arrangement would dismember Prussia, that it would separate East Prussia from the rest of Germany and turn it into "a German island floating in a Slavic sea." It would compel a German going by land from Berlin to East Prussia to cross Polish territory. Furthermore, he pointed out, the population of the city and district of Danzig, which exceeded 300,000, was overwhelmingly German, as was also the population in the narrow belt of territory around Marienwerder on the east bank of the Vistula.

On the other hand, Polish statesmen, backed by Clemenceau, maintained that either Germans must cross Polish territory to go by land to East Prussia or Poles must cross German territory in order to carry their commerce to the Baltic. Furthermore, they asserted, the rights and needs of the people in Poland ought to take precedence over those of the 1,500,000 in East Prussia. Danzig was the natural port of Poland and of the Vistula river basin, and had been for many centuries outside the political frontiers of Germany. The possession of the Marienwerder district was necessary in order that Poland might control the lower Vistula and the one direct railway between Danzig and the Polish capital, Warsaw.

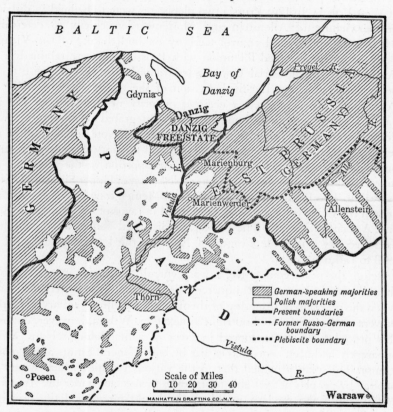

DANZIG AND THE POLISH CORRIDOR

Ultimately it was decided that in order to ensure Poland's economic interests in Danzig without actually annexing it to that republic, a district of about seven hundred square miles around the port should be established as a free city under the protection of the League of Nations. The Allies undertook to negotiate a treaty between Danzig and Poland which should bring Danzig within the Polish customs lines, should ensure to Poland free use of all waterways and docks necessary for Polish commerce together

with the control and administration of the means of communication between Poland and Danzig, and should give to Poland the conduct of the
foreign relations of the free city. The executive of Danzig was to be a high
commissioner appointed by the League of Nations.

In the treaty, therefore, Germany was compelled to recognize the independence of Poland and to renounce in the latter's favor about five sixths
of the former province of Posen and the greater part of the former province
of West Prussia. In East Prussia two plebiscites were to be held in districts
in the vicinity of Allenstein and Marienwerder, chiefly to determine
whether Poland should control territory on both banks of the Vistula.
Both districts later voted for union with Prussia and were retained practically intact. In industrial Upper Silesia a plebiscite was likewise to be
held; but in this case the final division of the district was favorable to
Poland. Germany received a decisive majority of the votes of the inhabitants, but the region, though a closely integrated economic unit, was
divided roughly in proportion to the number of votes each country received. The larger part of the population and territory went to Germany,
but Poland was given by far the greater proportion of the economic resources. Germany also surrendered a small section of Upper Silesia to Czechoslovakia. The Baltic cities of Danzig and Memel, together with a certain
area in the vicinity of each, were renounced in favor of the principal Allied
and Associated Powers. The former, as discussed above, was established
as a free city under the League of Nations; the latter was assigned in
1923 to Lithuania.

Before the peace conference, it was generally taken for granted among
the Allies that Germany's conquered colonies would not be returned, and,
when the question of disposing of them first came up in January, the great
powers of Europe favored outright annexation. Wilson, however, opposed
this procedure and pronounced in favor of a mandatory scheme which
apparently had been conceived earlier by both General Smuts and Colonel
House. This plan provided that to the various colonies which were "inhabited by peoples not yet able to stand by themselves under the strenuous
conditions of the modern world, there should be applied the principle
that the well-being and development of such peoples form a sacred trust
of civilization." The various colonies should, therefore, be distributed
among the powers as mandates which the powers should administer in
trust for the League of Nations, to which they must make an annual
report. Although French colonial circles were inclined to question the
practicability of the proposal, the only open opposition came from Australia, New Zealand, and the Union of South Africa. In the end, however,
the mandatory system was adopted. Germany renouncing overseas "all
rights, titles and privileges whatever in or over territory which belonged

to her or to her allies." Her former colonies were later distributed among Great Britain, France, Belgium, the Union of South Africa, Australia, New Zealand, and Japan as mandates of the League of Nations.

The fate of Germany's concession in Shantung caused an acute crisis at the conference. Early in the war Japan had joined the Allies and had captured the German fortress of Tsingtao; later, in 1917, Great Britain, France, and Italy had promised her Shantung and the German islands north of the equator. Definite engagements had thus been entered into which now arose to embarrass the conference. The Chinese government also had declared war on Germany, and at the conference the Chinese delegates demanded the restoration of Kiaochow to China. Wilson supported the Chinese in their demand and desired that Germany's rights in the Shantung peninsula should not be surrendered to Japan but should be returned directly to China.

But Japan was in possession of the district involved, and her delegates were inflexible in their demand for the concession. Taking advantage of the strained situation at the time of the withdrawal of the Italian delegation, they insisted that the Japanese claim to Shantung be granted at once, else they would leave Paris and refuse to sign the treaty or join the League. For a week the Shantung question monopolized the conference. Lloyd George and Clemenceau finally stated that they considered themselves bound by the pledges of 1917. Fearing that, in the face of these developments, the Covenant of the League of Nations might finally fail of adoption, Wilson yielded. It was agreed that the peace treaty should stipulate that Japan obtained the former German rights in Shantung. On the same day that the agreement was finally reached, however, Japan promised that she would return the Shantung district to China in full sovereignty, keeping only the economic rights which had formerly been granted to Germany, and the right to establish a settlement at Tsingtao. This promise was carried out by Japan in 1923.

LIMITATION OF ARMAMENTS

In the interest of the security of Germany's neighbors as well as in the interest of general disarmament, the peace conference deliberately sought to weaken Germany's military and naval forces and to limit her in the use of those which were actually left in her control. The treaty specifically stated that, after March 31, 1920, the army of the states constituting Germany "must not exceed one hundred thousand men, including officers and establishments of depots." There were to be neither military nor naval air forces. The great German general staff was to be abolished and might not be re-established in any form. The manufacture of arms, munitions, and other war material was strictly limited, and the importation or exportation of war material was forbidden. Neither the manufacture nor the importation of poisonous gases was permitted. Universal compulsory military service was abolished. In order to prevent the extension of military training to a greater number of men, by having a rapid turnover in the personnel of the army, the treaty stipulated that the enlistments of officers must be for at least twenty-five consecutive years and those of privates for at least twelve, and that the number of officers or privates discharged in any one year must not exceed 5 per cent of the total effectives.

Germany was definitely restricted in the use of her military forces even within her own frontiers. She was forbidden to maintain or construct any fortifications in her territory on the left bank of the Rhine, or on the right bank to a distance of fifty kilometers eastward. Those already existing were to be disarmed and dismantled. In this demilitarized area she was forbidden to maintain either temporarily or permanently any armed forces or to conduct any military maneuvers. Germany's violation of these articles would be regarded as a hostile act against the signatory powers. On the southern and eastern frontiers Germany must limit her system of fortified works to its existing state.

The German navy was restricted to six battleships, six light cruisers, twelve destroyers, and twelve torpedo boats, and she was forbidden to construct or acquire any warships except to replace units already in commission. Germany might not have any submarines, even for commercial purposes; and all existing submarines must be handed over to the Allied powers or destroyed. As in the army, so in the navy the personnel was limited. The fortifications, and harbor of Helgoland were ordered destroyed, never to be reconstructed.

Inter-Allied commissions of control were provided for in the treaty to supervise the execution of the disarmament clauses. They were given the right to establish their organizations in Berlin, to send agents into any part of Germany, and to demand information and aid from the German government. The upkeep and cost of these commissions of control and the expenses involved in their work were to be borne by Germany.

REPARATIONS

In a prearmistice note of November 5, 1918, the Allies had demanded that compensation should "be made by Germany for all damage done to the civilian population of the Allies and to their property by the aggression of Germans, by land, by sea, and from the air." Nevertheless, in the opening weeks of discussion at the peace conference, the British and French

delegates contended for the inclusion of all war costs in the amount which
Germany should pay, arguing that only thus would the settlement really
be based on justice. Wilson, on the other hand, maintained that the demands which might be made upon Germany were limited by prearmistice
agreements and that, consequently, only reparation of damage should be
collected, and not the costs of the war. Eventually the other three members
of the "Big Four" gave way and agreed that Germany's reparations obligations should be limited to what might be called actual damage, the costs
of the war being excluded.[2] The justification for the reparations demands
was set forth in the later famous or infamous Article 231:

> The Allied and Associated Governments affirm and Germany accepts the
> responsibility of Germany and her allies for causing all the loss and damage to
> which the Allied and Associated Governments and their nationals have been
> subjected as a consequence of the war imposed upon them by the aggression of
> Germany and her allies.

The next difficulty arose over the meaning of the term "damage" as distinct from "war costs." At first thirty-one different categories of damages
were considered, but the number was gradually reduced to ten upon
which there was general agreement except as to pensions and separation
allowances. Lloyd George vigorously urged the inclusion of these items,
and argued that there should be compensation for damage to families
behind the front as well as for damage to the houses at the front. "Payment for a destroyed chimney was not to be placed above compensation
for a lost life or a pension for a blinded or wounded soldier." The consent
of the "Big Four" for the inclusion of war pensions and separation allowances was finally gained by a memorandum submitted by General Smuts.
Next came the question of the amounts, periods, and method of payment to be required. The American delegates contended for a fixed and
reasonable sum. But the Allies could not agree on the amount which
Germany could pay, and they felt that she should pay all that she could.
In the end it was decided that it would be unwise politically to fix any
definite total in the peace treaty. Clemenceau asserted that whatever
amount might be agreed upon would fall far short of the expectations of
the French people and would bring the downfall of the government which
accepted it. Lloyd George, recalling the campaign arguments of the election of 1918, readily fell in with this view. A provisional solution was
therefore eventually agreed upon. Germany, by May, 1921, should pay in
gold or its equivalent a total of $5,000,000,000. Out of this amount the ex-
penses of the Inter-Allied army of occupation were first to be met, and

[2] A single exception was made in the case of Belgium; Germany was to pay all of her war
costs down to the signing of the armistice.

the balance then applied to the reparations account. The question of further payments was to be determined by that date, and the power to fix the final sum was to be vested in a Reparations Commission. In case of default by Germany in the performance of any of her reparations obligations, the commission might make recommendations as to the action to be taken in consequence of such default.

MISCELLANEOUS PROVISIONS

In addition to the provisions already discussed, the treaty when finally completed made a number of miscellaneous requirements of Germany. She consented to the abrogation of the treaties of 1839 which had established Belgium's neutrality, and also adhered to the termination of the regime of neutrality of the Grand Duchy of Luxembourg. She acknowledged and promised to respect strictly the independence of Austria, and agreed "that this independence shall be inalienable, except with the consent of the Council of the League of Nations."

In articles on waterways, the conference sought to provide access to the sea for landlocked countries of Europe by establishing international control over rivers which flowed through more than one country. International commissions were set up to control the Rhine, Oder, Elbe, Niemen, and Danube. In the control of three rivers considered as German—the Rhine, Oder, and Elbe—Germany was therefore placed in a minority. The treaty provided for free zones for Czechoslovakia in the harbors of Hamburg and Stettin. Finally, the Kiel Canal was to be free and open on terms of equality to the mercantile and war ships of all nations at peace with Germany.

Certain guarantees for the execution of the treaty of Versailles were stipulated in the treaty itself. German territory to the west of the Rhine, together with the bridgeheads, was to be occupied by the Allied troops for a period of fifteen years from the coming into force of the treaty. If the conditions of the treaty were faithfully carried out by Germany, at the expiration of five years the Cologne area would be evacuated; at the end of ten years, the Coblenz area; at the end of fifteen years, the Mainz area. If before the expiration of the fifteen years Germany should comply with all the undertakings resulting from the treaty, the occupying forces would be withdrawn immediately. If, on the other hand, the guarantees against unprovoked aggression by Germany were not considered sufficient by the Allied governments, the evacuation of the occupying troops might be delayed to the extent regarded as necessary for the purpose of obtaining the required guarantees.

THE SIGNING OF THE TREATY

On May 7, 1919, the draft treaty was presented to the German delegates who had at last been summoned to the conference, and they were informed that they would have three weeks in which to make written observations on the terms but that no oral discussions with the Allied delegates would be permitted. The counterproposals of the Germans reached the Council of Four on May 29, and were immediately submitted to ten Inter-Allied committees of experts for consideration. The Allied reply granted a few concessions, but in general left the treaty substantially unchanged. Germany was required to declare her willingness to sign the treaty, as modified, within five days, or the armistice would terminate and the Allies would take the necessary steps to enforce their terms. In Germany the feeling was most bitter, and the Scheidemann government resigned rather than sign the treaty. In the end, however, a new government, in which Gustav Bauer was chancellor and Hermann Müller foreign minister, agreed to accept it. Müller and Johannes Bell, minister for the colonies in the new German government, were appointed German plenipotentiaries for the formal signing.

Although none of the meetings of the conference had been held in the great palace of Versailles, arrangements were made to have the final ceremony in connection with the German treaty in the famous Hall of Mirrors in which, years before, the King of Prussia had been proclaimed German Emperor. There on June 28, 1919, the fifth anniversary of the assassination of the Austrian archduke, the final scene was enacted. When the delegates of all the Allied and Associated Powers were seated, at three o'clock the German delegates were admitted. "Müller was pale and nervous, Bell held himself erect and calm. They were led to their seats just opposite the table of rose and sandalwood on which the book of the Treaty was placed." Upon Clemenceau's invitation the German delegates signed. After them the other delegates signed in the alphabetical order of their countries according to the French names, President Wilson signing first for *Amérique du Nord*. While the signatures were still being affixed the guns began to boom outside. At 3:40 P.M. the ceremony was over. In the gardens, whose gorgeous fountains were playing for the first time since the outbreak of the war, cheering throngs greeted the delegates as they came from the historic ceremony.

THE SIGNIFICANCE OF THE TREATY FOR GERMANY

The effects of the treaty upon Germany were far-reaching. Of her territory in Europe she was deprived of more than 25,000 square miles; of her population she lost about 6,000,000. But her loss of raw materials was far greater and much more serious. Her prewar resources of iron, coal, oil, potash, lead, zinc, and foodstuffs were all greatly diminished. With Alsace-Lorraine went iron, petroleum, and potash; with the Saar basin went coal. With the removal of Luxembourg from the German industrial system went still more iron. With the lost regions in Upper Silesia, next to the Ruhr the most important industrial district in prewar Germany, went coal, zinc, lead, together with many foundries and mills. Altogether, Germany was compelled to surrender approximately 65 per cent of her iron-ore reserves, 45 per cent of her former coal wealth, 72 per cent of her zinc ore, 57 per cent of her lead ore, from 12 to 15 per cent of her principal agricultural products, and about 10 per cent of her manufacturing establishments.

Overseas, Germany lost an area of about one million square miles with a population of more than 12,000,000 natives. With this region went about 25 per cent of her prewar rubber supply, besides valuable oils and fibers. Her merchant marine, before the war totaling nearly 5,500,000 tons, was reduced to 400,000 tons. Many of the bases of her prewar foreign commerce, such as her special privileges, capitulations, and concessions in China, Siam, Morocco, Liberia, and Egypt, were destroyed. She forfeited many of her prewar commercial treaties with the Allied powers, was for a short period forbidden to discriminate against the commerce of any of the Allies, and in several respects had to grant without reciprocity most-favored-nation treatment to the Allies for a period of five years.

Possessing before the war the mightiest military machine in the world, she was reduced by the treaty to a peace army less than one eighth as large as her prewar establishment, and with no reserves. Her navy, from being second only to that of Great Britain, was reduced to comparative insignificance. Foreign armies were stationed in her territory, there to be maintained at her expense. Foreign commissions, likewise maintained at her expense, were given power to interfere in her economic and military life. On top of it all, she was committed to a reparations bill of unknown size which gave every indication of mounting into the tens of billions of dollars. It was a severe treaty, but it was in response to popular demand in the Allied countries, and should always be read in connection with the treaty which the Central Powers dictated to Russia at Brest-Litovsk.[3] Furthermore, it was President Wilson's idea that some of the treaty provisions would be more or less temporary, while the League of Nations would endure and eventually operate to correct the evils which might later appear.

[3] See pages 376–377.

The Treaties with Austria, Hungary, Bulgaria, Turkey

After the signing of the treaty of Versailles, other treaties were signed in 1919 with Austria and Bulgaria, and in the following year with Hungary and Turkey. In the drafting of the subsequent peace treaties, the treaty of Versailles served as the general model. Many of its clauses were transferred bodily into the later treaties, and many of its principles were simply modified to fit the other states.

THE TREATY OF ST. GERMAIN

The treaty with Austria took its name from St. Germain, near Paris, where it was signed. While the Germans were still considering their fate, the second of the peace treaties was presented to the Austrians on June 2, 1919. Like the Germans, they were given permission to make written observations. The Austrian delegates asserted that their state, "German Austria," was a new state, created after the armistice, and had never been at war with the Allies. It was just as much a successor state of the Habsburg empire, they declared, as Czechoslovakia, Poland, and the others. But they failed to convince the Allies, who insisted that Austria was an old state simply shorn of certain of its outlying provinces and endowed with a new government. Accordingly Austria was forced to drop the modifying "German" from her title and was further compelled to accept responsibility for the loss and damage inflicted upon the Allied powers "as a consequence of the war imposed upon them by the aggression of Austria-Hungary and her allies."

One reason why the Austrians had adopted "German Austria" as the official designation of their state was that it pointed the way toward their desired incorporation in the new German Republic. On racial and economic grounds the union seemed a natural arrangement, and, in general, it was approved by the American delegation. The French, Czechoslovaks, and Italians were all, for various reasons, opposed to Germany's annexing the Austrian territory, however, and they were able to influence the peace conference on this point. It was stipulated in the treaty that the independence of Austria was inalienable except with the consent of the Council of the League of Nations.

In dealing with central Europe, the peace conference was "placed in the position of executor of the Habsburg estate." Czechoslovakia, Poland, Rumania, Yugoslavia, Austria, Hungary, and Italy were the heirs, and by the time the conference assembled in January, 1919, they had already divided the territories of the Habsburgs in a rough, provisional fashion. The statesmen at Paris had a dual task. They had to adjust the conflicts which had begun between the different nationalities before they developed into actual war; and they had "to effect a definitive division of the Habsburg inheritance that would be just, practical, and conducive to the peace and security of Europe."

It must be emphasized that most of the provisions of the treaties were not drafted hastily by the statesmen of the great powers, but were rather the result of the careful investigation and study of a group of experts who were appointed for this purpose. When the report of a commission was unanimous, it was usually adopted without modification. Occasionally, however, when political considerations were involved or when a situation became especially acute, the "Big Four" took the whole problem into its own hands for settlement. Then "one might have seen President Wilson himself on all fours, kneeling on a gigantic map spread upon the floor and tracing with his finger a proposed boundary, other plenipotentiaries grouped around him, also on all fours."

As the result of boundary changes Austria lost not only her earlier subject peoples but even some of her own Germans as well. To Italy she ceded the Trentino, southern Tirol (although the latter included 250,000 Germans), Trieste, Istria, and two islands off the Dalmatian coast. To Czechoslovakia she lost part of Lower Austria, most of Austrian Silesia, Moravia, and Bohemia, with perhaps 3,000,000 Germans. To Poland she lost Galicia; to Rumania, Bukowina. The duchy of Teschen was divided between Poland and Czechoslovakia. To Yugoslavia she surrendered Bosnia and Herzegovina, together with the Dalmatian coast and islands. Austria shrank from an empire with a population of about 30,000,000 to a small landlocked state of only 6,500,000.

Most of the other provisions of the treaty were similar to those drawn up for Germany. Austria's army was reduced to 30,000 men; her entire navy was in the future to consist of only three police boats on the Danube. She must make reparation, the amount to be determined by the Reparations Commission. States which contained territory of the former empire, however, were required to assume a proportional amount of the Austrian prewar national debt. In order that Austria might have free access to the Adriatic, she was given the right to transport goods over the territories and in the ports formerly in the empire and was to receive in those territories and ports national treatment in respect to charges, facilities, and all other matters. On the other hand, she was obliged to concede to Czechoslovakia the right to send her own trains over certain Austrian lines toward the Adriatic. Although the Austrian assembly vigorously protested against the detachment of Germans in Bohemia and Tirol and against the prohibition of Austrian union with Germany, it eventually changed the name of the state from "German Austria" to "Austria," assented to the new boundaries and agreed to safeguard the rights of the racial, religious, and linguistic minorities of the republic. The treaty of St. Germain was finally signed on September 10, 1919.

THE TREATY OF TRIANON

Although it had been intended to open the peace negotiations with Hungary at the same time as with Austria, the signing of the Hungarian peace treaty did not occur until June, 1920. The chaotic domestic political situation in Hungary was the cause of this delay, for it was not until late in November, 1919, that a government was organized in Hungary which the Allies would recognize. In January, 1920, the first draft of the proposed treaty was presented to the Hungarian delegation headed by Count Apponyi.

The crisis which probably took up more time than any other one problem at the conference arose in connection with the Hungarian treaty. In the secret treaty of London Italy had been promised, in return for her entry into the war, the acquisition of certain territories around the head of the Adriatic and down the east shore, including the two ports of Trieste and Pola. But after the war the Italians were not content with the gains stipulated in the treaty of London. They demanded in addition the Hungarian port of Fiume, the population of which was declared to be for the most part of Italian blood. Furthermore, Italy had long aspired to the complete control of the Adriatic. Although Italy's former rival in the Adriatic had now disappeared, to many Italians it seemed that a new competitor for the control of that sea was being raised by the creation of Yugoslavia. But if Italy could secure the port of Fiume in addition to Trieste, Pola, and Valona, she would obtain practically a monopoly of the maritime trade of the Dalmatian coast and would greatly handicap the commercial expansion of Yugoslavia, whose only practicable port was Fiume. Consequently, Orlando and Sonnino put forward the Italian claims to that city.

On the other hand, the Yugoslav statesmen were insistent that Fiume and the Dalmatian coast should be awarded to Yugoslavia. They based their claim on nationality and self-determination, quoting figures to show that the population of the region was overwhelmingly Yugoslav [4] and that before the war practically every popularly elected official had been Yugoslav. In respect to Fiume itself they based their claim particularly on the fact that it was their only practicable seaport. Actually, nearly all the standard-gauge railways of Yugoslavia were in the latitude of Fiume and

[4] In Fiume itself the census of 1910 showed 24,000 Italians and 16,000 Yugoslavs. Serbia asserted that, if the population of Šušak, a suburb of Fiume, were counted, the Yugoslavs would have a majority in the municipal area.

had their only direct outlet to the sea at that port. To hand over Fiume to Italy, it was maintained, would be an intolerable subjection of the Yugoslavs to foreign control.

President Wilson gave his support to the Yugoslavs. He not only opposed Italy's annexation of Fiume; he even opposed the complete execution of the Adriatic terms of the treaty of London, which he claimed was not in harmony with the Fourteen Points. In fact, he himself drew a boundary, known as the "Wilson line," which cut down the London terms though it conceded to Italy for strategic reasons the three key positions of Pola, Lissa, and Valona. Orlando and Sonnino refused to accept it. Finally Wilson gave to the press a statement of his reasons for opposing Italy's claim to Fiume and appealed to "the people of Italy" to support his view. In protest the Italian delegates returned to Rome. But they realized that their continued absence from the conference would exclude Italy from the benefits of the treaty, and so, having found that the Italian people supported them in their opposition to Wilson, they returned to Paris. Orlando resumed his place in the Council of Four, but on June 19 his ministry fell, and he and Sonnino were succeeded in Paris by Nitti and Tittoni. The peace conference never succeeded in solving this problem but left it to be settled by direct negotiations between Italy and Yugoslavia.[5]

Aside from Fiume, however, the statesmen at Paris eventually succeeded in making some sort of provision for all former Hungarian territory. To Yugoslavia went Croatia-Slavonia and part of the Banat of Temesvar; to Rumania, the rest of the Banat, Transylvania, and some of the Hungarian plain to the west; to the Czechoslovak republic, Slovakia and territory to the east and south of the Carpathians inhabited by some 500,000 Ukrainians; to Austria, German West Hungary, the latter being the only case where one of the Central Powers was given additional territory. Hungary was reduced from a country with an area of over 125,000 square miles and a population of over 20,000,000 to a small landlocked state with only 35,-000 square miles of territory and about 8,000,000 inhabitants; while outside these greatly contracted frontiers dwelt some 3,000,000 other Hungarians. The territorial adjustments were difficult to reconcile with any one clear-cut principle.

The rest of the terms of the treaty were substantially the same as those of the treaty of St. Germain. Hungary particularly objected to the settle-

[5] In September, 1919, perhaps in imitation of Garibaldi's exploits in the nineteenth century, Gabriele d'Annunzio, an ultrapatriotic poet and soldier-aviator, seized Fiume with the aid of a small band of volunteers. In November, 1920, however, Italy and Yugoslavia signed the treaty of Rapallo recognizing Fiume as a free city, and Italian troops compelled D'Annunzio's forces to withdraw. Still later (1924), by another Italo-Yugoslav treaty, Fiume was annexed by Italy and Šušak, its chief suburb, by Yugoslavia.

ment of her boundaries without recourse to plebiscites and to the treaty's prohibition of a restoration of the Habsburg dynasty. Count Apponyi resigned from the Hungarian delegation as a protest against the refusal of the Allies to make desired modifications, but the delegation was reorganized, and the treaty of Trianon was eventually signed by Hungary on June 4, 1920, in the Grand Trianon Palace, adjoining the park of Versailles.

THE TREATY OF NEUILLY

The peace treaty with Bulgaria was signed at Neuilly-sur-Seine on November 27, 1919. Although she suffered far less shrinkage in territory than any other of the defeated powers, she did not escape altogether. Her most serious loss was western Thrace, which she had gained from Turkey in 1913 and which provided her only direct access to the Aegean. This she was compelled to surrender to the Allies, who handed it over to Greece. In the west she was obliged for strategic reasons to cede three small areas to Yugoslavia. These were awarded to the latter in order that she might control certain mountain passes and thus obtain greater security in time of war for her Nish-Saloniki railway. Slight alterations were made also in the Greco-Bulgarian boundary line. Bulgaria's military establishment was limited, like those of Germany, Austria, and Hungary, and her navy was surrendered. She was obliged to recognize her liability to make reparation, the amount in this case being fixed at $450,000,000, payable in thirty-seven years from January 1, 1921. As a result of the war and the treaty of Neuilly, Bulgaria became one of the least of the Balkan states in area, resources, population, and military power.

THE TREATY OF SÈVRES

The last of the peace treaties to be concluded at Paris, and the only one never to be ratified, was that with the Ottoman Empire, signed at Sèvres on August 10, 1920. During the war several secret agreements had been made by the Allies looking to the eventual partition of the Turkish lands. Roughly, according to these, Russia was to obtain Constantinople and European Turkey from the Straits up to a line running from Enos on the Aegean to Midia on the Black Sea. In addition, she was to have the islands of Imbros and Tenedos in the Aegean, all the islands in the Sea of Marmora, territory on the Asiatic shore of the Bosporus, the provinces of Erzerum, Trebizond, Van, Bitlis, and part of Kurdistan. The other Entente powers were to share in the partition. Great Britain was to secure southern Mesopotamia with Bagdad, and the two Mediterranean ports of Haifa and Acre; France, the coastal strip of Syria, the vilayet of Adana, and an extensive hinterland; Italy, the Dodecanese in the Aegean, and an area in southwestern Asia Minor in the vicinity of Adalia. Other agreements stipulated that the Arab population of the empire was to be freed and established as an independent Arab state, and that Palestine was to be internationalized. This disruptive program was never fully carried out, however, largely because of the Bolshevik revolution and the resultant uncertainty and differences of opinion which developed among the Allies as to the fate of those regions formerly assigned to Russia.

Eventually, under the provisions of the abortive treaty of Sèvres, Turkey surrendered sovereignty over practically all her non-Turkish populations. In Arabia the Kingdom of Hejaz was recognized as independent. Syria and Lebanon, Palestine, and Mesopotamia were to be entrusted to, or "advised and assisted" by, mandatory powers. Smyrna and its hinterland were to be administered by Greece for five years, at the end of which a plebiscite was to decide their future status. The Dodecanese and Rhodes were ceded to Italy, which by another treaty agreed to turn over the former to Greece. Other Greek islands in the Aegean, together with eastern Thrace up to the Chatalja line, were surrendered by Turkey to Greece. Turkey agreed to recognize the independence of an Armenian state to be constructed in the area of Erzerum, Trebizond, Van, and Bitlis, the frontiers of which were to be decided by the President of the United States. Kurdistan was to receive an autonomous government or, if a plebiscite so decided, independence. The Straits were to be internationalized and the adjoining territory demilitarized. Constantinople and a region in Europe up to the Chatalja line remained under Turkish sovereignty. Turkey was thus reduced to little more than a shadow of her former self, and became a small Asiatic state in the Anatolian uplands around Angora.[6]

The Minorities Treaties

In spite of the great advance toward nationalism which came as a result of the First World War, Europe was still far from organized into purely national states. So many considerations entered into the drafting of the new boundary lines that, even with the best of intentions, it was impossible to prevent the inclusion of racial minorities in some states. Along almost every frontier there were these minorities, a fact which gave considerable concern to the statesmen at Paris. To provide for this situation the "Big Four" decided to incorporate minimum guarantees for racial, linguistic, or religious minorities in the fundamental law of several of the European states. To this end, appropriate provisions were inserted in the peace treaties

[6] For the treaty of Lausanne which in 1923 supplanted the treaty of Sèvres, see pages 604–605.

with Austria, Hungary, Bulgaria, and Turkey, and special treaties for this purpose were signed by the principal Allies with Poland, Czechoslovakia, Rumania, Yugoslavia, and Greece.[7]

Although the minorities treaties differed slightly in details, they were very similar. In general, the various states agreed to assure full and complete protection of life and liberty to all their inhabitants without distinction of birth, nationality, language, race, or religion. All inhabitants were entitled to the free exercise, public and private, of any creed, religion, or belief the practice of which would not be inconsistent with public order or public morals. Such minorities were further granted the free use of any language in private business and in private schools, and the right to instruction in the public primary schools in their own language if they constituted a considerable proportion of the population. In some cases particular privileges, such as the right of Jews to observe their Sabbath as a holiday, were guaranteed. The protection of minority rights was placed in the hands of the League of Nations, and the guarantees might be modified only with the consent of a majority of the Council of the League.

The Conflict of Ideas

The contents of the peace treaties drafted at the close of the First World War clearly disclose the conflict which was waged within the peace conference between the diplomats and statesmen of the "practical" school, on the one hand, and those of the "idealistic" school, on the other. A comparison of the terms of the peace settlement with President Wilson's Fourteen Points [8] will reveal the extent to which the idealistic parts of his program were defeated.

Nevertheless, the statesmen of the idealistic school left their impress on the settlement. If the victors' desire for spoils deprived Germany of all her colonies and Turkey of much of her territory, the idealists dictated that those who gained control of these regions must hold them as mandates of a world society to which they must render account as stewards. If the desire for compensation or protection against Germany led to the demand for territory inhabited by an alien people, it encountered vigorous opposition. An examination of the map of postwar Europe discloses the marked advance which was made toward the coincidence of national and political

[7] Lithuania, Latvia, Estonia, and Albania later entered into engagements with the League of Nations to observe toward their minorities obligations more or less identical with those laid down in the minorities treaties.

[8] The Fourteen Points are enumerated on pages 377–378. It is interesting to note that Professor Geoffrey Bruun believes that "it is scarcely an exaggeration to say that the betrayal of the Fourteen Points had already been half-completed, with Wilson's knowledge and House's acquiescence, before the armistice was signed." See Geoffrey Bruun, *Clemenceau* (1943), pages 174–175.

frontiers. Despite the fact that there were some instances of arbitrary shifting of peoples from one state to another, such procedure was the exception rather than the rule. More frequently, when the will of the people was not fully known, it was determined through the use of a plebiscite. And in most cases where it was felt necessary, for strategic or economic or geographical reasons, to incorporate an alien people within the bounds of any state, the attempt was made to safeguard them in their political, religious, and linguistic rights by minorities treaties under the protection of the League of Nations. Finally, though the statesmen failed to decide wisely and ideally in every instance, they took steps to provide a future means of correcting and remedying their mistakes, for the League of Nations was an integral part of the peace treaties, the keystone of the postwar settlement.

The United States and the Peace Settlement

The fact that the League of Nations was inextricably woven into the peace settlement largely accounts for the determined opposition which the treaty of Versailles encountered in the United States, where the attack on the treaty was directed chiefly against Part I, which constituted the Covenant of the League of Nations. Within the Covenant the most bitter assault was made upon Aricle 10, in which members of the League guaranteed the territorial integrity and existing political independence of all the other members.

Many Americans denounced this article as an infringement on the right of Congress alone to declare war and to authorize the use of the military forces of the United States. Many feared that it might involve the country in war without any choice in the matter, that it transferred to the League "the right to send our boys into wars overseas." There was undoubtedly much misrepresentation and misunderstanding of the League and its powers, and Wilson upon his return to the United States decided to undertake a speaking tour throughout the country in behalf of the treaty and the League. In clear and eloquent addresses the President explained that the League could only advise members regarding steps to be taken against a recalcitrant state. Again and again he pointed out that, with the necessity for unanimous vote in the Council, the United States could not be led into a war against her will. In ratifying the Covenant, he explained, the United States did not assume any legal but only a strong moral obligation to enforce the sanctions of the League. Whether popular opinion would have been won to the support of the treaty had the President carried through his extensive speaking campaign will never be known, for on September 26, 1919, his strength failed him and he suffered a slight paralytic stroke.

Meanwhile, on September 5, the Senate had begun its formal consideration of the treaty, and in the course of the ensuing debates four points of view toward the League Covenant became evident: (1) nonratification, (2) ratification with far-reaching reservations, (3) ratification with mild reservations, (4) ratification without reservations. Wilson declared that the reservations proposed by Senator Lodge, chairman of the foreign relations committee, would seriously impair the League. Although willing to accept "reservations of interpretation" so long as they were not incorporated in the ratification, he vigorously opposed reservations in the ratification itself, and urged Democratic senators to vote against the treaty with Lodge's reservations. Consequently, in November and again in March, 1920, when votes were taken in favor of ratifying with reservations, the opposing votes of those Democratic senators who followed Wilson's advice prevented the two-thirds vote necessary for ratification.

Wilson was confident, however, that the majority of Americans were with him and not with the Republican senators who had proposed the reservations. It was his hope that the presidential election of 1920 might be made a popular plebiscite on the League, and that the Democrats might win such a victory as to enable them to secure ratification of the treaty without reservations. Although the election was in no sense a clear-cut plebiscite on the League of Nations, the Republicans interpreted their overwhelming victory in the election of President Harding as a popular mandate against the treaty and the League. The treaty of Versailles was therefore dropped, and the United States continued to be technically at war with Germany. Eventually, in August, 1921, the treaty of Berlin was signed with Germany. This treaty was in reality little more than an "index treaty," for its provisions merely referred to specific terms of the Versailles treaty which were either accepted or rejected as applicable to the United States. The provisions of the treaty of Versailles which the United States rejected were chiefly those dealing with the League of Nations, the boundaries of Germany, the fate of Shantung, and the trial and punishment of Germans for war atrocities. The provisions accepted and ratified by the United States included principally those dealing with colonies and mandates, restrictions upon Germany's military, naval, and air forces, war guilt and reparations, the financial and economic clauses, provisions concerning German ports, waterways, and railways, and the guarantees of execution.

It is obvious that the clauses of the treaty of Versailles which the United States ratified in its own treaty of Berlin were among those considered most harsh and iniquitous by the Germans, while those which the United States repudiated were, in the case of those establishing the League of Nations, the very provisions which were designed to ameliorate the harshness of the peace settlement. Unfortunately, in the postwar years most Americans believed that the United States government had repudiated the whole Paris peace settlement. They therefore thought that their country was in no way responsible for the postwar situation in Europe and accordingly was not called upon to take any action regarding such problems as reparations, the French invasion of the Ruhr, Hitler's rearmament of Germany, and his remilitarization of the Rhineland. Another unfortunate result of the United States' failure to ratify the treaty of Versailles was the absence of any American representative in the League of Nations and on the Reparations Commission.

Chapter XIV

THE PARIS PEACE SETTLEMENT:

UNFINISHED BUSINESS

THE statesmen at Paris did not reach definitive agreements on all the problems which they were called upon to solve. Some final boundaries were left to be decided by other agencies; certain features of the peace settlement were left to be administered or implemented by the League of Nations; and the ultimate decisions regarding Germany's payment of reparations were left to the Reparations Commission. Both the problem of maintaining peace among the nations and that of general national disarmament were bequeathed to the League of Nations. Something must therefore be said here about that organization.

The League of Nations

The League functioned through the instrumentality of an Assembly, a Council, and a permanent Secretariat. The Assembly was the representative body of the League and as such somewhat resembled the representative legislatures of national states, but with the essential difference that it had no real lawmaking power. It was the instrument by means of which the nations of the League conferred, advised, and deliberated, and in it each member state had one vote and not more than three representatives. Meetings were held annually in Geneva beginning in September. The Assembly was empowered to "deal at its meetings with any matter within the sphere of action of the League or affecting the peace of the world."

The Council was composed of one delegate from each of the states entitled to representation. The Covenant originally provided that the Council should have five permanent and four nonpermanent members, but the refusal of the United States to enter the League left only four permanent members. The total membership was thus only eight until in 1922 the Assembly increased the number of nonpermanent members to six. With the admission of Germany to the League in 1926, the number of permanent members was fixed at five and the number of nonpermanent members was increased to nine. In 1933 Japan and Germany gave notice of their

417

withdrawal from the League and ceased to be represented in the Council. One of these two vacancies was filled in 1934 when the Soviet Union was admitted to the League and assigned a permanent seat, but another vacancy was caused when Italy announced her withdrawal in December, 1937. Meanwhile, in 1933, the number of nonpermanent members had been increased to ten. In 1939, therefore, the Council consisted of three permanent members—France, Great Britain, and the Soviet Union—and ten regular nonpermanent members. The latter held seats for three-year terms, and a certain number of terms expired each year. The scope of the Council's powers was the same as that of the Assembly's, but the Covenant delegated to it certain specific tasks. It had the duty of formulating plans for the reduction of armaments, of advising on the means of protecting member states in time of foreign aggression, of mediating in case of international disputes, and of receiving reports from mandatory powers. In most cases the decision of the Council had to be unanimous.

The permanent Secretariat comprised a secretary-general and a large staff. The first secretary-general, Sir Eric Drummond, was named in the Annex to the Covenant, but subsequent secretaries-general were to be appointed by the Council with the approval of a majority of the Assembly. Chosen in this way, Joseph Avenol, a Frenchman who had served the League in various capacities including deputy secretary-general, succeeded Sir Eric as secretary-general in 1933. The secretary-general was assisted by two deputy secretaries-general and three undersecretaries-general. These offices were distributed among the great powers, the first secretary-general being British, the deputy and undersecretaries being chosen from the other great powers. The Secretariat, which was established in Geneva, required a personnel of several hundred men and women, who were gathered from more than forty different countries. In general it dealt with what might be called the civil-service duties of the League.

The constitution of the League of Nations was the Covenant, which might be amended by the unanimous vote of the members of the Council with a majority vote of the members of the Assembly. Any fully self-governing state, dominion, or colony not named in the Annex might become a member of the League by a two-thirds vote of the Assembly. At the time of the first meeting of the Council there were twenty-four members; ultimately the number increased to nearly sixty. A member might withdraw from the League after two years' notice of its intention so to do. Before the outbreak of the Second World War several had withdrawn, Japan, Germany, Italy, and Brazil being the most important.

The World Court

The Permanent Court of International Justice, commonly called the World Court, was also in a sense an agency of the League, which established it as directed in Article 14 of the Covenant. The court was composed of fifteen judges—not necessarily nationals of members of the League—chosen for nine-year terms by an absolute majority in the Council and the Assembly, each voting separately. The seat of the court was at The Hague, where the first ordinary session began on June 15, 1922. The court had both compulsory and voluntary jurisdiction, and eventually more than forty states agreed to the court's compulsory jurisdiction, some with reservations. In case of compulsory jurisdiction one state might summon another to appear before the court for trial, and, if the latter failed to respond, the court might give judgment by default. The jurisdiction of the court was voluntary when states having a dispute agreed to refer it to the court. The court had also the function of giving advisory opinions at the request of the Council or the Assembly, though this use of the court was open to some criticism on the ground that such advisory opinions were somewhat in the nature of international politics.

The International Labor Organization

To a certain extent the International Labor Organization, provided for by Part XIII of the treaty of Versailles and by similar sections in the other peace treaties of 1919–1920, was part of the machinery of the League of Nations. Although it was supported by the funds contributed by member states for the maintenance of the League, and although membership in the League entailed membership in the Labor Organization, the latter was completely self-directing. States might be members of the Labor Organization without being members of the League. The United States, for instance, became a member of the former in 1934, and various states which resigned from the League retained their membership in the Labor Organization. In 1939 there were about sixty member states.

The International Labor Organization (ILO) consisted of a General Conference, a Governing Body, and an International Labor Office. The first was analogous to the League Assembly; the second, to the League Council; the third, to the League Secretariat. The General Conference met annually and consisted of four delegates from each member state, one representing labor, one representing the employers, and two representing the government of the state. The work of the conference generally took one of two forms. It might draw up a recommendation in

the form of general principles for the guidance of national governments in drafting legislation, or it might formulate a draft convention in
more precise and detailed terms for ratification by the member states. Up
to 1939 some 133 recommendations and conventions had been drafted
by the annual labor conferences. These had to do with working hours,
woman and child labor, night work, sanitary conditions, unemployment,
public labor exchanges, rights of combination among agricultural workers, conditions of employment at sea, protection against occupational diseases, and the like. Many of the conventions were ratified, many were
not, at least by the industrial powers of the West, but before the outbreak
of the Second World War more than 700 ratifications had been received
from some fifty states.

Mandates and Minorities

As already pointed out, the mandatory system created by the peace conference was placed under the supervision of the League of Nations. By
the peace treaties Germany renounced in favor of the Allied powers all
her overseas possessions, and Turkey renounced the possession of her Arab
lands. All of the former and part of the latter were placed under the
mandatory system. Since the territories were widely distributed over
the globe and their peoples had reached varying degrees of civilization, the
mandates were ranged into three classes. Class A included Iraq, Syria
and Lebanon, Palestine, and Transjordan. These territories were considered to "have reached a stage of development where their existence as
independent nations can be provisionally recognized, subject to the rendering of administrative advice and assistance by a Mandatory until such
time as they are able to stand alone." In Class B were the six mandates
in central Africa, where a greater amount of supervision would be required, while Class C included Southwest Africa and the Pacific islands,
which, "owing to the sparseness of their population or their small size, or
their remoteness from the centers of civilization, or their geographical
contiguity to the territory of the Mandatory, and other circumstances, can
be best administered under the laws of the Mandatory as integral portions
of its territory," subject to certain safeguards in the interests of their native
population.

The distribution of the mandates was the work of the principal Allied
powers. In the C group, Southwest Africa was assigned to the Union of
South Africa; Samoa to New Zealand; Nauru to Great Britain, Australia,
and New Zealand jointly; other former German islands south of the equator
to Australia; and the former German islands north of the equator to Japan.
In the Class B mandates Kamerun (one sixth), East Africa (Tanganyika),

and Togoland (one third) were allotted to Great Britain; Kamerun (five sixths) and Togoland (two thirds) to France; and Ruanda-Urundi to Belgium. In the Class A mandates Palestine, Transjordan, and Iraq went to Great Britain, while France received Syria and Lebanon.

Annually the mandatory powers presented reports to the League regarding their mandates. These were examined by the Permanent Mandates Commission, which was composed of ten independent experts, the majority of whom were citizens of nonmandatory states. This commission presented its observations to the Council of the League. Each year both the Council and the Assembly discussed the working of the mandates, and an opportunity was provided for the public opinion of the world to bring influence to bear upon the mandatory powers to protect the rights of the natives under their control. On three occasions the Mandates Commission felt called upon to intervene in the administration of mandatory powers, but in general the mandatories sought to receive the approval of the League, and suggestions of the Mandates Commission proved effective.

The reconstruction of Europe following the war still left some thirty million of its inhabitants constituting racial minorities in various countries. Most of these people lived under the protection of the minorities provisions of fourteen postwar treaties, in which the League of Nations was named as guardian. Violations of the rights of minorities might be brought to the attention of the Council, and petitions might be sent to the League. The usual procedure in these cases was for the head of the section of the League dealing with minorities to attempt to reach a settlement directly with the government involved, but more than once cases were taken to the Council, and on two or three occasions they were referred to the World Court.

The League's handling of the minorities problem did not always meet with the universal approval of its members. At the meeting of the League Council in December, 1928, the German representative, Stresemann, questioned the effectiveness of the League's action in respect to minorities, and at the next two meetings of the Council the minorities question occupied a prominent place on the agenda. In 1934 Poland announced that she would no longer feel obliged to co-operate with the League in respect to minorities until some new general system for their protection had been developed. The whole system of protecting the rights of minorities was politically difficult, and the League, rather than try arbitrarily to impose its decisions upon the governments in question, sought to develop the spirit of toleration and conciliation.

Humanitarian Activities of the League

Less spectacular and less widely acclaimed in the press than the activities discussed above were the League's efforts to promote co-operation in matters of general humanitarian interest and concern. It supervised, for instance, the safe return to their homes of several hundred thousand prisoners of war; it helped to care for hundreds of thousands of Greek and Armenian refugees expelled from Turkey; it organized Europe's medical services to prevent the spread of typhus from Russia to the rest of the continent. It brought about the financial rehabilitation of Austria and Hungary, and gave financial assistance to other countries—notably Greece, Bulgaria, Estonia—in times of economic stress. It brought about regular international co-operation in the drafting of sanitary, antiepidemic, and quarantine regulations; in the suppression of traffic in women and in the study of comparative legislation for the protection of the life and health of children; in the reduction and restriction of the sale of opium; in the abolition of slavery and forced labor; in economic, financial, transit, and trade matters; in the extension of intellectual relations. In these fields of endeavor international effort was no longer feeble and spasmodic, for under the League's direction these questions were systematically and continuously studied.[1]

The League and the Preservation of Peace

Undoubtedly the chief purpose in the minds of those who formulated the League of Nations was the prevention of future international wars. To this end, the member states in accepting the Covenant agreed "to respect and preserve as against external aggression the territorial integrity and existing political independence of all members of the League" (Article 10); to concede it "to be the friendly right of each member of the League to bring to the attention of the Assembly or of the Council any circumstance whatever affecting international relations which threatens to disturb international peace or the good understanding between nations upon which peace depends" (Article 11); to resort to arbitration or judicial settlement in case of failure to settle satisfactorily any dispute suitable for submission to arbitration or judicial settlement, to carry out in full good faith any decision that might be rendered, and not to resort to war against a member which complied with such a decision (Article 13); to

[1] For the League's aid to Austria and Hungary, its administration of Danzig and the Saar, and its handling of various international disputes, consult the index under "League of Nations" or under the names of the countries or regions directly concerned.

submit to the Council any dispute likely to lead to a rupture which was not submitted to arbitration or judicial settlement (Article 15).

Penalties were stipulated for a member of the League which went to war in disregard of its agreements to resort to arbitration, mediation, or the World Court. All other member states agreed "immediately to subject it to the severance of all trade or financial relations" (Article 16). This was the so-called "economic weapon" and applied not only to the states involved but also to the nationals of those states. When the Covenant was adopted, it was expected that the League of Nations would be a universal organization. By 1935, however, when Article 16 was first invoked, not only the United States but Japan and Germany as well were nonmembers, so that at that time it was found to be exceedingly difficult to make economic sanctions as effective as expected. In addition to the "economic weapon" the Council might also "recommend" to the several governments concerned what effective military, naval, or air force the members of the League should severally contribute to the armed forces to be used to protect the covenants of the League. The members of the League agreed to adopt similar measures to protect a member state against a nonmember state which resorted to war against it.

The Geneva Protocol

The statesmen at the Paris peace conference passed on to the League of Nations the task of formulating plans for a general reduction of armaments. Accordingly a commission was appointed to make proposals, but the commission decided that no scheme for disarmament could be effective which did not provide some form of mutual security to be given in exchange. The League thereupon requested the commission to prepare a draft treaty embodying this idea of mutual security. The result was a draft treaty of mutual assistance, unanimously adopted by the fourth assembly in September, 1923. The security provided in this proposed treaty consisted of the assurance given by the signatory powers that, if a state were attacked, the rest of the signatory powers would come to its assistance. The question of deciding which state was the aggressor in case of war was delegated to the Council of the League. This draft treaty was circulated to all states whether or not they were members of the League, but it failed to receive the approval of Great Britain, the United States, and Russia—states which did not feel the need of collective security. Nearly all the replies pointed out the absence of a definition of aggression and criticized the policy of giving full power to the League Council to determine the aggressor state.

When, therefore, MacDonald and Herriot, premiers of Great Britain and France respectively, submitted to the fifth Assembly of the League a protocol for the pacific settlement of international disputes, they linked with disarmament and security a third feature, arbitration. This so-called Geneva Protocol (1924) provided that all legal disputes must go before the Permanent Court of International Justice and all nonlegal disputes must be submitted to arbitration. War was declared a criminal offense, and every state which resorted to war in violation of the undertakings contained in the Covenant or in the protocol became an aggressor. The definition of an aggressor state was thus made almost automatic, and one of the chief objections to the preceding treaty was overcome. The "sanctions" to be taken against an aggressor state remained those provided for in Article 16 of the Covenant—namely, economic boycott and possible military action. The definition of aggression, the system of arbitration, and the effective measures to be taken against an aggressor were supposed to create a threefold guarantee of security. The Geneva Protocol, however, had very much the same reception as the proposed treaty of mutual assistance and failed of adoption.

The Locarno and Paris Pacts

Nevertheless, the general principles of the Geneva Protocol were almost at once adopted in an attempt to provide collective security within a limited region, when Gustav Stresemann, German foreign minister, in 1925 offered France a pact of mutual guarantee and nonaggression. In Aristide Briand, French foreign minister, he found a kindred spirit who admitted that such an agreement might be possible under certain conditions. To formulate such an agreement representatives of Germany, France, Great Britain, Italy, Belgium, Poland, and Czechoslovakia gathered in the little Swiss town of Locarno where on October 16, 1925, they signed a treaty of mutual guarantee, usually referred to as the Locarno pact, four arbitration treaties between Germany on the one side and France, Belgium, Poland, and Czechoslovakia on the other, and two treaties of guarantee between France on the one side and Poland and Czechoslovakia on the other.

By Article 1 of the treaty of mutual guarantee, Germany, Belgium, France, Great Britain, and Italy, as a group and individually, guaranteed the inviolability of the existing frontiers between Germany and Belgium, and between Germany and France, and the demilitarization of the German Rhineland. By Article 2 Germany and Belgium, and Germany and France, mutually agreed in no case to attack, invade, or resort to war against each other except (1) in case of legitimate defense against a violation of Article 2 of the treaty, (2) in case of a "flagrant breach" of the agreements regarding the demilitarized zone, (3) in case of being directed by the League against a state which had first attacked another

member of the League. In case of a "flagrant violation" of either Article 1
or Article 2, the signatory powers agreed to come immediately to the
assistance of the injured party. In case of a doubtful violation, the question was to be considered by the Council of the League, and the signatory
powers agreed to fulfill their obligations as above if the Council was satisfied
that a violation or breach had been committed.

By the network of arbitration agreements Germany on the one side and
Belgium, France, Czechoslovakia, and Poland severally on the other engaged to settle by peaceful means all disputes of every kind. By the guarantee treaties which France signed with Czechoslovakia and Poland it was
agreed that in case Poland or Czechoslovakia or France should suffer
from a failure to observe the undertakings arrived at between them and
Germany, France and reciprocally Poland, or France and reciprocally
Czechoslovakia, should "lend each other immediately aid and assistance,
if such failure is accompanied by unprovoked recourse to arms."

In 1927 Briand, desiring to extend the network of treaties of arbitration and nonaggression, proposed to the United States a declaration by
the two powers renouncing war as "an instrument of national policy,"
and agreeing that a settlement of all disputes arising between them should
be brought about only by pacific means. The American secretary of state,
Frank B. Kellogg, suggested that instead of a bilateral treaty a similar
multilateral treaty should be drafted to include all states. In the course
of negotiations Kellogg's proposal was subjected to a number of reservations and interpretations, as a result of which it appeared that the nations
were agreed that all war was to be renounced except (1) in self-defense,
(2) against any treaty-breaking signatory state, (3) in the execution of
any obligation consequent upon the signing of any treaty of neutrality,
(4) in the case of Great Britain, in defense of certain strategic places which
were considered vital to the safety of the empire, (5) in fulfillment of the
obligations and responsibilities incurred by membership in the League of
Nations and by the signing of the Locarno agreements.

Subject to these reservations, which were not, however, incorporated
into the treaty, the plenipotentiaries of fifteen states gathered at the Quai
d'Orsay on August 27, 1928, and there signed a general treaty for the renunciation of war, the so-called pact of Paris. In it the powers solemnly
declared that they condemned recourse to war for the solution of international controversies, renounced it as an instrument of national policy
in their relations with one another, and agreed that the settlement or
solution of all disputes or conflicts which might arise among them should
never be sought except by pacific means. Immediately following the signing of the treaty, it was opened to the adherence of all states, and ultimately it was accepted by practically every country in the world. The

treaty was promulgated by President Hoover of the United States on July 24, 1929.

The Limitation of Naval Armaments

Although the Geneva Protocol, the League's projected preliminary to general disarmament, had not been accepted by the "safe" powers, the League did not abandon its efforts. Late in 1925 the Preparatory Commission for the Disarmament Conference was organized, consisting of representatives of all the great powers, including the United States and eventually Germany and Soviet Russia. This commission began its work at Geneva in May, 1926. During the succeeding years it struggled with the difficult problem of drafting a convention in which various blank spaces regarding the strength of effectives and matériel should be filled in later by the Disarmament Conference.

Meanwhile, some progress had been made in the limitation of navies by direct negotiations between the principal naval powers themselves. At the close of the First World War, with certain groups in the United States demanding that their country should have a navy second to none, it appeared for a time that Great Britain, Japan, and the United States were embarked upon a race for naval supremacy. To prevent such a development, the United States invited Great Britain and Japan to a conference to consider the possibility of limiting naval armaments. Since this question was found to be bound up with questions and problems concerning the Far East, however, the United States extended the scope of the conference to include these matters also, and invited not only Great Britain and Japan to send delegates, but France, Italy, China, Belgium, Portugal, and the Netherlands as well.

The Washington conference, in session from November 12, 1921, to February 6, 1922, resulted in the adoption of seven treaties which were designed to put an end to naval rivalry and to solve some of the difficulties in the Far East. Following the American proposal for a ten-year "naval holiday," two treaties were signed between the five most important naval powers: Great Britain, the United States, Japan, France, and Italy. The first treaty called for the scrapping of approximately 40 per cent of the capital ships already built or being constructed by the three great naval powers. For the future definite limits were placed upon the quota and tonnage of capital ships and aircraft carriers permitted to each state, the total tonnage being fixed at a ratio of approximately 5:5:3 for Great Britain, the United States, and Japan, and 1.67 for France and Italy. No new capital ships were to be constructed for ten years. The second treaty

ANOTHER "SCRAP OF PAPER"

The signing of the Briand-Kellogg pact, August 27, 1928.

outlawed the use of poison gas in warfare and restricted the use of sub
marines.

At the Washington conference Great Britain accepted the principle
of "parity" with the United States, but, when the latter sought to extend
the 5:5:3 ratio to all types of naval craft, an agreement was prevented
largely by differences of opinion regarding the size of cruisers and the
abolition of submarines. Another conference met in Geneva in 1927, upon
the invitation of the United States, but again it was found impossible to
reconcile the British program of a great number of small cruisers and the
American program of a small number of large cruisers. The failure of
the Geneva conference engendered considerable suspicion and ill will
between Great Britain and the United States. In 1929, however, something of a *rapprochement* was effected between the two countries, and
the British government invited the United States, France, Italy, and Japan
to participate in another naval conference in London in January, 1930. As
the Washington conference had abolished the competitive building of
capital ships, so it was hoped that the London conference might abolish
or allay competition in all other categories.

Although at London Great Britain, the United States, and Japan ultimately succeeded in reaching an agreement regarding the size of the various categories of their naval establishments, it proved impossible to conclude a five-power agreement because of differences between Italy and
France. The former demanded the right to have in all categories the parity
with France which had been granted her in capital ships at the Washington conference. This France steadily refused to concede, asserting that
to permit Italy parity with France would be to give Italy actual superiority
in the Mediterranean, since France had two seacoasts to defend. Both
France and Italy, therefore, declined to be bound by the general treaty
which was signed on April 27, 1930.

By the London naval treaty the existing holiday in capital ships was
extended until 1936. The total tonnage of the three principal powers in
cruisers, destroyers, and submarines was fixed, the United States being
granted substantial parity with Great Britain in all categories. Japan gained
parity in tonnage with these two in submarines, and in other categories
was permitted a ratio slightly better than the 5:5:3 agreed upon for capital
ships at Washington. These terms, it was believed, gave each of the three
powers sufficient naval strength to make a successful invasion of its home
waters by either of the others practically impossible.

The Geneva Disarmament Conference

During these years the League's Preparatory Commission for the Disarmament Conference had been working to pave the way for the calling of a general disarmament conference, and eventually, on February 2, 1932, the conference convened in Geneva with sixty nations, including the United States and the Soviet Union, represented. A number of difficult problems immediately confronted the delegates.

One was how to estimate effectives. The countries that employed conscription in general objected to the counting of trained reserves as effectives, while those which had volunteer armies maintained that reserves should be included in this category. Another problem was that of international supervision. France and her allies desired to have an elaborate system of international control established, but the other states maintained that the execution of any disarmament program must in general depend upon the good faith of the nations involved. The United States would not consent to any limitation of expenditures for armaments; Germany refused to approve any limitation of effectives unless trained reserves were included, and rejected the articles stating that existing treaties providing for the limitation of armaments should remain in force; Italy maintained that an agreement must be reached by all the naval powers on the proportions and levels of maximum tonnage.

France, still insistent upon her postwar thesis that security must precede disarmament, proposed that an international force, principally aircraft, should be created and placed at the disposal of the League for use in case sanctions had to be applied under Article 16 of the Covenant. This proposal found little favor among the other great powers. Germany, in turn, demanded general recognition of her "equality of right" to possess the same armaments as other countries. Soviet Russia suggested a progressive and proportional reduction of armaments with a view ultimately to their complete and rapid abolition. As none of these proposals was generally acceptable, a deadlock ensued. When the conference adjourned in July, the German delegation let it be known that it would not return to the conference until Germany's demand for equality had been granted. In December, 1932, the German claim to equality was recognized by the powers.

In February, 1933, the delegates resumed their labors at Geneva but by the end of the month, chiefly because of disagreements between the Germans and the French, another deadlock had resulted. French reluctance to grant Germany increased rights to rearm was greatly increased by the elevation to the chancellorship of the Reich of Adolf Hitler, who had long asserted his determination to scrap the treaty of Versailles. Disagreements therefore persisted regarding the steps to be taken to achieve disarmament, and in June, 1933, the conference again adjourned, this time until the following October. Meanwhile, it was hoped, informal discussions between the representatives of the great powers might eliminate some of the difficulties which prevented a general agreement. Eventually a tentative agreement was reached by Great Britain, France, Italy, and the United States, providing that for a period of four years no powers—Germany included—should increase their armaments. At the end of that period, however, Germany should be permitted to have such tanks, military airplanes, and other weapons forbidden by the treaty of Versailles as the other powers then retained. But Nazi Germany was determined to secure immediately the right to have a limited number of such "defensive" weapons—tanks and military airplanes—as the other great powers possessed.

On October 14, 1933, two days before the disarmament conference was to reconvene, the world was startled by Germany's announcement of her withdrawal from the conference and of her intended withdrawal from the League of Nations. It had become evident, the German foreign minister declared, that the conference would not bring about general disarmament in accordance with "the contractual obligations" of the powers, and that the "satisfactory fulfillment of Germany's recognized claim to equality" was therefore impossible. Since the latter constituted the condition upon which the German government had agreed to return to the conference in December, 1932, it was now compelled to withdraw.

The withdrawal of Germany brought the collapse of the conference. Although the rest of the delegates again convened on May 29, 1934, their views continued to fall generally into two incompatible categories. On the one hand, British, American, Italian, and other delegates made clear their desire to place disarmament first and to consider defensive security as resulting from it. On the other hand, the French and Russians—the latter, in view of the threat from Nazi Germany, being converted to collective security—argued for security first and disarmament second. On June 11 the League's disarmament conference, in despair of an agreement, adjourned for the last time; after more than two years of effort it had not succeeded in scrapping a single gun, tank, or airplane.

Germany's Default on Reparations Payments

Meanwhile, during the years when the world's statesmen were vainly endeavoring to carry out the Paris mandate regarding general disarmament, they were struggling—just about as vainly—to collect reparations from Germany in accordance with the terms of the treaty of Versailles.

It will be recalled that the peace conference decided that Germany must make compensation for all damage done to the civilian population of the Allied powers and to their property during the war, but that it did not stipulate the total amount which must be paid. This was left to be determined by a Reparations Commission.[2] After the peace conference, therefore, the first problem was to determine the total amount which Germany must pay and the system of payments which she must adopt.

Eventually, on April 28, 1921, the Reparations Commission notified Germany that she must pay $33,000,000,000,[3] in addition to Belgium's war debt. According to the schedule drawn up later, $12,500,000,000 of this amount was to bear interest at 5 per cent, and payments were to be made in fixed annuities of $500,000,000 plus variable annuities equal to a tax of 26 per cent on Germany's exports. Furthermore, despite Germany's claim to the contrary, the commission decided that Germany's total payments to date had not been more than sufficient to cover the expenses of the various Allied control commissions and armies of occupation. According to the Reparations Commission, Germany's total reparations indebtedness therefore still remained intact. An ultimatum was dispatched to Germany requiring her to accept without reserve the proposals of the commission under threat of Allied occupation of the Ruhr. On May 11, 1921, accordingly, Germany agreed to the total amount of reparations set by the commission and undertook to make payments according to the schedule the Allies had outlined.

A number of circumstances made it almost impossible for the German government to fulfill the obligations which it had assumed. In the first place, postwar Germany had no international credit; and, even if she had had, no countries in the world, with the possible exception of the United States, were in a position to advance her any large amounts immediately. She could not, therefore, settle the reparations demands at once by foreign loans. In the second place, owing to the Allied blockade which had so long cut her off from sources of raw materials and at the same time destroyed her prewar commercial system, Germany was faced with the necessity of buying extensively abroad, but was unable immediately to export an equivalent amount of goods. Her foreign trade, therefore, failed to bring into the country gold or foreign exchange which might have

[2] The Reparations Commission was originally intended to have one representative each from the United States, France, Great Britain, and Italy, with a fifth representative from time to time as the interests of other powers were directly involved. But the United States, because it did not ratify the treaty of Versailles, was not represented on the commission.

[3] The reparations figures given in this chapter in dollars are only approximate, for the German mark and Reichsmark (normally worth 23.81 cents) are here counted as four to the dollar.

been used to make reparations payments. On the contrary, the adverse balance of trade was draining from Germany the little gold that she had. The necessity of buying gold and foreign currencies to meet reparations obligations led, in turn, to increased inflation of German currency.

In the third place, Germany was handicapped by a tremendous "flight" of capital from the country. Capitalists were fearful lest their wealth be attached for reparations payments, and hastened to put as much of it as possible safely out of the clutches of the tax-gatherer. Considerably more than a billion dollars was thus placed beyond the reach of the government. The "flight" of German capital led to a still further inflation of the currency. This, in turn, coupled with the then existing inefficient fiscal system, resulted in a continuous national deficit which again compelled a resort to still greater inflation. Thus a vicious circle was created in the matter of currency inflation and depreciation. Finally, there existed in Germany a very definite lack of "the will to pay." This was especially true of the great industrialists, who with the depreciation of the mark waxed in power and arrogance. They appeared to defy the Allies, and refused to co-operate with their own government in any serious attempts to fulfill the terms of the treaty.

The combination of circumstances just discussed resulted eventually in Germany's failure to meet the cash payments or even to make full deliveries in kind according to the London schedule. Although the first payment of $250,000,000 was made, it was accompanied by a very decided decline in the value of the paper mark. By the end of the year Germany concluded that she could not continue to make full payments without the assistance of foreign loans or a resort to much greater inflation of the currency. She therefore raised the question of a moratorium. A partial moratorium was granted for 1922, but when Germany attempted to make her revised payments, the mark again sank rapidly in value. In July, 1922, Germany requested a moratorium on all cash payments until January, 1925.

As a result of Germany's demand for a total moratorium, the reparations problem resolved itself into a diplomatic conflict between the British and French governments. Fundamentally, the view of each in respect to the policy to be adopted toward Germany was based upon the economic situation in its own country, and the divergence which developed in the viewpoints of the two governments was caused chiefly by the changed economic situation in Great Britain.

For some time following the armistice, business had boomed in Great Britain, thanks to the immediate demand from European countries which had been cut off from the outside world by the war. But the boom collapsed in 1920 when exports fell off approximately 50 per cent. With the decline in exports, the volume of shipping fell off, and factories curtailed production. Business stagnation ensued, accompanied by wide-spread un-employment. British statesmen, therefore, were particularly eager that Germany, normally Great Britain's best customer, should regain her pros-perity and with it her ability to purchase British commodities. Therefore in 1922 they began to put forward the view that the economic restoration of Germany must precede the adequate payment of reparations.

On the other hand, France had emerged from the war with a devas-tated region of nearly thirteen thousand square miles. The chief economic problem for France, consequently, was to restore this devastated area to its former wealth-producing capacity. By the middle of 1922 she had spent $7,500,000,000 in reconstruction and pensions, and it was expected that this would ultimately be recovered from Germany. French states-men, therefore, did not look with favor upon Germany's demand for a moratorium. Poincaré, speaking for France, asserted that no moratorium should be granted unless "productive guaranties" were secured. Poincaré won out and, after Germany in November had demanded a total mora-torium for three or four years, the Reparations Commission, the British government dissenting, declared Germany in default. On January 10, 1923, the French government announced that a mission of control would be sent into the Ruhr.

The Ruhr Struggle and the Dawes Plan

Within a few days the whole Ruhr and Lippe region was occupied as far east as Dortmund by French and Belgian troops. Although the occu-pied area was only about sixty by twenty-eight miles in extent, it con-stituted the industrial heart of Germany. It was estimated that, at the date of the occupation, 80 to 85 per cent of Germany's coal, 80 per cent of her steel and pig-iron production, and 70 per cent of the goods and mineral traffic on her railways came from this territory. These facts constituted the basis of Poincaré's policy. By holding this small area, France and Bel-gium would either secure reparations payments at first hand or so paralyze the industrial life of Germany as to force her to agree to their terms.

The German chancellor, Cuno, believed that without German assist-ance France would be unable to operate the Ruhr industries, that the cost of the profitless occupation would force the French treasury into bank-ruptcy, and that thus the French would be compelled to withdraw in defeat from the territory. His unhappy guess as to the outcome led him to choose a policy of passive resistance, and the German government now proceeded to do everything that it could, short of open resistance, to op-pose French efforts. It ordered the inhabitants of the occupied area to pay no customs duties, coal taxes, or export duties which could come into

French hands, and forbade them to render any assistance to the French under threat of severe penalties. Finally, it entered upon a program of financial aid to all those—officials, railwaymen, miners, and industrial workers—who by reason of passive resistance lost their means of support.

Large numbers of men in the Ruhr were thrown out of employment, and food became scarce, the French allowing only sufficient to come into the district to ration the population. The German government was ruining itself to sustain passive resistance by paying allowances to expelled officials, to miners "on strike," and in a multitude of other ways. The deterioration of the mark was catastrophic. Not only the workmen in the Ruhr but, because of the decline of the mark and the cutting off of goods from that district, millions outside the Ruhr suffered as well. Ultimately the stranglehold which France held on German industry began to tell. Germany could not go on indefinitely without free access to this great center of her national industrial life. Unemployment in other parts of Germany soon resulted from the loss of products from the Ruhr. The mark continued its precipitate decline. Popular dissatisfaction with the complete failure of the policy of passive resistance brought the downfall of the Cuno ministry on August 12, 1923. A new cabinet was organized under Gustav Stresemann, who on September 26 announced that resistance had been abandoned.

On October 24, 1923, in a note to the Reparations Commission, Germany declared her willingness in principle to resume payments under the treaty of Versailles, and requested an examination of her capacity to pay. A committee of experts, headed by Charles G. Dawes of the United States and including representatives also from Great Britain, France, Italy, and Belgium, was accordingly appointed by the Reparations Commission. This committee made its report on April 9, 1924.

In brief, the so-called Dawes report embodied the following recommendations: (1) the Ruhr should be evacuated; (2) Germany should pledge certain revenues as security for payment of reparations; (3) the annual reparations payments should start at $250,000,000 and rise gradually over a four-year period to a normal figure of $625,000,000; (4) future payments should be increased or decreased according to an index of prosperity; (5) a foreign loan of $200,000,000 should be made as a foundation for Germany's fiscal system; (6) a central bank should be established with a fifty-year monopoly for the issue of paper money, subject to the control of an international board of seven Germans and seven foreigners. No change was made, however, in the total obligation for reparations payments placed upon Germany by the Reparations Commission in 1921. Germany accepted this report and on September 1 the plan began to operate. On July 31, 1925, the last French and Belgian soldiers left the Ruhr.

Inter-Allied War Debts and the Young Plan

Meanwhile, not unrelated to the problem of reparations was that of the Inter-Allied war debts, which were also a legacy of the First World War. During the early years of that conflict Great Britain, as the wealthiest of the Allies, advanced some billions of dollars in loans to Russia, France, Italy, and the lesser powers, and after the United States became a belligerent, the latter loaned approximately $10,338,000,000 to the Allies, including Great Britain, in return for their demand notes bearing interest at 5 per cent.

At the Paris peace conference the British proposed a general cancellation of all Inter-Allied debts; that is, Great Britain asserted her willingness to cancel the amounts owed her by the Allies if the United States would do the same. Such a step would of course have been to the advantage of Great Britain, for her loss in canceling the Allied debts to herself would have been more than offset by the cancellation of her debt to the United States and by the general stimulation to world trade which would have followed such a reduction of international debts. On the other hand, such a step would, for all practical purposes, have placed a war indemnity of over ten billion dollars on American taxpayers.

Nevertheless, it was argued by many Europeans and even by some Americans that, since the war against Germany had been a common struggle, and since the United States had entered the conflict late and lost relatively very few men, she should consider the loans to the Allies as her contribution to the common cause. It was further pointed out that an amount even greater than that advanced in loans was spent in the United States by the Allies during the war and hence that the United States should be satisfied with the great wealth which had come to her from her war-time activities and should not try to collect the war debts. Finally, it was asserted that, since Europe could not pay her war debts without flooding the United States with foreign commodities, collection of the debts would greatly harm American manufacturers and merchants.

At the peace conference President Wilson declined the British proposal, and eventually in 1922 the United States government officially requested all its debtors to take the necessary steps to fund their debts to the United States. Although the British still favored a general cancellation of both war debts and reparations claims, in the end the debtor states all entered into funding agreements with the United States. The amount actually funded, including the accrued interest, totaled approximately $11,500,-000,000. In principal and interest the debtor nations agreed to pay the United States over a sixty-two-year period a total of approximately $22,000,-

000,000. Even so, figured on the originally contracted rate of interest, approximately half of the total debt was remitted by the United States.

With Germany regularly making her reparations payments to the Allies under the Dawes plan, the Allies were able in turn to make their war-debt payments to the United States. Between September, 1924, and September, 1928, about $1,350,000,000 was paid to the Allies by Germany. Although the fact was not generally recognized at the time, Germany was enabled to make these reparations payments largely because during these years huge sums were being loaned to German interests by foreign bankers, chiefly American.

The Dawes report had, of course, limited itself merely to pointing out the amount which Germany could pay annually over a period of years. So far as Germany was concerned, she was still legally bound to pay $33,000,000,000 by the agreement which she had been forced to accept in May, 1921. But no one now considered it possible to exact any such amount, and so the next step in the reparations problem was to reach some new decision either as to a revised total which Germany must pay or as to the specific number of years over which the Dawes plan was to operate. A new committee of experts was accordingly appointed which included some of the best financial brains of the nations concerned and of the United States as well. Beginning in February, 1929, sessions of the committee were held in Paris under the chairmanship of Owen D. Young, one of the American delegates, who had played an important role in the drafting of the Dawes plan. As in the latter case, the committee soon became known from its chairman as the Young Committee. On June 7 the committee signed its report which in the early months of 1930 was ratified by the various governments.

The Young plan provided for thirty-seven payments by Germany averaging $512,500,000, to be followed by twenty-two further payments averaging $391,250,000. These were the equivalent of a cash payment of $9,000,000,000, in contrast with the $33,000,000,000 originally stipulated by the Reparations Commission. The Dawes plan had begun the process of removing the reparations problem from the political to the financial sphere; the Young plan carried the process still further by the creation of the Bank for International Settlements, which was to perform the banking functions necessary in the sequence between the initial payment of the annuities and the final distribution of the funds. The control of the management of the bank was placed in the hands of the central banks of the countries involved in the reparations settlement, including Germany. Obviously, the reparations problem was lifted out of the political sphere, and the former political method of handling what was purely an economic problem now became obsolete.

In contrast with the Dawes plan, the Young plan definitely fixed the number and the amounts of the annuities necessary for a final settlement. It removed the uncertainty attendant upon the operation of the index of prosperity. It abolished the system of external controls, gave Germany full financial autonomy, and left to her the obligation of facing her engagements on her own responsibility. Germany's payments, moreover, were fixed in relation to the sums owed by the Allied countries in war debts, and the *de facto* relationship between war debts and reparations was clearly recognized. If any of the creditor powers received any relief in its payments of war debts, during the first thirty-seven years Germany should benefit two thirds, and during the last twenty-two years the whole relief should be applied to the reduction of Germany's liabilities. Thus was destroyed the fiction that the problems of war debts and reparations were unconnected. Furthermore, it was agreed that the Inter-Allied occupation of the Rhineland should end. Evacuation began in September, 1929, and was completed by June 30, 1930. With the Allies and Germany at last in agreement regarding the number and amounts of the latter's future reparations payments, it was hoped that the settlement was "complete and final," and that at last the tortuous problem of reparations had been successfully solved.

The World Economic Depression

The Young Plan had been based on the assumption that world trade would expand both in volume and in value. Unfortunately, however, soon after the drafting of the plan came the Wall Street crash of 1929 and the beginning of an economic depression which brought in its train a drastic shrinking in the volume of world trade and a rapid and steady fall in commodity prices.

The causes assigned for the depression were about as varied as the interests and outlooks of those who examined the situation. By many the inadequacy of the world's relatively small supply of gold as a basis for national and international exchange was held responsible for the catastrophic decline in the price of commodities. By others the blame was placed upon the oversupply and consequently decreasing value of silver, which, it was asserted, greatly lessened the purchasing power of those countries—particularly China and India—which were on a silver basis. A world-wide surplus of agricultural products, it was further pointed out, inevitably brought a decline in the price of these commodities and therefore diminished the farmers' ability to purchase manufactured goods; while, at the same time, the postwar revolution in industry by the introduction of labor-saving machines decreased the man power needed in certain types of manufacturing and so through unemployment brought a decline in the purchasing power of the proletariat. The new machinery, on the other hand, vastly increased the output of manufactured goods, so that inevitably there came an overproduction and the closing down of factories, with further loss of purchasing power on the part of those who were dismissed. Extreme nationalism, with its erection of high protective tariffs and its resultant interference with the flow of international trade, also came in for bitter criticism. But, whatever were the causes of the depression, the year 1930 witnessed a marked slowing down of industry and an alarming increase in unemployment.

In 1931 the continued economic depression at last brought the financial collapse of certain countries of Europe, which found themselves unable to dispose of their surplus products at prices that would enable them to meet their international obligations. The incident which precipitated the financial crisis in central Europe occurred in Austria, where in June, 1931, the Creditanstalt, by far the largest private bank in the republic, came to the verge of collapse and had to be rescued by the Austrian government. The difficulties of the Creditanstalt shook foreign confidence in the solvency of central Europe as a whole and reacted on Germany, where a banking crisis was already developing, largely because American bankers were recalling their short-term credits.[4] Once again Germany seemed to face national bankruptcy. To prevent such a catastrophe, with all its attendant evils to the world, President Hoover, on June 20, 1931, proposed a suspension of all payments on reparations and intergovernmental debts for one year beginning July 1.

The situation in Germany, nevertheless, grew worse in July with the continued calling of short-term loans and the export of capital. Germans themselves, withdrawing money to hoard or to transfer abroad, precipitated a further crisis when on July 13 the Darmstädter und National-Bank, one of the largest financial institutions in the country, was forced to close its doors. This in turn evoked a governmental decree temporarily closing all banks and stock exchanges. In August a committee, headed by an American banker, Albert H. Wiggin, was convened by the Bank for International Settlements to study the German situation. This committee recommended that the existing short-term loans should be continued for a period of six months, and its recommendation was at once adopted by Germany's creditors, who negotiated a "standstill agreement" extending until February 29, 1932, all short-term credits.[5]

[4] In July, 1931, the short-term credits of Germany totaled approximately $3,000,000,000.

[5] In February, 1932, and yearly thereafter through 1939, the "standstill agreement" was extended. In 1940 short-term credits advanced by American banks had been reduced to less than $40,000,000.

This "freezing" of short-term loans in turn reacted disastrously on Great Britain, whose bankers were fatally handicapped by their inability to recall the short-term credits they had advanced to Germany. During August and September gold was rapidly withdrawn from London, particularly by Dutch, Belgian, and Swiss bankers who feared that British banks would not be able to meet their obligations, and that the British government might even be forced to abandon the gold standard. On September 21 continued withdrawals finally forced Great Britain to go off the gold standard, a step in which she was soon followed by many other countries both in Europe and throughout the world.

World economic conditions in general and German conditions in particular soon convinced the German government that it would be impossible to resume reparations payments at the end of the Hoover moratorium. Availing itself of a provision of the Young plan, it therefore requested the Bank for International Settlements to convene a special advisory committee of financial experts to investigate Germany's capacity to resume reparations payments in July, 1932. This committee reported that Germany would not be able to resume reparations payments at that time. The committee also took occasion to point out that a prompt adjustment of all intergovernmental debts to the existing world situation was the only lasting step capable of re-establishing economic stability and real peace, for the tremendous fall in commodity prices had obviously greatly increased the burden of all intergovernmental payments.

The End of Reparations and War-Debt Payments

On June 16, 1932, a reparations conference once more convened—this time at Lausanne—to decide upon "a lasting settlement" of the questions raised in the report of the most recent committee of financial experts, and to consider measures necessary to solve the other economic and financial difficulties which, it was felt, were responsible for and might prolong the existing world crisis. In the end an agreement was reached (July 9) that the reparations payments stipulated in the Young plan should be set aside and replaced by an obligation upon Germany to pay into a general fund for European reconstruction the sum of $750,000,000. To meet this obligation, the German government was to deliver to the Bank for International Settlements bonds to that amount.

The Lausanne agreement constituted one more recession in the series of ever-diminishing demands upon Germany for reparations. An Allied demand in 1921 that Germany assume an obligation to pay $56,500,000,000 was followed in the same year by the Reparations Commission's decision that the total figure should be $33,000,000,000. This stood legally as Germany's obligation until the Young Plan reduced it to an amount which was equivalent to a cash payment of approximately $9,000,000,000. Two years later came the Hoover moratorium, and then in July, 1932, the Lausanne agreement drastically revised Germany's obligations to a total cash payment of only $750,000,000, with the possibility that even this amount might never be paid.[6] Altogether, according to a competent and disinterested American calculation, Germany had paid under her reparations obligations a total of $5,396,250,000.

On the same day on which the Lausanne treaty was signed, Great Britain, France, Italy, and Belgium came to another agreement. By this so-called "gentlemen's agreement" these powers undertook not to ratify the Lausanne treaty until a satisfactory settlement had been reached between them and their own creditors. An effort was thus once more made to link the reparations question with the problem of Inter-Allied war debts, and to make the final solution of the reparations problem rest upon the willingness of the United States either to cancel or to reduce the debts due it from the Allies.

Although the Hoover moratorium in 1931 suspended all payments on war debts, the United States expected that with the expiration of the one-year period these payments would be resumed. Congress, in approving the moratorium in December, 1931, expressly declared that cancellation or reduction of any of the indebtedness of foreign countries to the United States was contrary to the policy of that body. On the other hand, the Allied governments maintained that the Lausanne agreement practically canceling Germany's reparations payments was made in the belief that the United States would consent to a revision of war-debts payments. In November, 1932, accordingly, Great Britain and France presented notes to the United States raising the question of debt revision. Both linked the questions of reparations and war debts, and both requested postponement of the payments due on December 15 as a preliminary to a general review of the debt agreements. In reply, President Hoover pointed out that the American government still held that "reparations are a solely European question in which the United States is not concerned," and that it refused to recognize that the Lausanne settlement of German reparations "was made in reliance upon any commitments given by this government."

Nevertheless, on December 15, 1932, only six states made their payments to the United States; five "deferred" them. In June and December, 1933, Finland alone made her payments in full; five states made merely "token" payments; and seven defaulted altogether. Although, in an effort

[6] Early in 1937 Chancellor Hitler announced the German government's repudiation of these reparations bonds.

to bring pressure on the debtor governments, the United States Congress, in April, 1934, passed the Johnson Act forbidding nationals of the United States to make loans to foreign governments in default on their debt obligations to the United States, on June 15, 1934, the only payment received was from Finland. And in the succeeding years she was the only country to make any payments whatever to the United States.

By 1934 it was becoming evident to most observers that the effort of the United States to collect some $22,000,000,000 of war debts and interest had broken down. Just as the attempts of the former Allies to collect reparations payments from Germany in amounts ranging from $33,000,000,000 to $9,000,000,000 had collapsed in the face of the impossibility of transferring such tremendous sums, so, it appeared, had American efforts suffered a similar fate. As the year 1932 saw the practical ending of the payment of reparations, so the year 1934 saw apparently the ending of payments of war debts to the United States by the Allied countries.

For this eventuality the United States was not entirely blameless. In the first place, although most of the original ten billion dollars had been transferred to the Allies in the form of commodities, the United States had refused to accept payment in kind from the debtor nations. In the second place, she had raised high tariff barriers against foreign commodities and had thus greatly handicapped the debtor powers in their efforts to secure American currency with which to make payments. In the third place, she had vigorously sought to increase her own export trade and in so doing had inevitably lessened the sale of goods abroad by the debtor nations. Finally, by subsidizing the American merchant marine, she had indirectly reduced the income of foreign shipping. All of these things the United States had a right to do, but in doing them she went far toward preventing the European powers from being able to meet their war-debt obligations. To many it seemed that the United States had as yet an incomplete understanding of her new position as a creditor rather than a debtor nation.

Political Effects of the World Depression

Meanwhile, the world economic depression had done more than merely smash the system of reparations and war-debt payments. It had profoundly affected the economic, social, and political life of most of the countries of the Western world. In the first place, one inevitable result of the depression was a tremendous increase in the number of unemployed, caused primarily by the closing down of factories as a result of the overproduction of goods and the inability of the masses to purchase them at the prices demanded. Although the unemployment problem affected every country

—with the possible exception of Soviet Russia—it was more general in the industrial countries, and most keenly felt in those which had most thoroughly rationalized their industries. Naturally, not only the millions actually unemployed, but also millions of their dependents as well, suffered deprivation and want and provided a fertile field for discontent with existing institutions.

But others felt the stern hand of the depression, too. Earnings and profits of practically all types of business enterprises seriously decreased or disappeared altogether. Dividends were reduced materially or were wholly omitted. Not only the great capitalists, who owned and controlled vast business interests, but also the more numerous members of the middle class—who had invested modest sums in shares of industrial companies—became alarmed at the threat to their economic security.

In most countries efforts were made by the governments to assist the unemployed. In some countries aid was given directly through unemployment payments or "doles"; in others, governments sought to aid the unemployed indirectly by the inauguration of projects calling for the construction of extensive public works. Efforts were made to "prime the pump" of business by giving employment directly to millions who would then become purchasers of goods, or by undertaking enterprises which, in the course of their construction, would create a demand for goods and thus indirectly give employment to various subsidiary industries.

Obviously, such government policies entailed severe drains upon national budgets, especially at a time when the ordinary channels of revenue were inclined to dry up. Accordingly, governments were forced to seek new sources of revenue whenever possible or to increase existing tax rates. This, of course, caused discontent among those classes upon whom the taxes fell. Furthermore, in efforts to maintain balanced national budgets, governments in some cases reduced the salaries of state employees and the interest on government bonds. Such policies inevitably created discontent among bondholders and state employees. Finally, in some countries the national budgets remained unbalanced and national debts increased enormously. The resultant popular fear of currency inflation or repudiation caused widespread alarm among the classes which would be most adversely affected.

With discontent so general, with so many different classes dissatisfied with conditions arising from the depression, it was inevitable that politics should be affected. As the succeeding chapters show, in practically every country where popular opinion was allowed to express itself and where the mass of the people had an opportunity to vote, the governments functioning at the time the depression began were turned out of office. The extent of the resultant political upheaval ranged from a mere change in the parties controlling the government to a veritable revolution such as occurred in Germany when the Nazis came into power. Furthermore, economic difficulties at home and the desire to get back to "normalcy" go far toward explaining why political leaders in the democratic countries were reluctant to resort to drastic measures to stop the aggressor nations in the early stages of what turned out to be the preliminaries of the Second World War.

Part Four

NATIONAL PROBLEMS AND EXPERIMENTS

BETWEEN TWO WORLD WARS

PRECEDING chapters have shown how the First World War released or engendered certain revolutionary forces which in 1917 and 1918 overturned the existing political regimes in one European country after another and brought into existence a number of new states. But the war also brought in its train tremendously heavy burdens and seemingly insuperable difficulties which in the postwar period caused the collapse of several national governments. The creation of new states and the establishment of new regimes in some of the older states in turn opened the way for the inauguration of political and economic experiments of a sweeping nature. The chapters in Part Four discuss somewhat fully the Communist, Fascist, and Nazi regimes in Russia, Italy, and Germany as well as in a number of the lesser states. But attention is also given to the serious problems which confronted those countries which continued to maintain liberal traditions and to the ways in which they met their difficulties without abandoning their long-cherished ideals. In other words, Part Four describes how the different countries of Europe reacted to the serious problems arising from the First World War.

Chapter XV

SOVIET RUSSIA

THE national reconstruction which occurred in so many countries as a result of the First World War saw the inauguration of new experiments in the political and economic life of Europe. The first of the great powers to embark upon such a new course was Russia, where, with the establishment of the Soviet regime, there developed a "dictatorship of the proletariat." In the succeeding years sweeping political, social, and economic changes were made. In the end private enterprise largely disappeared from the economic life of Russia, to be succeeded by a system which may be described as state capitalism or state socialism.

Lenin and Trotsky

During the first four years of the Soviet regime the reform program of the Bolsheviks was largely directed by Nicholas Lenin, whose tremendous will power and boundless energy so dominated the Bolsheviks that he might well have said, *"Le parti, c'est moi."* The real name of this "plump little man, with a high bulbous forehead, a snub nose, and bald head" was Vladimir Ilyich Ulianov. He was born in Simbirsk (now Leninsk) in 1870, the son of a district inspector of schools whose family descended from a stock of impoverished nobles. His elder brother, Alexander, was executed for his part in the attempted assassination of Alexander III in 1887, and doubtless Lenin was in sympathy with his views, for he himself was soon expelled from the University of Kazan because of revolutionary agitation. Later he passed the bar examinations in Petrograd, but soon gave up the practice of law, joined a secret organization of professional revolutionists, became a Social Democrat, and was even exiled for a time to Siberia because of revolutionary activities among the working classes of the capital. The split in the Social Democratic Party which occurred in 1903 was largely due to Lenin, who repudiated co-operation with the liberals and sought a violent outbreak of class war. During the revolution of 1905 he was again in Petrograd, but his role was rather unimportant, his chief endeavor being to incite violence and hostility against the Duma and the Constitutional Democrats. At the conclusion of the revolution he left the country, and from 1906 to 1917 lived abroad as a professional revolu-

447

tionary, giving himself exclusively to the work of revolutionary organization and secret propaganda.

In April, 1917, Lenin had returned to Petrograd, and had gradually gathered about him a group of followers: doctrinaire fanatics, masters of intrigue and propaganda, ambitious opportunists, sentimental visionaries, crazy degenerates, sincere idealists—yet withal many extremely energetic and capable men whose names later became prominent in Russian affairs. While Lenin unquestionably held first place in the Bolshevik Party, second place had soon gone to a new recruit, Leon Trotsky, who did not finally join the Bolsheviks until after the March revolution. Trotsky, whose real name was Leon Davidovich Bronstein, was a Russian middle-class Jew who had early become imbued with revolutionary ideas. Twice he had been exiled to Siberia, and twice he had escaped. As a Menshevik he had played a prominent role in the Petrograd Soviet of workers during the Russian revolution of 1905. The revolution of March, 1917, had found him in New York, where he had recently gone after having lived in exile for several years in Vienna and Paris, but he had hastened to return to Russia and had played a prominent part in the November revolution. As commissar for foreign affairs in the Soviet government he had signed the humiliating treaty of Brest-Litovsk because Lenin had believed that only by so doing could the Bolsheviks gain freedom to inaugurate undisturbed their extensive reforms.

Civil War and Foreign Intervention

But the Bolshevik hope of being left in peace to introduce their new regime in Russia was soon blasted, for both within and without the country numerous movements were at once begun for the purpose of driving the Bolsheviks from power. Many Russians—soon called White Russians because of their opposition to the Red Bolsheviks—believed that Bolshevism was but a passing phase in the Russian upheaval and hoped, by counter-revolutionary measures supported by the Allies, to be able to overthrow the Bolshevik regime. The Allies, in turn, feared that military supplies which had been landed at Murmansk, Archangel, and Vladivostok might be seized by the Central Powers. After Russia's signing of the treaty of Brest-Litovsk, therefore, Allied expeditionary forces were dispatched to these ports, and after the end of the war French forces seized Odessa and British forces occupied Russian Transcaucasia. Each of the regions seized at once served as a rallying ground for White Russians.

Menaced by innumerable revolutionary plots from within and threatened by Allied armies of intervention from abroad, the Bolshevik leaders depended for defense chiefly upon two agencies—the Cheka and the Red

Army. The Cheka was organized by Felix Dzerzhinsky immediately after the November revolution and it soon became an agency of terror. It was empowered to arrest, try, and shoot all who were considered dangerous to the Bolshevik regime. Thousands of tsarist sympathizers and bourgeois were ruthlessly put to death. The second agency, the volunteer Red Army, was organized by Trotsky, and it was developed during 1918 into a well-equipped, well-trained force, commanded for the most part by former tsarist officers whose loyalty to Russia led them to fight against what they looked upon as foreign invasion.

In 1919 the simultaneous advance of the White armies began, but they were all defeated and driven back. Perhaps the greatest single cause of their failure was the fact that the Russians came to view them as the agents of reaction who were seeking to restore lands to the landlords and the old system of privileges to the aristocracy. Furthermore, the advance of the White armies had been accompanied by looting, disorder, and a White Terror almost as ruthless as that of the Reds; and, as between Bolshevism and extreme military reaction, the Russian masses preferred the former temporarily as the lesser of two evils. The conduct of the counterrevolutionary armies and the bloody repressive measures of the White leaders also alienated popular sympathy in the Allied countries. By the close of 1919 all Allied forces had been withdrawn from European Russia, though the Japanese remained for a time in Vladivostok.

But the Soviet government was not yet freed from the need for military campaigns. The White forces of the south were actively supported by the French government, and during the early months of 1920 they once more moved northward in the Ukraine. At the same time the Poles, desiring to push their Russian frontier as far east as possible, began an invasion of Russia. In May they succeeded in occupying the city of Kiev. Again the Russians rallied to support the Soviet government, and the Poles were hurled back almost to Warsaw. Only the timely aid of the French prevented a debacle. In October a preliminary treaty brought peace between the two countries and a settlement of the boundary question. By this time the Soviet government had concluded similar treaties with Estonia, Lithuania, Latvia, and Finland, and was finally free to give its attention once more to the White armies in the south. By the close of the year 1920 European Russia was cleared of active counterrevolutionary armies.

The Russian Soviet Federated Socialist Republic

Meanwhile, the Bolsheviks had profoundly altered the political life of Russia. In 1918 a constitution, adopted by the fifth All-Russian Congress of Soviets, established the Russian Soviet Federated Socialist Republic

(R.S.F.S.R.), with Moscow as the national capital instead of Petrograd. Russia became a federal republic which was declared to be "a free socialist society of the working people of Russia." The right to participate in the government was given to citizens of both sexes who were eighteen years of age, provided they were productive workers, the housekeepers of productive workers, or soldiers or sailors. Local government was entrusted to rural and urban soviets. In villages the peasants, home workers, local teachers, and doctors met and elected the deputies of the local soviet. In cities deputies were elected to the urban soviet from the factories and shops according to the different types of industry. Housewives and independent handicraftsmen met ordinarily by districts. Until 1936 voting in these local elections was by show of hands rather than by secret written ballot. All representation above the village and city soviets was indirect, as shown in the accompanying diagram.

Supreme power in the R.S.F.S.R. resided theoretically in the All-Russian Congress of Soviets, composed of representatives chosen directly by the urban soviets in the ratio of one for every 25,000 voters, and by the provincial congresses in the ratio of one for every 125,000 inhabitants. A discrepancy in regard to representation was thus made in favor of the urban centers, where Communism had its greatest strength. The principal function of the All-Russian Congress was to elect the All-Russian Central Executive Committee, which was in theory responsible to it. This Central Executive Committee was "the supreme legislative, executive and controlling organ of the R.S.F.S.R." It convoked the All-Russian Congress and appointed the Council of People's Commissars, which was "entrusted with the general management of the affairs of the R.S.F.S.R." The Council of Commissars was a small group of members which resembled the ministry in a parliamentary state; its action was subject to annulment or approval by the Central Executive Committee.

The Union of Soviet Socialist Republics

For a time, after the November revolution of 1917, it appeared that Russia might be reduced in size to a territory little larger than that ruled by Ivan the Terrible in the sixteenth century. By the treaty of Brest-Litovsk she had been compelled to renounce her sovereignty over a great strip of territory in the west and over the whole of the Ukraine in the south. In the Transcaucasus her rule had been repudiated by Azerbaijan, Georgia, and Armenia, which had established themselves as independent states. In September, 1918, all Siberia had been organized under an anti-Bolshevik directorate at Omsk.

Nevertheless, with the exception of Poland and the new Baltic republics,

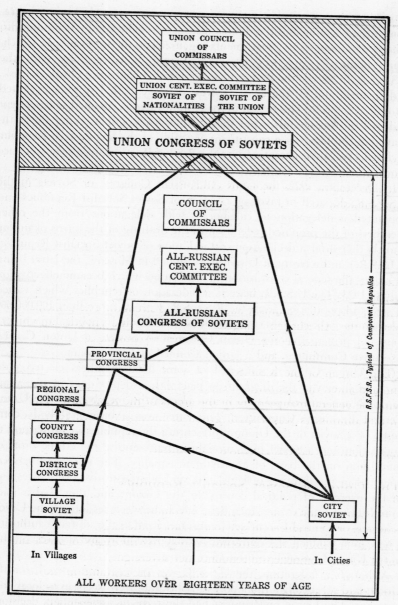

POLITICAL STRUCTURE OF THE U.S.S.R. UNTIL 1936

all of these apparently lost territories were soon regained. The reintegration of the Ukraine and the Transcaucasus was achieved by bringing into existence in those states governments organized on the soviet model, which, while nominally independent, entered into close relations with the R.S.F.S.R. In Siberia the Red armies succeeded in capturing Omsk, Tomsk, and Irkutsk, and all the territory west of Lake Baikal was incorporated into the R.S.F.S.R. The region to the east, however, remained independent and in 1920 was established as the Far Eastern Republic. After the withdrawal of the Japanese a constituent assembly of the Far Eastern Republic declared (1922) its absorption into the R.S.F.S.R. and Russia's control once more extended to the Pacific.

In December, 1922, the tenth All-Russian Congress of Soviets in the R.S.F.S.R. declared in favor of a Union of Soviet Socialist Republics and appointed a delegation to collaborate with delegations from the other members of the proposed federation in the drafting of the terms of union. Shortly thereafter a declaration of the Union of Soviet Socialist Republics (U.S.S.R.) and a treaty of Union were signed in Moscow, the latter being in reality the federal constitution of the Union which became effective on July 6, 1923. The U.S.S.R. became a federation of republics which varied in size and population from the R.S.F.S.R. with its more than 100,000,000 inhabitants to the smallest with less than one million. Its political machinery consisted principally of a Union Congress of Soviets, a Union Central Executive Committee, and a Union Council of Commissars.

The Union Congress consisted of some 1500 members elected indirectly as shown in the diagram on page 451, and met once in two years to decide on general policies. It also elected the members of the Union Central Executive Committee. The latter was a bicameral body composed of a Soviet of the Union representing the republics in proportion to population and a Soviet of Nationalities representing the ethnic units of the Union on the basis of approximate equality. The two chambers cooperated in the drafting of legislation and administrative ordinances and in the exercise of political control in the Union; and they had a joint presidium of some twenty members, which, between sessions of the Union Congress or Central Executive Committee, acted as the supreme authority. The Union Council of Commissars was appointed by and was responsible to the Union Central Executive Committee.

Although a federation, the U.S.S.R. was strongly centralized, for the Union had practically a monopoly of political power except as to local government. The Union government had the right to abrogate any decisions of the congresses of soviets, central executive committees, and councils of people's commissars in the constituent republics which infringed the treaty of Union. The federal character of the Union, therefore, was ex-

tremely limited, one Russian scholar asserting that the constituent republics retained merely the right to legislate on social insurance, public
health, education, minor courts, and agriculture except for land distribution.

The Soviet system of government as found in the separate republics and
in the union had three distinguishing characteristics. In the first place, the
Soviet state was controlled by only one class—the proletariat. During what
was expected to be merely a transitional stage from capitalism to pure communism the government of the Soviet Union was a dictatorship of the
proletariat; only the industrial workers and poor peasants had political
power. The ultimate goal, of course, was the abolition of all classes and
the destruction of the causes of class struggle. A second characteristic of
the soviet system was the extensive use of indirect representation and the
great distance which separated the voters from the supreme seat of authority. The peasants, who constituted perhaps 80 per cent of the people, were
six steps removed from the Union Council of Commissars, and the urban
proletariat were four. The third characteristic of the soviet system was the
complete lack of separation of powers. The same set of agencies was used
to perform all the functions of government—legislative, executive, administrative, and even, at times, judicial. The judiciary in the Soviet Union
was "not an independent organ of the government, but an administrative
department charged with the defense of the social order established by the
proletarian revolution."

The Role of the Communist Party

Behind the formal machinery of the Soviet government and so inter-
woven into its fabric that it was not always easy to disentangle the two was
the political organization of the Bolsheviks, the Communist Party.[1] Higher
offices in the government and in the party were largely interlocking. This
control of the higher offices was made possible largely because of the
close organization of the Communist Party and the political activity of its
members. Out of a population of approximately 160,000,000 in the U.S.S.R.,
only 2,500,000 were included in the party. But these members were subjected to a rigorous discipline. They were bound by the decisions of the
party and might be expelled from the organization for failure to accept
them. They were expected to be active in the trade unions and other organizations. In every soviet their aim was to organize the Communist members into efficient, disciplined groups for the purpose of winning control
by the election of Communist members to the higher positions. Candidates
for membership were required to pass through a probationary period before admission. The Communist Party, therefore, was "a carefully se-

[1] In 1918 the Bolsheviks changed their name officially to the Russian Communist Party.

lected body of active workers with a definite goal, who are willing to make great sacrifices for its success and who are bound together by a centralized discipline." The party, too, had various youth organizations. For the purpose of perpetuating the enthusiasm and sacrificial quality of the older Communists who suffered exile or imprisonment for their principles, three junior Communist societies were created. The Octobrists (eight to ten years of age), the Pioneers (ten to sixteen), and the Communist Youth (sixteen to twenty-three) ultimately came to have millions of members, drawn from both sexes.

Aside from the Communist Party no other parties were permitted. All opposition was suppressed. Freedom of speech and of the press was abolished. Even "movies" were subject to government censorship. Although the Cheka was formally abolished in 1922, a state political department was created to take its place. The new organization of espionage was usually referred to by its initials as the Ogpu, and according to some the only difference between it and the Cheka was the change of letters. In 1934 the Ogpu, in turn, was abolished, and its functions were entrusted to a commissariat of internal affairs, the NKVD, which was supposed to be organized along civil instead of semimilitary lines. Opposition continued to be crushed, however, by arbitrary imprisonment, exile to Siberia, or death.

Early Economic Experiments

Far more revolutionary than the changes introduced into the political system were those made in the economic life of Russia by the Communists during the first three years of their regime. The fundamental concept of their economic thought—prevention of the exploitation of the workers by the capitalists and landlords—demanded the nationalization of all land, forests, and minerals, together with all means of production, transportation, trade, banking, and insurance. These would then belong to the state, and under the soviet system the workers constituted the state. All profits which formerly went to landlords and capitalists would accrue to the state —in other words, to the workers. The surplus products of both peasants and proletariat would be turned over to state agencies from which each would in return secure those commodities which he needed; that is to say, money and wages would be abolished, and the state would take all output and in turn reward each according to his needs. In greatly simplified form, this was the economic system envisaged by the Communist leaders.

It had been the original intention of the Communists to nationalize only large industrial establishments at first, and then only after they had been concentrated in trusts. But this plan for gradual and systematic nationalization broke down almost immediately. Instead, there began a haphazard and punitive nationalization of all sorts of industries. But the workers were prepared neither by education nor by training to take over the responsibilities of management. There was little effort at co-ordination; each factory was run by its own committee independently of all others. Industrial chaos naturally ensued. In June, 1918, an attempt was made to develop a system of industrial administration under centralized control. Practically all industry was nationalized. Furthermore, all agencies of domestic and foreign trade, the merchant marine, and the banks were nationalized and their total assets confiscated. To control and co-ordinate the industrial life of the country the Supreme Economic Council was established. It was to see that all factories were supplied with necessary raw materials, fuel, and machinery, as well as the supplies and food needed for their workers. As might have been expected under the circumstances, the Supreme Economic Council proved altogether unable to accomplish so gigantic a task. Industrial production fell off alarmingly.

Meanwhile, the government had become involved in a struggle with the peasants. In accordance with the Communist economic plan, as briefly outlined above, the Soviet government in May, 1918, established a food dictatorship and ordered every peasant to turn over to the state all grain above a certain minimum needed for seed and for the consumption of his family. This at once encountered the opposition of the peasants, who either failed to understand or refused to adopt the role which had been assigned to them in the Communist economic scheme. If in return for the grain which they surrendered to the state they could have received an equivalent value in the manufactured goods which they needed, they might have acquiesced. But this was impossible, both because of the cutting off of the importation of manufactured goods from abroad and because of the demoralization of Russian industries at home. The peasants, therefore, refused to surrender their grain. When the government seized grain by force, the peasants resorted to passive resistance.

In 1920 the peasants reduced their acreage under cultivation until it was 29 per cent less than it had been in 1913. The smaller area sown and the decrease in available fertilizers and in effective agricultural tools, coupled with an unusually prolonged drought, combined to bring a tremendous reduction in available food supplies. The harvest in 1921 was only 42 per cent of the average in the four years immediately preceding the war. A severe famine resulted. Soviet authorities estimated that 30,000,000 people would need relief. The government fed millions, and appealed for foreign aid in the task. Some forty different foreign agencies undertook to feed the starving millions, but many died from starvation or epidemics.

The first large-scale communist experiment in history was headed for disaster. The industrial workers had failed to produce the manufactured goods needed by the peasants. The peasants, failing to obtain tangible goods in exchange for their grain, had curtailed their planting. This had contributed to produce a shortage of grain, and the government was now unable to provide adequate food supplies for the industrial proletariat. And unless the urban workers were supplied with food, they would certainly turn against the government. Outbreaks began to occur not only among the peasants but even among the proletariat, whose sympathy the government was beginning to lose. Cries of "Down with the Soviet Government!" began to be heard in workmen's meetings and demonstrations. Pure communism was doomed.

The New Economic Policy

In 1921 the Communists thus faced the possibility of losing their political power as a consequence of having antagonized the great body of peasants. They had made practically no headway in their efforts to win this class to their economic scheme, and so were forced to conclude that it was "easier to change their policy than to change the peasants." They decided that, while retaining complete control of the administration of the government, the means of transport, large-scale industry, and foreign trade, they would make a number of minor concessions in other phases of economic life. They began their economic retreat by inaugurating a "New Economic Policy" (Nep).

Perhaps the most important feature of this Nep was the abandonment of the system of requisitioning grain from the peasants and the substitution of a fixed tax. Whatever a peasant produced over and above the amount of his tax was his to retain or to dispose of freely in the open market. The incentive which had been destroyed by the communistic scheme was thus restored, and there at once followed a gradual increase in the area under cultivation. Existing conditions of land ownership, moreover, were stabilized. Although the Soviet government continued to insist that the state was the sole owner of the land and that the peasants were merely tenants, the right of usage and the right to dispose of products became so unrestricted that for all practical purposes the land belonged to the peasants. In 1925 the Nep was further extended to permit the renting of land for limited periods of time and the employment of a certain number of wage laborers. Some of the richer, more enterprising peasants (the kulaks) at once benefited.

In industry the Nep brought the denationalization of establishments employing fewer than twenty workers. With the exception of small factories and shops, however, the state still reserved to itself the monopoly of industrial production, though it introduced the principle of sweeping decentralization. Industries were organized into large independent units or "trusts," each with its board of managers acting as trustee of the state. In order to overcome the lack of capital, the Soviet government even granted foreign capitalists concessions for mining, manufacturing, transportation, trade, and agricultural activity.

In the realm of commerce, foreign trade remained a state monopoly, carried on through a number of organizations such as Amtorg in the United States and Arcos, Ltd., in Great Britain. Domestic trade was opened to private capital but was subject to taxation and, as it revived, to more and more state regulation. Private trade developed so rapidly that the government, beginning in 1924, began to exert great pressure against it in favor of state and co-operative agencies, with the result that many so-called Nep-men were forced out of business.

The re-establishment of banking and credit operations began with the opening of a state bank in November, 1921. This was followed after 1924 by the opening of other banks—municipal, agricultural, co-operative, savings—throughout the union. In 1921 insurance of private property was instituted as a state monopoly, and three years later life insurance was restored. A new currency was introduced (the *chervonets*), a gold reserve was accumulated, and in 1924 the new currency was stabilized on a gold basis. Money wages were once more paid, and the system of governmental rationing of the cities was abandoned. A monetary system of taxes was inaugurated and eventually a balanced national budget obtained.

To summarize, then, under the Nep the state retained control of production in the large and middle-sized industrial plants and completely monopolized foreign trade, but restored agriculture, small industrial establishments, and domestic trade to private enterprise, subject to some degree of state control. Russia's economic life, as a consequence, came to present a strange picture of intermingled state socialism, state capitalism, and private capitalism. Nevertheless, under it that economic life came to be almost fully restored; some branches indeed even rose above prewar levels of production.

The Rise of Joseph Stalin

Meanwhile, a bitter conflict had been going on within the ranks of the Communist Party. So long as Lenin was able to take an active part in the direction of Russian affairs, this conflict had been held in abeyance, for his prestige and influence were of such magnitude that his policies found ready acceptance among his followers. But after illness had removed him from active participation in Russian affairs early in 1922, and especially after his death in January, 1924, differences among the Communist leaders became pronounced and constituted the basis of a struggle to determine who should assume Lenin's position as head of the Communist Party.

Prominent among those who became involved in the struggle over policies and power were: Trotsky, the first commissar for foreign affairs and later organizer of the Red Army, a brilliant revolutionary leader, orator, and writer, the one looked upon by most foreigners as the logical successor of Lenin; Zinoviev, the organizer and head of the Communist or Third International, enthusiastic in his plans to carry out the international propaganda of Communist ideas in order to achieve the world proletarian revolution; Dzerzhinsky, a descendant of Polish-Lithuanian nobility, the organizer and head of the Cheka, skilled agitator and organizer of strikes who had twice suffered exile to Siberia under the tsarist regime; Stalin, the son of a Georgian shoemaker, a stalwart of the Communist "Old Guard" who had frequently suffered imprisonment and exile for his beliefs, former editor of the Communist newspaper *Pravda,* characterized by Lenin as "too cruel" and "too brutal" and as having concentrated too much power in his hands as general secretary of the Communist Party; Rykov, who as a young man had early come under Lenin's influence and had repeatedly suffered imprisonment and exile in his service, Lenin's private secretary, at one time head of the Supreme Economic Council, the successor of Lenin as president of the Council of People's Commissars; Kamenev, a former law student under President Millerand in France, vice-president of the Union Council of People's Commissars and chairman of the Council for Labor and Defense, suspected by Lenin of not being 100-per-cent Communist; Bukharin, an ardent supporter of Lenin, characterized as the "evangelist" of Communism, who from the words of his master had created "the gospel of Communism," yet considered by Lenin as having "stuffed his head too full of books." Within this small group there developed a powerful triumvirate composed of Stalin, Zinoviev, and Kamenev, the political genius of the group being Stalin. From this inner circle Trotsky was excluded, for he had joined the party only in 1917 and was looked upon as a newcomer by the "Old Guard," who consistently sought to discredit him.

Lenin's death at once precipitated a conflict within the party between a group led by the triumvirate and another led by Trotsky. The Stalin group believed that the capitalist regime outside Russia had become stabilized and that it was not likely to be overturned in the immediate future; the Trotsky opposition still clung to the hope of a world revolution "in our time." The former desired to cater to the interests of the peasants; the latter wished to emphasize the interests of the urban workers as being paramount in a proletarian state. The group led by Stalin maintained that

Russia's welfare demanded the assistance of foreign capital; the opposition denounced such a policy as treason to the Communist ideal. Briefly, the policies of the Stalin group were in the direction of stabilization; those of the opposition, in the direction of revolution. Late in 1924 Trotsky was defeated in the Communist Party congress. Early in 1925 he was dismissed as commissar for war and removed from the Council of Labor and Defense, and his active adherents were expelled from the army and navy.

Next the members of the triumvirate began to quarrel among themselves. Stalin was alarmed by the continued unrest among the peasants and advocated further concessions to win their support. He also advocated additional measures to attract foreign capital. Such concessions and measures were vigorously opposed by a Left group led by Zinoviev and Kamenev. In the party congress in 1925 Stalin, supported by Rykov, Dzerzhinsky, and Bukharin, succeeded in winning the support of the majority, and Zinoviev and Kamenev were ordered to discontinue their opposition. As they had humiliated Trotsky in the preceding year, so they themselves were now humiliated.

Trotsky then joined forces with Zinoviev and Kamenev in an attempt to oust Stalin and his group from control of the Communist Party. But again the Stalin group won out. In 1926 the Trotsky-Zinoviev opposition was ordered to submit to the party discipline or withdraw from the organization. When in the following year the opposition once more began its attacks, Trotsky, Zinoviev, Kamenev, and some fourscore of their associates were expelled from the Communist Party and sent into exile. But Trotsky from his place of exile in Turkestan continued his opposition, and during the winter of 1928–1929 his influence with the urban workers resulted in spasmodic agitation in the factories in his behalf. Eventually, on the ground that Trotsky was still carrying on illegal propaganda against the government, the latter exiled him from the union. In April, 1929, the Communist Party once more approved Joseph Stalin's leadership.

This heir to Lenin's power in Russia was born in 1879 in Gori, a town in the Caucasus. The son of a Georgian shoemaker, he had been christened Joseph Visserionovich Dzhugashvili. Destined by his parents for the priesthood, he had been sent to a theological seminary, but from this clerical institution he had been ultimately expelled because of his Marxian ideas. Soon thereafter he became a member of the Social Democratic Party, and in 1902 he was arrested and exiled to Siberia for his part in a demonstration at Batum. Although an exile in 1903, when the Social Democratic Party split, Dzhugashvili sided with Lenin and thus at once entered the ranks of the Communists.

In 1904 Dzhugashvili escaped from Siberia and returned to his home district under an assumed name, and during the ensuing decade his career was filled with repeated arrests, exiles, escapes, and new aliases. Of the latter, the one by which he became best known was Stalin (Steel), conferred upon him by his fellow Communists because of his strength, coolness, ruthlessness, and taciturnity. Always plotting, agitating, writing, or editing, he persistently worked against the tsarist regime from within Russia. Six times arrested and exiled, he five times escaped, thanks to his cleverness and to his physical powers of endurance. During the years after 1913, however, he was successfully kept in exile in northern Siberia within the Arctic Circle. Isolation, prison tortures, forced labor, and severe deprivation were the lot of this "man of steel."

Freed by the March revolution of 1917 with its political amnesty, and permitted to return to Petrograd, Stalin at once became active in organizing soviets. Not an impassioned and eloquent orator, he interested himself primarily in the practical affairs of organization and thus helped to rebuild the Communist Party. When the November revolution occurred, he became one of the first commissars in the new Communist government. During the period of White invasions, he played a prominent part in defense of the Communist regime, and to commemorate his success at Tzaritzin on the lower Volga, that city was rechristened Stalingrad. From 1920 to 1923 he was commissar of nationalities and left his impress upon the constitution of the U.S.S.R. with its Soviet of Nationalities. As secretary-general of the Russian Communist Party, Stalin directed and maintained discipline within that organization and ruthlessly eliminated all disruptive personalities. Quietly but solidly he built up a political machine which enabled him to dominate the party—and through it the Soviet Union.

The Five-Year Plans

During the struggle between Trotsky and Stalin the former had frequently denounced the latter on the ground that his policies were threatening Russia with a reversion to capitalism, permitting as they did the growth of Nep-men and kulaks. Although Trotsky and his followers were expelled from the party and in some cases even arrested or exiled, their attitude toward kulaks and Nep-men was actually adopted by the victorious Stalin, and a program of swift industrialization and ruthless elimination of these classes ensued in the years after 1928. Stalin's new policies became effective through the so-called Five-Year Plan (*Piatiletka*).

As early as 1925 the Soviet government had contemplated the introduction of a more organized and planned system of national economy. Eventually, on October 1, 1928, an official Five-Year Plan, prepared by the State Planning Commission (*Gosplan*), was inaugurated for the years

1928–1933. The fundamental aims of this first Five-Year Plan were: (1) to introduce modern technology; (2) to transform Russia from a comparatively weak agrarian country into a powerful industrial country which could be largely independent of capitalist countries; (3) to eliminate completely private capitalism; (4) to create a socially owned heavy industry which could provide machinery for industry, transport, and agriculture; (5) to collectivize agriculture and thus remove the danger of a restoration of capitalism inherent in the continued existence of individual farms; (6) to increase Russia's ability to defend herself in time of war.

The plan laid down a schedule for practically every phase of the country's activities—production, distribution, and finance. It called for an enormous amount of new industrial construction—huge tractor factories, gigantic agricultural machinery factories, immense steel plants, extensive hydroelectric works, and new railways. Agriculture was to be reorganized on a large-scale mechanized basis through the institution of huge state and collective farms. Through the organization of such farms it was planned to mechanize and socialize the agrarian system and thus at last bring agriculture, which had long been a stumbling block in the way of socialism, into the sphere of planned economic life.

The state farms were to be experiments in the application of the most modern mechanized methods of agriculture to huge expanses of fresh land. Managers were to be appointed by the grain trust, a state organization, and labor was to be hired on a wage basis. The state farms were to be financed by the government, and their total agricultural product would belong to the state. The collective farm, on the other hand, was to result from the combination of a number of peasants' small holdings into one large farm. In general the peasants were to retain their homes, gardens, cows, pigs, and chickens, but were to surrender their lands, machinery, and horses to common ownership. The peasants would then work together under the direction of an elected managerial board. After certain amounts were set aside for seeds and fodder, taxes and insurance, purchase of new machinery and construction of new buildings, debt payments, contributions for education and charity, and administrative expenses, the balance of income from the collective farm would be divided among the peasants in proportion to the amount of property which each contributed and the amount and quality of the work each had performed. This type of collective was called an "artel."

The inauguration of the plan inevitably raised a number of serious problems. Obviously, one was the matter of finance. The government planned to finance its undertakings chiefly by means of taxes, internal loans, profits from state trusts, and capital savings resulting from the reduced costs of production. To pay for the necessary importation of machinery and other needed articles from abroad, the government proposed to rely largely upon the export of the country's increased surplus of grain. In this connection a second problem was raised by the drastic decline in the world price of grain. Although in 1929–1930, for example, Russia's exports rose almost 50 per cent—thanks to increased production of grain—the world decline in prices prevented this increase from being reflected in the country's monetary income. To meet this unexpected crisis, the Soviet government ruthlessly stripped the country of articles which had export value, and the world beheld the curious anomaly of a people forced to live on short rations while millions of tons of grain were being exported from the land.

Another problem was that of securing an adequate number of well-trained engineers, technicians, and skilled workers. The plan called for the introduction of new specialized courses in schools and universities and for the establishment of many new technical and vocational schools. To solve the immediate problem, the services of foreign engineering firms and individual specialists were engaged. Foreign engineers and technicians became important, almost indispensable, cogs in Russia's industrialization machine. Still another problem was that of securing industrial efficiency from untrained or ill-trained workers. Machines were often injured and products ruined. The factory management itself was seriously handicapped by the necessity of discussing first with the workers any new plans they wished to inaugurate or orders which they wished to give. In the early period all incentive to speed and efficiency was largely lacking because of the policy of treating all workers alike.

The inevitable result of all these factors was that the scheduled decreased cost of production, increased efficiency of labor, and improved quality of goods were not attained. Although the quantity of goods produced in the ensuing years was frequently in excess of the control figures, the quality was usually below the required standards. Beginning with the year 1930, efforts were made by the government to remedy this situation. The Supreme Economic Council threatened severe punishment for individuals responsible for producing goods of low quality. Differential wage scales and piece work were introduced as an incentive to greater effort, and the work day was lengthened. To improve the efficiency of factory managements, their control over the workers was increased, and the authority of workers' committees was lessened.

Despite all handicaps and obstacles, the Five-Year Plan for industry moved steadily forward. In the case of many production schedules the five-year goal was attained within three years. In April, 1930, the 1100-mile Turkestan-Siberian Railway was completed more than a year ahead of schedule. The year 1932 saw a 900,000-horsepower hydroelectric plant, built at a cost of more than $100,000,000, dedicated at Dnepropetrovsk, and

A PRODUCT OF THE FIRST FIVE-YEAR PLAN

The dedication of the dam at Dnepropetrovsk in 1932.

the first blast furnace fired in the Magnitogorsk steel works, which was destined to become one of the largest steel plants in the world.

In agriculture astonishing changes were introduced. Principally in southeastern Russia, Siberia, and Kazakstan huge state farms were established on previously unused lands. These great farms averaged between 100,000 and 200,000 acres, and the largest, the "Giant," located in the northern Caucasus, put under the plow nearly 300,000 acres in 1930. Tens of thousands of tractors and hundreds of combines—great machines which reaped and threshed the grain at the same time—were put into service.

Great advances were made, also, in the collectivization of peasant holdings. Special inducements—such as lower taxes, easier credit facilities, precedence in the acquisition of machinery and manufactured goods—were offered to those who joined the collectives. On the other hand, heavier taxes and a ruthless requisitioning of grain at fixed prices were the lot of the more prosperous peasants, who were loath to merge their holdings in a collective. Ultimately the houses, livestock, and tools of thousands of these kulaks were confiscated, and they themselves were torn from their homes and banished to remote regions where they were compelled to work at hard labor. Thousands more were arrested and thrown into prison.

But collectivization by such methods had its evil side. Especially serious was the widespread slaughtering of livestock which occurred during the winter of 1929–1930, when peasants killed some 25 per cent of their cows, 33 per cent of their sheep, and 50 per cent of their hogs. This they did partly because they expected to lose them anyway as a result of forcible collectivization, and partly because the government's ruthless requisition of grain had the twofold effect of causing a shortage of foodstuffs for the peasants and fodder for their animals. This situation precipitated another conflict within the Communist Party. In 1929–1930, a Right group, led by Rykov, Bukharin, and Tomsky, attacked Stalin on the ground that his ruthless liquidation of the kulaks and his rapid and compulsory collectivization of peasant estates was altogether too radical. This so-called Rightist deviation was in turn crushed, however, much as had been the earlier Left opposition led by Trotsky.

Nevertheless, Stalin saw the dangers of the situation and in 1930 called a halt. Government decrees eliminated the worst abuses of the program of forcible collectivization. Peasants who had been collectivized by force were permitted to take back their property and become individual farmers once more if they wished. Additional inducements were soon held out to those who would voluntarily join, however, and it was decided that 5 per cent of the net income of each collective should be set aside yearly as a fund to reimburse peasants for animals and machinery which they had contributed to the enterprise. Gradually the tide turned again, and by the spring of 1931 more than 45 per cent of the peasant families were in collectives.

In 1930 the government decided that the Soviet economic year should coincide with the calendar year, and so it was decreed that the Five-Year Plan should include only four and one quarter years in order that it might close on December 31, 1932. With the official ending of the plan it became possible to form some judgment regarding its success. Great strides had certainly been made toward transforming Soviet Russia into a powerful industrial country. The Union was dotted with enormous new factories and magnificent new power plants. No other important country could show a rate of quantitative industrial progress to compare with that of the Soviet Union during these years. In the production of machinery, tractors, and petroleum the original plan had been exceeded. On the other hand, in certain industries, notably iron, steel, coal, and textiles, the production had failed to meet the schedule of the original plan. Furthermore, it had been discovered that huge industrial plants were far easier to construct than to operate efficiently.

In agriculture the plan, so far as acreage in state and collective farms was concerned, had been far exceeded. Nearly 30,000,000 acres had been organized into state farms, and more than 15,000,000 peasant households had been brought into the collective farms. Mechanization and collectivization of agriculture had made great advances. Nevertheless, here, too, not all the goals set up by the plan had been attained, for it had been found easier to bring the peasants into collective farms than to make them efficiently productive.

For the great mass of the Russians, perhaps the worst failure of the plan was in the matter of wages and living standards. Although money wages went up faster than had been contemplated, because of currency inflation prices became high in terms of the rubles which the Russians received for their products or labor. In the second place, there was a very real shortage of foodstuffs and of manufactured articles for daily consumption. The great majority of Russians were worse off in 1932 so far as food supply was concerned than they had been in 1927. In fact, the year 1932–1933 saw severe famine conditions in parts of Russia. Furthermore, consumption goods were sacrificed to the production of factories, power plants, and basic articles like steel, petroleum, and coal, with the result that many manufactured necessities of daily life became so scarce that they could not be generally obtained at any price. The first Five-Year Plan, nevertheless, undoubtedly constituted a landmark in Russian industrial history.

Early in 1934 the Communist Party congress approved an outline of a second Five-Year Plan covering the years 1933–1937. Under the second plan more attention was to be given to consumers' goods. Greater emphasis was to be laid, also, upon the efficiency of labor, the reduction in production costs, and the improvement in the quality of goods. The material welfare of the masses was one of the major concerns of the second period. Thousands of houses and apartments were to be erected in the industrial centers, together with theaters, clubs, stadiums, and parks. The crying need for such construction was caused by the great shift in population from farms to the cities, the number of industrial wage-earners having increased from 11,500,000 in 1928 to 23,500,000 in 1934. These figures likewise explain the Soviet problem of increasing efficiency in industrial production with workers many of whom were inexperienced. To help solve this problem provision was made in the second Five-Year Plan for still greater expansion of facilities for vocational and technical training. In the interests of greater efficiency a decree in 1934 abolished fixed minimum wages and ordered reductions for inefficient workers.

The results obtained under the second Five-Year Plan were distinctly encouraging. In the basic heavy industries—mining, iron and steel, petroleum, machinery, railway equipment, and the like—the specifications of the plan were generally exceeded. In fact, in 1934 the Soviet Union occupied second place in the world production of pig iron and third place in steel production, in each case ranking ahead of Great Britain. More encouraging still, perhaps, was the increase in workers' efficiency and the reduction in production costs; it was officially stated that labor productivity in 1937 was double that of 1929. Apparently the Russians had begun to master industrial technique. In agricultural production the gains were also notable. The grain harvest for 1933 was the largest in Russian history, that for 1934 was still larger, and that for 1935 again set a record. The last year saw record harvests, also, in sugar beets, tobacco, fruit, cotton, and flax. In 1937 agriculture was reported to be 93 per cent collectivized.

In contrast with the first Five-Year Plan, which imposed many privations upon the masses in order that the foundations might be laid for an industrialized country, the second Five-Year Plan began to bring to the Russian people some of the fruits of their long and arduous toil. This was evident, for instance, in the matter of foodstuffs. In 1935 the whole food-rationing system was abandoned, and all foodstuffs—meat, potatoes, butter, eggs, sugar, and the like—were made available to purchasers without restrictions. Moreover, prices were reduced by government decree. Nor were improvements in living standards limited to the matter of food. Since the industries producing textiles and footwear had exceeded their quotas under the plan, articles of wearing apparel were both more plentiful and lower-priced. In general, the retail stores were better supplied with goods than in previous years.

The peasants, too, participated in the rising standard of living. Higher official prices for farm products and freedom to sell surplus produce in the open market naturally increased their purchasing power. They thus found themselves in a position to buy in the village stores many consumers' goods which they had been unable to obtain in preceding years. And—what was equally important—more consumers' goods were available for purchase. It may therefore be stated with a fair degree of certainty that the real incomes of the Russian people and consequently their general standard of living rose during the early years of the second Five-Year Plan. The rate of improvement was checked in 1936, however, because of the greater emphasis upon military and naval armaments to meet the increasing Nazi menace.

In 1936 the Communist leaders announced that the Soviet state had largely achieved the first of its objectives in its march toward communism. The productive means of the country, it was asserted, had at length been almost entirely socialized. Private producers—both handicraftsmen and peasants—constituted only 5.6 per cent of the population in 1937. Thus, it was pointed out, with the socialization of industry and the collectivization of agriculture, there remained in Russia only one class—the workers. Among the peasants—the most difficult of the Russians to be absorbed into the communist state—there were, it was reported, no longer rich, middle-class, and poor. All had become "members of a collectivized and socialized agricultural society." Although the Communist leaders were doubtless slightly overenthusiastic about the extent of their achievements, it seemed fairly clear in 1936 that the struggle to establish in Russia a collectivized and mechanized system of agriculture had been largely won.

The Constitution of 1936

In view of this situation, apparently, the Communist leaders decided that it would be safe to remove some of the political restrictions and discriminations which were originally designed to protect the Communist regime from those classes which were unsympathetic. In February, 1935, therefore, the Union Congress of Soviets voted that the constitution of the Union should be amended to give more direct popular control of the political machinery. The Union Central Executive Committee, accordingly, appointed a constitutional commission with Joseph Stalin as chairman. This commission, instead of merely preparing amendments to the existing constitution, drafted a complete new document which was ultimately adopted with amendments by the Union Congress on December 5, 1936.

The new constitution changed Russia's political machinery slightly. The Union Congress of Soviets was abolished, and supreme power was lodged in the Supreme Council of the U.S.S.R., a bicameral legislature which was practically the former Union Central Executive Committee under a new name. A similar change was proposed for each of the constituent republics also. Much more significant were the modifications made in regard to franchise, method of voting, and system of representation.

In the new constitution every citizen at least eighteen years of age was given "the right to elect and be elected irrespective of his race or nationality, his religion, educational qualifications, residential qualifications, his social origins, property status and past activity." Candidates might be nominated by Communist Party organizations, trade unions, co-operatives, youth organizations, and cultural societies. Voting at elections was no longer by show of hands but by secret ballot. Moreover, the old system of indirect representation was completely abolished in favor of the direct election of deputies in all political units. That is to say, the peasant would now vote directly for those who should make his laws and would no longer be five steps removed from the supreme legislative body of the Union. Furthermore, the former discrimination against the peasants in favor of the proletariat was ended. Deputies to the Council of the Union, the popularly elected branch of the Supreme Council of the U.S.S.R., were to be elected from single-member constituencies in which all citizens whether peasants or urban workers had the same electoral privileges. Deputies to the Council of Nationalities were also to be chosen by popular election. A study of the diagrams on pages 451 and 469 will reveal the striking differences between the system of representation before and after 1936.

The new constitution, too, seemed to recognize some change in economic doctrines and policies. It still stated that the economic foundation of the U.S.S.R. consisted in the "socialist ownership of the implements and means of production" (Article 4), and that socialist ownership had either the form of state ownership or the form of co-operative and collective-farm ownership (Article 5). But alongside the socialist system of economy the law allowed "small private economy of individual peasants and handicraftsmen based on individual labor and excluding the exploitation of the labor of others" (Articles 9). That the Soviet Union had by 1936 departed from the ideals of pure communism seemed apparent in the statement that the "personal ownership by citizens of their income from work and savings, of home and auxiliaries pertaining thereto, of objects of domestic and household use, of objects of personal use and comfort, as well as the right to inherit private property are protected by law" (Article 10). This departure was further revealed by the declaration that in the U.S.S.R. "the principle of socialism is being realized: 'From each according to his ability, to each according to his work'" (Article 12). Apparently the earlier communist ideal of taking from each according to his ability and giving to each according to his needs had been abandoned.

Although the Communist leaders repeatedly emphasized the democratic

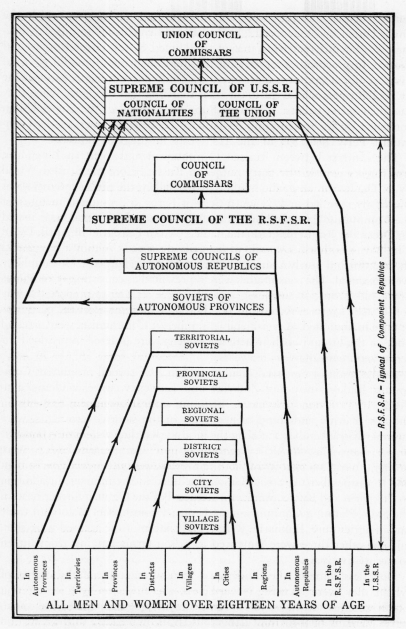

UNION COUNCIL
OF
COMMISSARS

SUPREME COUNCIL OF U.S.S.R.

| COUNCIL OF
NATIONALITIES | COUNCIL OF
THE UNION |

COUNCIL
OF
COMMISSARS

SUPREME COUNCIL OF THE R.S.F.S.R.

SUPREME COUNCILS OF
AUTONOMOUS REPUBLICS

SOVIETS OF
AUTONOMOUS PROVINCES

TERRITORIAL
SOVIETS

PROVINCIAL
SOVIETS

REGIONAL
SOVIETS

DISTRICT
SOVIETS

CITY
SOVIETS

VILLAGE
SOVIETS

R.S.F.S.R - Typical of Component Republics

In
Autonomous
Provinces

In
Territories

In
Provinces

In
Districts

In
Villages

In
Cities

In
Regions

In
Autonomous
Republics

In the
R.S.F.S.R.

In the
U.S.S.R

ALL MEN AND WOMEN OVER EIGHTEEN YEARS OF AGE

POLITICAL STRUCTURE OF THE U.S.S.R. AFTER 1936

features of the constitution of 1936, the next national election held in the Soviet Union, on December 12, 1937, disclosed that Russia's so-called democracy was far different from that of the United States, Great Britain, and France. In practically every one of the more than one thousand electoral districts, the voters were confronted with only one candidate. Most of the 91,113,153 voters who went to the polls therefore had no choice when they cast their secret ballots. When the Supreme Council of the Soviet Union convened for its first meeting on January 12, 1938, members of the Communist Party held 855 of the 1143 seats in the two houses.

The contrast between Russian Communism and Western Liberalism was further revealed by party purges in Russia before the Second World War. The fate of those who might dare to challenge Stalin's supremacy was startlingly revealed in 1934 when Sergius Kirov, a prominent member of the Communist Party and one of Stalin's close associates, was assassinated on December 1 in Leningrad (the name given to Petrograd in April, 1920). The Soviet authorities struck with terrifying speed. Within a few weeks the assassin and nearly a hundred others who were charged with complicity were executed. The conspirators were represented as consisting of remnants of the old Trotsky-Kamenev group who were seeking to prepare the way for Trotsky's return. Accordingly, a thoroughgoing purge of the party was at once inaugurated. A considerable number of Communists were arrested and, on the ground of their heretical beliefs, were ordered imprisoned for terms varying from five to ten years.

As the result of new trials inaugurated in 1936 several prominent Communist leaders, including Zinoviev and Kamenev, were condemned to death. In 1937 hundreds more, including several prominent generals in the Soviet army and some high officials in the state governments, were summarily tried and executed on the ground that they were either Japanese or German spies. In 1938 twenty-one more Communist leaders were brought to trial on charges of plotting to overthrow the Soviet government and to dismember the Soviet Union. Included in the number, in addition to Bukharin and Rykov, were a former head of the Ogpu, a former head of the State Planning Commission, and former commissars of foreign trade and of agriculture. Bukharin, Rykov, and sixteen of the accused were shot, and the other three were sentenced to prison terms ranging from fifteen to twenty-five years.

Doubtless some of the condemned men were guilty of the crimes of which they were accused. Nevertheless, the suspicion was strong that Stalin and his associates in the government had deliberately rid themselves of many of their most dangerous rivals by recourse to these treason trials. Apparently the struggle for control of the Communist Party and the Soviet government, begun even before Lenin's death and greatly intensified after 1924, had continued. And personal rivalries and disagreements between Stalin and his associates, on the one hand, and other Communist leaders, critical of the new bureaucracy, on the other, instead of being left for peaceful settlement by the popular vote of the Russian people, were liquidated with increasing frequency by resort to the firing squad. These events, many believed, revealed the wide gulf between the reputed democracy of the Soviet Union and that of the liberal countries of the West. Others maintained that they were proof, rather, that many of Stalin's enemies were willing to work with the Nazis, if necessary, to overthrow his regime and that those executed therefore had constituted what would have proved later to be "fifth columnists."

Education and Religion

Not unrelated to the political and economic life of Russia was the attitude of the Soviet government toward public education. Upon the schools the Communists relied for two important achievements. By them must be prepared the well-trained, skilled technicians who were expected to assume in the economic and administrative life of the Union the places left vacant by the overthrow of the bourgeoisie. In this sense there was in Russia a "race between education and catastrophe." Then, as Lenin pointed out, the Communist economic scheme was not possible without "an intellectual revolution." From this point of view the Communists looked to the schools to produce a generation which should be thoroughly versed in and loyal to the Communist ideal.

Just how these aims should be accomplished the Communists were not altogether sure, so that the Soviet Union came to constitute a great laboratory for educational experiments. On one thing they were determined, however: that the illiteracy of the tsarist period should be wiped out, that no more generations of Russian children should grow up in ignorance. Under the old regime the higher schools and in many places the secondary schools were closed to the workers and peasants. This the Soviet government would change. In the old days education was for the privileged classes only; henceforth it must be for the masses.

As already pointed out, the Five-Year Plans outlined programs of educational as well as industrial expansion. During the years 1928–1932 great strides were made in developing the public-school system, the aim being to make compulsory elementary education a fact and not merely a theory. By the close of the first Five-Year Plan nearly 22,000,000 children—three times the number in tsarist days—were enrolled in elementary schools; four fifths of all children between the ages of eight and fourteen were receiving education at the hands of the government; and illiteracy in the adult population had been to a considerable extent eliminated. An extensive system of vocational and technical training had also been developed, with factory schools to give instruction in the operation of machines and technical colleges for the training of engineers.

With the Communist Party officially atheistic and believing that religion is an "opiate of the people," it is not surprising that the position of the Orthodox Church in Russia was profoundly altered by the Soviet government. All lands belonging to the church or to monastic institutions were at once nationalized, and it was decreed that no ecclesiastical or religious association had the right to possess property. All church buildings became the property of the state. Many were transformed into schools or club-rooms, and some of the most famous cathedrals were turned into national museums. In general, however, buildings needed specifically for purposes of worship were turned over to associations of twenty or more persons for use free of charge.

The church was separated from the state, and government subsidies were abolished. The church was forced to depend henceforth, as in the United States, upon the voluntary contributions of its adherents. Public religious processions were forbidden, and the old church calendar—thirteen days behind that in use in the Western world—was abolished in favor of the latter. The church was deprived of its control of marriage and divorce, registration of births and deaths, and cemeteries. The control of all these was confided to the civil government. The schools were separated from the church, and it was originally decreed that Christian churches might not give organized religious instruction to minors under eighteen years of age. No religious instruction was permitted in any public or private school, but children in groups of three or less might receive religious instruction, provided it was given outside the schools and churches. Although the influence of the government was thus thrown against religion, attendance at religious services was unrestricted, except to members of the Communist Party.

Soviet Foreign Policy

For the sake of convenience and clarity the history of the Soviet Union's foreign policy will be discussed in relation to the different aims which seem to have predominated in successive periods since 1917. In the first three years after the November revolution the dominant aim of the Soviet government was to bring about the overthrow of all capitalist governments. During this period the Communist leaders were far from confident of their ability to retain control in Russia. To them a world proletarian revolution which should everywhere supplant capitalism by a Communist regime seemed absolutely essential to their own continuance in power. The Soviet government's foreign policy during these early years, therefore, may be characterized as primarily that of revolutionary propaganda.

To facilitate the carrying on of this propaganda the Communist leaders in March, 1919, founded the Third or Communist International (*Comintern*).[2] This organization was designed (1) to carry on an international propaganda of Communist ideas, (2) to unite and strengthen the Communist parties in all countries, (3) to win the leadership of all labor and socialist movements, and (4) "to accelerate the development of events toward world revolution." Once the revolution had been accomplished, the Third International was to direct the future efforts of the working classes. Its headquarters were set up in Moscow, and it was liberally subsidized by the Soviet government.

Sometimes through its own officials, but more often through the instrumentality of the Third International, the Soviet government during its first years attempted to launch anticapitalist offensives in various countries of Europe. It played a part in the Communist uprisings in Germany in 1918 and 1919, in the establishment of the Béla Kun regime in Hungary (1919), in the communistic experiments in Italy (1920), and in spasmodic outbreaks in some of the Baltic republics. Its efforts to establish strong connections with the workers of Great Britain, France, Austria, and Czechoslovakia, however, proved futile. Equally futile, too, were the government's efforts to win the good will and co-operation of the Asiatic peoples in the hope that they might be converted to Communism and a gigantic coalition be created against Western capitalism. Despite all efforts of the Soviet government and of the Third International, the world proletarian revolution failed to materialize.

At home, after three years of almost constant fighting against the forces of counterrevolution, the Communists found themselves at last in complete control, but in control of a Russia which, because of their communist experiments, was fast sinking into economic chaos. The New Economic Policy which Lenin thereupon decided to inaugurate at home was accompanied by a change in the Soviet government's policy abroad. In order to rescue Russia from its complete industrial and commercial collapse, there was need for the influx of capital, machinery, and experts from abroad. But these could hardly be obtained so long as Russia remained isolated among the nations. While not abandoning completely its purpose of undermining the capitalist governments by Communist propaganda, the predominant aim of the Soviet government next came to be the opening of trade relations with foreign countries as a means of hastening Russia's economic revival. A provisional trade agreement between Russia and Great Britain

2 For the First and Second Internationals, see pages 37–38.

was signed on March 16, 1921, and by the end of the year the Soviet government had succeeded in obtaining similar agreements with Germany, Norway, Austria, and Italy.

Nevertheless, Russia made little real progress toward regaining her former place in the states system of Europe. Six years after the November revolution she was still largely an outlaw nation. Her government was recognized *de jure* in Europe by only Poland, Germany, and the Baltic republics, and elsewhere in the world by only Turkey, Persia, and Afghanistan. In 1924 the dominant and openly declared aim of its foreign policy became, therefore, *de jure* recognition. It let it be known that it was prepared to conclude a commercial treaty on especially favorable terms with the first great power to grant it such recognition. On February 1 Ramsay MacDonald, head of the new Labor government in Great Britain, telegraphed unconditional *de jure* recognition of the Soviet government. Italian recognition came officially six days later, and in the following months the U.S.S.R. received the *de jure* recognition of Norway, Austria, Greece, Hejaz, China, Denmark, Mexico, Hungary, and even France. At the close of the year 1924 the Soviet government had been recognized by fifteen European states as compared with only six at its beginning, and every European great power had re-established diplomatic relations with it.

Meanwhile, the year 1925 had seen the successful conclusion of the Locarno negotiations among the other great powers of Europe. The Locarno treaties were looked upon in Moscow as a serious menace to Russia's position, and from 1926 to 1933 the Soviet government's primary aim in foreign affairs was the creation of a protective barrier of states which could not be drawn into any concerted attack upon Russia. So successful were the Communists in this phase of their foreign policy that by the summer of 1933 they had concluded pacts of neutrality and nonaggression not only with all their neighbors to the west and south but with a number of the other powers of Europe as well.

After 1933, because of alarm over the aggressive policies of Nazi Germany in the west and imperialistic Japan in the east, the Soviet government ceased to be content with nonaggression pacts and sought instead to obtain definite promises of aid in certain contingencies. In 1934, despite the fact that the Communists had professed to believe the League of Nations an organization of capitalist states conspiring against them, the Soviet Union joined the League, and thereafter worked for collective security. In the following year it concluded defensive military alliances against Germany with both France and Czechoslovakia.

In 1938, however, after the failure of Great Britain and France to prevent the dismemberment of Czechoslovakia, the Soviet government became suspicious that these powers were attempting to turn Hitler's aggression eastward toward Russia. In these circumstances the Communists decided to take such steps as might be necessary to postpone the Nazi-Soviet conflict as long as possible and accordingly signed a nonaggression pact with Nazi Germany in August, 1939. This step had, in Communist eyes, the double advantage of giving Russia added time to perfect her military preparations and at the same time of weakening Germany by leading her to become embroiled in a war with Great Britain and France.

The Eve of the Second World War

Shortly before the outbreak of the Second World War Russia launched her third Five-Year Plan (1938–1942), originally designed to raise the standard of living further by an expansion of the production of consumers' goods. The outbreak of war in Europe, however, forced changes in the plan. Although some increase in consumers' goods was permitted prior to 1941, greater emphasis was laid on the expansion of war industries. Efforts were made to develop regional economic autonomy, to utilize local resources to their utmost, and to eliminate wherever possible long hauls by train. These steps were designed not only to raise the country's general industrial efficiency but to enable it to continue its resistance in the face of any extensive invasion. As a result of this planned dispersal, by 1941 a considerable portion of the Soviet Union's industry was located east of the Volga; in fact, some 15 per cent of it was located east of the Urals. Furthermore, in answer to the increasing threat of war, the working day was lengthened to eight hours and the working week to six days.

Thanks to the three Five-Year Plans, the Soviet Union by 1940 was well on the way to becoming the second most important industrial country in the world. In that year its gross industrial output was reported as being five times as great as in 1929, twelve times as great as in 1913. In its production of railway locomotives, freight cars, trucks, tractors, and agricultural machinery it claimed to surpass any other European country. Its petroleum output was four times as much as that of the rest of Europe combined. It stood first in superphosphates, copper, and iron ore, and second only to Germany in the production of steel. Furthermore, it was claimed, of the ten important food and industrial crops, it led the world in acreage except in rice, corn, and cotton. During the Five-Year Plans the production of sugar beets and flax had increased nearly 200 per cent, potatoes nearly 300 per cent, cotton almost 400 per cent, and citrus fruits 160 times. Between 1932 and 1941 the production of milk had risen 50 per cent, and that of wool had doubled. In the latter year, too, the grain crop was 50 per cent greater than it had been in 1913.

In 1941 the Soviet Union, with its sixteen soviet socialist republics,[3] had a total population of 193,000,000. During the preceding fifteen years, according to semiofficial estimates, some 11,000,000 men had received full military training under the Soviet peacetime selective service law, and another 11,000,000 had received partial training. In 1939, as the war clouds darkened, the age of induction had been lowered from 20 to 19, and to 18 for those who had completed their high school education. During the thirties special attention had been given to mechanizing the army and to providing it with tanks, airplanes, and antitank and antiaircraft guns. At the same time, personnel was being trained in 63 schools for the land forces, 32 for the air forces, and 14 military academies. Russia in 1941 was much better prepared in leadership, man power, military equipment, and industrial and agricultural resources to withstand attack than she had been in 1914.

[3] These were the R.S.F.S.R., and the Ukrainian, White-Russian, Azerbaijan, Georgian, Armenian, Turkmen, Uzbek, Tadjik, Kazakh, Kirghiz, Karelo-Finnish, Moldavian, Lithuanian, Latvian, and Estonian soviet socialist republics.

Chapter XVI

FASCIST ITALY

THE second of the great powers to inaugurate a sweeping program of
political and economic reform during the years after the First World
War was Italy, where Fascism launched a counteroffensive against Communism and established what many called a "dictatorship of the middle
class." Fascism was often represented as "the last stand of capitalism," and
it is true that in Italy the means of production, though extensively regulated
and regimented, did remain for the most part in private hands with the
profit system continuing. Nevertheless, it will become obvious to the reader
of this chapter that the regime which Fascism introduced in Italy had
many characteristics in common with that which Communism established
in Soviet Russia.

Postwar Dissatisfaction with the Government

Probably the chief reason for Italy's embarking upon a new course in
1922 was that in the years immediately following the armistice a great
portion of the Italian people came to feel that their existing political regime was able neither to preserve and defend Italy's just national interests abroad nor to provide law, order, and efficient government at home.
More than the people of any other power, perhaps, the Italians entered
the First World War for the purpose of securing certain additions of
territory, and during the conflict their territorial ambitions further increased. They emerged from the war with the high hope and confident
expectation of territorial acquisitions which should meet their nationalistic
and imperialistic aspirations. Their first disappointment came in the case
of Fiume. The failure of the statesmen at Paris to award that city to Italy
bitterly disappointed the Italian people, and, when the Italian government later signed with Yugoslavia the treaty of Rapallo (November,
1920), recognizing the independence of the Free State of Fiume, and
used the Italian army to expel D'Annunzio's legionaries from that city,
the nationalists of Italy denounced the government for its weakness and
pusillanimity.

Their second disappointment had to do with Albania, where the plan
to make of the Adriatic an Italian lake called for the establishment of

477

Italian control. But the Italian forces which had entered Albania during the war were gradually forced back into Valona by the Albanians, and the Italian government was obliged to withdraw its troops and recognize Albanian independence. This withdrawal constituted for Italian nationalists an "inglorious page of our political and military history." A third disappointment came in the colonial sphere. After the war Italians aspired to territorial acquisitions in the eastern Mediterranean and in Africa. But by the treaty of Sèvres and complementary treaties, Greece got Smyrna which Italy coveted, and Italy was even forced to agree that the Greek-inhabited Dodecanese Islands, which she had occupied since 1912, should likewise be surrendered to Greece. In Africa Italy fared little better, for the German African colonies were granted as mandates to Great Britain, France, and Belgium. The Italian government was vigorously denounced for its inability to protect Italian national interests.

Nor were conditions within the country such as to win popular support for the government. Like so many other European countries, Italy faced a serious economic situation immediately after the war. Staggering national deficits succeeded one another yearly, and the national currency fell steadily to less than a third of its face value. Living costs, in terms of paper currency, accordingly rose far above their prewar level. Furthermore, many soldiers, returning to civil life at a time of industrial crisis, failed to regain their old jobs or to obtain new ones. Socialism profited by these circumstances. Demobilized soldiers, contrasting their actual conditions with the extravagant promises made to them by politicians in the last months of the struggle, were profoundly disillusioned and went over to socialism almost *en masse*. In the parliamentary elections of November, 1919, the Socialists practically doubled their numbers in the Chamber of Deputies, where they constituted a controlling force and helped to paralyze the government. Meanwhile, the emissaries of Russian Communism had been preaching strikes, the seizure of factories and the land, and the dictatorship of the proletariat. Influenced by the Russian revolution, the extreme Socialists abandoned their prewar law-abiding character and evolutionary methods and planned by revolution to transplant into Italy the soviet system.

The extremists sought to accomplish their ends by direct action, and as early as August, 1919, disorders broke out in the rural districts. During the war many had advocated land for the peasants, and it was in an attempt to bring this about by direct action that land-raiding was begun. In some instances former service men sought to obtain plots of idle land for cultivation; in others tenants refused to pay rent to the owners; while in still others rural laborers sought to introduce the eight-hour day. Outrages were perpetrated—people were killed, houses were burned, cattle were slaughtered, harvests were destroyed. Although the total amount of land seized was relatively small, the psychological effect on the property-owning classes was great.

In industry, too, strikes became frequent and occurred in such essential services as the railways, tramways, and postal and telegraph systems, and even in the light and food-supply systems of the large towns. The strike movement reached its peak in August and September, 1920, when more than 600 factories involving some 500,000 employees were suddenly seized by the workers. Throughout the country the "dictatorship of the proletariat" was hourly expected. The government, paralyzed by divisions in the parliament and embarrassed by difficulties abroad, was powerless to intervene. Anarchists and Communists sought to extend the scope of the movement and to give it definitely revolutionary aims, but their proposal was vigorously opposed by the more moderate element, and ultimately the factories were returned to their owners.

Although the crisis passed, sporadic strikes continued, and the fear which the short Communist experiment had engendered remained. The proletariat had failed to carry through its program, in fact had abandoned its attempt. Without permanently injuring the other classes, it had aroused their fear, hostility, and exasperation. Landlords and industrialists, who had looked in vain to the state for protection, denounced the supineness and inability of the government. All Italians who felt they had anything to lose by a Communist revolution urgently desired a firm government, and were ready to support any movement which might promise to provide it. And that there was dire need of some step to assure political stability seemed indicated by the fact that between June, 1919, and March, 1922, Italy had two parliamentary elections and four different prime ministers. The Chamber of Deputies as then constituted appeared to many to be utterly incapable of producing a stable majority which would maintain a strong government.

Mussolini and the Rise of Fascism

The group which benefited most from this situation was the new organization which had been founded by Benito Mussolini. This vigorous Italian was born in 1883, the son of a village blacksmith in northern Italy. His mother was a school teacher, and at the age of eighteen he himself became a teacher. Deciding that he needed further education, he later went to Switzerland, where he attended the Universities of Lausanne and Geneva, working to pay his expenses. While in Switzerland his innate organizing ability and his interest in socialism led him to participate in the founding of trade unions and the fomenting of strikes, activities for which he was ultimately expelled from the republic by the Swiss government.

Back in Italy he once more took up teaching. His continued interest in socialism, however, led him to become involved in agrarian disorders, and in 1908 he was arrested and temporarily imprisoned as a dangerous revolutionary. Later, after having been expelled from Trent by the Austrian government because of his irredentist propaganda, he drifted into journalism and in 1912 became editor of *Avanti,* the official organ of the Italian Socialist Party.

Upon the outbreak of the First World War Mussolini advocated Italian neutrality, urged the workers to resist being drawn into a "bourgeois" war, and preached preparation for a social revolution. Suddenly, in October, 1914, he changed his views and began to urge Italian intervention in the war. The Socialists thereupon repudiated him and forced him to resign from *Avanti.* In the following month he established in Milan the daily paper, *Il Popolo d'Italia,* which under his editorship became an interventionist organ. In September, 1915, when his class was called to the colors, Mussolini entered active service and served as a private on the Isonzo front. Early in 1917 he was wounded by the explosion of a trench mortar, and upon his recovery he procured exemption from further military service on the ground of being indispensable to the management of *Il Popolo d'Italia.*

At the conclusion of the war Mussolini, in March, 1919, issued a call for a meeting of former service men who "desire to express their attitude toward the country's postwar problems." A small group gathered about him—chiefly young men, mostly ex-Socialists—and under his leadership was founded the *Fascio di Combattimento* (Union of Combat). Its program of proposed political, economic, and religious changes was extremely democratic, even revolutionary, but at the same time strongly nationalistic. At first Fascism made little headway, however. In the parliamentary elections of 1919 it failed to elect a single candidate. Nevertheless, through pamphlets, speeches, and patriotic demonstrations the Fascisti denounced the government for its weakness both at home and abroad.

During the occupation of the factories Mussolini took no sides, though in the previous year he had approved a similar step. Following the collapse of the occupation, however, he threw the weight of his organization into a drive against the Communists. In northern and central Italy Fascist branches were established by ex-officers of the army and agents of the industrial and landowning classes. While Mussolini aroused enthusiasm by articles in his newspaper, *squadristi* of young men—wearing black shirts —were sent out to combat Communism. Guns, clubs, and castor oil were their weapons. The Giolitti government, wishing to destroy Communism, apparently connived with the Fascist forces; they were quietly supplied with arms, given free transportation on the railways, and rarely punished for their misdeeds. The growing strength of the Fascisti was revealed in the parliamentary elections of 1921, when they secured thirty-five seats in the Chamber of Deputies.

In 1921, too, Mussolini secured more followers when many of D'Annunzio's legionaries, expelled from Fiume, joined the Fascist movement. They added a more pronounced military and nationalistic element to Fascism and contributed certain Roman terms, symbols, and war cries. The fighting groups of "Black Shirts" rapidly increased during the first half of this year. Punitive expeditions, with their beatings, attacks on Communist and trade-union headquarters, and destruction of printing establishments continued. The Communists countered with ambuscades and mass attacks. Much blood was shed on each side during the conflict.

Great numbers now welcomed the new organization. To the employers it meant the restoration of discipline among workmen and the reduction of wages; to landowners, possible protection against further peasant outbreaks; to helpless and terrified professional men, middle classes, and intelligentsia, the restoration of law and order; to patriots, the purification of the civil life and the strengthening of the state. From all these classes young men hastened to enroll in the *squadristi*. Tired of violence and factional fights, the majority of Italians began to look to Mussolini to bring in an era of social peace. The failure of the Communist experiment, the weakness of the government, the subsidies of the rich, the revival of the middle class, the spread of patriotism, and the longing for a strong government, all these—together with Fascist willingness to resort to violence to attain its ends—contributed to bring success.

In November, 1921, the Fascist movement was transformed into the Fascist Party. A new and less radical program was drawn up. The succeeding months were spent in strengthening the party and in winning public opinion. The idea was spread abroad that Fascism had been responsible for the defeat of Communism, and that it alone stood between Italy and the return of that dread evil. The classes which had rallied to Fascism in order to rid the country of the threat of Communism now continued to support it for fear that the danger had not been permanently removed. The government remained unstable, weak, and inefficient. Its services were overstaffed, its budget unbalanced. Tremendous fiscal deficits piled up, and further currency inflation followed. Disorders continued at home, and the path of empire in Asia Minor and northern Africa was beset with difficulties. Ministerial instability discredited parliamentary government. During the summer of 1922 Fascism began its conquest of political power by the ejection of executive officials in the outlying provinces.

The "Fascistization" of the Government

During the fall of 1922 Mussolini repeatedly demanded that Facta, the premier then in office, either dissolve the parliament or resign in favor of a new cabinet which should include five Fascist ministers, but Facta refused to do either. In October, at a great congress of Fascisti in Naples, Mussolini delivered his ultimatum: "Either the government will be given to us or we shall seize it by marching on Rome." A ministerial crisis ensued. A tardy attempt was made to bring the Fascisti into the ministry by offering them certain positions. They declined. Instead they began their "march on Rome." The Facta government proclaimed a state of siege, but the king, in order to avoid civil war, refused to sign the decree. Instead he called upon Mussolini to form a new ministry. The government which the latter established on October 30 was a coalition in which the Fascisti were predominant.

Immediately upon assuming the premiership Mussolini demanded and received from the parliament what practically amounted to dictatorial powers until the end of 1923. Then followed the "fascistization" of the administrative offices of the government. Eventually a law was enacted giving the government authority to dismiss any civil servant who held political views contrary to those of Mussolini. Next came the "fascistization" of the parliament. An electoral reform bill was forced through the parliament, under the provisions of which the party obtaining the largest vote in a parliamentary election would receive two thirds of all the seats. In April, 1924, the plan was tested in a general election. The Fascist Party won over 60 per cent of the seats regardless of the provisions of the new electoral law, though the opposition declared that this was not accomplished without violence and intimidation. However that may be, the parliament was at any rate "fascistized." During 1925–1926 popular control of local government was also gradually abolished, and officials appointed by Mussolini's government in Rome took the place of popular government in all towns and cities.

Meanwhile, Mussolini's position as premier had been transformed into that of a dictator. He was freed from dependence upon the parliament and made responsible to the king alone. He was given permanent control of the national military, naval, and air forces. No item might be placed on the order of the day in either house of the parliament without his consent. The authority to issue governmental decrees with the force of law was placed in his hands. His title was changed to "Head of the Government," and the members of the ministry were made definitely subordinate to him.

All these changes were not accomplished without opposition, but wherever it appeared drastic steps were immediately taken to suppress it. Newspapers were so rigorously censored that eventually nothing but a Fascist press remained. Eventually university presidents and deans and public-school principals were required to be chosen from the Fascisti, and professors were dismissed for holding views contrary to Mussolini's. A secret police, the OVRA (*Organizzazione Volontaria per la Repressione dell' Antifascismo*), was established to ferret out those who plotted against the existing regime, and military tribunals were set up to try such offenders. Many were exiled to the Lipari Islands off the north coast of Sicily for holding political views contrary to Mussolini's.

In addition there was, especially in the early years, frequent resort to violence to suppress the opposition. Doubtless much of this was carried on by irresponsible elements in the party, but on at least one occasion members of the party in high standing became involved. In June, 1924, Giacomo Matteotti, a Socialist member of the Chamber of Deputies, was abducted and murdered, apparently because he had announced that he was going to expose the corruption of the Fascist minister of the interior. Although Mussolini, in an attempt to "purify" Fascism, at once removed from office all those known to be involved in the crime, they were later defended by high officers of the Fascist Party and escaped with almost no punishment.

The Fascist Party and "Doctrine"

The Fascist Party was a centralized, hierarchical organization. At its apex was the Fascist Grand Council presided over by Mussolini, *Il Duce* (the Leader). This council was the supreme Fascist organ, and Mussolini had the right to make appointments to it at will. The party consisted of some ten thousand branches (*fasci*), which were grouped into provincial federations with councils similar to the Grand Council. The secretary-general of the party was appointed by the king upon the nomination of Mussolini; the provincial secretaries were appointed by Mussolini on the nomination of the secretary-general; the local secretaries were appointed by the provincial secretaries. The control of the party was thus exercised from the top down rather than from the bottom up as in American political parties.

In order that Italy and Fascism might have a well-trained and disciplined youth, Fascism established four auxiliary organizations, the Fascist Wolf Cubs, the *Balilla,* the *Avanguardia,* and the *Giovani Fascisti,* for boys from six to eight, eight to fourteen, fourteen to eighteen, and eighteen to twenty-one respectively; and two, the *Piccole Italiane* and the *Giovane*

Italiane, for girls under and over twelve years respectively. In 1928 the government ordered the suppression of all non-Fascist institutions for the physical, moral, or spiritual training of Italian youth, and the ranks of Fascism were eventually closed except to "graduates" of the *Balilla* and *Avanguardia.*

Although, from 1923 on, the policies which were enacted into law by the Italian parliament were in general formulated and enforced by the leaders of the Fascist Party, the latter as such had no constitutional place in the Italian government. In 1928, however, the Fascist Party was written into the Italian constitution. By the provisions of the Electoral Reform Act of that year, discussed below, the Fascist Grand Council was given the legal right to draw up the list of candidates for the Chamber of Deputies. Later it was also given the right to nominate candidates for the office of prime minister and for the other high government positions. At the same time it was made the chief advisory body of the government on all questions of a constitutional character, such as proposed legislation affecting succession to the throne, the royal powers and prerogatives, the composition of the two houses of the parliament, the powers of the prime minister, and the relations between church and state. International treaties which involved changes in the national territory became subject to its deliberation. The Fascist Grand Council was changed, therefore, from a mere organ of the Fascist Party, unofficially consulted by the prime minister, into an openly recognized *de jure* part of the political machinery of the state.

Meanwhile, Fascism had been compelled to formulate a doctrine in order that it might have some articles of faith, for Mussolini repeatedly asserted that Fascism was a faith, "one of those spiritual forces which renovate the history of great peoples." He did not hesitate to claim that "innumerable signs point out Fascism as the doctrine of our age," and proclaimed that "never before have the nations thirsted for authority, direction, order as they do now." Fascism, he predicted, was "bound to become the standard type of civilization of our century for Europe—the forerunner of European renaissance."

Politically, the essence of the Fascist doctrine was the all-inclusive omnipotence of the state. "Everything in the state, nothing outside the state, nothing against the state." Apart from the state, according to Fascism, there was no scope for independent action either of individuals or of groups. Just as the past age had been that of the individual, the new age was to be that of the state. Fascism was thus the antithesis of democracy; it repudiated the right of the majority to rule. In place "of majorities and quantities" it sought to substitute the figure of *Il Duce,* "the Leader," which, of course, was but a euphemism for "dictator." In other words, Fascism stood for autocracy, not democracy.

Economically, Fascism's doctrine was colored by its early fight against the Communists and Socialists. It openly repudiated Marxian collectivism and denied the doctrine of historical materialism. It asserted that political, not economic, factors made history. Furthermore, it rejected the doctrine of the class struggle, which, it claimed, was "the natural outcome of the economic conception of history," and sought instead the fusion of all classes into "a single ethical and economic reality." In the corporative state, Fascism asserted, a unity of classes is realized, for in it the divergent interests are co-ordinated and harmonized. Obviously, Fascism was definitely opposed to the doctrine of *laissez-faire,* and asserted that the age of *laissez-faire* was nearing its end. In fact, Mussolini declared that, just as the nineteenth century had been the century of liberalism and *laissez-faire,* the twentieth century would be the century of authority.

The Fascist Syndical System

Mussolini's repudiation of *laissez-faire* is clearly revealed in the syndical system which he introduced into Italy. By the Collective Labor Relations Law of 1926 the government prescribed that occupational unions, or syndicates, should be organized in all types of economic activity. There were separate syndicates for employers and employees in each type of occupation except the professions and the arts, in which employers and employees belonged to the same syndicates. There were local syndicates in the municipalities, federations of syndicates in the provinces and regions, and at the top nine national confederations of syndicates, four for employers and four for employees in the fields of agriculture, industry, credit and insurance, and commerce, and one for professional men and artists.

These syndicates were given authority to enter into collective contracts regulating hours of labor, wages, apprenticeship, and the like. They had power over all workers and employers in a given industry and district regardless of whether the latter were members of the syndicates. The contracts which the syndicates made were binding upon all, and each syndicate had the right to exact an annual contribution to the common fund from all, whether members or not. Strikes and lockouts were illegal. When trouble arose between employer and employees, the syndicates to which they belonged sought an amicable settlement. In case of failure, the dispute was referred to the minister of corporations, an appointee of Mussolini. Failure here was followed by an appeal to one of the sixteen Italian courts of appeal, each of which had a labor section. From its decision there was no appeal.

This syndical system was designed to regulate the relations between workers and employers with a view to increasing the productive forces of the nation, and was thoroughly subordinated to Mussolini and the Fascist Party. The president and the council of each of the nine confederations were appointed by the government. The local syndicates were subject to the control of the provincial prefect if their activities were limited to a single province, or to that of the minister of corporations if they included two or more provinces. Although in theory the syndicates and federations were elective bodies, actually all syndical officials were appointed by the Fascist Party, subject to ratification by the minister of corporations, and might be removed whenever their work was unsatisfactory to party leaders.

The Corporative State

By the Electoral Reform Act of 1928 the syndical system was linked with Italy's political system. By that act the right to nominate all members of the Chamber of Deputies was given to the national confederations of syndicates and to certain legally recognized "cultural, educational, charitable, or propagandist" associations. The national confederations were authorized to propose 800 candidates and the other associations 200 more. These names were then to be sent to the Fascist Grand Council, which, with full power to accept or reject any name or even to choose one outside those submitted, should draw up a list of 400 candidates. This list was finally to be submitted to a plebiscite of the voters who, as a single national constituency, must vote "yes" or "no" on the list as a whole. Men twenty-one (or eighteen if they were married and had children) might vote if they paid syndicate dues or 100 lire in taxes, if they received pensions from the government, or if they belonged to the clergy.

The electoral scheme was given its first test early in 1929 when a plebiscite was held on March 24. During the preceding two weeks a campaign in favor of the Fascist nominees was conducted by means of speeches, proclamations, and posters. No opposition speeches were permitted. The question which was put to the electorate was: "Do you approve of the list of deputies chosen by the Fascist Grand Council?" Of the 9,460,727 male voters who composed the electorate, 8,663,412 voted in favor of the Fascist list. Only 135,761 had the temerity to cast their votes against it. Five years later a second election (March 25, 1934) had similar results. Of the 10,041,998 votes cast, only 15,265 were in the negative.

The final step in transforming Italy into a corporative state was taken in March, 1939, when the Chamber of Deputies was supplanted by the Chamber of Fasces and Corporations. This new legislative body consisted of the Duce, the members of the Fascist Grand Council and the

Fascist National Council, and the members of the National Council of Corporations. The latter, organized in 1934, consisted of representatives of employers, workers, and technicians in twenty-two branches of Italy's economic life based on cycles of production, and constituted, in the words of Mussolini, "the general staff of Italian economy." It was entrusted with the task of devising plans for Italy's self-sufficiency. The Chamber of Fasces and Corporations, therefore, represented politically the Fascist Party and economically the Italian corporative system. Members of the new national legislature were not popularly elected, had no fixed terms, and surrendered their seats when they were no longer members of the constituent bodies. The corporative system, according to Mussolini, was an attempt to advance in constitutional legislation along lines best calculated to promote smooth collaboration of all classes of society for the good of the state. It was, he declared, "the Fascist revolution's greatest legislative novelty" and an indication of "its great originality."

The Settlement of the Roman Question

Fascism inherited from its predecessors the long-standing problem of Italy's relations with the Vatican, a problem which Mussolini was especially eager to solve. In October, 1926, the Duce through an intermediary expressed to Pope Pius XI his strong desire to enter into negotiations for the purpose of eliminating the existing state of hostility between the church and the state. The delicate negotiations which ensued eventually resulted in an agreement between the papacy and the Italian government, and on February 11, 1929, a treaty, a concordat, and a financial convention were signed in the Lateran Palace by Cardinal Gasparri, papal secretary of state, and by Mussolini.

By the terms of the treaty Italy recognized the state of Vatican City under the sovereignty of the pope. The Vatican City was to have its own coinage system, postage stamps, wireless, and railway station, and the right to send and receive ambassadors. Its territory was always to be considered neutral and inviolable; freedom of access to the Holy See was guaranteed for bishops from all parts of the world; and freedom of correspondence with all states, even with states which might be at war with Italy, was assured. Furthermore, the privilege of extraterritoriality was granted outside the Vatican City to certain churches and buildings used by the Holy See for its administration. Finally, the person of the pope was declared to be as sacred and inviolable as that of the king.

In the concordat Italy recognized the Holy Catholic Apostolic and Roman religion as the only state religion in the country. The Italian government bound itself to enforce within its territory the canon law—that is to say, the laws relating to faith, morals, conduct, and discipline prescribed for Catholics by church authority. Matrimony was recognized by the state as a sacrament regulated by canon law, and thereafter, if certain regulations were observed, the state would recognize the legality of marriages performed by priests. Religious instruction, formerly excluded from the secondary schools, now became compulsory in both elementary and secondary schools, and was to be given by instructors selected by the bishops and maintained by the state. The election of bishops was also further regulated. Formerly they were appointed by the church subject to the approval of the state, which paid their salaries; thereafter the state's role would be restricted to the right of objecting to an appointee for political reasons. Ordained priests, moreover, were exempted from military obligations.

In the convention the pope accepted 750,000,000 lire ($39,375,000) in cash and 1,000,000,000 lire ($52,500,000) in 5-per-cent government bonds "as a definite settlement of all its financial relations with Italy in consequence of the fall of temporal power." Finally, the Holy See declared the Roman question irrevocably settled and therefore eliminated, and recognized the Kingdom of Italy under the House of Savoy, with Rome as the capital of the Italian state. On June 7 ratifications of the treaties comprising the settlement were exchanged in the Vatican by Cardinal Gasparri and Mussolini. Six months later the Chamber of Deputies voted that September 20, the anniversary of the taking of Rome in 1870, should be supplanted as a national holiday by February 11, the anniversary of the signing of the Lateran treaties.

Failure to Solve the Economic Problem

Mussolini likewise endeavored, but with less success, to solve Italy's general economic problem, also inherited from his predecessors. The seriousness of the problem rested chiefly on two basic facts: (1) the denseness of Italy's population, and (2) her lack of those natural resources which are essential to the upbuilding of a great industrial country. Italy lacked coal and iron, and even her agriculture failed to produce sufficient foodstuffs for her people. It is not surprising, therefore, that Italy was far from self-sufficient economically. She had long had a deficit in her foreign trade.

To overcome this situation, Mussolini called for a decrease in Italy's dependence upon foreign raw products. To this end, efforts were directed toward increasing the home production of foodstuffs by increasing the tillable area of the country, by draining swamplands and putting grasslands under the plow, and by increasing the yield through more intensive farming and the use of more modern scientific methods. By 1938 nearly twelve million acres had been reclaimed or were in the process of being reclaimed. At the end of the first decade of the "battle of the wheat," the production of wheat in Italy had increased by 70 per cent over that in 1922. At the same time, increases in the production of rice, corn, and oats ranged from 40 to 60 per cent, and further lessened Italy's need to import foodstuffs. Nevertheless, in the years just prior to the Second World War Italy still had a deficit in her production of foodstuffs. The possibility of freeing the country from dependence upon foreign fuel was no more favorable. Although hydroelectric projects were advanced until Italy stood first in Europe in this type of development, she was still forced to import large quantities of coal.

As a second part of his economic program, Mussolini sought to increase the production and export of Italy's manufactured goods, to expand her merchant marine, and to attract tourist trade. Under his new syndical system the number of days lost by strikes was greatly lessened, and the material forces of the nation were largely fused into "a single dynamo of production." As a result, Italy's industries expanded and her exports increased. Unfortunately, however, despite some increase in Italian mineral output, the country's dependence upon foreign metals rose with the acceleration of industrial production. To assist in the expansion of the Italian merchant marine, the government advanced subsidies to new lines. By the opening of the second decade of Fascist rule Italy had advanced to the place where she had, at least temporarily, a favorable balance of trade.

Inevitably, however, the world depression took its toll. In 1933 Italy once more had an adverse balance of trade. This disturbing situation, which grew steadily worse in 1934, was further aggravated by decreased income from tourists and from remittances from Italians living abroad. During the year 1934 the country therefore suffered increasingly heavy losses of gold. Finally, as a result of Mussolini's Ethiopian venture and his taking Italy into the Second World War, the Italian economic and fiscal system was of course completely wrecked.

Ultimate Failure of Foreign Policy

Although Mussolini failed to solve the nation's economic problem, there is little doubt that, during the first decade of his dictatorship, he raised Italy's international prestige. In the early years of the Fascist regime he was fortunate enough to recover for Italy some of the territories and concessions which had been lost through the "weakness" of preceding governments. The first gain came with the Dodecanese Islands which Italy had agreed to surrender to Greece by the Italo-Greek treaty of 1920. Mussolini maintained that this agreement was no longer valid because the treaty of Sèvres, with which it was linked, had lapsed. In the treaty of Lausanne (1923) Italy obtained legal recognition of her possession of the Dodecanese. A fortified naval base was at once constructed, and the foundation was laid for Italy's hoped-for predominance in the eastern Mediterranean.

Later in the year 1923 Mussolini delighted Italian nationalists by his spectacular action in the crisis arising out of the murder of an Italian who was head of the Delimitation Commission engaged in locating the boundary between Greece and Albania. On August 27 the head of the commission and four companions, of whom three were Italians, were killed on Greek soil near Janina. The Italian government at once presented an ultimatum to Greece, demanding among other things a strict inquiry with the assistance of the Italian military attaché and the payment of an indemnity of 50,000,000 lire. The other demands Greece offered to accept, but these two she regarded as "outraging the honor and violating the sovereignty of the state." Mussolini's answer was the bombardment and occupation of the Greek island of Corfu. The Duce announced that the occupation was only temporary, but many saw in the affair a strange similarity to the events of July, 1914.

Greece, acting under Articles 12 and 15 of the Covenant, immediately appealed to the League of Nations, but Salandra, the Italian representative on the Council, denied the competence of the League to deal with the affair. He asserted that the Delimitation Commission had represented the Council of Ambassadors, which should therefore handle the matter. Mussolini at first contended that the affair would be settled without outside interference, but popular indignation throughout the world led him to retreat to the position already taken by Salandra. The Council of Ambassadors stipulated that an Inter-Allied commission should supervise the investigation undertaken by Greece and that, if the Council of Ambassadors considered the commission's report warranted, it should assess damages. The commission reported that the persons guilty of the crime had not been discovered, and the ambassadors ordered Greece to pay to the Italian government 50,000,000 lire. The money was paid, and Corfu was evacuated on September 27. The government's seeming defiance of the League of Nations convinced Italian nationalists that the whole affair had been a distinct triumph for Mussolini.

The Duce's settlement of the Fiume question, while no less satisfactory to Italian nationalism, was much more skillfully and quietly accomplished. By the treaty of Rapallo (1920) Fiume had been made an independent free city. The arrangement was satisfactory neither to the Italians nor to the Yugoslavs, and it proved unworkable. Mussolini made suggestions regarding a new solution of the Fiume question, and eventually his suggestions were incorporated in the treaty of Rome, signed on January 27, 1924. By the provisions of this treaty the Free State of Fiume was divided between Italy and Yugoslavia. Fiume proper went to Italy. Port Baros, which had been originally constructed especially to handle the trade of Croatia and which was separated from Fiume by only a small stream, went to Yugoslavia. Another "catastrophic abandonment" of Italian interests was thus rectified.

Two years later Mussolini retrieved another lost position when, in 1926, Italy signed the treaty of Tirana with Albania, gaining economic concessions in return for guaranteeing "the *status quo,* political, juridical, and territorial, of Albania." The latter, furthermore, agreed not to conclude with other powers political and military agreements prejudicial to Italian interests. During 1927 internal improvements were carried out in Albania under Italian supervision and with Italian loans, and the Albanian army was reorganized by Italian officers. Later in the year Italy signed with Albania a twenty-year defensive alliance in which each agreed that, "when all the means of conciliation have been exhausted," she would come to the aid of the other in case of unprovoked attack. At last, it appeared, Italy had obtained the protectorate over Albania which Italian nationalists had been seeking ever since the outbreak of the First World War.

In 1927, too, Fascism sought to assert Italy's position as a great power in the western Mediterranean by securing the right to participate in the international regime at Tangier, a port in Morocco near the Strait of Gibraltar. In October of that year, on the eve of the opening of negotiations between France and Spain regarding the modification of the international regime in Tangier, three Italian warships made an ostentatious visit to that port. From Rome came the unofficial announcement that Italy as a Mediterranean power considered herself to be vitally concerned in the status of Tangier. There were not lacking those who perceived in Mussolini's gesture a striking similarity to the action of the German Kaiser William II when he precipitated the first Moroccan crisis in 1905.[1] Briand's policy of conciliation was in the ascendancy in Paris at this time, however, and Italy was invited to participate in the ensuing conference. A new agreement concerning Tangier was reached in 1928, and by it Italy was given a larger share in the administrative machinery of that city. Italy's position as a great power had been protected, and in Rome the outcome was looked upon as a great diplomatic triumph for Mussolini. His attempts to advance Italy's position in the Mediterranean still further by demanding naval parity with France at the London naval conference in 1930 [2] and in negotiations during the succeeding years were not, however, so successful. Nevertheless, Musso-

[1] See page 118.
[2] See page 428.

lini in the decade after 1922 undoubtedly did succeed in strengthening Italy's hold on the Adriatic, in increasing her prestige in the Mediterranean, and in extending her diplomatic and commercial influence in southeastern Europe.

Although Mussolini, without resort to war, thus made international gains for Italy, more and more Fascism exalted war instead of peace, maintaining that only war could keep man's energies at their highest pitch. War, it held, sets the mark of nobility on those nations which have the courage to face it. A nation must have "a will to power" and the desire for expansion. Life for the Fascisti must be "a continuous, ceaseless fight," and their aim must be to "live dangerously." According to Fascism, the pursuit of peace ran counter both to past experience and to "the tendencies of the present period of dynamism." "Equally foreign to the spirit of Fascism, even though they may be accepted for their utility in meeting special political situations, are all international or League organizations which, as history amply proves, crumble to the ground whenever the heart of nations is stirred deeply by sentimental, idealist, or practical considerations."

It is not surprising that Mussolini, dominated by such ideas, launched an offensive war and defied the League of Nations in his Ethiopian venture,[3] sent his troops to intervene against the legitimate republican government in the Spanish Civil War,[4] turned against the Western democracies and aligned himself with Hitler in the Rome-Berlin Axis,[5] sent his troops into Albania and annexed that country,[6] and seized what appeared to be an easy opportunity to expand the Italian empire by attacking France when the latter lay helpless before Hitler's blitzkrieg in 1940.[7] But the irony of the outcome was that Fascism's "will to power" brought not glory and empire but the end of Fascism and the execution of *Il Duce*.[8]

[3] See pages 641–644.
[4] See pages 564–566.
[5] See pages 645–646.
[6] See page 658.
[7] See page 674.
[8] See pages 707–708, 735.

Chapter XVII

LIBERAL AND NAZI GERMANY

G ERMANY emerged from the First World War defeated but with a new political regime which was distinguished for its liberalism and democracy. Although compelled to wrestle with almost insuperable problems, the liberal republic survived until it was fatally hit by the world-wide economic collapse of 1929. During the depression years which followed, conditions in Germany came to be not unlike those existing in Italy from 1920 to 1922, and the popular reaction in the former was very similar to that which had occurred in the latter. In 1933 Germany finally came into the control of the Nazis, who in their so-called Third Reich inaugurated a regime in many ways like that of the Fascists in Italy, one which was vastly different from that set up by the German constitution of 1919.

The Weimar Constitution

An understanding of the history of the German Republic requires some knowledge of the several political parties which played prominent roles and of their basic doctrines. The place of the former Conservative Party was taken in the republic by the Nationalist Party which consisted of the conservatives, the Pan-Germans, the militarists, and the majority of the Junker class. Its leaders openly avowed their monarchical sentiments. The Right wing of the old National Liberal Party organized itself into the People's Party, which, although it preferred monarchy, announced its acceptance of republican government. It was the party of "big business" and was ably led by Gustav Stresemann. The former Center Party survived the revolution and supported the democratic republic but it was strongly opposed to all attempts to establish a socialistic regime. Its outstanding leader was Matthias Erzberger. The Left wing of the old National Liberals united with the former Progressive Party to form the bourgeois Democratic Party. In addition to supporting the republic it denounced the "squirearchy" and the military bureaucracy. During the war the former Social Democrats had split so that in 1919 they were actually found in three political parties. The moderate Majority Socialists, led by Friedrich Ebert and Philipp Scheidemann, proposed a scientific and gradual policy of socialization to be accomplished through the ordinary channels of parliamentary government. The Independent Socialists, led by Hugo Haase, desired to establish socialism in Germany before popular elections were held, and accused the Majority Socialists of treason to the cause of socialism. The Communists, whose leaders—Karl Liebknecht and Rosa Luxemburg—were killed in January, 1919, wished to set up in Germany a state like Soviet Russia.

In the National Assembly, which was elected on January 19, 1919, the Majority Socialists held the most seats, followed by the Centrists, the Democrats, the Nationalists, the Independent Socialists, and the People's Party. Although the Majority Socialists elected by far the largest number of delegates to the assembly, they did not control a majority, so that a coalition now became necessary. When the National Assembly met at Weimar in February, 1919, the Majority Socialist government therefore gave way to the "Weimar Coalition," composed of Majority Socialists, Centrists, and Democrats, under the chancellorship of the Majority Socialist Scheidemann. Friedrich Ebert, who since the preceding November had served as chancellor, was then elected the first president of the German Republic.

The constitution, which the National Assembly drafted and finally accepted on July 31, 1919, largely incorporated the views of the "Weimar Coalition." Every member state had to have a republican constitution, and representatives had to "be elected by the universal, equal, direct and secret suffrage of all German citizens, both men and women, according to the principles of proportional representation." The chancellor and the ministers required for the administration of their offices the confidence of the Reichstag and had to resign if the latter by formal resolution withdrew its confidence. The republic was therefore a truly representative democracy.

The executive of the republic consisted of the president and the cabinet, composed of the chancellor and other ministers. The president was elected by the direct vote of the people, held office for seven years, and might be re-elected. Like the French president and the British king, the German president had little real power, every executive order requiring the counter-signature of the chancellor or some other minister. The chancellor, responsible to the Reichstag, was the one who determined the general course of policy and assumed responsibility therefor.

The national legislature consisted of two houses, the Reichstag and the Reichsrat. The former was composed of members elected for a term of four years by the direct vote of all men and women over twenty years of age. The Reichsrat, like the former Bundesrat, represented the states. In it each state had at least one vote, the larger states having one vote for each 700,000 inhabitants; but no state might have more than two fifths of all the votes. The Reichsrat functioned merely as a sort of "brake on legislation," and, contrary to the condition under the empire, the Reichstag was by far the more powerful branch of the legislature.

The Foes of the Republic

To draft and set up a republican form of government for Germany was one thing; to defend it against the onslaughts of domestic foes of the Left and Right was quite another. From the day of its proclamation the republic encountered the bitter opposition of the Communists. In December, 1918, in January, 1919, and again in March of the latter year the Communists instigated revolts in Berlin in attempts to overthrow it. In Munich another Communist uprising, provoked by a Nationalist's murder of Kurt Eisner, the Bavarian premier, actually led to the proclamation of a soviet republic in the spring of 1919. Eventually, however, all of these uprisings were quelled by the government.

Somewhat in proportion as the threat from the Communists declined in the early years of the republic, that from the reactionaries of the extreme Right increased. By 1920 the immediate danger from communism seemed to have passed, and in March, 1920, the reactionaries struck their first blow against the republic in what is known as the Kapp-Lüttwitz *Putsch*. General Baron von Lüttwitz, commander-in-chief of Berlin, suddenly seized the capital, and his confederate, Wolfgang von Kapp, was proclaimed chancellor. Because of the refusal of General Hans von Seekt, the chief of staff, to use the Reichswehr to protect President Ebert's government, it fled precipitately to Dresden and then on to Stuttgart. Nevertheless, the *Putsch* proved a miserable failure. Some of the monarchist leaders refused their active support, and the bulk of the army and of the propertied classes failed to rally to it. At the same time it encountered the determined opposition of the working classes, to whom President Ebert issued a passionate appeal to inaugurate a general strike. Necessities like water, gas, and electricity were suddenly shut off; railway and tramway services ceased. The revolutionary government was paralyzed and collapsed within a week.

During the next three years events in connection with the fulfillment of the peace treaty provided numerous opportunities for the reactionaries to criticize the republican regime and to seek to weaken and discredit it. The losses of territory by plebiscites, the Allied demand for the punishment of German "war criminals" (many of whom were looked upon as national heroes in the fatherland), the reparations and disarmament demands, the forced disbandment of the Bavarian *Einwohnerwehr* (citizen guard), all presented points of attack for the monarchists. A "stab in the back" legend was developed to the effect that all Germany's postwar ills arose from the military defeat, which in turn had been caused by the pre-armistice revolutionary intrigues of the present republicans. A campaign of agitation, centering in Bavaria, was directed against all who had played a part in the events leading to the signing of the Versailles treaty, and a series of political murders began which eventually claimed such distinguished figures as Matthias Erzberger, the Centrist leader, and Walther Rathenau, a Democrat who at the time of his assassination was minister for foreign affairs.

In 1923, when Germany was in chaos as a result of French occupation of the Ruhr and German passive resistance, various plots were hatched in Bavaria looking toward the overthrow of the Berlin government. One reactionary group under the leadership of Gustav von Kahr plotted the establishment of a directory which, backed by the military, would assume control of the Reich. Another group led by Ludendorff and Adolf Hitler, the latter destined to become the Nazi dictator of Germany, planned to march on Berlin, where Hitler would be proclaimed president under the military dictatorship of Ludendorff. Hitler's plans conflicted with those of Kahr, with the result that the two factions consumed their ardor in quarreling between themselves, and the "beer-cellar rebellion" of November 8 collapsed without having seriously threatened the republic. The chief conspirators were arrested and tried, but friendly courts let them off with lenient treatment.

The Currency Debacle

While statesmen of the Weimar Republic were engaged in a life-and-death struggle to prevent the destruction of the republic, they were forced to deal also with the baffling problem of a currency rapidly depreciating toward the vanishing point. The republic had inherited a currency which was already greatly inflated, thanks to the former imperial government's unwillingness to impose heavier direct taxes during the First World War. And the exigencies of the period of demobilization and readjustment, together with the necessity of making reparations payments, had brought further inflation, largely because German statesmen were reluctant to increase taxes. In the years immediately after the war the burden of taxation in Germany was only a quarter as heavy as the burden in Great Britain, only half as heavy as in France.

By May, 1921, the mark had declined to 60 (normally 4.2) to the dollar. This depreciation in turn operated to keep the national budget unbalanced, for taxes assessed with the mark at one figure were paid later with a mark depreciated below that figure. The continued deficits which resulted led to still more inflation. By November, 1922, the mark had sunk to 7000 to the dollar. The occupation of the Ruhr by the French and the

Wide World Photos

THE RESULT OF CURRENCY INFLATION

A Berlin firm's payroll in depreciated marks in August, 1923.

Belgians and the adoption by Germany of the policy of passive resistance, with the accompanying need for subsidizing the idle workers, started the mark upon its toboggan slide. By the close of January, 1923, it stood at 50,000 to the dollar. By the middle of November it had become practically worthless, being quoted in Berlin at 2,520,000,000,000 and in Cologne at about 4,000,000,000,000 to the dollar.

Many of the great industrialists of Germany tremendously increased their wealth and power during this inflationary period. Availing themselves of artificially cheap labor, extensive Reichsbank loans, and a rapidly falling currency, they piled up tremendous paper profits. With these they purchased substantial assets abroad, enlarged and modernized their plants at home, or paid off loans and bonded indebtedness. Thus the mighty capitalists and industrialists profited enormously by the inflation and showed no great concern to check it until the mark had become worthless.

When, however, farmers and merchants began to refuse to sell food for worthless currency, when "the catastrophe of currency developed into a catastrophe of the food and other supplies, which was worse than in the worst periods of the war," when plunderings and riots began to be of daily occurrence, the German government in desperation decided to create a new bank of issue and a new currency. In November, 1923, Hjalmar Schacht, general manager of one of Germany's largest banks, was appointed special currency commissioner with the task of stabilizing the mark and introducing the new currency. He stopped the printing presses and issued a new currency, which was stabilized at the old rate of 4.2 to the dollar. At the same time Finance Minister Luther by heroic measures balanced the budget and ended the need for inflation. Provision was made that the old depreciated marks might, until July 5, 1925, be converted into the new Reichsmark at the ratio of one trillion to one.

The economic and social results of this practical repudiation of the mark were terrific. The obvious effect of the devaluation was the destruction of savings, pensions, and insurance. Of what value were 100,000 marks invested in banks, bonds, or fixed annuities when the mark declined until it took 1,000,000,000 to buy a dollar's worth of food? The inevitable consequence of such a declining currency was the forced transfer of wealth from the creditor to the debtor class. Mortgages were lifted, bonds retired, and notes paid off with currency worth only an infinitesimal fraction of its face value. Undoubtedly the most lasting of the disastrous results of the currency inflation was the destruction or disintegration of a great part of the previously prosperous middle class. The support which the middle class later gave to Hitler was in no small measure the result of suffering and discontent engendered by the currency debacle.

Stresemann's Policy of Conciliation

Meanwhile, Germany had undertaken to implement a national foreign policy, the fundamental aim of which, inevitably, was to throw off the various limitations on her sovereignty in order that she might regain her prewar position of power and influence in world affairs. More specifically, she sought (1) to reduce and ultimately to escape from the reparations indemnity which she was obligated to pay, (2) to liberate her territory from foreign occupation, (3) to secure the removal of the Inter-Allied commissions of control, (4) to regain her freedom in military and naval matters, (5) to restore her right to fortify and protect the Rhineland, and (6) to emerge from isolation and once more hold a place as an equal among the great powers. Ultimately, she sought to redeem the Saar, to secure a union with Austria, to bridge the gap between Germany and East Prussia, and to regain at least some of her colonies.

Immediately after the war many German statesmen were inclined to look to the east for their country's salvation. They cordially hated the victorious Allies, spurned any move toward reconciliation with them, repudiated their dictated peace treaty, declined to adopt a policy of fulfillment, and hoped eventually, by forming an alliance with Russia, to be able to defy them and overthrow the treaty. The economic recovery of Germany they would hasten by re-establishing trade relations with Russia and by extending German economic control over the boundless resources of the Soviet Union. The most spectacular step taken in this policy of eastern orientation was the signing of the treaty of Rapallo with Russia in April, 1922. Germany accorded *de jure* recognition to the Soviet government, and each renounced all war claims and prewar indebtedness. The results of the attitude of defiance were unfortunate, however. Not only were none of the immediate ends of her foreign policy attained, but in 1923 Germany found herself further limited and weakened by the Franco-Belgian occupation of the Ruhr.

Those in Germany who favored a policy of western orientation believed that the republic's salvation was to be found only with the aid and co-operation of the Allies. They demanded a "policy of fulfillment and reconciliation." The one who more than all others developed a constructive foreign policy for Germany based on the idea of western orientation was Gustav Stresemann, who assumed the office of foreign minister in the critical days of August, 1923, and held it through ten shifting ministries down to his regrettable death on October 3, 1929. A member of the bourgeoisie, associated with big business, he belonged before the war to the

National Liberal Party. During the revolutionary days he formed the People's Party and became its leader. Content during the early years of the republic to follow a more or less negative policy of opportunism, his assumption of a share of the governmental burden of responsibility in 1923 led him to become increasingly constructive in his policies. Although the fundamental aims of Germany's foreign policy remained unchanged, under his guidance the republic chose the path leading toward at least apparent fulfillment and reconciliation as the best means to attain them.

Real gains came to Germany from Stresemann's policy. The Dawes Committee's investigation brought the settling of the method and amounts of reparations payments in accordance with the views of impartial experts, and the introduction of the Dawes plan brought financial assistance which made the economic rehabilitation of Germany possible. It led within a year to the military evacuation of the Ruhr. It secured for Germany admission to the League of Nations (1926) with a permanent seat on the Council. Early in the following year it brought the abolition of the Inter-Allied commissions of control, their duties being transferred to the League, of which Germany was now an influential member. In 1928 Stresemann secured the initiation of negotiations looking toward a new settlement of the reparations problem and the early evacuation of the Rhineland. As a result, the definite total which was fixed for German reparations liabilities was placed far below that originally fixed by the Reparations Commission in 1921; and it was agreed that all Allied forces of occupation should be withdrawn from the Rhineland by June 30, 1930.

Economic Recovery and Decline

Not unrelated to Stresemann's successful foreign policy was the rapid economic recovery which the republic experienced during the five years after 1924. Inflation had enabled Germany to compete for a time in the markets of the world with goods produced at home by labor unusually cheap, while at the same time it had enabled her industrialists to expand and modernize their plants with loans which were repaid with an almost worthless currency. By 1924, as the Dawes experts pointed out, Germany's industries and transportation system were in admirable physical condition. She soon reached the place where she again had a surplus of coal for export, and by 1927 her production of steel ingots was back nearly to the prewar figure. The rolling stock in her railways became superior in quality and condition to that of prewar days. The gross tonnage of her merchant vessels rose from 400,000 to 3,738,067 by 1928, and possessed the great advantage of being nearly all new.

German industrialists planned to resume their prewar commercial and

industrial relations and hoped to regain the place in the world's markets
which they had held in 1914. To hasten the republic's economic recovery
they introduced into German industrial life the "rationalization movement," to which they ascribed the rapid rise of American industry. Mass
production and industrial efficiency became their watchwords. Standardiza-
tion of products and materials, scientific planning and management, elimination of duplication and useless competition by the formation of trusts
and combines—these became their goals. Undoubtedly greater efficiency
was achieved. The average output per man was considerably increased

GERMANY BEFORE AND AFTER THE FIRST WORLD WAR

in various types of industry and even in agriculture. Furthermore, greater
protection was given to home industry by modifying the German customs
tariff act, and German interests abroad were advanced by the conclusion
of commercial treaties with all of the important powers. By 1929 the total
volume of industrial output in Germany exceeded that of 1913.

In 1929, however, it began to be apparent that the republic's rapid economic recovery could not continue. That recovery had been facilitated in
part by extensive loans which had been obtained from foreign bankers.
In 1929 the sources of these loans began to dry up. Continued economic
recovery required a further extension of German markets abroad. But
the high tariff walls raised by other countries, the successful competition
of the United States, Great Britain, and France, and the inability to regain

to any great extent the prewar markets in Russia, operated to prevent that necessary extension. Moreover, the loss of wages by those who were rendered superfluous in industry by the introduction of "rationalization," and the decrease in prices of agricultural products resulting from world overproduction, both brought a noticeable decline in the purchasing power of the home market. In 1929 German industrial activity began to decline, and unemployment began to rise. The resultant situation raised serious problems for the German government and inevitably reacted upon the political situation.

The Reichstag elections in May, 1928, when Germany was prosperous, had in general brought gains for those parties which supported the Weimar Republic. The Nationalists had lost heavily and the National Socialists had won only twelve seats. A Socialist, Hermann Müller, had become chancellor and a "grand coalition," consisting of the People's Party, Centrists, Bavarian People's Party (an offshoot of the Centrists), Democrats, and Social Democrats, had been organized under his leadership. But Social Democratic dissatisfaction with financial reforms which were pushed through the Reichstag in an effort to solve the republic's pressing economic problems after 1929 had brought the downfall of the Müller government in March, 1930. In the new government, headed by Heinrich Brüning, leader of the Centrists, the Social Democrats refused to participate.

The chief task of Brüning's government was to secure the adoption of a budget which would wipe out the steadily increasing national deficit, but conflicts between party, class, and local interests in the Reichstag constituted a serious handicap. Finally, in July, 1930, after the Reichstag had rejected the government's budget, President Hindenburg dissolved that body and called for new elections to be held in September. In the meantime, availing himself of the "emergency clause" (Article 48) of the constitution, the president inaugurated a financial program which differed little from the one the Reichstag had rejected.

Hitler and the National Socialists

The political group which benefited most from the economic depression and the growing spirit of unrest in Germany was the National Socialist Party, whose chief or *Führer* (Leader) was Adolf Hitler. This fanatical German leader was born (1889) not in Germany but in Austria, and was the son of a humble customs inspector of the Dual Monarchy. His formal education was somewhat limited, for he had been obliged to leave school at an early age because of financial difficulties. While yet a mere youth he went to Vienna for the purpose of studying architecture, but finding himself unable to enter the Painting Academy, he had had to be content with a position as draftsman and decorator. The Austrian capital Hitler had abhorred as a "racial Babylon," and it was during his years in Vienna, apparently, that he developed his bitter anti-Marxist and anti-Semitic hatreds.

Shortly before the First World War began, Hitler moved to Munich, where he worked as a house painter. During the war he fought in the Bavarian army as a private and later as a corporal, and was awarded the Iron Cross. Soon after the war he helped to organize in Munich the National Socialist German Workers' Party, and in February, 1920, a program of twenty-five points, formulated by Gottfried Feder, was adopted by the party. This early program, somewhat analogous to the early platform of the Italian Fascists, was modified by later pronouncements of Hitler and was ultimately much expanded in a volume of memoirs entitled *Mein Kampf* (My Struggle). In 1921 Hitler began to harangue the crowds in the Munich beer gardens, especially denouncing the Jews, the capitalists, the French, the treaty of Versailles, and the Weimar Republic. In 1923, as already pointed out, he co-operated with Ludendorff and others in an unsuccessful attempt to overthrow the German government, and was consequently sentenced to five years' imprisonment. After a prison term of only a few months, he was released but was forbidden for a time to make public speeches.

Hitler then devoted himself primarily to the task of organizing his followers, and in this work he closely followed the plans of Mussolini. The swastika, or hooked cross (卐), was adopted as the emblem of the National Socialist Party, which was further provided with an elaborate ritual and a military organization. Party members were required to pay small monthly dues and were permitted in turn to wear the party uniform—a brown shirt with a black swastika on an armband. Like Mussolini's *squadristi*, Hitler had his "storm troops" (*Sturmabteilungen*). In addition, the organization had its smaller group of "defense squads" (*Schutzstaffeln*), which constituted a sort of private police for protecting party leaders and for executing unusually difficult tasks. In order to reach the whole German people with the party program the country was organized into twenty-six districts, each in turn subdivided into "cells" to which a number of trained speakers were assigned. So far as organization was concerned, therefore, the National Socialists, or Nazis, were in a position to make great gains in the election of 1930.

Their program, too, was of such a nature as to attract large numbers of adherents in a time of national humiliation and economic depression. They were extremely nationalistic, seeking to unite all Germans in a common state, to regain for Germany her lost colonies and her parity with the other great powers in national armaments, to secure the cancellation of the peace treaties and thereby the refutation of war guilt and the repudiation of reparations obligations. They extolled the superiority of the Nordic Germans, denounced the Jews as foes of the fatherland, and threatened them with physical violence, civil and political degradation, and economic repression once the Nazis came into power. They advocated, too, certain social and economic reforms, notably the abolition of all unearned income, the confiscation of war profits, the nationalization of the great trusts and large department stores, the guarantee by the government of employment and decent living conditions for German citizens (Jews could not be citizens), the abolition of speculation in land, the inauguration of agrarian reform, and the shifting of tax burdens from the workers and lower middle classes to the rich. All these reforms and achievements were to be the fruits of the "Third Reich" [1] which the National Socialists aimed to establish.

At a time when the number of unemployed in Germany was close to 4,000,000, when the burden of taxation was becoming constantly heavier, when no ray of hope for a way out of the economic depression was visible, it is not surprising, perhaps, that great numbers were won to the National Socialist standard by the magnetic oratory of Adolf Hitler. Although labor, in general, remained deaf to the Nazi leader's siren song, millions of others who were alarmed at the prospect of pauperization responded. From the German youth great numbers of university students and university graduates, moved by their discontent with a situation which failed to provide employment for the educated classes, joined the Nazi ranks. From the professional classes many who suffered from the keen competition of the Jews in medicine, law, banking, and trade were cheered by the promise of the National Socialist anti-Semitic program. Unorganized retail shopkeepers and lesser capitalists, fearful of the encroachments of the great trusts, department stores, and chain stores, found hope in the Nazi plan to nationalize such enterprises. Even the peasants, burdened with debt and prevented by their concept of private property from supporting the Communists or Socialists, in many cases as a protest threw their support to the Nazis. Finally, the great ranks of the white-collar classes, unemployed or poorly paid, joined the Hitler movement almost *en masse*. When the votes were finally counted at the close of the election of September 14, 1930, therefore, it was found that the National Socialists had made tremendous gains. The 12 seats which they had held in the Reichstag at the time of its dissolution were now increased to 107, thus giving to the Nazis a strength in the national legislature second only to that of the Social Democrats.

---

[1] According to the Nazis the first Reich was the Holy Roman Empire and the second was created by Bismarck in 1871.

The Collapse of Parliamentary Government

Despite the losses of the middle parties, Brüning's government was enabled to continue in office through the support of the Social Democrats, who threw their strength to it on a vote of confidence. Again in December, 1930, however, President Hindenburg was compelled to resort to emergency decrees in order to put into effect the financial program of the government. But the national financial crisis grew steadily worse, and twice more in 1931 emergency decrees were issued in an attempt to increase income and reduce expenditures.

In order to spare the country the cost and excitement of a general election in a time of such economic distress, Brüning suggested to the various party leaders early in 1932 that President Hindenburg's term be extended beyond the legal seven years. In 1925 the aged Field Marshal Paul von Hindenburg had been elected as the candidate of the Right groups over the "Weimar Coalition" candidate, Wilhelm Marx, and the Communist candidate, Ernst Thälmann. Hitler opposed an extension of Hindenburg's term, however, and, since the president declined to use his emergency powers to prolong his own term, an election had to be held. Hindenburg and Hitler were the principal candidates in a campaign which witnessed a notable shift in party loyalties when contrasted with that of 1925. The Social Democrats and the Centrists, who on the former occasion had opposed Hindenburg's election as a menace to the republic, were now his most staunch and active supporters; while the Nationalists and the monarchists, who had put forward the marshal as their candidate in 1925, now became his most determined opponents. In the election of April 10, 1932, although Hitler received more than 13,400,000 votes, Hindenburg obtained a decisive majority and thus in his eighty-fifth year began his second term as President of the German Republic.

Seven weeks later Brüning resigned because Hindenburg—himself a landholder—opposed the chancellor's plan to carve up into small farms some of the large estates of East Prussia in order to provide relief for Germany's millions of unemployed. Throughout the republic, moreover, the feeling was becoming somewhat general that Brüning's system of governing by executive decrees—certainly not a parliamentary system—was a failure. The new chancellor chosen by Hindenburg was Colonel Franz von Papen, and the ministry which he selected was composed for the most part of nationalists and conservatives. Realizing that he could not hope to control a majority in the existing Reichstag, Chancellor von Papen had it dissolved immediately. Nothing, however, seemed to be able to stem the rising tide of Hitlerism. In the ensuing elections the Nazis gained a total of 230 seats, which gave them the largest number that any party had ever had in the history of the republic. Nevertheless, President Hindenburg rejected Hitler's demand that he be made chancellor.

To escape a vote of no confidence Papen at once dissolved the recently elected Reichstag and again called for elections. On this occasion the Nazis still retained first place in the Reichstag, but the Communists increased their total number of seats to 100 and came within striking distance of the strength of the Social Democrats. It appeared that the workers were deserting the moderate Social Democratic Party to join the ranks of the more radical Communists. President Hindenburg now invited Adolf Hitler to undertake to construct a government of national concentration, but the Nazi leader found himself unable to obtain the promise of majority support. The president in turn declined to entertain Hitler's proposal that he be appointed with dictatorial powers, and instead called to the chancellorship General Kurt von Schleicher, minister of defense in the Papen government. Schleicher's ministry, which was recruited largely from that of Papen, proved to be no more able to handle the situation than its predecessors. After less than two months in office General von Schleicher resigned on January 28, 1933.

The National Socialist Revolution

Two days later Adolf Hitler was appointed chancellor at the head of a ministry in which two of the appointments were highly significant. The important post of minister of the interior was given to Wilhelm Frick, one of Hitler's Nazi colleagues in the Munich *Putsch* of 1923. An appointment as minister without portfolio went to Hermann Göring, next to Hitler the most powerful personality in the Nazi movement. Göring had also participated in the "beer-cellar rebellion," and to escape punishment at that time he had fled to Italy, where he spent two years in studying Fascism.

In the hope of gaining ascendancy in the Reichstag the Führer dissolved that body and called for new elections. During the ensuing five weeks Hitler's government resorted to strong-arm methods against the opposition, particularly the Communists, the Social Democrats, and the Centrists. Opposition newspapers were suspended or suppressed; opposition meetings were forbidden or broken up; opposition speakers were denied access to the radio, which became a Nazi monopoly. Five days before the elections a fire—probably of Nazi origin—destroyed the Reichstag building. The Communists were at once accused of being the perpetrators of this act of vandalism, and hundreds of Communist leaders were arrested. By dwelling upon the dangers of a Communist-Socialist plot to overthrow the government, the Nazis sought to cause a wave of anti-Communist hysteria to sweep the country. An emergency decree of the president suspended all constitutional provisions guaranteeing personal liberty, freedom of the press, liberty to hold meetings, and even secrecy of the mails.

On March 5, 1933, stirred by the propaganda and excitement of the preceding week, more than 39,000,000 German citizens went to the polls. Although the German workers still showed their militancy and strength by polling 7,000,000 votes for the Social Democrats and 4,800,000 for the Communists, although the Catholic Center parties showed their opposition to the Nazi program of suppression and intimidation by casting 5,500,000 votes, the millions of ordinary "stay-at-homes" who participated in this election turned the tide in favor of the National Socialists. In the country as a whole the latter secured more than 17,000,000 votes, which, with the 3,000,000 votes of the Nationalists, who supported Hitler, gave the latter's government about 52 per cent of the popular vote. With 288 Nazi representatives and 53 Nationalists, Hitler controlled a majority of the 648 seats in the new Reichstag.

Wearing his Nazi uniform, Chancellor Hitler appeared before the newly elected Reichstag at its first session and demanded dictatorial powers for four years. In a single session the Reichstag rushed the enabling act granting these powers through the required three readings, and then adjourned indefinitely.[2] Adolf Hitler thus after more than a decade of fighting achieved by constitutional methods the great triumph toward which he had looked forward. He was now chancellor of Germany and possessed of power greater by far than even the "iron chancellor," Bismarck, had ever wielded.

Any attempt to appraise the forces which brought about the National Socialist revolution must take into account four or five major factors. Perhaps first in importance was the world economic depression. In the years from 1924 to 1929, when Germany was experiencing an economic recovery, the Nazi movement made relatively little headway. But the misery and suffering resulting from four years of economic depression inevitably caused in Germany as in every other country a reaction against those in power. A second factor was the resurgence of a militant German nationalism, carefully cultivated by Hitler's exaltation of German racial superiority. With the rise of nationalism came a strong reaction against the Weimar middle parties, which had pursued a policy of conciliation and fulfillment, and in favor of the Nazis, who promised to regain for Germany that proud place among the powers of the world which she had held before 1914.

A third factor in the situation was the temporary collapse of parlia-

[2] On January 30, 1937, the Reichstag extended this enabling act for four more years.

mentary government caused by the German multiparty system and the adoption of proportional representation under the Weimar constitution. As already pointed out, for more than two years before the elections of March, 1933, there was a deadlock in the Reichstag resulting from the fact that no party or group of parties controlled a majority. German labor, which in its own interest should have presented a common front against the Nazi menace, unfortunately became more divided than ever and accordingly weakened its power and contributed to the breakdown of parliamentary government. The German Communists, indeed, by their obstructionist tactics played directly into Hitler's hands. When a resort to government by presidential decrees failed to end the crisis, many became convinced that only a "strong man" could bring back to Germany the domestic peace and prosperity of prewar days.

This desire for a "strong man" was further increased by fear of the rising tide of Communism, which was winning millions of discontented and despairing workmen into its ranks. After the burning of the Reichstag building by alleged Communists, the anti-Communist feeling mounted almost to hysteria among the upper and middle classes, who saw in the Nazis a bulwark against the "Reds." Furthermore, fear of Communism and a desire to smash the power of German labor had led some of the great Rhineland industrialists, notably Fritz Thyssen, to subsidize the Nazi movement in the days when it might otherwise have collapsed.

Finally, Hitler's own contribution to the forces which brought the revolution must not be overlooked. The Nazi leader was apparently not particularly original in his methods or ideas, but he was certainly a skillful imitator. He undoubtedly understood the temper of the younger generation of Germans. He was an adept psychologist, a clever demagogue, and a master showman. At the same time, he was a resourceful agitator, a tireless worker, and an able organizer. With the conditions which existed in Germany and with Hitler's ability to exploit them to the full through popular propaganda, the outcome was almost inevitable, especially when the Nazis resorted to repression and intimidation in the weeks before the election.

The Totalitarian State

Vigorous measures were at once taken to create in Germany a totalitarian state in which there should be but one political party, the National Socialist. Some of the parties—notably the Communist, Social Democratic, and Democratic—were forcibly outlawed by the government; the others voluntarily dissolved. On July 14, 1933, Hitler's government decreed that the National Socialist Party was the only legal party in Germany, and that the formation of any new parties would constitute high treason. Furthermore, in order that the administrative offices of the republic might be filled with Nazis, a new civil-service law, applying to the federal, state, and municipal services, was promulgated, making it possible to dismiss all civil servants who were not acceptable to the central authorities.

The Nazi government also inaugurated a program designed to centralize all political authority in Berlin. Within a year it had progressed so far that on January 30, 1934—the first anniversary of Hitler's appointment as chancellor—the Reichstag passed unanimously Hitler's measure transferring the sovereign powers of the various German states to the Reich government. The legislative functions of the states were definitely abolished, and the governors appointed over the states by the Reich government were placed under the jurisdiction of the Reich minister of the interior. The formal abolition of the Reichsrat, which had originally been instituted to give the states parliamentary representation, occurred in February, 1934. Even the municipal governments were "co-ordinated." The burgomasters of the cities and the presidents of the villages were made appointees of the Reich minister of the interior. Full power to make all decisions was to rest with these appointed executives.

Steps were also taken to secure undisputed control of the German youth. In 1926 Hitler had organized the Hitler Youth, an organization which came to include boys from ten to twenty years of age. After coming into power Hitler created the position of "Leader of the Youth of the German Reich" and appointed to this office the director of the Hitler Youth organization. This new official was made head of all German youth organizations and was authorized to take over the administrative functions of all the governing bodies which had hitherto existed. Furthermore, no new youth organization or junior auxiliary of an adult organization might be formed without his consent. Late in 1936, in fact, it was decreed that all youth—boys and girls—within the Reich were to be included in the Hitler Youth organization.

Thus Hitler attained his goal of a completely centralized, totalitarian, or one-party, state. The federal, state, and local governments had been brought wholly under his control; the parliamentary system had been entirely destroyed; the various military organizations had been either absorbed into the Nazi ranks or suppressed; the German youth movements had been restricted and centralized under Nazi leadership. As in Italy all political life was centralized in and controlled by Mussolini's Fascist Party, so at last in Germany the political life of the republic was monopolized by the Nazis. "The National Socialist Party," Hitler announced, "is the state." The Nazi party flag—the black hooked cross in a white circle on a red field—in 1935 became the official flag of the Third Reich.

To expedite the creation of the totalitarian state, Hitler had utilized two different agencies: propaganda to popularize the Nazi regime, and force to suppress all opposition to it. The former was placed in the hands of Paul Joseph Goebbels as minister of propaganda and enlightenment; the exercise of the latter was confided to Göring, Prussian premier and minister of police. Freedom of speech and of the press was abolished, and even the secrecy of telephone conversations and of the mails was disregarded. The whole educational system was placed in the hands of the Nazis, and all teachers and officials known to be in opposition to the Hitlerite regime were removed. Many famous German scholars and scientists were deprived of their positions and forced to take refuge abroad. The *Gestapo* (*Geheime Staatspolizei*), a secret state police independent of the regular police, was created and placed under the command at first of Göring, later of Heinrich Himmler. To trace and fight all political activities dangerous to the state was declared to be its peculiar task. Thousands of Germans were arrested and placed in "concentration camps."

The "Co-ordination" of Germany's Economic Life

But the Nazi totalitarian program was not limited to the political realm alone. Steps were taken to bring Germany's economic life likewise into harmony with Nazi principles. In 1933 all the previously existing trade unions in Germany were suppressed, and in the following year all employers' associations were likewise dissolved. To replace these former organizations of workers and employers a new organization, the German Labor Front, was established to represent capital and labor in the realm of commerce, industry, and the professions. Under a new labor law, effective from May 1, 1934, collective bargaining, strikes, and lockouts were forbidden. The workers thus lost their ultimate safeguard against exploitation—the right to strike—and became dependent for their well-being upon labor trustees, political appointees of the Nazi government, who were given full authority to issue regulations, binding upon both workers and employers, "establishing the conditions for the concluding of wage agreements."

In its attitude toward agriculture the Nazi government was influenced to a considerable extent by its desire to realize national self-sufficiency (*Autarkie*). In view of Germany's experience during the First World War, the Nazis were particularly determined that the Third Reich should become completely independent of the outside world for its food supplies. The government, therefore, established for agriculture an organization called the Food Estate (*Nährstand*) under the direction of the Reich minister of agriculture. This organization introduced a sort of planned economy for agriculture and regulated the price and distribution of most foodstuffs. Despite their earlier promises of agrarian reform, the Nazis made no attempt to confiscate or to divide the great landed estates of the Junkers of East Prussia and Pomerania.

In the realm of foreign trade the Nazis encountered difficulties. The large export surplus which Germany had enjoyed at the time the Nazis came into power decreased—partly as a result of boycotts in foreign countries because of the Nazi anti-Semitic measures—until in 1934 it finally became an import surplus instead. The resultant drain on the gold reserves of the Reichsbank was so severe that they became depleted. Once more the fear of currency depreciation haunted the German people. Immediate and drastic steps were needed, and Hjalmar Schacht, president of the Reichsbank, was appointed minister of economics with dictatorial power. Three types of measures were taken by Schacht to meet the threatening situation: (1) default in whole or in part on foreign interest payments in order to stop one of the drains on Germany's gold, (2) rigid curtailment of imports into Germany from abroad in order to reduce another drain on the country's gold reserves, and (3) extensive subsidies to industries manufacturing for export in order that they might reduce their prices, increase their foreign sales, and thus bring gold or goods into Germany.

In German industry the years after 1934 saw a rapid recovery, production rising until by the opening of the year 1937 it was running 12 per cent ahead of the boom year 1928. This improvement was largely the result of credit-financed programs of rearmament and public works. To secure the funds for these extensive programs the government resorted to what amounted to a system of forced loans from banks, industries, and various organizations which had funds that might be used for investment. In other words, the German government went more and more into debt. The amount borrowed was not revealed, for after 1934 the Reich budget was not published.

In September, 1936, Hitler announced the inauguration of a Four-Year Plan designed to increase Germany's self-sufficiency. Since, however, Germany was at that time largely dependent upon foreign countries for all important industrial raw materials except coal, the plan placed upon German scientists what Hitler called a "stupendous task." Göring, the Nazi strong man, was placed in charge with plenary powers to issue all decrees necessary for the execution of the plan. Göring at once sought to hasten the development of certain synthetic products, notably rubber, oil, and fabric threads. In the interest of accelerating the rearmament program, efforts were made to increase the production of iron by the development of new methods for utilizing low-grade iron ore, by the more intensive exploitation of old mines, and by the salvaging of scrap iron. So far as trade and industry were concerned, Göring's attitude was expressed in his statement that there must be "cannon before butter." In 1938, on the fifth anniversary of Hitler's accession to power, official figures were released showing that the value of industrial production had doubled since 1933; steel production had mounted from 5,650,000 tons to 20,000,000; and the number of employed had increased from 12,580,000 to 18,370,000. Labor's share of the national income had declined, however, for wages and salaries had fallen from 56.9 per cent of the total in 1932 to 53.6 in 1938.

The "Co-ordination" of the Church

In Germany there were, before the National Socialist revolution, some twenty-nine major Protestant churches, a situation which did not accord with the totalitarian idea. Hitler desired instead that Germany should have one national church (*Reichskirche*) with one national bishop (*Reichsbischof*) at its head, and that it should be subordinate to the state. In order to forestall any possible interference by Hitler, the various Protestant churches took steps in 1933 to create an organization which should bring them all into one German Evangelical Church. The new constitution provided that the head of the new church should be a Lutheran bishop and that he should have co-operating with him a spiritual cabinet representing the non-Lutheran evangelical bodies. There was to be also one national synod to promulgate church legislation. Representatives of the twenty-nine Protestant churches chose as the first bishop of the new church Friedrich von Bodelschwingh, a clergyman widely known for his social-welfare work.

Unfortunately, Ludwig Müller, a Nazi army chaplain and one of Hitler's chief advisers on religious matters, desired to be bishop of the new church, and he at once issued a statement announcing that Nazi Protestants could not accept Bodelschwingh's election. His opposition led Hitler to interfere and a referendum on the new constitution was ordered, at which time delegates to the national synod and members of local church boards were also to be elected. In the days before the church elections the Nazis turned the full force of their political machine to the advantage of the Nazi Protestants. Press and radio publicity was limited to the pronouncements of the latter, and on the eve of the elections Hitler, in a radio address, once more raised the specter of Communism and appealed to the Protestants to elect representatives who would support the new political regime. The result was a foregone conclusion; the Nazi Protestants won by a landslide, and the national synod, when constituted, chose Ludwig Müller as Reich Bishop.

Extremists among the Nazi Protestants next sought to make a number of radical changes. They advocated the rejection of the Old Testament, the removal of crucifixes from the churches, and even a revision of the New Testament in such a way as to repudiate the divinity of Jesus Christ. To prevent such innovations in the church several thousand clergy, led by Martin Niemöller, organized the Pastors' Emergency League, which later gave way to the Confessional Synod, to which, rather than to Reich Bishop Müller, the opposition looked for direction in matters of doctrine and discipline. Hundreds of pastors were thereupon arrested, suspended, transferred, or deprived of their incomes because of their refusal to obey Müller. Eventually, in September, 1935, Hitler definitely placed the Evangelical Church under state control, and the minister for church affairs decreed that all groups which in the future attempted to interfere with state control of the church would be suppressed. Niemöller was finally sent to a concentration camp.

Meanwhile, in accordance with the Nazi totalitarian idea, Hitler, using Papen as his emissary, had sought and obtained a single concordat with the Holy See to replace the existing three concordats between the church and the governments of Prussia, Bavaria, and Baden. By the terms of the concordat Catholic clergy were forbidden to take any part in German politics, and the Vatican withdrew any support it had previously given to the German Center parties. All bishops and archbishops in Germany were to be German citizens and were to be appointed by the Holy See only after consultation with the German government. The Catholic religion in Germany was placed on an even footing with the Protestant faith and was guaranteed the same rights and privileges as the latter. The Nazi government recognized the Catholic Action as a nonpolitical organization under the leadership of which the Vatican might concentrate its efforts on the development of nonpolitical Catholic groups. Catholic schools, youth organizations, workers' associations, and cultural societies were to be unmolested so long as they did not concern themselves with politics.

As might perhaps have been expected, friction soon developed over the interpretation of certain articles of the concordat dealing with schools and youth organizations. In the last analysis, the Nazis were determined to limit the activities of the Catholic Action, to absorb the Catholic Youth Movement, to suppress the confessional schools, to destroy the Catholic workingmen's societies, and to abolish freedom of the Catholic press. Friction was further increased in 1935 when the Nazis charged that money and foreign exchange were being smuggled out of Germany by members of the Catholic secular and regular clergy contrary to German decrees. Millions of marks in fines were levied by the government. During 1936, despite the provisions of the concordat, the government continued its efforts to put an end to education by Catholic schools. By pressure upon parents the Nazis succeeded in reducing registrations for Catholic schools in some parts of southern Germany almost to the vanishing point. Ultimately the pope was led to protest, and to call upon German Catholics to rally to defend the freedom of the church. The government, nevertheless, in June, 1937, dissolved hundreds of Catholic schools in Bavaria, converting them into secular institutions. In the following year it was announced that not only the elementary schools of the church but the secondary schools as well were to be closed.

Anti-Semitism

But the woes of the Protestant and Catholic Christians of Germany were as nothing compared with those of the Jews. For years Hitler and his colleagues, in order to popularize their program and win members to the National Socialist Party, had carried on a bitter anti-Semitic campaign. It was not surprising, therefore, that the Nazi political victory in March was at once followed by numerous attacks upon Jews by Nazi storm troopers.

These early outbursts of physical violence were soon followed by many measures which, while not so violent, nevertheless made the Jews objects of persecution and deliberate discrimination. It was decreed that no person of non-Aryan descent [3] or married to one of non-Aryan descent could be eligible for appointment as an official of the national government, the states, the municipalities, or any kind of public or legal corporation, institution, or endowment. Non-Aryan civil servants were required to resign unless they had been already employed at the outbreak of the First World War or unless they had fought at the front or lost a father or son in the war. Likewise—subject to the same conditions—it was decreed that admission to the bar might be refused to Jewish lawyers, that Jews might be struck off the roll of patent-lawyers, that Jewish notaries should be "urgently advised" to refrain from exercising their calling. All Jewish judges were "invited" to apply for leaves without delay, and all Jewish court clerks and court attachés were ordered dismissed. Similar steps were taken in the medical profession, where Jewish doctors were deprived of the right to serve as panel doctors in the national health-insurance service [4] and were excluded from practice on clients of private companies insuring against illness. Various state and municipal authorities went so far as to issue orders expelling Jewish physicians from hospitals and forbidding Jewish nurses to practice.

---

[3] "Non-Aryan descent means descent from non-Aryan, and especially Jewish, parents or grandparents, even though only one of the parents or grandparents was of the Jewish religion."

[4] Great numbers of the younger physicians and many of the older ones received a large part of their professional income from their panel practice.

Tens of thousands of Jewish professional men, business men, teachers, writers, musicians, artists, and artisans felt the heavy hand of the Nazi regime as it ruthlessly deprived them of their accustomed means of livelihood.

In the realm of education it was decreed that Jewish students must not comprise more than 1.5 per cent of those entering schools, colleges, and universities, and that all Jewish students already attending such institutions should be dismissed in so far as their numbers exceeded 5 per cent of the total attendance. Jewish university professors and teachers in secondary schools were progressively dismissed from their positions and deprived of their licenses to teach or lecture. Even such a world-renowned scholar as Professor Albert Einstein, the physicist, incurred the wrath of the German Nazis. In an attempt to "extirpate the un-German spirit" from the public libraries, on May 10, 1933, the books of some 160 writers were burned at inquisitional stakes in various university towns. The seeds of anti-Semitism, so lavishly sown by Nazi agitators before 1933, thus bore abundant fruit.

Additional steps were taken in 1935 to define the status of Jews in Germany and to restrict them further in their political and social life. Jews were defined as those having more than two Jewish grandparents, and Jewish "hybrids" as those having less than three Jewish grandparents. Jews were specifically deprived of German citizenship. They were, however, to be subjects of the state; that is to say, although barred from voting and holding office, they would still have obligations to the state. A decree "for the protection of German blood and honor" forbade marriages between Germans and Jews and between Germans and Jewish "hybrids" who were half-Jews. In 1938 it was announced officially that the number of persons affected by these laws was between 800,000 and 1,000,000.

The government was apparently determined to hasten the emigration of Jews by bringing economic pressure to bear upon them. In April, 1938, for instance, all Jews possessing property worth more than 5000 marks in Germany or abroad were required to declare their holdings. This property, it was stated, would "be used in harmony with the needs of the German economy." Another decree forbade Jews to sell their property without official permission, or to open any new Jewish business or branch business. Later still another order deprived the Jews of access to their safe deposit boxes except in the presence of a Nazi observer. Still another decree deprived all Jewish physicians of their permits to engage in any medical practice after September 30, 1938. In November of that year, using as an excuse the assassination of a secretary of the German embassy in Paris by a Polish Jew, the Nazis subjected the German Jews to a brutal persecution. Thousands were arrested; many were reported executed. Jewish shops were looted, synagogues were burned, and the Jews collectively were fined

one billion marks. Nazi decrees closed all universities, high schools, theaters, and movies to Jews, and forbade them to engage in retail trade or
mail-order or commission business. Such persecution foreshadowed the
ruthless measures of the Nazis in an effort to exterminate all Jews under
their control during the Second World War.

Nazi Politics and Foreign Policy

It might reasonably have been expected that, after Hitler received dictatorial powers, he would not feel called upon to consult the German electorate. But this proved not to be true. Three times, when the nationalism
of the German people had been roused to a high pitch as a result of
some step taken by the Führer, elections or plebiscites were held to prove
the popular support of the Nazi regime. On one other occasion, after stirring events within the Reich, a plebiscite was held to show that Hitler's
deeds were sanctioned by the German people. The latter, therefore, though
ruled by a dictator, continued to have the privilege—the duty, according to
the Nazis—of expressing themselves in favor of the dictatorship through
popular elections.

The first of these elections was held to show that the Germans supported
Hitler in the first step in his foreign policy. As already pointed out, in
October, 1933, Germany withdrew from the Disarmament Conference,
the League of Nations, and the International Labor Organization because of the delay in granting the Reich equality in armaments.[5] At the
time that Hitler announced these steps the Reichstag was dissolved and
new elections were set for November 12. In the weeks preceding the
plebiscite Hitler pleaded with the Germans to cast their votes to show the
world that they were "solidly behind the stand formulated by me against
our country's accepting a position of inferiority to other countries." Of the
43,000,000 Germans who participated in the first national plebiscite and
election under the Nazi regime, more than 40,500,000 gave their approval
of the policy of the Reich government, and more than 39,500,000 voted in
favor of the Nazi list of Reichstag candidates.

Meanwhile, a dangerous cleavage was developing within the ranks of the
Nazis, who had been drawn from widely differing economic and social
groups. Anyone who seriously studied the Nazi program realized that it
contained goals that were distinctly in conflict one with another, and that,
when the time should come to put the program into effect, some of the
groups that had rallied to Hitler's standard would inevitably be disappointed. During the first half of the year 1934, the Left elements of the
party became restless because of Hitler's failure to carry into effect his

[5] See page 430.

earlier socialistic, anticapitalistic, and anti-Junker promises. Apparently Ernst Röhm, chief of staff of the Nazi storm troops, assumed leadership among the discontented elements of the party, who desired a "second revolution" which should carry into fuller effect the socialistic features of the original Nazi program.

According to Hitler's official statement, issued later, Röhm and a small group of ambitious storm-troop leaders spent some months in preparing for action. They feared that Hitler planned to lessen the importance of the storm troops and therefore plotted to forestall Hitler's action by seizing power for themselves. The discontented Left elements, they hoped, would rally to their side against the existing regime. On June 29, 1934, Hitler struck before the "plot" could be carried out. Apparently lists of those to be killed had been carefully prepared in advance, for Hitler's agents seemed to know exactly who were to be found. Within a few hours, in a reign of terror, seventy-four persons, according to the official statement, were summarily killed with little or no hearing. The complete list was never published. Hitler's defense of his summary action was that "I was responsible for the fate of the German nation and therefore I myself was the German people's Supreme Tribunal for those twenty-four hours."

Germany had hardly had time to calm down when on August 2, 1934, President Hindenburg died. Hitler at once assumed the functions of the president in addition to those of chancellor and thus became probably the world's most powerful ruler. He declined to assume the title of president, however, and requested that he be addressed as in the past as "Leader" or "Reich Chancellor." Desiring that the cabinet's action in combining the presidency and the chancellorship should have the approval of the German people, Hitler ordered another plebiscite to be held. Once again all the oratorical artillery of the Nazis was brought into action. A document described as the "political testament" of the late president, indicating Hindenburg's approval of Hitler's policies, was published on August 15. Two days later the chancellor made an appeal to the people in a national broadcast. Of the 43,529,710 ballots cast in the plebiscite, 38,362,760, or approximately 88 per cent, were in the affirmative.

Meanwhile, the Nazis had attempted to advance toward their goal of bringing all Germans into the Third Reich. Apparently in order that Germany might be undisturbed in her efforts to consummate the *Anschluss* with Austria and to redeem the Saar, the Reich government in January, 1934, had signed with Poland a ten-year nonaggression pact recognizing the inviolability of Germany's eastern frontiers. The Nazis then concentrated their attention on Austria and sought to "co-ordinate" that little German republic by a Nazi terror which culminated in the murder of the Austrian Chancellor Dollfuss and the abortive Nazi *Putsch* of July,

1934.[6] But the failure of the Austrians to support the *Putsch* and more especially Mussolini's prompt action in rushing Italian troops to the Austro-Italian frontier prevented the Nazis from seizing the Austrian government. In the Saar plebiscite in the following January, however, the Nazis were more successful, and in March, 1935, that German territory was incorporated in the Third Reich.[7] In other territory lost to Germany by the treaty of Versailles Hitler's policy was at first one of "Nazification." In 1935 the governments of Danzig and of Memel both came under the control of local Nazi parties which were linked with the Hitler organization in Germany.[8]

In the following year a third plebiscite was held after Hitler had made spectacular moves to regain full sovereignty for the Reich. In March, 1935, Hitler repudiated the military and naval restrictions of the treaty of Versailles, and in 1936 he remilitarized the Rhineland in defiance of the same treaty and of the Locarno pact as well. In the latter year, too, he denounced the clauses of the peace treaty which internationalized the Rhine, Elbe, Danube, and Oder rivers and the Kiel Canal. Confident, no doubt, that a plebiscite held under such conditions would be overwhelmingly favorable, Hitler called for elections in March, 1936. On this occasion nearly 45,000,000 voters went to the polls. After the votes were counted, it was announced that 99 per cent had been cast in favor of the Führer's foreign policy.

Although the Nazi foreign policy undoubtedly had emancipated and strengthened Germany as a military power, it had had an unfortunate effect upon her international position. By 1936 the Nazi drive against Communists and the Nazi program for eastern expansion had driven Russia into a Franco-Soviet military alliance; the Nazi attempt to absorb Austria had alienated Mussolini and facilitated a Franco-Italian *rapprochement;* and the Nazi rearmament program had alarmed Great Britain and forced her into what was practically an Anglo-Franco-Belgian alliance against Germany. In 1936 Germany stood practically isolated among the great powers of Europe.

But Hitler soon removed the chief cause of friction between Mussolini and himself. In July, 1936, Germany signed an agreement with Austria recognizing the independence of the latter and pledging herself not to interfere in Austria's domestic political life. Thereafter Mussolini and Hitler co-operated to a large extent in their foreign policies. Germany joined Italy in aiding the Spanish Insurgents, and Italy in turn supported Germany by signing the anti-Comintern pact which Germany and Japan

---

[6] See pages 573–574.
[7] See page 639.
[8] See page 589.

"THE SAAR IS GERMAN!"

Crowds in Saarbrücken giving the "Heil, Hitler!" after the announcement of the result of the Saar plebiscite.

concluded in November, 1936. The Rome-Berlin-Tokyo Axis was thus created.

Hitler next gained control of Germany's new military machine and prepared for a more active foreign policy. In February, 1938, he suddenly dismissed General von Fritsch, commander-in-chief, and thirteen senior generals in the army and air force, abolished the war ministry, and himself assumed the position of "supreme commander of the armed forces." At the same time he removed from the foreign ministry the experienced Baron von Neurath, who had held that position since before the Nazis came into power, and appointed in his place a pliant Nazi tool, Joachim von Ribbentrop. The "conservative" ambassadors to Italy, Japan, and Austria were also recalled. By this purge Hitler definitely strengthened the Nazi control of the Reich's army and foreign policy.

Evidence of an "activist" foreign policy was soon forthcoming. On February 12 occurred the famous interview between Hitler and Chancellor Schuschnigg of Austria in which the former by threats forced the latter to admit Austrian Nazis into his government. One month later came the overthrow of Schuschnigg's government and the absorption of Austria into the Third Reich,[9] which was thus increased in population to 74,000,000. The "activist" policy seemed to be highly successful; one more objective in Hitler's announced policy had been attained. On April 10, 1938, another plebiscite revealed that more than 99 per cent of the voters in Germany loyally supported Hitler.

With the German people thus apparently lending their support, the Nazis continued their aggressive foreign policy in the succeeding months. In September, 1938, they precipitated the Munich crisis,[10] as a result of which the Reich annexed the Sudetenland. Six months later, in March, 1939, Hitler destroyed Czechoslovakia altogether.[11] Bohemia and Moravia were for all practical purposes absorbed by the Reich, and Slovakia was made a dependent ally. In the same month, too, Hitler "redeemed" Memel by forcing Lithuania to cede that city to Germany.

Doubtless emboldened by these successes and confident of the superiority of the German military forces and *Luftwaffe,* Hitler next determined to continue the Reich's *Drang nach Osten* at the expense of Poland. Despite the warnings of Great Britain and France that they would enter the war if Germany attacked Poland, in September, 1939, Hitler launched an attack against that state.[12] By so doing he precipitated the Second World War, which eventually brought upon the German homeland destruction far worse than any suffered by that country since the Thirty Years' War.

[9] See pages 651–652.
[10] See pages 653–657.
[11] See page 658.
[12] See page 664.

Chapter XVIII

GREAT BRITAIN AND IRELAND

THE European great power which wavered least in its loyalty to the liberal tradition during the years following the First World War was Great Britain, which, more than any other country in Europe, displayed a deep attachment to political democracy and a continued concern for social justice. In the first decade after the war, for instance, two acts were passed to extend popular control of the government. The Representation of the People Act in 1918 conferred a parliamentary vote on all men twenty-one years of age who could qualify by six months' residence or by the occupation of business premises, and on all women thirty years of age who were local government electors or wives of such electors. The act also provided for the redistribution of representatives in accordance with the principle of single-member constituencies of approximately equal size, and the limiting of an elector's vote to not more than two constituencies. Ten years later the ballot was extended to all women on the same age basis as to men. These two acts, it was estimated, added nearly 13,000,000 new voters to the registers.

Social Legislation

Although in the first half of the nineteenth century Great Britain had begun to enact laws regulating hours and conditions of labor, she had been much slower than Germany to enact so-called social legislation. Nevertheless, during the period of Liberal government just before the First World War laws had been passed providing for workmen's compensation in cases of accidents or sickness, old age pensions, unemployment insurance, and labor exchanges.[1] In the interwar years the scope of these laws was further extended. The Unemployment Insurance Act was modified to cover all wage workers, except those in agriculture or household service; and when the operation of the act did not adequately meet the situation in times of unusual economic depression, the government itself contributed large sums to provide unemployment benefits—sometimes called "doles." Further social legislation was enacted. For example, a new act for widows', orphans' and old-age pensions, based on the prin-

[1] See pages 183–184.

ciple that the state, the employer, and the worker should each contribute to the fund, provided that every insured worker should receive a pension at the age of sixty-five, and that, if he died before that age, his widow and children should receive pensions. Furthermore, better schooling facilities were provided and underprivileged children were fed and provided with medical care.

Acts were also passed providing for the building of inexpensive houses with the aid of government subsidies. In the years between the two world wars approximately 4,250,000 dwellings (almost half as many as existed in 1919) were constructed. More than 40 per cent of them were financed wholly or in part by the national or local governments. In 1933, for instance, a five-year plan to replace 300,000 slum quarters with better dwellings was inaugurated by the national government and was largely completed before the outbreak of the Second World War. The new dwellings were more comfortable and convenient than the old, and helped to bring better health and more contentment to British workers. Generally speaking, Great Britain assured the bulk of her workers food, shelter, and medical care.

According to one investigator [2] who made studies of social and economic conditions in the manufacturing city of York in 1899 and again in 1939, workers' living standards had risen about 30 per cent. He found that the workers' real income had increased almost 40 per cent during the period, although the working week had been reduced on an average by from six to ten hours. The number of wage workers who lived near the destitution level had been halved, though in 1939 approximately 7 per cent were still in that category. The lot of children had greatly improved, especially in matters of health and education. Between 1899 and 1939 the child mortality rate had fallen from 160 to 54 per thousand. In 1899 no children of wage workers attended secondary schools; in 1939 about 1200 of them were in attendance. According to this investigator, these improvements in the living standards of workers and their families resulted chiefly from the government's social welfare measures. Still greater advances might have been made, had Britain not been seriously handicapped by a decline in her export trade.

Trade Decline and Unemployment

For a time after the armistice of 1918, thanks to the great demand for commodities in European countries long isolated from the rest of the world by the war, British trade prospered. But toward the close of 1920 the business boom collapsed, and in the next year exports fell off about one

[2] R. S. Rowntree, *Poverty: A Study of Town Life* (1901) and *Poverty and Progress* (1941).

half. During the succeeding years Great Britain's foreign trade never reached its prewar figure.

Various circumstances—some temporary, some permanent—accounted for Great Britain's plight. The war of 1914–1918 had impoverished the world's purchasing power so that, after the first spurt in buying, purchases were greatly curtailed. The situation was further aggravated by the inflation of many continental currencies at the very time when Great Britain was deflating her own. This situation worked to the great disadvantage of British manufacturers, who were forced to compete in foreign markets with goods produced where labor was relatively cheaper because of the depreciated currency in which it was paid. Furthermore, the war had ended in the creation of numerous new states, and each, led by an excessive national zeal, began to erect "political dams across the economic streams of Europe." National tariffs inevitably interfered with the flow of British goods to their accustomed markets.

The British coal industry was particularly hard hit. In prewar years Great Britain had been accustomed to export some 62,500,000 tons of coal annually, but the rapid development of new sources of power decreased the demand for raw coal. Germany's delivery of coal to France and Italy as part of her reparations payments further lessened the demand for British coal. But the staple industries were also seriously affected, in this case chiefly because the spread of the Industrial Revolution was depriving British industries of long-monopolized markets. The expansion of cotton manufacturing in India, China, and Japan, for example, was seriously felt in Lancashire. Outside Europe, Britain's exports of cotton cloth in the postwar years were only about half as great as before 1914. Old plants and antiquated methods, furthermore, handicapped many British industries in meeting competition. Because of the decline in export trade, factories were forced to curtail production. The volume of British shipping naturally decreased, and the demand for new ships for a time largely disappeared. The important shipbuilding industry was therefore also adversely affected.

With the collapse of Britain's commerce in 1921 came a rapid increase in unemployment. At the beginning of the year over one million were out of work; by the middle of the year the number had considerably more than doubled; and in subsequent years it rose as high as three million. The various British governments as they succeeded one another were inevitably compelled to wrestle with the problem of trade deficits and unemployment.

The Lloyd George Coalition

Great Britain emerged from the First World War with a coalition government. The exigencies of the war had brought a reorganization of the government in 1915, when Asquith had become the head of a coalition ministry composed of representatives of the Liberal, Conservative, and Labor parties. In 1916 a further change had occurred when Lloyd George forced Asquith out of the premiership and himself assumed the office. Politics had been "adjourned" in Great Britain for the duration of the war, so that the dissolution of Parliament which should regularly have occurred in 1915 had been postponed. When the armistice was signed, therefore, eight years had elapsed since the last election. It was high time for the electorate to be consulted. Parliament was at once dissolved, and new elections were set for December 14, 1918. Lloyd George appealed for the continuation of the war coalition. Asquith, however, denounced the coalition and entered the lists at the head of a party known as the Independent Liberals, and the Labor Party, declining longer to participate in the coalition, waged a campaign to increase its own parliamentary strength.

The result of the voting was an overwhelming victory for the Lloyd George coalition. Asquith's Independent Liberals managed to capture only 28 seats, but Labor increased its representation to 63. Lloyd George therefore had a large majority over all opposition groups. But the character of the majority must have given the Liberal leader pause, for it was made up five to two of Conservatives. In the reconstitution of the ministry in January, 1919, this fact was reflected. The proportion of Conservatives became so great that the coalition ceased to be predominantly Liberal in tone, and Great Britain was presented with the anomalous spectacle of an extreme Liberal at the head of a government consisting largely of Conservatives.

Lloyd George took two major steps in an effort to rehabilitate British trade and industry. On March 16, 1921, a provisional trade agreement was signed with Russia providing for the resumption of trade and commerce between the two countries pending the conclusion of a formal general peace treaty which should regulate their economic and political relations in the future. Later in the year the Safeguarding of Industries Act was passed to protect key industries which would be vital in the event of future war, and to protect British industry against the competition of cheap foreign commodities. For these purposes the act provided for a 33⅓ per cent duty to safeguard certain special industries, and for a tax on imports from countries with depreciated currencies. This partial abandonment of Great Britain's traditional policy of free trade aroused much opposition from Liberals and Laborites.

Meanwhile, as the years passed, Lloyd George discovered that the Conservative portion of his coalition was becoming restless. The good effect of the partial adoption of the Conservative policy of protection was nullified by his conclusion in 1921 of the Anglo-Irish treaty recognizing the Irish Free State. Conservative leaders, notably Bonar Law and Stanley Baldwin, moreover, were eager to secure freedom of action for their party and quietly fostered a movement looking toward secession. Finally, in October, 1922, the Conservative Party declared its independence and decided to enter the approaching electoral campaign as a separate party with its own leader and its own program.

With the defection of the Conservatives the coalition government was doomed. Lloyd George immediately resigned, and Bonar Law was called upon to head a new ministry. The government which the latter organized was drawn entirely from the ranks of the Conservatives and was the first homogeneous ministry since 1915. Parliament was dissolved, and new elections were called for November, 1922. In the ensuing campaign Lloyd George led what was known as the National Liberal Party, but Asquith and his Independent Liberals continued their active opposition and held aloof. The real struggle was between the Conservatives and the Laborites. Fear of the supposed radical tendencies of the Labor Party and hope of obtaining once more a one-party parliamentary government both helped to place the Conservatives in power with a majority over all opposition parties. Although the Conservatives won a great electoral victory, the achievement of the Labor Party was of even greater note. With the 142 seats which the Labor Party now controlled it became the second largest group in Parliament and therefore stepped into the position of "His Majesty's Opposition."

The Question of Free Trade or Protection

Bonar Law became prime minister in the new Conservative government, but ill health forced him to hand over the position to his lieutenant, Stanley Baldwin, in May, 1923. The latter, haunted by the specter of unemployment, resolved that some drastic step must be taken to revive British industry, and announced his determination to introduce a protective tariff on manufactured goods. But the Conservatives had taken office with the general understanding that they would embark upon no aggressive or radical program without further consulting the electorate. Such a radical departure from the long-accepted British policy of free trade, therefore, called for an appeal to the people, and Baldwin, recognizing this, dissolved Parliament and went to the country on the issue of protection.

The Conservatives argued that the whole world was erecting tariff barriers against British goods and that British duties might be utilized as a means of forcing reductions in these foreign tariffs. They asserted that the British Empire was economically sufficient unto itself and advocated Joseph Chamberlain's earlier scheme of imperial preference. They promised to keep raw materials on the free list, to place no tax on such foodstuffs as wheat and meat, and to reduce duties on tea and sugar. The opposition parties argued, on the other hand, that in an exporting country like Great Britain protection could not cure chronic unemployment. Among the Liberals personalities were subordinated in the face of Baldwin's attack upon their cherished free-trade principle, and a reconciliation, at least superficial, was brought about between the followers of Asquith and the Welsh leader. Although as a result of the election of 1923 the Conservatives still retained the largest number of seats, their former safe majority over all opposing parties was transformed into a decided minority. Labor maintained its position as the chief opposition party by raising its total representation in the Commons to 192. The reunited Liberals stood third with 158. A majority of the electorate appeared to favor the traditional policy of free trade.

Britain's First Labor Government

The outcome of the election entailed a change in the government. Clearly Baldwin had been rejected on the platform of protection, but on the other hand no single party now controlled a majority. Either a coalition or a minority government therefore became necessary. But none of the parties appeared anxious to merge its identity in a coalition again. The outcome was the resignation of the Baldwin ministry and the elevation of Ramsay MacDonald (January 22, 1924) to the premiership as the head of Great Britain's first Labor government.

But the change in government entailed no radical departure from well-established British policies by the introduction of anything suggestive of Bolshevism, for, in the words of MacDonald, "Our Labor movement has never had the least inclination to try short cuts to the millennium." In fact, one of the reasons why the Labor Party had increased so rapidly was the growing recognition by the British people of the essentially constitutional character of the movement. A second reason why nothing radical was to be expected in the way of legislation was the fact that Labor was dependent upon one of the other parties for the support necessary to enact any measure. Consequently Labor was compelled to defer its plans for nationalizing some of Britain's basic industries.

The Laborites were almost immediately confronted with an epidemic of serious strikes, but by their firmness in handling the strikers, who came from their own ranks, they gained the confidence and respect of the country at large. This confidence was retained by their handling of the fiscal problem, in which nothing especially radical was undertaken. The tax on cheap amusements was repealed, and, in spite of the vigorous protests of the protected interests, the protective duties inaugurated by Lloyd George were abolished.

MacDonald believed that British industry might be improved by further extending the markets for British goods in Russia, and that this extension could be obtained by recognizing the Soviet government. On February 1, 1924, only nine days after he became premier, he therefore gave *de jure* recognition. Two months later an Anglo-Soviet Conference convened in London for the purpose of negotiating a general treaty of amity and commerce to replace the provisional trade agreement of 1921, and to effect a settlement of the claims arising out of the Soviet government's repudiation of Russia's debts and the confiscation of private property. Two treaties were finally drafted and signed, the immediate effect of which would be the favorable treatment of British goods in Russian markets.

These Russian treaties were immediately attacked not only by the Conservatives but even by Lloyd George, who had been responsible for the first trade agreement of 1921. Without a majority to support him, MacDonald dissolved Parliament and appealed to the electorate. For the third time in two years the British voters were called upon for a decision. In this campaign both the Conservatives and the Liberals directed their attacks against Labor, and the latter's prospects were injured by the publication, shortly before the election, of a letter purporting to be from Zinoviev, the head of the Third International, urging British Communists to prepare the way for a revolution in Great Britain.

In the election of 1924, although Labor piled up a total of 5,500,000 popular votes, its parliamentary representation was reduced to 155. Since the Liberals elected only 36 members, the Conservatives were swept back into power with a top-heavy parliamentary majority of over two hundred, though they obtained less than a majority of the popular vote. With such a Conservative majority in the House, Baldwin of course returned to Downing Street, and MacDonald stepped down to his earlier position of leader of the opposition.

Five Years of Conservative Government

But the change in government brought no immediate improvement in Britain's economic situation. During the ensuing year the production of coal, iron ore, and pig iron, the basic industries of the kingdom, remained considerably below the prewar figure. In the hope of "safeguarding employment" and, incidentally, of satisfying certain British industrial interests, Baldwin returned to the tariff policy inaugurated by Lloyd George and afterward repealed by the Labor government. Over the protests of the opposition, who declared that he was violating his campaign pledges, a plan for partial protection was enacted.

The coal industry, in which the industrial depression was most pronounced, profited little from this scheme, however. The price of coal continued to fall, and the operators, in order to cut the cost of production, asked the miners to lengthen the working day from seven to eight hours and to accept a cut in wages. The miners refused to agree to these proposals, whereupon the operators availed themselves of a provision of the existing wage agreement to terminate it on July 31, 1925. In order to prevent a coal strike the government then subsidized the industry until May 1, 1926, pending a permanent settlement. Before that date a royal commission under Sir Herbert Samuel made an investigation of the coal industry. In its report it stated that three fourths of the coal raised was being produced at a loss. It recommended national ownership of the mines and an extensive reorganization of the industry. It declared that the coal industry was facing disaster and that wage reductions were necessary.

When the mine operators notified the miners that the existing wage agreement would end on May 1, the latter decided to strike. The Trades Union Congress, in order to assist the miners, thereupon called a sympathetic strike in certain vital industries, including the transport services and the printing trade. In popular belief Great Britain faced a "general strike," but this was hardly the case. Less than half of the six million trade-union members were called out, and it was specifically ordered that work should not cease in electric and gas, sanitary, and health and food services. The government at once declared a state of emergency and issued an appeal for volunteers to maintain the essential services. The generous response to this appeal more than any other factor contributed to the failure of the sympathetic strike.

The "general strike" lasted only nine days. On May 12 the Trades Union Congress announced the decision to end it with the understanding that negotiations would be resumed regarding the wages of miners. These, however, resulted in no agreement. In July Parliament passed the Mines Act providing for an eight-hour day in the coal industry, but the act produced no coal, and it became necessary to import large quantities from Germany and the United States. Finally, after more than seven months, the strike came officially to an end on November 19, 1926, with the complete surrender of the miners' unions. Their submission was forced by the exhaustion of their resources and by their inability to prevent numbers of miners from returning to work. With winter coming on, longer hours and lower wages seemed preferable to no work at all.

The Conservative Party, never particularly sympathetic with trade unions or the labor movement, availed itself of the state of public opinion and the exhaustion of labor after the great strike of 1926 to pass the Trades Disputes and Trades Union Act in the following year. By the terms of this law, a general strike became illegal, picketing was forbidden, and no member might be disciplined by a trade union for refusing to participate in an illegal strike. The Trades Dispute Act of 1906 was repealed in so far as it exempted trade unions from legal suit, and trade-union funds might be enjoined by the attorney-general. A blow was struck at the Labor Party by including a provision that trade unions might make political levies on their members only if the latter gave specific permission in writing. Formerly the law had stated that such levies might be made unless a member formally protested.

In foreign affairs the Conservative government largely continued the spirit of co-operation and conciliation so happily inaugurated by the Labor premier. Only in respect to Russia was the latter's foreign policy completely reversed. On May 12, 1927, in the alleged belief that certain secret documents which had disappeared from the British War Office had come into Russian possession, the government raided the offices of Arcos, Ltd., the headquarters of Russia's trading agency in Great Britain. Although the lost documents were not discovered, the government declared that considerable evidence was found of Russian military espionage in Great Britain and of other revolutionary activities in the British Empire. As a result, Parliament voted to sever all relations with the Soviet government.

Meanwhile, despite the establishment of many new industries in southern England and the noticeable shift of industrial population into that region, and despite the fact that London in general was prosperous, the economic condition of the country as a whole was unsatisfactory. The chief measures taken to meet the situation were designed to safeguard certain British industries from foreign competition and to relieve them from the burden of local taxation. By 1929 industries producing motorcars, silk and artificial yarns, clocks and watches, cinematograph films, gloves, cutlery, china, and rubber tires and tubes were being "protected by the back door." By the reform in local taxation the great basic industries were relieved to the extent of 75 per cent of the local taxes. In general, however, Baldwin advocated a policy of *laissez faire* toward business as a cure for unemployment.

Inevitably the problem of unemployment and rehabilitation of British trade was again the outstanding issue in the general elections of May,

1929. "The great need of the day," declared one influential journal, "is a positive policy for dealing with unemployment by promoting industrial recovery as well as by providing immediate work. The party that has the best unemployment policy deserves to be the next government." The elections brought an increase in Labor's representation in the Commons from 160 to 289, while the Conservatives declined from 396 to 259. Owing to the fact that the Liberal Party elected 58 candidates, however, no party controlled a majority. But it was apparent that the Conservatives had been rejected, and Stanley Baldwin at once resigned the premiership. On June 5, 1929, Ramsay MacDonald for the second time accepted the king's invitation to form a government.

The Second Labor Government

The second Labor government, like the first, was handicapped in carrying out its domestic policies by dependence upon either the Liberals or the Conservatives for support. In foreign affairs MacDonald returned to his earlier policy toward Soviet Russia. In December, 1929, full diplomatic relations were resumed with the Soviet government, on the latter's promise to abstain from subversive propaganda within the British Empire. This step led in April, 1930, to an Anglo-Russian trade treaty which provided for most-favored-nation treatment in commerce between the two countries. The treaty further stipulated that the general offices of the Russian trading corporation in Great Britain should be inviolate, thus obviating the possibility of another raid like that on the offices of Arcos, Ltd., in 1927. Finally, the treaty provided that the British government would guarantee a credit of $150,000,000 to be employed in financing Russian purchases in Great Britain during the ensuing two years.

Meanwhile, general business conditions in Great Britain improved not at all. Exports of manufactured goods declined in 1929. In 1930 the iron and steel trade fell to the lowest point in four years, and the depression in cotton manufacturing was considered the worst since the American Civil War. In 1930 the country's foreign trade declined by over $1,650,000,-000. Naturally, these figures were reflected in the growth of unemployment. When Labor took office the unemployed numbered approximately 1,000,000; within a year the number had increased to over 1,700,000; and early in 1931 it reached the highest point since the war with more than 2,600,000 out of work. The government was, in general, helpless to remedy the economic situation, but it did take care of those without work. It not only contributed tens of millions of dollars, as its share, to the unemployment insurance fund, but advanced hundreds of millions more in the form of loans to the fund, which went steadily further into debt.

The severe drain upon the British budget, resulting from increasing expenditures and decreasing tax receipts, became evident when the fiscal year 1929–1930 closed with a deficit instead of the contemplated surplus. The deficit in the following year was still greater, and that for the year 1931–1932 appeared likely to reach $600,000,000. The prospect of such a seriously unbalanced budget caused alarm both within and without the kingdom. Gold began to flow in large amounts from Great Britain to the Continent. London, which served as a bank of deposit for foreign funds, was fatally handicapped by the "standstill" agreement following the Hoover moratorium, which temporarily "froze" large sums that had been loaned by the Bank of England to Germany and other countries.

At this point came the report of the May Committee of financial experts which had been appointed to make recommendations to the chancellor of the exchequer. In order definitely to balance the budget the experts suggested some slight additional taxation, but particularly recommended severe reductions in expenditures for pensions, salaries, defense, public works, and social services. Laborites immediately denounced the report on the ground that approximately 90 per cent of the reductions suggested would be at the expense of the classes from which the Labor Party drew its chief support. Economies such as these, they claimed, did not constitute "a general sacrifice." They demanded, instead, that the deficit be met chiefly by increased taxation. When Ramsay MacDonald and Philip Snowden, chancellor of the exchequer, decided to accept the experts' recommendations, the Labor Party split, and the Labor government was forced to resign (August 24, 1931).

The National Governments: Economic Problems

MacDonald, apparently placing loyalty to Britain's welfare above loyalty to party pledges, organized a coalition ministry of Laborites, Conservatives, and Liberals which became known as the National government. Philip Snowden, J. H. Thomas, and Lord Sankey followed their leader into the new government, and for this step they and MacDonald were read out of the Labor Party.

In September, 1931, Snowden submitted a supplementary budget which in general followed the recommendations of the May Committee. Drastic economies were effected in national expenditures by decreasing the amount spent on social services, on army, navy, and air forces, and on government salaries. Meanwhile, the flow of gold from London had continued. Speedy action was needed, and on September 21 Parliament suspended the gold standard.

In October the National government went to the country in a general election, the outcome of which was an amazing triumph for the National government, which received 554 seats in a House of Commons of 615. This huge total was composed of 471 Conservatives, 68 National Liberals, 13 National Laborites, and 2 independents. The 267 seats which the Labor Party had held before dissolution were cut to 52. With the Conservatives so overwhelmingly returned it was thought that Stanley Baldwin might head a new government, but instead he gave MacDonald free rein to choose his ministers. The latter's fourth cabinet, as finally organized in November, 1931, consisted of eleven Conservatives, five National Liberals, and four National Laborites.

Three major domestic problems confronted the National government in the years that followed. The first was that of maintaining a balanced national budget. This it succeeded in doing for five years—at the cost of permitting Britain to fall behind Germany in the matter of armaments. Beginning with the so-called defense or rearmament budget for 1936–1937, despite considerable increases in taxes, huge expenditures for armaments resulted in unbalanced budgets. By 1938 the national debt had risen to the all-time high of £8,000,000,000.

The second problem with which the government wrestled was that of reducing the country's adverse balance of trade. One way to do this was to reduce imports, and a committee of the cabinet recommended a 10-percent tariff on a very wide range of manufactured and semi-manufactured articles. The new tariff was finally approved, and on March 1, 1932, after some eighty years of free trade, Great Britain again became a protectionist country. As a result of this step there did follow a considerable decrease in British imports.

A second way to reduce the adverse trade balance was to increase exports. One step had already been taken which it was hoped would help, namely, the abandonment of the gold standard with the subsequent depreciation of the British pound. This move was expected to lower the cost of production in Great Britain and thus enable British goods to compete on more favorable terms in world markets. In the hope of increasing still further the demand for British goods, the government sent a delegation to the Imperial Economic Conference which met at Ottawa during the summer of 1932. At this conference Great Britain made a number of treaties with various parts of her empire, as a result of which she gained slight advantages for some of her manufactured goods at the expense of nonempire countries. In exchange Great Britain gave the dominions an advantage by placing a duty on foreign wheat.

In subsequent years, by using the British protective tariff as a basis for bargaining, new reciprocal commercial agreements were negotiated with a number of countries for the purpose of increasing British exports, and

WASHINGTON MEETING ON ECONOMIC PROBLEMS, APRIL, 1933

Ramsay MacDonald (England), Cordell Hull (United States), Richard Bennett (Canada), Edouard Herriot (France).

these agreements were further supplemented by a system of import quotas designed to assure exports to some home industries and to control imports in favor of others. At the same time, to strengthen British business at home and to enable it to compete more efficiently abroad, the government adopted policies some of which strongly resembled those of the NRA and the AAA in the United States. Obligatory agreements to fix prices and wages, to control marketing, to abandon inefficient plants and out-of-date equipment, and to set up machinery for the self-regulation of industry were instigated or encouraged by the government. Financial assistance was granted to aid in the rationalization of some of the backward industries. Agricultural subsidies, processing taxes, protective tariffs, and import quotas were used to preserve the home markets against foreign competition. Nevertheless, the adverse trade balances in 1937 and in 1938 were the largest in British history.

The third major problem which faced the government during these years was the perennial one of unemployment. Despite all the efforts of the government to improve the situation, at the end of 1932 the number of unemployed had risen to the highest point reached at any time since the First World War, over 3,000,000 being out of work. By 1937 the number of unemployed had fallen below 1,500,000, but the depression of that year, referred to above, reversed the trend again. Not until men were absorbed in large numbers by expanding war industries and by the national military conscription act was the number of British unemployed materially reduced. Before the outbreak of the Second World War, in certain "depressed areas" in South Wales, in the north of England, and in Scotland the situation remained particularly bad.

The National Government: Politics

Politically, the position of the National government appeared to be weakening in 1934. In by-elections the Labor Party was usually able to reduce the immense majorities received by the National government in 1931. Probably most spectacular was the triumph of the Labor Party in the London County Council election in March, when Labor won a majority for the first time in its history, and displaced the Conservatives who had controlled the Council for a generation. In November Labor repeated its victory by extending its control from four to fifteen of London's twenty-eight boroughs. In other parts of the kingdom somewhat similar shifts in electoral strength were evident.

By clever political strategy in 1935, however, the Conservatives contrived to counter the trend toward Labor. A huge unofficial peace ballot taken earlier in the year had showed that at least 10,000,000 voters favored the

League of Nations and the use of economic sanctions against a warring nation. These millions might be expected to look with favor upon a government which had apparently dared to take the lead at Geneva in imposing sanctions upon Italy following her invasion of Ethiopia.[3] That Britain's Conservative foreign secretary had already conspired with Pierre Laval, French foreign minister, to sabotage those sanctions was not then apparent. On October 25, 1935, Stanley Baldwin, who had succeeded Ramsey MacDonald as prime minister in June of that year, dissolved Parliament and called for new elections. As was expected, the elections resulted in an easy victory for the National government, whose life was thus extended until 1940. As it turned out, in fact, a new Parliament was not elected again until 1945.

The year 1936 saw Great Britain confronted with a constitutional crisis for the first time since 1909–1910. The crisis was precipitated when Edward VIII, who had succeeded to the throne upon the death of his father on January 20, 1936, announced his intention to marry a twice-divorced American woman. Edward argued that his marriage was a private matter on which he was not limited by the advice of his ministers, but the Baldwin government maintained that it was a public act which was bound to affect seriously the monarch's standing not only in Great Britain but in the dominions overseas. Baldwin insisted that the elevation to the British throne of a twice-divorced woman would undermine the prestige of the crown to such an extent that he was doubtful "if anything could restore it."

The king's proposal that Parliament should legalize a morganatic marriage which would not raise his wife to the rank of queen and would exclude their children from the succession was also refused by the government. The House of Commons, realizing that the issue was fundamentally a question of whether the will of the king should prevail over the advice of the cabinet representing Parliament, supported Prime Minister Baldwin.

Faced by this impasse, Edward VIII on December 10 informed Parliament of his decision to renounce the throne. On the next day Parliament passed the Abdication Act giving effect to the king's abdication and regulating the succession to the throne. Edward VIII then gave his official assent to the measure, and that night left England. On December 12 the accession of King George VI and Queen Elizabeth was proclaimed in London. The new king's first act was to confer upon Edward a dukedom and the title of Duke of Windsor. Five months later (May 12, 1937) King George and Queen Elizabeth were crowned at Westminster Abbey in the presence of thousands of representatives of the kingdom, commonwealth, and empire.

[3] See page 642.

Shortly after the coronation Prime Minister Baldwin, who had been so much responsible for the change in monarchs, tendered his resignation and that of his cabinet, and retired from public life. A new ministry, dominated by the Conservatives but including also National Laborites and National Liberals, was organized on May 28 by Neville Chamberlain, son of the Joseph Chamberlain who had led the Unionist secession from the Liberal Party in 1886. Chamberlain at once announced a five-year plan of rearmament which called for an annual expenditure of £300,000,000 and which was to be concentrated on the production of aircraft, warships, air-raid shelters, and munitions. These expenditures seemed tremendous, but they were of course completely dwarfed by those of the Nazis, who since 1933 had been spending annually on an average five times as much for military preparedness. But Chamberlain's name is popularly connected not so much with his inadequate rearmament program as with his futile policy of "appeasement," a policy which is discussed in the later pages of this book.[4]

The British Commonwealth of Nations

According to Prime Minister Baldwin, the British government had been guided to a great degree during the constitutional crisis of 1936 by the advice of the various dominion governments. The fact that it had asked the assent of the dominion parliaments to the Abdication Act was in itself indicative of the change which had occurred since 1914 in the constitutional organization of the empire over which Great Britain had so long presided. During the First World War an imperial conference had recommended that the self-governing dominions be recognized as autonomous nations of an imperial commonwealth. Another conference in 1926 had actually declared (Balfour Report) that Great Britain and the dominions were "autonomous communities within the British Empire, equal in status, in no way subordinate one to another, . . . though united by a common allegiance to the Crown." A committee representing the "autonomous communities" had been appointed (1929) to recommend the steps that should be taken to carry into effect this declaration, and its report had been adopted by an imperial conference in 1930. This report had then been transformed into law by the action of the parliaments of Great Britain and the dominions. In accordance with this procedure the Statute of Westminster had been passed in December, 1931, by the British Parliament.

By the terms of this statute it was agreed that (1) no law passed by a dominion parliament could in the future be declared void because it was contrary to a law of Great Britain; (2) no law of the British Parliament

[4] See pages 651–658.

could apply to any dominion unless the latter specifically requested it; (3) no longer might the king on the advice of his British ministers set aside an act of a dominion parliament; (4) no change in the laws concerning succession to the British throne might be made without the consent of the dominion parliaments. As early as 1930 the dominions had successfully contended that their choice of governor-generalship should be accepted.

As the Statute of Westminster legalized the dominions' independence in their domestic affairs, custom and practice had brought a notable change in their status so far as international relations were concerned. The dominions came to have practical independence in their own foreign relations, being represented individually in the League of Nations, being allowed to administer mandates of the League in their own names, and having their own diplomatic representatives in many foreign capitals. Furthermore, they obtained the right to negotiate treaties for themselves and to refuse to ratify treaties entered into by Great Britain.

In other words, the British Empire in the years after 1914 had been transformed into something like a league of independent states bound together by a symbol, the crown, and co-operating through periodic imperial conferences of the prime ministers of the several states. Great Britain had thus ceased to be the ruling head of an empire and had become merely an equal member of the "British Commonwealth of Nations." That she still had the loyalty of these "independent states" in the Commonwealth was abundantly proved by the support which they gave her in the Second World War. Only Ireland remained neutral.

Ireland

The crisis which was provoked in Ireland at the time of the enactment of the third Home Rule Bill in 1914 has been discussed.[5] During the war the situation in Ireland had improved not at all. Irish demands became more radical, and, under the direction of Sinn Fein leaders, home rule came to mean for many not a parliament for an Ireland which would still constitute a part of the British Empire, but the establishment of a republic under which Ireland should be as independent of Great Britain as is the United States. This desire for independence resulted in an Irish revolt in 1916, planned in conjunction with the military leaders of Germany.

Although the rebellion was quickly suppressed, a very decided drift into the ranks of Sinn Fein continued. This was clearly revealed in the parliamentary elections of 1918 when the Sinn Feiners won an overwhelming victory outside Ulster. The newly elected Sinn Fein repre-

[5] See pages 187–189.

sentatives thereupon asserted that the elections constituted a mandate in favor of an independent republic, and proceeded to organize themselves into an Irish parliament, the Dail Eireann. In January, 1919, the latter elected Eamon de Valera "President of the Irish Republic." During the following months what practically amounted to a state of war existed between the "Irish Republic" and Great Britain.

In December, 1920, a fourth Home Rule Bill was passed by the British Parliament. This measure provided for two parliaments in Ireland, one for the six counties in northeast Ulster and one for the rest of the island. It reserved certain imperial services, notably the army, navy, foreign relations, customs, and excise, to the parliament at Westminster in which the two divisions of Ireland were still to be represented by duly elected though somewhat less numerous members. Northern Ireland at once accepted this plan and proceeded to carry it out. In Ireland, outside Ulster, however, the act was generally repudiated, for the Sinn Feiners refused to have anything to do with a scheme which seemed to make permanent the partition of the island.

Lloyd George therefore invited De Valera to confer with him regarding the possibility of some settlement, but the British proposals were rejected by De Valera. Nevertheless, Lloyd George extended a second invitation and in October, 1921, another conference convened, with Arthur Griffith, Michael Collins, Eamon J. Duggan, and Gavan Duffy representing the Sinn Feiners. After eight weeks of intermittent negotiations the signatures of the plenipotentiaries were eventually affixed to a treaty providing for the establishment of the Irish Free State. Under this agreement the Irish Free State was to have the same constitutional status in the British Empire as the self-governing dominions. The Free State was to have its own military forces, and its own armed vessels for the protection of revenue and fisheries. Certain harbor facilities were conceded by it to the imperial government, however, and the coast of Ireland was to be defended by the British fleet, pending an arrangement to be negotiated later. Northern Ireland was not to be included in the Free State if it declared its desire to continue under the act of 1920.

The treaty at once created a schism in the ranks of Sinn Fein. De Valera denounced it and urged its rejection. Arthur Griffith, on the other hand, asserted that the treaty would lay the foundation of peace and friendship between Ireland and England, that the end of the conflict of centuries was at hand. In the Dail the treaty was accepted, whereupon De Valera resigned from the presidency and Arthur Griffith was chosen to succeed him. A few days later De Valera and his followers withdrew from the Dail. The bare majority which remained set up a provisional government under the chairmanship of Michael Collins.

De Valera next plunged Ireland into civil war. The "Irregulars," as the men in his Irish republican army came to be called, subjected southern Ireland to an orgy of destruction, in the course of which the country was desolated. On August 12, 1922, came the unexpected death of Arthur Griffith, founder of Sinn Fein but since 1921 a loyal supporter of the Irish Free State treaty. Four days later Michael Collins, a Sinn Feiner who had turned his unbounded courage and energy to the defense of the Free

IRELAND TODAY

State, was ambushed and killed. But under the guidance of William Cosgrave and Kevin O'Higgins the provisional government resorted to vigorous measures to restore order. In the spring of 1923 De Valera finally admitted the impossibility of continuing the struggle, and ordered his followers to put aside their arms.

Some months before this, however, the Irish Free State had been legally established. In 1922 a provisional parliament had elected Cosgrave president of the provisional government, and had adopted a constitution. As in the other dominions, the executive authority was vested nominally in the king, represented by a governor-general. Actual executive power was placed in the hands of an executive council, directly responsible to the lower house of the legislature. The legislature was to consist of two houses, the Chamber of Deputies (*Dail Eireann*) and the Senate (*Seanad Eireann*). The latter was to be elected indirectly for twelve years, one fourth of the members being chosen every three years. The Chamber of Deputies was to be chosen by a system of proportional representation with universal suffrage. On December 6, 1922, the Irish Free State was established by royal proclamation.

In September, 1923, representatives of the Free State were received into the Assembly of the League of Nations; in October Cosgrave, president of the executive council, for the first time attended a dominion conference in London. Diplomatic representatives of the Free State were established in Washington, Geneva, Paris, Berlin, and Brussels, and a high commissioner took up his residence in London. In a reaction against the use of English, Gaelic was made compulsory for civil servants and for lawyers, and the Irish representative in the League of Nations Assembly was even instructed to make his speeches in Gaelic. Family and place names were Gaelicized, the best-known example being the change from Queenstown to Cobh. The difficulty of using Gaelic, however, prevented the universal adoption of the language. Irish nationalism did obtain some satisfaction, however, in the adoption of Irish coins and postage stamps.

In the summer of 1927 the world was shocked by the assassination of Kevin O'Higgins, vice-president of the executive council of the Free State and the "strong man" of the government. O'Higgins had been Cosgrave's chief lieutenant since the assassination of Collins and the death of Griffith. As minister of justice he had been largely responsible for the vigorous measures which had suppressed the Republican opposition. Although De Valera and his followers disclaimed any connection with the assassination, popular opinion throughout the world was inclined to place part of the responsibility for the deed upon the obstructionist tactics of the republican leader. Soon after this event De Valera changed his tactics. Until then he and his republican followers had refused to take the oath of allegiance to the British king and in consequence had been excluded from the Chamber of Deputies. In August, 1927, De Valera announced that he would take the oath and would undertake to become the head of a constitutional opposition.

Despite the very real material and nationalistic gains which came to the Irish as a result of Cosgrave's administration, the world depression inevitably affected the popularity of his government. As sentiment in practically all countries where democratic government prevailed turned against the parties in power during the years of the depression, so it was in Ireland. Furthermore, De Valera constantly appealed to the Irish with a very definitely anti-British—and therefore popular—program. The extreme republicans were attracted by his demand for the abolition of the oath of allegiance to the British king. Small landholders were won by his promise to withhold the land annuities which they were compelled to pay to the British government under the land-purchase agreements of earlier years. In the parliamentary election of 1932 De Valera's party, Fianna Fail, won the largest number of seats, and he was accordingly elected president of the executive council.

In July, 1932, De Valera withheld the payment of £1,500,000 due on the land annuities. This action the British government declared was a violation of a binding engagement of the Irish Free State, and the British parliament passed a law empowering the government to levy a duty up to 100 per cent on Irish goods coming into Great Britain, in order to secure funds equivalent to the defaulted land annuities. De Valera retaliated with Irish duties which were almost prohibitive on certain British goods, and a tariff war therefore ensued until 1936. In that year the Free State president practically admitted the failure of his plan by negotiating a trade agreement which removed the duty on British coal and gave the British practically a monopoly of the market for that commodity within the Free State. It also reduced the duties on a great number of other commodities usually imported from Britain and provided that one third of Ireland's cement should be purchased from British firms. In return Great Britain, although still retaining high duties on many Irish products, reduced them somewhat on livestock and meats.

Meanwhile, De Valera had been taking steps to emphasize the political independence of the Irish Free State. In May, 1933, the Chamber of Deputies passed a bill abolishing the oath of allegiance to the British king. Next the governor-general's approval was made unnecessary for the legalization of acts passed by the Irish parliament. The right of appeal from Irish courts to the British Privy Council was abolished. In 1935 no Free State delegate attended the celebration of the twenty-fifth anniversary of King George's accession to the throne. The absence of such a delegate was doubtless one more gesture designed to emphasize De Valera's determination to cut the Free State off from Great Britain. A similar gesture was made again in January, 1936, when King George died. The Irish Free State government took no step to proclaim King Edward VIII in Dublin and sent no official representative to the funeral of the deceased ruler. In December, 1936, during the constitutional crisis in Great Britain, the Chamber of Deputies abolished the office of governor-general and the British king's prerogatives in Ireland's domestic affairs. Although the Chamber gave its necessary official assent to the Abdication Act, in accordance with the provisions of the Statute of Westminster, the Free State government refused to proclaim the new king in Dublin or to send an official representative to his coronation in the following May.

In April, 1937, De Valera published a new Irish Free State constitution which proclaimed the Irish nation's "indefeasible and sovereign right to choose its own form of government, to determine its relations with other nations and to develop its life, political, economic and cultural, in accordance with its own genius and traditions." Nowhere in the constitution was there any mention of Great Britain or the British king. The new constitution provided for a titular president who should be elected by direct vote of the people for a seven-year term. Executive power was to be exercised, however, chiefly by a prime minister and cabinet responsible to the Chamber of Deputies. The parliament was to consist of a popularly elected Chamber of Deputies and an indirectly elected or nominated Senate. The proposed constitution was submitted to the voters and was approved by slightly more than 56 per cent of those who voted. The new constitution became effective on December 29, 1937, when the name of the Irish Free State was officially changed to Eire. On May 4, 1938, as the result of an agreement between De Valera and Cosgrave, leaders of the two largest political parties, Douglas Hyde, the seventy-eight-year-old poet, historian, and retired university professor, was elected President by acclamation. The son of a Protestant clergyman and himself a Protestant, Hyde had long been an ardent Irish nationalist.

Meanwhile, De Valera had turned his attention to the task of removing the causes of dissension between Eire and Great Britain and happily had found Prime Minister Chamberlain equally desirous of restoring amicable relations. After somewhat lengthy negotiations, on April 25, 1938, three agreements were signed in London between Great Britain and Eire. In the first Great Britain agreed to transfer to Eire the admiralty property and rights at Berehaven and the harbor defenses there and at Cobh and Lough Swilly. British forces, which had been stationed at these places by the terms of the treaty of 1921, were thereupon withdrawn, and Eire became responsible for her own defense. The second agreement provided that Eire should pay Great Britain £10,000,000 on or before November 30, 1938, as the final settlement of Britain's claim to land annuities. In addition Eire agreed to continue to pay £250,000 annually until 1987 in accordance with the Anglo-Irish agreement of 1925, which had to do with property damages incurred during the so-called "troubles." This convention also provided for the abolition of the special duties imposed by the British government in retaliation for the withholding of the annuities and for the abolition of the retaliatory customs duties levied by Eire. The third agreement was a trade treaty designed to restore to each of the signatories the favorable commercial position held prior to the recent tariff war. According to De Valera, all causes of difference between Great Britain and Eire were thus removed except the question of partition, which he still hoped would ultimately be adjusted. On May 27, 1938, Premier de Valera dissolved the Chamber of Deputies, doubtless with the expectation that, with Anglo-Irish relations thus happily adjusted, his party might benefit. His expectation was fulfilled, for the election of June 17, 1938, gave Fianna Fail a decisive majority over all the opposition groups.

The outbreak of the Second World War provided another opportunity to emphasize that Eire was independent of Great Britain. In contrast with the other members of the British Commonwealth of Nations, Eire at once declared her neutrality and remained out of the war. Throughout the conflict the inability of the British navy to use the ports surrendered to the Irish by Chamberlain in 1938 constituted a grave handicap in the battle of the Atlantic.

Chapter XIX

FRANCE AND SPAIN

FRANCE was the only great power on the Continent which in the postwar period continued to hold to the liberal tradition despite the many serious problems which confronted her. Though the uncertainties, anxieties, and hardships inevitably accompanying the attempts to solve these problems led many to advocate and support communism or fascism, the bulk of the French people stood loyally by their liberal republic. In France's neighbor, Spain, the postwar years saw a valiant attempt to introduce a liberal regime which resulted in the downfall of monarchy and the establishment of a republic. The Spanish liberals, however, were handicapped from the start by strong opposition from both the reactionary Rightists and the radical Leftists, and ultimately the republic succumbed to a civil war from which it emerged as a fascist state.

France

France emerged victorious from the First World War only to find herself beset by numerous and perplexing problems. Some of these were solved without too great difficulty, but others produced such differences of opinion among the French people that stalemate and national paralysis at times resulted. A careful study of French affairs clearly reveals that the forces and circumstances which led to the collapse of France in the Second World War were present and becoming increasingly effective in the years between 1919 and 1939.

THE PROBLEM OF RECONSTRUCTION AND FINANCE

At the close of the First World War Georges Clemenceau, who had become premier during the critical days of 1917, was still head of the government. National elections had been postponed in France during the war, and not until after the treaty of Versailles had been ratified by the French parliament did Clemenceau call for general elections. Then the National bloc, a coalition of most of the Right and Center parties, was organized by Alexandre Millerand to support the government, defend the treaty, and combat Bolshevism. In the elections in November, 1919, the National bloc won an overwhelming victory.

In the following month President Poincaré's term of office was to expire, and so on January 17 the National Assembly met to elect his successor. The two outstanding candidates were Clemenceau and Paul Deschanel, the latter long a member of the Chamber of Deputies and for years its president. Clemenceau was decisively defeated. Since the aged premier had made the presidential election a sort of vote of confidence on his work as premier, his defeat left him no alternative but to resign his office. He was succeeded by Millerand, the organizer of the National bloc. But the latter did not long retain the premiership. In September, 1920, President Deschanel resigned because of ill health and an unfortunate accident, and Millerand was chosen to succeed him. After some further ministerial changes the premiership was eventually assumed in January, 1921, by Aristide Briand, who was destined to play a prominent role in the diplomatic history of postwar Europe. Perhaps his most pressing immediate problem was to secure reparation payments from Germany commensurate with the cost of reconstructing northern France.

The restoration of this territory to its prewar state constituted a gigantic problem for France. During the war the French government had promised to reimburse its citizens for all direct and material losses occasioned by the war. With the cost of replacement of damaged and destroyed property averaging five times its estimated value in 1914, partly in consequence of the decline of the franc, the French government was thus called upon to expend billions in the work of restoration. But it was hoped and expected that whatever was spent for this purpose would ultimately be recovered from Germany under the treaty of Versailles. By the summer of 1921 great strides had been made in the work of restoration, in the course of which the French government had spent over 20,000,000,000 francs, but up to that time France had actually received nothing from Germany to apply on her reparations account.

It was inevitable that the reparations problem should become involved in French politics. Briand stood for a policy of reasonable moderation and conciliation. But with France's failure to receive reparations payments of any size, Frenchmen became restless. When at the close of 1921 Germany asked and was later granted a partial moratorium, the Nationalists, led by Raymond Poincaré and André Tardieu, took up cudgels against Briand, and in January, 1922, he was forced out of office and was succeeded by Poincaré. The latter's policy, culminating in the French occupation of the Ruhr and the subsequent appointment of the Dawes Committee, has already been traced.[1]

By 1924, however, a number of circumstances conspired to weaken Poincaré's position. The continued fall of the franc reacted against him,

[1] See pages 433–434.

as did the accompanying rise in the cost of living. The failure to secure reparations from Germany, the increase in the national debt, the heavier taxes being laid upon Frenchmen, and the inability of the government to balance the national budget gave his opponents numerous opportunities to attack him. Through the efforts of Briand a Left bloc was finally organized with the purpose of defeating Poincaré, and in the general parliamentary elections in May, 1924, the parties of the Left were returned in a majority, the Radical Socialists constituting the largest single group in the new Chamber.

The immediate result of this reversal in French politics was the downfall of both Premier Poincaré and President Millerand. That Poincaré should be forced to resign was, of course, quite to be expected but the leaders of the Left bloc resolved that Millerand also must resign because he had overstepped his presidential prerogatives by openly supporting the National bloc during the preceding electoral campaign. When, therefore, President Millerand called upon Édouard Herriot, leader of the Radical Socialists, to form a government, the latter declined. The president then invited another member of the Chamber to assume the premiership, but the latter's cabinet when presented failed to secure the support of the Chamber. An impasse was thus created which was surmounted only when President Millerand resigned his office on June 11. Gaston Doumergue, president of the Senate and a member of the Left group, was elected president, and Herriot then accepted the new president's invitation to form a cabinet.

Herriot's most difficult problem was that of national finance. Four factors united to produce a grave crisis in the French fiscal system: the tremendous increase in the service charges on the debt of France; the enormous current expenditures required for the reconstruction of the devastated area in the early years of the postwar period; the relatively insignificant amounts actually received in reparations payments prior to 1926; and the failure of the government's system of taxation to bring in revenue sufficient to balance the budget. During the five years before Herriot came into power annual deficits had added a total of 150 billion francs to the already gigantic national debt. The national currency had become greatly inflated, and the franc, normally worth 19.3 cents, had depreciated until by March, 1924, it was worth less than 5 cents.

In 1924 the French people began to show a reluctance to make further loans to the government, and holders of short-term bills displayed an unwillingness to renew their loans as they came due. But the government was unable to increase the national revenue materially because of the bitter conflict in the parliament over the method of taxation. The Left groups demanded a capital levy on the rich, heavier direct taxes, and a reduction of expenditures by a lowering of the interest rate on government bonds. The Right groups, on the other hand, demanded the imposition of more indirect taxes, heavier taxes on the middle classes, and a reduction of expenditures by the lowering of government salaries and wages. Parliament's inability to enact either of these programs in effect decreed a policy of currency inflation, with the result that increases in paper currency continued until, in April, 1925, the Chamber of Deputies forced the resignation of Herriot by refusing longer to support this procedure. In the ensuing fifteen months no less than six ministries followed one another in rapid succession while the fiscal impasse remained.

By May, 1926, an acute financial crisis had begun which culminated in a panic in the following July. The crisis brought a radical change in the government. Party lines were temporarily obliterated, and a ministry of National Union was organized to include six former premiers under the leadership of France's "strong man," Poincaré, who was given practically dictatorial powers in the realm of finance. Drastic measures were at once taken. New tax measures were enacted, increasing the amount of indirect taxes and shifting the burden somewhat from the wealthy to the middle classes. Extensive reforms in the administrative system reduced expenditures. The budget—the largest in the nation's history—was balanced, and the year 1926 closed with a surplus of over 1,500,000,000 francs in the treasury. The franc was gradually raised in value until, December 20, 1926, it stood at 25.19 to the dollar, where it was given *de facto* stabilization. With the franc at this value, the gold standard was restored in June, 1928. Renewed confidence in the government made it possible to reduce interest rates so that by 1928 the service charges on the floating debt had been decreased by over 300,000,000 francs yearly. Furthermore, the reconstruction of the devastated area was practically completed so that extraordinary expenditures for this purpose became negligible, while income from reparations payments under the Dawes plan increased.

In 1928 France had an opportunity to pass upon Poincaré's achievements in the parliamentary elections which were held in April. As in the elections four years earlier, the chief issue was Poincaré and his policies, but on this occasion the elections constituted a victory for his government. Poincaré continued to hold the premiership until ill health forced his resignation in July, 1929, when the removal of his strong hand from the helm of state brought a return of the republic's traditional ministerial instability.

THE PROBLEM OF ALSACE-LORRAINE

Meanwhile, another problem which had confronted French statesmen after the war was that of assimilating into a unitary state the provinces of

Alsace-Lorraine, whose institutions in the years after 1871 had come to differ from those of France. Under Germany the provinces had constituted a single political unit which, though ruled arbitrarily by the imperial government until 1911, had in that year been granted a local legislature with considerable power. But in a unitary state like France there was no place for provincial legislatures. In accordance with the French system of government Alsace-Lorraine in 1919 was divided into three departments, and the legislature was ignored. The inhabitants of the provinces were naturally reluctant to lose their local rights. Furthermore, they complained that officials sent out from Paris knew no German, the language most nearly akin to that spoken by the majority of the people.

The matter of language also caused ill feeling in the provinces. The great majority of Alsatians and Lorrainers spoke patois or dialects closely related to high German, which was used in printing and writing. With the return to France the official language of the schools of Alsace-Lorraine became French. It was required that during the first two years of the elementary schools French should be studied exclusively; after that three hours a week of instruction in German was also provided. The French government insisted that French should have a primary place in the school system and discouraged the use of German, despite the desire of many Alsatians for language equality.

The greatest dissatisfaction arose from the government's effort to change the religious and educational situation in Alsace-Lorraine. At the time when the provinces were taken from France in 1871, these matters were regulated by the concordat which Napoleon had concluded with the pope in 1801. Under this agreement the salaries of the clergy were paid by the government, which had a voice in their appointment, and education was almost entirely under the control of the church. The German government had respected these arrangements in Alsace-Lorraine when it annexed the provinces and had permitted them to continue. The result was that in Alsace-Lorraine the salaries of the clergy were paid by the local government, and the children were permitted to attend Catholic, Protestant, or Jewish schools in accordance with the religion of their parents. In the rest of France, on the other hand, subsequent anticlerical legislation had meanwhile altered the situation. Church and state had been completely separated, all religious instruction had been removed from the schools, and teaching by religious orders had been forbidden.

President Poincaré at the time of the recovery of Alsace and Lorraine had pledged the retention of their religious system, and the government of the National bloc had winked at the anomalous situation created in France when it permitted the religious and educational situation in Alsace-Lorraine to continue undisturbed. But the Left government which came into power in 1924 was definitely anticlerical, and determined to introduce in Alsace-Lorraine the same regime as existed elsewhere in France. When it attempted to disestablish the churches and to introduce secular schools, however, it encountered the active obstruction of the people. In the end the government had to recede from its stand. The churches were not disestablished, and the schools were not all secularized. In some places an "interconfessional" school system was introduced in accordance with which the children were to be sent for their academic instruction to a common school without regard to their religious beliefs but were to be separated for their religious instruction.

Many of those in Alsace-Lorraine who had welcomed French troops so enthusiastically as "liberators" who would bring in "a new era of liberty, prosperity, and happiness" later had serious doubts as to whether their return to France was altogether an unmixed blessing. In fact, stimulated by grievances and fears as well as by a highly financed propaganda, disgruntled elements of the Alsatian population were gradually won over to an autonomist movement which sought home rule or even separation from France. So serious did the situation become that in 1929 the Chamber of Deputies devoted itself for more than two weeks to a consideration of the problems connected with the administration of Alsace-Lorraine. In the succeeding years, however, and especially after the Nazis came into power in Germany, autonomist agitation largely ceased.

THE PROBLEM OF SECURITY

Meanwhile, too, French statesmen had been busily engaged in building a system of alliances to provide security for France. They were especially disturbed after the First World War by the specter of a discontented and revengeful Germany, for it took very little mathematical ability for a French statesman to prove that France's 39,000,000 would be no match for Germany's 62,000,000. Before the war, in order to counteract this situation, France had allied herself with populous Russia so that their combined man power and resources might be protection against their powerful neighbor, Germany. The loss of Russia as an ally, with the coming of the Bolsheviks in 1917, was a terrible blow for France, but at the peace conference her statesmen had sought to repair this damage by carrying through a program of security.

Although the French had obtained a number of the points for which they contended at the conference, they had not obtained all. As protection against another German invasion they had been obliged to accept, instead of French military control of the Rhine, a compromise which included Allied military occupation of the left bank of the Rhine for fifteen years, the permanent demilitarization of this area together with a strip of territory fifty kilometers wide on the right bank, and a tripartite guarantee treaty promising that the United States and Great Britain would come to the assistance of France in case of a future unprovoked attack by Germany. But this bulwark of protection was soon weakened. Although Great Britain ratified the guarantee treaty, the United States refused to have anything to do with it, and consequently the whole scheme fell to the ground, for Great Britain's adhesion to the treaty was contingent upon that of the United States.

French statesmen lost no time in crying over spilt milk. If they must now construct their own security alliance, they would proceed at once to do so. There was one country of western Europe which was as much concerned as France in the problem of her future security against Germany. Belgium after her terrible experiences of the war would be only too eager to obtain protection against their repetition; therefore to Belgium France now turned in a conciliatory spirit. Military conversations between the French and Belgian staffs culminated on September 7, 1920, in the signing of a military convention.

But France with Belgium alone could still not hope to cope with Germany. She must seek some greater power to take the place of her lost ally, Russia. With this in mind she turned to the new Polish Republic, largest of all the new states of Europe. If France needed security for her eastern frontier facing Germany, to no less a degree did Poland need a similar security for her western frontier, which had been established at the expense of Germany. If France had reason to fear for the stability of her German frontier, twice justified was Poland, for the loss of Upper Silesia, Posen, and West Prussia with their mineral and agricultural resources and their large German minorities was felt by the German nation more keenly than the loss of Alsace-Lorraine. Fear of German attack thus created a strong common bond between Poland and France. In the summer of 1920 during the crisis of the Russo-Polish campaign the French government sent a military mission to Poland and helped to save Warsaw from the Bolsheviks. Diplomatic negotiations next ensued, and a Franco-Polish treaty of alliance was signed on February 19, 1921. The treaty system thus far created by France provided that, if Germany should attack her, France would be aided by Belgium in the west and by Poland in the east.

But France was not yet content with the security which had been obtained, and turned next to Czechoslovakia, whose statesmen wished to guard against the union of Austria and Germany and against the restoration of either the Habsburgs or the Hohenzollerns. In 1924 a Franco-Czechoslovak treaty of alliance was formally signed in Paris. In 1926 she

signed with Rumania a treaty of friendship in which the two states promised to consult each other in all matters which might threaten their external security or which might tend to subvert the situation created by
the treaties of peace. The two states agreed to concert their policy in case
of any attempted modification of the political status of the countries of
Europe and to confer regarding the attitude to be taken in such an event.
In 1927 France signed an almost identical treaty with Yugoslavia.

This extensive system of alliances and friendship treaties conferred upon
France a position of leadership among those continental powers which
were, generally speaking, beneficiaries of the Paris peace settlement and
consequently vitally interested in the maintenance of the *status quo*. It was
hoped that as a bloc they would outweigh any power which might seek by
force to abrogate the terms of the peace treaties, and might therefore deter
such a power from military aggression. Furthermore, these treaties, it will
be recalled, were supplemented by the Locarno pact of mutual guarantee,
which bound Great Britain and Italy to aid France in case of a German
attack, and by the pact of Paris, which outlawed war as an instrument of
national policy. Thus, on paper, at least, France greatly strengthened her
national security during the years immediately following the First World
War.

Much of the credit for these diplomatic successes belonged to Aristide
Briand, who for more than seven years served as foreign minister. In 1931,
when President Doumergue's term of office expired, a large group of
senators and deputies of all parties united to urge Briand to stand as a
candidate for the presidency, and he finally consented. Two days later
the National Assembly elected not Briand but Paul Doumer President of
France. Doumer, a venerable self-made man and a representative of the
bourgeoisie, was at the time president of the Senate and had been president of the Chamber of Deputies. Briand's failure to be elected president,
like that of Clemenceau in 1920, seemed to many an indication that French
statesmen who play vigorous roles in politics arouse so many enmities
that they have great difficulty in being elevated to the presidency. For
some time Briand had been in poor health, and on March 7, 1932, shortly
before his seventieth birthday, he died. His impress on the public
mind is indicated by the fact that, though the international agreement to
outlaw war (1928) was officially known as the pact of Paris, it was popularly referred to throughout the world as the Briand-Kellogg pact. His
foresight is revealed by his eloquent advocacy of a European federal union
in 1930.

DEFLATION AND UNREST

Although France was slower to feel the world depression than most countries, by the time of the parliamentary elections of May, 1932, its effects upon French economic life had become abundantly evident. As in other countries during the depression, the vote went against those in office. The Left bloc won, with Herriot's Radical Socialists the largest single group in the new Chamber. In June, 1932, Herriot assumed the premiership, as he had done eight years earlier after a similar swing to the Left. In the meantime, on May 10, Albert Lebrun, then president of the Senate, had been elected president of the republic to succeed Doumer, who was assassinated on May 5.

In the succeeding years the rise and fall of ministries was generally connected with some phase of the republic's perplexing budgetary, fiscal, or economic problems. France, because of her adhering to the gold standard, found herself obliged to compete with devalued British pounds and American dollars. In consequence, her foreign trade greatly decreased, as did tourist expenditures which formerly brought into the country hundreds of millions of dollars. By bankers, exporters, and those catering to tourist trade the government was urged to devalue the franc once more in order to enable France to compete more successfully with foreign currencies. On the other hand, the *rentier* class, having learned by experience the effect of currency depreciation upon it, was unalterably opposed to any further experiments of that nature.

In general, the policy of French statesmen during the ensuing four years was that of deflation. That is, they sought by reductions in the wages of government employees, in the pensions of war veterans, and in the interest rate on government bonds to lessen the national expenditures, while at the same time they attempted by higher taxes to balance the budget and thus remove the necessity for increasing the national debt or inflating the currency. Such a policy inevitably incurred the opposition of many taxpayers, government employees, and war veterans. Furthermore, many in France argued that the government's fiscal system should be balanced not by deflation of the budget but by inflation of the currency. There was, accordingly, much dissatisfaction with the various attempts at deflation. Moreover, the government's revenues regularly fell below budgetary estimates, so that deficits continued and the national debt mounted. Alarm at this latter development in turn occasionally created fear of monetary inflation and a consequent run on gold. Altogether, the position of the premiers who succeeded one another during these years was far from enviable. Édouard Herriot, Joseph Paul-Boncour, Édouard

Daladier, Albert Sarraut, and Camille Chautemps, all Radical Socialists, held the premiership between June, 1932, and January, 1934.

During the winter of 1933–1934 the government became linked in the public mind with a pawnshop scandal which caused a loss of 200,000,000 francs to French investors. The failure of the police to find the absconder, Alexander Stavisky, led to charges of corruption against the administration of justice, and, when Stavisky killed himself, it was rumored that he had been shot by the police to prevent his revealing embarrassing information. Public demand for a complete reorganization of the government, accompanied by riots in the streets of Paris, eventually forced Chautemps out of office late in January, 1934.

But the disorders did not cease when he was succeeded by Daladier. Newspapers representing various elements in France, apparently seeking to embarrass the government, called upon their readers to gather for demonstrations on the day that the new cabinet was to appear before the Chamber of Deputies. On the one hand, royalists, war veterans, and members of various Right organizations were urged to gather for a demonstration "to oppose the thieves and this abject regime"; on the other, Socialists and Communists were incited to defend their interests against "the forces of fascism" which were said to be seeking to destroy democracy. On the night of February 6, 1934, while the crowds were milling about the Place de la Concorde and fighting the police, the floodlights suddenly went out. In the confusion that ensued police and troops, apparently without orders from their officers and under the impression that they were fighting in self-defense, began to use their pistols. Seventeen civilians were killed and more than six hundred were wounded. Of the police and military, one was killed and more than 1600 were wounded.

In view of these developments, the Daladier ministry was forced at once to resign. Prominent political leaders united in urging that former President Gaston Doumergue be made premier. In answer to their appeal this veteran statesman agreed to form a ministry on condition that he be given complete freedom in regard to his program and choice of ministers. Hailed as a "national savior," Doumergue arrived in Paris on February 8 and immediately organized a cabinet which included among its members six former premiers and Marshal Pétain. The new ministry inspired confidence, political harmony was attained, and government economies were introduced. But, when Doumergue sought to have the French constitution amended in order to increase his executive powers and to give the premier the right to dissolve the Chamber and call for new elections, fear of a movement toward dictatorial rule caused opposition and brought the fall of his ministry in November, 1934. Again came a rapid succession of governments, headed by Pierre-Étienne Flandin, Fernand Bouisson, Pierre Laval, and Albert Sarraut.

The reluctance of the Chamber of Deputies to vote new powers to the premiers during these years was caused, in part, by the fear that a movement toward a fascist dictatorship was under way in France. The one most suspected was Colonel François de la Rocque, leader of the *Croix de Feu,* an organization of war veterans, which was supported by many prominent French industrial capitalists. Colonel de la Rocque had been able by his oratory and personal magnetism to weld together an organization of several hundred thousand men. Although the *Croix de Feu* was the most important and most powerful of the various antirepublican organizations, there were several others, notably the royalist *Action Française* and *Camelots du Roi* and the nationalistic, anti-Communist *Cagoulards, Solidarité Française,* and *Jeunesse Patriote.*

THE POPULAR FRONT

In preparation for the parliamentary elections of 1936 the Radical Socialists, the Socialists, and the Communists organized the Popular Front. Although the parties differed among themselves on many points, on one fundamental they were agreed—that a united and militant front must be set up against the threat of fascism. Apparently the French electorate felt similarly, for the elections resulted in a decisive victory for the Popular Front. For the first time in French history the Socialists secured the largest number of seats in the Chamber of Deputies.

Their leader, Léon Blum, naturally anathema to the various political groups and organizations of the Right, was now called upon to assume the premiership. The opposition which he was bound to encounter was disclosed by a Rightist official circular: "This election clearly shows the extent of the Red menace and reveals the impossibility of parliamentary government." Blum sought to construct a ministry which would include representatives of all of the Popular Front parties, but the Communists declined to enter such a coalition. His cabinet, therefore, when it finally took over the reins of government on June 5, 1936, consisted of only Socialists and Radical Socialists.

At the time that the Blum government took office, France was seriously disturbed by "sit-down" strikes involving hundreds of thousands of workers who demanded collective labor contracts, wage increases, a forty-hour week, a two-week annual holiday with pay, and the right of the workers to present claims and complaints to the management. Immediately upon assuming office the new premier arranged a settlement between the workers and employers which granted wage increases. He also secured the enactment of legislation providing for a forty-hour week, holidays with pay, and collective labor contracts. Eventually the parliament empowered the government to provide by decree for the compulsory mediation and arbitration of industrial conflicts.

Legislation was enacted to carry out certain items of the Popular Front platform. The way was opened for the nationalization of the private armaments industry of France by a law providing that any concern engaged in the manufacture or sale of armaments could be expropriated at prices to be fixed by arbitration. Steps were also taken to "democratize" the powerful Bank of France by reducing the influence of the much-publicized "two hundred families." Legislation provided that each stockholder, regardless of the size of his holdings, should have a single vote, and that the composition and selection of the governing body of the bank should be altered so that all classes of French economic life would be represented and a majority of its members would be appointed by the government. Finally, in order to protect the French farmer from disastrous fluctuations in the price of wheat, a special office was created with authority to fix the price of that commodity.

In September, in an attempt to solve the republic's economic and fiscal problems, the government took the important step of reducing the gold content of the franc by about 30 per cent in order to align it with British and American currencies. Unfortunately for its hopes, however, the economic situation did not respond to devaluation as favorably as had been expected. It hoped that devaluation would bring the return of French capital in sufficient amounts to enable the government to meet its needs by floating loans. But here, too, it met disappointment, largely because the wealthy classes were opposed to the Socialist premier. In June, 1937, France still had an unbalanced budget, her bonds were selling below par, and the republic's credit was at the lowest point since 1926.

To meet the new crisis, Blum sought temporary dictatorial powers in the realm of finance like those conferred upon Poincaré in 1926. Although such powers were voted by the Chamber of Deputies, the more conservative Senate refused to pass the bill. In consequence, Blum resigned on June 20, 1937, after having established, in the words of one historian, "a record for energetic planning and parliamentary generalship unequaled in the history of the Third Republic." He was succeeded by Camille Chautemps, a leader of the Radical Socialists who had been a member of Blum's cabinet. The Socialists agreed to maintain the Popular Front government, and Blum and eight other Socialists accepted places in Chautemps' ministry. As in the case of Blum, the Communists gave the government their support.

On June 30 the parliament voted the Chautemps government, until August 31, 1937, the full powers which it had denied Blum. The new government thereupon gave up its attempt to maintain the French currency on a gold basis, and the franc immediately fell in value to about 3.75 cents. The budget deficit for 1937 amounted to about 8,000,000,000 francs, and the closing days of 1937 saw the franc again declining. The Socialists and the Communists demanded a controlled foreign exchange to solve the republic's monetary problem, but Georges Bonnet, the Radical Socialist finance minister, opposed such a solution. The Socialists then withdrew their support from the government, and Chautemps on January 14, 1938, resigned. For all practical purposes, the Popular Front was ended.

FRENCH WEAKNESS IN THE FACE OF NAZI GERMANY

During the ensuing weeks, when Hitler launched his *Drang nach Osten* by seizing Austria, France passed through a period of ministerial instability caused by the Socialists' opposition to Chautemps and the Senate's opposition to Blum, for, though the latter had largely abandoned his program of reform and wished to concentrate on national armament, the Rightists refused to co-operate with him. Not until April 10, 1938, after the *Anschluss* had been safely consummated, was a stable government of Radical Socialists and representatives of certain moderate groups organized under Édouard Daladier. And it did not augur well for France that her new premier was weak and indecisive and that her foreign minister, Georges Bonnet, was hostile to Soviet Russia, France's new-found ally against Nazi Germany. But by this time many French patriots were becoming alarmed at the growing threat to French security from across the Rhine, and, when Daladier demanded that party politics should yield to national politics, the parliament at once voted his government special powers.

Meanwhile, during the preceding decade, the government had been devoting special attention to the matter of national defense—and throughout this period the emphasis in France was on the word *defense*. Recalling the French success in holding back the Germans in the heroic battle of Verdun, the French high command had sought to transform the whole Franco-German frontier into a fortress more powerful even than Verdun. In 1930, under Tardieu's minister of war, André Maginot, French military engineers had begun the construction of a vast system of steel and concrete fortifications throughout Alsace-Lorraine which came to be known as the Maginot Line. The $500,000,000 expended on this line in the succeeding years seemed to indicate that the eyes of the French high command were turned toward the past, that French military leaders believed that in any future conflict the system of trench warfare and the slow war of attrition which had won in 1918 would inevitably win again. They revealed, too, though it seemed not to be evident to many observers, that France had abandoned the strategy of attack, which was the inevitable and necessary corollary of all the mutual assistance treaties which she had signed in the twenties.

It must be obvious to the reader of this chapter that conditions within France had conspired to weaken that country almost beyond repair. In the first place, the political leaders of France had failed to grasp the significance of the Nazi revolution or the determination of the Nazi leaders to remake the map of Europe; and, in the years when they should have been devoting their united efforts to preparing their country for defense, they had kept France weak by their continual maneuvering for personal political preferment. Moreover, the bitter antagonism between the Right and the Left had prevented the carrying out of a strong, nationally supported foreign policy and had militated against the execution of adequate measures for national defense. In some Frenchmen loyalty to groups had become stronger than loyalty to France. In fact, certain groups and certain prominent politicians—some of them under the influence of Otto Abetz, a German agent in Paris—had become definitely enamored of fascism. Through their anti-Communist eyes even Hitler's Nazism looked good. Many of the bourgeoisie had come to feel that "fascism was a sort of insurance against proletarianism." In the second place, during the period when capital and labor were sternly regimented in Germany in order that the nation's industry might pour out military equipment for use in a future war, French industrial and economic life had been repeatedly demoralized by strife between workers and employers.

Finally, those at the head of the French military forces had had little conception of the revolutionary changes introduced into warfare by airplanes and motorized equipment. They had failed to keep pace with Germany's production of these essential instruments of modern warfare, mistakenly putting their reliance in the defensive strength of a heavily fortified line. Furthermore, despite the German blow through Belgium in 1914, they had incredibly failed to extend the Maginot Line in its full strength along the Belgian frontier. The French commander-in-chief, General Maurice Gamelin, a cautious and unimaginative military leader, overrated the strength of the Maginot Line and underrated the striking power of the tank and the airplane. As for the French people, during the first decade after Versailles they had been impressed with the fact that France had the finest army in the world, and they continued to believe this even after Germany's rearmament had radically changed the situation. The outbreak of the Second World War, therefore, was to find France unprepared politically, industrially, militarily, and psychologically to fight through to victory.

Spain

In the quarter-century after the First World War the Spanish experienced more changes in the political structure of their state than any other people in western Europe. Constitutional monarchy, military dictatorship, democratic republic, bloody civil war, and corporate fascism followed one another at short intervals. During the years 1936–1939, moreover, the Spanish people were plagued by foreign intervention, during which the fascist dictators of Italy and Germany used Spain as a proving ground for their own military tactics and weapons. Whether the regime established in Spain as the result of civil war and foreign intervention was that desired by the majority of the Spanish people was open to grave question.

MILITARY DICTATORSHIP

The first of the revolutionary changes in the postwar period came on September 13, 1923, when General Miguel Primo de Rivera, with the approval of King Alfonso, overthrew the ministry, suspended the constitution, proclaimed martial law, and established himself as military dictator. Rivera was an army man of long standing. He had served with the Spanish troops in Cuba and the Philippines during the Spanish-American War; he had fought in Morocco in later years; and after 1915 he had been military governor of various districts of Spain. At the time of his *coup d'état* he held this position in Barcelona. As dictator, he at once dissolved the parliament, suppressed freedom of speech and of the press, and abolished trial by jury.

For the next few years Rivera ruled by strong-arm methods. Provincial legislatures were arbitrarily dismissed, leaders of the republican group were exiled, severe fines were exacted for minor offenses, and the censorship was tightened. In spite of these developments—or perhaps because of them—popular hostility toward the dictatorship increased instead of diminishing, and, unfortunately for King Alfonso, it tended to rise against the monarchy as well. After 1928 popular dissatisfaction grew rapidly. In 1929 a mutiny occurred in the army, and riots of university students and the working classes became frequent. Gradually Rivera was deserted by nearly all classes. The dictator became discouraged. Suffering from ill health, discovering that he had lost the confidence and support not only of his king but of the army as well, Rivera suddenly resigned his office on January 28, 1930, and left the country. On March 16 he died.

Upon Rivera's resignation, King Alfonso at once announced that the constitution of 1876 would be restored, the demands of university students and professors would be granted, all officers who had suffered at the dictator's hands would be given their former status, all political prisoners would be pardoned, and free and honest elections would be held late in 1930 for a new national parliament. The Socialists insisted, however, that the new government differed not essentially from that of Rivera, and before long shouts of "Down with the king and the monarchy!" began to be heard. The shouts were soon followed by the definite demand that a national assembly be called to draft a new constitution and to determine whether Spain should remain a monarchy or become a republic. In December a serious military uprising and a republican revolt were suppressed only after thousands had been arrested and martial law had again been proclaimed throughout the country.

In February, 1931, Alfonso restored the constitution and called for parliamentary elections to be held in March. So great was the popular demand for a constituent assembly rather than a parliament, however, that the government later suspended the call for the March elections. It announced instead plans for municipal and provincial elections in April, to be followed by the election of a constituent assembly. Apparently Premier Aznar and King Alfonso desired to learn popular sentiment by local elections before proceeding with plans for a constituent assembly. If so, they were not left in doubt. The municipal elections of April 12 constituted a veritable republican landslide. On the next day the Aznar government resigned, and a republican junta headed by Niceto Alcalá Zamora, leader of the unsuccessful republican revolt of December, 1930, issued an ultimatum stating that a revolution would be called if Alfonso refused to abdicate. That night the king without formal abdication left for France, merely suspending "the exercise of the royal power" until he should "learn the real expression of the collective opinion of his people."

THE ESTABLISHMENT OF THE REPUBLIC

Following the flight of the king, Zamora at once proclaimed a republic with himself as provisional president. A carefully selected cabinet of the best moderate republican and Socialist talent available took charge of the government, which was soon recognized by most of the leading powers. The republican government immediately guaranteed religious and civil liberty and recognized the rights of private property. It proclaimed an amnesty for all political prisoners and invited all exiles to return to Spain. It abolished all titles of nobility and arrested a number of former royal officials. It announced that it would inaugurate comprehensive agrarian reforms with a view to modernizing the system of land tenure and improving the methods of farming, which were hopelessly antiquated. It promised to hold elections for a national constituent assembly in the near future and modified the electoral system to make it conform with modern conditions. It extended the franchise to the clergy, but at the same time it abolished compulsory religious education in the public schools.

Elections for the constituent assembly were held in June, 1931, and resulted in an overwhelming victory for the Left Republicans and the Socialists. The assembly at once took up its task and, after nearly five months of consideration and debate, finally completed the republican constitution which on December 9, 1931, was adopted. Spain was declared "a republic of the workers of all classes," in which the franchise was extended to all men and women over twenty-three years of age. A single-chamber parliament (*Cortes*) was provided for, its members being elected directly for four years by popular vote. The president of the republic was to be chosen for a six-year term by an electoral college, consisting of the members of parliament and an equal number of electors chosen by the voters. Executive power was placed in the hands of a ministry directly responsible to the parliament. In other words, Spain became politically a democratic, parliamentary republic. In a move toward decentralization, the constitution provided that any area which desired autonomy might submit for the approval of the parliament a regional charter, and that the parliament in turn might delegate to the local authorities power to administer certain national laws.

Wide as was the break between Spain's former political system and that established in 1931, the departure from the former regime in social, cultural, and economic matters was perhaps even more pronounced. Spain was to have complete religious freedom and no state church. Education was to be secularized. Divorce was to be made easy, and illegitimate and legitimate children were to have equal rights. The state was to have authority (1) to expropriate, with compensation, all kinds of private property, (2) to socialize large estates, (3) to nationalize public utilities, and (4) to "participate in the development and co-ordination of industries." In general, therefore, all the wealth of the country was to be subordinated to the interests of the national economy. Spain, it appeared, was to be transformed from a semifeudal nation into a modern state with socialistic tendencies.

A special clause of the constitution provided that the first president of the Spanish Republic should be chosen by the national convention which had drafted the constitution. Accordingly, on December 10, 1931, Niceto Alcalá Zamora was elected to this office; on the next day he received the oath of office and took up his official residence in Alfonso's former palace. The provisional government at once resigned, and a new cabinet headed by Manuel Azaña took office. As has frequently been the case in the history of other countries, the constituent assembly did not resign upon the completion of its constituent duties, but continued to sit thereafter as the national parliament. The members of the assembly desired themselves to launch the program of reform which by laws should carry into effect the general principles laid down in the constitution. "We have finished the first step," said Premier Azaña. "We must now complete the revolution by drafting supplementary laws."

In January, 1932, the Jesuit order was dissolved; its property, valued at $30,000,000, was confiscated by the state and later ordered to be distributed for purposes of social welfare. In May, 1933, the drastic Associations Law was passed, stipulating that the heads of the various religious orders in Spain must be Spanish citizens and must submit to Spanish laws, and that the state reserved the right to pass upon their appointment. Members of religious orders were forbidden to teach anything except religion. Church schools were suppressed, and all teaching by members of religious orders was to cease. All church property was nationalized; although placed under the custody of the clergy, it was subject to the disposition of the government. All government support of priests was to cease after November 11, 1933. The pope at once issued a vigorous protest in an encyclical in which he condemned the separation of church and state and denounced the prohibition of teaching by religious orders.

The government also made a beginning of agrarian and labor reform. The great estates of Spain's grandees were confiscated, for the most part without compensation, and the parliament enacted a measure for distributing over fifty million acres of land held before the revolution by the king or under his royal grant. It was expected that a million Spaniards would be settled on these lands, and that they would be assisted with government subsidies. Furthermore, in the interests of the peasants and industrial workers alike, a new charter of economic independence and freedom was adopted, providing for a national schedule of working hours and wages and for mixed courts to settle labor disputes.

Finally, the problem of Catalan autonomy was settled to the apparent satisfaction of most of the Catalans. By the terms of an autonomy statute Catalonia in 1932 secured the right to have its own state government, which was given power to tax and to enact social legislation within certain restrictions. The enforcement of law and order in Catalonia was left to the local government, and the execution of national laws was in general confided to Catalan authorities. As further concessions to the national sentiment of the Catalans, they were granted the right to have a national anthem and their own flag. The Catalan language was made official in the province and was given equality with Castilian in official communications with the rest of Spain. On December 6, 1932, the Catalan parliament met for the first time since 1705.

THE STRUGGLE TO CONTROL THE REPUBLIC

But not all Spaniards were content with the course of events in the new republic. On the Right were the clericals, the royalists, and the landed aristocrats, who looked back with longing upon their positions and privileges in the old regime and who fervently prayed for the collapse of the republic and the return of the monarchy. On the extreme Left were the Syndicalists and Communists, who felt that the Spanish revolution had stopped altogether too soon, that the republican government should be displaced by a regime more like that in Soviet Russia. Abortive attempts to overthrow the government were made by both the royalists and the Communists in the years 1932 and 1933.

In November of the latter year the republic had its first parliamentary elections. The result was a disastrous defeat for the moderate Left parties which had been in control of Spain since the overthrow of the monarchy. The combined opposition of the Catholic Popular Action Party, led by the brilliant young editor José María Gil Robles, of the commercial, industrial, and financial leaders, and of the landlord classes—plus the universal tendency to vote against any government in office in time of economic depression—carried the day. The ensuing year was marked by a succession of minority governments which leaned more and more to the Right. The relations between the government and the Vatican were improved, legislation designed to ameliorate the lot of the clergy was passed, the educational measures and land reforms enacted in 1932–1933 were modified and weakened, and many grandees were permitted to return to their landed estates. The leaders of the Left became convinced that the parliament was undermining the republic and threatening to turn Spain back again to men who were monarchists at heart.

In October, 1934, a new ministry included three members of the Popular Action Party, which had been organized by men who in the national assembly had been frankly antirepublican and hostile to nearly every article in the constitution which was adopted. The Left parties at once called a general strike against what they claimed was a shift toward fascism in Spain. At the same time, Catalonia proclaimed itself a free and independent state. Open revolt spread rapidly through central and northern Spain, causing the death of thousands and the destruction of millions of dollars in property. But there was lack of solidarity among the Left elements and in many parts of the country relatively little support from the rural districts. The uprising in Catalonia was almost immediately crushed by the use of the army, the navy, and the civil guard. The Catalan statute was set aside and made subject to a thorough revision, while outstanding Catalonian leaders were held for trial by court-martial. In the reaction which followed, Socialist provincial governors and municipal councilors were throughout the country largely replaced by men loyal to the government at Madrid.

The Center and Right groups next sought to alter Spanish institutions to conform with their ideas, claiming that those who drafted the constitution had gone beyond the wishes of a majority of the Spanish people in matters relating to the church, education, and agrarian reform. In 1935 the government began to draft a number of constitutional amendments to carry out the policies of the Right. But ministerial instability continued, and when in December of that year the government was again overturned, President Zamora, who had apparently begun to fear for the safety of the liberal republic, appointed as premier a loyal moderate republican, dissolved the parliament, and called for new elections.

In the ensuing elections the score or more of political parties in Spain combined into two major groups. On the Left the Syndicalists, Communists, Socialists, Left Republicans, and Republican Unionists fought together as the Popular Front. They were determined to prevent the Rightists from securing control of the parliament lest they should liquidate completely the achievements of the republic. On the Right the Conservative Republicans, the clericals, and the royalists combined in an effort to prevent the triumph of those who were suspected of desiring to introduce a proletarian regime. The election resulted in a decisive majority in favor of the Left; within this coalition the Socialists won the most seats. Of all the parties, however, Gil Robles' Popular Action still had the greatest number of deputies.

1935

The premier, who was himself defeated in the election, at once resigned and was succeeded as head of the government by Manuel Azaña. The latter's ministry consisted of eleven Left Republicans and two Republican Unionists, the Socialists declining to participate in the government. Amnesty was at once proclaimed for 30,000 political prisoners and exiles. The Catalonian parliament, suspended since the revolt of October, 1934, reassembled, and steps were taken by the central government to restore Catalonian autonomy. Agrarian reform was again pushed, and thousands of tracts of land were distributed among the peasants. Anticlericalism once more surged to the front as scores of churches, schools, and convents were attacked and burned, and street clashes resulted in the death of some forty to fifty persons. In April, 1936, the parliament voted to remove President Zamora from office on the ground that he had exceeded his powers in dissolving the parliament, and Manuel Azaña was elected to succeed him as president.

CIVIL WAR

Meanwhile, the Popular Front government had been taking tardy steps to rid the army of officers whose loyalty to the existing regime was suspected. A decree stipulated that all officers known to have been politically active should be retired at once upon pensions. Some with monarchist or conservative sympathies were transferred to Spain's overseas possessions; General Francisco Franco, who had been chief of staff when Gil Robles was minister of war, was sent to the Canary Islands. In July the government further ordered the removal from their posts of many of the officers of the Foreign Legion in Morocco. These various measures threatened the control of Spain's military forces by the ruling clique of officers, and apparently led the latter to decide to overthrow the government. They knew that in a rebellion they could count on the support of most of the royalists, clericals, Conservative Republicans, and great landowners; and apparently they had the encouragement of Fascist and Nazi leaders in Italy and Germany.

On July 17, 1936, a number of regiments in Morocco raised the standard of revolt, and General Franco, the leader of the insurrection, flew to Morocco to take charge. In Spain garrisons in various parts of the country at once mutinied under the leadership of their generals. The Insurgents, it appeared, had the support of approximately 90 per cent of the officers and two thirds of Spain's organized military forces. In August, furthermore, they began to receive aid from Italy and Germany; ultimately thousands of well-trained officers and men from these countries joined the Insurgents as "volunteers."

The government, with only a small part of the organized military forces loyal to it, was obliged to turn to the Left-wing labor groups for assistance. In September, 1936, Francisco Largo Caballero, a Left-wing Socialist, became premier in a cabinet which for the first time included Communists. A Popular Militia of workers was hastily created, and thanks to its efforts Madrid and Catalonia were saved. But the Loyalist forces were unable to stop the advance of General Franco's disciplined units. In November the Insurgents were at the gates of Madrid, and the seat of the Loyalist government was transferred to Valencia. Germany and Italy thereupon extended *de jure* recognition to the Insurgent government which had been set up by General Franco at Burgos. But by this time the Popular Militia had been strengthened by antifascist volunteers from many foreign countries, and by supplies—particularly airplanes and tanks—presumably from

Soviet Russia. Although the Insurgents, or the Nationalists, as they came to call themselves, were unable to capture Madrid in either 1936 or 1937, in the latter year, aided by German and Italian planes, men, and munitions, they completed their conquest of northwestern Spain, and made plans to concentrate all of their forces against the Loyalist lines in the eastern part of the republic.

FOREIGN INTERVENTION

The outcome of the civil war in Spain was decided largely by the attitude of the major foreign powers. The fascist states—Italy, Germany, Portugal—assisted General Franco, on the professed ground that the triumph of the Loyalists would result in the establishment of another Bolshevik state in Europe. But Italy and Germany apparently saw advantages for themselves in the establishment of a fascist state on the "other" side of France. Mussolini by helping the Spanish Nationalists may have expected to advance Italy's program of controlling the Mediterranean, while Hitler apparently used the Spanish civil war to provide an opportunity for his military leaders to experiment with mechanized and aerial warfare in order to discover the best methods for a future blitzkrieg.

Soviet Russia appeared willing to assist the Spanish Loyalists, but the British and French governments seemed to be chiefly interested in preventing the struggle from developing into a general European war. The British people were divided in their views. Although the Laborites and trade unionists generally sympathized with the Loyalists, many others because of their economic investments and views were inclined to look with tolerance upon a Nationalist victory. The British government appeared to be attempting to follow a neutral policy. In France the Left groups favored the Spanish Loyalists, but the government—even when headed by Léon Blum—desired to avoid any steps that might open the way to a general war. The United States temporarily abandoned its traditional policy regarding the rights of legitimate governments in time of civil war, and forbade the export of munitions to either side, thus weakening the Loyalists who controlled the sea.

Not long after the civil war began, in August, 1936, France initiated negotiations looking toward a European agreement against intervention in the Spanish civil war. Eventually twenty-seven countries, including all the great powers of Europe, agreed to set up a committee in London to apply a policy of nonintervention. Early in 1937, on the suggestion of Great Britain and France, all of these countries further agreed to prohibit the flow of foreign "volunteers" to Spain and to this end decided to establish a system of international control. In March, by which time there were already 100,000 Italian soldiers in Spain in the guise of "volunteers," a naval cordon was thrown around Spain, and inspectors were stationed along the French and Portuguese land frontiers.

Eventually Great Britain and France pointed out that no improvement in the general European situation could be expected until the policy of nonintervention in Spain had been made fully effective by the withdrawal of foreign nationals from the Spanish armies. The question of the withdrawal of volunteers was therefore considered by the nonintervention committee, but the discussions were deadlocked by the fascist powers' demand that at the same time belligerent rights should be extended to the Nationalists. Ultimately, however, Italy and Germany agreed to accept in principle the British plan to defer the grant of belligerent rights until after "token" withdrawals of foreign fighters had been made from both sides. As was expected, the drafting of the specific plans for the actual withdrawals required long negotiations, and it was not until June, 1938, that the British plan for counting and evacuating the foreign volunteers was accepted by the nonintervention committee. The Loyalist government accepted the plan which had been drafted, but Franco's government raised so many objections to it that its reply constituted a rejection. In other words, Franco continued to have the assistance of large numbers of foreign troops.

VICTORY OF THE NATIONALISTS

Meanwhile, the Nationalists had pushed a threatening salient into the Loyalist lines defending Madrid, Valencia, and Catalonia, the point of the salient being only sixty miles from Valencia. Fearing that a Nationalist drive might divide Loyalist Spain and cut off Madrid and Valencia from Catalonia, the Loyalists late in October, 1937, had again moved the seat of their government—this time from Valencia to Barcelona. That they were justified in these fears soon became evident, for the Nationalists in the early months of 1938 drove eastward and on April 15 reached the sea south of Tortosa. The coast road connecting Barcelona with Valencia and Madrid was thus cut, and Loyalist Spain was divided.

For a number of months thereafter, thanks to the valiant efforts of the Loyalists, the military situation appeared deadlocked, but in December, 1938, the Nationalists with a well-equipped army of some 300,000 men again struck—this time toward Barcelona. The Loyalist forces, greatly inferior in guns, tanks, and airplanes, were unable to check the Nationalist advance. On January 13, 1939, Franco's forces crossed the Ebro, and twelve days later they reached the outskirts of Barcelona. Here they met no such determined fighting as they had encountered when they reached Madrid in November, 1936. The Loyalist government withdrew to Figueras, President Azaña fled to the Spanish embassy in Paris, and Barcelona surrendered without offering resistance on January 26.

With the extensive industries, munitions plants, and harbor facilities of Catalonia in the hands of the Nationalists, President Azaña and most of the cabinet ministers realized the futility of further resistance and urged the opening of negotiations with General Franco. Premier Negrín, a Right-wing Socialist who had succeeded Caballero as head of the government in May, 1937, was determined to continue the struggle, however, and in this determination was supported by the Cortes. But only central Spain with the two important cities of Madrid and Valencia still remained in Loyalist hands. To Madrid, therefore, Premier Negrín now returned by airplane, only to discover that the military leaders there believed that further resistance was useless.

On March 6 General Miaja, commander-in-chief of all remaining Loyalist forces, broadcast an appeal for peace. Then, following futile attempts to obtain a negotiated peace, General Miaja withdrew from Madrid, and on March 28, 1939, General Franco's victorious troops entered the capital unresisted. Already, on February 27, Great Britain and France had extended recognition to the Nationalist government in Burgos. The specter of a general European war rising out of foreign intervention in the Spanish struggle seemed at last to be definitely laid.

THE FASCIST CORPORATIVE STATE

Although during the civil war General Franco had received support from diverse groups within the country—royalists, landed aristocrats, army leaders, clergy, fascists—as early as April, 1937, he had adopted most of the program of the fascist Phalanx (*Falange Española Tradicionalista*) as his official program. In March, 1938, the Phalanx had issued a labor charter, and at the conclusion of the war the Nationalist government announced that this charter was thereafter to be applied throughout Spain. Labor unions were abolished, and strikes and lockouts were forbidden. All workers, including executives, were incorporated in vertical syndicates, restrictions were imposed on workers and employers alike, and each industry was organized under supervision of the syndicalist state, somewhat as in Italy under Mussolini.

Politically, Nationalist Spain was organized about the Phalanx Party, in which by a decree of July, 1939, officers and men of the army were incorporated as "affiliated members." At the head of the state stood the *Caudillo* (Leader)—General Franco—who on August 4, 1939, assumed "absolute authority" and became "responsible only to God and to history." Assisting him was the Phalanx National Council, part of whose members were named by the Caudillo, and the Phalanx Political Junta, the permanent governing body of the Phalanx, which had the right to present to the Caudillo any proposals it might think fit. In January, 1940, by the Law of Syndical Unity, all organizations representing economic or class interests —whether composed of employers or of workers—were incorporated in the Phalanx. The similarities between the Phalanx system of Spain and the Fascist system of Italy are readily apparent.

As might be expected, a number of decrees of a reactionary nature were issued. It was ordered, for example, that the grandees should be given back all land seized under the Agrarian Reform Law of 1932. The Catholic Church also regained many of the privileges which it had held in Spain before the downfall of the monarchy. Catholicism was made the official state religion, government subsidies were restored to the clergy, all confiscated property was returned to the Jesuits, civil marriage and divorce were prohibited, and religious instruction was required in all public schools, colleges, and universities.

While Franco took steps to reward his supporters, severe measures were invoked against those who had prominently supported the Loyalist government. A Law of Political Responsibilities, designed "to liquidate the political crimes of those who, through their acts or through their serious failure to act, have contributed to . . . the present plight of Spain," outlawed twenty-six specified organizations, including supporters of the Popular Front, autonomist organizations, and Masonic lodges. Even before the war ended, General Franco had stated that he had "more than 2,000,000 persons card-indexed, with proofs of their crimes and names of witnesses," and tens of thousands of new arrests were made immediately following the fall of Madrid.

Nationalist Spain's leaning toward the Axis powers was evident not only in its political and economic organization but in its foreign policy also. At the close of the civil war Franco's government signed Hitler's anti-Comintern pact, and in May, 1939, Spain withdrew from the League of Nations. The occasional demands of Spanish imperialists for the return of Gibraltar indicated that Spain under favorable circumstances might join the totalitarian states against the "possessing" powers, though financial weakness and need for physical rehabilitation militated against the country's hasty entrance into war in the immediate future. Throughout the Second World War she remained—formally, at least—an uneasy neutral.

Chapter XX

CENTRAL EUROPE AND THE

BALKANS

THE disruption of the once powerful Habsburg empire and the distribution of its territory and people among seven different states was one of the most spectacular of the many results of the First World War. Obviously, postwar central Europe differed radically from what it had been before 1914. Although the former Habsburg empire had long been a political anachronism, yet, stretching from the plains of the Vistula to the shores of the Adriatic and from the heart of the Alps to the bounds of Rumania, it had constituted a strong economic unit. Within its confines had been found grain fields, pasture-lands, and forests; oil wells and coal mines; iron, copper, lead, silver, and gold ores; breweries, distilleries, and sugar refineries; steel mills and textile factories; glassworks and potteries. All had been included within a common tariff union. This relatively balanced and unified economic organism was utterly disrupted by the nationalistic upheaval which followed the war.

Just as the Germans and Magyars, the ruling groups in the former empire, had bent all their efforts toward maintaining their predominance at the expense of the less fortunate nationalities, so now the liberated groups, particularly the Czechoslovaks, the Yugoslavs, and the Rumanians, directed their efforts toward protecting themselves against the vanquished. To check the outward thrust of Hungary's irredentism the surrounding states resorted to centripetal counteralliances. In this defensive movement the initiative was taken by Eduard Beneš, Czechoslovak foreign minister.

In 1920 Czechoslovakia and Yugoslavia signed a convention in which each agreed to assist the other in case of an unprovoked attack by Hungary. A Czechoslovak-Rumanian convention with practically identical terms was signed in April of the following year, and the so-called Little Entente was completed two months later by a Yugoslav-Rumanian alliance in which each agreed to aid the other if attacked by Hungary or Bulgaria. In 1933 a convention was signed with the purpose of transforming the Little Entente into a permanent "unified international organization." By the terms of this convention the earlier bilateral treaties between the members of the Little Entente were renewed for an indefinite period; a permanent council, consisting of the foreign ministers of the three states, was organized, and a permanent secretariat was established. Every political treaty and every economic agreement thereafter entered into by a member of the Little Entente was first to have the unanimous consent of the permanent council. This convention created in a sense—so far as international affairs were concerned—a new great power in Europe, with a population not far from 50,000,000 and with a combined military force of considerable size.

Austria

On October 21, 1918, the German deputies of the former Austrian Reichsrat had constituted themselves a provisional national assembly, and had declared the independence of German Austria. The bourgeois parties favored the establishment of a constitutional monarchy, but the workers demanded a republic and prepared to fight, if necessary, to get it. Elections in February, 1919, gave the Social Democrats the largest representation in the National Constituent Assembly, whose first act was to announce that Austria was a democratic republic. The Habsburgs were banished from the country, and all possessions of the dynasty were confiscated. On October 1, 1920, a constitution was adopted. Under it Austria became a federal republic with nine provinces, each with its own local diet. The national government had a bicameral legislature consisting of the Federal Council, elected by the diets, and the National Council, elected by popular vote. In 1929 provision was made for the popular election of the president also. Real executive power, however, resided in a ministry responsible to the National Council, which, furthermore, had authority to enact legislation over the veto of the upper house. The whole political structure rested on proportional representation and universal suffrage.

ECONOMIC AND FISCAL DIFFICULTIES

The disruption of the Habsburg empire had particularly unfortunate economic results for Austria. The latter, which inherited the populous capital of the former empire, was left with inadequate food supplies for her population and with insufficient coal and raw materials for her industries. She therefore faced the necessity of importing these commodities. But the free exchange of goods, which might have enabled her to pay for her imports by the exportation of her manufactured products, was prevented when each of the states of central Europe at once erected tariff barriers against its neighbors.

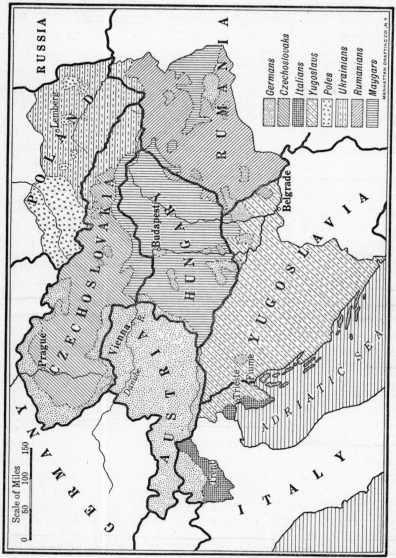

MANHATTAN DRAFTING CO., N.Y.

ETHNOGRAPHIC MAP OF THE FORMER DUAL MONARCHY, SHOWING THE SUCCESSION STATES, 1919–1938

By 1922 Austria's plight was so serious that Chancellor Ignaz Seipel proposed a currency and customs union with Italy as a cure for the republic's economic woes. But this proposal was so distasteful to Czechoslovakia that Beneš, the Czechoslovak foreign minister, did his utmost to persuade the League of Nations to save Austria from bankruptcy. In September, 1922, Seipel made a personal appeal to the League, stating Austria's willingness to accept a system of control if assistance were forthcoming, but warning that Austria unaided would constitute a grave danger to the peace of the world, a danger which it was the duty of the League of Nations to avert.

The League decided to undertake the financial rehabilitation of the little republic, and League experts worked out a plan essentially the same as the Dawes plan which was later drafted for Germany. On October 4, 1922, three protocols embodying the scheme were signed by representatives of Great Britain, France, Italy, Czechoslovakia, and Austria. The first protocol contained a solemn declaration that all the signatories would "respect the political independence, the territorial integrity, and the sovereignty of Austria," while the latter agreed not to alienate her independence and to "abstain from any negotiations or from any economic or financial engagement calculated directly or indirectly to compromise this independence." During the ensuing four years Austria was, so to speak, in the hands of a receiver. By June, 1926, however, the work of reconstruction had progressed to such a degree that the League's control of Austrian finances came to an end with that month.

During the next four years Austria managed to get along without great financial difficulties, but with the coming of the world depression her troubles once more began. In an attempt to meet the situation a tentative agreement was reached early in 1931 for the establishment of a customs union between Austria and Germany. But the nationalists of France, Czechoslovakia, and Poland—envisioning the consummation of the political union of the two countries which they so much feared—were immediately aroused, for to them the plan seemed to resemble the customs union which had helped Prussia to create the German political union in the nineteenth century. They therefore denounced the Austro-German proposal as contrary to the treaty of Versailles, the treaty of St. Germain, and the Geneva protocol of 1922. France and Great Britain brought the matter before the League of Nations, which in turn referred the question —one of interpreting treaty obligations—to the World Court for an advisory opinion. On September 5, 1931, the latter by an eight-to-seven vote decided that the proposed customs union was incompatible with the Geneva protocol of 1922. Again Austria had to turn to the League of Nations for help, and in the summer of 1932 a twenty-year loan of $42,000,000 was made to the republic through the Bank for International Settlements, but again with the proviso that Austria must not compromise her independence.

THE ANSCHLUSS QUESTION

To many the only solution for Austria's economic difficulties appeared to be union with Germany. Not all Austrians, to be sure, were thoroughly in sympathy with this idea. Some disliked the thought of being linked with a Germany so strongly Lutheran; others feared the dominance of aggressive and militaristic Prussia; while still others were disturbed by the prospect that their glorious Vienna might be relegated to the position of a second-rate provincial city like Munich. Those who favored the *Anschluss* argued, on the other hand, that all Germans should be in one state, that Austria's domestic markets would be greatly extended if she were part of Germany, and that, when it came to negotiating commercial treaties with foreign states, Austria as part of Germany could secure far better terms.

After 1931 the *Anschluss* question developed a new phase, largely because of the spectacular rise of Adolf Hitler in Germany. Even before the Nazi leader came into power at Berlin, a subdivision of his National Socialist Party was established in Austria, and the situation in the little republic became complicated by the organization of Nazi "Brown Shirts." Hitler's success in Germany in 1933 at once had its repercussion in Austria, where Austrian Nazis immediately began to work for the *Anschluss*. German Nazis, doubtless realizing that the outright annexation of Austria—which they had always advocated—would cause international complications, apparently determined to achieve the same end indirectly. Since the Austrian Nazis belonged to Hitler's party and took their orders from him, a Nazi political victory in Austria would bring the *de facto* union of the two republics. That this might be accomplished, the German Nazis spent millions of dollars on propaganda in Austria. Skilled agitators were sent into the little republic, while German Nazis dropped from airplanes over Austria and broadcast from Bavarian radio stations attacks upon Chancellor Dollfuss' government.

Eventually, on July 25, 1934, a small group of Austrian Nazis seized the government radio station and forced the announcer to broadcast a statement that the Dollfuss cabinet had fallen. Another group seized the chancellory, mortally wounded Dollfuss, and held other members of the cabinet captive. Apparently their plan was to force a reorganization of the government in order to give the Nazis prominent places in the new cabinet. Their plot was not well organized, however, and quickly collapsed. By July 28 the Austrian government had the situation well in hand, and on the next day a new cabinet was formed, headed by Kurt Schuschnigg, a Christian

Socialist colleague of the former chancellor and a member of Dollfuss' last cabinet. Between ten and fifteen of the Nazi leaders were eventually put to death, thus becoming Nazi martyrs, while hundreds were sentenced to prison terms of various lengths.

Events in Austria had their repercussions abroad, where it was widely believed that the German Nazis were back of the attempted revolt. Mussolini promptly mobilized troops along the Austrian frontier, as did also Yugoslavia. But Hitler's government carefully maintained a "correct" attitude, being as yet in no position to wage a war. It officially denied any connection with the Austrian revolt, closed the roads across the frontier into Austria, recalled the German minister in Vienna on the ground that he had overstepped his authority during the uprising, and dismissed the Nazi head of the radio station at Munich. Nevertheless, Austria's dependence upon outside support for the maintenance of her independence was made emphatically clear. Had it not been for Mussolini's swift dispatch of Italian troops to the Brenner Pass, the Nazi *Putsch* might have succeeded.

HEIMWEHR VERSUS SCHUTZBUND

But Austria was not disturbed merely by the German Nazis. In the second decade of its existence the republic was shaken by bitter conflicts between the urban proletariat and the rural classes. The republic comprised roughly two districts which were nearly equal in population though not in area. The eastern end, including Vienna, the plain between the capital and Wiener-Neustadt, and the ore-bearing districts of Styria, constituted a great industrial region. The rest of the republic was agricultural and was largely in the hands of peasant proprietors. As a consequence of these differences there had developed in postwar Austria a fairly clear-cut antagonism between the socialism of the factory and the individualism of the farm, between the skepticism of the city and the clericalism of the province— more specifically, between the "Reds" of Vienna and the "Blacks" of the countryside. The federalization of the republic had been caused chiefly by these differences, for decentralization had been demanded by the conservative Christian Socialists as a means of protection against the radical Social Democrats of the capital.

The enmity between the proletariat of Vienna and the peasants of the provinces led to the creation of two hostile military organizations, the *Schutzbund* and the *Heimwehr*. The former, with its strength in the industrial districts, came to have a well-disciplined membership of nearly 100,000 men, and managed to store in secret hiding places large quantities of arms and munitions for use in time of crisis. The rural Heimwehr, on the other hand, was a type of fascist organization which was not only strongly anti-Socialist but inclined to be monarchical as well. Financed to some extent by the wealthy Prince Ernst von Starhemberg, the Heimwehr ultimately enrolled some 60,000 well-armed men. Frequent clashes occurred between the rival bodies, and at times the government with its very small army had difficulty in maintaining order.

Ultimately the government's attitude toward this domestic conflict was influenced by its desire to prevent Austria from coming under the control of the Third Reich. At the close of the year 1933 Chancellor Dollfuss was looking for some way to strengthen his hand against the Nazis. The Social Democrats, the largest political group in Austria, would have been glad to unite with him in a common front against their common foe. But Mussolini, who had been supporting Dollfuss in his struggle to prevent the consummation of the *Anschluss,* apparently opposed an alliance with the Socialists and favored instead a government in Austria which should include the Heimwehr. The latter, in turn, made the destruction of the Socialists the price of their support. On February 12, 1934, police and Heimwehr men began raiding Social Democratic headquarters. When a general strike was called by Social Democratic leaders, Dollfuss at once outlawed the Social Democratic Party, declared martial law, ordered civilians with firearms to be executed, and began military measures against the Socialists. In the end the Social Democratic Party was completely suppressed.

Four weeks later the Austrian parliament without opportunity for debate—and with more than half of its members, including the Social Democrats, absent—approved a new constitution submitted to it by the Dollfuss government. An authoritarian corporative state was outlined. The word "republic" nowhere appeared in the new constitution, which abolished universal suffrage and political representation of the people. In one more European state democracy was crushed. Four years later Austria herself was crushed when Hitler absorbed the country into his Third Reich.

Czechoslovakia

On one of the last days of the First World War, October 18, 1918, Thomas G. Masaryk, head of the Czechoslovak Provisional Government in Paris, had issued the formal declaration of Czechoslovak independence, a step taken by Karel Kramář, head of the Czech National Committee, in Prague on the next day. The two provisional governments, the one in Paris and the other in Prague, had then co-operated in plans for the meeting of the first National Assembly, which, on November 14, 1918, unanimously proclaimed the republic and elected Masaryk President, Kramář premier, and Beneš foreign minister. On February 29, 1920, the National

Assembly approved a constitution, providing for a democratic parliamentary regime. The president of the republic was elected for a seven-year term by the National Assembly. On May 27, 1920, Masaryk was elected president.

Next to the revolution itself the greatest accomplishment of the republic, according to President Masaryk, was the land reform, which, in his words, constituted the "crowning work and the genuine realization" of the revolution. Before the reform, 2 per cent of the landowners of Bohemia owned more than 25 per cent of the land; less than one per cent of the landowners of Moravia owned nearly a third of the land; and in Slovakia about a thousand persons owned nearly half of the land. Most of these great estates owned by Germans had belonged to Czechs before the Bohemian Protestants were dispossessed by Emperor Ferdinand back in 1620. Land reform, therefore, had the double object of improving the lot of the peasants and righting a great historic wrong.

In April, 1919, a law providing for expropriation was passed. The maximum above which land might be expropriated was fixed at 375 acres for arable land and at 625 acres for other types. Peasant holdings were fixed usually at from 15 to 25 acres. By 1935 some 4,395,000 acres had been transferred to new peasant proprietors. A total of 1913 estates, including some 27 per cent of the tillable land of the country, had been involved. In place of a few hundred large agrarians, more than half a million peasants had become owners of land.

Undoubtedly the most difficult domestic problem of the republic arose from the great number of its racial minorities, about a third of the total population being Germans, Magyars, Ukrainians, Jews, or Poles. The rights of these minorities were protected by a minorities treaty signed by Czechoslovakia and by specific provisions of the Czechoslovak constitution which guaranteed the rights of all citizens without regard to language, race, or religion. Special schools for the minorities were provided, and official business might be transacted in a minority language in districts where 20 per cent of the populations belonged to that minority.

One phase of the minorities problem arose in Ruthenia, a province lying at the eastern tip of the republic. This province was assigned to Czechoslovakia by the peace conference to provide Czechoslovakia and Rumania with the direct connections which were considered essential to complete the territorial ring about Hungary. But the province was supposed to be granted extensive local autonomy. The population was composed largely of Ukrainians, who in 1919 were for the most part illiterate as a consequence of prewar Magyar oppression. The Czechoslovak government feared that a Ukrainian diet, if established at once, would be dominated by the well-organized Magyars and Jews rather than by the

Ukrainians, and therefore delayed establishing it. Although by 1922 more than half of the state officials of the district were natives of the district, the government's delay in granting full autonomy to Ruthenia caused bitter complaints.

The Czechs and Slovaks were officially regarded as forming one Czechoslovak nationality and as such constituted the racial majority in the republic. Nevertheless, the differences between them were marked. The Czechs had a very high degree of literacy and were inclined to be both socialistic in politics and agnostic in religion. The Slovaks, on the other hand, had in 1918 a high degree of illiteracy and as a conservative peasantry were for the most part loyal and pious Roman Catholics. It is perhaps not surprising, therefore, that friction developed between them. In the early years of the republic the Slovaks complained that the Czechs were monopolizing the administrative offices. The Slovak Popular Party (Catholic) began to demand semiautonomy for the province, and in 1924 went even so far as to hold meetings calling for a boycott of everything of Czech origin until the demand should be granted. Eventually, in 1929, a new local autonomy law went into effect and Bohemia, Moravia and Silesia, and Slovakia were given three local councils which were partly elected and partly nominated. By then, too, Ruthenia also had its own elected diet.

The aim of the government, under the direction of Masaryk and Beneš, was not only fair treatment of the minorities but such a union of all groups of the population that distinctions of majority and minority would not be felt. At first that policy seemed to succeed. In October, 1926, two Germans became members of the government, and three months later they were joined by two representatives of the Slovak Popular Party. Nevertheless, continued unrest in Slovakia led in September, 1929, to the dissolution of the parliament and to the Slovak Popular Party's decision to co-operate with the German and Magyar minorities in an effort to throw off Czech domination.

In 1932–1933 the German Nazi movement penetrated Czechoslovakia as it did Austria, and tended to interfere with the co-operation of the German parties in the parliament. The Czechoslovak government realized the menace of Hitlerism, with its Pan-German program, and sought, by restricting the use of the radio and prohibiting the circulation of many foreign newspapers from Germany and Austria, to handicap Hitlerite propaganda in the republic. Nevertheless, the Sudeten German (*Sudetendeutsch*) Party, which was organized under the leadership of Konrad Henlein to advance Hitler's program, polled the largest number of votes in the republic in the parliamentary elections of May, 1935. The Nazi movement, therefore, became a force to be reckoned with in Czechoslovakia.

Early in 1937 the government, in an effort to conciliate the three million Germans, whose presence within Czechoslovakia constituted the republic's chief minority problem, reached an agreement with them providing for cultural autonomy, a fair share of government contracts, a greater proportion of German officials, larger appropriations for social services, and an extension of the official use of German. Although these concessions appeared to satisfy the million or more members of the German Social Democratic Party and the German Agrarian League, Henlein refused to approve them on the ground that they fell short of the political autonomy which the Sudeten German Party demanded. It was the alleged sufferings of the Sudeten Germans which Hitler used as his excuse for dismembering Czechoslovakia in 1938.

In 1935 Masaryk, at the age of eighty-five, had resigned the presidency and his colleague, Eduard Beneš, had been chosen to succeed him. It was upon President Beneš and Premier Hodža that the impossible task of dealing with Hitler and Henlein fell in 1938. Happily for the "Father of Czechoslovakia," he had died before his country was destroyed.

Hungary

In Hungary, out of the political crisis which ensued with the disintegration of the Dual Monarchy, there finally rose to power one of the very few liberal aristocrats of the country, Count Michael Karolyi. Realizing that the collapse of Hungary was impending, Karolyi, in October, 1918, had pronounced in favor of peace and a federalized, moderately socialized republic. He openly negotiated with leaders of the non-Magyar and Social Democratic groups and finally succeeded in creating a Hungarian national council which became essentially a revolutionary body. This council, backed by the Budapest garrison, demanded Karolyi's appointment as prime minister, and, after revolutionary troops on October 31 had actually seized the government buildings, the king gave way and called upon Karolyi to head a ministry. Some two weeks later (November 13) King Charles issued a document—never countersigned—in which he renounced all participation in Hungarian affairs and recognized in advance future decisions regarding the form of the Hungarian state. With the way thus cleared, the National Council on November 16 proclaimed the Hungarian People's Republic.

With feverish haste long-overdue reforms were next initiated. Democratic federation, universal suffrage, secret ballot, proportional representation, freedom of speech and of the press, trial by jury, separation of church and state, genuine liberal education, expropriation of the large estates—all these were included in the aims of the new government. But Karolyi's program, liberal though it was, failed to win the support of the non-Magyars. The concessions came too late. No longer would the subject races be content with federation within a Hungarian republic. They now demanded complete independence or union with their kinsmen in neighboring states. Moreover, the Allies had no sympathy with Karolyi's plan to retain the subject peoples in a federalized Hungary and in March, 1919, ordered Hungarian troops to withdraw from Transylvania. Karolyi at once resigned his position as provisional president.

Meanwhile, radicalism had rapidly increased, fostered by the hardships resulting from the continued Allied blockade and by Bolshevik ideas brought back by soldiers returning from the Russian front. The Socialists and Communists decided to seize upon Karolyi's resignation as an occasion to set up a soviet state. Actual power came into the hands of the new commissar for foreign affairs, Béla Kun. This young middle-class Jew had been an active Socialist ever since his graduation from the Transylvanian University of Kolozsvár. During the war he had been an officer in the Austro-Hungarian army on the Galician front, where he had been taken captive in 1915. He was in Russia during the revolution of 1917 and became an ardent admirer of Bolshevism. Supplied with money from Russia, Béla Kun had returned to Hungary with the avowed object of overthrowing the People's Republic and of establishing soviet rule in its place.

All branches of the government now came into the hands of soviet officials, who assumed practically dictatorial powers. The immediate nationalization of large industrial establishments, railways, banks, and mines was ordered. A drastic land-reform scheme was adopted which nationalized the large estates without compensation. An elective soviet system was introduced, with the franchise limited to productive workers. Education was separated from church control and reorganized on a strictly proletarian basis. The Communists, comprising only a very small minority of the population, resorted to terror in order to maintain themselves in power.

But even Red Terror could not maintain them in power against the rising tide of opposition. The peasants refused to sell their produce for Bolshevik currency. The majority of the trade unionists, not extreme Communists at heart, turned against the new regime. The Allied powers demanded the resignation of the soviet government to make way for one elected by the people. A counterrevolutionary movement was inaugurated, and at Szeged in the French zone an opposition government was set up. A Rumanian army defeated the Hungarian Red Army and in August, 1919, captured Budapest. Béla Kun fled to Russia.

In November, 1919, counterrevolutionary forces, led by Nicholas Horthy, a rear admiral in the former Habsburg navy, entered the Hungarian capital. Early in 1920 elections were held for a national assembly. Sentiment for a monarchy was once more strong, and the first law enacted by the assembly restored the former monarchical constitution. Although Charles IV had never legally abdicated the throne, his return was temporarily prevented by the attitude of the Allies. Consequently, on March 1, 1920, the National Assembly elected Admiral Horthy to act as regent during the enforced absence of the king. Three weeks later an executive order formally declared Hungary a monarchy.

Influenced by the hope that the strong monarchical reaction in Hungary presaged an enthusiastic welcome to his return and by the belief that a *fait accompli* would receive no more than a formal protest from the Allied powers, King Charles suddenly returned to Hungary in March, 1921, and demanded back his throne. But Horthy declined to surrender his power until ordered to do so by the National Assembly, and the Little Entente powers and the principal Allies vigorously protested. The Hungarian National Assembly urged Charles to leave the country and so the ex-monarch reluctantly withdrew.

But Charles was neither convinced nor contented. In October, 1921, he made his second return to Hungary. Hungarian troops were dispatched against him, however, and he was defeated and taken prisoner. Horthy's government then demanded that Charles abdicate, but he resolutely refused to comply. Upon representations from the Allies, the ex-monarch and his wife were eventually delivered on board a British monitor in the Danube for removal to a definitive place of residence. The Allies demanded the deposition of Charles, but the Little Entente powers went further and demanded the permanent exclusion from the throne of the whole Habsburg dynasty. The Hungarian National Assembly was obliged to pass a law carrying these demands into effect. Hungary thus remained a monarchy, but with the election to the throne indefinitely adjourned.

Nevertheless, Hungary remained generally conservative in her institutions. Soon after proclamation of the monarchy an executive decree restricted the suffrage and called for open voting in most districts. In 1926 an upper legislative chamber was created, with forty life members and with the rest not popularly elected but drawn from the nobility, county and municipal councils, church organizations, universities, and commercial and industrial bodies. Not until 1938 was much progress made toward political democracy. In that year a law was finally passed extending the secret ballot to all constituencies and enfranchizing all men over twenty-six years of age, provided they met certain educational standards, and all women over thirty years of age, provided they were self-supporting or married to men qualified to vote. Although an agricultural country, Hungary experienced little in the way of agrarian reform during most of the postwar period, remaining a land of large estates. While nearly 40 per cent of the land was held in estates of more than 1400 acres each, the great majority of the peasants consisted of landless agricultural laborers or of owners whose tiny holdings placed them in practically the same category.

Among the lesser states of Europe, Hungary was probably the outstanding advocate of revisionism. From the day the treaty of Trianon was signed the spirited Magyars were ardent revisionists, for they deplored their loss of territory and the inclusion of some three million of their kinsmen within the frontiers of other states. Furthermore, they could not forget their pre-war dominant position as rulers of millions of Slavs, nor could the former landed aristocrats reconcile themselves to the loss of their vast estates in Transylvania and elsewhere. Their denunciation of the treaty of Trianon was vigorous, and their determination to overthrow the settlement established by that treaty was openly proclaimed by such nationalist organizations as the "Awakening Magyars."

When Hitler inaugurated his *Drang nach Osten* and sought the collaboration of some of the smaller states, he made a strong appeal to Hungarian revisionists by holding out promises of returning to Magyar control some of the regions which had once been in Hungary. Although the Budapest government sought for a time to combat Nazism, as the governments in Vienna and Prague had done, by 1939 Hungary had swung over to the Axis powers. In February of that year she signed Hitler's anti-Comintern pact, and two months later she announced her withdrawal from the League of Nations. With Austria and Czechoslovakia safely within the Reich's grasp, it appeared in 1939 that Hungary, too, was rapidly being brought under the economic and political influence of the German Führer.

Poland

History, which is frequently said to repeat itself, occasionally has a way of reversing itself. In the closing years of the eighteenth century Poland, partitioned by powerful Romanov, Hohenzollern, and Habsburg monarchs, disappeared as a state from the map of Europe. When at the close of the First World War those same proud dynasties were hurled from their thrones, the three separated portions of the Polish people once more became united, and their state again assumed an important position in the political system of Europe.

THE PROBLEM OF BOUNDARIES

Probably no other postwar territorial settlement in Europe led to so much actual fighting or to such bitter and prolonged controversy as did the definition of Poland's boundaries. The difficulties in connection with the problem of Danzig and the Polish Corridor have been discussed.[1] Just as the acquisition of the Polish Corridor led to animosity between Germany and Poland, the latter's seizure of Vilna caused bitter hostility in Lithuania.

Vilna had had a varied history. Capital of the medieval kingdom of Lithuania, it had passed under Polish influence when the two countries became united by the marriage of the Grand Prince of Lithuania to the young Queen of Poland in the fourteenth century. This union, further cemented by the Act of Lublin in 1569, lasted until the close of the eighteenth century, and during this period the Polish language and people came to dominate in the region about Vilna; in fact, the latter became a center of Polish culture. By the partitions of Poland, Vilna next passed under Russian control.

Following the overthrow of the tsar and the defeat of the Central Powers, the Lithuanians declared their independence and set up their own government in Vilna. In January, 1919, the Bolshevik army drove the Lithuanians out of Vilna, but the Bolsheviks in turn were driven out by the Poles, who then occupied the city themselves. No definite frontier between the two states was laid down by the peace conference, but the treaty of Versailles provided (Article 87) that the boundaries of Poland not established by that treaty should be "subsequently determined by the Principal Allied and Associated Powers." Acting under this authority, the Supreme Council on December 8, 1919, laid down a provisional boundary, the "Curzon line," which gave to Poland most of the territory in which the Poles predominated, but assigned the city and province of Vilna to Lithuania. Nevertheless, in 1920 irregular Polish troops drove the Lithuanians out of Vilna and in subsequent years efforts of the League of Nations to adjust the dispute to the satisfaction of both powers proved futile.

As Poland's seizure of Vilna antagonized Lithuania, her acquisition of part of Upper Silesia antagonized Germany. A plebiscite in that district, provided for in the treaty of Versailles, resulted in 707,605 votes for Germany and 479,359 for Poland, with 754 of the communes in favor of Germany and 699 in favor of Poland. The Poles at once claimed that they should be given those districts having Polish majorities, while Germany contended that the province was economically indivisible and that its fate as a whole should be decided by the majority. While the controversy continued to become more and more acute, a force of irregular Polish troops overran a large part of the territory. The matter was eventually referred to the League of Nations, which awarded the larger part of the population and territory to Germany, but gave Poland by far the greater proportion of the economic resources.

[1] See pages 398–400.

CENTRAL EUROPE, 1919–1938

The acquisition of eastern Galicia, like that of Vilna, resulted largely from the use of force. Although the inhabitants of western Galicia readily united in the establishment of the Polish Republic at the close of the war, the Ukrainians who constituted the bulk of the population in eastern Galicia were opposed to such a step. Many desired to unite with their kinsmen in the Ukrainian People's Republic, while others organized a national council in Lemberg and sought to establish an independent state. The Poles refused to recognize Ukrainian self-determination, immediately invaded the region, occupied Lemberg on November 5, 1918, and during 1919 completed their conquest of the province.

Between Russia and Poland the peace conference originally laid down a provisional frontier known as the "Curzon line," which was in general accord with the ethnographic situation. This, however, was not satisfactory to the Poles, who undertook a military campaign to regain their frontier of 1772.[2] The treaty which was finally signed with Russia at Riga in March, 1921, gave Poland an eastern boundary which, except for the territory that had become the new Republic of Lithuania, corresponded roughly with the one she had had just before the partition of 1795. The peace of Riga and the decision of the Council of Ambassadors to sanction the northern, eastern, and southeastern boundaries (1923) closed the period of acute controversy over Poland's frontiers. As finally stabilized, they included a territory four fifths as large as Germany, with nearly 29,000,000 inhabitants, many of whom, unfortunately, were of non-Polish nationalities. The frontiers were so drawn that in the first years of the republic, according to one Polish statesman, 75 per cent were "regarded as permanently menaced, 20 per cent insecure, and only 5 per cent safe."

THE CONSTITUTIONAL PROBLEM

Meanwhile, Poland had begun the organization of her political life in the hope of establishing a stable and efficient regime, and eventually, in March, 1921, a constitution was adopted. As in France, the president was to be elected for a seven-year term by a majority vote of the two legislative houses meeting together as a national assembly. The president was given no power over legislation, and in general his authority was greatly limited. Both houses of the parliament were to be elected directly by universal suffrage with an age requirement of thirty years for electors of the Senate. Real power in legislation was placed in the Chamber of Deputies (the *Sejm*), which was empowered to pass any measure over the veto of the Senate by a bare eleven-twentieths majority of those voting. Twenty months elapsed between the adoption of the constitution and the first parliamentary elec-

[2] See page 449.

tions held under it in November, 1922. A score or more of political parties then presented candidates, and at least fifteen of them succeeded in obtaining representation in the first Chamber of Deputies.

Poland was urgently in need of a strong, efficient government to deal with her serious economic and political situation. But the first parliament hindered rather than provided the efficiency needed. The multiplicity of parties produced ministerial instability, for no majority could be found that would consistently support a ministry. Governments changed in personnel and policies at frequent intervals, six ministries following one another within three and a half years. The policy of restricted expenditures, increased taxation, and cessation of inflation for the sake of fiscal reform was for two years prevented because the parliament would not support it. Agrarian reform was sacrificed to the interests of the great landed proprietors, capitalists, and rich peasants. Demands for new elections were heard on many sides. But Poland's constitution made it impossible for the government to dissolve the legislature and hold new elections without the consent of the Senate, and the latter, reluctant to face a new election, withheld its consent. An obstructive legislature and an obstructive constitution seemed to stand in the way of a strong government.

The political situation in Poland greatly disturbed Joseph Pilsudski, perhaps the most outstanding Polish patriot of his day. A veteran of the Russian revolution of 1905, he had suffered exile for his activities at that time. A determined opponent of the tsarist regime, he had left Russia on the very day that war was declared and had organized Polish legions to fight for the Central Powers in the First World War. Becoming convinced in 1917 that the latter did not intend to permit the establishment of a completely united and independent Poland, he had refused to fight longer against Russia and, in consequence, had been thrown into a Prussian prison in Magdeburg. From here he had been released by the outbreak of the German revolution, and had returned to Warsaw to help establish the Polish Republic.

In May, 1926, Pilsudski decided that the Polish political situation called for drastic action, and he and his followers marched on Warsaw somewhat as the Fascisti had marched on Rome. The premier and the president were forced to resign, and the constitution was amended in order to strengthen the executive control of the budget, provide the president with authority to dissolve the parliament with the consent of his cabinet, and give him power within limits to issue ordinances with the force of law. By the use of such presidential decrees steps were at once taken to balance the budget, stabilize the currency, reorganize the Polish Bank, and improve the national credit. In the ensuing years Pilsudski largely dictated the policies of the republic. Ministries came and went, but the premiers were regularly his lieutenants.

Pilsudski and his followers desired to reform the constitution in order to establish in effect a presidential dictatorship with a docile legislature. As early as 1929 they submitted such a project, but it was rejected by the parliament. They hoped that the elections of 1930 would give them the necessary control to accomplish their ends, but in this they were disappointed. In the spring of 1931 their project for constitutional reform was again presented and was again rejected. Once more in 1934 the government submitted its proposals, and this time, by methods which the opposition denounced as illegal, it secured the adoption of a new constitution, which was promulgated on April 23, 1935. Under the new frame of government the president appointed the ministers, who practically were responsible only to him; he convened, adjourned, and dissolved the parliament; he was head of the army, and appointed and dismissed the commander-in-chief and the inspector-general; he appointed one third of the members of the Senate, the others being chosen by a very limited electorate. The new basis of government obviously provided for a powerful executive. But the new electoral law provided for a complicated and far from democratic method of nominating and electing the Chamber of Deputies, and popular dissatisfaction with it led to a boycott of the elections of that year by a majority of the qualified electorate. On May 12, 1935, less than three weeks after the promulgation of the new constitution, Marshal Pilsudski, the outstanding exponent of strong government for Poland, died on the ninth anniversary of the bold coup by which he had seized control of the government.

THE PROBLEM OF MINORITIES

Poland contained within her borders the largest minorities population of all the countries of Europe. The most numerous minority group consisted of the Ukrainians. The latter insisted that the local autonomy which was extended to eastern Galicia was greatly restricted and not at all consonant with that stipulated by the peace settlement. Furthermore, they asserted that Poland was not observing her obligations under the minorities treaty but instead was carrying on a campaign to "Polonize" the eastern provinces. Although in 1924 some concessions were made in matters of language and schools, the Ukrainians continued to complain of the way they were treated, and at times even resorted to passive resistance by refusing to pay their taxes.

The second largest minority group consisted of the Jews. Unlike the other minorities, they were not segregated in one area, but constituted a large percentage of the population in all towns and cities. In the early years of the republic they were subjected to harsh treatment at the hands of the Poles, who denounced them as not being good patriots on the ground that they put personal profit above national welfare. In 1925, however, the government negotiated with representatives of the Jews an agreement which became known as the "Declaration of Warsaw." In consequence of the Jews' recognition of their duties to the republic, measures were introduced giving them the same linguistic privileges as had been granted to the border peoples, legalizing their observance of Jewish religious holidays, and recognizing their schools. The agreement went far toward removing the causes of friction between the government and one of the republic's most numerous minorities. Nevertheless, in the succeeding years, and especially after the rise of anti-Semitism in Germany in 1933, there were occasional anti-Jewish outbreaks in Poland. In fact, in 1936–1937 Jews in foreign countries were active in calling attention to the woes of their kinsmen not only in Germany but in Poland as well.

The third major minority group in Poland consisted of Germans, and between Poland and Germany friction was occasioned by the former's treatment of these Germans within her territory. Poland was eager to regain for Poles as much as possible of the land which had passed from Polish into German hands while Posen was in the German Empire, and in 1920 decided to cancel all contracts of tenants who held land from the former German government unless they could show clear legal titles. Germany appealed to the League, and the question went finally to the World Court, which decided that Poland must compensate the German colonists who had been evicted. Friction between Poland and Germany arose also from the complaints of the German minority in that part of Upper Silesia which was awarded to Poland in 1922. Germans here asserted that they were being subjected to mistreatment and unfair discrimination. The Polish government, it was alleged, failed to provide adequate protection to the Germans, who were exposed to terrorism at the hands of the Poles, particularly during political campaigns. Germans in Poland sought the sympathy of the German Republic, which on several occasions brought the Silesian troubles before the League. In fact, in 1939 Hitler used the "ruthless oppression of the Germans by the Poles" to whip up an anti-Polish hysteria in Germany on the eve of the Second World War.

THE PROBLEM OF AN OUTLET TO THE SEA

By the Paris peace settlement the only outlet to the sea which Poland received was Danzig, which was not included in Poland but was set up as a free city under the protection of the League of Nations.[3] Danzig had its own government, but the city's foreign relations as well as the protection of its nationals abroad were committed to Poland. The control of

[3] See page 399.

the port of Danzig was entrusted to a commission composed of an equal number of Poles and Danzigers with a neutral chairman, and Poland was given "free use and service of the port." Economically, during the first decade of its new regime, the free city prospered. Its importance as a port increased. In 1925 the total tonnage of seagoing vessels entering and leaving Danzig was about twice as much as in 1912, and the total import and export trade of the port for 1927 was more than four times as great as for any prewar year.

Poland was not entirely satisfied with this situation, however, and to free the republic from complete dependence upon Danzig, the construction of a new port was begun in 1925 at Gdynia on Polish territory in the extreme western corner of the Bay of Danzig. By 1929 what was formerly an obscure fishing hamlet had become a city of 15,000 inhabitants with a port capable of handling 2,000,000 tons of freight yearly. In 1930 the government inaugurated regular steamship service between Gdynia and New York, and opened a new railway between Gdynia and Bromberg on the southern edge of the Polish Corridor. In 1931 Poland turned to the bankers of her ally, France, and entered into an agreement with them to finance the building and operation of a railway to connect Upper Silesia with Gdynia. A direct line between the coal fields of Upper Silesia and Gdynia would greatly facilitate the exportation of Polish coal. By 1933 Gdynia had surpassed Danzig in total trading volume and had come to monopolize practically all of Poland's overseas passenger traffic. In 1939 its population totaled more than 125,000.

Poland's determination to create a great port of her own, however, caused considerable alarm in Danzig, which felt that its own economic position as the chief outlet for Polish commerce was threatened. In 1930 Danzig appealed to the League of Nations, seeking to have Poland compelled to use the port of Danzig either exclusively or preferentially for her sea-borne trade. But Poland refused to consider any arrangements involving the compulsory dependence of her trade upon Danzig, and steadily proceeded with the development of Gdynia. In 1933, however, a convention was signed between Poland and Danzig which stated definitely that Poland would direct 45 per cent of her foreign trade through Danzig and 55 per cent through Gdynia.

In the succeeding years the organization of a Nazi party in Danzig greatly disturbed the situation in the free city. The election of members of the Danzig Assembly on April 7, 1935, was preceded by an exciting electoral campaign in which some of the outstanding Nazi leaders of the Third Reich, including Göring, Goebbels, and Hess, participated. A Nazi campaign of terrorism, moreover, sought to intimidate the Socialists and Poles. The Nazis increased their representation in the Assembly, and gained

control of the Danzig government, and during 1936 and 1937 by administrative measures they transformed the government of the free city from
a democratic to a totalitarian regime. The Communist, Social Democratic,
German Nationalist, and Center parties were all dissolved or suppressed.
After October, 1937, the National Socialist Party was the only German
party permitted in the free city. Thus the Nazis eventually accomplished
in Danzig that co-ordination with the Third Reich which they had sought
but failed to achieve in Austria in 1934. But Hitler was not satisfied, and
his determination to absorb Danzig into the German Reich was the
immediate cause of the Second World War.

Greece

For repeated and spectacular reversals of political life, no state better
exemplified the unsettled conditions in the Balkans in the period between
the wars than Greece. The conflict between King Constantine and Venizelos
during the war sharply divided the Greeks into two hostile groups, and
after the king's forced abdication in 1917 Greek politics became subject
to sudden and unexpected shifts. The first of these shifts resulted from
the parliamentary elections of November 14, 1920. The unexpected death
of King Alexander in the preceding month injected into the campaign
the question of Constantine's return and made the elections a test of the
immediate relative popularity of Venizelos and the ex-monarch. The
premier's Liberal Party was decisively defeated, and Venizelos withdrew
from Greece. A popular plebiscite resulted in favor of the deposed monarch, who entered Athens amid great popular enthusiasm on December 19,
1920.

Unfortunately for Constantine, his presence on the throne came to be
connected in the public mind with the appalling Greek military disaster
of 1922.[4] His abdication was at once demanded by the military chiefs and
on September 27, 1922, Constantine surrendered his throne for the second
time in a little over five years. The Greeks then turned to Venizelos who
was recalled to the service of his country and sent to salvage all that was
possible for Greece at the Lausanne peace conference. The conflict between Constantine and Venizelos appeared to be settled in favor of the
latter.

The next shift which involved Venizelos arose from the question of
establishing a republic. Although Constantine's eldest son succeeded to the
throne as George II, sentiment in favor of transforming Greece into a
republic grew rapidly. Venizelos opposed the parliament's desire to depose
the king and advocated instead a popular plebiscite on the question. When

[4] See page 604.

the parliament persisted in its desire, Venizelos again withdrew from Greece, and in his absence the parliament voted to overthrow the Glücksburg dynasty. A popular plebiscite on April 13, 1924, then approved the establishment of a republic.

During the next four years conditions in Greece were far from stable. A succession of republican governments held office until Venizelos returned to his native land and in July, 1928, again became prime minister. In new parliamentary elections his Liberal Party secured about 90 per cent of the seats. The electorate, apparently weary of the endless succession of weak governments, had turned again to the country's only dominant personality. During the next four years Greece enjoyed a period of political stability and progress.

Along with the problem of securing political stability, Greece after 1922 was compelled to wrestle with the necessity of assimilating some 1,200,000 refugees who came to her chiefly from Asia Minor and eastern Thrace as a consequence of the Greek military disaster of 1922 and the resultant treaties with Turkey. The exigency which arose when the population of the country was thus suddenly increased by one quarter forced the republic to appeal to the League of Nations for assistance, but in the course of succeeding years the refugees were accommodated. The ultimate result for Greece was undoubtedly beneficial. Most of the naturally industrious Greeks from Asia Minor were settled in Greek Macedonia and western Thrace. New territories were put under cultivation, new crops were introduced, new industries were established, and the economic center of gravity in the republic was shifted in the direction of Saloniki.

But the effect of the influx of Greek refugees was not alone economic. It conferred a predominantly Greek character upon the republic's territory in Macedonia and western Thrace and thus, it was thought, removed from the agenda of international disputes the question of the racial composition of those districts, where for economic reasons both Bulgaria and Yugoslavia had long desired to establish themselves. Furthermore, the exchange of Greek and Turkish populations ended, for the immediate future at least, the century-long Greco-Turkish territorial conflict. In 1930 the two republics signed a treaty of friendship and arbitration and reaffirmed their acceptance of the territorial *status quo*. Three years later the two powers signed a ten-year pact of nonaggression, mutually guaranteeing the inviolability of their common frontiers.

In Greece as in other countries the world economic depression had its effect upon politics. In parliamentary elections held in the autumn of 1932 the Liberals lost heavily and the royalist People's Party gained accordingly. Panagis Tsaldaris, leader of the latter party, then became premier at the head of a royalist ministry. In 1935 fear that Tsaldaris was planning to restore the monarchy led to a republican revolt. Civil war broke out in Macedonia and Thrace, and the islands of Crete, Samos, Mytilene, and Chios went over to the revolutionists. Five warships in the harbor of Piraeus were seized by the rebels and forced to head for Crete, where the republican leader, Venizelos, was living. Vigorous measures were taken by the government, however, and in less than two weeks the revolt had been crushed. Venizelos fled from Crete. A few of the leaders were put to death, and a considerable number of the rebels were imprisoned.

That there was some basis for the fear of the republicans soon became evident, for in July, 1935, the parliament voted to have a plebiscite in which the electorate should decide whether to continue the republican regime. General George Kondylis, however, desired that a plebiscite should be held only after the republic had been abolished. On October 10, 1935, a military *coup d'état* led by Kondylis overthrew the government, whereupon bills were rushed through the National Assembly abolishing the republic and restoring the monarchical constitution of 1911. General Kondylis himself became premier and also regent until King George should return. On November 3 the plebiscite was held. Since the republicans felt that they could have little real influence on the outcome of the vote, in view of the fact that avowed monarchists were in control, they boycotted the plebiscite. The vote, therefore, proved to be almost unanimously monarchist. On November 25, 1935, George II, after an absence of some twelve years, returned to Athens as king. In April, 1936, King George appointed John Metaxas premier, and four months later Metaxas, after announcing that Greece was threatened by a Communist uprising, declared martial law, dissolved the National Assembly, and postponed elections indefinitely. From then until their country was conquered by the Axis powers in 1941, the Greeks lived under a dictatorship which was in its essentials fascist.

Yugoslavia

The kingdom of the Serbs, Croats, and Slovenes—after 1929 officially called Yugoslovia—comprised principally the descendants of three Slavic tribes which had pushed their way into the Danube valley and into the northwestern part of the Balkan peninsula in the seventh century. Despite their proximity and their kinship in race and language, however, the three peoples had never before 1918 constituted parts of the same state. Furthermore, with the Serbs looking eastward to Constantinople, and the Croats and Slovenes looking westward and northward to Rome, Vienna, and Budapest, the three groups in the course of centuries had developed many differences in customs, culture, and religion.

Nevertheless, a common racial heritage as Yugoslavs, a common hatred of the Habsburgs, and a vigorous nationalist propaganda emanating from Serbia had gradually brought the three groups to believe in a common nationality and to envisage their future in a common Yugoslav state. Existing differences were recognized, and the Corfu Manifesto of 1917, the so-called "birth certificate of Yugoslavia," seemed to take them all into consideration when it proclaimed to the world that the three peoples constituted a single nation; that their future state would be called "The Kingdom of the Serbs, Croats, and Slovenes"; that it would be "a constitutional, democratic, and parliamentary monarchy" under the ruling house of Serbia; that the new state would have a flag of its own and the three constituent members would in addition have their own flags, which would "rank equally" and might "be freely hoisted on all occasions"; that the two alphabets and the three religions prevalent among the Yugoslavs would likewise be of equal rank; that suffrage in the new state would be universal, equal, direct, and secret; and that the future constitution would be framed by a special constituent assembly elected by universal suffrage.

But the spirit of conciliation and co-operation, which the Corfu Manifesto so happily seemed to promise, failed to materialize. One question that famous document left to be decided, and the inability to settle it to the satisfaction of all caused continuous political unrest and repeated crises in the kingdom. Should Yugoslavia be a unitary or a federal state? Immediately after the collapse of the Central Powers and the disappearance of the Habsburg menace, the Yugoslavs split into two groups: those advocating a centralized state which should be in a general way an expansion of the former Serbian kingdom, and those demanding a federal state with a considerable degree of local autonomy. The leader of the former was Nikolas Pashich, the "grand old man of Serbia"; of the latter, Stefan Radich, the "uncrowned king of Croatia."

Although the latter's Croatian Peasant Party succeeded in electing fifty deputies to the Yugoslav constituent assembly, they refused to take their seats, so that Pashich was able to create a working majority. The Yugoslav constitution of June 28, 1921, therefore, provided for a centralized government which should apply equally to all parts of the country in order eventually to do away with localism and obliterate regional differences. Historic frontiers were erased, and provincial diets were supplanted by one national parliament (*Skupshtina*) in Belgrade. Local officials were to be chosen directly by the people, but in the conduct of their offices they were to be subject to national supervision exercised by the minister of finance and by prefects appointed by him.

The continued intransigence of the Croatian Peasant leader made parliamentary government difficult during the ensuing years, especially after the

THE BALKANS, 1923–1938

Croatian Peasant Party decided to permit its members to take their seats in the new parliament and after the country was later deprived of its most experienced statesman by the death of Pashich in December, 1926. Affairs came to a crisis on June 20, 1928, when Radich attacked a government proposal. Angered by the speech, a supporter of the government fired upon members of the Croatian Peasant Party, killing two and wounding several others. Among the latter was Radich himself, who died from the effects of his wound. The Croatian deputies thereupon withdrew from the parliament and set up a rival body at Zagreb, where they passed resolutions refusing to recognize laws enacted by the "rump" parliament at Belgrade.

King Alexander at length decided to resort to drastic measures and on January 5, 1929, he dissolved the parliament, abrogated the constitution of 1921, and called upon the commander of the guard division stationed in Belgrade to head the government. Yugoslavia was temporarily transformed into an absolute monarchy. Very definite efforts were made to wipe out particularism in the kingdom and to replace it by a genuine national sentiment. The use of the names of the separate races was frowned upon, the display of the flags of the separate peoples was prohibited, and the old historic boundaries were obliterated. Finally, in October, 1929, even the name of the state was changed by royal proclamation to the "Kingdom of Yugoslavia." After nearly three years of arbitrary rule, Alexander announced in September, 1931, that the dictatorship was ended, and a new constitution—not the work of a popularly elected constituent assembly but the product of the king and his advisers—was proclaimed.

The centralizing tendencies of King Alexander's government were apparently responsible for the assassination of the forty-five-year-old monarch. On October 9, 1934, the king disembarked at Marseilles on an official visit to France. As he and French Foreign Minister Barthou were riding together through the city, an assassin leaped upon the running board and shot the king dead. Investigations disclosed that the plot was the work of a Croatian terrorist organization headed by Ante Pavelich. In Yugoslavia Alexander's oldest son, a boy of eleven years, was proclaimed King Peter II, and a regency council was established.

Not until the Belgrade government became thoroughly alarmed at Hitler's *Drang nach Osten* and perceived how he used disaffection within Czechoslovakia to encompass that country's destruction, did it decide to make concessions to the Croatians. But on August 24, 1939, an agreement was finally reached between the Serbian and Croatian leaders, under the terms of which Croatia was to have its own legislative body at Zagreb and was to have full autonomy in all matters except foreign affairs, the army, foreign trade, state communications, public security, and religion. On September 23, 1939, the governor and the departmental heads of government of Croatia were appointed and Vladko Machek, Radich's successor as Croatian leader, announced that he was completely satisfied with the new arrangement. Unfortunately for the unity of the kingdom, however, the radical element among the Croatians still remained dissatisfied, and Hitler in 1941 was able to utilize this situation to his advantage.

Albania

To the west of Yugoslavia and Greece was Albania, the smallest and weakest of the Balkan states, with an area equal to that of Denmark but with only a quarter of the latter's population. The country, which gained its independence in 1913, was at that time a most backward and primitive region, having no railways and very few roads. Schools and newspapers were exceedingly scarce, and illiteracy was general. The population was for the most part agricultural or pastoral, organized on an almost feudal basis, and largely lacking in national sentiment. In fact, the question was raised then, and was subsequently repeatedly raised, whether there should be an independent Albania.

During the First World War the dismemberment of Albania was contemplated, but at the peace conference President Wilson steadily opposed its partition. Italy sought a mandate for the region, most of which she had occupied in the course of the war, but the military opposition of the Albanians led the Italians to recognize their independence and to withdraw from the country in the fall of 1920. Despite the desire of Greece and Yugoslavia to partition the country, Albania's independence was recognized by her admission to membership in the League of Nations in December, 1920. During the following year, while the question of boundaries was still unsettled, repeated incursions into Albania were made by bands from Yugoslavia, and disruptive revolutionary movements were encouraged and assisted with money, arms, and ammunition sent in from that country. This menacing situation was eventually ended by the League of Nations, which threatened to consider the application to Yugoslavia of Article 16 relating to economic sanctions.

Meanwhile, within Albania the question of future government was being settled. A monarchical regime had been originally set up with a German prince as ruler, but he had been forced to leave the country soon after the outbreak of the First World War. Early in 1920 a temporary regency council of notables was elected in place of the monarch, and a struggle for control ensued. After frequent changes in the government during a period of three years, Ahmed Zogu, a young tribal chieftain who from the age of sixteen had been fighting in the cause of the Albanian mountaineers, at length won out. In 1925 a national assembly was convoked, a republic proclaimed, and Zogu elected president for a seven-year term. The president had powers which made him essentially a dictator; in fact, in 1928 the National Assembly proclaimed him King Zog I.

The Albanian ruler's chief task was to create a modern state. To secure the capital which he so much needed, he entered into close relations with Italy. To secure an entering wedge for the economic domination of this weak state on the opposite shore of the Strait of Otranto, Italy gladly advanced the necessary funds. The treaty of Tirana (1926) granted Italy extensive economic concessions in Albania, and the Italo-Albanian defensive alliance (1927) drew the two states still closer together.[5] Albanian finances and the Albanian army were placed under the supervision of Italian experts. For all practical purposes Albania became an Italian protectorate and an outpost for Mussolini's desired economic penetration of the Balkans. Eventually, in April, 1939, Mussolini swept away all pretense, drove out King Zog, and had Victor Emmanuel proclaimed King of Albania.[6]

Bulgaria

The political history of Bulgaria after the First World War, although not so kaleidoscopic as that of Greece, was far from calm and uneventful. The military defeat of Bulgaria brought the immediate abdication and flight of King Ferdinand, who had been largely responsible for the country's joining the Central Powers, and the elevation to the throne of his young son, Boris III, who in succeeding years proved to be as democratic as his father before him had been autocratic. Military defeat likewise brought the downfall of the existing government and eventually (October, 1919) the elevation to the premiership of the leader of the Agrarian Party, Alexander Stambolisky. Under his guidance the Agrarian Party won a decisive victory in the parliamentary elections of March, 1920. Then followed a three-year period of Agrarian rule in which the role of Stambolisky differed not materially from that of dictator. The Agrarian leaders became ever more overbearing and intolerant. Freedom of the press was abolished, leaders of bourgeois parties were imprisoned, and universities were closed. Inevitably the bourgeoisie, the intelligentsia, and the military discovered a common bond in their hatred of the Agrarian regime. A conspiracy was entered into, and on June 9, 1923, all the ministers were suddenly arrested except Stambolisky, who was absent from the capital. A new government representing all opposition parties but the Communists was formed with Alexander Tsankov, a professor in the University of Sofia, as premier. Stambolisky was later captured and shot, and his parliament, on the ground

[5] For the terms of these agreements, see page 491.
[6] See page 659.

that it had been elected by fraud and violence, was dissolved. Thus ended the era of Agrarian rule.

A major threat to Bulgaria's political stability was the Macedonian revolutionary movement, which antedated the First World War. As early as 1893, when Macedonia was still included within the Ottoman Empire, agitation for autonomy had been begun by the Internal Macedonian Revolutionary Organization (IMRO). This agitation had eventually won the sympathy of the Bulgarians, who dreamed of a modern Macedonia which should be dependent upon Bulgaria for the defense of its territorial integrity, and be bound to her by ties of close kinship. But by the treaties of Bucharest (1913) and Neuilly (1919) Macedonia had been divided, most of it being allotted to Serbia and Greece.

After the First World War over 200,000 refugees and exiles from Greek and Serbian Macedonia had flocked into Bulgaria, where they formed a well-organized and well-armed group. These homeless masses constituted a grave domestic problem for Bulgaria, embarrassing the government's foreign policy by their constant demands for the redemption of their "Bulgaria irredenta," complicating the political situation by providing a fertile field for Communist propaganda, and frequently disturbing the ordered existence of the country by their brigandage. In that district of Bulgaria which was located near the convergence of the frontiers of Greece, Yugoslavia, and Bulgaria, the Macedonian *comitadjis* established a base of operations for guerrilla warfare, and their revolutionary activities repeatedly excited alarms and protests on the part of neighboring states. Numerous clashes occurred along the Greco-Bulgarian and Yugoslav-Bulgarian frontiers.

Another serious threat to the political stability of Bulgaria came from the Communists. In September, 1923, they launched an unsuccessful revolt to replace the monarchy with a soviet republic. In April, 1925, came a second Communist attempt when a bomb was exploded in the cathedral in Sofia at a time when most of the members of the government were in attendance. More than a hundred persons were killed and several hundred were injured, including Prime Minister Tsankov. A counterterror was at once inaugurated by the government; martial law was proclaimed; thousands were arrested; many were put to death.

In 1932 the Communists once more surged to the fore. In municipal elections in February and September of that year they won 19 of the 35 seats in the municipal council of Sofia. Fear of Communism now led the bourgeoisie to take defensive measures again. The League of Reserve Officers, which had played a leading role in overthrowing Stambolisky, called for a rallying of all forces opposed to Communism, and in 1934 Bulgaria finally succumbed to a dictatorship when the government was overturned by a *coup d'état* executed by a group of army officers and politicians. The new government outlawed all political parties, forbade all party activity, and took vigorous steps against both the Communists and the Macedonian revolutionists. Eventually King Boris established a royal dictatorship with Kiosseivanov, a personal friend, as premier.

As in so many of the states to the east of Germany, the Nazi movement penetrated Bulgaria. And, as in many other states, the government struck back; in 1938 and again in 1939 it ordered the dissolution of the Bulgarian Nazi Party. But, though officially suppressed, a pro-Nazi movement continued with another name under the leadership of former Premier Tsankov, who became increasingly revisionist in his views. Meanwhile, Hitler's government assiduously wooed Bulgaria. That it achieved some success seemed indicated by the announcement in Berlin on July 5, 1939, at the time when Premier Kiosseivanov was visiting Hitler, that Bulgaria and Germany realized they inhabited the same *Lebensraum* and understood the implications of that fact. The implications became more evident in 1940–1941.

Rumania

Rumania's acquisition of territory as a result of the First World War surpassed the fondest expectations of her extreme nationalists, for she emerged from the war with her territory practically doubled in extent. The least-expected territorial acquisition was Bessarabia, the district between the river Pruth, the river Dniester, and the Black Sea, which Russia had taken from Turkey in 1812. In December, 1917, after the Bolshevik revolution, a Supreme Council in Bessarabia proclaimed an independent Moldavian republic and requested the Rumanian government to send troops to preserve order and to provide protection against the Bolsheviks. In April, 1918, this Supreme Council voted for political union with Rumania but the Soviet government, claiming that this council was not a truly representative body and that it was intimidated by the presence of Rumanian military forces, refused to recognize the legality of the action. Nevertheless, on October 28, 1920, the principal Allied powers—France, Great Britain, Italy, Japan—signed a treaty recognizing Rumania's sovereignty over the district. Rumania's acquisition of Transylvania, Bukowina, and part of the Banat of Temesvar by the treaties of St. Germain and Trianon has already been mentioned. In these regions there lived perhaps twice as many Rumanians as in Bessarabia, and they brought to the kingdom a higher culture and a greater political self-consciousness than the latter. The assimilation of all these territories taxed the Rumanian administrative system to the limit.

In the first elections held in Rumania after the war the peasant groups won a large majority, and a coalition government was organized under a Transylvanian leader. The conservative elements of the country at once became alarmed because of proposed expropriation of land and the fear of Bolshevik propaganda, and King Ferdinand, who maintained that he had the right to appoint and dismiss his ministers regardless of the parliamentary situation, dismissed the peasant government. General Alexander Averescu, leader of the People's Party, was appointed prime minister. During the next eight years, despite the undoubted numerical superiority of the peasant electorate, the government was kept almost constantly in the hands of Averescu or John Bratianu, leader of the Liberal Party. During these years a program of agrarian reform was inaugurated in an effort to appease the peasants. Legislation enacted between 1917 and 1921 provided for the expropriation of all landed property of absentee and foreign owners, all the arable lands of the crown, and all large estates in excess of 1250 acres. By 1932 approximately 90 per cent of the land was in the hands of small peasant proprietors.

Meanwhile, despite agrarian reform, the peasants were becoming more and more restless because of their inability to obtain control of the government. In May, 1928, a peasant convention in Transylvania was attended by some 200,000 members of the National Peasant Party. Some had come equipped with arms, expecting that force would be employed, and the more spirited proposed a march on Bucharest. Plans for a rival National Peasant parliament and for a republican movement in Transylvania seemed to endanger not only the existing government but the monarchy itself. On November 4, 1928, the premier grudgingly laid down the reins of office, and the long rule of the Bratianus was broken. Two days later Julius Maniu, the peasant leader, became premier. Parliamentary elections confirmed the peasants' victory by returning an overwhelming majority for the National Peasant Party. It appeared that the half century of almost continuous rule by aristocratic landed and capitalistic classes had come to an end, that Rumania's 14,000,000 peasants had at last come into their own.

The years 1929 and 1930 saw an increasing sentiment in behalf of Prince Carol, who in 1925 had renounced his right of succession to the throne, choosing instead to keep his mistress, Magda Lupescu. At that time the Rumanian parliament had recognized as crown prince five-year-old Michael, Carol's son by his wife, the former Princess Helen of Greece. Upon the death of King Ferdinand in July, 1927, Michael had succeeded to the throne, with a regency to govern during his minority. But the exiled Carol was popular with the army, and his return and accession to the throne were favored not only by his brother, Prince Nicholas, but by the veteran politician, General Averescu, and by the National Peasant Party as well. In June, 1930, Carol arrived in Bucharest by airplane. The parliament at once annulled all acts which had been passed relating to his abdication, recognized him as having been the *de jure* king of Rumania since the death of his father, and proclaimed him as Carol II.

For some months after Carol's return the government remained in the control of the National Peasant Party. Then, from April, 1931, to May, 1932, Rumania was ruled by a thinly veiled royal dictatorship with Nicholas Iorga as premier. Financial difficulties ultimately brought the latter's resignation, however, and the National Peasant Party once more returned to power under Alexander Vaida-Voevod. The latter's chief contribution to Rumanian history was the conclusion of a nonaggression pact with Soviet Russia and the signing of a treaty in which the two states mutually guaranteed their existing frontiers.

Not all Rumanians favored cordial relations with the Soviet government, however. Vigorous opposition to the government's foreign policy came from the Iron Guard, a violently anti-Semitic organization which had developed in the postwar period and which had come to be fascist and pro-German in its outlook. Opposition of the Iron Guard brought the downfall of the Peasant government in November, 1933, and the assassination of the next premier, Ian Duca, one month later. In the ensuing years the Liberal government, headed by George Tatarescu, was compelled to wrestle with difficulties arising from the spread of fascism within the country. The fascist groups, subsidized by the German Nazis, denounced the government's efforts to find a working basis with Soviet Russia and assailed Rumania's pro-French, pro-Soviet orientation. The fascist denunciations became louder than ever after the conclusion of the Franco-Soviet and Czechoslovak-Soviet alliances (1935) and the Rumanian government's decision to construct a strategic railway to connect the Soviet Union with Czechoslovakia, Rumania's ally. But neither King Carol nor Premier Tatarescu favored the fascist program of converting Rumania into a Nazi outpost against Russia. In 1937, with aid from France and Czechoslovakia, they carried forward their rearmament program. At the same time the government took drastic action to curb fascist activities. Ultimately, in 1938, King Carol dissolved all political parties and inaugurated something in the nature of a royal dictatorship.

Cornelius Codreanu, leader of the Iron Guard, and hundreds of his followers were next arrested on charges of plotting to overthrow the government. The Iron Guard leader was sentenced to ten years' imprisonment, but on November 30, 1938, he and thirteen subordinates were killed "while attempting to escape from their prison guards." Thus the Iron Guard was deprived of its outstanding leader but at the same time provided with a "beloved martyr" whose death called for revenge. Thus, too, Rumania was weakened in the face of Hitler's *Drang nach Osten* by having among her citizens a considerable number who would be willing to co-operate with the German Nazis to bring about the downfall of Carol's government.

Balkan International Relations

During the period between the two world wars Balkan diplomats were busy in efforts to provide for the security of their various countries. The attempts of Rumania and Yugoslavia to obtain national security and to provide for the maintenance of the *status quo* in central Europe by uniting with Czechoslovakia in the Little Entente have already been discussed,[7] as has, also, the linking of the Little Entente with France.[8] But the Rumanian-Yugoslav convention of June 7, 1921, which finally completed the Little Entente, applied to the Balkans as well as to central Europe. Rumania and Yugoslavia had a common interest in Bulgaria's acceptance of the peace settlement, and the purpose of their treaty was stated to be the maintenance of both the treaty of Trianon and the treaty of Neuilly. Each state undertook to assist the other in case of an unprovoked attack by either Hungary or Bulgaria.

But Rumania, in view of the fact that her annexation of Bessarabia, though eventually sanctioned by the principal Allies, was not recognized as legal by the Soviet government, desired security not only against Bulgaria but against Russia as well. Soon after the First World War, therefore, Rumania initiated negotiations with Poland—also fearful of Soviet Russia—and in 1921 a Polish-Rumanian defensive alliance resulted. By the terms of this treaty, an unprovoked attack on the eastern frontier of either power would require the other to enter the war to assist the one attacked. When this alliance was renewed in 1926, it was extended to cover not only the eastern frontiers of the two states but all foreign aggressions.

The rise of Hitler and the success of the Nazis in Germany, the withdrawal of Germany from the League of Nations, and the subsequent collapse of the Geneva Disarmament Conference had their effect in the Balkans as they did in central Europe. As the result of negotiations initiated by Greece and Turkey, a movement was started to create an organization similar to the Little Entente in central Europe. What was envisaged was a general pact of nonaggression and guarantee to be signed by all the Balkan states. But Bulgaria, fearing that her adherence might prejudice her claim to an outlet on the Aegean Sea, declined to sign, and Albania, under Mussolini's influence, likewise declined.

[7] See pages 569–570.
[8] See pages 550–551.

On February 9, 1934, however, the foreign ministers of Greece, Turkey, Rumania, and Yugoslavia signed a pact agreeing to guarantee Balkan frontiers against aggression by any Balkan state, the pact to become effective against any Balkan state that might join an outside power that had committed an act of aggression against one of the signatories. The Balkan pact was obviously much more in the nature of a defensive alliance than a mere nonaggression pact. In Greece it at once encountered vigorous opposition, and the Greek parliament ratified it only with the reservations that the boundaries guaranteed were those internal to the Balkans and that under no circumstances were obligations arising from the pact to be so construed as to involve Greece in a war with Italy or any other great power. These reservations were accepted by the other signatories, though clearly they weakened the force of the pact. Provision was made for a permanent council, consisting, like that of the Little Entente, of the foreign ministers of the signatory powers.

Although Bulgaria had not joined the Balkan Entente in 1934, Hitler's seizure of Austria and the resultant fear of a Nazi *Drang nach Osten* drew Bulgaria and the Balkan Entente together in 1938. The former gave a pledge of nonaggression against any of the countries of the Balkan Entente, and in return the latter, on July 31, permitted Bulgaria to rearm and to remilitarize her frontiers with Greece and Turkey. This evidence of increasing solidarity in the Balkans was encouraging to those who hoped for continued peace in that part of Europe but, as in earlier times, that hope was eventually blasted by the interference of some of the great powers—in this case Germany and Italy in 1940.

Chapter XXI

THE EAST IN REVOLT

AFTER the First World War a widespread revolt against the domination of the West swept through northern Africa, western and central Asia, India, China, and Japan—in other words, through those regions of the world which, because of their type of civilization, are usually referred to as the East. In consequence, certain European powers emerged from the war only to find themselves almost immediately confronted or threatened in distant parts of the world with uprisings of native populations. Where these powers were forced to resort to military operations, the efficiency of their modern weapons usually brought victory. In some cases, however, European countries, in preference to actual war, made sweeping concessions to discontented peoples, and occasionally even military success was followed by measures designed to placate the conquered. Full political independence, extensive national autonomy, or a measure of local self-government was obtained by various non-European groups, accompanied in some instances by the abolition of capitulations, the cancellation of foreign privileges, and the grant of economic freedom. At the same time, though revolting against the West, the East showed a pronounced tendency deliberately and voluntarily to adopt many features of the civilization of the West.

Turkey

One of the first clear indications of this revolt of the West was the Turkish nationalist movement which repudiated the treaty of Sèvres,[1] opposed the loss of Turkish territory, threw off the servitude of capitulations, and then sought to modernize Turkey.

Although the sultan, in Constantinople within range of Allied warships, was ready to accept the dictated treaty of Sèvres, the Turkish Nationalists were not. Back in the hills of Anatolia, far beyond the reach of Allied guns, the spirit of Turkish nationalism and Moslem fanaticism were aroused by a veteran army officer, Mustapha Kemal, who demanded the retention by Turkey of all territory "inhabited by an Ottoman Moslem majority," a plebiscite in eastern Thrace, the security of Constantinople,

[1] For the provisions of the treaty of Sèvres, see pages 411–412.

and, by implication, the abolition of the capitulations. When the sultan, doubtless under Allied pressure, dissolved the parliament and denounced the Nationalists, the latter held a grand national assembly at Angora and organized a government with Mustapha Kemal at its head. By June, 1920, Nationalist armies were threatening the British on the Ismid peninsula, the French in Cilicia, and the Greeks in the Smyrna area.

In these circumstances Greek Premier Venizelos proposed, and the Allies approved, a Greek offensive against the Turks to compel them to accept the treaty of Sèvres, and Great Britain advanced a loan to the Greek government. Greek armies at once began operations and before the end of the year succeeded in defeating the Nationalists and in occupying extensive regions of Anatolia. During 1921 further military successes brought the Greek armies within two hundred miles of Angora, but their supreme attempt to capture the Nationalist capital failed.

Meanwhile, the Western powers had ceased to present a united front. In 1921 Soviet Russia recognized Mustapha Kemal's government and agreed to disavow the treaty of Sèvres. Italy, in return for the Nationalists' promise of economic concessions, evacuated the district of Adalia. And France, on October 20, 1921, signed a separate treaty with the Turkish Nationalist government, in consequence of which French troops were withdrawn from Cilicia. Furthermore, King Constantine's return to Greece in 1920 alienated even the British government, which refused to recognize the restored ruler and cut off its subsidies to the Greek government. When, therefore, the Turkish Nationalists launched a determined drive against the Greeks in the summer of 1922, it is perhaps understandable why they won a decisive victory. On September 9, 1922, the Nationalists entered Smyrna. Within a short time every Greek soldier in Anatolia was captured or driven off the mainland. Faced by this situation, the great powers invited Greece and Turkey to a conference to draft a new peace treaty with Turkey. Mustapha Kemal accepted their proposal, and an armistice was signed at Mudania on October 11.

The "revisionary" peace conference opened in Lausanne on November 20, 1922, and was attended by delegates of Great Britain, France, Italy, Japan, the United States, Russia, Greece, Rumania, Yugoslavia, and Turkey. The inclusion of Turkish delegates made this the only one of the peace treaties which was negotiated and not dictated. A draft treaty was finally completed and presented to the conference on January 31, 1923; but at the last moment the Turkish delegates asked for further time to consider, and at length definitely refused to sign. On April 24, however, the conference resumed its sessions, and three months later, after the Allies had yielded on enough points to satisfy the Turks, the treaty of Lausanne was signed on July 24, 1923.

The territorial extent of Turkey was slightly increased over what it was to have been according to the treaty of Sèvres. Although Mesopotamia, Arabia, Syria, and Palestine were still recognized as independent of Turkey, the latter advanced her frontier in Europe to the line of the Maritza River, plus a small district to the west of it in one place in order that she might control Karagach and its railway station. In the Aegean, Turkey retained the Rabbit Islands, off the entrance to the Dardanelles, and the islands of Imbros and Tenedos. The Dodecanese, Rhodes, and Castellorizo, Turkey ceded to Italy; and all her other Aegean islands to Greece. Turkey renounced all rights and titles over Libya, Egypt, and the Sudan, and recognized Great Britain's annexation of Cyprus. She also accepted articles for the protection of minorities similar to those signed by several of the European powers. On the other hand, she obtained the recognition by the signatory powers of the complete abolition of the capitulations in Turkey, suffered no restrictions of her military and naval forces, and was released from any claim on the part of the Allied powers to reparations on account of the First World War.

In separate conventions a number of other agreements were entered into which had the same force as the treaty itself. The "principle of freedom of transit and of navigation by sea and by air in the strait of the Dardanelles, the sea of Marmora, and the Bosporus" was recognized, and an International Straits Commission was to operate under the auspices of the League of Nations. Both shores of the Dardanelles and of the Bosporus were demilitarized, as were the islands off the entrance to the Dardanelles.

A Greco-Turkish convention stipulated that there should "take place a compulsory exchange of Turkish nationals of the Greek Orthodox religion established in Turkish territory, and of Greek nationals of the Moslem religion established in Greek territory." Exceptions were made in the case of the Greeks on the islands of Imbros and Tenedos and of those who were established in Constantinople before October 30, 1918, and of the Moslem inhabitants in the district in western Thrace which Greece had obtained in 1913 by the treaty of Bucharest. Other conventions provided for the demilitarization of a region on both sides of the Greco-Turkish and Turco-Bulgarian frontier lines. A comparison of the provisions of the treaty of Lausanne with the aims announced by the Nationalists reveals that the Turks obtained nearly everything for which they had fought—ethnographic frontiers, freedom from international servitudes, and national independence.

Meanwhile, on November 1, 1922, the Turkish Grand National Assembly had deposed Sultan Mohammed VI. Some three months after the signing of the treaty of Lausanne that same body, on October 29, 1923, proclaimed Turkey a republic and unanimously elected Mustapha Kemal the first president.[2] Despite the name "republic," however, Turkey in reality became a dictatorship. Kemal's People's Party was for years the only organized political group permitted in the country; and after 1927 Kemal, as president-general of the party, had the right to name all of the party's candidates for the National Assembly. But though the general government remained a dictatorship, laws were enacted to bring its judicial system into step with the Western world. A Supreme Court was established, and in 1926 all the old law codes, based primarily on the Koran, were supplanted by new civil, penal, and commercial codes which were based on European models. In 1932 Turkey became a member of the League of Nations.

The strong national spirit of Kemal and his associates led to efforts to free the Turks from non-Turkish influences. Cities were given new Turkish names, for example, Constantinople becoming Istanbul; Angora, Ankara; Smyrna, Izmir, and so on. The national capital was removed from the Bosporus, where it had been for centuries, and located at Ankara, which consequently grew from a small town into a modern city. To assist in the nationalizing movement, the language of the people was purified of Arabic influences. A national law in 1928 provided that in the course of the following fifteen years the Latin alphabet should supplant the old Arabic. Newspapers and books were ordered to cease publication in Arabic characters after January, 1929.

The religious institutions of the country also were fundamentally changed. In March, 1924, the National Assembly abolished the Turkish caliphate and exiled from the country all members of the former Osman dynasty. Four years later that same body decided that Islam should no longer be the state religion of Turkey, that in fact the republic thereafter should tolerate all religions on an equal footing. Although Islam continued to be the religion of the bulk of the Turks, republican officials were no longer required, upon taking office, to swear by Allah. Severe restrictions were placed on the teaching of religion—Mohammedan or Christian—in public or private elementary schools. Early in 1933, in order to force the Moslem clergy to have a more liberal training, the theological faculty and curriculum of the University of Istanbul were modified by the government. The next year the government again struck at the influence of the Moslem clergy by a decree forbidding the wearing of clerical garb except at religious rites. In 1935 Sunday rather than Friday, the Moslem's special day of prayer, was made the official day of rest.

Sweeping social changes were introduced by Kemal, especially in the position of women. In 1925 legal polygamy was abolished and divorce was

[2] In 1927, 1931, and 1935 he was re-elected to the presidency.

THE "WESTERNIZATION" OF THE EAST

Six of the seventeen Turkish women elected to the Grand National
Assembly in 1935.

made permissible. In the next year civil marriage was made compulsory, and the legal age for marriage was raised to seventeen for women and eighteen for men. Western clothing was introduced, the wearing of the fez was made illegal, and the wearing of the veil was made optional. Many occupations were opened to women. In 1929 women gained the right to vote in local elections and to hold office in municipalities; in December, 1934, an amendment to the constitution gave them the right to vote for and become deputies. In February of the next year seventeen women were elected to the Grand National Assembly. By another law passed in 1934 all persons were required to assume family names, which were to be registered with the authorities by January 1, 1935. The National Assembly suggested that Mustapha Kemal assume the surname "Atatürk" ("Father of the Turks"). This the president did.

In the realm of education considerable progress was made. Although handicapped by a shortage of money, teachers, and educational facilities, the government increased the number of schools to 7000 by 1936. Its goal was compulsory school attendance for all children between seven and sixteen years of age. Attempts were made to compel all Turks under forty years of age to take lessons in reading and writing, and beginning in June, 1931, literacy was in general necessary to obtain the full rights of citizenship. Nevertheless, although illiteracy, according to reports, had been reduced by half, in 1939 a considerable percentage of the population was still illiterate.

Some advance was made by Turkey in her economic life also. In this realm, too, Kemal's aim was modernization and Westernization. The government itself in many ways sought to assist directly in the economic upbuilding of the country. Special departments were established to study commerce, shipping, industry, and agriculture. Large appropriations for public works were made, railways and highways were constructed, and a strong central bank was established. To encourage infant industries, a protective tariff was adopted in 1929; and in succeeding years, in order to overcome the republic's adverse trade balance, a quota system of imports was inaugurated. State control or state ownership of various enterprises was secured. In 1936 a modern labor law was enacted requiring the compulsory arbitration of labor disputes, prohibiting strikes and lockouts, regulating woman and child labor, and providing for an eight-hour day, minimum wages, and social insurance.

To Westernize and industrialize the country further a five-year industrial plan was adopted in January, 1934, providing for the building of fifteen factories, twelve of which were to be owned and operated by the government. The new enterprises were designed, in part, to free Turkey from the need of importing certain types of manufactured goods. The government

announced that it had decided upon the adoption of a form of state capitalism and that, as rapidly as the resources of the government permitted,
private enterprises would be taken over. To make the raw materials of
the country more available, 1681 miles of railway were constructed by
1937, and plans called for the building of some thousands of miles of
additional railways in the ensuing years.

In 1934 the desire to free Turkey from foreign control again manifested
itself in several ways. In March the government announced its decision to
purchase the 450-mile Smyrna-Kassaba Railway, which was owned by
French interests. Later in the year the government made arrangements
to take over from the French companies their concessions for operating
the port facilities at Istanbul, and in 1935 it acquired the Istanbul Telephone
Company from British interests. Meanwhile, in 1934, the minister of public
works had announced that, in the future, enterprises undertaken by foreign capital in Turkey must register as Turkish companies, that no new
concessions would be granted to foreign companies having their headquarters abroad. Furthermore, in that same year a law went into effect
ousting all aliens from the professions, the trades, and jobs involving
manual labor. Only by becoming naturalized citizens of Turkey could
the thousands of persons affected escape the provisions of the law, regardless of the fact that they might have lived in Turkey for years.

Nationalism continued to exert an influence upon the republic's foreign policy, too. For a number of years Turkish newspapers strongly urged
the government to secure again its prewar right to fortify the Straits. Eventually, in 1936, after having sounded out the other powers, Turkey laid
before the states signatory to the treaty of Lausanne, and before the League
of Nations also, a formal request for the revision of those clauses of the
treaty relating to nonfortification of the Dardanelles and the demilitarized
zones. In July, 1936, an international conference, meeting at Montreux,
Switzerland, approved a new convention authorizing Turkey to proceed
with the fortification of the Straits immediately.

Nor were the Turks averse to seizing upon the exigencies of other states
to advance their nationalistic program. For some years they had insisted
that the Sanjak of Alexandretta in northwest Syria was inhabited chiefly
by Turks and should therefore be detached from that Arab state. Eventually,
in 1937, France, the mandatory power for Syria, so far gave way to Turkish
demands as to establish the sanjak as an independent state, which adopted
the name Republic of Hatay. But Turkey, having succeeded in detaching
the district from Syria, next desired to add it to her own territory. When,
in the summer of 1939, Great Britain and France were attempting to create
a bloc of powers to oppose Hitler's *Drang nach Osten*,[3] Turkey availed

[3] See pages 659–661.

herself of the international tension to attain this end. In order to secure a declaration of mutual assistance from Turkey, France was obliged to cede Hatay to Turkey, except for a small section inhabited by Armenians, which was returned to Syria. Alexandretta and Antioch thus became Turkish cities.

But Turkey's acquisition of these cities was not finally achieved by Kemal Atatürk. On November 10, 1938, the "Father of the Turks" died. Since the proclamation of the republic he had been its president, and to many observers he had seemed to be a dictator no less than Mussolini. Others, however, maintained that his dictatorship was merely a transition period between the old regime of the sultans and the Western democratic system which Atatürk hoped to see ultimately established in Turkey. Immediately after Atatürk's death the National Assembly chose as his successor his close friend and coworker in building the new Turkey, Ismet Inönü. The new president was a distinguished Turkish general and statesman. He had played a prominent role in the war against Greece (1920–1922), had represented Turkey at the Lausanne conference (1922–1923), and had for many years been prime minister during Atatürk's presidency. There seemed little doubt that Inönü would vigorously continue Atatürk's nationalist policy.

Meanwhile, Turkey's interest in pacts of nonaggression and security, so far as they affected her European boundaries, had been revealed by her treaty with Greece (1933) and by her joining the Balkan Entente (1934), both of which have already been discussed. But she was interested, too, in maintaining peace in Asia. In 1937 on Turkey's initiative a Middle Eastern Entente was established when a nonaggression treaty was signed by Turkey, Iraq, Iran (Persia), and Afghanistan. These four Moslem powers pledged themselves to guarantee security in the Middle East by fulfilling their obligations under the League Covenant and the Briand-Kellogg pact. They specifically promised to abstain from interfering in one another's affairs and undertook to prevent the formation within their territories of bands or associations seeking to disturb the peace of any of them. Thereafter Turkey was in a position to foster co-operation between the Balkan countries and those of the Middle East, for she was included in ententes with both groups of powers.

Egypt

At the close of the First World War, Egyptians insisted that their country be given its independence, and ultimately in 1922 that independence was recognized by the British government. The latter, however, reserved for future discussion (1) the security of British communications, (2) the defense of Egypt, (3) the protection of foreigners and minorities in Egypt, and (4) the Sudan.[4] Sultan Ahmed Fuad, in order to give formal expression to Egypt's new international status, on March 15, 1923, assumed the title of King Fuad I, and in April a constitution was enacted by a royal rescript. In the first general elections for the Egyptian parliament the Nationalist Party, led by Saad Zaghlul Pasha, won an overwhelming majority, and in January, 1924, the latter became premier. The Nationalists still demanded Egypt's complete freedom from Britain's control.

During the next decade the intransigence of the Nationalists caused friction between the British and Egyptian governments and ultimately the king suspended the constitution in 1930 and for a time his government wielded dictatorial powers. But in 1935 tension between Great Britain and Italy arising from the Italo-Ethiopian conflict gave the Egyptian Nationalists an excellent opportunity to bring pressure to bear upon Great Britain. Their nationalism was further aroused, moreover, by the apparent disregard with which Great Britain treated the Egyptian government in the military and naval steps which the former took in Egypt to prepare for a possible Italo-British clash, and by the fear that Egypt might be drawn into the Italo-Ethiopian conflict through Britain's actions. Eventually all parties in opposition to the government organized a "united front" under the leadership of the Nationalist Mustapha Nahas Pasha, to force the restoration of the constitution. Faced by the possibility of political chaos in Egypt, so important a strategic spot for Britain's activities in the Mediterranean, the British government surrendered to the Nationalist demands. On December 12, 1935, King Fuad issued a royal rescript restoring the constitution of 1923. This was his last important official act, for in April, 1936, he died, and was succeeded by his sixteen-year-old son, who was proclaimed King Farouk.

In the parliamentary elections following the restoration of the constitution the Nationalists won a decisive victory, and Mustapha Nahas Pasha became premier. Scenting the possibility of a still greater victory, the Nationalists next demanded a treaty of alliance with Great Britain which would recognize Egypt's complete independence. On August 26, 1936, such a treaty was signed in London. By the terms of the treaty (1) the administration of the Sudan reverted to the prewar status, (2) Great Britain agreed to withdraw her troops from Egypt except from the vicinity of the Suez

[4] The chief interest of both Great Britain and Egypt in the Sudan was economic, arising from the development of irrigation projects which make possible the extensive growth of cotton. Because the Assuan dam marked the limit of easy exploitation of the Egyptian Nile, and because of deterioration of the quality of Egyptian cotton in recent years, the Nationalists were eager to incorporate the Sudan in Egypt. This would entail the withdrawal of the British, for an Anglo-Egyptian condominium had governed the Sudan since 1899. In 1924 the British compelled Egypt to withdraw her troops from the Sudan.

Canal, (3) Egypt gave the British the right to use Alexandria and Port Said as naval bases and the right to move their troops through Egyptian territory in the case of war or the threat of war, (4) Egypt agreed to have her army instructed by the British and equipped with British arms, (5) both agreed that should either be at war the other would come to its assistance, (6) in recognition of Egypt's complete independence Great Britain agreed to replace her high commissioner by an ambassador and to support Egypt in her request for the abolition of capitulations and for membership in the League of Nations. The treaty was ratified by the Egyptian and British parliaments in November, 1936.

In May, 1937, a convention was signed at Montreux, Switzerland, by the capitulatory powers, providing (1) that after October 15, 1937, foreigners in Egypt would be subject to Egyptian-made law and taxation, and consular courts would surrender most of their powers to mixed tribunals, and (2) that after a transitional period the mixed tribunals would be abolished and in 1949 foreigners in Egypt would be subject to the Egyptian courts and laws in all matters. In the same month Egypt was admitted to membership in the League of Nations.

Syria and Lebanon

In western Asia at the close of the First World War most of the Arab regions of the former Ottoman Empire were entrusted to France and Great Britain as mandates of the League of Nations. The territory assigned to France, popularly referred to as Syria, stretched along the Mediterranean coast from Alexandretta to Tyre, and extended inland to the Jebel Druze in the south and northeastward across the Euphrates and Tigris rivers to a point north of Mosul. Although the whole region was placed under one French high commissioner, it was divided for administrative purposes. The Sanjak of Alexandretta—which included a considerable number of Turks—was given an autonomous regime. Lebanon, because of its large Christian population, had had a special administrative treatment under the Turks, and the French not only perpetuated this status but also enlarged the territory included in Lebanon.

Eventually, in 1928, the French permitted elections to be held for a constituent assembly which should draft a Syrian constitution, the understanding being that the adoption of the constitution would be followed by a Franco-Syrian treaty defining the relations between the two countries and giving Syria her place among the nations of the world. In the constituent assembly a substantial majority was held by the Syrian Nationalists, who wanted a completely independent republic. But the French were unwilling to permit the adoption of such a constitution, and so the high commissioner at first suspended and then adjourned the constituent assembly *sine die*. In May, 1930, a constitution promulgated by the high commissioner himself established a republic, subject only to the mandatory powers of the French government and to the latter's control of its foreign policy.

The success of anti-British agitation in Egypt in 1936 had its effect in Syria, where the Syrian campaign for independence was revived. When the French authorities sought to prevent trouble by ordering the dissolution of the Syrian Nationalist Party, violent street fighting broke out. A general strike by the Syrians finally compelled the French authorities to permit the establishment of a Nationalist cabinet. Léon Blum's government, which came into power in France in the summer of 1936, at once sought to bring about better relations with the natives and in the fall of that year signed with the Nationalist governments of Syria and Lebanon treaties of alliance and friendship which closely resembled the Anglo-Egyptian treaty of August, 1936. By the terms of these treaties both were to become independent nations at the end of a three-year transition period, and France was to sponsor their admission to the League of Nations. But the treaties were not ratified by the French parliament, and shortly before the outbreak of the Second World War the French high commissioner in Syria dissolved the Syrian parliament and suspended the Syrian constitution.

Palestine

Meanwhile, in their Palestine mandate the British had encountered great difficulties because of the irreconcilable differences of the Arabs and the Jews. In 1917 the British government, in the famous Balfour Declaration, had promised to establish in Palestine a national home for the Jewish people. Five years later the League of Nations assigned Palestine to Great Britain as a mandate, the terms of the mandate confirming the Balfour Declaration. In 1922 Sir Herbert Samuel, the first British high commissioner, promulgated a constitution for the mandated territory. The Arabs, who constituted about 80 per cent of the population, refused to participate in the elections for the legislative council, however, so that the high commissioner was compelled to resort to an appointed advisory council.

Although Arab opposition abated for a time, owing to the improvement of the economic condition of the country, as the years passed they again became restless. Despite a certain degree of government control of immigration, the number of Jews in Palestine steadily mounted until there were by 1929 some 160,000 in the territory—nearly twice the number there when the mandate was established. Furthermore, the Arabs denounced the agrarian legislation which had been enacted. Laws making it possible for the Jews to purchase large sections of the somewhat restricted area of arable land, so the Arabs declared, menaced the very foundations of their own economic existence. In August, 1929, the Arabs broke out in open rebellion and began an attack upon the Jews in Palestine which resulted in the death of more than two hundred and compelled the British government to rush forces to Palestine to restore order.

Despite the protests of the Jews, the British authorities for a time suspended immigration. In 1931, therefore, the Arabs became more conciliatory and displayed a willingness to co-operate in the election of a legislative council. When the project of such a council was accordingly revived, it next encountered the opposition of the Jews, who declared they would have nothing to do with it unless they were guaranteed at least an equality in membership with the Arabs. Once more the project had to be dropped.

Although some attempts were made by the British authorities to control the type of Jewish immigrant, by 1933 there were in Palestine, according to Jewish authorities, more than 200,000 Jews, and the amount of land held by the latter had increased twelvefold since the close of the war. One new Jewish city, Tel Aviv, was reported to have a population of 60,000 in 1933 and to be increasing at the rate of 12,000 a year. Meanwhile, in 1925, a Hebrew University had been opened in Jerusalem. Thanks to the influx of capital from abroad, to the increased application of scientific methods to agriculture, industry, and business, and to the aid of the Palestine Foundation Fund, Palestine was relatively unaffected by the world depression. Millions of dollars of Jewish capital flowed into the country, projects for electrification were started, Haifa was improved into a deep-water port, and a pipe line was laid to connect this port with the rich Mosul oil fields.

But the opposition of the Arabs continued. In 1936 anti-Jewish outbreaks again became serious. Clashes occurred which caused over three hundred fatalities, and increased British forces were sent to Palestine in an effort to restore order. To enforce their demand that further Jewish immigration be halted, the Arabs resorted to widespread strikes and to a campaign of civil disobedience. The British government then sent a royal commission to Palestine to investigate Arab and Jewish grievances. The Peel commission's report, published in July, 1937, declared that the aspirations of the 400,000 Jews and the 1,000,000 Arabs in Palestine were irreconcilable and the existing British mandate unworkable. It therefore recommended that Palestine be divided into three parts. Nazareth, Jerusalem, and a corridor from the latter to the Mediterranean at Jaffa should continue to be a British mandate; a section including about one third of Palestine should be converted into a Jewish state; and the rest of the territory should

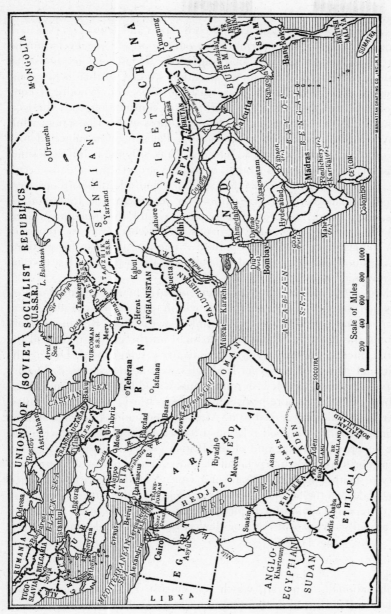

The Near and Middle East Between the Two World Wars

become an Arab state linked with Transjordan. The commission's proposals were vigorously denounced by both Arabs and Jews.

Although the British government at once approved the Peel commission's report, opposition was so strong in the House of Commons that it was voted to have the plan for partition studied further before final parliamentary action. Accordingly, early in 1938, the Woodhead commission was sent to Palestine to work out in consultation with the local communities there some detailed scheme. Almost without cessation, while the Woodhead commission was working, Palestine was subjected to a reign of terrorism and interracial fighting. Riots, sniping, bomb explosions, assassinations, banditry, and other outrages were of almost daily occurrence. British marines were landed at Haifa, and additional troops were ordered to Palestine. The grand mufti of Jerusalem, the leader of the Arabs, announced, however, that fighting would continue until Great Britain had accepted the Arab demands. In October, 1938, the report of the Woodhead commission was published rejecting the plan for partition on the ground that the practical difficulties in the way of such a division were insurmountable.

In May, 1939, the British government issued a new "Statement of Policy" which envisaged the establishment within ten years of an independent Palestine. The new state was to be linked with Great Britain in treaty relations; the Jews and Arabs were to share in the government, and the essential interests of both were to be effectively safeguarded. During the transitional period of ten years land sales were to be restricted. During the first five years 75,000 Jewish immigrants would be admitted into Palestine, but after that no more Jewish immigration was to be permitted unless the Arabs in Palestine agreed to it. After the Jews and Arabs in Palestine had finally established good relations between themselves, representatives of the people of Palestine and of the British government would together draft a constitution for independent Palestine. These proposals were satisfactory to neither Jews nor Arabs and violence and terrorism continued unabated. When the Second World War broke out, therefore, after twenty years of repeated efforts Great Britain seemed to be about as far as ever from a final settlement of the Arab-Jewish question in Palestine.

Iraq

Arab nationalism in Iraq, which was entrusted to Great Britain as a mandate in 1920, forced the latter to sign a treaty in 1927 agreeing to recognize the independence of Iraq within five years and to support her candidacy for admission to the League in 1932. Iraq, on her part, agreed to lease air bases to Great Britain and to turn over to a British military commission the training of the Iraqi army, which would use British equipment. Five years later the British mandate was ended, and Iraq became independent. The Mandates Commission in 1932 drew up a list of guarantees which Iraq had to accept before she could become a member of the League. These included protection of minorities, freedom of conscience and religion, recognition of rights acquired and debts contracted during the mandatory regime, and the guarantee of the rights of foreigners before the courts. Iraq promised, furthermore, in case of actual or imminent war, to aid Great Britain to the extent of her ability. On October 3, 1932, Iraq was admitted to the League as an independent power, and the European states surrendered their privileges under the capitulations.

Unfortunately for the orderly political progress of Iraq, King Feisal died in 1933. His son, who became King Ghazi, was less capable and less responsible, and the political situation thereafter deteriorated. In 1936 a *coup d'état,* brought about by the military, installed a Pan-Arab ministry, and Iraq became for all practical purposes a military dictatorship. The political situation was not improved when in 1939 King Ghazi was killed in an accident and was succeeded by his three-year-old son, who became Feisal II. It is not surprising that in the opening years of the Second World War Iraq became the scene of numerous plots and counterplots of the various belligerents.[5]

Iran (Persia)

Meanwhile, to the east of Iraq, the Persians had become imbued with the same nationalistic spirit which had led the Turks to rebel against the West. They had every reason to fear the extinction of their independence as a sovereign state, for the Anglo-Russian treaties of 1907 and 1915 had practically divided Persia between these two great powers. The withdrawal of Russian forces after the Bolshevik revolution gave little encouragement to Persian nationalists, since their place was taken by the British, and in 1919 an Anglo-Persian treaty made Persia dependent upon Great Britain in political and military matters.

The weak Persian government which consented to this treaty came to be regarded by Persian nationalists as an instrument of foreign rule. In February, 1921, this government was overthrown by a military revolution led by Riza Khan, who, like Mustapha Kemal, was a soldier who had risen from the ranks to be head of a small and efficient military force. Riza Khan at once became commander-in-chief of the Persian army and the

[5] See page 689.

real power in the government, which promptly denounced the Anglo-Persian treaty. Soon after the *coup d'état* of February, 1921, Riza Khan became minister of war, and, after making and unmaking several ministries, he finally assumed the premiership in October, 1923. The shah was induced to leave Persia for Europe, and on December 12, 1925, a Persian constituent assembly made Riza Khan hereditary shah with the title Riza Shah Pahlevi.

By this time the reconstruction of Persia had been largely accomplished. The Russian-officered Cossacks, British-officered South Persian Rifles, and Swedish-officered gendarmerie had given way to a well-organized and well-equipped national Persian army of some 40,000 men. With this force Riza Shah had succeeded in restoring order and in asserting the authority of the Teheran government over many tribes which had been enjoying *de facto* independence. In 1921 the Persian government had sought foreign assistance in its task of remodeling its public finances and promoting the economic development of the country, and in the succeeding years Riza Shah sought further to modernize Persia. The legal age for marriage for girls was made sixteen years, and women were given an equal right with men to secure a divorce. Railway construction was begun, highways were extended, an air force was created, and in 1932 a small Persian navy was placed in the Persian Gulf. The latter was connected with the Caspian Sea when a railway was opened shortly before the outbreak of the Second World War.

The attempt to throw off outside control continued. All foreign capitulations in Persia were abolished, and national tariff autonomy was secured. Foreign mission schools in the country were forbidden to teach Persian children in the primary grades. In 1931 the Persian government took over control of all the country's telegraph lines, which were formerly in the hands of the Indo-European Telegraph Department of the British India Office. In the next year the Junkers Aircraft Company, a German concern, was forced to discontinue its air services in Persia, largely because the Persian government placed difficulties in the way of a renewed concession; at the same time the government refused to allow the Imperial Airways Company of Great Britain to have landing fields in Persia on the route to India.

Finally, in November, 1932, the Persian council of ministers, presided over by Riza Shah, decided to cancel the concession of the Anglo-Persian Oil Company, a majority of whose stock was held by the British government. Great Britain at once denied Persia's right to cancel the concession, but proposed that the whole question be referred to the World Court. Persia refused to admit the competence of the court in a dispute between herself and a commercial company. Eventually the two countries agreed that direct negotiations regarding a new concession should be carried on between Persia and the Anglo-Persian Oil Company.

The Persian government ultimately won a victory in its dispute with the powerful British company and gained much better financial terms than she formerly enjoyed. Moreover, she made other nationalistic gains. The company's area of exploitation was drastically curtailed; it was to replace progressively its foreign employees by Persians; it was to spend some $50,000 annually educating Persians in Great Britain; and it was to sell oil to Persians and to the Persian government at a discount from the world prices. By many it was considered that Persia's victory in this dispute constituted an important precedent in the relations between "backward" nations and powerful concessionaries.

In 1935 Riza Shah officially changed the name of his country from Persia to Iran. Developments during the Second World War,[6] however, raised the question whether Iran was actually any more able to maintain its independence of the great powers than Persia had been a generation earlier.

India

Although nationalism had penetrated India before 1914, the First World War gave a great impetus to the nationalist movement there. The British government took steps to recognize the national awakening. In 1917 E. S. Montagu, secretary of state for India, announced that the British government was planning to increase the association of Indians in the administrative branches of the government and to develop gradually self-governing institutions. In 1918 the government issued a report on the reforms which had been drafted as a result of consultations between Montagu and Lord Chelmsford, the viceroy of India. The moderate parties in India accepted the scheme outlined, but the National Congress Party, the organ of the extreme nationalists, wholly condemned the proposals and demanded immediate and full autonomy.

For the time being, however, the constitutional question was eclipsed by the course of events in India, where Mohandas K. Gandhi, a Hindu social and religious reformer, became the spokesman and leader of the agitation and initiated a movement of passive resistance. The Indian government, alarmed by the unrest and revolutionary agitation, hurriedly passed certain emergency measures. These the Congress Nationalist press and politicians at once denounced as attacks upon popular liberties and as instruments of tyranny and oppression. A wave of excitement spread through the Punjab and reached its height when in April, 1919, the "Amritsar massacre" oc-

[6] See page 692.

curred. Military forces employed to disperse an unlawful gathering in Amritsar caused the death of about 400 Indians and the wounding of three times that number.

In Great Britain it was hoped that the admission of Indian claims to self-government would alleviate Indian unrest and Indian hostility. The Montagu-Chelmsford scheme of constitutional reform was accordingly pushed through Parliament and became the Government of India Act in December, 1919. This act applied not to the several hundred Indian principalities which had relations with the British government, but only to the 230,000,000 people living in British India.

The Government of India Act provided for decentralization through the establishment of provincial governments which should have charge of such matters as education, public health, agriculture, irrigation, criminal law, prisons, and labor legislation. For most administrative purposes, the provinces were treated as separate states within a kind of federation. Each of these provinces had a legislative council in which at least 70 per cent of the members were elected. All men over twenty-one years of age had the vote, provided they met certain property or occupational requirements, but these were of such a character that only about 5,350,000 persons had the franchise.

Within each province the functions of government were divided, under a system known as dyarchy, into reserved and transferred subjects. The reserved departments, including irrigation, land revenue, factory inspection, and police, were administered by the provincial governor and his executive council; the transferred departments, including public health, education, public works, and agriculture, were administered by ministers chosen from the provincial assembly and responsible to it. In this way it was planned to provide a field in which Indian leaders could be trained in the actual practice of government; and the dyarchical scheme was intended to be only transitory and experimental.

No dyarchy was provided for the central government, however, which consisted of the governor-general in council and two advisory bodies—the Legislative Assembly and the Council of State. The governor-general and his executive council remained directly responsible to the British Parliament for the government of India, but the two advisory bodies were chosen by very restricted Indian electorates. Those entitled to vote for the Legislative Assembly numbered less than a million men, while the electorate for the Council of State included less than eighteen thousand. The Legislative Assembly developed into the chief agency for crystallizing and voicing Indian opinion, and came to be something of a parliament without power.

The Government of India Act stipulated that ten years after its passage a parliamentary commission should go to India to inquire into the working of the plan and to report on the desirability of extending or modifying the degree of responsible government already existing. The British government accordingly appointed an interparty parliamentary commission under Sir John Simon, but the exclusion of Indians from the commission led to dissatisfaction among the Congress Nationalists.

During the early months of 1929 the Simon Commission made investigations in India, while Indian radicals did their utmost to awaken a widespread distrust of it and its objects. Gandhi again conducted a vigorous campaign against the use or sale of British cloth in India. In 1930 he inaugurated a new campaign of civil disobedience. Setting an example by himself violating the laws, he brought about a general defiance of laws in India. The collection of taxes was resisted, railway and street traffic was obstructed, and many Hindu officials resigned. Although Gandhi counseled his followers to avoid violence, disorders broke out, and in May, 1930, the government finally took the step of arresting and imprisoning Gandhi and a number of his more important followers.

In 1930 the report of the Simon Commission was published. The document carefully avoided any mention of dominion status or independence and appeared to seek an increase in the executive powers of the secretary of state for India, the governor-general, and the various provincial governors. It was thoroughly unsatisfactory to the Congress Nationalists. In an attempt to work out some compromise solution of the Indian problem the British government next called a number of round-table conferences to meet in London. But Hindus and Moslems disagreed on means of protecting the latter; British Indians and the native princes disagreed on the type of federation to be adopted; high-caste Hindus and the "untouchables" disagreed on the future status of the latter; and, finally, Britishers and Indians disagreed on the extent of self-government which India was to have. Ultimately the British government announced that it would itself work out a plan to solve the minorities problem, and that when it had done this it would summon another round table to draw up a new constitution for India.

In November, 1932, this conference convened in London for a final consideration of the projected Indian constitution, and when it adjourned a complete and definite form of government had at last been drafted. In March, 1933, the British government issued a white paper containing the new Indian federal constitution. Incorporated in the Government of India Bill, it was passed by the House of Commons and on August 2, 1935, became law.

Under her new constitution India still failed to attain dominion status, for the viceroy was to control defense and foreign relations and was to possess a number of emergency powers in case of domestic crises arising from conflicts over religion, minorities, currency, or justice to foreigners. British India was to have a central government and eleven provincial governments, and the general purpose of the constitution seemed to be to place the chief responsibility for domestic administration on the latter. In each of the self-governing provinces a ministry, selected from its legislature, was normally to conduct all provincial affairs, including even the maintenance of law and order. Over the ministry, however, was to be placed a British governor, as formerly, with special responsibilities. If circumstances demanded, the governor might take charge of any branch of the provincial government, might issue ordinances with the force of law, might even override the provincial legislature on appropriation bills. The electorate for the provincial legislatures, according to figures which were published, was to include some 38,000,000 men and women, and therefore marked a considerable extension of the franchise over that existing under the act of 1919. The Council of State, the upper house of the national legislature, was to have 150 members elected by the provincial legislatures, 100 members appointed by the princes, and 10 appointed by the government. The Legislative Assembly, the lower house, was to have 250 members elected directly by the voters, and 125 members appointed by the princes. The national electorate was to consist of some 6,000,000 voters, which likewise constituted an advance over the provisions of the act of 1919. Nowhere, of course, was universal suffrage provided. The new constitution, being a compromise, naturally pleased nobody. In general, the Indian view was that it in no sense substantiated agreements reached at the first two round tables. The Congress Nationalists at once decided to boycott the new regime.

When elections were held in the eleven provinces in 1937, however, the Congress Party participated and won a decisive victory, securing an absolute majority in six and a plurality in three of them. In March the All-India Congress Committee resolved that Congress ministers should accept office only if each governor would agree not to "use his special powers of interference or set aside the advice of ministers in regard to their constitutional activities." The provincial governors, however, declared it constitutionally impossible for them to accept this formula. On April 1, when the new constitution was formally introduced, a general strike and a protest demonstration were organized against it, but in seven provinces Congress leaders organized governments and in the succeeding months showed a desire to make their administrations function successfully.

In 1939, upon the outbreak of the Second World War, the Congress Party asked the British government to set forth Britain's war aims in regard to democracy and imperialism and to state their application to

India. The viceroy disappointed Indian Nationalists with his statement that at the close of the war the British government would enter into consultation with representatives of the various groups in India with a view to securing their aid and co-operation in framing modifications to the act of 1935. The Working Committee of the Congress Party thereupon called upon all Congress ministries to resign their offices.

China, Japan, and the First World War

Shortly before the First World War began, the Emperor of China—a boy six years of age—was deposed, and a republic was proclaimed (1912). Sun Yat-sen, who for years had worked to bring about the republic, was elected provisional president, but in the interest of Chinese harmony and unity he resigned in favor of Yuan Shih-k'ai, the last premier under the empire. The Chinese liberals, organized as the Nationalist Party (*Kuomintang*), were from the beginning suspicious of the new president and soon came into open conflict with him. While the Nationalists sought to establish in China a democratic regime, based upon a broad franchise, a strong parliament, and a relatively weak executive, Yuan aimed to set up a powerful executive and a weak parliament. Friction developed between the two groups, and, after an attempt had been made to overthrow Yuan, the latter ordered the unseating of the Nationalist members of the parliament (1913), and took steps looking toward the re-establishment of the monarchy. In 1916, before he had succeeded in doing this, he died, and after his death a succession of presidents held office in Peking. Although the Nationalists, denouncing the Peking government as illegal, in 1917 proclaimed a new provisional government in Canton and asserted that the latter was the only constitutional government in China, foreign powers continued to recognize and deal with the authorities in Peking. The real power in China fell more and more into the hands of various military chiefs (*tuchuns*), who devoted themselves primarily to the advancement of personal rather than national interests.

Meanwhile, in August, 1914, as has already been pointed out,[7] Japan demanded that Germany surrender her leased territory of Kiaochow and, when Germany refused to comply with this demand, Japan declared war upon her. In November the German base was surrendered to the Japanese. Not content with the acquisition of this former German stronghold on Chinese soil, the Japanese in January, 1915, presented to President Yuan a list of twenty-one demands designed to transform China into a Japanese protectorate. Menaced by a Japanese threat of war and well aware that the European powers were too preoccupied with their own affairs to intervene

[7] See page 348.

effectively in her behalf, China on May 25, 1915, finally signed two treaties which in a modified form embodied most of the points of Japan's original demands. The latter obtained special concessions in South Manchuria and Inner Mongolia. The Chinese Nationalists denounced the treaties and declared that they would never recognize their validity; the agreements, in fact, were never ratified by the Chinese parliament. Japan, nevertheless, claimed that her rights were valid because the treaties contained clauses providing that they should become effective on the date that they were signed.

In 1917 Japan further strengthened her position in China when she persuaded Great Britain, France, and Russia to agree to support at the peace conference Japan's claims to Shantung. Even the United States, after entering the war, became a party to an interchange of notes with Japan which resulted in the so-called Lansing-Ishii agreement. The two countries agreed that the Open Door policy should continue to be respected in China, but the United States was persuaded to recognize, in addition, that Japan had "special interests in China, particularly in that part to which her possessions are contiguous." Japan, it appeared, was trying to create a Monroe Doctrine of her own for the Far East.

In the early years of the war China had three times contemplated entering the conflict on the side of the Allies, but on each occasion the Japanese government—reluctant to have China build up an efficient army or participate in the eventual peace conference—had managed to prevent the step. After Japan's position in China had been strengthened by various agreements in 1917, however, she began to urge the latter to enter the struggle, and in this she was seconded by the United States. Eventually, in 1917, the authorities at both Peking and Canton declared war on Germany and Austria-Hungary.

At the peace conference China presented demands which included tariff autonomy, the abolition of extraterritoriality, the cancellation of foreign spheres of influence, the withdrawal of foreign troops, and the surrender of leased territories. The statesmen at Paris, however, held that they had no power to deal with these questions. On the other hand, the peace conference, shackled by secret treaty agreements, awarded the former German rights in Shantung to Japan. In China a widespread and vigorous boycott of Japanese goods was instituted, and Japanese trade in China suffered severely. China scorned the direct negotiations with Japan concerning Shantung which the peace conference recommended, and refused to sign the treaty of Versailles.

Nevertheless, some nationalist gains came to China as a result of the war. She obtained membership in the League of Nations by signing the treaty of St. Germain, and by a separate treaty with Germany she secured the cancellation of the latter's extraterritorial rights. Furthermore, China saw to it that treaties with the new states of Europe made no extraterritorial concessions.

The Washington Conference

The next real gains for China in her struggle for the recognition of her integrity and independence and for the abolition of all special privileges of foreigners in her territory came at the Washington conference on the limitation of armaments. In 1921 the United States government, besides wishing to check a possible naval race with Great Britain, desired to secure the satisfactory settlement of certain questions in the Pacific and the Far East. It therefore invited Japan, China, Great Britain, France, Italy, the Netherlands, Belgium, and Portugal to a conference at Washington. The conference sat from November 12, 1921, to February 6, 1922, and as a result of its deliberations a number of treaties were concluded. The two which had to do with naval disarmament have already been discussed.[8] The others dealt with questions which concerned the Pacific and the Far East.

Although China failed to obtain all that she demanded in the way of national rights, she made a number of gains. In a nine-power treaty the powers agreed to respect her territorial integrity and independence and again proclaimed the policy of the "open door." They also agreed to respect her rights as a neutral in time of war and promised not to support any agreements between their respective nationals which were "designed to create spheres of influence or to provide for the enjoyment of mutually exclusive opportunities in designated parts of Chinese territories." China, for her part, promised not to exercise or permit unfair discrimination of any kind on her railways. A second nine-power treaty permitted China to make an increase in her tariff rates and gave her greater control of the expenditure of the proceeds. A separate agreement between China and Japan, signed outside the conference, provided that Japan should return Shantung and all former German property rights in that province, and that China should reimburse Japan for the amounts which the latter had spent for railway and other improvements since 1914. In December, 1923, Shantung was restored to Chinese control.

Nationalist Efforts to Unite and Emancipate China

In the years after 1921 it appeared for a time that the Nationalists, who had established a constitutional government at Canton, might be the salvation of China. Their aim was not only to unite the whole country under one administration, but to emancipate it from all foreign restrictions as

[8] See pages 426–428.

well. For assistance against both Western imperialism and the opposing Chinese forces in the north they turned to the Soviet government, which was eager to assist in the fight against Western capitalism. Early in 1924 a Nationalist congress offered party membership to all Chinese Communists who were willing to accept the Kuomintang program.

By 1926, however, a serious schism had developed among the Nationalists, for the Right wing of the party was opposed to communism and desired to break with the Soviet government. Chiang Kai-shek, a successful general who became leader of the Nationalists after the death of Sun Yat-sen in March, 1925, threw his lot in with the Right wing of the party, repudiated communism, and began to persecute the Communist members of the Nationalist Party. Nevertheless, despite division within their ranks, the Nationalists successfully carried on their northward advance against the opposing military chiefs. In September, 1926, they captured Hankow and early in the following year Shanghai and Nanking. In April, 1928, Chiang moved his Nationalist government to the latter city, and, after Nationalist troops captured Peking in June of that year, the northern government was abolished, and Nanking was made the new national capital of China. The name of Peking (Northern Capital) was thereupon changed to Peiping (Northern Peace). In August the Nanking government was recognized *de jure* by the League of Nations, which accepted its representative at the meeting of the League Council in that month. By the close of the year 1928 the Nanking government had secured recognition from Japan and most of the Western states.

By this time the Nationalist government had begun its campaign to emancipate China from her international servitudes and had announced that it would abrogate all the "unequal treaties" as they expired. In 1928 the United States concluded a treaty restoring to China complete national tariff autonomy. Other Western powers took the same step, and the year closed with practically all countries recognizing Chinese tariff autonomy. Early in 1929 a new national tariff was put into effect by China, raising the basic rate from the former 5 per cent to 12½ per cent. A new criminal code and a new code of criminal procedure in accordance with Western ideas were introduced in September, 1928, and in October the Chinese government sent identical notes to all powers which still held extraterritorial privileges, asking them to take steps to abolish such privileges as soon as possible. Germany and Russia had already surrendered their extraterritorial rights, and late in 1928 Belgium, Italy, Denmark, and Portugal did the same. Again in April, 1929, the Chinese foreign minister, in a note to the foreign powers, requested action toward the relinquishment of the rights then held under treaties, so that steps might "be taken to enable

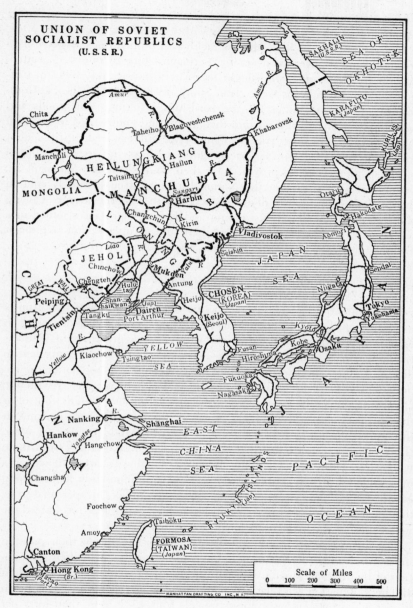

THE FAR EAST, 1920-1931

China, now unified and with a strong central government, to rightfully assume jurisdiction over all nationals within her domain."

Unfortunately for China, she was neither so unified nor possessed of so strong a central government as the Nationalist foreign minister asserted. Although Chiang earnestly sought to create a united and powerful Chinese state, his handicaps were great. South of the Yangtse Chinese Communists, taking advantage of the hardships resulting from floods and famines, won great numbers into their ranks and endeavored to establish a soviet regime. In other parts of China rival military leaders still sought to benefit from the central government's weakness by securing control of one or more valuable provinces for their own advantage. Worst of all, perhaps, was the fact that the Nationalist Party itself definitely split in the spring of 1931. Because of dissatisfaction with what they termed Chiang Kai-shek's "dictatorship," Kwantung and Kwangsi provinces joined in a rebellion against the Nanking government and set up a separate regime at Canton. Once more, it appeared, China was headed toward chaos.

Japanese Penetration of Manchuria

Meanwhile, the Japanese were availing themselves of every opportunity to strengthen their hold upon Manchuria. In 1931 what was described on maps as Manchuria consisted of the three eastern provinces of China—Liaoning, Kirin, and Heilungkiang—with a total area about equivalent to that of France and Germany combined, and with a population of approximately 30,000,000. The region was not closely integrated with the Chinese Republic but enjoyed a great degree of autonomy. The control of the district rested in the military power of the local war lord and not in the central government of China. The war lord and governor of Manchuria, Chang Tso-lin, had repeatedly declined to take orders from those who seized authority in Peiping, and had actually declared Manchuria's independence of China at various times. Chang apparently looked upon Manchuria as possessing extensive autonomy under his personal rule, though his son and successor, Chang Hsiao-liang, after 1928 recognized the sovereignty of the Chinese national government.

The Japanese were eager and determined to strengthen their position in Manchuria in order that they might continue and increase their exploitation of that region. Japan's own natural resources were not over-abundant and her population was relatively dense. Less in area than California, Japan proper had a population of approximately 65,000,000, more than forty per cent of which gained its livelihood directly from the soil. Unfortunately, however, less than one fifth of the country's area was tillable, so that the number of inhabitants in proportion to cultivated area was nearly four times as great as that in England. Even including Korea, the Japanese Empire had an area less in extent than Texas; yet it had to support a population of over 90,000,000, a population which was increasing by about one million annually. Obviously there was in Japan, therefore, a heavy pressure of population upon resources. The introduction of modern industrialism had afforded some relief from this pressure; but machines—if they were to be kept running—required plentiful supplies of raw products and profitable markets. Hence the Japanese were vitally interested in the future development of Manchuria.

It was almost inevitable that friction should develop between the imperialistic Japanese and the nationalistic Chinese. The interconnection of respective rights, the uncertainty at times of the legal situation, the increasing opposition between the conception held by the Japanese of their "special position" in Manchuria and the claims of the Chinese nationalists were a source of numerous disturbing incidents and disputes. Japan consistently sought to advance her interests in Manchuria by taking advantage of rights open to question. The Chinese authorities, on the other hand, repeatedly put obstacles in the way of the exercise of rights which unquestionably belonged to Japan. The tension between Chinese and Japanese in Manchuria continued to grow, while a movement of opinion in Japan began to advocate the settlement of all outstanding questions by the resort to force if necessary. That the group advocating a resort to force ultimately gained the ascendancy in Japan is made abundantly clear by events recorded in the next chapter.

Part Five

THE SECOND WORLD WAR

AND ITS AFTERMATH

ALTHOUGH mankind had emerged from the First World War fervently hoping that the new international order which the League of Nations was to establish would forever banish war from the face of the earth, by 1938 it seemed clear that forces were once more operating which would plunge the world into another great war. Crises followed one another with monotonous regularity as the tension between the powers constantly increased. In August, 1939, international relations were finally strained to the breaking point, and the nations plunged into the Second World War, from which they emerged shaken to their very foundations. The ensuing years saw part of mankind vainly seeking to re-establish life as it had been before the war, and part of it seeking to take advantage of the postwar chaos to spread its "revolutionary" doctrines. At the same time, hundreds of millions in the East sought with some success to throw off Western control in order that they might become free and independent peoples. The chapters in Part Five trace the tragic collapse of collective security, seek to give some idea of the terrible destructiveness of the Second World War, and show how the new postwar period was complicated by the conflict between "Communist totalitarianism" and "Western democracy."

Chapter XXII

THE COLLAPSE OF COLLECTIVE

SECURITY

THE fundamental causes which produced the First World War were not removed by that war nor by the peace settlement which followed it. Beginning in 1931, just as in the decade before 1914, conflicts of national interests arising from these causes produced international crises with monotonous regularity. The statesmen of the major world powers, instead of effectively utilizing the existing machinery of collective security to check the aggressor states, ignored or evaded their responsibility and resorted to the policy of "appeasement." But "appeasement" did not satisfy the aggressors, and tension between the powers increased steadily until it resulted in the Second World War.

Japan's Seizure of Manchuria

The crisis which lighted the powder train of events leading to the Second World War was occasioned by Japan's seizure of Manchuria in 1931–1932. Japanese imperialistic plans and aspirations in the twenties were revealed in the so-called Tanaka Memorial,[1] which purported to be a report to the emperor drawn up by General Baron Giichi Tanaka after a conference of high Japanese military and civil officials in Manchuria and Mongolia in 1927. The memorial pointed out that Japan's national existence required the conquest not only of Manchuria, Mongolia, and China, but of all Eastern Asia and the South Seas countries, and admitted that the achievement of this territorial expansion would entail the crushing of the United States.

The Japanese militarists were in a position to exert great influence upon the course of events, for in Japan the army and navy departments were practically independent of civil authorities and had the right to go directly to the emperor without regard for the cabinet. The army leaders had little sympathy for parliamentary rule and little respect for civil government. Beginning in 1931 they succeeded in largely dominating it, even

[1] See Carl Crow, *Japan's Dream of World Empire: The Tanaka Memorial* (1942).

to the extent of forcing it to defy the world. In fact, they did not hesitate upon occasion to resort to the assassination of high officials in order to advance their own policies. With this situation and state of mind in Japan, with China apparently on the verge of lapsing again into chaos, with the world as a whole in the throes of a disastrous economic depression which was hitting Great Britain and the United States particularly hard, it was small wonder, perhaps, that Japanese militarists should decide that the time was ripe for further advancing Japan's position in Manchuria. On the night of September 18, 1931, a section of the South Manchuria Railway near Mukden was destroyed by explosives, placed there—the Japanese army leaders asserted—by Chinese soldiers from neighboring barracks. The next morning the population of Mukden awoke to find their city in control of Japanese troops.

On September 19 the Chinese representative at Geneva, invoking Article 11 of the Covenant, placed the Manchurian situation before the Council of the League of Nations. The Japanese representative maintained that the incident was unimportant and could be settled by direct Sino-Japanese negotiations. The Council was loath to embark upon a course of vigorous action against Japan without assurance of the collaboration of the United States, but this was not forthcoming. The British representative, moreover, was also opposed to drastic action. Consequently, on September 22 the League Council merely called upon both China and Japan to withdraw their troops from the zone of conflict, and on the next day the United States sent identical notes of the same tenor to the two governments. Japanese military operations, however, continued in Manchuria.

When the Council reconvened on October 13, the United States government urged the League to exert all pressure and authority within its competence toward regulating the action of China and Japan; it stated that, acting independently, it would endeavor to reinforce what the League did; and it offered to appoint an observer to sit with the League Council if invited to do so. The Council thereupon invited the United States to participate in its deliberations. From the very outset Japan maintained that her military operations in Manchuria had no relation to anything but self-defense, and that she could not allow either their necessity or their appropriateness to be the subject of discussion.[2] Although the Council on October 24 passed a resolution calling upon Japan to evacuate the

[2] During the negotiations leading to the pact of Paris the American secretary of state, Frank B. Kellogg, had stated not only that the right of self-defense was inherent in every sovereign state and implicit in every treaty but that "every nation is free at all times and regardless of treaty provisions to defend its territories from attack and invasion, and it alone is competent to decide whether circumstances require recourse to war in self-defense." The United States Senate went even further by declaring that measures of self-defense might also involve military operations outside the territorial boundaries of the state.

occupied territory in Manchuria by November 16, 1931, the Japanese continued their military operations in Manchuria.

On November 16 the Council once more convened, but, apparently as a concession to Senate isolationists in the United States, the American government declined to have an observer sit with it. This change in policy appeared to indicate that the United States was faltering in its support of the League. During the ensuing three weeks futile efforts were made to draft a resolution which would reconcile the conflicting demands of the Chinese and Japanese governments. Finally, on December 10, 1931, the Council, acting on a proposal made by Japan, resolved to appoint a commission which should investigate the Sino-Japanese conflict in the Far East. This commission, which was composed of representatives of Great Britain, Italy, France, Germany, and the United States, with the British Earl of Lytton as chairman, soon became known as the Lytton Commission.

On January 7, 1932, the United States secretary of state, Henry L. Stimson, in identic notes to Japan and China, stated that the United States "does not intend to recognize any situation, treaty or agreement which may be brought about by means contrary to the covenants and obligations of the pact of Paris of August 27, 1928," and thus formulated the so-called Stimson doctrine of nonrecognition. The United States had invited the co-operation of the British and French governments in the promulgation of this doctrine, but the invitation had been declined. The British, having extensive investments in the Far East, were reluctant to send challenging notes to Japan unless there was a determination to back up the words by force. There was no indication that the United States was prepared to do this; in fact, it was opposed to the application of even economic sanctions. Accordingly, Great Britain did not join the United States at this time in announcing the doctrine of nonrecognition, and it again became obvious to Japan that no common Anglo-American front existed. And without the whole-hearted support of the United States and Great Britain the League of Nations was practically powerless.

Although Japan disavowed any intention of violating the territorial integrity of China, Japanese military authorities in Manchuria set up a friendly "administrative committee," which in February, 1932, issued a formal declaration of the independence of Manchuria and Inner Mongolia. Henry Pu-yi, who as emperor had been deposed by the Chinese in 1912, was then inaugurated as regent—later emperor—of the new state of Manchukuo. Next, in September, 1932, Japan and the latter signed a protocol in which Japan recognized Manchukuo as an independent state, and in return secured not only the right to station in Manchukuo "such Japanese forces as may be necessary" for the maintenance of the national security of either country, but Manchukuo's promise "to confirm and respect ... all rights and interests possessed by Japan or her subjects within the territory of Manchukuo by virtue of the Sino-Japanese treaties, agreements, or other arrangements, or through Sino-Japanese contracts, private as well as public." Manchukuo, it appeared, was to be a profitable Japanese protectorate.

Meanwhile, the Lytton Commission, with a group of expert advisers, had spent several months visiting Japan, China, and Manchuria, and had received extensive memoranda prepared by both the Japanese and the Chinese governments. In Manchuria, however, its investigations were gravely embarrassed by the fact that no one was allowed to come near it without a permit from the police. Thus, under the guise of protecting the members of the commission, Japan evidently sought to prevent it from obtaining first-hand information from those opposed to the new regime. But eventually, on October 2, 1932, the Lytton Report was published at Geneva. A number of conclusions were the result of its investigations, and based on these conclusions the commission recommended that a Sino-Japanese conference, with League help, should work out an agreement providing for the recognition of Japan's special interests in Manchuria, which should be autonomous under Chinese sovereignty.

In December, 1932, a Special Assembly of the League referred the Sino-Japanese dispute to a committee with the request that it draw up a plan of settlement. This committee eventually came to the conclusion that it could not formulate any plan which would be acceptable to both China and Japan, and proceeded to draw up a report on the dispute in accordance with Paragraph 4 of Article 16 of the League Covenant.[3] This exonerated China of blame for the course of events, denied that Japan's military measures as a whole could be regarded as measures of self-defense, asserted that the sovereignty of Manchuria belonged to China and that the "Government of Manchukuo" was made possible only by the presence of Japanese troops, declared that the presence of Japanese troops outside the zone of the South Manchuria Railway was incompatible with the legal principles which should govern the settlement of the dispute, and recommended the evacuation of all Japanese troops outside the treaty zones. Four recommendations were made. These provided in essence that the principles laid down by the Lytton Report should be executed through a committee which should supervise the subsequent Sino-Japanese negotiations. All League members were urged to continue nonrecognition of Manchukuo and to refrain from any action liable to prejudice the situation.

On February 24, 1933, the League Assembly met to consider the report

[3] This article read: "If the dispute is not thus settled, the Council either unanimously or by a majority vote shall make and publish a report containing a statement of the facts of the dispute and the recommendations which are deemed just and proper in regard thereto."

of this committee, and when the formal rollcall on approving the report was finally taken, forty-two member states, including all the great powers, voted "Yes"; Japan alone voted "No." Never before had such a universal vote of censure been passed upon any sovereign state. Yosuke Matsuoka, the Japanese representative, thereupon read a brief statement in which he expressed profound regret at the vote which had just been taken and emphasized that Japan had "reached the limit of endeavors to co-operate with the League regarding the Sino-Japanese dispute." With firm step he then withdrew from the Assembly, followed by the other members of the Japanese delegation. On March 27, 1933, the Japanese government gave notice of Japan's intention to withdraw from the League.

In that same month Japan's troops added still a fourth province—Jehol in Inner Mongolia—to her puppet state. Early in April they next launched a drive against the Chinese and advanced south of the Great Wall to within a few miles of Peiping and Tientsin. In May the Chinese government ordered its troops to evacuate Peiping, and shortly thereafter the "Peiping Political Council," composed of men holding moderate or pro-Japanese views, was constituted with administrative authority over an undefined area in North China. Negotiations were opened between this council and the Japanese, and on May 31, 1933, a truce was signed at Tangku, near Tientsin. By the terms of this truce it was agreed that Chinese troops should withdraw south and west of a line running roughly from Tientsin to Peiping and that Japanese troops should withdraw north of the Great Wall. These measures resulted in the creation between Manchukuo and China of a demilitarized zone administered by Chinese friendly to Japan —the possible future nucleus of another state with pro-Japanese sympathies. Apparently the Chinese government had been driven to realize the futility of struggling against Japanese military forces and had come to the conclusion that, to prevent the possible spoliation of China proper, it would have to recognize that Manchuria had gone the way of Burma, Annam, Tonkin, Formosa, and Korea.

Doubtless a punitive war, conducted jointly by all of the great powers of the West, might eventually have crushed Japan, compelled her to observe her treaty obligations, and forced her to withdraw from Manchuria. But such a conflict would have been a costly struggle and would have entailed sacrifices far greater than the peoples of the West were willing to make at that time. Possibly, had the great powers been able to suppress their economic rivalries long enough to subject Japan to the rigors of a general worldwide financial and commercial boycott in accordance with Article 16 of the Covenant, they might have compelled her to surrender her ill-gotten gains. But in 1931–1932 the whole world was in the depths of an economic depression of the first magnitude, and the statesmen of none of the great powers wished to embark upon a policy which would aggravate the economic distress within their own countries. Furthermore, even had the statesmen of the great powers within the League been willing to impose sanctions upon Japan, they would probably have been deterred from effective action by the knowledge that the United States was not a member of the League and would not participate in such sanctions. Finally, it is probably true that in the years 1931–1933 no Western people sufficiently resented Japan's conquest of Manchuria to be willing to wage war to prevent it, and no responsible statesman of the great powers went so far as to urge measures which might conceivably have precipitated such a war. Even Soviet Russia, which might have been expected to take a strong stand against Japanese domination of all of Manchuria, was primarily concerned in 1931–1932 with the success of her domestic economic program, and pursued during these years a policy which was distinctly pacific and defensive.

In the light of subsequent events it seems clear that the failure to enforce collective security in behalf of China was a fateful blunder. It is obvious now that the "appeasement" of Japan at the expense of China in 1931–1932 did not deter the former from further plans and acts of aggression. On the other hand, it seems likely that, if the great powers, including the United States, had resorted to an economic and financial boycott, supported if necessary by the might of their combined navies, Japan would have suffered an economic collapse, her military leaders would have been discredited, and her forces would have been withdrawn from Manchuria. Had these developments occurred, a great triumph for collective security would have been scored, and other potential aggressors would have been given reason to pause. But the inaction of the great powers in the face of Japan's aggression weakened the world's faith in collective security, encouraged other would-be aggressors to embark upon their plans, and brought upon the world further international crises.

Germany's Rearmament

The next country to break its treaty obligations and to flout the collective action of the great powers was Nazi Germany, whose dictator, Adolf Hitler, already inclined to be aggressive, was doubtless encouraged in this direction by the pusillanimous attitude of the powers in the face of Japan's seizure of Manchuria. Germany's withdrawal from the Disarmament Conference and her notice of withdrawal from the League of Nations late in 1933 have already been discussed.[4] These steps gave warning that Hitler was determined to abandon Stresemann's earlier policy

[4] See page 430.

of apparent collaboration in favor of a policy of recalcitrance and possibly of aggression.

The realization of this change in the spirit of German foreign policy at once had its effect on Europe's international relations. In June, 1934, the Soviet Union, Poland, and Rumania, in order to check Hitler's *Drang nach Osten,* mutually guaranteed their existing frontiers. Three months later the Soviet Union, apparently in order to be linked with fifty-seven other states in an organization for the defense of the *status quo,* accepted membership in the League of Nations. Russia thus became linked with the so-called satiated powers.

France, too, became active. In 1934 she opened negotiations with Italy in an effort to remove the postwar causes of friction between the two states. These negotiations were successfully concluded by Pierre Laval and resulted in the signing of a number of pacts and conventions in January, 1935. France ceded to Italy territory adjoining the latter's Libyan colony on the south and a strategic triangle of territory on the southern edge of Italy's Eritrea. In addition, she gave Italy a share in the railway from Jibuti in French Somaliland to Addis Ababa, the capital of Ethiopia. Another convention, dealing with the rights of Italians living in Tunis, was designed to remove Italy's dissatisfaction with the status of her citizens there. These various agreements went far toward removing the causes of ill feeling and friction between Italy and France, and resulted in Mussolini's moving into the French camp.

Meanwhile, it was widely suspected that Nazi Germany was secretly rearming despite her treaty obligations. That she did not openly defy the Allies in this matter may have been due to her belief that she should first accumulate a quantity of military supplies and to her fear that if she acted too soon the Allies might not permit the return of the Saar basin to Germany in accordance with the terms of the treaty of Versailles. But on January 13, 1935, a plebiscite was held in the Saar under the supervision of a League commission which resulted in an overwhelming vote in favor of the Saar's return to Germany. The Council of the League of Nations on January 17 accordingly awarded the entire Saar basin to Germany, and on March 1, 1935, the formal transfer of the district occurred.

A fortnight later, on March 16, Hitler proclaimed the rearmament of Germany. The Reich, he stated, would at once reintroduce compulsory military service and would increase the peace size of her army to more than 500,000 men. In justification of Germany's unilateral action in thus abrogating the treaty of Versailles, Hitler claimed that the treaty had already been nullified by the failure of the former Allies to carry out its promise of general disarmament. Protests against Germany's action were at once filed in Berlin by the British, French, and Italian governments. One month later the Council of the League of Nations formally condemned Germany for her unilateral repudiation of the disarmament clauses of the treaty of Versailles. But no steps were taken by the powers either singly or collectively to compel Germany to observe her treaty obligations. In fact, the British government by its own action soon gave evidence that it condoned Germany's breaking of the treaty. An Anglo-German agreement was reached (June 18, 1935) giving Germany the right to a navy 35 per cent as large as that of Great Britain and the right to have submarines, contrary to the limitations imposed upon her by the treaty of Versailles. To the French and many others it appeared that Great Britain, while taking steps to safeguard her own preponderance of power on the sea, was willing to permit Germany once more to become a military threat on the Continent.

France and the Soviet Union, meanwhile, had taken steps to meet the increased Nazi menace by signing (May 2, 1935) a five-year pact of mutual assistance. According to the agreement, France and the Soviet Union undertook to give each other mutual aid against unprovoked aggression involving violation of either's territory in case the League Council failed to reach a unanimous decision regarding the attack. A similar treaty was signed between the Soviet Union and Czechoslovakia a little later. Before the Franco-Soviet treaty was ratified, Germany called the attention of the powers to the fact that France was about to commit herself to obligations which were not reconcilable with the Locarno pact. Germany maintained that, in case of a Russo-German war, in the last analysis France reserved the right to decide at her own discretion who the aggressor might be. There seemed to be much justice in Germany's claim that the French agreement to aid Russia if the League Council did not agree on the aggressor was in contravention of the French promise in no case to attack, invade, or resort to war against Germany unless directed by the League.

In March, 1935, Hitler had given his solemn promise to observe the Locarno agreements which had been voluntarily initiated and signed by Germany ten years earlier. Nevertheless, the natural corollary of Germany's rearmament was that she should seize upon some favorable occasion to remilitarize the Rhineland. Such an occasion presented itself during the Italo-Ethiopian conflict when the Locarno front was broken. Timing his act to fall when the international situation was particularly tense because of contemplated petroleum sanctions against Italy,[5] Hitler on March 7, 1936, announced Germany's repudiation of the treaty of Versailles and the Locarno mutual-guarantee treaty. Simultaneously with his announcement, 20,000 German troops marched into the Rhineland.

[5] See page 644.

Five days later the signatories of the Locarno treaty—minus Germany —met and unanimously agreed that Germany's action was "a clear violation of Articles 42 and 43 of the treaty of Versailles and the Locarno pact." One week later the Council of the League of Nations also voted that Germany was guilty of infringing the Locarno treaty. Although demands for economic and financial sanctions against Germany were made by France, Poland, the Little Entente, and Soviet Russia, Great Britain opposed such a step. Under the Covenant sanctions were applicable only against a state which had illegally embarked upon a war. This Germany had not done. Many felt, moreover, that morally, if not legally, Germany had much to support her attempt to regain a status of national equality with the other great powers. Therefore, despite the fact that the Locarno treaty of mutual guarantee specifically stated that the signatory powers would come to the aid of the injured party in case of just such a "flagrant" violation of the demilitarized zone, no steps were taken to force the German troops out of the Rhineland. Once again it was shown that the powers could not agree on collective action to compel a state to observe its treaty obligations. This time the net result was a rearmed and militant Germany.

Italy's Conquest of Ethiopia

In the meantime the powers in the League of Nations had been engaged in a half-hearted attempt by collective action to prevent Mussolini from seizing Ethiopia. On December 5, 1934, Italian and Ethiopian border patrols had clashed at Ualual, an oasis in a disputed area between Ethiopia and Italian Somaliland. Ethiopia had immediately filed a protest with Italy and had requested that the affair be arbitrated in accordance with an Italo-Ethiopian treaty of 1928. Italy, however, had refused to arbitrate and had demanded instead a formal apology, an indemnity for Italian soldiers slain, and the arrest and punishment of the Ethiopian officers involved. There were not lacking those who believed that Mussolini was about to seize upon this incident to right another Italian "wrong" and to open the way for further Italian expansion.

Efforts were made to settle the dispute by peaceful means, however. On January 3, 1935, Ethiopia formally appealed to the League under Article 11 of the Covenant, but the League Council in its January meeting postponed its consideration of the incident until its next session, hoping that it might in the meantime be settled by direct negotiations between the two governments in accordance with their arbitration treaty. The arbitration commission's unanimous decision, announced on September 3, 1935, was that neither side was to blame for the Ualual clash, since each believed that it was fighting on its own soil. Obviously this report eliminated the incident as a pretext for Italian reprisals.

Meanwhile, on the suggestion of the League Council, Great Britain, France, and Italy had entered into negotiations for the purpose of facilitating a solution of the differences between Italy and Ethiopia. The negotiations were brought to a sudden end, however, when Mussolini rejected the Anglo-French proposal to entrust to Italy an economic mandate under the League for the financial and administrative organization of Ethiopia. Thereupon the British government decided to leave the dispute to the League and to invoke collective action and the use of sanctions against Italy if the latter attacked Ethiopia in violation of the League Covenant. Although France desired if possible to retain the newly won friendship of Italy even at the cost of permitting her to take part of Ethiopia, she wanted the support of Great Britain even more than that of Italy in case of another German war. Consequently, after the British government definitely determined to support collective action at Geneva, France was practically forced to take the same stand. When the League Council met in September, therefore, sanctions against Italy appeared to be almost inevitable unless Mussolini was willing to withdraw from his Ethiopian venture. That he was unwilling to do this seemed apparent when he refused to accept the recommendations of a League commission. On October 3, 1935, Italian troops invaded Ethiopia.

Four days later the League Council decided that "the Italian government has resorted to war in disregard of its covenants under Article 12 of the Covenant of the League of Nations," and thus, for the first time, declared a European great power to be an aggressor. The Council's decision was then referred to the Assembly, which at once concurred in the verdict and appointed a committee to consider what measures should be taken under Article 16 dealing with sanctions. By October 19 five proposals had been drafted. The first provided for immediately placing an arms embargo against Italy and lifting any existing embargo against Ethiopia. The second provided for financial sanctions. The third forbade the importation of all Italian goods. The fourth forbade the exportation to Italy of a list of key war materials, and the fifth provided that League members would try to replace imports from Italy by imports from states which normally had profitable markets in Italy. These proposals were accepted by most of the member states, and the Assembly committee eventually declared that all sanctions against Italy should be in effect by November 18, 1935.

Although, under Article 16, members of the League agreed immediately to sever *all* trade and financial relations with an aggressor state, unfortunately for the success of the League's first attempt to prevent aggression by the imposition of economic sanctions, the latter were not applied with full force. The export to Italy of certain commodities of which she had special need was not forbidden. The Canadian delegate to the League proposed that petroleum, coal, iron, and steel should be embargoed, but Pierre Laval, French foreign minister, and Sir Samuel Hoare, British foreign secretary, had already agreed to limit the application of sanctions even before the time came to apply them. Both were disturbed by Germany's rearmament and hoped to avoid giving Mussolini an occasion for collaborating with Hitler. Publicly, however, it was argued that an embargo on these special commodities could not be effective so long as the United States and Germany did not co-operate with the League. Accordingly, although the Canadian delegate's proposal was adopted "in principle," the embargo was not to come into force "until conditions for rendering it effective appear to be realized."

But, although President Roosevelt of the United States in October had placed an embargo on arms shipments to both Italy and Ethiopia, it was vigorously asserted in the United States that the neutrality resolution passed by Congress in 1935 gave him no authority to embargo petroleum, iron, or steel. In Europe it was argued that to forbid British and Dutch oil companies to ship oil to Italy would merely result in increased sales of oil to Italy by American companies. Furthermore, Mussolini had announced that the extension of sanctions to include petroleum would be regarded as an unfriendly act, that is, an act involving war; and the statesmen of England and France were determined to avoid war. Consequently, those supplies which Italy most needed for the successful prosecution of her war were not cut off.

While incomplete sanctions were being applied to Italy, the French and British foreign ministers sought to appease Mussolini, and the result of their efforts was the notorious "Hoare-Laval proposals" which were made in December. These envisaged the cession to Italy of areas in Ethiopia in the vicinity of Eritrea and Somaliland and the establishment of an extensive zone of expansion and colonization in southern Ethiopia in which Italy should have a monopoly of economic rights. Public condemnation of the plan was widespread and vigorous. Sir Samuel Hoare was forced to resign as foreign secretary and was succeeded by Anthony Eden, who was known for his loyal support of League measures and for his advocacy of the policy of sanctions. A few weeks later Laval, also, was forced to resign.

Late in January, 1936, Anthony Eden, the new British foreign secretary, urged the adoption of oil sanctions, but there was delay because of events in England and France and because the new French foreign minister,

Pierre Flandin, persuaded the League committee on sanctions to make one more attempt at conciliation before resort to the embargo. Consequently, action on the oil sanction was again deferred in order that a League committee might make a fresh appeal to Italy and Ethiopia to end the war on terms "within the League Covenant's framework." This appeal was sent on March 3, 1936, and stated that the committee would meet one week later to consider the replies. Before that date, however, Hitler's announcement (March 7) of the remilitarization of the Rhineland introduced a new element into an already complicated situation and definitely ended the possibility of France's supporting an oil embargo.

In Ethiopia, during these months, Italian forces had been carrying on operations, and eventually, in April, 1936, the primitive Ethiopian resistance collapsed in the face of Italian heavy artillery, tanks, airplanes, bombs, and poison gas. Emperor Haile Selassie, his armies demoralized and his retreat to the west cut off by disaffected tribal chiefs, on May 2 fled to French Somaliland, where he boarded a British warship. Meanwhile, 30,000 Italian troops in what was perhaps the greatest motorized column yet organized rolled slowly and steadily on by two main routes toward Addis Ababa. On May 5 they entered the Ethiopian capital and hoisted the Italian flag. In Rome, on the same day, Mussolini, in addressing a great victory celebration, announced "Ethiopia is Italian." Four days later the Duce decreed that all of Ethiopia was "placed under full and complete sovereignty of the Kingdom of Italy," and that the "title of Emperor of Ethiopia is assumed for himself and for his successors by the King of Italy."

Italy's annexation of Ethiopia presented a new problem—should the League recognize Italy's conquest as a *fait accompli* which it had failed to prevent, and now remove sanctions, or should it maintain that Italy had gone to war in disregard of her League obligations and continue economic sanctions against her, regardless of her victory? The British government favored the "common-sense" policy of abandoning sanctions. On the other hand, the Little Entente, the Balkan Entente, and the so-called neutrals all pronounced in favor of continuing sanctions. Ultimately, however, on July 4, 1936, the League Assembly adopted a resolution in which, while "remaining firmly attached to the principles of the Covenant ... excluding the settlement of territorial questions by force," it recommended that sanctions should end. Italy, it appeared, had won, and another crushing blow had been dealt to the belief in the efficacy of collective action to stop aggression.

The Rome-Berlin-Tokyo Axis

It was probably natural and perhaps even more or less inevitable that the three unsatiated great powers which had been disturbing the world by their aggressive acts in the years 1931–1936 should draw together for mutual support, especially in view of the fact that at the opening of the year 1936 each stood practically isolated as the result of its policies. Japan, because of her seizure of Manchuria, had been unanimously condemned by the League of Nations, from which she in turn had cut herself off by resigning in 1933. Italy, because of her invasion of Ethiopia, had been not only condemned but subjected to sanctions by the League, and these acts, in which Great Britain and France participated, had driven a wedge between Italy and them. Germany, too, had alienated the great powers of Europe. The Nazi attempt to absorb Austria by overturning Dollfuss' government in 1934 had antagonized Italy. Hitler's remilitarization of Germany in 1935 had resulted in a Franco-Soviet defensive alliance. And Germany's remilitarization of the Rhineland in 1936 had driven Great Britain into the arms of France. The former at once agreed to assist Belgium and France in case of a possible attack by Germany.

But in 1936 Germany took steps to emerge from her state of isolation. On July 11 she recognized the full sovereignty of Austria and agreed that the latter's political structure was an internal affair with which she would neither directly nor indirectly interfere. During that summer, moreover, Germany joined Italy in sending aid to General Franco in Spain, and their co-operation in a conflict which was described as one between fascist and communist ideologies further facilitated a *rapprochement* between Hitler and Mussolini. Finally, on October 25, Italy and Germany reached an accord which provided for (1) collaboration of the two states in all matters affecting their "parallel interests," (2) the defense of European civilization against communism, (3) economic co-operation in the Danubian region, and (4) the maintenance of Spain's territorial and colonial integrity. Germany recognized Italy's Ethiopian empire and in return was promised economic concessions in that part of Africa. In December an Italo-German trade agreement implemented the October accord by extending to Italian colonies the economic privileges which Germany already enjoyed in Italy and by dividing the river and rail traffic of the Danubian states in such a way as to benefit Hamburg and Trieste. Thus was created the so-called Rome-Berlin Axis.

But Hitler was not yet content. Further to strengthen the Reich's international position, especially with reference to Soviet Russia, Germany on November 25, 1936, signed a pact with Japan in which each promised to inform the other concerning the activities of the Comintern (Third International), to consult with the other concerning measures to combat its activity, and to execute these measures in close co-operation. There were many, especially in the Soviet Union, who believed that the anti-Comintern pact was not so innocuous as it appeared, that it perhaps contained secret clauses providing for military co-operation against Russia. However that may be, when, on November 6, 1937, Italy also adhered to the anti-Comintern pact, three of the important totalitarian and unsatiated powers were brought together in the so-called Rome-Berlin-Tokyo Axis.

Evidence of the spirit of co-operation which developed among these authoritarian states was forthcoming on several occasions. Italy's adhesion to the Rome-Berlin Axis was confirmed in 1937 by the Duce's statement that Italy could not give military assistance to protect Austria against a German attempt to consummate the *Anschluss,* by Mussolini's visit to Germany as Hitler's guest in September of that year, and by Italy's announcement of her withdrawal from the League of Nations in the following December. The cordial relations between the two Western powers and Japan were confirmed by Italy's recognition of Manchukuo as an independent state in November, 1937, and by Germany's similar action in May, 1938. Further evidence of the operation of the Rome-Berlin-Tokyo Axis seemed indicated in 1938 by Hitler's order that all German military advisers to the Nationalist government in China should leave that country. By 1938 the great powers, as in 1914, were once more coming to be divided into two increasingly antagonistic groups.

Japan's Invasion of China

Meanwhile, in the years after 1933, Japan had continued to strengthen her dominant position in the Far East and to announce with ever-increasing clearness and decision her thesis "that Japan, serving as only a cornerstone for the edifice of peace in eastern Asia, bears the entire burden of responsibilities." In April, 1934, the Japanese foreign office emphasized this viewpoint once more when it announced that the activities of the League of Nations for the rehabilitation of China, American loans to China, and the presence of foreigners as instructors in the Chinese army were considered by the Japanese government as tending to support in China resistance to Japan which threatened the peace of Asia. All of these measures, it was declared, were objectionable to Japan, and, if they were continued and supported by force, then "Japan herself may be compelled to resort to force." It seemed clear that Japan was determined to assert her exclusive right to control China in the interests of Japanese security and Japanese economic penetration.

THE "ROME-BERLIN AXIS"

The close co-operation between Fascist Italy and Nazi Germany was emphasized by Mussolini's visit to Hitler in September, 1937.

During 1935 Japan began to encroach upon several of China's northern provinces. In consequence of demands made upon the Nanking government, the governors of Hopei and Chahar provinces were removed, all branch offices of the Nationalist Party in North China were closed, all anti-Japanese organizations in Chahar were abolished, troops of the Nanking government were withdrawn from Hopei province and from the Chahar-Jehol frontier, and a new mayor, police commissioner, and garrison commander—all acceptable to the Japanese—were installed in Tientsin. In November, 1935, eighteen counties in and near the demilitarized zone along the Great Wall declared their independence and set up an autonomous state under a pro-Japanese commissioner. In the following month the Nanking government agreed to the establishment of a semi-independent regime in Hopei and Chahar provinces, which included Peiping, the old Chinese capital, and Tientsin, North China's commercial city. The newly organized government consisted chiefly of pro-Japanese members, and during 1936 it permitted the smuggling of Japanese goods into North China upon payment of only one eighth of the national tariff dues.

Despite measures taken by the Nanking government to guard against the possibility of popular opposition to its policy of appeasement, a strong nationalist and anti-Japanese sentiment developed in 1936 in China, thanks largely to the activities of Chinese students. So strong did this nationalist movement become that even the semi-independent Canton government in South China demanded that the government in Nanking should resist Japanese aggression with armed force. Of China's important military leaders, Chiang Kai-shek alone appeared to remain opposed to the adoption of a strong anti-Japanese program. In December, 1936, it was revealed that the Nationalist government had further agreed to suppress anti-Japanese movements, to engage Japanese advisers, and to reduce Chinese tariffs. In that month Nanking ordered twelve of the provincial governments to inaugurate an anti-Communist campaign in accordance with the Japanese desire to check the growing strength of the Communist forces in the northwest provinces of China. General Chiang himself proceeded to Shensi province because he was dissatisfied with General Chang Hsueh-liang's conduct of the campaign against the Communists.

But on December 12 by a sudden *coup d'état* Chang Hsueh-liang captured General Chiang and held him a prisoner. As conditions for release he demanded a declaration of war against Japan, the Nanking government's promise to recover all lost territories, and the readmission of Chinese Communists to the Nationalist Party. Although much about the coup remained a mystery, after a detention of two weeks Chiang Kai-shek was released, and he returned to Nanking bringing General Chang as a prisoner. In January, 1937, however, the latter received a full pardon for his part in the rebellion, and later in the month an agreement between the rebellious Shensi forces and the Nanking government permitted occupation of northern Shensi by Communist troops.

The Communist leaders declared their willingness to modify their social program and to place their armies under Chiang Kai-shek's command, if the Nationalist government would adopt an anti-Japanese policy and introduce a more democratic regime in China. During the first half of 1937 the Nanking government, with the whole of China united at least temporarily by a wave of nationalism, sought increasingly to re-assert its influence over North China officials. Undoubtedly the strong anti-Japanese sentiment in China and the apparently growing military strength of the latter were disturbing to Japanese military leaders, who planned to establish a pro-Japanese regime in China's five northern provinces.

As in Manchuria in 1931, the Japanese were able to arrange an "incident" at the appropriate time. On the night of July 7, 1937, a clash occurred a short distance west of Peiping between Japanese troops and units of the Chinese army. After some diplomatic temporizing by both the Chinese and the Japanese, the latter on July 19 made demands which the Nanking government refused to accept. Then, late in July, after an ultimatum, Japanese troops began an advance in the coveted northern provinces. Within a few days the eastern part of Hopei province, including Tientsin and Peiping, was effectively occupied, and provisional governments favorable to Japan were established. By the close of 1937 the Japanese had captured the capitals of Shansi and Shantung provinces and were well on their way to control of the five provinces north of the Yellow River. On December 14 a new pro-Japanese government was set up in Peiping, whose name had already been changed back to Peking (Northern Capital).

But the fighting had not been confined to North China. In August a campaign was also launched against the important commercial city of Shanghai, which, after three months of hard fighting, was captured on November 8, 1937. The Japanese next advanced up the Yangtse, and in December captured Nanking, the political capital of China. In an attempt to prevent the escape of fleeing Chinese soldiers, the Japanese resorted to indiscriminate attacks on all traffic on the Yangtse River above Nanking. During these attacks the United States gunboat *Panay*, although clearly marked to show that it was American, and three vessels of the Standard Oil Company were bombed and sunk by a Japanese airplane and four vessels of British registry were shelled. The survivors of the *Panay* were even attacked by machine-gun fire while they were attempting to reach shore.

Sharp protests and strong demands for satisfaction, made by President Roosevelt and by the British government, brought immediate and profuse apologies by Japanese officials, and the Japanese foreign office stated its readiness to pay compensation and to give guarantees against the recurrence of such incidents. The United States and British governments thereupon accepted the amends. But the relative indifference of Americans generally to the significance of the *Panay* incident may have convinced Japanese militarists that they had little to fear from the West, for the Japanese military in China continued to violate the rights of Americans and other foreigners residing in that country. They also continued their conquests. By the close of the year 1938 they held the great commercial cities of Tientsin, Peiping, Shanghai, Nanking, Hankow, and Canton. The Nationalist government of Generalissimo Chiang Kai-shek had, perforce, been moved to the interior city of Chungking.

Meanwhile, as in 1931, the Chinese government had appealed to the League of Nations against Japan. When the Assembly convened in September, 1937, China's appeal had been referred to the League's Far Eastern advisory committee, which unanimously condemned Japan as an invader and a treaty-breaker. It recommended that the Assembly should invite those members of the League which were signatories of the Washington nine-power treaty to meet as soon as possible to initiate consultation regarding the agreement to respect China's sovereignty, independence, and territorial integrity. Upon the League's invitation the representatives of nineteen nations therefore convened at Brussels in November, 1937, to consider what might be done to safeguard peace in the Far East. Japan declined to be represented at the meeting, however, and insisted that China was responsible for the existing conflict, that China, not Japan, was "violating the spirit of the pact against war." The delegates thereupon adopted a declaration characterizing Japan's military action in China as illegal, but China's appeal for the withholding of war materials and credits to Japan went unheeded. Late in November, just before adjourning indefinitely, the conference admitted that for the time being it could do nothing to reestablish peace.

In September, 1938, China again appealed to the League for assistance under the terms of Article 17 of the Covenant, which provided for the handling of disputes between a state in the League and one outside. The Council decided that Japan's invasion of China was a violation of the Briand-Kellogg treaty and of the nine-power treaty of 1922. It further decided that Article 16 regarding sanctions became applicable, but held that the time was not suitable for collective action. The net result of China's appeal was merely the Council's invitation to members of the League individually to support China. Once more collective security had been proved to be a broken reed. No group of states was willing to pay the price in life or wealth which would be necessary to save China from the invading armies of the Japanese.

Germany's Annexation of Austria

In the West, by 1938, the situation was such as to encourage Hitler, too, to embark upon his program of territorial expansion. Mussolini, who had earlier opposed the *Anschluss,* was now linked with Hitler in the Rome-Berlin Axis, and had even announced that Italy could not give military assistance to protect Austria against a German attempt to absorb that country. Furthermore, Italy was deeply involved in Ethiopia and in Spain and was therefore in no position to break with her partner in the Axis. France was passing through a period of ministerial instability and seemed also to be in no position to act effectively. In Great Britain a majority of the members of the Chamberlain government were in favor of a program of "appeasement" of Germany and Italy, so much so that Anthony Eden, who opposed "appeasement," was forced to resign as foreign secretary on February 20, 1938. In some quarters it was believed that the Chamberlain government looked with tolerance upon Hitler's desire to seize Austria.

The first step in Hitler's program of territorial expansion for Germany came on February 12, 1938, when an interview between the Austrian Chancellor Schuschnigg and Hitler occurred at the latter's Bavarian mountain chalet at Berchtesgaden. As the result of the Führer's threats, Schuschnigg was forced to appoint Arthur Seyss-Inquart, the Austrian Nazi leader, minister of the interior, and other Nazis ministers of justice and of foreign affairs. The Austrian chancellor still hoped to maintain the republic's independence, however, and on March 9 announced that a plebiscite on the question would be held in Austria four days later. Evidently he believed that the interval before election would be too short for the Nazis to mobilize their high-pressure speakers and terroristic methods effectively, and that the subsequent vote would prove to the world that the majority of Austrians had no desire to be absorbed by Germany.

But Hitler and the Austrian Nazis were determined that no plebiscite should be held under such conditions. On March 11 Seyss-Inquart presented Schuschnigg with an ultimatum demanding his resignation and the postponement of the plebiscite, threatening that otherwise German troops, already mobilized on the border, would invade Austria. Confronted by this situation, Schuschnigg, "in order to save bloodshed," canceled the plebiscite and resigned. Seyss-Inquart thereupon became head of the new cabinet, which at once invited the German government to send troops into Austria "to preserve order."

On March 12 Hitler returned to Linz, his former home in Austria. On the next day the German government issued a law declaring Austria to be a state of the German Reich. President Miklas resigned, and Chancellor Schuschnigg was placed under arrest. On March 14 Hitler arrived in Vienna, preceded by German mechanized and air forces, and was given an enthusiastic reception. "All Germany is living through this hour of victory—seventy-four millions in one united Reich," he shouted. "No threats, no hardships, no force can make us break our oath to be united forever." Although France and Great Britain lodged formal protests with Berlin, no state raised a hand in defense of Austria's sovereignty.

The absorption of Austria greatly strengthened Germany's position in central Europe and at the same time advanced her *Drang nach Osten*. She was now in direct contact with Italy at the Brenner Pass and also in direct touch with Yugoslavia and Hungary. Furthermore, domination in Austria gave the Third Reich military and economic control of practically all the communications of southeastern Europe. Czechoslovakia was almost isolated. Her trade outlets through Germany were at the mercy of the latter, and her communications by rail and river to the south and southeast could be severed almost at will. More important still, from a military standpoint, Germany by annexing Austria had placed herself in a position to outflank the powerful Czechoslovak defense system along the German frontier. Despite Hitler's pledge of March 11, 1938, that he would respect the integrity of the Czech nation, it is not surprising that the German Nazis next turned their attention to "alleviating the wrongs" suffered by their 3,500,000 kinsmen in Czechoslovakia.

The Dismemberment of Czechoslovakia

It has already been pointed out [6] that the Nazi movement had entered Czechoslovakia, where it was organized politically as the Sudeten German (*Sudetendeutsch*) Party under the leadership of Konrad Henlein. After Hitler's success in Austria the Sudeten German leader called upon all Germans in Czechoslovakia to join his party and succeeded in forcing various Germans to withdraw from the Czechoslovak ministry. Thereafter Henlein became ever more aggressive in his demands. In May, 1938, the tension both in Czechoslovakia and in Europe reached a high point when elections were held in the republic. Preceding the elections a vigorous campaign against Czechoslovakia was waged in the German press, and it was feared by many that the Nazi government might avail itself of some of the clashes between rival nationals in connection with the elections to go to the aid of the Sudeten Germans.

[6] See pages 577–578.

Although the French government urged Czechoslovakia to go to the limit of concession to the Sudeten Germans, it left no doubt that France would fulfill her military obligations if Czechoslovakia were attacked. Russia also stated her readiness to go to the aid of the Czechs, should the need arise. The British government kept in constant touch with Paris and sought to bring pressure at both Berlin and Prague in favor of peace. In the end the elections passed off without the feared German intervention. Of significance, however, was the fact that hundreds of thousands of Germans were at once put to work to construct a line of fortifications along the Rhine from Switzerland to the Netherlands. By many it was believed that these gigantic fortifications—called by Germans the West Wall—were designed to halt France in the west, should Germany later launch her *Drang nach Osten* against Czechoslovakia.

In July the British government, apparently adhering to Chamberlain's policy of "appeasement," asked Premier Hodža whether the Czechoslovak government would accept a British adviser in the dispute with the Sudeten German Party, and was informed that it would. Lord Runciman was then appointed as such an adviser, and both President Beneš and Premier Hodža stated that Czechoslovakia was prepared to go to the full limit of Lord Runciman's advice, provided the sovereignty of the state was protected. Ultimately, on September 7, the Czechoslovak government offered Henlein a plan, which, according to Lord Runciman, granted practically everything that the Sudeten Germans had earlier demanded.

Nevertheless, on September 12, 1938, in his final address to the hundreds of thousands gathered at the Nazi Party congress, Hitler demanded the "right of self-determination" for the Sudeten Germans of Czechoslovakia, and announced that, if the latter could not defend themselves, "they will receive help from us." The German Nazis, he declared, "will not remain indifferent for long if these tortured and oppressed creatures cannot defend themselves." Immediately after Hitler's address the Sudeten Germans, as though operated by a push-button from Nuremberg, began demonstrating in favor of union with Germany. Riots and clashes with the Czechoslovak gendarmerie ensued, and a number of casualties occurred. Events seemed to indicate that a situation was being created to provide an opportunity for German troops to invade Czechoslovakia in order to protect the "tortured and oppressed" Germans living in that republic. Such an invasion would place upon France and Russia the obligation to go to the aid of Czechoslovakia and so might precipitate a general European war.

In this highly critical situation Prime Minister Chamberlain of Great Britain, hoping to prevent war by "appeasing" Hitler, asked the German Führer for a personal interview, and on September 15 flew to Munich and proceeded to the Führer's mountain chalet at Berchtesgaden. Here Chamberlain learned that Hitler had decided that the Sudeten Germans should have the right to unite with the Reich, if they wished, and that he would aid them if necessary even at the risk of a general European war. The British and French governments thereupon decided that the only way to avoid a general European war was to accept the principle of self-determination. On September 19 they asked Czechoslovakia to agree to the immediate transfer to the Reich of areas inhabited by a population more than 50 per cent German. When Czechoslovakia suggested that the matter be submitted to arbitration, Great Britain and France, in what was practically an ultimatum, declared that she must accept Anglo-French proposals at once or bear the consequences alone.

This Anglo-French decision to desert Czechoslovakia was the result of several factors. In the first place, there was in both countries a popular desire to escape the horrors of a general European war. Moreover, neither England nor France was then prepared to deal effectively with an attack from the air, and Chamberlain and Daladier apparently envisioned the quick destruction of London and Paris by the much-advertised German Luftwaffe, should a general war be precipitated. In the second place, in both England and France there were influential groups which opposed a war in behalf of Czechoslovakia. In the former, certain elements looked upon Czechoslovakia as an "artificial" creation of the Paris peace conference, and believed that, so long as it existed as then constituted, it would continue to be a constant invitation to dismemberment by neighboring national states. In the latter, certain Rightist groups felt that a war with Germany would open the way for the French Leftists to secure control of France, and they preferred "appeasement" of Hitler at the expense of Czechoslovakia to the possible triumph of the Communists at home. In the third place, there was undoubtedly still held in some quarters in both countries the belief, which had been so assiduously cultivated by Hitler, that Nazism was a bulwark of strength protecting western Europe from Russian Communism, and that therefore it should be upheld even at some sacrifice. Finally, Hitler announced that once his demands upon Czechoslovakia were satisfied he would have no further territorial ambitions in Europe. Chamberlain and Daladier apparently still thought that some credence could be put in Hitler's pledged word, and consequently reasoned that the shift of the Sudeten Germans from Czechoslovakia to the Reich was not too high a price to pay for a satisfied Germany and a peaceful Europe.

Whatever may have been the reasons for Chamberlain's and Daladier's decisions, Czechoslovakia when faced by their final demand had little alternative but to give in. The Czech leaders had no wish to be blamed

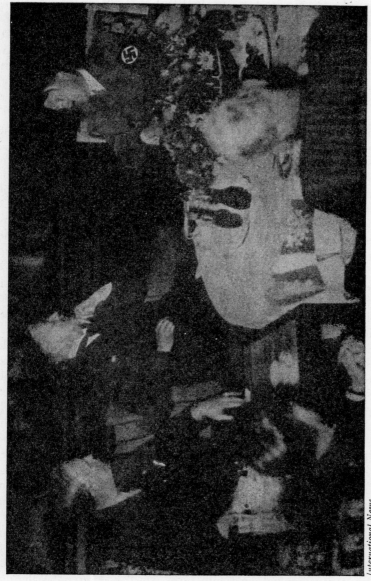

APPEASEMENT IN 1938

Chamberlain and Hitler at Berchtesgaden.

for precipitating a second world war. At the same time, they were reluctant to have their country saved by Soviet troops. On September 21 the Czechoslovak government accepted the Anglo-French proposals for the dismemberment of the republic. On the next day Chamberlain returned to Germany and at Godesberg in the Rhineland informed the Führer that Czechoslovakia had agreed to cede the German areas to the Reich. Hitler next demanded that all Czech armed forces, police, gendarmerie, customs officials, and frontier guards be withdrawn within ten days from most of the Sudeten German area, the evacuated territory to be handed over to Germany as it stood without any military, economic, or traffic establishments being damaged or removed. In certain other areas plebiscites were to be held before November 25.

On September 24 the government at Prague informed Chamberlain that Hitler's demands "in their present form" were "absolutely and unconditionally unacceptable," since they would deprive the republic of every safeguard for its national existence by admitting German armies deep into Czechoslovakia before the latter had been able to organize its defenses on a new basis, and because the whole process of moving the population would be reduced to panic and flight on the part of those who would not accept the German Nazi regime. Great Britain and France likewise held the demands to be unacceptable and agreed that no pressure would be exerted on Czechoslovakia to secure their acceptance. It appeared that Hitler might be compelled to carry out his threat to use force. And if he did, a general European war might result.

In these circumstances President Roosevelt of the United States made a direct appeal to Hitler urging an international conference to settle the controversy. At the same time Chamberlain, Daladier, and Roosevelt all appealed to Mussolini to use his influence with Hitler in the cause of peace. On September 28 Mussolini had a personal telephone conversation with Hitler, as the result of which the Führer agreed to an international conference to settle the Sudeten controversy. Chamberlain, Daladier, and Mussolini were invited to meet with the Führer at Munich on September 29. No representative of Soviet Russia, Czechoslovakia's most powerful ally, was invited. Nor was Czechoslovakia herself to be represented. On the appointed day the four statesmen reached an agreement regarding the Sudetenland which was essentially a complete surrender to Hitler's Godesberg demands. There was nothing for Czechoslovakia to do but submit to the Munich agreement. Early on the morning of October 1, 1938, German troops marched across the frontier. Two days later Adolf Hitler made a triumphal entry into Eger, which had served as the unofficial capital of the Sudeten Germans.

But the territorial losses to Germany were not the only ones suffered by Czechoslovakia. On the eve of Germany's entrance into the Sudetenland Poland demanded the evacuation of Czechoslovak troops from an area about Teschen, where most of Czechoslovakia's Poles lived. With a Polish army of some 200,000 men mobilized along the Czechoslovak frontier, the government at Prague on October 1, 1938, was forced to accept Poland's demands, and surrendered an area of some 400 square miles with a population of 240,000, of which 65 per cent were asserted to be Poles. The Hungarian government also demanded the cession of the area inhabited by Magyars, and Czechoslovakia agreed to negotiate the question. When the negotiations became deadlocked, however, the two countries agreed that their dispute should be arbitrated by Germany and Italy, and on Novem-

THE PARTITION OF CZECHOSLOVAKIA, 1938–1939

ber 2 the arbitrators awarded to Hungary approximately 4800 square miles of Czechoslovak territory with a population of about one million.

The crisis of September, 1938, had far-reaching effects on the international situation in Europe, for it largely wrecked the system of security which France had constructed on the Continent. Czechoslovakia, deserted by her strongest ally in the west, passed at once into the German orbit. Poland, Rumania, and Yugoslavia, with which France had long been linked in agreements to defend the *status quo* set up by the peace settlement, had every reason to question the value of collective security in general and of French commitments in particular. From Moscow came unofficial statements that the Soviet government considered its alliance with France as having come to an end. In fact, after Munich the Soviet government strongly suspected that the British and French had deliberately surrendered to Hitler in order to facilitate Germany's *Drang nach Osten* and thus precipitate a war between the Third Reich and the Soviet Union.

And despite Hitler's assertion that with the acquisition of the Sudetenland his territorial ambitions in Europe would be satisfied, events soon proved the contrary. Within a few months he seized upon the internal situation in Czechoslovakia to push his *Drang nach Osten* once more. In March, 1939, Hitler threw Germany's support to Joseph Tiso, leader of the Slovak Popular Party, which sought complete independence for Slovakia. On March 14, after an interview between Hitler and Tiso, the governments of both Slovakia and Ruthenia declared their independence. On March 14 President Hacha, who had succeeded Beneš upon the latter's resignation in October, 1938, and the Czechoslovak foreign minister were summoned to Berlin, and during discussions with Hitler President Hacha was persuaded—by what threats one can imagine—to place "the fate of the Czech people and the land trustingly in the hands of the Führer of the German Reich," to quote the language of the German communiqué. Early on the morning of the fifteenth Nazi troops occupied western Czechoslovakia. On March 16 Hitler announced that Czechia thereafter belonged to the territory of the German Reich and would be known as the "Protectorate of Bohemia and Moravia." Tiso invited Hitler to become the protector of Slovakia, also, which became a vassal state of the Reich, possessed of little more independence than Bohemia-Moravia. One result of Germany's military occupation of both Czechia and Slovakia was crystal-clear—she was now in a stronger position than ever to continue her *Drang nach Osten,* for she now had new bases from which she could strike either northward against Poland or southward against Hungary.

While these events were following one another in swift succession, on March 14 troops of the latter country had crossed the Ruthenian frontier, and two days later the Budapest government had announced the incorporation of Ruthenia in Hungary. Hitler also seized upon the confusion in Europe to redeem still another German area. On March 21 he demanded the immediate return to the Reich of the Memel territory. Lithuania was of course in no position to defy the Führer, and an agreement to this effect was at once signed in Berlin. Lithuanian troops and police were immediately withdrawn, and on March 23 Hitler arrived in Memel on board the battleship *Deutschland.*

Hitler's partner in the Rome-Berlin Axis now decided that he should strengthen Italy's position in the Balkans. For some time there had been serious differences of opinion between King Zog of Albania and Mussolini, and, persuasion having failed, the Duce resorted to force. Italian troops were landed in Albania, and on April 8, 1939, they captured Scutari and Tirana, from which King Zog and his family had already fled across the frontier into Greece. An Albanian constituent assembly then met and voted to abrogate the existing constitution and regime and to offer the Albanian crown to the King of Italy. On April 15 the Italian parliament decided that Victor Emmanuel's title thereafter should be "King of Italy and Albania, Emperor of Ethiopia," and on the following day the Italian king accepted the Albanian crown at the hands of the Albanian premier. Obviously Mussolini had improved his position in the Balkans should he thereafter decide to push his own *Drang nach Osten*.

The End of "Appeasement"

In his proclamation of March 16, 1939, stating the terms of his protectorate over Bohemia-Moravia, Hitler had justified his action not on the ground of self-determination, as he had done in the case of Austria and the Sudetenland, but on the basis of history and the principle of self-preservation. "Bohemia and Moravia," he proclaimed, "have for thousands of years belonged to the *Lebensraum* of the German people." Further, he explained, "It is in accordance . . . with the principle of self-preservation that the Reich is resolved to intervene decisively, to re-establish the bases of a reasonable Central European order, and to take all measures which in consequence arise."

This repudiation of his own principles and of the formal pledges he had given Chamberlain in September, 1938, seems at last to have convinced the British prime minister that no reliance could be placed upon any assurances that might come from the Führer. At the time of the Sudeten crisis Chamberlain had asserted that he would fight if it became clear that any nation had made up its mind "to dominate the world by fear of its force." It now seemed apparent that Hitler had undertaken to dominate, if not the world, at least Europe by his might or the fear of it, and many believed that the next victim of his aggression would be Poland or Rumania. Consultations were accordingly at once begun by Great Britain, France, Russia, and some of the states of eastern Europe regarding measures to be taken in case of such an eventuality.

The first step in the movement to "stop Hitler" came on March 31, 1939, when Great Britain and France announced that, "in the event of any action which clearly threatened Polish independence and which the Polish government accordingly considered it vital to resist with their national forces," they would at once lend Poland all support in their power. After Mussolini's seizure of Albania, Great Britain and France further announced on April 13 that they had extended to Greece and Rumania guarantees identical with that given Poland two weeks earlier. In May Great Britain and Turkey declared that "in the event of an act of aggression leading to war in the Mediterranean area, they would be prepared to co-operate effectively, and to lend each other all the aid and assistance in their power," and eventually, in June, the French and Turkish governments signed a declaration of mutual assistance analogous to that made by Great Britain and Turkey.

Meanwhile, the indications pointing to Poland's becoming the next storm center of Europe increased. In a manner which experience had taught was the usual prelude to Hitler's execution of some new stroke, the German press in March had begun reporting attacks upon Germans in the Polish Corridor and denouncing the intolerable terror to which the German minority in Poland was subjected. Next, Hitler on April 28 in a speech to the Reichstag reiterated an earlier demand that Danzig be returned to Germany and that the latter be given a motor road and a railway line through the Polish Corridor possessing the same extraterritorial status for Germany as the Corridor itself had for Poland. In return he stated his willingness, among other things, to give Poland a free harbor in Danzig, to regard the existing boundaries between Germany and Poland as final, and to conclude a new non-aggression treaty with Warsaw. On May 5 Poland denied the German demands for Danzig and for extraterritorial rights in the Corridor, but suggested a common guarantee of the existence and rights of the Free City and pointed out that Poland already allowed German citizens to travel across the Corridor without customs or passport formalities.

The Axis powers next made a countermove. In an apparent effort to strengthen themselves in the face of Great Britain's guarantee to Poland and the latter's resistance to German demands, or possibly in the hope of intimidating Chamberlain into returning to his policy of appeasement, Italy and Germany on May 22, 1939, signed a military alliance, which was at once implemented by conferences between German and Italian military leaders.

Meanwhile, it was obvious to most observers that the Anglo-French guarantees to Poland and Rumania were greatly weakened by the practical difficulty of sending military aid to eastern Europe. To solve this strategic problem the British government, under pressure from France, in April, 1939, had initiated negotiations for a mutual assistance pact with Russia similar to the Franco-Soviet pact of May, 1935. At the outset of the negotiations the Soviet government made clear that any such pact not only must provide for mutual assistance between Britain, France, and the U.S.S.R., but must also give to all the European states bordering on the Soviet Union a three-power guarantee against attack by aggressors. Furthermore, the pact must be accompanied by a military alliance, fully implemented by consultations of the general staffs of the three countries. Although the negotiations were continued until August, they failed to result in any Anglo-French agreement with Russia.

One of the principal reasons for this failure was the attitude of the Poles. The Warsaw government, fearful of Russia, was unwilling to accept any of the numerous proposals put forward as a basis for assuring effective Soviet-Polish co-operation in case of a German attack on Poland. The latter's attitude destroyed the possibility of any Anglo-Franco-Soviet agreement unless the Western powers were willing to proceed without regard to Poland's wishes. Though in 1938 they had done just that with Czechoslovakia in regard to Hitler's demand for the Sudetenland, they were unwilling to do so in 1939 in response to Russia's insistence that a military agreement with Poland was an indispensible condition for any Soviet pact with the Western powers.[7] The deadlock resulting from Poland's attitude lasted until August, when the political conversations were abandoned and the consideration of a military agreement was begun. The possibility of concluding such an agreement without a previous political understanding was remote, but the discussions continued until the announcement of the German-Soviet nonaggression pact in August.

For, while Russia had been negotiating—with little prospect of success—with Britain and France, she had also been seeking an understanding with Germany. On May 20 Foreign Commissar Molotov had proposed general political negotiations, and in June the Soviet government had let it be known that it desired a nonaggression pact with the Reich. Hitler had at first shown little interest and negotiations had lagged until August, when he began to push the matter urgently. By August 16 it had been agreed that a nonaggression pact would be signed and four days later Germany accepted the text as proposed by Russia. On August 23 a nonaggression pact and a secret accompanying protocol were signed in the Soviet capital. By the terms of the former, Russia and Germany agreed to refrain from any act of force against each other and to remain neutral should the other become "the object of warlike action on the part of a third power." The secret protocol divided Eastern Europe into German and Russian spheres, the dividing line running from the Baltic to the Black seas. In the north, Russia was to have a free hand in Finland, Latvia, and Estonia. In Poland, she was to annex the territory east of the Narew, Vistula, and San rivers. In the south, she was to regain Bessarabia which she had lost to Rumania at the close of the First World War. This agreement is more than faintly reminiscent of the one made at Tilsit in 1807 by Napoleon and Tsar Alexander I.

The motives which really actuated Hitler and Stalin in making these agreements cannot be known. Possibly Hitler hoped that an announcement of the signing of a Soviet-German nonaggression pact would cause Great Britain and France to repudiate their pledges to Poland as they had repu-

[7] Finland, Estonia, and Latvia also rejected the idea of a three-power guarantee.

diated those to Czechoslovakia in 1938. Then he would be in a position either to gain a bloodless victory once more or to wage a short victorious war against the Poles. In view of his well-known disregard for his pledges, perhaps he planned that once he had consolidated his realm in western Europe he could deal with Russia as he pleased. There is no evidence that he ever abandoned his idea of bringing the Ukraine under his control. Stalin, on the other hand, had probably come to the conclusion that Russia could expect no tangible assistance from France or Great Britain if Russia were attacked by Germany. Possibly he had decided, also, that it might be to Russia's advantage to have Germany become involved in a long and costly war with the Western powers, and thus give the Soviet Union time to strengthen its own military and industrial position to meet the eventual conflict with Nazi Germany which he believed to be inevitable. He may have been influenced, also, by the hope that Germany, France, Britain, and Italy might exhaust themselves in a general war in the West, and thus leave the Soviet Union the dominant power on the Continent.

The Crisis of August, 1939

On August 22, as soon as it had become known that the German-Soviet nonaggression treaty was to be signed, Chamberlain warned Hitler that that pact would in no way alter Great Britain's obligation to Poland, and stated that the British government was determined that there should be no misunderstanding on this point. He argued, however, that there was nothing in the German-Polish question which could not be settled without resort to force, and urged direct negotiations between Germany and Poland, possibly with the aid of a neutral intermediary. But he declared that any settlement which was reached should be guaranteed by other powers.

Hitler, in his reply on the following day, pointed out that Danzig and the Corridor were among the interests which it was impossible for the Reich to renounce. Germany was prepared to settle this problem with Poland "on a basis of a proposal of truly unparalleled magnanimity," but Britain's guarantee had made the Poles unwilling to negotiate and had encouraged them to unloose "a wave of appalling terrorism against the one and a half million Germans living in Poland." The British decision to assist Poland in case of war, Hitler maintained, could not change the Reich's determination to safeguard the interests of Germany. "The questions of Danzig and the Corridor must and shall be solved."

Two days later (August 25) Great Britain and Poland signed a five-year treaty for mutual assistance. On the next day Premier Daladier informed Hitler of France's determination to stand by Poland, but offered to cooperate in seeking a direct settlement between Poland and the Reich. Hitler replied that he saw no way of inducing Poland to accept a peaceful settlement, and once more restated his claims to Danzig and the Corridor. On August 28 Great Britain reiterated her contention that a reasonable solution of the German-Polish problem could be reached which would also safeguard Poland's essential interests, and declared that Poland had already agreed to enter into direct negotiations with the Reich on this basis, the settlement to be guaranteed by other powers. Great Britain hoped that Germany, too, would consent to such negotiations.

On August 29 Hitler declared that Germany was prepared to accept the British proposal for direct discussion, but explained that in the event of a territorial rearrangement in Poland, the Reich would no longer be able to give guarantees or to participate in guarantees unless the Soviet Union were associated therewith, and thus revealed that Germany had already made some commitment to Russia regarding the division of Polish territory. The German government, Hitler declared, accepted Great Britain's good offices in securing the dispatch to Berlin of a Polish emissary "with full powers," and it counted on the arrival of this emissary on the next day (August 30).

At 2:30 A. M. on August 30 the British government telegraphed its ambassador in Berlin to inform the Reich government that Hitler must not expect that the British government could produce a Polish representative in Berlin that same day. At 6:50 P. M. another telegram suggested that Germany adopt the normal procedure of handing the Polish ambassador the proposals for transmission to Warsaw. When Sir Nevile Henderson called on Foreign Minister von Ribbentrop to deliver this message, the latter "produced a lengthy document which he read out in German aloud at top speed." This document was a sixteen-point program [8] for the settlement of all German-Polish problems. When the British ambassador asked for the text of the proposals, he was informed that "it was now too late, as the Polish representative had not arrived in Berlin by midnight."

[8] The following are the main points in the proposals: the Free City of Danzig to return to the Reich; the Corridor to decide by plebiscite whether it should belong to Poland or to Germany, all domiciled there on January 1, 1918, or born there up to that date having the right to vote; the territory to be evacuated by the Polish authorities and armed forces and to be placed under the supervision of an international commission on which France, England, Italy, and the U.S.S.R. would be represented; Gdynia to be excluded from the plebiscite area; the plebiscite not to take place before the lapse of twelve months, and the question of ownership to be decided by a simple majority; if the plebiscite area went to Poland, Germany to have an extraterritorial traffic zone, one kilometer wide, in which to lay down a motor road and a four-track railway; if the area went to Germany, Poland to have an analogous communication with Gdynia; in this case, Germany to have the right to proceed to an exchange of populations; Danzig and Gdynia both to have the character of exclusively mercantile towns; an international commission of inquiry to examine complaints of both sides as to treatment of their minorities; Germany and Poland to guarantee the rights of the minorities by the most comprehensive and binding agreement; in the event of agreement on these proposals, both countries to demobilize immediately.

Apparently the German note of August 29 and the British reply of the thirtieth were not communicated to Poland until August 31. In the afternoon of that day the Polish government informed the British that it would authorize its ambassador in Berlin to inform the German foreign office that Poland had accepted Great Britain's proposals for direct negotiations. The Polish foreign minister stated, however, that the Polish ambassador would not be authorized to accept the proposals, which the earlier experience of the Austrian Chancellor Schuschnigg and the Czechoslovak President Hacha indicated might be accompanied by "some sort of ultimatum." Foreign Minister von Ribbentrop refused to see the Polish ambassador until the evening of the thirty-first. When at that time Ribbentrop learned that the Polish ambassador was authorized to receive Germany's proposals but had no plenary powers to negotiate, the interview was abruptly closed, and the German government at once broadcast its sixteen-point program, which had not yet been communicated officially to Poland. When the Polish ambassador tried to get in touch with Warsaw, he was unable to do so because all means of communication had been closed by the German government.

On that same evening Germany informed Britain that Hitler for two days had waited in vain for the arrival of a fully empowered Polish negotiator, and that therefore the German government regarded its proposals as having been "to all intents and purposes rejected." Apparently, as the British foreign secretary later pointed out, Hitler conceived of a negotiation between Germany and Poland as nothing more than the summoning of a Polish plenipotentiary to Berlin, at twenty-four hours' notice, to discuss terms not previously communicated to him. At this time, too, Germany at last provided Britain with the sixteen points in full, but before these could be considered Hitler had ordered the German army to advance across the Polish frontier. At about 5 A. M. on September 1, 1939, German airplanes began raining bombs upon numerous Polish cities. Later in the day Danzig by Hitler's order was incorporated in the Reich, and the Nazi leader in that city was appointed head of the civil administration. Great Britain and France thereupon immediately presented ultimatums to Germany stating that unless the latter suspended all aggressive action against the Poles and withdrew her forces from Polish territory, they would at once fulfill their obligations to Poland.

At 9 A. M. on September 3, after having received no reply to the ultimatum of September 1, the British ambassador in Berlin notified Germany that unless satisfactory assurances had been received by Great Britain by 11 A. M., a state of war would exist between the two countries. Such assurances were not given, and at 11:15 A. M. Chamberlain announced that Great Britain was at war with Germany. France made a similar announcement at 5 P. M. the same day. The Second World War had begun.

Chapter XXIII

THE PERIOD
OF NAZI BLITZKRIEG

IN 1939 Hitler at last resorted to military measures to continue his policy of territorial expansion of the Third Reich. In the resultant Second World War his armies conquered or occupied one country after another until by the middle of 1942 his power extended almost unbroken from the Atlantic to the Volga and from the Mediterranean and the Caucasus to the North Cape. For a short time he controlled an area larger by far than Napoleon's empire at its height.

Nazi and Soviet Aggressions in 1939

On September 1 Germany's motorized armies advanced into Poland from East Prussia, Pomerania, Silesia, and Slovakia, while German airplanes at once subjected Polish airdromes to severe bombardments. Within a week the "eyes" of the Polish army had been blinded by the destruction of its airplanes and its bases. Meanwhile, German bombers ranged constantly far and wide, behind the Polish lines, disrupting Polish communications and interfering with Polish concentrations, while German Panzer (armored) and motorized divisions pushed steadily forward.

At the end of the second week of hostilities the Poles had lost almost all of their western provinces, and Warsaw was practically surrounded. During the third week, while the Germans were attacking such advanced points as Brest-Litovsk and Lwow (Lemberg), the Polish armies in desperation hastily withdrew to the east and south in the hope that they might establish a front along the Dniester River where they could possibly be supported through Rumania by aid from France and Great Britain. But suddenly, on September 17, Soviet armies began advancing into Poland from the east. This move brought the collapse of all effective Polish resistance except at Warsaw, which heroically endured terrific artillery and air bombardments until September 27, when an armistice was concluded. Thus in the unbelievably short period of twenty-seven days was completed the military destruction of a nation of 34,000,000 people, inhabiting a country 150,000 square miles in extent, defended by an army of 1,500,000 men.

On September 28 Germany and Russia signed a new treaty defining the frontier of their interests in the former Poland. Generally speaking, the line roughly approximated the "Curzon Line" of 1919, and shifted to Ger-

KEY
░ To Germany
≡ To Russia
▨ To Lithuania
━ Former boundary of Poland

Scale of Miles
0   50   100   150

THE PARTITION OF POLAND, 1939

man control territory inhabited chiefly by Poles. In exchange for this additional territory, Hitler agreed that Lithuania should be considered in the Russian rather than in the German sphere. The territory given to Soviet Russia constituted an area of approximately 75,000 square miles, and, save in the province of Bialystok, a large part of the population was closely akin racially to the neighboring peoples in the Soviet Union. In October the newly acquired territory was organized as Western White Russia and the

Western Ukraine, and in November the former became part of the White Russian Soviet Socialist Republic and the latter was absorbed by the Ukrainian Soviet Socialist Republic. Thus at last Russia regained the territory which Poland had taken from her when the Communists were fighting against "White" armies and foreign intervention in 1920.[1]

Meanwhile, the Soviet government had brought the Baltic republics largely under its control. During September and October the foreign ministers of Estonia, Latvia, and Lithuania successively had been summoned to Moscow for conferences as a result of which each of the republics granted the Soviet Union the right to maintain land, sea, and air armed forces within its territory. Obviously the Baltic republics—once they had carried out the terms of these agreements—were powerless to prevent their permanent occupation by Russia. As a matter of fact, during the summer of 1940 the three states were finally absorbed by the Soviet Union.

Undoubtedly by the acquisition of these air and naval bases Russia greatly strengthened her defensive position in the west. But Soviet leaders felt that the security of Leningrad was still menaced as long as Russia did not fully control the sea and land approaches to that city. The Soviet government therefore in October, 1939, initiated negotiations with Finland, apparently expecting the latter to make concessions similar to those which had been made by the Baltic states. Finland acceded to most of Russia's demands, but refused to lease or sell to Russia the port of Hangoe, which, the Finns contended, would give Russia complete domination of their country. Negotiations eventually reached a deadlock and the Finnish delegation withdrew from Moscow. On November 29 the Soviet government broke off diplomatic relations, and on the next day Russian troops and airplanes crossed the border. On December 2 Finland appealed to the League of Nations, which on the fourteenth condemned the Soviet invasion and expelled the Soviet Union from the League.

Military developments seemed to indicate that the Soviet government had not actually expected to have to wage a war in order to enforce its demands upon Finland, and had not made adequate preparations to do so. Although the Russians launched attacks at various points, at first relatively little headway was made anywhere against the heroic Finns. By January, however, the Russians seemed to have gotten their forces better organized for the attack, and in that month they turned their attention particularly to the Karelian Isthmus, across which the Finns had constructed the Mannerheim Line. The weight of man power and munitions gradually turned the scale. On February 26 the Russians finally captured the fortress which served as the western anchor of the Mannerheim Line, and a few days later they were approaching Viborg. With their most powerful line broken,

[1] See page 584.

their second largest city about to fall into the hands of the enemy, and little prospect of securing from abroad sufficient assistance to stop the Russian "steam roller," the Finnish government sued for peace. At Moscow on March 12, 1940, Finnish plenipotentiaries accepted the Russian-dictated terms, which were much more severe than the demands made in the previous October.

The Allied Policy of Defense and Attrition

Meanwhile, there had been relatively little activity on the western front, although by the beginning of October, 1939, some 158,000 men of the British Expeditionary Force had arrived in France and had taken up their assigned positions. At the outset of the war the Western democracies adopted the principle of a unified command, and the French General Maurice Gamelin was given supreme control of the forces in France. He made little effort to smash the German West Wall, and was reported as saying that he had no intention of starting "a new Battle of Verdun." Gamelin's attitude was exactly what Hitler had gambled on, for at the time he launched his Polish invasion he had left on the west front only six combat-worthy divisions, none of which was armored. Hitler had maintained, in opposition to his own general staff, that the French would not attack. Had Gamelin launched an all-out offensive at that time, according to the German chief of the operations division, he could have smashed through to the Rhine.[2]

On the sea the war proceeded more nearly in accord with expectations, though here, too, it was largely defensive in nature on the part of the Allies. As in 1914, the overwhelming British sea power drove German shipping into home or neutral ports. Except in the Baltic the German flag practically disappeared from the seas. And, as in 1914, the Germans struck back with submarines. Nor did they delay in starting their "unrestricted" campaign. As early as September 4, 1939, the British passenger ship *Athenia* was sunk with 1400 persons on board, of whom more than 300 were Americans. Thereafter neutral as well as Allied shipping was sunk without discrimination by submarines, mines, and airplanes. Also, to prey upon Allied and neutral shipping, German pocket battleships slipped through the British blockade and roamed the high seas. Occasionally spectacular engagements occurred. In December, 1939, the British cruisers *Exeter, Achilles,* and *Ajax,* despite inferior armaments, outmaneuvered and outgunned the Reich's newest pocket battleship, the *Graf Spee,* and so damaged her that, on orders from Hitler, she was deliberately scuttled.

[2] O. J. Hale, "Adolf Hitler as Feldherr," *Virginia Quarterly Review,* Volume XXIV, page 210.

By this time it seemed to be clear that the Allies had decided to wage a war of attrition, relying upon the increasing pressure of economic strangulation to force Germany to her knees. To many observers there seemed to be a leisureliness about Allied long-range plans for the war that was extremely disturbing. The complacent assumption prevailed in high quarters that France was protected by the impregnability of the mighty Maginot Line and that Britain was safe behind her mastery of the sea. The eyes of most of those in authority appeared to be turned toward the past, and to believe that the system of trench warfare and the slow war of attrition which had won in 1918 must inevitably win again. They seemed blinded to the significance of the blitzkrieg which the German armored divisions and bombers had waged in Poland, and which was about to be unloosed against Norway.

Hitler's Seizure of Norway and Denmark

During the winter of 1939–1940 Hitler decided to seize Norway and Denmark, countries which had escaped being drawn into the First World War. These countries would provide him with valuable submarine and air bases for use against the British navy. Furthermore, their seizure would facilitate Germany's importation of much-needed Swedish iron ore by the use of the Norwegian port of Narvik and Norwegian territorial waters; would assure to Germans and deny to the British the foodstuffs which Denmark, particularly, produced; and, finally, would safeguard the Nazis against an attack from the rear when Hitler launched against the West the blitzkrieg which he was already planning.

On the night of April 9, 1940, German troops suddenly landed at the Norwegian ports of Narvik, Trondheim, Bergen, Stavanger, Egersund, and Arendal, and on the Oslo estuary, and early the next morning Denmark was similarly invaded by land and sea. Some of the "Trojan horse" troop transports, disguised as innocent merchant or ore ships operating through the territorial waters of Norway, had sailed from Germany at least a week before this blow was struck. Warships had been so dispatched as to reach all the Norwegian ports simultaneously, and the requisite air force had been carefully assembled to protect the troop transports against possible attack. But German military efficiency was not the sole explanation of the astounding success of the attack. Apparently the way had also been carefully prepared within Norway by the creation of a "fifth column" of Nazi sympathizers led by Major Vidkun Quisling and Colonel Konrad Sundlo. The easy conquest of the almost impregnable Oslo fjord was made possible because fake orders were sent to garrison commanders and naval units not to resist the Germans. At Narvik, in fact, the port was turned over to the Germans by Colonel Sundlo without resistance. Once more the world was given an example of Nazi success in boring from within.

King Christian and the Danish government at once submitted to German control, and Denmark became, temporarily, a German protectorate. But King Haakon and the Norwegian government decided to resist and fled from Oslo to avoid capture by the Germans. On the next day Germany insisted on the creation of a new government headed by Major Quisling and other Nazi sympathizers. King Haakon declined to accede to this demand, and was thereafter forced to flee from place to place to escape pursuing German airplanes.

The initial stroke of the Germans gave them a tremendous advantage over the Allies in the subsequent struggle for the control of Norway. In Oslo they possessed an excellent port to which they could ferry reinforcements protected by submarines and by airplanes operated from captured Danish and Norwegian air fields. Although they lost some transports as the result of Allied submarines and mines in the Skagerrak and Kattegat, they were able to land sufficient men and adequate military equipment for a swift campaign. Their chief objective was to open a route between their Oslo forces and the German units at Trondheim.

The Allied expeditionary forces were handicapped from the very outset. All the better ports were in the hands of the Germans, and the Allied troops were compelled to land in small ports without proper harbor facilities for handling heavy military equipment and without neighboring air bases. The chief Allied objective was to isolate Trondheim from rail communication with the German base at Oslo. Despite German superiority in the air, Allied forces were landed north and south of Trondheim, but they lacked both antiaircraft guns and fighter aircraft and before long their bases were nearly destroyed by German bombers. German mechanized units moved swiftly up from Oslo, encountering relatively little resistance, and on April 30 these units met the German forces pushing southward from Trondheim. From that moment the fate of the 12,000 Allied troops in central Norway was sealed. By May 3 they had been evacuated and the German control of southern Norway was assured. On June 9, 1940, the war in Norway ended with the capitulation of the Norwegian army and the flight of King Haakon and his government to London.

Hitler's victory in Norway had immediate political repercussions in Great Britain, where Neville Chamberlain's government at once fell from power. On May 11 Winston Churchill, who during the preceding years had repeatedly pointed out the disaster that awaited Britain unless she awoke and prepared for the coming conflict with Hitler, became prime minister. Included in his new government were outstanding representatives of all three

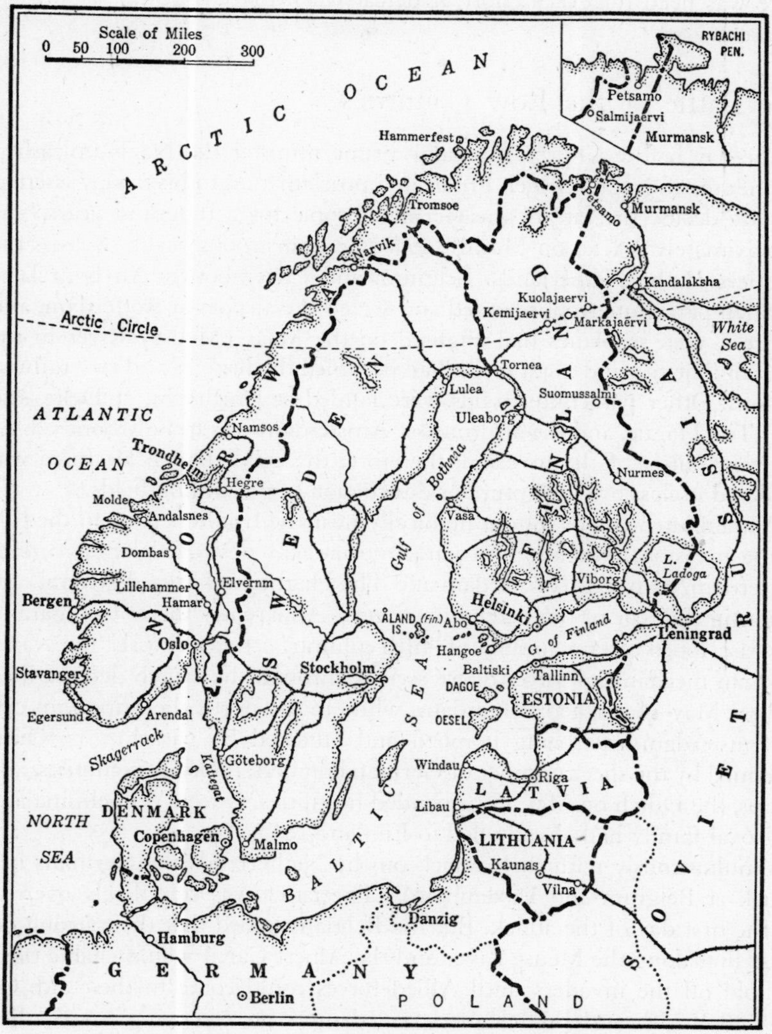

SCANDINAVIA AND THE BALTIC, 1939

British political parties. It was generally believed that Churchill would inject new life into Britain's military, economic, and diplomatic efforts. That there was need for every effort, if defeat was to be avoided, was already apparent.

The Battle of the Low Countries

The day before Churchill became prime minister the Nazis unleashed another terrific attack which Hitler in a proclamation to his troops asserted would "decide the fate of the German people for a thousand years." At approximately 3 A. M. on May 10, 1940, German troops began to cross the frontiers of the Netherlands, Belgium, and Luxembourg. An hour later German parachute troops landed and seized the airport of Rotterdam, and before 5 A. M. seaplanes had alighted on the Maas (Meuse) River in the heart of that city and Nazi forces had occupied the bridges and two railway stations. Other parachute troops were landed at Dordrecht, at Delft, and near The Hague, and the airdrome at Amsterdam was heavily bombed. At the very outset of the invasion, therefore, the small Dutch air force was rendered useless by the capture or destruction of its landing fields.

While Dutch troops fought heroically near the frontiers to stem the tide of the invasion, bombing and parachute attacks destroyed large parts of Rotterdam, damaged Amsterdam and The Hague, and caused general confusion in the rear of the defending armies. Apparently there was again in this case, too, a certain amount of "fifth column" activity to assist the Nazis. German mechanized forces drove swiftly through the Dutch defense lines and on May 14 reached Rotterdam, while to the north the important city of Amsterdam was being bombed and attacked by parachutists. Overwhelmed by the sheer number of German bombers, tanks, parachutists, and troops, the Dutch on May 15 suspended hostilities. Queen Wilhelmina and the royal family had already fled to England.

Simultaneously with their attack on the Netherlands the Germans had struck at Belgium and Luxembourg. The latter was completely overrun on the first day of the attack. But the Belgians hoped that their strong defense line along the Meuse River and the Albert Canal would enable them to hold off the invaders until Allied forces could come to their aid. On May 10 British and French mechanized units were moving toward Belgium on a front extending from the North Sea to the Moselle River. On the next day, however, the powerful Belgian fort commanding the passage of the Meuse River and the Albert Canal fell to the Nazis, and their capture of bridges over the Albert Canal permitted the Belgian defense line to be outflanked. One week after the opening attack German troops marched into Brussels, and Antwerp was thereupon at once abandoned by the Belgian forces.

But it was farther south that the Allies suffered a gigantic military disaster. As soon as the French forces had been lured forward to assist the Belgians, the Germans concentrated the full force of their terrific attack against the relatively weak but vital Sedan-Montmédy sector. On May 15 the Nazis crossed the Meuse north of Mézières at three points. On the next day the battle from Namur to Sedan became open warfare with motorized units and aircraft participating. By May 19 the German forces had opened a sixty-mile gap through the weaker extension of the Maginot Line. The German mechanized forces then pushed on. Protected by swarms of bombers, they captured Amiens on May 21, and then sped on to Abbeville near the mouth of the Somme. By completing this advance the Germans succeeded in isolating the Allied forces in Belgium and northern France from the main body of the French armies, and the Nazis envisaged the complete annihilation or capture of these forces.

From the south the Germans swiftly began to close in. The important port of Boulogne was occupied by their mechanized forces on May 23, and Calais was attacked on the twenty-seventh. Meanwhile, other German armies were constantly pounding the Allied forces in Belgium, where the northern flank was held by the Belgian army led by King Leopold. This army was subjected to terrific punishment. General Weygand, who had replaced General Gamelin, flew to King Leopold's headquarters to discuss the situation and was informed that the Belgians could not hold out without "substantial new assistance." But such new assistance could not, of course, be given. On May 28 the Belgian king, against the advice of his ministers, finally surrendered unconditionally, and ordered the Belgian army to cease fighting.

The collapse of Belgian resistance exposed the left flank of the Anglo-French forces in Belgium and made desperate the efforts to withdraw them through Dunkirk before their annihilation. On May 26 German armored formations were poised only twelve miles from the beaches of Dunkirk, prepared to destroy the Allied forces crowded into the beachhead. But Hitler, contrary to the advice of both his commander-in-chief and the chief of his general staff, forbade the commitment of these armored formations and assigned the task of destroying the Allied forces to the Luftwaffe. The German ground forces—minus armored formations—were held up for four days by the British at Calais; the British air force, aided by foggy weather, gained a superiority in the air in a limited area around Dunkirk; and the British navy mobilized some 220 war vessels and 650 other craft of all descriptions for evacuation purposes. Although the Allies admitted the loss of 12 destroyers and 20 other craft, War Secretary Eden announced that 350,000 of the 400,000 men in the British Expeditionary Force had been rescued before the Germans eventually captured Dunkirk on June 3. But the British army in Flanders had lost 30,000 men, 1000 guns, and all its mechanized equipment in what was characterized as a "colossal military disaster."

With the German capture of Calais and Dunkirk the first phase of the German drive on the western front was over. In twenty-four days Hitler's armies had overrun and conquered the Netherlands, Belgium, Luxembourg, and an important section of France extending from Montmédy to Abbeville north of the Somme and the Aisne. The victory was the most crushing German military triumph since Hindenburg's battle of Tannenberg. Not only had the channel coast opposite England fallen to the Nazis; all the ports in western Europe from Abbeville to Narvik beyond the Arctic Circle were now within their hands.

The Collapse of France

Meanwhile, the French had hastily prepared defensive positions extending roughly along the Somme, the Oise-Aisne Canal, and the Aisne to Montmédy at the western end of the Maginot Line. This new position was hopefully called by the populace the Weygand Line. On June 5, 1940, the Germans launched their new offensive against this line. The battle of France had begun. To meet the invader the French army stood practically alone, for most of the shattered British forces which had escaped from the Flanders trap were in England, recuperating and seeking new equipment to take the place of that abandoned in the hasty evacuation from Dunkirk. One British division held the extreme left of the French line south of Abbeville.

Although the French troops fought valiantly and tirelessly to stem the Nazi tide, they not only were decisively outnumbered by the attacking troops but were overwhelmed by German superiority in airplanes and tanks. By June 10 the Nazis had driven a wedge to the Seine near Rouen. On that day Mussolini, who had been becoming more and more bellicose with each advance of the Germans, took Italy into the war against France and Great Britain. This step removed all possibility of sending any of the million men guarding the Italian front to relieve the weary French soldiers before Paris. The Nazis began to encircle the capital, and the French government fled to Tours and then on to Bordeaux. In order that Paris might be spared the fate of Warsaw and Rotterdam, the government withdrew all troops and declared the capital an open city. German troops made a peaceful entry into the city on June 14.

Already on June 12 General Weygand had informed the French cabinet that the military situation was practically hopeless, and most of the ministers believed that the total occupation of France was therefore inevitable. Some urged an immediate armistice, but Premier Reynaud, who had suc-

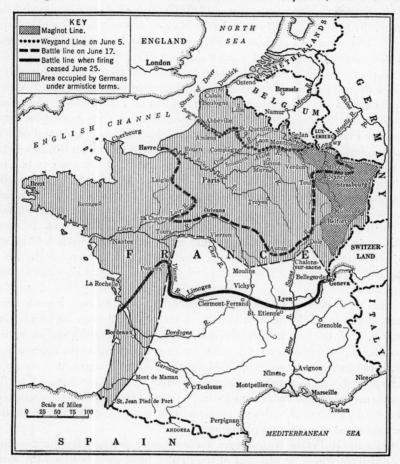

KEY
Maginot Line.
Weygand Line on June 5.
Battle line on June 17.
Battle line when firing ceased June 25.
Area occupied by Germans under armistice terms.

THE COLLAPSE OF FRANCE, 1940

ceeded Daladier in March, 1940, was determined that France should continue to fight as the ally of Great Britain, should never make a separate peace even if the government had to be transferred to northern Africa. But on June 16, after the German armies had captured Verdun, had begun to cut off the Maginot Line from the rear, and had penetrated it in frontal attacks from the north and east, Reynaud was forced to resign. His place as premier was taken by the 84-year-old Marshal Pétain.

Negotiations for an armistice were immediately begun, but it was not until June 21 that the French delegates were received by Hitler. On the afternoon of that day, in the railway coach at Compiègne in which Foch had handed the Germans the armistice terms in 1918, General Keitel read to the French the armistice terms of 1940. The French delegates signed these terms the next day, and two days later they signed another armistice with Italy. The order to stop hostilities was then given by Hitler, and fighting ceased on the battlefields of France on June 25, 1940.

By the terms of the Franco-German armistice, Nazi troops were to occupy all of France north and west of an irregular line from the Swiss frontier near Geneva to a point about twelve miles east of Tours, thence southwest to the Spanish frontier, the cost of the occupation and administration to be paid by France. This area constituted more than half of France and placed in German hands all French Atlantic ports. Except for the units required to maintain internal order, all French military and air forces were to be disarmed and demobilized. The French fleet was to collect in ports to be designated, there to be demobilized and placed under German or Italian control. All German prisoners held by France were to be surrendered, but French prisoners were to be held by Germany until the end of the war. France, furthermore, was to surrender any Germans on French territory whom the Reich government might designate, in order, apparently, that the Reich might arrest those anti-Nazi Germans who had sought refuge in France.

The Nazi blitzkrieg which demoralized and destroyed the French military forces at the same time destroyed the Third French Republic. On July 9, 1940, the two houses of the French parliament, meeting at Vichy outside the German-occupied zone, by overwhelming votes approved a draft resolution conferring upon Marshal Pétain full power to draw up a new constitution establishing an authoritarian regime. On the next day the same two houses, sitting as the French National Assembly, officially adopted the resolution, merely adding a proviso that the new constitution should be submitted to a national plebiscite.

On July 11 Pétain issued three constitutional decrees. By the first, he assumed the functions of Chief of the French State and abolished the position of President of France. By the second, he conferred upon the Chief of State plenary governmental powers both executive and legislative. By the third, he adjourned the Senate and Chamber of Deputies *sine die,* and decreed that they should thereafter be convened only on call of the Chief of State. On the next day he appointed what was considered a strongly fascist cabinet, and named former Premier Laval—who favored French "collaboration" with the Nazis—as vice-premier. Later by still another decree all high officials in France were required to swear fidelity to Pétain's person,

THE WEHRMACHT ON THE MARCH IN 1940
Nazi troops parading on the Champs-Élysées in Paris.

Acme Photo

and the Chief of State was given authority to punish any official who betrayed his duties. Thus by legal steps the Third Republic was converted into the Pétain dictatorship.

But not all Frenchmen approved the actions and policies of Pétain. General Charles de Gaulle, Reynaud's undersecretary of war, was one who did not. He believed that France, though conquered on the Continent, should still fight as the ally of Great Britain, continuing to use her navy, her air force, and her vast colonial realm. At the time of the collapse of the French army he was on a military mission in London, where on June 22 he had issued a radio appeal urging all Frenchmen outside France to continue the war against Hitler. The interest of France demanded, he declared, "that all free Frenchmen should fight wherever they are." After the signing of the armistice, General de Gaulle appointed himself leader of the French outside France and established a Provisional French National Committee. During August and September revolts against the Pétain government in favor of continuing the war in conjunction with Great Britain occurred in Chad, French Kamerun, French West Africa, French Equatorial Africa, and some of the scattered French islands.

The United States the "Arsenal of Democracy"

In September, 1939, the great majority of Americans had had certain definite ideas regarding the war which had broken out in Europe. One was that there was little doubt as to where "war guilt" lay. They had watched Hitler's increasing disregard of Germany's treaty obligations and had seen him become ever more and more aggressive. At the same time they had seen the leaders of Great Britain and France make numerous efforts to appease the Führer in order to prevent the outbreak of another war, even when such appeasement had entailed the destruction or dismemberment of weaker states. Most Americans were convinced, therefore, that the war was the direct outcome of Nazi principles and technique, and, since they abhorred these, most Americans were openly sympathetic with the Allies and hoped they would win what was feared would be a long war. But the great majority of Americans fervently hoped that the United States would not be drawn into this war as it had been in 1917. President Roosevelt, in a radio address on September 3, 1939, to some extent expressed these two ideas when he stated that he could not "ask that every American remain neutral in thought," but at the same time stated his hope and belief that "the United States will keep out of this war."

These two fundamental ideas of the American people were further expressed in a new Neutrality Act which was passed on November 4, 1939.

Under the Neutrality Act of 1937 the United States government was compelled to place an embargo on the shipment of implements of war to belligerent powers. Obviously, because of Britain's control of the sea, this act operated not to the detriment of Germany but to that of the Allies. Most Americans were willing to supply the Allies with the sinews of war if it could be done without involving the United States in war. The new act was designed to accomplish these two ends. The Allies were free to purchase war materials in the United States, but such materials might not be carried to a belligerent country in American ships. Furthermore, the act empowered the President to forbid American citizens and ships to enter combat areas in war zones. Thus, it was hoped, there would be no occasion for the United States to be dragged into this war as in 1917 because of the sinking of American ships by German submarines. Most Americans, it appeared, were willing to sit on the sidelines and watch the Allies defeat the Nazi dictator.

From this somewhat placid state the United States was rudely shaken by the startling developments in Europe in 1940. After the fall of France the feeling grew among Americans that Great Britain was their first line of defense against the Nazi and Fascist dictators, and that the British must be assisted with all aid "short of war." After Dunkirk the United States government turned back to American manufacturers—who rushed them to England—rifles, machine guns, field guns, and airplanes, which were needed to re-equip the evacuated British troops. In September, fifty over-age American destroyers were transferred to Great Britain in return for ninety-nine-year leases of naval and air bases in the islands of Newfoundland, Bermuda, the Bahamas, Jamaica, St. Lucia, Trinidad, and Antigua, and in British Guiana. By this transaction Great Britain was strengthened to defend her overseas lifeline and the United States secured advance bases for the defense of North America and the Caribbean.

While there was some difference of opinion among Americans regarding the policy of all aid to Great Britain "short of war," there were few who doubted that the United States should itself embark upon a sweeping program of national preparedness. In September, 1940, Congress passed and President Roosevelt approved the first American law to prescribe compulsory military service in time of peace. By the terms of the Selective Training and Service Act every male citizen who was between the ages of twenty-one and thirty-six was "liable for training and service in the land or naval forces of the United States." On November 18 the first groups of drafted men were inducted into the army. But men without weapons would, of course, be of little use in defending the country. During 1940 the government authorized the expenditure of more than $17,000,000,000 for a "two-ocean

navy" and for all the latest and most efficient weapons for land and air warfare, and in the first six months of 1941 more billions of dollars were voted
for similar purposes.

On December 29, 1940, President Roosevelt in a radio address pointed
out that the American people faced the possibility of an Axis victory, which
would mean "a new and terrible era in which the whole world, our hemisphere included, would be run by threats of brute force." In that address the
President defined what many considered a doctrine worthy to rank alongside the Monroe Doctrine, namely, that the American people were determined not to permit control of the seaways leading to their coasts to pass
into the hands of a power hostile to their own democratic way of life and
bent on its destruction. British sea power in the Atlantic was recognized
as a bulwark friendly to democracy, and in order that it should not be
destroyed an administration bill "to promote the defense of the United
States" was introduced in Congress in January, 1941.

This bill, which was popularly called the Lend-Lease Bill, after long debate in both houses of Congress finally became law on March 11. The act
authorized the President to manufacture for, exchange with, sell, lease, lend,
or in other ways make available any defense article to "the government of
any country whose defense the President deems vital to the defense of the
United States." Payment might be made by any means which the President
deemed satisfactory. The United States was to become the great "arsenal
of democracy."

The Battle of Britain

Meanwhile, spectacular though Hitler's military successes had been
against Poland, Norway, the Netherlands, Belgium, and France, they had
not attained for him his principal objective—the end of the war on his own
terms. Though Great Britain had seen five states, including her chief ally,
crushed in a few weeks by the mighty power of Hitler's war machine, she
was determined to fight on. "Bearing ourselves humbly before God," Prime
Minister Churchill had declared on July 14, 1940, "but conscious that we
serve an unfolding purpose, we are ready to defend our native land against
the invasion by which it is threatened. We are fighting by ourselves alone.
But we are not fighting for ourselves alone. . . . Should the invader come to
Britain," he warned, "there will be no placid lying down of the people in
submission before him. . . . We shall defend every village, every town, and
every city . . . ; we would rather see London in ruins and ashes than that it
should be tamely and abjectly enslaved. . . . Thus only, in times like these,
can nations preserve their freedom."

Already the British had struck one blow in an effort to protect themselves against Hitler's attack. Great Britain had reluctantly consented to France's withdrawal from the war on condition that the French fleet should be dispatched to British ports and remain there while negotiations were taking place. But the armistice terms which France signed stipulated, as already pointed out, that French warships should be collected in ports to be specified and be demobilized and disarmed under German or Italian control. The British feared that the situation on the seas might be seriously altered to Great Britain's detriment by the union of the French, Italian, and German fleets.

To prevent this eventuality, early on the morning of July 3, 1940, 2 French battleships, 2 light cruisers, 8 destroyers, a number of submarines, and about 200 smaller craft which lay in British harbors were seized by the British. At the same time, at the Egyptian port of Alexandria, a French fleet, consisting of a battleship, 4 cruisers, and a number of smaller vessels, had been immobilized as the result of negotiations with its commander. But at Oran, the French naval base in Algeria, the situation was not so easily handled. When the French admiral in command refused to comply with any of the alternatives offered him and declared his intention to fight, the British opened fire and all but destroyed his fleet. Thus Great Britain safeguarded her supremacy at sea, a supremacy which was to prove decisive in the battle of Britain.

In the ensuing struggle, Germany with a population of more than 80,000,000 held a distinct advantage over Great Britain, which without her overseas empire had only some 48,000,000. The British regular army at home consisted in July, 1940, of only 1,500,000 men. These were supported by another million "Home Guard" volunteers who had been hastily organized to destroy parachutists and other air-borne invaders. But the great bulk of the British troops were men who had never campaigned under actual war conditions, and many of them were incompletely armed and equipped. Moreover, the British suffered from a serious shortage of tanks, artillery, antitank guns, and even small arms. The German army, on the other hand, consisted of approximately 3,500,000 men, all well trained and fully armed and equipped. It was a veteran force, by most observers considered the best and most powerful in the world. It seemed rather certain that, if Great Britain in July, 1940, had been merely another country on the Continent, adjacent to France, she would have been invaded, overrun, and conquered by the Germans.

But, despite Hitler's declaration that there were "no more islands," Great Britain remained separated from the Continent by a moat of water twenty miles or more in width. To cross that moat with sufficient men and equipment to assure a successful invasion the Germans needed thousands of suitable landing craft. And, unfortunately for Hitler's dreams of conquest, the Germans did not have them. To overcome this lack they made a tremendous effort to assemble from all occupied Europe craft of any and all types, but the latter were blasted by the RAF while they still lay in their harbors. On this occasion Hitler was uncertain and loath to take the risk of ordering a cross-Channel invasion of England. Although preparations for the invasion were made, D-day for this operation was twice postponed and finally cancelled in the fall of 1940.

But the English Channel could not stop an invasion by the Luftwaffe, and Hitler pinned his hopes upon it. Although in some categories British airplanes were superior to the German in quality, there seemed little doubt that at the opening of the battle of Britain Germany possessed an air superiority of three or four to one in the number of warplanes. But the Germans possessed not only the advantage of a superior number of planes. Thanks to the conquests they had made, they held a great advantage geographically. Scores of new air fields in southern Norway, Denmark, the Netherlands, Belgium, and France gave German planes admirable bases for attacking the southern and eastern coasts of Britain. As a result, the latter was geographically and industrially much more vulnerable to air attack than Germany. Although the British had a highly organized air-defense system, consisting chiefly of fighter planes, antiaircraft guns, and balloon barrages, the effectiveness of these defenses against mass attacks by thousands of airplanes had yet to be proved.

Marshal Göring, head of the German Luftwaffe, believed that German planes by terrific offensives in which thousands of bombers would be used might overwhelm and eliminate the British air forces as they had those of Poland and the Netherlands. Then, once British air fields had been destroyed and British airplanes had been grounded or wrecked, the Germans would do to the industrial cities of Great Britain what they had done to Warsaw and Rotterdam. Factories, power plants, warehouses, business centers, means of communication, if necessary the homes of the people, would be destroyed, and Britain would collapse internally.

On the night of June 18–19, 1940, Göring launched his attack upon Britain when German warplanes bombed the Thames estuary and southern England. On the following night British airplanes struck back, bombing Hamburg, Bremen, Cologne, Düsseldorf, Frankfort, and other places. Thus was inaugurated the long-expected and much-dreaded air war between the Reich and Great Britain. Nightly the air-raid sirens screamed, and not only British civilians, who had never experienced the horrors of modern war on their own soil, but Germans, whose country had not known foreign invasion for more than a century, came to feel the terrors of war in the homeland. During the latter part of July the Germans increased the intensity of their air attack, and in August Germany announced that "systematic de-

THE RESULT OF A VISIT BY THE LUFTWAFFE

London burning on December 29, 1940.

struction" would soon start. Beginning in September the Nazi bombing attacks were greatly increased, and special efforts were made to destroy or "erase" London. German bombers, directed personally by Marshal Göring, unleashed furious attacks upon the British capital, dropping incendiary as well as explosive bombs. Fires in various parts of the city illumined the skies almost nightly, and much destruction resulted, not only in the industrial and commercial sections of the city but in the residential areas as well. Berlin announced that waves of bombers would continue to strike at London until the British people set up a government which would be willing to accept German terms.

But the Germans succeeded neither in destroying British morale nor in eliminating the British air force. The British based their defensive strategy on the conservation and replacement of planes and crews. By scattering their planes they prevented great losses on the ground when air fields were attacked. Although they lost some 900 planes between September, 1940, and May, 1941, a steady though almost insignificant flow of new planes from British factories enabled the RAF to continue to fight. On the other hand, British daring and skill in combat and superiority in quality of planes and in tactics enabled RAF pilots to destroy some 3000 German planes during these critical months. Obviously the British inflicted a high rate of attrition on the Luftwaffe.

Experts have pointed out the serious error in Göring's strategy in failing to concentrate the Luftwaffe's attack on British war industries. Half a dozen factories, whose location was unquestionably known to the Germans, held, it is said, the key to Britain's Spitfire output. If the Luftwaffe had systematically bombed these factories, the production of British fighter planes could have been almost eliminated. But the Germans long held stubbornly to the plan which had been successful in Poland. Not until 1941 did they modify their strategy and attempt to strike the British war effort at its industrial roots. "Then it was too late. The destructive power of the Luftwaffe had been sharply reduced; new camouflaged plants had been completed, and production of critical parts widely decentralized; and American Lend-Lease was functioning, with hundreds of . . . planes supplementing British output." [3] Although London, Coventry, Birmingham, Bristol, Liverpool, and other cities had suffered heavy property damage, they had not been "erased." Nor had the British air force been put out of the conflict.

[3] A. Carr, "The Five Fatal Mistakes of the Axis," *Harper's Magazine,* February, 1944, pages 219–223.

The Extension of the War into the Balkans

By this time the war had engulfed the Balkans where the First World War had originated. The Soviet Union had struck first. Obviously disturbed by Hitler's spectacular successes in the West in 1940, Russia had swiftly availed herself of the German-Soviet secret agreement of 1939 regarding Bessarabia. On June 26, 1940, the day after fighting ceased in France, Foreign Commissar Molotov presented Rumania with a twenty-four-hour ultimatum demanding the immediate cession to Russia of Bessarabia and northern Bukowina. After frantically seeking the advice of Hitler and Mussolini, who urged acceptance in order to prevent a new war, the Rumanian government acceded to the demands, and Russian forces at once occupied these additional territories. In the succeeding weeks Russia took steps to strengthen her position in the Baltic, too. In August Estonia, Latvia, and Lithuania were absorbed into the Soviet Union as constituent republics.

Hungary and Bulgaria, also, both showed signs of a determination to regain the territories which Rumania had taken from them. Troops were rushed to both frontiers, and the possibility of another Balkan war seemed imminent. This Hitler and Mussolini at the moment wished to avoid at almost all costs. The leaders of the Hungarian, Rumanian, and Bulgarian governments were summoned for conferences, and out of them eventually came a further partition of Rumania. Bulgaria received that part of the Dobrudja which Rumania had taken from her in 1913; and Hungary received the northern half of the province of Transylvania, all of which had been awarded Rumania by the treaty of Trianon in 1920.

Within Rumania the fascist Iron Guard [4] at once sought to take advantage of the new situation to overthrow King Carol, who had been hostile to their movement. Despite Carol's efforts to ingratiate himself with the Iron Guardists—by cutting all ties with the Western democracies, withdrawing Rumania from the League of Nations, establishing a totalitarian state in Rumania, and appointing as premier General Ion Antonescu, who was an Iron Guard favorite—the king on September 6, 1940, was forced to abdicate in favor of his son, who for the second time became King Michael. Antonescu decreed the establishment of an Iron Guard totalitarian state whose foreign policy would be in complete accord with that of the Rome-Berlin Axis. Early in October German troops entered Rumania and began the occupation of that country with the permission of Antonescu's government. Another state thus succumbed to Nazi forces and Rumania's lot appeared to be little better than that of Denmark. At last Hitler had reached

[4] See pages 600–601.

the Black Sea, one of the principal objectives which he had outlined in *Mein Kampf*.

The next aggressive step in the Balkans was taken by Mussolini who, apparently expecting an easy victory, on October 28, 1940, ordered his troops in Albania to advance into Greece. But the Greeks first halted the Duce's troops, then threw them on the defensive, and finally drove them back into Albania. During the first three months of 1941 the Greeks fought stubbornly on over difficult terrain toward Valona, Italy's chief Albanian port. The British, who had now secured naval and air bases on the Greek island of Crete, added to Mussolini's woes. British bombers and torpedo planes from Crete or from British aircraft carriers attacked Taranto and Naples and seriously interfered with the shipment of Italian troops and supplies across the Adriatic. By the spring of 1941 the Italian invasion of Greece had been turned into something of a debacle.

Meanwhile Hitler had been attempting through diplomacy to persuade the small states of central Europe and the Balkans to support the Nazis. In November, 1940, he had made some headway, for within a week Hungary, Rumania, and Slovakia had signed the tripartite agreement of September 27, 1940, which Germany, Italy, and Japan had made to facilitate the establishment of "a new order in Europe" and "in Greater East Asia." [5] Additional Nazi troops were soon sent to Rumania, and during the opening weeks of 1941 they were gradually concentrated on the frontiers of Bulgaria and Yugoslavia, apparently in the hope that pressure might force these states, also, to join the Axis powers and thus open the way to an attack upon Greece down the Struma and Vardar valleys. Hitler was eager to bring the Balkans entirely under his control in order to protect his southern flank during his projected invasion of Russia. On March 1, 1941, the Bulgarian government finally joined the Axis powers by signing the tripartite agreement in Vienna, and within a few hours Nazi forces were reported in occupation of Sofia.

After Bulgaria succumbed to Hitler's pressure and Nazi forces in consequence were able to concentrate on nearly all sides of Yugoslavia, the regent, Prince Paul, and Premier Cvetkovich apparently came to the conclusion that discretion would be the better part of valor. They knew that, if they defied Hitler and war resulted, the only route by which Yugoslavia could receive assistance and supplies was up the Vardar valley from Saloniki—and this route might be speedily cut by German mechanized forces. Furthermore, they feared that going to war against the Axis might mean the end of Yugoslavia, for Bulgaria would be quick to demand the territory which she had lost in 1913 and 1919, Mussolini would undoubtedly seek to extend Albania at Yugoslavia's expense, and dissident Croats might

[5] See page 740.

throw their lot in with the Nazis in the hope that a dismembered Yugoslavia might result in an independent Croat state. On March 25, 1941, the Yugoslav government formally signed the Axis tripartite pact in Vienna.

The news of this capitulation to the Axis was received in Yugoslavia—at least in the districts which had constituted Serbia and Montenegro—with anger and resentment, which finally culminated in a bloodless *coup d'état* in the early morning hours of March 27. The regency of Prince Paul and the

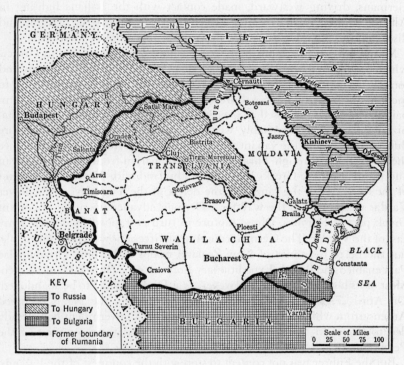

THE PARTITION OF RUMANIA, 1940

government of Premier Cvetkovich were both overturned. On the next day the seventeen-year-old son of former King Alexander was elevated to the throne as King Peter II, and General Dušan Simovich, commander of Yugoslavia's air force and leader of the coup against Cvetkovich, became premier. Although the new government announced that it would maintain a policy of strict neutrality as regarded the European war, it began to mobilize Yugoslav troops along the country's frontiers.

But Hitler struck before the Yugoslavs had time to complete their mobilization. On April 6 the Nazis launched invasions into both Yugoslavia and Greece, using their usual blitzkrieg pattern. With their overwhelming superiority in mechanized equipment and air force, they were able to carry out a campaign against Yugoslavia very much like the one they had waged against France in 1940. At various points the Yugoslav lines were pierced by "mechanized infiltration"; the Yugoslav armies were separated from one another and then encircled. At the same time a powerful German thrust down the Struma and into the Vardar valley effectively cut off the Yugoslavs from outside aid, even had such aid been available. Eventually the Germans, driving westward, made contact with the Italians fighting in Albania, and on April 17—after a twelve-day campaign—the defeated and disorganized Yugoslav army laid down its arms without conditions.

Meanwhile, the Germans had been pushing their invasion into Greece, which—aided by 60,000 British, Australian, and New Zealand troops and some heavy equipment from the Army of the Nile—was now compelled to meet blows from two major European powers. As in all their other campaigns, the Nazis possessed an overwhelming superiority in air and mechanized forces which inevitably weighed in the balance despite the more difficult terrain and the valiant stands of the Anzac troops. Almost at once the Nazis drove through Thrace from the Bulgarian frontier to the Aegean and thus cut off the Greeks from contact by land with Turkey. At the end of the third day of the campaign the defeat of the Yugoslavs in the lower Vardar valley opened the way for a German advance upon the important Greek port of Saloniki, whose capture in turn entrapped the Greek army east of the Vardar. The German conquest of Greece now seemed inevitable, but the fierce resistance of New Zealand troops at historic Thermopylae Pass enabled the British Expeditionary Force to evacuate 45,000 of its men. Most of its heavy equipment, however, as at Dunkirk, had to be abandoned. On April 27, 1941, after a three weeks' campaign, the Nazis occupied Athens, from which King George II and the Greek government had already fled to Crete. In the ensuing days they completed their conquest of the Peloponnesus.

But the Führer was not content to stop with the conquest of the Balkans. On May 20 he launched the first completely air-borne invasion in history against the strategic British-occupied Greek island of Crete, some sixty miles from the European mainland. Following a terrific attack by hundreds of bombing planes which prepared the way for them, thousands of Nazi troops were landed in Crete by parachutes, gliders, and transport planes. After a day of fighting with the British and Greek forces the Nazis, though having suffered heavy casualties, had gained a foothold on the island. Then followed a contest between air power and sea power. The British navy, though repeatedly attacked by Nazi dive bombers, shattered all German attempts to land troops and heavy equipment by sea, but hundreds of airplanes, shuttling back and forth between Greece and Crete, carried men, supplies, and light equipment to the Nazi "bridgeheads" on the island. By early June the Nazis had occupied most of Crete, the British without aerial protection being almost helpless. For the third time, however, they were able to carry out an overseas evacuation with some degree of success. Meanwhile, George II and his government had again fled, this time to Egypt.

British Dominance in the Middle East

While the Nazis were conquering the Balkans, it was thought by many that Hitler might next turn his attention to Syria and Iraq, both in order to obtain the coveted Mosul oil fields and to secure a military base for an advance on the Suez Canal. In Syria the French high commissioner appeared to be wholly in accord with the Vichy government's policy of collaboration with Hitler; and in Iraq, on April 4, the pro-British government was ousted by a *coup d'état* when the pro-Axis Rashid Ali Beg Gailani seized control. The coup seemed to presage ill for Great Britain, and to counter possible Axis penetration in this important oil-producing country the British on April 19 began to land troops at Basra, the Iraqi port on the Persian Gulf. Although by the Anglo-Iraqi treaty of alliance the British had the right to use the Iraqi "railways, rivers, ports, airdromes, and means of communication" in case of war, Rashid Ali objected. Hostilities broke out on May 2 when Iraqi troops attacked the British air base at Habbania, some sixty-five miles west of Bagdad, and Rashid Ali appealed to Hitler for aid.

Although Hitler dispatched some bomber and fighter planes to Iraq, utilizing Syrian airdromes as bases, he was apparently already preparing for his conquest of Crete and failed to send sufficient aid to enable Rashid Ali to gain superiority in the air. British and "Fighting French" airplanes not only attacked the Iraqi forces but also repeatedly bombed the airdromes in Syria which were being used by the Germans. At the same time British motorized units pushed steadily on toward Bagdad. Rashid Ali's government collapsed, the pro-Axis premier himself fled to Iran, and on June 1 all fighting between the British and the Axis-inspired Iraqi came to an end. The pro-British government, which had been overthrown in April, returned to power and Basra, Bagdad, and Mosul—the only Iraqi towns of any size—came into the hands of the British, who thus secured possession of the "backdoor to the Near East." Next British imperial and "Fighting French" forces invaded Syria and succeeded in occupying that country. With Palestine, Transjordan, Iraq, and Syria under their control, the British thus retained their dominant position in the Middle East, a position which was further strengthened in so far as the control of the Red Sea was concerned, by their conquest of Italian East Africa, which was completed in May, 1941.

The Deterioration of Soviet-German Relations

Although from the moment the German-Soviet nonaggression pact was signed Stalin and Hitler had been suspicious of each other, it was not until after the collapse of France that relations between Nazi Germany and Soviet Russia had begun to deteriorate. Stalin had disliked the German troops' use of Finland as a base for operations against northern Norway, while Hitler had not liked the Russian annexation of northern Bukowina, which had not been mentioned in the secret protocol of 1939. Stalin had also resented the German occupation of Rumania and the Axis guarantee to that country, which he considered was contrary to the interests of Russia. But his unwillingness to accept Hitler's ideas of Russia's proper sphere of influence was probably the immediate reason for the final break in the peaceful relations of the two countries.

After the air blitz against Britain had failed, Hitler in an interview with Foreign Commissar Molotov in Berlin on November 12, 1940, had proposed that Russia should sign a four-power treaty with Germany, Italy, and Japan, and had further proposed that Russia should center her territorial aspirations in the region south of the Soviet Union "in the direction of the Indian Ocean." Apparently the Balkans were to fall chiefly within the German sphere. To anyone familiar with Russia's many efforts to secure dominance in the Balkans and control of the Straits, it is obvious that Hitler's proposals would be unacceptable to the Soviet government. The latter had finally replied on November 25 that it would sign such a four-power pact only if it were accompanied by secret protocols providing that: (1) Russia should be guaranteed a base for her light naval and land forces on the Straits: (2) Bulgaria, recognized as being within Russia's geographical security zone, should sign a mutual assistance pact with the Soviet government; (3) the focal point of Russia's territorial aspirations should be recognized as lying south of Batum and Baku in the general direction of the Persian Gulf; (4) German troops should be withdrawn immediately from Finland; and (5) Japan should renounce her rights to concessions for coal and oil in Northern Sakhalin. The conflict between Germany's longstanding desire for a drive into the Balkans and Russia's equally longstanding ambition to control that region was obvious, and it is doubtful that Stalin ever expected Hitler to agree to such terms.

The Soviet reply reached Berlin on November 26, and three weeks later the Führer issued to his military leaders his secret directive for "Operation Barbarossa," which was designed "to crush Soviet Russia in a quick campaign" and "to establish a defense line against Asiatic Russia on a line running approximately from the Volga River to Archangel." Preparations for the campaign were "to be completed by May 15, 1941." This directive was of course not known to the Soviet government. Nevertheless, although on the surface Russia and Germany continued to be friends, clashes in policy developed. On January 17, 1941, Russia warned that the entrance of Nazi armed forces into Bulgaria would be considered "as a violation of the security interests of the U.S.S.R." But Germany had disregarded the warning and had occupied Bulgaria in March. On April 4, Molotov had informed Germany that Russia was about to sign a treaty of friendship and nonaggression with Yugoslavia, and "hoped that the German government, too, ... would do everything to maintain peace...." On April 6, the Nazis had invaded Yugoslavia, an action which Molotov characterized as "extremely deplorable."

Meanwhile, Stalin seems to have become convinced that a Nazi attack upon Russia was only a matter of time, and he had taken special steps to prepare for it. Diplomatically he had moved to prevent, if possible, a war on two fronts; on April 13, 1941, he had signed a treaty of neutrality and nonaggression with Japan. Industrially he had also taken steps to increase the military strength of the country. Production of war materials had been speeded up; the work-day had been lengthened from seven to eight hours; some of the vital industries in western Russia had been ordered moved to safer locations east of the Urals. Finally, in May, 1941, as though in anticipation of a crisis, Stalin himself for the first time assumed the premiership of the Soviet Union.

The Nazi Invasion of Russia

In June, 1941, Hitler began to make Nazi troop concentrations on the eastern front. In the north, German men, guns, and tanks were sent to Finland; in the south, the Rumanians were persuaded to mobilize on the Russian frontier. The Luftwaffe was largely shifted from the west to the east. Then without warning, without preliminary negotiations or an ultimatum, the Germans on June 22 advanced into Russia. In a proclamation to the German people the Führer promised that in the ensuing campaign the movement of German troops would be "in its extent and magnitude the greatest that the world has seen." There is little doubt that this phase of the war constituted one of the most gigantic duels in history; millions of men and thousands of tanks were hurled against one another along a battleline of some 1800 miles, while overhead thousands of planes struggled for mastery of the air.

The Nazi attack on Russia had its immediate effect on other countries. Prime Minister Churchill at once announced that, though he had not changed his views on communism, "any man or state who fights against

Nazism will have our aid." On July 13, 1941, Great Britain and the Soviet Union became formal allies. In July representatives of Great Britain and the United States flew to Moscow to ascertain what the Russians needed in the way of assistance, and late in September a formal conference in Moscow worked out plans for sending supplies to Russia by way of Archangel, Vladivostok, and Iran.

In order to safeguard a route to Russia by way of Iran the Allies were led to take drastic measures in that country. In August, 1941, Britain and Russia requested the shah to expel 3000 Germans from Iran. When the shah temporized, Russian and British troops entered the country and seized the railway lines and important oil centers. On September 9, the Iranian parliament finally agreed to surrender Axis nationals, expel the Axis legations, provide for transit facilities to Russia, safeguard the oil supply, and permit Allied military occupation of certain zones within the country. In the ensuing months the Trans-Iranian Railway and the motor highways were greatly improved by the Allies, and the routes through Iran came to play a vital part in providing Russia with much-needed British and American lend-lease supplies.

Meanwhile, the war in Russia had been proceeding. According to Hitler's original directive for the campaign, the zone of German operations was to be divided by the Pripet marshes into a northern and a southern sector. The main effort was to be made in the north. Soviet forces in White Russia and the Baltic states were to be annihilated and Leningrad and Kronstadt were to be captured. With the terrain in Russia generally similar to that in Poland, the Germans expected to execute on a much larger scale a blitzkrieg in which swift Panzer units would smash through the Russian lines in various places, then encircle the broken Red Army, and eventually annihilate it piece by piece. But the war in the north did not proceed "according to plan." Estonia was not completely overrun until September 5; Leningrad, although almost completely surrounded by besieging troops, never fell to the Nazis; and the Soviet armies were not encircled and annihilated.

In the area south of the Pripet marshes, according to the Führer's plan, German-Rumanian troops were to pin down the Soviet armies in Bessarabia while the main German force, advancing from Poland, was to capture Kiev and encircle and annihilate the Russian forces west of the Dnieper River. But here, too, operations did not proceed quite as the Nazis had expected. Nearly three months passed before Kiev was captured, and the Russian armies in the southwest were not enveloped and destroyed. But, during the period, the Soviet forces by their own admission lost 7000 tanks, 8900 large-caliber guns, and 5300 planes. Russia, the Führer publicly exulted on October 3, "is already broken and will never rise again." If he

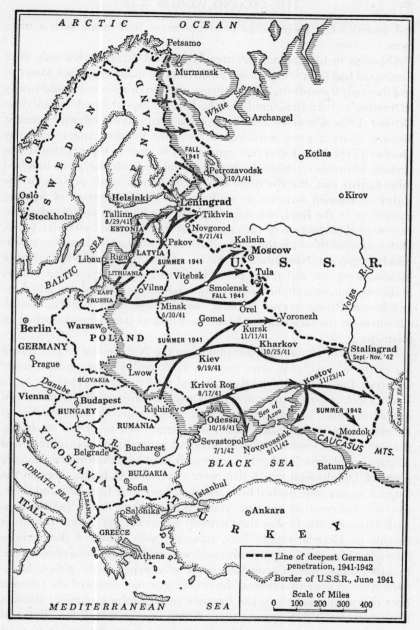

ARCTIC   OCEAN

○ Petsamo

● Murmansk

White Sea

○ Archangel

FALL 1941

○ Kotlas

● Petrozavodsk
10/1/41

Oslo ○
Stockholm ○

Helsinki ○

Tallinn
8/29/41

Leningrad
● Tikhvin

○ Kirov

ESTONIA

○ Novgorod
8/21/41

N O R W A Y

S W E D E N

F I N L A N D

Libau ○   Riga ○

○ Pskov   ○ Kalinin

● **Moscow**

U.   S.   S.   R.

LATVIA

SUMMER 1941

○ Vitebsk

● Tula

B A L T I C   S E A

LITHUANIA

○ Vilna

○ Smolensk
FALL 1941

○ Orel

EAST
PRUSSIA

○ Minsk
6/30/41

○ Gomel

○ Voronezh

Volga R.

Berlin ○   Warsaw ○

P O L A N D

SUMMER 1941

● Kursk
11/11/41

● Stalingrad
Sept.-Nov. '42

GERMANY

○ Prague

Kiev
9/19/41

● **Kharkov**
10/25/41

○ Lwow

SLOVAKIA

Danube R.

Vienna ○

○ **Budapest**

HUNGARY

○ Kishinev

Krivoi Rog
8/17/41

● Rostov
11/23/41

CASPIAN SEA

Sea of
Azov

SUMMER 1942

RUMANIA

○ Odessa
10/16/41

● Mozdok

○ Belgrade

○ **Bucharest**

Sevastopol
7/1/42

Novorossisk
9/11/42

CAUCASUS   MTS.

Y U G O S L A V I A

BULGARIA

B L A C K   S E A

Batum ○

A D R I A T I C   S E A

○ Sofia

○ Istanbul

ITALY

ALBANIA

○ Salonika

○ Ankara

GREECE

T U R K E Y

○ Athens

- - - - Line of deepest German
penetration, 1941-1942
〰〰 Border of U.S.S.R., June 1941

Scale of Miles
0   100 200 300 400

M E D I T E R R A N E A N   S E A

THE GERMAN INVASION OF RUSSIA, 1941–1942

had waited a few more weeks he might never have made such a statement.

Although in his original directive Hitler had declared that only after Leningrad had been taken should an attempt be made to capture Moscow, and that only a surprisingly fast collapse of Russian resistance could justify attempting to take Leningrad and the Russian capital simultaneously, on October 1 the Germans had launched a tremendous offensive against Moscow along a great semicircle some three hundred miles wide. By October 17 the Nazi forces had approached so close to the city that it was deemed advisable to move the Soviet capital to Kuibyshev, five hundred miles farther east. But the fierce Russian resistance, made possible by the ability of Russian factories to send an ever-swelling stream of fighting equipment to the front, not only surprised the German commanders but prevented their capture of the city. When this first Nazi offensive failed, Hitler, unmindful of the threat of a Russian winter, ordered another attack, which began on November 16. Seven of the eleven railways entering Moscow were cut, and at one point the Germans got within fifteen miles of the city. But, though the Germans meanwhile captured Odessa, Kharkov, and Rostov, Russia was not "broken," and Moscow was not taken. Instead, elsewhere on the far-flung battleline the Russians themselves launched an offensive.

A number of factors had contributed to the Nazi failure to put Russia out of the war with the same dispatch as Poland, France, and the lesser countries. For one thing, the Russians had plenty of space. Had any other country in Europe lost to an invader as much territory as the Germans conquered in Russia in 1941, it would have been completely overrun. Not so Russia. In the second place, Stalin was determined to permit no breakthrough by the German armies. The Soviet general staff, accordingly, had prepared a "defense in depth" into which the German armies repeatedly plunged, but through which they were never able to break. Though the Russian armies were pushed back and their lines were bent here and there, they avoided encirclement and remained intact. And the farther the Russians retreated, the farther the Germans advanced, the greater the strain became on German supply lines, especially since much of the territory through which the Germans advanced was deliberately devastated by the Russians themselves in accordance with a "scorched-earth" policy. Moreover, Russian guerrillas behind the invading armies menaced the German lines of communication. Soviet foresight in establishing many of Russia's newest and finest factories in eastern Russia or even east of the Urals and the swift transfer of some industries from the areas of invasion to safer regions to the east made possible the continued supply of Russian armies after the Germans had conquered regions previously considered the industrial heart of Russia. Space, time, weather, and Russian foresight and military skill all contributed to prevent the decisive victory which the Germans sought. In 1941 the Soviet armies punctured the myth of Nazi military invincibility.

When the German retreat in December, 1941, had threatened to become a rout, Hitler had summarily dismissed Field Marshal von Brauchitsch and had dismissed or relieved all but one of the older and experienced field commanders in the Russian theater of operations. He himself personally assumed command of the army, and thereafter held both the position of supreme commander of the German armed forces and commander-in-chief of the army. But the tasks which Hitler thus took upon himself were beyond his ability. Furthermore, in the succeeding years, which called for a greater effort on the home front than during 1939–1941, Hitler rarely left his military headquarters where he became less and less accessible. He lost personal touch with the military fronts, too, for between 1941 and 1945 he visited the armies at the front not more than twice. In the eyes of some military experts, Hitler's assumption of personal command in December, 1941, marked the turning point in the German conduct of the war.

The Battle of the Atlantic

Although the German attack upon Russia had compelled the Nazis to abandon their attempt to put Britain out of the war by the use of airplanes, they still hoped that the same end might be accomplished by their submarines. If the latter could successfully cut off the British from their overseas sources of supplies, England would be doomed.

To wage the battle of the Atlantic, Germany was more favorably situated than in the First World War. She had many more submarine and airplane bases, and they were more widely scattered—from Norway to the Pyrenees. It was much more difficult than in the previous conflict, therefore, for Great Britain to block German submarines by minefields, nets, and the like. Furthermore, many of the German submarines were larger and able to range farther than in the First World War. The Germans had still another advantage over 1917 in the ability of reconnaissance planes to inform submarine commanders of the location of British merchant ships which might otherwise escape detection.

On the other hand, the difficulty of the task of obtaining goods from abroad was greatly increased for Britain over what it had been in the First World War. In the first place, Hitler's conquest of Norway, Denmark, Holland, and France closed to the British some of their normal and near-by sources of supply. The longer hauls required to secure needed commodities from the New World or other overseas regions placed an added burden upon the British merchant marine. In the second place, Italy's entrance into the war against Britain practically closed the Mediterranean to British merchant ships, thus increasing the time and distance required for trips around the Cape of Good Hope to the Near and Middle East. At the same time Mussolini's determination to conquer Egypt and British East Africa made it more than ever necessary for the British to send supplies to those regions to meet the Axis threat. Great Britain, therefore, actually required more merchant ships than in 1917 to meet her needs.

Although British airplanes almost nightly bombed the most menacing German submarine bases on the Continent, the chief defensive measure against submarine attacks was the use of convoys protected by British warships. But the British were woefully short of destroyers, so that many convoys became relatively easy prey through lack of adequate protection. It was this desperate British need of added destroyers for convoy duty that led to the exchange of fifty over-age American destroyers for leases for United States air and naval bases in the western hemisphere in 1940. But the British were also handicapped in their convoy work by lack of some of the bases which they and the Americans had used effectively in the war against the German submarines in 1917. In 1938, Great Britain had surrendered all admiralty rights and harbor defenses in Eire, and, since Eire had declared her neutrality in the Second World War, the harbors of southern Ireland were closed to British warships.

By 1941 it was becoming apparent that the rate of destruction of British merchant ships was so great as to constitute a very real threat to Britain's ability to transport to her shores the foodstuffs and supplies without which she could not hope to continue the war. In May, 1941, the British admiralty revealed that German mines and air and sea raiders on British ships and ships in British service had, since the beginning of the war, sunk more than 1400 merchantmen, totaling more than 6,000,000 tons. Of this number 885 were British ships. It appeared that Britain's greatest difficulties in the battle of the Atlantic could be solved only if she obtained more merchant ships and more aerial and naval protection.

Meanwhile, the United States had begun to take steps to assist the British in the battle of the Atlantic. Early in 1941 the American Congress had passed the Lend-Lease Act to provide "the tools" for Britain to use in her struggle for existence. But it soon became clear to Americans that to produce the weapons of war was not enough. They must be put into Britain's hands if they were to be used in the fight in defense of democracy. The heavy toll of the German campaign against shipping, it appeared, might defeat the whole purpose of the Lend-Lease Act.

To assist in checking the ravages of the German submarines, the United

States navy therefore inaugurated a "neutrality patrol system" to warn peaceful shipping of the presence of raiding submarines and airplanes. Then, on April 9, 1941, Secretary of State Hull and the Danish minister to the United States signed an agreement giving the United States the right to establish air bases and other military and naval facilities in Greenland. For all practical purposes the island was placed under the protective custody of the United States for the duration of the war. American bases in Greenland would flank the "Great Circle" shipping route between North America and Britain and would greatly strengthen the American naval and air patrol eastward to within three miles of the Nazi-proclaimed blockade zone. The increased efficiency of the American patrol made possible the shifting to other zones of some British naval vessels which had been operating in the western Atlantic. Furthermore, since British shipyards were overcrowded with new construction and repair work, many British ships, even warships, were repaired in American drydocks.

On June 9, 1941, it was learned that a German submarine had deliberately sunk an American freighter in the mid-Atlantic far outside the combat zone. Passengers and crew had been left in open boats far from land. On June 14, President Roosevelt ordered the immediate "freezing" of the assets in the United States of Germany and Italy and eight other states occupied or controlled by them. Two days later the American government ordered the closing of all German consulates and bureaus of information in the United States because their "improper and unwarranted" activities were inimical to the welfare of the United States. On June 19, both Germany and Italy ordered American consulates in their countries closed, whereupon the United States ordered the closing of Italian consulates also. In June, American troops landed in Iceland "to supplement and eventually to replace" British forces which had occupied that island since May, 1940. Shortly thereafter the United States navy extended its "neutrality patrol" as far as that island, some 3000 miles from New York.

Obviously the United States was determined to aid Britain in her struggle to prevent a Nazi-dominated world. But obviously Americans, as well as other peoples, desired to know what sort of world was envisaged in case the Nazis were defeated. An answer was given in the so-called Atlantic Charter, issued (August 14, 1941) by President Roosevelt and Prime Minister Churchill as the result of a meeting which they held at sea off the coast of Newfoundland. In a manner somewhat reminiscent of President Wilson's Fourteen Points, these two leaders set forth the common principles in the national policies of the United States and Great Britain on which they based their hopes for a better future for the world. They declared that:

First, Their countries seek no aggrandizement, territorial or other;

Second, They desire to see no territorial changes that do not accord with the freely expressed wishes of the people concerned;

Third, They respect the right of all peoples to choose the form of government under which they will live; and they wish to see sovereign rights and self-government restored to those who have been forcibly deprived of them;

Fourth, They will endeavor, with due respect for their existing obligations, to further the enjoyment of all states, great or small, victor or vanquished, of access, on equal terms, to the trade and to the raw materials of the world which are needed for their economic prosperity;

Fifth, They desire to bring about the fullest collaboration between all nations in the economic field with the object of securing, for all, improved labor standards, economic adjustment, and social security;

Sixth, After the final destruction of the Nazi tyranny, they hope to see established a peace which will afford to all nations the means of dwelling in safety within their own boundaries, and which will afford assurance that all the men in all the lands, live out their lives in freedom from fear and want;

Seventh, Such a peace should enable all men to traverse the high seas and oceans without hindrance;

Eighth, They believe that all of the nations of the world, for realistic as well as spiritual reasons, must come to the abandonment of the use of force. Since no future peace can be maintained if land, sea, or air armaments continue to be employed by nations which threaten, or may threaten, aggression outside of their frontiers, they believe, pending the establishment of a wider and permanent system of general security, that the disarmament of such nations is essential. They will likewise aid and encourage all other practicable measures which will lighten for peace-loving peoples the crushing burdens of armaments.

A comparison of the Atlantic Charter and the Fourteen Points [6] reveals similarities and differences. One of the latter, especially significant, was the renunciation of any aim at territorial aggrandizement.

During the autumn of 1941 the United States further extended its aid in the battle against Nazi U-boats. In September its naval vessels began to assist in protecting convoys across the Atlantic. On the other hand, in order to prevent the increasing flow of lend-lease supplies to Great Britain, Russia, and the other Allies, German submarines redoubled their attacks on merchant ships, and began to seek out American destroyers engaged in patrol and convoy duty. When on September 4 an American destroyer was attacked by a German submarine, President Roosevelt announced that thereafter the navy "would shoot on sight" any Axis submarine observed anywhere in the Atlantic. In October, a second destroyer suffered some

[6] See pages 377–378.

loss of life in an engagement with a German U-boat and another was sunk with the loss of about one hundred of her crew.

In November, Congress repealed part of the Neutrality Act of 1939 in order to permit the arming of American merchant ships and to give them permission to carry cargoes into ports of belligerent countries. As the year 1941 drew to a close, therefore, it seemed quite possible that war might be precipitated between the United States and Germany by the course of events in the Atlantic. It was not in the Atlantic, however, but in the Pacific that the events occurred which plunged the United States into the Second World War. Those events are discussed in Chapter XXV. It must suffice here to point out that, after the Japanese attack on Pearl Harbor, both Germany and Italy on December 11 declared war on the United States.

Chapter XXIV

THE DEFEAT OF THE AXIS
IN EUROPE

U P to the autumn of 1942 Hitler's armies almost without interruption
had continued their successful conquest of Europe. In the closing
months of that year, however, thanks to the staying power of the British,
finally supplemented by the tremendous man power and industrial resources
of Russia and the United States, the German armies were halted. In 1943
they lost the initiative on all fronts. But Hitler conceived of no great
strategic idea to alter this situation and fell back upon the policy of living
upon "the capital sum of space" which the Germans had already conquered,
insisting upon an inelastic defense of all territory held. In the succeeding
years, however, they were driven out of their conquered lands and were
ultimately forced back behind the Reich's boundaries. In 1945 the forces
of the "United Nations" overran the devastated Fatherland, all German
military resistance collapsed, and Hitler and some of his close Nazi associates died amid the flames and ruins of the German capital.

A United Front

Among the chief factors which had contributed to the Nazi victories in
the first three years of the war were: (1) unity of command, which made
possible quick decisions on the conduct of military operations; (2) a large
and well-trained army, which enabled the high command to throw into
any one theater of the war greater man power than the enemy; (3) superiority in aircraft and mechanized equipment, which provided the Nazis
with the means to overwhelm their foes no matter how courageous the
latter might be; (4) possession of the initiative, which allowed the Germans
to choose where and when they would strike each overpowering blow.
Until all or most of these advantages had been shifted to the Allies, the
latter could have little hope of victory.

To this end the first step seemed to be the creation of a united front. On
January 1, 1942, twenty-six states, which had declared war against the Axis,
became the United Nations by signing in Washington a declaration in

Acme Photo

THE "BIG THREE" OF THE UNITED NATIONS
Stalin, Roosevelt, and Churchill at Teheran.

which each subscribed to the principles set forth in the Atlantic Charter, promised to employ its full resources, military or economic, against those members of the Axis and their adherents with which it was at war, and agreed not to make a separate armistice or peace with the enemies.

The achievement of general unity in the strategic sphere was, of course, fundamental to the whole Allied war effort. Strategic decisions rested with the heads of the various governments, and during December, 1941, important diplomatic conferences were held in Washington by Prime Minister Churchill and President Roosevelt, in Moscow by British Foreign Secretary Eden and Premier Stalin, and in Chungking by the British General Wavell, the American General Brett, and Generalissimo Chiang Kai-shek. As the basis of the Allied strategy it was agreed, in general, that the major foe was Germany, for it was argued with reason that, whereas the defeat of Japan would not necessarily entail the defeat of Germany, the defeat of the latter would inevitably bring the ruin of Japan.

To maintain and increase the close co-operation of the four major anti-Axis powers, more conferences were held in the succeeding years: at Washington in June, 1942; at Casablanca, French Morocco, in January, 1943; at Quebec in August, 1943; at Moscow in October, 1943; at Cairo, Egypt, and at Teheran, Iran, in November, 1943; again at Quebec in September, 1944; and at Yalta, Crimea, in February, 1945. As the result of these various conferences, attended in most cases by Churchill and Roosevelt and their military staffs and at Teheran and Yalta by Stalin as well, definite plans were made for the invasion of North Africa, for the invasion of Sicily and the knocking-out of Italy, for the general advance against Germany, and for the defeat of Japan.

Prime Minister Churchill had early pointed out that the first period of the global struggle that was initiated at Pearl Harbor must be one of consultation, combination, and preparation until the Allies had acquired the necessary overwhelming superiority in man power and equipment and the shipping tonnage to give the Allied armies power to cross the seas and oceans separating them from the enemy. The length of this period must depend, he had said, on the vigor of the effort put into production in industries and shipyards.

Although Great Britain, Russia, Canada, and Australia bent every effort to the increasing of their national production of war materials, it was realized that it must be the production of the United States which would decisively tip the scales against the Axis powers. With that thought in mind President Roosevelt ordered the American war-production schedules for 1942 set at 60,000 aircraft, 45,000 tanks, 20,000 antiaircraft guns, and 8,000,000 tons of merchant ships. Moreover, in order to shorten the war and speed the day of victory, the United States decided to expand tremendously the already existing lend-lease system and to make greater efforts to meet the needs of Soviet Russia. By the northern route through Murmansk and Archangel and by the southern route through Iran supplies were forwarded to the Soviet armies so that by October 31, 1943, Russia had received under lend-lease arrangements 7000 planes, 3500 tanks, and 195,000 motor vehicles.

The United States also played a decisive role in tipping the scales against the Axis in the matter of fighting man power. In 1942 the armed forces of the United States increased from slightly more than 2,000,000 to 7,000,000 men. By the close of 1942 more than 1,500,000 United States troops were in service outside the American continent. A combined chiefs-of-staff organization was established in Washington by the United States and Great Britain as a step toward the creation of suitable machinery for co-ordinating their military efforts. Eventually Anglo-American military co-operation reached the point where the armies of the two countries were so meshed in the European theater of war that they constituted one fighting force. By the fall of 1942 that fighting force was large enough and well enough equipped to enable the Allies to enter the second phase of the war as outlined by Churchill, namely, the period of liberation, in which territories lost to the Axis would be recovered.

The Expulsion of the Axis from Africa

The first indication of a definite turn in the tide of the war came in North Africa. Events in that theater had been subject to swift and startling changes ever since Mussolini had taken Italy into the conflict and had started out to conquer an empire at the expense of Great Britain. In September, 1940, the Italians had advanced to Sidi Barrani within the frontiers of Egypt, only to be hurled back by the British, who between December, 1940, and February, 1941, advanced as far as El Agheila, to the west of Bengasi. Then, in April, 1941, the Italians, reinforced by German divisions and commanded by the German General Erwin Rommel, struck with superior force and within a few days were once more back within Egypt. Seven months later the tables had again been turned when the British, themselves reinforced by a new armored division, assumed the offensive in November, 1941, and by the end of the year they were again back at El Agheila.

But by January, 1942, Rommel had received enough supplies to counterattack, and he succeeded in recapturing the important port of Bengasi. Four months later the Axis forces, having in the meantime gained a superiority in heavy tanks, heavy guns, and antitank guns, again drove to the east. At first the British held fast, and Rommel lost heavily in tanks, but in June, 1942, the British tank force was successfully ambushed and lost some

220 out of 300 tanks. Thus weakened, the British were forced to fall back. When they finally halted at El Alamein, they had retreated four hundred miles and had lost 80,000 men. The Axis forces were only sixty miles from Alexandria, whose fall was momentarily expected. In anticipation of a triumphal entry Mussolini hastened to North Africa.

But at El Alamein the British held a strong natural position, a front only forty miles wide protected on the north by the sea and on the south by the Qattara depression, in which tanks could not maneuver. Frontal attacks by Rommel's forces in July and again late in August, 1942, were successfully beaten back by the reinforced British. Meanwhile, the British Eighth Army had been given a new commander, General Sir Bernard Montgomery, and was being reorganized and re-equipped with the help of the United States. Huge convoys arrived with reinforcements and much-needed supplies, including heavier guns and heavier tanks. Rommel too received some fresh troops and added supplies, but by the fall of 1942 it was estimated that the Eighth Army had a superiority of four to one in guns and three to one in tanks and planes.

On the night of October 23, 1942, General Montgomery launched an attack designed to drive Rommel not only out of Egypt but out of Libya as well. It was no easy task to dislodge the Axis troops from their Alamein positions, and heavy losses were suffered on both sides. But on November 2 a furious armored battle was fought; Rommel's left flank was penetrated; and on November 3 a general Axis retreat began. By November 6 over 20,000 Axis prisoners had been counted, and 600 planes, 350 tanks, 400 guns, and thousands of vehicles had been captured or disabled. Four days later Rommel's forces had been driven back across the Egyptian frontier. Alexandria and the Suez Canal were again safe.

But General Montgomery did not halt his troops. On November 20 forces of the British Eighth Army entered Bengasi. Rommel tried to establish a line once more at El Agheila, the farthest point to which the British forces had ever penetrated in their previous advances into Libya, but, when Montgomery brought up his heavy guns and prepared for a second devastating barrage, the Axis retreat was resumed. On January 23, 1943, the victorious Eighth Army entered the port of Tripoli. The final battle for Egypt was over; the Italian empire in Africa was lost.

Meanwhile, far to the west the Allies had struck a surprise blow in accordance with plans decided upon at a conference between Churchill and Roosevelt in Washington in June, 1942. On November 7, shortly after Montgomery's break through the Axis position at El Alamein, the first of the great Allied amphibious undertakings was successfully carried through in French North Africa under the command of the American General Dwight D. Eisenhower. Convoys of more than 500 ships escorted by 350

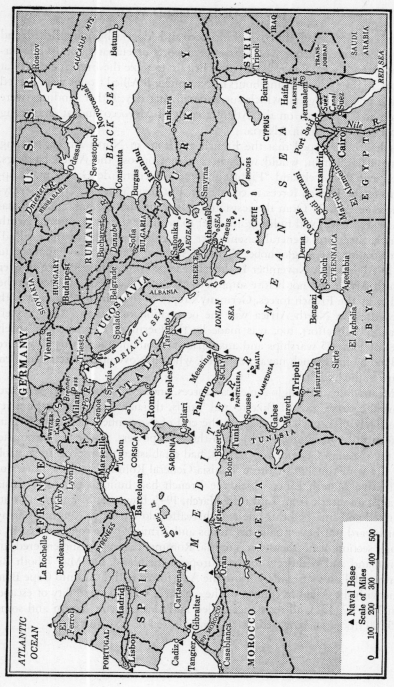

THE MEDITERRANEAN AREA IN THE SECOND WORLD WAR

▲ Naval Base
Scale of Miles
0   100   200   300   400   500

naval craft arrived off the coast of Morocco and Algeria, bringing British and American troops from widely separated ports of embarkation, while airborne troops were flown from Great Britain to seize the French air field at Oran. In the early morning hours of November 8 Allied troops were landed at the port of Algiers, which surrendered that day. Other landings were made at Casablanca on the Atlantic coast of Morocco and at the strong naval base at Oran in Algeria.

It had been hoped that the French garrisons in North Africa, totaling some 100,000 men, would welcome and not oppose the Allied landings. President Roosevelt and "Fighting French" General de Gaulle made appeals to the French forces to co-operate. But their appeals were not everywhere heeded. At Oran the resistance was somewhat serious, and at Casablanca there was stiff fighting. In order to facilitate the occupation of North Africa, therefore, General Eisenhower recognized as head of the civil administration the Anglophobe, Vichyite Admiral Darlan, who happened to be in Algiers. On November 11 the latter issued orders to cease fire all over North Africa, but not before some 2000 casualties had been inflicted on the Allies by the French forces. Germany's reply to French collaboration with the Allies in North Africa was the occupation of hitherto "unoccupied France." An effort, too, was made by the Germans to seize the French fleet of some 75 warships and auxiliaries at Toulon, but in this they were balked by the French naval personnel, who on November 27 scuttled their ships in the harbor.

Meanwhile, the Anglo-American forces, once established in Algiers, had started a drive toward Bizerte and Tunis, the naval base and capital respectively of French Tunisia. At the end of November they were within fifteen miles of Tunis, but by then the Axis powers, under the command of the German General von Arnim, had established themselves in control. At the same time, in southern Tunisia General Rommel held the powerful defensive Mareth Line, which the French had built to protect Tunisia against an attack from Libya. In March, 1943, however, Montgomery outflanked and smashed this line and thereafter slowly drove Rommel's army northward until eventually his troops and Arnim's were concentrated in a small section of northeastern Tunisia. Rommel thereupon surrendered his command and withdrew to the European mainland. On May 7 both Bizerte and Tunis surrendered, and the Axis forces withdrew onto Cape Bon. But with the Allies in control of the sea there was no possibility of escape. On May 12, 1943, all resistance ended and General von Arnim and some 225,000 troops surrendered. Africa was cleared of Axis forces.

The Collapse of Italian Fascism

Stalin had for some time been calling for the establishment of a second Allied front in Europe to relieve the Nazi pressure on Russia. Although he would have preferred the second front in western Europe, Churchill and Roosevelt, in a spectacular conference held at Casablanca in January, 1943, had decided to invade Sicily, and four months later, in May, at a similar conference in Washington, they agreed that the principal Allied objective in 1943 should be the knocking out of Italy.

In May, accordingly, the Allied air force directed the full weight of its attack against the small Italian islands between Sicily and North Africa, against the ports and air fields of Sicily itself, and against Naples, the chief supply base for Sicily in southern Italy. On June 12, 1943, the first tangible results of these bombings came when the Italian key island of Pantelleria, which virtually commanded the sea passage between Sicily and Tunis, was forced to surrender by Allied bombers even before any troops had been landed to attack it.

Four weeks later the Allied invasion of Sicily began with the landing of parachute and glider troops several miles back from the southern and eastern coasts. On the morning of July 10 this air invasion was followed by large-scale landings from an armada of 2700 vessels of all descriptions. The invasion was made on the southeast corner of the island, and in the first two days some 80,000 men and 300 tanks were put ashore. Eventually the expeditionary forces consisted of 150,000 American, British, and Canadian troops. Axis resistance was weak; by July 15 the bridgeheads were firmly established, and the advance northward began, the British Eighth Army up the east coast and the American Seventh Army north and northwest from the south coast. On July 22, in a surprise thrust across the island against only half-hearted resistance, the Americans captured the important port of Palermo. By the close of July the Axis force of nearly 100,000 men had been compressed into a small triangle in northeastern Sicily. Progress was slowed by Axis mines and demolitions and by stiff German resistance from hill positions dominating the roads. But the Allies pushed steadily forward and finally entered the port of Messina on August 17, 1943, whereupon all organized resistance in Sicily ceased.

Meanwhile, military events in North Africa and Sicily had had political repercussions in Italy. Italian military authorities were in despair and asserted that only greatly increased aid from Germany could save Italy. But Hitler apparently refused Mussolini's plea for such assistance and insisted instead that the Axis must withdraw to northern Italy. Mussolini returned from his interview with Hitler to find Rome greatly disturbed by its first air attack, which had occurred on July 18. The political effect of Hitler's refusal to send additional aid, the Allied gains in Sicily, and the prospect of further air raids on Rome was not long delayed. On July 24 the Fascist Grand Council demanded Mussolini's resignation. On the next day he was summoned to the royal palace, informed of his dismissal by the king, and arrested as he left. Marshal Pietro Badoglio, the victor in Ethiopia, was appointed by the king to succeed Mussolini as premier, and he at once decreed the formal dissolution of the Fascist Party. But he also announced that Italy would continue in the war.

For a time the Allies suspended their air attacks upon the Italian mainland in the hope that Badoglio might open negotiations. But when he made no such move, the air attacks were resumed on August 1, and air and naval forces began preparing the way for a landing in Italy. Coastal defenses were shelled, and important communications centers—Naples, Salerno, Taranto, Foggia, and others—were bombed. On August 13 a second raid was made on Rome. Almost immediately thereafter the Badoglio government opened secret negotiations with the Allies, and ultimately, on September 3, 1943, at Syracuse, a representative of the Badoglio government agreed to the terms of an armistice laid down by General Eisenhower. At the latter's insistence it was agreed that the armistice should be announced at the time the Allies considered most advantageous.

The Allied Invasion of Italy

A few hours before the armistice was signed, General Montgomery's Eighth Army had crossed the Messina Straits, landed on the Italian "toe," and begun advancing northward and eastward. Five days later, on September 8, a daring amphibious landing of American and British troops, under the command of General Mark W. Clark of the United States Fifth Army, was made at Salerno, southeast of Naples. From Rome Badoglio announced the armistice, instructed the Italian forces to cease all opposition to the Allies, and then moved the headquarters of the Italian government within the Allied lines.

Meanwhile, the fate of General Clark's Fifth Army at Salerno hung in the balance. For two weeks the Germans had been preparing defensive positions above Salerno Bay, and they had five divisions of troops in the vicinity. Soon the weight of German reinforcements against General Clark threatened to drive his forces into the sea. The situation was critical. But Allied air power, operating from Sicily and North Africa, dropped thousands of tons of bombs on the enemy forces while British dreadnoughts poured in shells from their powerful guns. At the same time, from the south, the Eighth Army pushed rapidly northward against the weak resistance of the retreating Germans. Eventually, on September 17, the two Allied armies made contact and established a continuous front along 225 miles from Salerno to the Adriatic. Two weeks later they entered Naples, and on October 13 the Badoglio government formally declared war upon Germany.

Thus in three months the Allies successfully carried out two major amphibious operations against the Axis forces; conquered Sicily, Sardinia, Corsica, and the Italian mainland to a line some thirty miles north of Naples; and brought about the overthrow of Mussolini, the collapse of Fascism, and the surrender of Victor Emmanuel's government. These achievements had secured for the Allies the bulk of the Italian navy and valuable air bases in Italy, especially the one at Foggia, from which the Allies could readily bomb Hungary and the Balkans. Indirect but valuable results of these successes, of course, were the freeing of the Mediterranean for the use of Allied shipping engaged in carrying supplies to Egypt, to India, and, via Iran, to Russia; the release of Allied naval units in the Mediterranean for use elsewhere; the drain upon German man power as Italian forces in France, the Balkans, the Aegean, and even Italy had to be replaced by loyal Nazi troops; and the enhancement of Allied prestige.

For months after the capture of Naples the Allies were stalled before the Germans' so-called Gustav Line, constructed along the Rapido and Garigliano rivers. Late in January, 1944, they tried to outflank this line or to force a German withdrawal from it by an amphibious landing of American and British forces in the vicinity of Nettuno and Anzio, but Allied troops from this Anzio beachhead, as it was called, were unable to isolate the German armies fighting to the south. Heavy German reinforcements were rushed to attack the beachhead in an effort to drive the Allied forces into the sea, but the Germans in turn failed to dislodge the Allies, and a stalemate resulted in this sector. Similarly, against the Gustav Line, despite terrific air bombardments of the monastery and town of Cassino in February and March, the Allies failed to make much progress.

On the night of May 11, however, the Italian front was galvanized into action when an all-out attack was launched along the Rapido and Garigliano rivers. Both rivers were crossed; the Gustav Line was breached; and on May 18 Cassino was at last taken. Four days later the Anzio beachhead forces also launched an attack, and on May 25 contact was made between these forces and the Allied Fifth Army advancing from the south. On June 3 the German line in the Alban Hills was pierced, and the way was opened for an advance upon Rome. The German General Albert Kesselring thereupon proposed that Rome be considered an open city and agreed to withdraw his troops. On June 4, 1944, in the face of only sporadic resistance, Allied troops entered the Eternal City, which thus became the first of Europe's capitals to be liberated from the Nazis.

In the succeeding weeks the Allies also liberated Perugio, Siena, Arezzo, and the important ports of Leghorn on the Ligurian Sea and Ancona on the Adriatic. The Germans, reinforced, made a determined effort to hold Pisa and Florence and the Arno River; they destroyed all the Florentine bridges across the Arno except one and blocked that by demolishing long-cherished buildings at each end. But on August 6, 1944, Allied troops stormed across the river into the heart of historic Florence. On September 2 Pisa, also, was captured, and the Nazis thereupon withdrew to their Gothic Line protecting the Po valley where they prepared to make a desperate stand against the victorious Allies. Though little headway was made by the latter in the succeeding months, they continued to exert strong pressure against the Gothic Line in order to prevent the Nazis from shifting troops to their other hard-pressed fronts.

Stalingrad and the Great Russian Offensives of 1943–1944

While in 1942–1943 the Western Allies were conquering North Africa, invading Italy, and bringing about the collapse of Fascism, events of even greater importance had been occurring in Russia. In 1942 the Germans had launched a double-pronged offensive, aimed at the capture of Baku on the Caspian and Stalingrad on the Volga. If these could be taken, the important Volga communications would be cut, and the bulk of the Russian forces operating to the north would be deprived of their access to the rich petroleum resources of the Caucasus. By the last of August the Germans were in the Caucasus and their Panzer divisions had reached the suburbs of Stalingrad with a superiority in men, tanks, and planes. Constantly their heavy artillery and planes bombed the city until its factories and apartments became mere rubble. But Stalin had ordered his namesake defended to the death and the Germans never succeeded in taking it. Nor did they capture Baku or the oil fields of the Caucasus. The days when they could advance irresistibly were past.

Instead, the Russians, timing their operations with those of the Allies in North Africa and using reserves brought from Siberia, in November, 1942, launched a great counteroffensive both north and south of Stalingrad. Before the close of that month Soviet troops had cut off from retreat the twenty-two divisions of Nazis besieging that city. On February 3, 1943, the last units of the half-starved and abandoned German forces surrendered. The German loss of materials at Stalingrad was far greater than the Allied

BATTLELINE
SEPT. 5, 1944

ROME TAKEN
JUNE 4, 1944

ALLIES LANDED
JAN. 22, 1944

NAPLES TAKEN
OCT. 1, 1943

BATTLELINE
NOV. 2, 1943

ALLIES LANDED
SEPT. 8, 1943

BRITISH LANDED
SEPT. 2, 1943

Scale of Miles
0 25 50 75 100

THE ALLIED ADVANCE IN ITALY, 1943–1944

losses at Dunkirk. Meanwhile, in their winter offensive of 1942–1943 the Russian forces had driven more than 400 miles westward from Stalingrad, had cleared the Germans out of some 185,000 square miles of Russian territory, and had again shattered the myth of Nazi invincibility.

During the next summer the Soviet armies retained their initiative, met some 218 Nazi and satellite divisions, drove them back with heavy losses, and liberated still more tens of thousands of square miles of Russian territory. When their summer offensive of 1943 closed at the beginning of November, the battle line in Russia extended roughly southward from Leningrad, which had been relieved in January, 1943, to a point east of Vitebsk, then south to a point east of Gomel, then in general along the east bank of the Dnieper River to the Black Sea.

Without letup, however, the Russian winter offensive of 1943–1944 succeeded the summer drive. On November 6, Kiev, the capital of the Ukraine, was recaptured by Soviet armies, which drove relentlessly westward until in January, 1944, they crossed into pre-1939 Poland south of the Pripet marshes. Other troops, operating to the southwest pushed the Germans back until by the end of March, 1944, the Russians had reached the Carpathian Mountains, where for sixty miles they stood along the former Czechoslovak frontier. Still others had crossed the Dniester River into pre-1940 Rumania. In April, Odessa was liberated and in May, Sevastopol and the Crimea were cleared of Nazi forces. Meanwhile, in the Leningrad area the Soviet armies had recaptured the south shore of the Gulf of Finland nearly to Narva in former Estonia, had opened the main railway from Leningrad to Moscow, and had driven to the east shore of Lake Peipus. The map on page 713 shows the extensive gains made by the Soviet armies in their offensives from November, 1942 to May, 1944. Thanks to the fighting prowess of the Russian soldiers, the strategic ability of the Soviet high command, the efficiency of the Red Army railway battalions in restoring lines of communication, the ability of Soviet factories to provide military equipment, and the great assistance of lend-lease supplies, which during 1943 had increased "from a trickle to a torrent," the German armies had been driven almost entirely out of the Soviet Union.

D-Day

By this time the United States and Great Britain were ready to open the second front in France which Russia had so long urged. The Allies at length were well supplied with the weapons of war, for, in addition to British production, between May, 1940 and September, 1943, American industry had produced and delivered 123,000 aircraft, 349,000 airplane engines, 53,000 tanks, 93,000 artillery weapons, and 1,233,000 motor trucks,

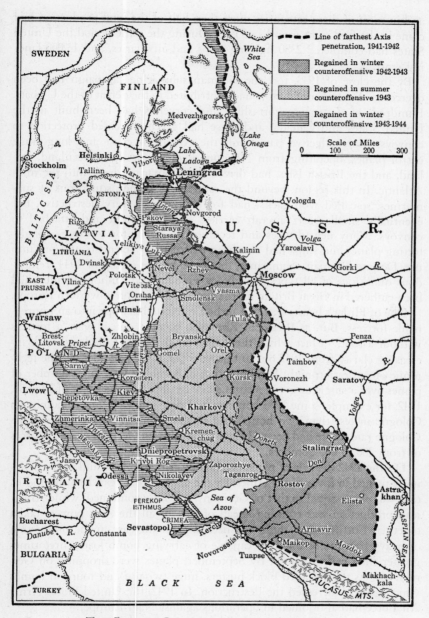

SWEDEN

White Sea

FINLAND

Medvezhegorsk

Lake Onega

Helsinki

Stockholm

Tallinn   Viborg   *Lake Ladoga*

Leningrad

BALTIC SEA   Narva

ESTONIA   *L. Ilmen*   Novgorod   Vologda

Riga   Pskov   Staraya Russa

LATVIA   Velikiye   **U.   S.   S.   R.**

LITHUANIA   Luki   Kalinin   *Volga*   Yaroslavl

Dvinsk   Nevel   Rzhev   Gorki   R.

EAST   Vilna   Polotsk   **Moscow**

PRUSSIA   Vitebsk   Orsha   Vyasma

Minsk   Smolensk

Warsaw

Brest-   *Pripet*   Zhlobin   Bryansk   Tula   Penza

Litovsk   R.   Gomel   Orel

P O L A N D   Tambov   R.

Sarny   Korosten   Kursk   Voronezh   **Saratov**

Lwow   Kiev

Shepetovka   Kharkov   *Volga*

Zhmerinka   Vinnitsa   Smela

CARPATHIAN   Dniester   Kremenchug   Donets   **Stalingrad**

Krivoi Rog   R.   Don

Jassy   Bessarabia   **Dniepropetrovsk**

Zaporozhye   Taganrog   Astra-

Odessa   Nikolayev   khan

R U M A N I A   **Rostov**   Elista

PEREKOP   *Sea of Azov*   CASPIAN SEA

ISTHMUS   Armavir

Bucharest   CRIMEA   Maikop   Mozdok

Danube R.   Constanta   **Sevastopol**   Kerch

BULGARIA   Novorossisk   Tuapse   Makhach-

kala

B L A C K   S E A   CAUCASUS MTS.

TURKEY

THE RUSSIAN COUNTEROFFENSIVES OF 1942–1944

and in most of these categories more than half of the total production had come in the first eight months of 1943. During the same period the United States had completed 2380 fighting ships and auxiliaries, and 13,000 landing craft.

By the close of 1943, too, the German submarine campaign had been overcome. A number of factors had contributed to the defeat of the U-boats. Hundreds of destroyer-escort ships and corvettes had been built in the United States and Canada, and these had given increased protection to convoys. More effective patrols off the American coast and long-range patrol planes, operating from Newfoundland, Labrador, Greenland, Iceland, and the British Isles, had driven the submarines back into the mid-Atlantic. In this region, beyond the range of airplanes, squadrons of submarines, so-called wolf-packs, had for a time been very destructive, but eventually small escort aircraft carriers had been built and attached to convoys. Many new devices and techniques—radar, for instance—for detecting planes and ships had also been perfected by scientists and put into use. Despite German submarines, therefore, by the spring of 1944 tremendous quantities of all types of military supplies and millions of men had been gathered in Great Britain for the projected invasion of western Europe.

One of Hitler's boasts was that he had converted Europe into an impregnable fortress. But, as President Roosevelt pointed out, it was "a fortress without a roof," a fact which the Allied air forces had disclosed with increasing clarity from 1942 on. In that year the RAF had adopted the technique of saturation night bombing, that is, bombing by a large number of planes over a single target in a short space of time. On the night of May 30, 1942, for example, some 1043 bombers had dropped 1500 tons of bombs on Cologne in less than two hours, and in the hundred days following the Cologne raid, there had been 43 large-scale raids on German cities by forces of from 200 to 600 bombers.

During 1942 the tide of plane production had definitely and overwhelmingly turned in favor of the Allies. By the close of that year, British production was about equal to that of Germany and Italy combined, while American production was running ahead of that of all the Axis powers taken together. Furthermore, there had been a great increase in the production of heavy four-motor bombers capable of carrying bomb loads three times greater than earlier planes. By September, planes were dropping on German targets the so-called block-busters, huge two-ton and four-ton bombs which greatly increased the destruction. In 1942, the United States Army Air Force had also joined in operations against Nazi Europe.

In 1943 the Allied air forces had greatly increased their bombing offensives. Thousands of tons of bombs had been dropped on the German industrial cities of Essen, Düsseldorf, Cologne, Hamburg, Wilhelmshaven,

Rostock, Lübeck, Berlin, Nuremberg, Munich, Karlsruhe, Mainz, and Frankfort; on the French cities of Lille, Le Creusot, and Rennes, and on the industrial suburbs of Paris; on the submarine bases of Lorient, St. Nazaire, Brest, Cherbourg, Dunkirk, and Rotterdam. In the first half of 1943 the RAF alone had dropped thirty-five times the weight of bombs dropped by the Luftwaffe over Britain in all its 1940–1941 attacks. In ten days beginning on the night of July 24, the RAF and the USAAF in eight raids had dropped upon the single city of Hamburg a total bomb tonnage far greater than that dropped on London during a period of nearly a year at the height of the Nazi air blitz. Hamburg had been nearly eliminated as a functioning port and production center. The destruction of power plants, railway junctions, canals, synthetic-petroleum and synthetic-rubber plants, and factories producing munitions, airplane engines, and aircraft undoubtedly had constituted a "softening up" of Germany.

At a conference at Teheran (November 28–December 1, 1943) Churchill, Roosevelt, and Stalin and their military staffs had mapped out plans for a concerted attack on Hitler's Fortress Europe during 1944. According to the announcement made at the close of their conference, they had agreed upon the scope and timing of operations which would be undertaken from the east, the west, and the south with the aim of annihilating the German forces. "No power on earth," they proclaimed, "can prevent our destroying the German armies by land, their U-boats by sea, and their war plants from the air. Our attacks will be relentless and increasing."

The Allies during the ensuing months devoted themselves to preparation, organization, and the further aerial softening-up of Fortress Europe. Many changes were made in the high command to make ready for the coming invasion of Europe, but only a few can be mentioned here. General Eisenhower, the successful supreme Allied commander in the Mediterranean, was appointed supreme Allied commander in western Europe, and General Sir Harold Alexander was made commander-in-chief of all Allied forces in Italy. General Montgomery was transferred from command of the British Eighth Army in Italy to command of all British ground forces in western Europe, and General Omar N. Bradley was made the senior commander of the United States ground forces in the same area. General Clark continued to command the Anglo-American Fifth Army in Italy, but General Sir Oliver Leese was put in command of the British Eighth Army, which was operating on the Adriatic flank of the Italian front. The Germans, for their part, appointed Field Marshal Rommel to head the Nazi anti-invasion command. Under his direction efforts were made by the Germans to strengthen still further the already "impregnable" Atlantic Wall.

Against this Atlantic Wall, on June 6, 1944, American, British, and Canadian troops stormed ashore on the beaches of Normandy as the vanguard of the greatest amphibious operation in all history. Brought to the coast in an invasion fleet of 3200 transports and landing craft, they were supported from the sea by 800 fighting craft of all sizes and from the skies by thousands of planes. While landings from the sea were made in four separate areas on the coast north of Bayeux and Caen, three divisions of Allied troops were also dropped behind the beaches by parachutes and gliders in what was probably the greatest air-borne operation yet undertaken. By the close of D-day, that is, at the end of the first twenty-four

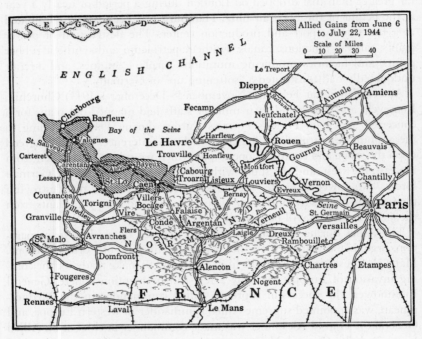

THE BATTLE OF NORMANDY, 1944

hours, 250,000 Allied troops had been successfully landed in Normandy. Their immediate task was to hold and consolidate their beachheads. This they did. By June 8 contact had been established between the sea-borne and air-borne troops. Despite the much-vaunted strength of Hitler's Atlantic Wall, it had been successfully breached. Allied sea, air, and land forces had carried through the "greatest and most successful combined operation of its type in military history."

It had been feared by many in Allied countries—and confidently believed by the Nazis—that any invasion force which might land on the beaches of western Europe could be wiped out or driven into the sea before it could consolidate its position or secure the necessary heavy mechanized equipment for a successful advance inland. What the outcome would have been had the Germans immediately rushed their armored divisions to the Allied bridgehead in Normandy can only be conjectured, for this they failed to do. Apparently Hitler and the high command believed that the landing in Normandy did not represent the main Allied effort. To this misconception the Allies had contributed in several ways. The pre-invasion bombings—carried on for a considerable period before D-day—had been deliberately scattered along the whole northwestern coast of France so as to give no accurate indication of the location of the projected landings. Then before and during D-day feints were made from England toward the Pas de Calais area by General George S. Patton's American Third Army, and on D-day an Allied naval demonstration was also made off that same coast. A feint was even made toward Norway by Allied planes and troops in Scotland. For weeks after D-day the Germans, in doubt as to the real purpose of the Allies, failed to transfer their troops from the Pas de Calais area to meet the invasion forces in Normandy.

It had also been feared in Allied circles that without an adequate harbor in Allied hands it would be impossible to land the heavy tanks and armored equipment that were necessary for a successful advance inland against an enemy who could easily and quickly move up such equipment over his land-based lines of communication. The ineffectiveness of landing forces without adequate harbor facilities had been strongly driven home by the Allied failures in Norway in 1940. And the terrible casualties which might accompany any attempt to capture a well-fortified harbor in enemy hands —even a futile attempt—had been startlingly revealed by an Allied attack on Dieppe in August, 1942. Furthermore, the disastrous effects which an Atlantic storm might have on the landing of men and supplies on open beaches was well recognized. To overcome these Allied handicaps, two artificial harbors had been constructed in England. Floating breakwaters and piers were towed across the Channel to anchorages off the newly won beaches in Normandy, and on the day after D-day thousands of men began constructing the harbors, which were designed for a total capacity larger than that of Cherbourg. Although a terrific storm on June 19–22 wrecked one of these harbors, the other continued to function and provided sheltered anchorages for Allied shipping and piers to expedite the flow of supplies and men. In the first four weeks after D-day more than 1,000,000 men, 183,500 vehicles, and 650,000 tons of supplies were landed despite German submarines, aircraft, mines, and other defensive weapons.

The Liberation of France and Belgium

Meanwhile, the Allied military operations had been proceeding ashore. In these operations the British and Canadian forces had been assigned a role which was primarily defensive while that of the Americans was offensive. The British seized and held the vital area around Caen, the hinge of the whole Allied position in Normandy. They thus protected the flank of the American troops, who struck inland across the peninsula and on June 18 reached the sea on the west side of the Cotentin peninsula. Cherbourg, on the tip of the peninsula, was thus isolated from the main German forces, and the American troops next stormed that city, which surrendered on June 26. Though the harbor had been wrecked by the Germans, Allied engineers here—as in Naples earlier—were soon at work preparing it for the use of Allied shipping. The capture of this important port made more secure the Allied foothold in Normandy and made more unlikely the success of any German attempt to expel the invaders from the Continent.

But for a time it seemed that the Nazis might manage to hold the Allies within the peninsula. For a month the latter made little apparent progress. Time was required, of course, for the Allies to build up reserves of men and matériel on the mainland. Nevertheless, even after they had landed more than a million men and hundreds of thousands of tons of supplies, the Germans continued successfully to localize the fighting within a small area. Allied casualties were heavy, and progress for a time was measured by yards. In the seven weeks after D-day the Allies suffered 105,765 casualties and gained only some 4800 square miles of territory.

Although the German armies appeared to be holding the Allies successfully, some disaffection and anti-Hitler sentiment had developed in the Reich, as indicated by an attempt to assassinate the Führer and the general staff on July 20, 1944. The plot was the work of a considerable number of military leaders, including a few generals on the general staff, and of certain key civilians. Although some of the generals present at the time of the bomb explosion died as the result of their injuries, Hitler himself escaped serious injury. The Nazis struck swiftly to purge Germany of anti-Hitler elements and to gain further control of the armed forces. Himmler, head of the Gestapo, was at once appointed "to make sure that there would be no second July 20." A court of honor was instituted "to inquire into the antecedents of field marshals and generals of the army to find out who took part in any way in the attempt," and during the succeeding weeks nearly 5000 persons—including some general staff officers and field commanders —were executed.

Meanwhile, on July 18 General Bradley's American First Army ulti-

THE LIBERATION OF PARIS IN 1944

General Charles de Gaulle and General Jacques Leclerc leading a parade on the Champs-Élysées.

mately had captured strategically important St. Lô. It next blasted a corridor through the German lines between St. Lô and Periers to Coutances (July 25–28), and then held the gap open while armored divisions of General Patton's American Third Army poured through. Suddenly the entire situation in France was changed from a war of position to a blitzkrieg. American spearheads at once struck south across the Breton peninsula, which was cut off when they reached the Loire River near Nantes on August 6. Other spearheads turned westward and, since the Germans had practically stripped Brittany to send reinforcements to Normandy, they met little opposition. The ports of St. Malo, Brest, Lorient, and St. Nazaire were soon invested.

The American armies now had plenty of room in which to maneuver, and spearheads were soon striking eastward toward Paris and northward toward the Seine. In conjunction with the British forces to the north an attempt was made to encircle the German Seventh Army southwest of Caen, but the Nazi armored units escaped, though German casualties were estimated at between 50,000 and 100,000. The remnants of the German Seventh Army next endeavored to withdraw across the Seine and to establish a new line behind that river. But by August 27 the Allies had established four bridgeheads across the Seine, and these obviously made such a line untenable.

While the Germans were thus hurriedly withdrawing and the Allies swiftly advancing in northern France, another blow was struck (August 15) at the German positions in that country when the American Seventh Army, consisting of American, French, and British forces, landed from the sea and from the air along a 100-mile stretch of the Mediterranean coast of France between Cannes and Toulon. Their purpose was to advance up the Rhone valley and sever communications between the Germans in France and those in Italy, and they met relatively light opposition. Within two weeks the important ports of Toulon and Marseilles were both captured. Although this Allied landing in the south came too late to be of much assistance to the operations in northern France, it did serve to demoralize still further the German defense.

To that demoralization the French themselves also contributed. Almost from the moment of the Allied landings in Normandy the French Forces of the Interior (FFI), or the *Maquis* as they were sometimes called, had been active in sabotage. German lines of communications had been disrupted, munition dumps blown up, troops ambushed, villages and towns wrested from Nazi hands. On August 12 the commander of the FFI had urged the underground units to strike hard at once to prevent reinforcements from reaching the Germans, and his forces had responded with alacrity. By August 22, it was announced, twenty-two departments in Brit-

tany and southern France had been liberated by the FFI, and all roads leading into Italy had come into their control. Everywhere the French tricolor
was being hoisted.

The most spectacular uprising of the FFI came in Paris, where a general
insurrection was ordered on August 19, when the Allied forces had advanced to within a score of miles of the capital. After four days of fighting
the German garrison in Paris was defeated. Although on August 23 the
German commander in the capital sought an armistice, on the next day
he repudiated it, resumed fighting, and threatened to destroy the city. The
FFI thereupon requested Allied aid, and General Patton sent to their
assistance the French General Jacques Leclerc with a French tank division
and some American troops. On August 25 the French capital, after four
years of Nazi occupation, was once more free.

But these stirring events in Paris did not retard the advance of the Allied
armies, which rushed to the north and the east. The very tactics that four
years earlier had swept the Germans on to Paris—plunging tank columns,
swarms of planes, mobile artillery, motorized assault forces—were now
turned against them. "Speed and power were welded into a weapon of
destruction. Tank columns kept thrusting far ahead, and it seemed a
mystery how they kept engines fueled, guns firing, men fed, and repairs
made." The roads of northern France, once the Allied vanguard had passed,
resembled vast conveyor belts, with trucks moving in endless streams, one
column going up and the other rolling back. Battlefields of the First World
War—the Marne, Château-Thierry, Verdun, Soissons, the Somme, Laon;
Reims, the Argonne, Sedan, Namur, Liége—where forces had been locked
in combat for weeks or months in the struggle of 1914–1918, were reached
and swiftly passed. Brussels was liberated on September 3 and the important port of Antwerp a few hours later. By the middle of September the
Allied armies had reached the German frontier in Belgium and Luxembourg and were facing the strong Nazi West Wall.

On the night of September 17 a bold attempt was made to outflank the
West Wall in the north when a large Allied air-borne force was dropped
in the Netherlands near Eindhoven, Nijmegen, and Arnhem. For days
these troops held on against heavy odds while the British Second Army in
Belgium battled its way northward toward them. Although the British
succeeded in moving the front up through Eindhoven and Nijmegen to the
south bank of the Lek River (the Dutch Rhine), German opposition was
so strong that they were unable to establish a bridgehead across this last river
barrier south of Arnhem. On the nights of September 25 and 26 the air-
borne force near the latter city was finally withdrawn, but, of the more
than 6500 men originally landed there, only 2000 got back. The failure of
this spectacular effort to outflank the West Wall appeared to leave the Allies

no alternative but to blast their way through the heavily defended, skill-fully constructed line. But that task was part of the battle of Germany, which is discussed later in this chapter.

At the close of what may be called the second battle of France, the com-bined operations of the Allied armies and the French Forces of the Interior had liberated nearly all of France, Belgium, and Luxembourg, and a part of the Netherlands. They had cost the Germans, according to Allied head-quarters, at least 750,000 men killed, wounded, and captured. Approxi-mately 400,000 prisoners had been taken, not counting the forces trapped in various invested ports. At the close of the battle the Allied forces stood, roughly speaking, on the German frontier from the Lek River in the north to the southern boundary of Luxembourg, and then on the west bank of the Moselle River south to the Belfort gap and the Swiss frontier.

The Collapse of Hitler's Satellite States

Meanwhile, in the east, terrific drives were being made by the Soviet armies on various sectors of their two-thousand-mile front extending from the Arctic to the Black Sea. Although at times during the summer and fall of 1944 the Russians were conducting several offensives simultaneously, for the sake of convenience and clarity each drive will be discussed as a unit as it was waged to the close of the year. In a general way, the eastern front was divided into four major sectors: (1) the Finnish front, extending from the Arctic to the Gulf of Finland, northwest of Leningrad; (2) the northern Russian front, extending from the Gulf of Finland southward to Vitebsk; (3) the central Russian front, confronting the German Fatherland Line and extending roughly from Vitebsk southward to the Pripet marshes; and (4) the southern Russian front, extending from the Pripet River west of the marshes south to Jassy in Bessarabia and then east to the Dniester River.[1]

On June 10, only four days after D-day in France, the Russians launched a strong offensive against the Finnish lines on the Karelian Isthmus. Nine days later the Finnish Mannerheim Line was breached, and on the next day Viborg (Viipuri) was captured. When it became obvious that Ger-many could not send aid to the Finns, President Ryti, who was committed to a continuance of the war, was forced to resign, and Field Marshall Man-nerheim was elected to succeed him. After the new government, on Russia's insistance, had broken relations with the Reich and had demanded the withdrawal of German troops from Finland, an armistice was signed on September 19 by the Soviet Union and Great Britain, acting on behalf of all

[1] See map on page 713.

the United Nations which were at war with Finland. The war was ended on that front.

Three days after the capture of Viborg, the second Russian offensive of the summer of 1944 was launched on the central front against the German Fatherland Line. With the fall of Minsk on July 3, the German defense system in White Russia was broken, and the weight and speed of the Russian offensive thereafter for a time swept aside all Nazi efforts to halt it. During August the Russians pushed on toward Warsaw but in the face of ever-stiffening resistance. The farther the Russians advanced, of course—and they had already advanced some four hundred miles on this front—the greater became their problem of supply and reinforcement, especially since the gauge of the railways in Poland had to be adjusted to accommodate Soviet rolling stock. Nevertheless, on September 14 they reached the Vistula and captured Praga, the Warsaw suburb on the east bank of that river. They failed, however, to establish a bridgehead across the Vistula, which the Germans were determined to hold as the last strong line of defense against an invasion of central Germany from the east.

One tragic result of the Russian failure to force the Vistula at this time came in Warsaw. As early as August 1, the Polish Home Army in Warsaw, an underground organization commanded by General Bor,[2] had risen against the Germans in that city. Whether General Bor's purpose was to liberate the city in the name of the Polish government in exile before the Russians reached Warsaw or whether he expected the speed of the Russian advance to continue so that aid would soon be forthcoming in the battle to free the Polish capital, is a matter of dispute. But long before the Russians had reached the Vistula, the Germans had launched strong tank attacks against the Polish Home Army. The failure of the Russians to force the Vistula again sealed the fate of the Polish capital for the time being. On October 2 the Home Army in that city gave up the struggle and surrendered to the Germans, who claimed that 200,000 Poles had lost their lives in the uprising. Many accused the Soviet government of deliberately failing to succor Warsaw in order to discredit and bring pressure upon the Polish government in exile, which was unwilling to recognize the Polish-Soviet boundary established in 1939.

However that may be, when the battle line in Poland became somewhat stabilized in September, it extended roughly from East Prussia to the Carpathians along the east banks of the Narew and Vistula rivers. Reserves of men and supplies would have to be built up and lines of communication

[2] General Bor's real name was Komorowski. He had commanded a cavalry brigade in the campaign of September, 1939, and afterwards he helped to organize the Polish underground army, of which he was appointed commander-in-chief by Premier Sikorski in July, 1943.

and transportation would have to be strengthened before Soviet troops could launch another effective drive on this front. A glance at the map, however, will reveal the vast extent of the Russian gains during some two months of fighting. The Germans had been hurled back in Poland beyond the line from which they had first launched their attack upon Russia in 1941.

The third Russian drive was launched on the northern front late in July. It had two major objectives: to push the Germans out of the Baltic republics and to protect the northern flank of the Soviet armies advancing into Poland. By the close of the year the Germans had been expelled from Latvia, from Estonia except for the Windau peninsula between the Gulf of Riga and the Baltic, and from Lithuania except for the district about Memel.

On the front south of the Pripet marshes the Soviet armies launched their fourth major offensive early in July. This offensive had two prongs. One struck southwestward with the apparent purpose of protecting the left flank of the armies advancing on the central front and of occupying Galicia with its extensive grain fields and oil wells. The second prong eventually turned southeastward into the Balkans with the purpose of driving the Germans out of that whole region, which Russia had for generations sought to make her own sphere of influence. By August 5, Soviet troops, driving southwestward, had captured Cholm, Lublin, Jaroslav, Przemysl, and Lwow (Lemberg), had taken the richest part of the Galician oil fields—thus depriving Hitler of one of his sources of natural petroleum—and Russian patrols were reported to be within thirty miles of Cracow, the gateway to central Germany. But as in 1915, so in 1944, the German defenses before that important industrial and strategic city held.

Stopped on the west, the Soviet armies on August 20 next launched a drive southeastward from Jassy in Bessarabia. The effect of the Russian advance was immediate in Bucharest. On August 23, King Michael dismissed the Antonescu government; appointed a new cabinet headed by his former aide, General Senatescu, and including both Maniu and Bratianu; ordered Rumanian troops to cease hostilities with the United Nations; and instructed them instead to fight at the side of the Allied armies to drive the Germans from Rumania and to liberate Transylvania from foreign occupation. Hostilities immediately broke out between German and Rumanian troops in Bucharest and Constanza and in the Ploesti oil fields, but on August 28 the Rumanian high command announced that all German resistance in Bucharest had ended. Three days later the Russians entered the Rumanian capital, and on September 13, 1944, an armistice was signed on behalf of the governments of the Soviet Union, Great Britain, and the United States.

In the meantime, Bulgaria had seen the handwriting on the wall and had been attempting to extricate herself from her position as a German satellite. On August 26 it was announced in Sofia that Bulgaria had withdrawn from the war, and on September 5, after a change in governments, Bulgaria proclaimed that she intended to carry out a "rigorous and unconditional policy of neutrality," that she would disarm all German forces in her territory, and that she considered as invalid her signature of the tripartite and anti-Comintern pacts. But these steps were not sufficient to satisfy Soviet Russia, which on the same day declared war on Bulgaria. The latter thereupon declared war upon Germany and asked Russia for an armistice. On September 16, Sofia was occupied by Soviet troops. On October 28, an armistice was signed with Bulgaria by representatives of the Soviet Union, Great Britain, and the United States. One more Hitler satellite state thus collapsed, and Bulgaria lost her gamble that she could secure Macedonia and Western Thrace by allying herself with Hitler's Third Reich.

The defection of Rumania and Bulgaria made the position of Nazi forces in Greece and the Aegean islands precarious. In September they began to withdraw and to move up the Vardar and Morava valleys toward Hungary. To hasten the Nazi withdrawal from Greece proper and, apparently, to prevent Russia from establishing a sphere of influence in that country, British forces landed at Patras in the northern Peloponnesus on October 4. They encountered only light German resistance as they advanced across the isthmus of Corinth, and ten days later Athens and its port of Piraeus were liberated. The northward advance continued, and with the help of Greek guerrilla forces most of the country was cleared of German troops by early November.

Meanwhile, the military forces of four countries had been co-operating to drive the Germans out of Albania and Yugoslavia. In the latter country patriot armies had never been completely suppressed by the Nazis, and now under the leadership of Marshal Tito they played a valiant role in the liberation of their country. They were assisted from the east by Bulgarian troops under Soviet command, from the Adriatic by British forces which were landed in Albania, Montenegro, and Herzegovina, and in the north by the Russian army moving west from Rumania. On October 20, Belgrade was liberated, and by the end of 1944, Albania, most of the Dalmatian coast, and eastern and southern Yugoslavia had been freed from Nazi domination. Only in the northwest, in Croatia and in Bosnia, did the Germans still retain control.

Farther north Russian and Rumanian armies had struck across the eastern Carpathians and the Transylvanian Alps into Hungary. With Soviet troops only fifty miles from Budapest, Horthy decided to seek an armistice. But Szalasy, leader of the Nazi Arrow Cross organization in Hungary, opposed such a step and was supported by German troops which had already occupied the capital. On December 16, Horthy was forced to resign and was interned in Germany. Szalasy thereupon headed a new government, appointed a regency council, and in an order of the day to the army announced: "Either we destroy or we will be destroyed." That the latter would be the outcome seemed indicated by the course of succeeding events, for the Russians continued to advance in Hungary and on November 4 the heavy guns of Soviet forces began to shell Budapest. The Nazis were determined to fight to the end in the Hungarian capital, however, and, though the city was ultimately surrounded and large sections of it were occupied by Russian troops, it was not until February 13, 1945, that Budapest was captured. Meanwhile, a Hungarian provisional government, chosen by a national assembly of delegates elected in the liberated territory, had announced a liberal political and agrarian policy and had promised to assist in the destruction of Hitlerism. On December 29 it had declared war on Germany. It also sought an armistice with the Allies, and on January 20, 1945, such a document was signed with Hungary by Russia, Great Britain, and the United States on behalf of the United Nations.

By this time, too, the liberation of Czechoslovakia had been begun. On the north Soviet troops from Poland had begun driving across the Carpathians into Slovakia and Ruthenia as early as September, 1944. Simultaneously other Soviet forces had advanced northward from Hungary. By the close of October, Ruthenia had been freed, and the Russians had begun to move westward into Slovakia. Operations here, however, were closely related to those in Hungary, and it was only after the fall of Budapest that substantial gains were made. But on April 4, 1945, the Russians captured Bratislava, the capital of Slovakia, and thus put the last and weakest of Hitler's satellite states out of the war.

Germany's Last Offensive

In the autumn of 1918, when it seemed likely that the Allies might soon be able to invade the Fatherland, German military leaders had forced the civilian government to sue for an armistice. If the decision had been left to the German high command in 1944, it is possible that in the fall of that year Germany might have again asked for a cessation of hostilities, for militarily the Third Reich was in a much more serious plight than the Kaiser's Germany had been in 1918. But the Nazi leaders well knew that their fate would be sealed when Germany surrendered, and consequently reasoned that they personally had everything to gain and nothing much to lose by forcing the German armies to fight on. The Nazi forces would therefore have to be utterly defeated and the Reich overrun by the Allies

Sovfoto

FROM STALINGRAD TO CENTRAL EUROPE

A Red Army patrol in the outskirts of Stalingrad, and Red Army troops
crossing the Danube on the way to Budapest.

before hostilities would cease. And before Germany could be invaded from the west, the allegedly impregnable West Wall would have to be smashed.

In the closing months of 1944 the Allies prepared for their eventual frontal attack. They lessened their supply problem by opening the Scheldt so that the extensive harbor facilities and railway connections of Antwerp could be utilized by the Allied armies facing the lower Rhineland. They cleared most of Alsace and Lorraine of German troops and reached the upper Rhine at Strasbourg. They captured Aachen and thus proved that important strategic bulwarks of the West Wall could be taken. The next stage in Allied activity in the west seemed likely to be a terrific smash across the Roer and Meuse rivers onto the Cologne plain. In fact, on December 16, 1944, General Bradley was at the supreme headquarters at Versailles for a conference on the details of the planned American winter offensive.

For some weeks, however, Hitler had been planning a counter-blow against the Allies, aimed at capturing Antwerp, driving a wedge between British and American armies, and annihilating the Allied forces to be surrounded in the area of Aachen-Liége. To the German commanders Hitler declared: "For months our entire industry has been working solely for this at the cost of the Eastern Front.... We must attack and start a war of movement once more." Surprise and speed, he declared, would be the most important factors, and the operation would be supported, he promised, by several thousand of the best and most modern German fighters which would secure, at least temporarily, air supremacy.

Thanks, in part, to their own careful planning and, in part, to failures of the United States military command, the Germans certainly achieved surprise when on December 16 they threw 250,000 men, 1200 tanks, and hundreds of new jet planes and V-bombs against a thin American line in the Ardennes held by only six divisions. German armored spearheads smashed through broken, difficult country and achieved a major breakthrough, advancing farther in a week than the Allied troops struggling toward Cologne had moved in the preceding three months of hard fighting. Despite the heroic resistance of American forces, especially at St. Vith and Bastogne, the Nazis drove on until they were within three miles of the Meuse near Dinant and Givet and less than that distance from the headquarters of the American First Army with its huge supply dumps and tanks of precious gasoline.

The Allied answer to this last gamble of the Germans was "the greatest and most rapid mobilization in history." All available reserves in the Central Army Group were used to strengthen the flanks of the penetration, and troops of the Northern Army Group were deployed to hold the line of the Meuse and the vital Liége area. When the German advance severed telephone communications between General Bradley on the south of the bulge and the headquarters of his First and Ninth Armies, the command of these armies and their supporting air forces was at once shifted to General Montgomery to the north of the bulge. The latter was able to contain the Germans and to prevent their advance upon Liége. At the same time the American Third Army was moved against the southern flank of the bulge and given the task of relieving the forces at Bastogne, which had refused to surrender. At the tip of the salient other American forces, aided by some units of the British Second Army, blunted the German attack and then turned it back. After the first week of the offensive, the weather cleared, and thousands of American and British planes assisted the Allied ground forces by bombing German concentrations and supply lines.

In less than two weeks the tide had turned. On December 28 Bastogne was liberated, and by the end of December nearly a third of the lost territory had been recovered. At the end of a month's hard fighting most of the bulge had been eliminated, though it was not until the end of January, 1945, that the lines were back where they had been on December 16. Both sides had lost heavily in men and equipment. Although the Germans had gained an initial tactical success and had imposed a delay of almost six weeks on the main Allied offensive in the West, they had failed to capture their primary objectives. They had lost 220,000 men, including 110,000 prisoners, and more than 1400 tanks and assault guns. To carry out the operation, moreover, the German high command had weakened the Reich in strategic reserves and resources which were needed to meet the powerful Soviet offensive which had begun.

The Battle of Germany

For, before the Belgian bulge had been completely obliterated, the Soviet armies had launched their expected winter offensive in Poland. The preceding four months had been utilized by the Russians to repair roads and railways through an area some 250 miles deep which they had conquered in their summer offensive of 1944. Time had been required, too, to bring up new weapons and men and to accumulate sufficient supplies for an extended offensive. At the close of their summer operations in Poland, it will be recalled, the Russians had stood roughly on a line running from the East Prussian frontier along the Narew and Vistula rivers to the Carpathians. On January 12, 1945, Stalin unleashed his new attack, which the Germans characterized as the "greatest of all time." Everywhere the Soviet forces, estimated at more than 3,000,000 men, seemed to move irresistibly forward.

By the middle of March the Russians had invaded Germany and held a line extending along the Oder River from its mouth, opposite Stettin, up to the Neisse River and along the latter toward the Czechoslovak frontier.

Silesia, except for beseiged Breslau, had been occupied, depriving the Germans of their second most important arsenal. Except for isolated forces near Gdynia, Danzig, and Königsberg, the Baltic had been cleared of Germans from Latvia to Stettin. According to Marshal Stalin, 800,000 Germans had been killed and more than 350,000 captured.

The next powerful blow against the Nazi homeland was delivered in the west, from which the German high command had transferred some twenty divisions to bolster the Reich's defense along the Oder River. With a decided superiority in men, supplies, mechanized equipment, and air power, the Western Allies—once the Belgian bulge had been eliminated—prepared to drive out or destroy the German armies on the left bank of the Rhine. Preceded and accompanied by terrific RAF and AAF blows, the initial attack was launched on February 8 by Canadian and British troops southeast of Nijmegen, who captured Cleve and Goch in the lower Rhineland. Immediately thereafter, on February 23, the American Ninth and First Armies swung into action, forced their way across the Roer, penetrated the German defense system, and made the whole West Wall vulnerable to envelopment from behind.

In the first of the ensuing envelopment movements the American Ninth Army cut behind the West Wall to the north, and on March 3 met the Canadians pushing southward. With the capture of much-battered Cologne three days later by the American First Army, the left bank of the Rhine from that city to the Netherlands was practically cleared of German troops.

The second enveloping movement began when forces of the American First Army struck up the Rhine from Cologne. So swiftly did they move that on March 8 they seized intact the Ludendorff bridge across the Rhine at Remagen just before the Germans planned to destroy it. This unexpected conquest was at once exploited by General Courtney H. Hodges to establish a bridgehead for the Allies firmly and securely on the east bank of the Rhine. In the meantime, the American Third Army west of the Moselle had been driving toward Coblenz, and on March 7 armored units reached the Rhine below that city. A junction was made by forces of the Third and First Armies with the result that the Rhine was cleared of German forces from Cologne to Coblenz.

The third of these enveloping movements came when the Third Army quickly drove to the west bank of the Moselle, crossed the river, and then slashed behind the German forces defending the Saar and the Palatinate against a frontal attack by the American Seventh Army. By March 23 the rich Saar Basin, the Reich's third most important coal and industrial district, had been seized, and German forces had been captured or driven out of the Palatinate except for a small bridgehead across from Karlsruhe.

The battle of the West Wall was one of the greatest Allied victories of

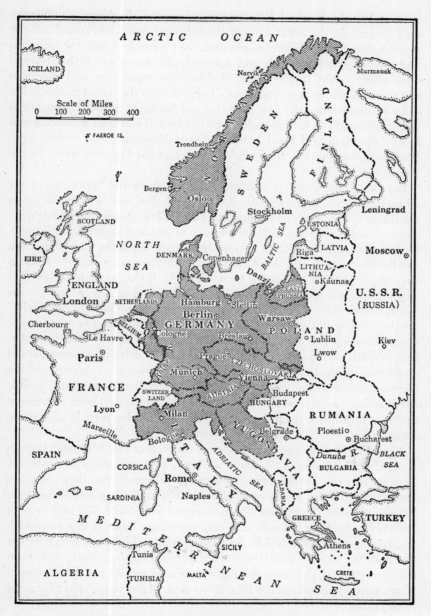

GERMANY AND GERMAN-HELD TERRITORY, JANUARY 1, 1945

the war. In a single month following the opening of the American offensive on February 23, the Allies had smashed through what was considered the world's most formidable defense system, over territory which the Germans had claimed was impassable and against fortifications which they boasted were impregnable. In the course of this achievement they had destroyed five German armies as military units. For 250 miles the Allied armies at last stood on the Rhine—the first time that any invading armies had achieved this feat since the days of Napoleon. Field Marshal Karl von Rundstedt was hastily removed, and Field Marshal Albert Kesselring was rushed from Italy to replace him as commander-in-chief of the German forces in the west.

But the Allies were not content merely to drive the Nazis out of the Rhineland. The American First Army already had one bridgehead across the Rhine at Remagen; on the night of March 22 the American Third Army stormed across the river in force south of Mainz and established a second. On the next night the Rhine was bridged again when the Canadian First, the British Second, and the American Ninth Armies crossed the river in the vicinity of Wesel, while the First Allied Air-borne Army in the greatest single air-borne operation of the war landed beyond the Rhine on the Westphalian plain. Thousands of Allied airplanes provided an "umbrella" for the crossing of the lower Rhine and struck behind the German lines at concentration points and communication centers. Within a week the American Seventh and the French First also joined the drive into Germany and established bridgeheads north and south of Mannheim. Apparently the German armies in the west, weakened to bolster the eastern front against the Russians, were powerless to hold the line. What had been considered the most formidable defense system in the world—the West Wall and the Rhine combined—was utterly destroyed.

As in France after the German break-through of the Weygand Line in June, 1940, there was in Germany in April, 1945, no longer any coherent front in the west. The German armies there did not retreat; they collapsed. During the first two weeks of April the Allies in the west took more than 550,000 prisoners. The Nazis who had started the Second World War with a blitzkrieg into Poland now saw that war being brought to a close with a blitzkrieg within the Reich. And the very superhighways which Hitler had built for his own armies were used to speed up the Allied advance. In less than three weeks from the night it crossed the Rhine, the American Ninth Army had crossed the Elbe River near Magdeburg, only fifty miles from Berlin.

Meanwhile, a number of enveloping movements had been successfully carried out by the Allied commanders. Spearheads of the American First and Third Armies enveloped the great industrial city of Frankfort, which

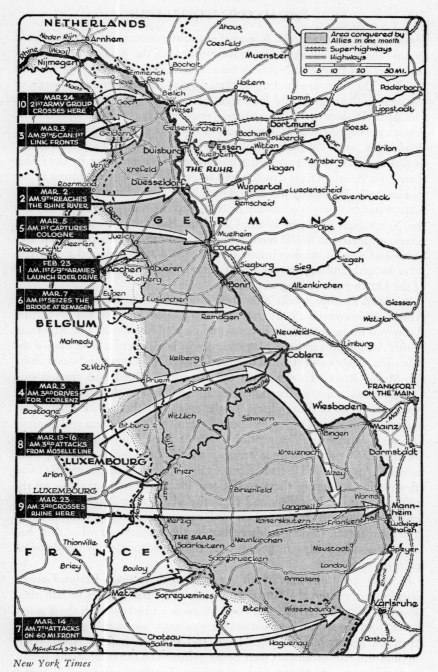

Ten Steps in Victory of the Rhine

was occupied on March 29. A second encircling movement was completed around the Reich's most valuable industrial area, the Ruhr, when units of the American First and Ninth Armies made a junction near Lippstadt on April 1. The Germans had made their largest concentrations of troops in the west in this region, and hard fighting ensued within the Ruhr pocket. On April 18, however, all organized resistance in the Ruhr ceased. The Americans captured 325,000 prisoners in the pocket, which made the Ruhr debacle the worst German defeat in the war, worse even than the disaster at Stalingrad. A third enveloping movement was carried out by the Canadian First Army, which struck north to cut off the German forces in the Netherlands. It reached the Ems River across from Emden and with the help of paratroopers successfully drove across the northern Netherlands to the North Sea. By April 19 the Canadians had compressed the German forces, estimated at 80,000 men, into the small but densely populated area south and west of the Ijsselmeer. In that area Amsterdam and Rotterdam were located, and apparently the Germans planned to deprive the Allies of the Dutch ports as long as possible.

By April 21, four weeks after their crossing of the Rhine in force, the Allies had conquered a large part of western Germany. The British Second Army was in the suburbs of Bremen and close to Hamburg. The American Ninth Army had captured Magdeburg and held a bridgehead east of the Elbe. The American First had captured Halle and Leipzig and stood along the Mulde River. To the south the American Third had crossed into Czechoslovakia, and farther south the American Seventh had captured the Nazi shrine city of Nuremberg. To the southwest the French First Army had taken Stuttgart. During this period German losses in men and matériel had been enormous. The central group of American armies alone had taken 842,864 prisoners since crossing the Rhine. During the first three weeks of April, Allied fliers had practically eliminated the Luftwaffe as an effective force. During these weeks, too, incontrovertible evidence of the inhuman cruelty, brutality, and depravity of German Nazi and military leaders was found in the prison and concentration camps captured by American forces. Claims made earlier by the Russians of what they had found in similar camps in the east were fully substantiated by the discoveries in the west.

In order not to interfere with the Russian drive upon Berlin, General Eisenhower ordered the American Ninth and First Armies to halt their advance at the Elbe and Mulde rivers to await a junction with the Russian forces from the east, a junction which was made by patrols at Torgau on April 25. Meanwhile, during March and the first half of April, while supplies and reinforcements were being gathered on the front facing Berlin, the Soviet armies had been active elsewhere. The Baltic area east of Stettin had been practically cleared of German forces with the capture of Gdynia, Danzig, and Königsberg. In the south, at the same time, Soviet forces had been moving west after their capture of Budapest, and on April 13 they had captured Vienna, the former capital of Austria.

Upon the capture of Vienna the Soviet armies on the Oder at once launched their final drive upon Berlin. On April 21, the assault upon the German capital began. Nazi fanatics called upon the inhabitants of the city to fight to the last man, and the ensuing struggle was bitter and destructive. But the Soviet forces were definitely superior in men and matériel, and they could not be stopped. On April 25, Marshal Gregory Zhukov's First White Russian Army and Marshal Ivan Konev's First Ukrainian Army completed the encirclement of Berlin and thereafter pressed their attack toward the heart of the capital.

The End of the War in Europe

Apparently the Nazis realized that the end was near. On April 24, Heinrich Himmler asked the Swedish government to arrange for him to meet General Eisenhower in order that he might surrender all German forces on the western front. But this offer, Himmler stipulated, was only for the Western Allies and did not include Russia. On April 26, the United States and Great Britain informed Sweden that the only acceptable terms were unconditional surrender to the three Allied governments on all fronts, and stated that the German forces should surrender to local commanders in the field. The final Nazi attempt to split the Allies thus failed.

The first of the ensuing mass surrenders occurred in Italy, where the American Fifth Army and the British Eighth Army had already launched a vigorous attack designed to drive the Germans beyond the Alps. The coveted key city of Bologna was captured on April 21; three days later the Allies crossed the Po River. Thereafter the Allied advance was swift and general as German opposition disintegrated and anti-Fascist Italian "Partisans" raised the standard of revolt behind the lines. By the end of April all important Italian cities, including Verona, Genoa, Milan, Venice, and Turin, had been liberated by the Allies and the Partisans. The futility of further Nazi resistance was recognized by the supreme German commander in Italy, General Heinrich von Vietinghoff, who on April 29 authorized the signing of an unconditional surrender for all German and Italian Fascist armies in northern Italy and southwestern Austria. The collapse of German resistance in Italy brought the death of Mussolini. On April 28, he and a few former Fascist leaders were captured near Como by Partisans, who quickly tried and executed them. Mussolini's body was taken to Milan, where it was hung by the heels to receive the scorn and vilification of the city's crowds—an ignominious end for the once proud, powerful, and ruthless Duce.

Hitler escaped an end quite so shameful as this. During the last months of the war, however, he had become a mental and physical wreck without the power to make decisions. In his last days, in the bunker beneath his Chancellery garden in Berlin, he blamed the army, the Nazi Party, the German people—everyone but himself—for the catastrophe which was engulfing the fatherland. Finally, on May 1 it was officially announced over the Nazi radio that, fighting to the last against Bolshevism, he had fallen for Germany. Apparently he had committed suicide. On the day before his death, Hitler, it was further announced, had appointed Grand Admiral Karl Doenitz, director of the German U-boat campaign, as his successor. The latter at once declared that he was "resolved to continue the struggle against the Bolsheviks." On May 2, however, the Russians captured Berlin, together with some 150,000 German soldiers, and avenged Stalingrad. On that same day, too, the British Second Army, which had taken Bremen, captured Hamburg and Lübeck. Two days later all German forces in the Netherlands, Denmark, and northwestern Germany, including Helgoland and the Frisian Islands, surrendered to Marshal Montgomery.

In southern Germany, meanwhile, the American Third and Seventh and the French First Armies had been driving steadily eastward into the so-called "National Redoubt." By May 5, Freiburg, Ulm, Regensburg, Augsburg, Munich, Innsbruck, Salzburg, and Berchtesgaden had all been captured, and the American Seventh Army had crossed the Brenner Pass to form a junction with the Fifth in Italy. The American Third Army drove on into Czechoslovakia and by May 6 had captured Pilsen and Karlsbad and was approaching Prague.

With practically all of Germany occupied by Allied forces and with most of the German armies already captured in the field, an all-inclusive unconditional surrender to the Western Allies and Soviet Russia was finally signed at General Eisenhower's headquarters at Reims in the early morning hours of May 7 by General Gustav Jodl on behalf of the German high command. The latter agreed to issue orders to all German military, naval, and air authorities to cease active operations on May 9 at 12:01 A. M. Greenwich time, to remain in positions occupied at that time, and not to scuttle or damage any ship, vessel, or aircraft. This surrender was formally ratified in Berlin on May 8 when a similar document was signed by Field Marshal General Wilhelm Keitel (who had presented the armistice terms to the French in 1940), General Admiral Hans George Friedeburg, and General Hans Jürgen Stumpff, commanders-in-chief respectively of the German army, navy, and air force.

And so Europe's most terrible war was brought to an end. As yet it is impossible to give an accurate picture of the gigantic toll of lives and wealth which it exacted; it will require years to make the necessary investigations and computations. The most reliable estimates of battle casualties placed the death toll at more than ten million men, with perhaps another ten million permanently disabled. The heaviest losses were sustained by Germany and Russia. American battle deaths in the war against the European dictators were placed at more than 160,000. In addition to battle casualties, however, millions of civilians had succumbed to disease or starvation or been murdered in Nazi concentration camps. The monetary costs of the war mounted to astronomical figures. The direct cost of waging the war was estimated at more than one trillion dollars, and to that figure would have to be added the cost of replacing destroyed or damaged property throughout Europe. Russia's loss as the result of the German invasion, for instance, was estimated at more than $100,000,000,000. The war which Hitler unleashed in Europe in September, 1939, undoubtedly took a greater toll of human and material resources than any other conflict in history.

But the Second World War did not end with the armistice in Europe. In 1941 the conflict had become a global war, and even after V-E day the fighting continued in the Far East.

Chapter XXV

JAPAN'S EARLY BLITZKRIEG

AND ULTIMATE COLLAPSE

AS early as 1894 Japan had begun to have dreams of an empire on the Asiatic mainland, and in the twentieth century she had succeeded in extending her economic and political control over extensive areas in Asia. By 1939 she had annexed Korea, established a puppet government in Manchuria, and obtained a strangle hold on China. The outbreak of the Second World War in that year, her military and political leaders thought, afforded Japan an exceptional opportunity to fulfill her long-cherished dream without the successful intervention of the Western powers, and in a highly successful blitzkrieg during 1941–1942 Japan extended her control over the areas which she had long coveted. But, unfortunately for Japan, she had clashed in 1941 with the United States, with the result that she was ultimately crushed by the tremendous industrial resources and naval and military might of that country. Japan emerged from the Second World War completely shorn of the overseas empire which she had so ruthlessly created.

The Situation in the Far East, 1939–1940

At the time Germany invaded Poland, Japan had already been engaged for more than two years in an undeclared war against China. By the opening of the year 1939 the Japanese had captured the great commercial cities of Tientsin, Peiping, Shanghai, Nanking, Hankow, and Canton, and had gained control of most of the main railways of that country. Outside the great cities, however, in practically every "occupied" province, Chinese guerrilla forces were operating only a few miles from the railway lines.

During the first half of 1939 Japanese forces seized the large and valuable Chinese island of Hainan, which dominated the coast of French Indo-China and lay in a position to menace the sea lane from Singapore to Hong Kong, and annexed the Spratley Islands, lying midway between Indo-China and Borneo. By these annexations Japan moved prophetically nearer the Netherlands East Indies, rich in petroleum and rubber.

When Hitler launched his invasion of Poland, Japan declared that she did not intend to become involved in the European conflict, but would "concentrate her efforts upon the settlement of the China affair." The war in Europe, it seemed, would certainly offer the Japanese an opportunity for increased freedom of action in the Far East if they could only force the Chinese Nationalist government to make peace. Events in 1939 demonstrated, however, that the Chinese could fight if they could continue to secure munitions and war supplies in sufficient quantities, but there remained to them only two major avenues of importation—from Indo-China and from Burma. The former was rendered useless when late in 1939 the Japanese cut the Hanoi-Nanning-Kweilin motor road. The second was closed when, after France's collapse in 1940, the Japanese forced Great Britain to suspend the transit of goods to China over the so-called Burma Road.

Germany's successful blitzkrieg in western Europe in May and June, 1940, had pronounced repercussions in the Far East, where Japan at once moved toward establishing her hegemony not only over the East Asiatic mainland but over the South Seas, too. "The present international situation is developing in a manner advantageous to Japan's national policy," declared the Japanese war minister on June 25. "We should not miss the present opportunity or we shall be blamed by posterity." In June, 1940, at the moment when Marshal Pétain was seeking to obtain an armistice with Germany, Japan forced France to agree that Japanese inspectors might be stationed at key points in Indo-China with power to supervise and control all traffic through that French colony. Moreover, Japanese troops moved up to the frontier of Indo-China, Japanese warships began patrolling its coast, and the Tokyo government called to the attention of Hitler and Mussolini Japan's claims for consideration in the disposal of French possessions in the Far East. Japan continued to exert pressure upon France, and eventually, on September 22, 1940, the latter agreed to permit the Japanese to establish three air bases in northern Indo-China and to maintain a limited number of troops at Haiphong, the chief port in that region.

The Immediate Antecedents of Pearl Harbor

With the European powers deeply involved in Hitler's attempt to establish his dominance in Europe, it appeared that the United States constituted the chief obstacle to Japan's dream of empire. As early as April, 1939, the former, by transferring the American fleet from the Atlantic to the Pacific, had taken one step to indicate disapproval of Tokyo's apparent determination to become more aggressive. Then, on July 26, as a step to place the United States in a position to use economic pressure, if necessary, to retard

Japan's plan for the "new order in East Asia," the American state department had given the six months' notice necessary to abrogate the existing Japanese-American commercial treaty. It was well known that for some time the United States had been the economic "lifeline" for Japan in her effort to conquer China. Four days after the French had been forced to admit the Japanese armed forces into Indo-China, President Roosevelt on September 26, 1940, placed an embargo on the export of all scrap steel and iron except to the western hemisphere and Great Britain. According to the Japanese press this American embargo made inevitable a clash between Japan and the United States. If Japanese expansionists considered that war was inevitable, then it must have been clear to them that such a war must be fought in the not distant future, for in 1940 the United States had embarked upon the building of a powerful "two-ocean" navy.

Japan's move in the diplomatic chess game came at once. On September 27, 1940, in Berlin, representatives of Germany, Italy, and Japan signed a ten-year military alliance in which they undertook "to assist one another with all political, economic, and military means when one of the three is attacked by a power at present not involved in the European war or in the Chinese-Japanese conflict." A second move came six months later when, on April 13, 1941, the Japanese and Soviet governments signed a five-year pact of nonaggression and neutrality. Following these treaties, Japan exerted further pressure upon France and, in June, 1941, forced the latter to sign military agreements which gave the Japanese an undoubted supremacy in Indo-China.

Again the United States and Great Britain protested. But this time they backed up their protests by acts. On July 25, 1941, both governments ordered Japanese assets frozen, and thus ended any important trade between their countries and Japan. The British government further announced its intention to cancel the existing trade treaties between Japan and Britain, India, and Burma. The United States followed this up on August 1 by placing an embargo on the export of aviation oil and gasoline, thus cutting off Japan from her oil supply in the United States. For some months Japan had been negotiating with the Netherlands East Indies in an effort to increase her supply of oil from those islands. Her negotiations had proved fruitless; in fact, following the United States embargo, the Netherlands East Indies suspended their trade agreement with Japan, thus threatening a further reduction of the latter's oil supply.

In August, Prince Konoye, the Japanese premier, urged a resumption of the Japanese-American negotiations which had been broken off in the preceding month. It was soon apparent, however, that the two governments were no nearer an agreement than before. The Japanese refused to retreat from the stand which they had taken earlier or to alter their policy

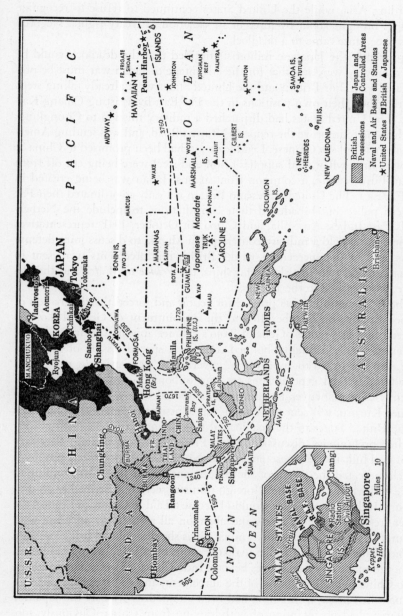

THE FAR EAST, 1939–1940

regarding Asia, while the United States continued to refuse to recognize changes brought about by force or in violation of treaty rights. Negotiations once more came to a deadlock.

Apparently the Japanese militarists decided that the deadlock could be ended only by war, and that for the advantage of Japan war must be precipitated soon. For Britain and the United States were already taking steps to strengthen their own positions in the Far East by assisting Chiang Kaishek. The United States had dispatched a military mission to Chungking, was helping to improve the reopened Burma Road, and was sending American fliers to aid the Chinese. Lend-lease aid had been promised to China at the very time when vital supplies of oil and steel were being cut off from Japan. Furthermore, a common front against Japan was being created in the Far East. The United States and Britain not only co-ordinated their Far Eastern policy but broadened their consultations to include the Netherlands East Indies, Australia, and China. In October, 1941, representatives of these states held a military conference in Manila to discuss joint defense plans, and in the succeeding weeks British reinforcements were sent to Singapore and two British capital ships, the *Prince of Wales* and the *Repulse,* were rushed to the Far East.

The Japanese militarists pressed for action and forced the resignation of Prince Konoye on October 16 and the appointment of General Tojo to succeed him as premier. General Tojo's cabinet appeared to indicate that the extremists had finally obtained control. A special session of the Japanese diet was called to approve the government's expansionist policy and to vote additional expenditures totaling billions of yen. Meanwhile, apparently as a maneuver to gain time, a special envoy, Foreign Minister Saburo Kurusu, was sent to Washington to assist the Japanese ambassador to the United States in the deadlocked negotiations.

After preliminary discussions with President Roosevelt and Secretary of State Hull, the Japanese envoys on November 20 presented proposals which indicated the extent of the concessions which Japan was willing to make and which the Japanese foreign minister secretly described as an ultimatum. If the United States would (1) cease all aid to China, (2) cancel the order freezing Japanese assets and abandon all restrictions on trade with Japan, (3) supply Japan with as much oil as she desired and bring pressure on the Netherlands East Indies to do the same, then Japan would (1) promise not to make any new moves beyond Indo-China, (2) evacuate southern Indo-China upon the signing of the agreement, and (3) evacuate all Indo-China when peace with China had been attained. Obviously the Japanese militarists had no intention of withdrawing from China. Obviously, too, their abandonment of further expansion outside China was to be bought only at the price of American aid to Japan in her conquest of China.

Whether the Japanese, once they had conquered and gained control of the resources of China, would stand by this agreement was a matter of conjecture. Meanwhile, Japanese troop concentrations in Indo-China were increased.

On November 24 the British government announced that, should Japan attack the United States, the latter would find Britain by her side in the ensuing war. Two days later the American proposals for a comprehensive settlement in the Pacific were presented to the Japanese envoys. If Japan would (1) recognize the integrity of Indo-China, (2) withdraw her forces from that country and from China, (3) abandon the puppet government of Wang Ching-wei and recognize that of Chiang Kai-shek, then the United States would (1) remove the restrictions on American exports to Japan, (2) offer a favorable trade agreement, and (3) assist Japan in the stabilization of her currency. The United States further proposed a joint declaration recognizing the principles of nonaggression, international cooperation, and equality of opportunity in the Pacific. Any such program was, of course, anathema to the Japanese militarists. War seemed imminent.

Japan's complete occupation of Indo-China was by this time well under way, and the movements of Japanese transports indicated that developments in Indo-China were preparatory to further moves. By the close of November strong Japanese naval forces were reported in the vicinity of the Japanese mandated islands. President Roosevelt conferred with the heads of the armed forces, and warnings of the imminence of war were sent to Hawaii and to the Philippines. On December 6, Roosevelt in a final effort to avert war sent a personal message to Emperor Hirohito assuring him that the United States had no intention of attacking Indo-China and undertaking to secure similar assurances from China, Thailand, Malaya, and the Netherlands East Indies if Japan would withdraw her forces. On the next day the Japanese envoys presented to the American government their country's formal reply to the proposals of November 26. It was a lengthy document, but its conclusion was that Japan could not accept the proposals as a basis of negotiations and that it would be impossible to reach an agreement through further negotiations.

Japan's Conquest of Empire

On Sunday morning, December 7, 1941, before the Japanese envoys had presented their formal reply to Secretary of State Hull, the Japanese without a declaration of war and as the result of plans and operations which must have taken weeks to execute, suddenly launched an attack upon Hawaii, followed by other attacks upon Guam, Wake Island, Hong Kong, the Philippines, Thailand (Siam), and Malaya. The attack on the American naval base at Pearl Harbor was the most important of these operations, and it was skillfully executed.

Despite the warnings of a possible surprise attack sent to the American army and navy commanders at Pearl Harbor, inadequate precautions had been taken to protect the sea and air forces stationed there. Admiral Kimmel and General Short apparently believed, as did high military and naval commanders in Washington, that the Japanese attack would probably be in the vicinity of Indo-China and the East Indies. A board of inquiry subsequently charged the commanders in Hawaii with being guilty of dereliction, and they were at once retired from active service. But this action could not compensate for the losses sustained by the United States navy. Nineteen naval vessels, including all eight of the battleships then in the harbor, were sunk or damaged so seriously as to be put out of action for some time. In addition 177 army and navy airplanes were destroyed, and 4575 casualties, of which 2343 were killed, were inflicted upon the navy and army personnel. The American aircraft carriers based at Pearl Harbor happened to be at sea and thus escaped damage. Nevertheless, at a cost of only a few aircraft and three midget submarines the Japanese in their first blow had succeeded in upsetting the naval balance in the Pacific to their great advantage.

On December 7, after the attack on Pearl Harbor, the Japanese government announced that it had been at war with the United States and Great Britain since dawn that morning, and on the next day it issued a formal declaration of war. On December 11, Germany and Italy gave their formal support to Japan's venture in the Pacific by declaring war on the United States, and on that same day the three Axis aggressors agreed to carry on war "in common and jointly," not to conclude either an armistice or a peace separately, and after the conclusion of the war to "collaborate closely . . . in order to realize and establish an equitable new order in the world." The Second World War had become indeed a global struggle.

A few hours after the attack on Pearl Harbor, Japanese planes from Formosa attacked Clark Field near Manila. Most of the American planes were caught on the ground, parked in rows, wing to wing, as they had been at Pearl Harbor. All the flying fortresses, recently arrived in the Philippines, and many of the pursuit planes were destroyed or severely damaged. Two days later Japan's air force further strengthened her hold on the sea by sinking the British battleships *Repulse* and *Prince of Wales,* which without air escort were seeking to intercept a Japanese convoy off the coast of Malaya. Thereafter, for some time, neither the United States nor Great Britain had naval or air power in the Far East capable of successfully challenging the Japanese. The two countries had been thrown back on their bases at Hawaii and Singapore, some 4000 miles apart.

THE JAPANESE ATTACK ON PEARL HARBOR

The destruction of the battleship *Arizona*.

With their control of the sea and the air the Japanese were able for a time to strike where and when they pleased with little fear of interference from the United States or Great Britain. The isolated American and British forces, which they thereafter attacked, could have no hope of aid or reinforcements from their homelands. Though they fought heroically, they were bound to be conquered or destroyed by the overwhelming naval, air, and military forces which the Japanese could concentrate where they pleased. In December Guam, Wake Island, and Hong Kong were captured, and Thailand, after a token resistance, surrendered and became a Japanese ally.

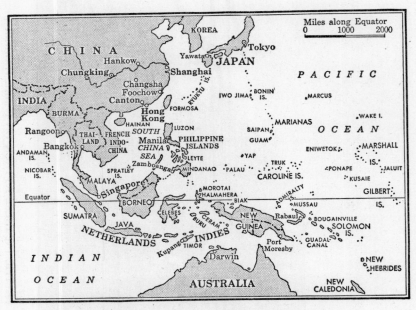

THE SCENE OF JAPAN'S BLITZKRIEG, 1941–1942

The Japanese next struck at Singapore from the rear. Their planes, using bases in Indo-China and Thailand, systematically destroyed the few British planes in northern Malaya and by the destruction of air fields in that region made it impossible to send air reinforcements to the British operating there. The latter fought valiantly and repeatedly tried to establish and hold a line across the Malaya peninsula. But the Japanese controlled the sea, and were therefore able to conduct an amphibious campaign. Repeatedly they compelled the British to retreat by landing a force some miles behind the line which the British had established. For some 400 miles the British fought a hopeless rearguard action, but eventually, on January 30, 1942, they fell back on Singapore. This $400,000,000 British naval base had not been designed to hold off a land attack, and on February 15, 1942, a British force of some 70,000 men surrendered to the Japanese. The conquest of Singapore gave the Japanese control of the easiest passage from the Pacific to the Indian Ocean; it gave them control of what had been regarded as the main defense of Sumatra and Java; and it released troops and planes for use on other battlefields.

Even while one force of Japanese was driving southward toward Singapore, another, operating from Thailand, was advancing westward into Burma. The latter, part of the British Empire, had recently been separated from the administration of India, but the political regime established was unsatisfactory to many Burmese, and there was much disaffection. The local population in many places, in fact, actively aided the Japanese by guiding them through hidden jungle paths to outflank the British and by destroying the latter's supplies and communications. At best only about two divisions of British forces were available to defend this region—which was larger than Germany—when the Japanese launched their attack into Burma in January, 1942. On March 9, Rangoon was captured and the invaders secured a major port of entry for supplies and reinforcements.

During the succeeding weeks the Japanese advanced northward up the Irrawaddy, Sittang, and Salween rivers. In this period the British forces were supplemented by two Chinese armies led by Chiang Kai-shek's American military adviser, General Joseph W. Stilwell, to whom was entrusted the defense of eastern Burma. But the ensuing developments were very much like those in Malaya. Repeatedly outflanked by the Japanese, the defenders were constantly compelled to fall back. In April the Japanese launched an unexpected drive northward from Thailand which cut behind the Chinese defenders and captured Lashio, the southern terminus of the Burma Road. At the same time a frontal attack from the south up the Irrawaddy valley split the Chinese forces, and on May 1, 1942, the Japanese captured Mandalay. Some of the British, at the sacrifice of their heavy equipment, managed to reach the security of India, and General Stilwell finally succeeded in extricating some of his forces, but Burma was lost and with it the last effective route for sending American and British supplies to Chiang Kai-shek.

By this time, too, the Japanese had largely conquered the rich Netherlands East Indies, one of their chief objectives. The forces which the Dutch could marshal to meet the invasion were none too formidable. They had an inexperienced army of 100,000 natives, built up from a nucleus of some 30,000 professional soldiers. This force was largely concentrated in Java. They also had some 400 planes, a few cruisers, and a number of destroyers and submarines. The American Asiatic squadron, consisting of one heavy cruiser and a number of destroyers and submarines, together with a British cruiser, an Australian cruiser, and some smaller British ships, had also been sent to the aid of the Dutch.

After capturing a few bases on islands to the north of Java, the Japanese in January, 1942, set out to invade that island, which occupied a key position in the East Indies, and for this purpose they sent a fleet of about a hundred transports and warships. This fleet was met in the Macassar

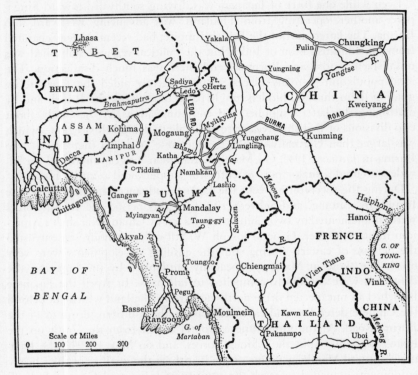

THE BURMA AREA

Straits by the Allied naval and air forces operating from Java, and in a six-day engagement (January 23–29, 1942), the latter succeeded in sinking or seriously damaging about a third of the Japanese ships. Temporarily checked in their direct advance upon Java, the Japanese next approached it obliquely. Immediately after the fall of Singapore they conquered Sumatra to the northwest of Java, and then, coming in from the other direction, they seized the island of Timor and the island of Bali at the eastern tip of Java. Late in February the Japanese fleet again advanced on Java, and the Allied fleet once more challenged the Japanese navy. In the course of a three-days' running battle most of the Allied ships were sunk; only four American destroyers managed to escape. The way was now open to Java, and the conquest of the island was swift. By March 9, 1942, organized resistance had collapsed, and Japan was in possession of an empire rich in foodstuffs, minerals, petroleum, and rubber, commodities which she greatly coveted and vitally needed.

Longest to hold out against the Japanese in the regions mapped out by them for immediate occupation were the Americans and their Filipino allies. Although the ultimate fate of these forces had been sealed by events at Pearl Harbor and Clark Field on December 7–8, 1941, some of the defenders of the Philippines held out until May 7, 1942. This long defense was possible in part because, after Manila had been neutralized, the Japanese did not exert their full strength against the Philippines until Singapore had fallen. It was made possible in part, too, by the advantages which the defenders had in terrain. General Douglas MacArthur soon consolidated his forces in the Bataan peninsula of the island of Luzon, the central defense of the archipelago, abandoning Manila to the Japanese. Bataan, with its steep, jungle-covered hills and deep ravines, was connected with the island proper by only a narrow neck of land, and enemy penetration was difficult. Furthermore, it could be protected from the sea to a considerable extent by the guns of the strongly fortified island of Corregidor, only three miles away.

The Japanese recklessly and heroically charged the American lines in mid-January, 1942, and again early in February. On both occasions, however, the machine-gun fire of the defenders and the electrically charged barbed-wire obstructions halted them. But General MacArthur's 40,000 men, mostly Filipinos, no matter how valiant, could not fight on indefinitely without replenishment of food, drugs, and matériel, and they were completely cut off from any such possibility. Eventually the defense was weakened by malnutrition, malaria, and other diseases. The defenders, decisively outnumbered and almost dead of fatigue, slowly retreated to the sea. A few hundred were evacuated to Corregidor, but on April 9, 1942, a force of some 35,000 surrendered. Resistance was continued by the forces at Corregidor, although many of the men there were sick and half-starved. A war of attrition was carried on by the Japanese, who ultimately succeeded in landing on the naval base. Further resistance was futile, and on May 7, 1942, the garrison of 12,000 also surrendered.

The commander who surrendered, however, was not General MacArthur but General Jonathan Wainwright. On February 22, President Roosevelt had ordered the former to leave Bataan and to establish his headquarters in Australia, where he was assigned the task of organizing the defense of that island. General MacArthur and his family, traveling by devious ways, managed to evade the Japanese, and arrived safely in Australia on March 17. There he became commander-in-chief of the Allied forces, and it was hoped that this shift presaged also a change from the defensive to the offensive for the Allies in operations in the Southwest Pacific.

The Checking of the Japanese in the South Pacific

Within a few months after Pearl Harbor the Japanese had achieved a series of successes against the Western powers that would previously have been thought impossible. They had captured Guam, Wake Island, and Hong Kong. They had occupied Indo-China and Thailand, had swept down the Malayan peninsula, and had taken the supposedly impregnable British naval base at Singapore. They had driven the Allies out of Burma and had cut the Burma Road to China. They had seized nearly every strategic point in the far-flung Netherlands East Indies, and had finally destroyed all organized resistance in the Philippines.

For a time it was feared that the Japanese might next invade Australia, for their seizure of Rabaul and northern New Guinea, outer defenses of Australia, as well as of Timor to the west and the Solomon Islands to the east, seemed to presage an invasion of that great island continent. From these various bases they sought to "soften up" the Australian air fields at Port Moresby in southeastern New Guinea and at Port Darwin in northern Australia. The Australians became very much alarmed. Some Australian forces were recalled from the Mediterranean area, and Prime Minister John Curtin appealed to the United States for help. American troops and supplies were rushed to the Fiji Islands, the New Hebrides, New Caledonia, and New Zealand to guard the routes to Australia, and an American expeditionary force was dispatched to the latter itself.

In May, 1942, the Japanese suffered what was probably their first major reverse in the war. A great concentration of Japanese shipping appeared in the Coral Sea, lying between northeastern Australia and the Solomon Islands. Whether its immediate objective was the conquest of Port Moresby, the occupation of New Caledonia and the New Hebrides, or a landing in Australia was not known. But a strong task force of the United States navy sailed forth to meet it. Though the two naval forces never made direct contact in the ensuing battle of the Coral Sea (May 7–8), American carrier-based planes, aided by land-based planes of General MacArthur's force, administered a decisive defeat to the Japanese and compelled them to withdraw. This battle "marked the high tide of Japanese conquest in the Southwest Pacific."

But the Japanese made one more aggressive move before they were completely checked. In June the largest concentration of Japanese naval strength yet assembled sailed east with the capture of Midway as its preliminary objective. Diversionary forces were sent northeastward to attack the Aleutian Islands, where they seized Attu and Kiska, but the main Japanese force struck toward Midway. The Japanese fleet was sighted on June 3, 1942, and thereafter for three days American seaplanes and land-based flying fortresses bombed the invaders, inflicting heavy losses. "The battles of the Coral Sea and Midway restored the balance of sea power in the Pacific to the United States." The latter was at last in a position to seize the initiative.

On August 7, 1942, a strong force of American marines, protected by an American-Australian naval task force, launched an attack against the chief Japanese positions in the Solomons. The Japanese were apparently taken by surprise, and by the night of August 8 the marines had seized the air field on Guadalcanal. On that night, however, the Allied naval force covering the landing operations was attacked off Savo Island by the Japanese, and in the ensuing engagement three heavy American cruisers and one Australian cruiser were destroyed. As a result of this disaster no cover could be given the American beachheads except what could be provided fitfully and by daylight from the American carrier force to the south, for the United States had launched the campaign with an irreducible minimum of heavy cruiser strength, which had now been wiped out.

Bitter seesaw battles ensued on Guadalcanal. The Americans were bombed by planes from Japanese bases to the north; they were shelled at night by light Japanese naval forces; they were persistently attacked by the Japanese troops still on Guadalcanal. But American engineers rushed to completion the landing strip on that island, and on August 20 American fighter planes landed on what was christened Henderson Field. Air reinforcements followed in the succeeding days. This was exceedingly fortunate for the Americans, for to the north the Japanese had been making a counter-concentration of ships and planes for the purpose of retaking Guadalcanal before it became too strong. On August 24, 1942, this Japanese naval and air force, nearly as powerful as that sent against Midway, swept down from the north. The most violent air engagement of the Pacific war to that date took place, and as a result the Japanese attempt to retake Guadalcanal was frustrated by the attacks of American carrier-based planes and bombers from Henderson Field.

By October 11, American naval reinforcements had arrived, and in an engagement following a surprise attack that night they avenged the disaster off Savo Island by sinking three Japanese cruisers, four destroyers, and one transport at a cost of only one destroyer. But the Japanese persisted in their efforts to retake the island. Steadily at night under cover of darkness they shipped in more men and supplies, and there were times when it looked as though they might overwhelm the American forces. Then once more the Japanese attempted to recapture Guadalcanal by a sweep from the north with battleships, carriers, cruisers, destroyers, and planes. In the terrific battle of Santa Cruz, which began on October 26 and was fought chiefly by the air forces, both fleets suffered heavily in the loss of carriers. But the Japanese were turned back; their powerful naval force never got near enough to Guadalcanal to fire a gun at it. Still a third time the Japanese sent a tremendous force against Guadalcanal, but a third time they were frustrated in a battle which raged on sea and in the air during November 13, 14, and 15. Heavy losses were inflicted on the Japanese task force, and most of the Japanese transports, deserted by their protecting warships, were sent to the bottom. Japan's drive to the south was checked; she had lost the initiative in that direction.

This was further revealed by the course of events in New Guinea, where the Japanese had established bases at Gona and Buna from which they apparently planned to advance upon Port Moresby, Australia's outlying base on the southern coast of that island. They first tried an amphibious operation, landing troops at Milne Bay at the southeastern tip of New Guinea on August 26, 1942. But they were at once attacked by General MacArthur's forces, and by the end of the month the area had been cleared of the Japanese and all their heavy equipment had been either destroyed or captured. The Japanese also attempted to advance overland upon Port Moresby. In this case they not only failed but the Allies drove them back and even captured their bases at Gona and Buna.

The Reduction of Japan's Outer Defense Area

Nevertheless, as the result of her sweep of conquest during the six months after Pearl Harbor, Japan had extended her domination over a tremendous land and sea area whose perimeter curved from northern Burma and India in the west to the waters north of Australia in the south, to the seas beyond the Ellice, Gilbert, and Marshall Islands in the east, and to Attu and Kiska in the Aleutian Islands in the north. This vast region, according to strategists, was divided into three major zones: the outer, secondary, and inner defense areas.

The outer defense area consisted of a screen of small islands with air and naval bases. As each of these island strongholds was linked to all the others by air and sea, any conceivable enemy concentration against one, it was thought, could be crushed by swift reinforcements from the rest. They therefore served as advance patrols to protect the vital parts of the expanded Japanese empire against any threat from American sea power. The secondary defense area consisted chiefly of southeast Asia—Indo-China, Thailand,

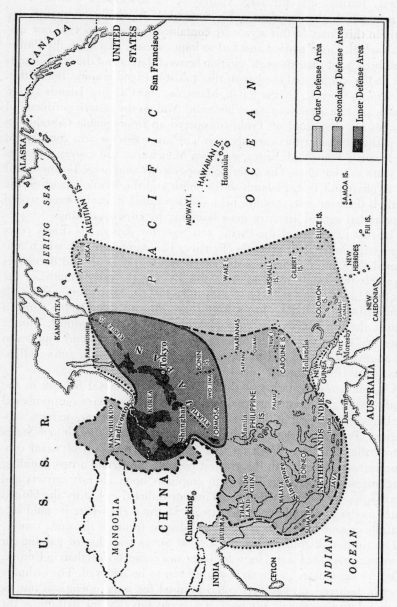

JAPAN'S DEFENSIVE AREAS

Outer Defense Area
Secondary Defense Area
Inner Defense Area

Malaya, Burma—and the large islands of the Southwest Pacific. New Guinea, which the Japanese never succeeded in wholly occupying, lay partly in this zone. In this area were contained the rich and vital raw materials which Japan needed and had so long coveted. In a sense the Philippines, because of their strategic location between Japan and the Netherlands East Indies, constituted the key to this valuable island empire. But within this area, to the east, lay the Palau, Marianas, and Caroline Islands as outposts against an American naval invasion. And on the eastern perimeter of the area lay the island of Truk, considered an impregnable Gibraltar in the pathway of an American advance. The inner defense area consisted of the Japanese homeland, Korea, southern Manchuria, and eastern China as far south as Shanghai. The outer defenses of this zone were Formosa and the Ryukyu and Bonin Islands to the south and the Kurile Islands to the north. If these outposts could be held, the homeland, it was believed, would be protected against effective mass bombing by enemy airplanes.

The first two years of the Pacific war were for Americans chiefly years of preparation for their eventual offensive. The immediate task which confronted the United States was that of establishing new air and fleet bases to protect the supply route to Australia. During the early months of the war the United States rallied its forces and established bases on many South Pacific islands, including Jarvis Island, the Phoenix Islands, the Samoan Islands, the Fiji Islands, the New Hebrides, and New Caledonia. Thus a protective screen was erected to safeguard the flow of men and supplies to the Southwest Pacific and to provide bases of operation for future offensives against the Japanese.

A second pressing task was that of restoring the naval balance in the Pacific. After the disaster at Pearl Harbor the Japanese navy outnumbered the United States fleet in the Pacific in every category except, perhaps, submarines. By two methods, attrition and construction, the United States altered that situation. Work on the "two-ocean" program of naval construction was rushed with the greatest possible speed, and a new building program was initiated in 1942 with emphasis upon aircraft carriers and submarines. By a construction program unparalleled in history the United States modernized and expanded its navy to the point where it could successfully engage hostile fleets on several distant fronts at the same time.

The third task confronting the United States was that of gaining air supremacy over the Pacific, for war in that vast ocean, no less than in Europe, called for supremacy in the air if victory was to be achieved. The ordinary types of fighters and bombers could be used for some operations but, in view of Japan's strategic situation, it was obvious that for striking at the Japanese homeland within the inner defense area something much more powerful and longer-ranged than ordinary bombers would be required.

Fortunately for the effectiveness of the American air war in the Pacific, the United States army air force had approved—even before Pearl Harbor—plans for the so-called B-29 bombing plane or superfortress, capable of carrying heavy bombloads to targets 1500 or even 2000 miles distant. After Pearl Harbor American industrial genius devoted itself to the production and perfection of this giant war machine.

At the conference between Churchill and Roosevelt at Washington in May, 1943, it was decided that General MacArthur and Admiral Chester W. Nimitz should move against the Japanese outer defenses, ejecting the enemy from the Aleutians and seizing the Marshalls, some of the Carolines, the remainder of the Solomons, the Bismarck Archipelago, and the northern coast of New Guinea. At the conference at Quebec three months later the specific routes of the advance were laid out. General MacArthur, to whose strategic command the army forces in the South Pacific had been added, was to continue his operations along the New Guinea coast to reach the Philippines by the autumn of 1944. Admiral Nimitz was to advance across the tremendous reaches of the Central Pacific, taking the Gilberts, the Marshalls, and the Marianas. It was believed that by the spring of 1945 the American forces would be able to land in the Ryukyus, on the very threshold of Japan.

By August 15, 1943, the Japanese had been forced out of Attu and Kiska in the Aleutian Islands as the result of American and Canadian operations during the first eight months of that year. In November, Tarawa and Makin in the Gilbert Islands were captured. Preceded by days of bombing from the air and from surface craft, designed to reduce the island defenses, American marines on November 20 stormed ashore on Tarawa in the face of a murderous fire from Japanese guns which had not been silenced by the preliminary bombing. In three days of hard fighting the marines wiped out the Tarawa garrison, though at a cost to themselves of 913 men killed and more than 2000 wounded. The capture of Makin was less difficult and was completed on November 22.

Japan's outer defense area with its system of supposedly interlocked bases was thus proved to be highly vulnerable, for her fighters in the Gilberts had been prevented from receiving any assistance from other Japanese island bases. Tarawa had an excellent air field, and Makin had wharves, a good anchorage, and a seaplane base. The capture of these two islands, therefore, provided facilities for American land-based planes and brought the Marshall Islands within easy bombing distance. In January the Marshalls were bombed on twenty-two consecutive days, and then, on January 31, 1944, a powerful sea and air attack began. On the next day beachheads were established, and by February 8 the whole Kwajalein atoll had been occupied. Apparently the Japanese had been taken by surprise.

Although more than 8000 Japanese were killed, the American losses on this occasion were only 286 dead and 82 missing. No American warships were sunk, and losses of aircraft were comparatively light. The next important step came on February 18 when Eniwetok, on the northwestern edge of the archipelago, was seized and with it a good air field extending American striking power some 300 miles farther toward the west. By the middle of April a score or more of the Marshall atolls were in American hands, and Japan's outer defense area in this part of the Pacific had been effectively reduced.

Four months later, on June 15, American marines and army troops landed on Saipan in the Marianas Islands, more than 3000 miles beyond Pearl Harbor. The Japanese here fought fanatically and not until after 21,000 men had been killed did their resistance collapse. The cost in American lives was heavy, too, for 2359 men of the invading forces were killed. By the close of July, Guam and Tinian had also been captured, and Truk and other Japanese bases in the Caroline Islands were largely isolated. On September 15, Admiral Nimitz' forces struck again, this time in the Palau Islands where marines and army troops landed on Peleliu, which had the best air field in the western Carolines and was only 500 miles from the Philippines.

Meanwhile, in the Southwest Pacific General MacArthur had been carrying on the campaign which had been committed to him. Without waiting for the final conquest of all of the Solomon Islands, which was not completed until early in 1944, MacArthur's American and Australian troops launched their drive westward. By the fall of 1943 the Americans in the Southwest Pacific had a superiority both on the sea and in the air, and it was MacArthur's intention to proceed along the coast of New Guinea by a series of envelopments. His forces were able to land where the Japanese were weakest and were able to isolate their stronger forces in places from which, because of American control of the sea and air, they could not be evacuated. By the end of May, 1944, Rabaul, Japan's strongest base in the Southwest Pacific, had been neutralized by landings on New Britain and in the Admiralty Islands (see map on next page), and all the Japanese bases on the north coast of New Guinea had been captured or isolated. In July, Noemfor Island was seized and on September 15, MacArthur's forces landed on Morotai, where they established a base less than 400 miles from Mindanao, the second largest island in the Philippines.

A glance at the map on page 753 will reveal that in consequence of American amphibious operations carried on in the Aleutians, in the Gilberts, in the Marshalls, in the Solomons, in the Bismarck archipelago, and in New Guinea, Japan's outer defense area in the Pacific had been almost completely eliminated. Although she still had some centers of resistance in that

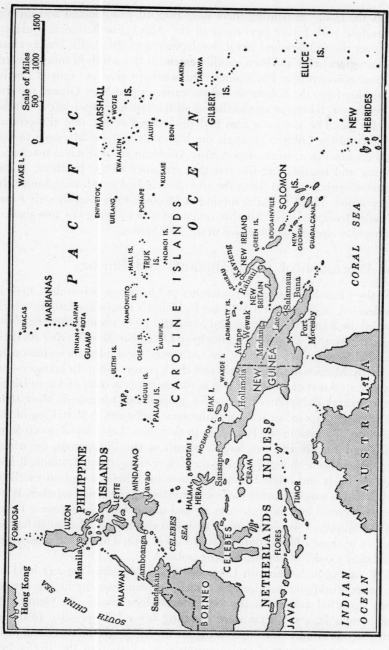

THE SOUTHWEST PACIFIC IN THE SECOND WORLD WAR

region, the troops remaining there were trapped and doomed and unable to interfere with future operations of the Allies. Furthermore, a glance back over the military and naval developments in the Pacific makes clear how two giant arms had been steadily extended thousands of miles toward the same objective, the Philippines. The southern arm had moved slowly but steadily from the Solomons and the eastern tip of New Guinea toward the northwest, taking or immobilizing all the Japanese bases in the Southwest Pacific. The northern arm had pushed irresistibly into the central Pacific from the Gilberts through the Marshalls and the Marianas to the Palaus, acquiring a string of powerful American air and naval bases and isolating and neutralizing the few that remained to the Japanese. These two arms, with a mailed fist at the end of each, had struck simultaneously on September 15, 1944, at Peleliu and at Morotai, each roughly only some 500 miles from the goal. All that remained was to bring the two mailed fists together on a single objective in the Philippines.

The Liberation of the Philippines and Burma

At the Churchill-Roosevelt conference at Quebec in September, 1944, it was decided, upon Admiral William F. Halsey's recommendation—which received the approval of Nimitz and MacArthur—to advance the date of the projected invasion of the Philippines from December 20 to October 20, 1944. Preceded by ten days of heavy air raids over the Philippines—Luzon in the north, Mindanao in the south, and the Viscayas group in between—on that day an American landing was made on the east coast of Leyte Island in the central Philippines by a major amphibious operation. More than 600 ships participated in what was the most ambitious undertaking of the American offensive in the Pacific up to that time. Leyte lay between Mindanao and Luzon, the two largest islands in the Philippines, on which the Japanese were thought to have their chief troop concentrations. It had some air fields and offered numerous sites for others. It had an excellent harbor which would provide facilities for bringing in needed supplies. With Leyte converted into an American air and supply base, the Japanese forces in the Philippines would be cut in two, and either flank of their defensive position in those islands could be rolled up at will. The Japanese troops in Mindanao would, of course, become isolated.

The American landing on Leyte obviously threatened Japan's hold on the entire Philippine archipelago, which, in turn, was the key to her recently acquired empire in the Netherlands East Indies. By October 22 three strong Japanese fleets were steaming toward Leyte—two from the west and one from home bases in the north. Although the two fleets from the west were discovered and vigorously attacked from the air as they

THE PHILIPPINE ISLANDS IN THE SECOND WORLD WAR

crossed, the one the Sibuyan Sea, the other the Sulu Sea, they continued on their course, the ultimate objective of which could not be immediately known to the American naval commanders. On the twenty-third Halsey's Third Fleet and Kinkaid's Seventh Fleet disposed themselves to watch the two available approaches to Leyte Gulf—San Bernardino Strait to the north and Surigao Strait to the South. Late in the day came news of the approach of the Japanese fleet from the north, whereupon Halsey's Third Fleet dashed northward to engage it, leaving Kinkaid's fleet to guard Leyte. Early in the morning of the twenty-fourth, Halsey's fleet attacked in the open sea to the east of Luzon. The Japanese immediately fled but suffered heavy losses, losses which would have been still heavier if Halsey had not been halted in his pursuit by ominous news from the Seventh Fleet.

Admiral Kinkaid had disposed the bulk of the latter to meet the southern-most Japanese fleet should it emerge from Surigao Strait, and had left only a sparse defending force of destroyers, escort carriers, and destroyer escorts to guard against the supposedly unlikely contingency of the central Japanese fleet's emerging from San Bernardino Strait. Kinkaid's heavy ships did their work well, for, when the southern Japanese fleet reached the narrow channel opening into Leyte Gulf, the Seventh Fleet opened fire and "crossed the enemy's T." The Japanese fleet thereupon retreated, shattered and beaten. Its losses might have been still heavier, too, except that suddenly Kinkaid received word that the central Japanese fleet had emerged from San Bernardino Strait, to the north of Samar, and was speeding down the east coast of that island toward the helpless American shipping in Leyte Gulf. Only the weak American defending force lay between it and its goal, but that force, after broadcasting the vital news to Halsey and Kinkaid, at once closed in action with the more powerful Japanese fleet, using smoke screens, torpedoes, and planes. This heroic action gained time but at the sacrifice of two destroyers, one destroyer escort, one escort carrier, and many lives. The sacrifice was not in vain, however, for the Japanese admiral, delayed by the action and knowing that Halsey and Kinkaid were rushing toward him with their more powerful ships, decided to abandon the attack. The American beachhead on Leyte and the shipping in the gulf were saved.

The battle for Leyte Gulf (October 23–25, 1944) had disastrous results for Japan's sea power in the Southwest Pacific. According to the official figures published by the United States high command, Japanese losses were 3 battleships, 3 aircraft carriers, 6 heavy cruisers, 4 light cruisers, and 8 destroyers sunk, and severe damage to a considerable number of other ships of all categories. American losses were 1 light aircraft carrier, 2 escort carriers, 2 destroyers, and 1 destroyer escort sunk.

The defeat of the Japanese naval forces in their attempt to interfere with American landings on Leyte decided the fate of that island. Although there was still much hard fighting, General MacArthur on December 25 announced that, except for mopping up, the campaign for Leyte had ended.

But already another landing had been made in the Philippines by American forces. On December 15 an amphibious force, after a circuitous 600-mile cruise from Leyte Gulf through Surigao Strait, the Mindanao Sea, and the Sulu Sea past enemy-held islands, had made a surprise landing against little resistance on the southwestern tip of Mindoro, one of the larger Philippine Islands just south of Luzon. This landing seemed to point the way to the ultimate invasion of southern Luzon, which was separated from the northern coast of Mindoro by only a narrow strait. And indications of an approaching invasion of Luzon from the south continued to multiply. Other amphibious landings on Mindoro advanced American positions northward on that island, and on January 5, 1945, United States troops seized the island of Marinduque, within ten miles of the southern Luzon coast, and less than 100 miles from Manila. American superfortresses, meanwhile, severely bombed the Japanese home islands, while planes of the American Pacific fleet raided Formosa and the Ryukyu Islands. Every effort was bent toward isolating the Philippines from Japanese bases to the north.

Then, on January 9, 1945, United States troops, led personally by General MacArthur and protected by a terrific naval and air bombardment, landed from a convoy of more than 800 ships, not in southern Luzon, but along the southern and southeastern coasts of Lingayen Gulf, approximately 100 miles north of Manila. The Japanese, apparently deceived by American feints toward southern Luzon, were not prepared to repulse the landing here. The American troops met only light opposition, quickly established a firm beachhead, and began their advance inland. In less than three weeks the Americans had captured the big air base at Clark Field and had pushed to within forty miles of Manila. On February 4, American troops smashed into the city, capturing Santo Tomas concentration camp and Bilibid prison and liberating some 4800 American prisoners and internees. By February 23, the last Japanese resistance was being mopped up within Manila, and on the following day the liberation of the city was completed. On February 27, in the battle-scarred capital of the Philippines General MacArthur formally returned civil control of the islands to President Osmeña.

With their conquests in the Philippines the Americans had invaded Japan's secondary defense area, and had established strategically located bases for its reduction. But much still remained to be done. The island of Luzon—larger than Bulgaria—had to be cleared of the Japanese, and the garrisons on the many other islands had to be captured or exterminated. The two tasks were carried on simultaneously. By the end of June the campaign in Luzon had been successfully ended and most of the larger and strategically important islands had been occupied. By that time, too, British, American, and Chinese troops as the result of long and difficult campaigns had succeeded in driving the Japanese out of Burma, and Lord Mountbatten's forces in southeastern Asia were closing in on Malaya and the Netherland East Indies. Australian troops were operating in southeastern Borneo, and Australian and Netherlands East Indian troops had seized Tarakan Island off northeastern Borneo. The Japanese secondary defense area was fast being overrun by the Allies.

The Attack on Japan

Even before the reduction of this secondary area had been completed, the Allies had begun carrying their attacks to Japan in the heart of the inner defense zone. As early as April, 1942, Tokyo and other Japanese cities had been bombed by American carrier-based planes commanded by General James H. Doolittle, but this attack had been an isolated exploit. It was not until more than two years later (June 15, 1944) that a "sizable task force" of American superfortresses flew from Chinese bases to make their first attack upon Japan, choosing as their target Yawata, the "Japanese Pittsburgh." But acceleration of these air attacks was painfully slow: two in June, two in July, three in August, two in September, four in October, and nine in November. One grave handicap was the arduous task of getting the necessary high-octane aviation fuel to the air bases in China, involving as it did transshipment in India and then a risky, gas-consuming 2400-mile round trip over the mountains by transport planes. The conquest of the Marianas, however, and the establishment of a superfortress base on Saipan greatly increased the possibility of bombing Japan.

On November 24, 1944, the superfortresses from Saipan inaugurated their attacks upon the Japanese home cities, and within eight days bombed aircraft factories and steel plants in Tokyo itself four times. Thereafter the number of attacks increased more rapidly: fourteen in December, and still more in January and February, 1945, when the Japanese homeland was attacked not only by B-29's but by hundreds of carrier planes of the American task force. During March the bombing of Japanese industrial centers— Tokyo, Nagoya, Osaka, Kobe—was particularly severe. Many square miles of the densely populated areas of these cities were laid waste by American explosive and incendiary bombs. The unpleasing prospect of having the industrial heart of their country scourged as other Allied planes had devastated Germany confronted the alarmed Japanese, whose industrial war machine was even more vulnerable than Germany's because it was more closely concentrated.

To secure additional bases from which to increase the air attacks upon

Japan, American marines on February 18, 1945, had landed on Iwo Jima, an important island (*jima* means island) southwest of the Bonin group, after it had first been subjected to sixty-nine consecutive days of aerial bombardment and to four days of terrific naval bombardment. Nevertheless, because of the difficult terrain—its volcanic hills were honeycombed with caves which could not be reached by bombs or shells—and the fanatical resistance of the Japanese garrison of 22,000–24,000, the conquest of Iwo was a tough job. Although the island was only eight square miles in extent, nearly a month of furious fighting was required to capture it. The conquest of Iwo provided the American air force with a valuable advanced base. Fighter planes from Iwo could protect B-29 bases in the Marianas from Japanese bombers; they could also fly to the Japanese mainland to protect the superfortresses. The capture of Iwo was the first American conquest of territory within the Japanese inner defense zone, but the price paid by the marines was high—19,938 casualties, of which 4189 were killed, constituting, it was said, the marines' worst ordeal in their 168-year history.

Two weeks after the end of Japanese resistance on Iwo other American forces on April 1 landed on Okinawa in the largest amphibious operation yet undertaken in the Pacific. They were protected by the guns of the American Fifth Fleet and by carrier planes, land-based planes, and superfortresses. Okinawa was the strongest of the Ryukyu chain of islands joining Japan and Formosa. It was only half as far from Japan as Iwo. American air and naval forces based on Okinawa could sever Japan's route to her empire in the south and west, could transform the China Sea into an American lake. The significance of all these facts was not lost on the Japanese, who repeatedly sent large forces of "suicide" planes to attack the invasion fleet. Hundreds of Japanese planes were shot down, but by the middle of June 33 American ships had been sunk and 45 damaged, chiefly by these kamikaze or suicide attacks. Meanwhile, ashore American forces battled against the fanatical Japanese resistance which continued in the southern end of Okinawa. Not until June 21 did organized resistance cease, and then only after the American forces had suffered casualties more than twice those suffered in capturing Iwo Jima. But in Okinawa the Americans at last had a sizable strategic base within the shadow of the Japanese homeland.

In April, fleets of Marianas-based B-29's had begun striking at Tokyo, Nagoya, and other Japanese industrial cities, protected in their attacks by land-based fighter planes which took off from Iwo Jima. In July, after the capture of Okinawa, air fields on that island also began to be crowded with bombers and fighters, which joined in the aerial assault on the Japanese islands and what was left of Japanese shipping. Japanese industries and communications rapidly crumbled under the mounting tempo of aerial bombardment, supplemented by the destructive power of Allied naval forces.

The Japanese had already suffered another naval disaster. Shortly after the Americans had landed on Okinawa strong Japanese fleet units had been sighted proceeding southward from Kyushu. On April 7 they were attacked in the East China Sea by American carrier planes, which sank one cruiser, four destroyers, and Japan's newest and largest remaining battleship, the *Yamato*. This disaster, coupled with that suffered in the battle for Leyte Gulf, so weakened the Japanese navy that it was powerless to challenge the American battle fleets successfully thereafter.

In July the fast carrier forces of the American Third Fleet, comprising the greatest mass of sea power ever assembled, set out to complete the destruction of the Japanese fleet and to conduct a pre-invasion campaign to destroy Japanese industries. Strikes were made by planes from the fleet's carriers and heavy units of the fleet shelled shore installations. On July 17 the Third Fleet was joined by units of the British Pacific Fleet and the first combined American-British bombardment of the Japanese homeland ensued. The Japanese seemed powerless to halt either the air or naval attacks. Between July 10 and August 15 the Allied forces sank or damaged 148 enemy combat ships, including the *Nagato,* one of Japan's two remaining battleships.

Plans were meanwhile being made for the invasion of the Japanese homeland. An assault on southern Kyushu in the fall of 1945 was to be followed by a second invasion of the Tokyo plain of eastern Honshu in the spring of 1946. It was known that Japan had an army of 2,000,000 in the homeland which was being steadily enlarged by withdrawals from the Asiatic mainland. It was known that she had been husbanding her waning air strength and she was thought to have still some 8000 planes of all types. If casualties in the conquest of Japan itself were in proportion to those suffered in taking Okinawa and Iwo Jima, the price in American lives would inevitably be high. The American high command contemplated no early or easy victory over the Japanese by the use of ordinary weapons of war. Since 1940, however, the full resources of American and British science had been working on the principle of atomic fission, and by the summer of 1945 had produced a new and terrifically destructive atomic bomb. It was thought that the use of atomic bombs might persuade the Japanese not to fight to a last-ditch national suicide.

The Atom Bomb and the End of the War

But before resort to atomic bombs, one last diplomatic effort was made by the Allies to secure an end to the war. On July 26, President Truman, Prime

JAPANESE SURRENDER ABOARD THE U.S.S. MISSOURI

Japanese Foreign Minister Mamoru Shigemitsu signs for his Emperor, as General of the Army Douglas MacArthur, U. S. A., Supreme Commander for the Allies broadcasts the ceremonies.

Minister Churchill, and Generalissimo Chiang Kai-shek, in a proclamation to the Japanese people, warned that prodigious forces were poised to strike final blows on Japan which would result in the utter devastation of the Japanese homeland. They demanded that the Japanese government should proclaim the unconditional surrender of its armed forces, and they stated the Allied terms: (1) the limitation of Japanese sovereignty to the islands of Honshu, Hokkaido, Kyushu, Shikoku, and minor islands; (2) Allied occupation of Japanese territory; (3) disarmament of Japanese military forces; (4) destruction of Japanese war industries; (5) trial and punishment of Japanese war criminals; (6) institution in Japan of freedom of speech, of religion, and of thought; (7) removal of obstacles to the revival and strengthening of democratic tendencies among the Japanese people. On July 29, however, the Tokyo radio reported that the Japanese Premier Suzuki had declared that the Allied proclamation would be ignored by the Japanese government.

To escape heavy casualties and to speed the end of the war, the American high command thereupon decided to use atomic bombs, and on August 6 one of these bombs was dropped on the military base of the Japanese city of Hiroshima. In a split second some 60 per cent of that city was obliterated. Said President Truman: "It was to spare the Japanese people from utter destruction that the ultimatum of July 26 was issued.... Their leaders promptly rejected that ultimatum. If they do not now accept our terms they may expect a rain of ruin from the air, the like of which has never been seen on this earth."

Thereafter the war came swiftly to a close. On August 8 the Soviet Union declared war against Japan in accordance with an agreement made at Yalta in February, and launched swift Red Army offensives into Manchuria and into southern Sakhalin. On August 9 a second atomic bomb was dropped on Nagasaki with even greater destructive force and fire than the Hiroshima bomb. On August 10 the Japanese government sued for peace. Four days later Japan declared her acceptance of the Allied terms, and on August 19 the instrument of surrender was presented to Japanese representatives by General MacArthur at Manila. On September 2 the formal surrender of the Japanese Imperial Government, the Japanese Imperial General Headquarters, and all Japanese and Japanese-controlled forces wherever located, was signed on board the United States battleship *Missouri* in Tokyo Bay. In a dramatic ceremony marking the final consummation of the victory of the United Nations, the last of the Axis powers laid down its arms, and the most extensive and destructive war in the history of mankind came formally to an end. The price of victory for the Americans was 170,596 casualties including 41,322 dead—almost as many in this one theater of operations as suffered by the American forces in the whole First World War.

Chapter XXVI

THE UNFINISHED PEACE
SETTLEMENT AND THE
"COLD WAR"

IN contrast with the relative speed with which the Paris peace conference was convened at the close of the First World War, nearly fifteen
months elapsed between the German signing of the armistice on May 7,
1945, and the convening of another Paris peace conference in July, 1946.
And even then no peace treaties were drafted by the conference for the two
major enemy states, Germany and Japan. This failure to complete the peace
settlement was undoubtedly the result of the clash in ideologies and policies
of the major Allied powers and to an increasing fear and suspicion which
led ultimately to what was called the "cold war" between the Soviet Union
and the United States. On the other hand, in marked contrast with the
delay in restoring formal peace to the world was the speed with which a
new international organization for the preservation of peace was launched
at the close of hostilities.

The United Nations

The Second World War, with its incredible waste of lives and wealth,
strikingly emphasized the shortsightedness of the world's statesmen in
failing to utilize the machinery of the League of Nations to halt aggression
in its initial stages. Moreover, it had brought to many Americans a growing
conviction that by their own abandonment of the League in 1919–1920 they
had contributed to the breakdown of collective security, a conviction that
became even more general after the United States was engulfed in the war
in 1941. To more and more Americans it became obvious that the "world
was growing smaller" and that a third world war would involve the United
States even more quickly and more disastrously than had the wars of 1914
and 1939.

Just as in the case of Woodrow Wilson, President Roosevelt became convinced that the war must lead to an international security system in which

UNITED NATIONS GENERAL ASSEMBLY

President Eisenhower Speaking Before the Assembly on December 8, 1953

the United States must take an active part. Soon after Pearl Harbor the United States department of state took up the task of drafting proposals for such a security system, and at Moscow in October, 1943, Secretary of State Hull presented proposals for a world organization to Foreign Secretaries Anthony Eden and V. M. Molotov, of Great Britain and Russia respectively, and to the Chinese ambassador to Russia. The results of their conversations and negotiations were eventually embodied in the Moscow Declaration, in which the governments of these four leading powers stated that they recognized the necessity of establishing a general international organization.

To implement this declaration representatives of the United States, Great Britain, Russia, and China met at Dumbarton Oaks in Washington from August 21 to October 7, 1944. The results of seven weeks of negotiations, added to the years of study which had already been devoted to the problem, were embodied in the Dumbarton Oaks Proposals for the establishment of a general international organization. It was agreed that these proposals should in turn be formally submitted to the governments of the United Nations to serve as the basis of discussion at a full conference at which the charter of the international organization would ultimately be drawn up.

On March 5, 1945, the United States government, on behalf of itself, Great Britain, Russia, and China, invited the governments of the other United Nations to send representatives to a conference, called to meet at San Francisco on April 25. It had been planned to have President Roosevelt address the opening session of this world security conference, but on April 12, while resting at his home at Warm Springs, Georgia, where he had gone to prepare his speech, President Roosevelt died suddenly of a cerebral hemorrhage. He of all the world's statesmen had done most to create and hold together the United Nations. What effect his death might have upon the future of that organization and upon the plans for world peace, none could foretell. But his successor, President Harry S. Truman, at once announced that Mr. Roosevelt's policies would be continued and that the San Francisco conference would open as scheduled.

The United Nations Conference on International Organization was held at San Francisco from April 25 to June 26, 1945, and was attended by representatives of fifty states which were at war with either Germany or Japan or both. In the Charter of the United Nations which was there drafted and adopted, the core of the Dumbarton Oaks proposals was retained with few alterations, but one entirely new section was added dealing with trusteeship for dependent peoples. The Charter came into force on October 24, 1945, following the deposit of the necessary number of ratifications.

The international machinery outlined in the Charter in many ways resembled that of the League of Nations.[1] The chief organs of the new organization are the following:

A General Assembly, composed of representatives of all member states, meeting in annual and special sessions, in which each state has one vote;

A Security Council, composed of representatives of eleven member states and so organized as to be able to function continuously. The United States, Great Britain, the Soviet Union, China, and France have permanent seats, while six states are elected for two-year terms by the General Assembly;

An International Court of Justice, to whose statute all members of the organization are parties;

A Secretariat, comprising an expert staff and headed by a secretary general as chief administrative officer;

A Trusteeship Council, consisting of the five great powers and such other states as administer trust territories, plus as many other states elected by the Assembly for three-year terms as may be necessary to ensure that the total number of members of the Trusteeship Council is equally divided between states administering and states not administering trust territories;

An Economic and Social Council, composed of representatives of eighteen member states chosen by the General Assembly for three-year terms;

A Military Staff Committee, composed of the chiefs of staff of the permanent members of the Security Council or their representatives with provision for the participation by other states when necessary.

The first five of these organs closely resemble in their composition and functions analogous bodies in the League of Nations, the Trusteeship Council being somewhat similar in purpose to the former Permanent Mandates Commission. The Economic and Social Council, however, is a new organ which was created to deal with matters which had formerly been handled by certain sections of the League Secretariat. Greater dignity and importance are given to economic and social questions by their being entrusted in this way to a special council elected by the General Assembly. The Military Staff Committee is, of course, something which the League of Nations did not have. The United Nations was expected to have military forces available for the maintenance of peace, and member states were expected to conclude agreements specifying in advance the numbers and types of forces to be made available to the Security Council. These armed forces would operate, when necessary, under the authority of the Security Council in accordance with plans made by it with the assistance of the Military Staff Committee. The new organization, it was hoped, would have more power to enforce its decisions than had the League of Nations. The primary responsibility for the maintenance of international peace and security was placed upon the Security Council, which would be in continuous session.

As might have been expected, the matter of voting in the latter body

[1] See pages 417–419.

caused considerable difficulty, but a compromise was finally reached which provided that: (1) each member of the Security Council should have one vote; (2) decisions of the Security Council on procedural matters should be made by an affirmative vote of seven members; (3) decisions of the Security Council on all other matters should be made by an affirmative vote of seven members, including the concurring votes of the permanent members, except that a party to a dispute should abstain from voting when the Security Council was engaged in the pacific settlement of disputes. In other words, the Security Council may informally discuss any dispute or difficulty without any power having a veto, and any member state may call that body's attention to a situation threatening the peace of the world without the veto interfering. But if a dispute moves beyond informal discussion to investigation or recommendation for peaceful settlement, there must be a formal vote in which the affirmative vote of seven must include the concurring votes of the five great powers unless one of the latter is a party to the dispute, in which case its vote is not counted.

The first session of the General Assembly convened in London on January 10, 1946, with fifty-one states represented. Paul-Henri Spaak of Belgium was chosen president of the Assembly and Trygve Lie of Norway was elected secretary general of the United Nations. The Assembly also elected six states—Australia, Brazil, Egypt, Mexico, the Netherlands, and Poland—as nonpermanent members of the Security Council, which held its first meeting on January 17 and immediately took up a number of important political problems connected with Iran, Greece, Indonesia, and Syria-Lebanon.[2] The Assembly, meanwhile, devoted itself to further organizational activities. Eighteen states, including the five great powers, were elected members of the Economic and Social Council; and fifteen judges were chosen, with the help of the Security Council, for the International Court of Justice, which met for the first time at The Hague in April, 1946. The Assembly decided that the Secretariat of the United Nations should be located in the United States, and eventually a permanent site was chosen in New York City. Thus a second experiment in world organization for the facilitation of international co-operation and for the prevention of war was hopefully begun.

Peace Negotiations and Another "Big Four"

Meanwhile, following the collapse of the Nazis and the military defeat of Germany, a three-power conference of the victorious powers had been held in Berlin (July 17–August 2, 1945) to consider the many problems

[2] For the United Nations' handling of various international problems, consult the index under "United Nations" or under the names of the countries or regions directly concerned.

arising from the outcome of the war. In the beginning the conference was attended by Premier Stalin, President Truman, Prime Minister Churchill, and their foreign ministers, Vyacheslav M. Molotov, James F. Byrnes, and Anthony Eden. Following Churchill's resignation as a result of the Labor Party victory in Great Britain,[3] however, Clement R. Attlee, the new British prime minister, and his new foreign secretary, Ernest Bevin, supplanted Churchill and Eden. Since the statesmen conferred at the Cecilienhof near Potsdam, their meeting came to be called the Potsdam Conference.

At this conference it was agreed to establish a Council of Foreign Ministers whose task should be the drafting of the peace treaties, first, with Italy, Rumania, Bulgaria, Hungary, and Finland, and eventually with Germany when the latter had established a government adequate for the purpose. At a subsequent conference in Moscow (December 16–26, 1945), Byrnes, Bevin, and Molotov agreed more specifically that the terms of the treaty with Italy should be drafted by the foreign ministers of Great Britain, the United States, Russia, and France; the terms of the treaties with Rumania, Bulgaria, and Hungary, by the foreign ministers of Great Britain, the United States, and Russia; and those of the treaty with Finland by the foreign ministers of Great Britain and Russia. The foreign ministers of France and the United States, it was further agreed, should have the right to attend all meetings of the council and to discuss treaty terms even in those cases in which they were not permitted to vote.

At the Moscow Conference it was also decided that, upon the completion of the draft treaties, a general peace conference consisting of representatives of the five great powers—Russia, Great Britain, the United States, France, China—and of the sixteen other states which had actively waged war with a substantial military force against the European states,[4] should be convened to consider the treaties and to make recommendations. Following this peace conference the states which had drawn up the original draft treaties should consider the recommendations of the conference and then formulate the final texts of the several treaties.

During the first seven months of 1946, therefore, the foreign ministers of the United States, Great Britain, Russia, and France, and their deputies, carried on negotiations in an attempt to reach agreement on the terms of the treaties to be presented to the future peace conference. Once more, as in 1919,[5] the peace negotiations were dominated by a "Big Four," which in 1946 consisted of Byrnes, Bevin, Molotov, and Georges Bidault, foreign minister of France, though the latter, like Orlando in 1919, played a some-

---

[3] See page 867.

[4] These sixteen states were Australia, Belgium, Brazil, Canada, Czechoslovakia, Ethiopia, Greece, India, the Netherlands, New Zealand, Norway, Poland, the Ukraine, South Africa, White Russia, and Yugoslavia.

[5] For the "Big Four" and peace negotiations in 1919, see pages 393–394.

what minor role. In the "Big Four" of 1946, however, there was probably a deeper distrust of one another's fundamental aims than in that of 1919, for Wilson, Lloyd George, Clemenceau, and Orlando had had at least one basic common bond in that they all represented capitalistic democracies. In 1946, on the other hand, the political and economic ideologies of the three "Western democracies" were far different from those of the Soviet Union. In consequence, the members of the "Big Four" in 1946 were soon caught in the vicious circle of fear and distrust—on the one hand, fear of Communism with its threat of "world revolution"; on the other, fear of "capitalistic imperialism" with its threat of "encirclement." Byrnes, Bevin, and Bidault accordingly sought national security against the alleged or suspected "plots of the Communists," while Molotov used his veto to try to check the "machinations of the greedy imperialists." Though not openly expressed, these fears were ever-present and the search for security by each side in turn only intensified national suspicions.

It is not surprising, perhaps, that, although agreement was readily reached on many points, the "Big Four" failed to come to a common understanding on several important matters, particularly the new Italian-Yugoslav boundary, the fate of Trieste, the disposal of Italy's colonies, Russia's claim to Italian reparations, the question of international control of the Danube, and the matter of withdrawing occupation forces from enemy states following the signing of the peace treaties. Usually the disagreement was between Molotov, on the one side, and Bevin and Byrnes, on the other.

The crisis which gained the greatest notoriety and which probably took up more time than any other one problem, in 1946 as in 1919, arose from the conflict over the boundary between Italy and Yugoslavia. In 1919, Italy, largely for strategic reasons sought a boundary which transgressed upon ethnic principles, and the city particularly involved was Fiume.[6] In 1946, Yugoslavia, from motives very similar to Italy's earlier, sought to push her boundary farther west in conflict with the ethnic situation, and the city involved was this time Trieste. In 1919, Wilson opposed Italy's demands and suggested a boundary which the Italians then denounced as grossly unfair but which in 1946 they themselves recommended as a just settlement. In 1946, Byrnes opposed Yugoslavia's demands for ethnic reasons and also, probably, because he was reluctant to see the important port of Trieste fall into the hands of a Russian satellite state.

The Trieste problem in 1946 likewise somewhat resembled the Danzig problem in 1919.[7] In the latter year Poland desired Danzig as an outlet to the sea, though Danzig's population of some 300,000 was overwhelmingly German. In 1946, Yugoslavia similarly desired Trieste as an outlet to

[6] For the Italian-Yugoslav crisis of 1919, see pages 409–410.

[7] For the Danzig problem in 1919, see pages 398–400.

the sea for her northwestern territories even though the city's 250,000 inhabitants were predominantly Italian. In 1919, France looked to Poland as a possible postwar ally, and Clemenceau therefore fought in the "Big Four" to have Danzig given to Poland. In 1946, Russia considered Yugoslavia as an ally and an outpost on the Adriatic, and Molotov consequently supported Yugoslavia's demand for Trieste. In 1946, as in 1919, a compromise was reached in the establishment of a Free City.

Ultimately in 1946, despite many disagreements in the "Big Four," full and almost complete peace treaties were drafted for each of the five minor defeated powers. Where agreement was not reached on any specific point alternative articles were prepared. The task of the peace conference of 1946, therefore, was to be that of accepting, rejecting, or amending articles already drafted by the "Big Four." The latter decided in advance, however, that the Council of Foreign Ministers must agree after the peace conference upon the specific and final terms of each treaty.

On July 29, 1946, the second Paris peace conference of the twentieth century was opened by French Foreign Minister Bidault. At the very first session of the plenary conference the smaller states revolted against domination by the "Big Four," but they won only slight concessions. In general, however, the small powers were better treated in 1946 than they had been at Paris after the First World War. For instance, in 1919 the full text of the treaty of Versailles was not presented to the small powers until the day before it was presented to the Germans, and then Clemenceau did not permit a vote on its acceptance or rejection. In 1946, the plenary conference, which included the small powers, was permitted to vote article by article on all five of the treaties. The defeated powers, too, were treated better in 1946 than in 1919, at least on the surface. Representatives of the five enemy states were invited to present their views to the plenary conference before the various commissions began their work, and speeches were accordingly delivered before the conference by the Italian and Rumanian premiers and by the Bulgarian, Hungarian, and Finnish foreign ministers. Although these speeches probably had little effect on the eventual treaties, the defeated powers were at least given a chance to be heard by the whole conference. Finally, the general public was better treated in 1946 than during the earlier peace conference. The 1919 meetings of the Council of Ten and of the "Big Four" were secret and even after the treaty of Versailles had been approved and presented to the German delegation, the full text was kept secret from people in the Allied countries. In 1946, on the other hand, the preliminary draft treaties were published at the time the peace conference opened, and all meetings of commissions as well as of the plenary conference were open to the press.

In 1946, as in 1919, most of the work of the peace conference was done by various commissions, but eventually on October 7 the latter had reports ready to submit to the plenary conference. In the ensuing days each national delegation was permitted one half-hour speech on each of the five treaties. Following these speeches the plenary conference started voting on the various articles of the peace treaties. Innumerable votes were taken and in general the outcome in each case was 15 to 6 in favor of the views of the Western powers and 15 to 6 against those of Russia or Yugoslavia. On the night of October 14 the last of the five treaties was approved, and on the next day the conference adjourned, following a farewell address by Bidault.

But it must be emphasized that the Paris peace conference of 1946 was only an advisory body and that the final treaties still had to be approved by those members of the "Big Four" which had signed the armistices with the respective enemy powers. About all that the conference had done, therefore, was to indicate by votes that, in general, those fifteen states which had capitalistic, democratic institutions uniformly supported Byrnes, Bevin, and Bidault against Molotov and that the Slav bloc of six states [8]—dominated by Russia with her communistic, totalitarian institutions—uniformly supported Molotov. The problem of unanimous agreement among the "Big Four" still remained unsolved.

In a last attempt to reach a solution another session of the Council of Foreign Ministers was held, this time in New York (November 4–December 12, 1946). On the majority of issues the agreements of the "Big Four" reached in that session were based upon recommendations made by the Paris peace conference. The five treaties were ultimately signed in Paris on February 10, 1947, by representatives of the enemy states and by representatives of the states which had participated in the Paris peace conference except the United States. Byrnes had already signed for the latter in Washington on January 20, the day before George C. Marshall succeeded him as secretary of state.

The Peace Treaties with Italy, Hungary, Rumania, Bulgaria, and Finland

The Italians, having signed an armistice with the Allies in 1943 and having indeed actually declared war on Germany in October of that year, were most unhappy over the peace treaty which they were obliged to accept. Under its territorial provisions Italy ceded four small and relatively unimportant areas along her northwestern boundary to France, the Dodecanese Islands to Greece, and her East Adriatic islands and most of the

[8] The Slav bloc consisted of Russia, White Russia, the Ukraine, Poland, Czechoslovakia, and Yugoslavia.

Istrian peninsula except Trieste to Yugoslavia. Trieste, which was to be established as a Free Territory, was lost to Italy. The latter further renounced all rights to Libya, Eritrea, and Italian Somaliland in Africa. The ultimate fate of these former Italian colonies was to be decided by the Council of Foreign Ministers, or, if the "Big Four" failed to agree, by the United Nations. But in the meantime they were to remain under British administration. Italy also surrendered all her rights in Albania, Ethiopia, and China.

Although no responsible statesman in 1946 had such fantastic ideas regarding reparation payments as were demanded from Germany after the First World War, Italy was required to make some payments in goods over a period of years: $100,000,000 to Russia, $125,000,000 to Yugoslavia, $105,-000,000 to Greece, $25,000,000 to Ethiopia, and $5,000,000 to Albania. She was also required to pay compensation for damage to Allied property in Italy to the extent of two thirds of its agreed value.

In the matter of war potential, Italy was drastically limited. Her army, including carabinieri, was reduced to 250,000 men, her air force to 25,000, and her navy to 22,500. She was permitted to have only 2 battleships, 4 cruisers, 4 fleet destroyers, 16 torpedo boats, and 20 corvettes, and she was forbidden to construct or acquire battleships, aircraft carriers, or submarines. Her air force was limited to 200 fighter planes and 150 transport and training planes, and she was forbidden to have any bombers. Extensive areas in Sardinia, Sicily, and Apulia, the strategic island of Pantelleria, and the Italian frontier areas along the boundaries with France and Yugoslavia were wholly or partially demilitarized. These restrictions were to remain in force until the treaty was modified by the Allies and Italy or, after Italy became a member of the United Nations, until agreement between Italy and the Security Council. The destruction of her empire and the limitation of her military, naval, and air forces, largely reduced Italy to the status of a third-rate power. In 1946 many Italians felt that for the second time in thirty years Italy had been betrayed by her "friends."

Many of the provisions of the peace treaties with Hungary, Rumania, Bulgaria, and Finland were in essence similar to those in the Italian treaty. The military, naval, and air forces of all four were strictly limited along the lines laid down for Italy. All four had to make reparation payments in goods over a period of years: Hungary—$200,000,000 to Russia and $50,-000,000 each to Czechoslovakia and Yugoslavia; Rumania—$300,000,000 to Russia; Bulgaria—$45,000,000 to Greece and $25,000,000 to Yugoslavia; Finland—$300,000,000 to Russia. Hungary surrendered all territorial gains made after January, 1938, and in addition ceded Czechoslovakia a small area on the right bank of the Danube opposite Bratislava. Rumania recognized her loss of Bessarabia and northern Bukowina to Russia and her loss of the southern Dobrudja to Bulgaria in accordance with treaties signed in 1940, but received back northern Transylvania which had been ceded to Hungary at that time.[9] Bulgaria, despite repeated efforts, failed to obtain a territorial outlet to the Aegean at the expense of Greece, but was allowed to retain the southern Dobrudja. Finland by her treaty lost to Russia the Karelian Isthmus, Viborg and its bay and islands, a number of islands in the Gulf of Finland, territory west, north, and northeast of Lake Ladoga, territory north of Markajaervi and Kuolajaervi, part of the Rybachi peninsula, and the district of Petsamo with its valuable mineral deposits and its outlet to the Arctic.[10] Furthermore, Finland leased Russia territory and water for a naval base on the Porkala headland in return for Russia's renouncing her earlier lease of Hangoe.

The European Recovery Program

The peace negotiations of 1945–1946 had repeatedly revealed the differences in ideologies and aims of Soviet Russia on the one hand and the Western democracies on the other. During those same years ideological clashes had also occurred over "democratic" elections in Bulgaria and Rumania, over Russia's removal of capital goods from Manchuria as "war booty," over the granting of "freedom and independence" to Korea, over Soviet pressure on Iran for oil concessions, and over Russia's demand for control of the Straits. Soon after the signing of the peace treaties the tension between Russia and the United States further increased as a result of the announcement of the "Truman Doctrine." Disturbed by the growing evidence of Soviet influence in the states of eastern and central Europe and by the possibility that Greece and Turkey might succumb to Communist pressure, President Truman on March 12, 1947, declared that "totalitarian regimes imposed on free peoples undermine ... the security of the United States," and asked the Congress to appropriate funds to aid Greece and Turkey to resist totalitarian pressure. Three months later the United States, in order to hasten the economic recovery of Europe—and decrease the likelihood of more countries turning to Communism—offered the so-called Marshall Plan. Russia and her satellite states rejected the plan, denounced it as American imperialism, and set out to wreck it. A "cold war" then ensued between Soviet Russia and the Western democracies, particularly the United States.

To anyone who knew the facts, however, the need for American economic aid to Europe was obvious. The physical destruction of European industry, transportation, and agriculture by the Second World War was

[9] See page 685.
[10] See map on page 671.

terrific.[11] In addition to outright destruction, however, there was also an invisible devastation caused by the war in deterioration of capital and man power and in economic dislocations. Deterioration of industrial and transport equipment inevitably resulted from obsolescence and from over-exploitation during the war years without adequate maintenance and replacement. A parallel deterioration of agricultural tools and equipment also occurred, accompanied by a deterioration of soil fertility. Moreover, the productive capacity of the people was reduced by war exhaustion, under-nourishment, and loss of technical skills.

In the immediate postwar years, consequently, Europe suffered acutely from a number of shortages of basic commodities. One was coal. Whereas Europe [12] had been self-sufficient with respect to coal before the Second World War, in 1947 it produced only 84 per cent of its prewar average, and to meet its most urgent needs had to import high-cost coal from the United States. Steel was another commodity essential for Europe's reconstruction but in 1947 Europe produced only 63 per cent of its prewar volume and was therefore in no position to meet its reconstruction requirements in the matter of steel. Shortages of machinery and equipment were serious everywhere but particularly in the devastated countries. These shortages in turn contributed to the delay in the Continent's industrial recovery. The lack of mine equipment, for example, impeded the increase in production of both coal and steel; and the lack of coal and steel, in turn, handicapped the manufacture of machinery. Europe's system of transport and communication, too, had suffered extensive damage during the war. This was particularly true of motor vehicles, railway rolling stock, and merchant marine. "Thousands of miles of railway lines, a great many railway and highway bridges (well over half of the prewar number in some countries), large and small stations, locomotive sheds, construction facilities, repair shops and other buildings, and harbor installations, as well, were either destroyed or incapacitated."

Furthermore, Europe's shortage of food was critical in the immediate postwar years. The chief factors causing the lack of food were shortages of fertilizers, machinery, farm equipment, and draught animals. Although UNRRA provided 23,000 tractors and 260,000 draught animals, it was estimated that these replaced less than 5 per cent of the loss of draught animals. The deterioration and depletion of the latter and of machinery, in turn, necessitated more hand labor than before the war to produce the same quantity of food. In many of the devastated areas, therefore, there

[11] The material in the first five paragraphs of this section is drawn chiefly from *Salient Features of the World Economic Situation, 1945–47* (1948), an economic report of the United Nations.

[12] In these paragraphs "Europe" denotes Europe excluding the Soviet Union.

occurred a shortage of farm labor. Moreover, the sharp decline in the production of insecticides and allied products in the devastated areas and the reduction in the capacity of chemical industries in Germany and Italy created a lack of these commodities so essential to agriculture. Europe was therefore forced to increase its importation of food over prewar days in order to feed its people, and even before the Second World War 25 per cent of the imports of western Europe had been foodstuffs.

In the United States, on the other hand, over-all industrial production had increased 80 per cent and agricultural output had expanded 36 per cent. In the third quarter of 1947 the production of the durable goods industries in that country was almost double that of prewar production. It was to the United States primarily that Europe had to turn to procure its needed commodities, and during the first half of 1947 United States exports were five times the dollar value of those in 1938. American imports, on the other hand, did not increase at any such rate so that the United States balance of payments indicated a surplus on account of goods and services of $16,700,000,000 in the two years after the war ended with Germany. The European countries did not have the dollar credits to meet this tremendous adverse balance, and the United States government was called upon to furnish aid to many governments, chiefly European, aid which totaled $16,600,000,000 by October 1, 1947.

But by the end of 1947 normal economic conditions were still far from re-established in Europe, and it had become apparent that postwar economic reconstruction would require a longer period of time and be more difficult to achieve than had been expected. Agricultural production, in particular, had received severe setbacks as the result of unfavorable weather conditions. The standard of living of the population of Europe was still far below prewar levels. And to make matters worse, no state of equilibrium had yet been achieved in the economies of European countries, which continued to be subject to inflationary pressures arising from continuing shortages in the face of huge reconstruction requirements.

In the summer of 1947, United States Secretary of State Marshall declared that the United States could not proceed much further with its assistance to Europe unless the countries there reached some agreement as to their requirements and as to their own contribution to European recovery. Any further American assistance, he declared, "should provide a cure rather than a mere palliative." On June 27, 1947, Bevin, Molotov, and Bidault conferred in Paris regarding the Marshall offer. Molotov's views differed from those of the other two. He dismissed the idea of an "all-embracing European economic plan" as unacceptable, suggesting that each country should merely state what it required from the United States. He denounced any plan which provided that German resources should be used for general European reconstruction before the reparations question was settled. He declared that the Marshall Plan indicated that economic recovery must result from co-operation with the great powers by states under their domination, and asked how the small states would be able to safeguard their national economies and their independence. Bevin and Bidault maintained that the United States had reasonably asked, as a prerequisite of further American aid, that the European countries should now state what they could do to help themselves and one another, and asserted that Great Britain and France intended to pursue the Marshall offer in collaboration with any state which wished to join them. Molotov thereupon warned that such a step "would lead to Britain, France, and that group of countries which follows them separating themselves from the other states, and thus the American credits would result in dividing Europe into two groups of states and creating new difficulties in the relations between them."

The British and French governments, nevertheless, sent invitations to all European countries, except Russia, Germany, and Spain, to a conference in Paris on July 12, and stated their belief that a temporary organization should be set up to gather the data on which a program covering both the resources and needs of Europe would be based. This conference was attended by representatives of sixteen states—Britain, France, the Netherlands, Belgium, Luxembourg, Austria, Denmark, Norway, Sweden, Eire, Greece, Italy, Portugal, Switzerland, Iceland, and Turkey. But Russia and her satellites—Poland, Finland, Rumania, Bulgaria, Yugoslavia, Albania, Hungary, and Czechoslovakia—held aloof, though it was reported that strong pressure had to be exerted by Moscow to keep some of them from attending. In the report on the European Recovery Program (ERP), made on September 22, 1947, the sixteen countries pledged themselves to take all feasible measures to bring their budgets into balance, to reduce inflationary pressures, and to stabilize their currencies as quickly as possible. Proposals were submitted to abolish abnormal restrictions on trade and to aim at a sound and balanced multilateral trading system. The report further outlined a four-year program for recovery which called for the restoration of a sound European economy by 1951, but which would entail a total deficit of $22,400,000,000 of which $19,300,000,000 would be required from the United States.

On December 19, 1947, President Truman requested the United States Congress to authorize an appropriation of $17,000,000,000 for the European Recovery Program from April 1, 1948 to June 30, 1952. Although there was considerable opposition to the program in the Congress, it was ultimately approved by both houses on April 2, 1948, with the title "Economic Cooperation Act of 1948." Two weeks later representatives of the powers participating in the European Recovery Program signed a convention in

Paris establishing a permanent organization, the Organization for European Economic Co-operation (OEEC). In June the Congress finally voted an appropriation of $6,030,710,228 for the period from April 1, 1948 to June 30, 1949. On April 5 the first shipments under the Marshall Plan had left American ports. Subsequent shipments were to include food, steel, coal, cotton, petroleum, farm machinery, mining machinery, electrical equipment, and motor trucks.

The results were encouraging. By June, 1950, the Economic Co-operation Administration (ECA)—the United States agency responsible for administering the ERP—announced, industrial production in countries of the OEEC had risen 20 per cent above that of 1938. Intra-European trade had also mounted above the prewar level and, according to the OEEC, price stability had been achieved in virtually all its member countries. By 1951 it appeared that the ERP had accomplished in three years nearly everything which had been expected in four. In the years 1947–1950 the total deficit in western Europe's current balance of payments had been reduced from $8,000,000,000 to $1,000,000,000. While exports had increased 91 per cent by volume, imports had risen only 22 per cent. In July, 1951, the industrial production of the OEEC countries was 50 per cent above the 1947 level. By the summer of 1951 Great Britain, Ireland, Sweden, and Portugal had announced that they would no longer need ERP assistance.

Unfortunately, in 1951 the effects of the outbreak of the Korean War began to be increasingly felt in western Europe. The outbreak of that war started prices rising again, and the decision of the Western democracies to gird themselves for a possible future conflict with the Communist world led to new agreements for collective security and to increased and accelerated rearmament. The latter, in turn, put a heavier burden on western Europe's economy and the dollar gap once more began to widen. The ECA administrator stressed the need for the United States to import more from Europe to relieve the dollar shortage, and in Europe the slogan, "Trade not Aid," began to be heard.

The fate of the ERP after June, 1952, received increasing consideration both in Europe and in the United States, for it seemed clear that some form of American assistance to western Europe would have to be continued after its expiration. Ultimately, in September, 1951, the United States Congress created the Mutual Security Agency (MSA) to co-ordinate the administration of all United States economic, military, and technical aid programs, with emphasis, it was expected, to be placed chiefly on assistance to increase the military strength of the Western democracies. Europe's economic recovery, it was obvious to all observers, was seriously handicapped by the division of the world into two hostile camps.

The Cominform

That Europe was to become split into two camps had become evident as early as October 5, 1947, when it was announced that a conference of the Communist parties of Bulgaria, Czechoslovakia, France, Hungary, Italy, Poland, Rumania, Russia, and Yugoslavia, held in Warsaw, had decided to set up an Information Bureau. The name "Cominform" was soon applied to this new Communist international organization, which to many seemed to resemble the former Comintern. It was obvious from the resolution setting up the Cominform that it was designed to counteract the European Recovery Program, which it characterized as "only the European part of a general plan of world expansion being carried out by the United States." To counter "this front of imperialists and nationalists," it asserted, all democratic countries must oppose it. The "great task awaiting the Communist parties . . . is that of preserving freedom and peace."

The organization of the Cominform might, perhaps, be called Russia's negative reaction to the European Recovery Program. What might be called the Soviet Union's positive reaction came with the organization of the Council for Economic Mutual Assistance at a conference of representatives of Bulgaria, Czechoslovakia, Hungary, Poland, Rumania, and Russia in Moscow in January, 1949. The announcement of the new organization stated that it was formed because the United States, Britain, and certain other western European countries had been boycotting commercially "the countries of the people's democracy" and Russia because they had failed "to submit to the Marshall Plan dictate, as this plan violated the sovereignty of countries and the interests of their national economies." The announcement stated that the new organization might be joined by other European countries which shared the principles of the Council for Economic Mutual Assistance, and in February Albania was admitted into the Council. The division of Europe thus became clear-cut.

The effects of the ensuing "cold war" between Russia and the Western democracies are easily discernible in the Allied treatment of Germany, Austria, and Japan.

The Allied Treatment of Defeated Germany

One significant difference between peace-making in 1946 and peace-making in 1919 was that after the Second World War the Allies gave their attention first to the drafting of treaties with the minor powers rather than, as in 1919, to the most important task, namely, the peace treaty with Germany. In 1946 the crucial question for all Europe—the fate of Germany—

was postponed. The reason given for the postponement was that a peace settlement could not be made for Germany until that country had a government ready to accept it and adequate to execute it. But undoubtedly behind the announced reason for delay were also the fears and suspicions of the "Big Four" and their realization of the difficulty which would confront them in agreeing upon terms.

As early as the Yalta Conference the Allies had begun to make plans for dealing with postwar Germany and during the succeeding years many conferences of the "Big Four" concerned themselves with Allied treatment of that country. At the time when knowledge of the terrible war destruction and ruthless treatment of conquered peoples by the Germans was fresh and the general desire to ward off the horror of a third world war was paramount, the Allies mapped out a program which called for severe punishment, extensive reparations, swift and sure destruction of German militarism and Nazism, and the drastic restriction of German industry in order to prevent the future rebuilding of war potential. But as the years passed without a definitive peace settlement, memories of German atrocities and destruction dimmed, the problem of sustaining life in disrupted and restricted Germany proved a burden for the Western powers, and the latter's fears and suspicions of the aims of Soviet Russia became intensified. Gradually some parts of the earlier-adopted program for dealing with the Reich were modified in order to lessen the burden on the Allies and to improve the lot of the Germans enough to prevent them and the other peoples of western Europe from falling a prey to Communism because of their economic hardships and dissatisfaction. In the interests of clarity, the Allied treatment of Germany will be discussed topically.

OCCUPATION ZONES

At Yalta, Churchill, Roosevelt, and Stalin had agreed that defeated Germany would be occupied by military forces of the United States, Great Britain, Russia, and France, each country in a separate zone, and that a central control council, consisting of the supreme military commanders of the four zones, with headquarters in Berlin, would provide for co-ordinated administration and control. As finally worked out, the American zone consisted of southeastern Germany, including Munich, Nuremberg, and Frankfort, and a small region on both sides of the Weser estuary, including Bremen. The Russian zone comprised the states of northeastern Germany up to the Oder and Neisse rivers, excluding Berlin but including Leipzig, Dresden, Chemnitz, Halle, Eisenach, and Magdeburg. The British occupied northwestern Germany, including Hamburg, the Ruhr area, and Cologne but excluding the American enclave about Bremen. The French took over the Rhineland south of Cologne, including the Saar Basin, an area which, though much smaller than that of the other Allies, was of vital concern to France.

By the middle of August, 1945, the Russians had relinquished parts of Berlin for occupation by the other Allies, and on August 30 the Allies in a proclamation to the German people announced the establishment of the Allied Control Council in the former German capital.

New York Times

THE OCCUPATION ZONES OF GERMANY

FUTURE BOUNDARIES

At the Yalta Conference, also, the "Big Three" had agreed that Poland, while surrendering to Russia most of the former Polish territory east of the "Curzon Line," must receive substantial additions of territory in the north and west, although the final delimitation of the western frontier must await the peace conference. At Potsdam the three Allies agreed in principle that East Prussia in the vicinity of Memel and Königsberg should be transferred to Russia and that all other former German territory east of the Oder and Neisse rivers should be under the administration of Poland and should not be considered as part of the zone of occupation in Germany. Although at Potsdam it was again agreed that the determination of the Polish-German boundary should await the peace settlement, it was later generally assumed by Russian and Polish statesmen that the territory under Polish administration was to be permanently Polish, and that the Oder-Neisse rivers would constitute Germany's eastern boundary.

POPULATION TRANSFERS

At Potsdam, the three Allies had recognized that the transfer to Germany of German populations remaining in Poland, Czechoslovakia, and Hungary would have to be undertaken, and in November, 1945, Allied representatives approved a plan for the transfer of some 6,650,000 Germans from those countries into the various occupied zones in Germany. This step was deemed necessary because of these states' fears of having any German minorities within their bounds. The German policy of using slave labor in the Reich during the war created another gigantic problem of transferring populations. It was estimated that in the twelve months after the armistice the Allies handled between 20 and 25 million people, some moving east and some moving west. Only a few glimpses of what occurred can be given here. To Hungary, Czechoslovakia, and Yugoslavia 4,000,000 displaced persons were returned; to Russia 2,000,000; to Poland more than 2,000,000; to France, the Netherlands, and Belgium, 800,000. In addition, 1,000,000 prisoners of war were repatriated to France, and great numbers to Italy. Even within Germany great shifts occurred; for instance, 5,000,000 persons went from the British to the Soviet zone and 1,700,000 from the Soviet to the British zone. These population movements probably dwarfed anything which had ever occurred in Europe in so short a period.

WAR CRIMINALS

In contrast with the little that was done after the First World War,[13] the Allies had meanwhile taken steps to bring the chief German war criminals to trial. An International Military Tribunal was established by the "Big Four" and by October 18, 1945, twenty-four German leaders had been indicted with participating in the plot against peace and humanity conceived by Hitler. The International Military Tribunal held its hearings for many months in Nuremberg and eventually in the autumn of 1946 condemned twelve men to death, three to life imprisonment, and four to prison terms of from ten to twenty years. Ley, former head of the Labor Front, had committed suicide soon after his indictment, and Gustav Krupp's trial had been postponed because of his ill health. Göring com-

---

[13] Almost no "war criminals" were punished after the First World War.

mitted suicide before his sentence was carried out, but on October 16 ten former German leaders,[14] including Ribbentrop, Keitel, Rosenberg, Streicher, Frank, Frick, and Seyss-Inquart, were hanged. Hess was sentenced to life imprisonment, but Schacht, Papen, and Fritzsche were acquitted, contrary to the desire of many foreigners and Germans. The Nuremberg Tribunal also condemned as criminal four Nazi organizations: the Leadership Corps, the Schutzstaffeln (SS), the Gestapo, and the Sicherheitsdienst (SD).

In addition to this spectacular trial of prominent war criminals in Nuremberg, the military governments of the four zones also conducted trials of hundreds of lesser criminals. Some military commanders were punished for the war crimes of troops under their command, some members of Hitler's ministry of justice were sentenced to prison, and many men—and some women—were hanged or imprisoned for their roles in connection with the terrible atrocities perpetrated on some millions of inmates of German concentration camps. In 1947, Friedrick Flick, Thyssen's successor as head of the Vereinigte Stahlwerke, the directors of the I. G. Farben Industrie, and the directors of the extensive Krupp industries were also brought to trial on charges of conspiring with Hitler to wage aggressive war and on charges of participating in the German program of slave labor and the plundering of occupied countries. Although all were acquitted on the charges of conspiracy with Hitler, they did not all escape on the other two counts. The United States military tribunal sentenced Flick to seven years' imprisonment, Alfred Krupp to twelve years in prison and to the confiscation of all of his property, and ten former Krupp officials and thirteen former directors or officials of the I. G. Farben concern to prison terms ranging from eighteen months to eight years.

DENAZIFICATION

At Yalta, it had been decided to wipe out the Nazi Party, laws, organizations, and institutions, and to remove all Nazi influences from the cultural and economic life of the German people. At Potsdam, it had been further decided that Nazi leaders, influential Nazi supporters, and high officials of Nazi organizations and institutions should be arrested and interned, and that all members of the Nazi Party who had been more than nominal participants in its activities should be removed from public and semipublic office and from positions of responsibility in important private undertakings.

In pursuance of these aims, the Allied Control Council in 1945 issued

---

[14] Martin Borman was tried and condemned in absentia, his whereabouts being unknown. Hitler and Goebbels had died during the battle of Berlin and Himmler had committed suicide in 1945.

directives repealing Nazi laws, liquidating Nazi organizations, removing Nazi sympathizers from public office, and providing for the denazification of schools. The occupying governments in all four zones undertook to investigate and try millions of Germans suspected of having been active in the Nazi Party. Thousands were given prison terms, sentenced to hard labor, or debarred from office. In some cases the Allies were assisted also by German courts; those in the American zone, for instance, gave prison sentences of various lengths to some men who had been high in the Third Reich. But the Allies discovered that at least one disadvantage resulted from sweeping denazification; so widespread had been membership in the Nazi Party that practically all trained leaders, executives, and administrators in Germany's political, economic, and cultural life were included and their removal from office frequently made it necessary to put men of less knowledge, ability, and training in their places. As the desire for rehabilitating Germany increased among the Allies, and particularly after tension between Russia and the Western powers developed, the enthusiasm for thoroughgoing denazification declined, and men who were known to have been Nazis or sympathizers with Nazism were frequently permitted to resume their former duties. In 1948 denazification proceedings were largely discontinued in all the zones.

Meanwhile, efforts had been made to eliminate Nazi doctrines from German education. Many educators from the Allied countries were sent to Germany to attempt to remold that country's educational system and indoctrinate the German youth in democracy. They were handicapped, of course, by a shortage of classrooms, teachers, and books, but more particularly by German adherence to Nazi principles. In November, 1947, a popular poll taken in the British zone showed that most Germans still believed that Nazism was "a good idea, but badly carried out under Hitler." Said the American adviser on cultural matters in June, 1948: "It is evident to me that Germany will have recovered economically long before she has recovered spiritually. She will have great economic power long before she has developed a democratic sense of responsibility for the use of that power."

DEMILITARIZATION

At both Yalta and Potsdam the Allies had announced their determination to destroy German militarism in order to ensure that Germany should never again be able to disturb the peace of the world. To this end they planned to disarm and disband all German armed forces, break up for all time the German general staff that had repeatedly contrived the resurgence of German militarism, remove or destroy all German military equipment, and eliminate or control all German industry that could be used for military production. The first three of these objectives were largely attained in all the zones by 1947. The fourth objective caused some disagreement among the occupying powers because of the difficulty of drawing the line between industries that were valuable for peace production and those that could be used to produce war supplies. When the problem of rehabilitating German economic life became acute, Great Britain and the United States were inclined to become more 'lenient in their definition of peace industry and to permit the continuation of some industries in their zones which France and Russia considered ought to be dismantled.

The conflict between France on the one hand and the United States and Great Britain on the other was well exemplified in views regarding the treatment of the Ruhr. On November 10, 1948, the United States and British military governments announced that, in the interest of greater efficiency and increased production, limited and temporary control of the Ruhr coal, iron, and steel industries would be turned over to German trustees pending the final determination of ownership by a future German government. An international authority, however, would regulate the distribution of the Ruhr's products. France at once protested against this Anglo-American decision, and contended that, in the interest of her own security, international control must be extended also to production. She was apparently able to force some modification in the Anglo-American plans, for eventually, in December, a London conference of the six powers interested in the Ruhr agreed to set up "The International Authority for the Ruhr," with sweeping powers to supervise the Ruhr's industries for an indefinite period. The main organ of this authority was to be a council representing the United States, Britain, France, Belgium, the Netherlands, Luxembourg, and Western Germany, with the three great powers and Western Germany having three votes each and the lesser states one each.

The international authority was given power to ensure that the resources of the Ruhr would in the future be used not for purposes of aggression but solely in the interests of peace. To that end it was agreed that there should not be allowed to develop ownership in the Ruhr coal, coke or steel industries, or trade and marketing agreements among such industries, which would institute excessive concentration of economic power; nor should persons who had been or might be found to have furthered the aggressive designs of the Nazis hold positions of ownership or control in the Ruhr industries. The authority was to divide the coal, coke, and steel production of the district so as to ensure adequate access to supplies of these products by countries co-operating in the common economic good, taking into account the essential needs of Germany. Although these agreements did not go far enough to satisfy some French leaders and were bitterly denounced for different reasons by both the Germans and the Russians, they were in line with earlier agreements of the chief Allied leaders.

ALLIED ECONOMIC CONTROLS

At Potsdam the Allied statesmen had decided that controls should be imposed on German economy to the extent necessary: (1) to carry out industrial disarmament; (2) to assure the production required to meet the needs of the occupying forces and to maintain in Germany average living standards no higher than those of other European countries; (3) to ensure the equitable distribution of essential commodities between the several zones so as to produce a balanced economy throughout Germany and reduce the need of imports; (4) to control German industry and commerce with the aim of preventing Germany from developing a war potential. German economy, it was further decided, should be decentralized to eliminate the excessive concentration of economic power as exemplified by cartels, syndicates, and trusts. Furthermore, in organizing the German economy primary emphasis should be placed on the development of agriculture and peaceful domestic industries. Productive capacity not needed for permitted production should be removed as reparations or destroyed.

Early in 1946 the Allied Control Council published its plan for the future level of German industry, the general effect of which was expected to be a reduction by 1949 to about half the level of 1938. Exports were planned as 3,000,000,000 marks (1936 value) for 1949, and approved imports were not to exceed that figure, though they had amounted to 4,200,000,000 marks in 1936. Certain specific decrees were issued. The production of synthetic gasoline, rubber, ammonia, aluminum, magnesium, certain chemicals, agricultural tractors, and machine tools was forbidden. Germany's steel production capacity was limited to 7,500,000 tons and the production of steel was not to exceed 5,800,000 tons in any year without permission of the Council. Furthermore, Germany was forbidden to construct ocean-going vessels and forbidden to export basic chemicals, vehicles, tractors, and heavy electrical or metallurgical equipment. These limitations on Germany's industry and commerce largely deprived her of her former means of payment for imports. With more need than in 1936 to import food, she would be less able to pay for it.

Ultimately the statesmen of the United States and Great Britain reached the conclusion that the Germans could not export enough to buy for themselves the food and raw materials which they needed so long as their industries were thus drastically restricted and their country was arbitrarily divided. And if the Germans could not become self-sufficient, the United States and Great Britain would be compelled to advance huge sums in subsidies to enable them to exist. Furthermore, unless Germany was possessed of a sound economy, it appeared, there could be no sound economy in western Europe. These statesmen thus found themselves forced to choose between two policies: (1) the continued limitation of German industry in order to prevent the revival of German military might; (2) the restoration of German industry to a higher level than earlier contemplated in order to make Germany self-supporting and able to contribute to the economic life of western Euope. Bevin and Byrnes decided in favor of the second course.

In August, 1947, the United States and Great Britain decided to revise the level of industry in their two zones up to that of 1936, in contrast with the 70–75 per cent of 1936 production permitted by the Allied Control Council's plan of 1946. Their hope was to make their two zones self-supporting, and new totals of production in the so-called restricted industries and in the total export trade were permitted. In return for the United States' assumption of most of the cost of subsidizing the German economy, the United States received the controlling voice in the agencies for deciding production and export policies in the two zones. Russia denounced the Anglo-American plan as an abrogation of the Potsdam agreement and the French, still thinking of security, also questioned the wisdom of the Anglo-American policy.

NATIONAL ECONOMIC DISUNION

The Potsdam Conference had decided that during the period of Allied occupation Germany should be treated as a single economic unit, and that essential German administrative departments, headed by state secretaries, should be established, particularly for finance, transport, communications, foreign trade, and industry. Such departments were to function under the direction of the Allied Control Council. But the French government which had not been represented at Potsdam, claimed that it was not bound by these decisions, and refused to approve the establishment of the central administrative machinery agreed upon at that conference. No progress, therefore, was made toward establishing the five German administrative departments needed for an economically unified Germany and in consequence freedom of interzone transportation, communications, and commerce was lacking.

The French, ever mindful of the three German invasions of their country in the preceding century, were primarily concerned with their own national security. They asserted that 65,000,000 Germans in one state, much smaller in area than in 1937 and with its industrial life drastically curtailed, would surely explode politically within a generation and once more produce war. They argued that, until a solution was found of the problem of the economic existence of the German people, it was necessary in the interests of the French national security to prevent the political unification of Germany.

In July, 1946, at a meeting of the Council of Foreign Ministers, Bevin suggested a plan for treating the economic resources of Germany as a whole without establishing the central administrative departments to which the French objected. Bevin maintained that there should be an equitable distribution of German resources throughout the four zones, that surplus resources in one zone should be made available to meet any deficit in the approved requirements of the other zones. Because Germany was not being treated as an economic unit, he pointed out, the British zone was not obtaining the benefit of surplus German resources of other zones. Surplus from the Soviet zone, he declared, was being taken as reparations. On this occasion Byrnes and Bidault approved Bevin's plan, but Molotov rejected it, claiming that its operation would be contrary to the reparations agreement made at Potsdam. Meanwhile, the Russian zone was largely closed to outsiders and shrouded in obscurity. For all practical purposes rivers and nearly all railways and roads ended at the so-called "Iron Curtain." Nevertheless, it was generally known that Russia had removed, and was continuing to remove, large quantities of machinery, tools, and other equipment from its zone as reparations.

REPARATIONS

At Yalta the "Big Three" had agreed that justice demanded that Germany should make compensation in kind to the fullest possible extent for all damage caused to the Allied nations. This general statement was made more explicit at Potsdam where it was decided that Russia's reparation claims should be met, in the first place, by removals from the zone of Germany occupied by Russia and from appropriate German external assets in Finland, Rumania, Bulgaria, Hungary, and eastern Austria. In addition, however, Russia should receive from the Western zones in Germany 10 per cent of such usable and complete industrial capital equipment as was unnecessary [15] for the German peace economy and a further 15 per cent of such capital equipment in exchange for an equivalent value of food and other commodities. Russia, in turn, agreed to settle Poland's reparation claims from her own share of reparations. The reparation claims of the United States, Great Britain, and other countries entitled to reparations, except Poland, were to be met from the Western zones and from appropriate German external assets in countries other than those reserved for Russia. The payment of reparations, it was agreed, should leave enough resources in Germany to enable her people to subsist without external assistance.

In January, 1946, an Inter-Allied Reparation Agency was created and

---

[15] The determination of what industrial capital equipment was unnecessary was made subject to the final approval of the zone commander in the zone from which the equipment was to be removed.

designated as the central organization for allocating German reparation assets among the states, other than Russia and Poland, which were to receive reparation payments. According to the original agreement reparations were to come from industrial capital equipment, German external assets in countries other than those assigned to Russia, merchant shipping, inland water transport, captured enemy supplies, and current production. The work of the Reparation Agency was greatly handicapped, however, by the disagreement which developed in the "Big Four" over the political and economic future of Germany, and reparation assets made available to the Agency for allocation were comparatively small. In November, 1947, the Agency estimated the total number of plants declared available for reparations by the military governors of the three Western zones as 858, valued at only 800,000,000 to 1,100,000,000 Reichsmarks, and expressed disappointment at the low amount of reparations thus declared available. The Agency discussed the possibility of obtaining additional reparations from existing stocks, current production, and services, but dropped the discussion following the disagreement in the Council of Foreign Ministers at London (November 25–December 15, 1947).[16]

By this date the four great Allies had definitely split on the question of the economic treatment of Germany. Russia held that reparations were essential to repair the economic losses suffered by the United Nations, especially by herself, at the hands of Germany and her satellites. But they were essential, also, she maintained, in order to reduce Germany's industrial war potential. Furthermore, Russia had found that the removal of capital assets from Germany to the Soviet Union was not so efficient as she had expected and had concluded that it would in some cases be preferable to leave factories in Germany and take their products as reparations. In other words Russia had begun to press for reparation payments from current German production.

The Western Allies, on the other hand, had become more and more angered at Russia's unwillingness to permit the economic unification of Germany and more and more concerned at the disruption that the removal of reparations was inflicting on the German economy. In August, 1947, the United States and Britain finally gave notice that no more plants in their zones would be made available for reparations until Western Germany's production had been built up and until Russia had become more cooperative in the matter of German economic unity. Molotov thereupon

[16] Up to the end of 1947 the Reparation Agency had had 261 plants or parts of plants made available to it for reparations, of which equipment from 234 had been allocated to different countries by April, 1948. Better progress had been made in the distribution of the German merchant fleet; by the middle of 1947 some 274 ships had been distributed to eighteen nations. The remaining German vessels, suitable only for scrapping, had been sold to the highest bidders.

appeared willing to accept Germany's economic unification provided that Russia obtained reparations from the current production of the Western zones. Marshall and Bevin, on the other hand, held that German ability to pay for imports must have priority over reparation payments, otherwise the United States and Great Britain, which had each been subsidizing German imports with almost $500,000,000 yearly, would find themselves "paying for the imports necessary to keep Germany alive while others obtain the reparations." When Molotov ultimately agreed that Germany's industrial production might be raised to twice the total originally planned, but insisted that 10 per cent of it should go for reparations, regardless of the effect on German self-sufficiency, the London Conference broke down and adjourned *sine die*.

RESTORATION OF LOCAL SELF-GOVERNMENT

At Potsdam it had been decided that the administration of affairs in Germany should be directed toward the decentralization of the political structure of the country and toward the development of local responsibility. To these ends it was agreed that democratic political parties should be allowed and encouraged throughout Germany, that local self-government should be restored on democratic principles as rapidly as consistent with military security, and that the representative and elective principles should be introduced into regional, provincial, and state (Land) administration as soon as justified by the successful application of these principles in local government. It was further decided that for the time being no central German government should be established.

Although at first the Germans seemed to be politically apathetic, eventually, four major political parties again appeared: Social Democrats, Christian Democrats, Free Democrats, and Communists. The Social Democratic Party, led in western Germany by Kurt Schumacher—a former Reichstag deputy who had spent ten years in Nazi concentration camps—had three main aims: unification of Germany under a central government with local administrative power delegated to the states, nationalization of basic industries, and preservation of personal and political liberty. The Christian Democrat Union, on the other hand, desired a federal type of government and the protection and encouragement of free enterprise, and the Right-wing branch of the party had a bourgeois hatred of Russia. The Free Democratic Party, the weakest of the four, advocated a unified but decentralized Germany, free enterprise, and friendship with Soviet Russia as well as the rest of the world.

The Communist Party, whose spokesman, Wilhelm Pieck, had been an associate of Karl Liebknecht and Rosa Luxembourg [17] and had later spent

[17] See page 494.

some years in exile in Russia, sought a unified Germany under a centralized government, a planned economy based on nationalization, and friendship with the Soviet Union. In the Russian zone the Communist Party was particularly active and in April, 1946, forced the Social Democratic Party there to join it in the Socialist Unity Party of Germany. Although Social Democratic leaders in the other zones repudiated this step, the Socialist Unity Party sought, somewhat futilely, to establish branches throughout Germany.

In 1946 the Germans were given their first opportunity to participate in the political life of their country when elections were held for the governments of the smaller political units. Later in the year and in 1947 they were also given an opportunity to elect the members of the various state legislatures. But no steps were taken to restore the national government in Berlin. This was one of the causes of dissension in the "Big Four" at their meetings in Moscow (March 10–April 24) and in London (November 25–December 15) during 1947. Molotov urged the establishment of German political unity as a prerequisite of economic unity and the removal of zonal barriers. But the Allied ministers proved unable to agree on how or when a central government should be formed. This inability to agree, in turn, seemed to indicate an indefinite postponement of any peace conference to deal with Germany, for Molotov insisted that the formation of a central government was also the prerequisite of such a conference.

THE BEGINNING OF WEST GERMAN UNIFICATION

Meanwhile, the Western Allies, despairing of achieving complete economic unification of Germany, had taken measures to unify their zones. In December, 1946, an agreement was signed by the United States and Britain, providing that their two zones should be treated in economic matters as a single area—"Bizonia." France and Russia were invited to join in the project, but both declined. Nevertheless, in 1948, despite formal protests from Russia charging violation of the Potsdam agreement, the United States, Great Britain, and France held conferences in London, attended also by representatives of Belgium, the Netherlands, and Luxembourg, to consider the merger of the French zone with Bizonia. The Americans and British were eager to integrate Germany in the European Recovery Program through increased German production; but the French feared that German economic recovery might again jeopardize French security.

Ultimately, however, the six powers agreed that, pending the eventual re-establishment of German unity, it was desirable for the West German people to establish for themselves political institutions which would enable them to assume full governmental responsibility, subject to the minimum requirements of Allied occupation and control. The military governors were therefore instructed to authorize the heads of the several German states in the three Western zones to convene a constituent assembly in September, 1948, to prepare a federal constitution for the approval of the states.

THE "BATTLE OF BERLIN"

Meanwhile, on June 20 the three Western powers had introduced a currency reform in their zones, replacing the Reichsmark—which had been inflated by the Nazis and later by the occupying powers—with the Deutschemark at a ratio of 10 to 1. Immediately the Russian military governor forbade the use of the Deutschemark in the Soviet zone and also in Berlin, on the ground that the city, although actually divided among the Big Four, lay well within the Russian occupation zone and economically formed part of that zone. He also announced that a new currency would be introduced in the Soviet zone and that after June 26 all other currencies would be banned both there and in Berlin. On June 23 the Western military governors announced that they would introduce the Deutschemark into their sectors of Berlin; on the next day the Soviet authorities stopped railway traffic between Berlin and the west because of a "technical disturbance." Eventually they threw an economic blockade around the Western sectors of the city of Berlin by cutting all rail and water routes which the Western powers had been using to bring supplies into the city.

The so-called battle of Berlin followed. The Western powers countered the Soviet move by instituting a spectacular "air lift" to Berlin, using hundreds of airplanes to carry thousands of tons of cargo to the city daily. At the height of the Allied effort planes arrived in the capital on an average of one every two minutes. The Western powers also cut off from the Russian zone of Germany coal, steel, and other supplies which had been coming from the west. Although the Soviet government appeared to stay carefully within its legal rights, it sought to handicap or restrict the Western powers in Berlin to such an extent that they would withdraw from the capital or make concessions to Russia elsewhere—perhaps abandon the plan for a separate West Germany or grant the Soviet government a share in the control of the industrially rich Ruhr.

Although the Allied use of airplanes to supply Berlin was spectacular, it could not permanently meet the needs of the 2,300,000 Berliners in the Western zones. It could not, for instance, supply the necessary fuel and raw materials to maintain the city's industries. Some factories had to close, and unemployment resulted. At the same time, industries in Russia's zone were affected adversely by the Allied counterblockade. Eventually the Western governments sought to solve the impasse by instituting negotiations directly with Stalin. From July 31 to August 27 the Western ambassadors held conferences in Moscow with Molotov, conferences which Stalin himself twice attended. The Russians wished to discuss the whole German situation, particularly the London decision to set up a Western German government at Frankfort. The West demanded the lifting of the Soviet Berlin blockade as a prelude to such general discussions. The Russians as a prerequisite to lifting the blockade in turn demanded that their German currency be recognized as the sole legal tender in the capital. At length it was agreed in principle that the Soviet mark should be the only currency in Berlin, and the technical questions of currency and the blockade were then turned over to the Allied Control Council, that is, to the four Allied military governors.

While conferences were being held by the Allied generals, Communist-inspired attacks on Berlin's assembly, the only branch of the city's government which had continued to function on a city-wide basis, early in September destroyed that body. The Communist members retained control of the city hall, which was in the Russian zone, and the non-Communist members of the assembly were forced to meet in the British zone. In December the Soviet military commander formally recognized the city administration set up by the Communist members of Berlin's assembly as the only legal municipal authority in the city. Friedrich Ebert, son of the Weimar Republic's first president, became burgomaster of the Communist administration in the Soviet zone of Berlin and he in turn declared that the Soviet military commander was the only authority recognized by his regime. His administration denied access to the city hall to members of the former administration.

In the three Western zones of Berlin, despite Soviet objections, popular elections were held on December 5 for a new municipal assembly. More than 86 per cent of the electorate went to the polls and their votes were distributed roughly 65 per cent to Social Democrats, 19 per cent to Christian Democrats, and 16 per cent to Free Democrats. The new assembly unanimously elected a burgomaster who proposed that, pending the ultimate unification of Berlin, the three Western zones of the city should be merged into a single administrative unit, that the Western military commanders should organize an Allied Control Council for this unit, and that in this unit the Western currency should be the only legal tender. On December 21 the three Western military governors decided to resume the sittings of the Allied Control Council, declaring that if the Soviet authorities should later decide to abide by the existing four-power agreements, the quadripartite administration of Berlin could be reactivated.

Meanwhile, later in September, 1948, the Western Allies had submitted the problem of the Soviet blockade of Berlin to the Security Council of the United Nations. In the succeeding weeks that body had sought to find a solution which would be acceptable to the four Allied powers, but without success. Not until May, 1949, after the Western powers had carried on their airlift for months and had revealed no inclination to recede from their stand on the issues, was the impasse ended. It was finally agreed through diplomacy that the Soviet blockade should be lifted on May 12 and that the Council of Foreign Ministers should once more convene to discuss the German and Austrian situations. Accordingly, the blockade came to an end. But the meeting of the diplomats of the four powers in Paris (May 23–June 20, 1949) brought no tangible results so far as peace treaties with Germany and Austria were concerned.

THE FEDERAL REPUBLIC OF GERMANY

In accordance with the decision of the Western powers at London a constituent convention for West Germany had convened in Bonn in September, 1948, and in May, 1949, it adopted what was called the "Basic Law for the Federal Republic of Germany." By the provisions of this constitution, Germany continued to be a federal state. The national parliament is a bicameral body consisting of the Bundestag (Federal Diet), elected for four years by popular vote, and the Bundesrat (Federal Council), representing the governments of the constitutent states. In the latter each state has at least three votes; the larger states have four or five. The delegates in the Bundesrat are bound by instructions from their respective state governments and must vote as a unit. The Bundesrat is not so powerful as the Bundestag and, in general, exercises a delaying power through its provisional veto.

The executive branch of the government consists of the president and the cabinet, which includes the chancellor and other ministers. The president, definitely less powerful than under the Weimar constitution, is elected for five years by a federal convention composed of the members of the Bundestag and an equal number of delegates from the state diets. The president's position resembles that of the British ruler; the real executive power resides in the federal chancellor, whose position is much stronger than it was under the Weimar constitution. Special provisions are designed to make it difficult for the Bundestag to overthrow him. Forty-eight hours must elapse between a motion to censure the government and the vote on that motion; surprise votes are thus prevented and time is available for the opposing parliamentary groups to marshal their forces. Furthermore, the Bundestag may express its lack of confidence only after it has elected a successor by a majority vote of its members. Since the Federal Republic has a multiparty system the chancellor may not easily be overthrown; although he may be supported by only a minority, the majority may be unable to agree on his successor. On the other hand, the chancellor may ask the Bundestag for a vote of confidence and, if he fails to receive it, the president, at his request, may dissolve that body and call for new elections. Finally, if the Bundestag rejects a bill declared by the cabinet to be urgent, by

Article 81 the president at the request of the cabinet and with the approval of the Bundesrat may declare a state of "legislative emergency," and if the Bundestag again rejects the bill it may be enacted by the Bundesrat without the consent of the lower house. The sole safeguard of the Bundestag is the provision that there may be only one six-month period of "legislative emergency" during the term of office of the same chancellor.

In the first parliamentary elections under the new constitution, held on August 14, 1949, the Christian Democrats, including the Christian Socialists (their counterpart in Bavaria) won 139 seats and the Social Democrats 131. The two major groups secured slightly more than two thirds of the popular vote, the other votes being divided among some thirteen parties. Of the latter the Free Democrats (mildly Rightist) won 52 seats, the Bavarian and German parties (both distinctly Rightist) each 17, and the Communists 15. On September 12 the Bundestag and Bundesrat in joint session elected as the first federal president Theodore Heuss, a member of the Free Democratic Party, who had been a newspaper editor, a university professor, and a member of the Reichstag in pre-Hitler days. Konrad Adenauer, the 72-year-old leader of the Christian Democrats, was then confirmed as the new chancellor, with a coalition ministry consisting of Christian Democrats, Christian Socialists, Free Democrats, and members of the German Party. On September 21 in a formal ceremony at the headquarters of the Western Allies the latter recognized the Federal Republic, ended their military government in Germany, and replaced their military governors by high commissioners, who still retained some power to supervise German affairs under the new Occupation Statute which came into effect.

THE GERMAN DEMOCRATIC REPUBLIC

Meanwhile, in the Russian zone of Germany another state had been set up. In 1948 a People's Congress had been elected under the auspices of the Socialist Unity Party and it in turn had elected a smaller People's Council. The latter had adopted a draft constitution in September, 1948, which, it was announced, would go into effect for all Germany at some future time. In May, 1949, following the adoption of the constitution for the Federal Republic of Germany, a congress was elected in the Russian zone—only one list of candidates was submitted—which approved the already-drafted constitution, but no steps were taken to establish a government in accordance with its provisions until after the West German government had been set up in Bonn. Then, following a vigorous Russian protest against the Bonn constitution, the People's Council of East Germany promulgated the new constitution on October 7.

Under the constitution of the German Democratic Republic, which proclaimed Germany an "indivisible, democratic republic," authority was vested in the People's Chamber, elected by universal, secret suffrage, and in the State Chamber, with much less power, representing the states. Although the judiciary was described as independent, the People's Chamber was given the power to dismiss the Supreme Court. The People's Council, chosen in 1948, at once became the new People's Chamber and the state legislatures appointed the delegates to the State Chamber. Wilhelm Pieck, leader of the Socialist Unity Party, was elected president by the two chambers and Otto Grotewohl, a former Social Democrat but now a member of the Socialist Unity Party, was chosen premier. On October 11 the German Democratic Republic was formally inaugurated with Berlin as its capital, and a statement was read informing the two chambers that the U.S.S.R. was turning over to it "the administrative functions which have thus far belonged to the Soviet military administration." For all practical purposes the new German Democratic Republic became another Communist state with a People's Front government similar to those found in the other Soviet satellite states in eastern Europe. The latter and the Soviet Union at once exchanged diplomatic representatives with the Berlin government.

On the basis of these steps in 1949 it appeared that Germany as a consequence of the "cold war" had been at least temporarily partitioned, and that gradually the life of the two halves was being reorientated. On the one hand, the Federal Republic, including some 75 per cent of Germany's postwar territory and more than two thirds of her population, constituted a democratic, parliamentary state with the freedoms found in the Western democracies, with which it was linked economically and militarily. On the other hand, the Democratic Republic, with about 25 per cent of the German territory and approximately one third of the German people, had a regime which closely resembled that found in the Soviet Union and the other Communist states. Such a division of Germany was contrary to the nationalistic trend of the nineteenth and twentieth centuries and certainly was contrary to the desires of the German people.

The Allied Treatment of "Liberated" Austria

The situation in Austria in the years after the defeat of the Nazi armies in many ways paralleled that in Germany, although it had been expected that Allied treatment of that state would be more lenient than it was of the former Reich. As early as October, 1943, the three great Allies had decided that Austria should be re-established as a free and independent state, and had then agreed that an Allied Commission should be charged with the task of recreating a central administration for Austria as quickly as possible after the country's resumption of normal political activities. The liberation of the country came in April and May, 1945, and the control machinery of the Allied Commission was approved in July. The most important organ was the Allied Council, consisting of the commanders-in-chief of the four occupying powers (France to be included, as in Berlin), which was to exercise supreme authority in all matters affecting Austria as a whole and to ensure uniformity of action in the four zones of occupation. The Allied Council on September 11, 1945, officially sanctioned the resumption of political activities by the Socialist, Communist, and People's parties. The Socialists were the former Social Democrats and the People's Party consisted chiefly of the former Christian Socialists with some adherents from the former Landbund and Heimwehr.

On November 25, 1945, a general election for a National Assembly, with former Nazis debarred from voting, resulted in the People's Party securing 85 seats, the Socialists 76, and the Communists 4. The results of the elections, so far as the popular vote was concerned, were approximately the same as those in the last free election in Austria in 1930. The National Assembly unanimously elected Karl Renner, a Socialist and former chancellor, as President of the Republic, and a new government was organized with Leopold Figl, the leader of the People's Party, as chancellor. On January 7, 1946, the four Allies recognized Austria as an independent state with the same boundaries as in 1937. The National Assembly restored the democratic constitution which had existed prior to 1934.[18] Elections in 1949 and in 1953 brought some decline in the strength of the People's Party. Figl continued as chancellor until April, 1953, when he was succeeded by Julius Raab, another leader of the People's Party, who presided over a coalition government. On December 31, 1950, the revered President Renner died at the age of 80; Theodor Koerner, another Socialist, was chosen to succeed him.

Meanwhile, the Allied military occupation of Austria had been established. Styria, Carinthia, and southern Tyrol were occupied by the British; Upper Austria, Salzburg, and northern Tyrol, by the Americans; Lower Austria, Burgenland, and the province of Vienna, by the Russians; and Vorarlberg, by the French. Vienna, like Berlin, was also split into four zones. The arable lands producing the main crops of cereals, potatoes, and beets were chiefly within the American and Russian zones, while the French and British zones were mainly mountain lands where agriculture consisted chiefly in raising live stock. The British zone included the iron mines and the headquarters of the iron and steel industry, but most of the engineering works were in the Russian zone. The French zone had timber and copper which the others needed, and oil was found only in the Russian zone.

18 For the Austrian constitution before 1934, see page 570.

Obviously, in both agriculture and industry the zones were complementary to one another and for economic recovery it was essential for Austria to function as a single unit.

Although in September, 1945, the Allied Council decided that freedom of transportation and communication should be restored throughout Austria in the near future, strict control on the demarcation lines continued. In January, 1946, the Allied Council decided that the free exchange between zones of surplus goods should be permitted but that each zone was to continue to be primarily responsible for its own self-sufficiency. The result was only a very limited movement of goods. Two months later it was decided that food rationing in all four zones should be identical, but neither the military nor political governments in the provinces were particularly ready to make available for Vienna foodstuffs from local resources. The old antagonisms between the "Blacks" and the "Reds" thus reappeared.[19] Hunger and starvation resulted.

As in the years immediately following the First World War,[20] Austria was forced to depend for her subsistence on aid from abroad. From April, 1945, to January, 1947, she received loans, credits, and relief assistance of about $281,000,000 from UNRRA, the United States, and Great Britain. After UNRRA came to an end on December 31, 1946, the country was dependent for assistance chiefly upon the United States. During 1947 numerous steps, official and unofficial, were taken in the latter country to help provide Austria with food, commodities, and foreign exchange, culminating in an emergency relief measure enacted by the American Congress to tide over France, Italy, and Austria until the European Recovery Plan—the so-called Marshall Plan—became operative. Austria was one of the sixteen states which had agreed to this plan, and benefited from the appropriation voted by the United States Congress in June, 1948.

The date of the final conclusion of a peace treaty with Austria seemed to retreat as the months and years passed. At a meeting of the "Big Four" in July, 1946, Byrnes proposed that a treaty should at once be drafted which would end the Allied occupation of Austria, but Molotov refused to accept his proposal, asserting that many Nazi laws were still in force in Austria, that the Pan-German movement there was still strong, and that hundreds of thousands of non-Austrians who had fought for Hitler had taken refuge in that country. Two years later the arrest of several hundred former Nazi Gestapo and SS men who had organized an underground Nazi movement in the British zone seemed to bear out these claims. At succeeding conferences of the "Big Four" one of the chief questions which delayed the Austrian peace settlement was that of determining what constituted German assets in that country. At Potsdam it had been decided that Russian claims

[19] See page 574.
[20] See pages 570–572.

to reparations should be met in part from appropriate German external assets in eastern Austria, but the four Allies proved unable to agree on a definition of German assets. During the period of the *Anschluss* German economic penetration of Austria had been far-reaching, and it was later estimated that, in all, Germans had seized about three fourths of Austria's total assets: mining, industry, banking, insurance, and property owned by Austrian state and public corporations. Russia insisted and the Western powers refused to concede that all these were legitimate German assets.

Again, at the Moscow Conference in 1947 the Allies failed to produce an Austrian peace treaty, being unable to agree on three major points: Russia's demand for $150,000,000 reparations from Austria, Russia's demand for the cession of Carinthia to Yugoslavia, and Russia's definition of German assets in Austria. A treaty commission was appointed to study these problems. But again at the London Conference which opened in November, 1947, the "Big Four" were no nearer agreement. By then it was obvious that Austria was strategically important in the struggle between Soviet Russia and the Western powers, and that the conclusion of a peace treaty with Austria was unlikely until the "cold war" should be ended. Although in the succeeding years Austria repeatedly requested the four Allied governments to resume work on the Austrian peace treaty and although from time to time the diplomatic representatives of the four powers did meet to discuss such a treaty, no apparent progress was made. Austria continued to be divided economically and occupied by Allied troops.

The Allied Occupation of Deflated Japan

There was much less difficulty in dealing with Japan at the close of the war than there was in the case of Germany or Austria, largely because, for all practical purposes, there was but one occupying authority, the United States.[21] The latter, immediately following the Japanese surrender, announced that though it would consider the wishes of the principal Allied powers "in the event of any differences of opinion among them, the policies of the United States will govern." The United States invited the powers directly interested in the postwar reconstruction of Japan to appoint members of a Far Eastern advisory commission, but Russia objected to its advisory nature and refused to participate. Byrnes, Bevin, and Molotov, at their conference in Moscow in December, 1945, eventually reached a compromise which provided for a Far Eastern Commission and an Allied Council for Japan.

The Allied Council sat in Tokyo and consisted of four members—one

[21] For an excellent brief discussion of the Allied occupation, see L. K. Rosinger, "The Occupation of Japan." *Foreign Policy Reports,* May 15, 1947.

each representing the United States, Russia, China, and one representing Great Britain, Australia, New Zealand, and India as a group. Its chairman was the American member—General MacArthur or his deputy. Its function was to consult with or advise the Supreme Commander for the Allied Powers (SCAP), General MacArthur, and it had no power to act. The Far Eastern Commission sat in Washington and included one representative from each of eleven governments concerned.[22] The functions of this body were to formulate policies, to review any directive issued to the supreme commander if requested by any member, and to consider other matters which might be referred to it by agreement of the participating powers. Theoretically the United States lost its predominant position, but actually directives to the supreme commander were issued according to the American interpretation of the commission's decisions, and General MacArthur generally applied the directives as he interpreted them. The irritation felt in some quarters over this situation was revealed by a speech made in Wellington, New Zealand, in February, 1948: "The Japanese emperor has renounced his divinity. It has been taken up by General MacArthur."

At Potsdam in July, 1945, the United States, Great Britain, and China had outlined their general aims for Japan [23] and these had later been accepted by Soviet Russia. Implicit in their announcement was the Allied decision to have the occupation authority operate through a continuing Japanese state and not, as in Germany, to displace the state. According to later American instructions to MacArthur, the Japanese emperor and government were to be subject to him, and he was to exercise his powers through them "to the extent that this satisfactorily furthers United States objectives." MacArthur might require changes in Japanese political machinery or governmental personnel or act directly if necessary. The American directive specifically stipulated that Japan was to be disarmed and demilitarized, the economic basis of her military strength was to be destroyed, and her war production was to cease. The large industrial and banking combinations which had controlled a great part of the country's trade and industry were to be dissolved. Democratic organizations in labor, industry, and agriculture were to be encouraged. Political prisoners were to be freed, ultranationalists were to be purged, civil rights were to be guaranteed, and the schools, laws, and government were to be reformed. Except for the decision to operate through the existing government, the program was much the same as that originally announced for Germany. This program was soon expressed in a series of directives issued by SCAP to the Japanese government.

[22] The states represented were: The United States, Great Britain, Russia, China, France, the Netherlands, Canada, Australia, New Zealand, India, and the Philippines.
[23] See page 766.

Immediately after the war the latter granted woman suffrage, lowered the voting age from 25 to 20 years, and permitted the organization of political parties, which had been dissolved in 1940. The most important of the new parties were the Liberal, Progressive, Social Democratic, and Communist. The first two represented the conservatives and sought to preserve as much as possible of Japan's old institutions. They had the support of most of the bankers and businessmen, the large landowners, the professional classes, and the peasant proprietors. The Social Democrats in their aims resembled the Labor Party in Britain. The Communists were not so extreme as those in Russia; they sought agrarian and industrial reforms but also promised the right of private ownership. The first postwar parliamentary elections in April, 1946, resulted in a conservative victory with the Liberal-Progressive bloc securing half the seats in the parliament.

Before the elections the government had issued the draft of a new constitution—reportedly drawn up by the staff of SCAP—to replace the undemocratic Japanese constitution of 1889. This was later ratified by the new parliament and was promulgated in November, 1946. Under this new constitution the emperor became merely the symbol of the state, deriving his position from the sovereign will of the people. All of his official acts required the approval of the cabinet which was made responsible to the parliament. A bill of rights was included, and war was "forever renounced as a means of settling disputes with other nations." On paper the constitution was a most liberal and progressive document. Whether under it the Japanese government would soon become the same, seemed open to some question. The first two premiers of the postwar period—Baron Kijuro Shidehara and Shigeru Yoshida—were members of the ruling circles which had long dominated Japan; the members of Japan's extensive bureaucracy of civil servants had, for the most part, been trained under the prewar regimes; and most of the Japanese apparently continued to revere the emperor despite his renunciation of divine status.

In the first general elections held (April, 1947) after the promulgation of the new constitution, although the conservative parties won more than a majority of the seats in each of the houses of parliament, the Social Democrats gained the largest number of any party. A shift in the ministry then occurred and Tetsu Katayama, the Socialist leader, became premier at the head of a coalition government. Because of dissension within his party, however, his ministry was forced to resign early in 1948 and Hitoshi Ashida of the Democratic (formerly Progressive) Party, who had been foreign minister under Katayama, became premier in a cabinet consisting of 6 Democrats and 8 Socialists. Although the Russian representative on the Allied Council demanded Ashida's dismissal on the ground that he had for seven years been president of a newspaper which was "one of the most notorious media for spreading the ideas of the Japanese military clique," Ashida remained in office until October, 1948, when, because of the indictment of two members of his ministry, he was forced to resign. Later Ashida himself was charged with accepting bribes. The Socialists refused to participate in a new coalition, and ultimately Shigeru Yoshida again became premier at the head of a conservative ministry of Liberals and Democrats.

Yoshida announced that his government contemplated the formation of a committee on un-Japanese activities and indicated that he meant activities of the extreme Left. The new premier dissolved the parliament and in the ensuing elections, held on January 23, 1949, his ultra-conservative Liberal Party won a decisive majority in the lower house. The moderate parties were rejected at the polls and Japan appeared to be dividing into ultra conservatives on the Right and Communists on the Left, for the latter increased their representation in the diet from 4 to 35 members. The Liberals were in a sense the successors to the men that had led Japan into war; they had shown their dislike of the Allied occupation and of the ideals of Western democracy; they had emphasized the necessity for a rebirth of Japanese nationalism. What their coming to power would entail for the occupation authorities remained to be seen.

Meanwhile, steps had been taken to demilitarize Japan. In 1945 military conscription was abolished as was also the general staff. Thousands of officers and men in the army, navy, or government were tried as war criminals and hundreds were convicted and put to death, including many generals and admirals. Ultimately, after a two-year trial, the International Military Tribunal for the Far East on November 12, 1948, sentenced seven Japanese to death by hanging, sixteen to life imprisonment, and two to prison terms. Included in the number were two former premiers, thirteen generals, one admiral, and former ministers and ambassadors. All but two were convicted of conspiracy to wage aggressive war for the domination of East Asia and the Pacific and Indian oceans. Those condemned to death were convicted, also, of breaches of the laws and customs of war. On December 22, after the refusal of the United States Supreme Court to intervene, the seven condemned to death were hanged. Some—Prince Konoye, for instance—saved the Allies the trouble of trials by committing suicide. Approximately 80,000 former army, navy, and military police officers were prohibited from holding public offices. Efforts were made, also, to remove from key positions in the government, the trades unions, and the school system those Japanese who had actively promoted war or who were considered subversive. By September, 1947, more than 570,000 persons had been "screened." In that month MacArthur announced the completion, too, of the purge of industrialists who had supported the militarists, though critics asserted that the top men had been often succeeded by their "lieutenants."

However that may be, the supreme commander declared in 1947 that the demilitarization of Japan had been largely completed.

Sweeping reforms were envisaged for Japan's economic life under the directives given to MacArthur by the United States government. Japan's prewar economy had been so organized as to reinforce militaristic concepts of government and foreign policy. The *Zaibatsu*, that is, the great financial-industrial-commercial holding companies, had controlled the country's economic life and had co-operated closely with the militarists in aggression. They had also largely prevented the rise of an independent middle class, which in most countries constitutes a liberalizing influence. In October, 1946, in accordance with the American directive and under plans drafted by SCAP, the stockholders of five of the most important *Zaibatsu*—Mitsui, Mitsubishi, Sumitomo, Yasuda, Fuji—voted to dissolve by transferring their securities to a commission which would sell them to the public. The companies in return would receive government bonds. A year later, in December, 1947, the parliament passed the Economic Decentralization Bill, designed to eliminate "concentrations of excessive economic power." It was estimated that some 500 of Japan's 93,000 corporations would be affected by this act but that these 500 controlled 65 to 75 per cent of Japan's industry. MacArthur believed that the free enterprise system could not be set up in Japan until the "traditional pyramid of economic power" had been destroyed. Whether SCAP could create a new financial-industrial ownership and prevent the new groups from repeating the *Zaibatsu* pattern remained to be seen. It could probably not secure much enthusiastic assistance in the task from the Japanese government.

Japan was of course expected to pay reparations and the first proposals were drafted by a commission headed by Edwin W. Pauley. These were used by the Far Eastern Commission to work out an interim program of removals which stipulated that arsenals, aircraft and light metal plants, steel capacity above 3,500,000 tons yearly, and much of the country's productive capacity in pig iron, shipbuilding, machine tools, and chemicals were to be removed. The problem of determining what each nation should receive was difficult, as was the question whether Russia's seizures in Manchuria should be considered "war booty" or reparations. A second reparations commission early in 1947 made milder recommendations than the Pauley commission, and in April of that year the United States announced that it would begin removals from Japan, with the largest share going at first to China.

As in Germany, the reparations problem was linked with disarmament and living standards. By a decision of the Far Eastern Commission in 1947 Japan's standard of living was to be that of 1930–1934, but her economy was to be changed to reduce her war potential much lower than in 1931.

As in Germany, too, the reparations problem was linked with American taxes, for the less Japan was able to pay for her necessary imports by her own exports, the more the United States would have to advance under its policy of deficit financing of occupied countries. With a population of more than 78,000,000 (1947) in an area less than that of California, Japan must necessarily be even more dependent upon exports to pay for her needed food supplies and raw materials than she was before the war. In 1947, however, her manufacturing output totaled only about 30 per cent of the 1930–1934 average, and in that year the United States began extending financial aid to Japan—in a sort of "small Marshall Plan"—for the purchase of needed raw materials and fibers for her textile mills. It seemed unlikely that the Japanese would have to make very heavy reparation payments.

Before the war Japanese industrial workers were denied the right to organize freely and worked in more or less enforced docility. The highest prewar union membership was only 420,000. By the close of 1946, however, the number of union members had increased to more than 4,400,000, most of them included in three different federations. Although the unions were deeply interested in politics—the Social Democratic Party won the most seats in the parliamentary elections of 1947—perhaps the chief cause of labor action was inflation. Despite the fact that it was the policies of SCAP which made possible the great increase in union membership, the infiltration of Communist leaders and the political pressure exerted by the unions apparently disturbed the supreme commander. In January, 1947, MacArthur forbade a proposed strike of some 2,500,000 employees, and in March, 1948, he announced that strikes such as the "co-ordinated work stoppage" planned by the union of communication workers could not be tolerated. Four months later the government announced that thereafter unions of government workers would possess neither the right of collective bargaining nor the right to strike, and in August, 1948, it further announced that all labor contracts and agreements concluded in the past were invalid. The Soviet delegate on the Allied Council protested to MacArthur and demanded that the ordinance be cancelled, and the American chief of the labor division of SCAP and some of his subordinates resigned in protest against what they considered MacArthur's new labor policy. Nevertheless, on November 30, the Japanese parliament passed legislation suggested by MacArthur outlawing strikes and collective bargaining by employees of the government or its enterprises, and in January, 1949, the Far Eastern Commission voted down the Soviet delegate's motion to condemn the law.

Although most Japanese landholdings were very small by American standards, before the war the landlord group dominated the rural economy. In 1936 nearly 70 per cent of the rural households consisted of tenants who, on an average, gave more than half their crops to the landlord as rent. In

December, 1945, MacArthur ordered sweeping changes "to destroy the economic bondage that has enslaved the Japanese farmers for centuries of feudal oppression." The Japanese parliament was dilatory, however, and not until October, 1946, were acceptable agrarian reform measures enacted. These provided that the government would purchase all tenant land owned by absentee landlords and all other landlord holdings above a certain size for resale to tenants, the latter to repay the government in thirty annual installments. Rural land commissions, which it was possible the landlords might dominate, were to decide what lands should be taken and to supervise the transfer. It was planned that more than 75 per cent of the land in tenancy would be sold, and by September, 1947, the government had purchased about 750,000 acres of land from absentee owners. But the Soviet delegate on the Allied Council characterized the land reform as only "a half-way measure" which was being unsatisfactorily administered because of opposition of the landowners. His view was supported by the British delegate and by an agricultural expert.

The Peace Treaty with Japan

In July, 1947, the United States had moved to secure a peace treaty with Japan by inviting the Far Eastern Commission to begin discussions under a two-thirds voting rule. Although the British Commonwealth nations accepted the American plan, Russia, probably realizing that she would be outvoted in the commission as she had been at the Paris peace conference in 1946, proposed that the Pacific "Big Four"—the United States, Great Britain, Russia, and China—should write the treaty as was done the year before for the lesser defeated powers in Europe by the Western "Big Four." But this proposal was rejected by the United States, probably for fear of a Russian veto. China offered a compromise that the Far Eastern Commission should draft the treaty with the "Big Four" holding a veto, but her proposal also was rejected.

For a time the matter of a peace treaty with Japan was allowed to drift, but Communist aggression in Korea revived the desire and determination of the United States to conclude a peace settlement for the Far East. In the autumn of 1950 the United States circulated an exploratory memorandum to the governments of fifteen countries particularly concerned in a Far Eastern settlement. This memorandum suggested that all nations at war with Japan might, if they wished, be parties to the treaty; that Japan should recognize an independent Korea and UN trusteeship under United States administration of the Ryukyu and Bonin Islands; that the future of Formosa, the Pescadores, South Sakhalin, and the Kuriles should be decided by Great Britain, Russia, China, and the United States, or, if they failed to reach a decision within one year, by the United Nations; that there should be co-operative responsibility between Japan and United States and perhaps other forces for the maintenance of internal peace and security in the Japan area; that reparations should be waived but that the Allies should keep Japanese property in their territory and be compensated for property lost in Japan.

Comments on this memorandum were received from most of the interested governments. As might have been expected, the Soviet government was the most critical. But the Chinese also expressed vigorous opposition to the suggested peace terms, and questions were likewise raised in Australia, New Zealand, and the Philippines, which all feared a resurgence of Japanese militarism. The Australian government declared that it would oppose any proposal permitting the unrestricted rearmament of Japan, although it agreed that Japan must be allowed "some capacity to defend herself against Communist aggression." The willingness of the United States to sign security pacts with Australia, New Zealand, and the Philippines, however, overcame the opposition of these states as far as it was based on the possibility of Japanese rearmament. By the summer of 1951 agreement on a draft treaty had been reached by most of the powers, though Russia, India, and the Philippines were not satisfied.

On July 12, 1951 a provisional peace treaty with Japan was published. It was immediately sent to the fifty-one countries at war with Japan, who were invited by the United States to a conference in San Francisco on September 4. India at once proposed that the treaty should be altered so that Japan should keep the Ryukyu and Bonin Islands, Formosa should go to China, and the clause permitting foreign troops to remain in Japan should be deleted. Although none of these proposals were incorporated, the text of a revised draft treaty, released on July 12, did contain a number of amendments resulting from other suggestions. With the release of this revised draft, the United States announced that, since the draft was the result of eleven months' negotiations with many nations, no further alterations of the text would be permitted at the San Francisco conference, which was for the conclusion and signature of the final text of the treaty and not for the reopening of negotiations on the terms. This conference, therefore, was to be of a quite different character from the one held in Paris in 1946.

On September 4 delegations from more than fifty states gathered in San Francisco for the Conference for the Conclusion and Signature of a Treaty of Peace with Japan. No delegates from India or Burma attended, and neither of the Chinese governments [24] had been invited to send representatives. On the other hand, contrary to general expectations, a Soviet delega-

---

[24] There was disagreement among the delegates as to which of the Chinese governments, the Nationalist government on Formosa or the Communist government on the mainland, represented China.

tion headed by Andrei Gromyko was present. At the outset, by a vote of 48 to 3 (Russia, Poland, Czechoslovakia), the draft rules of procedure submitted by Great Britain and the United States were adopted. In contravention of these rules, which forbade any further amendment of the draft, Gromyko immediately proposed a great number of changes in the treaty. In his speech he condemned especially the exclusion of the Ryukyu, Bonin, and other islands from Japanese sovereignty and the absence of provisions for the transfer of Formosa to China and for the return of Sakhalin and the transfer of the Kuriles to the Soviet Union. He argued that the treaty created conditions for the revival of Japanese militarism and opened the way for Japan's participation in aggressive alliances in the Far East. By an overwhelming vote, however, the conference overruled Gromyko's attempt to secure consideration of his proposals.

On September 8 the Japanese peace treaty was signed by the delegates of forty-nine states. But Gromyko and the delegates of Poland and Czechoslovakia declined to sign, Gromyko announcing to the press that the treaty was a draft for a new war which the Soviet Union could not support. Shigeru Yoshida, the Japanese delegate, on the other hand, expressed his people's "passionate desire to live at peace with their neighbors in the Far East and in the entire world." He did, however, appeal for the return to Japan of the Ryukyu and Bonin Islands and also of South Sakhalin and the Kuriles.

By the terms of the accepted treaty, (1) Japan recognized Korea's independence; (2) Japan renounced all claims to Formosa, the Pescadores, the Kuriles, Southern Sakhalin, and certain Pacific islands as well as her interests in the Antarctic and all special rights and interests in China; (3) Japan agreed to accept any United States proposal to the UN to place the Ryukyu and certain other American-occupied islands under UN trusteeship with the United States as sole administering authority; (4) all occupation forces were to be withdrawn from Japan within ninety days after the treaty came into force, but Japan might make bilateral or multilateral agreements with any Allied power or powers under which foreign troops could be retained within her territory; (5) Japan accepted the obligations of Article 2 of the UN Charter, that is, she agreed to settle all international disputes by peaceful means and to refrain from the threat or use of force against any state, but she was granted the right of self-defense which all UN members retained under Article 51 of the Charter; (6) Japan undertook to assist countries which had suffered war damage by making available Japanese skill and industry, but Japanese inability to pay reparations was recognized; (7) Japan agreed that China, though not a signatory, would be entitled to the benefits arising from Japanese renunciation of rights and interests in China; (8) Japan might conclude a bilateral peace treaty on the same or substantially the same terms with any state which, being a member of the UN and formerly at war with Japan, had not signed the present treaty; (9) the Allied powers recognized full Japanese sovereignty over Japan and its territorial waters; and (10) the return of captured Japanese military forces to their homes should be carried out to the extent not already completed.

In the absence of provisions stipulating heavy reparation payments and drastic limitations on national armaments, the peace treaty with Japan was in marked contrast with those concluded after the First World War, especially the treaty of Versailles. The treaty seemed to indicate that statesmen in 1951 realized better than they did in 1919–1920 the difficulties involved in exacting large reparation payments from any country. The treaty seemed to indicate, also, that the chief signatories were willing to take a calculated risk that the Japanese would not again become militaristic. It was hoped, apparently, that, if the treaty contained no restrictive provisions, the Japanese would have no reason to rebel against it and might therefore be willing to retain many of the reforms introduced under MacArthur's tutelage. In any case, rearmament would involve a very great burden for Japan, one which she would have great difficulty in carrying under her existing economic conditions. In fact, one of the unsolved problems seemed to be that of how Japan could survive economically without access to Manchuria's raw products and China's markets.

On the same day that the Japanese peace treaty was signed in San Francisco, the United States and Japan also signed a security pact agreeing (1) that the United States would have a right to deploy its land, sea, and air forces throughout the Japanese territory for the purpose of contributing to the maintenance of international peace and security in the Far East and to the security of Japan from armed attack from without; (2) that the United States would be allowed to help, at Japan's request, to put down any internal rebellions or disturbances instigated "by an outside power or powers"; (3) that Japan would not grant similar rights "of garrison or maneuver" to any third power without the prior consent of the United States; (4) that both governments would decide together when and how United States forces should be disposed; (5) that the pact would expire whenever both governments agreed that the strength of the United Nations or of other alliances was capable of maintaining peace in the area. The peace treaty and the accompanying security pact were both ratified by the Japanese parliament on November 18, 1951.

Chapter XXVII

SOVIET RUSSIA AND

HER SATELLITES

E AST of a line running roughly from Stettin on the Baltic to Trieste on the Adriatic, in the years immediately following the Second World War, were nine European states which came to follow in a general way the same foreign policy. The dominant state in this group was, of course, the Union of Soviet Socialist Republics. The others, which were forced or which chose to follow the Soviet foreign policy and even to adopt some of the features of Soviet internal institutions, constituted the so-called Russian satellite states.

The Union of Soviet Socialist Republics

As in so many other states in Europe, the period of the Second World War and the years following it saw several significant changes made in Soviet territory and institutions.

TERRITORIAL AND POLITICAL CHANGES

In 1939–1940 the Soviet Union was expanded by the absorption of Latvia, Estonia, and Lithuania, which became constituent republics in the Union, and by the addition of areas formerly in Poland, Finland, and Rumania. The latter areas were absorbed into already existing Soviet republics which were largely inhabited by populations of similar races. In 1945, following a plebiscite in Ruthenia, which was inhabited by Ukrainians, that territory, too, was transferred from Czechoslovakia to the Soviet Union and incorporated in the Ukrainian Soviet Socialist Republic.

At the close of the Second World War, therefore, the Soviet Union consisted of sixteen republics. In 1944, the Supreme Soviet of the Union had decreed that these constituent republics might enter into direct relation with foreign states and might conclude agreements and exchange diplomatic and consular representatives with them. They might also organize separate military formations. The armies which encircled Berlin in 1945, it will be recalled, were the First White Russian and the First Ukrainian. In international affairs, recognition of the change in the position of the constituent republics came with the admission of the White Russian and the Ukrainian Republics to the San Francisco Conference of the United Nations in 1945 and with their participation in the Paris peace conference in 1946.

In February, 1946, national elections to the two houses of the Supreme Soviet were held. Only one candidate was nominated for each seat and all were either Communists or representatives of a nonparty people's *bloc,* which appealed for a unanimous vote of confidence in the existing government. According to official statements, more than 96 per cent of the electorate voted and approximately 99 per cent approved the nominated candidates. Marshal Stalin tendered the resignation of his government to the new Supreme Soviet, which decided that thereafter the government should be called the Council of Ministers rather than the Soviet of People's Commissars. In the new ministry Stalin became prime minister and Molotov foreign minister.

WAR DESTRUCTION

The chief effect of the Second World War on Russia's economy was the vast devastation which it caused. The Soviet State Commission's report, published in September, 1945, revealed that the Axis armies had overrun an area inhabited by 88,000,000 people and, according to Marshal Stalin, had brought death to 7,000,000. The German-occupied territory included Russia's greatest single industrial region, her best agricultural land, and half of the nation's live stock.

Destruction by the invaders, moreover, was systematic and extensive in the entire Ukraine and in the Don Basin, for the Germans sought to deprive Russia of her newly created industries and to restrict her to the production of foodstuffs and raw materials for the great industrial empire which the Nazis intended to establish. They therefore methodically "destroyed industrial plants . . . flooded mines, gutted oil refineries, stripped factories and laboratories of machinery and tools, leveled homes to the ground, and destroyed means of transportation." They wrecked or partly wrecked 1,710 towns, and 31,500 industrial enterprises, which had employed some 4,000,000 workers. They ruined a considerable part of the country's railway system by destroying some 40,000 miles of permanent right of way, 4,100 stations, 15,000 bridges, 15,800 locomotives, and 428,000 cars. According to official reports of the UNRRA mission to the Ukraine, the industrial plants of Kiev, Kharkov, Dnepropetrovsk, Dneprostoy, and Odessa had been almost completely stripped of modern machinery and their buildings either razed or shattered. At Zaponozhnie the largest steel and iron plant of the Ukraine had been so completely destroyed that it would take three to four years to restore it. Of the workers' houses, the UNRRA mission stated, only 8 per cent remained.

Agriculture was also hard hit. According to the State Commission some 98,000 collective farms, 1,876 state farms, and 2,890 machine tractor stations were "ruined and ransacked." The losses in agricultural machinery were appalling: 137,000 tractors (30 per cent of the prewar total), 49,000 harvester-combines, 4,000,000 harrows, plows, and other soil-cultivating instruments, and 1,150,000 seeders and threshers destroyed or stolen. Furthermore, the Germans had killed or stolen 7,000,000 horses (34 per cent of the prewar total), 17,000,000 cattle (30 per cent of prewar), 20,000,000 hogs (71 per cent of prewar), 27,000,000 sheep and goats (29 per cent of prewar), and 110,000-000 poultry. They had also destroyed or burned, wholly or in part, 70,000 villages. In the occupied area as a whole 6,000,000 buildings were destroyed and 25,000,000 people made homeless. As a result, according to one investigator, the average number of occupants for each five-room dwelling unit in 1947 was thirty persons, compared with twenty in 1937. This situation, coupled with the neglect of the consumer-goods industries during the war, resulted in living standards far below even the low standards of the prewar period.

Russia's total direct loss as a result of the German invasion was estimated as the equivalent of $128,000,000,000. These tremendous losses, especially of capital goods, went far to explain Soviet Russia's insistence upon reparation payments from the defeated Axis powers as well as her reportedly ruthless seizure of capital goods and other commodities in the countries occupied by her armies in the postwar period.

One has but to consider the fate of Stalingrad and its factories to realize that the Russians were faced by a herculean task of rehabilitation following the expulsion of the Axis forces from their land. Nevertheless, they set resolutely to work to bring their country back economically to the place it had been when "the enemy interfered with their long-range plans." In this task they were aided by the wartime expansion of industry, which had occurred in the region east of the Volga, where new plants had been constructed and to which, according to reports, some 1,300 large factories had been moved from the invaded areas. In the first half of 1945, for instance, the industrial output of the eastern areas—almost entirely in the heavy industries—was twice as great as in 1941; in the Volga area, 240 per cent greater; in the Urals, 260 per cent greater; in Siberia, 180 per cent greater.

NEW FIVE-YEAR PLANS

Not content with merely repairing the damage inflicted by the Nazis, however, the Russians in 1946 embarked upon another Five-Year Plan in which the immediate aim was to regain the ground lost as a result of the war and the long-term goal was a great increase in national production over the prewar period. The government still clung to its policy of giving primacy to heavy industry or, as Stalin phrased it, the "production of the means of production." By the final quarter of 1947 the country's industrial production as a whole equalled the average quarterly output of 1940, although in some categories—notably cement, timber, copper, steel, tractors, and steam turbines—this was not true. In 1948, the third year of the fourth Five-Year Plan, however, the prewar production level was reached in iron and steel, according to the State Planning Commission. In 1950, the final year of the plan, the production of basic materials and fuels had increased above that of 1940 as follows (in millions of metric tons): steel, from 18.3 to 27.3; pig iron, from 14.9 to 19.2; coal and lignite, from 166 to 261; petroleum, from 31 to 38. In the same period the production of electric power had increased in billions of kilowatt hours from 48 to 90. Shortages were still reported in iron and steel, however, and there were official complaints about slow progress in the Baku oil fields and in some individual industries. But according to official reports, the total national income for 1950 was 64 per cent above that for 1940, considerably above the goal originally set.

In the production of consumer goods and in agriculture the gains were not so striking. As in the first Five-Year Plan, consumer goods were deliberately sacrificed to produce capital goods. In agriculture only cotton, among the major agricultural products, exceeded the objectives of the fourth Five-Year Plan. Grain acreage in 1950 was reported as 20 per cent above that for 1940. Although the number of livestock was 4 per cent above 1940, it was below the planned goal. According to a study published by the UN Economic Commission for Europe, the agricultural production in Russia during these years had "probably not quite kept pace with the rise in population." In the hope of increasing it, steps were taken in 1950 to consolidate smaller collective farms into larger units. Initiated in the province of Moscow, where 6,000 farms were consolidated into less than 2,000, the movement spread into other areas to such an extent that by the end of the year the number of collective farms in the Soviet Union had decreased from some 254,000 to 215,000.

Although the fourth Five-Year Plan was completed in 1950, details of the fifth plan for the years 1951–1955 were not disclosed and approved until October, 1952, and they were then ratified, not by the Supreme Soviet, but by the Communist Party congress. The aim of the fifth plan was to increase the total volume of investment in industry to twice that made in 1946–1950, and to increase the gross industrial output by 70 per cent. But the planned production increases were not the same for all industries; heavy industries were to increase by 80 per cent but light industries by only 65 per cent. The number of industrial workers, also, was to expand from 39,200,000 to 45,100,000, and labor productivity was to increase by 50 per cent over 1950. In agriculture the plan called for an increase in the gross grain harvest from 125 million metric tons in 1950 to 175–190 in 1955. Most of this increase was expected to come from higher yields which, it was hoped, might be brought nearer to the best European levels in the more fertile Soviet regions. Large increases in the output of chemical fertilizer were therefore planned. The goals for livestock were percentage-wise more modest than for grain.

In October, 1952, Georgi Malenkov reported on the progress of the fifth Five-Year Plan. One can never be certain of the meaning of Soviet production figures and percentages, for the basis upon which calculations are made is sometimes altered without clear explanation. Nevertheless, even allowing for some exaggeration, the figures were generally encouraging to the Communists. According to Malenkov, the investment in industrial plants in Russia in 1952 was 77 per cent greater than in 1940 and the output of the heavy industries was 170 per cent above the prewar figure. The production of machines and equipment generally, which may include some military equipment, was reported as three times that in 1940. In some categories it was still higher. The output of petroleum equipment, for instance, was said to be 4.3 times that of 1940 and that of metallurgical machinery 5.4 times. In 1952 the number of industrial workers had increased to 41,700,000 and productivity had risen 18 per cent above 1950. The dispersion of industry had continued and the Volga valley and the Ural Mountains region had become the heart of Soviet heavy industry. In this connection the completion of the Volga-Don Canal in 1952 was significant. In May, 1954, Malenkov announced that in the preceding three years industrial output had increased 45 per cent, that in the year 1953 the Soviet Union had produced 38,000,000 tons of steel and 320,000,000 tons of coal, in both cases twice as much as was produced in 1940.

In agriculture the consolidation of collective farms had continued and in 1952 the number had been reduced to some 97,000. There was, however, no great indication of increased efficiency resulting from the consolidation. Progress toward the livestock goals of the plan appeared to have been slow except for hogs. Nevertheless, according to the figures released, the number of cattle had increased by 1,800,000 head in 1951–1952 and the number of sheep and goats by 12,000,000. Meat production, it was reported, had increased by 709,000 tons in the years 1946–1951. But the Russian people were promised by 1955 a 90 per cent increase in meat supplies over those available in 1950 and a 300 per cent increase in dairy products. One large-scale agricultural project envisaged was the draining of the Pripet Marshes in White Russia which, it was estimated, would bring into cultivation some 12,000,000 acres of high quality agricultural land.

During 1953 and 1954, however, it was admitted that Russian agricultural production was insufficient for the population's food needs and the raw material needs of light industry. The most serious shortages were said to be in meats, potatoes, and vegetables. The central committee of the Communist Party attributed the situation to mismanagement on state farms and to lack of guidance by party, government, and agricultural bodies. A new directive set increased targets for livestock and poultry and for acreages of grass, corn, fodder, silage crops, and vegetables. At the same time, the directive moderated some of the government's policies for collective farms to provide incentives for more production. In March, 1954, Vice-Premier Krushchev publicly censured various high officials for the "sorry state of affairs" in agriculture, and subsequently thousands of agronomists, engineers, technicians, and other specialists were dispatched in an attempt to overcome the "serious shortcomings" of the collective farms.

The percentage increases in consumer goods were not so impressive as those in the heavy industries. The total increase over production in 1940 was given as 60 per cent, but this was partly offset by an increase of some 8 per cent in population. Nevertheless, if the war or immediately postwar years are taken as a basis, improvement was marked. Consumer goods produced in 1952 were three times those in 1944 and 2.4 times those in 1946. There were considerable increases in fabrics and footwear and greater supplies of consumers' durables, notably furniture, radios, televisors, watches, bicycles, and cameras. Furthermore, in the view of one observer, the food supplies in state and co-operative stores in the towns and cities were perhaps more ample than at any time since 1928. Retail trade in 1952, it was reported, had doubled since 1948 and foreign trade, chiefly with the countries of the so-called democracies, was three times that of the prewar years.

In the matter of housing, Malenkov admitted that the Russians "still have an acute housing shortage everywhere." While the rate of home construction under the fourth and fifth Five-Year Plans was high in relation to prewar times, in view of the wartime destruction and the growth of population it was not enough to bring any rapid relief to the extremely overcrowded urban population of the country.

It was obvious to those who examined the figures released regarding the progress of the fifth Five-Year Plan that there were failures to reach goals and that in no way did the Soviet industrial and agricultural production match that in the United States. Nevertheless, as one careful student of Soviet affairs pointed out: [1]

The 1955 goals for basic industries speak eloquently against any complacency in the free world: 44 million tons of steel, 373 million tons of coal, 70 million tons of oil, 162 billion kilowatt-hours of electric power. Even if some of these goals,

[1] Oleg Hoeffding in *Foreign Policy Bulletin*, April 1, 1953, page 8.

and those of industries dependent on them, are not fully met, the fact remains that the U.S.S.R. is expanding its industrial potential at a rate not matched by the United States, let alone Western Europe.

THE NINETEENTH COMMUNIST PARTY CONGRESS

In the early years of the Soviet regime Communist Party congresses were held somewhat frequently; during the struggle for power after Lenin's death they had been held yearly. After Stalin had become the acknowledged dictator of Russia, however, these congresses had been held more infrequently, and up until 1952 none had been held since before the Second World War. In August, 1952, it was announced that the nineteenth all-Union congress of the party would be held in October to hear reports, pass on the fifth Five-Year Plan, and reorganize the party. During the intervening weeks regional party conferences elected some 1,200 delegates, among whom were Premier Stalin, all the members of the existing politburo, all the deputy premiers, and the principal members of the government. Present, also, when the congress convened, were delegates from the Communist parties of forty-four other countries so that this nineteenth congress somewhat resembled a meeting of the former Comintern.

The opening keynote address at the congress (October 5–14) was made by V. M. Molotov, and other major speeches were delivered by G. M. Malenkov, L. P. Beria, A. I. Mikoyan, N. A. Bulganin, and War Minister Vassilievsky. Seventy-two-year-old Stalin did not take an active part in the congress, but he did make a short closing address. The general tenor of the speeches was that the Soviet Union had only peaceful intentions, but that the Western democracies were imperialistic and aggressive, that the United States in particular was seeking world domination, and that the other states in NATO were only "unequal partners" and "poor relations" of the United States. But the delegates were assured that the Soviet Union was no longer isolated as it had been after Munich, since it now had as allies the Chinese People's Republic, the German Democratic Republic, and the people's democracies of Europe. They were further assured that the Union's domestic economy and foreign trade were expanding satisfactorily, and that, despite her peaceful intentions, Russia's economy could be quickly put on a war footing. Finally, they were told that the Soviet army had been revolutionized and its battle potentialities sharply increased, and that the fifth Five-Year Plan would provide for supplies of the most modern weapons "considerably greater than during the last war."

The congress adopted a number of proposed changes in party organization. On the ground that the Mensheviks had been annihilated and that therefore there was no longer rivalry between Bolsheviks and Mensheviks, the official name of the party was changed from "All-Union Communist

Party of Bolsheviks" to "Communist Party of the Soviet Union." The party membership, Malenkov announced, had increased from 2,500,000 in 1939 to more than 6,882,000 in 1952. Seventy-one new party statutes were presented, made necessary, it was explained, by various evils within the party which must be ruthlessly eradicated by expulsion of those guilty of them. The chief evils cited were lack of discipline among party leaders, the covering-up of mistakes and shortcomings, the frustration of criticism, nepotism, and favoritism. The proposed statutes were adopted.

In the party reorganization the politburo and the orgburo (organization bureau) were abolished and replaced by a single body, the presidium of the central committee, consisting of twenty-five members, among whom were Stalin, Molotov, Malenkov, Beria, Mikoyan, and Bulganin. A new and considerably enlarged central committee was elected which was headed by Stalin and included all the members of the former politburo. In the light of an article published by Stalin shortly before the meeting of the congress, the latter voted to set up a committee of eleven to reshape the party's program, which had not been revised since 1919. Among those appointed to the revision committee were Stalin, Malenkov, Beria, Molotov, and Kagonovich. The proposed fifth Five-Year Plan was unanimously adopted by the congress.

That Stalin still held the party reins seemed obvious. He was made chairman of the presidium of the congress, chairman of the new party presidium which supplanted the former politburo and orgburo, head of the party secretariat, and chairman of the committee to revise the party program. Furthermore, it seemed that the article which he had published shortly before the congress convened had more influence on the party than all of the speeches delivered at the congress.

THE PASSING OF STALIN

Nevertheless, it had been believed for some time that Stalin was not in good health, for his public appearances had become more and more infrequent. The world was not taken completely by surprise, therefore, when it was announced on March 4, 1953, that Stalin had suffered a stroke three days earlier which had affected his brain and that he was seriously ill. On the next day the seventy-three-year-old Soviet premier and head of the Communist Party of the Soviet Union died.

For a quarter of a century Joseph Stalin had been the practically unchallenged dictator of Russia. The son of a lowly Georgian shoemaker, he had risen to be probably the most powerful individual in the world. A non-Russian, he had become one of the greatest figures in all Russian history. By his policies and actions he had converted a backward agrarian country into the second strongest industrial power on earth. He had prepared the

Soviet Union to meet Hitler's "inevitable" attack and in the Second World War his armies and air force had eventually hurled back the Germans and freed Russia from possible Nazi domination. His achievements had been great.

On the other hand, he had oppressed the church and had forced scholars and scientists to conform to his edicts. In the years after he became dictator he had liquidated most of the leading figures of the November Revolution, who were still living, when they had dared to differ with him over policies. In the course of his collectivization program millions of peasants had been ruthlessly punished for opposition or had died as a result of the consequent famine. He had, according to reports, enslaved millions in his forced labor camps. Finally, at the end of the Second World War, when the Russians had won the respect and admiration of the United Nations by their heroic sacrifices and magnificent victories, he had turned these sentiments into suspicion and fear by his destruction of free governments in the states which his armies had overrun in eastern Europe. As the result of his policies, the world at the time of his death was engaged in a tremendously costly and threatening armaments race, which everywhere handicapped efforts to raise living standards.

Outside of Russia it was believed by many—perhaps hoped—that Stalin's death would weaken the Soviet Union from within, that a struggle for power such as followed Lenin's death might plunge the country into chaos. There was no immediate evidence of this, however. On March 6 a joint statement of the central committee of the Communist Party, the council of ministers of the Soviet Union, and the presidium of the Supreme Soviet announced a new government, the principal appointments being Malenkov, Stalin's right-hand man, premier, Beria, Molotov, Bulganin, and Kagonovich deputy premiers, Voroshilov chairman of the presidium of the Supreme Soviet (technically the president of the Soviet Union), Beria minister of internal affairs, Molotov foreign minister, Bulganin war minister, and Mikoyan minister of internal and external trade. It was also announced that the central committee of the Communist Party would thereafter have a single presidium of ten members instead of thirty-six. Among the ten were Malenkov, Beria, Molotov, Voroshilov, Bulganin, Kagonovich, and Mikoyan. Quite obviously those who had played leading roles in the nineteenth congress of the party were to carry on in Stalin's place, at least temporarily. The "big three" of the group appeared to be Malenkov, Beria, and Molotov.

On March 15 the government changes announced on March 6 were unanimously approved by the Supreme Soviet. In an effort, perhaps, to centralize power, there were many mergers of ministries, the number of ministries being reduced from fifty-one to twenty-six. In an address to the

Supreme Soviet at that time Premier Malenkov declared that the measures to reduce and unify the leadership had been agreed on while Stalin was still alive and that their execution had been merely accelerated by his death. On the question of the Soviet Union's foreign policy, he declared that it would aim at maintaining and consolidating peace, at insuring the defense and security of the country, at collaboration and trade with other countries, and at strengthening the ties of friendship with China and the people's democracies. He asserted, finally, that there was no question in Soviet relations with other states which could not be settled by peaceful means on the basis of mutual agreement.

In an attempt, perhaps, to win popular support for the new government, an amnesty decree issued on March 27 ordered the immediate release from prison of all persons serving terms up to five years, of persons serving longer terms if they were pregnant women or women with children under ten years of age, women over the age of fifty, or men over fifty-five. Also to be released were persons serving terms for "official" or "economic" crimes. Other persons serving terms longer than five years were to have their sentences reduced by half. Junior officials sentenced for exceeding their authority or failing to use it, state store clerks sentenced for cheating customers, factory directors sentenced for producing substandard goods, and workers sentenced for absence without leave were expected to benefit by the decree. In another apparent effort to win popular support, price reductions were ordered on items of food, cloth and clothing.

Nevertheless, despite surface indications of harmony among the top Communist leaders, on July 10 came the startling announcement that the central committee of the Communist Party had expelled Lavrenti Beria and that the presidium of the Supreme Soviet, in view of Beria's criminal anti-state actions, had removed him from his posts as deputy premier and minister of internal affairs and had referred his crimes to the supreme court of the U.S.S.R. Simultaneously, *Pravda,* the party newspaper, accused Beria of being "an agent of international imperialism," "an adventurist," and "a foreign hireling." Beria, a Georgian, who had joined the Bolsheviks in March, 1917, had since 1938 been head of the ministry of internal affairs. In other words, for some fourteen years he had been Stalin's right-hand man in control of the secret police. Obviously the accusation that he had tried to "subvert the Soviet state in the interest of foreign capital" was open to serious question. More plausible, probably, was the charge that he had attempted to "place the ministry of internal affairs above the government and the Communist Party." Even more credible, however, was not the charge but the fear of those associated with him in the post-Stalin government that he might use the secret police, as Stalin had done, to ensure the supremacy of one particular man. On December 15, 1953, it was an-

Sovfoto

STALIN'S IMMEDIATE SUCCESSORS
Molotov, Voroshilov, Beria, Malenkov

nounced that Beria and six other former officials in ministries of internal affairs—four of them from Georgia or the Ukraine—had been investigated and would be tried by the Soviet Supreme Court on charges of high treason and anti-Soviet activities. All, it was declared, had admitted their crimes. Eight days later the seven men were sentenced to death for high treason and were shot.

In the view of some competent observers, Beria's arrest and execution constituted a victory for "collective leadership," for those who were "determined to prevent the emergence of a new dictator à la Stalin." Whether or not this was true, in the opening months of 1954 Premier Malenkov seemed to be playing the prominent role in Soviet affairs formerly played by Stalin. Meanwhile, in the six months after Beria's arrest, numerous changes had been made in the governments and Communist Party organizations in many of the constituent republics, and a new man, Nikita Krushchev, had been elected first secretary of the central committee of the Russian Communist Party. What all these shifts signified was not clear. But apparently they did not provide the basis for a Malenkov dictatorship, for on February 8, 1955, the world was startled by the news that Malenkov had submitted his resignation as premier to the Supreme Soviet. The premiership required, said Malenkov, great experience "and I am conscious of my inadequate experience." He also confessed his "guilt for short comings in agriculture." Malenkov was at once succeeded as premier by Nikolai Bulganin, whose former place as minister of defense was taken by Nikita Krushchev. Again, as after Lenin's death, it appeared that a struggle for power was occurring among the Communist leaders.

RUSSIA AND MANCHURIA

During and after the Second World War it was repeatedly stated in Russia that the Soviet Union needed a long period of peace in order to rehabilitate its devastated regions and to carry through successfully its plans for further industrializing and modernizing the country's economy. The paramount aim of Soviet foreign policy, therefore, was said to be the safeguarding of the security of Russia in order that the country might be left in peace to accomplish these tasks. But, as Foreign Minister Molotov stated in May, 1946, it is difficult at times to draw a line between the desire for security and the desire for expansion. There seemed to be evidence to indicate that Russia's foreign policy was designed not only to extend the area indirectly dominated through the Communist parties of other states but to increase the area actually brought under the direct control of the Soviet government itself.

Russia's desire for open imperialistic expansion seemed to be most evident in Asia. At Yalta, in return for the Soviet promise to enter the war

against Japan within three months after Germany surrendered, Stalin secured Roosevelt's and Churchill's promises that the rights lost by Russia
in Manchuria by the treaty of Portsmouth in 1905 would be restored, that
southern Sakhalin would be returned, that the Japanese Kurile Islands,
off the east coast of Siberia, would be ceded to the Soviet Union, and that
the existing status in Outer Mongolia, a Soviet protectorate, would be
preserved. The Kurile Islands and southern Sakhalin—Japanese territory—
were occupied by Russian troops in 1945.

So far as China was concerned, the agreements reached at Yalta were
subsequently incorporated in treaties with the Soviet Union in August,
1945. In consequence of these treaties, the Chinese Eastern and the South
Manchurian railways were united into the Chinese Changchun Railway,
which became the common property of the Soviet Union and the Chinese
Republic and was to be operated by them jointly under the management of
a Soviet citizen. After thirty years the railway was to pass to Chinese ownership without compensation. Port Arthur was made a naval base for the
joint use of the two countries. It was to be controlled by a commission
dominated by Russia, which was entitled to erect the necessary installations
for its defense and to maintain Soviet military, naval, and air forces there.
In this case, too, after thirty years all Russian equipment and public property in the area were to be transferred to China without compensation.
Dairen, which by 1945 had been enlarged to handle trade and shipping
second only to Shanghai in Eastern Asia, was made a free port, open to the
trade and shipping of all countries, and piers and warehouses were to be
leased to Russia. The Soviet Union thus reacquired approximately the
position in the Far East which imperialistic tsarist Russia had had prior
to the Russo-Japanese War of 1904.

In August, 1945, the Soviet armies overran Manchuria with little opposition. Japan's capital investments in that region, valued at more than one
billion dollars, were considered as war booty by the Soviet government,
which proceeded to strip the region of machine tools and electrical equipment and, in some cases, of entire factories. Following the establishment of
the Chinese People's Republic, however, Russian policy changed abruptly.
The two Communist states became allies, former Japanese properties in
Manchuria were turned over to China, and some of the Russian concessions
gained in the treaty of 1945 were surrendered by the Soviet government
(See page 988).

RUSSIA AND KOREA

In view of Russia's attempt to penetrate Korea prior to 1904, her activities in that country after the Second World War were open to suspicion
of being imperialistic, though Russian statesmen declared that they were

designed merely to establish in Korea "a true democratic and independent country, friendly to the Soviet Union, so that in the future it will not become a base for an attack on the Soviet Union."

On August 8, 1945, Russian forces landed in northern Korea and began mopping up the Japanese, whose regime was immediately liquidated. Korean committees of law and order were given authority to function under Soviet command, and on August 25 the "Executive Committee of the Korean People" took over the administrative powers of the former Chosen government-general. This Executive Committee, in turn, under the guidance of the Soviet authorities began to construct its organs of government. In February, 1946, the All-Korean People's Interim Committee of North Korea [2] was formally established in Pyongyang, the northern capital, to replace the Executive Committee. The final step in organizing the government of North Korea came in February, 1947, when a national assembly convened and approved the actions of the People's Interim Committee, adopted a national economic plan, chose a presidium and a supreme court, and confirmed the composition of the People's Committee of Northern Korea. In the meantime political parties had appeared, but in 1946 the United National Democratic Front was created, outside of which no political activity was permitted. Meanwhile, too, a people's militia of more than 100,000 men, armed with captured Japanese equipment and trained by Soviet officers, provided a force which could be used to maintain the Communist regime in power even if the Soviet army withdrew.

The economy of Northern Korea was largely copied from Soviet Russia. Lands and property of Japanese and Korean landlords were confiscated and transferred without charge to some 725,000 landless peasants or small holders. The new holders obtained their land in perpetual usufruct only, however, and it was not transferable. Banks, factories, and means of transport and communication which had belonged to "Japanese aggressors and to traitors to the Korean people" were also taken over by the people's committees and put under direct government control. Soviet technicians and managers directed and supervised the progress of economic rehabilitation. By the close of 1947, obviously, Northern Korea had become a Communist state. And this state contained some 88 per cent of all Korea's industries and practically all the timber, high-grade coal, nitrate deposits, and developed water power. Through its ability to control water power it was in a position to handicap the economic development of South Korea.

At the Cairo Conference (November 22–26, 1943) Roosevelt, Churchill, and Chiang Kai-shek had agreed that their three states were "determined

---

[2] At Yalta and Potsdam decisions were taken providing that the Soviet forces should accept the Japanese surrender north of the 38th parallel, and the United States forces should accept it south of that line. American forces did not land in Korea until September 8, 1945.

that in due course Korea shall become free and independent." Later, at the Moscow Conference (December 16–26, 1945), an agreement had been reached upon the procedure by which Korea was to gain her independence, but in the ensuing two years no implementation of the plan occurred because Russia and the United States could not agree on "the Korean democratic parties and social organizations" which their joint commission was supposed to consult. In September, 1947, the United States proposed an election in both zones of Korea, supervised by the United Nations, for a provisional legislature and government. The Soviet Union rejected this proposal and the United States then placed the case of Korea before the General Assembly of the United Nations. In November, 1947, the General Assembly voted that elections should be held in both zones under the observation of the United Nations and that a bizonal provisional government should be set up with United Nations assistance. The Soviet government's motion that the United Nations order both the Russian and American occupation troops out of Korea by January 1, 1948, was rejected, whereupon Russia declared she would not admit United Nations emissaries to the northern zone.

Nevertheless, in accordance with the United Nations resolution elections were held in Korea outside the Soviet zone on May 10, 1948, under the observation of a United Nations commission. The national assembly thus elected, representing about two thirds of the Korean people, drafted a republican constitution and elected Syngman Rhee as president. On August 15, the third anniversary of the country's liberation from Japan, the Korean Republic was proclaimed in Seoul, the capital.

The United States and China at once extended *de facto* recognition to the government of the Korean Republic, and on December 10 the United States agreed to provide at least $300,000,000 aid to the republic in the ensuing years through the Economic Co-operation Administration. Plans were made for the extensive nationalization of transportation, communication, and the major industries. In December the United Nations Assembly by a vote of 48 to 6 recognized the Seoul government as Korea's only legitimate government, and appointed a permanent commission to work for the unification of Korea and the withdrawal of occupation troops. In October the Soviet government had ordered the gradual evacuation of its troops from Korea and on December 30, 1948, it was announced in Moscow that all Russian troops had been withdrawn. Early in January, 1949, the United States took similar steps and by the end of June all American troops had been withdrawn except a small advisory mission.

But the government of neither of the Korean states was satisfied with the 38th parallel and both claimed jurisdiction over the entire peninsula. Each apparently had underground forces in the territory of the other, and after the withdrawal of American troops the rival Korean armies fought something of an undeclared war along the 38th parallel. How in June, 1950, the North Koreans, probably encouraged by Russia, finally launched an all-out invasion against the Korean Republic is discussed in Chapter XXXI. Following the signing of the armistice at the close of the Korean War in 1953, the Soviet government expressed its willingness to help in the peaceful reconstruction of North Korea. It promised to make a one billion rouble grant to North Korea for the latter's use in the industrial construction and reconstruction of the country.

RUSSIA AND IRAN

The desire for territorial or economic expansion appeared to motivate, also, the Soviet government's policies toward Iran. As early as 1944 Russia asked for oil concessions in northern Iran at the same time that American and British oil companies were seeking new concessions in the southeastern part of that country. But Iran declined to grant such concessions during the war, whereupon Russia apparently brought pressure upon the government in Teheran and was accused of even encouraging a separatist movement in Iranian Azerbaijan. The problem was brought before the United Nations, but two agreements between Russia and Iran in April, 1946, seemed to settle the matter without action by that body. The first provided for the complete withdrawal of Russian troops from Iranian territory; the second, subject to ratification by the Iranian parliament, provided for the formation of a joint Soviet-Iranian oil company to operate as a monopoly for fifty years in developing the petroleum resources in a strip of territory across northern Iran.

Elections for a new parliament which should ratify or reject the Soviet-Iranian oil agreement were held early in 1947 and gave a substantial majority to the government which had signed the agreement. But in March came the announcement of the so-called Truman Doctrine, which committed the United States to combat the extension of Soviet influence throughout the world, and in the succeeding months pressure was applied on the Iranian government from all sides. During the summer it was announced that Iran would receive from the United States some $30,000,000 worth of surplus army equipment, together with a $25,000,000 credit with which to pay for it; and in September the United States ambassador to Iran stated that his country would defend Iran's freedom to make her own choice in matters of foreign commercial proposals. Finally, on October 6, 1947, the United States signed a pact with Iran providing for an American military mission to "enhance the efficiency of the Iranian army." Two weeks later the parliament in Teheran voted overwhelmingly against ratifying the Soviet-Iranian agreement for a joint oil company. The Soviet government at once declared that the Iranian government had "treacherously violated its undertakings," made a strong protest against its "hostile actions," and declared that it "must be responsible for any consequences." In February, 1948, the Iranian parliament voted to purchase $10,000,000 worth of arms from the United States.

RUSSIA AND THE STRAITS

What appeared to be a preliminary move to the demand for some concessions from Turkey, also, was the Soviet government's decision in March, 1945, to denounce the Turkish-Soviet nonaggression pact of 1925. Many suspected that the Soviet government was about to attempt to improve Russia's position at the Straits, a suspicion which was justified in August, 1946, when the Soviet government demanded that the Montreux Convention be modified to put the Dardanelles under the control of the Black Sea powers—Turkey, Russia, Rumania, Bulgaria—and that the fortification of the Straits be placed under joint Russo-Turkish control. Russia thus once more sought to realize her age-long desire to control the Straits, a control which had been promised her by the Allies during the First World War. Turkey opposed any Russian encroachment on the Straits and was supported in her stand by Great Britain and the United States. Turkey's desire to protect herself against pressure from Russia had led her to keep her army mobilized even after the end of the war, despite the heavy drain on her national treasury. To assist the Turks to maintain their military position, President Truman requested and the United States Congress approved in April, 1947, an appropriation of $100,000,000 to help Turkey in her military needs. As in the case of so many other world problems, Soviet-Turkish relations seemed destined to be involved in the "cold-war" between the United States and Russia. Six years later, however, after Stalin's death, the Soviet government in a note to Turkey on May 30, 1953, renounced Russia's claims to Turkish territory and to special privileges in the Dardanelles.

RUSSIA'S SATELLITE STATES IN EUROPE

Little effort was made by the Soviet government to conceal its desire to control indirectly through Communist parties the states lying along Russia's western boundary, for Stalin himself publicly justified it on the ground that the Germans had invaded Russia through Finland, Poland, Rumania, Bulgaria, and Hungary, and had been able to do so because governments hostile to the Soviet Union had existed in those countries. With the Red Army's successful advances in 1944 and the destruction of Germany's military and political power in 1945, the states in Eastern Europe which came to be characterized as "Russian satellites" fell almost inevitably within the Soviet sphere. Their economic and military weakness made it practically impossible for them to oppose Russia effectively just as it had prevented their successful resistance to the political, economic, and military pressure exerted earlier by Germany. In all of these satellite states except Finland, by the close of 1948, regimes had been established which were dominated directly or indirectly by Communists.

In the view of Soviet writers, three factors had helped to establish the new order in these Eastern European states. The first was the elimination of the former ruling groups because of their policy of collaboration with the Nazis. There is little doubt, certainly, that each of these countries at the outbreak of the Second World War was being governed by a political group which feared Communism and leaned more or less toward Fascism or Nazism. During the war their ruling classes had collaborated with Germany, and the latter's defeat inevitably involved them in total discredit. In fact, the strongly Leftist character of the resistance movements in some of the states was probably the outgrowth of popular revolt against the continuation of their Rightist, anti-Russian, often corrupt and inefficient governments. The second factor, according to Soviet writers, was the leading role played by Communists in the resistance movements, which produced national fronts against Fascism and its economic basis, big landownership and capital. Again, it is undoubtedly true that in all these satellite states, at the close of the war, there were set up coalition or "Front" governments of one kind or another in which Communists played important roles. Indeed, in some of the countries—notably Poland, Yugoslavia, Bulgaria, and Czechoslovakia— former Comintern officials actually returned during or in the closing days of the war to help organize the national Communist movements and to build strong party blocs around them of Leftist and patriotic resistance groups. The third factor which contributed to the establishment of the new order in these states, according to Soviet writers, was the moral, diplomatic, economic, and—they might have included—military support given by the Soviet Union. Without this factor, they admit, these countries would have succumbed to internal and external Fascist pressure.

In other words, the strongest factor in the creation of these "new-type democracies" was the influence of Communist Russia, exerted not through the revolutionary establishment of a Soviet system in the various states, as attempted in Germany and Hungary in 1919, but through a variety of "Front" coalition governments. In these "Front" governments a Communist usually took over the ministry of the interior, and then as unobtrusively as possible he gradually transformed the police and other security forces of the state into a Communist instrument. A similar process was usually carried out in the trade unions, also. At some point in the growth of Communist power and influence, the non-Communist ministers in the government became faced with the choice either of seeking to stop the

Communist expansion of power and thus opening themselves to the Communist charge of "disrupting national unity" or of finally acquiescing in the Communist seizure of power. In all the states except Finland they

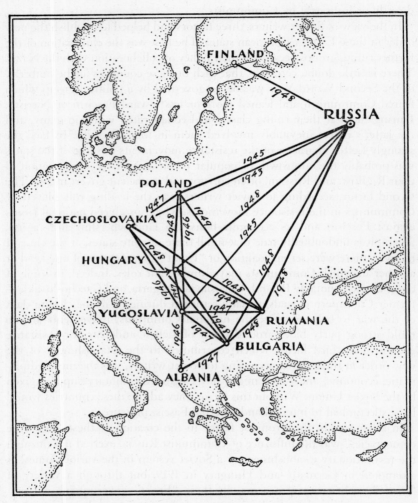

RUSSIA'S NETWORK OF ALLIANCES, 1949

finally acquiesced. The liquidation of the chief opponents of Communism, on the ground that they were "traitors," "collaborators," or "conspirators," then followed and in the end the states for all practical purposes became Communist. Meanwhile, the satellite states had been linked together with

Russia and with one another by a network of alliances and mutual assistance pacts.

In 1948 the world was given a dramatic example of the value to Russia of her satellite states and of the close co-operation of the latter with the Soviet Union in international affairs. At Paris in 1946 the Western powers had insisted that an article should be included in the peace treaties with Hungary, Rumania, and Bulgaria stating that a conference of the interested states would be convened to establish a new permanent international regime of the Danube. Russia had maintained that the question of internationalizing the Danube should not be included in these treaties since it concerned other Danubian states also, but she had been voted down. It was decided that such a conference should be held and that it should be attended by representatives of Great Britain, France, Russia, the United States, and the six riparian states—Czechoslovakia, Hungary, Yugoslavia, Bulgaria, Rumania, and the Ukraine.

This conference eventually met in Belgrade from July 30 to August 18, 1948. At the very first session it became obvious that Russia would dominate the gathering. The Soviet government submitted the draft of a new convention which accepted the principle of free navigation for the commercial vessels of all countries, but which called for a revision of the international machinery for enforcing this principle and regulating traffic on the river. The prewar commission, which represented Belgium, France, Great Britain, Greece, Italy, Rumania, Yugoslavia, Czechoslovakia, Germany, Austria, Bulgaria, and Hungary, was to be replaced by one composed of representatives of the riparian states alone. Russia thus sought to exclude the Western powers from any control of the Danube, while the latter sought by opposing Russia's draft to retain some hold on that river as a means of penetrating the "Iron Curtain."

But just as the Western powers at the Paris peace conference had been able to carry through their program and defeat Russia's usually by a 15 to 6 vote, so now the Soviet government with a solid block of seven votes was able to defeat every proposal of the Western powers and force the adoption of the Russian Danubian convention. Great Britain, France, and the United States refused to sign the convention, and the United States government stated: "The unhappy subservience of the Danube peoples to Soviet imperialism was never more clearly manifest than at this conference. There was an evident Soviet determination to perpetuate its economic and political enslavement of the Danube peoples."

Poland

Perhaps the most conspicuous instance of Russia's determination to set up a friendly government in a neighboring state occurred in Poland. In prewar days the government of this state had usually been hostile to or suspicious of the Soviet Union. Poland had invaded Russia in 1920 and had pushed her boundary far east of the "Curzon Line" suggested by the Paris peace conference. She had formed an alliance with Rumania against Russia and had long declined to sign a nonaggression pact with the latter. After Hitler came to power she had even declined to participate in a French-sponsored Eastern Locarno, designed to safeguard the frontiers in eastern Europe, although the Soviet government expressed its willingness to do so. Finally, at the time of the Franco-British attempt to secure Russia's participation in an anti-Hitler pact in 1939, the Poles had resolutely refused to give the Soviet Union permission to send troops into their territory even to help defeat Germany in case the latter attacked Poland.

Following the collapse of Poland in September, 1939, a Polish government-in-exile was constituted in France, the creation of a Polish army of volunteers to fight on the side of the Allies was begun, and contact was soon established with an underground movement within Poland. When Germany conquered France in 1940 the Polish government moved its interim capital to London. Although the Poles were naturally more hostile than ever toward Russia because of the latter's participation in the partition of their country in 1939, it appeared for a time in 1941 that the basis for a future friendly collaboration might be laid. In July of that year, after the Nazi invasion of Russia, a treaty was signed between the Polish government in London and the Soviet Union in which the latter recognized that the Soviet-German treaties of 1939 regarding territorial changes in Poland had "lost their validity."

The Polish government in London at once interpreted this statement to mean that Russia's incorporation of Polish White Russia and the Polish Ukraine into the Soviet Union was invalidated, a view with which the Soviet government did not agree. The Moscow government apparently had in mind a settlement in which the territory east of the "Curzon Line" would remain in Russia and in which Poland would be compensated by the absorption of territory to the north and west which the Germans had taken from Poland in the eighteenth century. When the London government steadfastly refused to accept this view, relations between it and Russia deteriorated. The Soviet government did not long delay to take steps to create in Poland a regime friendly to Russia. During the winter of 1941–1942 a Russian plane dropped in Poland behind the German lines, Boleslaw Bierut, a former leader of the underground Communist organization in prewar Poland. In 1942 he helped create an organization in Poland in opposition to the underground movement directed by the Polish government in London.

In 1943, following the London government's request that the International Red Cross investigate the alleged slaying by Russia of some 10,000 Polish officers at Katyn near Smolensk in 1940, Moscow severed diplomatic relations with the Polish government. Russia maintained that the officers had been killed by the Germans and that the Polish government's request for an investigation indicated that the latter was only too willing to believe the "slanderous campaign hostile to the Soviet Union launched by the German Fascists." But in 1944 the Soviet government made one last effort to reach an agreement with the London Poles. On January 15, Moscow reaffirmed its view that the restoration of eastern Poland to Russia in 1939 had rectified "the injustice committed by the Riga Treaty of 1921," and again contended that "Poland must be reborn, not by means of the seizure of Ukrainian and White Russian lands, but through the restoration to Poland of lands which belonged to her from time immemorial and which were wrested from Poland by the Germans." The London Polish government's failure to accept Russia's proposals led the Soviet government to announce its belief that that government did not desire to establish good-neighbor relations with the Soviet Union.

Later in 1944, however, Prime Minister Stanislaw Mikolajczyk, leader of the Polish Peasant Party, who had become head of the London Polish government in 1943, went to Moscow to confer with Stalin regarding the re-establishment of friendly relations between their two countries. In the conference it became apparent that friendly relations would be resumed by Russia only if the London government repudiated the undemocratic Polish constitution of 1935, and agreed to Russia's proposals regarding Poland's new boundaries. Mikolajczyk, who had himself voted against the constitution of 1935, tried to persuade his government to accept these proposals but failed. He thereupon resigned the premiership and was succeeded in that office by a Russophobe Pole.

Meanwhile, early in 1944 Bierut and others of his pro-Russian underground group in Poland had gone to Moscow and had there set up the Polish National Council and the Polish Committee of National Liberation. When the Soviet armies rolled back the Germans in 1944, this Committee took charge of the areas liberated. Eventually, following the advance of the Red Armies, it established itself in the Polish city of Lublin. In January, 1945, following Mikolajczyk's futile efforts at a Polish-Russian reconciliation, the Polish National Council in Lublin announced the establishment of the Provisional National Government of the Polish Republic, with

Bierut as President and Edward Obsubka-Morawski as prime minister. On January 5 the Soviet government extended diplomatic recognition to the new regime, and following the liberation of Warsaw the new Polish government transferred its seat to the national capital. On April 21, 1945, the Warsaw government and the Soviet government signed a twenty-year defensive alliance against Germany.

With Russia recognizing the Lublin government and Great Britain and the United States recognizing the London government, it was imperative, in the interests of Allied military collaboration, that the two governments should be fused if possible. To this end, at the Yalta Conference in February, 1945, Stalin, Churchill, and Roosevelt agreed that the Lublin government should be broadened by the inclusion of democratic leaders from both inside and outside the country, and authorized the appointment of a three-man Allied commission to facilitate the reorganization. The new government would be pledged to hold free elections as soon as possible on the basis of universal suffrage and the secret ballot, with all democratic parties having the right to put forward candidates. Upon its reorganization, it was agreed, the United States and Great Britain would enter into diplomatic relations with the Warsaw government.

In June, 1945, the Allied commission held consultations in Moscow with representatives of the Warsaw Provisional Government, democratic leaders from Poland, and democratic leaders from abroad, including Mikolajczyk. As a result of these consultations Obsubka-Morawski's government resigned and was replaced by a Government of National Unity headed by him but including from abroad Mikolajczyk as vice-premier and minister of agriculture and Jan Stanczyk, a former leader of the Socialist Party, as minister of labor and social welfare. The new government, a majority of which consisted of men favorable to Soviet Russia, announced that it accepted the Yalta decisions and was prepared to hold free elections with a secret ballot, and the British and United States governments, accordingly, extended to it diplomatic recognition. The London government, no longer recognized by the three great powers, for all practical purposes ceased to exist.

Although the new ministry was called the Government of National Unity, its members were not united on the policies to be followed. The promised elections for the constituent diet were delayed until January, 1947, and then were accompanied by accusations of the government's use of terror, arrest, fraud, and suppression of freedom of speech and the press. Mikolajczyk's Peasant Party declined the invitation of the other parties in the government to form an electoral bloc with a single list of candidates. The Communists and Socialists thereupon began to accuse the leaders of that party of being reactionary, of being "Churchill's agents," and of having returned from London to conduct an opposition within the Government of National Unity. They further asserted that the Peasant Party had become the haven of those undemocratic Rightists whose own parties had been outlawed. The elections resulted in an 8 to 1 victory in the popular vote for the government bloc; Mikolajczyk's Peasant Party won only 28 out of 444 seats.

The new diet elected Bierut to be President of Poland and he, in turn, asked a leader of the Polish Socialist Party to form a cabinet. The latter included representatives of five political parties which were favorable to Russia. No member of the Polish Peasant Party was included. In October, 1947, because of alleged threats against his life, Mikolajczyk fled from Poland; thereupon the Left wing of his party, which had failed in an attempt to oust him from control earlier in the year, took complete charge. In February, 1948, the new leader of the party announced the abandonment of Mikolajczyk's policies and promised the fullest support of alliances with the Soviet Union and the other Slavic countries. Thereafter there was no important political group actively opposed to collaboration with Russia. The diet, meanwhile, had denounced Mikolajczyk as a traitor to Poland, deprived him of his seat in the diet, and banished him for life.

After 1948 the political situation moved closer to that of the Soviet Union when, after purging themselves of a number of Rightist leaders, notably Vladislav Gomulka, secretary of the Communist Party, and Edward Osubka-Morawski, former Socialist premier in the Lublin and Warsaw governments, the Communists and Socialists merged into the United Workers Party. In 1949 Soviet Marshal Konstantin Rokossovsky was sent to be Polish minister of defense and marshal of the Polish armies. Gomulka was thereupon dropped from the Communist central committee and was replaced by Rokossovsky. Later in the year he was expelled from the party, and in 1951 he and others were tried and ultimately imprisoned.

In 1952 a new Polish constitution was unanimously adopted by the diet, and the official name of the state was changed to the Polish People's Republic. The office of the president was abolished, his former duties being entrusted to a small State Council by which the diet was completely overshadowed. The State Council had authority to call elections, convene the diet, initiate legislation, issue decrees with the force of law, and declare martial law. Moreover, it supervised the national councils, which were the sole organs of state authority in all the political units of the republic. In October a new diet was elected from only one list of candidates, and in November, 1952, President Bierut was chosen premier. In many respects Poland's political situation thus came to resemble that of the Soviet Union, and thereafter as a satellite she followed more and more the "Moscow line."

Territorially, the new Poland was quite different from that which existed before 1939. The Yalta Conference had accepted Russia's contention that

Poland's eastern frontier should, in general, be based on the "Curzon Line." But in the Soviet-Polish treaty of August 17, 1945, settling the frontier, Russia ceded to Poland two districts—near Lwow and near Brest-Litovsk—besides several other small deviations from that line. It had also been decided at Yalta that Poland should receive substantial additions of territory in the north and west, though the final delimitation of Poland's western frontier should await the peace conference. At Potsdam, however, it was agreed that, pending this final determination, the former German territories east of a line running from the Baltic Sea immediately west of Swinemunde, and then along the Oder River to the confluence of the western Neisse River and along the latter to the Czechoslovak frontier (excluding only a portion of East Prussia around Königsberg and Memel, which was to be administered by Russia) should be under the administration of Poland and should not be considered as part of the zone of occupation in Germany. This boundary, which both Polish and Russian leaders soon considered permanent, gave the new Poland three fine outlets to the sea at Danzig, Gdynia, and Stettin, and gave her also all of the valuable industrial resources of Upper Silesia. These boundary changes, however, reduced Poland's prewar area by 20 per cent.

The territory added to Poland obviously contained a large German population, and the Potsdam Conference had decided that the transfer to Germany of the German population in Poland would have to be undertaken. By 1949 some 5,000,000 of the 8,000,000 Germans living within the new Polish boundaries had been transferred to Germany. Many of them had been allowed to take with them only such possessions as they could carry and a very small amount in currency. At the same time hundreds of thousands of Poles had been transferred into Poland from Germany and from former Polish territories incorporated in Russia. The transfer of both Polish and German populations inevitably occasioned grave hardships and losses to both. Probably the worst wartime sufferers in Poland, however, were the Jews, for in 1946 the Polish premier announced that of 3,200,000 Jews in prewar Poland, only 80,000 were left. Poland's heavy population losses during the war, together with the changes in boundaries, reduced her population from 35,000,000 in 1939 to 24,000,000 in 1945.

Following the Second World War, Poland was faced with problems of economic and social rehabilitation far greater than those which confronted her in 1919. These resulted primarily from the vast amount of material destruction which had occurred during the war [3] and from the forced transfer and shifting of a large part of the Polish population. Nevertheless, Presi-

---

[3] According to a United Nations economic report, in Poland 30 per cent of the railway lines, 70 per cent of the large bridges, 42 per cent of the locomotives, 92 per cent of the passenger cars, and 98 per cent of the freight cars were either destroyed or removed.

dent Bierut declared that the leaders of the new Poland aimed to change their country from an agricultural into an industrial power. According to him, before 1939 only some 1,500,000 persons had been employed in industry while 70 per cent of the population had "existed in misery" on their inadequate earnings from tiny farms and farm labor. To remedy the latter condition, a program of land reform was initiated in 1944 which entailed the confiscation of land belonging to Germans or to traitors and criminals and estates consisting of more than 125 acres of arable land. Some of the farms confiscated were distributed among landless peasants and those holding tiny plots, but much of the land formerly owned by German Junkers became state farms, which in 1954 included 12.8 per cent of all Poland's farmland. Many landless peasants, it was hoped, would become industrial workers.

The latter development was dependent, of course, upon the expansion of Poland's industry. This expansion, in turn, was greatly facilitated by Poland's acquisition of the relatively undamaged industrial resources of Upper Silesia and by some industrial equipment received as reparations from Germany. By 1949 Upper Silesia, plus other newly acquired territory, had increased Poland's production of steel by 25 per cent, of cotton goods by 33 per cent, of coal, cement, paper, sugar, and engineering goods by approximately 50 per cent, and had doubled the coke output. Poland eventually passed Italy in per capita industrial output and threatened to catch up with France in the industrial race.

In January, 1946, all industries employing more than 50 workers (a limit subsequently raised to 100 and in some industries to 400) were nationalized. After nearly six years of German occupation all Polish industry, according to reports by some foreign observers, was disorganized and awaited government operation. Most of the former owners and managers had either refused to co-operate with the Germans and had therefore lost their factories and often their lives, or they had collaborated with the Nazis and had thus disqualified themselves as owners in the eyes of Polish patriots. Poland's postwar economy came to be a combination of state and privately owned enterprises, something like the situation which had existed in Russia under the Nep. Foreign trade was largely, but not wholly, controlled by state departments, co-operatives, or state-sponsored companies.

By 1950, as the result of the Three-Year Plan inaugurated in 1947, industrial production was reported as 100 per cent and agricultural production as 67 per cent above that in 1946. Socialization of industry and of retail trade had increased considerably, but collectivization of farms had lagged. In 1950 a Six-Year Plan was begun which called for a yearly output of 100,000,-000 tons of coal by 1955, an increase of industrial production by another 95 per cent and of agricultural production by 45 per cent. Particular emphasis was to be placed on collectivization in agriculture. Nevertheless, because of the woeful inefficiency of the state farms, in comparison with those of the kulaks and even with the small peasants, in the matter of agricultural production, the Polish government was actually somewhat wary of collectivization. In the five-year period, 1949–1954, only some 7 per cent of the country's farmland was brought into collectives. The individual peasant holders, owning some 80 per cent of the land and live stock, in 1954 still constituted the predominant factor in Poland's agricultural economy.

In the summer of 1953, as in some of the other satellite states, strikes and anti-Communist demonstrations occurred in Poland following the outbreak of violence in the German People's Republic in June of that year. Serious demonstrations were also reported three months later in consequence of the government's suspension or "deposition" of the Cardinal Archbishop of Warsaw and the arrest and imprisonment of other Roman Catholic clergy. In 1954 Bierut relinquished the premiership to Joseph Cyrankiewicz and became first secretary of the party's central committee.

Czechoslovakia

Czechoslovakia is an example of a state which, although it willingly linked itself with Russia in foreign policy, nevertheless was ultimately forced to adopt institutions in its internal life which were in line with Communist ideology but distasteful probably to a majority of its own citizens. Its adoption of a Communist regime in 1948, like its loss of the Sudetenland ten years earlier, came as the result of the policies of the great powers who were maneuvering to their own advantage.

It will be recalled that following the Munich settlement of 1938, Eduard Beneš had resigned the presidency of Czechoslovakia and left the country. From then until the outbreak of the Second World War he lived abroad, chiefly in England and the United States. Upon the outbreak of the war in 1939, Beneš returned to Europe and, as he had done during the First World War, organized the Czechoslovak National Committee whose immediate purpose was to build up a new Czechoslovak army to fight against Germany. This National Committee refused to recognize the legality of either the Munich settlement or the government set up in Prague under Hitler's protection, and in 1942 it received British, Russian, French, and American recognition as the legal government of Czechoslovakia. In June of that year Beneš' government and the Soviet government signed a twenty-year defensive alliance against Germany and that treaty became the "central pillar" of Czechoslovakia's foreign policy.

After the German slaughter of Czech intellectuals in 1941–1942, no outstanding leaders arose within Bohemia and Moravia so that the Czechs were able to do little in the way of organized resistance during the war. But in Slovakia—supposedly an ally of the Third Reich—a resistance movement did arise against the Nazis. Delegates of the movement made contact with Beneš late in 1943 and plans were made for a rising to take place either when the Russian army called for it or when the Germans occupied Slovakia. Such a rising occurred in August, 1944, when German troops entered Slovakia. A large part of the organized Slovak army joined the patriots, and a Slovak National Council—50 per cent of whose members were Socialists or Communists—took over political control of liberated regions. Delegates of this Council conferred with the Czechoslovak government in London and announced that there was no fundamental difference of view between them and that government regarding the national future of their country.

In the spring of 1945, President Beneš returned to Czechoslovakia and set up temporary headquarters in Kosice. In April, after consultation with Stalin, he appointed a new government in which Zdenek Fierlinger, former Czechoslovak ambassador to Russia and a Left-wing Socialist with strong pro-Soviet leanings, was prime minister. Eventually, in May, 1946, elections were held for a constituent assembly, and as in prewar days several parties participated and elected candidates. Of the 310 seats, however, the Czech and Slovak Communist parties won the largest number (114), and President Beneš thereupon requested Klement Gottwald, the Communist leader, who had once been a member of the executive committee of the Third International, to organize a ministry. In June, Beneš was unanimously re-elected President of the Czechoslovak Republic, and in the following month the constituent assembly approved Gottwald's National Front ministry, which included representatives of the Communist, Social Democratic, National Socialist, People's, and Slovak Democratic parties.

The new Czechoslovakia differed from that existing before 1938 in area and population. Territorially, it was slightly smaller, for Ruthenia—inhabited by Ukrainians—in 1945 voted to join the Ukrainian Soviet Socialist Republic and was permitted to do so. Racially, the new Czechoslovakia was somewhat more homogeneous, for the great powers at Potsdam had agreed that the German population in Czechoslovakia should be transferred to Germany. These transfers were made, for the most part, in 1945 and 1946, and in the Sudetenland nearly 2,000,000 Czechs from other parts of the republic and from abroad were settled. Czechoslovakia also wished to have her Magyar population transferred to Hungary but, though Russia approved, the other members of the "Big Four" refused to assent and left the matter to be settled by negotiations between Czechoslovakia and Hungary. Since the latter was opposed to receiving into her territory all her kinsmen from across the border—perhaps because she wished to retain a basis for future "revisionist claims"—only some 20 per cent of Czechoslovakia's Magyars were transferred.

Minus its Ukrainians, most of its Germans, and some of its Magyars, it was hoped that the new Czechoslovak Republic might be less plagued than its predecessor by the problem of minorities. But the Slovak problem persisted. The attempt to draft a new constitution for the republic was blocked for more than two years by the Slovak demand for all the advantages of regional autonomy while having full participation in the central government's direction of national affairs. The Slovak Democratic Party, which received more than two thirds of the votes of Slovakia in 1946, contained former supporters of Tiso who had both separatist and fascist tendencies. In September, 1947, a widespread "plot" was discovered to assassinate President Beneš and restore an independent Slovak state with the co-operation of leading remnants of the former Tiso regime who had escaped abroad. Several prominent members of the Democratic Party were incriminated; some were arrested; others were forced to resign from government offices; and at least two had their parliamentary immunity suspended. In April, 1948, a number of members of the Slovak Democratic Party, including a former deputy premier of the republic, were given prison sentences.

The economic life of postwar Czechoslovakia came to differ markedly from that existing prior to 1939. Although the country's industrial system was practically unscathed by the war, its structure had been severely dislocated by the Nazis. Even before the Beneš government returned to Prague, it had announced a program of nationalization, and by four decrees in October, 1945, some 65 per cent of the country's industrial capacity was nationalized and Czechoslovakia was transformed into one of the leading socialist countries in the world. At that time, generally speaking, no business with fewer than 150 workers was nationalized but scarcely any employing more than 500 escaped. Small industries, retail trade, apartment houses, office buildings, and hotels were left in private ownership.

In October, 1946, a Two-Year Plan was adopted for the years 1947–1948 and had as its chief objectives a wider distribution of industry over the country and a shift in the balance of industrial development away from some of the light industries, in which highly-skilled German workers had formerly been engaged, to the heavy industries in which the Czechs hoped to play an important international role in southeastern Europe. The success of this Two-Year Plan, however, was contingent upon the receipt of foreign credits, especially from the United States, for it was largely from the latter that some of Czechoslovakia's basic needs for equipment must be filled. Unfortunately for the Czechs, the obtaining of further aid from the West was handicapped by the international struggle between the United States and the Soviet Union.

Meanwhile, during the first two years after the war the National Front had functioned with little difficulty. There was no Czechoslovak party which was fundamentally anti-Communist, those of prewar days having been liquidated and the bases of their power removed by nationalization decrees and population transfers. Furthermore, there was no Right wing in Czechoslovakia as there was in France and no anti-Communist Left wing like the Labor Party in Britain. The other parties in the National Front were primarily non-Communist rather than anti-Communist. The party which held the balance was the Social Democratic, and for two years it voted nearly always with the Communists.

There was in Czechoslovakia during these years what has been called a compromise between Eastern Socialism and Western Democracy. An Eastern orientation in foreign policy was dictated for the republic by all that had happened to it in the preceding decade. To the Czechs it seemed apparent that Russia was the only power that could guarantee them security against a resurgent Germany. At the same time a Western orientation in internal affairs, particularly in respect to political democracy and intellectual and personal freedom, was dictated by the history and temperament of the Czech people.

To many, however, it seemed obvious that this compromise within the republic could endure only if a similar compromise could be reached between the Western powers and Russia, and the deterioration which occurred in the international field in 1947 inevitably affected Czechoslovakia. Because the latter at the Paris peace conference in 1946 had voted on every major issue with the Soviet bloc, she apparently lost the good will of the United States government, which in September of that year cancelled $40,000,000 worth of credits already granted and suspended negotiations for an additional loan. Failure to obtain American credits in turn seriously handicapped Czechoslovakia's Two-Year Plan, for the Czechs aimed to overcome their serious man-power shortage by mechanization and had planned to buy much of their needed machinery in the United States with proceeds from loans.

When the Marshall Plan was offered, therefore, the Czechs at once announced their intention to participate in it and to send their delegates to Paris to join in the projected negotiations. In the Anglo-Saxon press suggestions were thereupon forthcoming that Czechoslovakia was going to disengage herself from the Slav bloc. Russia apparently feared that Czechoslovakia might indeed be won over to the side of the Western powers, in which case the Soviet Union would be deprived of an increasingly important source of industrial goods at the very time when the United States was determined that Russia should receive no further reparations in capital goods from western Germany. The Soviet government, accordingly, insisted that Czechoslovakia refuse to attend the Paris conference and continue to align herself with the Slav bloc. "The Marshall offer brought down Czechoslovakia as an independent, sovereign state."

The conflict between the Western powers and Russia next made itself felt in the internal affairs of the little republic, for the Communist parties of Czechoslovakia now launched upon a program of extra-parliamentary steps and even direct action to secure greater control. Ministers who opposed their policies were denounced as "reactionaries," mass meetings of factory workers were held, and strikes were even called in some of the nationalized factories. For a time the Social Democrats resisted Communist pressure and aligned themselves with the other non-Communist parties, but in September, 1947, this alignment was broken when a Social Democratic delegation, headed by Fierlinger, unexpectedly concluded a Socialist-Communist pact. A crisis thereupon occurred in the Social Democratic Party; Fierlinger was repudiated by the Western wing and was succeeded as president of the party by the reportedly more moderate Bohumil Lauš-man, who was at once denounced by the Communists.

In 1948 the latter sought to tighten their control of the police, the army, the trade unions, and the radio, probably with a view to controlling the next parliamentary elections which were scheduled to be held in the early summer. In an effort to prevent such steps, the non-Communist parties in February demanded that the minister of the interior cease purging the police of non-Communists. When no reply was made by him, twelve members of the ministry—representing the National Socialist, the People's and the Slovak Democratic parties—resigned on February 20, apparently hoping to force an immediate general election. Premier Gottwald at once denounced these opposition ministers as "traitors" and demanded that President Beneš permit him to form a new government. The latter recognized Gottwald's right to head a new ministry but stated that he would not approve the exclusion from it of any party which had been in the previous government. On February 24, Communist "action committees" seized the ministries which had been held by the resigned ministers and a considerable show of armed force was made by marching Communists in the capital. On the same day the Social Democratic Party decided to support Gottwald and thus assured him of a parliamentary majority. On the next day the General Confederation of Labor—Communist-controlled—announced that it would call a general strike unless President Beneš approved Gottwald's new ministry. Faced, he feared, by the prospect of national industrial paralysis and perhaps even civil war, Beneš gave in, and accepted a cabinet consisting of

CZECHOSLOVAKIA'S LAST DEMOCRATIC STATESMAN

Eduard Beneš

twelve Communists, four Social Democrats—including both Laušman and Fierlinger, and eight others who were either members of minor parties or considered to be non-party. One of the latter, Jan Masaryk, son of the founder of Czechoslovakia, continued as foreign minister, declaring, "I have always gone with the people and I shall continue to do so."

Gottwald's new government set out to consolidate its power and to remove from the civil service, from government departments, from the judicial system including the supreme court, and from schools and universities those considered "not representative of the working classes." The minister of education decreed that a portrait of Stalin should be hung in every classroom, and announced that school teaching must be political throughout its course. The minister of justice declared that the "action committees" should be the supreme organs on cultural and political matters. Professors and even the rector of the 600-year-old Charles University were removed. Obviously the personal and intellectual freedom and the political democracy which both Masaryk and Beneš had cherished and sought to preserve in Czechoslovakia were being destroyed.

On March 10 came the startling news that Jan Masaryk had committed suicide by jumping from a window of his apartment. In Western countries some asserted that his death was the result of his depression over the destruction of democracy in his native land; others suspected that he had actually been murdered by Communists. Communist leaders in Czechoslovakia, on the other hand, attributed his death to illness and to depression caused by "recriminations from the West" for his part in the February crisis. It may have been caused by his belief that his failure to secure American economic assistance contributed to the collapse of the Czechoslovak democracy. At least it is known that a few weeks before his death Masaryk had lamented: "The United States treats us as though we had already been sold down the river, but we haven't—yet."

In the succeeding months events indicated Czechoslovakia's progressive conversion into a totalitarian socialist state. By April 6, it was announced, some 8,300 persons had been affected by the political purge. In April, further laws intensified the nationalization of the country's industry and trade until only about 8 per cent remained in private hands, and plans were made to confiscate land holdings in excess of 125 acres for allotment to landless peasants. In that month, too, the Social Democrats and Communists agreed to amalgamate into one party after the May elections. On May 9, the constituent assembly at its final session adopted a new constitution on the recommendation of Premier Gottwald, and three weeks later the National Front received nearly 90 per cent of the valid ballots cast in the parliamentary elections of May 30. Early in May, President Beneš had informed Gottwald of his intention to resign his office, partly because of political developments and partly because of his ill health. On June 7, he formally resigned—some said because he was determined not to approve the new constitution. One week later parliament by a show of hands elected Klement Gottwald to be the third President of the republic. Another Communist, Antonin Zapotocky, was chosen premier to succeed Gottwald and the two most important political positions in Czechoslovakia thus came into the hands of the Communists.

For some time Beneš had been in ill health. In the summer of 1947 he had suffered a stroke, and after the Communist coup of February, 1948, he had retired to his country home in Sezimovo Usti. During the summer his health continued to fail and he died on September 3. After a state funeral in Prague his body was buried, as he wished it to be, in a quiet corner of his garden in Sezimovo Usti. Thirty-four of his sixty-four years had been devoted to active service in behalf of the Czechoslovaks. For thirty years, except for a brief interlude following the Munich settlement, Beneš had served the republic as foreign minister or as President. During the period between the wars he had been one of the outstanding diplomats of Europe. Nevertheless, twice within a decade he had seen his country betrayed by great powers which were her professed friends or allies, first by France and Britain in 1938 and then by Soviet Russia in 1948. A firm believer in Western democracy, he had twice resigned after that type of democracy had been destroyed in his country by Nazis or Communists. Much as he was loved by the Czechoslovaks, some felt that he had lacked the necessary will power and confidence for effective political leadership in a time of great crisis. However that may be, the deaths of Beneš and Masaryk undoubtedly deprived Czechoslovakia of her two most notable exponents of true democracy.

In the succeeding years the Communists sought to belittle the roles of Masaryk and Beneš in Czechoslovak history, going so far, in 1953, as to order the destruction of all statues and monuments to former President Masaryk. Anti-government demonstrations at that time indicated the great difficulty which the Communists were having to crush the spirit of those who still clung to the ideals of Western democracy. That there was even a certain amount of anti-Russian nationalism within the Communist Party seemed indicated, too, by the repeated purges, treason trials, and executions which occurred. In 1949 President Gottwald admitted that an organized underground to "re-establish capitalism" existed in Czechoslovakia, and at that time more than 100,000 members were expelled from the Communist Party.

As in Russia, the Czechoslovak purges were no respecters of members in high standing. In 1950 Vladimir Clementis, an old-guard Slovak Communist, was dismissed as foreign minister on the ground of his anti-Soviet nationalism. In 1951 the powerful and ruthless secretary-general of the party, Rudolf Slansky, was arrested on charges of high treason. Finally, in November, 1952, fourteen purged Communists, including Clementis and Slansky, were tried and convicted. These two and nine others were hanged, and three were sentenced to life imprisonment. In March, 1953, the sudden death of President Gottwald brought further political changes. Premier Zapotocky was elevated to the presidency and Siroky succeeded him as premier. Both had been nominated by the central committee of the Communist Party.

Meanwhile, the success of a new Five-Year Plan (1949–1953) had been retarded by opposition and sabotage among workers and peasants. The unrest among the former was dramatically revealed by demonstrations and riots in Pilsen in June, 1953, which were so serious that the Czechoslovak security police with armored cars had to be called in to suppress them. It was less dramatically emphasized by the continued decline in the production of finished goods. At the same time, in 1953 President Zapotocky admitted that there was a serious shortage of foodstuffs in the country as a result of the low production of the new collective farms which constituted some 30 per cent of the arable land. A year later it was announced that the start of the second Five-Year Plan would be delayed until 1956 to bring it into line with Russia's fifth plan.

At the close of the year 1953 one careful observer of the Czechoslovak situation declared that the Czechoslovaks were "so disgruntled and disillusioned that but for the unpleasant nearness of the Soviet troops, especially the tanks and airplanes, just across the borders of . . . the country, Czechoslovakia might soon be in a state of revolutionary chaos." The government successfully countered this situation, however, by repeated purges and treason trials in 1954.

Hungary

Hungary's first postwar government was organized in December, 1944, by a group of Hungarian Communists who had been living in Moscow, some of them since the fall of Béla Kun's regime in 1919. This government was a coalition, known as the Hungarian National Independence Front, which consisted of representatives of the Communist, Socialist, Smallholders, National Peasant, and Bourgeois Democratic parties, and of the trade unions. The Smallholders championed the interests of the lesser landowning peasants; the Socialists, those of the urban industrial workers; the National Peasants, those of the landless agrarian proletariat; and the Bourgeois Democrats, those of the "progressive bourgeoisie." The premier was General Béla Miklos, who had commanded the First Hungarian Army but had gone over to the Russians when Regent Horthy had issued his proclamation of surrender in October, 1944.

The program of the new government included the following points: recognition of all the orthodox democratic liberties; radical land reform and measures in favor of peasant proprietors and agricultural laborers; social legislation for industrial workers; nationalization of mines and sources of power; state ownership or control of some large industries; state support for artisans and small industries; and respect for the principle of property as such. In March, 1945, the government revoked all anti-Jewish laws, ordered the immediate release of all persons sentenced or on trial under these laws, and proclaimed the full equality of all citizens.

Miklos' Independence Front coalition governed Hungary during the difficult period while the war was being fought in that country. In April, 1945, following further Russian successes, the government moved to Budapest and a regular civilian administration was restored. Eventually, on November 4, 1945, general elections were held throughout the country. The parties of the original Independence Front—minus the Bourgeois Democrats, who had been relegated to the opposition—announced in advance that whatever the outcome might be, the four-party coalition would continue. The elections resulted in the Smallholders securing 246 seats, the Socialists 71, the Communists 67, and the National Peasants 22. They were therefore a distinct victory for the moderate, middle-class-farmer party and were considered to reflect something of a revulsion of feeling against the Communists who had created and largely dominated the Independence Front. A new coalition ministry was thereupon organized with Zoltan Tildy, leader of the Smallholders, as premier and with other representatives of the Smallholders receiving the important portfolios of foreign affairs and defense. In February, 1946, following the abolition of the monarchy and the proclamation of a republic, the National Assembly chose Tildy to be President of the Republic and Ferenc Nagy, Tildy's successor as head of the Smallholders Party, as premier.

In the elections of 1945 there had been no opposition parties of importance, with the result that most opposition votes had been cast for the Smallholders Party which was the one farthest to the Right. As a consequence, anti-government tendencies frequently found support within the ranks of the Smallholders Party, which in March, 1946, expelled nineteen members of parliament from the party as reactionaries. But the Communists were not satisfied with this purge and continued to demand the expulsion of all Right-wing members of that party. In January, 1947, the press reported a plot to overthrow the government in which many members of the Smallholders Party were involved. Premier Nagy asserted that the Smallholders, Social Democratic, and Communist parties had all been infiltrated by some of the plotters, but Communist leaders put the blame on the Smallholders entirely. Hundreds, including army officers and members of parliament, were arrested. In February twenty-five more deputies were expelled from the Smallholders Party, and Béla Kovacs, secretary-general of the party, was arrested by Russian military authorities, who later claimed that he had confessed his guilt as a conspirator, though they declined to submit copies of the documents to the Western powers. In March three ministers, members of the Smallholders Party, were dismissed from the government.

In May, while Premier Nagy was in Switzerland on a vacation, Moscow informed the Hungarian government that it was willing to hand over evidence of Kovacs and others which implicated many leading members of the Smallholders Party. Nagy became alarmed, resigned the premiership, and refused to return to Hungary, whereupon he was expelled from his own party which announced that it planned to rid itself not only of those implicated in the conspiracy against the state but even of those who might have given it moral support. Lajos Dinnyes, a member of the Smallholders Party and former minister of defense, was appointed prime minister to succeed Nagy.

On August 31, Hungary had parliamentary elections for the second time since the collapse of the Horthy regime. In addition to the four coalition parties, which decided in advance to maintain the Independence Front, there were six opposition parties, formed chiefly by members of parliament who had been elected in 1945 but who had subsequently been expelled or had seceded from their parties. A new electoral law disfranchised certain classes of citizens—Germans, sympathizers with the Nazis who had fled the country and not returned until after 1945, and those who were considered to have a fascist or counter-revolutionary past. Including the 150,000 Germans, the total number of disfranchised was announced as 330,000, or 6 per cent of the electorate. Despite Nagy's appeals—over the United States' radio—for Hungarians to boycott the elections, the number of votes cast was greater than in 1945, and of the votes 3,042,919 went to the four Independence Front parties and 1,955,419, or about 40 per cent, to the opposition parties. The Communists stood first with 1,113,050 votes but second place went to the opposition Democratic Peoples Party, supported by the lower clergy and by some of the religious orders. In view of its vicissitudes in the preceding six months, it is not surprising, perhaps, that the Smallholders Party stood third, slightly ahead of the Social Democrats. In the reorganized government, Dinnyes continued as premier but the Communists took over one more portfolio, that of foreign affairs.

The succeeding months witnessed some steps toward the destruction of non-Communist parties. In November, 1947, Zoltán Pfeiffer, leader of the extreme Rightest Independence Party, fled to the United States, and his party was ordered disbanded by the government. In the early months of 1948 arrests of those charged with disloyalty continued—political and business leaders, journalists, police officers. Right-wing members of the Social Democratic Party were expelled or resigned and ultimately in March, 1948, that party passed a resolution urging fusion with the Communists and the further exclusion of some forty more Right-wing leaders and officers. The program of the resultant United Workers Party called for an abandonment of the coalition government, an intensified war on capitalism, the nationalization of the schools, and the removal from them of all religious teaching.

Late in July, 1948, President Tildy's son-in-law, the Hungarian minister to Egypt, was arrested shortly after his return to Budapest on charges of spying and treason. Under the circumstances, Tildy announced, he himself felt that he could no longer command the confidence of his fellow citizens and accordingly resigned as President of Hungary. No attempt was made by the majority of parliament to dissuade him from this step, and in his place Arpad Szakasits, a pro-Communist Socialist leader of the new United Workers Party, who was then vice premier in the cabinet, was elected President on August 3. Thus another Smallholders Party leader was eliminated from the government and his place filled with one sympathetic with the Communists.

In the ensuing months the position of the Smallholders Party was further undermined. Early in December, 1948, it was revealed that the minister of finance, a Smallholder, had fled to Switzerland and resigned, and that five under-secretaries of state, also Smallholders, had also resigned. The party's political committee thereupon condemned Premier Dinnyes for his careless handling of double-dealing "bourgeois elements" within the party and forced his resignation, also. Dinnyes, a middle-class lawyer, was succeeded as premier by another Smallholder, Istvan Dobi, a "dirt farmer" who had been a resistance leader among the peasants during the Nazi occupation. The Smallholders political committee next declared that the party must be purged of all its bourgeois followers who had dressed themselves up as Leftists. A number of members of parliament thereupon resigned from the party, and it appeared that this once-dominant group might be largely liquidated. Finally, on February 2, 1949, the leader of the Democratic Peoples Party dissolved what had been Hungary's largest opposition group and fled the country, claiming that he had been threatened by Matyas Rakosi, a Communist leader, because he would not take a stand against Cardinal Mindszenty.

On February 1, the third anniversary of the proclamation of the Hungarian Republic, the official name of the state was changed to the Peoples Republic of Hungary. The government coalition likewise changed its name from Independence Front to Peoples Front. But Rakosi, the Communist deputy premier, apparently continued to wield the real power in Hungary.

Meanwhile, changes had been made in Hungary's economic life. The country had suffered severely as the result of both German and Russian military occupation. In the actual fighting Budapest, particularly, was hard hit and extensively damaged. Then, when the Germans were forced to retreat, they took with them food stocks, gold reserves, consumer goods, machinery, and railway equipment, and, so far as they could, wrecked what they were compelled to leave behind. One third of the country's capital in mining and industry, it was estimated, was destroyed during the war. Next, the exhausted and ravaged country was called upon to support a large Soviet army of occupation and to make reparations payments. Foodstuffs were requisitioned by the Russians as needed and factories producing materials desired by the Russian army were commandeered by them. On top of all other economic woes the country's monetary system was ruined; in May, 1946, the pengo, normally worth 20 cents in American money, was quoted at 400,000,000 to the dollar and was rapidly sinking in value. This fantastic inflation was finally ended in August of that year with the introduction of a new currency unit, the forint, which could be exchanged for 400,000,000,000 pengos. To insure the success of this new currency, the government announced, it would be necessary for the state to play a greater role in the economic life of the country.

Before the war the Hungarian government had owned the nation's railways, river and sea shipping, and some steel mills and factories producing machinery. During the years 1946–1947 the government had extended state ownership by nationalizing coal mines, power plants, heavy industry, and food-processing enterprises. After the political upheaval of May, 1947, the principal banks of the country were also nationalized, and in 1948 the nationalization of all industries employing more than 100 workers brought state ownership or control of the country's industry to 90 per cent.

Strong economic ties bound Hungary to the Soviet Union. In part this resulted from Russia's seizure of German assets in Hungary which she took as payments on German reparations. Using these German assets as its contribution, the Soviet government insisted on the formation of five corporations concerned with bauxite, oil, refining, railways, and civil aviation, owned jointly by the Russian and Hungarian governments. The board of directors of each corporation consisted of equal numbers of Russian and Hungarian citizens, but the general manager of each such joint enterprise was a Russian. But Russia's strong position in Hungary's economy was also the result of the latter's obligation to pay $200,000,000 in reparations to the Soviet government. In January, 1948, an estimated 15 per cent of the latter's current industrial production was going to the Soviet Union, but in June—in response to a plea from Hungary—the Soviet government cut its reparation demands by half.

In the meantime, long-delayed agrarian reform which was so much needed in Hungary had at last been brought about. Even before the war ended the provisional government had published a land reform act. Properties belonging to former members of Nazi or other Fascist organizations were confiscated, and all landholdings of others above 1,420 acres were ordered surrendered with some compensation. Smaller holdings were ordered reduced to a maximum of 142 acres. The land thus taken over by the state was to be distributed, first, to farm employees of the confiscated estates; next, to other landless agricultural workers; and the rest to small holders, the maximum area to be held being fixed at 21 acres. The land was to be paid for by the recipients over a period of twenty years. By 1948 about 640,000 families had received allotments, though many of them held only "dwarf farms."

It had been anticipated that the new small farms would prove to be less efficient economic units than the former large estates, and the government encouraged the development of agricultural co-operation. By 1949 there were said to be some 2,000 collective farms and a hundred state farms in Hungary. Although until 1949 no great pressure had been exerted on the peasants to join the collectives, the richer peasants—like the kulaks in Russia—had opposed the movement and some sympathy with the individualism of the richer peasants had existed in the ministry of agriculture. It was for this reason, apparently, that in October, 1948, scores of officials in that ministry were sentenced to punishment for sabotage and corruption. After 1949 pressure in favor of some kind of agricultural collectivization increased; by the close of 1953 some 25 per cent of the arable land was in collective farms.

Probably, in view of the government's agrarian policy, it was inevitable that state and church should clash after the Communists gained the ascendancy in Hungary. The Catholic Church had been the largest landowner in the country, possessing in 1944 some 1,370,000 acres, and it had lost more than a million of these acres by expropriation. Although the government agreed to pay the church an annual grant of some $8,000,000 for its religious, charitable, and scholastic establishments, the church never acquiesced in the state's agrarian policy. As late as 1948 Joseph Cardinal Mindszenty, the primate of Hungary, in a pastoral letter had referred to the injustices of the land reform. The Communists considered such a document an attack upon one of their most popular measures and resented the cardinal's action. They also resented his failure to recognize the republic and his openly avowed preference for the restoration of the Habsburgs.

The conflict between church and state finally developed into an acute crisis because of the government's educational reforms. In 1947 the government extended the prewar four-year elementary school curriculum to eight years and made these eight years of education compulsory, a big advance over the prewar situation. To meet the changed situation new textbooks were published by the state which, though accepted by the non-Catholic denominational schools, were rejected by the Catholic Church. The church's attitude therefore provided the government with a reason or an excuse for nationalizing all schools. The churches were invited to participate in negotiations, and the Calvinist and Lutheran churches, to which some 30 per cent of the Hungarians adhere, issued declarations in favor of such negotiations. Cardinal Mindszenty's reply, however, was considered uncompromising and unsatisfactory by the government. Ultimately the two Protestant churches approved a nationalization plan from which six Protestant secondary schools were exempted and under which the Protestant churches would receive financial grants from the state for twenty years. A similar compromise was suggested to the Catholic Church, but Cardinal Mindszenty in another pastoral letter rejected the principle of the scheme. Nevertheless, the school nationalization law was passed in 1948, affecting some 6,669 schools and 25,896 teachers. After the enactment of the law the minister of education again sought to negotiate—this time with the heads of various Catholic orders—but the primate declared that these heads had no authority and so the negotiations collapsed.

The uncompromising attitude of Cardinal Mindszenty in defense of what he considered the Catholic Church's traditional rights inevitably won for him the hatred of the Communists, who declared that the Catholic Church served as the protector of all those who were opposed to the government. Using the "confession" of a village priest that he had incited to murder under the influence of pastoral letters and instructions from the cardinal primate, the government launched an attack against the latter. Finally, on December 28, 1948, it announced that the cardinal and thirteen others, mostly churchmen, had been arrested on charges of treason, espionage, and foreign currency abuses. In February, 1949, Cardinal Mindszenty was tried before a people's court in Budapest and in the course of the trial he stated—whether voluntarily or under duress was a matter of dispute—that "I am guilty in principle and in detail of most of the accusations made, but I cannot accept the conclusion of having participated in a plot to overthrow the democratic regime." The court found him guilty on all charges and sentenced him to life imprisonment, with the loss of civil rights and all property. In practically all countries outside the "Iron Curtain" strong protests were voiced against the trial and conviction of the cardinal, and the pope excommunicated all those connected with the prosecution. Nevertheless, by 1950 the Catholic Church in Hungary had lost both its landed estates and the right to maintain its system of schools.

In the succeeding years changes in the government eliminated Arpad Szakasits as president and Istvan Dobi as premier, the latter being succeeded by Matyas Rakosi, secretary-general of the Communist Party. Vigorous efforts were made to nationalize and collectivize agriculture and to exalt heavy industry. Both policies encountered great opposition and much sabotage, accompanied by arrests, an increase in concentration camps, and a decline in living standards. In July, 1953, however, after anti-Communist riots and demonstrations in East Germany had revealed widespread popular dissatisfaction with Communist policies, the Communist regime in Hungary suddenly moved to conciliate the masses. The politburo was reorganized and Rakosi's government resigned. The new premier, Imre Nagy, another Russian-trained Communist, announced a program subordinating industry to agriculture, permitting individual trade and individual farms, granting amnesty, liquidating concentration camps, and promising higher living standards—a sort of Hungarian Nep. In 1954 Rakosi, head of the party politburo, formally approved this new economic policy.

Rumania

Russia's increased influence in the Balkans is well exemplified by the course of events in Rumania. In August, 1944, when the Russians were rapidly advancing on Bucharest, King Michael dismissed the pro-Hitler government of General Antonescu and appointed a coalition cabinet consisting of the National Democratic Bloc under General Sanatescu. This bloc included the National Peasant, the National Liberal, the Socialist, and the Communist parties, and two smaller groups—the Plowmen's Front and the Patriots' Union—which co-operated with the Communists. The new government announced that it would purge the administration of all pro-Nazi elements, try war criminals, fulfill the armistice terms, and introduce agrarian reforms which would embrace all estates of more than 125 acres.

Inevitably the members of a coalition government such as Sanatescu's came to disagree over policies. The Peasant Party led by Julius Maniu and the Liberal Party led by Constantin Bratianu formed the moderate Right wing of the government and represented a large part of the Rumanian people. On the extreme Left were the Communists, representing some 5 per cent of the people, and the Plowmen's Front and Patriots' Union. These Left-wing groups desired to go much further than the moderates in introducing agrarian and financial reforms, and in general had the support of the Soviet government. The Socialist Party stood between the moderates

and the extreme Leftists. Differences within the cabinet led eventually to
the breakup of the National Democratic Bloc and the formation of the
National Democratic Front by the Socialists and the three extreme Left
groups. Although the Democratic Front was given increased representation
in the cabinet, it did not secure majority control, and popular disorders
organized by extremist leaders continued to embarrass the government.
Suddenly, in February, 1945, A. Y. Vyshinsky, Russian vice-commissar for
foreign affairs, arrived in Bucharest and demanded that the government be
thoroughly reorganized. Although King Michael objected, he could secure
no help from the Western Allies, and so on March 6 a new cabinet, with
Petru Groza, leader of the Plowmen's Front, as premier, and George Tartarescu, a former premier under Carol, as deputy premier, came to power.

Under the Groza regime the Peasant and Liberal parties were permitted
no part in the government and were prevented from presenting their views
in the press or at public meetings. Although the Socialist Party was given
cabinet posts, they went to members who were known to be pro-Russian,
and ultimately, in March, 1946, the head of that party was ousted in favor
of the pro-Russian leader, Stefan Voitec. Meanwhile, in 1945 the economic
position of Russia in Rumania had been strengthened by a trade agreement
and by the creation of five joint Soviet-Rumanian corporations interested
in oil, transportation, civil aviation, banking, and lumber, the Soviet government taking over German assets in Rumania in accordance with the
armistice terms. It is not surprising that on August 9, 1945, Russia recognized the Groza government.

But the United States and Great Britain delayed recognition and in
August, 1945, King Michael requested Groza to resign so that a government satisfactory to the three great Allies might be created. When Groza
refused to step down, Michael appealed to these great powers for assistance.
The latter, as a result of their deliberations at Moscow in December, 1945,
advised King Michael that the Rumanian government should be reorganized to include one member each from the Peasant and Liberal parties,
that it should hold free parliamentary elections on the basis of universal
suffrage and a secret ballot as soon as possible, and that it should guarantee
freedom of press, speech, religion, and association. It was agreed that when
the desired assurances had been received from the Rumanian government,
it would be recognized by the United States and Great Britain.

Representatives of the Peasant and Liberal parties were admitted to the
cabinet in January, 1946. The Groza government then pledged itself to fulfill the conditions set forth at Moscow and announced that elections would
be held in May, whereupon it was recognized by the United States and
Great Britain. But elections were not held until November 19, 1946, and
then they were preceded by organized terrorism which brought, for in-

stance, an attack upon the secretary of the National Peasant Party and the killing of a colleague when they attempted to hold a political meeting. The National Democratic Front, consisting of the Communists, the Plowmen's Front, the Socialists, and the Tartarescu National Liberals, won 80 per cent of the votes in an election which foreign observers asserted was based on "wholesale falsification of the results by the government authorities."

In the ensuing months hundreds were arrested in an attempt, apparently, to suppress all opposition to the government's policies. In July it moved against the strongest opposition group, the National Peasant Party, when it arrested its president, Julius Maniu, and five prominent National Peasant deputies on charges of plotting to overthrow the government. Ten days later the party was ordered dissolved. In November, Maniu and a colleague were convicted of treason and sentenced to life imprisonment, while other peasant leaders received lesser penalties. During Maniu's trial evidence seemed to implicate the National Liberal Party and its leader, Tartarescu. In November the chamber of deputies adopted a motion accusing the latter and the three other Liberal Party members of the cabinet of complicity in treason. All four at once resigned and Tartarescu later announced his withdrawal from public life. Of the four new ministers appointed, two were Communists and one a Socialist. Meanwhile, in October, the Social Democrats had approved a merger with the Communists to form the United Workers Party.

In December, Premier Groza utilized King Michael's request for the government's permission to marry a Danish princess to demand the king's abdication. On December 30, an announcement in Michael's name stated that, in view of the political, economic, and social changes which had occurred in Rumania, the institution of monarchy no longer corresponded to the new situation and that therefore the king was abdicating and resigning all his prerogatives not only for himself but for his successors. Parliament at once passed unanimously a law proclaiming for Rumania a "People's Republic" and chose a state council of five to act as executive pending the drafting of a new constitution. Elections for a constituent assembly in March, 1948, gave the government bloc 405 of the 415 seats. In April, a new constitution was approved, a Soviet-type of presidium was set up, and another government, headed by Groza and having only two of its twenty-one ministers non-Communists, took over. In August, 1948, a secret state police was established under the ministry of the interior, and all religious denominations and the teaching of religion were placed under state control. The new constitution provided for the nationalization of industry, transport, and means of communication, and in June, 1948, parliament transferred all industrial establishments, banks, insurance companies, and transport facilities to the state.

Economic conditions in Rumania continued to be bad. Her economy, already damaged by war destruction, was subjected to the further strain of having to produce sufficient quantities of specified commodities to fulfill her $300,000,000 reparations obligation to Russia, and to provide food for the Russian army of occupation. The joint Soviet-Rumanian corporations, too, by 1952 increased to thirteen, appeared to operate primarily "as a one-way conveyor belt for exports to Russia." Furthermore, the government's efforts to expropriate and collectivize the land met the bitter opposition and passive resistance of the peasants, though by the close of 1953 approximately 22 per cent of the country's arable land was reported as being in collective farms. On top of everything, between 1947 and 1953 inflation twice led to devaluation of the currency.

Whether to provide scapegoats for Communist failures in Rumania, or to tighten Communist control of the country, or to put into power those who would more ruthlessly execute Communist policies, significant changes were made in the government and party in 1952. Vasile Luca, vice premier and finance minister, who had forced upon Rumania the unfavorable trade treaties and the joint Soviet-Rumanian corporations and had in general been responsible for the country's economic policy, was removed from the ministry of finance and expelled from the central committee of the party. At the same time Ana Pauker, the foreign minister, was dismissed from that office, dropped from the politburo and the party secretariat, and eventually arrested. Teohari Georgescu, minister of the interior, was also expelled from the central committee. Vasile Luca and Ana Pauker were accused of obstruction because of their opposition to currency reform and collectivization. On June 2 the National Assembly supplanted Petru Grozu as premier by raising Gheorghe Gheorghui-Dej, secretary general of the Rumanian Communist Party, to the premiership. Thus, in 1952 in both Hungary and Rumania the head of the Communists openly took over political power.

Nevertheless, the year 1953 witnessed events which indicated both dissatisfaction with the Communist regime and efforts by the latter to placate the peasants and workers. In August the prime minister admitted that the attempted industrialization of Rumania had been at the expense of agriculture and promised that more attention would be given to the production of food and consumer goods in an effort to raise living standards. Increases in food rations were announced. To conciliate the peasants, a reduction of taxation was made and all deliveries from peasants to the state which were in arrears for the year 1952 were cancelled. Later in the year a reorganization of the ministries having to do with foodstuffs became effective, and during 1954 still more changes in party organization were made.

Bulgaria

Soviet influence was also strong in Bulgaria in the postwar period. The arrival of the Russian army in Sofia had been followed by the overturn of the Bulgarian government and the creation of the Fatherland Front, a strongly pro-Russian coalition consisting of Communists, the Zveno National Union (a pressure group of army reserve officers and businessmen), the Agrarian National Union, and the Socialists. The Communists received the key ministries of the interior and justice, though the premiership went to Kimon Georgiev, leader of the Zveno National Union. The new government maintained the regency established after the death of King Boris in 1943, with a veteran Communist as one of the regents.

The Fatherland Front at once inaugurated a program which called for the liquidation of the legislation of the former pro-Nazi regimes and the institution of people's courts to try war criminals. The term "war criminal" was broadly interpreted and some 11,000 persons were brought to trial. The regents and cabinet members who served between March 1, 1940, and September 1, 1944, together with many former members of parliament, were among the more than 2,000 persons who were convicted and executed.

In their Yalta Declaration of February, 1945, the great powers offered their joint aid in the restoration of political order in the former Axis satellite states and pledged their assistance in the formation of democratic provisional regimes and the holding of free elections. The acts of the Fatherland Front in trying to destroy the Agrarian National Union and in depriving the leader of the Socialists of his newspaper were held to be inconsistent with the Yalta formula. So, too, was the scheme to have all political parties run as a single ticket in the elections scheduled for August 26, 1945. The Agrarians and Socialists felt sure that together they would win a majority in free elections, and in protest six members of the cabinet resigned. The United States and Great Britain thereupon stated that they would not recognize as democratic any government resulting from such elections, and the latter were accordingly postponed.

Three months later on November 18, 1945, elections were finally held but because of the electoral procedure and the police pressure of the government the Agrarian and Socialist parties refused to nominate candidates. The single Fatherland Front ticket therefore received some 88 per cent of the votes cast, the seats were distributed according to a prearranged bargain among the groups which had participated, and the composition of the ministry remained unchanged. But the United States declared that it would not accept elections held under such conditions as measuring up to the Yalta formula and both it and Great Britain withheld recognition.

At Moscow in December, 1945, the three great powers agreed that prior conditions for recognition were the inclusion in the government of two additional members of the opposition groups who were truly representative of those groups and willing to work with the government. The leaders of the Agrarian and Socialist parties, however, made their entering the government contingent upon two conditions: first, that the Communists should surrender the portfolios of the interior and justice and, second, that new free elections should be held. The Georgiev government refused to accede to these demands, whereupon the United States and Great Britain claimed that Bulgaria had not met the conditions laid down at Moscow. Russia supported the Georgiev government's action, however, and an impasse regarding recognition resulted.

At the time of the death of King Boris his young son had been elevated to the throne to succeed him as King Simeon II, but a regency council had been appointed to rule during the latter's minority. During 1945–1946 sentiment in favor of abolishing the monarchy began to develop, especially after a kindred South Slav state, Yugoslavia, proclaimed a republic late in 1945. Eventually the Bulgarians were called upon to vote on the question and in a referendum held on September 8, 1946, they voted decisively against the monarchy. A Bulgarian People's Republic was thereupon proclaimed. A few weeks later (October 27) in general elections for a constituent assembly, carried out in an atmosphere of terror, the Fatherland Front won 364 seats out of 465, the Communist Party alone obtaining 277. In the reorganized government George Dimitrov, a former secretary of the Comintern, became prime minister.

During 1947 steps were taken to destroy political opposition to the Communist regime. In June, Nikola Petkov, leader of the opposition Agrarian Party, was arrested on charges of "preparing for an armed *coup d'état*" and the assembly deprived twenty-three Agrarian deputies of their seats. Despite protests from the Western great powers, or perhaps because of them, Petkov was convicted and hanged. Others, including army officers, were given long prison sentences. In August, the assembly finally ordered the Agrarian Party dissolved because of its "terrorist, sabotage, and diversionary acts." Thus the Communists strengthened their dominant position in the republic. In December a new constitution was adopted and promulgated with a presidium, in which the Communists held a safe majority, as the supreme governing body. During 1948 the liquidation of the opposition parties continued, culminating in November in the arrest and imprisonment of nine Socialist deputies. By the close of the year, it was reported, not a single Bulgarian democratic leader remained at liberty.

The death of Premier Dimitrov in July, 1949, and that of his successor six months later led to the elevation of Vulko Chervenkov, the Communist

Party secretary general, to the premiership. The succeeding four years have been referred to as "Chervenkov's years," and apparently during them the economic structure of Bulgaria was radically altered. Collectivized farms, for instance, rose from 6.2 per cent to 60.5 per cent of the country's arable land, and the number of collectivized households increased to 53 per cent of all the peasant households. The "socialist sector" of Bulgarian agriculture came to be predominant in the country's production. But the extreme poverty of Bulgaria's peasants after four years of intense collectivization seemed indicated by the government's concessions in the autumn of 1953. Income-tax arrears and all taxes, fines, and other debts to the government up to December, 1952, were cancelled and all collective farm debts to machine and tractor stations were remitted up to August 31, 1952. At the same time, concessions were announced to the "private sector" of agriculture, contrary to the government's policy in preceding years. In fields other than agriculture, private enterprise in industry, transport, trade, and other forms of business was eliminated. According to official figures, the country's industrial production rose 250 per cent in the years 1948–1953, the period of Bulgaria's first Five-Year Plan. Unfortunately for the standard of living, however, emphasis was placed on the heavy industries, though in September, 1953, Chervenkov explained that the rates of development of heavy and light industry should be altered to increase the production of consumer's goods.

But Chervenkov's more conciliatory attitude in 1953 was revealed in other than economic affairs. In that year the Bulgarian Orthodox Church was permitted to elect a patriarch for the first time since 1395, and—still more amazing—it was allowed to elect a Western-educated Bulgarian bishop who was known for his anti-Communist views. The prime minister's conciliatory attitude was also revealed in his pronouncements on foreign affairs. In true Communist style, however, the elections for the Bulgarian National Assembly in December, 1953, presented the voters with a single list of candidates drawn up by the Communist-controlled Fatherland Front. Moreover, possibly indicating party unrest, Chervenkov announced in March, 1954, that nearly 50,000 Communists had been expelled from the party since 1948.

Albania

The course of events in Albania during the Second World War was somewhat like that in Yugoslavia. During the period of Axis domination resistance groups appeared and as they grew stronger these groups not only fought the Germans but inaugurated a civil war among themselves. Eventually the Communist-controlled forces, commanded by Enver Hoxha, emerged as the strongest element and when the Germans evacuated Albania in the fall of 1944, Hoxha was able to occupy Tirana and set up a government. In November, 1945, his regime was recognized as the provisional government of Albania by Great Britain, the United States, and Russia. In December Hoxha's Democratic Front Party won the national elections, and the resultant constituent assembly on January 11, 1946, formally deposed King Zog and proclaimed the People's Republic of Albania.

The new republic became a Communist state. In 1945 an agrarian law provided for the confiscation of all land and by the close of 1946 some 200,000 landless peasants or smallholders had received parcels of it. The constitution of 1945 declared that all mineral deposits belonged to the people and laws were subsequently passed nationalizing mining, industry, and banking. The little republic appeared too weak to stand alone economically, and in 1946 Albania and Yugoslavia signed a far-reaching agreement to co-ordinate their economies. Yugoslavia's expulsion from the Cominform (see page 941), however, brought a drastic change in this situation. Diplomatic relations between Yugoslavia and Albania were broken, and Albania sought aid by joining the Soviet Council for Mutual Economic Assistance. Although Albania is certainly one of Russia's satellites, perhaps because of her physical isolation from the Soviet Union the latter never signed a treaty of mutual assistance with her as it did with its other satellites. This isolated Communist bridgehead on the Adriatic, politically unstable and economically bankrupt, is now strategically almost useless to Moscow. Nevertheless, in an apparent effort to show its friendship with Albania, the Soviet Union raised its legation there to the status of an embassy in 1953.

Finland

Of all the Russian satellite states Finland was probably the most closely connected with Western thought and culture, and the principle of liberty governed by law was perhaps more deeply and generally rooted there than in the other seven. One of the main problems of Finnish statesmen in the years after 1944 was so to conduct themselves as to give Russia as little excuse as possible to intervene in Finnish internal affairs. Consequently when in 1944 the Soviet army had smashed the Mannerheim Line and captured Viborg, a political conflict had developed within Finland. President Risto Ryti was determined to keep Finland in the war on the side of Nazi Germany; the bulk of the Finns and Field Marshal Mannerheim, on the other hand, realized the futility of further resistance. Ryti had been forced to resign, Mannerheim had been elected President to succeed him, and in

September, 1944, Finland had signed an armistice with Russia. In fact, in the following March the Finnish government had even declared war on Germany.

Parliamentary elections held in the spring of 1945 appeared to reveal some desire to orient Finland to the new European situation. Less than half of the deputies in the preceding diet were re-elected and the Right group lost its majority control. On the other hand, the new Popular Democratic Union, a Communist organization, won 49 of the 200 seats and the Social Democrats won 50. The Agrarian Party, a conservative group, held the balance of power in the coalition government which Premier Juho K. Paasikivi formed, though ten of the eighteen ministers were chosen from the Left.

The Communists in their platform had demanded a partial nationalization of industry, but no drastic new measures were enacted. Even before 1939, however, the railways and important power plants were state-owned as also were the principal ore deposits and 40 per cent of the country's forest land. Despite the fact that 90 per cent of the land already belonged to individual farmers, the need for resettling some 45,000 Finnish families from the areas ceded to Russia led to further land reform. Owners of 62 acres or more were forced to turn over to the state portions of their holdings, ranging from 10 per cent for those in the lowest category to 60 per cent for those owning 500 acres. For all practical purposes, the land was confiscated, since it was paid for in inflated currency but at 1940 prices.

The Communists in 1945 had also demanded a limited prosecution of those responsible for Finland's joining the Axis in the war. This part of their program was carried out. A special People's Court was established to try Finland's war criminals, and in February, 1946, former President Ryti and seven former ministers, including Vaino Tanner, leader of the Social Democrats, were sentenced to imprisonment for terms ranging from two to ten years. The punishment inflicted, however, was far less severe than that meted out in most of the former Nazi satellites. In 1946 the Soviet prosecutor at the Nuremberg trials presented evidence of Field Marshal Mannerheim's collaboration with the Nazis, and soon thereafter, ostensibly because of his poor health, Mannerheim resigned as President of Finland. Paasikivi was elected to succeed him.

Aside from the resettlement of the Finns displaced by the cession of territory to the Soviet Union, Finland's chief postwar problem was the payment of reparations to Russia. As originally drawn up, more than half of the reparations payments were to be made by deliveries of machinery and ships. But the production of these commodities was dependent upon the import of raw materials which, in turn, was dependent upon Finland's ability to obtain foreign loans. The Soviet government did take some steps to assist the Finns. A trade treaty, made in August, 1945, was designed to relieve some of Finland's shortages, and concessions regarding rail and coastal transportation in the areas which Russia had annexed were designed to reduce Finland's transportation difficulties. In June, 1948, after the conclusion of a military assistance pact between Finland and Russia [4] and shortly before elections were to be held for a new diet, the Soviet Union reduced its remaining reparations claims on Finland by 75 per cent.

With the growing tension between Russia and the Western powers in 1948 there were evidences that the Communists might seek greater control in Finland, although President Paasikivi in April declared that no attempts to stage a Communist coup in that country had any chance of success. In May the diet passed a vote of no confidence in the Communist minister of the interior, Yrjo Leino, on the ground that he had been responsible for a police regime since 1945, and President Paasikivi dismissed him when he refused to resign. Some 100,000 workers, by strikes, attempted to force the appointment of another Communist to succeed Leino, and in the reshuffle of the cabinet a member of the Popular Democratic Union, favorable to the Communists, was appointed. The wife of Leino—who was, incidentally, the daughter of the president of the Finno-Karelian Soviet Socialist Republic—was also appointed minister without portfolio.

In the parliamentary elections in July, 1948, the Communist-dominated Popular Democratic Union fell from first to third place in the number of seats held in parliament. The Agrarians stood first with 56 seats; the Socialists were second with 55; and the Popular Democrats (Communists) elected only 38 members in contrast with the 51 which they had held before the elections. Not until four weeks later was it possible to organize a government. The Agrarians refused to join a two-party coalition for fear that the Popular Democrats would start strikes, and the latter declined to be in a coalition unless they received the foreign ministry and the ministries of interior and trade. Ultimately, on July 29, Karl Fagerholm, former president of parliament, became premier in an all-Socialist minority cabinet, which remained in office until March, 1950, when it was replaced by an Agrarian Party government headed by Urko Kekkonen. The latter believed in a neutralist policy for Finland, and for Scandinavia generally, in which the republic would have friendly relations with the Soviet Union. Meanwhile, in February, 1950, Paasikivi had been re-elected President of Finland. In the parliamentary elections of 1951 and 1954 the Communists gained slightly in their number of seats but still won less than either the Social

---

[4] The pact provided that in case Finland, or the Soviet Union through Finnish territory, became the object of an armed attack by Germany or any state allied with Germany, Finland would fight within her frontiers to repel the attack, if necessary with the assistance of or jointly with the U.S.S.R. which pledged itself to help Finland. Each state further agreed not to conclude an alliance or join a coalition against the other and to observe the principle of nonintervention in the internal affairs of the other.

Democrats or Agrarians, who once more established a coalition ministry.

In 1952 Finland completed her heavy reparations payments to Russia. The two states then made a trade agreement which enabled Finland to exchange manufactured goods for needed raw materials from Russia. Two years later a Finnish-Soviet trade agreement for the years 1956–1960 was signed, providing for further increases in Finnish exports to Russia. The two republics also agreed to change their legations to embassies.

East Germany

The German Democratic Republic, set up in the Soviet zone of occupation in 1949, must be included among Russia's satellites. This state with some 18,850,000 inhabitants, almost a quarter of whom were refugees from the regions east of the Oder-Neisse line, became organized politically very much after the Soviet pattern. In August, 1952, power was further centralized when the five existing provinces (*Länder*) were broken up into fourteen districts, each administered directly by the central government. Although, formally, there were four political parties besides the Socialist Unity Party, generally speaking they kept in step with the latter. In the parliamentary elections of 1950 and 1954, for instance, there was but one slate of candidates and on the surface, at least, most of them were not members of the Socialist Unity Party. In practice, however, most of these elected representatives supported Communist policies. The most important government ministers and higher officials of the republic, moreover, were members of the Socialist Unity Party.

In 1950 the latter adopted a revised constitution along Communist lines, and the Moscow-trained Walter Ulbricht became secretary-general. As in Russia and the other satellites, there were party and government purges. By the middle of 1951 more than 200,000 members of the Socialist Unity Party had been expelled. The other parties, too, were apparently forced to do some purging of their own in 1952–1953.

Also, as in the Soviet Union, the Communists utilized youth movements to progress toward their goals. The Free German Youth (*Freie Deutsche Jugend*) was organized under the headship of Walter Ulbricht in close association with the Socialist Unity Party. By 1950 the FDJ included about a million young people aged 14 to 24 and nearly that many more aged 6 to 14 years. In the schools more and more Communists were placed as teachers. Books not in conformity with Communist ideas or programs were purged and others emphasizing the history of Communism, Leninism, Stalinism, and anti-Anglo-American imperialism were introduced. The aim of the government was to have enough young people pass through these Communist-directed schools to ensure soon a "correct Marxist atmosphere" in the German Democratic Republic. Church-maintained schools, however, were abolished and Christian youth organizations were forbidden. In fact, in 1952–1953 there were increasing evidences of Communist oppression of the church.

In foreign policy, too, the German Democratic Republic was a faithful follower of the Moscow line. In 1950 the republic joined the Soviet Council for Economic Assistance, and signed trade treaties with some of the other satellites. Its foreign minister in 1950 attended the Prague conference of East European foreign ministers where, under Molotov's direction, the satellite governments joined with the Soviet Union in formulating statements of policy regarding Germany. The German Democratic Republic cooperated with Russia in attempting to prevent West Germany from being rearmed and becoming more closely integrated with the West. On the other hand, in November, 1950, Premier Grotewohl in a statement reaffirmed the republic's close ties with the Soviet Union. The influence of the latter could be seen in the republic's agreements with Poland and Czechoslovakia. More Communist than German was the treaty (1950) with Poland in which the two states agreed on an "inviolable frontier of peace" at the Oder-Neisse line, the German Democratic Republic thus recognizing the loss of some 39,000 square miles of territory which had been German before 1939. In a similarly magnanimous spirit, the republic signed a joint statement with Czechoslovakia recognizing that the "resettlement" of Germans from Czechoslovakia was final.

As in Russia, after some preliminary preparations the German Democratic Republic eventually adopted a Five-Year Plan (1951–1955), designed to double the production levels of 1936 by 1955. Again, emphasis was placed on the development of heavy industry. In 1953 it was reported that Soviet stock companies, after having turned over to the republic sixty-six basic industrial enterprises in 1952, still owned 15 per cent of the republic's industrial capacity, nationalized companies 62 per cent, and private companies 23 per cent. The first two categories held the key positions in the economy; only in the production of consumer goods did private enterprise play much of a part. Wholesale trade was reported in 1953 to be in the hands of state-owned distributing centers. In retail trade there were state stores, cooperative societies' stores, and privately-owned stores, the first two types accounting for about 60 per cent of the trade. Collectivization of farms was also introduced; in 1954 it was officially announced that there were 4,655 such farms, which included some 1,767,000 acres.

The Soviet Union exploited the German Democratic Republic as it did its other satellites. Part of this exploitation was in the form of reparations. According to Moscow the republic by May, 1950, had paid $3,658,000,000 on its $10,000,000,000 account. At that time the Soviet government announced that it was cutting in half the balance and that the remaining $3,171,000,000 might be paid in fifteen yearly installments. But the United States high com-missioner claimed that the U.S.S.R. had already taken some $18,000,000,000 from East Germany as the result of looting, dismantling, seizure of current production, and recognized reparations. It seemed obvious that in 1953 the economic hardships of the people of the German Democratic Republic were much greater than those in the German Federal Republic. The most important foodstuffs were still rationed and, as in Russia in the early days of the Communist regime, the rationing was graded according to the types of work done.

Unsatisfactory conditions and the loss of freedom—economic, political, intellectual, social, and religious—undoubtedly accounted for the great stream of refugees who fled from the German Democratic Republic into Western Germany, a stream which accelerated in 1952–1953. They accounted, also, for the rather extensive demonstrations and riots which occurred in the eastern sector of Berlin and in other cities of the republic in June, 1953, riots which were serious enough to necessitate the use of Soviet troops and tanks to suppress them. The speed and smoothness with which they were suppressed, however, and the numerous executions and imprisonments which followed gave added proof that the German Democratic Republic was one of Russia's satellites.

In the succeeding weeks the Communists adopted a policy of concession and repression. Almost immediately the Socialist Unity Party promised increased wages, lower work norms, higher pensions, better housing, more schools, kindergartens, and theatres, relaxed travel restrictions, and reduced train fares for low income workers. At the same time Premier Grotewohl promised a revision of the republic's Five-Year Plan to place less emphasis on heavy industry and more on the production of consumer goods—a policy, in the words of the deputy premier, of "butter instead of cannon." A beginning was made, also, of returning some of the smaller nationalized enterprises to their former owners and some foodstuffs which had been hoarded by the government were released in an attempt to quiet the unrest. It was even reported that the Soviet Union would reduce substantially its demands for reparation payments from East Germany in order that the latter might the more readily raise the living standards of its people.

On the other hand, four weeks after the riots the minister of justice of the republic was arrested and replaced by one who had a record of imposing harsh punishments. The minister of transport was reprimanded by the politburo for his capitulation to the June rioters and an official associated with him was expelled from the party because he had actually supported the demonstrators. Wilhelm Zaisser, minister of state security, was dropped from the government and purged from the politburo because of his "defeatism," and the editor of the leading Communist newspaper in East Germany was similarly dropped from the party's central committee and purged from the list of "candidates" for the politburo. Finally, in conformity with the Communist party reorganization in Russia, the office of secretary-general of the Socialist Unity Party was abolished, though Ulbricht as first secretary of the central committee apparently retained his place as party leader. When in July United States President Eisenhower offered $15,000,-000 worth of food supplies to relieve food shortages in East Germany, Soviet Russia indignantly rejected the offer on the ground that it was an imperialist attempt to stir up trouble in the German Democratic Republic. And when hundreds of thousands of East Germans went to West Berlin to secure free food packages, the East German Communist government eventually brought pressure to bear upon its people to stop their going. In 1954 arrests, imprisonments, and executions still occurred. Events seem to indicate how difficult it is to overthrow or rebel against a Communist government, with its control of heavy armaments and its ubiquitous secret police.

On January 1, 1954, the most important of the provisions of an agreement signed on August 23, 1953, between Russia and East Germany came into effect. Thirty-three Soviet-owned industries were returned to East Germany, reparations payments were abolished, the occupation costs were reduced, and East German postwar debts to Russia were cancelled. It was estimated that the returned industries employed about 16 per cent of the East German workers and accounted for 32 per cent of the republic's industrial production. The great uranium works in Saxony, however, were not returned.

Following the failure of the Berlin conference of the great powers early in 1954 to agree upon a solution of the German problem, the Russian government announced its decision to recognize the German Democratic Republic as a sovereign state which should have the right to decide all questions of internal and external policy, including its relations with the rest of Germany. The Soviet government also declared that the Occupation Statute fixed by Great Britain, France, and the United States for West Germany was incompatible with the national rights of the German people and actually impeded German reunification. The Western great powers and West Germany, however, asserted that the Soviet declaration was apparently intended only to create the impression that sovereignty had been granted the German Democratic Republic. They contended that the Soviet Union still retained effective control of East Germany and they therefore refused to recognize that the latter was a sovereign power. The government of the Federal Republic of Germany, they maintained, was the only freely elected and legally constituted government in Germany. The schism between the Western powers and Russia was thus once more emphasized.

Chapter XXVIII

THE SO-CALLED GREAT POWERS
OF WESTERN EUROPE

IN the decade before the First World War most historians considered that there were six great powers in Europe, though Italy was usually included in the number more because of her ambitions than because of her potentialities. From this number the First World War definitely eliminated Austria-Hungary and the Second World War apparently removed Germany, Italy, and France. Though the latter was included in the "Big Four" discussions in the years after 1945, she usually played a secondary role. In fact, if present and future industrial and military power and not past history were taken as the sole basis for judgment, it is doubtful if there were in the world after 1945 more than two great powers, the United States and the Soviet Union. Aside from the latter, however, the European state which played the most important role in the postwar years was Great Britain.

Socialist Britain

The First World War seriously undermined Great Britain's economic position in the world; the Second weakened it so much more that the problem of paying for the needed imports of raw materials to sustain the country's industrial system and foods to preserve a reasonable standard of living for the country's population appeared to be almost insoluble. This problem was handed to the leaders of the Labor Party shortly before the Second World War ended.

THE LABOR PARTY IN POWER

In marked contrast with the victory which Lloyd George and his coalition won at the close of the First World War was the decisive electoral defeat which Winston Churchill suffered just after the end of the war with Nazi Germany. In the parliamentary elections held on July 5, 1945—the first since 1935—the Labor Party won 393 out of 640 seats, and for the first time in British history gained a clear majority in the House of Commons. Churchill was accordingly succeeded by Clement Attlee, leader of the Laborites, who included in his cabinet appointments Herbert Morrison,

Ernest Bevin, Arthur Greenwood, Hugh Dalton, Sir Stafford Cripps, and Sir William Jowett, all prominent Laborites.

The defeat of the Conservatives was nowhere considered a repudiation or denial of Churchill's incomparable services as wartime leader. There was in Britain, however, a widespread conviction that a fuller life was the reward which should come to the masses for their wartime sacrifices and that this fuller life should provide houses, social security, guaranteed jobs, agricultural reforms, greater educational opportunities, and adequate health insurance. Apparently the majority of the British felt that these objectives were more likely to be attained under a Labor government than under the Conservatives who had been in power since the crisis of 1931.

THE BAFFLING PROBLEM OF INTERNATIONAL PAYMENTS

The most difficult problem which the Labor government faced—profoundly important, too, because all others were directly or indirectly dependent upon it—was that of bringing into balance Britain's international expenditures and income. Britain's dependence on the import of foods and materials for her factories was long standing. These imports, before the Second World War, had been paid for by British exports, receipts from overseas investments, and by other items of invisible income—shipping receipts, and insurance and banking returns. Britain's war effort, however, not only had undermined the pattern of her peacetime production but had changed her from a creditor to a debtor nation. Furthermore, by June, 1945, she had sold £1,118,000,000 of her overseas capital holdings and had lost a large part of her merchant-marine tonnage. As a consequence of all these factors, in 1946 not only were Britain's exports reduced to 41 per cent of the prewar level, but her net invisible income was changed from a surplus of £232,000,000 in 1938 to a deficit of £176,000,000.

Only American lend-lease had enabled Britain to carry on during the war, and with the sudden end of lend-lease in 1945 she was faced with the necessity of paying for her imports. It was estimated that Britain would have to increase her exports at least 50 per cent above the 1938 figure to do so. Obviously, however, much time would be required to return the British productive machine to its normal peacetime pattern, to say nothing of increasing the production and export of goods above the 1938 level. Meanwhile, the gap between British overseas earnings and payments was bridged by United States and Canadian credits and by other temporary borrowings. But if Britain were not to live on foreign loans indefinitely, the gap between her expenditures for necessary imports and her income from exports would have to be narrowed.

In the first year and a half after the end of the war the British made rapid progress in the recovery of production and exports. By the middle of 1946 nearly 30 per cent more workers were employed in export industries than in 1938, and by the fourth quarter of that year the volume of exports had risen to 111 per cent of 1938. But in 1947 the unprecedented rise in world food prices hit Great Britain especially hard. The same volume of British exports bought less imports in 1947 than in 1945, and the purchasing power of United States credits declined rapidly as American prices became more and more inflated. The government made determined efforts to reduce imports. The importation of gasoline, newsprint, and American movies was reduced, and the importation of American tobacco was stopped altogether. In August, 1947, Prime Minister Attlee presented a so-called "austerity program" which called for substantial cuts in overseas expenditures, further restrictions on the consumption of goods in Britain, and an all-out drive to increase production and exports. Wartime rationing of food, gasoline, and foreign travel allowances was restored.

Nevertheless, largely because of an unexpected fuel shortage in February of 1947, the rate of expansion of British exports slowed down, so that the volume of exports in the fourth quarter of that year rose to only 117 per cent of 1938. The discouraging result was that whereas Britain had a total net deficit in international payments of £380,000,000 in 1946, it rose to £675,000,000 in 1947. Although in January, 1948, exports were 28 per cent above the 1938 figure, in February, Sir Stafford Cripps, minister of economic affairs, admitted that the export situation had become more critical for Britain in the preceding few months because it was proving more and more difficult for her to increase the sale of her goods abroad. Basically, in the years 1945–1948, the British people were living beyond their means, a fact which Cripps emphasized when he declared: "We must either export and earn enough to pay for our food and raw materials, or do without." Although the British in 1948 were being denied many of the products which they themselves produced, it seemed likely that a still greater per cent of the country's manufacturing capacity might have to be devoted to exports.

In 1949 it became obvious that the efforts to bridge the gap between exports and imports, though increasingly successful in much of the world, were failing so far as the United States was concerned. By the middle of that year Britain's gold and dollar reserves had fallen below the $2,000,000,000 considered to be the minimum safe margin. In July, therefore, the government ordered a halt in all new purchases from the United States and Canada in an effort to safeguard the nation's reserves. Finally, in September, 1949, when the gold and dollar reserves had fallen to $1,340,000,000, the government devalued the pound sterling from $4.03 to $2.80, in the hope that the cheaper pound would stimulate exports to the dollar area. In the ensuing months Britain's economic recovery was dramatic, partly because of the devaluation, partly because of renewed prosperity in the United States, and partly because of Marshall Plan aid. The country's gold and dollar reserves doubled in the year following devaluation, rising to $2,756,000,000 by October 1, 1950. Rearmament abroad created more demand for British goods and in November, 1950, exports reached an all-time record. With the dollar deficit gradually reduced and ultimately converted into a surplus Britain announced that she would no longer need Marshall Plan aid after January 1, 1951. On June 30 of that year the country's gold and dollar reserves reached a postwar peak of $3,867,000,000.

Unfortunately for Britain, circumstances beyond her control soon changed this happy situation. As a consequence of the wave of inflation which the Korean War caused, higher commodity prices raised the cost of British imports. Thus, since the prices of British manufactured goods could not be raised correspondingly, the basis for another payments and dollar crisis was laid. In the third quarter of 1951 Britain lost $598,000,000 of her gold and dollar reserves because of the renewed and increasing adverse balance of trade. Churchill's Conservative government, which had come into power on October 26, at once announced a program designed to cut imports drastically. Nevertheless, the dollar crisis grew progressively worse. By January 1, 1952, the gold and dollar reserves had fallen to $2,335,000,000, and four months later they were down to $1,662,000,000. But during the summer and fall of 1952, in consequence of the forced reduction of imports, the decline in reserves was halted. By October 1 they were back to $1,895,000,000 and six months later, on April 1, 1953, they had risen to $2,167,200,000.

But the problem was far from solved. In December, 1953, the OEEC explained that Britain's problem was to achieve "a substantial increase of exports, particularly to countries outside the sterling area," a rather obvious conclusion. As a matter of fact, Britain's industrial production for 1953 was 6 per cent higher than in 1952, and by the end of 1953 the volume of exports was 10 per cent higher than a year earlier. The OEEC asserted, however, that Britain's rise in industrial production since 1950 had lagged behind that of other OEEC countries; unfortunately, according to a government report, Britain's industrial output per man in 1953 was little more than in 1951 and the rate of increase was frequently below that of Britain's competitors. Nevertheless, in 1954 Britain established a new high record both for the value and the volume of her exports, and the country's industrial output rose nearly 6 per cent.

This problem of international payments seemed likely to continue to be a baffling one for Britain, since it was largely affected by circumstances and conditions in other countries, particularly the United States, over which she had no control. Some felt that Britain's salvation lay, not in still better tillage of the land and still larger exports, but in large-scale emigration.

THE BEGINNING OF NATIONALIZATION

Linked with the plans to increase the production and export of British goods was the Labor Party's program of nationalization, for the Laborites contended that the modernization of industry and the attainment of full industrial capacity could be reached, in some cases, only through nationalization. Under private enterprise some of the older British industries had failed to remechanize as new machines were invented in the twentieth century, with the result that their products had been forced out of the world markets by those of more efficient competition in other countries. In the election campaign of 1945 the Laborites had therefore stated that their ultimate purpose was the establishment in Britain of a Socialist commonwealth. They had proposed to nationalize the Bank of England, the fuel, power, iron, and steel industries, and inland transport.

During its first year in power, the Labor government energetically pushed its program to convert Britain into a Socialist commonwealth. The Bank of England was nationalized, with compensation to its stockholders; government interest rates were lowered in order to give the state greater control over credit; and bills were passed to control investment. During the first year, too, Labor nationalized civil aviation and introduced a bill to nationalize the coal industry. The government maintained that the need to nationalize the coal mines was paramount, pointing out that since 1913 the industry had been declining, partly because of mine exhaustion but largely because of obsolete machinery and the use of antiquated methods. In July, 1946, the nationalization bill was passed and a National Coal Board took over the management of the mines on January 1, 1947. A national tribunal decided that the government should pay the owners some £165,-000,000, which the latter regarded as a reasonable figure.

In the first year of its ownership of the mines the government had a trying experience. When the latter assumed control, the stocks of coal on hand were nearly 3,000,000 tons less than they had been a year earlier, despite the need for more coal because of the increased scale of industrial production. This coal shortage, combined with the coldest winter in fifty years, and the partial breakdown of transportation, brought on a national crisis during the winter of 1946–1947. Many factories were closed, train services were reduced, street lighting was curtailed, and even many homes were deprived of electricity because of the lack of coal. Ultimately the crisis passed, however, and vigorous efforts were then made to increase the country's coal production to 200,000,000 tons in 1947. Although the goal was missed by only 300,000 tons, critics of socialism pointed out that the price of coal was higher in 1947 than in 1946 and that, even so, the government lost money on the year's operations. The Coal Board maintained, however, that the success of nationalization could not be decided in one transitional year. In 1948, Britain's coal production rose to 208,500,000 tons and the amount available for export was increased. The goal for 1949 was set at 223,000,000 tons.

In 1947, Parliament passed the Transport Act nationalizing the country's railways, canals, and trucking services. On January 1, 1948, the British Transport Commission took charge of all inland transport, and planned eventually to reorganize the country's entire transportation system by eliminating unnecessary duplication and arranging to have railways, trucks, and canals complement one another instead of competing for business. In November, 1947, the House of Commons had also approved the government's proposal to nationalize the iron and steel industry as of "May 1, 1950, or later." The act to nationalize Britain's iron and steel companies was eventually passed in November, 1949, but at that time the transfer date was not set. A year later a vote to proceed with the nationalization encountered strenuous opposition but was carried by a slim margin. The Iron and Steel Corporation was then organized and the nationalized companies were transferred to it in February, 1951. The individual companies as such were not dissolved but all the stock was transferred to the new corporation at prices fixed by the government. The original firms retained their own names and legal entity and, to a large extent, the same boards of directors. They were free to compete. Meanwhile, the progress of nationalization in Great Britain was a matter of considerable interest and concern to many outside that country, who were watching to see whether Britain could prove in practice that socialism and democracy could be compatible.

THE PROGRAM OF SOCIAL WELFARE

One thing at least was certain; under the socialist Labor government Britain greatly expanded the social insurance and social welfare programs which had been inaugurated by the Liberals in the years 1906–1914. During the Second World War the famous Beveridge Report, a study of social insurance in Great Britain, had been published in November, 1942. In 1944, the Churchill government had proposed to provide for unemployment and sickness insurance, health service, widows' pensions, retirement pensions, family allowances, orphans' allowances, maternity grants, and death grants by a scheme which would be compulsory for every citizen of Great Britain, so that all would have security "from the cradle to the grave." Before the election of 1945 a ministry of national insurance had been created to supervise the new program, though the program itself had not yet been adopted when the Churchill government fell.

In 1946, the Labor government introduced into Parliament the National Insurance Bill and the National Health Service Bill. The former expanded and strengthened the existing system of social insurance. The latter was designed to provide for socialized medicine and the program was ultimately inaugurated in July, 1948. By the provisions of the act all public hospitals and clinics were nationalized, and every Briton was assured medical and dental care, hospital treatment, home nursing, ambulance service, drugs, medical supplies, and other aids to physical well-being. Physicians and dentists were to receive from the government a basic salary plus a fee for each patient treated, and were to be permitted to continue some private practice if they desired. The so-called social-security charter, it was hoped, would free British citizens of their worst economic anxieties in sickness, in unemployment, and in old age.

Although the Labor government was not responsible for its enactment but only for its execution, another measure provided for improved educational facilities in Britain. Passed during the war, a new Education Act, effective on April 1, 1945, aimed to give British children and youth better schooling, better paid teachers, and better facilities. Those in the lower grades who showed outstanding ability were to receive scholarships to enable them to attend secondary school and college. More technical schools were established to provide the country with needed technologists, research specialists, scientists, engineers, and skilled machinists and electricians. In 1947 the school-leaving age was raised from fourteen to fifteen years.

The Labor government also sought to improve the housing situation in Britain. During the war some 500,000 houses had been destroyed and some 4,000,000 others had been damaged. Before 1939 over 300,000 houses were being built annually and this construction had stopped during the war, thus further creating a shortage. In addition, the great rise in the marriage rate during and just after the war increased the demand for shelter. Before Labor came to power the government had formulated a housing plan in which it was estimated that between three and four million new houses would be needed to satisfy shortages, and to eliminate slums, obsolescence, and overcrowding. Labor's task was to carry through the housing plan, but success here was handicapped to a considerable extent by the need to import lumber and other building materials at a time when the government was desperately seeking to reduce imports. Meanwhile, the national government and some municipalities embarked on extensive plans for slum clearance and the erection of new apartments and dwellings. To assist in this task the government passed another measure, the Town and Country Planning Act, which gave the state authority not only to control and restrict a landowner's freedom to build on his land but to prevent him from charging an unreasonable price for it in case it was needed for the site of government building projects. The national government also granted subsidies for houses built by local authorities.

POLITICAL DEVELOPMENTS SINCE 1945

Although the postwar years were difficult for most Britons, the majority of them seemed to support the Labor government in its attempts to solve the nation's problems, if one may judge from the many by-elections which the party won following its coming into power. Inevitably, of course, hardships and privations caused some discontent, and the Conservatives tried to capitalize upon it. The coal crisis of 1947 they attributed falsely to the nationalization of the mines (which did not occur until January 1, 1947), and Churchill moved a vote of no-confidence. The motion was defeated. Later in 1947 the harshness of the government's austerity program apparently engendered more serious opposition. Municipal elections held in 388 towns and cities outside London resulted in a Conservative net gain of 625 seats and a Labor net loss of 652 seats. Churchill thereupon declared that the results showed that Labor had lost its popular support, and called for a general election. But the government pointed out that Labor had won all five of the by-elections in 1947, and refused Churchill's demand. On February 24, 1949, despite Churchill's active campaign in behalf of the Conservative candidate, the Labor Party won its forty-eighth successive by-election without losing a single seat to the Conservatives, a record unparalleled in British history.

One step which was taken by the Labor government appeared likely to alter the political situation in the country. In 1947 the House of Lords had delayed the enactment of the government's bill to nationalize the railways, even though the measure had been passed by the House of Commons. Apparently fearing that the Conservative Lords might use their existing right to hold up for two years Labor's contemplated measure for nationalizing the iron and steel industry, the government in the fall of 1947 introduced a bill to reduce from two years to one the period of time which the Lords might delay the enactment of any measure passed by the Commons. Despite strong opposition from the Conservatives, the bill was passed by the Commons on December 10, 1947, and was sent to the Lords who could constitutionally delay its enactment until December, 1949. At that time, however, the bill was passed by the Commons for the third time and, though also defeated by the Lords for the third time, it became a law. The power of the Lords to delay legislation passed by the Commons was thus reduced to one year.

Since the maximum term of the House of Commons is five years except in time of great national crisis, parliamentary elections were due during the first half of 1950. Early in February Parliament was dissolved and the election of a new House of Commons occurred on February 23. During the election campaign neither the Laborites nor the Conservatives frankly discussed the real economic remedies which Britain's situation called for. Generally speaking, the Laborites talked somewhat less about further nationalization, defended their program of social welfare, and sought to identify the Conservatives with British mass unemployment in the years before the Second World War. The Conservatives, on the other hand, consistently called the Laborites Socialists and talked much of the Socialist road to ruin. At the same time, however, they seemed to promise even more social benefits than the Laborites, and advocated no general reversal of nationalization except in the case of inland transport. Many expected the Conservatives to win control of the House of Commons, for, in an election in which more Britons voted than ever before, it seemed inevitable that some of the dissatisfaction caused by the country's difficulties and by the government's austerity program would be turned against the Labor Party. Although this expectation proved to be true and Labor's representation in the Commons was reduced from 391 to 315, the Labor Party still held an overall majority of six. The Conservatives increased their representation from 216 to 294, but this was not enough to enable them to take over the government. Labor's program, it appeared, still had wide support.

The smallness of the government's majority, however, militated against its embarking upon any comprehensive program of contentious measures. About the only step of this sort was the completion of the nationalization of the steel industry, which the Conservatives threatened to undo when they came into power. Meanwhile, the Labor Party was being weakened from within. Sir Stafford Cripps, chancellor of the exchequer, resigned because of ill health in October, 1950, and six months later Ernest Bevin, foreign secretary, resigned shortly before his death on April 14, 1951. Furthermore, the Laborites became divided over the urgency of the rearmament program which, it was estimated, would cost some $13,160,000,000 in the three years beginning April 1, 1951. With rearmament given top priority in the budget introduced in April the government sought to curtail some expenditures by placing ceilings on the cost of social services and on food subsidies and by imposing a charge on spectacles and dentures, which had previously been provided free under health insurance. In protest against these actions and against the scale and speed of rearmament, Aneurin Bevan, who had been health minister and director of the national health insurance program, resigned from the government, and was accompanied by two other ministers.

Meanwhile, too, conditions within the country were not conducive to the government's popularity. During the first half of 1951 the cost of living rose rapidly as a result of the resurgence of inflation following the outbreak of the Korean War. Moreover, the impact of rearmament and the reappearance of shortages of goods led the government to reimpose some of the controls which had previously been rescinded or relaxed. And, on top of all this, as pointed out above, another gold and dollar crisis was developing. It is not surprising, therefore, that when the government dissolved Parliament again in October, 1951, it was widely believed that the Conservatives would win a sweeping victory. Actually, however, in the election of October 25 the Conservatives received fewer popular votes than the Labor Party, though they did increase their representation in the House of Commons to 321 and secured an overall majority of seventeen. Though the Labor Party secured more popular votes, its representation fell to 295. Seventy-six-year-old Winston Churchill, therefore, succeeded Attlee as prime minister and thereafter he and the Conservatives had the task of trying to solve Britain's difficult economic problems.

The change in ministries could bring no startling change in Britain's economic situation, even though many Britons had been roused to expect better times if only the Laborites could be removed from power. Because of the country's international payments crisis, the Churchill government was compelled in 1952 to order further cuts in imports, lower rations, new controls, in a word, more austerity. In its first budget, in 1952, the government ordered a cut of some 40 per cent in food subsidies, by means of which British consumers since the war had been partly protected from the rising prices of basic food imports. The result was a sharp increase in the cost of living. But the budget introduced in 1953 was more encouraging. No new taxes were proposed, some reductions were made in income taxes and purchase taxes, and the excess profits tax was abolished as of January 1, 1954. At the same time, payments for old age relief and allowance for dependent relatives were increased slightly.

The Conservatives were pledged to denationalize the steel industry and truck transportation and to decentralize the nationalized coal mines, but they moved toward these goals slowly and cautiously. It was not until November, 1952—more than a year after they took office—that they introduced a bill to denationalize the steel industry. On May 14, 1953, the bill became law. Under the new act the securities of the companies which had been nationalized were transferred from the Iron and Steel Corporation to the Holding and Realization Agency which was to dispose of them to private bidders. The individual firms would then again be independent although the guidance on central policy enforced by the Iron and Steel Corporation was not entirely dropped. An Iron and Steel Board—similar to the board which had supervised general policy from 1946 to 1948—was set up to supervise the industry. The first chairman of the new board had been chairman of the earlier board and the first vice chairman had been general secretary of the steelworkers' trade union. The nationalized steel industry, meanwhile, had done well in production, establishing new high records for output in January and February, 1953, partly as a result of operations of a new steel plant in South Wales said to be the most modern in the world. Financially, in the year ending on September 30, 1952, the industry had earned a profit, before taxes, of £64,426,216.

The bill to denationalize road haulage (truck transportation) became a law on May 6, 1953, and freed long-distance haulage—forty miles or over—from restrictions on private ownership. The act was to be given effect by offering for sale to any bidder the 40,000 vehicles which the Transport Commission owned, after the undertakings operated by the government had been divided into "units." The purchasers would form road haulage firms or would expand their current haulage operations and would thereafter operate freely under the normal rules and regulations governing road haulage.

Meanwhile, on February 6, 1952, George VI had died at the age of fifty-six. Although he had been in ill health and had undergone an operation some months earlier, his death came unexpectedly and was a shock to the world. Never trained for the throne and handicapped physically for carrying out many of the royal duties, he had loyally assumed the kingship at the time of the crisis occasioned by the abdication of Edward VIII in 1936. He had been held in deep affection in Britain and the Commonwealth and, like his father before him, had been admired as a king who served his people to the end. His older daughter, who had been assuming many of her father's public obligations as his health failed, was in Kenya on her way to a royal tour of Australia and New Zealand at the time of his death. She at once returned to London by plane and was publicly proclaimed Queen Elizabeth II on February 8.

The twenty-five-year-old queen had been trained for years to fill the position for which she was destined. Intelligent, capable, and charming, her coronation on June 2, 1953, seemed to provide the British with the first great occasion for happiness and rejoicing since before Munich. A holiday spirit pervaded gayly decorated London where millions of coronation pilgrims, for days before and after the great pageant, gave the most sustained demonstration of loyalty to the Crown that the nation had ever seen. "For the first time the people as a whole, carried into Westminster Abbey by television and radio, seemed to realize that the coronation was not an event only of this time and of this country but . . . 'the vivid repetition of a great historic act.'" Though in their hearts they probably knew that they still faced almost unsolvable economic problems, for the time being their morale was lifted and they were proud of the spectacle of unity, loyalty, and splendor which they presented for all the world to see.

BRITAIN'S NEW QUEEN
Elizabeth II, with Her Husband, the Duke of Edinburgh

BRITISH EMPIRE CHANGES

British economic difficulties together with the increasing strength of nationalism in the East forced many changes in Britain's imperial position in the postwar years. The need to reduce the financial burdens of empire was the cause of Britain's withdrawal from Greece and Turkey in favor of the United States [1] and, at least partly, the cause of her concessions to Egypt, her surrender of her mandate in Palestine, her grant of practical independence to India and Burma, of dominion status to Ceylon, and of greater self-government to the Federation of Malaya.[2] The maintenance of British troops in these territories had cost money. Winston Churchill denounced the Labor government for "scuttling" the British Empire, but Sir Stafford Cripps maintained that "only in the old conception of the word" was the empire being liquidated, that the British overseas territories were being developed, "which is a much better situation."

Although the great value of the Mediterranean-Suez Canal route to the Middle and Far East had been re-emphasized to the British by their temporary loss of control of this "lifeline" during the Second World War, the strategic importance of this route was lessened somewhat by the reduction of British imperial responsibilities. But that the British were not prepared to forego entirely their control of this lifeline their interest in the fate of the Italian colonies disclosed. Furthermore, although they lost some of their footholds in the eastern Mediterranean, they developed a new strategy which placed its principal reliance on a network of air bases in Cyprus, Kenya, Tanganyika, and Transjordan rather than primarily on naval bases as in the days before the development of air power.

The Fourth French Republic

Although France experienced the disaster of military defeat and occupation by enemy troops during the Second World War, thanks to the continued fighting of the British and to the entrance into the war of Russia and the United States she emerged from that conflict as one of the victorious powers. She found herself free to decide her own political future and free, too, to wrestle with her own national problems.

THE EFFECTS OF THE WAR ON FRANCE

Although France did not suffer from the war so grievously as many other countries, her life was disrupted and some of her institutions destroyed. Her population, already decimated by the First World War, was further

[1] See page 928.
[2] For these changes in the East, see pages 950, 955, 964–965, 969–973.

reduced. It was conservatively estimated that more than 1,500,000 French were killed as the result of military operations and subsequent bombing or died from hunger or other causes directly related to the war. This loss was a severe blow to a country which in 1939 was already suffering from under-population, and it resulted in a serious postwar labor shortage. Material war damage in France was estimated at $21,000,000,000, approximately twice that suffered in the First World War. Most serious were the destruction or damage to buildings, the disruption of the republic's transportation and communication systems, the depletion of the country's supply of industrial machine tools and agricultural equipment, and the loss of nearly 42 per cent of the nation's merchant shipping. The resultant problem of rehabilitating the economic structure of the country was great and it was rendered still greater by the need to import heavily from abroad.

Furthermore, during the war the French currency became greatly inflated as a result of the payment of 631,866,000,000 francs to the Germans. The country's monetary circulation increased from 114,000,000,000 francs in 1939 to 620,000,000,000 francs in the fall of 1944. Postwar France accordingly inherited an inflated cost-of-living index which, aggravated by the country's inability to finance necessary imports and its decreased domestic production in the immediate postwar years, grew progressively worse. The price level at the end of the war was 3.7 times the prewar level; at the end of 1946 the figure was 8.5 times; in January, 1948, it was 13.5 times. Such changes in the cost of living inevitably caused labor unrest, strikes, and disputes over the relative merits of various policies proposed to halt inflation.

Finally, the war destroyed the French constitutional structure and the question of restoring that structure or creating another by means of a new constitution faced the French people. There was no unanimity of views regarding the nature of the political and economic structure which France should have in the postwar period. This clash of views was further accentuated as the result of developments within France during the period of German occupation.

THE RESISTANCE MOVEMENT DURING THE WAR

In the years 1940–1944 those who opposed the dictatorial Vichy government set up by Marshal Pétain in 1940, who rejected the policy of French collaboration inaugurated by Pierre Laval and others, and who fervently hated all Nazis, had sought to undermine and sabotage the German and Pétain regimes. Gradually within France eight or more resistance groups had been organized in different parts of the country. At the risk of their lives, indeed sometimes at the cost of their lives, leaders and members of these groups—men, women, young people—had carried on an unremitting campaign against the Vichyites and the Nazis.

By the spring of 1943 it had become obvious to the resistance leaders that their movements would be strengthened by union. Accordingly in that year the National Council of Resistance (CNR), representing eight resistance groups, was founded. In March, 1944, some three months before D-day in France, the CNR drafted a Resistance Charter as a program for postwar France. Politically, the charter called for the continued unity of the resistance groups after liberation, the punishment of traitors who had actively collaborated with the Nazis,[3] and the maintenance of freedom of the press, conscience, and assembly. Economically, it demanded the nationalization of large banks, insurance companies, and "the great means of monopolized production." The economic program of the CNR was not greatly different from that of the British Labor Party.

DE GAULLE'S PROVISIONAL GOVERNMENT

Meanwhile, following the Allied successes in North Africa in the fall of 1942, the "Fighting French" movement, which had been inaugurated by General Charles de Gaulle in 1940, had been crystallized into something resembling a provisional government when the French Committee of National Liberation, a sort of ministry, was established in Algiers under the chairmanship of De Gaulle. Later the French Consultative Assembly, a sort of unofficial legislative body, was also set up in Algiers. Félix Gouin, a Socialist leader, was chosen president of the Assembly, which made recommendations from time to time on matters relating to policy.

Immediately after D-day the name of the French Committee of National Liberation was changed to the Provisional Government of the French Republic. Following the liberation of Paris, General de Gaulle staged a triumphal entry on August 25, 1944, and was enthusiastically welcomed as *"l'homme du 18 juin, 1940*—the symbol of courage, resistance, and hope." Political initiative appeared to lie with this "Fighting French" leader. Recognizing the strength and importance of the CNR, De Gaulle at once reorganized his Provisional Government to include six resisters, of whom Georges Bidault, chairman of the CNR, became foreign minister. This reorganized Provisional Government was then recognized as the *de jure* government of France by Great Britain, the United States, and the Soviet Union, and the administration of Paris and Central France was turned over to it. The membership of the Consultative Assembly was increased to 246, of which the CNR was given 149, a clear majority, and early in November it convened in Paris and again chose Félix Gouin as its president.

---

[3] In 1945 Pétain was sentenced to death, national degradation, and the confiscation of his property for intelligence with the enemy, but General de Gaulle, at that time Provisional President of France, commuted the death sentence to life imprisonment. Laval and some others were sentenced to death for treason and were executed.

During the ensuing months the Provisional Government was compelled to struggle primarily with the economic problems which faced France, and its chief objective was to obtain the man power, transport, coal, and other materials needed for the revival of production. But in attaining this objective it was handicapped by the continuance of the war until May, 1945. The fact that nearly all kinds of essential supplies became more scarce after the Provisional Government was established than they had been under the Nazi regime naturally caused disappointment, misunderstanding, and some discontent among the French. So, too, did the fact that De Gaulle's cabinet at first supported relatively conservative policies on nearly every important political and economic question which arose. Nevertheless, even his government eventually nationalized the commercial airlines, the factories producing airplane motors, some of the coal mines, the Renault automobile works, the Bank of France, and the big deposit banks. It also provided for the establishment of works committees in all factories employing more than 100 workers (the number was reduced to 50 in 1946). These committees consisted of representatives elected by the workers and presided over by the employer or his representative, and they were given extensive rights to deal with matters concerning increased production and the workers' welfare. They had also the right to know about the economic position of the enterprise—its profits, for example—and to have two representatives sit on its board of directors. The influence of the labor elements in the CNR was thus made felt.

With the ending of the war in Europe a growing sentiment in France demanded the re-establishment of government by elected representatives and the election of a President of the Republic. In response to this demand the election of a National Assembly by universal suffrage occurred on October 21, 1945. At that time the electors were also called upon to answer "Yes" or "No" to the question: Shall the National Assembly draft a new constitution for France? In this first national election with universal suffrage, 82 per cent of the registered electors voted almost unanimously in favor of a new constitution. By this action and by the overwhelming defeat which they administered to Rightist parties and to the Radical Socialists— long the chief party of the conservative middle class—the French repudiated "the political institutions and leaders associated with the defeatism that led to Munich and Vichy."

The three political parties which won most of the seats were the Communists, who advocated the Russian political and economic systems, the Socialists, who resembled the British Laborites, and the Popular Republicans, members of the *Mouvement Républicain Populaire* (MRP). The MRP was a new, predominantly Catholic party which had grown up during the period of resistance. Consisting in the beginning primarily of Catholic trade unionists and young Catholic Leftists, it had grown greatly in strength after liberation by adding many liberals and Rightists who had opposed the former collaborationists but who also opposed the goals of the Socialists and Communists. The MRP advocated the nationalization of certain key industries but with the retention of individualistic patterns of life based on private property. Since in the new Assembly the Communists held 151 seats and the Socialists and Popular Republicans each 142, it seemed clear that most of the French held views that were considerably to the Left of De Gaulle's. Nevertheless, the French Assembly unanimously elected the latter President of the Fourth Republic.

DISAGREEMENTS OVER A NEW CONSTITUTION

As soon as the Assembly's constitutional commission began its work, differences between De Gaulle and a majority of the Assembly developed. The general believed that in the Fourth Republic the President should be a strong executive and should have approximately the same powers as those possessed by the President of the United States. The MRP supported De Gaulle on this point, and also advocated a bicameral legislature which should be limited in its powers to overthrow the cabinet. The Communists, who opposed any system of political checks and balances, advocated an honorary President with an all-powerful unicameral legislature which should choose the ministry and designate its program. This would be more like the British than the American system of government. In January, 1946, the Socialists decided to support the Communist viewpoint. To De Gaulle it appeared that if the Communist-Socialist type of constitution were adopted he would become a mere figurehead as President, and on January 21, 1946, he resigned in protest. Félix Gouin was elected to succeed him. He at once organized a cabinet consisting of Socialists, Communists, Popular Republicans, and one Independent, with Georges Bidault as foreign minister. His government further advanced the policy of nationalization. In three months measures were enacted nationalizing all sizable coal, gas and electric, and insurance companies.

Eventually the constitutional commission completed its task and on April 9, 1946, the text of the new draft was laid before the Assembly. It provided for a one-house National Assembly which was empowered to enact laws, to elect the President of the Republic, and to choose the premier. The President was to have only honorary functions as under the Third Republic and the premier's powers were to be confined to the execution of the laws. The National Assembly was to be elected for five years by universal suffrage, and during the first half of its term it could be dissolved only by a resolution passed by a two-thirds majority of its members. The new document obviously provided a powerful legislature with little in the way of checks and balances. The proposed constitution was adopted by the Assembly by a vote of 309 to 249, the Popular Republicans opposing it and the Communists and Socialists approving it.

The draft constitution was next submitted to the people in a referendum on May 5, 1946. In this referendum less than 37 per cent of the electorate voted for it and more than 41 per cent opposed it, with nearly 20 per cent abstaining from taking any stand. The Communists had been the most vociferous campaigners for the new constitution, and apparently many of the French mistrusted their motives and suspected them of being too closely linked with Moscow. Many voted against the constitution, therefore, because they thought it did not provide sufficient safeguards against attempts to set up a single-party system of government as in the Soviet Union.

It had been expected that the elections on June 2, 1946, would be for a legislative body. As it turned out, however, it was again necessary to choose an Assembly not only to enact laws but to draft a constitution. As a result of the new elections the Assembly was somewhat less Leftist than its predecessor, for the Popular Republicans received 1,000,000 more votes than they had received in 1945, and secured the largest number of seats. The MRP held 161, the Communists 145, and the Socialists 115. The new Assembly elected Georges Bidault, a Popular Republican, President of France, over the opposition of the Communists. The latter agreed, however, to enter another coalition government under Bidault, who organized a ministry consisting of Popular Republicans, Communists, Socialists, and one Independent, with the Communist Thorez and the Socialist Gouin both deputy premiers.

In the second Assembly the Socialists co-operated with the Popular Republicans rather than with the Communists in the drafting of the constitution. The second draft provided for a bicameral parliament consisting of a National Assembly and a Council of the Republic. But the latter, chosen indirectly by a somewhat complicated system, was primarily a consultative body with chiefly delaying and supervisory functions. It could force the National Assembly to reconsider acts but could not stop their passage; and it could call attention to laws which it held to be unconstitutional but it could not force their repeal. The President of France was to be elected by the parliament for a seven-year term. Although he was largely a figurehead, he was given the right to request the National Assembly to reconsider a bill, and his advice had to be sought before the government could ask for a dissolution of parliament. On the matter of dissolution, the new constitution provided that after the National Assembly had been in existence eighteen months it might be dissolved if it passed two votes of no confidence within eighteen months. Fundamentally, however, the National Assembly was supreme, legislatively speaking; the cabinet was responsible to it alone.

A referendum on the second draft constitution was held on October 13, 1946, and the vote in metropolitan France resulted roughly in 9,000,000 for the constitution, 8,000,000 against it, and 8,000,000 abstentions. Actually, fewer voted for the second draft than had voted for the first. But since fewer also voted against it than voted against the first, it was adopted with the approval of about 36 per cent of the electorate.

Four weeks later elections for the new National Assembly gave the Communists and their allies 183 seats, the Popular Republicans 164, the Socialists 105, the Radical Socialists and their allies 64, the extreme Rightist PRL (*Parti Républicain de la Liberté*) 72, and other parties 23. After the Communist Thorez and the Popular Republican Bidault had both been rejected by the Assembly, on December 12 Léon Blum—generally regarded as a great and unselfish statesman of the highest integrity—was chosen almost unanimously to be premier in a stop-gap government. On January 16, 1947, Vincent Auriol, a veteran Socialist, was elected the first constitutional President of the Fourth French Republic, whereupon Blum submitted his resignation and was succeeded as premier by Paul Ramadier, another Socialist. The latter's ministry was a coalition of Socialists, Communists, and Popular Republicans. With a constitution, a President, a bicameral legislature, and a ministry, the Fourth French Republic was at last launched.

THE REAPPEARANCE OF OLD PROBLEMS AND OLD CONFLICTS

But the position of French premiers in the ensuing years was not an enviable one. As in prewar days the electorate was split into many parties or groups and political leaders were chiefly preoccupied with party struggles. Conflicts between the extreme Right and the extreme Left once more developed, fears of communism or fascism were again expressed, and ministerial instability in the Fourth French Republic resembled that in the Third. Between January 22, 1947, and May 21, 1953, for instance, France had thirteen ministries. The basic problem of each successive premier was to manage his multiparty cabinet in a way to offend none of the parties composing his government, which during the early years of this period consisted of Socialists, Popular Republicans and Radical Socialists, a coalition which came to be called the "Third Force." But since frequently, almost usually, the parties in his ministry were in conflict over some major policy, financial aid to Catholic schools, for example, or direct versus indirect taxes, attempts to hold them together often brought political inaction, if not national paralysis. No French leader seemed able to resolve the fundamental political and economic differences of the French parties. Consequently, in the words of one foreign observer, parliamentary government in France appeared as "an interregnum of dissent between spells of chaos."

There seems little value to be gained from tracing the rise and fall of every premier during these years.

Numerous problems, indeed, presented opportunities for conflict among the political parties. Many of them, in the last analysis, had a bearing on the national budget. For instance, the reconstruction of the devastated areas of the country, the cost of postwar social policies, the conduct of the long and ruinous war in Indo-China, and the rearmament of France to meet her obligations to the European Defense Community, all increased the total national expenditures (the budgets for 1952 and 1953 reached all-time highs) and, without some counter action, entailed an unbalanced budget. Thereupon inevitably ensued a conflict between political parties as to the proper method of balancing it, whether by decreasing expenditures in some other categories, the social service or the civil service, for example, in order to hold the total down or by increasing the income from taxes enough to cover the larger expenditures. And when it came to the consideration of increased taxes, as in the years between the wars [4] conflicts followed between the Left and Right as to the types of taxes to be imposed, and usually the budget went unbalanced. In consequence the government had frequently to resort to loans, the republic went more into debt in terms of francs, and the currency became further inflated. In 1952 the republic's monetary circulation reached the record figure of more than 2,000,000,-000,000 francs.

So, despite the government's repeated efforts to initiate deflation by imposing some price and wage ceilings, inflation therefore continued. For instance, from September, 1949, to the end of 1951 French retail prices rose 33 per cent, and one year later they were over 40 per cent higher than in December, 1951. The resultant lag of wages and salaries behind the rising cost of living in turn brought unrest among the workers and resulted in conflicts between labor and management and occasional strikes. The latter, in turn, were at times exploited by the Communists and, whether so exploited or not, contributed to handicap the rise of industrial production. Furthermore, the rise in prices of French goods led those engaged in export trade or in catering to tourists to demand measures to enable them to compete more successfully with other countries, and led to the devaluation of the franc. By 1953 the official rate of the franc stood at 350 to the dollar (in 1926 Poincaré had stabilized it at 25 to the dollar), though at times it was sold on the free market at as high as 475.

Despite ministerial and financial instability during the years after the Second World War, however, France happily experienced some economic recovery, thanks in part to aid from the United States. By the middle of 1952 the republic's industrial index was 39 per cent above that of

[4] See pages 547, 548, 552.

1938. The production of coal in the restored and modernized mines reached a new high, though it was still insufficient for domestic needs. The steel produced in the first nine months of that year was 50 per cent more than for the same period in 1938, though the 7,000,000 tons seem pitifully small by American standards. The output of electricity, as a result of new hydroelectric plants, was far above the prewar level. Automobile factories, too, established new high records for the number of cars manufactured.

On a comparative basis, however, the French industrial situation was not so encouraging. "Since 1929," declared former Premier Reynaud in 1953, "American production has doubled. In Great Britain and Western Germany it has increased by over 50 per cent. Our production has increased by only 8 per cent." Whereas the basic industries, modernized and re-equipped under the Monnet plan, were efficient and capable of meeting foreign competition, the great bulk of France's industrial and commercial undertakings were small, under-equipped, and inefficient. As a result, their prices were too high to enable France to compete effectively in the export market. French agriculture, too, despite a 12 per cent increase in production since 1938, was still on the whole inefficient. A third of the farms were estimated in 1953 to be uneconomic. The French agricultural community was said to pay only about 13 billion francs in taxation but to receive 16 billion francs in subsidies and about 100 billion francs in the guise of legal privileges of various kinds. In 1953 French imports of agricultural products were twice the amount of her exports. That year saw France in a difficult foreign trade position. In the previous year her dollar deficit had almost doubled.

In the view of many observers, a thorough-going fiscal reform and the introduction of a system which would successfully prevent tax evasion would go far toward solving the republic's budgetary difficulties. A sound fiscal system might make it easier for France to improve her industrial plants further, which still suffered from undermechanized and antiquated methods of production. And such improvements, in turn, might bring sufficient reductions in the prices of French products to enable them to compete more successfully in world markets. But the state of public opinion, the political supremacy of the National Assembly, and an Assembly profoundly divided on economic policy made it practically impossible for successive premiers even to attempt to carry out any coherent economic policy.

And the course of French internal politics in the years beginning with 1951 gave no grounds for optimism regarding any improvement in the political situation. In the years during which the "Third Force" had been governing a new political party had appeared on the scene. This was De Gaulle's Rally of the French People (*Rassemblement du Peuple Français*). The RPF, as it was popularly called, was organized in 1947 and drew its support chiefly from parties of the Right, from the conservative clergy, and from prewar nationalists. It called, among other things, for a new constitution and "the re-establishment of authority in the state," and it was accused of being antirepublican.

In 1951 the "Third Force" in the hope of preventing the RPF from securing enough seats to control the Assembly and in the hope of reducing the number of Communist deputies, enacted a new electoral law. The latter stipulated that deputies were to be elected by majority votes from departmental lists, and provided for the possibility of alliances between parties something like the system introduced in Italy in 1953.[5] Since no party would associate itself with the Communists and De Gaulle announced that the RPF would make no alliance with any other party, the new law was expected to operate to the advantage of the parties of the "Third Force." This it did. In the election of June 17, 1951, fifteen political parties nominated candidates, though some of them formed blocs. A new grouping of moderate and Rightist parties was made, for instance, which called itself the "Fourth Force." As a result of the election, in which nearly 80 per cent of the electorate voted, although the Communist Party declined by only 2.1 per cent in its popular vote its representation in the Assembly fell from 187 to 103. The RPF secured 118 seats, but obviously not enough to control the government. The "Third Force" parties came through with 283 seats, and the new "Fourth Force" group won 98 seats.

A long ministerial crisis followed the elections of June, 1951, for the parties of the "Third Force" were deeply divided on at least two major issues. One was that of granting subsidies to Catholic schools, a practice initiated by the Pétain dictatorship but discontinued with the fall of the Vichy government. The Socialists and Radical Socialists, both long anticlerical parties, looked upon any such moves as an attack on the republic itself. The Popular Republicans, on the other hand, favored aid to the Catholic schools. But to complicate the situation still further, the Socialists were estranged from the Radical Socialists on economic and social policy. Ultimately the Socialists decided not to participate in the government though they were willing in general to lend their support. In the government which René Pleven formed on August 11, therefore, the Radical Socialists were the only lay party and the Popular Republicans constituted the most Left-wing party on economic and social questions. Eventually, in September, the "Third Force" came to an end; the usual political alignments were broken when the Assembly voted to re-establish the school subsidies. On this occasion the Socialists joined the Communists in opposition and De Gaulle's RPF united with the rest of the Assembly to pass the measure. Thereafter the political shift was more to the Right.

The longest ministerial crisis of the Fourth Republic occurred in 1953.

[5] See page 900.

Premier René Mayer sought to stop the constant increase in governmental expenditures and demanded special powers to make administrative reforms and economies. He made the matter a question of confidence, and when he lost the support of the National Assembly he was forced to resign on May 21. In the ensuing weeks the Assembly refused to accept one man after another as the new premier. Not until President Auriol had summoned eleven former premiers or designated premiers and nine leaders of as many political parties to meet with him to seek a solution of the crisis did the Assembly finally approve Joseph Laniel as premier on June 26.

Laniel was a business man and a farmer. He had been one of the leaders of the Maquis during the war and had been a deputy for twenty years. He was a conservative leader of Reynaud's Independent Party and was obviously a compromise candidate. His policy statement to the Assembly was short; he made no promises and asked for no exceptional powers. On July 8, however, the National Assembly approved the government's bill for financial reform and did grant him special powers until December 31 to issue decrees on rent control, social security, administration, transport, and "the reintroduction of free competition in industry and commerce." Following the end of a wave of strikes—the most extensive since 1936— the government issued many decrees covering administrative reform, taxes, and prices. A budget was adopted for 1954 but it again showed a deficit, this time of 416,000,000,000 francs.

The National Assembly was called upon to choose a successor to President Auriol, and the ensuing contest strikingly revealed the many cross currents and the resultant difficulty in getting action in the French parliament. Thirteen ballots were required before a new president was elected on December 23, 1953; on no previous occasion since 1875 had more than two been necessary. None of the outstanding candidates could be elected. The new president was René Coty, a 71-year-old senator who was practically unknown before his election.

In the ensuing months Laniel's government was increasingly criticized for its support of the European Defense Community (EDC) treaty, its failure to reach a definitive settlement with Viet Nam, and its inability to end the long war in Indo-China.[6] Following the defeat of the French forces at Dien Bien Phu in May, 1954, and the National Assembly's rejection of the government's request not to condemn its policy in Indo-China, Laniel's ministry resigned on June 12. Six days later Pierre Mendès-France, a trained economist and a former finance minister, was chosen premier by the National Assembly.

Mendès-France announced that he had three immediate objectives: a settlement in Indo-China, a decision by the National Assembly concerning

[6] For these matters, see pages 979–981, 1015.

the EDC treaty, and the formulation of an economic recovery and expansion program. He soon attained some of these objectives. On July 20 an agreement for an armistice in Indo-China was reached at the Geneva conference of the great powers. Two days later Mendès-France announced that shortly thereafter the administrative independence of Laos, Cambodia and southern Viet Nam would be completed. By a large vote the Assembly thereupon approved the Indo-China settlement.

Soon after this parliamentary victory for his government the premier started out to do what premiers in the preceding two years had never dared to do, that is, obtain a decision on the EDC treaty from the National Assembly. After vainly seeking to persuade the other signatories of the treaty to accept a number of amendments, he brought the treaty before the Assembly but did not make its ratification a matter of confidence. Eventually, on August 30, 1954, the Assembly—with practically all parties divided on the matter—rejected the EDC treaty by a vote of 319 to 264. But the premier had, at any rate, obtained a decision.

At the time he took office Mendès-France had promised the Assembly to submit "a coherent and detailed program for economic recovery," for the realization of which he would ask the necessary powers. Earlier in August he had presented for a vote of confidence a request for a free hand, until March, 1955, to take necessary steps for the rejuvenation and expansion of French industry. He desired authority (1) to cut tariffs on imports, (2) to eliminate domestic trade restrictions in order to increase competition, and (3) to make tax adjustments and increase government investment in certain industries in order to stimulate new production. Though there was some opposition from the Right, the premier won approval of the Assembly by a decisive vote. At the very end of the year he again won by a narrow margin a vote of confidence and approval of the Paris treaties admitting a rearmed Germany into the North Atlantic Treaty Alliance. Although this was considered a great achievement, some believed that his government would fall in 1955 on some domestic question.

THE FRENCH UNION

Meanwhile, in the years after the Second World War French statesmen had had to wrestle not only with problems within continental France but with those arising in the republic's overseas territories. Throughout this world's third largest "empire," with its 73,000,000 inhabitants, swept the same dynamic nationalism which had manifested itself elsewhere in the worldwide revolt of the East against the West. In an effort to solve France's new imperial problem the constitution of 1946 created the French Union, based upon the principle that French overseas territories are a part of the French Republic, with which they are joined as more or less equal members.

Within the French Union four types of territories were recognized: (1) Overseas Departments, (2) Associated States, (3) Overseas Territories, (4) Associated Territories. The seven Overseas Departments include Algeria, which constitutes three departments, and Martinique, Guadeloupe, Réunion, and French Guiana. These departments have the same rights and privileges as those of continental France, and their inhabitants are full-fledged French citizens. The Associated States consist of Tunisia, Morocco, and Indo-China (Viet Nam, Laos, and Cambodia), which are considered semi-independent countries linked with France by treaties. The Overseas Territories include French West Africa, French Equatorial Africa, French Somaliland, Madagascar, French settlements in the South Sea Islands, New Caledonia, St. Pierre and Miquelon, and the Comoro Islands, all of which are governed from Paris. The Associated Territories, Togoland and Kamerun, were received by France as mandates at the close of the First World War and are now held under trusteeship agreement with the United Nations.

The political machinery of the French Union consists of a President, a High Council, and an Assembly. The President of the French Republic is the President of the Union. The High Council, something like a ministry, is presided over by the President, and its members are appointed partly by the French government and partly by the overseas territories. Half of the deputies in the Assembly are chosen by the French National Assembly and half by overseas assemblies. The Assembly of the Union is not a legislative body, however. It has authority only to recommend legislation and to propose motions to the French National Assembly.

Despite their attempt to introduce a new type of "democratic colonialism," the French subsequently had serious trouble in their overseas territories. This was particularly true in Indo-China where the French were forced to conduct a disastrous and costly war against a nationalist, even though Communist-led, uprising.[7] But in North Africa, too, France was forced to stand on the defensive against the mounting nationalist movements in Tunisia, Algeria, and Morocco, each of which demanded liberation from colonial rule. Although Algeria was juridically considered "an integral part of France" and as such elected deputies to the French National Assembly, the Algerian natives became increasingly nationalistic and advocated the establishment of an Algerian republic. The fact that the former Italian colony of Libya was recognized as an independent kingdom by the United Nations in 1951 only contributed to French difficulties in Algeria.

Morocco, nominally a sovereign state over which France exercised a protectorate by virtue of a treaty (1912) with the Sultan of Morocco, became a serious problem when in 1950 the Sultan requested a revision of the

[7] See pages 978–981.

protectorate treaty in order to hasten the independence of his country. Ultimately, in 1952, the French government accepted the principle of conversations looking toward the greater independence of Morocco—within the framework of the treaty of 1912. But a crisis developed in the latter part of the year when the Sultan, in a speech, demanded the formal abrogation of the protectorate. Riots broke out and the French on December 10, 1952, ordered the Nationalist and Communist parties in Morocco dissolved and their leaders arrested.

Continued disorders, however, led the French government to depose the Sultan in August, 1953, and to send him and his two sons into exile. On the next day a new Sultan, Mohammed ben Arafa, was enthroned and he announced that he planned to make Morocco a modern state. In September he signed decrees delegating part of his legislative power to a mixed council of viziers and French officials and later approved a new French program of reform. The latter was designed to provide municipal commissions consisting of an equal number of French and Moroccans and regional assemblies composed in a similar manner. These reforms gave the Moroccans a greater participation in their own affairs and at the same time gave French residents the same share in the management of Morocco as the Moroccans. In October the Sultan agreed to an entirely elective instead of a partly nominated Council of Government. Subsequently, judicial reforms instituted, for the first time in Morocco, law courts independent of the executive, and other plans called for the establishment of local representative institutions.

In Tunis, although in 1951 the French, in collaboration with the leading nationalist party, introduced reforms aimed at bringing the nationalists into the actual administration of the protectorate, the latter considered these measures as only a beginning which should be followed by further steps toward autonomy. Subsequent Franco-Tunisian negotiations proved futile, however, and an impasse resulted. Eventually, in 1952, the Tunisian cabinet appealed to the United Nations to settle the Franco-Tunisian dispute. This step was considered illegal and contrary to the treaty of 1881 by the French, who arrested some of the nationalist leaders. Tunisian riots, in turn, led to the further proclamation of martial law by the French and to the arrest of the Tunisian premier and three of his cabinet members.

Shortly thereafter the Bey of Tunis disavowed the violence of the extremists and appointed a moderate premier who accepted in principle a plan of reforms proposed by the French, and the latter thereupon released the former premier and his associates. But this did not conclude the Tunisian affair. Thirteen Arab states decided to submit the problem to the UN even though the French delegate announced that the relations between Tunisia and France were purely an internal matter and not within the realm of the UN. Though the Soviet bloc threw its support to the Arabs, in

December, 1952, the UN General Assembly rejected the Arab motion of direct UN intervention. In the face of continued Tunisian unrest and terrorist activities, however, Premier Mendès-France in July, 1954, proposed a program designed to give Tunis greater internal autonomy while safeguarding French national interests.

The Italian Republic

During the years after 1943 the Italians threw off the Fascist yoke, joined the Allies in the war against Hitler, rejected their monarchy under the House of Savoy, drafted and put into effect a republican constitution, and by popular vote aligned themselves with the Western powers in the "cold war" which had developed between the latter and Soviet Russia.

BADOGLIO'S GOVERNMENT

Mussolini's downfall in July, 1943, it will be recalled, was followed by King Victor Emmanuel's appointment of Marshal Pietro Badoglio as premier. Badoglio's government at once set out to destroy the Fascist regime. The Fascist Party was dissolved and the Fascist Grand Council and the Chamber of Fasces and Corporations were abolished. The minister of finance was instructed to liquidate Fascist Party funds, and any assets which had belonged to the party were transferred to the state. Plans were made for the destruction of Mussolini's corporative state, with the retention of only the system of syndicates, which were to be reorganized on an elective basis. It was decided also to punish those who had been responsible for the suppression of freedom in Italy, members of Fascist organizations, and those who had taken part in the March on Rome, and a High Court for the Punishment of Fascist Crimes was set up for this purpose. In the succeeding months many were tried and sentenced to death or imprisonment for their activities under Mussolini. On the other hand, Mussolini's political prisoners were liberated and many who had lived in exile because of their views were permitted to return to Italy.

Badoglio's government was for all practical purposes a military dictatorship with the king's blessing. The dictatorial nature of the government was revealed in one of its first acts which forbade the activities of political parties. Despite the government's efforts, however, six major parties were organized in the autumn of 1943. From Left to Right these were: Communists, Socialists, Actionists, Labor Democrats, Christian Democrats, and Liberals. Confronted by a government which forbade all political activity, these parties temporarily ignored their differences and united in a common front in what came to be officially called the Committee of National Liberation (CLN). In October, 1943, Committees of National Liberation were set up in various cities and towns of liberated Italy. Ultimately the parties in the CLN agreed to oppose the dictatorial Badoglio government and to seek the abdication of Victor Emmanuel on the ground that he was responsible for the misfortunes of the nation. But Victor Emmanuel refused to abdicate voluntarily and the Allies, especially Britain, maintained that fundamental constitutional changes should not be made until the Italian people could be freely consulted at the termination of the war.

Badoglio next sought to organize an all-party government under his continued premiership. The Communists, Socialists, and Actionists refused to consider such a step, however, and an impasse resulted. This was solved by the return to Italy from Russia of Palmiro Togliatti, a founder of the Italian Communist Party, and by his insistence that the winning of the war should come first and that constitutional changes could wait. Victor Emmanuel, too, helped to solve the impasse by announcing that on the day the Allies entered Rome he would voluntarily withdraw from public life and appoint Crown Prince Humbert as Lieutenant of the Realm. This announcement by the king enabled the Socialists and Actionists to accept Badoglio's proposal of an all-party government, which was organized in April, 1944. But Badoglio's second government was not long in power. In May, the Allies launched their great offensive in Italy and on June 5, Allied troops entered Rome. On the next day, Victor Emmanuel, as he had promised, withdrew from public life and appointed his son Humbert as Lieutenant with power to exercise all royal prerogatives. When Badoglio for the third time attempted to form a new government to include representatives of the Roman CLN he failed because of the opposition of CLN leaders from Rome and Naples.

THE EMERGENCE OF ALCIDE DE GASPERI

Following Badoglio's failure, Ivanoe Bonomi, a pre-Fascist premier and more recently head of the Rome underground National Liberation Committee, formed a ministry which consisted of CLN nominees. Before accepting the premiership, however, Bonomi forced Crown Prince Humbert to guarantee that a constituent assembly would be summoned at the close of the war and secured a new formula for the oath of allegiance which did not commit the ministers to support the House of Savoy. Friction shortly developed within Bonomi's government when the Socialists and Actionists proposed that the Italian government should be built on the central, regional, and district Committees of National Liberation somewhat as the Communist government of Russia had been erected on the system of soviets. This idea Bonomi rejected, a ministerial crisis ensued, and in December, 1944, Bonomi formed a new cabinet with the Socialists and Actionists in opposition. It was not the opposition of these parties, however, but the end of the war which brought Bonomi's downfall.

The military successes of the Allies in 1945 and the collapse of the Third Reich brought the surrender of all Nazi and Fascist forces in Italy in May, 1945. The end of hostilities in Italy in turn brought a further reorganization of the government, for most of the parties in the CLN now wanted as premier one who had taken a leading part in the resistance movement. The North Italian Liberation Committee demanded one who had been active in the resistance movement in the North. The northern leader who enjoyed the widest prestige was Ferruccio Parri of Milan, who had been known to the partisans as "General Maurizio." The impact of the northern CLN upon the Roman CLN resulted on June 17, 1945, in the elevation of Parri to the premiership as the head of the first government of reunited Italy. All parties were represented in Parri's cabinet.

But with the war over and Italy liberated, it was natural that six parties holding such divergent views should sooner or later clash. In November, 1945, the Liberal and Labor Democrat ministers resigned and thus still another political crisis was precipitated. The Right and Left were fairly evenly balanced, and the crisis was finally solved by the elevation to the premiership of a leader from the center group, the Christian Democrat Party, the successor of the Catholic Popular Party of pre-Fascist days. The new premier was Alcide de Gasperi who had been a member of the three preceding governments. He had opposed Mussolini, had been imprisoned for a time, and after his release had worked under an assumed name in the Vatican library, writing an account of Leftist tendencies among Catholics. In December, 1945, De Gasperi formed a coalition government with the Socialist leader, Pietro Nenni, as deputy premier.

THE REJECTION OF THE MONARCHY

The way was now open for the promised opportunity to decide regarding the future of the monarchy in Italy. It was agreed that Italy's first democratic election since before the Fascisti came to power should be held on June 2, 1946, and that on that same day a referendum should be held to decide whether Italy should remain a monarchy or become a republic. Crown Prince Humbert, it was announced, would respect the free decisions of the Italian people. The outcome of the June elections, in so far as the monarchy was concerned, was to some extent foreshadowed by municipal elections in March which showed a decided republican trend. It seemed likely that the monarchy under the House of Savoy was doomed. Perhaps hoping that the elimination of himself as monarch might help change the trend toward a republic, Victor Emmanuel on May 9, 1946, signed a formal act of abdication and he and the queen sailed into exile in Egypt, where he died in December of the following year. Immediately after his father's abdication, the Crown Prince proclaimed himself King Humbert II, but De Gasperi's government in approving the title carefully omitted the traditional phrase "by the grace of God and the will of the people."

On June 2, 1946, the elections for a constituent assembly and the referendum on the monarchy were held simultaneously. The referendum showed that a slight majority of the men and women who voted favored a republic. King Humbert at first showed some reluctance to accept the results of the referendum as final but on June 13 he left for Spain whither his wife and children had already preceded him. In the elections for the constituent assembly, three parties captured most of the 556 seats; the Christian Democrats won 207, the Socialists 115, and the Communists 104. When the constituent assembly convened it elected Enrico de Nicola, a member of the Liberal Party before 1924, to be provisional President of the Italian Republic until a definitive head of the state should be chosen in accordance with the constitution which the assembly was to draft. Alcide de Gasperi was again chosen premier and foreign minister and the first Italian republican government—consisting of representatives of the Christian Democrats, Socialists, Communists, and Republicans—was sworn in by President de Nicola on July 14, 1946.

THE REPUBLICAN CONSTITUTION

At the outset the new Italian Republic was confronted with five major problems: (1) the conclusion of a peace settlement with the Allies; (2) the drafting of a republican constitution; (3) the attainment of political stability within the republic; (4) the choice between Western and Eastern orientation in its foreign policy; (5) the restoration of the country's economic life. The peace settlement with Italy has already been discussed.[8] Despite De Gasperi's pleas at the Paris peace conference in 1946, Italy by the peace treaty lost territory in Europe and all her overseas empire, was required to pay $360,000,000 in reparations, and was restricted in respect to her army, navy, and air force. Although many Italians were bitter over the treatment which their country had received at the hands of the Allies, Italy signed the treaty in February, 1947, and the constituent assembly ratified it on July 31 of the same year.

Meanwhile, the assembly in addition to legislating for Italy had been struggling with the problem of a new constitution. Party conflicts, ministerial changes, and labor unrest handicapped it, but ultimately, in December, 1947, it adopted the final text of the constitution of the Italian Republic, which came into force on January 1, 1948. This new constitution declared

[8] See page 775.

Italy to be "a democratic Republic founded on work," in which sovereignty belonged to the people. Popular sovereignty was to be exercised principally through universal suffrage and the direct election of both houses of the parliament. Members of the Chamber of Deputies were to be elected from single-member constituencies of approximately 80,000 population; those of the Senate, from each of the nineteen new large political units, the "regions," one senator for approximately every 200,000 inhabitants in each region. The President of the Republic was to be elected by the two houses of the parliament, sitting in joint assembly, with the participation of three delegates elected by the council of each region. The President constituted the titular head of the state, but the real executive power was lodged in a premier and ministry which required the confidence of the two chambers. The new constitution provided for a democratic, parliamentary, unitary republic.

ITALY IN THE "COLD WAR"

It was hoped by many that once the Italians had adopted a constitution for their republic, political stability might be achieved, for in the first five years after the overthrow of the Fascist regime Italy was plagued with ministerial instability. In the period between Mussolini's downfall and the referendum in favor of a republic the country had six different ministries, and during the first two years of the republican regime there were five more changes in the government. The latter were caused chiefly by the inability of the four parties represented in De Gasperi's government of July, 1946, to agree on national policies. In the beginning of this period the Communists and Socialists were bound by a unity-of-action agreement and seemed determined to use their position to turn Italy from the West toward Russia. In January, 1947, however, a split occurred in the Socialist Party when Giuseppe Saragat, president of the constituent assembly, and some forty Right-wing Socialist members of the parliament seceded from the party. The Saragat Socialists opposed continued close co-operation, amounting almost to fusion, with the Communists, and their refusal to support De Gasperi's government which included Communists led to the organization of a new ministry which the Saragat Socialists and the Republicans declined to join. The absence of these two groups, however, resulted in a government in which the opposing views of the Christian Democrats and Communists were evenly balanced and this situation, in turn, frequently produced a deadlock and prevented the government from taking decisive steps. But the fiscal and economic conditions in the republic called for action, and finally in May, 1947, De Gasperi again resigned.

Ultimately, on May 31, after both Nitti and Orlando had failed to form a government, De Gasperi resumed the premiership at the head of a ministry consisting largely of Christian Democrats and nonparty experts. For the first time since the collapse of Fascism there were no Communists or Socialists in the government. During the succeeding months, therefore, Left-wing criticism of the government greatly increased, doubtless fostered in part by the severe inflation which had pushed prices up to 58 times the prewar level by July, 1947. But in many cases criticism was accompanied by political violence, strikes, and the threat to use armed force. A general strike, called in Rome in December, proved a failure, however, and after its collapse De Gasperi organized his fifth government, increasing its strength in the parliament by including moderate Republicans and Saragat Socialists.

With the adoption of the new constitution a few days later, the life of the constituent assembly came to an end and preparations were made for electing the members of the two houses of the parliament on April 18, 1948. By this time the "cold war" between the Soviet Union and the United States was being waged with full force, and Italy inevitably became involved. The question was whether she would join the Western or Eastern bloc of powers. During the pre-election campaign Christian Democrats and others supporting De Gasperi emphasized the importance of Italy's participation in the Marshall Plan and the advantages which the country had already obtained from generous American aid, and argued that a Communist victory in the elections would undoubtedly result in cutting Italy off from this much-needed foreign assistance. Indeed, statements made in the United States, as well as that country's policy toward Czechoslovakia, indicated quite clearly that Italy could expect little assistance from America if she "went Communist." Communist and other Left-wing speakers, on the other hand, declared that Italy would receive Marshall-Plan aid regardless of the outcome of the elections, and that, anyway, American economic assistance was actually only camouflaged penetration by American capitalists. On the eve of the election, apparently to swing the voting against the Communists, the United States, Britain, and France announced their readiness to discuss the return to Italy of Trieste. The Catholic Church, too, threw its powerful influence unreservedly against the Communists. The voting was unusually heavy, more than 26,000,000 Italians going to the polls, and the Christian Democrats received more than 12,000,000 votes. With 307 seats, they secured an absolute majority of the 574 seats in the Chamber of Deputies. To some extent the outcome was the result of the going to the polls of many voters, not normally interested in politics, who cast their ballots in favor of the middle parties and "law and order." On May 11, 1948, the two houses of the parliament elected, as Italy's first constitutional President, Luigi Einaudi, governor of the Bank of Italy, who had been vice-premier and minister for the budget in the existing government. Once more

De Gasperi formed a new ministry, in which the Christian Democrats held a majority of the posts but in which Saragat became vice-premier and Carlo Sforza, long an implacable foe of Fascism, minister for foreign affairs.

ITALY SINCE 1948

In the United States and Britain the Christian Democratic success in the elections of 1948 was interpreted to mean that the majority of Italians had decided that their country should be linked with the Western powers rather than with Soviet Russia, and in the succeeding years Italy did, in fact, become closely linked with the Western democracies. In 1949 she ratified the North Atlantic treaty and thus became a member of NATO. In the same year she participated in the drafting of the statute of the Council of Europe, and in 1952 she ratified the Schuman Plan for the pooling of the coal and steel output of Western Germany, the Netherlands, Belgium, Luxembourg, France, and Italy. She co-operated in the drafting of the treaty setting up the European Defense Community and early in 1951 announced that three divisions would be her initial contribution to the European army. In July of that year Italy formally requested the Allies to revise the arms clauses of the Italian peace treaty. These limitations, the treaty provided, were to remain in effect until modified by the Allies and Italy, or, after Italy had become a member of the United Nations, until agreement between Italy and the Security Council. Italy's admission to the UN, however, had been vetoed by Soviet Russia.

In September, 1951, the American, British, and French governments declared that the restrictions and disabilities to which Italy was subject under the peace treaty no longer accorded with the actual situation and stated their willingness to give favorable consideration to Italy's request to remove them. These restrictions and discriminations had no further justification, they asserted, and they affected Italy's capacity for self-defense. Despite Russia's denunciation of this action of the Western powers, it seemed apparent that Italy would be allowed and encouraged to rearm so that she could protect herself and play her assigned role in the North Atlantic Treaty Organization. In part because of increased military expenditures, the Italian government operated with budgetary deficits in 1952–1953 and 1953–1954.

During the years 1948–1953 De Gasperi's government sought to maintain financial stability, encourage industrial progress within Italy, and introduce some reforms. During this period, thanks to government policies, Italian currency remained stable. That there was industrial progress was indicated by a new national steel-production record of 3,000,000 tons in 1951, by the development and utilization of natural gas resources in northern Italy, by the rapid growth of petroleum refining, by the expansion of the country's chemical industry, and by the construction of new hydroelectric plants.

Although industrial production generally rose above the 1938 level, however, it apparently was not enough to compensate for Italy's increase in population or to overcome the republic's serious adverse balance of trade. But it was hoped that, as a member of the newly-organized European Coal and Steel Community, Italy might benefit from lower prices and more abundant supplies of those two key commodities.

Agrarian reform laws were passed in 1950, applying particularly to southern Italy where the need was both social and agricultural. As originally conceived, the program was to involve some 3,000,000 acres or 5 per cent of the country's arable land, on which it was hoped that 150,000 families might perhaps be settled. It was estimated that approximately 8,000 landowners might be affected but they were to receive compensation in cash and 5 per cent government bonds. There was to be no drastic abolition of private ownership and no compulsory collectivization. Rather, the aim was to break up large, poorly managed estates, to create numerous small peasant holdings, to encourage and support reclamation, and to introduce better land-use methods. But progress in carrying out the program was slow and the number benefiting directly was small. Peasant dissatisfaction and unrest continued, as was indicated by agrarian riots in 1952.

Politically, during these years, there seemed to be in Italy some contraction of the center elements and a polarization toward the extreme Right and Left. The strength of the Communists and Left Socialists has already been noted. The two Rightist reactionary groups which increased in strength during these years were the Monarchists, led by Achille Lauro, a Neapolitan shipping magnate, and the neo-Fascist Italian Social Movement (*Movemento Sociale Italiana* or MSI) in which the former Fascist, Marshal Rudolfo Graziani, was prominent. Local elections in 1951 and 1952 indicated a decline in the strength of De Gasperi's Christian Democratic Party.

In the hope of preventing a disastrous ministerial instability which might result if no party or working group of parties secured a safe parliamentary majority in the Chamber of Deputies to be elected in 1953, De Gasperi's government in October, 1952, introduced a bill to alter the electoral system. As later amended, the bill provided that, because of the increase in population since 1947, the number of seats in the Chamber should be increased from 574 to 590 and that, if any party or group of parties associated in a single list secured more than 50 per cent of the popular votes in a parliamentary election, it would receive 380 seats. The remaining 210 seats would be divided among the opposition parties in proportion to the popular vote each received in the national election. If there were no majority the seats would be divided among the several parties on the basis of a rough proportional representation. This bill was strongly suggestive of the Acerbo Act forced through parliament in 1923 by Mussolini.[9] Although there was great opposition to the bill in both the Chamber of Deputies and the Senate on the part of the Right and Left parties, De Gasperi eventually made its acceptance in both houses a question of confidence and it finally became a law on March 31, 1953.

Four days later both houses of parliament were dissolved, although Senate elections were not normally due until April, 1954, and general elections were set for June 7 and 8. The leaders of the Christian Democratic, the Democratic Socialist (Saragat Socialists), the Republican, and the Liberal parties, which had supported the electoral reform bill, agreed to fight the electoral campaign as a democratic center group and hoped as a bloc to receive at least 50.1 per cent of the popular vote and a resultant safe majority in the Chamber.

Conditions were not quite so favorable for a Christian Democratic victory in 1953 as they had been in 1948, however. In the latter year expectations of benefits from Marshall Plan aid were great; in 1953, despite continued economic assistance from the United States, many apparently failed to see how the aid had benefited them personally. In 1948 hopes were high that Trieste might be returned to Italy because the United States, Britain, and France had announced their readiness to discuss its return; in 1953, although the United States and Britain had transferred to Italy most of the civil administration in their occupation zones, Italy had not yet been able to annex the city and adjoining areas which she wished. And the fact that the United Nations had appointed Italy as a trustee of former Italian Somaliland for ten years seemed in no way to lessen the disappointment over Trieste. Furthermore, there was dissatisfaction with the government's failure to solve the persistent unemployment problem, to reform the national tax structure by reducing indirect taxes (which supplied about 80 per cent of the government's revenue), or to take adequate measures to meet the housing shortage.

In the elections of June 7 and 8, 1953, some 27,000,000 voters, or 93 per cent of the electorate, went to the polls. The center bloc, whose parties had received 62.7 per cent of the votes in 1948, received only 49.85 per cent in 1953 and thus failed by a few thousand votes to secure the necessary majority to give it the coveted 380 seats in the Chamber of Deputies. Each of the parties in the coalition declined percentage-wise from its vote in 1948. On the other hand, the Monarchists and the neo-Fascists increased their percentages from 4.8 in 1948 to 12.68 in 1953, and the Communists and Left Socialists increased their vote from 31.3 per cent of the total to 35.3 per cent. In the subsequent apportionment of seats the center bloc was allotted 303, the Left opposition 218, and the Right opposition 69, so that De Gasperi's coalition

[9] See page 482.

had a majority of 16 seats in the Chamber. In the Senate the center bloc won 125 of the 237 seats. Although the center bloc's majorities in each house thus appeared sufficient to enable De Gasperi to organize a new government, observers in the Western democracies were somewhat disturbed by the gains of the Right and the Left. Parties in both of these groups had opposed the Western policy of joint rearmament under NATO, though for different reasons.

On June 29 De Gasperi's government resigned but agreed to continue to deal with current affairs temporarily. A week later President Einaudi requested the former premier to try to form another government and on July 15 he submitted his eighth consecutive ministry, composed entirely of Christian Democrats. The Democratic Socialists, Liberals, and Republicans, perhaps because of their losses in association with the Christian Democrats in the June elections, declined to continue that association. But De Gasperi's government, in order to have a majority, needed the support of either their 38 deputies or that of the 40 Monarchist deputies. Consequently, when on July 28 a vote of confidence was taken and the Monarchists—who opposed De Gasperi's pro-Western foreign policy—voted with the opposition and the deputies of the three minor center parties abstained from voting, De Gasperi failed to secure a majority. He therefore at once resigned and President Einaudi was faced with the task of choosing another to try to organize a government.

To many observers it appeared that the next premier must be either a Left-wing Christian Democrat who might win the support of the Left-wing Socialists or a Right-wing Christian Democrat who might be satisfactory to the Monarchists. On August 2 President Einaudi asked former Vice Premier Attilio Piccioni, a Right-wing Christian Democrat to try to form a government. His choice apparently displeased the Democratic Socialists and Republicans but, since Piccioni strongly favored European integration and co-operation with the West, he could not win the support of the Monarchists. He therefore failed to form a government. Einaudi next invited Guiseppe Pella, minister of the budget in De Gasperi's last government, to organize a ministry. He formed a cabinet consisting, with one exception, of Christian Democrats, which he admitted was of a transitory nature but which lasted until January, 1954.

During this period Italy made a serious effort to regain control of Trieste. Premier Pella declared that the Allied tripartite declaration of 1948 stating American, British, and French willingness to discuss the return of that city to Italy should be implemented. On October 6, 1953, he announced that, while Italy's adherence to NATO remained the basis of her foreign policy, it might be difficult to get the EDC treaty ratified by the Italian parliament if Italy did not receive satisfaction over the question of Trieste. Two days later the United States and Great Britain sent a joint statement to Rome and Belgrade declaring that since it had been impossible to find a solution of the Trieste question acceptable to both Italy and Yugoslavia because of Soviet obstruction in the UN Security Council, they had decided to end the Allied military government in Zone A and to turn over its administration to the Italian government. The Anglo-American governments had come to the conclusion that the division of the Trieste area along the zonal border was the only practical course. They apparently expected protest and criticism but believed that Yugloslavia and Italy would ultimately acquiesce in the decision.

The Italian government at once accepted the Anglo-American proposal as an important step toward a definitive solution of the Trieste question but did not waive Italy's rights to territory outside Zone A. But Russia declared that the handing over to Italy of the administration of this zone would be a violation of the Italian peace treaty. Yugoslavia likewise asserted that such action would be a "unilateral violation" of the peace treaty and proclaimed that "in no circumstances" would she accept the situation which would result from the Allied withdrawal from Zone A. Yugoslav troops and tanks were ordered into Zone B, administered by Yugoslavia, and Marshal Tito stated that any movement of Italian troops into Zone A would be considered an act of aggression. In November the Italian flag was hoisted over the Trieste town hall in defiance of the Allied military government. When it was hauled down by the police, Italian riots started in the city—deliberately provoked and partly organized from Italy, according to the British foreign secretary—and six persons were killed and many injured before they were suppressed. In Rome, Milan, and other cities anti-American and anti-British demonstrations occurred. But the United States and Great Britain stood firm for law and order and regular diplomatic procedure, and ultimately Italy accepted an Allied proposal for a five-power conference on Trieste. Shortly thereafter Marshal Tito expressed Yugoslavia's willingness to attend such a conference and proposed that the city of Trieste should go to Italy and the Slovene-populated hinterland should go to Yugoslavia. In December Yugoslavia and Italy agreed to withdraw their troops from along the common frontier, and it was hoped in Allied circles that eventually the two countries would agree on a division of the territory.

So long as the Trieste crisis existed Premier Pella received the support of his parliament, but when that question was set aside for a solution by the diplomats, Pella was deserted by the Left wing of his party because of his failure to advance the Christian Democratic program of social reform, and had to resign on January 5, 1954. He was succeeded by Amintore Fanfani, a Left-wing Christian Democrat, who headed a government which, with two exceptions, consisted of Christian Democrats. But within a few days his government, too, was rejected by the Chamber of Deputies. The Christian Democrats having failed several times to get parliamentary support for a purely Christian Democratic government—Center, Right, or Left in political complexion—finally gave up the attempt at a one-party government, and agreed to a coalition with four Democratic Socialists and three members of other center parties in a government headed by the Sicilian, Mario Scelba. Perhaps his outstanding achievement was the settlement of the Trieste dispute with Yugoslavia on October 5, 1954. In effect the Free Territory was divided between Italy and Yugoslavia in accordance with the existing zonal boundary and Allied troops were withdrawn.

West Germany

On the basis of population, resources, industrial production, and military potential, the Federal Republic of Germany should probably be included among the so-called great powers of western Europe. Much smaller territorially than the prewar German Republic, it still had in the postwar period a population (about 50,000,000) exceeding that of either France or Italy. Although terrifically battered by Allied wartime bombing and deprived of valuable mineral and industrial resources, especially in Upper Silesia and the Saar, by October, 1952, West Germany had so far restored her factories that her industrial production was 59 per cent above that for the same area in 1936 and the German Federal Republic ranked next to Great Britain as an industrial power. There was certainly great need for Germany's industrial recovery, for, with the addition to her former population of ten million refugees and transferees from eastern Europe and the loss of former agricultural lands in eastern Germany, she was forced to import 40 per cent of her food supplies, and needed to export manufactured goods to pay for them.

From the day of its creation the German Federal Republic undoubtedly had three major goals: (1) to escape from the restrictions placed upon Germany as a consequence of her defeat by the Allies, or, in other words, to regain her national sovereignty; (2) to regain her former place among the great powers of Europe; (3) to re-unite Germany in a democratic state. In her attempt to attain these goals she was aided by the "cold war" which had developed between Russia and the Western democracies in 1947 and by Communist aggression in Korea in 1950 and the resultant desire of the Western powers to build up and strengthen collective security for the free world.

Within a few weeks after the outbreak of the Korean War the foreign ministers of France, Great Britain, and the United States in September,

1950, agreed: (1) to end the state of war with Germany by legislation; (2) to reinforce their troops there and to treat any attack against the Federal Republic or on Berlin as an attack on themselves; (3) to help in creating mobile police formations in the West German *Länder* (states) which would be at the call of the federal government in an emergency; (4) to empower the federal government to set up a foreign ministry and enter into diplomatic relations with foreign countries "in all suitable cases"; (5) to revise the Occupation Statute, and to remove or relax the Allied controls; (6) to revise the agreement on prohibited and restricted industries and in the meantime to allow cargo ships of any size to be built for export, and the steel production limit of 11,100,000 tons annually to be exceeded "where this will facilitate the defense of the West."

In March, 1951, a start was made in the execution of these agreements when the three powers authorized the German Federal Government to establish a foreign ministry and embassies in any country where it already had consulates, except in France, Great Britain, and the United States. In the latter the channel for relations between Germany and themselves would continue to be the high commission, and texts of all international agreements made by Germany would still be subject to high commission scrutiny and disapproval if found prejudicial to a German peace treaty. Within Germany federal and state legislation was freed from the necessity of prior high commission approval.

During 1951, too, nearly all restrictions on German industry were abolished except in respect to military equipment, atomic energy, and aircraft. The Allied high commission handed over to the federal government the control of all internal economic policies, requiring only that the republic complete the decentralization and decartelization programs already begun, and later transferred to the federal government the control of foreign trade, also. In 1952 the German Federal Republic achieved a favorable balance of trade. Following the lifting of all restrictions from West German shipping and shipbuilding, the republic once again began to participate in ocean trade and transport. By April, 1953, West Germany's merchant navy, almost totally destroyed as a result of the war, had risen to 1,840,000 tons, with nearly a million more tons of new ships being built in her shipyards.

For the republic's economic recovery the German people—resourceful, industrious, well educated, and trained in technology—were much responsible. But so, too, were the Western democracies, not only for lifting restrictions from West German economy but for giving much needed assistance. Between the end of the war and the middle of 1951, according to Chancellor Adenauer, the Western powers advanced some $4,000,000,000 (mostly from the United States) of which some $2,200,000,000 was a gift (again, mostly from the United States). Further to lighten West Germany's economic burdens, nineteen countries in February, 1953, agreed to scale down the republic's prewar foreign indebtedness from some $3,375,000,000 to $1,825,000,000.

Meanwhile, during 1951 various events had indicated West Germany's gradual return to her place among the nations. In May of that year the German Federal Republic was admitted to full membership in the Council of Europe [10] and Chancellor Adenauer attended the committee of ministers. In the next month it was also admitted to membership in the International Labor Organization. In July Great Britain ended her state of war with Germany and three months later the United States did likewise. By the end of the year the republic was a member of UNESCO and of OEEC.

In September, 1951, the Allied high commission had been instructed to negotiate agreements as soon as possible with the federal government to replace the Occupation Statute and to bring West Germany into the European Defense Community (EDC).[11] Because of conflicting national views and policies, however, many months were consumed in negotiations before the contractual convention between the Western powers and the German Federal Republic was signed in Bonn on May 26, 1952, and the six-power treaty creating the EDC was signed in Paris the next day. The linking of the general agreement with the projected European army was a concession to French desires, for obviously the German Federal Republic would acquire juridical equality with other nations and an end of the Allied occupation only by agreeing to enter the Atlantic defense community and by contributing armed forces to the proposed European army under NATO's control.

When the general agreement and the related conventions should come into force, however, the Occupation Statute with its powers of intervention in the internal affairs of the Federal Republic would be revoked, and the Allied high commission would be abolished. The three Western powers would retain only such special rights as could not at that time be renounced because of the special international situation of Germany, rights relating particularly to the stationing and security of Allied armed forces in Germany. The mission of these forces would be the defense of the free world including the Federal Republic and Berlin. Although the powerful German Social Democratic Party opposed ratification of these instruments, they were both eventually approved in 1953 by the federal parliament. To become effective, however, they required the ratification of all of the other signatory powers and, unfortunately for the plans of many in Europe and America, the French National Assembly in August, 1954, rejected the EDC treaty and thus defeated the whole project. Whether subsequent plans to admit Federal Germany into NATO and permit her to have a national

[10] See pages 1010–1011.
[11] See pages 1013–1015.

army would be blocked by some state other than France remained to be seen.

Undoubtedly one of the major desires of the German people after 1947 was a reunited fatherland. Social Democratic arguments against ratification of the Bonn and EDC agreements were that they would destroy the chances for German unification, because the Soviet Union would never permit the creation of a reunited Germany if that Germany were to be rearmed and allied with the West. On the other hand, Chancellor Adenauer argued that Western integration of the Federal Republic would create such a position of strength, politically and economically, that Eastern Germany would automatically be pulled into a unified, democratic Reich. Adenauer's government, moreover, sought not only the unification of East and West Germany but demanded the return of East Prussia, the area east of the Oder-Neisse line, the Saar coal basin, and small border districts annexed after the Second World War by Belgium and the Netherlands.

So far as the former Allies were concerned, both the Soviet Union and the Western democracies theoretically stood for a unified Germany. But the situation in Germany seemed to be similar to that in Korea.[12] On the surface there was inability to agree on what constituted democratic parties and free, democratic elections. But basically the Soviet government feared a unified, rearmed Germany allied with the West, and the Western democracies were determined to prevent the unification of Germany by any methods which might result in a reunited Reich, with all its resources and manpower, coming into control of a Communist government.

The Communist countermove to the Bonn and EDC treaties was to urge the unification of Germany and the withdrawal of all occupation troops. During the years 1951–1953 Soviet Russia and her satellite, the German Democratic Republic, took the initiative in keeping unification before the Germans in an apparent effort to influence the west Germans not to sign or ratify the Bonn and EDC treaties. Early in 1951 Premier Grotewohl of the East German government appealed directly to the West German Bundestag for a meeting of representatives of the two states to draft a constitution, arrange for elections, and establish a united Germany, which should be followed by a peace treaty and the withdrawal of all occupation troops. Nothing came of this appeal. In September of the same year the People's Chamber of East Germany made about the same appeal. But when the German Federal government laid down fourteen principles upon the basis of which it would accept the East German proposals and itself proposed that the territories east of the Oder-Neisse line be included in the voting, nothing came of this appeal either. In February, 1952, the Democratic Republic in its first formal note to the Big Four powers requested

[12] See page 826.

that the United States, the Soviet Union, Great Britain, and France sign a peace treaty with Germany to speed unification.

Meanwhile, upon the request of Chancellor Adenauer, Great Britain, France, and the United States had asked that a UN commission should investigate the possibility of holding free elections in Germany. The East German government at once protested that German elections were a local matter in which the United Nations should have no concern. Ultimately Poland refused to serve on the UN commission and the East German government refused to reply to the commission's requests for opportunity to investigate conditions in East Germany. The Communist attitude toward the UN and German unification was similar to its attitude toward the UN and Korea in 1947.

In March, 1952, the Soviet government sent notes to the Western powers suggesting the bases on which a peace treaty with Germany should be drafted. During the exchange of notes in the ensuing weeks it became obvious that the United States objected to several of the bases laid down by Russia and also insisted that a treaty could be signed only with a government of unified Germany based on free elections. In August the Soviet government in another note to the Western powers accused them of violating agreements with Russia by signing a peace treaty with West Germany and by including the latter in an aggressive military alliance. But it suggested a four-power conference to discuss a German treaty and the creation of a government for all Germany. The Western powers, however, contended that such a four-power conference should limit itself to a discussion of free elections. Again nothing came from the exchange of notes. The year closed with all parties in the East German People's Chamber signing a declaration favoring four-power negotiations to achieve "a peaceful solution to the German problem."

In April, 1953, the East German People's Chamber in a message to the British House of Commons reiterated its desire for the early calling of a four-power conference to draft a German peace treaty and provide for German reunification "on the basis of peace and democracy." Whether influenced by this message or not, three weeks later Prime Minister Churchill in a speech on foreign affairs in the British House of Commons declared his belief that a conference on the highest level should take place in privacy between the leading powers without long delay. But President Eisenhower's view was that there should be more evidence of Russia's general good faith before the United States government committed itself to such a high-level international conference. Because of the latter's stand it was decided that a preliminary conference of the heads of the United States, British, and French governments should be held in Bermuda before a four-power conference including Russia should convene. A long ministerial crisis in

FEDERAL GERMANY'S FIRST CHANCELLOR
Konrad Adenauer

France, however, delayed the Bermuda conference and by the time the French crisis was resolved Prime Minister Churchill had been advised by his physicians to abandon his projected journey to Bermuda and to lighten his duties.

In view of Churchill's withdrawal from active duties, the idea of the Bermuda conference was abandoned and it was decided to hold instead a conference of the foreign ministers of the three states in Washington in July. This conference decided to propose a meeting of the foreign ministers, instead of the heads, of the Big Four states to discuss "the first steps which should lead to a satisfactory solution of the German problem." The three Western governments at once sent nearly identical notes to the Soviet government officially inviting Russia to such a conference, to begin about the end of September, to discuss the organization of free elections in all Germany and the conditions for the establishment of a free all-German government with freedom of action in internal and external affairs. Concessions were made to the United States in thus limiting the meeting to foreign ministers instead of heads of states and to a specific, limited agenda dealing only with Germany. The Soviet government did not reply to the three-power invitation until early in August and then, although it formally accepted the invitation, it made so many charges against the Western powers and suggested so many other subjects to be included in the agenda that it was impossible to arrange a conference in September. Eventually, in January, 1954, the Big Four foreign ministers did meet in Berlin, but no progress was made in plans for reuniting Germany.

The reason that the Western powers had suggested that the conference be held late in September was that it might come after the German parliamentary elections scheduled for September 6, so that nothing said or decided at that conference should embarrass or handicap Chancellor Adenauer in his efforts to hold his majority control in the Bundestag. Local elections in 1951 and 1952 had shown slight gains for the Social Democrats and for the Rightist parties at the expense of Adenauer's Christian Democrats. There was a mounting popular desire for German reunification upon which the opposition parties sought to capitalize. Kurt Schumacher, the aggressive postwar leader of the Social Democrats, had died in August, 1952, but the party, led by Erich Ollenhauer, carried on its same attack on Adenauer because, they said, he placed German integration with the West before German reunification.

A strong resurgence of German nationalism also apparently encouraged many former Nazis to re-enter politics and led some of the Rightist parties deliberately to seek Nazi support. In was reported, for example, that there was a distinct rise in pro-Nazi orientation among adherents of the Free Democratic and German parties. In January, 1953, British occupation authorities arrested Werner Naumann and seven other former Nazi leaders as ringleaders of a group which was anti-West in views and was plotting to regain power in Germany. Naumann had been nominated in Hitler's will to succeed Goebbels as propaganda minister. In February the federal government banned the German Free Corps as a neo-Nazi organization and arrested five of its leaders. But during the summer of 1953 the German Supreme Court released Naumann and his associates as well as the leaders of the Free Corps, and Naumann became a candidate for a seat in the Bundestag on the ticket of the German Reich Party.

Meanwhile, in an attempt to decrease the likelihood that a great number of splinter parties might elect members to the Bundestag and thus complicate the problem of majority rule, the Christian Democrats, Free Democrats, and Social Democrats in June had pushed through the Bundestag a new electoral law, somewhat as was done in Italy before the 1953 parliamentary elections. The German law was complicated but in essence it provided that no party should be represented in the Bundestag unless it received at least 5 per cent of the total popular vote or elected at least one candidate in the district elections.

The outcome of the parliamentary elections in West Germany on September 6, 1953, was quite different from that in Italy earlier in the year. Chancellor Adenauer's Christian Democrats secured an absolute majority over all other parties, and the government coalition won 307 of the 487 seats. Four political parties, including the Communist and the German Reich parties, secured no seats at all. In October Adenauer was re-elected by a decisive majority in the Bundestag and again organized a coalition ministry. He announced that his government's prime aim would be the restoration of German unity in collaboration with the Western powers, and declared that Germany would never recognize the Oder-Neisse frontier. Six months later, on July 17, 1954, Theodore Heuss was re-elected president of the Federal Republic for another five-year term.

Chapter XXIX

THE LESSER STATES OUTSIDE
THE "IRON CURTAIN"

I
N Europe outside the "Iron Curtain" there were after the Second World War a dozen so-called lesser powers. In the post-war period efforts were made by the Western great powers to organize these states into some kind of a common front against Russia but, although most of the states finally entered with Britain, France, and the United States into a defensive alliance, some of the others—notably Switzerland and Sweden—preferred to follow a policy of neutrality. On this matter the Scandinavian countries divided.

The Scandinavian Monarchies

In the twentieth century, as has already been pointed out, socialism had become an influential force in the political and economic life of the three Scandinavian monarchies. The Socialists in these countries nevertheless believed firmly in the democratic process, in the fundamental freedoms of speech, press, assembly, and worship, and in the rights and dignity of the individual. In the years after the Second World War they were, therefore, among the strongest bulwarks in Europe against Communism.

Although Denmark did not suffer so much during the war as some of the other occupied countries, she did not escape unscathed. She lost half her merchant shipping, and her stocks of raw and finished industrial materials were nearly wiped out. In addition, the Germans drew heavily on the National Bank of Denmark for occupation costs. Altogether, it was estimated, the German occupation cost Denmark 12,000,000,000 crowns.

From the beginning of the occupation there had been some resistance to the Germans, but it was not until the last two years that the country's regular political parties joined the movement. Ultimately party leaders and other key persons made secret plans for a government to take over when the Germans should be obliged to withdraw. When that moment arrived in May, 1945, a new cabinet came into power and the prime minister declared that the Danish constitution was once more in force. Denmark had a multiparty system, and in the period after the war the same political parties were prominent as before 1940. Parliamentary elections were held in 1945, 1947, 1950, and 1953. In all of them the Socialists won by far the largest number of seats but not a majority. From 1947 to 1950 they constituted a minority government. During these years Denmark definitely aligned herself with the West, participating in ERP and NATO. Steps were taken also to increase the armed forces to meet the needs of EDC. In 1950 differences over the means of raising funds for the country's increased defense forces led to the resignation of the Socialist government, which was succeeded by another minority government consisting of Agrarians and Conservatives. This coalition, with the tolerent support of the Socialists, remained in office until after the plebiscite of May 28, 1953, in which the Danes voted on whether to change their constitution. At that time the voters adopted the recommendations of an all-party commission and by amendments to the Danish constitution (1) altered the provisions regarding royal succession so that King Frederick's daughter, Princess Margrethe, might succeed, (2) abolished the upper house of parliament, (3) lowered the voting age from twenty-five to twenty-three, and (4) converted Greenland from a colony to an integral part of Denmark. In the first elections held under the amended constitution in September, 1953, the Social Democrats won 74 out of a total of 175 seats, but none of the seven parties won a majority. A Social Democratic minority government was then again organized.

Norway suffered at the hands of Hitler much more than did Denmark. Her losses resulted from the military campaigns of 1940, the Allied bombing of targets in the country, the sabotage activities of the resistance movement, the ruthless German devastation of Finnmark, and the sinking of some 43 per cent of the nation's merchant marine. It was estimated that Norway's real capital was reduced by about 5,600,000,000 crowns. Furthermore, the Germans, in order to finance their purchases of Norwegian goods and their extensive military works in the country, had forced the Bank of Norway to advance 11,200,000,000 crowns and had thus brought on inflation. During the war, Norwegian underground resistance to the Germans had grown steadily until it became a nation-wide movement under the direction of a secret central council. King Haakon's government in London had maintained a close and constant contact with this underground leadership on the home front, and at the close of the war the king, upon his return in 1945, was hailed by all the political parties as the symbol of the Norwegian fight against Nazism. The country's quislings were quickly arrested and in the succeeding two years tried in the Norwegian courts. Vidkun Quisling himself and some of his more notorious followers were condemned to death, and others received sentences ranging from fines to life imprisonment.

In the country's first postwar elections the Labor Party received 76 of the 150 seats in parliament, obtaining for the first time a clear majority of its own. The new Labor premier had been a distinguished leader in the underground home front during the war. He declared that the Labor Party was socialistic and aimed at a socialist society but admitted that it had no popular mandate authorizing a general socializing movement. Although the nationalization of existing businesses was not an immediate goal of the government, it did pursue a policy of establishing new enterprises and purchasing shares in existing ones. In the parliamentary elections of October, 1953, the Labor Party increased its popular vote but, because of a revised electoral system, its majority of seats over all other parties was reduced to six. On the other hand, the Communists—who lost in popular support—won three seats, whereas previously they had had none.

By 1952 Norway's recovery from the economic dislocations occasioned by the war was encouraging. Her merchant fleet had been more than restored, as had practically all of her war-damaged housing. By 1951 her industrial output had risen some 40 per cent above that of 1938, and her per capita consumption of electricity was said to be the highest in the world. In 1952 the parliament passed a number of laws designed to implement a ten-year plan for the economic development of northern Norway through the expansion of regional industries, particularly fishing, farming, mining, and manufacturing. Like Denmark, however, Norway was plagued by the problem of international payments. Before the war the country had obtained a large part of its imports from sources other than the western hemisphere, and until this pattern could be resumed the problem of international payments seemed likely to continue.

Like Denmark, too, Norway aligned herself with the West in NATO and the European Defense Community. Both countries extended the period of compulsory military service, Norway aiming at trained and fully equipped armed forces totaling 270,000 men.

Sweden was one of the few European countries which escaped being embroiled in the Second World War. During that war the government became an enlarged coalition, and among the people a remarkable degree of national unity was preserved. There was no serious questioning of the government's policy of neutrality and all parties supported the substantial increases in national armaments. Nevertheless, Sweden did suffer some economic losses from the war. She lost 40 per cent of her merchant marine, an important source of earnings for balancing her international payments. There was, too, an excessive cutting of the nation's forests. The country's industrial plant and equipment also suffered deterioration, and its customary source of supply for much of its iron and steel, chemicals, and textiles—Germany—was lost. Sweden, therefore, had to rely more upon the United States for these commodities, and therefore was soon confronted with a dollar problem.

Although the Socialists won half the seats in the lower house of the Swedish parliament and a majority in the upper house in the elections of 1944, it was not until the summer of 1945 that the wartime coalition government gave way to a Socialist ministry headed by P. A. Hansson. The latter denied that his government had plans for complete socialization, insisting that the main principle of its program was that the means of production must be used as effectively as possible. "Whenever private enterprise proves to be used effectively, it will have our support," he declared, "but if it fails in any field, we shall have to find other forms of production or distribution." Following the death of Hansson in 1946, Tage Erlander—who was considered less conservative than his predecessor—became premier. The parliamentary elections of 1948 did little to weaken his position, but to broaden the base of his government in 1951 he persuaded the Farmers' Party to join it in a coalition. Parliamentary elections in 1952 gave this coalition a decisive majority over all other parties.

Even in the years before the First World War a considerable amount of socialization had existed in Sweden. The state had long owned some forest areas and waterfalls; the first railways had been constructed by the state; and the telephone and telegraph systems had been merged under government ownership. By 1948 the state owned about 20 per cent of the forests, a large share of the waterfalls, and the main electrical power lines. More of the private railway lines had been acquired and added to the state's system. All radio facilities, the domestic air service, the national bank, the munitions and armaments factories, and the telephone factories were also government owned. In addition, the state held all or most of the shares in a number of other industrial corporations, notably, pulp factories, saw mills, iron works, and mines. Sweeping agrarian reforms, designed to make agriculture more profitable, were enacted by the parliament in 1947, and additional family allowances and old-age pensions were made effective on January 1, 1948. In the postwar period, however, Sweden was increasingly confronted with economic difficulties, arising largely from the unexpectedly slow recovery of devastated Europe, the country's growing dependence upon the United States for essential supplies which its exports to that country did not pay for, and the impossibility of converting its earnings from other areas into hard currencies. In September, 1951, however, Sweden was able to dispense with Marshall Plan aid.

The difficult economic situation in which the Scandinavian countries found themselves after the war led them to consider the possibility of some kind of inter-Scandinavian economic co-operation. The foreign ministers of Denmark, Norway, Sweden, and Iceland [1] in 1947 did recommend the appointment of a committee of experts to investigate the possibility of some sort of economic union, but no tangible results followed. Nevertheless, a Scandinavian parliamentary council was established in 1952, consisting of representatives of the cabinets and parliaments of the four countries, which was to meet annually and to make recommendations regarding the solution of common problems. The so-called Nordic Council, in July, 1954, inaugurated a common labor market for the four countries.

During 1948 the Scandinavian countries considered, also, the possibility of establishing a defensive military alliance. All three were apparently willing to conclude such an alliance, but Sweden and Norway differed in their views regarding its relation to the North Atlantic pact. Sweden desired an alliance for Scandinavian self-defense but one which would be neutral in case of war among the great powers. Norway, in order to receive arms and assurances of aid from the Western powers, desired to have the Scandinavian alliance linked with the North Atlantic pact. In January, 1949, the projected Scandinavian alliance foundered on Sweden's determination to stick to her traditional policy of neutrality.

The Benelux Countries

After the Second World War Belgium, the Netherlands, and Luxembourg embarked upon a program designed to increase their mutual trade and to remove the obstacles to their eventual economic union. Before 1939 the tiny Grand Duchy of Luxembourg had been united with Belgium in a customs union, and on January 1, 1948, the Netherlands joined Belgium and Luxembourg in an enlarged customs union. The ultimate goal of the three states was a full economic and monetary union, which it was hoped might finally be brought into being. Beginning in 1947 the three states came to be referred to collectively as Benelux. By 1954 more than 98 per cent of all nonagricultural goods moved within the Benelux countries free of any governmental restrictions. In the same year it was agreed that there should be free capital transfers within the countries. Belgium, for instance, floated loans in the financial markets of the Netherlands.

On March 17, 1948, the Benelux countries and Great Britain and France signed the treaty of Brussels in which all five states agreed to co-ordinate their economic activities, endeavor to raise the standards of living of their peoples, and afford all military and other assistance to any one of their

---

[1] In 1944, Iceland, whose inhabitants are of Scandinavian origin, had severed her union with Denmark under a common sovereign and had become an independent republic.

number in case of an armed attack. For the purpose of better co-operating they further agreed to create a Consultative Council which should function continuously. Provision was made for other countries, also, to accede to the treaty. In January, 1949, the foreign ministers of these five states, meeting in London, issued a statement giving approval to the creation of a Council of Europe, which ultimately developed into a full scale attempt to integrate all western Europe (see pages 1010-1019).

The two dominant states in Benelux, of course, were Belgium and the Netherlands, the latter popularly referred to as Holland.[2] Economically, Holland suffered severely as a result of the Second World War, her loss of national wealth being estimated at one third, not counting losses in the Dutch East Indies. Within the Netherlands itself about 10 per cent of the arable land was inundated, nearly 100,000 houses were completely destroyed, about 50 per cent of the country's merchant marine and 40 per cent of the inland fleet were lost, and the transport system was almost completely disorganized. But postwar recovery was encouraging. Within a few months the flooded lands had been reclaimed; by the middle of 1946 transportation was again functioning; and by 1948 production in gas, electricity, and shipbuilding exceeded prewar levels. Full-scale revival, however, was hampered by the slowness of Germany's recovery, by the decline in British purchases, and by the disruption of trade with the Dutch East Indies, rent by civil strife.[3] Nevertheless, the situation so improved that in January, 1953—before the disastrous flood of that year—the Dutch announced that they could dispense with American financial aid.

Political democracy had been slower to develop in Holland than in some of her neighbors. It was not until 1917 that manhood and womanhood suffrage at the age of twenty-five was introduced for the election of the lower house of parliament. In the years between the wars the kingdom had had a multiplicity of parties which had made parliamentary government difficult. In the elections of 1937, for instance, twenty parties had entered candidates and ten had secured representation in the lower house. The three major parties were the Roman Catholics, the Socialists, and the Calvinist Anti-Revolutionaries. Prior to 1939 the Socialists were unwilling to join a coalition government so that during the interwar years Holland had had a series of Right-wing cabinets. During the Second World War, Queen Wilhelmina's government had functioned from London but after the country was liberated parliament lowered the voting age to 23 years in preparation for new elections.

[2] Holland is only one—but the largest and richest—of the eleven provinces in the Kingdom of the Netherlands.
[3] See pages 973-979.

In the parliamentary elections after the war the strength of the leading political parties changed relatively little. But the Labor Party (Socialist) gave up its earlier aversion to participating in a coalition government, and after the war joined with the Catholic Party to organize ministries. Until 1948 the premier was a Catholic but after that he came from the Labor Party. The co-operation of the Catholics and Laborites assured the government the two-thirds majority needed to enact constitutional changes in connection with the establishment of the Netherlands Indonesian Union.[4] It also ensured the continued influence of the Labor Party, with its social welfare program, on the government's policies.

Meanwhile, on September 4, 1948, the beloved Queen Wilhelmina, after a successful reign of fifty years, had abdicated in favor of her daughter, who succeeded her as Queen Juliana. The latter, in her speech from the throne in September, 1953, declared that the Netherlands considered economic integration one of the necessary steps in the creation of a European community, and asserted that her government would support the work of the Council of Europe, the OEEC, and other inter-governmental organizations. In fact, in January, 1954, the Netherlands parliament completed its ratification of the European Defense Community treaty.

Belgium experienced a rapid economic recovery following the Second World War. Its valuable resources at home and in the Congo enabled it to move ahead with limited help from abroad. Successive governments carried out a rigorous deflation program, stabilized wages and prices, and expanded social legislation to include practically all workers. If currencies had been freely convertible into gold or dollars as in "the good old days," Belgium would have been on a self-sustaining basis. As it was, however, the country was handicapped by inability to convert sterling receipts into dollars and by the further fact that former nondollar sources of supplies for her foods and industrial raw materials were no longer available so that she had to turn to the United States for supplies. Since most of Belgium's exports were shipped to nondollar countries, she had in 1947 a trade deficit of $374,000,000 with the United States as compared with annual deficits of some $16,000,000 in prewar years.

In the period between the wars, Belgium had had six political parties, of which the Catholic, the Liberal, and the Socialist were the largest. The Catholic Party included diverse economic groups but was dominated by conservatives; the Liberal Party was essentially bourgeois, but its Right wing was so strong that the Liberals often joined with the Catholics to form a government. The Socialist Party had originally been Marxist in its ideology, but under Émile Vandervelde in the twenties and Paul-Henri Spaak in the thirties it had abandoned its revolutionary program and had come

4 See page 978.

to resemble the Labor Party in Britain. On the extreme Left was the Communist Party, created in 1923 by a militant group which had seceded from the Socialist Party. On the extreme Right there were two fascist parties; the Flemish Nationalist Party, which was financed in the thirties by Germany; and the Rexist Party, which included in its ranks high army officers and big businessmen, and which was generously supported by subsidies from many Belgian industrialists. As the result of parliamentary elections in 1939 the lower house consisted of 73 Catholics, 64 Socialists, 33 Liberals, 17 Flemish Nationalists, 9 Communists, and 4 Rexists. The government at the time of the Nazi invasion in 1940 consisted of Catholics, Socialists, and Liberals under the premiership of Hubert Pierlot, a conservative Catholic. This government, somewhat reduced in numbers, functioned from London during the period of Nazi occupation.

On February 17, 1946, Belgium had her first postwar parliamentary elections. The Flemish Nationalist Party and the Rexist Party had been outlawed and some 300,000 to 400,000 persons, condemned for or suspected of collaboration with the Nazis, were denied the right to vote in the elections. In the elections the Catholics obtained 92 of the 202 seats in the lower house. The Socialists won 69, the Communists 23, and the Liberals only 17 seats. After a considerable period of ministerial instability the government was temporarily stabilized in August, 1946, under the premiership of Camille Huysmans, a Socialist, who held the office until March, 1947, when Paul-Henri Spaak, the Socialist leader, organized a government which was an alliance between the Socialists and the Catholics. His cabinet rested on a coalition of the kingdom's two most powerful parties which together commanded nearly all the seats in the two houses of parliament. For the first time since 1915, except for a short interval, the Liberal Party was not in the government.

The question of King Leopold's restoration to the throne still remained to be settled. In September, 1944, after the Nazis had taken him as a prisoner of war to Germany, the Belgian parliament had elected his brother, Prince Charles, as Regent of the Kingdom. Following the liberation of Leopold III at the end of the war, conferences were held at Salzburg between the king and Belgian political leaders, during which the king apparently asked that the condemnation passed upon him in 1940 be retracted.[5] This the Belgian leaders refused to do and the king's return to Belgium in 1945 was prevented by the government with the support of the parliament. The Socialists, Communists, and most Liberals wanted Leopold to abdicate in favor of his son, Prince Baudouin, while the Catholics advocated a plebiscite on the question of his restoration. A referendum in 1950 showed 58 per cent

[5] The Belgian cabinet, which had fled from the country, in 1940 had repudiated King Leopold's action in surrendering as traitorous.

of the voters favoring the king's return. When his return provoked strikes, riots, and the threat of civil war, however, Leopold agreed to permit his son to rule as prince royal until his twenty-first birthday. Leopold III finally abdicated on July 16, 1951, and his son succeeded him as King Baudouin I.

The provisions of the EDC treaty, which Belgium approved in 1954, were held to affect Belgian sovereignty, so that a revision of the country's constitution became necessary. Such a revision, in turn, necessitated the dissolution of parliament and the holding of a general election. As the result of the voting in April, 1954, the Catholic (Christian Social) Party lost its majority in both houses of parliament, and in consequence a Socialist prime minister took office at the head of a Socialist-Liberal coalition.

Switzerland and Ireland

During the Second World War, Switzerland was eventually surrounded by Axis-controlled territory and her normal economic life was greatly disturbed. Although the republic's flourishing economy had largely been built on the principles of liberty, private property, and private initiative, economic planning became inevitable, emergency measures were inaugurated without popular approval gradually bringing the country's economy to a great extent under government control. At the end of the war the Swiss were divided in their views on this situation.

Two popular referendums were held in May, 1946, and a third in July, 1947, in an effort to reach some conclusion on the policy to be followed. In the first two the more radical and far-reaching program of the Socialists was repudiated; in the third, a compromise solution—favored by the Federal Council and the parliament—was adopted by a majority of the 87 per cent of the electorate voting. As a result, though the regime of emergency powers was ended, the state was constitutionally empowered to provide for the development of social welfare, the economic security of the community, and the equitable settlement of labor conditions. It was further authorized to take necessary measures to protect endangered parts of the country or branches of industry, to preserve the peasantry and agriculture from the harmful effects of cartels, and to deal with problems arising from unemployment, economic crises, and war. In economic matters *laissez-faire* was thus abandoned in favor of some degree of government control.

The dispute over centralization entered the field of taxation, also. Normally direct taxes were levied by the cantonal governments, which passed on to the federal government amounts fixed by quotas. During the Second World War, however, the federal government had been granted emergency powers to levy direct taxes, powers which had been extended until the end of 1949. There appeared to be much opposition to this levying of direct taxes by the federal government, but after some political maneuvers, the latter called for a popular referendum on the proposal to extend its authority to do so until December, 1954, by which time it was hoped that permanent financial reforms could be worked out to meet budgetary needs. This proposal was carried by more than a 2 to 1 vote. In December, 1953, however, the Swiss voters in a referendum rejected the government's proposed constitutional amendment providing that direct federal taxes be levied on a permanent basis. Apparently they preferred to return to their earlier long-established emphasis on the powers of the cantonal governments.

In Eire, as already pointed out,[6] the government had declared its neutrality at the outbreak of the Second World War. Twice during the conflict, moreover, De Valera had been able to block British conscription in Northern Ireland and when United States troops were landed in that territory in 1942, De Valera had protested. Throughout the conflict the government of Eire had maintained its normal relations with Hitler's Reich, and the latter's diplomatic staff in Eire had been of considerable assistance to the Nazis in obtaining information helpful in the struggle against Britain. Moreover, the cities of Eire by not dimming their lights at the time of Hitler's air blitz against the British had given the Nazis indirect assistance in locating their targets in Britain.

In 1948, after sixteen years in office, De Valera was finally forced to relinquish the premiership. Parliamentary elections held on February 6 of that year, though they gave his Fianna Fail Party the largest number of seats in the Chamber of Deputies, left his party in a minority. The other five parties and most of the Independents combined against him and on February 18 he was succeeded as prime minister by John A. Costello, a member of the Fine Gael Party, whose ministry was a coalition of all five parties. The new prime minister declared that social, economic, and educational matters would be his government's chief concern, and that economic conditions must take priority over all political and constitutional matters. Meanwhile, on June 16, 1945, Sean O'Kelly, a member of Fianna Fail, had been elected President of Eire to succeed Douglas Hyde.

Despite Costello's statement on the relative unimportance of constitutional matters for Eire, in the fall of 1948 his government took steps to repeal the External Relations Act of 1936, which constituted the last formal tie between Eire and the British king. Under the terms of this act, Britain's King George signed letters of credence of representatives of Eire going abroad. Costello asserted that under the act Eire was neither within the British Commonwealth nor an independent republic and that its repeal would clarify Eire's status as a sovereign independent state. On December 21, 1948, President O'Kelly signed the Republic of Ireland Bill, which

[6] See page 543.

repealed the External Relations Act, declared that the state should be described in English as the Republic of Ireland, and transferred to the President of the Republic the British king's function in connection with the state's external relations.

The reciprocal rights of Eire's citizens living in Britain and British citizens residing in Eire were provided for by actions of the British and Eireann governments. Representatives of both governments declared that everything would be done to develop the closest economic co-operation, but Eireann statesmen declared that there could be no military alliance with Britain so long as Ireland remained divided.

In June, 1951, De Valera returned to the premiership after new parliamentary elections had failed to give Costello's coalition a majority, but three years later general elections in May, 1954, again put Fianna Fail in a minority position and Costello once more became prime minister in a coalition government. Meanwhile, in 1952 O'Kelly had been re-elected President of the Republic of Ireland.

The Two Iberian "Police States"

It is probably something more than mere coincidence that among the states of western Europe the only ones that were "police states" in the years after the Second World War were Spain and Portugal.

FRANCO SPAIN

Although the sympathies of Franco Spain were undoubtedly with the Axis powers during a great part of the Second World War, the country's political wounds and economic exhaustion prevented it from actively entering the conflict. Officially the Spanish government adopted a policy of neutrality at the start; then, with Hitler's spectacular successes in 1940, it changed to one of "nonbelligerency"; and finally, after the tide of battle had manifestly turned in favor of the Allies, in October, 1943, Spain re-adopted her policy of neutrality. During the period of nonbelligerency Spain illegally seized the international zone of Tangier, dispatched the "Blue Division" of some 17,000 to 18,000 men to fight against Russia, sent at least 20,000 Spaniards to work in Germany, permitted Axis submarines and destroyers to use Spanish ports, supplied Hitler with strategic war materials and used her own ships to transport these materials as well as Axis agents, allowed Germany to operate an extensive spy and sabotage system from Spanish territory, and secretly planned with Germany to attack Gibraltar and Morocco and to close the Mediterranean to the British.

On the other hand, Franco did give some assistance to the Western Allies, though for the most part it was of a negative character. He did not interfere with the Allied landings in North Africa; he twice refused to permit German troops to cross Spain. At the same time he let thousands of French volunteers cross the country to join the Allied forces in North Africa; he permitted an Allied spy system to operate in Spain; he allowed some 1,500 Allied airmen to escape internment and permitted Americans to retrieve secret equipment from downed planes; and, finally, under Allied pressure, he embargoed the export of wolfram—desperately needed by Germany for the manufacture of arms. After the war Franco surrendered to the Allies millions of dollars worth of official or semi-official German assets and returned to Germany for trial over three hundred Nazi officials, agents, or technicians.

After the end of the war Franco, on the surface at least, sought to push the Phalanx Party somewhat into the background; the party salute, for instance, was abolished as a form of greeting. In June, 1945, he declared that the Phalanx Party no longer wielded political power or made political decisions. In July he appointed the secular head of the Catholic Action foreign minister, and thus linked that well-organized group officially with his regime. The new foreign minister announced that Spain's system of government was moving toward new forms of popular representation and would eventually co-ordinate with the political systems of the Anglo-Saxon countries. Tens of thousands of political prisoners had been released during the war years, and on October 20, 1945, a government decree granted amnesty to all such prisoners convicted before the end of the civil war. In 1943 the Cortes had been re-established, but with all its members appointed directly or indirectly by the government, and in 1945 Franco in an official speech declared that he hoped the Cortes would examine and the nation approve a law for the monarchy's restoration. To many it appeared that the Caudillo (leader) was seeking to regularize his regime in the eyes of the Western world.

But apparently Franco's talk about the restoration of the monarchy was chiefly for effect. When Don Juan, the thirty-three-year-old third son of Alfonso XIII, sought to open negotiations with Franco in 1946, the latter proved to be unenthusiastic. In fact, five university professors and five members of the Cortes who had signed a letter supporting Juan, were at once dismissed. Unofficial negotiations between Juan and Franco eventually failed, apparently because the Caudillo refused to give up his powers. On March 31, 1947, Franco announced that Spain was to become a monarchy with a Council of the Kingdom and himself as Chief of State. The former was to consist of twelve members, most of them ex officio; only three members were to be chosen by the Cortes. In case of the incapacity or death of the Chief of State, the government ministers and the Council of the Kingdom, meeting jointly, should decide by a two-thirds vote who was to be proposed to the Cortes as king or regent. In effect the proposed law would make Franco virtual king of Spain and would give his appointees the right to choose his successor.

Don Juan at once denounced Franco's proposal as an attempt "to turn the dictatorship of an individual into his rule for life, consolidating his precarious claims and wrapping in the mantle of monarchy a regime based on arbitrary government." Gil Robles, leader of the earlier Catholic Popular Action Party,[7] from his residence in exile also denounced Franco's proposal, declaring that Catholicism was based on justice and truth, neither of which he could see in the existing Spanish regime. The Cortes, nevertheless, on June 7 passed the bill as proposed by the Caudillo, who called for a popular plebiscite on the law. A referendum was held on July 6, 1947, and resulted in 14,145,163 in favor of the law and 722,656 against it. Franco thus seemed securely settled in his position as Chief of State.

But Spain still remained a police state whose political opposition was ruthlessly hounded and summarily dealt with by military courts. In the early months of 1948 sixteen Spaniards were sentenced by a court martial to prison terms ranging up to twenty-five years on charges of attempting to re-establish the Socialist Party; seventy other Spaniards were sentenced by court martial to prison terms up to thirty years for being leaders in a quasi-military movement; the former chief of Franco's air force was sentenced to detention for expressing royalist views at a private gathering; and four high-ranking Spanish nobles were fined 25,000 pesetas each for holding or helping to organize private monarchist meetings without the permission of the police. In October of the same year eight men were sentenced to death and sixty-four others to terms of imprisonment on charges of activity against the state. Obviously, no challenge to the decisions of Franco and his advisers was to be countenanced.

Toward the close of 1948 Spain had what were called the first "popular elections" since 1936, when municipal councils were elected in three stages. On November 21 about one third of the councillors were chosen by heads of families and other adult males who were domestically and economically independent. One week later another third were elected by the officers of the syndicates, and one week later still, on December 5, those councillors already elected chose the remaining third from lists submitted by Franco's provincial governors. Obviously, "democracy" in Spain—even on the municipal level—differed from that found in Britain, France, and the United States.

After the Second World War, Spain found herself in a largely unfriendly world but a world which was reluctant to take any steps to remove the Franco regime. The United Nations Charter by indirection specifically barred Spain from membership in the United Nations. In 1946 the United

[7] See page 562.

States, Great Britain, and France declared that there could not be full and cordial association with Franco Spain and expressed the hope that the Spaniards might "soon find means to bring about the peaceful withdrawal of Franco." Poland charged in the UN Security Council that Spain was likely to endanger international peace and suggested that UN members should sever diplomatic relations with that state. Russia wished for drastic action to restore popular government in Spain, but the United States and Britain were reluctant to force Franco from power lest he be succeeded by a government under Communist influence. The attitude of the great powers continued to be similar to that shown during the civil war in 1936–1939.

The Security Council finally decided to appoint a committee to consider the situation and this committee reported that no act of aggression had been proved nor had any threat to peace been established. It recommended that the matter be submitted to the UN Assembly with the recommendation that diplomatic relations with Spain be severed by all UN members. Russia thought this action was too mild and vetoed it. Later in the year the Spanish question was raised in the UN Assembly. The United States and Great Britain argued against intervention in the internal affairs of a nation, and ultimately a compromise was adopted by the Assembly recommending that member nations should withdraw their heads of missions without severing relations and that Spain should be excluded from all UN functions. The UN action had little effect on Franco's position at home.

On the other hand, the intensification of the cold war after 1948 and the outbreak of the Korean War led to a distinct improvement in Spain's international position. In 1949 the United States lifted its embargo on private loans to that country, and shortly thereafter $35,000,000 was advanced by American bankers and businessmen, chiefly to finance the purchase of surplus American cotton. After the outbreak of the Korean War the United States Congress voted loans to Spain on a much larger scale. The changing attitude of many states was further revealed in November, 1950, when the UN General Assembly revoked its resolution of 1946 calling for the withdrawal of ambassadors and ministers from Spain and her exclusion from specialized agencies of the United Nations. Shortly thereafter both the United States and Great Britain sent ambassadors to Madrid. In 1952 Spain was finally admitted into UNESCO. In that same year, too, Franco was further forgiven for his past acts. In 1945 Great Britain, France, the United States, and Russia had sought to punish him for having unlawfully seized the internationalized city of Tangier in 1940. In 1952, however, the Control Council of that city, representing eight countries, yielded to Franco's demand and voted to return to the statute of 1923. By so doing they permitted Spain extensive participation in the rule of the city, including control of the police.

Meanwhile, United States military authorities had become convinced of

Spain's strategic importance in the defense of Western Europe. In May, 1951, perhaps to test international sentiment on the subject, the American ambassador in Madrid expressed the hope that the Western countries would allow Spain to take her place in the common front against Communism. The general outcry which was raised against this suggestion in many western European countries and even in the United States, however, apparently convinced the United States government that Franco Spain's inclusion in the North Atlantic Treaty Organization or in the Western European Union was not likely to be soon welcomed or permitted. Subsequently, exploratory talks were initiated between the United States and Spain, aimed—according to the American secretary of state—not at Spain's association with NATO but at a bilateral agreement between the two powers. Six months later a United States mission was sent to Spain to survey air and naval bases which might be leased by the former. Finally, in September, 1953, three agreements were signed between Spain and the United States making Spain eligible for American economic, technical, and military aid from the Mutual Security Administration and authorizing the United States to develop, build, and use jointly with Spanish forces certain military airfields and naval facilities in Spain. The latter, however, were to remain under Spanish sovereignty and command. During 1954 assistance to Spain totaling $226,-000,000 would be furnished by the United States. Commenting on the agreements, which were to remain in force for at least ten years, Franco declared that Spain had emerged triumphantly from the international conspiracy to isolate her. The agreements were ratified unanimously by the Spanish Cortes in November, 1953.

Internally, in 1953 a further step was taken in the organization of management and labor when, on November 1, a decree was issued requiring an advisory council of employer and employed to be set up in all commercial undertakings having 1,000 or more employees. The councils were to consist of the owner or manager as chairman and from four to twelve employees, and were to be established eventually in all undertakings employing more than fifty persons in one place of business. These councils were strongly reminiscent of those set up in Germany by Hitler in 1934 (see page 510). Meanwhile, a great spread had developed between prices and wages, and the standard of living in Spain was recognized as the lowest in western Europe.

PORTUGAL

Portugal, Spain's neighbor in the Iberian Peninsula, must also be classified as a police state with authoritarian characteristics, though, compared with Franco's regime in Spain, that of Salazar in Portugal is mild and humane indeed. Salazar's regime, which has lasted a quarter-century, had its background in events which occurred in Portugal shortly before the First World War. The republic established at that time failed to bring political stability, and great strikes, frequent riots, and occasional insurrections and coups prepared the way for the establishment of a military dictatorship. In 1926, the military marched into Lisbon, seized the government offices, disbanded the parliament, dissolved all political and trade-union organizations, suppressed freedom of the press, and imprisoned, banished, or deported to the colonies all who protested. General Antonio Oscar de Fragosa Carmona was elected to the presidency and ruled as dictator.

General Carmona was baffled by the national economic and fiscal conditions which confronted him, and in 1928 he persuaded Antonio de Oliveira Salazar, a university professor of economics, to come to his assistance. As minister of finance Salazar introduced drastic reforms and gradually became the dominant factor in the government, though Carmona continued as President. In 1932, Salazar assumed the premiership and in the next year he gave Portugal a new constitution which laid the legal basis for an authoritarian regime. Political nonconformists found themselves subject to special extralegal security police and were from time to time sent to detention camps without means of redress. Press censorship was continued. The general temper of Salazar's regime may be further judged by the fact that the Portuguese government sympathized and co-operated with Franco and his Insurgents during the Spanish civil war and by the fact that in 1940 it signed a concordat with the pope reconfirming the Catholic Church in possession of properties which had belonged to it before the separation of church and state.

Although as a neutral Portugal profited by the Second World War, the economic hardships following the war inevitably engendered criticism and discontent. By 1947, the currency had been inflated to about four times that of 1939. Prices rose and the cost of living increased to between 200 and 300 per cent of 1939. Wages, however, were not permitted to rise proportionately so that living costs were high out of all proportion to earnings. In 1947 strikes began to occur. In April a number of university students were arrested for having been involved in activities against the security of the state. In June, Admiral José Mendes Cabeçadas, the original head of the military triumvirate which sponsored the coup of 1926, and ten army officers and nineteen university professors and lecturers were dismissed from the service because of their part in conspiracies against the state. When the ex-officers were arrested and detained pending trial, Admiral Cabeçadas claimed for himself and his friends the benefits of habeas corpus, but in November, the government refused to grant the petition. Although the professors were later reinstated, the military men were held for trial by a court martial. Cabeçadas sought to inform his old colleague in revolt, President

Carmona, that the Portuguese constitution was being consistently flouted, but apparently to no purpose. In June, 1948, a court martial sentenced the admiral to one year's imprisonment and nine others to eighteen months for their parts in the military revolt of April, 1947.

In 1949 Portugal had two elections. In the first the aged General Carmona, after the opposition candidate withdrew, was elected for his fourth seven-year term. In the second Salazar's National Union Party won all 120 seats in the national assembly; neither the monarchists nor the Left-wing groups had entered candidates. In April, 1951, President Carmona died at the age of eighty-one. In the ensuing presidential campaign two men opposed General Craveiro Lopes, the candidate approved by the National Union Party. One was disqualified by the supreme court nine days before the election; the other withdrew from the contest six days later. General Lopes was elected president. Again in November, 1953, as in the parliamentary election of 1949, the National Union Party won all 120 seats in the national assembly. Twenty-eight opposition candidates stood for election but were defeated.

Portugal is a member of NATO but not of the UN. Under the Marshall Plan she received some $50,000,000 which improved her economic situation. In 1951 she granted the United States more bases in the Azores and by the end of that year an American military mission was helping to equip and train the Portuguese armed forces.

The "Truman Doctrine" Countries

On March 12, 1947, President Truman of the United States in an address to the American Congress declared that "totalitarian regimes imposed on free peoples undermine the foundations of international peace and hence the security of the United States," and asserted his belief that it must be the policy of the United States "to support free peoples who are resisting attempted subjugation by armed minorities, or by outside pressure." At that time he asked the Congress to appropriate funds for the assistance of Greece and Turkey, and to give permission for American military and civil personnel to go to those countries. Actually, what the President was suggesting was that the United States should assume Great Britain's role in the Near East and seek to prevent Russia from reaching the Mediterranean by bolstering up the two non-Communist states which lay between her and that sea, namely, Greece and Turkey. These two countries, therefore, may well be classified as "Truman Doctrine" countries.

GREECE

That conditions in Greece were alarming in 1947, there was little doubt. The turbulent course of Greek history in the years immediately following that country's liberation from the Germans was the result primarily of the interplay of three forces: (1) the Greek resistance movement within the country, (2) the Greek government-in-exile, and (3) Great Britain's interest in Greece and the Near East.

Developments within Greece in the years 1941–1944 were very similar to those within France during the period of German occupation. In Greece, although there were several resistance movements, the largest and most effective organization was the EAM (National Liberation Front) with its military force, the ELAS (National Popular Liberation Army). Although in the beginning the EAM was organized and led chiefly by Communists, within a short time it had attracted such widespread support that it was in fact a National Liberation Front. At the peak of its power it was reported to have enrolled approximately one third of the population of the country. Its announced aim was to liberate Greece and assure the establishment of a truly representative and democratic postwar government. When Italy capitulated in 1943 the EAM obtained much war material from the surrendering Italian forces, with the result that ELAS greatly increased in numbers, became practically a regular army, and took over control of some three fourths of the country.

Meanwhile, after George II fled from Greece in April, 1941, he had eventually established his government, which was essentially a continuation of the Metaxas dictatorship, in Cairo. Metaxas himself had died, and the government in 1941 was headed by Premier Emmanuel Tsouderos. Though King George in 1942 announced the end of the dictatorship, the Tsouderos government remained strongly conservative, and it is not surprising, therefore, that when the three chief resistance groups made two basic demands upon it—that George II should not return to Greece until after a plebiscite and that the EAM should be represented in the government—Premier Tsouderos rejected both demands. The rejection was made contrary to the advice of the Greek cabinet but, it was said, on the advice of Churchill's government.

The policy of the British government toward Greek affairs appears to have been influenced primarily by two factors: extensive British investments in the Greek public debt and in Greek enterprises, and a British desire to check Soviet Russia's southward advance into the Balkans and the Mediterranean. Apparently Churchill and his advisers believed that British economic and strategic interests in Greece would be more likely to be advanced by King George's Rightist government-in-exile than by the Leftist

EAM. From 1943 on the British became increasingly anti-EAM and distributed arms and supplies to forces opposed to the ELAS.

Eventually, in September, 1944, a Greek government of national unity, which included representatives of the EAM, was formed in Cairo by George Papandreou, who was acceptable to the British. Three weeks later he, in turn, asked that British troops be dispatched to Greece, on the ground that an EAM–ELAS coup could be expected after the withdrawal of the Germans. On October 5 the British began their occupation of the country. Following the return of Papandreou's government to Athens a crisis arose because Rightists demanded the disarming of the ELAS. When the British General Scobie threw his support to the Rightists by calling for the disbandment of all guerrilla forces, the EAM ministers resigned from the cabinet; and the EAM central committee called for a protest mass meeting in Athens on December 3 and for a general strike on the following day. Government police fired upon the mass meeting, killing 23 and wounding 142. By December 5 British troops had begun fighting ELAS in Athens, and hostilities continued as heavy British reinforcements arrived. On January 11, 1945, however, a truce was concluded and subsequently the Varkiza Agreement was signed by representatives of the EAM and of the Greek government. By the terms of this settlement all arms were to be surrendered by ELAS within two weeks, the Communist Party and the EAM were to be recognized as legal political organizations, and the government was to grant an amnesty for all political crimes committed during the civil war.

But the amnesty was largely nullified by the harsh measures of the anti-Communist government forces and by local Rightist bands, so that—according to United Nations investigators—many guerrillas who might otherwise have laid down their arms and returned home were undoubtedly forced to retain them and flee to the hills in self-defense. Communist leaders, at the same time, urged their followers to keep their arms and to go underground or flee to Albania, Yugoslavia, or Bulgaria. As a result of this Communist policy, the military strength of ELAS was gradually re-established, and the subsequent internal conflict between the Greek Left and Right became linked with the general rivalry between Russia and the Western powers in the Balkans.

While the Greek people were still emotionally stirred by the civil war and further alarmed by fears of aggression by the pro-Soviet countries to the north, the government called for parliamentary elections. The EAM believed that a free vote would not be permitted and requested the Security Council of the United Nations to send a commission to Greece "to note that democratic conditions do not exist, and that the White terror continues." The Security Council took no action, but Great Britain, the United States, and France decided to send a mission of observers. In the elections on March 31, 1946, the royalist groups received the votes of about 710,000 of the 1,850,000 registered electors. So far as the parliament was concerned, Rightist parties won 234 of the 354 seats, the royalist People's Party alone securing 191 seats.

Eventually, on April 18, 1946, Constantine Tsaldaris, leader of the People's Party, formed a government consisting entirely of royalist ministers. On September 1, 1946, a plebiscite on the return of George II was held and resulted in a majority in favor of the return of the king. Most of the voters feared the Communists and hated the Bulgarians and their Slav supporters, the Russians; and apparently they hoped for strong Allied support against these foes if the king were restored. They therefore chose George II, despite his record of dictatorship, as the lesser of two evils. On September 28, 1946, the latter returned to Athens and for the third time mounted the throne of Greece.[8]

The land over which the king returned to rule was in dire straits. Before the war it was one of the poorest countries in Europe, and it had emerged from German occupation as one of the most thoroughly devastated areas in the world. In the period after the liberation it had received some $700,- 000,000 worth of foreign aid, chiefly from UNRRA, Great Britain, and the United States, but the country had failed to show any significant signs of economic recovery. When, in December, 1946, the premier went to Washington seeking a new loan from the United States, he learned that such a loan would be contingent on the establishment of a more competent government in Greece. In January, 1947, Tsaldaris therefore gave way as premier to a more moderate member of the People's Party, Dimitrios Maximos, who formed a ministry representing the Right and Center parties in parliament.

Meanwhile, after the king's return the scale of guerrilla activities had increased, and during the winter of 1946-1947 the "Democratic Army," consisting primarily of former members of ELAS, grew steadily from some 3,000 men to an estimated 13,000 in February, 1947. The Greek army appeared to be unable to destroy the guerrilla forces, partly because it lacked equipment and training for guerrilla fighting and partly because the rebels fled into Albania, Yugoslavia, or Bulgaria when pursued. At this time, when the Greek government was having difficulty in handling the Communist-led rebellion, Great Britain on February 24, 1947, informed the United States that, because of her own difficult economic situation, she would be obliged to end her economic assistance to Greece and Turkey on March 31, and to withdraw her troops from Greece soon thereafter. American statesmen believed that Britain's withdrawal would create a vacuum which Russia would quickly fill unless the United States acted at once. President

[8] On April 1, 1947, George II died and was succeeded on the throne by Paul I, his brother.

Truman therefore asked the Congress for emergency legislation authorizing the expenditure of $400,000,000 to enable Greece and Turkey to survive as "free nations." More than half of the amount, it was planned, would go for military supplies.

But since Greece had failed in the past to progress toward economic recovery in a measure commensurate with the amount of foreign aid received, the United States required the Greek government to undertake a series of economic and social reforms and to consult American advisers before making decisions which might effect the American aid program. In May, 1947, the first contingent of the military section of the American mission was sent to Greece and on July 14, 1947, Dwight P. Griswold, chief of the mission, and the first group of 130 civilian experts arrived in Athens. In August the first installment of arms, munitions, planes, trucks, food, and clothing for the Greek army arrived at the Piraeus, and Griswold announced the award of contracts to American companies for the rebuilding of highways, railways, and the principal ports of Greece. While the United States disclaimed any desire to intervene in Greek political affairs, American spokesmen informed Greek leaders that the United States would welcome a broader political regime. On August 23, the Maximos government resigned, and eventually a new one was created by Sophoulis, the Liberal leader, which consisted about equally of Liberals and members of the People's Party, with Tsaldaris as vice premier and foreign minister.

The United States also took steps to make the Greek military forces more effective against the guerrillas. In September, 1947, it agreed to supply the necessary materials to increase the Greek army to 200,000 men. In October it was announced that United States officers would be attached not only to the general staff of the Greek army but also to operational units. In November an agreement was reached for a joint Greek–United States army staff. In February, 1948, General James Van Fleet was appointed chief of the United States advisory and planning group. Thereafter steady gains were made by Greek forces against the guerrillas until in August, 1948, the guerrilla chief was forced to flee across the frontier into Albania.

By the fall of 1949 the guerrillas were finally defeated. Three factors primarily accounted for the government's success: (1) American equipment and financial support, which enabled Greece to put a larger army in the field; (2) the appointment of General Alexander Papagos, the Greek leader in 1940–1941, as supreme commander; (3) Yugoslavia's break with the Cominform (see page 941) and the subsequent refusal of Marshal Tito to permit Yugoslav aid and asylum to be given the Greek guerrillas.

Following the end of civil war in Greece, American officials wished to begin rapid and extensive economic reconstruction. They desired a rigorous reduction of government expenditures in order that more funds might be available for investment in industry and agriculture, and that as a result some of the glaring inequalities between the rich and the poor might be alleviated. But this program encountered at least the passive resistance of the civil service employees, the army, and King Paul and an influential group of the Athenian ruling class. On top of all this, the outbreak of the Korean War interfered, for it at once led to the abandonment of the proposals to reduce Greek military expenditures, which had been an essential part of the American economic plan.

A continuing obstacle to Greek recovery was the ministerial instability which prevailed down to 1953. Because of innumerable political parties and jealousies and ambitions of Greek political leaders, the kingdom had had some twenty-five changes in the ministry during the postwar period. Partly in consequence of American pressure, however, the proportional system was replaced by the majority system in the election of November, 1952, which resulted in a landslide victory for the reactionary Greek Rally Party, led by General Papagos. The latter had pledged his government to an honest administration, wide national economies, the revival of provincial life, the improvement of agricultural conditions, and full employment. His contemplated reforms seemed likely to encounter the opposition of some of his most influential supporters, but if Premier Papagos could hold his majority in line for the four-year term economic benefits might result.

In 1953 provision for increased co-operation between the United States and Greece was made in a pact signed on October 12 authorizing the United States to improve and use jointly certain airfields and naval installations in Greece. The Soviet government protested that the pact changed Greek territory into a base for the "aggressive NATO *bloc*" and created a threat to peace and security in the Balkans. It further declared that Greece had begun to carry out measures in preparation for a new war by permitting United States armed forces to be based in her territory. Greece rejected the Soviet protest.

But Greek co-operation was not limited to the United States. Negotiations were initiated among the Greek, Turkish, and Yugoslav governments which resulted in 1953 in a treaty of mutual friendship. This was followed in August, 1954, by the signing of an alliance and military convention by the same three countries, the text of the alliance having been first approved by the NATO Council. This twenty-year mutual defense treaty provided that the three states would: (1) settle disputes by peaceful means; (2) treat aggression "against one as an aggression against all"; (3) exchange mutual defense aid; and (4) establish a permanent ministers' council. Since the pact also called for consultation in the event of aggression against any NATO power, it indirectly tied Yugoslavia to NATO. Greece and Yugoslavia also signed an agreement for the construction of joint defenses along the Greek and Yugoslav frontiers with Bulgaria and Albania.

During 1954 the Greek government began to press for the incorporation of the island of Cyprus into the kingdom. According to Prime Minister Papagos, the government could no longer ignore the demand of the 400,000 Greeks in Cyprus to link their fate with that of all other Greeks. The Greek government preferred to reach a peaceful bilateral settlement with Great Britain, but threatened to bring the issue before the United Nations General Assembly. The British government maintained, however, that the UN Assembly had no powers to discuss a question which lay within the jurisdiction of a member government, and that the question of the status of Cyprus was such a question. Furthermore, it was asserted, "nothing less than continued sovereignty over the island could enable the United Kingdom to carry out its strategic obligations in Europe, the Mediterranean, and the Middle East." The British government did announce, however, that it had decided to introduce in Cyprus in the near future constitutional provisions for a legislature—partly nominated and partly elected—and for an executive council to take charge of departments. Nevertheless, in August, 1954, Greece requested the UN Assembly to order a plebiscite on the question of uniting Cyprus with Greece. The Assembly, however, postponed any decision on the request.

TURKEY

In the case of Greece the aid which President Truman called upon the American Congress to grant was to be used primarily to help the government of that country to suppress armed minorities within its borders, minorities which had the moral and material support of Communists in neighboring states. In the case of Turkey, on the other hand, there was no serious threat from any minority within the country. The aid which the United States was called upon to extend here was for the purpose of enabling Turkey to modernize and strengthen her armed forces so as better to resist "outside pressure" which was being brought to bear to force her to grant Soviet Russia a dominant position at the Straits.[9]

Throughout the war Russia had been dissatisfied with Turkey's attitude, especially in regard to the Straits, and even before the war ended the Soviet government had denounced its treaty of friendship and nonaggression with that country. Soon after the end of hostilities Russia demanded a revision of the Montreux convention governing the status of the Straits. During the war Turkey had kept a large army mobilized as a deterrent to German invasion, and after the threat from that country had passed she continued

[9] See page 828.

to maintain her armies on a war footing because of the fear of Soviet Russia. It had been possible for a nation of less than 19,000,000 inhabitants to sustain an army of more than 500,000 men largely because it had sold chrome and other critical materials to the belligerents for high prices and because it had received extensive foreign aid, especially from Great Britain. In 1947 the latter's announcement of her intended withdrawal of economic and financial support to Turkey was followed, as already indicated, by President Truman's request for American aid to the Ankara government.

By the subsequently signed agreement between the latter and the United States it was provided that an American mission by consultation with Turkish representatives should determine the state of Turkish military equipment in order that the United States should provide those military necessities which Turkey herself was not in a position to procure. The American mission decided that approximately $90,000,000 should be spent on the armed forces, $5,000,000 on arsenals and repair facilities for motorized equipment, and $5,000,000 on repairing and building roads. In September, 1947, American aid began to arrive—antiaircraft weapons, warning systems for defense against air attacks, planes, tanks, motor vehicles, and supplies of ammunition and ordnance equipment. Since, it was said, the United States was supplying Turkey with war surplus material at 10 per cent of its original cost, the latter was destined to receive a considerable quantity of supplies. But in 1948 expenditures for defense still constituted 48 per cent of Turkey's national budget.

Whether the Turks constituted one of the "free peoples" of the world in the Western sense of that word, however, was in 1948 still open to question. In the quarter-century prior to 1946 Turkey had had only one political party—the People's Party, founded by Mustapha Kemal.[10] Tentative experiments had once or twice been made with a two-party system, but they had been abandoned. The Communist Party had been outlawed, and in 1946 two attempts to establish Socialist parties had been suppressed. Nevertheless, there was in Turkey a growing popular opposition to the continuation of the one-party system, and in November, 1945, President Inönü proposed the replacement of the single-party rule by a parliamentary system. In 1946 a former premier was permitted to launch the Democratic Party, which criticized the restrictions on civil liberties and private enterprise, and demanded free, secret, and direct elections and the more rapid democratization of the country. The new party expected to be organized in time for elections in the spring of 1947, but the government unexpectedly advanced the date for voting to July, 1946. As the result of these elections the Democrats secured only 63 members out of 465 so that the People's Party still remained

[10] For conditions in Turkey between the wars, see pages 604–610.

strongly entrenched in the government. A member of that party became premier, and Inönü, the head of that party, was re-elected President by the National Assembly.

The Democratic Party had drawn its support chiefly from the younger members of the People's Party who held moderate Left-wing views. Another opposition party was created by older Right-wing members. This was the Nationalist Party which, on the whole, was inclined to be economically, politically, and religiously reactionary. The Nationalists questioned the wisdom of the secularization policies introduced earlier by Atatürk and were apparently supported by the Moslem clergy. In new parliamentary elections held in May, 1950, however, the Democratic Party won an overwhelming victory, securing 408 seats in the National Assembly to 69 for the People's Party and only one for the Nationalists. Most of the Democratic victors were newcomers to the National Assembly. Djelal Bayar, the leader of the Democratic Party, was elected president to succeed Inönü, and Adnan Menderes was chosen to be premier in a cabinet in which eleven of the fifteen members had never sat in the National Assembly.

President Bayar was primarily a civilian, in contrast with Atatürk and Inönü, both of whom had been military men. As a young man he had been a banker but had given up his business career to participate in the Young Turk movement which had brought about the revolution of 1908. Under Mustapha Kemal he had been minister of economy until 1924 and again in 1932. Between times he had been head of a bank. In 1937 he had become premier but had resigned in 1939. He was concerned that Turkey should be further liberalized and that Turkish business should be freed from state control and allowed to develop under private enterprise. Premier Menderes had been educated at the American College at Izmir. He had served for many years in the National Assembly, had been considered a moderate, and because of his interest in agriculture, had been a member of the government commission on land reform. The political change in 1950 seemed to indicate that Atatürk's transition period for training new leaders and preparing the way for liberal parliamentary government had at length borne fruit in a middle-class government.

Premier Menderes announced four major aims: (1) the attainment of a balanced budget by economies in state expenditures; (2) the "acceleration" of the economic system; (3) the preparation of an over-all plan; (4) the liberation of production from governmental and bureaucratic interference. Much of the money saved by economies elsewhere was to be directed into agriculture, which still constituted the cornerstone of the country's economy. Tractors, better seeds, improved techniques, and the training of village leaders in agricultural institutes were needed. It was hoped that reductions could be made in the item of national defense, by far the largest item in the budget, and that the reductions might be made up by American aid. The republic had already received some $117,000,000 in Marshall Plan aid and in 1952 she received more than $58,000,000 from the Mutual Security Administration for military expenditures.

Considerable economic and social progress occurred in Turkey in the postwar period. In 1945 a land reform act transferred state and ecclesiastical lands, reclaimed and uncultivated lands, and private lands in excess of some 240 acres to landless peasants and Turkish immigrants from Soviet Russia and the Balkans. By 1949 the government's program of reclamation and irrigation had begun to show results in the added acres which were under cultivation. Compared with the average of 19,026,700 acres under cereal production in 1946–1950, for example, the area in 1952 was some 24,710,000 acres. And increased yield resulted in a total cereal production in 1953 more than double that of the prewar years. Turkey was, in consequence, converted from an importer to an exporter of cereals.

In 1947 the Turkish government reversed its earlier policy regarding the investment of foreign capital in the country, and removed all restrictions on the entry of such capital and on the withdrawal of profits. In 1954, for instance, contracts were signed with British business companies for the building of grain elevators and for the construction of a dam and hydroelectric power station. In that year, too, the National Assembly passed a bill granting to foreign firms the right to prospect for and exploit oil in Turkey. But Premier Menderes planned not only to give foreign capital security but to give domestic industry the incentive of free competition. By 1953 the manufacture of alcoholic beverages and 49 per cent of the state merchant shipping had been returned to private enterprise, the state match monopoly had been abolished, and salt production for export had been turned over to private companies. But Turkey in 1953 was still plagued with an adverse balance of trade, diminishing though it was. In that year it curtailed the free list of imports, restricting them to those essential for the country's economic development. With a view to reducing the adverse balance of trade it imposed tariff duties on other commodities.

In May, 1954, Turkey once more had parliamentary elections. This time three parties entered candidates: the Democratic Party, which stood on its four-years record; the People's Party, which sought to find flaws in the government's record; and the Republican Nation Party, a recently organized Right-wing party, which seemed to favor religious reaction and advocated constitutional reform to that end. The first two parties both wanted to preserve the Atatürk reforms; both desired Turkey to develop along Western lines; both favored the republic's alignment with the West in NATO, the UN, and the Balkan alliance. But the party in power was aided by the prosperity of the farmers—80 per cent of the electorate—and won about 63 per cent of the votes. Menderes therefore continued as premier.

In the postwar years Turkey became closely integrated in the various organizations for collective security set up by the Western powers. In 1949 she became a member of the Council of Europe; in the Korean War she contributed troops in the interest of collective security; in 1952 she was admitted into the North Atlantic Treaty Organization; in 1953 she joined with Greece and Yugoslavia in a defense alliance, which was made more binding in 1954 by the political and military agreements signed at Bled. In addition, Turkey in 1954 signed a treaty with Pakistan, supplementing a friendship treaty of 1951, which provided for consultation between the two states concerning the best means to preserve peace and security but which contained no military clauses. In a sense Turkey thus served as an anti-Communist bridge connecting the Balkans with the Middle East.

Yugoslavia, Ex-Satellite of the Soviet Union

Yugoslavia's refusal meekly to become an Axis satellite like Hungary, Rumania, and Bulgaria had led in 1941 to a German invasion, a ruthless crushing of the people, and dismemberment of the country. Italy and Hungary had both seized Yugoslav territory, Albania and Bulgaria had been given parts of the kingdom, and two puppet states—Croatia and Montenegro—had been established with Axis quisling governments. Particular vengeance had been wreaked on the Serbs; thousands had been put to death by Ante Pavelich (the Axis puppet in Croatia), by the Hungarians in the territory which they had seized, and especially by the occupying Germans.

Although the Yugoslav army had officially surrendered unconditionally to the Germans on April 17, 1941, fighting never completely ceased. The first resistance group to emerge was led by Dragha Mihailovich, and was known as the Chetniks. This group consisted primarily of Serbs, favored a continuation of the monarchy, and was bitterly anti-Communist. In the back country and in the hills the Chetniks continued the military struggle against the Axis and compelled the latter to keep a considerable occupation force in Yugoslavia. Mihailovich was eventually raised to the rank of general and was appointed minister of war by King Peter's government-in-exile.

Following the German invasion of Russia a second resistance group, the Yugoslav Army of Liberation or the Partisans, appeared in Yugoslavia led by Josip Broz, a Croatian Communist "trained in the university of revolution," who went under the nickname of Tito. The latter's group, too, came originally from the Serbian section of Yugoslavia but Tito's greater activity and uncompromising hostility to the Axis gradually drew adherents from other parts of the country. The Partisans were largely Communist in leadership but Tito tried to conceal this by an appeal to a progressive nonparty patriotism. Unfortunately for Mihailovich, his hatred for the Communists led him and his Chetniks to begin collaborating in 1942 with Italians against the Partisans and eventually in 1944 even with the Nazis. Because of Stalin's support of Tito and because of the greater effectiveness of the Partisans against the Axis forces—they tied down in Yugoslavia during 1943–1944 between ten and twenty German divisions—the Allies sent supplies chiefly to "Marshal" Tito.

With the spectacular Russian military successes of 1944 and the increasing prospect that his country might soon be freed of German troops, King Peter took steps to align the resistance movements in Yugoslavia with his government-in-exile and thus, incidentally, to improve the likelihood of his return as the country's monarch. On June 1, 1944, he appointed Ivan Subasich, former governor of Croatia, to head his cabinet and authorized him to negotiate with Tito and Mihailovich. Eventually an agreement was signed by Tito and Subasich which provided that a plebiscite would be held to determine whether King Peter should return, that in the meantime a regency council would be appointed by the king and a provisional government would be formed to include ministers from each federal unit of Yugoslavia, that a constituent assembly would be elected within three months after the liberation of the country, and that until the convocation of the constituent assembly all legislative functions in Yugoslavia would be exercised by the Council of National Liberation, a Partisan body. Although Peter objected to some of these terms, in March, 1945, he appointed the regency council and the latter called upon Marshal Tito to form a new government. The new ministry included representatives of all linguistic and religious groups in Yugoslavia with Tito as prime minister. Subasich was foreign minister and five other former ministers in Peter's government-in-exile were given portfolios.

It was not long, however, until Tito and Subasich, holding altogether different views regarding the political and economic future of Yugoslavia, were unable to co-operate in the government. In August, 1945, Marshal Tito declared that the monarchy was completely incompatible with the new regime which was being developed in the country; two months later, Subasich resigned from the government because of Tito's attitude. General elections, with universal suffrage for all over eighteen, in November, 1945, resulted in Tito's National Front candidates winning over 80 per cent of the seats in each of the two chambers of the new National Assembly. The latter thereupon unanimously proclaimed the Federal People's Republic of Yugoslavia, consisting of six states: Serbia, Croatia, Slovenia, Bosnia-Herzegovina, Montenegro, and Macedonia. It also passed laws prohibiting the return of the king, intrusting the functions of the President of the Republic to a presidium, and gave Marshal Tito's ministry a vote of confidence. In December, 1945, Great Britain and France recognized the new Yugoslav government and in April, 1946, the United States did the same. A year later King Peter and his close relatives were deprived of their nationality and their property was ordered confiscated.

In the trials of "war criminals," "collaborators" or "conspirators," which were conducted in Yugoslavia beginning in 1946, the one which attracted most attention was that of Dragha Mihailovich, who was condemned to death and shot on July 17, 1946, despite protests from Great Britain and the United States. A number of others who had played prominent roles just prior to the Second World War were also shot or given prison sentences. In October, 1947, for instance, Dragoljub Yovanovich, leader of the Serbian Peasant Party, was sentenced to nine years' penal servitude for conspiracy against the government, and in the following February leaders of the Croatian Peasant Party, accused of being members of an illegal "Machek center," were similarly sentenced. Even leaders of the Catholic Church in Yugoslavia were arrested because of former collaboration with the Germans or because of opposition to the People's Republic. In 1948 the arrests of those accused of conspiring against the People's Republic still continued.

Yugoslavia's economy, which was backward before the Second World War, was completely disrupted by German occupation and exploitation, added to the inevitable war damage and looting. The systematic destruction of communications during the war by the resistance groups and by Allied bombing resulted in a situation which greatly hampered the rehabilitation of the country after hostilities ended. Even before the war a considerable part of Yugoslavia's economy had been state-owned; under Tito the state's part was greatly increased. By 1948 only about 10 per cent of the country's economic activities—limited largely to handicrafts, some retail trade, and agriculture—was left in private hands. Even in agriculture some steps had been taken to establish village co-operatives and the use of agricultural machinery rented by the state. In April, 1947, a Five-Year Plan for economic development during the years 1947–1951 was adopted, and like Russia's first Five-Year Plan it stressed the expansion of capital goods rather than the production of consumer goods. It was also designed to scatter industries into some of the less developed states, notably, Macedonia, Montenegro, and Bosnia-Herzegovina.

But the success of Tito's Five-Year Plan was very seriously endangered by the deterioration of relations between Yugoslavia and Russia which occurred in 1948. In the spring of that year the Russian Communist Party had criticized Tito and other Yugoslav Communist Party leaders because of their disregard of class differentiation in the peasant villages, their toler-

ance of unrestricted peasant landownership, their renunciation of the Marxist theory of classes and class war, and their behavior toward the Soviet
Union in the same manner as toward bourgeois states. But, in the words
of the Cominform announcement of June 28, the Yugoslav Communist
leaders, "instead of honorably accepting this criticism and setting out on
the road of Bolshevik correction of the errors committed, received the
criticism with resistance and hostility, and set out on the anti-party road of
categorical and general denial of their errors." Accordingly, the Cominform
Bureau, meeting in Rumania, expelled Yugoslavia and moved the headquarters of the Cominform from Belgrade to Bucharest.

Fundamentally, the issues in the break between the Cominform and
Yugoslavia seemed to be two. In the first place, Tito had evidently discovered that the success of his Five-Year Plan was dependent upon the
peasants and had accordingly reversed his attitude toward them just as
Lenin had done in introducing his Nep in Russia in 1921. In the words of
the Yugoslav Communist Party statement, "to force collectivization on
peasants while such tasks as industrialization are still in their early stages
... would provoke a political struggle that might disorganize the country's
economy." But Tito's reversal of policy seems to have come at a time when
Moscow was urging more drastic moves in the field of land policies, and a
clash in policies therefore resulted. For reasons connected with his own
country's welfare, Tito apparently refused to agree with the move planned
in Moscow and imposed on the Cominform parties. In other words, Tito
on this matter was in 1948 more a nationalist than an internationalist, and
there was in Russia's program no place for the development of a strong
nationalism in her satellites.

The second issue between Yugoslavia and the Cominform apparently
was whether the governments of Russia's satellites were to be subservient
to Moscow in their internal and foreign policies. The Russian Communists apparently expected the Communist leaders in their Cominform states
to be obedient and, when criticized, to recant and submit. Early in 1948,
for instance, Premier Dimitrov of Bulgaria had spoken favorably of an
Eastern European Federation, but when he had been rebuked by *Pravda,*
the Soviet Communist Party newspaper, he had thanked it for its "timely,
valuable and useful warning" and had abandoned his idea. Similarly, in
September, 1948, Vice Premier Wladslaw Gomulka of Poland, the active
leader of the Polish Communist Party, after having been repudiated as
leader by the party's executive committee because he supported a peasant
policy in Poland similar to Tito's, recanted and adopted the "party line."
It is possible that the Cominform's criticism and expulsion of Tito were
designed to serve as a warning to any other Communist leaders who might
be inclined to adopt a nationalist viewpoint.

In the ensuing months economic pressure was brought to bear against Yugoslavia by the members of the Cominform, which either reduced their trade with that country or boycotted it altogether. In January, 1949, for instance, Yugoslavia was excluded from the Council of Economic Mutual Assistance although she desired membership. Apparently the Soviet economic blockade was designed to bring Yugoslavia to her knees or at least to discredit Tito to such an extent that he might be driven from power by the discontented Yugoslavs. Tito was, perforce, compelled to turn to the Western democracies, particularly Great Britain and the United States, for aid. In the succeeding four years he received economic assistance to the extent of some $267,000,000, and obtained it without having political strings attached. Yugoslav trade, in consequence of the break with the Cominform, became completely reoriented.

But Tito's Five-Year Plan had to be scaled down and extended over a longer period. The cost of the import of capital equipment from the West, even with some assistance from the West, placed a heavy strain on Yugoslavia's economy. Furthermore, the need for increased rearmament after 1949 diverted manpower and materials from the original Five-Year Plan. In the ensuing years defense expenditures averaged twice what they had been before 1948, taking in 1953 some 20.5 per cent of the country's national income. Nevertheless, by 1952 a new machine-tool factory and a new steel plant were in production and in that year most Yugoslav industries had reached or surpassed the prewar level of production. By November, 1952, according to Tito, the state had invested $5,633,000,000 of its own funds in rebuilding and modernizing the country since the war. In June, 1953, however, it was announced that the great financial expenditures for heavy industries had caused stagnation in those producing consumers' goods and that a program of investment in industries producing the latter would be initiated.

As already pointed out, Yugoslavia did not follow Soviet Russia's lead in her agricultural program. Yugoslav land was not all nationalized. The size of holdings was limited, however, at first to approximately 85 acres but in 1953 to only 25 acres. A few state farms were established, and after 1948 some efforts were made by pressures of one sort or another to persuade or force peasants to organize collective farms, but in 1952 individual peasants still controlled 75 per cent of the agriculture. In that year, finally, the forced sale of agricultural products to the state at fixed prices was abolished and some controls and restrictions were removed in an effort to provide greater incentive to production. According to Marshal Tito, in the autumn of 1953, as a result of the government's decision to allow peasants to withdraw from the collectives and to sell their products in the open market the number of collective farms had decreased from about 6,000 to 2,000. But

Wide World photo

YUGOSLAVIA'S ANTI-RUSSIAN PRESIDENT
Marshal Tito

he pointed out the need for increased food supplies to take care of the country's increasing population and urged the peasants to "invest" their own efforts to match the government's investment in the manufacturing of farm equipment and in irrigation projects.

In January, 1953, Yugoslavia replaced her Soviet-type constitution of 1946 by one which was designed to remove the "tyranny of the administrative apparatus over the social initiatives of the workers" which was the root cause of "Soviet despotism," according to Yugoslav Communist leaders. The national parliament remained bicameral, with the lower house, the Federal Council, popularly elected. But the old upper house, the Council of Nationalities, was replaced by the Council of Producers, representing the agricultural, industrial, and craftsmen's groups. The former presidium was abolished as was also the cabinet. The latter was replaced by the Federal Executive Council, chosen by the parliament. The new constitution provided for a President to be chosen by the two houses of parliament in joint session as in France during the Third Republic. The President of the Republic was also to be president of the Federal Executive Council, supreme commander of the armed forces, and chairman of the National Defense Council. On January 14, 1953, Marshal Tito was elected the first President of the Republic. Even before 1953 the federal government had transferred to the six constituent states direct control of heavy industry, public utilities, and social welfare within their borders, and had increased their control of education, finance, industry, and local transport.

In international affairs Marshal Tito after the break with the Cominform at first tried to pursue a policy of neutrality in the "cold war." But after the Soviet Union and its satellites renounced their alliances with Yugoslavia in 1949, and especially after the North Korean attack on the Korean Republic in 1950, he apparently reassessed Yugoslavia's international position. Events in Korea seemed to indicate that, though Soviet Russia might not wish to become involved in a general war, she might not be averse to having her satellites attack Yugoslavia, and the satellites in various ways constantly conducted a "war of nerves" against Tito's republic. Desire for economic and military assistance from the West undoubtedly prompted Tito to turn more and more toward the Western democracies, and the desire of the latter to build as strong a defensive bulwark as possible against any future Soviet aggression led the West to seek to strengthen Yugoslavia.

In 1949 the United States changed its economic policy toward Yugoslavia and lifted its embargo on all except military goods. In that year and the next it gave financial assistance to Tito through loans and through Marshall Plan aid. It supported the successful move in 1949 to seat Yugoslavia on the UN Security Council in place of the Ukraine. In 1949–1950 Great Britain also negotiated commercial agreements with Yugoslavia providing for the exchange of British manufactured goods for Yugoslav raw materials. In 1952 Great Britain, the United States and France advanced millions of dollars to Tito to cover Yugoslavia's trade deficit. At length, in 1951–1952, the United States undertook to provide military supplies, equipment, and service for the Yugoslav armed forces and to provide tanks, heavy artillery, and jet aircraft in 1952–1953. Yugoslavia, Tito declared in May, 1953, would never forget the support of the Western democracies in the most difficult moment of her history. But when, in January, 1954, Milovan Djilas, chairman of the Yugoslav Communist Party and a vice-president of Yugoslavia, was expelled from the central committee of the party because articles which he had written were charged with being of a "revisionist character" pleasing to certain quarters in the West, President Tito denounced his error and asserted that, though Yugoslavia was drawing closer to Western democracy, this was only in international matters and not on internal questions.

Meanwhile, Yugoslavia's relations with her non-Communist neighbors had improved. In 1949 Yugoslavia and Italy signed their first postwar trade treaty and reopened their frontiers which had been closed since 1949. Although in 1953 relations between the two countries became strained by Italy's attempts to secure Trieste, in 1954 moderation prevailed on both sides and the Trieste area was eventually divided in a way satisfactory to the two countries. Meanwhile, relations between Yugoslavia and Greece had improved after the former in 1949 gradually closed her frontiers to Greek insurgents and thus contributed to the end of the civil war in Greece. Eventually, as already pointed out, Yugoslavia, Greece and Turkey signed a tripartite defensive alliance in 1953, aimed at placing 70 military divisions in the field against any Soviet attempt to reach the Mediterranean. This was supplemented by more specific political and military agreements in 1954. The extent to which Yugoslavia had become an ex-satellite of the Soviet Union is revealed by Marshal Tito's description of Russia as "the largest imperialist power with the most reactionary conceptions of relations between nations."

Nevertheless, the year 1953 saw—at least on the surface—a lessening of the tension between Russia and her satellites on the one hand and Yugoslavia on the other. Russia, Hungary, and Bulgaria resumed diplomatic relations with Yugoslavia, and in the Danube Commission the Russian and satellite delegates joined in electing a Yugoslav to the post of secretary, which had formerly been held by a Russian. The commission also approved a Yugoslav proposal to move the headquarters of the commission from Galatz in Rumania to Budapest. Relations continued to improve in 1954, too, with limited trade relations restored between Yugoslavia and Russia and Bulgaria and with discussions begun for a revival of trade relations with the whole bloc of countries behind the Iron Curtain.

Chapter XXX

NATIONALISM IN THE EAST

IN the closing years of the nineteenth century, nationalism—which had played such an important role in the history of Europe—began to penetrate the East. In the period between the two world wars it had manifested itself in a growing revolt against the domination of the West, which had forced several European governments to make concessions to the natives of their overseas possessions. In the years after the Second World War this wave of nationalism became a veritable flood which swept away many of the long-established systems by means of which the West had ruled the East. Political independence, dominion status, or more self-government were won by many of the Eastern peoples, whose subsequent efforts to rule themselves were, however, in some cases complicated by Communist attempts to overthrow their new governments.

The Arab League

Even before the First World War the Arabs had begun to be imbued with nationalism, and during that war—encouraged by British promises of independence and the establishment of an Arab kingdom—the Arabs had fought on the side of the Allies to escape from Turkish domination. At the close of the war Arab nationalists were bitterly disappointed when, instead of being allowed to establish an independent Arab kingdom, most of the Arabs were distributed in various small states which were handed over to Great Britain and France as mandates of the League of Nations. In the years between the wars, Arab nationalists continued their struggle, now waged against their former allies, and made some gains. Iraq and Egypt were able to achieve their independence, but with the exception of Saudi Arabia and Yemen the rest of the Arab lands remained under European domination. Independence of all Arabs from foreign control and the formation of a united Arab nation continued to be the basic aims of Arab policy.

To advance these aims, on March 22, 1945, representatives of Egypt, Iraq, Transjordan, Saudi Arabia, Syria, Lebanon, and Yemen, meeting in Cairo, established the Arab League. The League, representing some 45,000,000 Arabs, would have a Council, in which each member state would have one vote, which would supervise the enforcement of conventions concluded among its members and would study means of collaboration with other international organizations. Recourse to force for the settlement of disputes between members was forbidden, and decisions of the Council in disputes brought before it—not affecting the independence, sovereignty, or territorial integrity of member states—would be binding. The League was to be open to other independent Arab states, and, until Palestine gained its independence, the League Council would appoint an Arab representative for Palestine. The permanent secretariat of the League was set up in Cairo.

The aims of the League were declared to be the strengthening of friendship between members, the co-ordination of their political action, and the safeguarding of their independence. In 1946 the Council approved a proposal to grant common citizenship to Arabs of all Arab states, and in the following year the states in the League concluded a cultural treaty designed to draw the Arab countries together. This provided for the exchange of students, professors, and teachers, for the encouragement of educational visits among the different states, and for co-operation in maintaining and revising the Arab cultural heritage.

The League sought to influence the course of political events by presenting the Arab viewpoint and, if necessary, by bringing pressure to bear on non-Arab states. In 1946 it voted to support Egypt's demands for the early withdrawal of British troops, and in the following year it supported that country's demands for the union of the Sudan with Egypt under the latter's king. It also resolved to work for the independence of Libya, and planned to co-ordinate the efforts of all nationalist parties to obtain full independence for Tunisia, Algeria, and French and Spanish Morocco. It tried to prevent the partition or federalization of Palestine and sought to establish it as an independent Arab state. It threatened to bring economic pressure to bear against states which voted for the partition of Palestine, using especially the power of certain of its member states to handicap foreign countries in their production or transportation of petroleum within Arab territories. The influence of the Arab League seemed to account, in part, for the vacillating policy of some of the great powers in regard to the future of Palestine.

The League, however, had internal weaknesses arising from the rivalry existing between the Hashimite family and the family of King Ibn Saud of Saudi Arabia. King Abdullah represented the aspirations of the Hashimites and he was supported by Transjordan and Iraq, which were ruled by his family. Ibn Saud, who in 1924 had added Abdullah's father's kingdom of Hejaz to his realm, represented the opposition to the Hashimites, and to some extent at least he was supported by Syria and Lebanon which were anti-Hashimite. The Arab situation was further complicated by King Farouk of Egypt who was anti-Hashimite but who also apparently had ambitions of his own. This inherent disunity of the Arabs helps to explain their ineffective war against Israel in 1948, which is discussed below. Although the Arabs failed to prevent the establishment of Israel, the Arab League continued to play a role in international affairs, especially in the United Nations where its members usually constituted a bloc.

Egypt and the Sudan

At the close of the First World War, it will be recalled, Egyptians had insisted that their country be given its independence, and ultimately that independence had been recognized by the British government.[1] A treaty between Great Britain and Egypt had provided, however, for the stationing of British troops in the latter country. During the Second World War, Egypt had been saved from Axis subjugation largely by British empire troops operating within her borders in accordance with the terms of that treaty. But at the close of the war demands were made by Egypt that all British troops be evacuated and that negotiations should be initiated regarding the future of the Sudan.[2] Anti-British riots and violence occurred and the Arab League even announced that its member states would fight on the side of Egypt should war with Britain ensue.

In May, 1946, the British Labor government announced that it would withdraw from that country all British naval, military, and air forces. As evidence of its good intentions, on July 4, 1946, the Union Jack was lowered from the Cairo citadel where it had flown for some 64 years, and the Egyptian national flag was hoisted in its place. Three questions still remained, however, to be negotiated by the British and Egyptian governments: (1) the schedule to be followed by the British in evacuating their troops, (2) the future of the Anglo-Egyptian defensive alliance of 1936, and (3) the status of the Sudan. These negotiations were further complicated by Sudanese demands that they should be free to set up an independent democratic government of their own which would decide their country's future relations both with Egypt and with Great Britain.

Ultimately, in October, 1946, a draft treaty and two draft protocols were initialed by the representatives of Egypt and Britain. These so-called Sidkey-Bevin drafts provided for the cancellation of the treaty of 1936 [3] and for the establishment of a new defensive military alliance between the two countries, by the terms of which Egypt assumed only limited obligation. Whereas Great Britain would come to the aid of Egypt in case of any armed attack, Egypt would assist the British only if they became involved in war as the result of an attack on countries adjacent to Egypt. In respect to the

[1] See page 610.
[2] For the importance of the Sudan, see the footnote on page 611.
[3] See page 611.

Sudan, they provided that Egypt and Britain would set up a joint council to watch the progress of the Sudanese toward self-government and to recommend eventually suitable arrangements for ascertaining the wishes of the Sudanese regarding their political status. Although the Egyptian cabinet and Chamber of Deputies approved the Sidkey-Bevin drafts, the Nationalists, led by Mustapha Nahas Pasha, declared that they would launch a passive resistance campaign against any government which signed them. Further negotiations were carried on until March, 1947, when they broke down because Egypt refused to accept Britain's proposal of eventual self-government for the Sudanese, who should then be free to choose independence or association or union with Egypt.

Following the collapse of Anglo-Egyptian negotiations the British took steps to facilitate the development of autonomous political institutions in the Sudan. Eventually in May, 1952, a self-government statute was adopted by a Sudanese legislative assembly. Under it the Sudan was to have a bicameral parliament. Of the fifty members of the upper house, twenty were to be named by the governor-general and thirty were to be elected. The prime minister was to be chosen from the members of the lower house and his cabinet was to be responsible to the parliament. The British governor-general, however, was still to retain wide powers, being responsible for foreign affairs, the civil service, and the approval of the speakers of the two houses of the parliament. In case of a constitutional breakdown, he was to have full legislative and executive authority. On October 22, 1952, the British government approved the statute.

By this time in Egypt the Nationalists had once more gained control of the parliament and Mustapha Nahas Pasha had become premier, with the avowed aims to abrogate the Anglo-Egyptian treaty of 1936, to drive the British out of the Suez Canal zone, and to unite the Sudan with Egypt. In fact, in 1951 the Egyptian parliament had unilaterally abrogated the treaty of 1936 and proclaimed Farouk "King of Egypt and the Sudan." The British had countered by increasing their military forces in Egypt and seizing the Suez Canal. Generally disturbed conditions within Egypt, coupled with widespread governmental corruption and an increasing antagonism to King Farouk, led in July, 1952, to a *coup d'état* by army officers under General Mohammed Nagib, which deposed Farouk, suppressed political parties, suspended the constitution, and ultimately proclaimed Egypt a republic. General Nagib became president and Colonel Gamal Abdel Nasser premier.

The army officers desired to settle all Anglo-Egyptian disputes as quickly as possible because they believed that these disputes prevented Egypt's cooperation with the West and also caused instability within Egypt. In the interest of settling the dispute over the Sudan Nagib's government agreed to self-determination for the Sudanese, and this in turn made possible a new Anglo-Egyptian agreement on the Sudan which was signed in February, 1953. A Sudanese constituent assembly was to draft a permanent constitution and electoral law and to decide whether the Sudan should be linked with Egypt or be independent. In elections held during November and December, 1953, the National Unionists won a decisive majority of the seats, and on January 6, 1954, the leader of that party, Ismail el-Azhari, who had been educated at Beirut University and had served for many years in the Sudan ministry of education, was chosen the first prime minister of the Sudan. Under the agreement of February, 1953, the Sudan would now enter the transitional stage of self-government which was to end in union with Egypt or independence after a period of not more than three years, provided that by that time that country's army, police, and administration had been Sudanized.

In 1954 Anglo-Egyptian negotiations regarding the Suez Canal zone were again undertaken and this time, despite difficulties, they eventuated in an agreement which was signed on October 19. Both sides made concessions in the effort to remove sources of mistrust and friction and in the belief that an agreement would improve relations between Egypt and Britain and would contribute to the maintenance of peace and security. By the terms of the agreement, (1) British forces would be withdrawn from the canal zone within twenty months, (2) Egypt would assume responsibility for the base and would permit Egyptian and British firms to maintain and operate some of the installations, (3) Britain would be allowed to return to the base in case of an armed attack on Egypt or any other Arab state or on Turkey, (4) Egypt and Britain would consult in case of a threat of attack on any of these states, (5) the agreement would last seven years. This settlement, declared Premier Nasser, constituted "a turning point in the history of Egypt," and inaugurated "a new era of friendly relations . . . between Egypt and Britain and the Western countries."

For some time there had been dissension within the group of army officers who had led the revolution in 1952. Apparently there was rivalry and jealousy between Nagib and Nasser. At any rate, on November 14, 1954, President Nagib was relieved of office and placed under surveillance on the ground that he had planned with the Communists and the Muslim Brotherhood to undo the revolution. The cabinet decided that Premier Nasser should take over the duties of the head of the state but that the office of president should remain vacant for the time being. What the future held for Egypt seemed open to question.

The United Kingdom of Libya

To the west of Egypt lies an area of some 700,000 square miles—mostly desert—with a population of some 1,250,000, which before the Second World War was part of the Italian "empire." Generally speaking, Libya consisted of two major divisions, Tripolitania and Cyrenaica, in both of which Islam is universal and Arabic the dominant language. In Italian efforts to conquer the region more protracted resistance was encountered in Cyrenaica than in Tripolitania, partly because Egypt offered the Cyrenaican fighting men a refuge when hard pressed. During the Second World War a Libyan Arab Force of Cyrenaicans was organized on its own initiative to fight the Italians in the name of Emir Idris, leader of the Moslem religious fraternity of the Senussi. This force returned to Cyrenaica as "liberators" with the British Eighth Army in 1942. Because the Tripolitanians were liberated without much effort on their part, the Cyrenaicans regarded themselves as the more patriotic Libyans.

In the immediate postwar years the British set up separate military administrations for Cyrenaica and Tripolitania. In the peace negotiations the great powers were unable to agree upon the fate of Italy's former colonies and so, in accordance with the peace treaty with Italy, the question was referred to the UN General Assembly. The political committee of the Assembly in 1949 proposed that Libya should become independent after ten years, that in the meantime the British should administer Cyrenaica for that period and Tripolitania for two years, and that from 1951 to 1959 Italy should serve as trustee for the latter. Largely because of the opposition of the Arab states to Italy's return as a trustee, the proposals were defeated in the Assembly, however. Instead, the latter voted that a unified Libya should become independent by January 1, 1952, and that meanwhile a UN commissioner should administer the region.

A Libyan national assembly drafted a constitution providing for a federal democratic kingdom with Emir Idris as king. On December 24, 1951, final powers were handed over to the legally constituted Libyan government by the British administrators. Libya's first parliamentary elections were held on February 19, 1952, and the inaugural meeting of the parliament occurred in Benghazi, the capital of Cyrenaica, on March 25. To alleviate the rivalry between Tripoli and Benghazi, the parliament reconvened in the former city on April 27. Thus a people, who for two thousand years had been subjects of larger political organisms, had their national aspirations at last recognized.

Syria and Lebanon

In the years between the wars, Syria and Lebanon had been constantly disturbed by the struggle between Arab nationalism and French imperialism.[4] Although eventually, in 1936, France had signed treaties with the Syrian and Lebanese governments looking toward their full independence at the end of a three-year transition period, on the eve of the Second World War the French high commissioner had dissolved the Syrian parliament and suspended the Syrian constitution. In 1941, however, British imperial and "Fighting French" forces had launched an invasion of Syria to oust the pro-German Vichyite regime functioning there, and at that time the commander of the "Fighting French" in the Middle East, had proclaimed the independence of Syria and Lebanon. Later in the year the "Fighting French" authorities had terminated the French mandate, and the two states had become sovereign, independent republics. In 1945 they were invited to attend the San Francisco Conference of the United Nations.

Nevertheless, contrary to the desire of the Syrian Nationalists, French and British troops continued to occupy Syria and Lebanon after the end of the Second World War, and in the summer of 1945 fighting occurred in Damascus and elsewhere between French troops and Syrians. Late in that year the French and British governments, which appeared to be suspicious of each other's motives in regard to Syria, signed an agreement providing for the withdrawal of their forces from both Syria and Lebanon, leaving only sufficient troops to guarantee security until the United Nations decided on the organization of collective security in that region. The Syrians and Lebanese were wholly dissatisfied with what they considered the dilatory nature of this agreement, and in February, 1946, they asked the UN Security Council to recommend the total and simultaneous evacuation of British and French troops from their countries. Although the Council took no decisive action, in the next month the French and British agreed to complete their evacuation by late summer. The evacuation was carried out as announced, and a national holiday was observed in Syria to mark the departure of all foreign troops. In November Syria was elected a nonpermanent member of the UN Security Council.

The Syrians, who are primarily Moslem Arabs, established a parliamentary government, but in the years immediately after the war were largely dominated by some twenty to forty families drawn from the four main towns. The Lebanese, a slight majority of whom are Arab-speaking Christians, also established a parliamentary republic. Their small state, only about

[4] See pages 612–613.

a third the size of Belgium, owed its separate existence largely to memories of the ill-treatment of its Christians by Moslems in the nineteenth century.

Iraq and Jordan

Arab nationalism among the Iraqi, which in the period between the wars had forced Great Britain to recognize Iraq as an independent state rather than as a mandate, in 1948 was again aroused against the British. In a new treaty of alliance with Iraq, signed in January, 1948, Great Britain gave up her part ownership and management of the Iraqi railways as well as her rights in the management of the port of Basra. She also turned her air bases in Iraq over to the latter, though they were to be available for British use until peace treaties became effective with all ex-enemy powers—which might be a considerable time. A joint defense board, with equal Iraqi and British representation, was to co-ordinate defense policy, and Iraq agreed to standardize her armaments with those of Britain and to employ Britons if foreign military instructors were required. All facilities were to be given in Iraq to British forces in case of war or the threat of war. Although this treaty was readily signed by Iraqi representatives in Britain, in Iraq violent opposition to it appeared and the treaty was rejected. By 1953 Iraqi nationalists were demanding nationalization of Iraqi oil and the abrogation of Britain's right to maintain air forces in the country.

In Transjordan, too, concessions to nationalism had to be made. In the period between the wars this sparsely settled Arab state was a British mandate of the League of Nations, administered by the British high commissioner for Palestine and Transjordan. But the postwar period saw this small country transformed from a mandate to an independent kingdom linked with Britain merely in an alliance. An Anglo-Transjordan treaty, concluded in 1946 and modified in 1948, provided for a mutually defensive alliance between the two countries and for the stationing of British armed forces in Transjordan. On May 25, 1946, the independence of the country was formally proclaimed under King Abdullah. After the incorporation of the Arab remnant of Palestine the name of the state was changed to the Hashimite Jordan Kingdom, usually referred to as Jordan.

Palestine and Israel

The conflict which raged in Palestine from 1918 to 1939 between Jewish Zionism and Arab nationalism and which complicated Great Britain's task as a mandatory power there has already been described in some detail.[5]

[5] See pages 613–616.

But after twenty years of repeated efforts to solve the Palestinian question, when the Second World War broke out Great Britain seemed to be about as far as ever from a final settlement of the Arab-Jewish conflict. In fact, from a strategic and diplomatic viewpoint the situation had become even more difficult for Britain. Further development of Arab nationalism, the growing solidarity of the Arab states as indicated by the organization of the Arab League and the latter's support of the Palestinian Arab demands, and the presence of millions of Moslems in India and Egypt, all these factors—plus Britain's need for bases and Moslem support in the Middle East—forced the British government to give careful consideration to Arab demands. At the same time, the continued propaganda of the Zionists, the terrible sufferings of the Jews at the hands of the Nazis, and the ardent desire of a million or more European Jews to find a haven of refuge somewhere, convinced world opinion that something must be done for the Jews. President Truman of the United States, for instance, in 1945 urged the British government to admit 100,000 Jews to Palestine at once, a step which was vigorously opposed by the states in the Arab League and by Moslem organizations in India.

Britain was eager to associate the United States with her in the settlement of the Palestinian question, and consequently invited the latter to join in setting up an Anglo-American Commission of Enquiry to examine the question of European Jewry and to review the Palestinian problem in the light of that examination. The report of this commission was published as a British Blue Book on May 1, 1946. It recommended, among other things, that 100,000 Jews be admitted into Palestine as rapidly as conditions would permit, but pointed out that Palestine alone could not meet the emigration needs of Jewish victims of Nazi persecution. It therefore further recommended that Great Britain and the United States, in association with other countries, should endeavor immediately to find new homes for Jewish refugees. The report was at once denounced by both Jews and Arabs.

Palestine continued to be torn by acts of terrorism and violence, chiefly at the hands of the Jewish underground. These culminated on July 22, 1946, in the wrecking of the King David Hotel in Jerusalem, headquarters of the British Army in Palestine and of the secretariat of the Palestinian government. Scores were killed, including several high British officials. The Jews, Prime Minister Attlee contended, were adopting in Palestine "some of the very worst of the methods of their oppressors in Europe." In the late summer of 1946 the British were forced to take drastic military and naval measures to cope with Jewish terrorism as well as to prevent the illegal entry of Jews into Palestine.

During the summer of 1946 British and American officials met in London to examine and discuss the Anglo-American commission's report. Out of their discussion came a recommendation for a Palestinian constitution providing for federalization. This was followed by the British government's calling of a roundtable conference to meet in London, to be attended by representatives of the Palestinian Arabs and Jews and by representatives of the states in the Arab League. Since the Palestinian Arabs and Jews refused to attend the conference, nothing was accomplished. The British then made one more effort to reach an agreed solution by putting forward new proposals in February, 1947. When these were rejected outright by both Jews and Arabs, the British government decided to refer the whole problem of Palestine to the United Nations.

At a special session of the General Assembly of the United Nations a special committee was organized to investigate the Palestinian problems, and this committee, after visiting Palestine and a number of refugee camps in Europe, made its report on August 31, 1947. The majority recommended the establishment of two independent states, one Jewish and the other Arab, neither to include Jerusalem, which would be under international administration. During the General Assembly debates on the Palestine problem, Great Britain announced that, regardless of the Assembly's action, she was surrendering her mandate and planning to complete the evacuation of her troops in the summer of 1948. Thanks largely to the support of the United States and Russia, particularly of the former, the Assembly on November 29, 1947, voted in favor of partition. There was rejoicing among the Jews but consternation and disappointment among the Arabs, who threatened to use force to prevent the execution of the plan.

Recruits for guerrilla operations in Palestine were enlisted in all the Arab countries, but the Arab League apparently decided not to use its national armies until after the British had withdrawn their forces. Although for some years the Jews had been directing their underground forces against the British troops and officials in Palestine, there had during this period been little conflict between the Jews and the Arabs. With the announcement of the partition and Arab opposition to it, however, open conflicts between the two groups began. During the next three months widespread disorders resulted in the gradual breakdown of economic life. Arab hostility to the United States and its possible effect on American oil and other interests in the Middle East apparently provoked an anti-Zionist reaction in Washington. Suddenly, on March 19, 1948, the United States representative in the Security Council announced that his country's support of partition was withdrawn. He proposed instead a temporary United Nations trusteeship for the whole country. The Security Council accordingly called another special meeting of the General Assembly for April 16.

Meanwhile, in Palestine the Jewish military position had steadily improved, so that by the middle of May there was a well-defined area of Jewish control which included the most important parts of the territory assigned to the Jewish state by the partition plan. On May 14, when a UN commission was attempting to negotiate a truce in Palestine and when the General Assembly was debating the idea of a trusteeship, the establishment of the State of Israel was proclaimed in Tel Aviv. At once, without even notifying the American delegation in the General Assembly, President Truman announced that the United States recognized this "provisional government as the *de facto* authority of the new state of Israel." At midnight of May 14 the British mandate in Palestine ended.

On the following morning the regular armed forces of Egypt, Transjordan, Iraq, and Syria advanced into Palestine. Within a week the Jews had been driven from the northern outskirts of Jerusalem, the Egyptians had occupied Gaza and Beersheba, the Syrians were fighting south of Lake Galilee, and Tel Aviv had been bombed several times from the air. An American demand that the Security Council should declare that a "breach of peace" within the meaning of Article 39 of the UN Charter existed in Palestine was rejected, but the Council did vote to call on all governments and authorities to issue cease-fire orders to their military forces. Open fighting in Palestine ended on June 11, when a four-weeks truce became effective. By that time the Arabs had occupied a substantial part of the area allotted them and had forced the unconditional surrender of the Jewish quarter of the Old City of Jerusalem. The Arab quarters of New Jerusalem remained in Jewish hands, however.

A tentative plan for a settlement, put forth by Count Folke Bernadotte, the United Nations mediator, was flatly rejected by both Jews and Arabs, and on July 9 fighting was resumed. This time the Jewish forces gained at the expense of the Arabs. The Security Council again issued a cease-fire order with threat of sanctions attached; the Arabs, under considerable pressure from Britain, complied, and fighting again came to an end. Some 300,000 Arabs had by this time fled for safety from Jewish areas to neighboring Arab states, and on July 22 the provisional government of Israel decided in principle not to allow the general return of these refugees to their homes. During the rest of 1948 fighting and cease-fire orders alternated with a monotonous regularity. Nonmilitary violence continued, too, and culminated on September 17 in the murder of the UN mediator, Count Bernadotte, by members of the so-called Stern gang of Jews. But by August, 1949, thanks largely to the efforts of Ralph Bunche, the acting UN mediator, armistices had been signed between Israel and each of her four Arab neighbors and hostilities had "officially" ended.

By this time it was obvious that the Arabs had failed, first, in their efforts to prevent the partition of Palestine and the establishment of an independent Jewish state, and, second, in their efforts to reduce the size of Israel to a minimum. The Arabs, especially those in Egypt, were inclined to blame

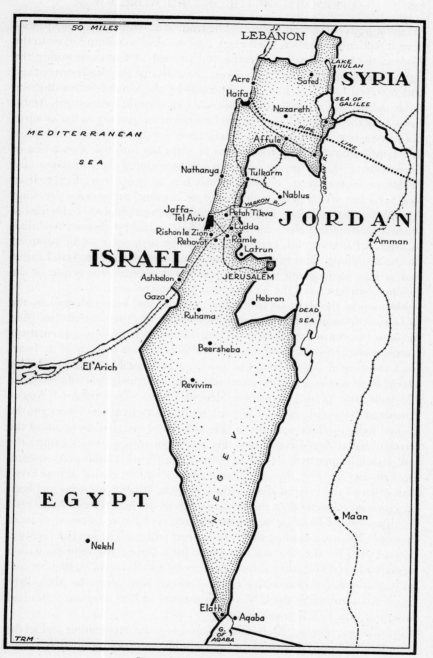

ISRAEL AND HER NEIGHBORS

the great powers for their failure. "The trouble is," complained one prominent Egyptian newspaper, "that every time we deal a crushing blow to the Zionists the big countries intervene and prevent us from continuing the fight." There was some feeling among the Arabs that they had been tricked and betrayed by Great Britain, influenced by the United States. But the Arab failure was certainly the result, also, of disunity among the Arabs. For a time the latter had been united by a common hostility to the Zionists, but after a few months this unity had been destroyed by internal rivalry and family disputes. This rivalry was brought out into the open when in September, 1948, one group of Arabs had announced the formation of a "Palestine Government" at Gaza which was recognized by Egypt, Iraq, and Syria but which was characterized as "strange and serious" by King Abdullah of Transjordan. The rivalry was further emphasized in December when a meeting of Palestinian Arabs in Jericho had proclaimed Abdullah as king of Palestine and Transjordan, and the parliament of Transjordan had unanimously approved the decision to unite the two. The Arab League was at least temporarily weakened when it denounced the action of the Jericho conference and the Transjordan parliament.

Meanwhile, the territory controlled by Israel had been enlarged by the military operations of Israeli troops. Meanwhile, too, preparations had been made to transform the provisional government of Israel into a permanent constitutional regime. On January 25, 1949, elections were held in Israel for a constituent convention. The moderate socialist Maipai Party, led by David Ben-Gurion, the provisional prime minister of Israel, won 46 of the 120 seats; the Leftist opposition Mapam Party, which opposed Anglo-American "imperialism" and favored an Eastern orientation, won 19; the United Religious bloc won 16; the Heruth Party, the political organ of the terrorist Irgun Zvai Leumi, won 14; and eight minor parties gained the rest. Israel, it appeared, would have to struggle with a multiparty system. On February 17, 1949, the Israeli constituent assembly elected as first President of Israel the veteran Zionist leader, Chaim Weizmann, who had been provisional president since the proclamation of the new state in May, 1948. By this time the Israeli government had received the recognition of more than thirty states, including most of the great powers. The interim constitution adopted for the new state provided for a democratic republic with a figurehead president, elected for five years by a unicameral legislature, and with ministerial responsibility to the national legislature. In May, 1949, Israel was admitted to the UN, and by the end of 1950 sixty-one states had recognized the Israeli government.

But the neighboring Arab states refused to grant recognition and so the boundaries between them and the new republic were not legally fixed. Israel barred Jordan's access to the Mediterranean and, after the latter incorporated the Arab remnant of Palestine, Jordan barred Israel's most direct route from Tel Aviv to Jerusalem and held the Jewish quarter of the Old City. Arab-Israeli relations were further disturbed by Israel's refusal to permit the return of the Arabs who had fled from Palestine in 1948. These refugees, numbering 881,000 in 1952, were compelled to live on relief in the Arab countries where they had taken refuge. In 1953 and 1954 clashes along the borders between Israel and the adjoining Arab states were frequent.

Israel's chief domestic problem was to improve her economic life so that it could support an increasing population. In the five years after 1948 some 700,000 immigrants poured into Israel. Millions of dollars in aid were received from American and other agencies to assist in housing projects and in economic development. By 1953 the area under cultivation had been increased five-fold and food production four-fold; iron, copper, and phosphate mines had been opened; modern industrial establishments for the production of chemicals, textiles, and metal and food products had been built; and a merchant marine had been launched.

Iran

The nationalistic efforts under Riza Shah Pahlevi to modernize Iran and to force better terms from Western capitalism in the years between the wars have already been outlined (see pages 617–619). Although some progress was made, in the period after the Second World War most of the Iranians were still desperately poor, undernourished, and uneducated. Approximately 80 per cent of the country's 16,500,000 people were dependent on agriculture, but only 10 per cent of the land was cultivated and 15 per cent used for grazing. Agricultural development had been handicapped by scarcity of water and by unfavorable climate. But it had also been handicapped by an absentee-landlord system which took from the peasant some 80 per cent of his production and by agricultural methods which were wholly out-of-date.

Shah Mohammed Riza Pahlevi, who had succeeded his father on the latter's abdication in 1941, and some of his more enlightened advisers sought at the close of the Second World War to change some of these conditions. Eventually, with the advice of American consultant firms, a Seven-Year Plan to increase the country's agricultural and industrial production and raise living standards was adopted in 1949, and the parliament allocated all oil revenue for the ensuing seven years to finance the contemplated capital improvements. The next step was to secure the parliament's ratification of the 1949 supplemental agreement to the Anglo-Iranian Oil Company (AIOC) concession, by the terms of which Iran's share in the company's earnings would be about doubled.

But throughout 1950 the parliament deferred action and in the face of the determined opposition the government finally withdrew the agreement. The processing of oil at the AIOC refinery at Abadan, the largest refinery in the world, constituted Iran's largest single industry, employing in all its operations some 100,000 Iranians. But those who opposed ratification of the new agreement pointed out that the British government received more in taxes on AIOC profits than Iran did in royalties, and although the new agreement would increase Iran's share, opponents of ratification wanted Iran to obtain even more. Some demanded that Iranians should have a greater share in the management of the company; others demanded nationalization of the company altogether. Mohammed Mossadegh, leader of the National Front which had twice prevented ratification of the 1949 agreement by the parliament, proclaimed that nationalization would cure all the country's ills, that Iran's disasters lay solely in the existence of the Anglo-Iranian Oil Company. But Premier Ali Razmara, who shared the shah's reform ambitions, believed it necessary to co-operate with the West to implement the Seven-Year Plan and stanchly opposed all demands for nationalization. In consequence, on March 7, 1951, Razmara was murdered, "a martyr to reason and compromise." On April 28 the parliament then voted unanimously to nationalize the oil industry and two days later Mossadegh became premier. In his initial broadcast as the new premier he declared that all Iran could live in ease and affluence once the oil was nationalized.

The Iranian oil situation now became an international problem. The United States sought to persuade Great Britain to accept nationalization and attempt to work out some reasonable settlement with Iran, to take the long view—even at some sacrifice to herself—of the regional interests of the Middle East in order to prevent the extension of the Soviet empire into Iran. But the British believed that surrender to Iranian demands would only encourage extremists in the Arab oil-producing countries to denounce the oil agreements which had been negotiated with them, that it would open the way to endless blackmail of the West. The British did accede, however, to the American request not to use military force without prior consultation with the United States. Instead, Great Britain took the case to the International Court of Justice to try to force Iran to arbitrate with the oil company. She also appealed to the UN Security Council. Mossadegh flew to New York to present Iran's case, and the council postponed a decision. In June, 1952, Mossadegh presented Iran's case before the International Court, claiming that the court had no jurisdiction, and the court a month later ruled that the dispute did fall outside its jurisdiction.

Upon Mossadegh's return from The Hague, he demanded dictatorial powers from the parliament but was refused. His consequent resignation was followed by widespread riots, fomented by his supporters and by the Communist Tudeh Party, and a few days later he was reappointed premier and given special powers to rule by decree for six months. His first decree as dictator was to impose a 20 per cent tax on landowners, half of the tax to go to the tenant farmers and half to village councils for local needs and improvements. He further attacked the feudal agrarian system by forbidding work without wages and levies on peasants. On the other hand, he stopped the agrarian program of the shah, who wished to sell the royal estates to the peasants on easy terms. He became more autocratic as time passed. In September he purged the judges in the civil courts and dissolved all special courts; in October, 1952, he rid himself of the Senate, which had showed some opposition to him.

Meanwhile, after Anglo-Iranian negotiations had become deadlocked, Iranian troops in September, 1951, had seized the Abadan refineries and those members of the British staff not already withdrawn were ordered to leave. During the early months of 1952 the International Bank for Reconstruction and Development attempted to find a basis for resuming the production of oil, but to no avail. Mossadegh, in turn, sought to find purchasers for Iranian oil and when the British announced that the oil was theirs and could not be sold, he closed the British consulates within Iran. In August the Iranian government informed Great Britain that it was willing to reopen negotiations with the AIOC within the framework of the nationalization law, but it attached conditions which the British would not accept. Counter proposals by Prime Minister Churchill and by President Truman were in turn rejected by Mossadegh, and in October Iran finally broke off diplomatic relations with the British. In February, 1953, new Anglo-American proposals were made to Iran, but they were rejected one month later by Mossadegh who, however, still left the door open for negotiations. Earlier in the year Mossadegh had informed the Soviet government that Iran, planning to nationalize the Iranian fisheries industry, would not extend the Soviet-Iranian fishery agreement which expired on January 31. Russia accepted the Iranian decision but reminded Iran of the latter's obligation not to grant a fishing concession to any other foreign power in the next twenty-five years.

In the first half of 1953 Mossadegh further increased his power. In January he demanded and received a one-year extension of his position as dictator. During February tension between the more moderate shah and his nationalistic premier increased to the point that the shah considered leaving the country, and for a time Iran was greatly disturbed by demonstrations—pro-shah or pro-Mossadegh. The premier sought to restrict the shah's authority, declaring that he should reign but not rule. By July, Mossadegh, through his National Front deputies, had managed to destroy the Chamber of Deputies' quorum and was thus able to rule about as he pleased. In August, a referendum held in the provinces resulted, it was announced, in an overwhelming demand for the dissolution of the Chamber.

But the Iranians had been promised that nationalization of the AIOC would bring them prosperity. Although in 1953 Iran sold some oil at 50 per cent discount to Japanese and Italian purchasers, the loss of the oil royalties had not only destroyed all gains expected from the Seven-Year Plan but had crippled the country's economy and contributed to a spiral of inflation. Even the United States showed its disapproval of Mossadegh's intransigence, when in July, 1953, President Eisenhower refused the premier's request for more economic aid on the ground that if Iran would settle with the British it could exploit its own rich resources and would not need outside help.

In August, after an abortive attempt of the shah to replace Mossadegh as premier by General Fazollah Zahedi, the monarch and his wife fled by airplane to Rome. Mossadegh at once sent troops to occupy the royal palaces and the parliament building and ordered the arrest of all opposition deputies and of about 100 others charged with complicity in the royal plot. But apparently the anti-Mossadegh, pro-shah sentiment was stronger than he expected. On August 19 the troops turned against their officers and the mobs shifted to the support of the shah. After pitched battles and mob violence, causing the death of hundreds and the burning of a number of buildings, the pro-shah forces gained control of Teheran and arrested Mossadegh. Three days later the shah returned to his capital, explaining that when the constitution was violated, the Chamber dissolved, the army disintegrated, and the treasury funds dissipated, then the law had to be carried out. It appeared that the hereditary ruler and the army sought to maintain the constitution whereas the prime minister, who began with a reputation as a democrat, had attempted to set up a personal dictatorship. In November the former premier was brought to trial on charges of defying the shah, attempting to overthrow the regime, and illegally dissolving the Chamber of Deputies. In the ensuing weeks the supreme court was re-established, the Senate was re-convened, the shah resumed the distribution of crown lands to the peasants, and in November Premier Zahedi announced that state lands also would be distributed to the peasants and workers.

Soon after his appointment the new premier had expressed the hope that the oil problem could be settled with due regard for the nationalization law and Iranian national aspirations. In December, 1953, diplomatic relations were resumed between the Iranian and British governments and it was announced that they would negotiate a settlement of the oil problem. In April, 1954, a consortium was organized, consisting of the Anglo-Iranian Oil Company and one Dutch, one French, and five American oil companies. Negotiations between representatives of this consortium and of the Iranian government eventually brought an agreement which was signed on September 19. Under the provisions of this agreement, subsequently ratified by the Iranian Chamber of Deputies, two companies would be formed—one to concern itself primarily with exploration and production, the other with refining. Five of the seven directors of each would be named by the consortium and two by Iran. The latter, in turn, agreed to pay the AIOC £25,000,000 in ten years, beginning on January 1, 1957, and the other oil companies were to pay the AIOC for their share in the consortium.

India and Pakistan

Under the Government of India Act, which became effective in 1937, Indians had reached the point where at the outbreak of the Second World War a limited electorate controlled the eleven provincial ministries and chose a majority of both houses of the Indian national parliament, but did not control the national government.[6] The act had failed to grant India dominion status, however, and was therefore unsatisfactory to the Congress Nationalists. Soon after the outbreak of the war, because they felt that Britain's assurances regarding India's future independence were too vague, the Congress Nationalists had instructed all Congress ministries to resign their offices and a policy of noncollaboration in the war effort was begun.

In 1942, after the Japanese had advanced nearly to the frontiers of India, Churchill sent Sir Stafford Cripps to that country to propose that at the conclusion of the war India should receive dominion status with the right of secession. Cripps nearly succeeded in bringing the Congress Nationalists and the Moslem League into agreement with Britain, but failed—many believed—because of Churchill's interference in the negotiations. Cripps' failure was succeeded by an outbreak of anti-British sentiment and violence which culminated in the government's arrest of all important Congress leaders. Not until 1945 were these political prisoners released. The Moslem League, which had not participated in the Congress Party's anti-British agitation, meanwhile inaugurated a campaign for the establishment of an

6 See pages 621- 623.

independent Indian Moslem state, Pakistan. The situation in India which confronted the British Labor government when it came into power in 1945 was thus far from appealing.

Nevertheless, in September of that year Prime Minister Attlee announced that his government would act in accordance with the spirit and intention of the Cripps offer, and again in December the British government stated that it regarded as a matter of the greatest urgency the setting-up of an Indian constitution-making body, by which the Indians would decide their own future as an independent state. When only mutinies, strikes, and the defiance of authority ensued in India, a Cabinet mission was dispatched to that country, where it consulted with the leaders of the various important groups and ultimately convened a conference to discuss a possible constitution. But the Indian leaders were unable to agree upon the framework of their future government, so the Cabinet mission in May, 1946, put forward a plan of its own, by means of which a constitution could be drafted by the Indians for the Indians. An essential part of the new proposal was the immediate establishment of an interim government to administer India while the new constitution was being drafted by a constituent assembly. With the exception of the viceroy, this new government was to consist of Indians, resting on the support of the popular parties as disclosed in the Indian elections of 1945.

Instead of proceeding at once to implement this plan for giving India dominion status, extremist Moslems and Hindus resorted to a bloody reign of terror against each other which brought the death of thousands of Indians. Jawaharlal Nehru and Mohammed Ali Jinnah, leaders of the Congress and Moslem groups respectively, were unable to agree upon an interim government, so that it was not until September, 1946, that such a government was created, and then it was selected by the Congress Party alone. Efforts of the viceroy, Lord Wavell, to persuade Jinnah to bring the Moslem League into the government failed, and ultimately the viceroy "virtually thrust the Moslem League into the cabinet." Friction between Moslems and Hindus continued, however, and the constituent assembly convened in December, 1946, without the Moslems, who feared that the Hindus would use their majority ruthlessly in the assembly. By February, 1947, it appeared that no compromise was possible and a new outbreak of violence was momentarily expected. On February 20, Prime Minister Attlee—apparently in the hope of breaking the impasse in India—announced that the British government intended to transfer power into responsible Indian hands and to withdraw from India not later than June, 1948. At the same time Lord Mountbatten was named to serve as Britain's "last viceroy" of India.

Attlee's startling announcement apparently forced some measure of cooperation upon the Moslem and Hindu leaders in India, for under Mount-

THE FIRST PREMIER OF THE UNION OF INDIA

Jawaharlal Nehru

batten's guidance the Congress Party, the Moslem League, and the Sikhs agreed upon a policy of partition. The British government thereupon announced that it intended to transfer power to Indian authorities on a dominion status on August 15, 1947. An Indian Independence Act, ratifying agreements thereafter rapidly reached between Mountbatten and Indian leaders, was passed by the British parliament in July to become effective on August 15. This act eliminated the word "Emperor" from the British king's title, removed British control from the whole of India, and provided for the partition of India into two dominions—the Union of India, in which Hindu majorities prevailed, and Pakistan, where Moslems constituted a majority. It returned paramountcy to the princely states of India and renounced all British treaties with their rulers. Pakistan was to include Baluchistan, Sind, the Northwest Frontier Province, West Punjab, and East Bengal. The provisional division of the last two provinces was made subject to revision by a boundary commission. The existing national legislature for all India was abolished, and the legislatures of India and Pakistan were to have all authority possessed by any dominion under the Statute of Westminster.[7] At the outset the constitution under which each dominion would function would be based on the Government of India Act of 1935,[8] but each would have authority to alter this act by legislative action. The two states had the option of seceding from the British Commonwealth after June, 1948. On August 15 the transfer of power occurred as planned, and six months later the last British troops left India.

In the Union of India, Lord Mountbatten served as governor-general until June, 1948, when he was succeeded by an Indian. Nehru became the first prime minister, and outlined a moderate socialist program of economic and industrial development, the abolition of the landlord system, the expansion of educational opportunities, and the enactment of a bill of rights. "Untouchability" for some 50,000,000 of the lowest social caste of Hindus was abolished, and all rights of citizenship in the dominion were granted them. New Delhi remained the capital of India and English was made the official language. India became a federal republic in which provincial governments and legislatures conduct local affairs. Nationally, there is a president but real executive power is in the hands of a cabinet responsible to the parliament which is elected by all aged 21 or over. In the UN the new dominion received the membership of the former empire.

In Pakistan, Jinnah, president of the Moslem League and author of the Pakistan plan, became the first governor-general and another Moslem the first premier. The port city of Karachi was designated as the temporary capital of Pakistan, and English was adopted as the official language of the

7 See page 536.
8 See page 621.

government. But the plan of government envisioned by Jinnah for this dominion was non-Western, being based on Moslem religion and law as set forth in the Koran. Pakistan was at once admitted to membership in the United Nations and soon established diplomatic missions abroad. This dominion seemed to have one inherent weakness, however. It consisted of two separate blocks of territory, nearly a thousand miles apart, whose inhabitants were of different race and spoke different languages. Whether their common adherence to Islam would hold them together remained to be seen. The appointment of the premier of East Bengal to succeed Jinnah as governor-general, upon the latter's death in September, 1948, may have been designed to strengthen the ties between the two halves of Pakistan.

Most of India's hundreds of semi-independent princely states affiliated with either India or Pakistan in matters of defense, foreign affairs, and communications, with the princes continuing to govern locally. But not everywhere did events move smoothly. In Kashmir, where Moslems constituted more than 75 per cent of the 40,000,000 inhabitants, a Moslem uprising, supported by invading tribesmen from Pakistan, proclaimed a provisional government which promised to hold a plebiscite on the question of joining India or Pakistan. The Hindu maharajah, Sir Hari Singh, however, acceded to India, and Sikh troops were flown from the latter to defend the Kashmir capital. When hostilities broke out India referred the matter to the UN Security Council which in the summer of 1948 sent a commission to investigate the situation. Although the commission persuaded both India and Pakistan to give a cease-fire order to their forces in Kashmir, the political question remained unresolved.

In the summer of 1952, however, an agreement was concluded between the Indian and Kashmir governments providing, among other things, that (1) Kashmir was to have a head of state elected by its constituent assembly instead of an hereditary maharajah, but his election was to be confirmed by the president of India; (2) Kashmir was to have a state flag but the Indian flag was to fly in Kashmir as the flag of the Union; (3) Kashmir was to be integrated financially into the Republic of India; and (4) Kashmir was to recognize the jurisdiction of the Indian supreme court. The Kashmir constitution was accordingly amended to provide for a head of state elected for a five-year term. The maharajah abdicated and his son was then elected head of state.

During 1953, however, a split developed among the leaders in the Kashmir government. The premier, Sheikh Abdullah, appeared to advocate more independence from India rather than closer integration; the deputy premier, after conferences with Nehru in Delhi, pronounced in favor of Kashmir's accession to India. In August the head of state suddenly dismissed Sheikh Abdullah as premier and appointed the deputy premier in his place. In 1954 the Kashmir constituent assembly, with fifteen members absent, unanimously approved the 1952 agreement, and the Kashmir premier announced that the accession of Kashmir to India was final and irrevocable.

In 1954, also, steps were initiated which seemed designed to bring the annexation of those enclaves in India which had long been held by France and Portugal. Economic and political pressure was exerted against the enclaves and, after elected representatives of the French settlements had voted in favor of the step, France on November 1, 1954, transferred her enclaves to the Union of India. It seemed inevitable that Portugal would have to do the same.

Meanwhile, Hyderabad, a princely state with a population of 16,000,000 and an area nearly as large as Great Britain's, was completely surrounded by the Union of India and from the geographical point of view should have acceded to that dominion. Although a large majority of Hyderabad's population was Hindu, the ruling prince was a Moslem. He apparently had no desire to join his state with Hindu India, while most of his subjects had no wish to be linked with Moslem Pakistan. The prince apparently sought to enter into friendly relations with India but to remain outside the Union with freedom to conduct his own foreign affairs. During the early months of 1948 negotiations were carried on between the Indian and Hyderabad governments, but to no avail. In June, Nehru declared that economically and geographically Hyderabad was an integral part of India which could not tolerate in its midst a unit which could not be assimilated. Three months later two Indian divisions began an invasion of Hyderabad which resulted in the prince's announcement (September 17) of his government's capitulation to India's demands.

As many observers had feared, the withdrawal of the British political and military forces from India was followed by the outbreak of violent conflicts between Hindus and Moslems. In each sector of the divided Punjab, for instance, the majority sought forcibly to expel the minority, and millions of persons were uprooted from their homes. Scores of thousands were reported killed in the mob violence which occurred. In an attempt to bring an end to the conflicts the aged Gandhi again embarked upon a fast which was broken on the sixth day when he received assurances from various communal leaders that peace would again prevail. But on January 30, 1948, Mahatma Gandhi was killed by a Hindu. Thus the great Indian leader, who more than any other person had dramatized for the world the struggle for Indian independence and who had always advocated the use of nonviolent methods, died at the hands of an Indian assassin shortly after the attainment of Indian independence. Ultimately in 1950, however, an agreement was signed by the premiers of India and Pakistan guaranteeing the protection of religious minorities in both countries.

The Union of Burma

East of India, across the Bay of Bengal, lay before the Second World War the British dependency of Burma. This state, with an area three times the size of Great Britain and a population of some 15,000,000, had been separated from India and granted a degree of self-government by the Government of Burma Act in 1935. The political regime established at that time had failed to satisfy many of the Burmese, however, and when the Japanese invaded Burma in 1942 the local population in many places had actively aided them, lured on by the Japanese promise of "independence." Though Burmese enthusiasm for the Japanese soon evaporated during the period of occupation and though a Burmese patriot army of 10,000 men was eventually raised to aid the Allies in expelling the Japanese, extreme nationalists in the country at the close of the war were demanding independence. In June, 1945, the British governor of Burma assured the Burmese that one of his government's main objectives was to ensure that Burma attained full self-government as soon as possible. In December, 1946, Prime Minister Attlee declared that it was for the people of Burma to decide their own future and to draft their own constitution.

Thereafter political events moved rapidly. A constituent assembly was elected in Burma in April, 1947, and practically its first decision when it met in June was that Burma should be an independent sovereign republic to be known as the "Union of Burma." Three months later the constituent assembly unanimously adopted a new constitution drafted in accordance with this decision, and on October 17, 1947, a treaty was signed between Great Britain and Burma to regulate matters arising out of the transfer of power. Britain recognized the Union of Burma as a fully independent, sovereign state and agreed to remove all British troops from that country as soon as possible after the transfer of power. Burma, on her part, agreed that Great Britain should provide instructional and other staff for service with the Burmese military, naval, and air forces and agreed not to receive a defense mission from any state outside the British Commonwealth. She further agreed that British military aircraft should have the right to fly over and to use prescribed airfields in her territories. To assist Burma financially, Great Britain cancelled £15,000,000—about one third of Burma's debt to Britain—and Burma agreed to pay the balance without interest in twenty yearly installments. In December, 1947, the Burma Independence Bill was passed by the British parliament, and on January 4, 1948, Burma became an independent country. In the succeeding months the Union of

Burma was admitted to membership in the United Nations and in the International Labor Office.

From the very beginning of its existence, however, the new republic was handicapped by revolts in various parts of the country. Communists denounced Burma's independence as a sham and sought to overthrow the government. The Karens, a racial minority of some 2,000,000 concentrated in a region northeast of Rangoon, demanded autonomy or independence. And the People's Volunteer Organization, consisting of former members of the anti-Japanese resistance forces who had not been rehabilitated, continued resistance tactics against the new Burmese government and tended to join the Communists. Finally, early in 1950, after the Communist successes in China, some 12,000 Chinese Nationalist troops took refuge in Burma where they plundered the countryside. By 1953 the government had largely reduced the native revolts to sporadic guerrilla activities, but the Chinese Nationalist forces were more difficult to defeat. In March, 1953, Burma brought their activities before the UN, which passed a resolution demanding their withdrawal. Subsequent negotiations among Burma, Formosa, and Thailand provided for their evacuation through Thailand. It was announced by the supervising committee in May, 1954, that most of the Chinese Nationalists had been evacuated.

The Dominion of Ceylon

Ceylon, an island in the Indian Ocean off the southern tip of India, with an area more than that of Belgium and Holland combined, and with a population of more than 5,000,000 at the time of the outbreak of the Second World War, had been taken from Holland by the British during the French and Napoleonic wars. From that time it had been ruled as a crown colony, and its exports of tea and rubber had contributed to British prosperity. In 1942 it was feared that the Japanese might seek to capture the island, and British empire forces were rushed to its defense. At the same time the British governor of Ceylon, seeking to rally the Ceylonese to the Allied cause, declared: "Ceylon has suddenly become a bastion ... of the sore-pressed citadel of freedom. It is not too much to say that the eyes of the world are upon us."

Perhaps the Ceylonese felt that if they were a bastion of freedom they should have more control of their own government. At any rate, when Sir Stafford Cripps was in India in 1942, the Ceylonese sought to send a deputation to discuss constitutional matters with him, but Cripps stated that the question of Ceylon's status was outside the province of his mission. A year later, however, the British colonial secretary declared his government's intention to examine the possibility of granting Ceylon full responsible government in matters of internal civil administration after the war. A royal commission subsequently recommended self-government for Ceylon with eventual full dominion status. On May 15, 1946, the British granted Ceylon a constitution providing for a bicameral parliamentary government with full powers to make laws except those discriminating against any community or religion. The British government's assent would be required, however, for bills relating to defense and external affairs, and the power to amend or revoke the constitution was retained by the British government.

Elections for the Ceylonese parliament were held on September 22, 1947; the first Ceylonese cabinet was sworn in four days later; and on February 4, 1948, Ceylon became a self-governing dominion in the British Commonwealth of Nations. Treaties between the Ceylonese and British governments provided for mutual military assistance for the security of their territories, for defense against external aggression, and for the protection of essential communications. Ceylon granted Britain the right to base such naval and air forces and to maintain such land forces in Ceylon as might be required for the above purposes. Obviously Ceylon's "dominion" status was not the same as that of Canada or Australia. But the developing nationalism in Ceylon seemed to be indicated by an announcement in October, 1953, that thereafter at official functions the Union Jack would no longer be flown but only the Ceylonese flag. In July, 1954, with the approval of Queen Elizabeth, a Ceylonese became governor-general.

The Federation of Malaya

In Malaya before the Second World War the British held a colony, the Straits Settlements (Singapore, Penang, Malacca), and had established a protectorate over four federated and five unfederated native states. During the war these states were all conquered and held by the Japanese. Shortly after the latter surrendered the British government announced its decision to form a Malayan Union of the nine federated and unfederated states and the two British settlements of Penang and Malacca. The fullest opportunities would be provided, it promised, to the peoples of Malaya to take a direct part in the civil administration, and facilities would be established to enable them to fit themselves for government posts. Singapore was to be established as a separate British colony. In January, 1946, Malcolm MacDonald, son of the first Labor prime minister, was appointed governor-general of the Malayan Union and Singapore, and Sir Edward Gent was appointed governor of the Malayan Union.

In March, 1946, however, a Pan-Malayan Congress resolved that the creation of a Malayan Union and Malayan citizenship would destroy nine sovereign states and was contrary to the principle of the sanctity of treaties.

Moreover, it resolved, the new agreements made with the British government by the sultans of the native states were executed without the knowledge of their subjects, were contrary to democratic principles, and were
null and void. At the request of the Pan-Malayan Congress the sultans
did not attend the ceremony installing Governor Gent, nor did the Malay
members attend the first meeting of the governor's advisory council. Later
in the year the congress resolved that the transference of jurisdiction and
sovereign rights from the states to the British crown was illegal, and at a
conference of the sultans the latter decided to protest against the contemplated Malayan Union. They proposed instead a federation with a central
body to decide matters of common interest to the nine constituent states
but with each state having local autonomy. In May no sultans attended the
ceremony of installing MacDonald as the first governor-general of the
Malayan Union and Singapore.

During 1946 and 1947 negotiations were carried on by the British government with the sultans and the United Malays' National Organization, and
ultimately an agreement was reached. The Federation of Malaya, a British
protectorate, would be established to include the eleven states originally
included in the proposed Malayan Union. The central government of the
federation would consist of a high commissioner, a federal executive council, and a federal legislative council. The high commissioner would act as
the representative of the British crown in matters of defense and foreign
relations, and would advise the sultans in all matters of government except those relating to the Moslem religion and Malayan custom. The federal legislative council would consist of the high commissioner, 14 official
members, and 34 unofficial members, selected to give the fullest representation to economic and social interests. Each of the constituent states would
have a state executive council and a council of state with legislative powers.
A British representative for each state would have the power of advice in
state matters. The native rulers thus won some concessions from the British.
On January 21, 1948, the nine rulers of the Malay states signed a treaty which
established the Federation of Malaya, and on February first the new constitution was inaugurated and Sir Edward Gent was sworn in as the first
high commissioner. The Federation had a population of 4,867,491, of which
2,130,493 were Malay and 1,880,452 were Chinese.

During the summer of 1948 Malaya was rocked by violent outbreaks
which were ascribed to Communists, for there was an active Communist
Party in Malaya, consisting chiefly of Chinese, and many organizations
were said to have been subverted by it. On June 12, the federal government
declared illegal the Pan-Malayan Federation of Trade Unions and ten other
trade-union organizations. After many had been murdered and much property destroyed by guerrillas and terrorists, a state of emergency was declared

throughout the federation and British aircraft and troops were sent in to restore order. Apparently the terrorists sought to paralyze the economic life of the federation, and their movement was aided by the widespread apathy or actual resentment of the Malayan Chinese, by the isolation of the plantations and mines, and by the almost limitless opportunities for ambush afforded by the jungle. In the succeeding five years, according to official figures, the terrorists suffered 8,363 casualties, the government forces 1,563, and civilians 4,095. The struggle was still going on in 1954, but it was believed the government was winning out. A Malayan army was being organized, full citizenship rights were offered to Chinese and Indians, settlements were being provided for Chinese squatters, greater self-government was being extended to rural communities, and programs for the social and economic betterment of the masses were being drafted.

Indonesia

Before 1939 the Netherlands East Indies, with an area of some 723,681 square miles and a population of 72,000,000, consisted of Java, Sumatra, Borneo, Celebes, half of New Guinea, and many small islands. Even before the First World War a nationalist movement had developed in the islands and had been greatly influenced by the Congress Party of India. In the period between the wars, socialist and communist ideas had begun to influence the native workers, and labor disputes and strikes had resulted. By 1934 the Dutch had imprisoned all outstanding nationalist leaders, who did not secure their freedom until they were released by the Japanese when they conquered the Dutch Indonesian empire in 1942. During the period of Japanese occupation hatred for the white man was systematically and effectively cultivated by Japanese propagandists, and an intense nationalism was aroused. Perhaps to counteract the Japanese, Queen Wilhelmina in December, 1942, announced her intention, after the liberation of the Netherlands, to hold a joint consultation regarding the structure of the future Netherlands kingdom. She visualized, she said, a commonwealth in which all the Dutch colonies, together with the Netherlands, should participate, with freedom for each part to conduct its internal affairs.

Two days after the surrender of the Japanese forces in the Netherlands East Indies, Achmed Soekarno, a former political prisoner of the Dutch, who had collaborated with the Japanese occupation forces in Java because of their promise of independence for the Indonesians, proclaimed the Republic of Indonesia. The Netherlands government characterized this new state as a Japanese puppet government and refused to have any official relations with it. In Java extreme nationalists organized the Indonesian People's Army and, contrary to the desires of Soekarno's government, declared war on the Dutch. When the government at The Hague announced that it would not be forced into negotiations with the Indonesians, the Dutch governor-general of the Netherlands East Indies resigned. The progressive Lieutenant-Governor-General Hubertus van Mook thereupon announced that the Dutch realized that the old colonial system should go and that the Indonesians should have an ever-increasing share in the government. Fighting meanwhile continued between the Indonesian People's Army and British land, sea, and air forces, which had been assigned the task of reoccupying the islands.

In December, 1945, the Dutch lieutenant-governor-general returned to The Hague and in a broadcast explained that developments in Indonesia were "manifestations of an international spirit that will no longer tolerate subjugation by force of one people by another." Deeds were demanded, he declared, and a solution must not take too long. In February, 1946, the Netherlands government, under British pressure, published its proposal for the constitutional future of Indonesia, the main features of which were the establishment of the Commonwealth of Indonesia, in which the internal affairs would be managed independently by the Commonwealth's own institutions. The Commonwealth would be a partner in the kingdom, and the central institutions of the latter would consist of representatives of its constituent parts.

In September, 1946, a Netherlands commission arrived in Java to negotiate a settlement with the Republic of Indonesia; on October 1 a conference was opened; two weeks later a truce was agreed upon, based on the stabilization of existing military positions; and on November 15, 1946, the Dutch and Indonesian delegates initialed the so-called Linggadjati Agreement. The latter provided that (1) the Republic of Indonesia would include Java, Madura, and Sumatra; (2) by January 1, 1949, a United States of Indonesia, consisting of the Republic of Indonesia, Borneo, and the eastern part of the archipelago to be known as the Great East, would be formed on a federal basis, and its constitution would be drafted by a constituent assembly; (3) also, by January 1, 1949, a Netherlands Indonesian Union would be established, consisting of two parts—the Kingdom of the Netherlands and the United States of Indonesia—with the queen of the Netherlands at its head, to look after foreign relations, defense, and, so far as necessary, finance. This agreement marked a victory for the progressive section of Dutch opinion led by Lieutenant-Governor-General van Mook, but at The Hague it met a storm of opposition from the conservative and reactionary groups. Nevertheless, it was eventually signed in March, 1947, by the Netherlands and the Indonesian Republic.

It was one thing to reach an agreement, but it was quite another for the two parties to implement it when each distrusted the other. Negotiations were begun to set up an interim government to function until the establishment of the United States of Indonesia, but the discussions made little progress. On May 27, 1947, the Dutch commissioner-general presented five demands which amounted to a practical ultimatum, and the Indonesian government in reply suggested arbitration as provided by the Linggadjati Agreement. The Dutch refused to arbitrate. The Indonesian premier on his own initiative offered several concessions, but he was repudiated by his own party. The United States government then intervened and urged the Indonesian government to co-operate without delay in the formation of an interim government, and Great Britain urged the same. On July 8 and again on July 17 the new Indonesian premier accepted all the Dutch demands except one, and the British government suggested to the Dutch a compromise proposal on that one. But the Dutch adopted an increasingly menacing attitude, and on July 21 Dutch forces began military operations against the Republic of Indonesia to "end the intolerable situation" and to "guarantee" law and order.

On July 31, 1947, on the request of India, the UN Security Council began a consideration of the Indonesian situation, and on the next day the Council called on both parties to end hostilities and to settle their dispute by peaceful means. Both sides agreed to issue cease-fire orders. But a Security Council committee of observers reported that under the guise of mopping-up operations, the Dutch were continuing their advance and that therefore the cease-fire order had never been obeyed by either side. On August 25 an American proposal that the Security Council should tender its good offices to the Dutch and Indonesians for a peaceful settlement was adopted and accepted by both governments. A UN commission, consisting of the United States, Belgium, and Australia, was appointed, and in December it began discussions with the Dutch and Indonesians. The commission's proposals were accepted by the Indonesians, but the Dutch rejected them.

In January, 1948, the Dutch premier came to Batavia and announced that immediate steps would be taken to form an interim government, adding that "Holland reserves the right to resume her freedom of action if satisfactory results are not soon achieved." In the face of this ultimatum another agreement was reached on January 17, 1948. Five months later, however, the UN commission reported to the Security Council that the Dutch and Indonesians still remained divided by the same issues as formerly: (1) the ways and means by which the United States of Indonesia should come into being; (2) the place of the Republic of Indonesia in the federation; and (3) the allocation of powers between the federation and the Netherlands Indies Union. Negotiations between the Dutch and Republican delegations under the auspices of the UN commission broke down in June, 1948.

By December, 1948, the Dutch had created a number of states out of territory of the Republic of Indonesia, and to many it appeared that they were seeking to reduce the Indonesian Republic, which originally included 80 per cent of Indonesia's population, to the status of a relatively small and weak unit in a future federation. By military force and political action they had reduced the republic's territory to a fraction of its original size, and they continued to surround it with a naval blockade which, according to the UN commission's report in July, 1948, had prevented the economic rehabilitation of Indonesia.

The Dutch apparently believed that the UN Security Council was so divided that they could safely ignore its resolutions and its commission. Although the Soviet Union was strongly pro-republican and Australia, Syria, and Colombia were inclined to favor the republic, the colonial powers—Britain, France, and Belgium—seemed loath to support strong measures against another colonial power. The United States and China sought to maintain an intermediate position and strove to achieve some compromise. But the policy of the United States appeared at times to be vacillating, probably because that country was involved in the "cold war" with Russia and was committed to the economic recovery of western Europe and the creation of the North Atlantic alliance. Indirectly, the United States strengthened the Dutch in their struggle with the Indonesian Republic by granting $422,000,000 to the Netherlands and $84,000,000 to the Dutch-controlled area in Indonesia under the Marshall Plan.

On December 3, 1948, the UN commission reported that its efforts to bring about negotiations between the Dutch and the republic had been fruitless, that no political negotiations under its auspices had occurred in the preceding five months. Two days later the Dutch mission left Batavia for home. Two weeks later, in violation of the truce agreement of January, 1948 (the so-called Renville agreement), and after dispatching to the Republic of Indonesia an ultimatum with a time-limit so short that it could not be met, the Dutch launched a surprise air-borne invasion of the republic and captured President Soekarno and other high republican political and military leaders. The Dutch premier explained that republican truce violations had made any peaceful settlement impossible. Once again, as in July, 1947, "police action" was undertaken by the Dutch to "end an intolerable situation."

In 1949 the United States government gave its support to the Indonesians more whole-heartedly than it had done in 1947. When the Security Council reconvened in January of that year the United States representative condemned the Netherlands, and proposed the re-establishment of the republican government at Jogjakarta; the progressive withdrawal of Dutch troops to the Renville truce lines and later from all of Java, Sumatra, and Madura; the creation of a new UN commission; general elections in Indonesia by October, 1949; complete sovereignty for the United States of Indonesia by April, 1950. Meanwhile, a strong popular reaction against the attitude of the Dutch had made itself felt in most countries. In the Asiatic world this sentiment was crystallized when, on the invitation of Prime Minister Nehru of India, representatives of nineteen African, Asiatic, and Far Eastern states [9] convened at New Delhi to consider the Indonesian problem. By a unanimous vote these states, which represented approximately half of the world's population and a third of the members of the United Nations, on January 23, 1949, adopted a resolution similar to the January proposals of the United States but more drastic in that it called for a somewhat faster schedule to be followed.

Soon after the adjournment of the New Delhi conference the Security Council adopted a resolution calling for (1) the immediate release of the Indonesian political prisoners; (2) the immediate return of Jogjakarta and its environs to the Indonesian Republic; (3) a three-power UN commission to supervise elections and recommend areas from which the Dutch should withdraw; (4) the formation of a federal interim government by March 15, 1949; (5) elections in October, 1949; and (6) the establishment of the United States of Indonesia by July, 1950.

The pressure of international opinion as exemplified by these resolutions, the desire of the other members of Benelux and NATO to have the Netherlands help increase the economic and military strength of Western Europe, plus the tremendous financial burden of maintaining an army of more than 100,000 men in Indonesia all combined to bring a change in Dutch policy. The imperialistic minister for overseas territories was forced to resign from the Netherlands government, which announced that it would convene a round-table conference with the Indonesians to consider the whole problem.

Under the mediation of a UN commission a compromise settlement was reached providing for the return of the Indonesian republican government to Jogjakarta, the discontinuance of military operations, and the release of all political prisoners arrested in the republic since December 17, 1948. President Soekarno and other members of the Indonesian government returned to Jogjakarta on July 6, 1949, and the cessation of hostilities occurred on August 1. Three weeks later the round-table conference opened at The Hague, with the UN commission in attendance. On November 2, 1949, the final act of the conference was signed. The solutions agreed upon were based

[9] The states which sent representatives were Afghanistan, Australia, Burma, Ceylon, Egypt, Ethiopia, India, Iran, Iraq, Lebanon, Pakistan, the Philippines, Saudi Arabia, Syria, and Yemen. China, Nepal, New Zealand, and Siam sent observers.

on those originally reached in the Linggadjati and Renville agreements, but with one major difference—the new agreements provided for the immediate transfer of sovereignty.

The real, complete, and unconditional transfer of sovereignty to the Republic of the United States of Indonesia, consisting of sixteen states including the former Republic of Indonesia, took place in a formal ceremony at The Hague on December 27, 1949. The new state included all the former Netherlands East Indies except Dutch New Guinea, whose final status was left to be decided by future Netherlands-Indonesian negotiations. A Netherlands-Indonesian Union, under the Netherlands ruler, was created for the voluntary co-operation of the two states in fields of mutual interest, particularly foreign affairs and defense. The Union Statute stipulated that a permanent secretariat would be established and that conferences of ministers would be held at least twice a year. All decisions, however, would require unanimity and would have to be approved by the respective parliaments before becoming effective. For all practical purposes the Netherlands and the United States of Indonesia became two separate states with a common sovereign.

Achmed Soekarno was elected president of the new federal republic and Mohammed Hatta became its first premier. Almost at once, however, numerous revolts occurred in some of the constituent states, and in order to strengthen the new regime national leaders in August, 1950, adopted a new provisional constitution. This abolished the federal system of government and created a centralized unitary state for all Indonesia, with ten provinces instead of sixteen states. At the same time the name of the state was changed to the Republic of Indonesia. In September, 1950, the republic was admitted to membership in the United Nations. During 1951 most military remnants of the war for independence disappeared; the Dutch completed the withdrawal of their troops, and the UN commission which had been mediating between the Netherlands and Indonesia was discharged.

But Indonesian nationalism continued to have its effect on Indonesian affairs. In 1951 a premier was defeated because he was considered too moderate in his dealings with the Dutch in regard to New Guinea. He was succeeded by a Moslem leader who called for the nationalization of major industries and the Java Bank, all Dutch owned, and for agrarian reform so that Indonesians might take over land held by foreigners. But this premier was in turn rejected in 1952 because he accepted Mutual Security aid from the United States, which certain nationalist groups feared would compromise Indonesia's ability to pursue an independent foreign policy. And Ali Sastroamijojo, who became premier in July, 1953, declared that the most urgent question of foreign policy was revision of relations with the Netherlands. A year later, in August, 1954, Indonesia and the Netherlands did, in fact, sign a protocol abolishing the Netherlands-Indonesian Union. Disagreement over the sovereignty of Dutch New Guinea still remained unsettled, however, to plague relations between the two countries.

Indo-China

In 1939 French Indo-China consisted of Laos, Cambodia, Tonkin, Annam, and Cochin-China. The first four were protectorates; Cochin-China was a colony. The population of Indo-China totaled about 23,000,000, of which the Annamites constituted about 72 per cent, although they inhabited only about 10 per cent of the area, chiefly the plain and coastal regions of Annam, Tonkin, and Cochin-China. As in the Netherlands East Indies, nationalism had gained a foothold in Indo-China even before the First World War. During the Second World War the Japanese occupied Indo-China, but they left the pro-Axis Vichy government in nominal control until March, 1945. At that time they interned the French and recognized an autonomous state of Viet Nam (the ancient name for Annam), consisting of Annam, Tonkin, and Cochin-China, with Bao-dai, the former emperor of Annam, as ruler.

Meanwhile, in 1942 the underground Annamite Communists had organized the Viet Minh, or League for Viet Nam's Independence, headed by Ho Chi Minh, a Russian-trained Communist. Following the collapse of Japan, the Viet Minh Party proclaimed Viet Nam to be a democratic republic and Emperor Bao-dai abdicated. In March, 1945, De Gaulle's government had approved a new statute for Indo-China, providing that it would become a federation of Indo-Chinese states with local autonomy within the French Union, and at the close of the war the French were prepared to put these plans into effect. In October, 1945, the French and Vietnamese leaders agreed to cease fighting in order that negotiations might be carried on, but the latter were determined that Indo-China should have not autonomy but independence within the French Union. Negotiations broke down, fighting was resumed, and French reinforcements poured into Indo-China.

But the unexpected strength of the Vietnamese forces led the French in March, 1946, to recognize the Republic of Viet Nam as a "free state" having its own government, parliament, army, and finances, but forming part of the Indo-Chinese Federation and French Union. As in the case of the Republic of Indonesia, however, when it came to implement this agreement, difficulties arose and negotiations broke down. Fighting became widespread in the north and the French poured in more reinforcements until some

150,000 troops were stationed in the country. During the ensuing years hostilities between the French and the Viet Minh forces continued without a decision.

Meanwhile, the French sought to organize a nationalist movement under former Emperor Bao-dai to counteract the Vietnamese movement led by Ho Chi Minh, and eventually an agreement was reached between the French and Bao-dai. Viet Nam was to be independent in internal matters, maintain a national army, and have limited diplomatic representation of its own, but was to remain within the French Union and permit France to have troops within its territory. In Cambodia and Laos, the two non-Annamite countries of Indo-China, the anti-French nationalist movement was not so strong. Both accepted autonomy within the French Union, with French officials serving as advisers and with French high commissioners possessing authority over affairs concerning French nationals.

It soon became apparent that Bao-dai, who in 1949 declared himself chief of state of Viet Nam and whose government was soon recognized by the United States and Great Britain, was failing to unite the Vietnamese under his leadership. The greater part of the nationalists remained either allied to Viet Minh or held aloof from the struggle. In an effort to impress the nationalists and to increase the prestige of the French-sponsored governments in Viet Nam, Laos, and Cambodia, the United States invited them to participate as independent nations in the signing of the Japanese peace treaty in San Francisco in September, 1951. Nevertheless, the attempt to organize all the progressive anti-Communist Vietnamese into an alliance with the French and Americans to repel the forces of Viet Minh proved unsuccessful, despite minor concessions made to the Viet Nam government by France from time to time. The fact that the former was not truly independent was strikingly emphasized in May, 1953, when the French without prior consultation with Bao-dai's government devalued the Vietnamese currency in terms of French francs.

In 1953 the pressures on the French government to grant full independence to the Indo-Chinese greatly increased. The premier of Viet Nam demanded that the treaty of 1949 be scrapped and that Viet Nam be given greater independence. The Cambodian government demanded independence as the price of Cambodian resistance to Viet Minh, and in June the king of that country went into voluntary exile in protest against French delay in granting independence. The United States apparently held the view that French colonialism was handicapping the fight against Communism and urged concessions to the nationalists. Finally, within France a powerful sentiment seemed to favor reducing the republic's commitments in Indo-China or withdrawing altogether. In July, therefore, France offered to begin round-table negotiations to increase the independence of Viet

Nam, Cambodia, and Laos, and within three months she had signed agreements with Cambodia and Laos which gave these two states practical independence within the French Union.

In Viet Nam, however, probably because of Bao-dai's realization of the
need of French military assistance against the forces of Ho Chi Minh,
progress toward "complete independence" was somewhat slower. Conversations between Emperor Bao-dai and the French government in August, 1953, did result in the latter's pledge to grant Viet Nam full independence and in Bao-dai's pledge of Viet Nam's free association in the
French Union. But pledges alone did not satisfy the Viet-Namese nationalists who in a congress in October resolved that the relations between Viet
Nam and France should be based upon a treaty of alliance to be ratified by
the Viet-Namese national assembly.

But progress toward the military defeat of Ho Chi Minh's forces was
even slower than that toward complete independence for Viet Nam. At
the opening of the year 1954 the French-supported government of Bao-dai
had effective control over only a small part of the country; Communists
controlled from 75 to 85 per cent of the area. Despite more than seven years
of bitter and sanguinary battles, despite French annual expenditures of
close to one billion dollars to carry on the struggle, despite greatly increased military aid from the United States, despite France's weakening
of her army in Europe and her appalling loss of officers, the French seemed
in a worse position than ever. And the factor that particularly militated
against French success was Viet-Namese nationalism. Ho Chi Minh's
soldiers, apparently, were far less influenced by the fact that their leader
was a Communist than by the feeling that they and he were fighting for
home and country against foreign imperialist troops.

During the first six months of 1954 Ho Chi Minh's forces continued to
make gains not only in Viet Nam but even in Cambodia and Laos. Eventually French military misfortunes culminated in a "disaster" at Dien Bien
Phu on May 7 when the French fortress there, manned by some 10,000
soldiers, fell to the Viet Minh forces. But the latter continued their advances
elsewhere to such an extent that the French were also forced to evacuate
the whole southern zone of the Red River delta, the rich region in the vicinity
of Hanoi.

By this time the situation had ceased to be merely military; it had become
linked with the whole complex of diplomatic and political questions being
discussed at the Geneva conference on the Far East which had been in
progress since April 26.[10] As the result of negotiations carried on there a
cease-fire was agreed upon in July, 1954, and an armistice line was established in Indo-China which divided Viet Nam approximately at the 17th

[10] For a discussion of the Geneva conference, see pages 1001–1004.

parallel, leaving about 12,750,000 people under Viet Minh rule in the north and about 9,300,000 under Viet Nam rule in the south. In a declaration signed by the powers at the conference, including France, the latter's pledge to withdraw her troops from Viet Nam, Laos, and Cambodia and to respect the independence, and sovereignty, unity, and territorial integrity of the three states was formally noted. The end of French colonial rule in Indo-China seemed to be indicated.

The Chinese People's Republic

Although in 1943 Great Britain, the United States, the Netherlands, and Norway surrendered their extraterritorial rights in China, Chinese nationalism continued to be handicapped by a serious division among the Chinese people. The conflict between the Kuomintang, or Chinese Nationalist Party, and the Chinese Communists, as it had existed in 1929–1936, has been discussed.[11] For a time, beginning in 1937, the two groups had co-operated to present a common front against the Japanese, but during the Second World War Chiang Kai-shek's hostility to the Chinese Communists frequently led him to use a large portion of his forces against them rather than against the Japanese. When the war ended in the Far East the relationship between the Chinese Nationalists and Communists was one of "passive belligerency."

At the time of Japan's surrender, the Nationalist armies were largely concentrated in southwest China, and the Communist forces, being situated in the north and northeast, were able to take over Japanese equipment and to extend their positions before the Nationalist forces arrived. Furthermore, in 1945 the Chinese Communists moved into Manchuria to meet the advancing Russian armies and were consequently in a position to take over that region when the Soviet armies withdrew.[12] They were not inclined to give up their favorable positions to the "reactionary" Nationalists without a struggle, and open hostilities between the Chinese Communists and Nationalists resulted.

The United States recognized the Chiang Kai-shek government as the legitimate government of China, but it was eager for the cessation of hostilities there, and hoped that a conference between Nationalist and Communist leaders might work out a solution which would bring about national unification. To aid in the Chinese negotiations, President Truman, in December, 1945, sent General George C. Marshall, former army chief of staff, to China as his special envoy. Marshall succeeded in obtaining

[11] See pages 625–628, 648.
[12] For the Sino-Soviet treaty regarding Manchuria and Outer Mongolia, see page 824.

a truce between the hostile Chinese groups and the convening of an all-party consultation conference in Chungking. This conference rewrote and liberalized a draft constitution, originally drawn up in 1936, but never adopted, and agreed that a National Assembly should meet to consider it.

Although both the Nationalists and the Communists issued a cease-fire order in January, 1946, neither side apparently observed it. The efforts of the Nationalists to reoccupy Manchuria were handicapped by Communist control of the Peiping-Mukden railway and by Russia's refusal to allow Nationalist troops to land at Dairen or Port Arthur. Tens of thousands of Chiang Kai-shek's forces were ultimately flown in by United States transport planes, however, and after a vigorous campaign the Nationalists succeeded in occupying most of southern Manchuria. In June the Generalissimo announced a fifteen-day truce to permit negotiations for a settlement, with Marshall as arbiter, but the Communists rejected this proposal and accused the United States of interfering in China's internal affairs.

In July, 1946, Chiang Kai-shek's government, without consulting the Communist Party, announced that the National Assembly would convene in Nanking in November. Since the Communists did not attend the meeting, the Assembly was dominated by the Nationalists. The Right wing of the Nationalist Party sought to introduce some reactionary changes in the draft accepted earlier in the year by the all-party conference, but Chiang Kai-shek insisted upon the adoption of the agreed-upon draft, which was finally passed unanimously. On December 31, 1946, the Generalissimo promulgated the Republican Constitution of China, the eleventh to have been promulgated since the overthrow of the empire in 1912, to become effective one year later. In November, 1947, a general election was held to choose the first National Assembly under the new constitution, but Manchuria and North China except for Peiping and Tientsin did not take part because they were under Communist control.

The sessions of the Chinese National Assembly, the great majority of whose members were appointees of Nationalist Party organizations, were devoted chiefly to ratifying the constitution and to electing a new President and Vice President of the Chinese Republic. Attempts by the Assembly to exercise legislative power, to amend the constitution, and to impeach some high officials proved futile. The constitution was ratified unchanged, and Chiang Kai-shek, after announcing he was not a candidate, was elected President by an overwhelming vote. The only successful revolt on the part of the members came in the election of the Vice President when General Li Tsung-jen was finally chosen despite opposition of Chiang Kai-shek and the old guard Nationalists, who favored Sun Fo, the son of Sun Yat-sen.

How far the son had departed from his father's democratic ideas seemed indicated by the former's demand, after his defeat, that the Nationalist Party should adopt the Soviet system of discipline and organization to restore the dominance of the party machine.

Meanwhile, the years 1947–1948 had seen disaster after disaster overtake the Nationalist army at the hands of the Communists. Manchuria was largely lost, and Communist forces occupied large areas in Hopei, Shantung, Shansi, Shensi, and Honan provinces. In the early months of 1948 some 110,000 Nationalist troops were captured or destroyed, and immense quantities of arms and munitions were thus secured by the Communists. Much, if not most, of the equipment used by the Chinese Communists consisted, it was said, of supplies captured from the Nationalists, whose armies seemed riddled with corruption, inefficiency, and nepotism. According to William C. Bullitt, a strong advocate of American military assistance to China, half the Nationalist generals and a third of the other officers were incompetent or corrupt or both.

General Marshall, at the time he was recalled as President Truman's special envoy to China in January, 1947, in order to become American secretary of state, declared that the chief obstacle to peace in China was "the complete and almost overwhelming suspicion with which the Chinese Communist Party and the Kuomintang regard each other." Although he believed that Chiang Kai-shek's government was in effect the National Party, which in turn was dominated by a group of military and political reactionaries who opposed the formation of a real coalition, yet the exigencies of the "cold war" with Russia led him as secretary of state to approve further American aid to the Generalissimo. There was among many groups in the United States a feeling that a non-Communist China was as essential for the welfare of the democratic countries as a non-Communist Greece and Turkey. General Claire Chennault, commander of the China Air Task Force during the war, for instance, told the American Congress that China was the "key to peace" or to victory if war came. In response to this sentiment, President Truman in 1948 added to the European Recovery Program aid for China, and the Congress approved an appropriation of $420,000,000 to stop the deterioration of the Chinese economy.

Nevertheless, during the second half of that year and the first two months of 1949 the situation steadily deteriorated in so far as the Nationalist government at Nanking was concerned. By the end of October, 1948, Mukden had been captured by the Communist armies, and with it not only large stocks of arms but the general control of Manchuria. Three months later the Communists had also captured Tientsin, Peiping, and Suchow, and had advanced to the Yangtse River in many places. Meanwhile, in November,

1948, the Nanking government had been reorganized with Sun Fo becoming prime minister; the Chinese National Assembly had urgently appealed to the United States for aid; and Mme. Chiang Kai-shek had flown to Washington to place the situation before President Truman personally. But the Chinese Nationalist appeals proved fruitless. Apparently the United States government had decided to disengage itself from the policy of supporting Chiang Kai-shek, a policy which had been ineffective in stemming the tide of the Communist military advance, and had excited an Americanophobia among millions of Chinese. Apparently, too, it had come to feel that should the Soviet government seek to intervene in China, the Chinese nationalism which had become so anti-American would then be turned against the Soviet Union. In January, 1949, the United States terminated its program of military training of the Chinese Nationalist armies, and in February the United States Navy began the withdrawal of American marines from the Chinese mainland.

During the early weeks of 1949 political developments within China moved swiftly for a time. On January 14, General Mao Tse-tung, the Communist leader, broadcast his peace terms which among other things included the punishment of Generalissimo Chiang Kai-shek and prominent Nationalists as war criminals. One week later Chiang, who for more than two decades had headed the Nationalists, announced his retirement as president in "the hope that hostilities may be brought to an end and the people's sufferings be relieved." Following the Generalissimo's withdrawal to southern China, Vice President Li Tsung-jen became Acting President of the republic. Li sought to treat with Mao Tse-tung and eventually in April did succeed in opening negotiations with the Communists in Peking (the name restored to the city by the Communists), but to no avail.

Before the month was out Mao Tse-tung's forces again began to advance. On April 23 Nationalist troops and officials evacuated Nanking, which was at once occupied by the Communists. By the close of May the latter had also captured the important cities of Hankow and Shanghai. On September 30, 1949, while their troops were fighting their way toward Canton, the Chinese Communists proclaimed the Chinese People's Republic, with its capital at Peking and with Mao Tse-tung, chairman of the central committee of the Chinese Communist Party, holding a position equivalent to that of president in other republics. In October Canton fell to the Red armies, and by the end of 1949 effective Nationalist resistance on the Chinese mainland had ceased. Early in 1950 Hainan Island and the Chusan Islands were also captured by the Communists, whose government by the close of January, 1950, had received the recognition of India, Pakistan, Burma, and Israel in Asia and of the Soviet Union, Great Britain, Norway, Denmark,

Sweden, and Finland in Europe. Finally, in May, 1951, by an agreement for the "peaceful liberation of Tibet" that vast region was also brought under effective Chinese Communist control.

In outward form the structure of the Peking government continued to conform with the coalition idea used by Mao Tse-tung during his earlier years. There continued to be a "united front" government which was called an alliance of "workers, peasants, petty bourgeoisie, and national bourgeoisie." In fact, however, the Chinese Communists soon established in China a thorough-going Communist totalitarianism, complete with political centralization, sweeping censorship, propaganda and indoctrination, ubiquitous security police, innumerable arrests and executions, confiscation and redistribution of land, tentative attempts at collectivization, a gradual destruction of private enterprise, and a five-year plan of industrialization.

Eventually, in January, 1953, a committee to draft a constitution was set up under the chairmanship of Mao Tse-tung. In June, 1954, the text of the draft was published and was found to be modelled closely on the Russian constitution of 1936 except in the matter of the headship of the state. The Chinese draft provided for a Chairman (President) of the Republic, a largely honorary position but one which carried with it the power to propose the name of the prime minister. Mao Tse-tung became the first Chairman of the Republic and Chou En-lai, Chinese foreign minister, assumed the premiership. In September, 1954, the first All-China People's Congress of more than 1,100 elected delegates opened in Peking and was addressed by Chairman Mao Tse-tung, who informed them that their tasks were national unity, winning support of friends in all nations, building a great socialist state, defending international peace, and furthering the cause of human progress. They were urged to be honest and modest, earnest and industrious that in the course of "several five-year plans" they might transform their "economically and culturally backward" land into a great industrialized country with a modern culture. They should, he declared, learn from "the advanced experience of the Soviet Union."

Meanwhile, evidence indicated that a working unity existed between the Chinese People's Republic and the Soviet Union. In 1949 the latter made vigorous but futile efforts to have the Peking government recognized by the United Nations as the legitimate government of China. In 1950 the two states signed a treaty of alliance in which it was agreed that they would act in concert in defense of China against Japan or against any power associated with Japan, a phrase which was thought to mean the United States. Both states guaranteed the independence of the Mongolian People's Republic, and they simultaneously recognized the Communist Viet Minh regime in Indo-China. Obviously the two Communist states co-operated in the Korean War, with the Soviet government supplying aircraft and other

RED CHINA'S DICTATOR
General Mao Tse-tung

weapons for the Chinese fighting forces. They co-operated, too, in plans for the rehabilitation of North Korea after the war. Finally, early in 1954, Soviet Foreign Minister Molotov persuaded the Western great powers to include representatives of Communist China in the important conference which was to meet in Geneva later in the year to discuss the whole Far Eastern question.

Also, in 1950, notes were exchanged between the Russian and the Chinese Communist governments recognizing that the Sino-Soviet treaty and other agreements of August, 1945,[13] were no longer valid. It was now agreed that after the signing of a peace treaty with Japan, and in any case not later than 1952, Russia would transfer to China all her rights in the administration of the Chinese Changchun Railway and that Soviet troops would be withdrawn from Port Arthur. Russia further agreed to hand over to the Chinese without compensation property acquired from the Japanese in Manchuria, and extended to the Chinese government a $300,000,000 credit at one per cent interest. In accordance with the agreements of 1950 the Chinese Changchun Railway was transferred to China in 1952 but, because "conditions dangerous for peace and favorable for the reiteration of Japanese aggression" had arisen, China agreed to permit Soviet troops to remain in Port Arthur until peace treaties with Japan had been concluded.

In various parts of China Sino-Soviet companies were established and Soviet technicians and advisers—estimated at 80,000—played an increasing role in the management of China's enterprises. To assist China in her five-year plan, inaugurated in 1952, Russia agreed to increase her shipments of capital goods. In September, 1953, Mao Tse-tung, expressed to Premier Malenkov China's gratitude for the Soviet government's agreement to extend economic and technical aid in the construction and renovation of many of the country's enterprises. Later in the year a Russian delegation joined in celebrations to mark the completion of steel mills and a new blast furnace which, it was claimed, would enable China to build her own ships, railways, and bridges.

But events seem to indicate that Mao Tse-tung had no intention of transforming China into a servile Russian satellite. At the close of negotiations which had begun in Peking in September, 1954, between representatives of the Soviet and Chinese governments a joint communiqué announced, among other things, that (1) Russia would hand over to China on January 1, 1955, all her shares in joint Sino-Soviet companies; (2) Soviet troops would be evacuated from Port Arthur, which would be transferred to China by May 31, 1955, without compensation; (3) the Soviet government would grant China a long-term credit, would aid the latter in constructing 155 new industrial enterprises, and would increase deliveries of

[13] See page 824.

equipment for industrial enterprises already planned; (4) the two countries would soon begin the construction of two railways to supplant overland trade routes from China to Alma Ata and Ulan Bator. The communiqué further announced "complete unity of views" on co-operation between the two countries and on the international situation.

The Chinese Nationalists on Formosa

Late in 1949, after the Chinese Communists had captured the various cities on the mainland to which the Nationalists had successively moved their government, the latter finally withdrew to Formosa where Taipei was chosen as the capital of Nationalist China. Because the Chinese Reds then lacked effective air and sea power, it was believed that on Formosa—one hundred miles from the mainland—the Nationalists might maintain themselves. Early in 1950 Chiang Kai-shek again took over the political helm of Nationalist China, displacing Acting President Li despite the latter's objections. He also resumed control of the Nationalist military forces, consisting of some 600,000 men—defeated, disorganized, unpaid, and largely unequipped.

Formosa, with an area about one third that of Ohio, had been under Japanese rule from 1895 until 1945. But in the latter year, in accordance with the Cairo Declaration, the island had been transferred to China and a Nationalist general had been appointed governor. The population of Formosa was estimated as approximately 6,000,000 in 1949, and during that year it was increased by the influx of a million civilians from the mainland and the Nationalist army. Pressure of population on resources seemed inevitable. To lessen this pressure the government sought by agrarian reform measures to increase incentive and agricultural production. Land rentals were drastically reduced, land formerly owned by Japanese corporations was sold to tenants, and eventually holdings of absentee owners were purchased for sale to tenants. American ECA funds, moreover, were made available for the importation of fertilizer. Beginning in 1951 Formosa once more had rice to export.

Meanwhile, the Chinese Nationalist government remained practically as it was in 1948, with the terms of the legislative body being extended from year to year. Eventually, in March, 1954, Chiang was re-elected president for another six-year term. Li Tsung-jen, former vice president and acting president during 1949–1950, from abroad denounced the election as illegal, and General Chen Cheng, the Chinese Nationalist premier, was elected vice president in his place.

The political future of Formosa soon became a matter for heated debate. The United States government at first held the view that the issue should be settled by the Chinese themselves. In January, 1950, accordingly, President Truman announced that the United States would not give military assistance or advice to the Chinese Nationalists on Formosa. But this decision was extremely unpopular with many Americans, and it was ultimately changed after the outbreak of the Korean War, which is discussed in the next chapter.

The Chinese Communists, controlling all the Chinese mainland with its hundreds of millions of inhabitants, maintained that the Cairo Declaration had stated that Formosa was to be returned to China, and that it was therefore a legitimate part of the Chinese People's Republic. In August, 1954, the Central Council of the People's Republic called for "determined action to liberate" Formosa, and Premier Chou En-lai declared that the "occupation" of the island by the United States "absolutely cannot be tolerated." On the other hand, in September, 1954, President Chiang Kai-shek in a public address announced that Chinese Nationalist preparations for a counter-attack against the Communist mainland were almost complete. Minor hostilities between the Chinese Communists and the Chinese Nationalists occurred in the summer and autumn of 1954, and the possibility that a clash between the two Chinese governments might eventually lead to a general war was feared by many. In January, 1955, President Eisenhower requested, and was granted by the United States Congress, authority to use the American armed forces at his discretion to defend Formosa and the Pescadores against Communist aggression.

Chapter XXXI

COLLECTIVE SECURITY ON ·TRIAL

FIVE years after the conclusion of the Second World War collective security was once more challenged, this time by a military attack on a state established under the protection of the United Nations from an area outside that organization. Again, as in 1931, the challenge came in the Far East, but the subsequent course of events indicated that in 1950 some of the great powers, at least, were determined that such challenges should no longer be met by a policy of inactivity and appeasement. The succeeding years witnessed not only a resort to arms by the United Nations to throw back the forces of aggression but far-reaching and systematic efforts to strengthen and integrate the military and economic resources of the free world.

The Korean War

It has already been pointed out how, because of Soviet Russia's policy of obstruction in the United Nations and in Korea, the latter was not permitted to become a single unified state.[1] As a consequence, there were established in the peninsula the Republic of Korea, a democratic state which controlled the territory south of the 38th parallel and had its capital at Seoul, and the Korean People's Republic, a Communist state which controlled the area north of that parallel and had its capital at Pyongyang. The former was recognized by most of the states in the United Nations as the legitimate government of Korea and had the support of the United States; the latter enjoyed the recognition and support of the Soviet Union and its satellites. The governments of both republics claimed jurisdiction over all of Korea, and a state of undeclared war, with occasional minor clashes, prevailed along the 38th parallel. Although until the close of 1948 Russian forces had occupied the northern territory and the United States forces the southern, in 1949 the forces of both states were withdrawn, leaving the two republics to defend themselves with their own armed forces. It was generally recognized, however, that Russia had built up in the Korean People's Republic a far stronger and better equipped force than that possessed by the Republic of Korea.

Perhaps it was inevitable that sooner or later one of the Korean states

[1] See page 826.

should seek to unify the peninsula under its own government. Several factors may have played a part in influencing the North Koreans to make the first attempt. They may have realized that, after the withdrawal of United States troops, the outnumbered and lightly armed South Koreans would be unable to withstand the Communist armies from the north. Statements of responsible persons in the United States that South Korea could not be successfully defended against an attack from the north and that Korea was not essential to the security of the American defense line in the Pacific may, also, have convinced them that the United States would not undertake a campaign to free South Korea if the Communists once conquered it in a swift campaign. Finally, the North Koreans may have been encouraged to make the attack by the Soviet Union. The latter may have hoped thus to extend Communist influence throughout Korea or, if prevented from doing this by the intervention of the democratic powers, to weaken the latter so much economically and involve their forces so deeply militarily in Korea that they would be seriously handicapped in their efforts to create a strong army under the North Atlantic pact.[2]

Whatever the motives behind the move, on June 25, 1950, North Korean troops in overwhelming force and strongly supported by Russian-made aircraft and tanks crossed the 38th parallel and pushed on toward Seoul. Once more collective security was challenged and the question was whether the states of the United Nations would remain inactive as those of the League of Nations had when Japan sought swiftly to occupy Manchuria in 1931. By many it had long been felt that the immediate train of events which led to the Second World War had started with the failure of the United States and the League of Nations to take up Japan's challenge at that time. In 1950 much depended upon the attitude of the United States.

President Truman at once decided that "the United States must do everything within its power, working as closely as possible with the United Nations, to stop and throw back this aggression," and at once took steps to bring the situation quickly before the UN Security Council. On the very afternoon that the war began in Korea the Council adopted a resolution declaring that North Korea had committed a breach of peace and calling for the immediate cessation of hostilities and the withdrawal of the North Korean forces to the 38th parallel. It further requested all UN members to give every assistance to the UN "in the execution of this resolution and to refrain from giving assistance to the North Korean authorities."[3]

The United States government believed that the attack on South Korea

---

[2] See page 1008.

[3] At that time the Soviet government was boycotting the UN because of the latter's failure to recognize the People's Republic of China, so no Soviet delegate was present.

resembled the pattern of aggression which had led up to the Second World War. The possibility of active Russian or Chinese intervention to support the North Koreans was not ignored, but it was felt that the risks involved in stopping the aggression were less than the dangers involved in failure of the United States and the United Nations to take action. On June 26, therefore, the United States government decided that its navy and air force should be ordered to provide the fullest possible cover and support to the Republic of Korea (ROK) forces south of the 38th parallel. At the same time, in order to remove any temptation for the Chinese Communists to enter the war—and perhaps to placate Chiang Kai-shek's supporters in the United States—it was decided to order the United States Seventh Fleet to prevent any attack on Formosa and to call upon Chiang to cease any military action against the Chinese Communists. The American fleet was ordered to "neutralize" Formosa. On June 27 the UN Security Council adopted a resolution calling on the states members of the UN to give all necessary assistance to the South Korean Republic.

Meanwhile, the ROK forces had been driven back and were trying to form a line at the Han River just south of Seoul. On June 29 General Mac-Arthur, the Allied supreme commander in the Far East, reported that the South Koreans had already suffered casualties of nearly 50 per cent, and the United States joint chiefs of staff decided that stronger measures were needed, not only to help the ROK forces but to ensure evacuation of American nationals. United States ships and planes were thereupon authorized to strike military targets in North Korea, and the use of army service troops in South Korea and of certain combat units to protect a port and an airfield in the general area of Pusan was also authorized. These decisions were facilitated by the Soviet government's refusal to accede to the American request that it "use its influence with the North Korean authorities to withdraw their invading forces." Instead, Moscow had put all the blame for the situation in Korea on the South Koreans and "those who stand behind their back."

On June 30, after a personal reconnaissance in Korea, General MacArthur reported that the only assurance of holding the line of the Han River and regaining lost ground lay in the use of American combat troops. He urgently asked, and received the same day, the President's authorization to start the building up in Korea of two divisions from American troops in Japan for an early counter-offensive. Shortly thereafter American troops were being sent by airlift to Pusan in South Korea. Thus, six days after the start of the Communist aggression, orders committing United States troops to the struggle to provide collective security had been given to General Mac-Arthur. The attitude and actions of the United States government in this crisis were in marked contrast with those at the time of the Japanese aggression in Manchuria in 1931.[4]

On July 7 the UN Security Council approved an Anglo-French resolution which, among other things, recommended a unified command of United Nations forces and requested the United States—the country which had taken the lead in sending forces to combat the Communist aggression—to designate the commander. In compliance with the Council's directive President Truman at once named General MacArthur as commander-in-chief of all the UN forces in Korea. These consisted at first of only Americans and South Koreans, but ultimately ground, naval, or air forces were sent by Australia, Belgium, Canada, Colombia, Ethiopia, France, Great Britain, Greece, Luxembourg, the Netherlands, New Zealand, the Philippines, South Africa, Thailand, and Turkey. Hospital units were sent by Denmark, India, Italy, Norway, and Sweden.

Meanwhile, in Korea the first six weeks of the fighting had witnessed the steady retreat of the UN forces. The strength of the North Koreans had been underestimated by military observers, including even MacArthur, who had at first apparently thought that two United States divisions might be enough to turn the tide. But the superior numbers and the armored equipment of the North Koreans prevailed, and ultimately drove the UN forces into a 4,000 square-mile beachhead protecting the supply port of Pusan at the southern end of the Korean peninsula. It was feared that the forces of the UN might be driven out of Korea but this situation was swiftly changed on September 15 when some 50,000 United States marines and infantry made a successful amphibious landing at Inchon, on the west coast of the peninsula near Seoul. Ten days later the UN forces recaptured that capital city, and by the end of the month, all organized North Korean activities had ceased south of the 38th parallel. The aggressors had been hurled back.

On September 30 the South Korean parliament passed a resolution asking the United Nations to continue their advance beyond the 38th parallel. Whether to cross or not cross that parallel raised many questions. If the UN forces did not cross it and crush the aggressors, it was argued, the North Korean Communists would have an opportunity to reorganize their forces preparatory to another invasion. Moreover, not to cross it would appear to entail a divided Korea for an indefinite period. On the other hand, the crossing of the 38th parallel might provide an argument to bolster the Communist claim that the United States was embarked on an imperialist venture, an argument which might have considerable weight in the Asiatic world. Furthermore, such a crossing might incite the Chinese People's Republic to move its troops into Korea from Manchuria, might indeed precipitate a third world war.

[4] See pages 634–638.

THE SCENE OF THE KOREAN WAR

Even while the debate was being carried on, however, South Korean troops crossed the parallel and pushed northward. On October 7 the UN General Assembly approved a resolution which by implication authorized the crossing of the parallel by UN forces, and two days later UN forces crossed it in strength north of Kaesong. By October 20 they had captured Pyongyang, the capital of the Korean People's Republic, and a month later they were approaching the Yalu River, which constituted the boundary between Manchuria and Korea.

In North Korea along the Yalu River were power installations which had been started by the Japanese in 1937. After the Second World War these had become the joint property of Korea and China, and they supplied electric power for steel works, coal mines, and an aluminum plant in Manchuria. There were indications that the Chinese Communists were fearful that these power installations would fall into the hands of a hostile state and many observers believed that they would use their forces to protect them. From Western European governments came suggestions that a buffer zone be created along the Manchurian frontier and that no attempt be made to clear the North Korean troops from that border zone.

On November 24, however, General MacArthur announced a large-scale UN offensive, designed to "end the war, restore peace and unity in Korea, enable the prompt withdrawal of UN military forces, and permit the complete assumption by the Korean people and nation of full sovereignty and international equality for which the war was fought." But suddenly Chinese Communist troops in great numbers were hurled into the conflict on the side of the beaten North Korean army. Again the tide of battle turned. Outnumbered and outmaneuvered, the UN forces were halted and then thrown back. MacArthur at once notified the UN that Chinese Communist troops numbering more than 200,000 men now faced the UN forces in Korea, thus posing issues which would have to be resolved by the United Nations and within the chancelleries of the world. The American representative on the UN Security Council thereupon denounced the Chinese People's Republic as an aggressor.[5]

In December, 1950, Pyongyang was recaptured by the Communists. The UN forces withdrew to positions near the 38th parallel and regrouped for a new defense of Seoul. But the weight of the Chinese Communist forces continued to be felt. Early in January, 1951, the United States Eighth Army was compelled to withdraw from Seoul in the face of overwhelming attacks by Chinese infantry, supported by tanks and artillery. The South Korean government again fled from Seoul to Pusan. Before the month was out the

[5] After much discussion and delay a United States resolution declaring the Chinese People's Republic was engaged in aggression in Korea was adopted by the UN General Assembly on February 1, 1951.

Communist forces had once more crossed the 38th parallel. For a time it seemed that the long retreat of the summer of 1950 might be re-enacted, but ultimately the Communist advance was stemmed. The UN forces first halted their retreat and then gradually turned to the offensive again. On March 14, 1951, Seoul was recaptured for the second time by South Korean forces. By the end of the month UN troops were once more back approximately to the 38th parallel. In April that parallel was again crossed in a limited offensive.

For some time it had been apparent that General MacArthur's views on how to conduct the war in Korea and to provide American security in the Far East differed from those of the government of the United States and those of other members of the United Nations. The policy of the United States was to limit the war to Korea, to convince the Communist leaders by UN fighting that it was useless for them to continue their aggression, and thus lead them to be willing to negotiate. The bombing of Manchuria or China and the use of Chiang's Chinese Nationalist troops, it was believed, might result in the spreading of the conflict or even to a third world war. General MacArthur, on the other hand, felt that his conduct of the war was seriously handicapped by these restrictions, and although he had been instructed to clear all statements of a political nature with the government in Washington, he failed to do so. On April 11, 1951, President Truman unexpectedly relieved him of all his Far Eastern commands on the grounds that he did not agree with the official policies of the United States and the United Nations and was thus unable to give wholehearted support to them. General Matthew B. Ridgway, commander of the United States Eighth Army in Korea, was appointed to succeed MacArthur as the supreme commander in the Far East.

But the change in commanders had little effect on the military situation in Korea. Fighting continued, but General Omar Bradley, chairman of the United States joint chiefs of staff, announced in May that it was not the objective to drive the Communist armies out of North Korea but to inflict maximum casualties so that the Communists would be persuaded to negotiate. In June Trygve Lie, secretary general of the UN, declared that a new effort should be made to arrange a cease-fire approximately along the 38th parallel. This, he maintained, would fulfill the main purpose of the Security Council's resolutions of June and July, 1950. If no armistice could be arranged, he asserted, members of the UN should contribute additional forces for the war in Korea. It soon became obvious that both the Russian Soviet government and the Chinese People's government favored some such step, and ultimately, on July 10, 1951, cease-fire negotiations began at Kaesong.

But it soon became equally obvious that, though the Communists were ready to begin negotiations for a truce, they were in no particular hurry to reach an agreement on its terms. On question after question there were prolonged and seemingly futile discussions. Month after month passed without final agreement. And meanwhile fighting—but not all-out fighting—continued on the battlelines, with little result except to increase steadily the casualties on both sides. In some circles among the citizens of the free countries patience wore thin and demands for drastic action by the UN were vigorously voiced. But, seemingly, most of the free world preferred to negotiate as long as any hope of a cease-fire remained, and so intermittently the negotiations continued. Eventually, after some 158 meetings of the top negotiators and hundreds of meetings of their subordinates, the truce document was completed and signed by United Nations and Communist representatives. All military action in Korea and its surrounding waters halted at 10 P. M. on July 27, 1953, a little more than two years after the negotiations had started. As a result of the war the United Nations forces had suffered a total of 1,474,269 casualties (dead, wounded, captured, or missing), of which the South Koreans had suffered 1,312,836 and the United States, 144,173. The total Communist casualties were estimated at 1,540,000, of which the North Koreans had suffered 520,000 and the Chinese 900,000.

By the terms of the truce both sides, having ceased fire, were to withdraw two kilometers from the final battleline to form a neutral zone between the opposing armies. Both sides accepted restrictions on troop reinforcement and airfield construction, and a commission consisting of representatives of India, Sweden, Switzerland, Poland, and Czechoslovakia was to see that these restrictions were observed. All prisoners on both sides who wanted to return were to be repatriated at once and the others were to be placed in custody of a neutral commission, consisting of representatives of the above-mentioned states, with India providing troops to guard the prisoners. Communist and UN teams were to have opportunities to try to persuade reluctant prisoners to accept repatriation, with the neutral commission certifying any changes of mind. Finally, a high-level political conference was to convene within ninety days after the beginning of the truce to "settle through negotiation the questions of the withdrawal of all foreign troops from Korea, the peaceful settlement of the Korean question, etc." On August 5 the first prisoners of war were exchanged, and the exchange was completed on September 6. Four days later Indian troops began taking over custody of prisoners of both sides who had refused to be repatriated: 22,606 held by the UN and 1,578 held by the Communists. "Explanations" to the prisoners began on October 15 and ended on December 23. Neither side succeeded in changing the decisions of any large percentage of the men interviewed. More than 22,000 prisoners refused to be repatriated. On January 23, 1954, these prisoners were freed.

casualties   1,474,269
S. Korean   1,312,836
U.N.   161,433
U.S.   144,173
other U.N.   17,260

Futile Attempts to Negotiate a Political Settlement in the Far East

To most observers it appeared extremely unlikely that a final political agreement regarding Korea could be easily reached. President Syngman Rhee of the Korean Republic appeared eager to unify Korea by military measures if diplomacy did not quickly achieve it, and, with the South Korean forces in 1953 far stronger than the North Korean (the reverse of the situation in 1950), many believed that the Russian and Chinese Communists would be reluctant to withdraw their forces. On the other hand, President Rhee feared that should both the Chinese and the United Nations actually withdraw their forces from Korea, the Chinese armies, just across the Yalu River, might sometime again launch an all-out offensive and conquer all Korea before the UN forces could effectively come to the Korean Republic's assistance. To overcome Rhee's fears and possibly to deter the Chinese Communists from attempting any such coup, the United States on August 8 signed with the Korean Republic the draft of a mutual security pact with a provision giving the United States the right to station troops in Korea similar to that in the security pact between Japan and the United States.[6] Furthermore, the sixteen countries which had fought under the UN flag in Korea pledged themselves to take up arms again in case of any new Communist attack on Korea.

On the question of the political unification of Korea, both the Communists and the United Nations were in agreement. The problem appeared to be whether in 1953 they could agree any better than in 1947 [7] on the method of achieving this end and on the meaning of "free elections." Finally, it appeared likely that the abbreviation, "etc.," in the truce agreement would cause disagreements not only between the United Nations and the Communists but among the United Nations themselves. Involved in this abbreviation seemed to be the fundamental question of the relation between the Western world and the People's Republic of China. Twenty-seven nations had recognized the Communist government in Peking and were apparently willing to admit it into the UN, but in the United States a great body of opinion, official and unofficial, opposed both of these steps. Shortly before the signing of the truce the United States Congress had unanimously adopted a resolution opposing Communist China's admission to the UN.

Meanwhile, on August 17, 1953, the General Assembly of the United Nations had convened in order to arrange the political conference on

[6] See page 811.
[7] See page 826.

Korea provided for in the armistice agreement. At the outset a Russian proposal to invite representatives of Communist China and North Korea to participate in the debate on the political conference was rejected. Another Russian proposal that the conference should consist of representatives of the United States, Great Britain, France, Russia, Communist China, India, Poland, Sweden, Burma, North Korea, and South Korea was also voted down. A British proposal that India should be represented was likewise defeated, chiefly because of the opposition of the United States. In the end, the Assembly decided that all states which had borne arms under the UN flag, together with South Korea, should be entitled to representation. It then voted that the Soviet Union should be invited to take part in the conference, "provided the other side desires it." Arrangements regarding the place of meeting of the conference were to be made by United States and Communist representatives.

Talks between the United States and Communist envoys on the proposed Korean conference began in Panmunjom on October 26, 1953. Disagreements on many subjects at once arose. Eventually, on December 12, after the Communists had rejected a "final" plan proposed by the United States, the American envoy broke off the discussions. Although, a month later, the Communists proposed the resumption of the negotiations at Panmunjom, apparently both sides realized that the approaching meeting of the foreign ministers of the Big Four was the real place where a decision would be reached.

On January 25, 1954, the Big Four Council of Foreign Ministers—consisting this time of John Foster Dulles (United States), Anthony Eden (Great Britain), Georges Bidault (France), and Vyacheslav Molotov (Russia)—met in Berlin to discuss the whole complex of East-West differences. As was generally expected, the ministers failed to reach agreement on a plan to unify Germany, on an Austrian peace treaty, or on the question of European security. In fact, so far as Europe was concerned, no agreements were reached. Apparently the Russians had decided to hold fast to their positions in the West. In respect to the Far East, however, an agreement was reached, based on a proposal made by Molotov at the opening of the conference. When the meeting adjourned on February 18 the ministers had decided that a conference of representatives of the United States, Britain, France, the Soviet Union, and the People's Republic of China would be convened in Geneva in April for the purpose of reaching a peaceful settlement of the Korean question and of discussing the Indo-Chinese situation. In deference to Secretary of State Dulles' desire, it was at the same time announced that the Geneva conference in no way implied recognition of the Communist regime in China.

Although the Big Four at Berlin had voted to limit the Geneva conference to the five great powers, on April 26, 1954, the conference convened
with delegations from twenty states present to discuss the fate of Korea.
Represented were the sixteen United Nations countries which had sent
troops to defend Korea, the Soviet Union, the Chinese People's Republic,
South Korea, and North Korea. The North Korean foreign minister at
once proposed the withdrawal of troops within six months from both parts
of Korea and the unification of Korea on the basis of free elections to a
national assembly, the elections to be supervised by an all-Korean commission composed of members elected by the North and South Korean parliaments. The North Korean proposals immediately received the full support
of Chou En-lai, premier of the Chinese People's Republic, and of Vyacheslav Molotov, Russian foreign minister.

John Foster Dulles, American secretary of state, opposed the North Korean proposals, however, declaring that they ignored the United Nations
and gave no more than equality to South Korea although the latter contained some 75 per cent of the Korean people. He pointed out also that
whereas the Chinese Communist forces, if they withdrew across the Yalu
River, would still be within easy striking distance of Korea, the UN troops,
if they withdrew, would be a considerable distance away. Representatives
of most of the states present at the conference supported the American
view, and both French Foreign Minister Bidault and British Foreign Secretary Eden insisted that any Korean elections must be internationally
supervised. The Canadian foreign minister went so far as to characterize
the North Korean proposals as completely unworkable, unfair, and unacceptable.

In the ensuing discussions the representatives of the three Communist
states spent much of their time attacking the United States. They accused
the latter of planning to create "an aggressive *bloc* which is in conflict with
Asian peoples," of attempting to set Asians against Asians, of refusing to
recognize the Chinese people's right to choose their own system of government, of having launched a war of intervention against North Korea in
1950, of violating the Korean armistice agreement by concluding a defense
pact with South Korea, of having invaded Formosa and converted it into
a base for aggressive activities against the Chinese mainland, and of using
the Indo-Chinese war as a pretext for establishing an aggressive southeast
Asia defense pact, thereby threatening to start a new world war. But the
Communists failed to split the sixteen UN nations, many of whose representatives staunchly defended the United States against these accusations.

Eventually, on June 15, the sixteen non-Communist representatives announced that further discussion of the Korean question would serve no

useful purpose so long as the Communists rejected the two fundamental principles which the sixteen nations considered necessary for a solution. These principles were (1) that the United Nations was fully and rightfully empowered to extend its good offices to seeking a peaceful settlement in Korea, and (2) that, in order to establish a united, independent, and democratic Korea, genuinely free elections must be held under UN supervision for a national assembly in which representation must be in direct proportion to the indigenous population of Korea. It thus seemed apparent that again in 1954 the unification of Korea was blocked, as it had been in 1947, by the unwillingness of the Communists to permit a free election under the supervision of a United Nations commission.

But the Geneva conference not only failed to wipe out the division of Korea; it approved a settlement which recognized, at least temporarily, the division of another country between Communist and non-Communist regimes. Part of the purpose of the Geneva conference was to end, if possible, the long war in Indo-China. This problem was considered by representatives of France, Great Britain, Soviet Russia, the United States, the Chinese People's Republic, Laos, Cambodia, and both Bao Dai's government and the Viet Minh government in Viet Nam. From May 8 till July 20 the delegates of these nine governments debated the Indo-Chinese situation, often in closed session, before an agreement could be reached.

Various proposals for a settlement were advanced by France, Viet Nam, Viet Minh, Russia, and Great Britain. As in the case of Korea, there was a sharp contrast in the views and opinions expressed by the Communist and non-Communist delegates. As in the case of the discussions in Korea, too, the Communist representatives went out of their way to attack the United States, going so far as to assert that the Americans had from the start aimed at gradually ousting the French from Indo-China, turning that region into an American colony, and making it a base for the conquest of the countries of southeast Asia. The charge of Chinese intervention in Indo-China, the Communists maintained, was only an American fiction and slander designed to cover up their own intervention.

Nevertheless, despite such fulminations some progress toward a settlement was made. On May 29 all of the delegates accepted the British proposal that military representatives from the two commands, that is, France and Viet Nam on the one side and Viet Minh on the other, should meet to discuss the regrouping of units in Viet Nam as the first step toward an armistice. On June 19 the delegates also agreed that representatives of the commands of the two sides should meet immediately to study the problem of cessation of hostilities in Cambodia and Laos and should report to the conference within twenty-one days their conclusions and recommendations.

Meetings of these military representatives were held on June 24 and July 7.

Ultimately, on July 20, the conference agreed on the terms of a cease-fire. According to the agreement, Viet Nam was to be divided by an armistice line at the 17th parallel, though the Communists had originally demanded the 13th. The powers, in the so-called Geneva Declaration, recognized that the demarcation line was not to be interpreted as a political or territorial boundary, and inhabitants in Viet Nam were to be allowed freely to choose in which zone they wished to reside. French forces in the Red River delta, which included the important cities of Hanoi and Haiphong, were to be evacuated within ten months, and two enclaves south of the 17th parallel were to be evacuated by Viet Minh troops within eight months. The introduction of foreign troops and munitions into either zone of Viet Nam was forbidden, no foreign military base should be established in either, and neither zone should constitute part of any military alliance or be used for the resumption of hostilities. Free elections by secret ballot were to be held throughout Viet Nam in July, 1956, under the supervision of an international commission appointed by a committee representing India (chairman), Poland, and Canada.

International armistice commissions were also to be provided for Laos and Cambodia by representatives of the same three powers. All Viet Minh troops were to be withdrawn from Laos and elections were to be held in that state in August, 1955. Cambodia and Laos pledged themselves never to take part in an aggressive policy, never to allow their territory to be utilized for such a policy, and never to make an agreement to enter into a military alliance not in conformity with the UN charter. The conference powers agreed that no foreign bases were to be established in Cambodia or Laos except for two small bases in Laos where a limited number of French troops might be stationed.

France pledged herself to respect the independence and sovereignty, unity, and territorial integrity of Viet Nam, Cambodia, and Laos, and the powers signatory of the Geneva Declaration likewise pledged themselves not to interfere in the internal affairs of the three countries. The United States, which did not sign the Geneva Declaration, pledged itself not to threaten or use force to disturb the conditions envisaged by the Geneva settlement and to view "with grave concern" any renewal of aggression in Indo-China.

In the government established in the region north of the 17th parallel Ho Chi Minh became prime minister and at once promised that his government would respect the various armistice agreements. In the region south of that parallel the prime minister of Viet Nam denounced the armistice agreements and ordered flags to be flown at half mast. The French commissioner-general announced that France considered the southern Viet Nam government as the only one linked with France by past agreements, but declared that French policy would be based upon the principles of total independence and complete support of Viet Nam. Viet Nam independence, he asserted, like that of Laos and Cambodia, would be achieved by the end of 1954. On September 7, 1954, in fact, in a formal ceremony the residence of former French governors-general at Saigon was handed over to the South Viet Nam government. Some three months later, on December 29, 1954, France and the Indo-China states signed agreements giving South Viet Nam, Laos, and Cambodia what was described as full financial and economic independence also.

The Geneva settlement in Indo-China was regarded by many observers as a serious defeat for the West in the Far East. It undoubtedly enhanced the prestige of the Chinese People's Republic and lessened that of the United States and the other Western powers. The agreement, it was felt, strengthened the Viet Minh cause to such an extent that the Communists were very likely to win control of the government of a united Viet Nam in the elections scheduled for 1956. Moreover, in control of China, North Korea, and North Indo-China, the Communists seemed to be in an admirable position to direct their campaign of propaganda and subversion against Thailand, Burma, Malaya, and even India. This threatening situation gave added impetus to the search for collective security in the Far East which had been going on since the Communist attack on South Korea in 1950.

Security Measures in the Far East

Communist aggression in Korea had worldwide repercussions. Without hesitation the foreign ministers of France, Great Britain, and the United States, meeting in New York in September, 1950, agreed that the most urgent problem before them was that of strengthening the defenses of the free world in Asia and in Europe. In the attempt to solve this problem the United States took the lead, seeking to bind countries together by mutual defense pacts and extending military and economic assistance to innumerable states in an effort to build up their ability to resist aggression. In some cases the desire to increase the effective strength of the anti-Communist world entailed a clear-cut reversal of former United States policies.

In the Far East, for example, the United States attitude of nonintervention in case of an attempt by the Chinese Communists to take over Formosa was completely altered. Immediately following the Communist attack on the Republic of Korea President Truman declared that since it had become clear that Communism had passed beyond the use of subversion to conquer independent nations and would now use armed invasion and war, a Communist occupation of Formosa would be a direct threat to the security of the Pacific area. He therefore ordered the United States Seventh Fleet to prevent any attack on that island. Then, early in 1951, the United States agreed to extend American military aid to the Chinese Nationalist government to enable it to ensure the internal security and self-defense of Formosa, and an American military mission was dispatched to supervise the use of that aid. In addition, economic and technical assistance to the extent of hundreds of millions of dollars was provided Chiang in the years following the outbreak of the Korean War. Apparently it was believed in Washington that in case a third world war should develop in the Far East Chiang and his Nationalist forces might be useful against Communist China.

Similarly, the United States attitude became more favorable to the French efforts to restore order in Indo-China, where for some years the French had been fighting a war against a native resistance movement led by the Russian-trained Communist, Ho Chi Minh. The French claimed that Ho Chi Minh's forces were being supported in part by the Chinese Communists, who provided training, technicians, and American equipment which had been captured earlier from Chiang Kai-shek's forces on the mainland. They argued that in Indo-China the French were fighting the battle against Communism the same as the UN forces were in Korea, and pointed out that they had paid and were paying a heavy price in lives and money in order that Communism might there be checked.

Immediately after the Communist attack on the Korean Republic President Truman announced that military aid to the forces of France and the "associated states" of Indo-China—Viet Nam, Laos, Cambodia—would be speeded up and that a military mission would be despatched to provide close working relations with those forces. In December, 1950, military aid conventions were signed between the United States and the "associated states." Without the ever-increasing flow of war materials from the United States in the ensuing years, the French forces in Indo-China could probably not have held out as long as they did.

Steps were also taken by the United States to create a network of mutual defense pacts in the Pacific area. On August 30, 1951, the United States and the Republic of the Philippines signed a treaty in which both nations expressed their common determination to defend themselves against attack and their joint recognition that an armed attack in the Pacific area on either would be dangerous to the peace and security of the other. Two days later Australia, New Zealand, and the United States also signed a mutual defense treaty, which provided that an attack on any one of the three states or on territories under their jurisdiction in the Pacific area would be recognized as a danger to all three parties and that each would act to meet it in accordance with its constitutional practices and with UN principles. In 1952 the Pacific

Council of Ministers of Australia, New Zealand, and the United States (ANZUS) was established to carry out Pacific defense planning under the three states' mutual security pact. Finally, on September 8, 1951, at the time of the signing of the Japanese peace treaty, the United States entered into a far-reaching and long-time security pact with the Japanese government, the terms of which have been outlined.[8]

But with the increasing successes of the Viet Minh forces in Indo-China in 1953–1954 the establishment of some more general East-West system of collective security against the continuous expansion of Communism seemed to many to be called for. This was especially the view of the United States government which in 1954 emphasized the strategic importance of Indo-China and American determination that it should not be lost to the Communists. But most of the Asiatic powers felt that France's war in Indo-China was a struggle to preserve her colonial prerogatives and therefore declined to join the United States in any armed intervention; Great Britain also declined to join on the ground that such action would further alienate Asiatic opinion from the West. Since the United States was unwilling to intervene in Indo-China alone, Viet Minh successes continued and the Geneva armistice, favorable to the Communists, resulted.

But the United States was still desirous of creating some kind of Southeast Asia security organization to deter the Communists from further aggression and proceeded with plans to that end. Ultimately, in September, 1954, the representatives of the United States, Great Britain, France, Australia, New Zealand, the Philippines, Thailand, and Pakistan met in Manila to draft a Southeast Asia defense treaty. Great Britain had wished to have more Asiatic countries included, but India, Burma, Indonesia, and Ceylon had declined to attend. These states believed that peaceful co-existence with Communist China and Communist Russia was possible, and feared that a military partnership with the West might aggravate their already delicate relations with those countries. Prime Minister Nehru of India, in fact, declared that the Manila conference "was likely to reverse the trend of conciliation released by the Indo-China settlement." From the Asiatic mainland, therefore, only Thailand and Pakistan sent representatives.

Nevertheless, on September 8, 1954, the representatives of the powers present in Manila signed a Southeast Asia defense treaty in which the eight countries agreed to co-operate to strengthen defense, to develop economic measures for social well-being, and to counter subversion from without. They further agreed, in the event of armed attack or aggression in the "treaty area" against any designated state or territory, to take action in

[8] See page 811.

accordance with their constitutional processes, and, in the event of threats other than by armed attack, to consult on necessary measures. The "treaty area" was defined as Southeast Asia, including Thailand, Pakistan, Cambodia, Laos, and South Viet Nam, and the general area of the Southwest Pacific south of 21°30′ north latitude. Formosa was excluded from the area. The United States signed the treaty with the understanding that its agreement regarding armed attack or aggression applied only to Communist aggression. To implement the treaty the powers decided to establish a council as part of the Southeast Asia Treaty Organization (SEATO).

The powers at Manila also signed a declaration of principles, the Pacific Charter, in which they stated that they upheld the principle of equal rights and self-determination of peoples, and pledged themselves to strive by every peaceful means to promote self-government and to secure the independence of all countries desiring it and capable of undertaking its responsibilities. At the same time, they asserted their determination to prevent or counter any subversive attempts in the treaty area to destroy their sovereignty or territorial integrity.

Although SEATO was hailed by some as the first multilateral defensive alliance to link the East and the West against Communist aggression, it is obvious that it was at best a small organization with only two minor Asiatic powers included. Not included were Japan, India, Burma, Indonesia, Formosa, and South Korea. It is obvious, also, that most of the military strength, if it were ever used, would have to be furnished by the West. But Britain and France thought that economic aid was the most potent weapon against Communism, and they were reluctant to accept commitments in SEATO which would imply drawing a line in Southeast Asia and agreeing to go to war if the Communists crossed it. Accordingly, none of the members of SEATO was really obliged to do anything against aggression except to "consult" and "act in accordance with constitutional processes." No provision was made for the pooling of military strength or for any unified command. SEATO was, therefore, no such close and binding organization as that which had been earlier created in the North Atlantic Treaty Organization.

The North Atlantic Treaty Organization

During the discussions and debates which preceded and followed the dismissal of General MacArthur as the supreme commander in the Far East it was made abundantly evident that the United States and the states of Western Europe, although determined to oppose aggression in the Far East, were likewise resolved not to be turned aside from their endeavor to build up collective security in Europe. In fact, the war in Korea undoubtedly gave added impetus to the plans for the political, economic, and military integration of the states of the North Atlantic area.

Even before the outbreak of the Korean War it had begun to be felt both in western Europe and in the United States that military support by the latter was just as essential for world peace as its economic support was for European reconstruction. In June, 1948, the United States Senate adopted the so-called Vandenberg resolution which recommended, among other things: (1) that the United States encourage the development of collective security arrangements, (2) that it associate itself with such arrangements when they were based on full self-help and mutual aid and when they affected the security of the United States, and (3) that it make clear, in advance, that any armed attack by an aggressor nation upon a peace-loving nation whereby the security of the United States was affected would be combatted by the latter.

In October, 1948, the Canadian and the Brussels-pact governments [9] announced their readiness to negotiate a collective security treaty with the United States, and eventually, on April 4, 1949, the North Atlantic treaty was signed in Washington by the foreign ministers of twelve states—Great Britain, France, Belgium, the Netherlands, Luxembourg, Italy, Portugal, Norway, Denmark, Iceland, Canada, and the United States. The treaty contained six main points: (1) signatories renounced war as an instrument of policy except as provided by the United Nations Charter; (2) they were obligated to take military or other action forthwith in case of an armed attack against any signatory nation; (3) each signatory would decide for itself what constituted an armed attack and what immediate action it would take to fulfill its obligation; (4) the treaty would run for twenty years; (5) it would create a North Atlantic Council with powers to establish other committees; (6) the co-operation of certain other states would be welcomed.

In accordance with the terms of the North Atlantic treaty the North Atlantic Treaty Organization (NATO), consisting of one representative of each of the signatory powers, was established and held its first meeting in September, 1949. In that same month the Congress of the United States approved the creation of a military assistance program fund of $1,000,000,000, with which to finance shipments of arms to the pact countries from United States surpluses. In 1950 NATO approved integrated defense plans for the entire North Atlantic area and the United States signed bilateral agreements for arms shipments to all member countries which requested aid. It also agreed upon the necessity for concentrating on "the creation of balanced collective forces"; that is, the states agreed that each should concentrate on contributing its best resources for the common defense. It seemed to be ex-

[9] See pages 916–917.

pected that the United States would be responsible for strategic bombing, Great Britain and the United States for naval forces, France and Great Britain for tactical aviation, and the continental powers chiefly for ground forces.

The Communist attack on the Korean Republic in 1950 increased the desire to provide effective security through NATO. The United States Congress appropriated an additional $3,500,000,000 for the military assistance program, and NATO approved plans for the further integration of Western defenses and the appointment of a supreme Atlantic pact commander. In December, 1950, General Dwight D. Eisenhower, who had been supreme Allied commander in Western Europe in 1944–1945, was appointed to head NATO's armed forces. In April, 1951, he formally assumed command at the Supreme Headquarters of Allied Powers in Europe (SHAPE), which were located near Paris.[10] As the result of the decision of the North Atlantic Council meeting at Ottawa in September, 1951, Greece and Turkey, in whose defense against Soviet aggression the free peoples of the world were vitally concerned, were invited to become members of NATO. This invitation was ratified by the various governments and the number of NATO members was thus increased to fourteen. Despite the fears of some of the smaller Western European powers, the North Atlantic defense area was thus extended eastward to the Aegean and Black seas and to the Caucasus.

In February, 1952, the North Atlantic Council, meeting at Lisbon, decided to create a permanent operating organization, with a secretariat and an established headquarters, and subsequently the NATO headquarters were set up at Paris, near SHAPE. In the expanded organization the North Atlantic Council remained the most powerful organ, deciding upon the general policies of NATO in so far as the ministers had powers to make such decisions. A second organ was the permanent council, consisting of state ministers, which was to sit "continuously" at NATO headquarters. The secretariat would perform for NATO duties like those of the former secretariat of the League of Nations or that of the United Nations. A general military committee was established to represent all member states, but a special standing group, staffed by British, French and United States officers, to which the Supreme Allied Commander was responsible, was set up in Washington.

Meanwhile, progress was being made in the task of building up NATO's military force. Early in 1954 there were 28 or 29 ready active divisions under arms in Western Europe, plus 31 more in Greece and Turkey. Yugoslavia,

---

[10] He was succeeded in 1952, after he had resigned to run for the presidency of the United States, by the American General Matthew B. Ridgway who, in turn, was succeeded in 1953 by the American General A. M. Gruenther.

which was not a member of NATO but seemed more and more inclined to co-operate with it, had about 32 small divisions. In air strength the goal of 4,000 tactical aircraft by the close of 1952 had been practically met, chiefly by contributions of the United States, though the figure included some 1,500 planes which were assigned to the home defense of France and Britain and were not technically under the control of the Supreme Allied Commander. Some 120 airfields and a large network of signal communications facilities were in use. The goals for air and naval forces for 1953 had been substantially met, and in December, 1953, the NATO Council had set goals for 1954 calling for some increase in the numerical strength of forces and a very substantial improvement in their quality and effectiveness.

According to military experts, the NATO forces in 1954 were strong enough so that the Soviet opportunity for a surprise attack had passed and the day of the "push-over" had ended. It was believed that, because of the West's superiority in both atomic and hydrogen bombs, any Russian attack on territories of the NATO countries would be punished severely and that Russians would pay heavily for any gains. It was hoped that this fact would serve as a deterrent to any Soviet attack. On the other hand, it was recognized that NATO strength was as yet inadequate to win a war against Russia or even to defend Europe for long. If the treaties signed with West Germany in October, 1954 [11] were ratified, however, the latter's twelve divisions and new airforce would materially increase NATO's military strength.

Attempts to Integrate Western Europe

The Communist aggression in Korea gave added impetus, also, to the movement to bring about a closer political, economic, and military integration of Western Europe than yet existed. A slight beginning of political integration had been made in 1948 when the Benelux countries and Great Britain and France had signed the Brussels treaty and had given approval to the creation of the Council of Europe.[12]

THE COUNCIL OF EUROPE

On May 5, 1949, ten powers—Belgium, Denmark, France, Great Britain, the Irish Republic, Italy, Luxembourg, the Netherlands, Norway, and Sweden—formally signed the Statute of the Council of Europe, which inaugurated a sort of small-scale United Nations. In its organization the Committee of Ministers was analogous to the Security Council; the Consultative Assembly resembled the General Assembly; and a Secretariat was estab-

[11] See pages 1018–1019.
[12] See page 917.

lished at Strasbourg, the seat of the new international organization. In 1951 the German Federal Republic was also admitted to membership in the Council. It had become clear, said the chairman of the Committee of Ministers, that Europe could not exist without Germany, nor Germany without Europe. German Federal Chancellor Adenauer, attending the Committee of Ministers for the first time on May 2, 1951, declared that Germany would work in the Council toward the integration of Europe as the only way to resist pressure from Eastern Europe and from Asia.

In November, 1951, after American spokesmen had indicated that they hoped Western Europe might work out some plan for federation, Paul Reynaud of France proposed a union of all Western Europe, which, with the help of Great Britain and the United States, would be able to build a defense against the danger of encroachment by the Soviet Union. But some of the states in the Council of Europe were apparently reluctant to join a European federation unless Great Britain were included for fear it might come to be dominated by Germany. But the British government, even under Churchill—who had frequently preached European unity without specifying that he excluded Britain—reiterated its stand that Great Britain, because of her relations with her dominions, could not enter a European federation.

The development of plans for the European Coal and Steel Community (ECSC) and the European Defense Community (EDC), both discussed below, led the Council of Europe to concern itself with the task of deciding what its role should be relative to such specialized bodies. Beginning in 1951 two desires of the Assembly were discernible. First, it wished to emancipate itself from the control of the Committee of Ministers in order to have something more than a mere deliberative and advisory role. This desire of the Assembly, which in reality was a move toward the creation of a European federation, had the support of the United States but encountered the obstacle of the national sovereignty of its member states. The second desire of the Assembly was to make the Council of Europe the framework into which the various specialized bodies, the ECSC, the EDC, and any others which might be set up, could be fitted. That the Council of Europe would develop into a Federation of Western Europe in the near future seemed doubtful, however.

THE EUROPEAN COAL AND STEEL COMMUNITY

The possibility of an economic integration of Western Europe was chiefly connected with the so-called Schuman Plan, suggested by French Foreign Minister Robert Schuman in May, 1950. He proposed that the coal and steel production of France, Germany, and the other Western European nations should be pooled under a common authority. The Benelux countries and Italy joined with France and Western Germany to give shape to this proposal, but Great Britain declined to participate. A draft treaty embodying the plan set up the European Coal and Steel Community, and was ultimately signed on April 18, 1951.

Under the constitution of the European Coal and Steel Community executive power was entrusted to the High Authority, a sort of cabinet with nine members. A second organ, the Council of Ministers, consisting of one representative from each participating government, had the function of harmonizing the action of the High Authority with the general economic policies of the participating states. The High Authority was responsible to the Assembly, in which France, Germany, and Italy had eighteen delegates each, Belgium and the Netherlands ten each, and Luxembourg four. The Assembly might by a two-thirds vote censure the High Authority, and such a vote of censure would entail the resignation of all the members of that body and the immediate appointment of new members. Finally, the High Court of seven judges had power to adjudicate upon complaints brought against the High Authority by a member state, the Council of Ministers, an association of producers, or an enterprise. The court also had power to annul any decision or recommendation, should the High Authority abuse or exceed its powers or contravene the treaty or the law.

The primary concern of the European Coal and Steel Community was the creation of a single market within which free trade in coal and steel should prevail, and the powers conferred on the High Authority were chiefly designed to assure the six-country area free competition. Illegitimate competitive devices, particularly temporary or local reductions of price in order to secure a monopoly, were forbidden, as was also any price discrimination according to the nationality of the purchaser. Every enterprise was compelled to publish its schedule of prices and its conditions of sale, and the High Authority was given power to fix maximum or, in a time of a crisis, minimum prices for any coal or steel products. In case of a depression the High Authority had the right to fix production quotas, or to impose a tax on production by an enterprise in excess of an assigned limit and use the proceeds to subsidize enterprises which were underemployed. In its operations the ECSC would be somewhat like a cartel.

The importance of the projected European Coal and Steel Community seemed indicated to some extent by the fact that it was at once denounced by the Communists and characterized by them as the "pact of the cannon kings." Undoubtedly, a coal and steel pool of six West European countries under one administration would create a strong industrial potential in Europe to rival the Eastern bloc's Council for Economic Mutual Assistance.[13] The coal production of the six Western countries would equal Russia's production, and their joint steel production would exceed by several million

[13] See page 782.

tons annually that of the whole Eastern bloc. The Communists of Germany, France, and Italy at once undertook to defeat the ratification of the Schuman Plan.

Nevertheless, the Schuman Plan treaty was ratified by the six states involved, and came into force on July 25, 1952. It was decided that Luxembourg should be the ECSC's headquarters until the future of the Saar had been decided. In August the High Authority held its first meeting, with Jean Monnet, the French economic expert who with Schuman had been co-author of the plan, as chairman. In September the first meeting of the Council of Ministers was held under the chairmanship of Chancellor Adenauer of Germany, and the Assembly met and elected Paul-Henri Spaak, former Belgium premier, as president. The first task of this supranational organization was to level barriers within the ECSC, which had a total annual production of some 41,000,000 tons of steel and 235,000,000 tons of coal. In January, 1954, the High Authority revealed that, since the opening of the common market, deliveries of coal between countries in the community had increased by 20.4 per cent, of iron ore by 14.7 per cent, and of scrap iron by 66 per cent. At the same time the Assembly approved a four-year capital investment policy designed to reduce retail prices, especially of steel, and to improve working and living conditions. In April, 1954, the United States and the ECSC signed an agreement by which the former was to make a 25-year loan of $100,000,000 to the ECSC for the modernization and development of its resources.

THE PROJECTED EUROPEAN DEFENSE COMMUNITY

To some extent, the movement to integrate the armed forces of Western Europe was launched by Winston Churchill who in a speech before the Consultative Assembly of the Council of Europe in August, 1950, had called for a real defensive front in Europe in which all members of the Council of Europe, including Germany, should bear their share. The Assembly had thereupon voted for "the immediate creation of a unified European army under the authority of a European minister of defense, subject to proper European democratic control and acting in full co-operation with the United States and Canada." But under the existing statute of the Council of Europe the Assembly was forbidden to discuss defense, so that its action on Churchill's proposal was ineffective.

In October, 1950 however, the so-called Pleven Plan was suggested by French Premier René Pleven in the hope of achieving some compromise between French fear of a remilitarized Germany and NATO's desire to have Western Germany contribute to its armed forces. Pleven proposed the creation of a European Defense Community (EDC) with a European army under a European minister of defense, who would be responsible to a European authority and would carry out the directives of a council of ministers composed of members of the participating countries. The European army, which would be financed by a common budget, would be used in accordance with obligations assumed under the North Atlantic treaty. The participating countries which already had national armies would retain control over that part of their armed forces which was not incorporated in the common force, but the Pleven idea was that a supranational army would gradually but irrevocably supersede the national armies.

The German Federal Republic was invited to participate in a conference at Paris on the formation of such a European army. Although Kurt Schumacher, the German Social Democratic leader, asserted that the Pleven Plan offered no basis for discussion, in February, 1951, a German representative attended the conference which included delegates also from France, Italy, Belgium, and Luxembourg. The French foreign minister emphasized the plan as a permanent solution of the "anachronistic and absurd divisions" of Europe, and asserted that Atlantic defense and European defense were not incompatible. The European army should be an integral part of the Atlantic force, and in the early stages of the plan decisions regarding the use of the European army would be the sole prerogative of the North Atlantic Treaty Organization. The conference decided that the heads of the five participating delegations should serve as a committee to work out the details of the plan.

In July, 1951, the delegations again met and agreed that the armed forces of the five countries set aside for European defense should be fused under a common supranational authority, political and military, the organs of which should be similar to those of the ECSC. Relations with NATO should be close and the military Authority should conform to the views and directives of SHAPE. Finally, in November, six countries—the Netherlands now joined the original five—agreed in a joint report, which they submitted to the North Atlantic Council, that a combined European army should be created as quickly as possible and placed under the command of General Eisenhower.

According to the EDC plan the six nations would pool all their ground, air, and sea forces—with certain specific exceptions—and would control this combined army by means of a European Authority staffed by and responsible, through a Council of Ministers, to all six powers. The European army would be paid and equipped from a common budget, made up of contributions from all six states augmented by United States aid. The forces to be excluded from control of the Authority would be (1) forces of the member states which were needed for service in their respective overseas territories, (2) forces engaged in "international" duties, as in Korea, Austria, and Berlin, and (3) forces needed for internal security. Each state, it was agreed, might exchange personnel between its troops in the European army and its overseas units, providing no diminution of the over-all European strength would result.

On May 27, 1952, the foreign ministers of France, the German Federal Republic, Italy, Belgium, the Netherlands, and Luxembourg signed the European Defense Community treaty, its military and financial protocols, and a protocol dealing with relations between NATO and EDC. The foreign ministers of the EDC states and of Great Britain and the permanent representatives of the NATO states also signed two additional protocols on the assistance to be given by EDC signatories to NATO members, and *vice versa,* in case of armed aggression. Generally speaking, all land and air forces of the six member states, except those needed in overseas territories and for special international commitments, would be under the control of SHAPE.

The European Defense Community would not come into force until all six states had ratified the treaty. The basic aim, of course, was to obtain German armed forces to aid in the defense of Europe without permitting the German Federal Republic to have a national army which might become dangerous to the peace of Europe again and which, as a national army, would undoubtedly raise French fears of a resurgent and aggressive Germany. Within Germany there was much opposition to the ratification of the EDC treaty. But the ratification of the latter was a prerequisite of the coming into effect of the convention between the Allies and Germany [14] providing for the abolition of the Occupation Statute with its authorization of Allied intervention in the internal affairs of the Federal Republic. Both houses of the German parliament approved the EDC treaty in 1953 but, despite considerable pressure from the United States government, both France and Italy delayed taking action. Eventually, in France fears of a rearmed Germany outweighed the desire for European integration, and on August 30, 1954, the French National Assembly took the decisive step of rejecting the treaty. This brought to an end all hopes of establishing the European Defense Community as originally projected.

WEST GERMANY'S ADMISSION TO NATO
AND THE WEST EUROPEAN UNION

As early as December, 1950, the powers of the North Atlantic Treaty Organization had agreed that a German contribution to Western defense was necessary, and France, Great Britain, and the United States had been invited to explore the matter. Discussions had been opened between the three Allied high commissioners and German Chancellor Adenauer, who had agreed that the defense of Europe called for the participation of West

[14] See page 906.

Germany. Many French statesmen, however, feared to permit the national rearmament of Germany lest German militarism be revived and France once again find herself confronted by a powerful and aggressive neighbor. It was in the hope of overcoming this French reluctance that Premier Pleven had put forth his plan for a European Defense Community. The rejection of the EDC treaty by the French National Assembly in August, 1954, was a blow to those who sought to strengthen the military forces of the West by bringing West Germany into some common military organization.

But the statesmen of the Western powers were determined to salvage as much as possible of that European defense unity, including Germany, which had been earlier envisaged. On September 20, speaking before the Consultative Assembly of the Council of Europe, Mendès-France proposed that the Western defense problem be solved by an extension of the Brussels Treaty to include Federal Germany and Italy, with a central authority to exercise control over manpower and armaments. He pointed out that one of the main objections in France to the EDC treaty was the absence of Britain, and that his proposed solution would meet that objection.

Mendès-France's suggestion was explored in negotiations between various sets of diplomats, in the course of which a number of compromises were made by one side and the other. Eventually the representatives of France, Great Britain, the United States, Canada, Italy, West Germany, the Netherlands, Belgium, and Luxembourg convened in London on September 28 and there on October 3, 1954, initialed numerous agreements, protocols, and annexes. The latter provided in principle for bringing a practically sovereign, rearmed West Germany into NATO and a West European Union under strict military safeguards but without the supranational controls included in the rejected EDC. Premier Mendès-France declared that he would throw all the authority of his government behind the London agreements and, although attacked by former Foreign Minister Schuman and the Popular Republicans, on October 12 he won a decisive vote of confidence in the National Assembly on their acceptance in principle.

But the agreements reached in principle at London had to be translated into specific detailed treaties for signing and for ratification. In the interests of France and doubtless in the hope of increasing the likelihood of eventual ratification of the subsequent treaties by the National Assembly, the French premier declared that before he would sign any of these detailed treaties a Franco-West German agreement must first be reached regarding the Saar. The value of the Saar to France and the status of the Saar after the First World War have been discussed earlier in this vol-

THE WESTERN "BIG THREE" IN 1954

Foreign Secretary Eden, Premier Mendès-France, and Secretary of State Dulles in Paris

ume.[15] After the Second World War the French had organized the Saar as an autonomous state with a constitution that provided for close economic ties with France and also prevented pro-German political parties from campaigning. After a series of conferences between Adenauer and Mendès-France, which for a time kept the fate of the London settlement in grave doubt, on October 23 a Saar agreement was reached. By the terms of this agreement (1) the Saar would be "Europeanized" under a commissioner (not a Frenchman, German, or Saarlander) named by the Western European Union; (2) the Saarlanders would be permitted to vote on the agreement and pro-German parties would be permitted to campaign; (3) assuming approval of the plan by the Saarlanders, an election would be held in the Saar for a legislature, with a change in the Saar's status not permitted as an issue; (4) the settlement of October 23 would be subject ultimately to the terms of a German peace treaty. It is obvious that Adenauer and Mendès-France both made concessions in order to reach this agreement.

With the Saar problem out of the way, the representatives of fifteen states gathered later on the same day at the Quai d'Orsay in Paris where four sets of agreements were signed. One was the Saar agreement outlined above, which was signed by France and West Germany. In a second treaty France, Britain, the United States and West Germany signed a new and shortened version of the 1952 Bonn convention.[16] The new agreement like that of 1952 revoked the Allied Occupation Statute and abolished the Allied high commission. It granted West Germany immediate and virtual sovereignty; the only right reserved to the Big Three was that of stationing troops in the Federal Republic and in Berlin for the "defense of the free world."

In a third document France, Great Britain, Belgium, the Netherlands, and Luxembourg—signatories of the Brussels treaty of 1948—[17] agreed to invite West Germany and Italy to join an expanded Brussels treaty organization which was to be officially called thereafter the Western European Union (WEU). This organization was greatly strengthened by Britain's commitment not to withdraw her forces from the continent without the permission of the other signatories. It was also strengthened by being given two functions not possessed by the Brussels treaty organization: (1) the right to fix the maximum size of the continental members' contributions to NATO and (2) the right to control all continental, and especially West German, manufacture of arms. No military increases would be permitted without the unanimous consent of the members of the Western

[15] See pages 396–397.
[16] See page 906.
[17] See pages 916–917.

European Union. Unlike the proposed EDC, however, it would have no authority to set up a supranational arms procurement agency and arms pool.

Finally, in a fourth document the fourteen states in NATO signed an agreement inviting West Germany to join the North Atlantic Treaty Organization with the right to raise a 500,000-man force which would be integrated with the other NATO forces only at the highest levels. In effect, a powerful national German army would be created. To prevent its independent deployment, however, increased powers were given to the supreme NATO commander over all NATO continental armies, including the West German, and over their placement, logistic arrangements, and supplies.

Thus, on paper at least, the Federal Republic of Germany was to emerge once more as an almost fully sovereign state linked with the other Western powers in three international organizations, the Council of Europe, the Western European Union, and the North Atlantic Treaty Organization. Thus, on paper at least, the armed forces of NATO were to be greatly increased by the addition of the large army and airforce which West Germany was to be permitted to have. But the Paris agreements required for their fulfillment the approval of many national parliaments, and whether they would receive the necessary ratifications by each of the signatory powers still remained to be discovered. Some ground for optimism was found, however, in the fact that the French National Assembly—after much pressure and with much reluctance—finally ratified the Paris agreements by a vote of 287 to 260 on December 30, 1954.

The Awaited Verdict

At the time this chapter was written collective security was still on trial, and the final verdict was far from certain. In the Far East the situation seemed to indicate a favorable outcome in the conflict between aggression and collective security. The Korean Communists, striking suddenly and with superior forces, in June, 1950 had overrun most of the Republic of Korea. Had the latter been left unaided to defend itself, there appears to be little doubt that it would have been conquered. But the armed forces of the United Nations went to its assistance, hurled back the invaders, and cleared the territory south of the 38th parallel of enemy troops. Then, in November, 1950, the Chinese Communists became aggressors. Their armies entered the fray in overwhelming numbers, and again the capital and some of the territory of the Korean Republic were occupied. But once more the United Nations armies stopped the aggressors, drove them north of the 38th parallel and apparently convinced them that a truce might be desirable. The truce obtained in July, 1953, constituted a victory for the United Nations. Though at considerable cost in men and money, they forced an aggressor to call off a war. Moreover, the United States, in the hope of discouraging further aggression in the Far East, signed a series of security pacts with Australia, New Zealand, the Philippines, and Japan, and initiated the loosely organized Southeast Asia Treaty Organization.

In the West the success or failure of collective security seemed to some to depend on the success or failure of efforts to bring about the political, economic, and military integration of Western Europe. The best that seemed likely to be achieved in the realm of political integration, however, was a close co-operation among a limited number of sovereign states in a small United Nations. But the prospects of some degree of economic and military integration seemed better. Both the Schuman Plan and the Pleven Plan, to be sure, were attacked by certain groups within Germany and France, and the latter was, in fact, rejected by the French. But the European Coal and Steel Community became effective in 1952, and it was widely hoped that the agreements signed in Paris in October, 1954, would ultimately be ratified and an integrated West European military force, including West Germany, would come into being.

By 1954 considerable progress had been made in strengthening the forces of collective security through the North Atlantic Treaty Organization. To a large extent this was a consequence of the fact that Communist aggression in Korea had spurred the United States to make tremendous increases in its own armed strength and in its assistance to the armed forces of other nations. There seemed little doubt that at the close of the year 1954 the total armed forces of the free world were far greater, not counting those in Korea, than they had been when the aggressors launched their attack. And, in the words of General Eisenhower, the first Supreme Commander of NATO's armed forces, if the nations in NATO would stop their haggling over minor points of national interest or prestige and would achieve a closer unity—political, military, and economic—the collective security of the free world could be assured.

Although at times progress seemed painfully slow, it appeared possible that eventually through NATO the balance of Soviet and non-Soviet power would be improved by the linking together of more than 350,000,000 people, whose industrial and military potential for the conduct of modern war would be great enough to neutralize the strength of the Soviet world. And thus collective security—achieved through NATO—would, the free world fervently hoped, create, in the words of former President Truman, "a shield against aggression and the fear of aggression."

SELECT BIBLIOGRAPHY

No attempt has been made to include in this bibliography all of the thousands of books which deal in one way or another with the history of Europe since 1870. The author has sought (1) to list enough books on each topic so that some of them will almost surely be found in any college or public library; (2) to include the biographies, memoirs, and reminiscences of those who played roles in the history recorded so that readers may be able to humanize the necessarily brief outline in the text; and (3) to call attention, where possible, to books on both sides of various controversial questions so that those who wish may have an opportunity to form their own opinions on these questions. For more complete bibliographies, including works published in foreign languages, the reader is referred to:

Gooch, G. P., *Recent Revelations of European Diplomacy* (1940); Kerner, R. J., *Slavic Europe, A Selected Bibliography in Western European Languages* (1918); Langer, W. L., and Armstrong, H. F., *Foreign Affairs Bibliography: A Selected and Annotated List of Books on International Relations, 1919–1932* (1933); Lewin, P. E., *Best Books on the British Empire* (1943); Mudge, I. G., *New Guide to Reference Books* (1929); Pinson, K. S., *Bibliographical Introduction to Nationalism* (1935); Ragatz, L. J., *A Bibliography for the Study of European History, 1815–1939* (1942–1945); Sacks, B., *Bibliography for Europe between 1815 and 1914* (1946); Savord, R., *World Affairs. A Foreign Service Reading List* (1946); Scott, F. D., and Rockefeller, A., Jr., *The Twentieth Century World: A Reading Guide* (1948); Temperley, H. W. V., and Penson, L. M., *A Short Bibliography of Modern European History, 1789–1935* (1936); Walsh, W. B., *Russia under Tsars and Commissars: A Readers' Guide* (1946); Woolbert, R. G., *Foreign Affairs Bibliography: A Selected and Annotated List of Books on International Relations, 1932–1942* (1942).

The following collections of source materials and readings are available for the period: Chandler, A. R., *The Clash of Political Ideals: A Source Book on Democracy, Communism, and the Totalitarian State* (1940); Cook, A. N., *Readings in Modern and Contemporary History* (1937); Cooke, W. P., and Stickney, E. P., *Readings in European International Relations Since 1879* (1931); Hall, W. P., and Beller, E. A., *Historical Readings in Nineteenth Century Thought* (1928); Langsam, W. C., *Documents and Readings in the History of Europe Since 1918* (1939); Robinson, J. H., and Beard, C. A., *Readings in Modern European History,* Vol. II (1909); Scott, F. J., and Baltzly, A., *Readings in European History Since 1814* (1930); Spahr, M., *Readings in*

Recent Political Philosophy (1935); Stearns, R. P., *Pageant of Europe: Sources and Selections from the Renaissance to the Present Day* (1947); Walsh, W. B., *Readings in Russian History* (1948).

For the very recent period much material may be found in such annuals as *The Statesman's Year Book, The New International Year Book, The Annual Register, Political Handbook of the World,* and *Survey of International Affairs,* and in such periodicals as *Foreign Affairs, Political Science Quarterly, The Journal of Modern History, The Journal of Central European Affairs, The Round Table, Fortnightly Review, Nineteenth Century,* and *Contemporary Review,* and in the publications of the Royal Institute of International Affairs, the Foreign Policy Association, and the United States Department of State.

Chapter I. Industrialism, Imperialism, and World Politics

ECONOMIC HISTORIES: Ashton, T. S., *The Industrial Revolution; A Study in Bibliography* (1937); Bogart, E. L., *Economic History of Europe, 1760–1939* (1942); Barnes, H. E., *An Economic History of the Western World* (1937); Bowden, W., *et al., An Economic History of Europe Since 1750* (1937); Clough, S. B., and Cole, C. W., *Economic History of Europe* (1946); Day, C., *Economic Development in Europe* (1942); Gibbins, H. de B., *Economic and Industrial Progress of the Century* (1903); Heaton, H., *Economic History of Europe* (1936); Nussbaum, F. L., *A History of the Economic Institutions of Modern Europe* (1933); Whittaker, E., *A History of Economic Ideas* (1940).

SCIENCE AND INVENTION: Beard, C. A., *The Industrial Invention* (1929); Byrn, E. W., *The Progress of Invention in the Nineteenth Century* (1900); Cressy, E., *Discoveries and Inventions of the Twentieth Century* (1930); Dampier-Whetham, W. C., *A History of Science* (1929); Gray, G. W., *The Advancing Front of Science* (1937); Jeans, Sir J., *The Growth of Physical Science* (1948); Kaempffert, W. B., *Invention and Society* (1930); Kaempffert, W. B., *Popular History of Invention,* 2 vols. (1924); Mumford, L., *Technics and Civilization* (1934); Murray, R. H., *Science and the Scientists* (1925); Pledge, H. T., *Science Since 1500* (1947); Slosson, E. E., *Creative Chemistry* (1938); Usher, A. P., *History of Mechanical Invention* (1929); Williams, H. S., *Story of Nineteenth Century Science* (1900).

THE NEW INDUSTRIAL REVOLUTION: Burn, D. L., *Economic History of Steelmaking, 1867–1939* (1940); Burnham, T. H., and Hoskins, G. O., *Iron and Steel in Britain, 1870–1930* (1944); Chase, S., *Men and Machines* (1929); Epstein, R. C., *The Automobile Industry, Its Economic and Commercial Development* (1928); Giedion, S., *Mechanization Takes Command* (1948); Howe, H. E. (ed.), *Chemistry in Industry* (1924); Johnson, E. A. J., *Some Origins of the Modern Economic World* (1936); Knauth, O., *Managerial Enterprise* (1948); Knowles, S. C. A., *Industrial and Commercial Revolutions During the Nineteenth Century* (1926); Luckiesh, M., *Artificial Light* (1920); MacGregor, D. H., *Evolution of Industry* (1912); Meakin, W., *The New Industrial Revolution* (1928); Ross, V., *The Evolution of the Oil Industry* (1920); Rugg, H. O., *The Great Technocracy* (1933); Stocking, G. W., and Watkins,

M. W., *Cartels or Competition* (1948); Wallace, A. R., *Wonderful Century* (1898); Wile, F. W. (ed.), *Century of Industrial Progress* (1928).

TRANSPORTATION AND COMMUNICATION: Berglund, A., *Ocean Transportation* (1931); Bowen, F. C., *A Century of Atlantic Travel* (1930); Brown, C. L. M., *The Conquest of the Air* (1927); Gibson, C. R., and Cole, W. B., *Wireless of To-Day* (1923); Gilfillan, S. C., *Inventing the Ship* (1935); Holland, R. S., *Historic Airships* (1928); Manus, T. F., and Beasley, W., *Men, Money, and Motors: The Drama of the Automobile* (1929); MacPherson, L. G., *Transportation in Europe* (1910); Maginnis, A. J., *The Atlantic Ferry* (1892); Nixon, S. J. C., *The Invention of the Automobile* (1936); Sherrington, C. E. R., *A Hundred Years of Inland Transportation, 1830–1933* (1934); Talbot, F. A., *Railway Conquest of the World* (1911); Talbot, F. A., *Steamship Conquest of the World* (1912).

MODERN CAPITALISM: Edwards, G. W., *The Evolution of Finance Capitalism* (1939); Einzig, P., *World Finance, 1914–1935* (1935); Emden, P. H., *Money Powers of Europe in the Nineteenth and Twentieth Centuries* (1938); Feis, H., *Europe: The World's Banker, 1870–1914* (1930); Fraser, H. F., *Foreign Trade and World Politics* (1926); Hobson, J. A., *The Evolution of Modern Capitalism* (1917); Hobson, C. K., *The Export of Capital* (1914); Sée, H. E., *Modern Capitalism* (1926); Soule, G., *Introduction to Economic Science* (1948).

IMPERIALISM: Hobson, J. A., *Imperialism; A Study* (1938); Langer, W. L., *The Diplomacy of Imperialism*, 2 vols. (1935); Moon, P. T., *Imperialism and World Politics* (1926); Ragatz, L. J., *March of Empire* (1948); Reinsch, P., *World Politics at the End of the Nineteenth Century* (1900); Simonds, F. H., and Emeny, B., *The Great Powers in World Politics* (1939); Townsend, M. E., and Peake, C. H., *European Colonial Expansion Since 1871* (1941); Tucker, I. St. J., *History of Imperialism* (1920); Woolf, L. S., *Economic Imperialism* (1920); Woolf, L. S., *Imperialism and Civilization* (1928).

EUROPE IN AFRICA: Ballard, C. R., *Kitchener* (1930); Brown, R., *The Story of Africa and Its Explorers*, 4 vols. (1911); Buell, R. L., *The Native Problem in Africa*, 2 vols. (1928); Crowe, S. E., *The Berlin West African Conference, 1884–85* (1942); Hailey, W. M., *An African Survey* (1939); Hallberg, C. W., *The Suez Canal: Its History and Diplomatic Importance* (1931); Harris, N. D., *Europe and Africa* (1927); Hoskins, H. L., *European Imperialism in Africa* (1930); Johnston, H. H., *Livingstone* (1891); Johnston, H. H., *The Opening Up of Africa* (1911); Johnston, H. H., *A History of the Colonization of Africa by Alien Races* (1913); Keith, A. B., *The Belgian Congo and the Berlin Act* (1919); Keltie, J. S., *The Partition of Africa* (1895); Little, H. W., *H. M. Stanley* (1890); Livingstone, D., *Missionary Travels and Research in South Africa* (1858); Livingstone, D., *The Last Journals of David Livingstone* (1875); Lucas, C., *The Partition and Colonization of Africa* (1922); Mitchell, Sir L., *The Life of the Right Honourable Cecil John Rhodes, 1853–1902*, 2 vols. (1910); Middleton, L., *The Rape of Africa* (1936); Morel, E. D., *Red Rubber* (1907); Morel, E. D., *The Black Man's Burden* (1920); Raphael, L. A. C., *The Cape to Cairo Dream: A Study in British Imperialism* (1936); Stanley, H. M.,

Through the Dark Continent (1878); Stanley, H. M., *How I Found Livingstone* (1913); Stanley, H. M., *The Congo and the Founding of Its Free State,* 2 vols. (1885); Theal, G. M., *The Portuguese in South Africa* (1896); Woolf, L. S., *Empire and Commerce in Africa* (1919).

EUROPE IN THE FAR EAST: Bain, H. F., *Ores and Industry in the Far East* (1927); Bienstock, G., *The Struggle for the Pacific* (1937); Blakeslee, G. H., *The Pacific Area* (1929); Douglas, R. K., *Europe and the Far East* (1928); Fletcher, C. B., *The Problem of the Pacific* (1919); Harris, N. D., *Europe and the East* (1926); Millard, T. F., *The New Far East* (1907); Morse, H. B., and MacNair, H. F., *Far Eastern International Relations* (1931); Owen, D. E., *Imperialism and Nationalism in the Far East* (1929); Scholefield, G. H., *The Pacific; Its Past and Future* (1919); Treat, P. J., *The Far East, A Political and Diplomatic History* (1935); Vandenbosch, A., *Dutch East Indies* (1934); Vinacke, H. M., *History of the Far East in Modern Times* (1941).

JAPAN: Allen, G. C., *Modern Japan and Its Problems* (1928); Baelz, E., *Awakening Japan* (1932); Dyer, H., *Japan in World Politics* (1909); Gowen, H. H., *Outline History of Japan* (1927); Gubbins, J. H., *The Making of Modern Japan* (1922); Hershey, A. S. and S. W. *Modern Japan* (1919); Latourette, K. S., *The History of Japan* (1947); Matsunami, N., *The Constitution of Japan* (1930); McLaren, W. W., *Political History of Japan, 1867–1912* (1916); Murdoch, J., *A History of Japan* (1926); Okuma, S., *Fifty Years of New Japan* (1909); Orchard, J. E., *Japan's Economic Position* (1930); Porter, R. P., *Japan; The Rise of a Modern Power* (1918); Reischauer, E. O., *Japan Past and Present* (1947); Uyehara, S., *Industry and Trade of Japan Since 1868* (1926).

CHINA: Bau, M. J., *The Foreign Relations of China* (1921); Bau, M. J., *The Open Door Doctrine in Relation to China* (1923); Bland, J. O. P., and Backhouse, E., *China Under the Empress Dowager* (1910); Chen, S. and Payne, R., *Sun Yat-sen: A Portrait* (1946); Clements, P. H., *The Boxer Rebellion* (1915); Dingle, E. J., *China's Revolution, 1911–1912* (1912); Holcombe, A. N., *The Chinese Revolution* (1930); Hughes, E. R., *The Invasion of China by the Western World* (1938); Keeton, G. W., *Development of Extraterritoriality in China,* 2 vols. (1928); Kent, P. H., *Passing of the Manchus* (1912); Koo, V. K. W., *The Status of Aliens in China* (1912); Latourette, K. S., *The Chinese, Their History and Culture,* 2 vols. (1946); Latourette, K. S., *The Development of China* (1946); Lattimore, O. and E., *The Making of China: A Short History* (1947); Overlach, T. W., *Foreign Financial Control in China* (1919); Smith, A. H., *China in Convulsion,* 2 vols. (1901); Tai, E. S., *Treaty Ports in China* (1918); Williams, T., *A Short History of China* (1928); Van Dorn, H. A., *Twenty Years of the Chinese Republic* (1932); Willoughby, W. W., *Foreign Rights and Interests in China,* 2 vols. (1927).

Chapter II. Social Changes, Problems, and Programs

PROGRESS IN MEDICINE: Clark, P. F., *Memorable Days in Medicine* (1941); De Kruif, P. H., *Microbe Hunters* (1926); De Kruif, P. H., *The Fight for Life* (1938); Drinkwater, H., *Fifty Years of Medical Progress, 1873–1922*

(1924); Duclaux, E., *Pasteur* (1920); Fishbein, M., *Frontiers of Medicine* (1933); Galdston, I., *Progress in Medicine: A Critical Review of the Last Hundred Years* (1940); Haagensen, C. D., and Lloyd, W. E. B., *A Hundred Years of Medicine* (1943); Hartzog, H. S., *Triumphs of Medicine* (1927); Mettler, C. C., *History of Medicine* (1947); Paget, S., *Pasteur and After* (1914); Riesman, D., *Medicine in Modern Society* (1939); Shryock, R. H., *The Development of Modern Medicine* (1947); Sigerist, H. E., *Civilization and Disease* (1943); Sigerist, H. E., *Medicine and Human Welfare* (1945); Truax, R., *Joseph Lister, Father of Modern Surgery* (1944); Vallery-Radot, R., *Pasteur* (1923).

FOOD AND POPULATION: Chamberlain, J. S., *Chemistry in Agriculture* (1926); Collins, J. H., *The Story of Canned Food* (1924); Davidson, J. B., *Agricultural Machinery* (1931); Kranich, F. N. G., *Farm Equipment for Mechanical Power* (1923); Rogin, L., *Introduction of Farm Machinery* (1931); Ross, E. A., *Standing Room Only?* (1927); Steward, J. F., *The Reaper* (1931); Weber, A. F., *Growth of Cities in the Nineteenth Century* (1899); Wright, H., *Population* (1923); Yates, P. L., *Food Production in Western Europe* (1940).

SOCIALISM, SYNDICALISM, AND ANARCHISM: Bebel, A., *My Life* (1925); Beer, M., *The Life and Teaching of Karl Marx* (1929); Berlin, I., *Karl Marx; His Life and Environment* (1948); Bernstein, E., *Ferdinand Lassalle as a Social Reformer* (1893); Bernstein, E., *Evolutionary Socialism! A Criticism and Affirmation* (1909); Bober, M. M., *Karl Marx's Interpretation of History* (1927); Brockway, F., *Socialism over Sixty Years: The Life of Jowett of Bradford, 1864–1944* (1947); Cathrein, V., *Socialism, Its Theoretical Basis and Practical Application* (1904); Cole, G. D. H., *Socialism in Evolution* (1938); Croce, B., *Historical Materialism and the Economics of Karl Marx* (1914); Eltzbacher, P., *Anarchism* (1908); Ensor, R. C. K., *Modern Socialism as Set Forth by Socialists in Their Speeches, Writings, and Programs* (1910); Footman, D., *The Primrose Path: A Life of Ferdinand Lassalle* (1946); Goldendach, D. B. (ed.), *Karl Marx and Friedrich Engels* (1927); Harley, J. H., *Syndicalism* (1912); Hook, S., *Towards the Understanding of Karl Marx* (1933); Kautsky, K., *Economic Doctrines of Karl Marx* (1925); Laidler, H. W., *Socialism in Thought and Action* (1930); Le Rossignol, J. E., *From Marx to Stalin: A Critique of Communism* (1940); Lorwin, L. L., *Syndicalism* (1914); Lorwin, L. L., *Labor and Internationalism* (1929); Lubac, H. de, *The Un-Marxian Socialist: A Study of Proudhon* (1948); Macdonald, J. R., *The Socialist Movement* (1911); Markham, S., *A History of Socialism* (1931); Marx, K., *Capital*, 3 vols., (1906–1909); Marx, K., *Karl Marx and Friedrick Engels: Selected Correspondence, 1846–1895* (1943); Mehring, F., *Karl Marx, The Story of His Life* (1936); Orth, S. P., *Socialism and Democracy in Europe* (1913); Pipkin, C. W., *Social Politics and Modern Democracies*, 2 vols. (1927); Proudhon, P. J., *What is Property?* (1876); Proudhon, P. J., *Proudhon's Solution of the Social Problem* (1927); Rühle, O., *Karl Marx* (1929); Russell, B., *Roads to Freedom* (1920); Sombart, W., *Socialism and the Social Movement* (1909); Spargo, J., *Syndicalism, Industrial Unionism and Socialism* (1913); Steklov, I. M., *History of the First International* (1928); Wagner, D. O., *Social Reformers* (1934); Webb, S. J., *et al., Socialism and Individualism* (1908); Zenker, E. V., *Anarchism: A Criticism and History of the Anarchist Theory* (1898).

FEMINISM: Anthony, K., *Feminism in Germany and Scandinavia* (1915); Booth, M., *Women and Society* (1929); Bres, R. F., *Maids, Wives and Widows* (1918); Hale, B., *What Women Want: An Interpretation of the Feminist Movement* (1914); Hecker, E. R., *Short History of Women's Rights* (1914); Mencken, H. L., *In Defense of Women* (1922); Reed, R., *The Single Woman* (1942); Schmalhausen, S. D. (ed.), *Woman's Coming of Age* (1931); Schreiner, O., *Woman and Labor* (1911); Walsh, C. M., *Feminism* (1917); Zahm, H. G., *Woman in Science* (1913).

Chapter III. The German Empire

GENERAL: Barker, J. E., *Modern Germany* (1907); Barker, J. E., *The Foundations of Germany* (1919); Bülow, Prince von, *Imperial Germany* (1917); Dawson, W. H., *The Evolution of Modern Germany* (1919); Dawson, W. H., *The German Empire, 1867–1914,* 2 vols. (1916); Fife, R. H., *The German Empire between Two Wars* (1916); Gooch, G. P., *Germany* (1925); Henderson, E. F., *A Short History of Germany,* 2 vols. (1916); Howard, B. E., *The German Empire* (1906); Krüger, F. K., *Government and Politics of the German Empire* (1915); Lichtenberger, H., *Germany and Its Evolution in Modern Times* (1913); Oncken, H., *Germany Under Wilhelm II* (1913); Schevill, F., *The Making of Modern Germany* (1916); Shuster, G., and Bergstraesser, A., *Germany: A Short History* (1944); Snyder, L. L., *From Bismarck to Hitler; Background of Modern German Nationalism* (1935); Taylor, A. J. P., *The Course of German History: A Survey of the Development of Germany Since 1815* (1946); Ward, A. W., and Wilkinson, S., *Germany, 1815–90,* 3 vols. (1916–1918).

SPECIAL TOPICS: Cerf, B., *Alsace-Lorraine Since 1870* (1919); Crothers, G. D., *The German Elections of 1907* (1941); Friedjung, H., *The Struggle for Supremacy in Germany* (1935); Hazen, C. D., *Alsace-Lorraine under German Rule* (1917); Kolbeck, M. O., *American Opinion on the Kulturkampf, 1871–1882* (1942); Muncy, L. W., *The Junker in Prussian Administration under William II, 1888–1914* (1944); Nowak, K., *Germany's Road to Ruin; The Middle Years of the Reign of Emperor William II* (1932); Perris, G. H., *Germany and the German Emperor* (1912); Phillipson, C., *Alsace-Lorraine* (1918); Tims, R. W., *Germanizing Prussian Poland* (1941).

ECONOMIC PROGRESS: Brook, W. F., *Social and Economic History of Germany from William II to Hitler, 1888–1938* (1938); Clapham, J. H., *Economic Development of France and Germany, 1815–1914* (1921); Dawson, W. H., *Protection in Germany* (1904); Dawson, W. H., *Industrial Germany* (1912); Farrell, H. H., *The Franco-German War Indemnity and Its Economic Results* (1913); Hauser, H., *Germany's Commercial Grip on the World* (1918); Helfferich, K., *Germany's Economic Progress and National Wealth, 1888–1915* (1915); Hoffman, R., *Great Britain and the German Trade Rivalry, 1875–1914*

(1933); Howard, E. D., *The Cause and Extent of the Recent Industrial Progress of Germany* (1907); Snow, C. D., *German Foreign Trade Organization* (1917); Stolper, G., *German Economy, 1870–1940* (1940); Veblen, T., *Imperial Germany and the Industrial Revolution* (1915).

SOCIALISM AND SOCIAL LEGISLATION: Anderson, E., *Hammer or Anvil: The Story of the German Working-Class Movement* (1945); Ashley, W. J., *The Progress of German Working Classes* (1904); Bernstein, E., *Ferdinand Lassalle as a Social Reformer* (1893); Brandes, G., *Ferdinand Lassalle* (1911); Dawson, W. H., *Bismarck and State Socialism* (1891); Dawson, W. H., *German Socialism and Ferdinand Lassalle* (1899); Dawson, W. H., *The German Workman* (1906); Dawson, W. H., *Social Insurance in Germany* (1911); Howe, F. C., *Socialized Germany* (1915); Lowie, R. H., *The German People: A Social Portrait to 1914* (1945); Shirokauer, A., *Lassalle* (1932).

FOREIGN POLICY: Anderson, P. R., *The Background of Anti-English Feeling in Germany, 1890–1902* (1939); Benson, E. F., *The Kaiser and English Relations* (1937); Bernhardi, F. von, *Germany and the Next War* (1914); Brandenburg, E., *From Bismarck to the World War* (1933); Carroll, E. M., *Germany and the Great Powers, 1866–1914* (1939); Coolidge, A. C., *The Origins of the Triple Alliance* (1926); Gooch, G. P., *Franco-German Relations* (1923); Hale, O. J., *Germany and the Diplomatic Revolution, 1904–1906* (1931); Hammann, O., *World Policy of Germany, 1890–1912* (1925); Langer, W. L., *European Alliances and Alignments, 1871–1890* (1931); Mitchell, P. B., *The Bismarckian Policy of Conciliation with France, 1875–1885* (1936); Pribram, A. F., *The Secret Treaties of Austria-Hungary, 1879–1914,* 2 vols. (1920–1922); Rohrback, P., *German World Policies* (1915); Sarolea, C., *The Anglo-German Problem* (1912); Schmitt, B. E., *England and Germany, 1740–1914* (1916); Simpson, J. (ed.), *The Saburov Memoirs or Bismarck versus Russia* (1929); Sontag, R. J., *Germany and England: Background of Conflict, 1848–1894* (1938); Wedel, O. H., *Austro-German Diplomatic Relations, 1908–1914* (1932).

IMPERIALISM AND NAVALISM: Aydelotte, W. O., *Bismarck and British Colonial Policy: The Problem of South West Africa, 1883–1885* (1937); Calvert, A. F., *The German African Empire* (1916); Earle, E. M., *Turkey, the Great Powers and the Bagdad Railway* (1923); Hurd, A. S. and Castle, H., *German Sea Power* (1913); Langer, W. L., *The Diplomacy of Imperialism,* 2 vols. (1935); Lewin, P. E., *The Germans and Africa* (1914); Norem, R. A., *Kiaochow Leased Territory* (1936); Rudin, H. R., *Germany in the Cameroons, 1884–1914* (1938); Schnee, H., *German Colonization Past and Present* (1926); Taylor, A. J. P., *Germany's First Bid for Colonies, 1884–1885; A Move in Bismarck's European Policy* (1938); Townsend, M. E., *The Origins of Modern German Colonialism* (1921); Townsend, M. E., *The Rise and Fall of Germany's Colonial Empire* (1930); Wertheimer, M. S., *The Pan-German League, 1890–1914* (1924); Wolf, J. B., *The Diplomatic History of the Bagdad Railroad* (1936); Woodward, E. L., *Great Britain and the German Navy* (1935).

BIOGRAPHIES AND MEMOIRS: Bebel, A., *Reminiscences,* 2 vols. (1910–1914); Bismarck, O. von, *Reflections and Reminiscences,* 3 vols. (1898–1922):

Bülow, Prince von, *Letters* (1930); Bülow, Prince von, *Memoirs,* 4 vols. (1931–1932); Busch, M., *Bismarck, Some Secret Pages of His History,* 2 vols. (1898); Davis, A. U., *The Kaiser as I Knew Him* (1918); Dombrowski, E., *German Leaders,* (1919); Egelhaaf, G., *Bismarck* (1922); Gauss, C. (ed.), *The German Emperor as Shown in His Public Utterances* (1915); Hammer, S. C., *William the Second* (1915); Hohenlohe, Prince, *Memoirs,* 2 vols. (1906); Hulderman, B., *Albert Ballin* (1922); Ludwig, E., *Kaiser Wilhelm II* (1925); Morrow, I. F. D., *Bismarck* (1943); Nowak, K. F., *Kaiser and Chancellor* (1930); Ponsonby, F., *Letters of the Empress Frederick* (1929); Robertson, C. G., *Bismarck* (1918); Shaw, S., *William of Germany* (1913); Tirpitz, A. von, *My Memoirs,* 2 vols. (1919); Tisdall, E. E. P., *She Made World Chaos. The Intimate Story of Empress Frederick of Prussia* (1940); Weigler, P., *William I: His Life and Times* (1929); Wile, F. W., *Men Around the Kaiser* (1913); Wilhelm II, *The Kaiser's Speeches* (1903); Wilhelm II, *Letters from the Kaiser to the Czar* (1920); Wilhelm II, *The Kaiser's Memoirs* (1922); William II, *My Early Life* (1926); Zedlitz-Trutzschler, R., *Twelve Years at the Imperial German Court* (1923).

Chapter IV. The Third French Republic

GENERAL: Bainville, J., *The French Republic, 1870–1935* (1936); Bodley, J., *France,* 2 vols. (1902); Bourgeois, E., *History of Modern France, 1815–1913,* 2 vols. (1919); Bracq, J. C., *France under the Republic* (1916); Brogan, D. W., *France Under the Republic: The Development of Modern France, 1870–1939* (1940); Coubertin, P. de, *The Evolution of France under the Third Republic* (1897); Guérard, A. L., *French Civilization in the Nineteenth Century* (1914); Guignebert, C. A. H., *A Short History of the French People,* 2 vols. (1930); Hale, R. W., Jr., *Democratic France. The Third Republic from Sedan to Vichy* (1941); Hanotaux, G., *Contemporary France,* 4 vols. (1903–1909); Lawton, F., *The Third French Republic* (1909); Maillaud, P., *France* (1943); Recouly, R., *The Third Republic* (1928); Seignobos, C., *The Evolution of the French People* (1932); Thomson, D., *Democracy in France: The Third Republic* (1946); Tilley, A. A., *Modern France, A Companion to French Studies* (1922); Vizetelly, E. A., *Republican France, 1870–1912* (1913); Wolf, J. B., *France, 1815 to the Present* (1940); Wright, C. H. C., *History of the Third French Republic* (1916).

SPECIAL: Acomb, E. M., *French Laic Laws, 1879–1889* (1941); Bertaut, J., *Paris, 1870–1935* (1936); Brabant, F. H., *The Beginning of the Third Republic in France. A History of the National Assembly (February–September, 1871)* (1940); Bury, J. P. T., *Gambetta and the National Defense, A Republican Dictatorship in France* (1936); Collins, R. W., *Catholicism and the Second French Republic* (1923); Charpentier, A., *The Dreyfus Case* (1935); Dreyfus, A. and P., *The Dreyfus Case* (1937); Fetridge, W. P., *Rise and Fall of the Paris Commune in 1871* (1871); Hale, L. A., *People's War in France, 1870–1871* (1904); Hayes, C. J. H., *France, A Nation of Patriots* (1930); Herzog, W., *From Dreyfus to Pétain; The Struggle of a Republic* (1947); Jellinek, F., *The*

Paris Commune of 1871 (1937); Kayser, J., *The Dreyfus Affair* (1931); Lissagaray, P. O., *History of the Commune* (1886); Mason, E. S., *The Paris Commune* (1930); McKay, D. C. (ed.), *The Dreyfus Case* (1937); Muret, C. T., *French Royalist Doctrines Since the Revolution* (1933); Phillips, C. S., *The Church in France, 1848–1907* (1936); Sabatier, P., *Disestablishment in France* (1906); Siegfried, A., *France, A Study in Nationality* (1930); Simon, J., *The Government of M. Thiers,* 2 vols. (1879); Wright, G., *Raymond Poincaré and the French Presidency* (1942).

POLITICS: Barthélemy, J., *Government of France* (1924); Poincaré, R., *How France Is Governed* (1914); Sait, E. M., *Government and Politics of France* (1920); Soltau, R. H., *French Parties and Politics, 1871–1930* (1930).

ECONOMIC AND SOCIAL: Bernstein, S., *Beginnings of Marxian Socialism in France* (1933); Clapham, J. H., *Economic Development of France and Germany, 1815–1914* (1937); Clough, S. B., *France: A History of National Economics, 1789–1939* (1939); Golub, E. O., *The Méline Tariff: French Agricultural and Nationalist Economic Policy* (1944); Haight, F. A., *A History of French Commercial Policies* (1941); Lorwin, L. L., *The Labor Movement in France* (1912); Lorwin, L. L., *Syndicalism in France* (1914); Meredith, H. O., *Protection in France* (1904); Moon, P. T., *The Labor Problem and the Social Catholic Movement in France* (1925).

IMPERIALISM AND FOREIGN AFFAIRS: Anderson, E. N., *The First Morocco Crisis, 1904–1906* (1930); Barlow, I. C., *The Agadir Crisis* (1940); Carroll, E. M., *French Public Opinion and Foreign Affairs, 1870–1914* (1931); Giffin, M. B., *Fashoda, The Incident and Its Diplomatic Setting* (1930); Gooch, G. P., *Franco-German Relations, 1871–1914* (1923); Knight, M. M., *Morocco as a French Economic Venture; A Study of Open Door Imperialism* (1937); Langer, W. L., *The Franco-Russian Alliance, 1890–1894* (1929); Langer, W. L., *The Diplomacy of Imperialism, 1890–1905* (1935); Michon, G., *The Franco-Russian Alliance, 1891–1917* (1929); Morel, E. D., *Morocco in Diplomacy* (1912); Power, T. F., Jr., *Jules Ferry and the Renaissance of French Imperialism* (1944); Priestley, H. I., *France Overseas: A Study of Modern Imperialism* (1938); Roberts, S. H., *History of French Colonial Policy, 1870–1925,* 2 vols. (1929); Schuman, F. L., *War and Diplomacy in the French Republic* (1931); Sloane, W. M., *Greater France in Africa* (1923); Southworth, C., *The French Colonial Venture* (1931); Stuart, G. H., *French Foreign Policy, 1898–1914* (1921); Tardieu, A., *France and the Alliances* (1908); Wienefeld, R. H., *Franco-German Relations, 1878–1885* (1929).

BIOGRAPHIES AND MEMOIRS: Adam, G., *The Tiger: Georges Clemenceau, 1871–1929* (1930); Brush, E. P., *Guizot in the Early Years of the Orleanist Monarchy* (1929); Bruun, G., *Clemenceau* (1943); Calman, A. R., *Ledru-Rollin and the Second French Republic* (1922); Clemenceau, G., *In the Evening of My Thoughts,* 2 vols. (1929); Deschanel, P., *Gambetta* (1920); Dreyfus, P., *Dreyfus, His Life and Letters* (1937); Gambetta, L., *Gambetta: Life and Letters* (1909); Huddleston, S., *Poincaré* (1924); Hyndman, H. M., *Clemenceau* (1919); Jackson, J. H., *Clemenceau and the Third Republic* (1947); Jackson, J. H., *Jean Jaurès: His Life and Work* (1943); Lecomte, G. C., *Georges Clemen-*

ceau: The Tiger of France (1919); Martet, J., *Georges Clemenceau* (1930); Marzials, F. T., *Life of Léon Gambetta* (1890); Marzials, F. T. (ed.), *Memoirs of M. Thiers, 1870–1873* (1915); Michon, G., *Clemenceau* (1931); Pease, M., *Jean Jaurès* (1917); Poincaré, R., *Memoirs,* 4 vols. (1926–1930); Porter, C. W., *The Career of Theophile Delcassé* (1935); Rambaud, A. N., *Jules Ferry* (1903); Remusat, P. de, *Thiers* (1889); Stannard, H., *Gambetta* (1921); Tabouis, G., *The Life of Jules Cambon* (1938); Thomson, V., *Briand, Man of Peace* (1930); Weinstein, H. R., *Jean Jaurès, A Study of Patriotism in the French Socialist Movement* (1936).

Chapter V. The Kingdom of Italy

GENERAL: Croce, B., *History of Italy, 1871–1915* (1929); Deecke, W., *Italy, A Popular Account of the Country* (1899); Foerster, R. F., *The Italian Emigration of Our Times* (1919); Gualtieri, H. L., *Labor Movement in Italy* (1946); Hentze, M., *Pre-Fascist Italy: The Rise and Fall of the Parliamentary Regime* (1939); Lowell, A. L., *The Governments of France, Italy, and Germany* (1914); Marriott, J. A. R., *Makers of Modern Italy* (1931); McClellan, G. B., *Modern Italy* (1933); Orsi, P., *Modern Italy, 1748–1922* (1923); Salomone, A. W., *Italian Democracy in the Making: The Political Scene in the Giolittian Era, 1900–1914* (1945); Salvatorelli, L., *A Concise History of Italy* (1940); Sedgwick, H. D., *A Short History of Italy, 476–1900* (1905); Sforza, C., *The Real Italians: A Study in European Psychology* (1942); Spriggs, C. J. S., *The Development of Modern Italy* (1943); Sturzo, L., *Italy and the Coming World* (1945); Tittoni, T., *Modern Italy* (1922); Trevelyan, J. P., *A Short History of the Italian People* (1920); Underwood, F. M., *United Italy* (1912); Wallace, W. K., *Greater Italy* (1917); Zimmern, H., and Agresti, A., *New Italy* (1920).

THE VATICAN QUESTION: Halperin, S. W., *The Separation of Church and State in Italian Thought* (1937); Halperin, S. W., *Italy and the Vatican at War* (1939); Johnson, H. J. T., *The Papacy and the Kingdom of Italy* (1926); Orlando, V. E., *Rome versus Rome* (1937); Parsons, W., *The Pope and Italy* (1929); Wallace, L. P., *The Papacy and European Diplomacy, 1869–1878* (1948).

IMPERIALISM AND FOREIGN AFFAIRS: Askew, W. C., *Europe and Italy's Acquisition of Libya* (1943); Barclay, T., *Turco-Italian War* (1912); Glanville, J. L., *Italy's Relations with England, 1896–1905* (1934); Lapworth, C., *Tripoli and Young Italy* (1912); McClure, W. K., *Italy in North Africa* (1913); Tittoni, T., *Italy's Foreign and Colonial Policy* (1914); Villari, L., *The Expansion of Italy* (1930).

BIOGRAPHIES AND MEMOIRS: Crispi, F., *Memoirs: The Struggle for Italian Independence to the Crisis Concerning the Alliances,* 3 vols. (1912–1914); Giolitti, G., *Memoirs* (1923); Robertson, A., *Victor Emmanuel III* (1925); Stillman, W. J., *Francesco Crispi* (1899).

Chapter VI. The United Kingdom and the British Empire

GENERAL: Barker, E., *Britain and the British People* (1943); Brebner, J. B., and Nevins, A., *The Making of Modern Britain* (1943); Ensor, R. C. K., *England, 1870–1914* (1936); Farrer, J. A., *England Under Edward VII* (1922); Fay, C. R., *Great Britain from Adam Smith to the Present Day* (1928); Gretton, R. H., *A Modern History of the English People, 1880–1910*, 2 vols. (1913); Innes, A. D., *History of England and the British Empire* (1914); Jackson, J. H., *England Since the Industrial Revolution* (1936); Klingberg, F. J., *Main Currents in English History* (1943); Low, S., and Sanders, L. C., *Political History of England, 1837–1901* (1907); Marriott, J. A. R., *England since Waterloo* (1913); Marriott, J. A. R., *Modern England, 1885–1932* (1934); McCarthy, J., *Short History of Our Own Times*, 4 vols. (1879–1905); Meech, T. C., *This Generation*, 2 vols. (1928); Oman, C. W. C., *England in the Nineteenth Century* (1923); Somervell, D. C., *Modern Britain, 1870–1939* (1941); Somervell, D. C., *English Thought in the Nineteenth Century* (1929); Trevelyan, G. M., *British History in the 19th Century and After, 1782–1919* (1937); Walpole, S., *History of Twenty-Five Years, 1856–1880*, 4 vols. (1904–1908); Wingfield-Stratford, E. C., *The Victorian Sun-Set* (1932); Wingfield-Stratford, E. C., *The Victorian Aftermath, 1901–1914* (1933).

GOVERNMENT AND PARTIES: Adams, G. B., and Schuyler, R. L., *Constitutional History of England* (1941); Allyn, C., *Lords versus Commons* (1931); Belloc, H., and Chesterton, C., *The Party System* (1911); Blease, W. L., *Short History of English Liberalism* (1913); Brinton, C. C., *English Political Thought in the Nineteenth Century* (1933); Cecil, H., *Conservatism* (1912); Christie, O. F., *The Transition to Democracy, 1867–1914* (1934); Fyfe, H., *The British Liberal Party* (1928); Gaus, J. M., *Great Britain; A Study of Civic Loyalty* (1929); Gooch, R. K., *The Government of England* (1939); Hobhouse, L. T., *Liberalism* (1911); Humphrey, A. W., *History of Labour Representation* (1912); Jennings, W. I., *The British Constitution* (1941); Keith, A. B., *The Constitution of England from Queen Victoria to George VI*, 2 vols. (1940); Kent, C. B. R., *The English Radicals* (1899); Laski, H. J., *Parliamentary Government in England* (1938); Lowell, A. L., *Government of England*, 2 vols. (1912); Marriott, J. A. R., *The English Constitution in Transition, 1910–1924* (1925); Morris, H. L., *Parliamentary Franchise Reform in England from 1885 to 1918* (1921); Ogg, F. A., *English Government and Politics* (1936); Park, J. H., *English Reform Bill of 1867* (1920); Seymour, C., *Electoral Reform in England and Wales, 1832–1885* (1915); Slesser, H., *A History of the Liberal Party* (1944); Thomas, J. A., *The House of Commons, 1832–1901* (1939); Trevelyan, C., *From Liberalism to Labour* (1921); Violette, E. M. (ed.), *English Constitutional Documents since 1832* (1936); Wilkinson, W. J., *Tory Democracy* (1924); Williams, W. E., *The Rise of Gladstone to the Leadership of the Liberal Party, 1859–1868* (1934); Woodward, E. L., *The Age of Reform, 1815–1870* (1938).

ECONOMIC AND SOCIAL: Aberconway, C. B. B. M., *The Basic Industries of Great Britain* (1927); Ashley, W. J., *British Industries* (1903); Blanshard, P., *Outline of the British Labor Movement* (1923); Barou, N., *British Trade Unions* (1947); Beer, M., *A History of British Socialism* (1940); Bowley, A. L., *Wages and Income in the United Kingdom Since 1860* (1937); Brown, B. H., *The Tariff Reform Movement in Great Britain, 1881–1895* (1943); Clapham, J. H., *An Economic History of Modern Britain*, 3 vols. (1926–1938); Cole, G. D. H., *The Common People, 1746–1938* (1938); Cole, G. D. H., *British Working Class Politics, 1832–1914* (1941); Cole, G. D. H., and Postgate, R., *The British People, 1746–1946* (1947); Cole, G. D. H., *A Short History of the British Working Class Movement, 1789–1927*, 3 vols. (1925–1927); Cole, M., *Beatrice Webb* (1946); Cole, M., *Makers of the Labour Movement* (1948); De Schweinitz, K., *England's Road to Social Security* (1943); Ernle, Lord, *English Farming, Past and Present* (1936); Fay, C. R., *English Economic History, Mainly Since 1700* (1940); Fuchs, C. J., *The Trade Policy of Great Britain* (1893); Green, F. E., *History of the English Agricultural Labourer, 1870–1920* (1920); Haggard, H. R., *Rural England*, 2 vols. (1902); Hayes, C. J. H., *British Social Politics* (1913); Hearnshaw, F. J. C. (ed.), *The Social and Political Ideas of Some Representative Thinkers of the Victorian Age* (1923); Heath, F. G., *British Rural Life* (1911); Holyoake, G. J., *History of Coöperation in England*, 2 vols. (1906); Jones, G. P., and Pool, A. G., *A Hundred Years of Economic Development in Great Britain* (1948); Lowndes, G. A. N., *The Silent Social Revolution; An Account of the Expansion of Public Education in England and Wales, 1895–1935* (1937); Pease, E. R., *History of the Fabian Society* (1916); Perris, G. H., *Industrial History of Modern England* (1914); Postgate, R. A., *A Pocket History of the British Working Class* (1942); Rostow, W. W., *British Economy of the Nineteenth Century* (1948); Seebohm, M. E., *The Evolution of the English Farm* (1927); Slater, G., *The Making of Modern England* (1915); Stamp, D. L., *The Land of Britain; Its Use and Misuse* (1948); Wagner, D. O., *Church of England and Social Reforms since 1854* (1930); Webb, S. and B., *History of Trade Unionism* (1920).

BIOGRAPHIES AND MEMOIRS: Asquith, H. H., *Fifty Years of British Parliament*, 2 vols. (1926); Beeley, H., *Disraeli* (1936); Benson, E. F., *Queen Victoria* (1935); Buckle, G. E. (ed.), *Letters of Queen Victoria* (Second Series) 3 vols. (1926–1928); (Third Series), 3 vols. (1930–1932); Burdett, O., *Gladstone* (1927); Cecil, G., *Life of Robert, Marquis of Salisbury*, 4 vols. (1921–1932); Chamberlain, A., *Politics from Inside, An Epistolary Chronicle, 1906–1914* (1936); Clarke, E., *Benjamin Disraeli* (1926); Cunliffe, J. W., *Leaders of the Victorian Revolution* (1934); Disraeli, B., *Letters*, 2 vols. (1929); Dugdale, B. E. C., *Arthur James Balfour*, 2 vols. (1937); Edwards, W. H., *The Tragedy of Edward VII* (1928); Garratt, G. T., *The Two Mr. Gladstones* (1936); Garvin, J. L., *Life of Joseph Chamberlain*, 3 vols. (1932–1934); Gavin, C., *Edward the Seventh, A Biography* (1941); Gladstone, H., *Gladstone After Thirty Years* (1928); Grey, Viscount, *Twenty-Five Years*, 2 vols. (1925); Guedalla, P., *The Queen and Mr. Gladstone* (1933); Haldane, Viscount, *Before the War* (1920); Haldane, Viscount, *The Autobiography of Richard Burdon Haldane* (1929); Hall, W. P., *Mr. Gladstone* (1931); Jeyes, S. H., *Mr. Chamberlain* (1903);

Kebbel, T. E., *Lord Beaconsfield and Other Tory Memoirs* (1907); Lee, S., *Queen Victoria, A Biography* (1903); Lee, S., *King Edward VII,* 2 vols. (1927); Marriott, J. A. R., *Queen Victoria and Her Ministers* (1934); Maurois, A., *Disraeli; A Picture of the Victorian Age* (1928); Monypenny, W. F., and Buckle, G. E., *Life of Benjamin Disraeli, Earl of Beaconsfield,* 6 vols. (1910–1920); Morley, J., *The Life of W. E. Gladstone,* 3 vols. (1903); Morley, J., *Recollections,* 2 vols. (1917); O'Connor, T. P., *Lord Beaconsfield* (1884); Petrie, C., *The Chamberlain Tradition* (1938); Petrie, C., *Joseph Chamberlain* (1940); Petrie, C., *The Life and Letters of the Right Hon. Sir Austen Chamberlain* (1940); Raymond, E. T., *Life of Arthur James Balfour* (1920); Raymond, E. T., *Mr. Lloyd George* (1922); Raymond, E. T., *Disraeli* (1925); Sitwell, E., *Victoria of England* (1947); Somervell, D. C., *Disraeli and Gladstone* (1926); Spender, H., *The Prime Minister, Lloyd George* (1920); Spender, J. A., *The Life of the Right Hon. Sir Henry Campbell-Bannerman,* 2 vols. (1924); Spender, J. A., and Asquith, C., *Life of Lord Oxford and Asquith,* 2 vols. (1932); Stapledon, G., *Disraeli and the New Age* (1943); Strachey, G. L., *Eminent Victorians* (1918); Strachey, G. L., *Queen Victoria* (1921); Sylvester, A. J., *The Real Lloyd George* (1946); Traill, H. D., *The Marquis of Salisbury* (1891); Trevelyan, G. M., *Grey of Fallodon, The Life and Letters of Sir Edward Grey, afterward Viscount Grey of Fallodon* (1937); Walpole, S., *The Life of Lord John Russell,* 2 vols. (1889); Zetland, L. J. L. D., *Lord Cromer* (1932).

THE IRISH QUESTION: Balfour, A., *Aspects of Home Rule* (1912); Barker, E., *Ireland in the Last Fifty Years, 1866–1916* (1919); Benns, F. L., *The Irish Question, 1912–1914* (1928); Clarkson, J. D., *Labor and Nationalism in Ireland* (1925); Colvin, I., *Carson the Statesman* (1935); Dicey, A. V., *England's Case Against Home Rule* (1887); Ervine, S., *Parnell* (1925); Eversley, G. J. S. L., *Gladstone and Ireland* (1912); Hackett, F., *Ireland, A Study in Nationalism* (1918); Haslip, J., *Parnell; A Biography* (1937); Leamy, M., *Parnell's Faithful Few* (1936); MacDonagh, M., *Home Rule Movement* (1920); McNeill, R., *Ulster's Stand for Union* (1922); Mansergh, N., *Ireland in the Age of Reform and Revolution* (1940); Mansergh, N., *Britain and Ireland* (1942); Morris, J. E., *Great Britain and Ireland, 1845–1910* (1914); O'Brien, R. B., *Life of Charles Stewart Parnell,* 3 vols. (1899); O'Connor, J., *History of Ireland, 1798–1924,* 2 vols. (1925); Parmiter, G. de C., *Roger Casement* (1936); Parnell, K., *Charles Stewart Parnell* (1914); Phillips, W. A., *The Revolution in Ireland, 1906–1923* (1926); Pomfret, J. E., *The Struggle for Land in Ireland, 1800–1923* (1930); Redmond-Howard, L. G., *John Redmond; The Man and the Demand* (1911); Sheehan, D. D., *Ireland Since Parnell* (1921); Turner, E. R., *Ireland and England in the Past and at Present* (1920).

FOREIGN POLICY: Benson, E. F., *The Kaiser and English Relations* (1936); Chang, C. F., *The Anglo-Japanese Alliance* (1931); Churchill, R. P., *The Anglo-Russian Convention of 1907* (1939); Dennis, A. L. P., *The Anglo-Japanese Alliance* (1923); Egerton, H. E., *British Foreign Policy* (1917); Gooch, G. P., and Masterman, J. H. B., *A Century of British Foreign Policy* (1917); Heindel, R. H., *The American Impact on Great Britain: 1898–1914* (1940); Hoffman, R., *Great Britain and the German Trade Rivalry* (1934);

Knaplund, P., *Foreign Policy* (1935); Lutz, H., *Lord Grey and the World War* (1928); Marder, A. J., *The Anatomy of British Sea Power* (1940); Montgelas, M., *British Foreign Policy under Sir Edward Grey* (1928); Nicolson, H., *Portrait of a Diplomatist* (1930); Pribram, A. F., *England and the Great Powers, 1871–1914* (1931); Seton-Watson, R. W., *Disraeli, Gladstone and the Eastern Question* (1935); Seton-Watson, R. W., *Britain in Europe, 1789–1914: A Survey of Foreign Policy* (1937); Sontag, R. J., *Germany and England: Background of Conflict, 1848–1894* (1938); Tyler, J. E., *The British Army and the Continent, 1904–1914* (1938); Ward, A. W., and Gooch, G. P. (eds.), *Cambridge History of British Foreign Policy, 1783–1919*, 3 vols. (1922–1923); Woodward, E. L., *Great Britain and the German Navy* (1935).

BRITISH IMPERIALISM: Adams, J. T., *Empire in the Seven Seas: The British Empire, 1784–1939* (1940); Barker, E., *Ideas and Ideals of the British Empire* (1941); Bodelsen, C. A., *Studies in Mid-Victorian Imperialism* (1925); Boulger, D. C. de K., *England and Russia in Central Asia*, 2 vols. (1879); Chapman, M. K., *Great Britain and the Bagdad Railway, 1889–1914* (1948); Currey, C. H., *British Colonial Policy, 1783–1915* (1916); Egerton, H. E., *Short History of British Colonial Policy* (1918); Gretton, R. H., *Imperialism and Mr. Gladstone, 1876–1887* (1923); Gull, E. M., *British Economic Interests in the Far East* (1943); Hallberg, C. W., *Suez Canal* (1931); Holdich, G. H., *The Indian Borderland, 1880–1890* (1909); Knaplund, P., *Gladstone and Britain's Imperial Policy* (1927); Knaplund, P., *The British Empire, 1815–1939* (1941); Maxwell, H., *A Century of Empire, 1801–1900*, 3 vols. (1909–1911); Newton, A. P., *A Hundred Years of the British Empire* (1948); Shuster, W. M., *Strangling of Persia* (1912); Trotter, R. G., *The British Empire-Commonwealth* (1932); Weinthal, L. (ed.), *The Story of the Cape to Cairo Railway*, 4 vols. (1923); Williamson, J. A., *Builders of the Empire* (1925); Williamson, J. A., *Short History of British Expansion*, 2 vols. (1930); Wilson, A. T., *Suez Canal* (1933).

EGYPT: Blunt, W. S., *Secret History of the English Occupation of Egypt* (1907); Boulger, D. C., *Life of Gordon*, 2 vols. (1896); Cromer, Lord, *Modern Egypt*, 2 vols. (1908); Hodges, A., *Lord Kitchener* (1936); Low, S., *Egypt in Transition* (1914); Martin, P. F., *The Sudan in Evolution* (1921); Milner, Lord, *England in Egypt* (1920); Traill, H. D., *England, Egypt, and the Sudan* (1900).

SOUTH AFRICA AND THE BOER WAR: Brand, R. H., *The Union of South Africa* (1909); Brookes, E. H., *The History of Native Policy in South Africa* (1927); Dawson, W. H., *South Africa* (1925); De Wet, C. R., *Three Years' War* (1902); Doyle, A. C., *Great Boer War* (1903); Hobson, J. A., *The War in South Africa* (1900); Hole, H. M., *The Making of Rhodesia* (1916); Kruger, P., *Memoirs* (1902); Leyds, W. J., *The Transvaal Surrounded* (1919); Lovell, R. I., *The Struggle for South Africa; 1875–99* (1934); Maurice, J. F., and Grant, M. H., *History of the War in South Africa, 1899–1902*, 4 vols. (1906–1910); Millan, S. G., *Rhodes* (1933); Newton, A. P., *Select Documents Relating to the Unification of South Africa*, 2 vols. (1924); Plomer, W., *Cecil Rhodes* (1933); Spender, H., *General Botha* (1916); Theal, G. M., *South Africa* (1900); Walker, E. A., *A History of South Africa* (1928); Williams, B., *Cecil Rhodes*

(1921); Worsfold, W. B., *Lord Milner's Work in South Africa* (1906); Worsfold, W. B., *Union of South Africa* (1912).

THE OTHER DOMINIONS: Birkenhead, Earl of, *Story of Newfoundland* (1920); Condliffe, J. B., *Short History of New Zealand* (1925); Hall, H. D., *The British Commonwealth of Nations* (1920); Hall, W. P., *Empire to Commonwealth, Thirty Years of a British Imperial History* (1927); Jebb, R., *Imperial Conference, A History and a Study,* 2 vols. (1911); Jenks, E., *History of the Australasian Colonies* (1912); Jenks, E., *The Government of the British Empire* (1918); Keith, A. B., *Imperial Unity and the Dominions* (1916); Keith, A. B., *Responsible Government in the Dominions* (1928); Lipson, L., *The Politics of Equality: New Zealand's Adventures in Democracy* (1948); McInnis, E., *Canada: A Political and Social History* (1947); Martin, C. B., *Empire and Commonwealth* (1929); Muir, R., *Short History of the British Commonwealth,* 2 vols. (1922–1923); Reeves, W. P., *State Experiments in Australia and New Zealand* (1925); Rusden, G. W., *History of New Zealand,* 3 vols. (1895); Rusden, G. W., *History of Australia,* 3 vols. (1908); Scholefield, G. H., *New Zealand in Evolution* (1909); Spender, J. A., *Great Britain, Empire and Commonwealth, 1886–1935* (1936); Turner, H. G., *First Decade of the Australian Commonwealth* (1911); Tyler, J. E., *The Struggle for Imperial Unity, 1868–1895* (1938); Wise, B. R., *Making of the Australian Commonwealth, 1889–1900* (1913); Wittke, C. F., *A History of Canada* (1941); Wrong, G. M., *Canada* (1924).

INDIA: Allan, J., et al., *The Cambridge Shorter History of India* (1934); Chirol, V., *India* (1921); Cross, C., *The Development of Self-Government in India, 1858–1914* (1922); Curzon, Lord, *British Government in India,* 2 vols. (1925); Dodwell, H. H., *A Sketch of the History of India from 1858 to 1918* (1925); Dutt, R. C., *Economic History of British India,* 2 vols. (1916); Trotter, L. J., *History of British India under Queen Victoria,* 2 vols. (1886).

Chapter VII. The Lesser States of Western Europe

THE SCANDINAVIAN MONARCHIES: Arneson, B. A., *The Democratic Monarchies of Scandinavia* (1939); Bain, R. N., *Scandinavia, A Political History of Norway, Denmark, and Sweden, 1513–1900* (1905); Birch, J. H. S., *Denmark in History* (1938); Childs, M., *Sweden, The Middle Way* (1936); Cole, M., and Smith, C. (eds.), *Democratic Sweden* (1939); Drachmann, P., and Westergaard, H., *Industrial Development and Policies of the Three Scandinavian Countries* (1915); Eppstein, J. (ed.), *Denmark* (1945); Gathorne-Hardy, G., *Norway* (1925); Gjerset, K., *History of the Norwegian People,* 2 vols. (1915); Grimley, O. B., *The New Norway* (1938); Hallendorf, C., and Schück, A., *History of Sweden* (1929); Howe, F. C., *Denmark, A Co-operative Commonwealth* (1921); Jensen, E., *Danish Agriculture: Its Economic Development* (1937); Keilhau, W. C., *Norway in World History* (1944); Larsen, K., *A History of Norway* (1948); Leach, H. G., *Scandinavia of the Scandinavians* (1915); Lindahl, E., *The National Income of Sweden, 1861–1930* (1937); Manniche, P., *Denmark, A Social Laboratory* (1939); Montgomery, G. A., *The Rise of Modern Industry in Sweden* (1939); Nansen, F., *Norway and the Union with Sweden* (1905); Rothery, A. E., *Denmark: Kingdom of Reason* (1937); Stefansson, J., *Denmark and Sweden, with Iceland and Finland* (1917); Stomberg, A. A., *A History of Sweden* (1931); Thomas, D. S., *Social and Economic Aspects of Swedish Population Movements, 1750–1933* (1941); Westergaard, H. L., *Economic Development in Denmark Before and During the World War* (1932).

HOLLAND AND BELGIUM: Barnouw, A. J., *Holland under Queen Wilhelmina* (1923); Barnouw, A. J., *The Making of Modern Holland* (1948); Cammaerts, E., *Belgium* (1921); Cammaerts, E., *Albert I* (1935); Cammaerts, E., *Keystone of Europe; History of the Belgian Dynasty, 1830–1939* (1939); Clough, S. B., *History of the Flemish Movement in Belgium* (1930); Corti, Count, *Leopold I of Belgium* (1923); Edmundson, G., *History of Holland, 1361–1913* (1922); Ensor, R. C. K., *Belgium* (1915); Essen, L. van der, *Short History of Belgium* (1920); Goris, J.-A. (ed.), *Belgium* (1945); Holden, A., *Uncle Leopold, A Life of the First King of the Belgians* (1936); Jitta, A. C. J., *Holland's Modern Renascence* (1930); Lichtervelde, L. de, *Leopold of the Belgians* (1929); Linden, H. van der, *Belgium; The Making of a Nation* (1920); Omond, G. W. T., *The Kingdom of Belgium and the Grand Duchy of Luxemburg* (1923); Putnam, R., *Luxemburg and Her Neighbors* (1919); Reed, T. H., *The Government and Politics of Belgium* (1924); Shepherd, H. L., *The Monetary Experience of Belgium* (1936); Vandenbosch, A., *The Dutch East Indies* (1934); Vlekke, B. H. M., *Evolution of the Dutch Nation* (1945).

SWITZERLAND: Brooks, R. C., *Government and Politics of Switzerland* (1918); Brooks, R. C., *Civic Training in Switzerland* (1930); McCrackan, W. D., *Rise of the Swiss Republic* (1901); Martin, W., *History of Switzerland* (1931); Oechsli, W., *History of Switzerland, 1499–1914* (1922); Rappard, W. E., *The Government of Switzerland* (1937); Rougemont, D. de and Muret, C. T., *Switzerland: The Heart of Europe* (1941).

SPAIN AND PORTUGAL: Atkinson, W. C., *Spain: A Brief History* (1934); Braganca Cunha, V. D., *Revolutionary Portugal, 1910–1936* (1939); Brandt, J. A., *Toward the New Spain* (1933); Chapman, C. E., *A History of Spain* (1948); Clark, H. B., *Modern Spain, 1815–1898* (1906); Cooper, C. S., *Understanding Spain* (1928); Crabitès, P., *Unhappy Spain* (1937); Hume, M. A. S., *Modern Spain, 1788–1898* (1900); Livermore, H. V., *A History of Portugal* (1947); Madariaga, S. de, *Spain* (1943); Manuel, F. E., *The Politics of Modern Spain* (1938); McCabe, J., *Spain in Revolt, 1814–1931* (1931); Ramos Oliveira, A., *Politics, Economics and Men of Modern Spain, 1808–1946* (1946); Peers, G. A., *The Church in Spain, 1737–1937* (1938); Sedgwick, H. D., *Spain: A Short History of Its Politics, Literature and Art* (1923); Sencourt, R., *The Spanish Crown, 1808–1931* (1932); Stephens, H. M., *Portugal* (1898); Stewart, E., *Twenty-Nine Years; A Biography of Alfonso XIII* (1931); Strobel, E. H., *Spanish Revolution, 1868–1875* (1898); Trend, J. B., *The Origins of Modern Spain* (1934); Verduin, A. R., *A Manual of Spanish Constitutions, 1808–1931* (1941), Young, G., *Portugal, Old and Young* (1917).

Chapter VIII. The Russian Empire

GENERAL: Alexinsky, G., *Modern Russia* (1913); Beazley, R., *et al., Russia from the Varangians to the Bolsheviks* (1918); Berard, V., *The Russian Empire and Czarism* (1905); Chaninov, B., *A History of Russia* (1930); Curtiss, J. S., *Church and State in Russia: The Last Years of the Empire, 1900–1917* (1940); Dorosh, H., *Russian Constitutionalism* (1944); Drage, G., *Russian Affairs* (1904); Fortescue, A., *The Orthodox Eastern Church* (1911); Fortescue, A., *The Uniate Eastern Churches* (1923); Gurko, V. I., *Features and Figures of the Past* (1939); Hare, R., *Russian Literature from Pushkin to the Present Day* (1947); Kornilov, A., *Modern Russian History from the Age of Catherine the Great to the End of the Nineteenth Century* (1943); Kovalevsky, M. M., *Russian Political Institutions* (1902); Kucharzewski, J., *The Origins of Modern Russia* (1948); Leroy-Beaulieu, A., *The Empire of the Tsars*, 3 vols. (1893–1896); Makeef, N., and O'Hara, V., *Russia* (1925); Masaryk, T. G., *The Spirit of Russia*, 2 vols. (1919); Pares, B., *History of Russia* (1947); Parry, A., *Russian Cavalcade. A Military Record* (1943); Platonov, S. F., *History of Russia* (1925); Pokrovsky, M. N., *Brief History of Russia* (1932); Pratt, H. G., *Russia from Tsarist Empire to Socialism* (1937); Price, M. P., *Russia Through the Centuries* (1943); Thompson, H. M., *Russian Politics* (1896); Tompkins, S. R., *Russia Through the Ages* (1940); Vernadsky, G. V., *Political and Diplomatic History of Russia* (1936); Vernadsky, G. V., *A History of Russia* (1944); Williams, H. W., *Russia of the Russians* (1914); Wolfe, L., *A Short History of Russia* (1942).

THE ROMANOVS: Bing, E. J. (ed.), *The Secret Letters of the Last Tsar* (1938); Botkin, G., *The Real Romanovs* (1931); Graham, A., *Tsar of Freedom; The Life and Reign of Alexander II* (1935); Hanbury-Williams, J., *The Emperor Nicholas as I Knew Him* (1920); Lowe, C., *Alexander III of Russia* (1895); Radziwill, E., *Behind the Veil at the Russian Court* (1914); Radziwill, E., *Nicholas II: The Last of the Tsars* (1931).

ECONOMIC AND SOCIAL: Baring, M., *The Russian People* (1914); Hindus, M. G., *The Russian Peasant and the Revolution* (1920); Mavor, J., *Economic History of Russia*, 2 vols. (1925); Maynard, Sir J., *The Russian Peasant and Other Studies* (1942); Miller, M. S., *The Economic Development of Russia, 1905–1914* (1926); Mirsky, D. S., *Russia: A Social History* (1932); Palmer, F. H. E., *Russian Life in Town and Country* (1904); Pavlovsky, G., *Agricultural Russia on the Eve of the Revolution* (1930); Raffalovich, A. (ed.), *Russia; Its Trade and Commerce* (1918); Robinson, G. T., *Rural Russia under the Old Régime* (1932); Turin, S. P., *From Peter the Great to Lenin: A History of the Russian Labour Movement* (1935); Wallace, D. M., *Russia* (1912); Wiener, L., *Interpretation of the Russian People* (1915).

SUBJECT PEOPLES: Allen, W. E. D., *The Ukraine: A History* (1940); Brandes, G., *Poland, A Study of the Land, People, and Literature* (1903); Dubnow, S. M., *History of the Jews in Russia and Poland*, 3 vols. (1916–1920); Dyboski, R., *Outlines of Polish History* (1931); Fisher, J. R., *Finland and the*

Tsars (1901); Friedlaender, I., *The Jews of Russia and Poland* (1905); Greenberg, L., *The Jews in Russia,* Vol. I. *The Struggle for Emancipation* (1944); Hrushevsky, M., *A History of Ukraine* (1941); Lewinski-Corwin, E. H., *Political History of Poland* (1917); Orvis, J. S., *Brief History of Poland* (1916); Reade, A., *Finland* (1917); Sergeevsky, N. D., *Finland* (1911); Singer, I. (ed.), *Russia at the Bar of the American People. A Memorial of Kishinef* (1904); Wuorinen, J. H., *Nationalism in Modern Finland* (1931).

REVOLUTION VERSUS REPRESSION: Barbusse, H., *Stalin* (1935); Breshko-Breshkovskaia, E. K., *Hidden Springs of the Russian Revolution* (1930); Carr, E. H., *Michael Bakunin* (1937); Footman, D., *Red Prelude* (1945), the assassination of Alexander II; Graham, S., *Stalin* (1931); Hecht, D., *Russian Radicals Look to America, 1825–1894* (1947); Herzen, A., *Memoirs,* 4 vols. (1924–1925); Kennan, G., *Siberia and the Exile System,* 2 vols. (1891); Korff, S. A., *Autocracy and Revolution in Russia* (1923); Kravchinskii, S. M., *Underground Russia* (1892); Kravchinskii, S. M., *The Russian Peasantry* (1894); Kravchinskii, S. M., *Career of a Nihilist* (1901); Kropotkin, P. A., *Memoirs of a Revolutionist* (1899); Lenin, N., *The Revolution of 1905* (1931); Levin, *The Second Duma: A Study of the Social-Democratic Party and the Russian Constitutional Experiment* (1940); Levine, I. D., *The Man Lenin* (1924); Levine, I. D., *Stalin* (1931); Lévy, R., *Trotsky* (1920); Marcu, V., *Lenin: Thirty Years of Russia* (1928); Miliukov, P. N., *Russia and Its Crisis* (1905); Mirsky, D. S., *Lenin* (1931); Nevinson, H. W., *The Dawn in Russia* (1906); Olgin, M. J., *The Soul of the Russian Revolution* (1917); Pares, B., *Russia and Reform* (1907); Perris, G. H., *Russia in Revolution* (1905); Pobiedonostev, K. P., *Reflections of a Russian Statesman* (1898); Rappoport, A. S., *Pioneers of the Russian Revolution* (1918); Scudder, J. W., *Russia in the Summer of 1914: Her Pressing Problems* (1920); Shub, D., *Lenin: A Biography* (1948); Trotsky, L., *My Life* (1930); White, W. C., *Lenin* (1936); Wolfe, B. D., *Three Who Made a Revolution: A Biographical History* (1948).

MEMOIRS AND REMINISCENCES: Appleton, N., *Russian Life and Society; As Seen in 1866–67 by Appleton and Longfellow* (1904); Burroughs, H. E., *Tale of a Vanished Land. Memories of a Childhood in Old Russia* (1930); Colton, E. T., *Forty Years with the Russians* (1940); Dolgorouky, S., *Russia Before the Crash* (1926); Gilliard, P., *Thirteen Years at the Russian Court* (n.d.); Joubert, C., *The Truth About the Tsar and the Present State of Russia* (1905); Kokovtsov, V. N., *Out of My Past* (1935); Maiskii, I. M., *Before the Storm* (1944); Maud, R., *One Year at the Russian Court, 1904–1905* (1918); Morley, H. (ed.), *Sketches of Russian Life* (1866); Narishkin-Kurakin, E., *Under Three Tsars: The Memoirs of the Lady-in-Waiting* (1931); Pares, Sir B., *A Wandering Student* (1947).

FOREIGN POLICY: Alexinsky, G., *Russia and Europe* (1917); Izvolsky, A. P., *Recollections of a Foreign Minister* (1921); Kerner, R. J., *The Urge to the Sea. The Course of Russian History* (1942); Korff, S. A., *Russia's Foreign Relations during the Last Half Century* (1922); Langer, W. L., *The Franco-Russian Alliance, 1890–1894* (1929); Langer, W. L., *The Diplomacy of Imperialism,* 2 vols. (1935); Sazonov, S. D., *Fateful Years* (1928); Stieve, F., *Izvolsky and the World War* (1926); Zabriskie, E. H., *American-Russian Rivalry in the Far East: A Study in Diplomacy and Power Politics, 1895–1914* (1946).

EXPANSION OF RUSSIA: Baddeley, J. F., *The Russian Conquest of the Caucasus* (1908); Curzon, G. N., *Russia in Central Asia* (1889); Lobanov-Rostovsky, A., *Russia and Asia* (1933); Price, M. P., *Siberia* (1912); Rambaud, A., *The Expansion of Russia* (1904); Ravenstein, E. G., *The Russians on The Amur* (1861); Semyonov, Y., *The Conquest of Siberia: An Epic of Human Passions* (1944); Skrine, F. H., *Expansion of Russia, 1815–1900* (1915); Sumner, B. H., *Tsardom and Imperialism in the Far East and Middle East, 1880–1914* (1943); Vamberry, A., *Central Asia and the Anglo-Russian Frontier Question* (1874); Wright, G. F., *Asiatic Russia*, 2 vols. (1902).

RUSSO-TURKISH WAR: Harris, D., *A Diplomatic History of the Balkan Crisis of 1875–1878. The First Year* (1936); Holland, T. E., *The European Concert in the Eastern Question, A Collection of Treaties and Other Public Acts* (1885); Maurice, J. F., *The Russo-Turkish War of 1877* (1905); Rupp, G. H., *A Wavering Friendship: Russia and Austria, 1876–1878* (1941); Stojanovic, M. D., *The Great Powers and the Balkans, 1875–1878* (1939); Sumner, B. H., *Russia and the Balkans, 1870–1880* (1937); Temperley, H. W. V., *The Bulgarian Atrocities, 1875–1878* (1931); Wirthwein, W. G., *Britain and the Balkan Crisis, 1875–1878* (1935); Woodward, E. L., *The Congress of Berlin* (1920).

RUSSO-JAPANESE WAR: Asakawa, K., *The Russo-Japanese Conflict* (1904); Dennett, T., *Roosevelt and the Russo-Japanese War* (1925); Hershey, A. S., *International Law and Diplomacy of the Russo-Japanese War* (1906); Kuropatkin, A., *The Russian Army and the Japanese War*, 2 vols. (1909); Murray, D., *The Official History of the Russo-Japanese War*, 5 vols. (1908–1910); Price, E. B., *Russo-Japanese Treaties of 1907–1916 concerning Manchuria and Mongolia* (1933); Volpicelli, Z., *The China-Japan War* (1896); Volpicelli, Z., *British Official History of the Russo-Japanese War*, 6 vols. (1910–1916); Witte, S. I., *The Memoirs of Count Witte* (1921).

Chapter IX. The Austro-Hungarian Dual Monarchy

GENERAL: Cohen, V., *The Life and Times of Masaryk the President-Liberator; A Biographical Study of Central Europe Since 1848* (1941); Drage, G., *Austria-Hungary* (1909); Gayda, V., *Modern Austria* (1915); Jászi, O., *Dissolution of the Hapsburg Monarchy* (1929); Léger, L., *History of Austro-Hungary from the Earliest Times to the Year 1889* (1889); Rumbold, Sir H., *The Austrian Court in the 19th Century* (1909); Schierbrand, W. von, *Austria-Hungary* (1917); Steed, H. W., *The Hapsburg Monarchy* (1919); Taylor, A. J. P., *The Hapsburg Monarchy, 1815–1918: A History of the Austrian Empire and Austria-Hungary* (1941); Whitman, S., *Austria: A History to 1898* (1899); Wiskemann, E., *Czechs and Germans; A Study of the Struggle in the Historic Provinces of Bohemia and Moravia* (1938).

HUNGARY: Apponyi, A., *The Memoirs of Count Apponyi* (1935); Capek, T., *The Slovaks of Hungary* (1906); Eckart, F., *A Short History of the Hungarian People* (1931); Forster, F. A., *Francis Deák* (1880); Hevesy, A. de,

Nationalities in Hungary (1919); Knatchbull-Hugesson, C. M., *Political Evolution of the Hungarian Nation,* 2 vols. (1908); Kosáry, D. G., *A History of Hungary* (1941); Seton-Watson, R. W., *Racial Problems in Hungary* (1908); Seton-Watson, R. W., *Corruption and Reform in Hungary* (1911); Teleki, P., *Evolution of Hungary* (1923); Vámbéry, A., and Heilprin, L., *The Story of Hungary* (1886); Yolland, A. B., *Hungary* (1917); Zarek, O., *The History of Hungary* (1939).

FOREIGN POLICY: Goričar, J., and Stowe, L. B., *The Inside Story of Austro-German Intrigue* (1920); Pribram, A. F., *Austrian Foreign Policy, 1908–1918* (1923); Pribram, A. F., *Secret Treaties of Austria-Hungary, 1879–1914,* 2 vols. (1920–1922); Rupp, G. H., *A Wavering Friendship: Russia and Austria, 1876–1878* (1941); Schmitt, B. E., *The Annexation of Bosnia, 1908–1909* (1937); Seton-Watson, R. W., *The Southern Slav Question and the Hapsburg Monarchy* (1911); Seton-Watson, R. W., *German, Slav, and Magyar* (1916); Taylor, A. H. E., *The Future of the Southern Slavs* (1917); Wedel, O. H., *Austro-German Diplomatic Relations, 1908–1914* (1932).

FRANCIS JOSEPH: Bagger, E., *Francis Joseph, Emperor of Austria* (1927); Corti, E. C., *Elizabeth, Empress of Austria* (1937); Ernst, O., *Franz Joseph As Revealed by His Letters* (1927); Ketterl, E., *The Emperor Francis Joseph I* (1929); Larisch von Moennich, M. L. E., *Her Majesty Elizabeth of Austria-Hungary* (1934); Mahaffy, R. P., *Francis Joseph I* (1915); Margutti, A., *The Emperor Francis Joseph and His Times* (1921); Redlich, J., *Emperor Francis Joseph of Austria* (1929); Tschuppki, K., *Francis Joseph* (1930); Vivian, H., *Francis Joseph and His Consort* (1917).

Chapter X. Turkey and the Balkans

GENERAL: Brailsford, H. N., *Macedonia, Its Races and Their Future* (1906); Duggan, S. P. H., *The Eastern Question: A Study in Diplomacy* (1902); Durham, M. E., *Twenty Years of the Balkan Tangle* (1920); Forbes, N., *et al., The Balkans; A History of Bulgaria, Serbia, Greece, Rumania and Turkey* (1915); Gewehr, W. M., *The Rise of Nationalism in the Balkans* (1931); Kohn, H., *History of Nationalism in the East* (1929); Marriott, J. A. R., *The Eastern Question: An Historical Study in European Diplomacy* (1940); Miller, W., *The Balkans* (1923); Murray, W. S., *The Making of the Balkan States* (1910); Newbigin, M. I., *Geographical Aspects of Balkan Problems* (1915); Panaretoff, S., *Near Eastern Affairs and Conditions* (1922); Pribichevich, S., *World Without End: The Saga of Southeastern Europe* (1939); Schevill, F., and Gewehr, W. M., *The History of the Balkan Peninsula from the Earliest Times to the Present Day* (1933); Schmitt, B. E., *The Annexation of Bosnia, 1908–1909* (1937); Seton-Watson, R. W., *The Rise of Nationality in the Balkans* (1917); Sloane, W. M., *The Balkans: A Laboratory of History* (1920); Tyler, M. W., *The European Powers and the Near East, 1875–1908* (1925); Villari, L. (ed.), *The Balkan Question* (1905).

ALBANIA: Chekrezi, C. A., *Albania, Past and Present* (1919); Robinson, V.,

Albania's Road to Freedom (1942); Swire, J., *Albania: The Rise of a Kingdom* (1929).

BULGARIA: Beaman, A. H., *Stambuloff* (1895); Black, C. E., *The Establishment of Constitutional Government in Bulgaria* (1944); Dicey, E., *The Peasant State* (1894); Gleichen, E., *Bulgaria and Roumania* (1924); Harris, D., *Britain and the Bulgarian Horrors of 1876* (1939); Huhn, A. E. von, *The Kidnapping of Prince Alexander of Battenberg* (1887); Koch, A., *Prince Alexander of Battenberg* (1887); MacDonald, J., *Czar Ferdinand and His People* (1913); Madol, H. R., *Ferdinand of Bulgaria* (1933); Monroe, W. S., *Bulgaria and Her People* (1914); Panaretoff, S., *Bulgaria and Her Neighbors* (1917); Protich, S., *Aspirations of Bulgaria* (1915); Temperley, H. W. V., *The Bulgarian Atrocities, 1875–1878* (1931); Todorov, K., *Balkan Fire Brand* (1943), autobiography of a Bulgarian soldier and statesman for years 1889–1943.

GREECE: Chester, S. B., *Life of Venizelos* (1921); Forster, E. A., *A Short History of Modern Greece, 1821–1940* (1941); Gibbons, H. A., *Venizelos* (1923); Hibben, P., *Constantine I and the Greek People* (1920); Jebb, Sir R. C., *Modern Greece* (1901); Kaltchas, N., *An Introduction to the Constitutional History of Modern Greece* (1940); Levandis, J. A., *The Greek Foreign Debt and the Great Powers, 1821–1898* (1944); Martin, P. F., *Greece of the Twentieth Century* (1913); Mavrogordato, J., *Modern Greece, 1800–1931* (1931); Miller, W., *A History of the Greek People, 1821–1921* (1922); Miller, W., *Greece* (1928); Sergeant, L., *Greece in the Nineteenth Century: A Record of Hellenic Emancipation and Progress, 1821–1897* (1897).

RUMANIA: Brilliant, O., *Roumania* (1915); Clark, C. U., *Greater Roumania* (1922); Clark, C. U., *Bessarabia, Russia and Roumania on the Black Sea* (1927); Gleichen, E., *Bulgaria and Roumania* (1924); Iorga, N., *History of Roumania* (1925); Mitrany, D., *Roumania, Her History and Politics* (1917); Parkinson, M. R., *Twenty Years in Roumania* (1922); Riker, T. W., *The Making of Roumania* (1931); Seton-Watson, R. W., *A History of the Roumanians* (1934).

SERBIA AND MONTENEGRO: Buchan, J. (ed.), *Yugoslavia* (1923); Harding, B., *Royal Purple* (1935), an historical novel; Petrovitch, W. M., *Serbia* (1915); Stead, A., *Servia by the Servians* (1909); Stevenson, F. S., *A History of Montenegro* (1912); Temperley, H. W. V., *History of Serbia* (1917).

TURKEY: Allen, W. E. D., *The Turks in Europe* (1920); Blaisdell, D. C., *European Financial Control in the Ottoman Empire* (1929); Castle, W. T. F., *Grand Turk; The Last Years of the Ottoman Empire* (1943); Creasy, E. S., *History of the Ottoman Turks*, 2 vols. (1906); Eliot, C. N. E., *Turkey in Europe* (1908); Eversley, G., *The Turkish Empire, Its Growth and Decay* (1923); Graves, P. P., *The Question of the Straits* (1931); Graves, P. P., *Briton and Turk, 1878–1940* (1941); Liman von Sanders, O. V. K., *Five Years in Turkey* (1927); Mears, E. G., *Modern Turkey, A Politico-Economic Interpretation, 1908–1923* (1924); Miller, W., *The Ottoman Empire and Its Successors, 1801–1936* (1936); Paneth, P., *Turkey; Decadence and Rebirth* (1945); Parker, J. and Smith, C., *Modern Turkey* (1940); Pears, E., *Turkey and Its People* (1912); Pears, E., *Life of Abdul Hamid* (1917); Phillipson, C., and Buxton, N., *The*

Question of the Bosphorous and Dardanelles (1917); Poole, S. L., *Story of Turkey* (1922); Shotwell, J. T., and Deák, E., *Turkey at the Straits* (1940); Ward, B., *Turkey* (1942); White, W. W., *The Process of Change in the Ottoman Empire* (1937).

THE BALKAN WARS: Ashmead-Bartlett, E., *With the Turks in Thrace* (1913); Durham, M. E., *The Struggle for Scutari* (1914); Gueshoff, I., *The Balkan League* (1915); Howard, H. N., *The Partition of Turkey, 1913–1923* (1931); Rankin, R., *The Inner History of the Balkan War* (1914); Schurman, J. G., *The Balkan Wars, 1912–1913* (1916); Stickney, E. P., *Southern Albania or Northern Epirus, 1912–1923* (1926); Young, G., *Nationalism and War in the Near East* (1915).

Chapter XI. The Outbreak of the War in 1914

HOPES OF PEACE: Allen, D., *The Fight For Peace* (1930); Angell, N., *The Great Illusion* (1913); Beales, A. C. F., *History of Peace* (1931); Bloch, J. S., *The Future of War . . . Is War Now Possible?* (1899); Brailsford, H. N., *War of Steel and Gold* (1914); Bury, J. B., *The Idea of Progress* (1920); Coulton, G. G., *Main Illusions of Pacifism* (1916); Higgins, A. P., *The Hague Peace Conferences and Other International Conferences Concerning the Laws and Usages of War* (1909); Hull, W. I., *The Two Hague Conferences* (1908); Key, Ellen, *War, Peace, and the Future* (1914); Marvin, F. S., *Century of Hope* (1919); Scott, J. B., *The Hague Peace Conferences*, 2 vols. (1909); Veblen, T., *An Inquiry into the Nature of Peace* (1919).

CAUSES OF WAR: Bakeless, J., *Economic Causes of Modern War* (1921); Hayes, C. J. H., *Essays on Nationalism* (1926); Krehbiel, E., *Nationalism, War and Society* (1916); Liebknecht, K., *Militarism* (1917); Mahan, A. T., *Armaments and Arbitration or the Place of Force in the International Relations of States* (1912); Millis, W., *Martial Spirit* (1931); Muir, R., *Nationalism and Internationalism* (1916); Nicolai, G. F., *The Biology of War* (1917); Powers, H. H., *The Things Men Fight For* (1916); Reisner, E. H., *Nationalism and Education since 1789* (1922); Smith, M., *Militarism and Statecraft* (1918).

THE CRISIS OF 1914: Barnes, H. E., *The Genesis of the World War* (1928); Benson, E. F., *The Outbreak of War, 1914* (1934); Bloch, C., *The Causes of the World War* (1935); Durham, M. E., *The Sarajevo Crime* (1925); Ewart, J. S., *The Roots and Causes of the Wars, 1914–1918*, 2 vols. (1925); Fabre-Luce, A., *The Limitations of Victory* (1926); Fay, S. B., *The Origins of the World War*, 2 vols. (1928); Kautsky, K., *The Guilt of William Hohenzollern* (1920); Lutz, H., *Lord Grey and the World War* (1928); Montgelas, Count M., *The Case for the Central Powers* (1925); Renouvin, P., *The Immediate Origins of the War* (1928); Rumbold, Sir H., *The War Crisis in Berlin: July–August, 1914* (1940); Schmitt, B. E., *The Coming of the War: 1914* (1930); Scott, J. F., *Five Weeks* (1927); Seton-Watson, R. W., *Sarajevo: A Study in the Origins of the Great War* (1926); Stieve, F., *Isvolsky and the World War* (1926); Wegerer, A. von, *A Refutation of the Versailles War Guilt Thesis* (1930); Willis, E. F.,

Prince Lichnowsky, Ambassador of Peace: A Study of Prewar Diplomacy, 1912–1914 (1942); Wilson, H. W., *The War Guilt* (1928).

MEMOIRS AND RECOLLECTIONS: Asquith, H. H., *Genesis of the War* (1924), by the British prime minister in 1914; Bertie, F. L. B., *A Diary of Lord Bertie*, 2 vols. (1924), by the British ambassador at Paris in 1914; Bethmann-Hollweg, T. von, *Reflections on the World War* (1920), by the German chancellor in 1914; Buchanan, Sir G., *My Mission to Russia*, 2 vols. (1923), by the British ambassador to Russia in 1914; Churchill, W. S., *The World Crisis, 1911–1918*, 4 vols. (1923–1927), by the British first lord of the admiralty in 1914; Grey, E., Viscount of Fallodon, *Twenty-Five Years, 1892–1916*, 2 vols. (1925), by the British foreign secretary in 1914; Lichnowsky, Prince K. M., *Heading for the Abyss* (1928), reminiscences of the German ambassador to Great Britain in 1914; Paléologue, G. M., *An Ambassador's Memoirs*, 3 vols. (1924–1926), by the French ambassador to Russia in 1914; Poincaré, R., *The Memoirs of Raymond Poincaré*, 2 vols. (1926–1928), these volumes cover the years 1912–1914; Poincaré, R., *The Origins of the War* (1922), by the President of the French Republic in 1914; Sazonov, S. D., *Fateful Years, 1909–1916* (1928), by the Russian foreign minister in 1914; Schoen, W. E., Freiherr von, *The Memoirs of an Ambassador* (1922), by the German ambassador to France in 1914; Tirpitz, A. von, *My Memoirs*, 2 vols. (1919), shows the influence of the German naval staff; Wilhelm II, *The Kaiser's Memoirs, 1887–1918* (1922), throws a psychological light on the Kaiser but is of little historical value.

DOCUMENTS: Bridge, Major W. C. (ed.), *How the War Began in 1914, Being the Diary of the Russian Foreign Office* (1925), the diary of Baron Schilling, confidential assistant to Sazonov; Cooke, W. H., and Stickney, E. P., *Readings in European International Relations since 1879* (1931); Dugdale, E. T. S. (ed.), *German Diplomatic Documents, 1871–1914*, 4 vols. (1928–1931), selections from *Die grosse Politik der europäischen Kabinette, 1871–1914*, the monumental German publication of foreign correspondence; Headlam-Morley, J. W. (ed.), *Foreign Office Documents, June 28th–August 4th, 1914* (1926), this is Volume XI of *British Documents on the Origins of the War, 1898–1914*, edited by G. P. Gooch and H. W. V. Temperley; Montgelas, M., and Schücking, W. (eds.), *Outbreak of the World War: German Documents Collected by Karl Kautsky* (1924); *Official Files Pertaining to Pre-War History*, 3 vols. (1920–1921), a fuller edition of the Austrian "Red Book" of 1914; *Official German Documents Relating to the World War*, 2 vols. (1923), documents dealing with the responsibility for the war, published by the Investigating Committee of the Reichstag; Romberg, G. von, *Falsifications of the Russian Orange Book* (1923), reveals the deceptions by which the Russian government sought in 1914 to hide its responsibility for the war; Scott, J. B. (ed.), *Diplomatic Documents Relating to the Outbreak of the European War*, 2 vols. (1916), contains the official documents issued by the different European countries just after the outbreak of the war; Scott, J. B. (ed.), *The German White Book Concerning the Responsibility of the Authors of the War* (1924), notes exchanged between the German and Allied governments during the Paris peace conference relative to the responsibility for the outbreak of the war.

Chapter XII. The First World War

GENERAL: Buchan, J., *A History of the Great War,* 4 vols. (1922); Chambers, F. P., *The War Behind the War, 1914–1918: A History of the Political and Civilian Fronts* (1939); Cruttwell, C. R. M., *A History of the Great War, 1914–1918* (1934); Frothingham, T. G., *A Guide to the Military History of the World War* (1920); Hayes, C. J. H., *A Brief History of the Great War* (1926); Liddell Hart, B. H., *A History of the World War, 1914–1918* (1935); McPherson, W. L., *A Short History of the Great War* (1920); McPherson, W. L., *The Strategy of the Great War* (1919); Pollard, A. F., *A Short History of the Great War* (1928); Simonds, F. H., *A History of the World War,* 5 vols. (1917–1920); Stallings, L. (ed.), *The First World War: A Photographic History* (1933); Thompson, P. A., *Lions Led by Donkeys* (1927); Woods, W. S., *Colossal Blunders of the War* (1930).

SPECIAL AREAS OR BATTLES: Abbott, G. F., *Greece and the Allies, 1914–1922* (1922); Ashmead-Bartlett, E., *The Uncensored Dardanelles* (1928); Buxton, N. and C. R., *The War and the Balkans* (1915); Churchill, W. S., *The Unknown War* (1931), the east front; Emin, A., *Turkey in the World War* (1930); Essen, L. van der, *The Invasion and the War in Belgium* (1917); Golovin, N. N., *The Russian Army in the World War* (1931); Gordon-Smith, G., *From Serbia to Jugo-Slavia* (1920); Graves, R., *Lawrence and the Arabian Adventure* (1928); Healy, T., *More Lives than One: An Account of the Author's Experiences with the Australian Army at Gallipoli and in France during the First World War* (1944); Heckscher, E., *et al., Sweden, Norway, Denmark, and Iceland in the World War* (1930); Ironside, Sir E., *Tannenberg: The First Thirty Days in East Prussia* (1925); Kannengiesser, H., *The Campaign in Gallipoli* (1928); Kluck, A. von, *The March on Paris, 1914* (1920); Lawrence, T. E., *Revolt in the Desert* (1927); Liddell Hart, B. H., *Colonel Lawrence: the Man Behind the Legend* (1934); Liman von Sanders, O., *Five Years in Turkey* (1927); McEntee, G. L., *Italy's Part in Winning the World War* (1934); Noel-Buxton, E., and Leese, C., *Balkan Problems and European Peace* (1919); Page, T. N., *Italy and the World War* (1920); Salandra, A., *Italy and the Great War: From Neutrality to Intervention* (1932); Seton-Watson, R. W., *Roumania and the Great War* (1915); Thomas, L. J., *With Lawrence in Arabia* (1924); Trevelyan, G. M., *Scenes from Italy's War* (1919); Tyng, S., *The Campaign of the Marne, 1914* (1935); Villari, L., *The War on the Italian Front* (1932).

THE WAR ON THE SEA: Alexander, R., *The Cruise of the Raider "Wolf"* (1939); Carr, W. G., *By Guess and by God* (1930), submarine activities; Corbett, J. S., and Newbolt, H., *Naval Operations,* 5 vols. (1920–1931); Domville, C., *Submarines and Sea-Power* (1919); Dorling, H. T., *Endless Story* (1931), an account of the activities of British destroyer squadrons; Fawcett, H. W., and Hooper, G. W. W. (eds.), *The Fighting at Jutland* (1929); Fisher, J. A., *Memories and Records,* 2 vols. (1920); Forstner, G. G. von, *The Journal of Submarine Commander von Forstner* (1917); Gibson, L., and Harper, J. E. T., *The Riddle of Jutland* (1934); Gibson, R. H., and Prendergast, M., *The German*

Submarine War, 1914–1918 (1931); Guichard, L., *The Naval Blockade* (1930); Hashagen, E., *The Log of a U-Boat Commander, or U-Boats Westward!* (1931); Jellicoe, J. R., *The Crisis of the Naval War* (1920), the antisubmarine campaign of 1917–1918; Jellicoe, J. R., *The Grand Fleet, 1914–1916* (1922); Jellicoe, J. R., *The Submarine Peril* (1934); Lauriat, C. E., Jr., *The Lusitania's Last Voyage* (1915); Newbolt, Sir H., *A Naval History of the War, 1914–1918* (1920); Pochhammer, H., *Before Jutland: Admiral von Spee's Last Voyage* (1931), discusses the battles at Coronel and the Falkland Islands; Puleston, W. D., *The Dardanelles Expedition* (1927); Scheer, R., *Germany's High Sea Fleet in the World War* (1920); Thomas, L., *Count Luckner, the Sea Devil* (1927); Thomas, L., *Raiders of the Deep* (1928).

THE WAR IN THE AIR: Lehmann, E. A., and Mingos, H., *The Zeppelins* (1928); Raleigh, Sir W. A., *The War in the Air*, 6 vols. (1922–1937); Rawlinson, Sir A., *The Defense of London, 1915–1918* (1923); Treusch von Buttlar-Brandenfels, H., *Zeppelins over England* (1932); Turner, C. C., *The Struggle in the Air, 1914–1918* (1919).

ESPIONAGE AND PROPAGANDA: Aston, Sir G. G., *Secret Service* (1930); Berndorff, H. R., *Espionage!* (1930); Bruntz, G., *Allied Propaganda and the Collapse of the German Empire in 1918* (1938); Crozier, J., *In the Enemy's Country* (1931); Hardie, M., and Sabin, A. K. (eds.), *War Posters Issued by Belligerent and Neutral Nations, 1914–1919* (1920); Landau, H., *All's Fair* (1934); Lasswell, H. D., *Propaganda Technique in the World War* (1927); Nicolai, W., *The German Secret Service* (1924); Playne, C. E., *Society at War, 1914–1916* (1931); Ponsonby, A., *Falsehood in Wartime* (1928); Read, J. M., *Atrocity Propaganda, 1914–1919* (1941); Squires, J. D., *British Propaganda at Home and in the United States from 1914 to 1917* (1935); Stuart, Sir C., *Secrets of Crewe House* (1920); Thomson, Sir B., *The Allied Secret Service in Greece* (1931); Viereck, G. S., *Spreading Germs of Hate* (1930); Wild, M., *Secret Service on the Russian Front* (1932); Yardley, H. O., *The American Black Chamber* (1931).

SPECIAL TOPICS: Chamberlin, Waldo, *Industrial Relations in Wartime Great Britain, 1914–1918* (1940); Cocks, F. S., *The Secret Treaties and Understandings* (1918); Cook, E., *The Press in War-Time* (1920); Dewar, G. A. B., *The Great Munition Feat, 1914–1918* (1921); Foulkes, C. H., *Gas! The Story of the Special Brigade* (1934); Fradkin, E., *Chemical Warfare* (1929); Fuller, J. F. C., *Tanks in the Great War* (1920); Liddell Hart, B. H., *Reputations Ten Years After* (1928); Martin, W., *Statesmen of the War in Retrospect, 1918–1928* (1928); Maurice, Sir F., *Lessons of Allied Co-operation: Naval, Military, Air, 1914–1918* (1942); Miller, H. W., *The Paris Gun* (1930); Molony, W., *Prisoners and Captives* (1933).

BIOGRAPHIES, MEMOIRS, RECOLLECTIONS: Asquith, H. H., *Memories and Reflections, 1852–1927*, 2 vols. (1928); Aston, Sir G. G., *The Biography of the Late Marshal Foch* (1929); Beaverbrook, Lord W. M. A., *A Politician and the War: 1914–1916* (1928); Brusilov, A. A., *A Soldier's Notebook* (1930); Bruun, G., *Clemenceau* (1943); Charteris, J., *Field Marshal Earl Haig* (1929); Churchill, W. S., *The World Crisis, 1911–1918*, 4 vols. (1923–1927); Corday,

M., *The Paris Front* (1934); Djemal, A., *Memoirs of a Turkish Statesman, 1913–1919* (1922); Eisenmenger, A., *Blockade: The Diary of an Austrian Middle-Class Woman, 1914–1918* (1932); Falkenhayn, E. von, *General Head-quarters and Its Critical Decisions* (1919); Foch, F., *Memoirs* (1931); French, G.,*The Life of Field Marshal Sir John French* (1931); French, Sir J., *1914* (1919); Galet, E. J., *Albert, King of the Belgians, in the Great War* (1931); Giolitti, G., *Memoirs of My Life* (1923); Hamilton, Sir I., *Gallipoli Diary,* 2 vols. (1920); Hindenburg, P. von, *Out of My Life,* 2 vols. (1921); Hoffmann, M., *War Diaries and Other Papers,* 2 vols. (1929); Joffre, J. J. C., *Personal Memoirs,* 2 vols. (1932); Lecomte, G. C., *Georges Clemenceau: The Tiger of France* (1919); Liddell Hart, B. H., *Foch: The Man of Orléans* (1932); Lloyd George, D., *War Memoirs of David Lloyd George,* 6 vols. (1933–1937); Luden-dorff, E., *Ludendorff's Own Story, August 1914–November 1918,* 2 vols. (1920); Madelin, L., *Foch* (1929); Mercier, D. J., *Cardinal Mercier's Own Story* (1920); Morgenthau, H., *Ambassador Morgenthau's Story* (1919), wartime Turkey as seen by the American ambassador; Recouly, R., *Joffre* (1931); Robertson, Sir W., *Soldiers and Statesmen, 1914–1918,* 2 vols. (1926); Speranza, F. C. (ed.), *The Diary of Gino Speranza: Italy, 1915–1919,* 2 vols. (1941), reflects conditions in Italy during the war; Townshend, Sir C., *My Campaign in Mesopotamia* (1920); Wavell, General Sir A., *Allenby: A Study in Greatness* (1941); Whit-lock, B., *Belgium: A Personal Narrative,* 2 vols. (1919); Witkop, P., *German Students' War Letters* (1929).

    THE UNITED STATES AS A NEUTRAL: Baker, N. D., *Why We Went to War* (1936); Baker, R. S., *Neutrality: 1914–1915* (1935); Bernstorff, J. von, *Memoirs of Count Bernstorff* (1936); Bernstorff, J. von, *My Three Years in America* (1920); Clapp, E. J., *Economic Aspects of the War: Neutral Rights, Belligerent Claims and American Commerce in the Years 1914–1915* (1915); Dumba, K., *Memories of a Diplomat* (1932); Gerard, J. W., *My Four Years in Germany* (1917); Gwynn, S. (ed.), *The Letters and Friendships of Sir Cecil Spring-Rice,* 2 vols. (1929); Hendrick, B. J., *Life and Letters of Walter H. Page,* 3 vols. (1922); Landau, H., *The Enemy Within: The Inside Story of German Sabotage in America* (1937); Lansing, R., *War Memoirs* (1935); Lyddon, W. G., *British War Missions to the United States, 1914–1918* (1938); Millis, W., *The Road to War: America, 1914–1917* (1935); Morrisey, A. M., *The American Defense of Neutral Rights, 1914–1917* (1939); Peterson, H. C., *Propaganda for War: The Campaign Against American Neutrality, 1914–1917* (1939); Robinson, E., and West, V., *The Foreign Policy of Woodrow Wilson, 1913–1917* (1917); Scott, J. B. (ed.), *President Wilson's Foreign Policy* (1918); Scott, J. B., *A Survey of International Relations between the United States and Ger-many, August 1, 1914–April 6, 1917, Based on Official Documents* (1917); Seymour, C., *American Diplomacy during the World War* (1934); Seymour, C., *American Neutrality, 1914–1917: Essays on the Causes of American Inter-vention in the World War* (1935); Seymour, C., (ed.), *The Intimate Papers of Colonel House,* 2 vols. (1926–1928); Seymour, C., *Woodrow Wilson and the World War* (1922); Sharp, W. G., *The War Memoirs of William Graves Sharp, American Ambassador to France, 1914–1919* (1931); Tansill, C. C.,

America Goes to War (1938); United States Department of State, *Diplomatic Correspondence with Belligerent Governments Relating to Neutral Rights and Duties,* 4 vols. (1915–1918).

THE UNITED STATES AS A BELLIGERENT: American Council on Public Affairs, *The Food Front in World War I* (1944); Ayers, L. P., *The War with Germany: A Statistical Summary* (1920); Bailey, T. A., *The Policy of the United States toward the Neutrals, 1917–1918* (1942); Bassett, J. S., *Our War with Germany* (1919); Beamish, R. J., and March, F. A., *America's Part in the World War* (1919); Clarkson, G. B., *Industrial America in the World War: the Strategy Behind the Lines, 1917–1918* (rev. ed., 1924); Creel, G., *How We Advertised America* (1920); Daniels, J., *Our Navy at War* (1922); Davison, H. P., *The American Red Cross in the Great War* (1919); Frothingham, T. G., *The American Reinforcement in the World War* (1927); Frothingham, T. G., *The Naval History of the World War,* Vol. III (1926); Gleaves, A., *A History of the Transport Service* (1921); Harbord, J. G., *The American Army in France* (1936); Hurley, E. N., *The Bridge to France* (1927); Liggett, H., *A.E.F.: Ten Years Ago in France* (1928); McMaster, J. B., *The United States in the World War,* 2 vols. (1918–1920); MacQuarrie, H., *How to Live at the Front* (1917), handbook published for American soldiers; March, P. C., *The Nation at War* (1932); Mock, J. R., *Censorship, 1917* (1941); Mock, J. R., and Larson, C., *Words That Won the War: The Story of the Committee on Public Information, 1917–1919* (1939); Moore, S. T., *America and the World War: A Narrative of the Part Played by the United States from the Outbreak to Peace* (1937); Mullendore, W. C., *History of the United States Food Administration, 1917–1919* (1941); Palmer, F., *Newton D. Baker,* 2 vols. (1931); Palmer, F., *Our Greatest Battle* (1919), the Meuse-Argonne; Patrick, M. M., *The United States in the Air* (1928); Paxson, F. L., *America at War, 1917–1918* (1939); Pershing, J. J., *Final Report to the Secretary of War* (1919); Pershing, J. J., *My Experiences in the World War,* 2 vols. (1931); Sims, W. S., and Hendrick, B. J., *The Victory at Sea* (1920); Thomas, S., *History of the A.E.F.* (1920); Van Every, D., *The A.E.F. in Battle* (1928); Viereck, G. S. (ed.), *As They Saw Us* (1929), the work of the American forces discussed by Allied and German generals.

THE BOLSHEVIK REVOLUTION IN RUSSIA: Alexandra, Empress Consort of Nicholas II, *Letters of the Tsarina to the Tsar, 1914–1916* (1923); Buchanan, Sir G. W., *My Mission to Russia,* Vol. II (1923); Bunyan, J., and Fisher, H. H. (eds.), *The Bolshevik Revolution, 1917–1918* (1934); Chamberlin, W. H., *The Russian Revolution, 1917–1921,* 2 vols. (1935); Carr, E. H., *The Bolshevist Revolution, 1917–1923,* 3 vols. (1951–1953); Chernov, V., *The Great Russian Revolution* (1936); Florinsky, M. T., *The End of the Russian Empire* (1931); Fülöp-Miller, R., *Rasputin: the Holy Devil* (1928); Golder, F. A. (ed.), *Documents of Russian History, 1914–1917* (1927); Hill, C., *Lenin and the Russian Revolution* (1947); Hindus, M. G., *The Russian Peasant and the Revolution* (1920); Judas, E., *Rasputin, Neither Devil Nor Saint* (1942); Kerensky, A. F., *The Catastrophe* (1927); Kerensky, A. F., *The Prelude to Bolshevism* (1919), the Kornilov revolt; Kirby, L. P., *The Russian Revolution* (1940); Lenin, N., *Preparing for Revolt* (1929); Marcu, V., *Lenin: Thirty*

Years of Russia (1928); Marye, G. T., *Nearing the End in Imperial Russia* (1929); Meyendorff, Baron A. F., *The Background of the Russian Revolution* (1929); Miliukov, P., *History of the Second Russian Revolution* (1920); Mintz, J., *How Moscow Was Won in 1917: A Chapter in the History of the Revolution* (1941); Mirsky, D. S., *Lenin* (1931); Nicholas II, *The Letters of the Tsar to the Tsarina, 1914–1917* (1929); Pares, Sir B., *The Fall of the Russian Monarchy: A Study of the Evidence* (1939); Rodzianko, M. V., *The Reign of Rasputin: An Empire's Collapse* (1927); Shub, D., *Lenin: A Biography* (1948); Trachtenberg, A. (ed.), *Lenin: Toward the Seizure of Power,* 2 vols. (1932); Trotsky, L., *From October to Brest-Litovsk* (1919); Trotsky, L., *The History of the Russian Revolution* (1934); Trotsky, L., *Lenin* (1925); Trotsky, L., *My Life* (1930); Vulliamy, C. E. (ed.), *The Red Archives* (1929); Wheeler-Bennett, J. W., *Brest-Litovsk: the Forgotten Peace, March, 1918* (1939); Wolfe, B. D., *Three Who Made a Revolution: A Biographical History* (1948); Youssoupoff, F. F., *Rasputin* (1927).

WAR AIMS AND PEACE EFFORTS: Andrassy, Count J., *Diplomacy and the War* (1921); Czernin, O., *In the World War* (1920); Dahlin, E., *French and German Public Opinion on Declared War Aims, 1914–1918* (1933); Dickinson, G. L. (ed.), *Documents and Statements Relating to Peace Proposals and War Aims, 1916–1918* (1919); Forster, K., *The Failures of Peace: The Search for a Negotiated Peace during the First World War* (1941); Harding, B., *Imperial Twilight* (1939), includes the Austro-French peace negotiations of 1917; Manteyer, G. de (ed.), *Austria's Peace Offer, 1916–1917* (1921); Nekliudoff, A. V., *Diplomatic Reminiscences before and during the World War, 1911–1917* (1920); Scott, J. B. (ed.), *Official Statements of War Aims and Peace Proposals, December 1916 to November 1918* (1921); Slice, A. van der, *International Labor, Diplomacy, and Peace: 1914–1919* (1941).

THE DISINTEGRATION OF AUSTRIA-HUNGARY: Baerlein, H., *The Birth of Yugoslavia,* 2 vols. (1922); Bauer, O., *The Austrian Revolution* (1925); Beneš, E., *My War Memories* (1928); Burian, Count S., *Austria in Dissolution* (1925); Čapek, K. (ed.), *President Masaryk Tells His Story* (1935); Cohen, V., *The Life and Times of Masaryk, the President-Liberator: A Biographical Study of Central Europe Since 1848* (1941); Gillie, D. R., *Joseph Pilsudski: The Memories of a Polish Revolutionary and Soldier* (1931); Glaise von Horstenau, E., *The Collapse of the Austro-Hungarian Empire* (1930); Jászi, O., *The Dissolution of the Hapsburg Monarchy* (1929); Jászi, O., *Revolution and Counter-Revolution in Hungary* (1924); Karolyi, Count M., *Fighting the World: The Struggle for Peace* (1924); Kerner, R. J., *The Jugo-Slav Movement* (1918); Masaryk, T. G., *The Making of a State* (1927); Nowak, K. F., *The Collapse of Central Europe* (1924); Opočenský, J., *The Collapse of the Austro-Hungarian Monarchy and the Rise of the Czechoslovak State* (1928); Papoušek, J., *The Czechoslovak Nation's Struggle for Independence* (1928); Pilsudski, J., *The Memories of a Polish Revolutionary and Soldier* (1931); Polzer-Hoditz und Wolframitz, A. Count of, *Emperor Karl (Charles IV, King of Hungary)* (1928); Selver, P., *Masaryk* (1940); Seton-Watson, R. W., *Masaryk in England* (1943); Steed, H. W., *Through Thirty Years* (1924); Street, C. J. C., *President*

Masaryk (1930); Strong, D. F., *Austria, October, 1918–March, 1919: Transition from Empire to Republic* (1939); Tormay, C., *An Outlaw's Diary,* 2 vols. (1924); Windisch-Graetz, L., *My Memoirs* (1921), by a member of the Austrian foreign office in 1918.

THE DOWNFALL OF THE HOHENZOLLERNS: Baumont, M., *The Fall of the Kaiser* (1931); Bevan, E., *German Social Democracy during the War* (1919); Bouton, S. M., *And the Kaiser Abdicates: The German Revolution, November 1918–August 1919* (1921); Bruntz, G. G., *Allied Propaganda and the Collapse of the German Empire in 1918* (1938); Frölich, P., *Rosa Luxemburg: Her Life and Work* (1940); Hafkesbrink, H., *Unknown Germany: An Inner Chronicle of the First World War Based on Letters and Diaries* (1948); Lutz, R. H. (ed.), *The Causes of the German Collapse in 1918* (1934); Lutz, R. H. (ed.), *Fall of the German Empire, 1914–1918: Documents of the German Revolution,* 2 vols. (1920); Lutz, R. H., *The German Revolution of 1918–19* (1922); Maximilian, Prinz von Baden, *The Memoirs of Prince Max of Baden,* 2 vols. (1928); Rosenberg, A., *The Birth of the German Republic* (1931); Scheidemann, P., *The Making of New Germany: The Memoirs of Philipp Scheidemann* (1929); Ströbel, H., *The German Revolution and After* (1923).

THE END OF THE WAR: Maurice, Sir F., *The Armistices of 1918* (1943); Menne, B., *Armistice and Germany's Food Supply, 1918–1919: A Study of Conditional Surrender* (1944); Rudin, H., *Armistice, 1918* (1944); Scott, J. B. (ed.), *Preliminary History of the Armistice* (1924); Shartle, S. G., *Spa, Versailles, Munich: An Account of the Armistice Commission* (1941).

THE COST OF THE WAR: Bogart, E. L., *Direct and Indirect Costs of the Great World War* (1919); Brittain, V., *Testament of Youth* (1933); Clark, J. M., *The Costs of the World War to the American People* (1931); Dumas, S., and Vedel-Petersen, K. O., *Losses of Life Caused by War* (1923); Folks, H., *The Human Costs of the War* (1920); Grebler, L., and Winkler, W., *The Cost of the World War to Germany and to Austria-Hungary* (1940); Hirst, F. W., *The Consequences of the War to Great Britain* (1934); Kohn, S., and Meyendorff, Baron A. F., *The Cost of the War to Russia* (1932); Shotwell, J. T., *What Germany Forgot* (1940), the cost of the war to Germany.

Chapter XIII. The Paris Peace Settlement: The Treaties

THE PARIS PEACE CONFERENCE: Albrecht-Carrie, R., *Italy at the Peace Conference* (1938); Bonsal, S., *Unfinished Business* (1944) and *Suitors and Suppliants: The Little Nations at Versailles* (1946); Dillon, E. J., *The Inside Story of the Peace Conference* (1920); Harris, H. W., *The Peace in the Making* (1920); Haskins, C. H., and Lord, R. H., *Some Problems of the Peace Conference* (1920); House, E. M., and Seymour, C. (eds.), *What Really Happened at Paris: The Story of the Peace Conference, 1918–1919, by American Delegates* (1921); Huddleston, S., *Peace-Making at Paris* (1919); Lansing, R., *The Peace Negotiations: A Personal Narrative* (1921); Luckau, Alma, *The German Delegation at the Paris Peace Conference* (1941); Marston, F. S., *The Peace Conferences, 1919: Organization and Procedure* (1945); Nicolson, H., *Peace-making,*

1919: Being Reminiscences of the Paris Peace Conference (1933); Noble, G. B., *Policies and Opinions at Paris, 1919* (1935); Palmer, F., *Bliss, Peacemaker: The Life and Letters of General Tasker Howard Bliss* (1934); Riddell, G., *Lord Riddell's Intimate Diary of the Peace Conference and After, 1918–1923* (1933); Schiff, V., *The Germans at Versailles* (1930); Seymour, C. (ed.), *The Intimate Papers of Colonel House,* Vol. IV (1928); Shotwell, J. T., *At the Paris Peace Conference* (1937); Temperley, H. W. V. (ed.), *A History of the Peace Conference of Paris,* 6 vols. (1920–1924); Thompson, C. T., *The Peace Conference Day by Day* (1920); United States Department of State, *Papers Relating to the Foreign Relations of the United States: The Paris Peace Conference, 1919,* 4 vols. (1942–1943).

THE BIG FOUR: Bailey, T. A., *Woodrow Wilson and the Lost Peace* (1944); Baker, R. S., *Woodrow Wilson and the World Settlement,* 3 vols. (1922–1923); Brunn, G., *Clemenceau* (1943); Clemenceau, G., *Grandeur and Misery of Victory* (1930); Dodd, W. E., *Woodrow Wilson and His Work* (1932); Johnson, G. W., *Woodrow Wilson, the Unforgettable Figure Who Has Returned to Haunt Us* (1944); Lansing, R., *The Big Four and Others of the Peace Conference* (1921); Lloyd George, D., *Memoirs of the Peace Conference,* 2 vols. (1939); Loth, D., *Woodrow Wilson—The Fifteenth Point* (1941).

THE TREATY OF VERSAILLES: Baruch, B. M., *The Making of the Reparation and Economic Sections of the Treaty* (1920); Birdsall, P., *Versailles Twenty Years After* (1941); Burnett, P. M., *Reparation at the Paris Peace Conference from the Standpoint of the American Delegation,* 2 vols. (1940); Carnegie Endowment for International Peace, *The Treaties of Peace, 1919–1923,* 2 vols. (1924); Ebray, A., *A Frenchman Looks at the Peace* (1927); Jessop, T. E., *The Treaty of Versailles: Was It Just?* (1942); Keynes, J. M., *The Economic Consequences of the Peace* (1920); Miller, D. H., *The Drafting of the Covenant* (1928); Nitti, F. S., *The Wreck of Europe* (1922); Nowak, K. F., *Versailles* (1929); Scott, A. P., *An Introduction to the Peace Treaties* (1920); Stegeman, H., *The Mirage of Versailles* (1928); Tardieu, A., *The Truth about the Treaty* (1921).

THE LESSER TREATIES: Almond, N., and Lutz, R. H. (eds.), *The Treaty of St. Germain* (1934); Bethlen, I., *The Treaty of Trianon and European Peace* (1934); Deák, F., *Hungary at the Paris Peace Conference: The Diplomatic History of the Treaty of Trianon* (1942); Donald, Sir R., *The Tragedy of Trianon* (1928); Howard, H., *The Partition of Turkey, 1913–1923* (1931); Seton-Watson, R. W., *Treaty Revision and the Hungarian Frontiers* (1934).

THE UNITED STATES AND THE PEACE SETTLEMENT: In addition to the books on President Wilson listed above, the following are valuable: Bailey, T. A., *Woodrow Wilson and the Great Betrayal* (1945); Bartlett, R. J., *The League to Enforce Peace* (1944); Burlingame, R., and Stevens, A., *Victory Without Peace* (1943); Dickinson, T. H., *The United States and the League* (1923); Fleming, D. F., *The United States and the League of Nations* (1932); Foley, H. (ed.), *Woodrow Wilson's Case for the League of Nations* (1923); Lodge, H. C., *The Senate and the League of Nations* (1925); Schriftgiesser, K., *The Gentleman from Massachusetts: Henry Cabot Lodge* (1944).

Chapter XIV. The Paris Peace Settlement: Unfinished Business

THE LEAGUE OF NATIONS: Bassett, J. S., *The League of Nations: A Chapter in World Politics* (1928); Beer, M., *The League on Trial* (1933); Burton, M. E., *The Assembly of the League of Nations* (1941); Cecil, E. A. R., Viscount, *A Great Experiment: An Autobiography* (1941); Conwell-Evans, T. P., *The League Council in Action* (1929); Davis, H. E. (ed.), *Pioneers in World Order: An American Appraisal of The League of Nations* (1944); Howard-Ellis, C., *The Origin, Structure and Working of the League of Nations* (1928); Institute on World Organization, *World Organization: A Balance Sheet of the First Great Experiment* (1943); Jones, R., and Sherman, S. S., *The League of Nations: From Idea to Reality* (1927); League of Nations, *Ten Years of World Co-operation* (1930); Marburg, T., *Development of the League of Nations Idea,* 2 vols. (1932); Morley, F., *The Society of Nations* (1932); Rappard, W. E., *The Quest for Peace since the World War* (1940); Slocombe, G. E., *Mirror to Geneva: Its Grandeur and Decay* (1938); Wilson, F., *The Origin of the League Covenant* (1928); Zimmern, A., *The League of Nations and the Rule of Law, 1918–1935* (1936).

THE WORLD COURT: Bustamante, A. S. de, *The World Court* (1925); Hudson, M. O., *The Permanent Court of International Justice* (1934); Lindsey, E., *The International Court* (1931)· Wheeler-Bennett, J. W., *Information on the World Court, 1918–1928* (1929).

THE INTERNATIONAL LABOR ORGANIZATION: Barnes, G. N., *History of the International Labour Office* (1926); Oliver, E. M., *The World's Industrial Parliament* (1925); Shotwell, J. T. (ed.), *The Origins of the International Labor Organization,* 2 vols. (1934); Wilson, F. G., *Labor in the League System* (1935); World Peace Foundation, *The International Labour Organization* (1931).

MANDATES AND MINORITIES: Azcárate, P. de, *League of Nations and National Minorities: An Experiment* (1946); Gerig, B., *The Open Door and the Mandates System* (1930); Junghann, O., *National Minorities in Europe* (1932); Mair, L. D., *The Protection of Minorities* (1928); Margalith, A. M., *The International Mandates* (1930); Molony, W. O., *Nationality and the Peace Treaties* (1934); Robinson, J., et al., *Were the Minorities Treaties a Failure?* (1943); Rouček, J. S., *The Working of the Minorities System under the League of Nations* (1929); White, F., *Mandates* (1926); Wright, Q., *Mandates under the League of Nations* (1930).

THE UNITED STATES AND THE LEAGUE: Berdahl, C. A., *The Policy of the United States with Respect to the League of Nations* (1932); Fleming, D. F., *The United States and the World Court* (1945); Hudson, M. O., *The Permanent Court of International Justice and the Question of American Participation* (1925); Jessup, P. C., *The United States and the World Court* (1929); Kellor, F. A., and Hatvany, A., *The United States Senate and the International Court* (1925).

SECURITY PACTS: Ferrell, R. H., *Peace in Their Time* (1952); Glasgow, G., *From Dawes to Locarno, 1924–1925* (1925); Miller, D. H., *The Geneva Protocol* (1925); Miller, D. H., *The Peace Pact of Paris* (1928); Myers, D. P., *Origin and Conclusion of the Paris Pact* (1929); Noel-Baker, P. J., *The Geneva Protocol for the Pacific Settlement of International Disputes* (1925); Shotwell, J. T., *War as an Instrument of National Policy and Its Renunciation in the Pact of Paris* (1929); Wheeler-Bennett, J. W., *Disarmament and Security since Locarno* (1932); Wheeler-Bennett, J. W., *Information on the Renunciation of War, 1927–1928* (1928); Wheeler-Bennett, J. W., and Langermann, F. E., *Information on the Problem of Security, 1917–1926* (1927).

DISARMAMENT: Boggs, M. W., *Attempts to Define and Limit "Aggressive" Armament in Diplomacy and Strategy* (1941); Buell, R. L., *The Washington Conference* (1922); Engely, G., *The Politics of Naval Disarmament* (1932); Harris, H. W., *Naval Disarmament* (1930); Hindmarsh, A., *Force in Peace: Force Short of War in International Relations* (1933); Hoag, C. L., *Preface to Preparedness: The Washington Disarmament Conference and Public Opinion* (1941); Ichihashi, Y., *The Washington Conference and After* (1928); Lefebure, V., *Common Sense about Disarmament* (1932); Myers, D. P., *World Disarmament* (1932); Sloutzki, N. M., *The World Armament Race, 1919–1939* (1941); Williams, B. H., *The United States and Disarmament* (1931).

REPARATIONS: Angas, L. L. B., *Germany and Her Debts* (1923); Bergmann, C., *The History of Reparations* (1927); Borsky, G., *The Greatest Swindle in the World: The Story of the German Reparations* (1942); Dawes, C. G., *A Journal of Reparations* (1939); Dawes, R. C., *The Dawes Plan in the Making* (1925); Frasure, C. M., *British Policy on War Debts and Reparations* (1940); Keynes, J. M., *The Economic Consequences of the Peace* (1920); Keynes, J. M., *A Revision of the Treaty* (1922); Kuczynski, R. R., *American Loans to Germany* (1927); Lichtenberger, H., *The Ruhr Conflict* (1923); Lloyd George, D., *The Truth about Reparations and War Debts* (1932); Long, R. E. C., *The Mythology of Reparations* (1928); Moulton, H. G., and McGuire, C. E., *Germany's Capacity to Pay* (1923); Myers, D. P., *The Reparation Settlement* (1929), the Young Plan; Schacht, H., *The End of Reparations* (1931); Sering, M., *Germany under the Dawes Plan* (1929); Wheeler-Bennett, J. W., *The Wreck of Reparations* (1933), the 1932 Lausanne agreement; Wheeler-Bennett, J. W., and Latimer, H., *Information on the Reparation Settlement* (1930), the Young Plan.

WAR DEBTS: Bass, J. F., and Moulton, H. G., *America and the Balance Sheet of Europe* (1921); Dexter, P., and Sedgwick, J. H., *The War Debts: An American View* (1928); Fisk, H. E., *The Inter-Ally Debts* (1924); Moulton, H. G., and Pasvolsky, L., *War Debts and World Prosperity* (1932); Moulton, H. G., and Pasvolsky, L., *World War Debt Settlements* (1926).

WORLD DEPRESSION: Einzig, P., *The Sterling-Dollar-Franc Tangle* (1933); Einzig, P., *The World Economic Crisis, 1929–1932* (1932); Hodson, H. V., *Slump and Recovery, 1929–1937* (1938); Kranold, H., *The International Distribution of Raw Materials* (1939); League of Nations, *World Production and Prices, 1925–1933* (1934); Patterson, E. M., *The World's Economic Di-*

lemma (1930); Robbins, L. C., *The Great Depression* (1934); Somary, F., *Changes in the Structure of World Economics since the War* (1931); Stamp, J. C., *The Financial Aftermath of War* (1932); Varga, E., *The Great Crisis and Its Political Consequences* (1935); Wright, Q. (ed.), *Unemployment as a World Problem* (1931).

Chapter XV. Soviet Russia

GENERAL: Basily, N. de, *Russia under Soviet Rule: Twenty Years of Bolshevik Experiment* (1938); Best, H., *The Soviet Experiment* (1941); Chamberlin, W. H., *Collectivism, a False Utopia* (1937); Chamberlin, W. H., *The Russian Enigma* (1943); Dallin, D. J., *The Real Soviet Russia* (1944); Davies, J. E., *Mission to Moscow* (1941); Duranty, W., *Duranty Reports Russia* (1934); Duranty, W., *The Kremlin and the People* (1941); Duranty, W., *USSR: The Story of Soviet Russia* (1944); Eastman, M., *Stalin's Russia and the Crisis in Socialism* (1940); Fischer, M., *My Lives in Russia* (1944); Florinsky, M. T., *Toward an Understanding of the U.S.S.R.: A Study in Government, Politics, and Economic Planning* (1939); Griffith, H., *This is Russia* (1944); Loukomski, G., *The Face of Russia* (1944); Lyons, E., *Assignment in Utopia* (1937); Schlesinger, R., *The Spirit of Post-War Russia: Soviet Ideology, 1917–1946* (1946); Utley, F., *The Dream We Lost: Soviet Russia Then and Now* (1940); Webb, S. and B., *Soviet Communism: A New Civilization?*, 2 vols. (1936); Webb, S. and B., *The Truth about Soviet Russia* (1942).

INTERVENTION AND COUNTERREVOLUTION: Aleksandrov, G. F., *et al.*, *History of the Civil War in the U.S.S.R.*, 2 vols. (1946); Alioshin, D., *Asian Odyssey* (1940), by an officer in Kolchak's army; Bunyan, J. (ed.), *Intervention, Civil War and Communism in Russia, April–December 1918: Documents and Materials* (1936); Coates, W. P. and Z. K., *Armed Intervention in Russia, 1918–1922* (1935); Cudahy, J., *Archangel: The American War with Russia* (1924); Denikin, A. I., *The White Army* (1930); Graves, W. S., *America's Siberian Adventure* (1931); Maynard, Sir C. C. M., *The Murmansk Venture* (1928); Stewart, G., *The White Armies of Russia: A Chronicle of Counter Revolution and Allied Intervention* (1933); Strakhovsky, L. I., *Intervention at Archangel* (1944); Varneck, E., and Fisher, H. H. (eds.), *The Testimony of Kolchak and Other Siberian Materials* (1935).

PARTY AND GOVERNMENT: Bukharin, N., and Preobrazhensky, E., *The A.B.C. of Communism: A Popular Explanation of the Program of the Communist Party of Russia* (1922); Gurian, W., *Bolshevism: Theory and Practice* (1932); Harper, S. N., *The Government of the Soviet Union* (1938); Popov, N., *Outline History of the Communist Party of the Soviet Union*, 2 vols. (1935); Rosenberg, A., *A History of Bolshevism* (1934); Strong, A. L., *The New Soviet Constitution: A Study in Socialist Democracy* (1937); Towster, J., *Political Power in the U.S.S.R., 1917–1947: The Theory and Structure of Government in the Soviet State* (1948); Vishinsky, A. Y., *The Law of the Soviet State* (1948).

SECRET POLICE AND TERROR: Agabekov, G., *Ogpu* (1931); Brunovskii, V. K., *The Methods of the Ogpu* (1931); Cederholm, B., *In the Clutches of the Tcheka* (1929); Popov, G. K., *The Tcheka: the Red Inquisition* (1925); Tchernavin, T., *Escape from the Soviets* (1934); Tchernavin, V. V., *I Speak for the Silent Prisoners of the Soviets* (1935).

LENIN AND STALIN: Barbusse, H., *Stalin: A New World Seen through One Man* (1935); Bigland, E., *The Riddle of the Kremlin* (1940); Graham, S., *Stalin: An Impartial Study of the Life and Work of Joseph Stalin* (1931); Krupskaya, N. K., *Memories of Lenin,* 2 vols. (1930), by his widow; Levine, I. D., *The Man Lenin* (1924); Levine, I. D., *Stalin* (1931); Lyons, E., *Stalin: Czar of All the Russias* (1940); Marcu, V., *Lenin: Thirty Years of Russia* (1928); Mirsky, D. S., *Lenin* (1931); Rochester, A., *Lenin on the Agrarian Question* (1942); Shub, D., *Lenin: A Biography* (1948); Souvarine, B., *Stalin: A Critical Survey of Bolshevism* (1939); Veale, F. J. P., *The Man from the Volga* (1932), Lenin; Vernadsky, G., *Lenin, Red Dictator* (1931); Werner, M. R. (ed.), *Stalin's Kampf: Joseph Stalin's Credo Written by Himself* (1940); Yaroslavsky, E., *Landmarks in the Life of Stalin* (1942).

AGRICULTURE AND INDUSTRY: Baykov, A., *The Development of the Soviet Economic System* (1947); Beauchamp, J., *Agriculture in Soviet Russia* (1931), the state farms; Chamberlin, W. H., *Russia's Iron Age* (1934); Chamberlin, W. H., *The Soviet Planned Economic Order* (1931), the first Five-Year Plan; Coates, W. P. and Z. K., *The Second Five-Year Plan of Development of the U.S.S.R.* (1934); Dobb, M., *Soviet Economic Development Since 1917* (1948); Fischer, L., *Machines and Men in Russia* (1932); Hirsch, A., *Industrialized Russia* (1934); Hubbard, L. E., *The Economics of Soviet Agriculture* (1939); Hubbard, L. E., *Soviet Labour and Industry* (1943); Iakovlev, I. A., *Red Villages: The Five-Year Plan in Soviet Agriculture* (1931); Rukeyser, W. A., *Working for the Soviets* (1932); Russian Economic Institute, *U.S.S.R. Economy and the War* (1942); Scott, J., *Behind the Urals: An American Worker in Russia's City of Steel* (1942); Turin, S. P., *The U.S.S.R.: An Economic and Social Survey* (1944); Yugow, A., *Russia's Economic Front for War and Peace: An Appraisal of the Three Five-Year Plans* (1943); Yugow, A., *et al., Management in Russian Industry and Agriculture* (1944).

EDUCATION AND RELIGION: Anderson, P. B., *People, Church and State in Modern Russia* (1944); Bolshakoff, S., *The Christian Church and the Soviet State* (1942); Casey, R. P., *Religion in Russia* (1946); Counts, G. S., and Lodge, N. P. (trs.), *"I Want to Be Like Stalin"* (1947), a training manual for teachers; Evans, S., *Churches in the U.S.S.R.* (1943); Fülöp-Miller, R., *The Mind and Face of Bolshevism: An Examination of Cultural Life in Soviet Russia* (1928); Harper, S. N., *Civic Training in Soviet Russia* (1929); Harper, S. N., *Making Bolsheviks* (1931); Hecker, J. F., *Religion and Communism* (1935); King, B., *Changing Man: The Soviet Education System of the U.S.S.R.* (1937); Mehnert, K., *Youth in Soviet Russia* (1933); Moscow Patriarchate (comp.), *The Truth about Religion in Russia: Compiled by the Moscow Patriarchate* (1944); Struve, G., *Twenty-Five Years of Soviet Russian Literature* (1944); Timasheff, N. S., *Religion in Soviet Russia: 1917–1942* (1942).

FOREIGN POLICY: Beloff, M., *The Foreign Policy of Soviet Russia, 1929–1941,* 2 vols. (1946–1949); Borkenau, F., *et al., World Communism: A History* of the Communist International (1939); Coates, W. P. and Z. K., History of Anglo-Soviet Relations (1944); Dallin, D. J., Soviet Russia's Foreign Policy, 1939–42 (1942); Davis, K. W., The Soviets at Geneva: The U.S.S.R. at the League of Nations, 1919–1933 (1934); Fischer, L., The Soviets in World Affairs, 2 vols. (1930); Gankin, O. H., and Fisher, H. H., The Bolsheviks and the World War: The Origin of the Third International (1940); Laserson, M. M. (comp.), The Development of Soviet Foreign Policy in Europe 1917–1942: A Selection of Documents (1943); Molotov, V. M., Soviet Foreign Relations (1940); Moore, H. L., Soviet Far Eastern Policy, 1931–1945 (1945); Murphy, J. T., Russia on the March: A Study of Soviet Foreign Policy (1941); Pares, Sir B., Russia and the Peace (1944); Pope, A. U., Maxim Litvinoff (1943); Pusta, K. R., The Soviet Union and the Baltic States (1942); Ross, M., A History of Soviet Foreign Policy (1940); Taracouzio, T. A., War and Peace in Soviet. Diplomacy (1940); Trotsky, L., The First Five Years of the Communist International (1946).

SPECIAL TOPICS: Asquith, M., Famine: Quaker Work in Russia, 1921–1923 (1944); Binder, P., Russian Families (1942); Bulygin, P., The Murder of the Romanovs (1935); Dallin, D. J., and Nicolaevsky, B. I., Forced Labor in Soviet Russia (1947); Field, A. W., Protection of Women and Children in Soviet Russia (1932); Fisher, H. H., The Famine in Soviet Russia (1927); Halle, F. W., Woman in Soviet Russia (1933); Newsholme, A., and Kingsbury, J. A., Red Medicine: Socialized Health in Soviet Russia (1933); Podolsky, E., Red Miracle (1947), the growth of medicine in Soviet Russia; Serebrennikov, G. N., The Position of Women in the U.S.S.R. (1936); Smith, E. S., Organized Labor in the Soviet Union (1943); Telberg, G. G., and Wilton, R., The Last Days of the Romanovs (1920); Trotsky, L., The Revolution Betrayed (1937).

Chapter XVI. Fascist Italy

GENERAL: Binchy, D. A., Church and State in Fascist Italy (1942); Bonomi, I., From Socialism to Fascism (1924); Borgese, G. A., Goliath: The March of Fascism (1937); Ebenstein, W., Fascist Italy (1939); Elwin, W., Fascism at Work (1934); Finer, H., Mussolini's Italy (1935); Hambloch, E., Italy Militant: A Study in Economic Militarism (1939); Hentze, M., Pre-Fascist Italy: The Rise and Fall of the Parliamentary Régime (1939); King, B., Fascism in Italy (1931); McGuire, C. E., Italy's International Economic Position (1926); Massock, R. G., Italy from Within (1943); Matthews, H. L., The Fruits of Fascism (1943); Minio-Paluello, L., Education in Fascist Italy, 1922–1940 (1946); Nathan, P., The Psychology of Fascism (1943); Nenni, P., Ten Years of Tyranny in Italy (1932); Nitti, F. F., Escape (1930); Salvemini, G., The Fascist Dictatorship in Italy (1927); Schneider, H. W., Making the Fascist State (1928); Schneider, H. W., and Clough, S. B., Making Fascists (1929); Sforza, C., The Real Italians (1942); Sillani, T. (ed.), What is Fascism and Why? (1931); Treves, P., What Mussolini Did to Us (1940); Walter, K., The Class Conflict in Italy (1938); Williamson, B., The Treaty of the Lateran (1929).

THE CORPORATIVE STATE: Field, G. L., The Syndical and Corporative

Institutions of Italian Fascism (1938); Goad, H. E., *The Making of the Corporate State* (1932); Haider, C., *Capital and Labor under Fascism* (1930); Pitigliani, F., *The Italian Corporative State* (1934); Salvemini, G., *Under the Axe of Fascism* (1936); Schmidt, C. T., *The Corporate State in Action: Italy under Fascism* (1939); Schmidt, C. T., *The Plough and the Sword: Labor, Land, and Property in Fascist Italy* (1938); Schneider, H. W., *The Fascist Government of Italy* (1936); Steiner, H. A., *Government in Fascist Italy* (1938).

BENITO MUSSOLINI: Fiori, V. E. de, *Mussolini, the Man of Destiny* (1928); Kemechy, L., *"Il Duce": The Life and Work of Benito Mussolini* (1930); Macartney, M. H. H., *One Man Alone: The History of Mussolini and the Axis* (1944); Megaro, G., *Mussolini in the Making* (1938); Mussolini, B., *My Autobiography* (1928); Mussolini, B., *My Diary, 1915–1917* (1925); Pini, G., *The Official Life of Benito Mussolini* (1939); Sarfatti, M. C., *The Life of Benito Mussolini* (1925); Seldes, G., *Sawdust Caesar: The Untold History of Mussolini and Fascism* (1935).

FOREIGN POLICY: Booth, C. D. G., and Bridge, I., *Italy's Aegean Possessions* (1928); Currey, M. I., *Italian Foreign Policy, 1918–1932* (1935); Macartney, M. H. H., and Cremona, P., *Italy's Foreign and Colonial Policy, 1914–1937* (1938); Morgan, T. B., *Spurs on the Boot* (1941); Packard, R. and E., *Balcony Empire* (1942); Monroe, E., *The Mediterranean in Politics* (1938); Villari, L., *The Expansion of Italy* (1930).

Chapter XVII. Liberal and Nazi Germany

THE WEIMAR REPUBLIC: Angell, J. W., *The Recovery of Germany* (1932); Bieligk, K. F., *Stresemann* (1944); Brunet, R., *The New German Constitution* (1922); Daniels, H. G., *The Rise of the German Republic* (1928); Halperin, S. W., *Germany Tried Democracy: A Political History of the Reich from 1918 to 1933* (1946); Hoetzsch, O., *Germany's Domestic and Foreign Policies* (1929); Ludwig, E., *Hindenburg and the Saga of the German Republic* (1935); Luehr, E., *The New German Republic* (1929); Mendelssohn-Bartholdy, A., *The War and German Society: The Testament of a Liberal* (1937); Morgan, J. H., *Assize of Arms: Being the Story of the Disarmament of Germany and Her Rearmament, 1919–1939* (1945); Mullins, C., *Leipzig Trials* (1921), war criminals; Olden, R., *Stresemann* (1930); Oppenheimer, H., *The Constitution of the German Republic* (1923); Quigley, H., and Clark, R. J., *Republican Germany* (1928); Rheinbaben, R. von, *Stresemann, the Man and the Statesman* (1929); Schacht, H., *The Stabilization of the Mark* (1927); Scheele, G., *The Weimar Republic: Overture to the Third Reich* (1946); Scheidemann, P., *The Making of New Germany: The Memoirs of Philipp Scheidemann* (1929); Spiecker, K., *Germany: From Defeat to Defeat* (1944); Stresemann, G., *Gustav Stresemann: His Diaries, Letters and Papers*, 3 vols. (1935–1940); Tschuppik, K., *Ludendorff: The Tragedy of a Military Mind* (1932); Vallentin, A., *Stresemann* (1931); Weterstetten, R., and Watson, A. M. K., *The Biography of President von Hindenburg* (1930); Wheeler-Bennett, J. W., *Wooden Titan: Hindenburg in Twenty Years of German History, 1914–1934* (1936); Ybarra, T. R., *Hindenburg, the Man with Three Lives* (1932).

THE DOWNFALL OF THE WEIMAR REPUBLIC: Abel, T. F., *Why Hitler Came into Power* (1938); Armstrong, H. F., *Hitler's Reich: the First Phase* (1933); Brecht, A., *Prelude to Silence* (1944), an explanation of why the "good" Germans permitted Hitler to seize power; Butler, R., *The Roots of National Socialism* (1942); Clark, R. T., *The Fall of the German Republic* (1935); Feder, G., *Hitler's Official Programme and Its Fundamental Ideas* (1934); Florinsky, M. T., *Fascism and National Socialism* (1936); Heberle, R., *From Democracy to Nazism: A Regional Case Study on Political Parties in Germany* (1945); Hoover, C. B., *Germany Enters the Third Reich* (1934); Knickerbocker, H. R., *The German Crisis* (1932); Knight-Patterson, W. M., *Germany From Defeat to Conquest, 1913–1933* (1945); Kraus, H., *The Crisis of German Democracy* (1932); Lengyel, E., *Hitler* (1932); Lutz, R. H., *The Reichstag Election of March 5, 1933* (1943); Menne, B., *The Case of Dr. Bruening* (1943), an indictment; Rauschning, H., *The Voice of Destruction* (1940); Reed, D., *The Burning of the Reichstag* (1934); Scandrett, J. J. M., *The Nazi Disease* (1939); Strasser, O., *History in My Time* (1941); Thyssen, F., *I Paid Hitler* (1941); Watkins, F. M., *The Failure of Constitutional Emergency Powers under the German Republic* (1939).

THE THIRD REICH: Brady, R. A., *The Spirit and Structure of German Fascism* (1937); Dodd, W. E., Jr., and M. (eds.), *Ambassador Dodd's Diary, 1933–38* (1941); Ebenstein, W., *The Nazi State* (1943); Fraser, L., *Germany Between Two Wars: A Study of Propaganda and War Guilt* (1945); Garratt, G. T., *The Shadow of the Swastika* (1938); Guillebaud, C. W., *Economic Recovery of Germany from March, 1933 to the Incorporation of Austria* (1939); Hambloch, E., *Germany Rampant: A Study in Economic Militarism* (1939); Holt, J. B., *Under the Swastika* (1936); Institute on Jewish Affairs, *Hitler's Ten-Year War on the Jews* (1943); Krieger, S., *Nazi Germany's War against the Jews* (1947); Kuczynski, J., *A Short History of Labor Conditions in Germany under Fascism* (1944); Landau, R., *Hitler's Paradise* (1941); Lichtenberger, H., *The Third Reich: Germany under National Socialism* (1939); Loewenstein, K., *Hitler's Germany: The Nazi Background of the War* (1939); Nathan, O., *The Nazi Economic System* (1944); Neumann, F. L., *Behemoth: The Structure and Practice of National Socialism* (1942); Pollock, J. K., *The Government of Greater Germany* (1940); Rauschning, H., *The Revolution of Nihilism* (1939); Roberts, S. H., *The House That Hitler Built* (1938); Schuman, F. L., *The Nazi Dictatorship: A Study in Social Pathology* (1935); Shirer, W. L., *Berlin Diary: The Journal of a Foreign Correspondent, 1934–1941* (1941); Sington, D., and Weidenfeld, A., *The Goebbels Experiment* (1943); Warburg, G., *Six Years of Hitler: The Jews under the Nazi Regime* (1939).

HITLER AND HIS ASSOCIATES: Bayles, W. D., *Caesars in Goose Step* (1940); Baynes, N. (ed.), *Hitler's Speeches,* 2 vols. (1942); Behrend, H., *Real Rulers of Germany* (1939); Bondy, L. W., *Racketeers of Hatred: Julius Streicher and the Jew Baiter's International* (1946); Combs, G. H., *Himmler, Nazi Spider*

Man (1942); Dutch, O., *The Errant Diplomat: The Life of Franz von Papen* (1940); Dutch, O., *Hitler's Twelve Apostles* (1940); Frange, G. W. (ed.), *Hitler's Words: Two Decades of National Socialism, 1923–1943* (1944); Heiden, K., *Der Fuehrer: Hitler's Rise to Power* (1944); Heiden, K. (ed.), *Der Führer: Speeches and Writings, 1919–1941* (1941); Hitler, A., *My Battle* (1943); Koeves, T., *Satan in Top Hat* (1941), a biography of Franz von Papen; Lochner, L. (ed.), *The Goebbels Diaries* (1948); Ludecke, K. G., *I Knew Hitler* (1937); Mühlen, N., *Schacht, Hitler's Magician* (1939); Murphy, J., *Adolf Hitler: The Drama of His Career* (1934); Pope, E. R., *Munich Playground* (1941); Riess, C., *Joseph Goebbels* (1948); Schwarz, P., *This Man Ribbentrop* (1943); Semmler, R., *Goebbels: The Man Next to Hitler* (1947); Singer, K., *Göring: Germany's Most Dangerous Man* (1940); Strasser, O., *Hitler and I* (1940); Wagner, L., *Hitler: Man of Strife* (1942).

THE GESTAPO SYSTEM: Heiden, K., *The New Inquisition* (1939); Karst, G. M., *The Beasts of the Earth* (1942), the Dachau concentration camp; Lorant, S., *I Was Hitler's Prisoner* (1935); Seger, G., *A Nation Terrorized* (1935); Stein, L., *I Was in Hell with Niemoeller* (1942); Wallner, P., *By Order of the Gestapo: A Record of Life in Dachau and Buchenwald Concentration Camps* (1941); Winkler, E., *Four Years of Nazi Torture* (1942).

EDUCATION AND RELIGION UNDER THE NAZIS: Brennecke, F., *The Nazi Primer* (1938), required reading for Hitler Youth; Carmer, C. (ed.), *The War Against God* (1943); Duncan-Jones, A. S., *The Struggle for Religious Freedom in Germany* (1938); Frey, A., *Cross and Swastika: The Ordeal of the German Church* (1938); Hartshorne, E. Y., *The German Universities and National Socialism* (1937); Kneller, G. F., *The Educational Philosophy of National Socialism* (1941); Micklem, N., *National Socialism and the Roman Catholic Church* (1939); Power, M., *Religion in the Reich* (1939); Wolf, A., *Higher Education in Nazi Germany, or Education for World Conquest* (1944); Ziemer, G., *Education for Death: The Making of the Nazi* (1941).

Chapter XVIII. Great Britain and Ireland

BRITISH INTERNAL AFFAIRS: Benham, F., *Great Britain under Protection* (1941); Brand, C. F., *British Labour's Rise to Power: Eight Studies* (1941); Briffault, R., *Decline and Fall of the British Empire* (1938); Bromfield, L., *England: A Dying Oligarchy* (1939); Cartland, B., *The Isthmus Years* (1943); social history of England between the two wars; Dalton, H., *Practical Socialism for Britain* (1935); Davison, R. C., *British Unemployment Policy: The Modern Phase Since 1930* (1938); Dickie, J. P., *The Coal Problem, 1910–1936* (1936); Fyfe, H., *Behind the Scenes of the Great Strike* (1926); Graves, R., and Hodge, A., *The Long Week End: A Social History of Great Britain, 1918–1939* (1941); Greenwood, G. A., *England Today: A Social Study of Our Time* (1926); Heaton, H., *The British Way to Recovery* (1934); Hill, A. C. C., Jr., and Lubin, I., *The British Attack on Unemployment* (1934); Hutt, A., *The Post-War History of the British Working Classes* (1938); Jennings, W. I., *The British Constitution* (1941); Lawrence, F. W. P., *The Gold Crisis* (1931);

Loveday, A., *Britain and World Trade* (1931); Lubin, I., and Everett, H., *The British Coal Dilemma* (1927); McHenry, D., *His Majesty's Opposition: Structure and Problems of the British Labor Party, 1931–1938* (1941); Marriott, Sir J. A. R., *Modern England, 1885–1939: A History of My Own Times* (1943); Masterman, C. F. G., *England after War* (1922); Morton, W. A., *British Finance, 1930–1940* (1943); Pigou, A. C., *Aspects of British Economic History, 1918–1925* (1947); Priestley, J. B., *An English Journey* (1934), a readable description of England's "depressed areas" in 1933; Siegfried, A., *England's Crisis* (1931); Snyder, R. K., *The Tariff Problem in Great Britain, 1918–1923* (1944); Somerville, D. C., *Between the Wars* (1948); White, J. L., *The Abdication of Edward VIII: A Record with All the Public Documents* (1937).

BIOGRAPHIES AND MEMOIRS: Arthur, Sir G., *Concerning Winston Spencer Churchill* (1941); Bolitho, H., *King Edward VIII: An Intimate Biography* (1937); Bolitho, H., *King George VI* (1938); Broad, L., *Winston Churchill* (1941); Buchan, J., *The People's King* (1935); Edwards, J. H., *David Lloyd George, the Man and the Statesman*, 2 vols. (1929); Feiling, K., *The Life of Neville Chamberlain* (1946); Glasgow, G., *MacDonald as a Diplomatist* (1924); Gore, J., *King George V* (1941); Guedalla, P., *Mr. Churchill* (1942); Hamilton, M. A., *Arthur Henderson: A Biography* (1938); Hamilton, M. A., *England's Labour Rulers* (1924); Hodgson, S., *The Man Who Made Peace: Neville Chamberlain* (1938); Johnson, A. C., *Anthony Eden: A Biography* (1939); Johnson, A. C., *Viscount Halifax* (1941); Kraus, R., *The Men Around Churchill* (1941); Kraus, R., *Winston Churchill* (1940); Mallet, Sir C. E., *Mr. Lloyd George: A Study* (1930); Paneth, P., *King George VI and His People* (1944); Petrie, C., *The Chamberlain Tradition* (1938); Roberts, C. E. B., *Stanley Baldwin, Man or Miracle?* (1937); Snowden, P., *An Autobiography*, 2 vols. (1934); Steed, H. W., *The Real Stanley Baldwin* (1930); Strauss, P., *Bevin and Co., the Leaders of British Labour* (1941); Thompson, E. R., *Mr. Lloyd George* (1922); Tiltman, H. H., *J. Ramsay MacDonald, Labour's Man of Destiny* (1929).

BRITISH FOREIGN POLICY: Carr, E. H., *Britain: A Study of Foreign Policy from the Treaty of Versailles to the Outbreak of the War* (1939); "Cato," *Guilty Men* (1940), an indictment of the "appeasers"; Churchill, W. S., *The Gathering Storm* (1948); Coates, W. P. and Z. K., *History of Anglo-Soviet Relations* (1944); Eden, A., *Foreign Affairs* (1939); Jerrold, D., *Britain and Europe, 1900–1940* (1941); Kennedy, J. F., *Why England Slept* (1940); Langford, R. V., *British Foreign Policy: Its Formulation in Recent Years* (1942); Medlicott, W. N., *British Foreign Policy since Versailles* (1940); Scarfoglio, C., *England and the Continent* (1939); Seton-Watson, R. W., *Britain and the Dictators: A Survey of Postwar British Policy* (1938); Sipple, C. E., *British Foreign Policy since the World War* (1932); Willert, Sir A., *Aspects of British Foreign Policy* (1928).

COMMONWEALTH RELATIONS: Dawson, R. M., *The Development of Dominion Status, 1900–1936* (1937); Elliott, W. Y., *The New British Empire* (1932); Muir, R., *The British Commonwealth: How It Grew and How It Works* (1941); Wheare, K. C., *The Statute of Westminster, 1931* (1933).

IRELAND: Béaslaí, P., *Michael Collins, Soldier and Statesman* (1937); Collins, M., *The Path of Freedom* (1923); Curtis, E., *A History of Ireland* (1938); Good, J. W., *Ulster and Ireland* (1919); Gwynn, D. R., *De Valera* (1933); Harrison, H., *The Neutrality of Ireland: Why It Was Inevitable* (1942); Healy, T. M., *Letters and Leaders of My Day*, 2 vols. (1929); Hull, E., *A History of Ireland and Her People* (1926); Ireland, T., *Ireland, Past and Present* (1942); Jones, F. P., *History of the Sinn Fein Movement and the Irish Rebellion of 1916* (1917); Kelly, R. S., *Ireland's Bloodless Revolution, 1932–1936* (1936); Kohn, L., *The Constitution of the Irish Free State* (1943); McManus, M. J., *Eamon de Valera* (1946); MacNeill, R., *Ulster's Stand for Union* (1922); Mansergh, N., *The Government of Northern Ireland* (1936); Mansergh, N., *The Irish Free State* (1934); O'Connor, B., *With Michael Collins in the Fight for Irish Independence* (1930); O'Connor, F., *Death in Dublin: Michael Collins and the Irish Revolution* (1937); Paul-Dubois, L., and Gill, T. P., *The Irish Struggle and Its Results* (1934); Phillips, W. A., *The Revolution in Ireland, 1906–1923* (1926); Quekett, Sir A. S., *The Constitution of Northern Ireland* (1928); Ryan, D., *Unique Dictator: A Study of Eamon de Valera* (1936); Talbot, H. (ed.), *Michael Collins' Own Story* (1923); Wells, W. B., and Marlowe, N., *A History of the Irish Rebellion of 1916* (1916); a careful, detailed study.

Chapter XIX. France and Spain

FRENCH INTERNAL AFFAIRS: Bates-Batcheller, T., *France in Sunshine and Shadow* (1944); Daniels, H. G., *The Framework of France* (1937); Davis, S. C., *The French War Machine* (1937); Fox, R. W., *France Faces the Future* (1936); Fraser, G., and Natanson, T., *Léon Blum, Man and Statesman* (1937); Hale, R. W., Jr., *Democratic France: the Third Republic from Sedan to Vichy* (1941); Hayes, C. J. H., *France: a Nation of Patriots* (1930); Huddleston, S., *France* (1927); Huddleston, S., *Poincaré: A Biographical Portrait* (1924); Joseph-Maginot, M., *He Might Have Saved France* (1941); Lazareff, P., *Deadline: The Behind-the-Scenes Story of the Last Decade in France* (1940); Leeds, S. B., *These Rule France: The Story of Edouard Daladier and the Men Around Him* (1940); MacDonald, W., *Reconstruction in France* (1922); Maillaud, P., *France* (1943); Peel, G., *The Economic Policy of France* (1937); Riethinger, A., *Why France Lost the War: A Biological and Economic Survey* (1940); Rogers, G. H., *The Process of Inflation in France, 1914–1927* (1929); Saposs, D. J., *The Labor Movement in Post-War France* (1931); Sharp, W. R., *The Government of the French Republic* (1939); Siegfried, A., *France: A Study in Nationality* (1930); Simon, Y., *The Road to Vichy 1918–1938* (1942); Spengler, J. J., *France Faces Depopulation* (1938); Stokes, R. L., *Léon Blum: Poet to Premier* (1937); Tissier, P., *I Worked with Laval* (1942); Torrès, H., *Pierre Laval* (1941); Vaucher, P., *Post-War France* (1934); Werth, A., *France in Ferment* (1935); Werth, A., *The Twilight of France* (1942); Weyer, E., *The Decline of French Democracy: The Beginning of National Disintegration* (1940); Winter, G., *This Is Not the End of France* (1942).

FRENCH FOREIGN POLICY: Cameron, E. R., *Prologue to Appeasement*

(1942); Daladier, E., *In Defense of France* (1939); Micaud, C. A., *The French Right and Nazi Germany, 1933–1939: A Study of Public Opinion* (1944); Ormesson, W. d', *France* (1939); Street, C. J. C., *The Treachery of France* (1924); Thomson, V., *Briand, Man of Peace* (1930); Werth, A., *France and Munich: Before and After the Surrender* (1939).

SPAIN: Alvarez del Vayo, J., *Freedom's Battle* (1940); Arraras, J., *Francisco Franco: The Times and the Man* (1938); Barea, A., *The Forging of a Rebel: An Autobiography* (1946); Brandt, J. A., *Toward the New Spain* (1933); Brenan, G., *The Spanish Labyrinth: An Account of the Social and Political Background of the Civil War* (1943); Casado, S., *Last Days of Madrid* (1939); Davis, F., *My Shadow in the Sun* (1940), civil war; Deakin, F. B., *Spain Today* (1924); Dundas, L., *Behind the Spanish Mask* (1943); Elstob, P., *Spanish Prisoner* (1939); Foltz, C., Jr., *The Masquerade in Spain: A Report Unmasking the Rulers of Modern Spain* (1948); George, R. E. G., *Spain's Ordeal* (1940); Hamilton, T. J., *Appeasement's Child: The Franco Regime in Spain* (1943); Jellinek, F., *The Civil War in Spain* (1938); Knoblaugh, H., *Correspondent in Spain* (1938); Last, J., *Spanish Tragedy* (1939); Loveday, A. F., *World War in Spain* (1939); Madariaga, S. de, *Spain* (1943); Manuel, F. E., *The Politics of Modern Spain* (1938); Mendizabal Villalba, A. O., *The Martyrdom of Spain* (1938); Morrow, F., *Revolution and Counter-Revolution in Spain* (1938); Peers, E. A., *Catalonia Infelix* (1938); Peers, E. A., *Spain in Eclipse, 1937–1943* (1943); Peers, E. A., *The Spanish Tragedy, 1930–1936: Dictatorship, Republic, Chaos* (1936); Regler, G., *The Great Crusade* (1940); Rogers, F. T., *Spain: A Tragic Journey* (1937); Rolfe, E., *Lincoln Battalion: The Story of the Americans Who Fought in Spain in the International Brigades* (1939); Salter, C., *Try-out in Spain* (1943); Smith, R. M., *The Day of the Liberals in Spain* (1938); Young, G., *The New Spain* (1933).

Chapter XX. Central Europe and the Balkans

THE DANUBE BASIN: Basch, A., *The Danube Basin and the German Economic Sphere* (1943); Crane, J. O., *The Little Entente* (1931); Evans, J. D. E., *That Blue Danube* (1935); Fodor, M. W., *Plot and Counter-Plot in Central Europe: Conditions South of Hitler* (1937); Gedye, G. E. R., *Heirs to the Hapsburgs* (1932); Gulick, C. A., *Austria From Hapsburg to Hitler,* 2 vols. (1948); Hanc, J., *Tornado across Eastern Europe* (1942); Hertz, R., *The Economic Problem of the Danubian States: A Study in Economic Nationalism* (1947); Lengyel, E., *The Danube* (1939); Macartney, C. A., *Problems of the Danube Basin* (1942); Machray, R., *The Little Entente* (1929); Pasvolsky, L., *Economic Nationalism of the Danubian States* (1929); Seton-Watson, R. W., *Eastern Europe Between the Wars, 1918–1941* (1945).

AUSTRIA: Ball, M. M., *Post-War German-Austrian Relations: The Anschluss Movement, 1918–1936* (1937); Basch, A., and Dvořáček, J., *Austria and Its Economic Existence* (1925); Bitterman, M., *Austria and the Customs Union* (1931); Bullock, M., *Austria, 1918–1938: A Study in Failure* (1939); Frischauer, W., *Twilight in Vienna, the Capital without a Country* (1938);

Fuchs, M., *Showdown in Vienna: The Death of Austria* (1939); Germains, V. W., *Austria of Today* (1932); Gregory, J. D., *Dollfuss and His Times* (1935); Hardy, C. O., and Kuczynski, R. R., *The Housing Program of the City of Vienna* (1934); Kleinwächter, F. F. G., *Self-Determination for Austria* (1929); League of Nations, *The Financial Reconstruction of Austria* (1926); Macartney, C. A., *The Social Revolution in Austria* (1926); Macdonald, M., *The Republic of Austria, 1918–1934: A Study of the Failure of Democratic Government* (1946); Rothschild, K. W., *Austria's Economic Development Between the Two Wars* (1947); Rüdiger, E., *Between Hitler and Mussolini: Memoirs of Ernst Rüdiger Prince Starhemberg* (1942); Schuschnigg, K., *My Austria* (1938); Schuschnigg, K., *Austrian Requiem* (1946); Sheridan, R. K., *Kurt von Schuschnigg* (1942).

CZECHOSLOVAKIA: Bartusek, L., *Happy Times in Czechoslovakia* (1940); Beneš, E., *Eduard Beneš in His Own Words: Three Score Years of a Statesman, Builder and Philosopher* (1945); Bilek, B., *Fifth Column at Work* (1945); Borovicka, J., *Ten Years of Czechoslovak Politics* (1929); Čapek, K., *et al., At the Cross-Roads of Europe: A Historical Outline of the Democratic Czechoslovakia* (1938); Crabites, P., *Beneš, Statesman of Central Europe* (1936); De Colonna, B., *Czechoslovakia Within* (1938); Grant Duff, S., *Europe and the Czechs* (1938); Hitchcock, E. B., *"I Built a Temple for Peace": The Life of Eduard Beneš* (1940); Holland, C., *Czechoslovakia: The Land and Its People* (1931); Kerner, R. J. (ed.), *Czechoslovakia: Twenty Years of Independence* (1940); Lechner, O., *As We Saw It in Prague: Twelve Discussions and a Letter, 1933–1939* (1943); Lowrie, D. A., *Masaryk of Czechoslovakia* (1938); Mackenzie, C., *Dr. Beneš* (1946); Mackworth, C., and Stransky, J., *Czechoslovakia* (1944); Polišensky, J. V., *History of Czechoslovakia in Outline* (1948); Seton-Watson, R. W., *A History of the Czechs and Slovaks* (1943); Seton-Watson, R. W. (ed.), *Slovakia, Then and Now: A Political Survey* (1931); Seton-Watson, R. W., *Twenty-Five Years of Czechoslovakia* (1945); Street, C. J. C., *President Masaryk* (1930); Textor, L. E., *Land Reform in Czecho-Slovakia* (1923); Thomson, S. H., *Czechoslovakia in European History* (1943); Vondracek, F. J., *The Foreign Policy of Czechoslovakia, 1918–1935* (1937); Wiskemann, E., *Czechs and Germans: A Study of the Struggle in the Historic Provinces of Bohemia and Moravia* (1938); Young, P., *Czechoslovakia, Keystone of Peace and Democracy* (1938).

HUNGARY: Apponyi, Count S., *et al., Justice for Hungary* (1928); Bethlen, I., *The Treaty of Trianon and European Peace: Four Lectures Delivered in London, November, 1933* (1934); Deák, F., and Ujváry, D. (eds.), *Papers and Documents Relating to the Foreign Relations of Hungary, Vol. I, 1919–1920* (1939); Donald, Sir R., *The Tragedy of Trianon* (1928); Eckhart, F., *A Short History of the Hungarian People* (1931); Gower, R., *The Hungarian Minorities in the Succession States* (1937); Jászi, O., *Revolution and Counter-Revolution in Hungary* (1924); Kaas, A., and Lazarovics, F. de, *Bolshevism in Hungary: The Bela Kun Period* (1931); Kosáry, D. G., *A History of Hungary* (1941); League of Nations, *The Financial Reconstruction of Hungary* (1926); Macartney, C. A., *Hungary and Her Successors, 1919–1937* (1938); Seton-Watson, R. W., *Treaty Revision and the Hungarian Frontiers* (1934); Street, C. J. C., *Hungary and Democracy* (1923).

POLAND: Buell, R. L., *Poland: Key to Europe* (1939); Devereux, R., *Poland Reborn* (1922); Dyboski, R., *Poland Old and New* (1926); Goodhart, A. L., *Poland and the Minority Races* (1922); Gorecki, R., *Poland and Her Economic Development* (1935); Halecki, O., *A History of Poland* (1943); Humphrey, G., *Pilsudski: Builder of Poland* (1936); Janowsky, O. I., *People at Bay: The Jewish Problem in East Central Europe* (1938); Machray, R., *The Poland of Pilsudski, 1914–1936* (1937); Mackiewicz, S., *Colonel Beck and His Policy* (1944); Murray, M. (ed.), *Poland's Progress, 1919–1939* (1944); Patterson, E. J., *Pilsudski, Marshal of Poland* (1935); Reddaway, W. F., *Marshal Pilsudski* (1939); Rose, W. J., *Poland* (1939); Schmitt, B. E. (ed.), *Poland* (1945); Segal, S., *The New Poland and the Jews* (1938); Shotwell, J. T., and Laserson, M. M., *Poland and Russia, 1919–1945* (1945); Slocombe, G., *History of Poland* (1940); Symonolewicz, K., *Studies in Nationality and Nationalism in Poland Between the Two Wars* (1944).

DANZIG AND THE POLISH CORRIDOR: Baginski, J., *Poland and the Baltic: The Problem of Poland's Access to the Sea* (1943); Donald, Sir R., *The Polish Corridor and the Consequences* (1929); Leonhardt, H., *Nazi Conquest of Danzig* (1942); Machray, R., *The Polish German Problem* (1942); Martel, R., *The Eastern Frontiers of Germany* (1930); Mason, J. B., *The Danzig Dilemma* (1945); Smogorzewski, C., *Poland, Germany and the Corridor* (1930).

GREECE: Alastos, D., *Venizelos: Patriot, Statesman, Revolutionary* (1942); Andrew, Prince of Greece, *Towards Disaster* (1930); Eddy, C. B., *Greece and the Greek Refugees* (1931); Gibbons, H. A., *Venizelos* (1920); Hibben, P., *Constantine I and the Greek People* (1920); Ladas, S. P., *The Exchange of Minorities* (1932); League of Nations, *The Greek Refugee Settlement* (1926); Macartney, C. A., *Refugees* (1931); Mavrogordato, J., *Modern Greece: A Chronicle and a Survey, 1800–1931* (1931); Mears, E. G., *Greece Today: The Aftermath of the Refugee Impact* (1929); Miller, W., *Greece* (1928); Morgenthau, H., *I Was Sent to Athens* (1929); Phocas-Cosmetatos, S. P., *The Tragedy of Greece* (1928); Toynbee, A. J., *The Western Question in Greece and Turkey* (1922).

YUGOSLAVIA: Adamic, L., *My Native Land* (1943); Adamic, L., *The Native's Return: An American Immigrant Visits Yugoslavia and Discovers His Old Country* (1934); Baerlein, H., *The Birth of Yugoslavia*, 2 vols. (1922); Beard, C. A., and Radin, G., *The Balkan Pivot: Yugoslavia* (1929); Buchan, J. (ed.), *Yugoslavia* (1923); Ellison, G, *Yugoslavia: A New Country and Its People* (1935); Graham, S., *Alexander of Yugoslavia* (1939); Laffan, R. G. D., *Yugoslavia since 1918* (1929); Lodge, O., *Peasant Life in Jugoslavia* (1942); Sforza, C., *Fifty Years of War and Diplomacy in the Balkans: Pashich and the Union of the Yugoslavs* (1940).

ALBANIA: Bareilles, B., Durham, M. E., *et al., Albania and the Albanians*

(1920); Chekrezi, C. A., *Albania, Past and Present* (1919); Stickney, E. P., *Southern Albania or Northern Epirus in European Affairs, 1912–1923* (1926); Swire, J., *King Zog's Albania* (1937).

BULGARIA: Anastasoff, C., *The Tragic Peninsula* (1938); Christowe, S., *Heroes and Assassins* (1935); Leslie, H., *Where East Is West: Life in Bulgaria* (1933); Logio, G. C., *Bulgaria Past and Present* (1936); Londres, A., *Terror in the Balkans* (1935); Pasvolsky, L., *Bulgaria's Economic Position, with Special Reference to the Reparation Problem and the Work of the League of Nations* (1930); Swire, J., *Bulgarian Conspiracy* (1939).

RUMANIA: Bolitho, H., *Roumania under King Carol* (1940); Cabot, J. M., *The Racial Conflict in Transylvania* (1926); Clark, C. U., *Bessarabia* (1927); Clark, C. U., *United Rumania* (1932); Deák, F., *The Hungarian-Rumanian Land Dispute* (1928); Dragomir, S., *The Ethnical Minorities in Transylvania* (1927); Evans, I. L., *The Agrarian Revolution in Roumania* (1924); Hoven, Baroness H. von der, *King Carol of Romania* (1940); Ionescu, T., *Some Personal Impressions* (1920); Iorga, N. A., *History of Rumania* (1925); Janowsky, O. I., *People at Bay: The Jewish Problem in East-Central Europe* (1938); Mitrany, D., *The Land and Peasant in Roumania* (1930); Rakovsky, C. G., *Roumania and Bessarabia* (1925); Rouček, J. S., *Contemporary Roumania and Her Problems* (1932); Szasz, Z., *The Minorities in Roumanian Transylvania* (1927).

BALKAN INTERNATIONAL RELATIONS: Geshkoff, T. I., *A Road to Peace in Southeastern Europe* (1940); Kerner, R. J., and Howard, H. N., *The Balkan Conferences and the Balkan Entente, 1930–1935* (1936); Konacs, F. W. L., *The Untamed Balkans* (1942); Newman, B., *Balkan Background* (1944); Padelford, N. J., *Peace in the Balkans: The Movement towards International Organization in the Balkans* (1935); Rouček, J. S., *Politics in the Balkans* (1939); Stavrianos, L. S., *Balkan Federation: A History of the Movement toward Balkan Unity in Modern Times* (1944).

Chapter XXI. The East in Revolt

GENERAL WORKS ON THE NEAR AND MIDDLE EAST: Arberry, A. J., and Landau, R., (eds.), *Islam Today* (1943); Ben-Horin, E., *The Middle East: Crossroads of History* (1943); Boveri, M., *Minaret and Pipe-line: Yesterday and Today in the Near East* (1939); Breasted, J. H., *The New Orient*, Vol. I (1933); Chirol, Sir V., *The Occident and the Orient* (1924); Dutcher, G. M., *The Political Awakening of the East* (1925); Hocking, W. E., *The Spirit of World Politics* (1932); O'Leary, D. E., *Islam at the Crossroads: A Brief Survey of the Present Position and Problems of the World of Islam* (1923); Puryear, V. J., *International Economics and Diplomacy in the Near East* (1935); Spender, J. A., *The Changing East* (1926); Toynbee, A. J., *Survey of International Affairs, 1925: Part I, The Islamic World Since the Peace Settlement* (1927); Toynbee, A. J., *The Western Question in Greece and Turkey: A Study in the Contact of Civilizations* (1922).

TURKEY: Allen, H. E., *The Turkish Transformation* (1935); Armstrong,

H. C., *Gray Wolf: Mustapha Kemal* (1933); Ellison, G., *Turkey Today* (1928); Hālidah Adïb, K., *Turkey Faces West* (1930); Ikbāl, Alī Shāh, *Kamal: Maker of Modern Turkey* (1934); Jackh, E., *The Rising Crescent* (1944); Jarman, T. L., *Turkey* (1935); Krüger, K., *Kemalist Turkey and the Middle East* (1932); Luke, H., *The Making of Modern Turkey* (1936); Mikusch, D. von, *Mustapha Kemal* (1931); Ostroróg, L., *The Angora Reform* (1928); Price, C., *The Rebirth of Turkey* (1932); Toynbee, A. J., and Kirkwood, K., *Turkey* (1927); Webster, D. E., *The Turkey of Atatürk* (1939); Wortham, H. E., *Mustapha Kemal of Turkey* (1931).

EGYPT: Harris, M., *Egypt under the Egyptians* (1925); Howell, J. M., *Egypt's Past, Present and Future* (1929); Newman, E. W. P., *Great Britain in Egypt* (1928); Royal Institute of International Affairs, *Great Britain and Egypt, 1914–1936* (1936); Symons, M. T., *Britain and Egypt: The Rise of Egyptian Nationalism* (1925); Young, G., *Egypt* (1927); Youssef Bey, A., *Independent Egypt* (1942).

PALESTINE AND SYRIA: Antonius, G., *The Arab Awakening* (1939); Armstrong, H., *Turkey and Syria Reborn* (1930); Hanna, P. L., *British Policy in Palestine* (1942); Kallen, H. M., *Zionism and World Politics* (1921); Lowdermilk, W. C., *Palestine, Land of Promise* (1944); Luke, H. C., and Keith-Roach, E., *The Handbook of Palestine and Trans-Jordan* (1930); Mc-Callum, E. P., *The Nationalist Crusade in Syria* (1928); Main, E., *Palestine at the Crossroads* (1937); Preiss, L., and Rohrbach, P., *Palestine and Trans-jordania* (1926); Royal Institute of International Affairs, *Great Britain and Palestine, 1915–1936* (1936); Samuel, M., *On the Rim of the Wilderness* (1931); Sereni, E., and Ashery, R. E., *Jews and Arabs in Palestine* (1936); Sidebotham, H., *Great Britain and Palestine* (1937); Stein, L., *Syria* (1926); Stoyanovsky, J., *The Mandate for Palestine* (1928); Van Ess, J., *Meet the Arab* (1943).

IRAQ AND PERSIA: Elwell-Sutton, L. P., *Modern Iran* (1941); Foster, H. A., *The Making of Modern Iraq* (1935); Ireland, P. W., *Iraq: A Study in Political Development* (1938); Main, E., *Iraq* (1935); Merritt-Hawkes, O. A., *Persia: Romance and Reality* (1935); Millspaugh, A. C., *The American Task in Persia* (1925); Ross, Sir E. D., *The Persians* (1931).

INDIA: Andrews, C. F. (ed.), *Mahatma Gandhi: His Own Story* (1930); Andrews, C. F., *Mahatma Gandhi's Ideas* (1930); Anstey, V., *The Economic Development of India* (1931); Coatman, J., *India: The Road to Self-Government, 1908–1940* (1943); Duncan, A., *India in Crisis* (1931); Dutt, R. P., *The Problem of India* (1943); Fischer, L., *Empire* (1943); Gandhi, M. K., *The Story of My Experiments with Truth*, 2 vols. (1927–1929); Gandhi, M. K., *Gandhi's Autobiography* (1948); Mitchell, K. L., *India Without Fable* (1942); Nehru, J., *Toward Freedom* (1941); Rolland, R., *Mahatma Gandhi* (1924); Simon, Sir J., *India and the Simon Report* (1930); Singh, A., *Nehru, the Rising Star of India* (1939); Whyte, Sir F., *India: A Bird's-Eye View* (1943).

GENERAL WORKS ON THE FAR EAST: Blakeslee, G. H., *The Pacific Area* (1929); Breasted, J. H., *The New Orient*, Vol. II (1933); Buss, C. A., *War and Diplomacy in Eastern Asia* (1941); Close, U., *The Revolt of Asia* (1927); Hudson, G. F., *The Far East in World Politics: A Study in Recent*

History (1937); Millard, T. F. F., *Conflicts of Policy in Asia* (1924); Park, No-Yong, *Retreat of the West* (1937); Vinacke, H. M., *A History of the Far East in Modern Times* (4th ed., 1941).

CHINA IN REVOLUTION: Berkov, R. H., *Strong Man of China* (1938), Chiang Kai-shek; Chang, H., *Chiang Kai-shek: Asia's Man of Destiny* (1944); Clark, E. T., *The Chiangs of China* (1943); Clark, G., *The Great Wall Crumbles* (1935); Gannes, H., *When China Unites: A History of China's Struggle for National Independence, 1840–1938: An Interpretive History of the Chinese Revolution* (1938); Hedin, S., *Chiang Kai-shek, Marshal of China* (1940); Holcombe, A. N., *The Spirit of the Chinese Revolution* (1930); Hsü, L. S. (comp.), *Sun Yat-sen: His Political and Social Ideals* (1933); Lattimore, O. and E., *The Making of Modern China: A Short History* (1944); MacNair, H. F., *China in Revolution* (1931); Peffer, N., *China: The Collapse of a Civilization* (1930); Pringle, J. M. D., and Rajchman, M., *China Struggles for Unity* (1939); Restarick, H. B., *Sun Yat-sen* (1931); Sharman, L., *Sun Yat-sen* (1934); Van Dorn, H. A., *Twenty Years of the Chinese Republic* (1932); Wu Chao Chu, *The Nationalist Program for China* (1929).

CHINA AND THE POWERS: Buell, R. L., *The Washington Conference* (1922); LaFargue, T. E., *China and the World War* (1937); Norton, H. K., *China and the Powers* (1927); Pollard, R. T., *China's Foreign Relations, 1917–1931* (1933); Willoughby, W. W., *China at the Conference* (1922); Willoughby, W. W., *Foreign Rights and Interests in China,* 2 vols. (1927).

JAPAN BEFORE 1931: Carus, C. D., and McNichols, C. L., *Japan: Its Resources and Industries* (1944); Eckstein, G., *In Peace Japan Breeds War* (1943); Hishida, S., *Japan among the Great Powers* (1940); Ishii, Viscount K., *Diplomatic Commentaries* (1936); Lederer, E., and Lederer-Seidler, E., *Japan in Transition* (1938); Lory, H., *Japan's Military Masters* (1943); Mitchell, K. L., *Japan's Industrial Strength* (1942); Moulton, H. G., and Ko, J., *Japan* (1931); Norman, E. H., *Japan's Emergence as a Modern State* (1940); Takeuchi, T., *War and Diplomacy in the Japanese Empire* (1935); Tanin, O., and Yohan, E., *Militarism and Fascism in Japan* (1934); Wildes, H. E., *Japan in Crisis* (1934); Young, A. M., *Imperial Japan: 1926–1938.*

Chapter XXII. The Collapse of Collective Security

INTERNATIONAL RELATIONS, 1919–1939: Armstrong, G. G., *Why Another World War? How We Missed Collective Security* (1941); Birdsall, P., *Versailles Twenty Years After* (1941); Butler, H., *The Lost Peace* (1942); Cuff, S. H., *The Face of the War, 1931–1942* (1942); Foot, M., *Armistice, 1919–1939* (1940); Graham, S., *From War to War, 1917–1940: A Datebook of the Years Between* (1940); Haines, C. G., and Hoffman, R. J. S., *The Origins and Background of the Second World War* (1943); Jordan, W. M., *Great Britain, France, and the German Problem: 1918–1939* (1944); Kain, R. S., *Europe: Versailles to Warsaw* (1939); Lee, D. E., *Ten Years: The World on the Way to War, 1930–1940* (1942); Marriott, J., *The Tragedy of Europe* (1941); Orton, W. A., *Twenty Years' Armistice, 1918–1938* (1938); Rayner, R. M., *The Twenty*

Years Truce (1943); Schuman, F. L., *Design for Power: The Struggle for the World* (1941); Schwarzschild, L., *World in Trance: From Versailles to Pearl Harbor* (1942); Spender, J. A., *Between Two Wars* (1943); Wolfers, A., *Britain and France Between Two Wars: Conflicting Strategies of Peace since Versailles* (1940).

JAPAN'S SEIZURE OF MANCHURIA AND INVASION OF CHINA: Bisson, T. A., *American Policy in the Far East: 1931–1940* (1940); Borton, H., *Japan since 1931* (1941); Byas, H., *Government by Assassination* (1942); Chamberlin, W. H., *Japan in China* (1940); Chamberlin, W. H., *Japan over Asia* (1938); Crow, C. (ed.), *Japan's Dream of World Empire: The Tanaka Memorial* (1942); Grew, J. C., *Ten Years in Japan* (1944); Hindmarsh, A. E., *The Basis of Japanese Foreign Policy* (1936); Kawakami, K. K., *Manchoukuo, Child of Conflict* (1933); Lattimore, O., *Manchuria, Cradle of Conflict* (1935); League of Nations, *The Verdict of the League* (1933); Moore, F., *With Japan's Leaders: An Intimate Record of Fourteen Years as Counsellor to the Japanese Government, Ending December 7, 1941* (1942); Saito, H., *Japan's Policies and Purposes* (1935); Tang Leang-li (ed.), *The Puppet State of Manchukuo* (1935); Timperley, H. J., *Japan, a World Problem* (1942); Wang, Ching-chun, *Japan's Continental Adventure* (1941); Willoughby, W. W., *The Sino-Japanese Controversy and the League of Nations* (1935).

CHINA ON THE DEFENSIVE: Bate, D., *Wang Ching-wei, Puppet or Patriot* (1941); Bertram, J. M., *First Act in China: The Story of the Sian Mutiny* (1938); Carlson, E. F., *Twin Stars of China* (1940); Chinese Ministry of Information, *China Handbook, 1937–1943* (1944); Clegg, A., *Birth of New China* (1943); Koo, V. K. W., *China after Five Years of War* (1943); Lin Yutang, *The Vigil of a Nation* (1945); Linebarger, P. M. A., *The China of Chiang K'ai-shek: A Political Study* (1941); MacNair, H. F., *The Real Conflict between China and Japan: An Analysis of Opposing Ideologies* (1938); Smedley, A., *China Fights Back* (1938); Snow, E., *Red Star over China* (1938); Taylor, E., *The Struggle for North China* (1941).

ITALY'S CONQUEST OF ETHIOPIA: Badoglio, P., *The War in Abyssinia* (1937); Martelli, G., *Italy Against the World* (1937); Potter, P. B., *The Wal Wal Arbitration* (1938); Rey, C. F., *The Real Abyssinia* (1935); Royal Institute of International Affairs, *Abyssinia and Italy* (1935); Sandford, C., *Ethiopia under Haile Selassie* (1944); Steer, G. L., *Caesar in Abyssinia* (1937); Work, E., *Ethopia, a Pawn in European Diplomacy* (1935).

GERMANY'S *DRANG NACH OSTEN:* Armstrong, H. F., *When There Is No Peace* (1939), the Sudeten crisis; Beneš, V., and Ginsburg, R., *Ten Million Prisoners* (1940), the Nazi invasion of Czechoslovakia and the results; Birchall, T., *The Storm Breaks: A Panorama of Europe and the Forces That Have Wrecked Its Peace* (1940); Brooks, C., *Can Chamberlain Save Britain? The Lesson of Munich* (1938); Chamberlain, N., *In Search of Peace* (1939); Churchill, W. S., *Step by Step: 1936–1939* (1939); Churchill, W. S., *While England Slept: A Survey of World Affairs, 1932–1938* (1938); Churchill, W. S., *The Gathering Storm* (1948); Dean, V. M., *Europe in Retreat* (1939); Einzig, P., *Appeasement before, during, and after the War* (1942); Fuchs, M., *Show-*

down in Vienna: The Death of Austria (1939); Gafencu, G., *The Last Days of Europe* (1948); Gedye, G. E. R., *Betrayal in Central Europe* (1939); George, G. J., *They Betrayed Czechoslovakia* (1938); Grant Duff, S., *A German Protectorate: The Czechs under Nazi Rule* (1942); Hadley, W. W., *Munich Before and After* (1944); Hodson, S., *The Man Who Made the Peace: Neville Chamberlain* (1938); Hutton, G., *Survey after Munich* (1939); Johnson, A. C., *Anthony Eden* (1939); Lennhoff, E., *The Last Five Hours of Austria* (1938); Loewenstein, K., *Hitler's Germany: The Nazi Background to War* (1939); Mendelssohn, P. de, *Design for Aggression* (1947); Namier, L. B., *Diplomatic Prelude, 1938–1939* (1948); Ripka, H., *Munich Before and After* (1939); Schuman, F. L., *Europe on the Eve: The Crisis of Diplomacy, 1933–1939* (1939); Walker-Smith, D., *Neville Chamberlain* (1940); Wiskemann, E., *Czechs and Germans: A Study of the Struggle in the Historic Provinces of Bohemia and Moravia* (1938); Wolfe, H. C., *The German Octopus* (1938).

THE CRISIS OF 1939: Benson, O. E., *Through the Diplomatic Looking Glass: Immediate Origins of the War in Europe* (1939); Fisher, H. A. L., et al., *The Background and Issues of the War* (1940); Henderson, Sir N., *Failure of a Mission: Berlin, 1937–1939* (1940); Schuman, F. L., *Night over Europe: The Diplomacy of Nemesis, 1939–1940* (1941); Seton-Watson, R. W., *From Munich to Danzig* (1939); Tolischus, O. D., *They Wanted War* (1940); Wegerer, A. von, *The Origins of World War II: A Brief Survey of the Beginnings of the Present War, on the Basis of Official Documents* (1941); Wiskemann, E., *Prologue to War* (1940).

DOCUMENTS: France, *Papers Relative to the Events and Negotiations Which Preceded the Opening of Hostilities Between Germany on the One Hand, and Poland, Great Britain, and France on the Other* (1940). Gantenbein, J. W. (ed.), *Documentary Background of World War II, 1931 to 1941* (1948); valuable. Germany, *Documents on Events Preceding the Outbreak of the War* (1940). Great Britain, *Documents Concerning German-Polish Relations and the Outbreak of Hostilities Between Great Britain and Germany on September 3, 1939* (1939). Poland, *Official Documents Concerning Polish-German and Polish-Soviet Relations, 1938–1939* (1940). Royal Institute of International Affairs, *Documents on International Affairs, 1939–1946*, Vol. I. *March–September, 1939* (1951). Sontag, R. J., and Beddie, J. S. (eds.), *Nazi-Soviet Relations, 1939–1941* (1948); documents from the archives of the German foreign office. Toynbee, A. J. (ed.), *Documents on International Affairs, 1939–1946*, Vol. I. *March–September, 1939* (1951); also includes significant documents showing Nazi plans for aggression, 1936–1938. U.S. Department of State, *Documents on German Foreign Policy, 1918–1945*. Series D, Vols. I–V (1949–1953); from the archives of the German foreign office. U.S. Department of State, *Germany and Czechoslovakia, 1937–1938* (1949); official German documents. U.S. Department of State, *The United States and Italy, 1936–1946* (1946). Woodward, E. L., and Butler, R. (eds.), *Documents on British Foreign Policy, 1919–1939* (1951).

MORE RECENT BOOKS: Carr, E. H., *German-Soviet Relations between the Two World Wars, 1919–1939* (1951); a critical but brief study by a British political scientist. Ciano, Count G., *Ciano's Hidden Diary, 1937–1938* (1953); deals with the Spanish Civil War and Munich. Ciano, Count G., *The Ciano Diaries* (1946); covers the years 1939–1943. Esch, P. A. M. van der, *Prelude to War: The International Repercussions of the Spanish Civil War, 1936–1939* (1952); based on documents in European archives and on the press and periodicals of the chief states. Laffan, R. G. D., *et al.*, *Survey of International Affairs, 1938*, Vol. II., *The Crisis over Czechoslovakia, January to September, 1938* (1951); excellent. Langer, W. L., and Gleason, S. E., *The Challenge to Isolation, 1937–1940* (1952); American diplomacy from Munich to the destroyer deal. Namier, L. B., *Europe in Decay: Study in Disintegration, 1936–40* (1950); excellent study by a British historian. Rossi, A., *The Russo-German Alliance, August 1939 to June 1941* (1950); a readable account by a former Italian Communist. Schmidt, P., *Diary of Hitler's Interpreter: The Secret History of German Diplomacy* (1951); by Hitler's and Ribbentrop's chief interpreter, 1935–1945. Wiskemann, E., *The Rome-Berlin Axis: A History of the Relations between Mussolini and Hitler* (1949); interestingly written. Craig, G. A., and Gilbert, F. (eds.), *The Diplomats, 1919–1939* (1953); by seventeen experts. Hilger, G., and Meyer, A. G., *The Incompatible Allies. A Memoir-History of German-Soviet Relations, 1918–1941* (1953). Langer, W. L., and Gleason, S. E., *The Undeclared War, 1940–1941* (1953); American diplomacy. Salvemini, G., *Prelude to World War II* (1953); an indictment of Britain's Conservative government. Tetens, T. H., *German Plots with the Kremlin* (1953).

Chapters XXIII–XXIV. The Nazi Blitzkrieg and Defeat

GENERAL ACCOUNTS: Baldwin, H., *Great Mistakes of the War* (1950); by the military expert of the *New York Times*. Brown, F., and Manditch, L., *The War in Maps: An Atlas of the New York Times Maps* (1946). Churchill, W., *The Second World War*, 6 vols. (1948–1953); by the British wartime premier. Commager, H. S., *The Story of the Second World War* (1945); a selection of accounts designed to depict the war as it looked and felt at the time. Graves, P. P. (ed.), *A Record of the War* (1940 ff); published quarterly. Horrabin, J. F., *Atlas History of the Second World War*, 9 vols. (1941–1945). Hutchinson, W., *Pictorial History of the War*, 26 vols. (1939–1945). Ingersoll, R., *Top Secret* (1946); a postwar analysis of the Allied commanders and strategy in western Europe. Liddell Hart, B. H., *The German Generals Talk* (1948); based on conversations with surviving German generals. McInnis, E., *The War*, 6 vols. (1940–1946); written yearly during the war— excellent for contemporary atmosphere. O'Neill, H. C., *A Short History of the Second World War and Its Social and Political Significance* (1951); by a famous British military analyst. Root, W., *The Secret History of the War*, 2 vols. (1945); biased and undocumented. Sinderen, A. van, *The Story of the Six Years of Global War* (1946); a chronicle by months. Wilmot, C., *The Struggle for Europe* (1952); a history of World War II in western Europe by an Australian.

BIOGRAPHIES AND BIOGRAPHICAL SKETCHES: Bradley, O. N., *A Soldier's Story* (1951); valuable for its gallery of military portraits. Bullock, A., *Hitler: A Study in Tyranny* (1953); comprehensive, clear, well-written biography. Chatterton, E. K., *Leaders of the Royal Navy* (1940). Davis, K. S., *Soldier of Democracy; A Full Length Biography of Dwight Eisenhower* (1945); eulogistic. DeWeerd, H. A., *Great Soldiers of World War II* (1944); by an editor of the *Infantry Journal*. Frye, W., *Marshall: Citizen Soldier* (1947). Gilbert, F. (ed.), *Hitler Directs His War: The Secret Records of His Daily Military Conferences* (1950). Guderian, H., *Panzer Leader* (1951). Hagood, J., *et al.*, *These Are the Generals* (1943); brief sketches of United States generals. Halder, F., *Hitler as War Lord* (1950); by the former chief of German general staff. Hart, W. E., *Hitler's Generals* (1944); by a former German officer who was anti-Nazi. Hatch, A., *General Ike* (1944). Hinsley, F. H., *Hitler's Strategy* (1951); based on records of his War Council. Karslake, H., *Leaders of the Army* (1940); British. Mellor, W. B., *Patton: Fighting Man* (1946); reveals an effort to be objective. Miller, F. T., *Eisenhower, Man and Soldier* (1944). Moorehead, A., *Montgomery: A Biography* (1947). Nicolay, H., *Born to Command: the Story of General Eisenhower* (1945). Payne, R., *The Marshall Story: A Biography of General George C. Marshall* (1951). Pollard, A. O., *Leaders of the Royal Air Force* (1940). Steel, J., *Men Behind the War* (1942); in Europe and Asia. Stokes, D. H., *Men Behind Victory* (1944). Wellard, J., *General George S. Patton, Jr., Man Under Mars* (1946); eulogistic. Weygand, M., *Recalled to Service* (1952); the story of both France and General Weygand from the outbreak of World War II until the Allied landings in Africa. Hitler, A., *Hitler's Secret Conversations, 1941–1944* (1953); reveals Hitler's confused mind.

THE WAR IN POLAND AND FINLAND: Anders, W., *An Army in Exile: The Story of the Second Polish Corps* (1949); by its commander. Bryan, J., *Siege* (1940); the Nazi attack on Warsaw. Elliston, H. B., *Finland Fights* (1940). Finland, *The Finnish Blue Book: The Development of Finnish-Soviet Relations during the Autumn of 1939, Including the Official Documents and the Peace Treaty of March 12, 1940* (1940). Hollingworth, C., *The Three Weeks' War in Poland* (1940). Langdon-Davies, J., *Invasion in the Snow* (1941); the Russo-Finnish war of 1939–1940. Mowrer, L., *Arrest and Exile* (1941); experiences of Poles transported from Lemberg to Siberia by Russia in June, 1940. Ullman, S. de, *The Epic of the Finnish Nation* (1940). Wierzynski, K., *The Forgotten Battlefield* (1944); the war in Poland. Wuorinen, J. H., *Finland and World War II, 1939–1944* (1948); edited by an American.

THE WAR IN NORWAY: Broch, T., *The Mountains Wait* (1942); by the mayor of Narvik. Buckley, C., *Norway: The Commandos, Dieppe* (1952). Curtis, M. (ed.), *Norway and the War, September, 1939–December, 1940* (1940); a collection of documents. Hambro, C. J., *I Saw It Happen in Norway* (1940); by the president of the Norwegian parliament. Johnson, A., *Norway, Her Invasion and Occupation* (1948); by an American professor. Koht, H., *Norway, Neutral and Invaded* (1941); by the foreign minister of

Norway. Lapie, P. O., *With the Foreign Legion at Narvik* (1941). Torris, M. J., *Narvik* (1933); by one who fought there.

THE GERMAN CONQUEST OF HOLLAND AND BELGIUM: Belgian-American Educational Foundation, *The Belgian Campaign and the Surrender of the Belgian Army, May 10–28, 1940* (1940); exonerates the Belgian king. Belgian Ministry of Foreign Affairs, *Belgium: The Official Account of What Happened, 1939–1940* (1941). Cammaerts, E., *The Prisoner at Laeken: King Leopold—Legend and Fact* (1941). Chatterton, E. K., *Epic of Dunkirk* (1940). Divine, A. D., *Dunkirk* (1945); a thrilling account of the role of the ships and boats. Doorman, P. L. G., *Military Operations in the Netherlands from 10th–17th May, 1940* (1944). Falaise, H. de la, *Through Hell to Dunkirk* (1943). Kleffens, E. N. van, *Juggernaut over Holland* (1941); by the Dutch foreign minister. Masefield, J., *The Nine-Days Wonder* (1941); beautifully written account of the Dunkirk evacuation. Netherlands, *Netherlands Orange Book* (1940). Rhodes, A., *A Sword of Bone* (1943); the British retreat to the coast and evacuation of Dunkirk. Williams, D., *Retreat from Dunkirk* (1941); personal experiences.

THE COLLAPSE OF FRANCE: Armstrong, H. F., *Chronology of Failure: The Last Days of the French Republic* (1940). Barlone, D., *A French Officer's Diary (23 August 1939–1 October 1940)* (1942). Bloch, M., *Strange Defeat* (1949); an examination of the causes of defeat, by a history professor who joined the resistance movement. Blum, L., *For All Mankind* (1946); the Socialist leader's explanation of France's collapse. Bois, E. J., *Truth on the Tragedy of France* (1941); criticizes the government officials. Chambrun, R. de, *I Saw France Fall* (1940); by Laval's son-in-law. Cot, P., *Triumph of Treason* (1944); by a former French minister. Draper, T., *The Six Weeks' War: France, May 10–June 25, 1940* (1944). Gerard, R. M., *Tank-Fighter Team* (1942); the battle of France. Giraud, A., *The Grave Diggers (I—Gamelin, Daladier, Reynaud; II—Pétain)* (1943). Lattre de Tassigny, Marshal de, *The History of the French First Army* (1953); by its commander. Malaquais, J., *War Diary* (1944); the French army before June, 1940. Marshall, S. L. A., *Armies on Wheels* (1941); a study of the significant campaigns from May, 1940 to the fall of 1941. Maurois, A., *Why France Fell* (1941); by a distinguished French writer. Simone, A., *J'Accuse!—The Men Who Betrayed France* (1940). Torres, H., *Campaign of Treachery* (1942); attacks pro-Nazi Frenchmen. Vilfroy, D., *War in the West: The Battle of France, May–June, 1940* (1942), by a French officer. Werth, A., *The Last Days of Paris* (1940).

VICHY FRANCE: Brooks, H. L., *Prisoners of Hope* (1942); report on life in Vichy. Flanner, J., *Pétain: The Old Man of France* (1944). Huddleston, S., *Pétain: Patriot or Traitor* (1951); a defense by a British journalist. Langer, W. L., *Our Vichy Gamble* (1947); an account of United States' relations with Vichy France, authorized by the State Department. Laval, P., *The Diary of Pierre Laval* (1948); Laval's defense, written while in prison before his execution. Lorraine, J., *Behind the Battle of France* (1943); the collaborationists.

Marchal, L., *Vichy: Two Years of Deception* (1943). Martel, F., *Pétain: Verdun to Vichy* (1943); an indictment. Mikés, G., *Darlan: A Study* (1943). Montmorency, A. de, *The Enigma of Admiral Darlan* (1943). Sadleir, M. (tr.), *Pétain-Laval: The Conspiracy* (1942). Thomson, D., *Two Frenchmen: Charles de Gaulle and Pierre Laval* (1951); interpretative biographies. Tissier, P., *The Government of Vichy* (1942). Torres, H., *Pierre Laval* (1941); critical.

DE GAULLE AND THE FIGHTING FRENCH: Aglion, R., *The Fighting French* (1943). Barrès, P., *Charles de Gaulle* (1941). Cattain, G., *Charles de Gaulle* (1945). Gaulle, C. de, *The Speeches of General de. Gaulle,* 2 vols. (1942–1943). Hassenstein, A. A., *A Giant in the Age of Steel: The Story of De Gaulle* (1944). Kerillis, H. de, *I Accuse de Gaulle* (1946); an indictment by a former member of the Chamber of Deputies. Riveloup, A., *The Truth about De Gaulle* (1944).

THE BATTLE OF BRITAIN: Ayling, K., *R.A.F.: The Story of a British Pilot Fighter* (1941). Beauman, B. (ed.), *The Airmen Speak* (1941): personal experiences told by officers and men of the RAF. Bolitho, H., *Combat Report: The Story of a Fighter Pilot* (1943). Bonnell, J. S., *Britons Under Fire* (1941). Dade, H. A., *To His Refugee Son* (1942); letters of an Englishman to his son in America during the blitz. Daniell, R., *Civilians Must Fight* (1941); concise, simple, dramatic description of an air attack on London. Eade, C. (comp.), *The War Speeches of the Rt. Hon. Winston Churchill,* 3 vols. (1953); they go back to 1938. Forbes-Robertson, D., *The Battle of Waterloo Road* (1941); the life of a typical London family during the blitz. Gleed, I., *Arise to Conquer* (1943); by a pilot of the RAF. Great Britain, Air Ministry, *The Battle of Britain* (1941); from August 8 to October 31, 1940. Great Britain, Air Ministry, *Bomber Command* (1941); the British air offensive against the Axis, 1940–1941. Great Britain, Air Ministry, *Coastal Command* (1943); air force attacks on German ships. Great Britain, Ministry of Information, *Roof over Britain: The Official Story of Britain's Anti-Aircraft Defenses, 1939–1942* (1943). Grey, C. G., *The Luftwaffe* (1944). Lee, A., *The German Air Force* (1946); perhaps the best general discussion. Leska, G., *I Was a Nazi Flier* (1941); the diary of a German flight sergeant. Michie, A. A., and Graebner, W. (eds.), *Their Finest Hour* (1941). Michie, A. A., *The Air Offensive Against Germany* (1943). Pile, F., *Ack-Ack* (1950); the story of Britain's air defense. Reynolds, Q., *A Londoner's Diary* (1941). Robertson, B., *I Saw England* (1941); by the London correspondent of *PM.* Strachey, J., *Digging for Mrs. Miller* (1941); the story of an ARP warden. Underdown, T. H. J., *Bristol under Blitz: The Record of an Ancient City and Her People during the Battle of Britain, 1940–41* (1942).

THE WAR IN THE BALKANS: Amery, J., *Sons of the Eagle: A Study in Guerilla War* (1949); in Albania. "Athenian," *The Greek Miracle* (1942). Casson, S., *Greece Against the Axis* (1942); by a British officer. Easterman, E. L., *King Carol, Hitler, and Lupescu* (1942). Greek Office of Information, *The Campaign in Greece and Crete* (1943). Greek Office of Information, *Diplomatic Documents Relating to Italy's Aggression against Greece; The*

Greek White Book (1943). Hetherington, J., *Airborne Invasion* (1943); the battle of Crete. Howell, E., *Escape to Live: Memoirs of the Campaign in Crete and Greece* (1947); by a British officer. Lavra, S., *The Greek Miracle* (1943). Mackenzie, C., *Wind of Freedom: The History of the Invasion of Greece by the Axis Powers, 1940–1941* (1943). Mitchell, R., *The Serbs Choose War* (1943). Montgomery, J. P., *Hungary: The Unwilling Satellite* (1948); of Nazi Germany. Papagos, A., *The Battle of Greece, 1940–1941* (1949); by a Greek general. Patmore, D., *Balkan Correspondent* (1941); an account of Rumanian politics, 1939–1941. St. John, R., *From the Land of Silent People* (1942); the campaign in Yugoslavia, Greece, and Crete. Tobin, C. M., *Turkey, Key to the East* (1944); explains Turkey's neutrality in the war. Waldeck, R. G., *Athene Palace, Bucharest* (1943); Rumania in 1940–1941. Wason, B., *Miracle in Hellas: The Greeks Fight On* (1943); by an American correspondent. White, L., *The Long Balkan Night* (1943); 1940–1941. Wisdom, T. H., *Wings over Olympus: The Story of the Royal Air Force in Libya and Greece* (1942).

THE WAR IN RUSSIA: Allen, W. E. D., and Muratoff, P., *The Russian Campaigns of 1944–1945* (1946). Borodin, G., *Red Surgeon* (1944); a biography. Caldwell, E., *All-Out on the Road to Smolensk* (1942); by an American correspondent. Cassidy, H. C., *Moscow Dateline* (1943); reports from Russia, 1941–1943, by an Associated Press correspondent. Ehrenburg, I., *The Tempering of Russia* (1944); the war to the battle of Stalingrad, by a Soviet correspondent. Fadeev, A., *Leningrad in the Days of Blockade* (1946); by a Russian. Fineberg, J. (tr.), *Heroic Leningrad: Documents, Sketches and Stories of Its Siege and Relief* (1945). Fischer, G., *Soviet Opposition to Stalin* (1952); the story of Russian "defeatists" who aided the Germans. Graebner, W., *Round Trip to Russia* (1943); explains why and how the Russians fought so bravely. Grossman, V., *The People Immortal* (1944) and *With the Red Army in Poland and Byelorussia* (1945); by a *Red Star* correspondent. Hughes, P., *Retreat from Rostov* (1946). Isakov, I. S., *The Red Fleet in the Second World War* (1947); by a Soviet admiral. Kerr, W., *The Russian Army: Its Men, Its Leaders, Its Battles* (1944). Kovpak, S. A., *Our Partisan Course* (1947); the Russian guerrillas. Lesueur, L., *Twelve Months That Changed the World* (1943); October, 1941–October, 1942. Mehring, W., *Timoshenko: Marshal of the Red Army* (1942). Plievier, Theodor, *Stalingrad* (1948). Poliakov, A., *Russians Don't Surrender* (1942) and *White Mammoths: The Dramatic Story of Russian Tanks in Action* (1943); accounts of fighting in 1941–1942. Ponomarenka, P. K., *et al., Behind the Front Lines: A Chronicle of Soviet Guerilla Activity Behind the German Lines* (1945). Skomorovsky, B., and Morris, E. G., *The Siege of Leningrad* (1944). Stalin, J., *The Great Patriotic War of the Soviet Union* (1945); Stalin's speeches and orders of the day. Stroud, J., *The Red Air Force* (1943). Thorwald, J., *Flight in Winter: Russia Conquers—January to May, 1945* (1951); a bitter book written from the German viewpoint. Tikhonov, N., *The Defense of Leningrad* (1943). Voyetekhov, B., *The Last Days of Sevastopol* (1943); a vivid account. Voznesensky, N. A., *The Economy of the*

USSR during World War II (1948); based on official data. Weaver, D., *On Hitler's Doorstep* (1943); the German campaign in Russia to September, 1942, reported by a Swedish correspondent. Werth, A., *Leningrad* (1944); *Moscow War Diary* (1942); *The Year of Stalingrad* (1947); by an English correspondent. Zacharoff, L., *The Voice of Fighting Russia* (1942); a vivid picture of the war in Russia both on the battlefront and behind the lines. Anders, W., *Hitler's Defeat in Russia* (1953); a Polish general examines the reasons for it.

THE BATTLE OF THE ATLANTIC: Armstrong, W., *Battle of the Oceans* (1944); the British merchant marine. Cant, G., *The War at Sea* (1942); by a naval expert. Carse, R., *Lifeline: The Ships and Men of Our Merchant Marine at War* (1944). Chatterton, E. K., *Fighting the U-boats* (1942) and *The Royal Navy from September, 1939 to June, 1943,* 3 vols. (1942–1946). Coale, G. B., *North Atlantic Patrol* (1942). Edwards, K., *The Royal Navy and Allies from July, 1943 to September, 1945,* 2 vols. (1947–1948). Grenfell, R., *The Bismarck Episode* (1949); the exciting chase and destruction of Germany's most powerful battleship. Halstead, I., *Heroes of the Atlantic* (1942); a tribute to the merchant navy. Herman, F., *Dynamite Cargo* (1943); a convoy to Russia. Johnston, G. H., *Battle of the Seaways: From the Athenia to the Bismarck* (1942). Karig, W., *et al., Battle Report,* Vol. II. *The Atlantic War* (1946); from U.S. official sources. Leeming, J., *Brave Ships of World War II* (1944); both British and American. Low, A. M., *The Submarine at War* (1942). Martienssen, A., *Hitler and His Admirals* (1949); a documented account of Germany's war at sea. Masters, D., *Up Periscope* (1943); British submarines. McCoy, S. D., *. . . Nor Death Dismay* (1944); the merchant marine. Monsarrat, N., *Corvette Command* (1944). Morison, S. E., *History of United States Naval Operations in World War II,* Vol. I. *The Battle of the Atlantic: September, 1939–May, 1943* (1947); practically an official history. Puleston, W. D., *The Influence of Sea Power in World War II* (1947). Reynolds, Q., *Convoy* (1942). Rogers, S., *Enemy in Sight* (1943); stories of naval operations. Shaw, F. H., *The Merchant Navy at War* (1944). Spaight, J. M., *Blockade by Air: The Campaign Against Axis Shipping* (1942). U.S. Office of Naval Intelligence, *Führer Conferences, 1939–1940* (1947). Woodward, D., *The Tirpitz, and the Battle for the North Atlantic* (1953). Zim, H. S., *Submarines* (1942).

THE UNITED STATES AND THE WAR: Alsop, J., and Kintner, R., *American White Paper: The Story of American Diplomacy and the Second World War* (1940). Alsop, S., and Bradon, T., *Sub-Rosa—The OSS and American Espionage* (1946). Chamberlin, W. H., *America's Second Crusade* (1950); an attack on President Roosevelt's policies. Deene, J. R., *The Strange Alliance* (1947); an account of co-operation between the OSS and the NKVD, by the head of the U.S. military mission in Moscow, 1943–1945. Ford, C., *Cloak and Dagger: The Secret Story of the OSS* (1946). Hull, C., *The Memoirs of Cordell Hull,* 2 vols. (1948); the United States secretary of state. Hynd, A., *Passport to Treason* (1943); Nazi activities in the United States. Janeway, E., *The Struggle for Survival: A Chronicle of Economic Mobiliza-

tion in World War II (1951). Johnson, W., *The Battle Against Isolation* (1944); discusses the Committee to Defend America by Aiding the Allies. King, C., *Atlantic Charter* (1943). King, E. J., *Fleet Admiral King* (1952); memoirs by U.S. admiral. Lavine, H., and Wechsler, J., *War Propaganda and the United States* (1940); a study of pressure groups. Marshall, G. C., Arnold, H. H., and King, E. J., *The War Reports* (1947); by the heads of the U.S. armed forces. Morton, H. V., *Atlantic Meeting* (1943); background of the Atlantic Charter. Nelson, D. M., *Arsenal of Democracy: The Story of American War Production* (1946); by the chairman of the War Production Board. Riess, C., *Total Espionage* (1941); Axis espionage in America. Sherwood, R. E., *Roosevelt and Hopkins: An Intimate History* (1948); revealing. Stettinius, E. R., Jr., *Lend-Lease: Weapons for Victory* (1944); by the American administrator. Stettinius, E. R., Jr., *Roosevelt and the Russians: The Yalta Conference* (1949); by the then U.S. secretary of state. Treffousse, H. L., *Germany and American Neutrality, 1939–1941* (1951); a study of Germany's policies toward the U.S. U.S. Department of State, *Peace and War: United States Foreign Policy, 1931–1941* (1943). Welles, S., *Seven Decisions that Shaped History* (1951); wartime decisions by President Roosevelt. Cole, W. S., *America First; The Battle Against Intervention, 1940–1941* (1953).

THE WAR IN AFRICA: Aglion, R., *War in the Desert: The Battle for Africa* (1941). Austin, A. B., *Birth of an Army* (1943); the American Tunisian campaign. Belot, R. de, *The Struggle for the Mediterranean, 1939–1945* (1951); by a French admiral. Butcher, H. C., *My Three Years with Eisenhower* (1946); diary of Eisenhower's naval aide. Clark, M. W., *Calculated Risk* (1950); an account of the war in North Africa and Italy, by an American general. Clifford, A. G., *The Conquest of North Africa, 1940–43* (1943); the British Eighth Army. D'Arcy-Dawson, J., *Tunisian Battle* (1943); the British First Army. Gerard, F., *Malta Magnificent* (1943); its two years of resistance. Great Britain, Ministry of Information, *The Army at War: Tunisia* (1944). Hill, R., *Desert Conquest* (1943); the British Eighth Army. Houghton, G. W., *They Flew Through Sand* (1943); the RAF in Libya. Liddell Hart, B. H., *The Rommel Papers* (1953); valuable. Marshall, G. C., *Report of the Chief of Staff of the U.S. Army to the Secretary of War (July 1, 1939 to June 30, 1943)* (1943). McMillin, R., *Rendezvous with Rommel* (1943); the British Eighth Army. Montgomery, Viscount, *El Alamein to the River Sangro* (1949); by the British commanding general. Morison, S. E., *History of United States Naval Operations in World War II*, Vol. II. *Operations in North African Waters, October, 1942–June, 1943* (1947); practically official. Pyle, E., *Here Is Your War* (1943); the American forces in Africa. Schmidt, H. W., *With Rommel in the Desert* (1952); by his aide de camp. Wordell, M. T., and Seiler, E. N., *Wildcats over Casablanca* (1943); American navy planes. Young, D., *Rommel, the Desert Fox* (1950); includes a discussion of the general's part in the plot to kill Hitler.

THE INVASION OF ITALY: Badoglio, P., *Italy in the Second World War* (1948); by the Italian chief of staff in 1940. Brown, J. M., *To All Hands: An Amphibious Adventure* (1943); the landing in Sicily. Gibson, H.

(ed.), *The Ciano Diaries, 1939–1943* (1945); diaries of Mussolini's son-in-law who was Italian foreign minister. Heller, F., *Twilight of the Gladiators: Italy and the Italians, 1939–1943* (1944); by a Swedish journalist. Linklater, E., *The Campaign in Italy* (1951). Macartney, M. H. H., *One Man Alone: The History of Mussolini and the Axis* (1944). Majdalany, F., *The Monastery* (1946); an excellent account of the battle for Monte Cassino. Mussolini, B., *The Fall of Mussolini: His Own Story* (1948); written by the Duce after his downfall to justify his actions. Packard, R., and E., *Balcony Empire: Fascist Italy at War* (1942); by American correspondents in Rome, 1939–1941. Pyle, E., *Brave Men* (1944); Sicily and Italy. Shapiro, S. B., *They Left the Back Door Open* (1945); the Allied campaign in Sicily and Italy. Skorzeny, O., *Skorzeny's Secret Missions: War Memoirs of the Most Dangerous Man in Europe* (1950); by the Nazi who kidnapped Mussolini for Hitler. Starr, C. G., *From Salerno to the Alps: A History of the Fifth Army, 1943–45* (1948); by an American officer. Strabolgi, J. M. K., *The Conquest of Italy* (1944). Thruelsen, R., and Arnold, E., *Mediterranean Sweep* (1944); aerial warfare. Tregaskis, R., *Invasion Diary* (1944); Sicily and Italy.

THE ALLIED AIR OFFENSIVE AGAINST FORTRESS EUROPE: Ayling, K., *Bombers* (1944). Carlisle, N. V. (ed.), *The Air Forces Reader: An Account of the American Air Forces in Action* (1944). Charlton, L. E. O., *The Royal Air Force and U.S.A.A.F. from July, 1943 to September, 1945*, 2 vols. (1946–1947). Craven, W. F., and Cate, J. L. (eds.), *The Army Air Forces in World War II*, 4 vols. (1948–1951); with more to come. Hermann, H., *Luftwaffe: Its Rise and Fall* (1943). McCrary, J. R., and Scherman, D. E., *First of the Many* (1944); by one who bombed Germany. Pollard, A. O., *Bombers Over the Reich* (1941). Redding, J. M., and Leyshon, H. I., *Skyways to Berlin: With the American Flyers in England* (1943). Straubel, J. H. (ed.), *Air Force Diary* (1947); the U.S. Army Air Force. U.S. Army Air Forces, *Target, Germany: The Army Air Forces' Official Story of the VIII Bomber Command's First Year over Europe* (1943).

THE WAR IN THE WEST, 1944–1945: Allen, R. S., *Lucky Forward: The History of Patton's Third U.S. Army* (1947); by Patton's intelligence operations officers. Brown, J. M., *Many A Watchful Night* (1944); the Normandy landing. Chaplin, W. W., *The Fifty-two Days* (1944); following D-day. D'Arcy-Dawson, J., *European Victory* (1945); from the Normandy landing on. Edwards, K., *Operation Neptune* (1945); an account of the combined sea operations which covered the invasion of Europe on D-day. Eisenhower, D. D., *Report by the Supreme Commander to the Combined Chiefs of Staff on the Operations in Europe of the Allied Expeditionary Force, June 6, 1944 to May 8, 1945* (1946). Eisenhower, D. D., *Crusade in Europe* (1948); contains interesting material not in his official report. Guignand, F. F. de, *Operation Victory* (1947); by Montgomery's chief of staff. Gunther, J., *D Day: What Preceded It; What Followed It* (1944). Hagen, L. E., *Arnhem Lift: A Diary of a Pilot Glider* (1945). Harrison, G. A., *Cross Channel Attack* (1951); a detailed integrated account of D-Day. Heaps, L., *Escape from Arnhem* (1946); by a Canadian paratrooper. Lerner, D., *SYKEWAR: Psycho-*

logical Warfare Against Germany, D-Day to V-E Day (1950); valuable, but not easy reading. Marshall, G. C., *Report of the Chief of Staff of the U.S. Army to the Secretary of War (July 1, 1943 to June 30, 1945)* (1945). Marshall, S. L. A., *et al., Bastogne: The First Eight Days* (1946); based on interviews with survivors. Melville, A., *First Tide: "D" Day Invasion, June 6, 1944* (1945). Merriam, R., *Dark December* (1947); the battle of the Bulge. Montgomery, Viscount, *Normandy to the Baltic* (1947); rather dry reading. Morgan, Sir F., *Overture to Overlord* (1950); the beginnings of the plans for the invasion of Normandy. Munro, R., *Gauntlet to Overlord: The Story of the Canadian Army* (1946); by a leading Canadian war correspondent. Norman, A., *Operation Overlord: The Allied Invasion of Western Europe* (1952). Patton, G. S., Jr., *War As I Knew It* (1947); reveals the temperament and viewpoint of the commander of the American Third Army. Pyle, E., *Brave Men* (1944). Rowan-Robinson, H., *Onward from D-Day* (1946). Speidel, H., *Invasion, 1944: Rommel and the Normandy Campaign* (1950); by Rommel's chief of staff. Tobin, R. L., *Invasion Journal* (1944); Normandy. Wallace, B. G., *Patton and His Third Army* (1946); by a military man. Wertenbaker, C. C., *Invasion* (1944); Normandy.

NAZI TREATMENT OF OCCUPIED EUROPE: Apenszlak, J. (ed.), *The Black Book of Polish Jewry* (1944); treatment by the Nazis. Basch, A., *The New Economic Warfare* (1941); Germany's manipulation of trade and politics in other countries. Berg, M., *Warsaw Ghetto* (1945); a diary. Christensen, S., *Norway Is My Country* (1943); life in Nazi-occupied Norway. Curie, E., *et al., They Speak for a Nation: Letters from France* (1941); from those living under Nazi control. Davies, R. A., *Odyssey Through Hell* (1946); treatment of the Jews in Eastern Europe. Goris, J.-A., *Belgium in Bondage* (1944). Gudme, S., *Denmark, Hitler's "Model Protectorate"* (1942). Hlond, August, Cardinal *et al., The Persecution of the Catholic Church in German-Occupied Poland* (1941). Kernan, T., *France on Berlin Time* (1941); by an American who was publisher of the Paris *Vogue*. Lemkin, R., *Axis Rule in Occupied Europe* (1945); dispassionate. Lorraine, J., *The Germans in France* (1947). Malaparte, C., *Kaputt* (1946); evidence by an Italian Fascist on the brutal atrocities of the Nazis. Mentze, E., *5 Years: The Occupation of Denmark in Pictures* (1946). Moën, L., *Under the Iron Heel* (1941), a restrained, factual eye witness account of the Nazi occupation of Belgium. Nikitin, M. N., and Vagin, P. I., *The Crimes of the German Fascists in the Leningrad Region: Materials and Documents* (1946). Paulmer, P., *Denmark in Nazi Chains* (1942). Polnay, P. de, *The Germans Came to Paris* (1943); an account of life in Paris from June, 1940, to the latter part of 1941. Reveille, T., *The Spoil of Europe* (1941); Nazi methods of exploiting conquered countries. Shoskes, H., *No Traveler Returns* (1945); Poland. Shub, B., *Starvation over Europe: Made in Germany* (1943). Sledzinski, W., *Governor Frank's Dark Harvest* (1946); Poland. Somerhausen, A., *Written in Darkness: A Belgian Woman's Record of the Occupation, 1940–1945* (1946). *Soviet Government Statements on Nazi Atrocities* (1946); official. Weinrich, M., *Hitler's Professors* (1946); the part played by German scholars in the destruction of Jews and Poles. Zywulska, K., *I Came Back* (1951); by a Polish woman who spent 20 months in a Nazi extermination camp.

THE RESISTANCE MOVEMENTS IN OCCUPIED EUROPE: Brown, A., *Michailovitch and Yugoslav Resistance* (1943). Fast, H. M., *The Incredible Tito* (1944). Goffin, R., *The White Brigade* (1944); the Belgian underground. Höye, B., and Ager, T. M., *The Fight of the Norwegian Church against Nazism* (1943). Huot, L., *Guns for Tito* (1945); by an American officer who helped get supplies to Tito. Jones, W., *Twelve Months with Tito's Partisans* (1946). Jong, L. de, and Stoppelman, J. W. F., *The Lion Rampant; The Story of Holland's Resistance to the Nazis* (1943). Karski, J., *Story of a Secret State* (1945); the Polish resistance movement. Kessel, J., *Army of Shadows* (1944); French resistance movement. Liebling, A. J., *The Republic of Silence* (1947); resistance in France. Millar, G. R., *Maquis* (1945); French resistance movement. Myklebost, T., *They Came as Friends* (1943); Norway's reaction to the Germans. Nyquist, R. B., *Sons of the Vikings* (1943); underground warfare against the Nazis in Norway. Orska, I., *Silent Is the Vistula* (1946); experiences inside Warsaw during and after the abortive uprising of 1944. Padev, M., *Marshal Tito* (1944). Rootham, J., *Miss Fire: The Chronicle of a British Mission to Michailovich* (1946). Sava, G., *The Chetniks* (1942); Yugoslavia. Sudjic, M., *Yugoslavia in Arms* (1943); the resistance movement. Tenenbaum, J., *Underground: The Story of a People* (1952); the Polish Jews during German occupation. Wachsman, Z. H., *Trail Blazers for Invasion* (1943); underground activities of the Nazi-conquered countries. Woodman, D., *Europe Rises* (1943); resistance movements in Nazi-occupied countries.

NAZI GERMANY IN WARTIME: Andreas-Friedrich, R., *Berlin Underground* (1947); by a member. Boehm, E. H. (ed.), *We Survived: The Stories of Fourteen of the Hidden and the Hunted of Nazi Germany*. Burney, C., *The Dungeon Democracy* (1946); a German concentration camp. Deuel, W., *People Under Hitler* (1942); report by an American journalist. Dulles, A. W., *Germany's Underground* (1947); by the head of the U.S. OSS in Switzerland. Flannery, H. W., *Assignment to Berlin* (1942); Germany in 1941. Fraenkel, H., *The Other Germany* (1943); discusses the "good" Germans. Fredborg, A., *Behind the Steel Wall* (1944); by a Swedish correspondent. Gaevernitz, G. v. S. (ed.), *They Almost Killed Hitler* (1947); based on the personal account of one who made a daring attempt to kill Hitler. Gisevius, H. B., *To the Bitter End* (1947); the conspiracy against Hitler. Hassell, U. von, *The Von Hassell Diaries, 1938–1944* (1947); by a member of the German underground. Jansen, J. B., and Weyl, S., *The Silent War: The Underground Movement in Germany* (1943). Pihl, G., *Germany: The Last Phase* (1944); life within Germany as seen by a Swedish journalist. Rothfels, H., *The German Opposition to Hitler: An Appraisal* (1948). Rousset, D., *The Other Kingdom* (1947); the concentration camps. Seydewitz, M., *Civil Life in Wartime Germany* (1945). Smith, H. K., *Last Train from Berlin* (1942); the state of the German home front in the winter of 1941–1942.

Trevor-Roper, H. R., *The Last Days of Hitler* (1947); the results of a careful investigation by a British scholar.

MISCELLANEOUS: Baker, R. L., *Oil, Blood and Sand* (1942); the Middle East. Denny, H., *Behind Both Lines* (1942); prison camps. Gordon, D. L., and Dangerfield, R., *The Hidden Weapon: A Story of Economic Warfare* (1947). Howe, T. C., *Salt Mines and Castles: The Discovery and Restoration of Looted European Art* (1946). Kirk, G., *The Middle East in the War: A Survey of International Affairs, 1939–1946* (1953); objective and documented. Linebarger, P. M. A., *Psychological Warfare* (1948). Loeffe, W., *Spionage* (1950); activities of a German counter-spy. *The New Yorker Book of War Pieces* (1947); some of the finest descriptive reporting of the war. Riess, C., *Total Espionage* (1941); the Nazi system. Sayre, J., *Persian Gulf Command* (1945). Singer, K. D., *Duel for the Northland* (1943) and *Spies and Traitors of World War II* (1945); the former is an account of German espionage in Scandinavia. Vail Motter, T. H., *The Middle East Theatre: The Persian Corridor and Aid to Russia* (1952). Weizsacker, E. von, *Memories of Ernst von Weizsacker* (1951); apologia of a German war criminal who participated in the Anschwitz atrocities.

Chapter XXV. Japan's Early Blitzkrieg and Ultimate Collapse

THE FAR EAST, 1931–1941: Abend, H., *Chaos in Asia* (1940). Clayton, E. L., *Heaven Below* (1944); by an eye-witness of events in China until early in 1942. Hanson, H., *"Humane Endeavor"; The Story of the China War* (1939). Harcourt-Smith, S., *Fire in the Pacific* (1942); the background of Japan's ambitions and military adventures. Hauser, E. O., *Honorable Enemy* (1941); psychological analysis of the Japanese people. Matsuo, K., *How Japan Plans to Win* (1942); originally published in Japan in 1940 as *The Three-Power Alliance and a U.S.-Japanese War*. Maurer, H., *The End Is Not Yet* (1941); Chinese resistance. Quigley, H. S., *Far Eastern War, 1937–1941* (1942); a record of the war and a survey of American relations with China and Japan. Snow, E., *The Battle for Asia* (1941); the war in China, 1937–1941. Whelan, R., *The Flying Tigers: The Story of the American Volunteer Group in China* (1942); before the United States entered the war.

THE IMMEDIATE BACKGROUND OF PEARL HARBOR: Beard, C. A., *American Foreign Policy in the Making, 1932–1940: A Story in Responsibilities* (1947); critical of Roosevelt. Beard, C. A., *President Roosevelt and the Coming of the War, 1941* (1948); blames him for the war with Japan. Bisson, T. A., *America's Far Eastern Policy* (1945); a valuable survey. Davis, F., and Lindley, E. K., *How War Came: An American White Paper: From the Fall of France to Pearl Harbor* (1942); sympathetic with the Roosevelt administration. Feis, H., *The Road to Pearl Harbor: The Coming of the War Between the United States and Japan* (1950); chiefly an account of diplomacy. Hornbeck, S. K., *The United States and the Far East: Certain Fundamentals of Policy* (1942); by an authority on the Far East. Hull, C., *The Memoirs of*

Cordell Hull, 2 vols. (1948); Roosevelt's secretary of state. Johnstone, W. C., *Why Japan Chose War* (1942); by an American professor. Kase, T., *Journey to the "Missouri"* (1950); the causes and influences leading to Japan's actions in 1941, by a Japanese diplomat. Millis, W., *This Is Pearl! The United States and Japan—1941* (1947); disagrees with Beard's books listed above. Mook, H. J. van, *The Netherlands Indies and Japan: Battle on Paper, 1940–1941* (1944); by the Dutch lieutenant governor-general. Morganstern, G., *Pearl Harbor: The Story of the Secret War* (1947); violently anti-Roosevelt. Rauch, B., *Roosevelt, From Munich to Pearl Harbor: A Study in the Creation of Foreign Policy* (1950); an able defense of Roosevelt's policy. Sanborn, F. R., *Design for War: A Study of Secret Power Politics, 1937–1941* (1951); maintains that Roosevelt plotted war. Tansill, C. C., *Back Door to War* (1952); a hostile account of Roosevelt's foreign policy. Taylor, G. E., *America in the New Pacific* (1942); explains how the United States became involved in the war. United States, Department of State, *Papers Relating to the Foreign Relations of the United States: Japan: 1931–1941* (1943) and *Prelude to Infamy: Official Report on the Final Phase of U.S. Japanese Relations, October 17 to December 7, 1941* (1943).

JAPAN'S CONQUEST OF EMPIRE: Bailey, D., *We Built and Destroyed: An Account of the Fall of Malaya and Singapore* (1944). Bayler, W. L. J., *Last Man Off Wake Island* (1943). Belden, J., *Retreat with Stilwell* (1943); from Burma. Braly, W. C., *The Hard Way Home* (1947); an account of Japanese prison camps in the Philippines. Brown, W., *Hong Kong Aftermath* (1943); a record of experiences in a Japanese prison in Hong Kong. Chennault, C. L., *Way of a Fighter: The Memoirs of Claire Lee Chennault* (1949); Commander of the Flying Tigers. Clark, T. B., *Remember Pearl Harbor!* (1942); by an eyewitness of the attack. Devereux, J. P. S., *The Story of Wake Island* (1947). Donahue, A. G., *Last Flight from Singapore* (1943); by an American in the RAF. Franklin, A. and G., *One Year of Life: The Story of H.M.S. Prince of Wales* (1944). Gallagher, O. D., *Action in the East* (1942); Malaya and Burma. Glover, E. M., *In 70 Days: The Story of the Japanese Campaign in British Malaya* (1944). Hersey, J., *Men on Bataan* (1942); MacArthur's defense. Hotz, R. B., *With General Chennault: The Story of the Fighting Tigers* (1943); over Burma and China. Miller, E. B., *Bataan Uncensored* (1949); a former U.S. colonel tries to assess the blame for the catastrophe. Morrill, J., and Martin, P., *South from Corregidor* (1943); an account of navy men who escaped to Australia. Playfair, G., *Singapore Goes Off the Air* (1943); an account of the siege and fall. Raleigh, J. M., *Pacific Blackout* (1943); the war in the Netherlands Indies in 1942. Redmond, J., *I Served on Bataan* (1943); by an American army nurse. Romanus, C. F., and Sunderland, R., *Stilwell's Mission to China* (1953); also Burma and India. Romulo, C. P., *I Saw the Fall of the Philippines* (1943); by a Filipino officer. Scott, R. L., *God Is My Co-Pilot* (1943); by an American flyer in Burma and China. Stilwell, J., *The Stilwell Papers* (1948); by an American general in China and Burma. Thompson, V., *Postmortem on Malaya* (1943); an explanation of why it fell so quickly. Wagg, A., *A Million Died* (1943); the

Burma campaign. Wainwright, J. M., *General Wainwright's Story* (1946); by MacArthur's successor as commander in the Philippines. White, W. L., *They Were Expendable* (1942); the Philippines campaign. Morton, L., *The Fall of the Philippines* (1953); official history of the defeat of the U.S. forces in 1941–1942.

GENERAL ACCOUNTS OF OPERATIONS AGAINST THE JAPANESE: Cant, G., *America's Navy in World War II* (1943) and *The Great Pacific Victory* (1945); from Pearl Harbor to Tokyo. Edmonds, W. D., *They Fought with What They Had: The Story of the Army Air Force in the Southwest Pacific, 1941–42* (1951). Eichelberger, R. L., *Our Jungle Road to Tokyo* (1950); by a U.S. general. Halsey, W. F., and Bryan, J., 3rd, *Admiral Halsey's Story* (1947); a first-hand but not unbiased account. Haugland, V., *The AAF Against Japan* (1948); from Pearl Harbor to Tokyo. Hough, F. O., *The Island War* (1947); by a major in the marines. Howard, C., and Whitley, J., *One Damned Island after Another: The Saga of the Seventh* (1947); air-force operations. James, D. H., *The Rise and Fall of the Japanese Empire* (1951). Jensen, O., *Carrier War: Task Force 58 and the Pacific Sea Battles* (1945); written during the war. Karig, W., *et al., Battle Report:* Vol. I. *Pearl Harbor to Coral Sea* (1944); Vol. III. *Pacific War—Middle Phase* (1947); Vol. IV. *The End of An Empire* (1948); Vol. V. *Victory in the Pacific* (1949); from U.S. official sources. McInnis, E., *The War,* 6 vols. (1940–1946); written yearly during the war. O'Sheel, P., and Cook, G. (eds.), *Semper Fidelis: The U.S. Marines in the Pacific, 1942–1945* (1947); by the marine corps combat correspondents. Pratt, F., *The Marines' War: An Account of the Struggle for the Pacific from Both American and Japanese Sources* (1948); by an American naval historian who had access to United States and Japanese documents. Wertenbaker, G. P., *5000 Miles Toward Tokyo* (1946); naval air force.

SPECIAL AREAS OR BATTLES: Appleman, R., *et al., Okinawa, the Last Battle* (1949); official account. Ayling, K., *Old Leatherneck of the Flying Tigers* (1945); General Chennault in China. Burchett, W. G., *Wingate's Phantom Army* (1947); in Burma. Cave, H. B., *et al., Long Were the Nights: The Saga of PT Squadron "X" in the Solomons* (1943). Coale, G. B., *Victory at Midway* (1944). Fergusson, B., *Beyond the Chindwin: Being An Account of the Adventures of Number Five Column of the Wingate Expedition into Burma* (1945); to expel the Japanese. Field, J. A., Jr., *The Japanese at Leyte Gulf* (1947); based on a cross-examination of Japanese officers. Ford, C., *Short Cut to Tokyo: The Battle for the Aleutians* (1943). Handelman, H., *Bridge to Victory* (1943); the reconquest of the Aleutians. Henri, R., *Iwo Jima: Springboard to Final Victory* (1945); excellent photographs. Hoffman, C. W., *Saipan: The Beginning of the End* (1950) and *The Seizure of Tinian* (1951); by a U.S. officer. Hough, F. O., *The Assault on Peleliu* (1950); by a U.S. officer. Johnston, G. H., *The Toughest Fighting in the World* (1943); New Guinea. Johnston, S., *Queen of the Flat-Tops: The U.S.S. Lexington and the Coral Sea Battle* (1942). Kahn, E. J., Jr., *G.I. Jungle* (1943); New Guinea. Matthews, A. R., *The Assault* (1947); an account of the first twelve days in Iwo Jima. Mears, F., *Carrier Combat* (1944); off Guadalcanal. Merillat, H. L., *The Island: A History of the Marines on Guadalcanal* (1944). Miller, J., Jr., *Guadalcanal: The First Offensive* (1949); an account of the ground operations. Morison, S. E., *History of United States Naval Operations in World War, II:* Vol. III. *The Rising Sun in the Pacific, 1931–April, 1942;* Vol. IV. *Coral Sea, Midway, and Submarine Actions, May 1942–August 1942;* Vol. V. *The Struggle for Guadalcanal, August 1942– February, 1943;* Vol. VI. *Breaking the Bismarcks Barrier, 22 July 1942–1 May 1944;* Vol. VII. *Aleutians, Gilberts and Marshalls, June 1942–April 1944;* Vol. VIII. *New Guinea and the Marianas, March 1944–August 1944* (1948–1953); official history. Mountbatten, Earl of Burma, *Southeast Asia, 1943–1945: Report to the Combined Chiefs of Staff* (1951); by the British commander in that area. Owen, F., *The Campaign in Burma* (1946). Rolo, C. J., *Wingate's Raiders* (1944); British efforts to expel the Japanese from Burma. Shalett, S., *Old Nameless* (1943); naval action off Savo and Guadalcanal. Sherrod, R., *Tarawa: The Story of a Battle* (1944) and *On to Westward* (1945); the fighting on Tarawa, Saipan, Iwo Jima and Okinawa. Tregaskis, R., *Guadalcanal Diary* (1943); by a war correspondent. Vetter, E. G., *Death Was Our Escort* (1944); early fighting in New Guinea. Wilson, E. J., *et al., Betio Beachhead: U.S. Marines' Own Story of the Battle of Tarawa* (1945); by marine combat correspondents. Wolfert, I., *Battle for the Solomons* (1943) and *Torpedo 8: The Attack and Vengeance of Swede Larsen's Bomber Squadron* (1943); both deal with the Solomon Islands fighting. Woodward, C. V., *The Battle for Leyte Gulf* (1947); excellent.

MISCELLANEOUS: Bell, F. J., *Condition Red: Destroyer Action in the South Pacific* (1943). Cope, H., and Karig, W., *Battle Submerged* (1951); based on the activities of individual American submarines. Hubler, R. G., and DeChant, J. A., *Flying Leathernecks: The Complete Record of Marine Corps Aviation in Action, 1941–44* (1944). Huie, W. B., *Can Do! The Story of the Seabees* (1944). Kenney, G. C., *General Kenney Reports* (1949); by the head of MacArthur's air force. Lawson, T. W., *Thirty Seconds over Tokyo* (1943); by one who participated in the Doolittle raid. Olds, R., *Helldiver Squadron: The Story of Carrier Bombing Squadron 17 with Task Force 58* (1944). Pratt, F., *The Navy Has Wings* (1944); U.S. naval aviation. Rickenbacker, E., *Seven Came Through* (1943); experiences on a rubber raft for twenty-one days in the Pacific. Roscoe, T., *United States Submarine Operations in World War II* (1950); a definitive one-volume study. Sherman, F. C., *Combat Command: The American Aircraft Carriers in the Pacific War* (1950); by a U.S. admiral. U.S. Strategic Bombing Survey, *The Fifth Air Force in the War against Japan* (1947) and *The Effects of Air Attack on Japanese Urban Economy* (1947). White, W. L., *Queens Die Proudly* (1943); a flying fortress in the Southwest Pacific.

THE ATOM BOMB: Hersey, J., *Hiroshima* (1946); the moving stories of six survivors. Laurence, W. L., *Dawn Over Zero: The Story of the Atomic Bomb* (1946); by the science reporter of the *New York Times*. Miller, M., and Spitzer, A., *We Dropped the A-Bomb* (1946); by a radio operator who flew over

both Hiroshima and Nagasaki.   Magai, T., *We of Nagasaki* (1951); the story
of eight survivors of the atom bomb.

Chapter XXVI. The Unfinished Peace Settlement and the "Cold War"

THE UNITED NATIONS: Arne, S., *United Nations Primer* (1945); the
genesis of the organization.   Besterman, T., *Unesco: Peace in the Minds of Men*
(1951); aims and achievements.   Dolivet, L., *The United Nations: A Handbook on the New World Organization* (1946); an excellent brief treatment.
Evatt, H. V., *The United Nations* (1948); by an Australian statesman.   Good-
rich, L. M., and Hambro, E., *Charter of the United Nations. Commentary and
Documents* (1946).   Huxley, J., *UNESCO: Its Purpose and Philosophy* (1947).
Murray, G., *From the League to the UN* (1948).   United Nations, *Yearbook of
the United Nations* (1948 ff); a valuable official source.   Vandenbosch, A. and
Hogan, W. N., *The United Nations: Background, Organization, Functions,
Activities* (1952).   World Peace Foundation, *International Organization*
(1947 ff); a valuable quarterly containing an account of the activities of the UN.
PEACE NEGOTIATIONS, 1945–1946:   Byrnes, J. F., *Speaking Frankly*
(1947); by the United States secretary of state during 1945–1946.   Dallin, D.,
The Big Three (1945); conflict in foreign policies of Russia and the United
States and Britain.   Holborn, L., *War and Peace Aims of the United Nations,*
2 vols. (1943–1948); official statements during the war of the political leaders of
the Allies.   Ivanyi, B. G., and Bell, A., *Route to Potsdam: The Story of the Peace
Aims, 1939–1945* (1945); Allied peace aims and problems.   Kalijarvi, T. V.
(ed.), *Peace Settlements of World War II* (1948).   Laserson, M., *Russia and
the Western World* (1945); optimistic.   Nenoff, S., *Two Worlds, U.S.A.—
U.S.S.R.* (1946).   Neumann, W. L., *Making the Peace, 1941–45: The Diplomacy of the Wartime Conferences* (1949); brief, objective, based on documents
and memoirs.   Pick, F. W., *Peacemaking in Perspective* (1950); brief account
of international conferences, 1945–1949.   Ratchford, B. U., and Ross, W. D.,
Berlin Reparations Assignment: Round One of the German Peace Settlement
(1948); by two Americans who helped decide on Germany's level of industry.
U.S. Department of State, *Paris Peace Conference, 1946—Selected Documents*
(1948); valuable source.   Ziff, W. B., *Two Worlds; A Realistic Approach to
the Problem of Keeping the Peace* (1946); the problem of Soviet-American
relations.
EUROPEAN RECOVERY PROGRAM: Balogh, T., *The Dollar Crisis;
Causes and Cure* (1950); by a British economist.   Harris, S. E., *The European
Recovery Program* (1948); by an American professor of economics.   Kindle-
berger, C. P., *The Dollar Shortage* (1951), its nature, causes, and possible remedies, discussed by a British writer.
THE "COLD WAR":   Burnham, J., *The Struggle for the World* (1947);
advocates fierce opposition to Russia's program.   Carr, E. H., *The Soviet Impact on the Western World* (1947); by a distinguished British writer.   Clay, L.,
Germany and the Fight for Freeedom (1950); by the military governor of the

U.S. zone in Germany. Dean, V. M., *Russia: Menace or Promise* (1947) and *The United States and Russia* (1947); by the Foreign Policy Association's expert on Russia. Dennett, R., and Johnson, J. E. (eds.), *Negotiating with the Russians* (1951); by negotiators for the West. Fisher, H. H., *America and Russia in the World Community* (1946); objective. Harris, S. E., *The European Recovery Program* (1948); by an American professor of economics. Lippmann, W., *The Cold War* (1947); a brief criticism of U.S. foreign policy. MacCurdy, J. T., *Germany, Russia, and the Future* (1945); a psychological study by a British professor. Morrell, S., *Spheres of Influence* (1946); an analysis of the Big Three struggle. Nenoff, S., *Two Worlds, U.S.A.—U.S.S.R.* (1946). Norborg, C., *Operation Moscow* (1947); believes Soviet-American agreement is impossible. Roberts, L., *Home from the Cold Wars* (1948). Ward, B., *The West at Bay* (1948); by a brilliant English writer. White, T. H., *Fire in the Ashes: Europe in Mid-Century* (1953); an appraisal of American policy since 1948.

THE ALLIES AND GERMANY: Davidson, B., *Germany: What Now? Potsdam, 1945—Partition, 1949* (1950). Friedman, W., *The Allied Military Government of Germany* (1947). Hill, R., *Struggle for Germany* (1947); urges the Western powers to build up Germany. Holborn, H., *American Military Government: Its Organizations and Philosophy* (1947). Morgenthau, H., Jr., *Germany Is Our Problem* (1945); the much-discussed proposals of the former U.S. secretary of the treasury. Noth, E. E., *Bridges over the Rhine* (1947); a French warning to the Allies not to let the Germans divide them. Plischke, E., *History of the Allied High Commission for Germany: Its Establishment, Structure, and Procedures* (1951). Pollock, J. K., and Meisel, J. H., *Germany under Occupation: Illustrative Materials* (1947); official documents and statements. Price, H., and Schorske, C. E., *The Problem of Germany* (1947); economic, social, and cultural. Riess, C., *The Berlin Story* (1952); from 1945 to 1952. Röpke, W., *The Solution of the German Problem* (1947); suggestions by an anti-Nazi German professor. Settel, A. (ed.), *This is Germany* (1950); a good analysis of conditions under the occupation. Stolper, G., *German Realities* (1948). U.S. Department of State, *Occupation of Germany: Policy and Progress, 1945–46* (1947); official report. Warburg, J. P., *Germany, Bridge or Battleground* (1947); an excellent account of the Allied policies in Germany. Zink, H., *American Military Government in Germany* (1947); by a professor of government who was a participant.

THE NUREMBERG TRIALS: Belgion, M., *Victor's Justice* (1949); critical of the trials. Calvocoressi, P., *Nuremberg: The Facts, the Law and the Consequences* (1948); by an English lawyer. Gilbert, G. M., *Nuremberg Diary* (1947); by an American who was prison psychologist at Nuremberg. Glueck, S., *The Nuremberg Trial and Aggressive War* (1946); by a Harvard professor of criminal law. International Military Tribunal, *Trial of Major War Criminals: Proceedings*, 40 vols. (1947–1949). Jackson, R. H., *The Case Against the Nazi War Criminals* (1946) and *The Nuremberg Case, As Presented by Robert H. Jackson, Chief of Counsel for the United States* (1947). Kelley, D. M., *22 Cells in Nuremberg* (1946); by the official United States psychiatrist. Mendelssohn, P. de, *The Nuremberg Documents: Some Aspects of German War Policy, 1939–1945* (1946). United States Chief of Counsel for Prosecution of Axis Criminality, *Nazi Conspiracy and Aggression*, 8 vols. (1946) and *Nazi Conspiracy and Aggression: Opinion and Judgment* (1947).

CONDITIONS IN POSTWAR GERMANY: Bach, J., *America's Germany* (1946); one of the better books on postwar Germany. Bourke-White, M., *"Dear Fatherland, Rest Quietly"* (1946); pictorial history of Germany in collapse. Byford-Jones, W., *Berlin Twilight* (1947); an account of postwar life in Berlin. Howley, F., *Berlin Command* (1950); by the commander of the United States sector. Joesten, J., *Germany: What Now?* (1948); includes sketches of German postwar political leaders. Klemme, M., *The Inside Story of UNRRA: An Experience in Internationalism. A First Hand Report on the Displaced Persons of Europe* (1949). Knappen, M., *And Call It Peace* (1947); German conditions described by an American historian in the AMG. Knauth, P., *Germany in Defeat* (1946); conditions in 1945. Kulischer, E. M., *Europe on the Move* (1948); a documented account of population movements. Lewis, H. O., *New Constitutions in Occupied Germany* (1948); discussion and documents. Peters, W., *In Germany Now: A Diary of Impressions in Germany, August–December, 1945* (1946). Rodnick, D., *Postwar Germans: An Anthropologist's Account* (1948); excellent. Schechtman, J. B., *European Population Transfers, 1939–1945* (1946); a careful study of the resettlement of Germans by the Nazis. Spender, S., *European Witness* (1946); an appraisal of German intellectuals by a British writer. Stern, J., *The Hidden Damage* (1947); the German civilians after the war.

THE ALLIES AND JAPAN: Brines, R., *MacArthur's Japan* (1948); by the head of the Associated Press in Japan. Busch, N. F., *Fallen Sun* (1948); an estimate of the results of U.S. occupation, by a writer for *Life*. Cohen, J. B., *Japan's Economy in War and Reconstruction* (1949); covers the years 1937–1948. Colbert, E. S., *The Left Wing in Japanese Politics* (1951). Farley, M. S., *Aspects of Japan's Labor Problems* (1950); the labor movement under the occupation. Fearey, R. A., *The Occupation of Japan: Second Phase, 1948–1950* (1950); by a member of the U.S. State Department. Gayn, M., *Japan Diary* (1948); experiences in Japan and Korea in 1945–1946. Kato, M., *The Lost War* (1946); an indictment of Japan's military leaders by a Japanese journalist. Kelley, F. and Ryan, C., *Star-Spangled Mikado: Japan under American Occupation* (1947); a somewhat critical appraisal by an American and a British journalist. La Cerda, J., *The Conqueror Comes to Tea. Japan Under MacArthur* (1946); readable, gossipy, but not documented. Lauterbach, R. E., *Danger from the East* (1947); critical of MacArthur's success. Markham, E. M., *The Allied Occupation of Japan* (1948); official declarations and directives and their effects. Reel, A. F., *The Case of General Yamashita* (1949); an indictment of the U.S. military commission by one of the general's defense lawyers. Reischauer, E. O., *The United States and Japan* (1950); a consideration of U.S. occupation policy and the possibility of a democratic Japan. Royal Institute of International Affairs, *Japan in Defeat* (1945); good discussion of Japanese institutions and possibilities. Textor, R. B., *Failure in Japan* (1951); critical of the achievements of the occupation.   U.S. Department of State, *Occupation of Japan: Policy and Progress* (1946); official.   Van Aduard, E. J. L., *Japan: From Surrender to Peace* (1953); a panegyric of MacArthur.   Wakefield, H., *New Paths for Japan* (1948).   Willoughby, C. A. and Chamberlain, J., *MacArthur—1941–1951* (1954); the man and the legend.

Chapter XXVII. Soviet Russia and Her Satellites

POSTWAR CONDITIONS IN SOVIET RUSSIA: Arakelian, A., *Industrial Management in the USSR* (1950); a brief discussion.   Balzac, S. S., *et al.* (eds.), *Economic Geography of the U.S.S.R.* (1949); a Soviet work.   Basseches, N., *Stalin* (1952); a biography by a former Viennese correspondent in Moscow, weak on period after 1937.   Beck, F., and Godin, W., *Russian Purge and the Extraction of Confession* (1951); by a German scientist and a Russian historian.   Berman, H. J., *Justice in Russia* (1950); an analysis of the elements comprising Soviet law.   Counts, G., and Lodge, N., *The Country of the Blind: The Soviet System of Mind Control* (1949); by American students of Soviet Russia.   Crankshaw, E., *Russia and the Russians* (1948); a valuable interpretation by an Englishman.   Crankshaw, E., *Cracks in the Kremlin Wall* (1951); a penetrating analysis of the weaknesses of the Soviet Union in the cold war.   Dallas, D., *Dateline Moscow* (1952); a picture of the Soviet capital between 1947 and 1950.   Deutscher, I., *Stalin: A Political Biography* (1949) and *Soviet Trade Unions: Their Place in Soviet Labour Policy* (1950); by a British specialist on Soviet Russia.   Duranty, W., *Stalin & Co., the Politburo: The Men Who Run Russia* (1949); by one who lived many years in Soviet Russia.   Ebon, M., *Malenkov: Stalin's Successor* (1953); a careful preliminary study.   Fischer, L. (ed.), *Thirteen Who Fled* (1949); life stories of Russian refugees.   Frazier, R., *Malenkov* (1953); somewhat unrestrained.   Herling, A. K., *The Soviet Slave Empire* (1951); based on testimony of Soviet victims.   Inkeles, A., *Public Opinion in Soviet Russia* (1950); how the government seeks to control it.   Jasny, N., *The Socialized Agriculture of the USSR: Plans and Performance* (1947); a critical analysis of Soviet farming since collectivization.   Kalme, A., *Total Terror: An Exposé of Genocide in the Baltics* (1951); by a Latvian school teacher who suffered under both Russians and Nazis. Kirk, L., *Postmarked Moscow* (1952); bitter comments on everyday Moscow by a U.S. ambassador's wife.   Lauterbach, R. E., *These Are the Russians* (1945) and *Through Russia's Back Door* (1947); experiences and conversations of an American correspondent in 1945–1946.   Lipper, E., *Eleven Years in Soviet Prison Camps* (1951); by a German woman Communist.   Magidoff, R., *In Anger and Pity* (1949); conditions in Russia described by an expelled foreign correspondent.   Magidoff, R., *The Kremlin vs. the People* (1953); a discussion of tensions within Russia by a correspondent long in Moscow.   Maynard, Sir John, *Russia in Flux* (1948).   Members of the Overseas Press Club of America, *As We See Russia* (1948); chapters of varying value.   Milhailov, N., and Pokshishevsky, V., *Soviet Russia: The Land and Its People* (1948); by Soviet geographers.   Murray, N., *I Spied for Stalin* (1951); an interesting picture of Soviet society as seen by the daughter of a high ranking NKVD official. Nyaradi, N., *My Ringside Seat in Moscow* (1951); a picture of political and social life in Moscow in 1947 written by a former minister of finance in Hungary. Petrov, V., *Soviet Gold* (1949); by a former inmate of a slave-labor camp in the Kolyma gold fields. Pirogov, P., *Why I Escaped* (1950); by a Russian aviator who deserted in 1948. Rounds, F., Jr., *A Window On Red Square* (1953); excellent reporting and reflection resulting from a stay in Russia in 1951–1952. Schueller, G., *The Politburo* (1951); a comprehensive and detailed study. Schwartz, H., *Russia's Soviet Economy* (1950); a valuable factual survey. Schwarz, S. M., *Labour in the Soviet Union* (1951); a study of the transformation of the Soviet worker into a semi-serf. Schwarz, S. M., *The Jews in the Soviet Union* (1951); by a former member of the democratic Russian government of 1917. Shore, M. S., *Soviet Education, Its Psychology and Philosophy* (1947). Simmons, E. J. (ed.), *USSR: A Concise Handbook* (1947); excellent. Smal-Stocki, R., *The Nationality Problem in the Soviet Union and Russian Communist Imperialism* (1950); the Soviet problem of dominating non-Russian nationalities. Smith, W. B., *My Three Years in Moscow* (1950); experiences and reactions of the U.S. ambassador in Moscow, 1946–1949. Steinbeck, J., *A Russian Journal* (1948); with excellent photographs. Stevens, L. C., *Russian Assignment* (1953); the two years' experiences of a U.S. admiral in Russia. Baldwin, N. R. (ed.), *A New Slavery, Forced Labour: The Communist Betrayal of Human Rights* (1953). Curtiss, J. S., *The Russian Church and the Soviet State, 1917–1950* (1953). Deutscher, I., *Russia After Stalin* (1953); an attempt to forecast. Fainsod, M., *How Russia Is Ruled* (1953); a careful description and analysis of the power structure of Soviet Russia. Gruliow, L. (ed.), *Current Soviet Policies: The Documentary Record of the 19th Communist Party Congress and the Reorganization after Stalin's Death* (1953).

POSTWAR SOVIET FOREIGN POLICY: Carman, E. D., *Soviet Imperialism: Russia's Drive Toward World Domination* (1950); since 1939. Communist International, *Blueprint for World Conquest: The Official Communist Plan* (1946); excerpts from documents. Dallin, D. J., *Soviet Russia and the Far East* (1948); before and after the Second World War. Ebon, M., *World Communism Today* (1948); a dispassionate report on the situation in the various countries. Laserson, M. M., *Russia and the Western World* (1946); seeks to provide historical perspective. Possony, S. T., *A Century of Conflict: Communist Techniques of World Revolution, 1848–1950* (1953); a penetrating analysis. Rothstein, A. (tr.), *Soviet Foreign Policy during the Patriotic War: Documents and Materials*, 2 vols. (1946); covers 1941–1944. Snow, E., *Stalin Must Have Peace* (1947); by a veteran American correspondent. Umiastowski, R., *Poland, Russia, and Great Britain, 1941–1945: A Study of Evidence* (1947); critical of Russia and Great Britain. Beloff, M., *Soviet Policy in the Far East, 1944–51* (1953).

THE SATELLITES—GENERAL: Bartlett, V., *East of the Iron Curtain* (1950); the fate of the peasants, aristocracy, and middle class. Beamish, T., *Must Night Fall?* (1950); a discussion of postwar developments in Poland, Rumania, Bulgaria and Hungary by a British Conservative. Betts, R. R. (ed.),

Central and South East Europe, 1945–1948 (1950); developments in the Soviet satellite zone. Dewar, M., *Soviet Trade with Eastern Europe* (1951); brief. Gluckstein, Y., *Stalin's Satellites in Europe* (1952); especially good for economic changes and for the Stalin-Tito conflict. Gyorgy, A. *et al., Soviet Satellites: Studies of Politics in Eastern Europe* (1949); a discussion of social reforms. Lehrman, H., *Russia's Europe* (1948); behind the "Iron Curtain" in Central Europe. MacEoin, G., *The Communist War on Religion* (1951); an indictment of Soviet policy toward organized religion, especially in the areas of postwar control in eastern Europe. Seton-Watson, H., *The East European Revolution* (1951); discusses developments in the "Iron Curtain" states. Shearman, H., *Finland—The Adventures of a Small Power* (1950); by an Irish economic historian. Stowe, L., *Conquest by Terror* (1952); an authoritative and readable account of satellite Europe. Waddams, H. M., *Communism and the Churches* (1950); a study of the situation in Russia, Albania, Bulgaria, Czechoslovakia, Hungary, Rumania, and Yugoslavia. Warriner, D., *Revolution in Eastern Europe* (1950); a brief British account dealing with Poland, Czechoslovakia, Hungary, Yugoslavia, and Bulgaria. Meyer, P., *et al., The Jews in the Soviet Satellites* (1953); scholarly and objective.

POLAND: Anderson, F., *What I Saw in Poland, 1946* (1946); by an UNRRA representative. Brant, I., *The New Poland* (1946); brief description of conditions in 1944–1945 by an American correspondent. Cary, W., *Poland Struggles Forward* (1949); conditions in 1947 described by an American. Ciechanowski, J., *Defeat in Victory* (1947); a denunciation of Anglo-American concessions to Russia, by the Polish ambassador to the United States, 1941–1945. Czapski, J., *The Inhuman Land* (1952); a Polish study of Soviet treatment of the Poles. Gronowicz, A., *Pattern for Peace* (1951); a defense of the Oder-Neisse line as Poland's frontier. Jordan, Z., *Oder-Neisse Line: A Study of the Political, Economic and European Significance of Poland's Western Frontier* (1952). Kerstein, E. S., *Red Star Over Poland: A Report from Behind the Iron Curtain* (1947); conditions seen by an American. Kusnierz, B., *Stalin and the Poles* (1949); a Polish indictment. Lane, A. B., *I Saw Poland Betrayed* (1948); by the U.S. ambassador to Poland, 1945–1947. Mackiewicz, J., *The Katyn Wood Murders* (1951); a Polish journalist finds the Soviets guilty. Mikolajczyk, S., *The Rape of Poland: Pattern of Soviet Aggression* (1948); by the leader of the Peasant Party who fled from Poland in 1947. Scaevola, *A Study in Forgery: The Lublin Committee and Its Rule Over Poland* (1945); hostile account. Shotwell, J. T., and Laserson, M. M., *Poland and Russia, 1919–1945* (1945); contains a good discussion of the period 1939–1945. Strong, A. L., *I Saw the New Poland* (1945); sympathetic with the Lublin Poles. Umiastowski, R., *Poland, Russia, and Great Britain, 1941–1945: A Study of Evidence* (1946); hostile to Russia and Britain. Wojciechowski, Z. (ed.), *Poland's Place in Europe* (1947); Polish historians argue in favor of Poland's new western boundaries. Sharp, S. L., *Poland: White Eagle on a Red Field* (1953); a scholarly examination of the weaknesses of Poland's position as an independent state. Stern, H. P., *The Struggle for Poland* (1953); the years 1941–1947.

CZECHOSLOVAKIA: Brown, J., *Who's Next?* (1951); insights into

Communist coup in Czechoslovakia in 1948, apparently by a Czech.   Diamond, W., *Czechoslovakia Between East and West* (1947); developments, 1945–1947. Hindus, M., *The Bright Passage* (1947); optimistic account of Czechoslovakia written before the Communist coup.   Lockhart, R. H. B., *Jan Masaryk: A Personal Memoir* (1951); a brief estimate by a friend.   Mackenzie, C., *Dr. Beneš* (1946); perhaps the best biography in English.   Ripka, H., *Czechoslovakia Enslaved: The Story of the Communist Coup d'État* (1951); by a Czech scholar and former cabinet minister.   Schmidt, D. A., *Anatomy of a Satellite* (1952); how the Communists took power in Czechoslovakia.   Stransky, J., *East Wind Over Prague* (1951); a former Czech official's attempt to show how the Red Army paved the way for the Communist coup.

HUNGARY: Fabian, B., *Cardinal Mindszenty: The Story of a Modern Martyr* (1949); by a Hungarian exile.   Mindszenty, J. Cardinal, *Cardinal Mindszenty Speaks* (1949); official public letters and declarations collected by Mindszenty and ordered to be published if he should be arrested.   Nagy, F., *The Struggle Behind the Iron Curtain* (1948); by the Hungarian premier who fled in 1947.   Orme, A., *Comes the Comrade* (1950), a day by day record of Russian actions in Hungary in 1944–1945.

RUMANIA: Bishop, R., and Grayfield, E. S., *Russia Astride the Balkans* (1948); Soviet policy in Rumania.   Lee, A., *Crown Against Sickle: The Story of King Michael of Rumania* (1950).   Markham, R. H., *Rumania Under the Soviet Yoke* (1949); by a *Christian Science Monitor* correspondent.   Roberts, H. L., *Rumania: Political Problems of an Agrarian State* (1951); since the First World War.

EAST GERMANY: Loewenthal, F., *News from Soviet Germany* (1950). Nettl, J. P., *The Eastern Zone and Soviet Policy in Germany* (1951); an excellent study.   Schaffer, G., *Russian Zone of Germany* (1948); an eye-witness account of life in the Soviet zone.   U.S. Department of State, *East Germany under Soviet Control* (1952).   Klimov, G., *The Terror Machine: The Inside Story of Soviet Administration in Germany* (1953); by an escaped Russian official.

Chapter XXVIII. The So-Called Great Powers of Western Europe

SOCIALIST BRITAIN: Bocca, G., *Elizabeth and Philip* (1953); chatty. Brady, R. A., *Crisis in Britain: Plans and Achievements of the Labour Government* (1950); a good summary of the problems and achievements of Britain's "middle-way socialism."   Clarke, C. F. O., *Britain Today: A Review of Current Political and Social Trends* (1951); an impartial account with considerable insight.   Clemens, C., *The Man from Limehouse: Clement R. Attlee* (1946); deals particularly with the years 1939–1946.   Cowles, V., *No Cause for Alarm* (1949); an account of social and political evolution under the British Labor government.   Cowles, V., *Winston Churchill: The Era and the Man* (1953); a lively, shrewd, and original study.   Dutt, R. P., *Britain's Crisis of Empire* (1950); a British appraisal of Britain's overseas problems.   Estorick, E., *Chang-*

ing Empire: Churchill to Nehru (1950); a biographical approach to the problem. Estorick, E., *Stafford Cripps: Master Statesman* (1949); eulogistic but well-informed. Evans, T., *Bevin of Britain* (1946); brief biography of the former Labor foreign secretary. Hutchison, K., *The Decline and Fall of British Capitalism* (1950); an account of the rise of Labor from 1880 to 1949. Jenkins, R., *Mr. Attlee: An Interim Biography* (1948). Kahn, A. E., *Great Britain in the World Economy* (1946). Laffitte, F., *Social Security: The Fullest Summary of the Beveridge Proposals and Their Implications for the People of Britain* (1944). Mansergh, N., *The Commonwealth and the Nations* (1949); an analysis of changes in the British Commonwealth since 1939. Maillaud, P., *The English Way* (1946); penetrating appraisal of the British people by a Frenchman. McCallum, R. B., and Readman, A., *The British Election of 1945* (1946); excellent explanation and interpretation. Munro, D. (ed.), *Socialism, The British Way* (1948); a discussion of the achievements of Attlee's government. Murphy, J. T., *Labour's Big Three* (1948); Attlee, Bevin, and Morrison. Nicholas, H. G., *The British General Election of 1950* (1951); a study of the campaign, press attitude, forecasts and results. Paish, F. W., *The Post-War Financial Problem, and Other Essays* (1951); in Britain. Somervell, D. C., *British Politics Since 1900* (1950); a readable survey. Taylor, R. L., *Winston Churchill* (1952); entertaining and well documented, but suffers from being extremely laudatory. Watkins, E., *The Cautious Revolution: Britain Today and Tomorrow* (1950); a full and informative account of Britain, 1945-1950. Williams, F., *Socialist Britain* (1949); a study of England under Labor. Williams, F., *Ernest Bevin; Portrait of a Great Englishman* (1952). Windrich, E., *British Labour's Foreign Policy* (1952); the author believes that it is different from that of the Liberals or Conservatives. Broad, L., *Winston Churchill, 1874–1951* (1952). Fitzsimons, M. A., *The Foreign Policy of the British Labour Government, 1945–1951* (1953); critical. Nicolson, H., *King George the Fifth: His Life and Reign* (1953); excellent account of the king's public life.

THE FOURTH FRENCH REPUBLIC: Cowan, L. G., *France and the Saar, 1680–1948* (1950); objective. Earle, E. M. (ed.), *Modern France: Problems of the Third and Fourth Republics* (1951); an excellent collection of papers. Ehrmann, H. W., *French Labor From Popular Front to Liberation* (1947); deals chiefly with the period 1936–1941. Einaudi, M., *et al., Communism in Western Europe* (1951); particularly good for French and Italian Communism since World War II. Goguel, F., *France Under the Fourth Republic* (1952); by a professor at the University of Paris. Malraux, A. and Burnman, J., *The Case for De Gaulle* (1948); a biased account of the aims and possible effects of the Gaullist movement. Pickles, D. M., *France Between the Republics, 1940–1945* (1946); a brief guide to French politics. Rossi, A., *A Communist Party in Action: An Account of the Organization and Operations in France* (1951); by a former member of the secretariat of the Comintern. Russell, F. M., *The Saar: Battleground and Pawn* (1951); covers the period from 1914 to 1951. Taylor, O. R., *The Fourth Republic of France: Constitution and Political Parties* (1951); a concise and satisfactory coverage of the subject. Wright, G., *The Reshaping of French Democracy* (1948); excellent discussion by an American professor who was with the U.S. embassy in Paris, 1945–1947. Pickles, D., *French Politics: The First Years of the Fourth Republic* (1953); a careful and thorough study.

THE ITALIAN REPUBLIC: Croce, B., *Croce, the King, and the Allies: Extracts from a Diary by Benedetto Croce, July 1943–June 1944* (1951); throws light on the question of continuing the Italian monarchy. Einaudi, M., *et al., Communism in Western Europe* (1951); particularly good for French and Italian Communism since World War II. Grindrod, M., *The New Italy: Transition from War to Peace* (1947); a concise, factual account, published by the Royal Institute of International Affairs. Macartney, M. H. H., *The Rebuilding of Italy* (1945); the problems facing Italy after the war, discussed by a well-known British writer. Einaudi, M., *Christian Democracy in Italy and France* (1952). Hughes, H. S., *The United States and Italy* (1953); an excellent book on contemporary Italy.

WEST GERMANY: Clark, D., *Again the Goose Step: The Lost Fruits of Victory* (1949); observations of an American correspondent in occupied Germany. *Germany's Parliament in Action: the September 1949 Debate on the Government's Statement of Policy* (1950); gives a good idea of the atmosphere in West Germany at that time. Middleton, D., *The Struggle for Germany* (1949); the postwar German situation as seen by the head of the *New York Times* bureau in Berlin. Muhlen, N., *The Return of Germany: A Tale of Two Countries* (1953); a report on conditions in Federal and Communist Germany. Office of the U.S. High Commissioner for Germany, *Report on Germany* (1952); 9th quarterly report, covering Oct. 1 to Dec. 31, 1951. Tetens, T. H., *Germany Plots with the Kremlin* (1953); believes United States policy toward Germany is hazardous and ill-conceived.

Chapter XXIX. The Lesser States Outside the "Iron Curtain"

THE SCANDINAVIAN MONARCHIES: Arneson, B. A., *Democratic Monarchies of Scandinavia* (1949). Childs, M. W., *Sweden: The Middle Way* (1947). Cole, M., and Smith, C., *Democratic Sweden* (1939); an excellent discussion of Swedish social democracy. Friis, H. (ed.), *Scandinavia Between East and West* (1950); a comprehensive and authoritative account of social conditions. Galenson, W., *Labor in Norway* (1949); particularly industrial labor. Herlitz, N., *Sweden: A Modern Democracy on Ancient Foundations* (1939); excellent. Hinshaw, D., *Sweden: Champion of Peace* (1949). Howe, F. C., *Denmark: The Cooperative Way* (1936). Kenney, R., *The Northern Tangle; Scandinavia and the Post-War World* (1946); deals chiefly with the years 1939–1944. Larsen, K., *A History of Norway* (1948); by an American historian. Moller, J. C., and Watson, K., *Education in Democracy: The Folk High Schools of Denmark* (1944). Royal Institute of International Affairs, *The Scandinavian States and Finland* (1951); a concise informative report by specialists. *Social Denmark: A Survey of the Danish Social Legislation* (1946); authoritative. Strode, H., *Sweden: Model for the World* (1949); a readable survey. Walker, R., *A People Who Loved Peace: The Norwegian Struggle Against Fascism* (1946).

THE BENELUX COUNTRIES: Barnouw, A. J., *The Pageant of Netherlands History* (1951); an attempt to present the spirit of the peoples of the Low Countries. Goris, J.-A. (ed.), *Belgium* (1945); a symposium on its history and institutions. Hamilton, C., *Holland Today* (1950); brief. Kennedy, J. P., and Landis, J. M., *The Surrender of King Leopold, with an Appendix Containing the Keyes-Gort Correspondence* (1950); favorable to the king. Landheer, B. (ed.), *The Netherlands* (1944); a symposium by Dutch or descendants of Dutch. Landheer, B., *The Netherlands in a Changing World* (1947); by a Netherlands official. Mason, H. L., *The Purge of Dutch Quislings: Emergency Justice in the Netherlands* (1952); by an American professor who was a U.S. Army intelligence officer in the Netherlands, 1944–1946. Miller, J. K., *Belgian Foreign Policy between Two Wars, 1919–1940* (1951); a preliminary but incomplete account. Riemens, H., *The Netherlands: Story of a Free People* (1944); by a secretary of the Dutch embassy in Washington. Roberts, K., *And the Bravest of These* (1946); Belgian conditions, including a discussion of the problem of King Leopold.

SWITZERLAND: Brooks, R. C., *Civic Training in Switzerland* (1930). Rappard, W. E., *The Government of Switzerland* (1937); by a Swiss authority. Rougemont, D. de and Muret, C. T., *Switzerland: The Heart of Europe* (1941). Siegfried, A., *Switzerland: A Democratic Way of Life* (1950).

SPAIN AND PORTUGAL: Alba, V., *Sleepless Spain* (1948). Barea, A., *The Forging of a Rebel: An Autobiography* (1946); an excellent account of Spanish history, 1923–1939, by a Spanish Socialist. Bragança Cunha, V. D., *Revolutionary Portugal, 1910–1936* (1939). Cleugh, J., *Spain in the Modern World* (1953); by a pro-Franco Briton. Feis, H., *The Spanish Story: Franco and the Nations at War* (1948). Foltz, C., Jr., *The Masquerade in Spain* (1948); discusses the group behind Franco. Hayes, C. J. H., *Wartime Mission in Spain, 1942–1945* (1945), by the United States wartime ambassador to Franco Spain. Hoare, S., *Complacent Dictator* (1947); by the British wartime ambassador to Franco Spain. Hughes, E. J., *Report from Spain* (1947); by an American Catholic who was a press attaché in the U.S. embassy in Madrid, 1942–1946. Livermore, H. V., *A History of Portugal* (1947); the best book in English. Lovejoy, A. F., *Spain, 1923–1948* (1949), a pro-Franco account by a British businessman. Pattee, R., *This Is Spain* (1950); a well-documented pro-Franco presentation. U.S. Department of State, *The Spanish Government and the Axis* (1946); official German documents.

GREECE AND TURKEY: Bisbee, E., *The New Turks: Pioneers of the Republic, 1920–1950* (1951); a sympathetic and informative account of post-Kemalist Turkey by a former professor at Robert College. Burr, P., *My Turkish Adventures* (1951); observations on present day Turkey by a school teacher at the American Girls College at Istanbul. Byford-Jones, W., *The Greek Trilogy: Resistance, Liberation, Revolution* (1946); by a British writer. Gomme, A. W., *Greece* (1945). Leeper, R. W. A., *When Greeks Meet Greeks* (1950); by the British ambassador to the Greek government, 1943–1946. McNeil,

W. H., *The Greek Dilemma: War and Aftermath* (1947); an objective analysis of the Greek political situation, 1944–1946. National Liberation Front, *White Book, May 1944–March 1945* (1945); official and unofficial documents for the period 1944–1945. Paneth, P., *The Glory That Is Greece* (1945); events in Greece, 1941–1944. Sarafis, S., *Greek Resistance Army: The Story of ELAS* (1951); by a military commander of ELAS. Smothers, F., *et al., Report on the Greeks* (1948); the situation after one year of American aid. Stavrianos, L. S., *Greece: American Dilemma and Opportunity* (1952); critical of American policy in Greece under the Truman Doctrine. Tomlin, E. F., *Life in Modern Turkey* (1946). Woodhouse, C. M., *Apple of Discord: A Survey of Recent Greek Politics in Their International Setting* (1948); by the chief of the Allied military mission. Kousoulas, D. G., *The Price of Freedom: Greece in World Affairs, 1939–1953* (1953); by a Greek who fought in the underground.

YUGOSLAVIA: Armstrong, H. F., *Tito and Goliath* (1951); Tito's rise, the break with the Cominform, and subsequent conditions. Bilainkin, G., *Tito* (1950); by a British correspondent who interviewed Tito. Clissold, S., *Whirlwind: An Account of Marshal Tito's Rise to Power* (1950); by a British press attaché in Yugoslavia. Dedijer, V., *With Tito Through the War* (1951); part of a Partisan wartime diary. Dedijer, V., *Tito* (1953); an authorized biography. Fotitch, C., *The War We Lost: Yugoslavia's Tragedy and the Failure of the West* (1948); criticism of the Allied policy toward Tito, by a former Yugoslav diplomat. Kerner, R. J. (ed.), *Yugoslavia* (1949); valuable. Korbel, J., *An Ambassador's Report on Tito's Communism* (1951); by the Czechoslovak ambassador to Yugoslavia, 1945–1948. Markham, R. H., *Tito's Imperial Communism* (1947); by a former correspondent of the *Christian Science Monitor*. Martin, D., *Ally Betrayed: The Uncensored Story of Tito and Mihailovich* (1946); strongly anti-Tito. Mihailovic, *General Mihailovich: The World's Verdict* (1947). Radin, G., *Economic Reconstruction in Yugoslavia: A Practical Plan for the Balkans* (1946); an account by experts. St. John, R., *The Silent People Speak* (1948); sympathetic with Tito's Yugoslavia. Ulam, A. B., *Titoism and the Cominform* (1952); based largely on material published in Yugoslavia and some of the satellite states. White, L., *Balkan Caesar: Tito versus Stalin* (1951); hostile to Tito. Pattee, R., *The Case of Cardinal Aloysius Stepinac* (1953); an indictment of Tito.

Chapter XXX. Nationalism in the East

THE ARAB WORLD: Antonius, G., *The Arab Awakening* (1946). Graves, P. (ed.), *Memoirs of King Abdullah of Transjordan* (1950). Hourani, A. K., *Syria and Lebanon* (1945); a careful analysis. Issawi, C., *Egypt: An Economic and Social Analysis* (1947). Khadduri, M., *Independent Iraq* (1952); an account of politics since 1932. Rivlin, B., *The United Nations and the Italian Colonies* (1950); a brief but valuable discussion. Royal Institute of International Affairs, *Great Britain in Egypt* (1952). Stark, F., *The Arab Island: The Middle East, 1934–1943* (1945). Twictchell, K. S., *Saudi Arabia* (1947). Van Ess, J., *Meet the Arab* (1943); by one who lived among the Arabs for many years.

Izzeddin, N., *The Arab World: Past, Present and Future* (1953); an Arab view-point toward world affairs.

PALESTINE AND ISRAEL: Barbour, N., *Palestine: Star or Crescent?* (1947); by a student of the Middle East. Bentwich, N., *Israel* (1953); an objective account by a former British mandate official. Crossman, R., *Palestine Mission: A Personal Record* (1947); by a British Laborite who was a member of the Anglo-American Commission appointed in 1945. Crum, B., *Behind the Silken Curtain* (1947); Palestine discussed by an American member of the Anglo-American Commission of 1945. Dunner, J., *The Republic of Israel: Its History and Its Promise* (1950); an introductory work. García-Granados, J., *The Birth of Israel* (1948); by a member of the UN Special Committee on Israel. Gaury, G. de, *The New State of Israel* (1952); a discussion of political, economic, and cultural conditions and problems. Hurewitz, J. C., *The Struggle for Palestine* (1950); a scholarly study of the problem since 1936. Joseph, B., *British Rule in Palestine* (1948). *Palestine: Land of Israel* (1948); excellent photographs. Matthews, C. D., *Palestine—Mohammedan Holy Land* (1949). *Palestine: A Study of Jewish, Arab, and British Policies*, 2 vols. (1947); by a number of scholars and experts. Rosenne, S., *Israel's Armistice Agreements with the Arabs States* (1952); a legal interpretation of the documents of 1949. Royal Institute of International Affairs, *Great Britain and Palestine, 1915–1945* (1947); a good survey. Schechtman, J. B., *The Arab Refugee Problem* (1952). Stone, I. F., *This Is Israel* (1948). Weizmann, C., *Trial and Error: The Autobiography of Chaim Weizmann* (1919); Israel's first president. Lilienthal, A. M., *What Price Israel* (1953); critical of the Zionists.

THE MIDDLE EAST: Bullard, R., *Britain and the Middle East: From the Earliest Times to 1950* (1951); a brief survey. Eliot, G. F., *Hate, Hope and High Explosives: A Report on the Middle East* (1948); by an American military commentator. Frye, R. N. (ed.), *The Near East and the Great Powers* (1951); a collection of papers presented at the Harvard conference on the Middle East in 1950. Lenczowski, G., *The Middle East in World Affairs* (1952); good for the period since 1914. *The Middle East: A Political and Economic Survey* (1950); a useful compendium of social, economic, and political information. Payne, R., *The Revolt of Asia* (1947). Royal Institute of International Affairs, *The Middle East: A Political and Economic Summary* (1948). Seton-Williams, M. V., *Britain and the Arab States: A Survey of Anglo-Arab Relations, 1920–1948* (1948); by a former member of the British ministry of information. Fisher, S. N. (ed.), *Evolution in the Middle East: Reform, Revolt and Change* (1953); a symposium.

IRAN: Haas, W. S., *Iran* (1946). Lenczowski, G., *Russia and the West in Iran, 1918–1948* (1949); provides excellent background. Mehdevi, A. S., *Persian Adventures* (1953); description of life in Iran by the American wife of an Iranian. Najafi, N., *Persia Is My Heart* (1953); sympathetic but revealing account of conditions by a member of the minor nobility. Thomas, L. V. and Frye, R. N., *The United States and Turkey and Iran* (1951). Wilber, D. N., *Iran: Past and Present* (1948); the latter part deals with the period since Riza Shah.

INDIA AND PAKISTAN: Ahmad, N., *The Basis of Pakistan* (1947). Bright, J. S. (ed.), *Selected Writings of Nehru, 1916–1950* (1950). Brown, W. N. (ed.), *India, Pakistan, Ceylon* (1951). Brown, W. N., *The United States and India and Pakistan* (1953); a pessimistic account of the two states by an American professor. Campbell-Johnson, A., *Mission with Mountbatten* (1953); by the press officer of the last viceroy of India. Choudhary Rahmat Ali, *Pakistan: The Fatherland of the Pak Nation* (1947); by the founder of the Pakistan National Liberation Movement. Cousins, N., *Talks with Nehru: India's Prime Minister Speaks Out on the Crisis of Our Time* (1951); a brief record of conversations held with Nehru. Fischer, L., *The Life of Mahatma Gandhi* (1950). Jones, G. E., *Tumult in India* (1948); a *New York Times* correspondent's description of conditions in India, 1946–1947. Joshi, G., *The Constitution of India* (1951). Kothari, S., *India's Emerging Foreign Policies* (1951); doubtful of the wisdom of India's having remained within the Commonwealth. Mellor, A., *India Since Partition* (1951); a brief account by a British newspaper man. Nehru, J., *Independence and After: A Collection of Speeches* (1950); by India's first prime minister. Roosevelt, E., *India and the Awakening East* (1953); based on a journey in 1952. Spencer, C., *Nehru of India* (1948). Symonds, R., *The Making of Pakistan* (1950); sympathetic. Vakil, C. N., *Economic Consequences of Divided India* (1950). Wallbank, T. W., *India in the New Era* (1951). Bowles, C., *Ambassador's Report* (1954); a competent and readable appraisal of India by a U.S. ambassador. Birdwood, Lord, *India and Pakistan: A Continent Decides* (1954); informative.

INDONESIA AND SOUTHEAST ASIA: Bailey, S. D., *Ceylon* (1952). Boeke, J. H., *The Evolution of the Netherlands Indies Economy* (1946). Dobby, E. H. G., *Southeast Asia* (1951). DuBois, C. A., *Social Forces in Southeast Asia* (1949). Gerbrandy, P. S., *Indonesia* (1950); by a former Dutch premier who opposed granting independence. Jennings, I., *The Constitution of Ceylon: Ceylon as a Dominion* (1950). Lasker, B., *Human Bondage in Southeast Asia* (1950); helps one to understand developments in this area. Middlebrook, S. M., and Pinnick, W. A., *How Malaya Is Governed* (1949); a concise manual. Mills, L. A., *et al.*, *The New World of Southeast Asia* (1949); by eight experts. Mook, H. J. van, *The Stakes of Democracy in Southeast Asia* (1950); by the former Dutch lieutenant-governor-general. Robequain, C., *The Economic Development of French Indo-China* (1944). Sjahrir, S., *Out of Exile* (1949); letters from a prominent Indonesian leader to his wife while he was imprisoned or interned, 1934–1941, by the Dutch. Talbot, P. (ed.), *South Asia in the World Today* (1950). Thayer, P. W. (ed.), *Southeast Asia in the Coming World* (1953); an outstanding symposium. Thompson, V., and Adloff, R., *The Left Wing in Southeast Asia* (1950); a study of the radical movements. Vandenbosch, A., *The Dutch East Indies* (1934). Wolf, C., Jr., *The Indonesian Story: The Birth, Growth and Structure of the Indonesian Republic* (1948); by a former American vice-consul at Batavia. Kahin, G., *Nationalism and Revolution in Indonesia* (1952); the most detailed study in English. Bro, M. H., *Indonesia: Land of Challenge* (1954); first-hand observations.

CHINA: Ballantine, J. W., *Formosa: A Problem for United States Foreign*

Policy (1953); clear statement by a former State Department director of Far Eastern affairs. Bate, H. M., *Report from Formosa* (1952); sympathetic with the Nationalist cause. Belden, J., *China Shakes the World* (1949); a discussion of the social and political conditions which contributed to the victory of the Communists. Bodde, D., *Peking Diary: A Year of Revolution* (1950); diary of a United States student in Peking, 1948–1949. Chang, C., *The Third Force in China* (1952); by the anti-Chiang liberal who drafted the Chinese constitution of 1946. Compton, B. (ed.), *Mao's China: Party Reform Documents, 1942–44* (1952); party resolutions and policy-setting speeches by Mao Tse-tung and other party leaders. Elegant, R. S., *China's Red Masters: Political Biographies of the Chinese Communist Leaders* (1951). Fairbank, J. K., *The United States and China* (1948); a scholarly discussion of the problem of Sino-American relations. Fitzgerald, C. P., *Revolution in China* (1952); a penetrating examination of the Communist regime. Flynn, J. T., *While You Slept* (1952); denounces America's postwar policy toward China as responsible for Communist successes. Forman, H., *Report from Red China* (1945); somewhat sympathetic with the Chinese Communists. Hsiung, Shih-i, *The Life of Chiang Kai-shek* (1948). Hunter, E., *Brain Washing in Red China* (1951); a study of totalitarian re-education in China. Latourette, K. S., *The American Record in the Far East, 1945–1951* (1952); a brief objective account of policy and blunders. McCammon, D. S., *We Tried to Stay* (1953); experiences of a Mennonite missionary in Nationalist and Communist China. Moraes, F., *Report on Mao's Red China* (1953); by a lawyer who visited China in 1952. Payne, R., *China Awake* (1947); an account of conditions 1944–1946 by a former teacher in China. Payne, R., *Mao Tse-tung* (1950); an appreciative account of the Chinese Communist leader. Riggs, F. W., *Formosa under Chinese Nationalists Rule* (1952). Rosinger, L. K., *China's Wartime Politics, 1937–1944* (1944); good for Kuomintang-Communist relations. Schwartz, B. I., *Chinese Communism and the Rise of Mao* (1951); a scholarly study based largely on Chinese and Russian sources. Stockwell, F. O., *With God in Red China* (1953); by the last Methodist missionary to leave China. Strong, A. L., *The Chinese Conquer China* (1949); by a Communist sympathizer. U.S. Department of State, *United States Relations with China, with Special Reference to the Period 1944–1949* (1949); an official White Paper. Utley, F., *Last Chance in China* (1947); a pro-Chiang, anti-Soviet book. Vinacke, H. M., *The United States and the Far East, 1945–1951* (1952); a brief summary of events and an illuminating analysis of the historical forces which produced them. Feis, H., *The China Tangle: The American Effort in China from Pearl Harbor to the Marshall Mission* (1953); a brilliant discussion of a controversial subject. Hutheesing, Raja, *The Great Peace: An Asian's Candid Report on Red China* (1953); by the brother-in-law of Indian Premier Nehru. North, R. C., *Moscow and Chinese Communists* (1953); how Russia was related to the Communist success in China.

Chapter XXXI. Collective Security on Trial

THE KOREAN WAR: Green, A. W., *The Epic of Korea* (1950); a brief survey of the first three postwar years. Gunther, J., *The Riddle of MacArthur: Japan, Korea and the Far East* (1951); readable and sometimes penetrating. Higgins, M., *War in Korea* (1951); by a war correspondent. Kahn, E. J., *The Peculiar War* (1952); the Korean War described by a newspaper reporter. Kim, A. D., *I Married a Korean* (1953); informative, first-hand account of life in rural Korea. Marshall, S. L. A., *The River and the Gauntlet: The Defeat of the Eighth Army by the Chinese Communist Forces November, 1950, in the Battle of the Chongchon River, Korea* (1953). McCune, G. M., *Korea Today* (1950); conditions prior to the outbreak of war in 1950. Meade, E. G., *American Military Government in Korea* (1951); by a participant in that government who claims that the U.S. failed to carry out effectively a reform program. Office of the Chief of Military History, Dept. of the Army, *Korea-1950* (1952). Oliver, T., *Why War Came in Korea* (1950); by a supporter of President Rhee. Riggs, R. A., *Red China's Fighting Hordes* (1951); by a U.S. Army officer. Rovere, R. and Schlesinger, A. M., Jr., *The General and the President* (1951); an account of the MacArthur controversy of 1951. Jacobs, B., *Korea's Heroes* (1953); the exploits of Medal of Honor winners.

NATO: *Atlantic Alliance: Nato's Role in the Free World* (1952); a brief study of aims, organization, and achievements. Boyd, A., and Metson, W., *Atlantic Pact, Commonwealth and United Nations* (1949); origins and significance of the pact. Hoskins, H., *The Atlantic Pact* (1949); an introduction. Middleton, D., *The Defense of Western Europe* (1952); an explanation of why NATO will be the pivot in Western Europe's turn against Soviet aggression. Royal Institute of International Affairs, *Atlantic Alliance: Nato's Role in the Free World* (1952); excellent. Roberts, H. L., and Wilson, P. A., *Britain and the United States, Problems in Cooperation* (1953); a joint report by British and Americans.

COUNCIL OF EUROPE: Boyd, A., and F., *Western Union: A Study of the Trend Toward European Unity* (1949). *European Movement and the Council of Europe* (1949); the aims and steps leading to the Council of Europe. Hawtry, R. G., *Western European Union* (1949). Reynaud, P., *Unite or Perish: A Dynamic Program for a United Europe* (1951); by a former French premier.

INDEX

The following abbreviations are used in this index: First World War (1WW), Second World War (2WW), World Wars (WW's).